CW00663336

MANCHESTER
THE CITY YEARS

BY THE SAME AUTHOR

HISTORICAL/FACTUAL

From Maine Men To Banana Citizens (1989), Temple Press

The Pride of Manchester (with Steve Cawley, 1991), ACL & Polar

Manchester: The Greatest City (1997 & 2002), Polar Publishing

Farewell To Maine Road (2003), Polar Publishing

Manchester City Hall Of Fame (2005), Hamlyn

Manchester City The Complete Record (2006), Breedon Books

Manchester City: 125 Years Of Football (2006 & 2007), At Heart Publications

Manchester: A Football History (2008 & 2010), James Ward

The Big Book Of City (2009), James Ward

FICTION

Atkinson For England (with Mark Brown, 2001), Empire

BIOGRAPHY

Football With A Smile: The Authorised Biography of Joe Mercer, OBE (1993 & 1994), ACL & Polar

Joe Mercer, OBE: Football With A Smile (2010), James Ward

TELEVISION

The History Of Football (2007), Channel M

MANCHESTER
THE CITY YEARS

GARY JAMES

PUBLISHED BY

First published in Great Britain in 2012 by
James Ward
PO BOX 822, HALIFAX, HX1 9FX

www.manchesterfootball.org

info@manchesterfootball.org

© Gary James 2012

The right of Gary James to be identified as author of this work has been asserted in
accordance with Section 77 of the Copyright, Designs and Patents Act 1988
A catalogue record for this book is available from the British Library.

All rights reserved. No part of this publication may be reproduced or stored in a retrieval system,
or transmitted, in any form or by any other means, electronic, mechanical, photocopying, recording or
otherwise without prior permission in writing of the copyright holders, nor be otherwise circulated in any
form or binding or cover other than in which it is published and without a similar condition being
imposed on the subsequent publisher.

Designed by Trevor Hartley

ISBN 978-0-9558127-7-4

James Ward 7774

Printed & bound in Great Britain by Butler Tanner & Dennis, Frome, Somerset

Contents

	The Journey	7
	Acknowledgements	12
	The Beauty Awakes	15
1857-1880	Football Arrives	21
1880-1887	On The Move	35
1887-1892	Ardwick Association Football Club	47
1892-1899	Promoting Manchester	57
1899-1902	Meredith – The First Star	75
1902-1904	Manchester's Success	85
1904-1907	Scandal	105
1907-1915	Rebuilding The Blues	119
1915-1923	Royal City	137
1923-1928	Records and Wembley	151
1928-1934	Wild Success	171
1934-1939	The Championship Arrives	191
1939-1951	Living With The Enemy	203
1951-1956	Wembley Double	219
1956-1965	Losing Supremacy	237
1965-1968	Mercer and Allison	257
1968-1970	European Challenge	281
1970-1973	Premature End	301
1973-1976	Seventies Success	317
1976-1979	Glamour City	335
1979-1983	Buy Now Pay Later	351
1983-1986	McNeill's Bargain Buys	377
1986-1989	Relying on Youth	389
1989-1992	Developing City	405
1992-1996	Premier Blues	421
1996-1999	We're Not Really Here	449
1999-2003	Looking To The Future	477
2003-2007	Premier Home	505
2007-2009	Double Takeover	521
2009-2011	Wembley Glory	545
2011-2012	Worthy Champions	579
	Subscribers	606

Earliest Known Fixture: 13 November 1880 (as St. Mark's, West Gorton) V Macclesfield Baptist Church

Formation: St. Mark's football team evolved out of the church's cricket side. Some cricket matches took place in the 1860s and the cricket team are known to have played regularly on a competitive basis by 1875.

Honours:

European Cup Winners' Cup
Winners: 1970

Football League First Division/Premier League (first tier)
Winners: 1936–37, 1967–68, 2011-12
Runners-up: 1903–04, 1920–21, 1976–77

FA Cup
Winners: 1904, 1934, 1956, 1969, 2011
Finalists: 1926, 1933, 1955, 1981

League Cup
Winners: 1970, 1976
Finalists: 1974

**Football League Second Division/
Football League First Division (second tier)**
Winners: 1898–99, 1902–03, 1909–10, 1927–28, 1946–47, 1965–66, 2001–02
Runners-up: 1895–96, 1950–51, 1936–37, 1999–2000

Football League Second Division (third tier)
Play-off winners: 1998–99

Full Members Cup
Finalists: 1986

Charity Shield
Winners: 1937, 1968, 1972
Runners-up: 1934, 1956, 1969, 1973, 2011
The 2012 shield match had yet to occur at time of publication.

FA Youth Cup
Winners: 1986, 2008
Finalists: 1979, 1980, 1989, 2006

Records:

Most League Goals By An Individual In A Season: 38
Tommy Johnson, Division One 1928-29
Most Capped Player: Colin Bell (England 48)
Most League Appearances: Alan Oakes 561 (plus 3)
Most League Goals: Eric Brook & Tommy Johnson 158
Oldest Player: Billy Meredith, 49 years 245 days
(V Newcastle United, FA Cup semi-final, March 1924)
Youngest Player: Glyn Pardoe, 15 years 314 days
(V Birmingham City, Division One, April 1961)

Top Ten Average Attendances:
47,044, 2011-12
46,830, 2003-04
45,880, 2010-11
45,512, 2009-10
45,192, 2004-05
42,899, 2008-09
42,856, 2005-06
42,725, 1947-48
42,126, 2007-08
41,687, 1977-78

Top Five Highest Home Attendances:
84,569 (FA Cup V Stoke, 1934) – remains a record for any League club.
79,491 (V Arsenal, 1935) – was a Football League record at the time.
78,000 (V Manchester United, 1947) – remains the highest Manchester derby attendance.
76,166 (V Cardiff, 1924) – was a record for any game staged in Manchester at the time.
76,129 (V Everton, 1956) – ground developments meant this was the last home crowd over 76,000.

Five of the top ten highest footballing attendances in Greater Manchester are for Manchester City home fixtures. Three are for Manchester United home games (all of which were staged at City's Maine Road ground during 1948-49), and two are for neutral fixtures (one of which was at Maine Road).

The Journey

On Monday 14th May 2012 I stood amongst a crowd in excess of 100,000 to witness Manchester City's Premier League homecoming parade. By that time I had dedicated over a couple of years of my life to writing this book and, as I waited for the team to pass, I thought about City's history and the journey the Blues had taken to get here.

Football success is usually measured in trophies won, games played and so on, but on that Monday evening as I waited I realised that the homecoming parade itself was perhaps one of the most significant moments in the Club's history, just as City's very first homecoming in 1904 had been.

Back in 1904 the press focused on the size of the crowds, the welcome received and, most significantly as far as I am concerned, the unifying aspect of City bringing national footballing success to Manchester for the first time.

The 1904 homecoming saw fans of all ages, social backgrounds and stature join together to celebrate as one. This made City a Mancunian institution and one which was able to boast that it was Manchester's club. For decades afterwards neutrals talked of City as 'the popular club of Manchester' or 'Manchester's premier team'. City's first success was seen as the defining moment when football began to matter to Manchester.

City's pre-eminent position lasted until after World War Two. Record crowds and incredible success during the Thirties suggested the Blues would always be the dominant force locally, however under former Blue Matt Busby Manchester United became a true force in the Fifties. The Blues had to share the attention but then, as United grew stronger, City declined.

A new Blue spirit emerged in the mid-Sixties under Joe Mercer, Malcolm Allison and Chairman Albert Alexander and that rekindled the spirit, drive and ambition the Club had experienced pre-war. Incredible success followed but by the mid-1980s a succession of errors caused City to decline as a force.

There were some bright moments during the Eighties and Nineties but overall City were heading in a downward spiral. Everything connected with the Club seemed to be focused on the short term. A point best demonstrated by the erection of a new stand at the Platt Lane end of Maine Road in 1992-93, the first Premier League season. The old stand sat over 9000 spectators, the new one held less than 5,000 limiting any potential the Club may have had to grow during the Premier League era.

The stand did include the stadium's first executive boxes, but there were many issues with the overall look and feel of the place. The stand's link up with the Main Stand was messy to say the least and included a number of stanchions, while there was a large void beneath the terracing of the entire new stand. Proper planning would have created a hospitality lounge to allow additional income, but instead the space was used for storage and investigations a few years later proved that the cost of converting this space would have been excessive to say the least. A short term move limited the Club's long term growth.

There were, of course, serious issues on the pitch during the nineties. City plummeted down the divisions competing at the third level of English football for the first time in 1998-99.

As City struggled Manchester United grew at a pace. They benefitted hugely from the riches success in the Premier League era brought and the gap between Blue and Red grew to be the largest it had ever been.

Under Joe Royle a new spirit ensured the City fight back began midway through the 1998-99 season. Promotion to the second level was achieved in dramatic fashion at Wembley in 1999. A day when City looked dead and buried ended with two late goals to equalise the play off final and force a period of extra time. The drama didn't end there however as extra time ended goalless forcing promotion to be determined by a penalty shoot-out. Goalkeeper Nicky Weaver performed brilliantly to guarantee promotion.

The new found spirit lifted the Blues onwards and

Fans celebrating at Old Trafford, 2008.

upwards first under Joe Royle and then under new manager Kevin Keegan. A move to the present stadium followed in 2003 – for which City had to give up Maine Road (valued at a figure of around £27m) and pay around £30m in fitting out the new home, plus a rental based on gate receipts.

Playing at the new stadium was expected to see City push forward and re-establish themselves as one of the game's elite. However, football had changed significantly since the formation of the Premier League and the gap between the richest clubs and the poor was immense. Despite a loyal and dedicated support the Blues struggled financially. The sale of Shaun Wright-Phillips for £21m in 2005 was evidence that City were unable to compete with England's wealthiest clubs. Thirty years earlier the Blues had been one of the Country's elite, able to buy whoever they wanted at any price, now they were a selling club.

The future looked bleak. A life of mid-table obscurity with the occasional cup run, maybe reaching a quarter-final, at best. A couple of particularly woeful FA Cup quarter final defeats (at home to West Ham and away to Blackburn) brought home the realisation that this was as good as it gets to some fans.

In 2007 everything seemed to change as former Thai Prime Minister Thaksin Shinawatra bought the Club. Immediately the atmosphere lifted and the incredibly loyal City fans became positive once more, but Shinawatra's ownership hit problems. Negative headlines surrounded his every move by 2008, while financially he seemed unable to take the Blues forward in the way he had planned. Rumours of City heading towards administration even circulated.

It was with immense relief that in 2008 Shinawatra then made the best decision of his time at City (on a personal level this eclipsed him buying four copies of my *Manchester A Football History* book and paying cash for them!). He sold the Club to Sheikh Mansour from Abu Dhabi and the Blues have never looked back.

Activities on the pitch improved significantly and ultimately led to FA Cup glory in 2011 and the Premier League title in 2012. These events were hugely important and the ones that gained worldwide headlines, but behind the scenes the entire Club was transformed.

As with an iceberg everyone focused on the visible peak, but down below an even more substantial City existed. It is this area below the surface that will ultimately ensure the Blues remain a viable, sustainable and successful club for the long term. This unseen area is developing at a pace.

While standing on Deansgate the day after the Blues had won the 2011-12 Premier League title I thought of the steps along City's journey. Like most fans, transfer deadline day 2008 was a landmark moment when we all heard the news of the takeover. However, it was almost three weeks later when the takeover directly affected me. Back on Saturday 20th September 2008 I had been asked by Executive Chairman Garry Cook if I would come into the stadium to talk with someone about the history of the Blues.

I had no idea who I was to meet or what I was to be asked, but Garry Cook made it clear that this would be of interest. Intrigued I set off and drove to the stadium.

City were due to play Portsmouth the following day and so, apart from a few people ensuring the usual preparations were being made, the stadium was empty. I waited for what seemed like an eternity before Garry Cook appeared. He took me to the Chairman's Lounge and as we walked he explained who I was to meet. He said: "In the Lounge will be representatives of Sheikh Mansour, the man who is buying City. They're finalising details right now, but Khaldoon Al Mubarak, who will be the new Chairman, wants to meet you to talk about the Club.

"They've done lots of research of course, but he wants to hear first-hand about the Club and he wants to have a proper look around the stadium. Don't hold anything back. Tell him the truth, the absolute truth. Let him know the good and the bad."

Cook stressed the significance of the chat and his comments encouraged me enormously.

After the introductions I was asked to sit down at a table with Khaldoon and the others. His first question was a simple but very important one: "How and why was this football club created?" For me this was a landmark moment. Obviously, anyone buying a football club should know about its history, but this was the first time in all my years writing and researching that anyone in a senior position had asked that question. Interestingly, I was told that Thaksin Shinawatra had passed on a copy of *Manchester A Football History* – this must have been one of the copies he had bought only a few weeks earlier.

It could be argued that every previous chairman and director already knew the answer and therefore did not need to ask, but I know that could not be said for all of them. Khaldoon's question encouraged me enormously that the takeover would be right for City. Simply asking that question proved to me that the Abu Dhabi investors were not buying a 'plaything' as the media often suggested. Some suggested they cared little for City's history, but Khaldoon proved with his very first question on his very first day at Manchester City that he was interested. He did care.

During the afternoon Khaldoon asked a variety of historical questions some of which, quite frankly, surprised me. He had obviously performed his research because he asked what the various elements of City's old club badge signified, such as the red rose, as well as those on the modern day eagle badge, for example. He also demonstrated a great deal of interest in the story of Bert Trautmann and asked Garry Cook to ensure Bert was invited to the stadium as soon as possible.

Everything I experienced that day encouraged me enormously that the Abu Dhabi takeover was good for Manchester City. The takeover was not for personal glory, evidenced by the reluctance of Khaldoon, Sheikh Mansour and others to take the acclaim in the manner that some former owners and chairmen had. Nor was the takeover a result of some rich guy looking at a Premier League table and saying "I want that one" as some implied.

Sheikh Mansour bought Manchester City because the Club offered great potential for growth; had a large and dedicated support; was based at a modern stadium; was surrounded by an area that offered great investment potential; and had been underperforming for years.

As mentioned earlier, ever since the formation of the Premier League, in fact for over a decade before, the Blues had been lagging behind their traditional rivals in terms of investment both on and off the pitch. Off the pitch, apart from a brief period under the chairmanship of Francis Lee when he tried to ensure investment matched needs and ambition, a make-do and mend approach had dominated. This meant that year after year, the Blues dropped further behind. However, that under-investment eventually became a significant reason for Sheikh Mansour to invest.

In many ways it's ironic that all those years of pain and failure for City actually created the conditions that enabled the Blues to be purchased so enthusiastically by Sheikh Mansour and his team.

The question 'why City?' has been asked on numerous occasions by supporters of other clubs who wish theirs had been chosen, but Garry Cook explained to me his simple view why City was chosen above many other, possibly more successful clubs: "It's a bit like property. If you've got two houses next to each other and one's worth a million quid, and it's beautiful and you turn the key and you're in and the furniture's there and it's all beautiful. It's all done for you. Great. You just hope the value increases.

"The other house. The one next door is a bit tatty, a bit run down. It needs an extension, and the gardens need fixing. But if you can pick it up for £350,000 you know you can put in another £300,000, making a total spend of £650,000 but suddenly it's worth a million. These people are businessmen and it's really not that difficult to understand why City. But I would add they are passionate about the game.

"So, do you buy Arsenal, Man United, Chelsea, Liverpool, Newcastle, or the gem – the needle in a haystack? Look at that. It's got everything. Who's running it? Let's go and have a chat. It's got the city, property, history, heritage... that sounds good. We can have some fun with that. People have mystified some of this, but I always say 'keep it simple and keep going.'"

Some initially suggested Liverpool may have been a better purchase: "Buy Liverpool? But how much would you have had to pay and what would be the growth?"

Liverpool, and they were not alone, had a history of success and achievement. Any improvement in success would only have had minimal impact, whereas with City any trophy success would be a significant improvement.

I asked Khaldoon the obvious question during an interview in May 2010: "Why City? Well there were many factors that came into the decision. I think from Sheikh Mansour's perspective this team presented value for money for several reasons. Number one is that this team had a rich history. A rich heritage with a strong fan base.

"Number two - this is a team that has underperformed, so there was a considerable upside. Number three - from a value proposition you're talking that it represented good financial value from the point of acquisition. So all in all it was a great mix. It had the right ingredients from a financial perspective, in terms of football history, in terms of future potential upside in both the financial side and football."

There is no doubt that this is an investment and no one should be fooled into thinking this is merely a plaything with money being thrown at it willy-nilly. Every £1 spent has to be spent wisely and the value of the Club has to improve to carefully thought out plans. The ultimate aim has to be to make Manchester City the most valuable football club in the world.

To achieve that aim the Club has to be successful both on the pitch and off it. The football world and British media tend to focus on activities on the pitch and player purchases. That is understandable but only one piece of a very large jigsaw puzzle.

Due to the efforts being made off the pitch I am convinced that one day, possibly in ten years (or 'maybe in another generation' as the song 'Boys In Blue' puts it),

Manchester City will be held up as the example of how a football club should be run. City will be the benchmark for others to follow. Hopefully this will be because of success on the pitch, but more significantly I believe it will be because of their planning, structure, facilities, youth development, sustainability and, most important of all, their community developments.

For me the first major public example of City becoming the choice for the current generation came when I stood on Deansgate the day after the Premier League title was won. I looked around and took it all in. There were people of all ages, all backgrounds, and ethnic mix. There were office types, labourers, pensioners, hoodies, mothers, fathers, boys, girls and babies in their prams and pushchairs. Every generation and sector of society appeared to be there.

There were youths sitting on 'phone boxes, lads on traffic lights clinging on for their lives. Others climbed up on to other vantage points such as the veranda at Kendal's. Restaurant staff, some of east European birth, rushed out on to the streets as the parade bus came near to share in this moment of Mancunian pride.

This brought the realisation home to me that City's 2012 success was likely to have a similar impact to the 1904 FA Cup success. That day Manchester united in its support of the Blues and, in 2012, it felt as if the population had once more viewed City's success as theirs. Of course, there are now two successful teams bearing the Manchester name whereas, in 1904, the Blues had been the only one to achieve national success. Nevertheless, the manner of City's victory and the scenes witnessed on both the Sunday and at the parade seems to have created a situation whereby the Blues' success is perceived as in the long term best interests of Manchester and football.

The 2012 bus journey started with a capacity 20,000 in Albert Square. In 1934 when Pathe News claimed there were over a million people on the streets for City's second FA Cup success, Albert Square was packed without any capacity restrictions. That day fans young and old, male and female sang a well-known City song of the period "Who Said City Couldn't Play Football" – in 2012 a similarly mixed group sang the modern day anthem "Blue Moon."

After various activities in Albert Square, the parade made its way along Princess Street, down Portland Street, Chepstow Street, Great Bridgewater Street, Albion Street (close to where the 1904 parade started at Central Station), Whitworth Street West, and then up Deansgate. The homecoming travelled all the way up Deansgate, part of which (from Peter Street) also formed part of the first trophy parade.

Thousands lined the streets with an estimated 80,000 on Deansgate alone. Some simply had to be there because of the manner of City's victory the previous day. Others had waited their entire lifetime for this moment.

Parents lifted their babies up as the bus drove past with Vincent Kompany lifting his baby, the Premier League trophy, for them all to see.

The route continued into St Mary's Gate and, while the original 1904 route had continued up Market Street, the 2012 tour turned at Corporation Street, went on through Exchange Square and ended between Urbis (the new National Football Museum) and the Printworks. Although it is doubtful any one on the bus or stood in the streets surrounding this area realised, finishing outside the Printworks was appropriate from a historical perspective as it was in the Old Boar's Head that used to stand on that site that in 1894 the newly formed Manchester City gained admittance to the Football League. That day the streets were packed with partying Mancunians for reasons explained later in this book, as they were again in 2012.

This was Manchester in all its glory.

The Club has always been a proud ambassador for Manchester. In many ways its highs and lows have matched Manchester's own peaks and troughs. City's successes and failures have been felt by Mancunians of all types. Every Mancunian throughout history has known what it's like to suffer hardships and that's why Manchester City is so representative of the city. Mancunian reality – warts and all.

I've always known this to be true, but in recent years some have claimed that City is a club with 'no history'. That clearly insults the hundreds of players and thousands of fans who have been a part of City life for so long. It also insults Manchester. To say City has 'no history' suggests that one million on the streets in 1934 were an irrelevance, or that Manchester's first major success in 1904 was insignificant, or that England's record club attendance of 84,569 didn't happen.

Every football club has history of course. However, as some footballing figures continued to repeat this angle following the 2008 takeover, I decided it was time to prove the Club had history by updating my full history of the Blues. My 1997 publication *Manchester The Greatest City* had been out of print since it was updated in 2002, and so I investigated ways of bringing that story up to date.

I took the original main narrative from that book, reviewed it all, rewrote significant sections, and then added new material focusing on the early years that led to the birth of the Club and on the last decade or so.

The format of the book was to change somewhat and so I decided to amend the title to be more reflective of City's current position. *Manchester The Greatest City* was so named for two reasons – one was my love of Manchester and everything about the place, and the other was to emphasise City's significance. As time

Champions, 2012.

wore on I realised that the name implied that the Blues were the 'greatest' football team to be called City. That is, I believe, a fact, but it doesn't really fit with the Club's aspirations. I dug out my old notes from when I first selected the title *Manchester The Greatest City* and looked at the options I had back then.

Manchester The City Years leapt out as an appropriate name as this version of the book has been designed to follow the Club's story in a seasonal manner. There are chapters covering key periods and each contains a seasonal review.

The new title was selected fairly early in the 2011-12 season and was registered with the appropriate authorities. Then in December 2011 journalist Martin Samuel wrote an article focusing on Alex Ferguson in which he commented: "He will not wish to hang around for Manchester: the City years." Although this came some time after the name had been registered, it demonstrated that the new title could prove significant if the Blues were to begin to dominate football locally.

At that time I had no idea that the League title would arrive. I hoped it would of course, but knew that whether it did or it didn't the book would be welcomed by fans. The original *Manchester The Greatest City* came out during the Blues' relegation season to the third tier of English football and yet sold out completely within 12 months.

I hope you enjoy the book as much as I've enjoyed reliving so much of City's history. Start wherever you want. Although the story is, in the main, a chronological one the book has been written with the hope that fans will dip in and out whenever they get a spare moment. I guess most are going to start with the 2011-12 season, but once you've done that open the book at any random page and see what you discover.

Finally, I'm sure there will be some who continue to mention the 'No History' line over the coming years. If they do show them this book. Tell them about Beastow, Furniss and Maley. Show them Meredith making his name and finding success years before he helped United find their first successes. Tell them about Hyde Road bursting to the seams, of record crowds being set at Maine Road and of Manchester's first Wembley final. Point out how great Frank Swift, Eric Brook, Sam Cowan, Fred Tilson and Peter Doherty were. Give them the lowdown on Bert's broken neck. Explain to them how Mercer, Allison & Alexander brought the glory days back. Recreate Tueart's overhead kick. Follow John Bond's Blue & White army and then the youthful team of the late Eighties. Explain how fans felt with the demise of the Kippax, or of Maine Road itself. Relive the anguish and joy of Wembley 1999 and the rebirth that followed. Tell them about survival and the importance of City's Academy, and then bring the story right up to date with Wembley 2011 and QPR 2012.

Enjoy the journey through City's amazing history.

Gary James
10th August 2012

Acknowledgements

As with every book I write there are many, many people who have helped during the production of this book. I have been very fortunate over the years that so many people have been interested enough to help me develop my research, or have made themselves available for interviews and discussions about Manchester's Blues.

No one could ever write a book of this size and scope without support along the way and I am personally very grateful for any support provided.

Obviously, I must thank Manchester City and its directors & employees throughout the period of my research. When they authorised my original history of the Blues - *Manchester The Greatest City* - in 1997 they allowed me to tell the story with a free hand and I was able to tell the story as it deserved to be told. Warts and all. That approach has continued with this volume and I am delighted that at no time have I been asked to censor any comment.

I would also like to thank the 100s of people I've interviewed in recent years. Some of their words appear in this book, others were used to form an opinion of a particular period or story. I performed specific interviews with the following (some have been interviewed on multiple occasions both during and after their period at City):

Chairmen: Khaldoon Al Mubarak, Eric Alexander, David Bernstein, Francis Lee, Peter Swales and John Wardle. I also held discussions with Thaksin Shinawatra during his period of ownership that have helped form an opinion. Albert Alexander, the only other City chairman during my life, passed away while I was still a young boy and I never got the opportunity to talk City with him.

Directors/senior officials: Chris Bird, Jim Cassell, Garry Cook, Peter Fletcher, Bernard Halford, Vicky Kloss, Sarah Lynch, Alistair Mackintosh, Brian Marwood, Simon Pearce, Dave Pullan, Steve Sayer, Jon Stemp, Dennis Tueart and Graham Wallace.

Managers: Malcolm Allison, John Benson, John Bond, Tony Book, Sven-Göran Eriksson, Jimmy Frizzell, Johnny Hart, Brian Horton, Billy McNeill, Roberto Mancini, Joe Mercer, Phil Neal and Joe Royle. Further discussions have been held with Peter Reid, Howard Kendall, Kevin Keegan and Stuart Pearce.

Players: Ken Barnes, Peter Barnes, Colin Bell, Ian Bishop, Ian Bowyer, Ian Brightwell, Frank Carrodus, Roy Cheetham, Kenny Clements, Joe Corrigan, Steve Daley, Andy Dibble, Paul Dickov, Roy Dixon, Willie Donachie, Edin Dzeko, Fred Eyre, Fionan 'Paddy' Fagan, Steve Fleet, John Foster, Trevor Francis, Dietmar Hamann, Ron Healey, Andy Hinchcliffe, Bobby Kennedy, Paul Lake, Roy Little, Steve Mackenzie, Rodney Marsh, Ian Mellor, Paul Moulden, Alan Oakes, Gary Owen, Glyn Pardoe, Neil Pointon, Paul Power, Niall Quinn, Kevin Reeves, Micah Richards, John Riley, Mike Summerbee, George Smith, Bert Trautmann, Patrick Vieira, Dave Wagstaffe, Dave Watson, David White, Alex Williams and Johnny Williamson.

Supporters, media and other footballing figures: Bill Cronshaw, Kevin Cummins, Lee Dixon, Keith Durham, Sir Tom Finney, George Graham, Ricky Hatton, Paul Hince, Harry Hughes, Alan Johnson, Kevin Kennedy, Eddie Large, Martin Lewis, Ian Manford, Jason Manford, Janice Monk, John Motson, Ian Niven junior, Fran Parker, Will Perry, Mike Pickering, Roger Reade, James H Reeve, Sean Riley, Colin Savage, Helen 'the bell' Turner, Jimmy Wagg, Dave Wallace and Sue Wallace.

Inevitably there are many other people who I've interviewed or discussed City with over the years. Some have asked to remain anonymous, while others are mentioned in the text at relevant moments in this book. I am grateful to them all for their assistance. I have enjoyed my discussions, visits, and contact with them all.

Significant support has also come from the BFI, British Pathe, Manchester Central Library, Manchester Evening News, National Football Museum, the Northwest Film Archive, the newspaper archive of the British Library at Colindale, the Reporter Group and Tameside Libraries.

In addition I have received great support, assistance and inspiration from: Len Balaam, Mike Barnett, Ian Barton, Julian Baskcomb, Noel Bayley, Stewart

Beckett, Ashley Birch, Frank Borson, Colin Bottomley, Harry Bramble, Bryan Brett, Peter Brophy, Tony Bugby, John Bullock, Pete Bulmer, John Burfield, Richard Burgess, Andy Burton, Mark Bushell, David Butler, Julia Byrne, Sean Cable, Dave Cash, Dennis Chapman, Doug Cheeseman, Simon Clarke, Simon Clegg, David Concannon, Johnny Crossan, Phil Crossley, David Djordjevic, Geoff Donkin, Rob Dunford, Eddie Dunne, Garth Dykes, Phill Gatenby, Ray Goble, Peter Godkin, Bob Greaves, Rod Hall, Derek Hammond, Trevor Hartley, Tony Heap, Andrew Heydeman, Martin Hewitt, Mark Hodkinson, Paul Hodkinson, Eddy Hogg, Jane Hogg, Pete Hollins, Geoff Homer, Brian Horsnell, Brian Houghton, Ian Howard, Greg Hughes, John Hughson, Geoffrey Ireland, Alan Jubb, Mike Kelly, Mark Kennedy, George Kirby, Josh Langton, Paul Leach, Tony Lees, Peter Lupson, Andy Lyons, Jean-Francois Maille, Iain McCartney, Malcolm McAlpine, Sarah McBriar, John Maddocks, Alistair Mann, Clare Marsden, David Masey, David Meek, David Mercer, Norah Mercer, Glen Midgley, David Miller, David Mooney, Andy Morris, Tommy Muir, Chris Nield, Phil Noble, Andy Noise, Mike Pavasovic, Kevin Parker, Geri Parlby, Heidi Pickup, John Pickstone, Alan Potter, David Powter, Chris Prince, James H Reeve, Stuart Renshaw, Simon Richardson, David Ricketts, Steve Rigby, Norman Rucker, David Scally, Maynard Scott, Ray Shepley, Ken Smallwood, Ian Smith, Tor Sønsteby, Graham Stringer MP, Paul Taylor, Graeme Thompson, David Ticehurst, Paul Toovey, Richard Tucker, Ric Turner, Andy Walsh, Andy Ward, Cros Ward, David Whalley, Richard Whitehead, Mark Wilbraham, Chris Williams, Steve Worthington and Bob Young.

Inevitably, thousands of individual newspaper editions have been consulted during my research. These include: The Bury Times, Manchester Courier, Manchester Evening Chronicle, Manchester Evening News, Manchester Weekly Times, Oldham Evening Chronicle, The Reporter Group, Rochdale Observer, Salford Chronicle, Stockport Express & Advertiser, Cheshire County News, Daily Dispatch, Umpire News, the Hornet, Athletic News & the Sporting Chronicle. Plus of course all modern day national newspapers, football magazines, and club-based material. I would also like to thank all the journalists, photographers, and officials who have helped chronicle the game throughout the history of the Blues. The majority of photographs come from Manchester City Football Club, the Manchester Evening News, Edward Garvey, Anna James, Sharon Latham, Richard Tucker and the author. Special thanks to MCFC for allowing me to use their recent imagery.

I would particularly like to thank Kevin Moore and his staff and officials at the National Football Museum including Peter Evans, Peter Holme, Alex Jackson, David Pearson, Andy Pearce and Jon Sutton. It is a wonderful museum and one everyone should visit.

As always, Trevor Hartley has performed miracles with the layout of this book and its cover. In addition, I would like to say 'thanks' to my family for their continuing support.

I am certain there are many other people who have helped along the way. If I have overlooked your contribution please don't feel slighted in any way. I'm sure you can appreciate the amount of effort that has taken place over many, many years to produce this book and, inevitably, I haven't always been able to keep track of every contribution. Undoubtedly, there will also be a number of people who assist me in one form or another the moment this book is printed. Again, if you fall into this category thank you.

I hope you enjoy reading *Manchester The City Years* and that it gives you a great understanding of the Blues entire history. I know it is inevitable some mistakes will have crept in, but I sincerely hope there are not too many. If you do find any then please contact me via the publishers.

Thanks,

Gary James

Twitter: @garyjameswriter

Facebook.com/garyjames4

Mario Balotelli and Yaya Toure celebrate Yaya's FA Cup final winner, 2011.

The Beauty Awakes

"After a journey, they come to an overgrown palace where, following a confrontation between the forces of good and evil, the Prince awakens Aurora with a kiss. The spell is broken."

The English National Ballet's version of *Sleeping Beauty*, 2011

When Sergio Aguero scored the final goal in the dying seconds of the last game of the 2011-12 Premier League campaign, the roar from the Etihad Stadium terraces was incredible. The goal gave Manchester City the Premier League title for the first time since the League had been restructured in 1992, but it actually brought much more to the Blues. It brought back pride, spirit and a sense of incredible achievement. This was a goal that told the world that Manchester City had finally woken. The sleeping beauty was awake once more.

Winning the Premier League 44 years after the Blues last top flight title was a major achievement considering how low the Club had dropped in the Nineties, and how far from success they appeared to be only a mere five years earlier.

Back in 2007 Manchester City's Chief Executive openly admitted that the Blues needed investment. He travelled the world searching for an investor – any investor it seemed to fans – as City found it increasingly more difficult to challenge. The birth of the Premier League in 1992 had created a situation over time where

four clubs seemed to dominate and everyone else was left some way behind hoping for, at best, a decent run in one of the domestic cup competitions. It was an awful situation to be in and one that never seemed likely to change.

Similar sized clubs, such as Aston Villa, had been taken over by wealthy overseas businessmen while the Blues were left behind, hoping for investment. Then in 2007 a takeover did occur.

Thaksin Shinawatra, a former Thai Prime Minister, saw the potential City offered and he launched a bid for the Club, ultimately receiving backing from existing shareholders to take over the Club in its entirety. This meant that he, and his family, owned City and could do whatever they wanted with it. Some fans were concerned but, as with the proposed takeover of Manchester United by Michael Knighton in 1989, the vast majority welcomed Thaksin with open arms and believed they had, at long last, found someone who could bring the glory days back to the Blues.

Shinawatra made plans and he seemed keen to

spend a few years at least developing City into a world renowned name. His critics later suggested his thinking had all been short term, but some of his initial actions suggested he aimed to be at City for a few years at least.

Within a year of Shinawatra's purchase however, it all began to go wrong. The former Thai Prime Minister's political record was being investigated, as was his financial situation. None of this had anything to do with football, but it began to drag the Blues down. Then Shinawatra began to suffer financially as assets were seized and restrictions imposed. Supporters began to worry that City would suffer or worse, be forced into administration.

Fortunately, before the situation could deteriorate further Shinawatra finally managed to appoint Garry Cook to provide hands-on management of the Blues for him. Cook had his own long term vision of what he believed Manchester City should aspire to and he worked hard on documenting his plans. Those plans were often ridiculed in the media; for example he talked of City winning the Premier League within ten years and held a view that City could become renowned around the world. However, Cook believed in them and was determined to make them happen.

As Shinawatra's financial situation became more of an issue it was clear City needed further investment. Shinawatra's trusted advisors began talking with contacts in the middle east and elsewhere looking for investment. The owner still wanted to retain the majority shareholding and felt he could find an investor who would support him. Cook believed this would be unlikely. He felt anyone investing in City at this stage would want to own the Club outright.

Ultimately, the search for an investor found a man who had been keen to invest in English football for some time, HH Sheikh Mansour bin Zayed Al Nahyan of Abu Dhabi. Sheikh Mansour's advisers had been looking at a variety of Premier League football clubs, but none of them seemed perfect. Then they found a club with a loyal fan base; a great modern stadium; a wonderful history; and a club that was at the heart of its community. They met with Shinawatra's people and then with Garry Cook. Cook performed a presentation in which he talked through his ideas for the growth of City.

Further discussions occurred in which the opportunities were fully considered. These focused on the fact that City had been underperforming for three decades and yet support had remained high, and on the potential for growth in Manchester. The links with Manchester City Council helped of course. In particular the City Council's desire to see investment come to east Manchester to help regenerate a depressed area of the city.

It was, and still is, often ignored but the takeover by Sheikh Mansour was to see considerable investment in the area around the stadium and in Manchester as a whole.

Sheikh Mansour appointed the dignified and respectable Khaldoon Al Mubarak as Chairman of Manchester City and, together with Garry Cook who remained the key figure at the Club on a daily basis, the Blues were transformed beyond all recognition within a very short time. New players were brought in, facilities were improved or constructed from scratch, and the whole place finally began to match the ambitions of the fans and, most significantly, the Club's earlier history.

Following the takeover of the Club in 2008, various senior footballing figures and media-types incorrectly claimed that the Blues were a club with 'no history', yet City did have a 'history' of notable landmarks and successes. It may seem churlish to highlight that the Blues found success in European competition before Liverpool – and Michel Platini's own Juventus - and that they won their first major trophy four years before Manchester United found major success; 26 years before Arsenal and an incredible fifty years before Chelsea. City also topped the attendance charts at various points throughout their existence and, even today, they are still able to boast the record club attendance.

Where City struggled – and struggled they have – was in the period from 1981 through to the late 2000s. Despite what the media and others may say, it is actually these three decades that have been out of character for the Blues. Sadly, in an era when media coverage of football reached new heights and 24 hour sporting TV channels searched for sound bites and stories, it was City's struggles – or at least their ability to make life difficult for themselves – that defined the Club.

This generation of failure affected even those most passionate about the Club. They may not have recognised it at the time but supporters, City personnel and others with a close affinity to the Blues began to believe that the Club was destined to live a life of failure or, at best, valiant near-misses.

Media faces who were portrayed as loyal City fans couldn't help focusing on this angle. Author Colin Shindler wrote about the Blues as perennial underdogs, while broadcaster Stuart Hall talked of City's home from 1923 to 2003 Maine Road as The Theatre of Base Comedy. Although said with affection, it really gave the world a view of City and, in truth, helped establish the Blues as a side where mediocrity was expected.

Fortunately, deep inside Manchester City there was a soul that had remained. The Club may well have fallen into a deep sleep, but there was still life in there somewhere. Like a sleeping beauty waiting for her prince charming, City needed to be awoken from its long slumber and re-appear in public as beautiful as ever.

Previously, City had their ups and downs of course, but that was no different to other major sides. Every generation experienced trophy success at some point and the magic of supporting a side like City was the knowledge that the good days were always likely to follow those of struggle. It hadn't been like that for thirty years. The Club fell into its coma in the early eighties – midway through the 1981-82 season appears to be the point when City's directors started cutting back and focusing on downsizing rather than speculating.

Prince Charming, actually Sheikh Mansour from Abu Dhabi, arrived in 2008 and Manchester City was given the kiss of life.

The Sheikh, his advisors and dedicated team of achievers recognised the Club's understated beauty. The years of slumber had taken their toll and they knew that to re-establish the Blues at the level they'd previously been at needed resources and effort – considerable effort. Everything had to be improved to even stand a chance of awakening the Club.

Enormous investment had to be made, both in player acquisition and in developing the Club as a whole. This wasn't because City was a plaything for Middle Eastern royalty as some claimed, it was because the Club was woefully inadequate. As a football club City had struggled, but as a business the Blues were in a critical state. This situation had to change.

The investment in all areas lifted City from its slumbers but, significantly, this investment was aimed at creating a sustainable football club for the future. The aim was not to win a trophy as quickly as possible by buying the best players, it was to develop the whole club to provide a platform that would allow success over many years.

Those acting for the new owner made it abundantly clear at their first meeting with staff that they were in this for the long term and, in Abu Dhabi terms, the long term is usually viewed as a period lasting closer to eighty years than five years. For a Club that tended to think that a manager deserved a long service medal if he lasted a couple of years, that was very encouraging. When they unveiled their plans for the area around the stadium, to be known as the Etihad Campus, their commitment was abundantly clear.

The media may focus on events on the pitch, but it is the long term planning that will ultimately make Manchester City a successful force for many future generations to enjoy.

The first tangible on the pitch success came in 2010-11. That season City won the FA Cup and qualified for the Champions League.

The FA Cup Final ended with many typical scenes. The players danced on the pitch and posed for team photographs. The Manager held the FA Cup aloft. The fans sang their songs of celebration and waved their flags. But this was not like the FA Cup finals of recent years. This was different. This signified much more

than simply winning one – albeit a very important – competition. This success came at the end of 35 years of missed opportunities. Over three decades of hurt for fans.

When City's coaching staff grabbed a banner reading "00 Years" everyone knew that this was a real life changing moment. This was the point when a club's habit of self-destruction was turned on its head.

Winning the FA Cup would inevitably be a significant step forward for any club, but for Manchester City this was a serious statement of intent. Finally, after 35 years without major trophy success at the highest levels of the game, the 'noisy neighbours', as Manchester United's manager Alex Ferguson had termed them, had at last cause to be vocal. Significantly, it felt as if this was merely the starter for a gourmet meal.

City's success was incredible. At the end of his first full season in charge Roberto Mancini had guided the Blues to FA Cup glory, Champions League qualification, and their highest end of season placing since the late 1970s. In fact you have to go back to 1903-04 to find a comparable season for Manchester City – that year the Blues won the FA Cup and were runners-up in the League, although City did win two trophies in the 1969-70 season.

At the start of the 2010-11 season the Club had set a target to finish third in the League, thereby gaining automatic qualification for the Champions League. The football world at large had suggested City's target was fourth place but it was actually third. Third guaranteed Champions League football, fourth merely brought possible entry into the qualifying round and that uncertainty was not what the Blues needed. They needed confidence.

Winning the FA Cup and qualifying for the Champions League was the first on the pitch indication that City was waking from its slumber. In general terms City were on track and achieving the plans the Club had made shortly after the takeover in 2008, but the beauty was still not fully awake.

The plans for this period had been discussed within three months of the takeover when Garry Cook performed a presentation to all staff in the Commonwealth Suite at the stadium. During the presentation he talked, at a high level, of the plans and ambitions for the Blues. That day he announced that every effort would be made to turn the Club around and admitted that for the wider world it would be activity on the pitch that they would be judged on. He then outlined that City aimed to develop across all areas year on year.

Focusing on football, he explained the aims for the rest of the 2008-09 season, and those for 2009-10. Overall, apart from a few worrying moments in both seasons, City were to achieve their aims, but the most significant on the pitch developments were always planned to occur after the 2009-10 season.

Cook outlined that qualifying for the Champions League and finding trophy success was the ultimate aim for 2010-11, followed by consistent development year on year after that. At the time, some staff felt this was unlikely but they loved the ambition of it all.

A little over two years later, the first stages of the plan agreed at the highest level had been realised. Little of the actual planning was public knowledge at the time, because that was not a sensible way to ensure the plan worked. Too many times in the past football clubs, particularly City, had talked of what they would do but ultimately failed to deliver. Following the 2008 takeover the decision was taken to plan, deliver and then let people see how the Club improved. Deliver first, talk second.

The successes of 2010-11 were very important and allowed supporters to earn bragging rights. After all, as the 2011-12 season commenced, City were one of only two remaining Premier League sides that had actually found major trophy success the previous season.

Understandably, some claimed City's success owed everything to the enormous transfer fund they had available. Clearly that is an argument with some justification, but for thirty years fans had been told that City's failure had been the cause of the high-spending of the late Seventies/early Eighties. The suggestion was that the Blues had bought success but that they had also bought failure for thirty years.

In reality City's expenditure in recent seasons has been a necessary evil. The Blues have been playing 'catch-up' and the investment they've made since 2008 still represents an under-investment over the last three decades in comparison with many teams they were on a par with at the start of that period.

The Abu Dhabi investment has led to the Blues progressing year on year. In 2009 City reached the quarter-finals of the UEFA Cup and finished tenth; in 2010 they reached the semi-finals of the League Cup and finished fifth; in 2011 they won the FA Cup and finished third in the League. Progress year after year at an incredible rate.

Of course, City's 2011 success did not mean that the Blues were certain to challenge year after year in the way that Liverpool did in the Seventies and Eighties, or Manchester United have in the last two decades, but it did indicate that City were back on course after three decades of relative under-achievement.

By the summer of 2011 the Blues were heading in the right direction, but the 2011-12 season would perhaps see if the Club was able to develop further. They needed to mount a sustained challenge for the game's top honours once more if they were to persuade the world that City were now a force. The FA Cup success could not be a one off. The beauty had to regain full consciousness.

Inevitably, there was a lot of focus on City's 2011-12 Champions League campaign. A lot was expected of Roberto Mancini's side, however the UEFA draw gave the Blues a very tough group that included eventual finalists Bayern Munich, regular Champions League challengers Villarreal, and the developing Italian side Napoli. Everyone agreed it was by far the toughest group and the Blues failed to progress despite amassing ten points – a figure which would ordinarily guarantee progression.

Although City performed admirably in the Champions League, some suggested the Blues were not quite the force the media hyperbole had suggested. This, of course, ignored the fact that the Blues had performed better than many other, longer established, European competitors.

The talk of City failing was ill-advised as the Blues' Premier League campaign proved. Mancini's men became the team to watch. Throughout the opening months of the 2011-12 season they thrilled and brought a real buzz to every ground they visited. For the entire season they were never out of the top two positions.

The best result of the opening months came at Old Trafford on 23rd October. Despite the Blues already impressing game after game, many in the media assumed this would be the day when City would be 'found out', while some connected with United openly stated that Mancini's side had yet to face a team capable of challenging. They had, of course, overlooked the fact the Blues had defeated Tottenham, a team that maintained a challenge throughout the season and eventually finished fourth, 5-1 at White Hart Lane.

At Old Trafford the Blues swept United aside with ease. As most City fans would stress throughout the season, that day it could have been ten for the Blues. In the end Mancini's side had to feel satisfied with a derby record equalling 6-1 scoreline.

The victory cemented the Blues' place at the top. From October through to March they topped the table, game after game, week after week, setting records along the way.

The season was not quite as straight forward as everybody wanted it to be. However, the Blues did go on to win the title in the most dramatic and ultimately satisfying way possible on the last day of the campaign.

The manner of City's victory that day became news around the world. Everyone wanted to talk about the Blues' success and what it actually meant. Was this a turning point in Manchester's history? Were the Blues to be a force for decades? Was this the end of Manchester United's dominance?

In his press conference Alex Ferguson congratulated City but added: "It'll take them a century to get to our level of history." It was an amazing comment considering the pace of City's development since Sheikh Mansour's takeover. It also paid little attention to the history of Manchester football as the Blues had been the dominant force for at least the first sixty years or so, plus at other key points. There have also been periods when City and United were neck and neck, or spells when one has been almost dead and the other found glory. Sometimes the Reds were the force, sometimes the Blues.

The gap between United and City became significant during the modern era as the Reds found tremendous success and the Blues struggled. Those successes catapulted United into a position of financial strength which, in turn, allowed them to buy players while City and other sides struggled to survive. The Reds' grew at an incredible rate after 1992 and the formation of the Premier League. That's what created such a gulf. That means it took United around twenty years to reach their current level of success and financial strength. As City are growing and developing at a much faster rate it is possible that they could match Ferguson's achievements in a similar timeframe. It took United a lot less than 100 years to go so far ahead of City, and so it seems likely that with appropriate planning the Blues could match United in a lot less than the 100 years Ferguson suggested.

Regardless of whether City do match United's success in the long term, it is important that all Blues remember that the developments in recent years are only the early stages of the plan. Garry Cook, who sadly left City during the 2011-12 season, was often mocked for talking of his aspirations for the 'project' as it was termed. Yet, his plans and aims could, by the summer of 2012, be seen to be achievable. They may have been ambitious, but that ambition has already meant that City have won the two biggest prizes in domestic football – some would argue that the Premier League is the biggest prize in world club football of course due to its stature and presence around the globe.

The journey, of course, continues. Hopefully, further success will follow. For the moment it is worth standing back to recognise that the Club has finally awoken from its sleep. Less than five years earlier, the Blues were going nowhere fast. Now they have found real trophy success and are speeding towards further glory that, if all goes to plan, will eclipse all that has gone before.

Most significantly, City's success on the pitch has come a little earlier than perhaps it ought to have done. The owner, via Chairman Khaldoon Al Mubarak and a dedicated team of personnel, is reshaping all aspects of the Club in a bid to create a sustainable football club for the future. They have been creating some incredible plans in all areas of the business and backroom operation, including the development of players. If all goes to plan these should reap rewards in years to come. Unlike most other football clubs the Blues' leaders are

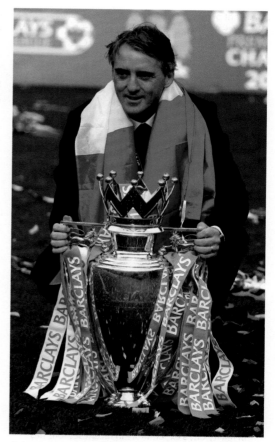

Roberto Mancini won his second trophy in his second full season at City.

planning for the long term, not merely a season at a time like many clubs, including the 'old' City, often do.

Some have suggested the Club has lost its soul in a quest for glory and the riches success brings, but the truth is that community continues to play its part. City remains the community club of Manchester but it is also becoming known throughout the world for its community activities. Facilities have been opened for disadvantaged youngsters in various countries as the Blues try to leave a legacy everywhere they visit.

Community has been a key focus for the Club since its birth. It has always been there, but the Club's present day successes and investment have enabled that to reach a new level.

With success on the pitch and in the community it is fair to say that Manchester City is alive and well. The Club is destined for a bright future.

The Beauty has awoken from its slumber.

1857-1880
Football Arrives

"A match was played between the Baptist Church (Macclesfield) and St. Mark's (West Gorton) on Saturday on the ground of the latter, and resulted as follows: Baptist 2 goals, St. Mark's 1 goal."

A report of the first known game, played 13th November 1880, from the *Gorton Reporter*

Football clubs are always created for a purpose, but as time goes by the exact reason or reasons why a club first existed are often forgotten. The early pioneers move on, and the history of the club relies on those left behind to keep the stories alive. Often stories become confused. The very nature of the sport is the game itself and so for some the history means little. The focus, understandably, is on the club's ambition and, hopefully, next achievements.

The early history of Manchester City Football Club has become confused at various points over the years with myths developing and information forgotten. There are several reasons why City's early history was not properly recorded with the most significant of these being the destruction of key records. In 1920 a fire destroyed all official material, and some seventy years later an infamous clear out occurred during the period of Peter Swales as chairman.

Significant attempts have been made by a variety of historians to properly record the birth of the Club and it is only with the support, interest and efforts of several people that a consistent story has become established. It must be stressed however that no one can say with absolute certainty what the spark was that created the football team, who the actual founder was, and why the Club was created. What follows here is a view based on all available sources. It has been checked and verified, but due to lack of hard evidence from the period no history can ever be described as a factual record of everything that occurred.

The early history of City must be seen in context with the history of Manchester itself, indeed the whole history of the Club has always been closely linked with the development of the World's first industrial city. During the period 1800 to 1851 the population of the Manchester area trebled to 1,063,000, within another fifty years it had reached 2,149,000. Immigrants came from rural England, Ireland, and continental Europe, especially Germany and Italy. They were attracted by the Cotton industry and the developing engineering businesses of the region.

The Manchester region was seen as possessing great opportunities. This was true for some, but for others conditions were harsh, extremely harsh. Large numbers of back-to-back houses were built across Manchester with volume rather than quality the main concern. The conditions were often appalling for the area's workers.

As time progressed rural areas surrounding the city centre were developed. 'Coronation Street' style terraced houses were built on the rural land surrounding the City centre with areas such as Ardwick Green, Bradford, Longsight and Gorton becoming densely populated suburbs of the growing city. These terraces were better than those that existed in the main city centre but some were shoddily constructed, and most were built with density, and therefore profitability, the main aim. Families were packed into these areas at a rapid pace with multiple families often occupying houses with only two bedrooms.

Ardwick Green, Bradford, Gorton and so on were towns or villages in their own right in the early to mid 1800s, but by the end of the century they were in effect part of Manchester's general urban sprawl. This stretched from Reddish Lane at the eastern edge of Gorton, through to the city centre, and on to the developing Trafford in the west.

With the growth of urban Manchester came social inequality, poor conditions and all the ills of the period. The main issue for many was alcohol. On what seemed like every corner of the area's terraced streets, public houses were developed to give the men a break from the pressures of their grim industrial lives. As well as the regular public houses known by the majority of Mancunians today, there were also beer shops and residential properties where the inhabitants would sell beer as a sideline – or indeed a main activity – without proper license or control.

Hyde Road, the main thoroughfare from Manchester to the Cheshire town of Hyde (very much a separate conurbation back then), some eight miles away, was one of the city's busiest roads, and a prime example of how Manchester had developed. Industry, terraced housing,

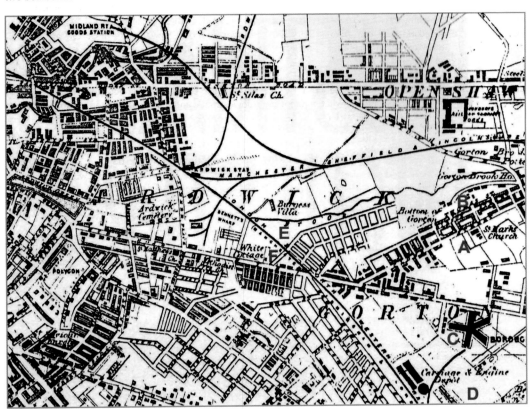

Bradshaw's c.1870 plan of Manchester shows (A) St. Mark's Church, (B) Brooks & Doxey's Union Ironworks, (C) the Gaol, where Sam Kirkman lived, (D) the site of Kirkmanshulme CC (where the football team played in 1881-82, (E) the site of City's Hyde Road ground (1887-1923), & (F) White Cottage - the Hyde Road Hotel was built on this site.

The original Isaac Holden plan for St. Mark's Church.

churches and plenty of 'pubs' could be found along its route.

Along the Hyde Road, a short distance from the city centre, was Gorton or more specifically Gorton and West Gorton. Viewed at the time as two separate districts, both Gortons remained independent urban districts for several years. In 1890 West Gorton was absorbed into the city with Gorton following in 1909.

Gorton had a long history and possessed an identity separate to that of Manchester until the twentieth century, however West Gorton was somewhat different. Virtually the whole of West Gorton had developed from nothing during the 1800s. It was as if someone had looked at a map of the area, seen the gap between Gorton in the east and Ardwick in the west and thought "that'll make a good place for factories and housing."

Buildings were thrown up at a rapid rate. It seems apparent that those responsible for the developments were more intent on maximising land usage than on social well-being. Others did care, however, and a man called Jabez Ashworth arrived in West Gorton in 1857 determined to develop a moral fibre to the area. Previously, he had set up a chapel in Droylsden, moving it to larger premises on Edge Lane in 1853.

He moved to West Gorton in 1857 and on 10th November that year he issued a circular outlining plans to raise money. He focused on Gorton Brook which, at that time, was basically the top end of Clowes Street, roughly where the modern day Pottery Lane meets Gorton Lane. This was the main developed area of West Gorton. Ashworth: "Gorton Brook is a thriving though somewhat isolated village in the Township of Gorton, and parish of Manchester, situate between Hyde Road and Openshaw, close to Ashbury Station. There are excessive Iron, Chemical, Cotton and Paper Manufacturers in the neighbourhood. The population is about two thousand. Opportunities for public worship and instruction being much needed."

Ashworth's work was continued in 1861 when Reverend Richard Adams arrived. He issued a paper entitled "Proposed New Church For Gorton" on 13th January 1862 which documented the first significant steps in the development of what was to become St. Mark's Church. 28 year old Adams, who lived at newly developed 5 Cromwell Street between Hyde Road and Clowes Street, announced he was setting up weekly Sunday services at the nearby former Zion Chapel. These commenced on Sunday 19th January 1862.

Adams efforts were fruitful and within weeks the weekly services were proving popular. The success encouraged him to begin negotiating with local businessmen and landowners. Later in 1862 he issued another circular: "The parish of West Gorton is large in extent and population. It extends from near the railway arch on Hyde Road to Denton on the one part, and to Droylsden on the other part. The population is estimated at between nine and ten thousand, and is rapidly increasing. To meet the wants of this large population there is church accommodation for not more than one twentieth part, and it is proposed to remedy the evil by erecting a New Church on Colonel Clowes's property at West Gorton, where building is daily in progress.

"Land sufficient for the Church has been given by Colonel Clowes without cost, and Mr Beyer has headed the subscription list with a munificent donation of one thousand pounds."

The donation from Charles Frederick Beyer was important. By 1862 Beyer was one of the founders of the engineering firm Beyer Peacock, set up in 1854, and he was one of the key figures behind the transformation of the Gorton area from a rural landscape into an area of major industry. Significantly, he was also a German national and, like many of the people in the area, had arrived in Manchester because of the opportunities the region presented. With a mix of nationalities, religious beliefs and classes there was often tension in the area but Richard Adams made it clear from the outset that his aim was to create something for the good of all: "Rich and poor, old and young, of all classes and denominations are invited to lend a helping hand in this work."

A photograph of Arthur Connell, c1884, located by Glen Midgley and Tony Lees.

Both Adams and Beyer worked hard to establish a community spirit and were key figures, President and Treasurer respectively, behind what was termed a Gorton Brook Working Men's Association. Adams described the 48 strong group as: "A number of working men who at present form part of a congregation worshipping in St. Mark's Schoolroom, Gorton Brook."

Adams, with other members of that group, aimed to raise £4,000 for what he described as his: "great desire that a new Church should be erected. To help forward this desire Colonel Clowes has generously given the land, and Mr Beyer has generously given £1,000, and the working people who worship together have united to imitate according to their means such a munificent example."

As housing and factories were being thrown up on the rest of Colonel Clowes' land efforts were made to increase fundraising and raise publicity. Renowned architect Isaac Holden was appointed. Previously he had designed St Peter's in Ancoats and the Palatine Building next to Chetham's in the city centre.

On 14th March 1864 a concert was held to mark the commencement of the new church's construction. This was followed on 30th April 1864 (originally planned for 13th April) by a special ceremony which saw Shrewsbury MP and civil engineer Henry Robertson officially lay the foundation stone. Robertson was also a sleeping partner in Beyer Peacock and after the official ceremony finished he matched Beyer's £1,000 donation.

The festivities that day were significant. As part of the activities a bottle was placed under the stone containing three Manchester daily newspapers, coins and a document detailing those involved. Sadly, none of this was salvaged when the church was demolished over a century later.

Over the following year or so £3,880 was spent building the church and boundary walls. Alongside these developments baptisms and other parish activities continued to take place in the school room.

Finally, on Thursday 30th November 1865 the new St. Mark's Church was consecrated by the first Bishop of Manchester James Prince Lee. Around the church there were still signs of a rural community, but this was vanishing as streets were being laid out and names being selected. The road that St. Mark's was officially positioned on became Clowes Street in honour of the landowner Colonel Clowes.

A few days later, on 5th December, Irishman Arthur Connell arrived on a permanent basis. He would ultimately become the first rector of St. Mark's and is recorded as either Curate or Incumbent on baptismal records until August 1866 when he is finally recorded as Rector.

It was later claimed that Connell had been curate at High Harrogate when he received a letter from John Edwards, the Rector of a church in Bradford (Manchester) close to the present day Etihad Stadium. Edwards and Connell had trained together and Edwards clearly felt his friend would be perfect to fill the vacancy created when Richard Adams left the parish in December 1864, although Adams returned to perform some activities until February 1865. His departure could have disrupted plans significantly, however Edwards believed Connell was the right man to fill the gap.

Edwards' letter told Connell that West Gorton would give him a "fair field for ministerial usefulness." Connell came to Gorton as a result of the letter, preached as Adams had done at St. James' Church on a Sunday morning and then at St. Mark's in the evening. Connell's first known St. Mark's baptism came in August 1865.

Connell later claimed that he had believed "the call to be from God" and the obvious need in West Gorton influenced him to resign from his position at Harrogate to develop his work in Gorton. He was, it has to be stressed, of course a deeply religious man and held views typical of similar church leaders at that time. His sermons, inevitably, carried very serious views on faith, other religions, morality and society, some of which would be out of place in the 21st century. Nevertheless, it is fair to say that his arrival in Gorton brought a recognition that the church could provide hope for the area.

In 1931 a Gortonian by the name of Sam Kirkman gave his memories of the West Gorton area to the *Reporter* newspaper. Kirkman was born in 1860 in the turret of Belle Vue Gaol, Hyde Road. His father was a warder at the prison and the young Kirkman's life revolved around the streets and fields of the Clowes Street area. He attended both St. Mark's church and school during the late 1860s and 1870s, and went on to complete an apprenticeship in 1881 at an engineering works, Brooks & Doxey's Union Ironworks, that ultimately became highly significant in the development of Manchester City Football Club.

As part of his article on the Manchester Martyrs and the killing of Police Sergeant Charles Brett on Hyde Road in September 1867 – one of Manchester's most significant 19th Century incidents – Kirkman described the scene from the gaol, which at that time stood on the southern side of Hyde Road, through to Clowes Street in September 1867: "On the opposite side of Hyde Road from the [gaol's] turret stood the old Horse Shoe Inn, and right across from there was open ground, reaching across to what was then called Gorton Brook – the 'Top of Gorton' end of Clowes Street. Looking right across from the house, a big tree stood close to Clowes Street.

"Hyde Road then was like a country road, right away to Ardwick Green, which at the time was a big pond."

Arthur Connell, his wife Anna, daughters Anna and Georgina and youngest child Arthur, were actually living on Hyde Road at number 457 around this time, but as the area became more developed during the 1870s they moved to North Road, close to Kirkmanshulme Lane on the southern side of Belle Vue.

As Hyde Road and the Clowes Street area developed the rural scenes outlined by Kirkman were replaced. The building work caused other problems and in 1866 a letter appeared in the *Manchester Courier* outlining the situation on Clowes Street itself where work was ongoing to pave the street: "our working men having to travel these roads daily may well curse their mismanagement, when they often get up to their ancles (sic) in mud, or run the risk of falling and breaking their limbs over rubbish left on the footpath."

The letter went on to talk about shoddily erected buildings and streets: "At present the township is notorious for its jerry buildings, few, if any, properly drained; streets without any light, where people have to grope their way through mud and dirt, at the risk of life and limb."

Four years later, in January 1870, a similar letter suggested little had changed: "The first noticeable peculiarity which will strike the visitor is mud, the presence of which can easily be accounted for by the fact that West Gorton possesses one and a half properly laid out streets."

Mud was only one concern. There were other much more serious issues facing West Gortonians as the area grew. Many male inhabitants of West Gorton were spending too much time in the area's pubs and beer houses, while most children seemed to focus their energies on unsavoury activities. Sometimes the men

and the boys would have shared experiences but these tended to be on activities that the wider public would frown upon. One such activity was bare knuckle fighting. This was highly popular on waste land near both Clowes Street and Hyde Road and would take place between men of varying ages and watched by large crowds of men and boys. Sam Kirkman himself admitted to both watching and then participating in these sessions.

He also talked of another significant threat to the social well being of the area during the late 1860s and early 1870s - 'Scuttling'. Kirkman told the *Gorton Reporter* stories about Gorton-based Scuttlers meeting rivals from Bradford or Miles Platting: "They would be drawn up not in echelon but in mass format. They would approach nearer and nearer. Then the leader would shout their battle cries. The weapons were belts, slings, sticks and stones. Both sides would give a yell as the police came on the scene, then the two armies would scatter in all directions to meet some other day."

Conditions were harsh for the young men of the area and they found that Scuttling brought a release. The Scuttlers developed a community spirit of their own at a time when the community at large seemed to care little for their well being.

With West Gorton growing at an incredible rate and the problems intensifying, someone had to do something. Someone had to focus on making things better. Ultimately, St. Mark's Church became established at the centre of the community. The church offered activities to improve the well being of parishioners. It seems Rector Arthur Connell encouraged leading parishioners to establish community activities. His aim may have been to spread religious influence, but for the parishioners the focus on community activities improved everyday life for many.

A new St. Mark's school was established and prospered. Thomas Goodbehere, a mechanical draughtsman at Brooks Union Ironworks (later Brooks & Doxey's), was highlighted as the school's manager and by the mid 1870s, it was viewed as being of a higher standard than all other schools within the Gorton area. In 1931 Sam Kirkman, born in 1860, talked of attending the school at the age of nine or ten. Discipline was high, maybe it needed to be, and Kirkman didn't seem to enjoy the experience: "My troubles began when I was sent to St. Mark's School, Clowes Street, Gorton. Going was bad enough, but returning was worse. It often ended with a flogging… Mr Connell was the rector and Mr. 'Cocky' Bradbury the schoolmaster."

Kirkman admitted that he regularly found himself in trouble. His problems continued at St. Mark's Church itself: "The Church wardens sat behind us with long thin sticks in their hands, and if I just turned my head to whisper to the lads next to me down came the stick on my innocent head. How I longed for the end of the sermon. It always sounded something like 'hear endeth'. That was a joyful sound, and never did soldiers stand to attention quicker than I did when the congregation rose to their feet."

Perhaps his age had something to do with it, but those connected with the church must have felt that the boys and young men of the area had to be brought into line. Kirkman did also talk positively of prize giving ceremonies and of the time he was "awestruck" when he was given a prize by local businessman Charles Beyer.

The school helped provide formal education and a moral code, but the area needed more. While Arthur Connell, his wife Anna, and daughters Anna and Georgina (Arthur junior had emigrated to Canada by 1881), continued their quest to make the St. Mark's community strong in spirit and mind, other prominent parishioners became involved. One of the men who achieved most for West Gorton as a whole in the long term, was William Henry Beastow.

Beastow, along with Goodbehere, was a significant figure at Brooks & Doxey's Union Ironworks on Thomas Street (now Wenlock Way), the neighbouring street to Clowes Street. He did not own the company, but it is clear that many of his ideas and aims were similar to some of the philanthropic mill owners of the period. It seems every moment of his free time was dedicated to the people of West Gorton. He became an overseer of the poor, a member of the Gorton Local Board of Health, a sidesman at St. Mark's, and as time progressed a councillor for West Gorton. Later he represented the area on Manchester City Council, and he also became president of the National Friendly Society and a freemason.

During the early 1870s he lived at 155 Hyde Road and by the end of the decade he had moved to 178 Clowes Street. By that time he knew well the hardships, issues and general problems his neighbours faced. He played his part in many of St. Mark's key activities and he was also keen to establish better conditions and a community spirit for all. He joined various organisations and looked to see what he could do to help focus minds on positive matters. In 1874 he joined the Ashbury's Masonic Lodge and went on to be Master of the Lodge in 1882. He was also the key figure behind the West Gorton Working Men's Institute. This had been set up following the failure of another organisation – the West Gorton Working Men's Conservative Club – and the Institute had taken over their club room and furniture.

In January 1877 Beastow's organisation was also forced to close. At the time he explained the organisation's history and reason for closure: "[we] made it into a Working Men's Club, thinking it would be taken over by working men generally, so that they could come here - instead of going to worse places – where they could obtain enjoyment of a rational character. Well,

about 14 men joined out of about 30,000 inhabitants."

Despite the failure of the Institute Beastow remained committed to improving conditions and developing a community ethos. It is clear Beastow's aim was to help the average man but maybe his efforts were aimed at the wrong ages? Perhaps he needed to focus on the younger men of the parish, or maybe he needed the support of a more formal local organisation?

He visited local employers to try and convince them to focus on social activities for their workforce. He was reported in the local newspaper: "I have met some of the principal employers and they said 'We will help the working men when the working men attempt to help themselves', and I do not blame them for if you look around this vast neighbourhood we have not a place where you can send your children even to a drawing class, and if the working men will not come forward we cannot blame the employers for this state of things."

As time went by he became more involved with St. Mark's Church and, ultimately, he began to focus on the church's community activities. It seems he became, in effect, the chairman of the St. Mark's Cricket Club.

Some cricket activity occurred during the 1860s – brief match reports exist for games in 1867 and 1868 – and it is possible that the first actual cricket match took place during the new church's first summer of 1866. Cricket was known to occur at the southernmost point of the St. Mark's parish many years earlier. For instance Longsight Cricket Club was established in 1848 and was based for its first few decades at Albert Grove, Longsight. It is therefore possible a St. Mark's cricket team was established as soon as the church was officially up and running. Maybe Rector Arthur Connell had experienced successful cricket clubs during his time at Harrogate. The church he had come from is, to this day, opposite a large grassed area where sport is regularly played.

 *A St. Mark's CC result reported in August 1876.*

Research continues into the St. Mark's parish's first sporting activities but it is clear that the cricket club grew, and that during the 1870s frequent match reports appeared in the local newspapers for both a first team and a junior team. Beastow, together with another member of the Ashbury's Masonic Lodge James Moores, presided over the cricket meetings. Moores, it should be stressed was also a St. Mark's Church sidesman, and his brother played for the cricket team. Also worth highlighting that Beastow's son and stepson were appearing in the junior cricket team by the summer of 1879.

The cricket team seemed to prosper, particularly once the junior side became established. Beastow must have been pleased that progress was finally being made in establishing a positive spirit amongst some of the young men of the parish.

Despite the improvements, many of the area's problems were not going away. The visits Arthur Connell and his family made to households within the parish demonstrated the issues – domestic violence, poverty, alcoholism, hunger, gang warfare… and so it went on.

Crime was an issue, often punished hard. In January 1874 a West Gorton man named James Clarke was sentenced to three months in prison with hard labour for stealing a shirt from a clothes line. It was not the most serious of crimes but it indicated that the authorities felt they had to clamp down on behaviour like this. A much more worrying crime took place in October of that year when a nine year old boy stabbed 13 year old Telegraph Messenger and Clowes Street resident Arthur Robbins. Various explanations were suggested, but the upshot was that this was not perceived as a particularly unusual activity and was, perhaps, to be expected. Local newspapers carried many stories of violence, crime and domestic issues during the 1870s.

Clowes Street residents faced these issues daily. An example was given in the *Gorton Reporter* during April 1874 when it reported the story of Joseph Beard, a beer seller on Clowes Street. On Sunday 22nd March 1874 at 3.05pm a local named Jane Aldred was spotted knocking on Beard's door. The door opened and a bottle containing a pint of beer was handed to her in exchange for two pence. Although this may not sound too much of an issue, this was illegal trade taking place on a Sunday. The deal had been seen by a policeman. When constable Hartley confronted the beer seller later that day the seller offered him a five shillings bribe. The case went to court and the beer seller was fined 40 shillings for selling the beer (this would normally have been 20 shillings but it was not his first such offence) and 50 shillings for the attempted bribe.

Regardless of the way alcohol is viewed today, back in the 1870s it was a major issue affecting every area of life. Think of the devastating effect of drug addiction and related criminal activity on an area – that's how alcohol affected life in areas of West Gorton and Manchester in general.

In 1932 Sam Kirkman, who had returned from a period in the States, remembered that pubs and beer houses were plentiful and often violent in Clowes Street: "Tom Connors was a famous wrestler and kept a beer house in Clowes Street about fifty years ago. I have seen some rough houses in various parts of America, but [the roughest] I ever saw was when Connors kept this beer house."

The Connells, together with Beastow and some

Clowes Street.

of the other senior parishioners, tried to improve all aspects of West Gorton life. The "St. Mark's Mutual Improvement Society" was making significant progress during the 1870s, and by the end of 1877 a women's group was established by Georgina Connell, Arthur's youngest daughter, with much success. A few months later St. Mark's opened a new church hall to provide the community with a decent meeting place.

Arthur was working extremely hard at this time as he tried to tackle many issues. He also asked the church authorities if he could be provided with a curate to help manage his workload, but this was rejected. In 1878 the tone of articles in the local press suggested he was suffering with stress and related ailments. Despite this he ploughed on and, together with his family, took on more activities.

In 1879 Arthur set up soup kitchens and a relief fund. On its first day of operation in January 300 people queued for soup, bread and other food, and within a week over 1500 gallons of soup, 1000 loaves of bread and ten tons of coal had been distributed from the church. The *Gorton Reporter*, talked of parishioners milling around the church: "crowds of poor, famished-looking creatures pressed to that place, where soup and bread were provided in order to satisfy the cravings of nature."

That same year it seems Arthur's oldest daughter Anna discussed with William Beastow and Thomas Goodbehere the idea of forming a Working Men's club. Maybe this had been a long held intention of Arthur's and Anna thought she should try to make it happen.

Anna had been working as a Governess in Coppull, near Preston, during the early 1870s and maybe in the late 1860s. It's possible she only returned to West Gorton when her father's workload and stress levels increased. From 1879 she is mentioned in the local press often, suggesting that had she been in the parish earlier in the decade she would have been as active as she was afterwards. She is often mentioned in relationship to St. Mark's School, suggesting her Governess experience allowed Arthur to concentrate on some of the area's other concerns.

For Anna, the setting up of a Working Men's club seems to have been something she was determined to see work. Yet, as Beastow had seen earlier in the decade, the men were reticent, and only a handful turned up at the first few Tuesday night sessions. Anna persevered, knocking on doors in a bid to encourage attendance, and eventually, after considerable effort, the working men's meetings became popular. With Beastow's direct involvement in both the men's meetings and the cricket team it seems the two organisations could have worked together.

Progress was being made across the parish, but the Scuttling and some of the other issues were not going away.

In May 1879 the *Gorton Reporter* claimed that more than 500 young men had been involved in a battle a short distance from West Gorton in an area reported as Bradford-cum-Beswick which, in truth, was an area between West Gorton and the modern day Etihad Stadium. Another report from this period appeared in the *Ashton Reporter* under the title 'Openshaw V. Gorton'. The following extract describes the scenes close to Clowes St:

"According to one of the witnesses the bother commenced soon after breakfast and was on more or less all day. When Constable Wilson arrived on the scene, a little before Seven o'clock in the evening, he found gathered on one side of Gorton Brook some lads and lasses from Openshaw and on the opposite side of the brook a similar gang of lads and lasses belonging to Gorton. They were engaged in the delightful occupation of storming each other.

"Some of them, said the officer, had their belts off, but they were not sufficiently close to be able to use them. This is bad, but the state of terrorism excited by the scuttlers' conduct is worse. In explanation of the fact that rowdyism was allowed to go on for so long a time, it was stated that the people living in the vicinity were afraid to inform the police, as they know that the result would be that their windows would be broken.

"This will give to those people who happily live in districts where scuttling is unknown some idea of what it means."

Scuttling had plagued the east Manchester districts of West Gorton, Openshaw, and Bradford throughout the 1870s and 1880s. It had been a real menace throughout the developing years of the area. Almost two decades after Scuttling first plagued West Gorton the journalist Alexander Devine defined those involved and their

activities in a September 1890 *Manchester Guardian* article: "A scuttler is a lad, usually between the ages of 14 and 18, or even 19, and scuttling consists of the fighting of two opposed bands of youths, who are armed with various weapons."

Devine himself was a social pioneer. In 1887 he established a working lads' club in Hulme and performed voluntary work with disaffected youths across Manchester throughout the decade. He believed the Scuttlers were suffering from a Society that cared little for what happened to these young men. He tried to explain: "They go to work at twelve or thirteen years of age and during the day they are employed. But at night what becomes of them? They have no homes worthy of their name in which to spend their time; but are thrown on the streets or other less desirable places, exposed to all kinds of temptations, the victims for which crime and mischief of all kinds is hunting."

West Gortonian Sam Kirkman held similar views, though he himself seemed to come from a caring family. In 1931 he explained: "The combatants hailed from the badly-lighted slum districts of those days. There was nothing for the lads but the streets. No picture houses, no billiard halls. What could anyone expect?"

He added: "I am not sure but I sometimes think the lads of those days were much hardier and more tougher than the lads of today. Most of them would be at work at 6 o'clock in the morning, after, in some instances, a three or four miles walk to work. When the workman's trams started in 1877 they were a godsend to many."

In the 1880s and 1890s as scuttling became an issue across Manchester and Salford, Devine helped bring Scuttling to the attention of the wider population. Ultimately he helped improve the situation enormously. However, it appears that the West Gorton scuttles were more of an issue in the 1870s, before widespread efforts to tackle the problem with the formation of Lads clubs and so on.

William Beastow, Thomas Goodbehere, James Moores and the Connells and a few other key local figures seemed to search for activities for all members of the West Gorton community during the 1870s. This included activities to release aggression in a more productive manner than the Scuttles and, it was hoped, those activities aimed specifically at the men of the parish would help develop a strong community identity. The Scuttles had developed the wrong community identity, although whether those participating in the activity felt that is not certain.

For many of the Scuttlers the sense of belonging – replicated in gang warfare in the modern era and in football hooliganism in the Sixties to Eighties – that the fights brought meant that they had a cause to believe in. They fought for their turf and though the locals would rather they did not fight in their name, it is fair to say that some form of identity was being established. The aim had to be to focus the Scuttlers' attention on more worthwhile activities, and to develop a positive identity for the young men of the area to rally around.

The formation of the Working Men's Meetings and related activities encouraged by Anna Connell, William Beastow and Thomas Goodbehere clearly helped focus minds, but whether the meetings played any part in the sporting direction of the parish is not clear. It seems highly unlikely as the Cricket Club predated the meetings by over a decade, but it is true to say that through William Beastow both organisations received a consistent message and direction.

In November 1880 the cricketers – significantly the junior cricketers - played football for the first reported occasion.

It should be stressed that since 2005 much has been made of the role of Anna Connell in the formation of the football club, however extensive research by the author and by Paul Toovey, suggests that the football club evolved out of the cricket club, and not Anna's men's meetings. However, it is fair to say that every activity undertaken under the name St. Mark's was linked in some way and that the Connells would have been, at the very minimum, supportive.

In the author's earlier research and writing it was accurately reported that the football club had evolved out of the cricket club, but there was confusion over the origin of the cricket team. Based on research in the 1970s by Tony Heap, many earlier works suggested the cricket team was formed in 1879 directly from the Working Men's Meetings. However, Toovey's research proved it was in existence much earlier.

Further research has now identified that some games occurred within 19 months of St. Mark's 1865 consecration. As Tony Heap did not have access to this material when he was researching in the mid 1970s he reached the understandable assumption that the cricket team came out of the Men's Meetings due to the involvement of Beastow. However, evidence available in recent years has made it obvious that the cricket team predated the Men's Meetings.

Beastow appears to be the main consistent authoritative figure connected with St. Mark's sporting activities during the mid to late 1870s, but that does not mean he should be regarded as the founder. It emphasises the point that the Club was borne out of actions by a variety of individuals during those formative years.

Another figure who seemed to be involved throughout this period was James Moores. Moores, like Beastow, worked on a variety of initiatives within Gorton, including the Gorton Local Board Of Health, and he was also an active member of St. Mark's Church. He was also a freemason – his involvement with Ashbury's Masonic

Lodge predated Beastow's – and his name is linked to the cricket club and football club for several years. It is possible that Moores may have played cricket for St. Mark's like his brother.

Moores, Beastow and the players appear to be the only consistent figures in the development of St. Mark's sporting activities, but the environment the Connells created allowed these initiatives to develop.

By the late 1870s the cricket club had proved relatively successful. Its junior players were the same age as Sam Kirkman and, also, many of the people engaged in scuttling. Whether cricket could actually focus minds away from scuttling is not clear. In any case, it only kept the young men engaged during the summer months. What about the rest of the year?

Without labouring the point general church activities were unlikely to give the young men the excitement they craved. A long drawn out game of cricket would also seem unappealing to some of the young men, particularly those that needed the kind of buzz scuttling gave them. Someone clearly saw football as an activity that could prove a more attractive proposition.

Despite considerable research it has been impossible to say with certainty who came up with the idea of playing football. At this time Association Football was not widely known. Much is made of Newton Heath (Manchester United) being formed in 1878 but, as with the St. Mark's players, there is no evidence of any football activity taking place until November 1880 (one week after St. Mark's to be precise).

An article in the *Manchester Evening News* in 1890 suggested that Mancunians first became interested in football in 1878 when Manchester FC faced the famous Queen's Park side in a friendly, although the details of that meeting seem a little confused as Queen's Park's own sources show that they had arranged games with two other football sides – Birch and Arcadians in 1878 – but not Manchester FC. Significantly, Birch adopted association football when former Queen's Park player J Strang arrived in 1877.

1877-78 was actually the first to see a Manchester side enter the FA Cup, and there was also a high profile match between Manchester and Stoke. It is highly possible that this game, played in January 1878, was actually one that caused the residents of West Gorton to sit up and take notice of the association game as it actually occurred on the edge of the St. Mark's parish, close to the homes of some of the young boys who would ultimately play for St. Mark's football team.

The match was staged at the original Longsight Cricket ground on Albert Grove, the next street to the St. Mark's rectory, close to Kirkmanshulme Lane and only about 100 yards from the Connell family's residence in North Road.

According to reports there was "a large assembly of spectators" and it seems likely that at least one of the St. Mark's cricketers would have watched that match. This was not the first significant football match to be played in the area as in December 1876 the famous Sheffield side arrived at the original Longsight Cricket ground for their first ever match in Manchester. They also played Manchester, though the side was termed 'Manchester Association' for this match.

Only around 500 spectators watched the Manchester-Sheffield game due to exceptionally poor weather, but the *Sheffield Daily Telegraph* did report: "we feel certain that all who saw the match on Saturday were pleased with the play, and will not willingly miss another opportunity of being present if possible. With fine weather and good matches, there is no reason why association football should not in time be as popular and well supported in Manchester as it is now in Glasgow and Sheffield. The time may or may not be far distant, but eventually the brutal rough Rugby rules will give way before the more artistic and superior game adopted by the association."

Those words suggest that the residents of West Gorton may have been encouraged and influenced by these matches and others, such as when

FOOTBALL.

SHEFFIELD v. MANCHESTER.

The following is the Manchester team for this match, which will be played on the ground of the Longsight Cricket Club, Manchester, on Saturday next:—J. F. Richardson (goal), A. B. Potter (Eton), G. A. Jones (half backs), F. J. Haigh (back), S. G. Smith, Notts (captain), A. Mason (Shropshire Wanderers), T. A. C. Hampson (Oxford), J. A. Railton, jun. (Forest School), C. F. Edwards (Shropshire Wanderers), H. Ellis (Forest School), R. A. Thorp. Mr. C. Mason umpire.

NOTTS. F.C. v. MANCHESTER ASSOCIATION.—The Notts. F.C. journeyed over to Manchester last Saturday to try conclusions with the only Association club in that locality. Their train arrived somewhat late, and it was not until 3.50 p.m. that they kicked off from the Pavilion goal. The ground, situated at Longsight, was very bad, and also slippery, owing to its general damp character. The ball was well returned by Barnet (one of the Royal Engineers, stationed in Manchester), who dribbled most neatly throughout the match, and the game went on for some time in neutral territory, until good play by Schofield sent the ball behind the visitors' goal line. The latter then made one or two fruitless attacks on their opponents' stronghold, R. Greenhalgh sending the leather over the Manchester goal, and H. Cursham, after it had travelled all over the ground, at length succeeding in placing it between the posts. Smith then kicked off for the home contingent, when Mason and Railton showed some good play for Manchester, as did Oliver and H. Cursham for Notts., the latter player making an ineffectual shot at goal. Barnet then was to the fore, and all but scored for the home team; but H. Greenhalgh's goal keeping was too safe. After this Manchester secured a corner kick through some good play on the part of Smith, Jessop was now conspicuous by some long kicks for Nottingham, who soon gained a second corner kick, and afterwards a third, the latter being the result of a capital run by H. Cursham. After this Man-

Landmark matches on the edge of the St. Mark's parish in 1876 (top) and 1878 (bottom).

Nottinghamshire (Notts County) played Manchester there in February 1878.

Whether these games had a direct bearing is impossible to say, but it does seem likely that at least one of the St. Mark's cricketers, possibly Edward Kitchen who lived very close to the venue, or one of the more authoritative figures such as Beastow, Moores or maybe even one of the Connells was present at one of the matches.

Typically, football was a sport that developed through public schools and universities and was not an activity that most ordinary Mancunians or Gortonians would have participated in. However, someone involved with St. Mark's first game must have come up with the idea and that means the individual responsible must have known enough about the match to have been able to persuade the others to give it a try. There is a possibility that William Beastow or James Moores may have introduced the game, although that appears unlikely.

If the person who introduced the sport was one of the players then it has to be either someone present at those Manchester matches – worth recalling that both Sheffield and Stoke were viewed as major footballing sides who were seen as ambassadors and role models by many young men - or someone who knew about the sport who had recently moved into the area.

It is known that the first captain was William Sumner and that suggests he was able to guide the others in areas of team play, but that does not mean he actually came up with the idea of playing football. Nevertheless, his arrival in West Gorton around 1879 coincides with St. Mark's move into football.

Sumner was an engineering student lodging in Gorton by this point and was also a member of the St. Mark's cricket club. In later years Sumner also played for Manchester FC, and appeared for them in a FA Cup tie against Stoke in November 1883 and possibly was in the squad that travelled to Queen's Park for the first FA Cup tie ever held in Scotland that same season.

Genealogist Glen Midgley has been researching Sumner's life, and that of the other members of the Club's formative years, and has uncovered the details of his family life and career. Midgley has discovered that Sumner was born on 21st December 1860 and that he was from the Barton area.

The facts of his early life suggest he was as likely to suggest the game of football as many of the other original players, however Midgley believes that he may have had genetic leadership skills. Certainly, the other players looked upon Sumner as a true leader.

As with so many football clubs it seems unlikely that the specific person who introduced football to St. Mark's will ever be properly identified. Perhaps that's how it should be because the Club succeeded because of many,

many individuals. It would be unfair to specifically credit any individual as the founder or the one who created the football team.

Little factual evidence exists of discussions taken and attempts made during this period. Any records that did exist at St. Mark's have long since vanished. It is known that detailed records of all parish activities were kept, but as the parish magazine did not exist until 1883, there is nothing publicly available other than comments in local newspapers and personal diaries. The *Gorton Reporter* provides a good commentary on the parish's activities, although sporting activities tended to take a back seat as far as journalists were concerned.

Most histories of the Blues prior to 1997, and some since, claim the Club's first pitch was on Clowes Street itself. This seems unlikely as most of the Clowes Street area was already occupied by housing and industry by 1880.

The initial match report talks of the first reported game taking place in Longsight, but that seems to be a red herring based on the location of the St. Mark's rectory at the time. This appears to be merely confusion on the part of the newspapers involved as the rectory was actually at 17 North Road, Longsight (in an area south of Belle Vue). It is probable that all communication in relation to the football club was sent with the rectory address at the head of all correspondence.

As stated in *Manchester The Greatest City* (1997) the first true clue of where the ground could have been comes from the *Book Of Football* published in 1905. This states that the site of the first pitch had been developed between 1881 and 1905 into Brooks & Doxey's Union Ironworks. Maps from the period show that the only possible location for the first game was on land immediately north of St. Mark's Church on Thomas Street (present day Wenlock Way), a road running parallel to Clowes Street. The site now forms part of the car park for the former ICL/Fujitsu office block and was in the 1880s part of the Union Ironworks complex.

After detailed research in the mid-1990s for *Manchester The Greatest City* the conclusion was reached that this was the site of the first pitch. Maps from the late 1880s show sufficient land next to the original factory for a football pitch.

This land at Brooks & Doxey's was certainly an extremely short walk from the church, and so could easily have been the Club's first pitch. It is highly likely the players themselves would have changed in the Church, or its schoolroom, and been able to walk along William Street – the road St. Mark's actually faced on to – to the land.

Comments by Sam Kirkman in 1931 seem to support this view. As *Manchester The Greatest City* first suggested, this site formed part of Brooks & Doxey's Union Ironworks where William Beastow was employed.

Kirkman: "Brooks & Doxey's covers a lot more ground than it did when I was serving my time. On the left or Hyde Road side there was what we called 'Farmer's Field'. It was then railed round and kept under cultivation. To the right there was open ground up to the works of Messrs Pearn's. It was on this ground where boxing and wrestling took place at night."

Kirkman goes on to explain that the fights were popular: "I well remember a fight there one Sunday morning with the leader of another gang of young fellows. It was a big attraction for the residents of Thomas Street. There were houses all along the other side. There was soon a crowd and a ring made, and it was a good fight while it lasted."

Ignoring the violence, the confirmation that this space was utilised for entertainment, spectator events and sporting activity also fits with a newspaper report from April 1879. The article suggests it was a regular hang-out area for the young men and women of the area and potentially it may have been used by the St. Mark's cricket team as well. Under the headline "One lad stabbed by another at cricket", the unfortunate story was told of violence between West Gorton youngsters. A 14 year old was stabbed by a 15 year old on this site: "the lads were playing cricket along with some others in a field behind Thomas Street."

Although after almost three decades of research I have yet to prove conclusively where this first pitch was, it is my opinion that the Brooks & Doxey's land referred to by Kirkman was the Club's first pitch. William Beastow and the young players will have been aware of the potential of the land. It has to be remembered that in 1880 this land was nothing more than wasteland, but it was enough to allow the fledgling club to play its first reported game there on 13th November 1880. The first opponents were the Baptist church from Macclesfield.

The pitch markings would have been questionable – reports from later in the decade suggest local residents knew about rugby but not association football – nevertheless the game itself was a major achievement.

The first known game was staged on a pitch that contained goal posts with a tape across the posts to form the goal – common practice at the time. It was played between sides containing twelve players each. This may have been to accommodate all those who arrived with the Macclesfield side, or it may have simply been agreed some time in advance. It doesn't really matter as it was the game itself that was important. It does show however that football as we know it today could not have been imagined back in 1880.

A brief report, probably submitted by either James Moores, William Beastow or one of the players, appeared in the *Gorton Reporter*. A review of that newspaper's sports coverage makes it clear that the attempts by William Beastow and the players to stage the first game must have been great as none of the other match reports detailed under the heading 'Football' refer to Association Football. All the other 'football' matches reported are rugby football games featuring local sides – Reddish, Failsworth Rangers, Newton Heath Rovers, Newton Heath, Blackley, Sandfield Hornets, and St. Mary's (Failsworth). This suggests that football was very much the minor sport despite the occasional visits from the well known Sheffield and Stoke clubs to the area. Rugby remained the area's key winter activity.

As the opponents for St. Mark's first known game came from another church it suggests contacts via the religious community may have helped identify another potential group of footballers. However, the Macclesfield side were Baptists not Church of England.

St. Mark's was very much a local side for local people, similar in many ways to a present day pub team. The idea of bringing together the young men of the area and to use football as a release from the pressures of the world's first industrial city seemed to work from the first game onwards. That first known game, a 2-1 defeat, was staged at 3.15pm on 13th November 1880.

A couple of Cheshire based newspapers including the *Cheshire County News* carried much more detailed reports. These reports were headed "Baptist V St. Mark's, Longsight" but it is clearly the West Gorton club. As mentioned earlier, during its first few seasons match reports occasionally referred to Longsight either in the side's name or as the venue for a match.

From the Macclesfield-based report it has been identified that St. Mark's took an early lead with the historic first goalscorer being James Collinge. It should be recorded that both Collinge's parents had passed away at some point between 1869 and 1881 and that, together with his elder sister – 21 year old Martha – James took on responsibility for the family. It is known that in 1880 three of James' siblings were aged 11, 14 and 16. Life was hard for the Collinges and James' involvement with St. Mark's football team must have helped him find a brief escape from some of the pressures he faced.

By simply staging St. Mark's first recorded football game many of the aims of William Beastow, James Moores, the Connells and others were satisfied.

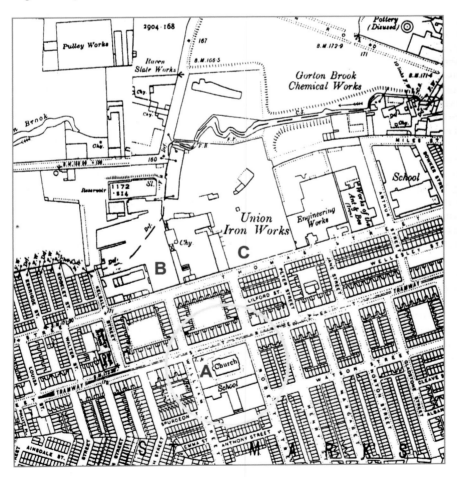

A 1905 map of the Clowes Street area showing (A) St. Mark's Church & school and the site of (B) Farmer's Field and the recreation space (C) where sporting activities took place. Over time both (B) and (C) were covered by Union Iron Works buildings but in 1880 both these areas were undeveloped and (C) is the most likely location of the St. Mark's first pitch.

TRUE BLUES
The first twelve

The historic first twelve, with an indication of their age (based on census material) were:

Charles Beastow (18)

Born in Hulme as Charles Frederick Cooper in 1862. The adopted son of William Beastow who was occasionally known by his original name in St. Mark's match reports. He also reverted back to Cooper when he married James Moores' daughter in 1888.

William Sumner (19)

An engineering student who performed the role of captain.

Frederick Hopkinson (18)

Born 22nd Sep 1862 in West Gorton, but baptised in Clitheroe where his family had lived before he was born.

Walter Chew (15)

Born April 1865 in Hulme.

Henry Heggs (21)

Born on 14th July 1859 as Alfred Henry Heggs, but known as Henry, in Barton St Mary, Gloucestershire.

William Downing (19)

Born first quarter of 1861 at Bramhall.

Richard Hopkinson (21)

Born 20th February 1859 in Clitheroe.

Edward Kitchen (18)

Born 13th July 1862 at Woods Moor, Bramhall.

Archibald MacDonald (20)

An iron moulder.

John Pilkington (17)

Born during 1863 in Manchester.

John Beastow (18)

William Beastow's son, born in 1862 in Manchester.

James Collinge (18)

Born 1862 in Heywood.

There is a little uncertainty over **Archibald MacDonald**. In match reports he is recorded as A MacDonald, and the only person matching that name of the right age range is Archibald MacDonald. If this is true then he is the only member of the team living outside of the West Gorton area when the 1881 census was taken. Paul Toovey's research has identified another possible player – Alexander McDonald. This 'A McDonald' was a 16 year old cooper living in Ancoats. However, as Archibald was an iron moulder it seems more likely that he may have been in contact with William Beastow or even been employed at the Union Ironworks.

BAPTIST v. ST. MARK'S LONGSIGHT.—A very pleasant and exciting game was played between the above clubs on Saturday last, at Longsight, near Belle Vue. The Longsight captain winning the toss, elected to play against the wind. The ball was set in motion at 3-15 by the Baptist captain. The Longsight forwards soon settled to work, and in a very few minutes were rewarded for their exertions by scoring the first goal, which was made by Collinge. The ball being again started, the Baptist men played more carefully, and, after a few unsuccessful shots at goal, W. Potts got possession of the ball, and running it up shot the ball in the centre of the goal, where Hornby, who was in waiting, very cleverly passed it under the tape, thus making matters equal. Both sides now strove hard to gain supremacy, the ball travelling rapidly from one end of the field to the other, Hornby and Taylor making themselves the most conspicuous by the neat way in which they passed their opponents. The Longsight men still kept working hard, H. Heggs and R. Pilkington especially. Wallworth, now getting possession, passed to Hornby, who made a shot which was well stopped by Sumner. The Baptist forwards now rushed the ball up, and one of the Longsight team kicking it behind, resulted in a corner kick for the Baptist, which was entrusted to W. Pott, who shot the ball right in the centre again, where Bickerstaff breasted the ball in, thus making the second goal for the Baptist. Shortly afterwards the Longsight men got a corner kick, but failed to score from it. A few minutes afterwards half-time was called, when ends being changed the Longsight men exerted themselves still more to make matters equal, but with very little success, Pilkington made a good shot, which, however, did not score. A very close and exciting scrimmage now took place in Baptist quarters lasting over five minutes, which was ended by Bennett sending the ball right away. H. Heggs, however, soon brought it back again by an excellent run up the side, passing four of the Baptist men in succession; just as he was going to deliver the ball he was charged and the ball taken from him, and returned to the Longsight end, where Hornby made another shot which just flew over the tape. Time getting short, the Longsight men worked strenuously, and getting near to the Baptist goal, Kitchen made a shot which fell wide by about a yard. Scrimmages now became the order of the day, during one of which time was called, leaving the Baptist winners by two goals to one.

BOLLINGTON v. MANCHESTER WANDERERS, 2ND TEAM. —This match was played at Bollington on Saturday last, and resulted in a victory for the home team by six goals

A thirteenth young member of the St. Mark's parish, **William Hardy** (20, occupation was as a striker at the ironworks), performed the role of Umpire. There were two umpires who controlled the game with both sides providing one each.

Frederick and Richard Hopkinson were brothers and their father, Richard Hopkinson senior, was a senior member of the St. Mark's congregation and played the organ for the church. William Beastow's son John and his stepson Charles were both key members of the side.

It is interesting to note that the majority of players were under the age of twenty and that they had, in the main, been born in Manchester, although the majority of their parents had been born away from Manchester. This suggests that the aim of creating an organisation to help unite and develop a community spirit within the West Gorton area, and to give the young men of the parish something to focus on were achieved to some extent with the first game.

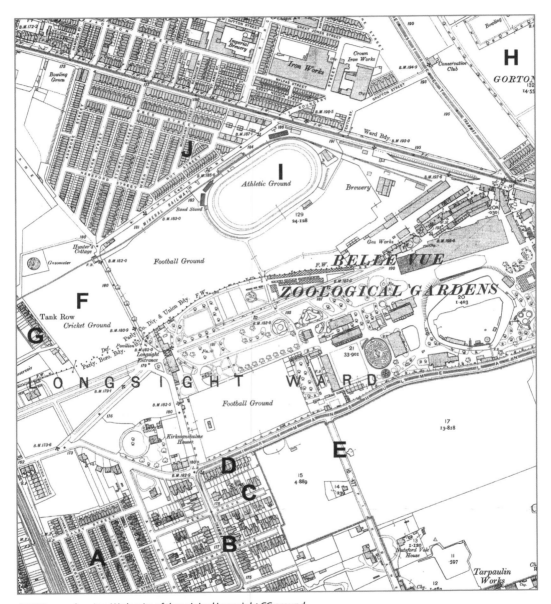

A 1905 map showing (A) the site of the original Longsight CC ground,
(B) St. Mark's Rectory, (C) & (D) addresses where Lawrence Furniss lived,
(E) Pink Bank Lane (ground somewhere on Pink Bank Lane in 1884-85),
(F) Kirkmanshulme CC (ground 1881-1882), (G) Edward Kitchen lived
at number 4, (H) Queen's Road ground (1882-84), (I) 1889 Floodlit
Manchester derby played here and (J) site of the former Belle Vue Gaol.

1880-1887
On The Move

"Like many famous organisations, Manchester City began in a small way. It came into existence in the year 1880, and the father of the club was Mr. W. Chew... The first field was situated just off Clowes Street – the site is now covered by Messrs. Brooks & Doxey's works."

Comment on the first season, from the *Book Of Football* (1905)

1880-1881 The First Season

Two weeks after the first known game St. Mark's staged their second reported match. They managed a goalless draw with a team called Arcadians from Harpurhey, one of two ambitious sides that two years earlier had managed to persuade Queen's Park to travel from Scotland to face them. In between St. Mark's first two known fixtures the young men had been occupied with practice sessions in their free time. It is not known who organised these or how often they took place, but it is likely that captain William Sumner took the lead role.

Those sessions gave the young men a focus and, who knows, maybe games were staged between various groups from St. Mark's and the Clowes Street area. For many in the vicinity the game of football would still have been an odd pursuit, but by staging the first match and

then performing the training sessions Sumner and the others would have provoked interest. Football would have seemed rather exciting in comparison with the slower local activities of cricket and rugby, although Scuttling and bare-knuckle fighting would continue to provide a buzz for some. Sadly, match reports were inconsistent in their reporting and line ups are not known for every game, so it is impossible to gauge if interest grew immediately or over time.

To date newspaper reports have been identified for nine matches that season, with the last known game taking place at Stalybridge on 19th March 1881. This was actually the Club's first victory but the home side, Stalybridge Clarence, could only find eight of their regular players. Three volunteers from the crowd filled the positions and, by half time, the makeshift Clarence side were leading by a single goal. Not surprising really as one of the players drafted from the crowd was actually a player called Booth who captained Broadbottom.

Richard Hopkinson turned the game round for the Gortonians with a couple of quick goals - the first after a neat dribble along the right wing and the second direct from a corner. James Collinge scored a third for St. Mark's, while the match report credited the captain Sumner and goalkeeper Kitchen as the side's 'men of the match'. St. Mark's won the game 3-1.

The first season's playing record was: Played 9, Won 1, Drawn 3, Lost 5, Goals For 5 & Goals Against 23

It is impossible to say for certain that this was the Club's complete match record but it does give a fair reflection of the season's progress.

1881-1882 Keeping Faith

By the start of the cricket season discussions would have taken place on the significance of football to the cricketers and the wider public. William Beastow and James Moores, as the Club's two senior figures, would have discussed with the young men the advantages of football. They would, undoubtedly, have discussed the achievements of the side's first football season with Arthur Connell and, potentially, with his eldest daughter Anna via the Working Men's Meetings.

As with the formation of the Club, the decision to continue must have been considered at length by a variety of individuals. Captain William Sumner and Frederick Hopkinson, who was acting as secretary, would have felt significant progress had been made on the pitch, especially after the Stalybridge victory, while William Beastow and James Moores would have been encouraged by the social implications of what the Club was achieving. It is known that 18 players appeared in the Club's first reported nine games, while others acted as umpires. This was proof that football could help to keep the young men occupied to an extent and away from negative, perhaps destructive, activities.

During the summer of 1881 a decision was taken to move to a more professional playing surface. They selected the Kirkmanshulme Cricket Club ground, a five acre site on Redgate Lane, close to the large Belle Vue Zoological Gardens. Edward Kitchen, one of the players from the first game and an important figure in the running of the Club, lived next to the cricket ground at 4 Tank Row and it seems likely he was the player who first suggested the location. He would have walked past it every day and may have known committeemen and others connected with Kirkmanshulme C.C.

The venue was like many other cricket grounds with a pavilion and possibly a few benches for spectators, but that would have been it as far as facilities were concerned. Nevertheless, this was still better than the Club's first home.

The playing surface would have been far superior to the original pitch, at least until the footballers started to use it. In one of St. Mark's games during the inaugural season of 1880-81, the *Reporter* newspaper highlighted that the ground was "in a very sloppy state, and consequently the falls were very numerous." That game ended with the season's heaviest defeat - a 7-0 drubbing by Hurst from Ashton-Under-Lyne - and probably the most embarrassing day for the embryonic club. If St. Mark's wanted to achieve a good image, the players could not afford to be humiliated either on the pitch or because of the pitch.

At the cricket ground, the Club are known to have played a total of twelve games during the 1881-82 season. Those matches included the first meetings with Newton Heath. On the anniversary weekend of St. Mark's first reported game, 12th November 1881, the two sides met for the first time. The game, played at North Road, Newton Heath, attracted an attendance of around 3,000 (according to details recorded many years later).

The 'Heathens', who went on to become Manchester United in 1902, defeated West Gorton (St. Mark's) 3-0 in what was described as a 'pleasant game'. I wonder what the reporter would make of 21st Century derby matches! Two goals were scored in the first half, one being an own goal by one of West Gorton's 'backs'. It is not reported who scored the goal, all the *Ashton Reporter* match report says is that the player was "attempting to stop a shot by E. Thomas".

One of the significant aspects of the way this game was reported which has created some confusion over the years concerns the Club's name. It was recorded as West Gorton (St. Mark's) as opposed to St.Mark's (West Gorton) and that change has caused some to suggest that the church were unhappy in some way with the Club. There was a suggestion that the Club was attracting players from outside of the parish and that was an issue, but none of this now appears to be correct. The church appeared to be happy with the way the side was developing and, if anything, the selection of Kirkmanshulme Cricket ground actually meant the team were playing fairly close to the St. Mark's rectory. The move potentially increased the opportunity for spreading the church's work and that may be why the person sending in the match reports to the local newspaper changed the emphasis.

The week after the first meeting with Newton Heath, West Gorton achieved their first victory of the season with St. Mark's parishioner John Pilkington providing the only goal – "during a tight scrimmage Pilkington made a splendid shot, which the goalkeeper was unable to stop" - in the away game with Arcadians.

The Arcadians were continually having to defend as the St. Mark's men put in their best attacking display so far. They even had a goal disallowed: "the ball striking

Modern day Gorton Park on the site of the Club's ground from 1882-84. This is the only former home still being used for football.

the cross-bar, and fell in a slanting position, which the goalkeeper then knocked back into play. The West Gorton appeal for a goal was, however, disallowed by the Arcadians' umpire."

The year ended with a 3-0 defeat at Broadbottom on New Year's Eve. The fact that Gorton only managed to field nine players appears to be the reason why the match was so one sided especially as, only two months later, the home fixture between the two clubs ended 3-0 in West Gorton's favour. It is fair to say however that the St. Mark's men were rather inconsistent.

On 14th January they defeated Haughton Dale 8-1, with James Collinge scoring a remarkable five goals, yet two weeks later were embarrassed by a 6-0 defeat at Hurst. It has to be explained that Hurst were one of the region's better sides and that in 1883 they became the region's third, after Manchester FC and Birch FC, to enter the FA Cup. In comparison the West Gorton (St. Mark's) side was still coming to terms with football. Many of the players had only played the occasional game and some were merely St. Mark's parishioners who, to be frank, should never have walked onto a football pitch. These people, though, were the life of the Club. They raised funds and performed many of the supportive tasks, organising away games for example, and therefore had a right to participate in the games. Without them West Gorton (St. Mark's) would have died.

The only other game worth noting in the Club's second season was the return match with Newton Heath

at the Kirkmanshulme Cricket ground. Gorton gained revenge for the 3-0 defeat in their first encounter, as they overturned Newton Heath 2-1. Gorton had managed to take the lead, via Charles Beastow, as early as the eighth minute, and then had to hold off the Heathens who had been awarded a couple of consecutive corners. The second actually lead to Gorton's second goal. James Collinge obtained possession in front of the Gorton goal then proceeded to run the full length of the pitch, before sending the ball flying between the Heathens' posts amid loud cheering.

The score remained 2-0 until late in the game when, according to reports, the Heathens baffled the home 'keeper Edward Kitchen by performing several good passes before the ball entered the goal. Exactly how baffled Kitchen was we don't know, but we do know that this game was well attended.

Years later the attendance that day was reported as 'around 5,000', although it would be unfair and ridiculous to suggest that this was the actual attendance. It seems incredible that around a sixth of Gorton's population would have been able to attend a game which, at that point, was not regarded as a 'derby' or an important fixture whatsoever. Nevertheless. it does provide an indication that West Gorton (St. Mark's) were becoming popular.

The Club still appeared to be part of the St. Mark's Cricket Club. It certainly did not appear to be a separate organisation at this point. A month after the Club's final reported football match of the 1881-82 season both William Beastow and James Moores talked of the advantages engaging in healthy activities such as cricket and football could bring. This event, held on 15th April 1882, marked the opening of the cricket season but it seems likely that for some it also marked the end of the football season. The two are hard to separate at this stage in the Club's development.

According to legend, the Kirkmanshulme C.C. asked the footballers to find another ground around this time as their playing surface had been badly damaged, or at least they felt that it was no longer the perfect pitch you would expect for a gentlemanly game of cricket. Maybe damage had been caused by the large attendance at the Newton Heath game, West Gorton's last at the ground, or maybe it was simply because of the general wear and tear on the pitch, who knows. It is known though that West Gorton (St. Mark's) were now desperate for a new ground - any ground!

1882-1883 A Bit Parky!

The whole of Gorton was still expanding rapidly. New streets were being established all the time, while various factories and industry to support the railways were providing employment for the increasing population. In fact the only area of Gorton not growing was the amount of land available for recreational activities, thus making it exceptionally difficult for West Gorton (St. Mark's) to find the perfect venue.

It is at this point where the history of the Club became confused over the years and there is still some uncertainty. Match reports cannot be found for all games, while various early club histories, newspaper articles and even the memories of those involved had conflicting information. Some grouped activities over several seasons into a simple paragraph suggesting the Club cut all ties with St. Mark's, moved to a new pitch and merged with another team. Some of this confusion has been – and continues to be - repeated in authoritative football literature.

We know that the Club moved to land off Queen's Road, approximately three quarters of a mile east of Clowes Street, along the Hyde Road. The venue was occasionally reported as 'Clemington Park' in the local *Reporter* newspaper, but it was a very basic area of land. In 1930 Fred Johnson in *Manchester City Football Club – A Souvenir History* briefly explained why this rather open and undeveloped area of land was given grander names from time to time: "The 'official reporter' of the Club, calling largely upon his imagination, styled the scene of their operations 'Clemington Downs'. However, in later years it did blossom into a public park."

Johnson's was the first history of City and was followed by David Williams' *Famous Football Clubs*

- *Manchester City* booklet published in the 1940s. According to Williams "A West Gorton club, playing in Scarlet and Black, had got going in Queen's Road, West Gorton, however, and the pitchless St. Mark's men threw in their lot there. In later years this ground developed into a park, but it looked more 'parky' than anything else in those days."

Williams' mention of scarlet and black and his comments about the St. Mark's men joining another West Gorton side adds some mystery to the Club's story. Johnson's book also talks of those colours and, as if emphasising the uncertainty, his commentary also suggests that those colours belonged to a team that the St. Mark's men joined, rather than being a team that followed a merger: "The Club wound up its career after a short season on the Kirkmanshulme cricket ground. Prior to this, however, some other pioneer enthusiasts for the Association game had started the West Gorton club (colours: scarlet and black), their ground being in Queen's Road, West Gorton; and several former St. Mark's players joined."

Although Johnson consulted Walter Chew, who by 1930 was treasurer of the Manchester FA, the information concerning the scarlet and black wearing West Gorton side that some of the St. Mark's men joined does not appear to link up with information available in 2012. Chew was one of the Club's key figures in 1882, but evidence suggests there was no merger in 1882.

It is known that the Club played at least four home games at Queen's Road during 1882-3. The last of these matches came on 24th February 1883 when West Gorton (St. Mark's) defeated Middleton 1-0.

By this time Walter Chew was the side's captain, taking over from William Sumner when he was injured in a 1-1 draw at Marple on 2nd December 1882. It was a sad loss to the Club as Sumner had been the guiding light, as far as the players were concerned, throughout the opening years. He was undoubtedly a talented player and went on to appear for Manchester FC. He also appeared in a very significant FA Cup tie for his new side which saw Stoke defeated 2-1 in November 1883.

Sumner's injury was one of a number of issues during the season. The Club struggled to make a complete team for four of the known ten games played. The reason is unclear but it is known that another side, Belle Vue Rangers, was in existence and that some of the St. Mark's men played for that team. In fact a player by the name of W Chew was recorded as the captain of Rangers when it appeared in the local press the previous season. It is fair to assume that this was Walter Chew, however one Rangers' game in January 1882 (away at Hurst Park Road) took place on the same day as Chew is also reported to have played a home game for West Gorton. Walter did have a brother William who was appearing for West Gorton (St. Mark's) at this time, so it's

TRUE BLUE
Walter Chew

When Walter Chew passed away in 1948 he was described as the founder by some reporters. David Homer, a member of the Club's Maine Road ground committee for many years and whose own family involvement with the Blues stretches back over several generations, met Chew at games: "I can remember sitting next to Walter Chew during the war when I sat with my Dad immediately behind the Ground Committee Box at Maine Road. We sat in the front row of a small section of about 12 seats in B Block. All I can remember was that he was very old – he'd have been about eighty and I was not yet a teenager of course. He was greatly respected and well known. He seemed to be a good friend of my Grandpa. He used to talk about the early days and of football in general, but it is my regret that at that age I didn't listen as eagerly as I would do now. I only wish - knowing what I know now - that I had paid more attention!"

possible the two players were listed as W Chew in games when only one of them appeared.

In 1882-83 match reports for both sides suggest 'W Chew' was Walter and from the games known to have occurred there appears to be no clash - he either appeared for West Gorton or for Belle Vue Rangers. Other St. Mark's players appeared for Rangers during 1882-83 were Edward Kitchen, Edward Groves and Edward Bower.

1883-1884 Emerging Facts

Although there does not appear to have been a merger in 1882-83, research by the author Paul Toovey in 2008 suggests there was a merger the following year. Toovey was the first modern historian to piece together a view of what seems to have occurred.

During 1883 Walter Chew and Edward Kitchen, as two of the most prominent players for West Gorton (St. Mark's) and Belle Vue Rangers, appear to be the main figures behind a merger of the clubs. This appears to be the merger referred to by both Johnson and Williams, but whether the side wore scarlet and black is open to debate. Both men talked of the side that the St. Mark's men joined as wearing scarlet and black, and it's possible the shirt colours remained post-merger. But we cannot be certain that the merged West Gorton wore those

colours. It is fair to assume that as these colours were specifically mentioned in 1930 – 47 years after they may have been worn - and that Johnson discussed the early years with Chew that these were accurate. Although it has to be stressed that both Johnson's and Williams' books do contain other errors or conflicting information from this period.

Whatever kit was worn, on 6th October 1883 the first reported game following the merger saw the newly named West Gorton defeat Hurdsfield 4-3. The name reflected the fact that the side no longer claimed to be part of St. Mark's church in any shape or form. It seems that transition had occurred during the previous season. Some St. Mark's men continued to play for the Club, which fielded two teams, and other players would have lived within the parish, but the organisation was no longer seen as part of the church, or indeed the St. Mark's Cricket Club. It had a life of its own.

Two days after the merged Club's first reported game the *Manchester Courier* included a small piece about William Sumner joining Manchester but it also suggested all West Gorton football activity was over: "I am informed that Sumner who played for West Gorton last season, and which club has broken up, will play for Manchester Association next Saturday against Macclesfield, and his services will add greatly to the strength of the club."

Despite this report West Gorton continued to play and correspondence appeared in the newspaper over the following weeks from the Club's committee, including a letter from P. Howarth of 201 Yew Tree Terrace, the honorary secretary of the merged club. Considering the letters and commentary that supports those pieces it does seem fair to assume that West Gorton was the newly merged side.

There is proof that West Gorton played at least 16 games in 1883-84 (Johnson claims there were 20) with seven of those being played at Queens Road (present day Gorton Park). The final home match of the season saw West Gorton defeat Gorton Villa 7-0 in a game that was now perceived as the Club's main derby match, although it appears to be the only meeting between the two clubs. No doubt two progressive sides from the same district would have met again that season, unfortunately no evidence exists to say they did.

> **WEST GORTON ASSOCIATION FOOTBALL CLUB.**
> *To the Editor of the Manchester Courier.*
>
> Sir,—From what source "Dribbler" gets his information I can't tell, but it is "quite wrong." At the beginning of the present season several of the older members of the West Gorton club notified their intention of giving up the game, whilst others left the club to join another. The Belle Vue Rangers then cast off their name, and joined with the remaining members of the West Gorton club, thus keeping the club from breaking up, so that there is no hankering about it. With this I hope "Dribbler" will be satisfied.—Yours, &c.,
> P. HOWARTH, Hon. Sec.
> 201, Yew Tree-terrace, Gorton-lane, Gorton, Oct. 29.

Gorton AFC in 1884. The man on the far right is believed to be William Beastow. The man sat next to him with a beard and holding a cane is Richard Peacock. It appears that the first player on the back row (far left) is Lawrence Furniss and that Edward Kitchen is sat on the left of the middle row. James Moores is possibly the man in the lighter suit.

There were other notable highs, including a 2-1 victory over Bentfield which brought an end to their two year unbeaten run, but also a few concerns. In January the Queens Road pitch was reported as being unfit for football being "five to six inches deep in mud" but the game actually went ahead because there was "great interest in the game." Another match saw Furness Vale Rovers leave the pitch 15 minutes before the game's official end because West Gorton had dared to question the legitimacy of a Furness goal.

These issues were typical of most games at the time, and it demonstrates that even after four seasons of local football the game was still developing. Something else that seemed to be developing was the Club's support. It is difficult to know with absolute certainty what level of support the side was getting, but one report talks of 600 spectators being present.

When the season ended those that had previously been with St. Mark's, primarily Walter Chew and Edward Kitchen, seem to have considered their future. The reasons are unclear. Maybe the merger caused friction between the members of the two former clubs' committees, and thus made team selection extremely difficult. Maybe the social aspects that had encouraged the creation of the St. Mark's team in the first place had somehow become lost somewhere in the process.

It is worth noting that, while the future of the side seemed unclear, steps were being taken locally to formalise football in the region. According to a *Manchester Evening News* article in 1890, the Manchester & District Football Association was first suggested in May 1884. Apparently, a meeting was held in which representatives of all Manchester's leading clubs took place. Those representatives were Manchester, Levenshulme, Hurst, Hurst Clarence, Greenheys, Dalton Hall and Hurst Park Road. Neither Newton Heath (Manchester United) or West Gorton (City) were considered to be of sufficient stature at that first meeting. Ultimately, both clubs did become affiliated to the Manchester FA when it was properly constituted.

This season did also provide an interesting connection with the Club's later incarnation as Manchester City. On 16th February 1884 West Gorton won 5-1 at Greenheys but the significant point, as far as the Blues' history is concerned, is that Greenheys home ground was on Dog Kennel Lane – the road that would soon be renamed Maine Road. The ground appears to have been located close to the site of modern day Claremont Road school and this means that West Gorton played at Maine Road almost 60 years before City moved there.

1884-1885 Black Kit

Looking back it is difficult to say with certainty how the Club was structured during this period, but when West Gorton's first reported game of the 1884-85 season took place Edward Kitchen was not listed as a first team player. That game was staged on 4th October and former St. Mark's men Walter Chew, Edward Bower and Edward Groves were listed. It is possible Kitchen was a member of the squad of course, however an announcement in the *Gorton Reporter* on 25th October 1884 suggests Kitchen was the key figure behind a demerger of the West Gorton club: "The members of the old West Gorton Association Football Club have pulled together and, with the assistance of a few other players, have formed a new club under the name of 'Gorton Association'. A suitable ground has been secured near Belle Vue Station. Mr E Kitchen, Railway Cottages, Longsight has been appointed secretary. He is arranging matches for both first and second teams."

A similar notice appeared in other newspapers including one of the main sporting 'papers of the day *The Umpire*. This suggests that ambition was high.

Kitchen and the other St. Mark's men reformed the Club, following the demerger, under a more ambitious title of Gorton Association Football Club. This is another significant moment in the development of the football club and the steps that followed need to be properly recognised as a defining moment in the growth of the club that was eventually to become Manchester City.

Before pursuing the Gorton AFC story further, it's worth pausing to highlight what happened to the men left at Queens Road. Over the following couple of years they renamed the club West Gorton Athletic, recorded as taking place in 1885 by Manchester FA material although the *Athletic News* claimed the team was known as West Gorton, and moved to land close to the Gorton Brook Hotel at the top of Clowes Street. Records show that in 1885 the secretary was Thomas Allen, a resident of Thomas Street and a former team mate of Chew at the start of the 1884-85 season. By 1887 the side was playing at Church Lane, Gorton and used the New Inn on Gorton Lane as their headquarters. It is also recorded that they wore a kit of red and white quarters in 1887.

The demerged Gorton AFC's new ground was, like so many other venues of the period, a piece of local wasteland. It was positioned off Pink Bank Lane, not too far from the St. Mark's rectory on the southern side of the Belle Vue Gardens. It had been suggested by 26 year old forward – and St. Mark's Church regular - Lawrence Furniss. Over the following sixty years, Furniss was to become one of the most influential men driving the Club forward.

With Furniss' knowledge of the land (he lived nearby), and a few negotiations with the landlord,

A reproduction shirt commissioned by the Manchester City Experience in 2005 to mark the 125th anniversary of the first reported game.

Gorton AFC were able to move forward. An annual rent of £6 was set and Edward Kitchen was free to organise fixtures.

Around this time Gorton took the first step towards organised football by applying to join the newly formed Manchester & District Football Association. It cost them 10 shillings and sixpence to do so, but it was money well spent as Gorton were moving forward. For the first real moment in their history it seems as if the Club were making sensible plans for the future of the Club. In the past the purpose had been to provide worthy activities, and so simply playing sport was the achievement. Now, with a little careful planning over the following years, Gorton aimed to be at the forefront of Manchester football.

This new ambition may suggest that the Club's original community roots were now forgotten or an irrelevance, but this was not the case. In fact 1884 brought all of those original motives back but now the focus was to be on the whole of Gorton, not simply the parish of St. Mark's or West Gorton. This point is emphasised by the involvement of William Beastow, James Moores and one of Gorton's most significant figures Richard Peacock. Peacock, along with Charles Beyer (who contributed significant funds to aid the building of St. Mark's Church and school), was a founder of the renowned engineering firm of Beyer-Peacock. He was to become the MP for Gorton in the 1885 General Election and, significantly, he contributed to almost every area of Gorton life in one way or another. One of his contributions was a sum of £5 to Gorton AFC during its first season - this was substantial when it's considered that the Club's expenses that year were to total nine pounds and sixpence and that all other income came to approximately the same amount as Peacock had donated.

It seems Peacock may have been more involved than that and his contributions to the Club were recognised when he appeared on the Club's first known team photograph.

It is worth noting that the community aspect of the Club was significant once more. Several of the original St. Mark's church and school figures were involved in Gorton AFC, while the senior committee men, and driving forces behind the Club, were James Moores and William Beastow. By this time Moores was the senior church warden at St. Mark's and a member of the Union Iron Works Board of Directors, while Beastow also maintained influential positions at both organisations. Both the welfare of the community and the leisure pursuits available were important in helping to establish a satisfied workforce.

According to various historians over the years Beastow presented the Club with a complete set of Black jerseys emblazoned with a white cross in October 1884. Official records do not state categorically that Beastow presented that kit, however he does seem to have been the most likely member of the Club to have done so. Whether it was Beastow or not, it is true that he would undoubtedly have wanted to provide a clear identity for the Gorton team. Why was black chosen as the predominant colour? This is unknown, however if it is accurate that scarlet and black had been the colours of the merged side in 1883-84, then it is possible that the side decided to keep one of those colours as part of their identity. This is all pure speculation, but West Gorton Athletic are known to have worn red and white in the years that followed, could Gorton have chosen to keep the black and West Gorton chosen the scarlet from the original kit? Highly speculative of course.

There are many mysteries tied up with Gorton's new kit. Over the years much has been made of the white cross and what it signifies. Some have suggested it proves the link with St. Mark's Church was still there

(indeed some of the original plans for the church appear to utilise a cross styled in this manner), others have suggested it ties in with Ellice Hopkins' White Cross League but this seems highly unlikely.

Another possibility is that this demonstrates a link with the Masonic community of the Gorton area. William Beastow, and for that matter James Moores, were key figures in the Ashbury Masonic Lodge. Moores involvement in the Masonic community predated Beastow's slightly, but both were instrumental in the development of the Ashbury Lodge following its warrant of constitution in 1873. In 1882 Beastow became the Master of the Lodge. Significantly, the Ashbury Lodge met at the Justice Birch Hotel – the venue for several Gorton AFC functions.

White crosses of the style worn on the Gorton shirt have been emblems within the Masonic community, and have been connected with the Knights Templar and Knights Hospitalier. They are known as cross pattee but have been referred to as Maltese crosses in City related material in the past.

Cross pattee have appeared on various non-sporting products over the years. They have also appeared in connection with churches. The existing Holy Trinity Church in Failsworth has several crosses, similar to that worn on the Gorton shirts, carved into stonework around the church. This church was built over twenty years after Gorton adopted their new kit, but it does perhaps provide evidence that some religious organisations in the Manchester area also used the cross.

It is worth noting however, that several sporting organisations wore similar crosses around this time. One of Gorton's opponents, Earlestown AFC, played in white shirts with a black cross pattee during the same period. The shirt looks like a negative of the Gorton kit. In addition, some significant employers in the region did as well and, potentially, the one with most in common with William Beastow and the Gortonians was the engineering company Crossley Brothers. Crossley's were based a short distance away on Pottery Lane and

A pattee cross at Holy Trinity, Failsworth.

Brooks & Doxey's Union Iron Works at the turn of the century. It's possible some of the older men had played for the Club during the 1880s. The land close to the chimney on the right may have been the site of the Club's first pitch in 1880.

used a very similar version of the white cross as part of their logo when they set up a car manufacturing base close to Gorton Park in the early 1900s. The cross was used to symbolise their Christian views and their belief in sobriety.

Ultimately, we may never know the true meaning of the cross on the Gorton shirt. Based on material provided by Freemason's Hall it is known that this style of cross was not an official emblem of the Ashbury Lodge, that was the square and compass. Various Masonic libraries have been consulted during research for this book and Freemason's Hall has provided significant information on Beastow's membership. It was suggested that the use of the white cross could be linked with the Masonic Knights Templar. However, they have been unable to trace Beastow's membership of that organisation.

Regardless of why the cross was familiar enough to be considered appropriate, it does seem likely that Beastow, and maybe Moores, included the emblem to signify that Gorton AFC followed aims similar to those of St. Mark's Church and the Ashbury Masonic Lodge, such as respect, understanding, kindness, tolerance, support and high moral standards. Ignoring the political and religious aspects of links to either the church or the Masonic community, those aims were ones Beastow and Moores would have wanted the side to follow. They also managed to weave their way through into the fabric of what was later to become Manchester City.

It is not known specifically which game saw Gorton

adopt the shirts for the first time. The first known home game after the shirts are believed to have been presented was a 3-0 victory over Gorton Villa on 15th November 1884, a week after the second team had defeated Eccles' second team 4-2.

Although performance on the pitch was important to the Club by this point, it should be highlighted that the community aims that had helped establish it during the late 1870s were still important. The area continued to be plagued by many of the problems Beastow, the Connells and the other senior St. Mark's figures had wanted to tackle in the 1870s, and so there was still a great deal of activity both within the general St. Mark's community and the football team. 1884-85 was an important season as one of the more headline grabbing scuttling cases was reported in the Manchester press. It was recorded that on 7th December 1884 gangs from Gorton and Openshaw fought with sticks, broken bottles and stones in Gorton itself. In January 1885 five of the young men were charged with rioting – three were aged 16, one 17 and one 18 - but from a football perspective it is significant that two of the ringleaders were sixteen year olds from the site of City's initial birth (Clowes Street and Thomas Street). The area desperately needed the Club to continue its development and provide a positive distraction for the youths. Clearly, they could not all play for the side, but they could support the Club or help in other ways. Gorton AFC still hoped to be a Club for the people.

Match reports have not been located for all games

played during 1884-85, but it is known that Gorton appeared in a 16 first team games and a further 17 second team matches. Those 16 first team games included the Club's first Manchester & District Challenge Cup (later known as the Manchester Senior Cup) tie which ended in a 1-0 defeat by the renowned university side of Dalton Hall.

Despite that defeat, the 1884-85 season can be said to have been a major success for the Club. It marked a triumphant return to the Club's aims and roots. The Annual Dinner was held at the Justice Birch Hotel. A report from the local newspaper provides an interesting insight into the structure of the Club:

"GORTON ASSOCIATION FOOTBALL CLUB"
"The first Annual Dinner in connection with the above club was held on Monday evening, 20th April 1885, at the Justice Birch Hotel, Hyde Road, where there was a good attendance. Mr. and Mrs. Pitt served an excellent dinner, and it was thoroughly enjoyed. Afterwards, Mr. James Moores presided, and Mr. W.H. Beastow was vice-chairman. The loyal toasts were honoured, interspersed with the songs 'Heats Of Oak' by Mr. Chew, and 'The Old Brigade' by Mr. F. Hopkinson. The toast, 'The Manchester & District Association', was heartily received and acknowledged by Mr. Colbert, the President of the Manchester & District F.A., who was in attendance as the guest-of-honour."
"Mr. F. Hopkinson read the Annual Report, which stated that the club, though only formed in October last, had made considerable progress. It has a membership of about twenty-five active members, with a promise of a good increase next season. The first team last season played 16 matches, 7 of which were won, 7 lost, and 2 drawn; number of goals scored 31, as against 21 scored by their opponents."
"In conclusion, the Report said that, financially, there was a balance on the right side, and all that is required for the success of the club is a good ground. Other toasts then followed, and songs were given by Messrs. F. Hopkinson, Furniss, Barber and others, the evening being very agreeably spent. Mr. R. Hopkinson ably officiated as Pianist."

Virtually all the names mentioned in that article were linked with the Club's earliest formation as St. Mark's, and it's interesting that Frederick Hopkinson chose to sing 'The Old Brigade'. Was there a feeling that the Club - which was once again made up mostly of St. Mark's parishioners - was now back on course after a season or so of strife?

A profit of £1 8s 8d was made, however the Club would have made a near £4 loss had Richard Peacock's £5 donation not been made. The following season he made a smaller donation of £2 10s but Samuel Brooks, the owner of Brooks & Doxey's Union Ironworks, contributed a further £1 1s. This proved that the support of several key figures within the community remained.

1885-1886 The Bull's Head

During the summer of 1885 Gorton moved from the rough and ready Pink Bank Lane. It is not known whether the Club was forced to move or whether Gorton were dissatisfied with the quality of the venue, but the year-end accounts for 1885-86 show that the Club was given £2 compensation for loss of ground. This suggests they had to move.

Their new venue was land owned by the Bull's Head Hotel on Reddish Lane on the very eastern edge of Gorton. This was approximately three miles from the Club's birth place. Years later the Club's first histories talked of the landlord of the Bull's Head charging the footballers £6 per annum to use the pitch and change in the public house, but the accounts show they actually paid £4 17s 6d in 1885-86.

Regardless of the amount paid, the new venue allowed Gorton to develop further. Two of the original players, Walter Chew and Edward Kitchen, remained significant committeemen. According to some sources Chew took over as secretary from Kitchen, however the 30th August edition of the *Athletic News* recorded that Kitchen, living at 39 Birch Street by this point, remained the key figure. Perhaps Chew took over during the season?

The captain for 1885-86 was Lawrence Furniss – a man destined to remain influential through to the 1940s.

As with previous seasons match reports do not exist for every game played. Evidence in the *Gorton Reporter* mentions 13 first team games, however the *Athletic News* carried information on other games. Significantly, the matches reported in the *Athletic News* that did not appear in the *Reporter* were high scoring Gorton defeats – for example in October Denton defeated Gorton 5-0 at the Bull's Head and the following month Farnworth Standard beat Kitchen's side 7-0.

At this time in football history club secretaries were responsible for submitting reports of their games

LINCOLN CITY v. MEXBORO'.—Played at Lincoln on Saturday, the home team winning by four goals to nothing.
GOLDEN HILL v. STOKE FREE WANDERERS.—Played at Golden Hill and resulted in a draw.
DENTON v. GORTON.—At Gorton, and resulted in a win for Denton by five goals to none.
DERBY ST LUKE'S beat NOTTINGHAM WANDERERS by eleven goals to none.
BURNLEY UNION STAR (2nd) v. PADIHAM (2nd).—Star, two goals ; Padiham, one.

A convincing Denton victory in October 1885.

to the media and, inevitably, if a secretary forgot to send a report in, or missed a deadline, then it would not appear. Also, some secretaries would despatch reports to their local 'paper but not nationals. It is highly plausible that Kitchen, Chew and the other Gortonians would keep the *Gorton Reporter* informed of most games, but that opposition secretaries would issue reports elsewhere. Maybe the Denton and Farnworth Standard secretaries always kept the *Athletic News* informed.

There will undoubtedly be match reports focusing on Gorton in other regional newspapers, for example in Bolton and Stockport, submitted by opposition secretaries.

From the reports known to exist it is clear Gorton, though developing, were still lagging behind most of their contemporaries, such as Hurst and Newton Heath who treated the Manchester Cup as a very serious competition and one they had to win. A sustained run in that competition brought attention to clubs and Newton Heath, West Manchester, and Hurst were gaining fame as a result. In 1885-86 Gorton fell at the first hurdle once again, losing 2-1 away to Pendleton Olympic.

Some clubs also saw the FA Cup as a step in their development and 1885-86 was to be the third consecutive season Hurst appeared, while Manchester FC had appeared twice and Birch once. Within three years Newton Heath, West Manchester, Hyde, Denton and Heywood Central would also enter the national competition.

1886-1887 Making Progress

By the 1886 close season Walter Chew was secretary and he hoped the 1886-87 season would see the stature of the Club improve. As early as 9th May 1886, he advertised in the Manchester produced national sports 'paper *The Umpire* saying that Gorton had several dates available for first and second team matches in the 1886-87 season.

Gorton clearly still had a long way to go, but they had enthusiasm and spirit. Through men like Chew, Kitchen and Furniss the Club had commitment and, at last, the 1886-87 season saw the side progress past the first round of the Manchester Cup.

The victory was obviously significant but this cup tie had also been one the team had to win as their

TRUE BLUE
Edward Kitchen

A player in the first game and secretary during 1884-86.

opponents were arch-rivals and former bedfellows West Gorton Athletic.

A crowd of 1,000 at the Bull's Head ground witnessed Gorton take a 3-0 lead by half time. The final score was 5-1, with two of the goals scored by Jack Hodgetts.

The second round pitted Gorton away to Newton Heath - a team that had featured in every Manchester Cup final so far - and although the Gortonians were determined to win they were, quite simply, overpowered with the Heathens winning an easy tie 11-1. Gorton's consolation goal came in the final minute.

Despite the second round defeat, the Manchester Cup of 1886-87 is important as it shows the increase in Gorton's desire to succeed. Reports show that the Gorton players were far from happy at succumbing to Newton Heath. They took defeat badly, so badly that the *Reporter* newspaper tried to cheer the Gortonians up by looking into the future: "Perhaps in another season or two Gorton will be able to avenge itself. It is as yet but a young club, and there is plenty of time to show of what stuff its members are made."

By the summer of 1887 it is understood that Gorton were faced with a rent increase at the Bull's Head, although it is not known exactly how much was demanded, nor if the Gorton committee seriously considered staying. The ground was not in an ideal location - it was closer to the rather less developed Reddish than Gorton centre - and even though it was probably Gorton's best venue to date, it was far from perfect. If the Club had any kind of ambition it needed to search for a better site in a densely populated district. Its roots were in West Gorton and many felt the Club should return home.

1880-1887 SUMMARY

Club Names: 1880 St. Mark's (West Gorton), 1881 West Gorton (St. Mark's), 1883 West Gorton & 1884 Gorton AFC

Secretary/Managers: 1880-83 Frederick Hopkinson, 1883-84 appears to be P Howarth, 1884-86 Edward Kitchen & 1886-89 Walter Chew (some reports suggest Chew took on the role of secretary at some point during 1885-86).

ARDWICK
ASSOCIATION FOOTBALL CLUB.

HYDE ROAD HOTEL,

ARDWICK. August 23rd, 1887.

Sir,

Having formed a Club under the above title, and secured a Ground situate between the L. & N. W. Railway and Galloways' Works, in Bennett Street, Hyde Road, we have decided to hold a Meeting in connection with the same, at the above Hotel, on *Tuesday Next, the 30th inst.*, at 8 p.m., prompt.

The bearer of this Circular will be glad to give you all particulars you may require respecting the prospects of the Club.

Hoping you will give this your favourable consideration,

We are, Sir,

Yours respectfully,

W. CHEW, } Hon. Secs.

J. H. WARD, } *Pro Tem.*

N.B.—Your attendance at the Meeting will be greatly esteemed.

1887-1892
Ardwick Association Football Club

"The defeat of Bolton Wanderers by Ardwick in the Manchester Cup competition probably surprised no one more than Ardwick people themselves. Certainly the eleven have done one or two fine performances during the season, but nothing to lead their most sanguine supporter to believe them capable of defeating such a team as the Wanderers. However, they did so, and, what is more, did it by playing better football than their opponents. This is the second time David Weir's men have won the cup, and the victory will do much to enhance the reputation of the team."

Commentary on the 1892 Manchester Cup Final, from the *Athletic News*

1887-1888 A Professional Approach

Gorton needed a home. Ideally they wanted to be close to their roots. Opportunities were limited until Kenneth McKenzie, the Club captain, solved the problem when he realised that some wasteland close to his home could be converted into a perfect home. McKenzie lived in Bennett Street, Ardwick, and every lunch he took a short cut from Bennett's Timber Yard, off Hyde Road, through the L&NWR railway arches, and across the wasteland to an opening on Bennett Street close to Galloway's Boilerworks.

In the early 1880s this area was already well known to the young men of West Gorton as a result of illegal activity that took place there. Scuttling was still an issue within the district, however the illegal acts that took place in this area were often regarded more as entertainment rather than violent, although a modern day view would be somewhat different. The entertainment found on this site was bare knuckle fighting and gambling. Former St. Mark's pupil and Brooks & Doxey's employee Sam Kirkman talked of the site during the early 1930s: "The meeting place was some low-lying ground near the railway behind the Galloway's Boilerworks. These fights were the real thing with the 'raw uns'. The combatants were stripped from the waist upwards."

Kirkman went on to talk of specific fights including

one which saw a "bruiser type" take on a much smaller and thinner man who must have been desperate for money. Kirkman watched the smaller man "get battered." He also described a police raid which saw the crowd scatter in all directions, while the police grabbed younger crowd members hoping they would give the names of the men who fought and those that had organised the bout.

Whether McKenzie had ever attended any of the fights staged on this land is open to debate, but he certainly believed the land could become Gorton's home. He spoke with the committee and they visited the site. At first they must have been appalled by the low-lying ground. It was uneven, had little if any grass, and water had gathered creating an immense puddle (pond was too grand a word for the dirty, polluted, water-filled holes that occupied this area of industrial wasteland) - but with a little imagination they began to see what could be achieved.

With this site Gorton would be able to develop the Club's first all enclosed ground. True it would take a considerable amount of effort but, after seven years of relative struggle the Gortonians were prepared to do whatever was necessary to find their own enclosure.

The young Lawrence Furniss searched to find the owners of the land and, after a little investigation, discovered that it belonged to the Manchester, Sheffield and Lincolnshire Railway Company. After an initial letter from Walter Chew to Edwin Barker, the company's estate agent, negotiations began. Eventually, Furniss and Chew managed to agree seven months' rental for the sum of £10, and the Gortonians spent considerable time and effort in turning this barren patch into a pitch fit for football. By the end of August 1887 the pitch was ready. It may not have been the ideal playing surface, after all for most of the summer the Club had been busy levelling it, but it was now home.

Around this time discussions took place as to the name of the Club. It was felt that a new home deserved a new beginning and, in any case, the Club was no longer within the Gorton boundary. Instead of trying to retain the Gorton moniker, the Club members decided to adopt the name of the district they had now moved to, and so during the summer of 1887 Gorton Association Football Club became Ardwick Association Football Club.

Some historians incorrectly believe Association was similar to names like Wanderers or Rovers or, even, City, but the truth is that the word Association was only used to differentiate between the sport of rugby, normally recorded as football, and association football. There was already an Ardwick Football Club in existence, playing at Slade Lane, but this club was a rugby club. Ardwick A.F.C. was named to differentiate the sports.

Another aspect often misunderstood over the years concerns the Club's location. Some have suggested

the Club had moved entirely away from its roots by this point, and that the new 'Hyde Road Ground', as it was to become known, was several miles from the Club's origins. This is simply not true. The Hyde Road Ground was several miles from the Bull's Head pitch, but it was actually closer to Clowes Street and St. Mark's Church than any of the other grounds apart from perhaps the first two pitches (the land near Clowes St. and Kirkmanshulme C.C.). In a sense the Club came home, although it was within another district it was merely a third of a mile from the St. Mark's Church itself and, as Sam Kirkman outlined in the early 1930s, it was a site well known by the young men of the area.

Although it was so close to the church, the Club decided to make a large public house, the Hyde Road Hotel, its headquarters. This public house had been built during the great development of the area which had seen it transformed in a similar manner to the Clowes Street area. Kirkman, looking back on the 1870s, remembered: "Hyde Road then was like a country road, right away to Ardwick Green, which at the time was a big pond. Where the car depot [present day bus depot] now stands was Bennett's Timber Yard, and on the same side nearer to the railway arch stood a house covered with oyster shells."

His comment about oyster shells sounds a little bizarre but on maps from this period the site that would later be occupied by the Hyde Road Hotel was occupied by a building called 'White Cottage' – could this have been the oyster shell house?

With the agreement of the Hyde Road Hotel licensee, Richard Stephenson, all the important meetings of the period were held there and, on match days, the hotel served as Ardwick's changing rooms - and scene of celebrations (or commiserations) afterwards. With Stephenson's support the Club decided to promote itself and raise awareness by inviting any interested party to the Club's inaugural meeting. A circular was handed out in the Ardwick and Gorton area to publicise the event.

With this kind of formal notification the local population could not fail to understand the ambition of the Club. Local councillor, and member of the influential local brewing family, Stephen Chesters-Thompson was invited to become Honorary President of the Club. Over the course of the next thirty years Chesters Brewery would play a major role in the establishment of the Club, while also gaining considerable revenue from, first, Ardwick's use of the Hyde Road Hotel, then exclusive rights to supply all the bars within the ground.

Stephen Chesters-Thompson.

48

NEWTON HEATH v. ARDWICK DISTRICT

This match was played at Belle Vue Gardens last night before a tremendous crowd, the "gate" being for the benefit of the Hyde Explosion Fund. There were twenty of the Wells's lights round the ground, but still there seemed to be some difficulty in seeing the ball at times, especially when it was off the ground. It was stated that there had been quite 6,000 tickets sold, and the gates were crowded for over two hours before the time for starting, so that there would be quite 10,000 people present, and it ought to result in a considerable addition to the fund. Mr. Charles Jennison kicked off, and R. G. Barlow was referee. The game was not a success as an exhibition of football, but still at times there was some good bits of play, which were applauded by the spectators, who seemed to be quite enthusiastic. The chief feature of the match was the cheering when the ball was kicked either over the bar or outside, as most of the spectators were sure it went through. The scoring done was four goals by Newton Heath and one by the District, but, unfortunately for the former, one of theirs was put through his own goal by Powell. Score :—Newton Heath, three goals ; Ardwick and District, two goals.

A report of the first floodlit Manchester derby in 1889.

Another move made during this period was into the world of professional football. Any club with ambition had to attract the best players, and so Ardwick decided to turn professional. In actual fact they chose to pay existing first team player Jack Hodgetts five shillings a week to play, rather than seek other more famous players, nevertheless it is an important move in the history of the Club, and clearly shows how far they had progressed since formation a mere seven years earlier.

Hodgetts, although glad of the money, was a little perturbed by the treatment he received from the other players. Some cold-shouldered him and believed he felt above himself. It was nothing to do with Hodgetts as a person it was more the principle. It wasn't long however before the committee realised that the situation would have to change for the good of the Club. They reached a decision to allow the rest of the first team players to claim expenses and, to keep the peace, they reached a maximum figure of five shillings per man. They were officially able to retain their amateur status, while enjoy the luxury of expenses. Everybody was happy.

It is believed the Club also wore blue for the first time this season. It is not known whether Gorton continued to wear the black kit with a white cross from 1884 until 1887 or whether another kit was selected. However, records at Manchester United's club museum show the colours the region's main sides submitted to the Manchester FA for the 1887-88 season. According to those details Ardwick wore Royal Blue & White vertical stripes. These details do seem accurate when compared with the information documented on the region's other sides and other information on Ardwick, such as the use of the Hyde Road Hotel as headquarters.

Considering all available evidence, it appears that Ardwick did adopt blue and white, albeit royal blue rather than pale blue, from the start of their existence. In later years people would claim that the selection of blue was linked to Masonic influence, however the fact that the first form of blue worn was royal blue rather than pale blue suggests this is a red herring.

With the Blue and Whites full of ambition, a grand opening fixture was arranged for 10th September 1887. Ardwick's first opponents were to be Salford A.F.C. yet for some unknown reason they failed to arrive at the Hyde Road ground. A band had been hired and a crowd of over five hundred had turned up, only to discover that Ardwick's birth was to be a farce. Over eighty years later, Francis Lee made a famous quote about the possibility of the Club winning 'Cups for cock-ups'. He was talking about the Club's 1970s ability to make the easy difficult, but he could have been referring to almost any period in the Club's history. It seems that this 'grand opening' was the first but by no means the last 'own-goal'.

The following week the ground was used for a match - this time Hooley Hill from Denton defeated Ardwick 4-2 in a game played in 'delightful weather' according to a newspaper report. Even so, the quality of the Hyde Road playing surface was quite poor - one of Ardwick's goals was scored from the midst of a puddle, despite the fact that it had not rained at all. Later in the season Ardwick's 8-1 demolition of Hyde in the Ashton & District Cup had to be replayed due to complaints from the Hydonians that the ground was unfit for football. The replay took place at Hyde with Ardwick dominating the game so much that the home side continually sent the ball as far away as possible. The match report commented on the amount of times the ball had to be retrieved from the field next to the Hyde ground. Not surprisingly Ardwick easily beat the Hydonians 3-1.

Gradually Ardwick - who were nicknamed the Brewerymen because of their connections with Chesters Brewery - gained passionate support. Perhaps a little too passionate at times. On 26th November 1887, at the end of a 1-0 defeat by Edenfield, the Hyde Road crowd were reported to have "stoned the visitors off the field." Secretary Walter Chew sent a letter to the *Gorton Reporter* denying the incident, nevertheless the local 'paper stood by their report. Interestingly, Jack Hodgetts, who passed away in 1922, was famous for telling his friends about games like this where supporters stoned the away side, although in Hodgetts' version it was always the Ardwick team that were on the receiving end of the supporters' wrath.

Ardwick's passionate supporters followed them to many away games during this first season, most noticeably the Manchester Cup first round tie at Lower Hurst (Ashton-Under-Lyne). Despite losing 3-2 the Ardwick fanatics gave their side great encouragement

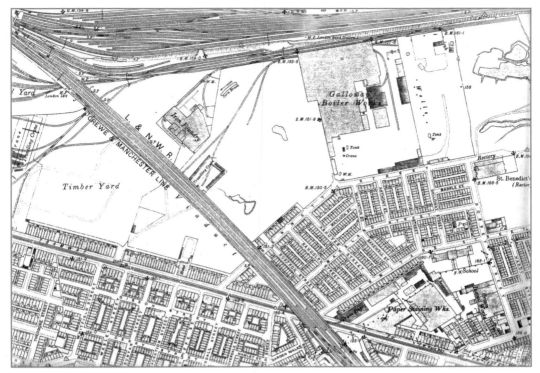

The wasteland between the railway line and Galloways often staged bare-knuckle fights. In 1887 Kenneth McKenzie thought it would make a good home for Ardwick AFC.

and continually shouted "Play Up, Ardwick!" - could this have been the Club's first chant?

All in all the first season was not a great success. Off the field the Club lost £13 despite gate receipts of £47 9s 9d. On it Ardwick achieved a few notable results, but also struggled against, in many cases, weak sides (Astley Bank defeated Ardwick 13-0!). Also, the Hyde Road pitch had not stood up to the rigours of the football season, nevertheless it still had better prospects than any of the other venues used in the 1880s, and with the right financial backing Ardwick knew they could develop the ground as and when required.

1888-1889 Allison's Cures

During 1888 and 1889 significant progress was made. With the help of Chesters, Ardwick built a grandstand capable of holding 1,000 spectators, and for the sum of £5 15s the Club's first pay box - turnstile was not an appropriate name - was erected. With the new pay box the Club raised £213 gate money – a massive increase on the previous season - with income exceeding expenditure by roughly £39. Amazingly only 5 shillings

had been spent on medical requirements. Perhaps a pint of Chesters was the Ardwick team's cure-all.

In addition the Club attracted a number of wealthy backers to complement the Chesters' money. John Allison became one of Ardwick's main benefactors in September 1888.

On 26th February 1889 Ardwick featured in a friendly with Newton Heath at Belle Vue, close to Hyde Road. The game was a floodlit charity match in aid of the Hyde Colliery disaster and raised £140 with an attendance of around 12,000. The result was a 3-2 defeat even though the Ardwick side was strengthened by the inclusion of players from other local sides. Nevertheless it perhaps proved that the gulf between the Heathens and Ardwick was narrowing.

1889-1890 Illuminated Ardwick

The 1889 floodlit game with the Heathens was a significant spectacle, and Lawrence Furniss and John Allison seemed keen to create more spectacular moments for the Club and its loyal band of supporters.

With the Football League now in operation those

connected with Ardwick realised how far they could take the Club and, although most of Ardwick's fixtures remained friendlies, they adopted a more professional approach. As 1889-90 developed, the progression was there for all to see.

On 30th December 1889 the Ardwickites defeated Hurst, one of the early giants of the game locally, 7-0 at Hyde Road to complete the double over the Ashton side and, by the time of the meeting with Newton Heath on 1st February 1890, Ardwick were described in the press as a team: "just rising to a higher standard in the football world."

In February 1890 the *Manchester Evening News* featured two of Manchester's leading clubs – Newton Heath and West Manchester. It talked of their strengths and achievements to date, but ended with a verdict that encouraged everyone at Hyde Road: "It is more than probable that in the course of time both will have to give way to Ardwick, a club which has capital management behind it, and what is more some good talent in its midst."

At last the media were noticing that Ardwick were moving up a gear. The following month there was another significant step forward. On 1st March Ardwick managed a thrilling 6-4 victory over Manchester FC. The *Manchester Evening News* was extremely positive: "No more interesting meeting than that between Ardwick and Manchester ever took place in local Association circles for both are regarded as coming clubs. We have more than once had a good word to say for Ardwick, and there is nothing to alter the opinion that they are a club of undoubted promise."

That promise encouraged the Club to organise several fixtures with sides that brought a challenge. One was a high profile meeting with Football League side Everton on 10th March 1890. This was exactly the kind of spectacle Furniss and Allison wanted and the committee turned this into the Club's first known home floodlit game. Despite appalling conditions and heavy rain on a miserable Monday night Stephen Chesters Thompson, the Club's President, performed the kick off before an impressive crowd of 5,000. Impressive because the ground at this stage contained cover for very few fans.

Ultimately, even though Ardwick had brought in a player from Derby County and one from Notts County to supplement the side, Everton won this first ever meeting of the teams 3-0. Nevertheless, this had been a major step forward for the Club and the fact the side had brought in Wells Lights to illuminate the pitch and generate a real spectacle for fans proved that Ardwick was innovative.

The added illumination of the pitch however may have raised an issue that caused Ardwick to make an announcement in the days that followed. According to the *Manchester Evening News*: "Ardwick has 'come on'

marvellously and they promise next season to become even more important. They are proposing to attempt during the summer to grow grass on their ground. At present it is as bare as a brick-kiln, and on wet days, the players simply wallow in the mud."

Both in terms of facilities and playing squad Ardwick recognised they had to improve if they were ever to reach the standard the local media felt they could. The following May, while the grass grew at Hyde Road, Furniss and Allison looked beyond the confines of Manchester to search for quality professionals. They journeyed to Scotland where, in next to no time, they signed the brilliant Dundee based goalkeeper Douglas. They had to rely on the services of an agent, P. Allen, who received £10 commission, but nevertheless they had finally signed a player of quality.

While in Scotland they raided the Ayr squad, signing Robson, Campbell, and McWhinnie, and signed Young from Glasgow Northern. Back in England, they obtained the services of several Bolton Wanderers players - 'Wally' Rushton, Milne, McWhirter, Haydock, Whittle and Pearson. They were also fortunate to sign the English International, Davie Weir, from the Trotters.

All this activity helped the Club progress and it seems that the involvement of John Allison had brought this new ambition. Unfortunately, the new approach also created a certain amount of controversy for a team that many regarded as 'young upstarts'.

1890-1891 The Brewery Men

In the summer of 1890, Ardwick spent over £600 re-turfing and draining the playing surface, while also improving access by agreeing with Chesters to open up an additional entrance by the path at the side of the Hyde Road Hotel. Chesters also increased the number of bars within the ground. Looking back it is relatively easy to understand the reasoning behind Chesters involvement in the Club - any venue where 5,000 men regularly congregated must have stood a decent chance of selling large quantities of alcohol - yet it is also essential that the Ardwick view is considered. Without the close partnership with Chesters the Club could easily have gone under. They would certainly not have been able to develop the ground in the fashion they had. The two organisations benefitted greatly by their partnership.

With the support of Stephen Chesters-Thompson and Chesters Brewery Ardwick were developing at a great rate. 1890-91 was to prove to be one of the Club's most important seasons. The professional approach, as suggested in 1889-90, seems clear in a team photograph, rediscovered by Paul Toovey in 2009, showing the side looking like most other well-organised clubs of the period.

The photograph suggests the side wore pale blue and white quartered, sometimes incorrectly referred to as halved, shirts and navy blue shorts. A quartered football shirt at this time was one in which both the front and back would be split into two with opposing colours on front and back. For example, the Ardwick shirt had a white right breast and pale blue left breast. On the back the colours were reversed.

The FA Cup holders Blackburn Rovers wore Cambridge Blue and white quartered shirts during this period. Whether there was any connection isn't clear but the Rovers were known as one of the leading clubs after winning the FA Cup for three successive seasons in the 1880s and then again in 1890. Another success followed in 1891.

Most of the progressive sides in the Manchester area looked at the more northern Lancastrian sides as the ones to emulate. When the Ardwick Blue & Whites signed Walker from another major Lancastrian side Burnley they immediately found themselves on the Football League's blacklist. Apparently Ardwick had poached the player. In those days transfer agreements between Football League clubs and those still on the outside were not in existence. Ambitious teams like Ardwick wanted to sign the best.

In December 1890, the Football League tried to counter Ardwick's activities by introducing a rule that forbade League clubs from organising fixtures against clubs found guilty of poaching. Ardwick, found guilty, were prohibited from arranging lucrative fixtures against any League club - a move that would penalise any ambitious club.

The 'Brewery Men' had even paid the player £5 to travel to Manchester in an attempt to sign him. League clubs were told not to do business with the 'upstarts' from Manchester and those that did - such as Preston who arranged a fixture with Ardwick - were officially censured.

Ardwick were much more than a football club. As early as 1890 they began holding annual sporting events for the local community.

After two months of struggle, Ardwick apologised and offered Walker back to Burnley. Interestingly, there is no trace of Walker ever actually turning out for Ardwick's first team. Ardwick were removed from the blacklist and allowed to continue their quest for big time fixtures. They desired a place in football's hierarchy and in 1890-91 they entered the FA Cup for the first time. In a qualifying match they defeated Liverpool Stanley 12-0 with the impressive Davie Weir scoring an hat trick yet, for some unknown reason their next game in the competition did not take place. They were due to face a team from Bolton called Halliwell away from home but no record exists to show that the match actually took place. Perhaps Ardwick managed to arrange a more lucrative fixture at Hyde Road. Whatever occurred, Halliwell did go through to the next round.

By this time Walter Chew, one of the players from the Club's first known game back in 1880, had resigned from the committee. It appears he relinquished his position in November 1890 and, if this is true, it is possible he felt a little concerned with the approach Ardwick were now taking. Chew had been a passionate committeeman from the Club's earliest days and he remained a supporter throughout his life, but it may be that he felt he could no longer actively contribute to an outfit that was becoming more professionally minded day-by-day. Chew was, by this point, an important member of the Manchester FA's Committee. It seems likely that he felt he had more to offer Manchester at a regional level than at a club-specific level. Worth recalling that he was still only 25 at this point and that there are no indications that he was dissatisfied with any individual – Lawrence Furniss remained a friend, John Allison was a Manchester FA Vice-president and, according to the *Athletic News* annual Stephen Chesters-Thompson was Honorary President of the same organisation.

In April 1891 a major landmark was reached when the Brewerymen overcame Newton Heath 1-0 in the Manchester Cup final. The influential Ardwick captain Davie Weir scored in the seventh minute to give the unfancied Ardwickites the trophy. According to match reports the game was rather even, although Ardwick did actually have another goal disallowed. Nevertheless, the victory finally made the footballing fraternity sit up and notice the Brewerymen. Newton Heath had featured in every Manchester Cup final since inception, and were clearly one of the biggest Manchester sides, whereas Ardwick had struggled to shake off the image of a small time club. By winning the Manchester Cup Ardwick were able to declare 'We've arrived!'

Success in the trophy fuelled the committee's ambition and at the 1891 Football League AGM Ardwick - along with Darwen, Newton Heath, Nottingham Forest, Stoke, and Sunderland Albion - applied for the first time to join the 'big boys' when the League was expanding

The Ardwick team of 1890-91 wearing the quartered shirts. Coloured by Tim Ashmore.

from 12 to 14 clubs. In those days election to the League was based on a voting system. Each existing League side would vote and in 1891 the two sides with the highest number of votes were to be admitted.

All the applicants, with the exception of Ardwick, were members of the Football Alliance - a league originally set up to rival the Football League – and Ardwick's inexperience of formal competition was expected to work against them. There was also a real possibility that those interested in seeing a Manchester side join the League would be frustrated simply because the vote could be split – this was a genuine concern and may ultimately have had a bearing on the following year's applications.

Incredibly, the election saw a very impressive performance for Ardwick. They managed to secure four votes and ended up receiving more votes than any of the other non-elected sides. Darwen and Stoke both received seven votes and were accepted into the League. Significantly, Ardwick's local rivals Newton Heath finished bottom without gaining a single vote. The potential the Ardwickites offered was starting to be recognised.

According to the *Athletic News* annual the Club had played fifty games in 1890-91, winning 29 and drawing seven. It claimed the side had netted 152 goals and conceded 97. The annual also includes a fixture list that

showed that on 15 April 1892 the Brewerymen planned to face the famous Scottish side Celtic in a friendly.

Ardwick were moving forward at a rapid rate.

1891-1892 A Second Manchester Cup

Although attempts to join the Football League ended in failure, Ardwick did find themselves accepted into the Alliance for the start of the 1891-92 season. Apart from local knock-out competitions and the occasional appearance in qualifying rounds of the FA Cup, this was Ardwick's first attempt at organised football. It was their chance to move away from the image of a team fit for friendlies, but nothing else, into a world where they could achieve their many aims. Newton Heath were the only other Manchester side in the Alliance, and so it was quite a feat for the Brewerymen to enter that league.

By joining the Alliance the Club had to ensure it was a formal organisation. The Club submitted their basic organisational details to the Alliance and some of these appeared in that season's *Athletic News* Annual. It was recorded that Ardwick's kit comprised of "white shirts and navy blue knickers" but sadly it is not clear when the side swapped their blue and white quartered shirts for plain white shirts.

During the pre-season they had developed the

ground further - the Club boasted that it had "stand accommodation for 3,000 spectators", and had strengthened the side with Archie Ferguson from Heart of Midlothian, Hugh Morris from Chirk, with Bob Milarvie transferring from Newton Heath. In addition they played two pre-season friendlies at Hyde Road the first a 2-2 draw with West Manchester, the second a 2-1 win over Gainsborough Trinity. Ardwick believed they were ready for the Alliance.

The season started at home to Bootle with a crowd of approximately 6,000. Although Ardwick went in at half time only one goal up, they had dominated the first half with Whittle providing the goal, Weir having one disallowed for offside, and McWhinnie heading over.

The second half was more of a mixed game with Bootle equalising early on, quickly followed by a second while Ardwick's Robson lay injured - The Umpire newspaper described that he had been "badly kicked". Ardwick were determined to put in a good performance in front of the Hyde Road crowd and, after much pressure, Davies equalised. More Ardwick pressure followed and in the final quarter McWhinnie provided an excellent pass to Morris who sent the ball through for the home side's third goal.

Ardwick then allowed Bootle to score straight from the kick off. Apparently, Bootle charged down the pitch and provided Grierson with the opportunity of scoring from a low shot, and so a game that Ardwick hoped to win ended in an exciting 3-3 draw. Nevertheless it was an indication that perhaps Ardwick were ready for this kind of organised approach to football.

Overall in the Alliance that season, Ardwick did achieve a great deal. Although they only finished seventh out of twelve clubs, they had defeated Walsall Town Swifts 6-0 at Hyde Road, and drew the home derby game with Newton Heath 2-2. In fact the 1891-92 season was probably the first real season of rivalry between the two Manchester clubs. Prior to the Alliance, Ardwick's main 'derby' rivals were all minor clubs from the Gorton area - indeed they continued to play friendlies against Gorton Villa up until 1893 - however, once the two sides met in the Manchester Cup final of 1891, and then

The Manchester Cup, the first trophy ever won by the Club.

faced each other in the Alliance, they were meeting as equals. Their first season as opponents in the Alliance allowed the large Manchester population to have a choice - Newton Heath or Ardwick. Although Newton Heath had been the more successful club so far, Ardwick were perhaps seen as being more progressive and were already the better supported of the two. Perhaps these points had been recognised at the League AGM.

The Hyde Road derby attracted a crowd of over 10,000, whereas the Heathens home game at North Road was watched by around 4,000. Even the Hyde Road derby attendance was bettered by Ardwick on two other occasions in the Alliance that season.

Ardwick managed to prove their pedigree and position as one of the strongest clubs in the Manchester area when they defeated the touring Canadians – a national XI – 3-1 in December. Unfortunately, the planned friendly with Celtic had to be cancelled but they did beat both Renton from the Scottish League and the Football League's Notts County during April 1892.

The team selected to play Fairfield in February 1892. Note that the Manchester St Bride's goalkeeper was John Edward Chapman, the future chairman of City.

They ended April with an impressive 5-1 victory over another League side Stoke and there had also been a 1-1 draw with Everton. These games may have been staged as part of a concerted effort to convince the existing League sides of the potential of the Ardwickites, and it is clear that the Brewerymen's reputation was developing rapidly. Helped in no small way by success in the Manchester Cup for the second year running.

To win their second Manchester Cup the side convincingly defeated Football League side Bolton Wanderers 4-1, although the game itself had to be delayed. Two minutes before it was due to start the two sides entered the Newton Heath pitch at North Road, only to discover that they were both wearing their regular white shirts and dark blue shorts. A quick search around the ground failed to find an alternative strip, and so a man was sent in a hansom cab to fetch different colours. He returned thirty minutes later with a set of red and black shirts. Whether these were the side's regular second strip is not clear. Presumably they were, otherwise the old blue and white quartered shirts may have been worn.

The game eventually kicked off at 4:05, with Ardwick having most of the play throughout the first half. However, "just as the whistle was about to be blown", according to a contemporary match report, Munro scored for Bolton. Within a minute Hugh Morris made it 1-1. Not long after the interval Captain Davie Weir, a former Bolton player who had been dropped then reinstated for fear that he would not try against his old club, dribbled from the half way line, before firing a shot past the Bolton goalkeeper. From a Weir free-kick, John Milne scored Ardwick's third, and then a few minutes later Bob Milarvie sent the ball goalwards for what seemed like a certain goal, only to see Davie Weir poach the fourth Ardwick goal - who said the captain wouldn't try against his old club?

Ardwick had now reached a point in their history where they could look back with pride. The Club no longer had to worry about finding a ground, or a game for that matter. They were on the up and up.

TRUE BLUE
Lawrence Furniss

A player with Gorton, Ardwick's first secretary, a City director and chairman, and the first man to be awarded the presidency of City for life. Without Furniss Manchester City would not exist.

1887-1892 SUMMARY

Best Cup Run: Ardwick won the Manchester Cup in 1891 & 1892; appeared in the FA Cup Qualifying Round 1 in 1890-91 & 1891-92. They withdrew from the Qualifying Round 2 in 1891

Highest League Attendance: c.13,000 Newton Heath, 19/12/91 (Alliance League)

Highest Cup Attendance: c.11,000 Newton Heath, 03/10/91 (FA Cup)

Secretary/Managers: 1886-89 Walter Chew (some reports suggest Chew became secretary during 1885-86) & 1889-93 Lawrence Furniss

Seasonal Record:

Season	League	Posn	FA Cup	Other	Leading Scorer	Average Attendance
1890-91			Q2			
1891-92	Alliance	12	Q1		Morris 10	6,800

1892 - 93.

Ardwick Association Football Club

SEASON 1892-93.

Available to

UNCOVERED STANDS (BOYS)

MS4 496

No. 50

Name John Bicek

Address 6 ... Ardwick

Sec.'s Signature

NOT TRANSFERABLE, and if
found to be used by anyone other than the person
whose name it bears, the ticket will be withheld.

Shotlin & Co., Printers, 67, London Road, Manchester.

1892-1899
Promoting Manchester

"The confidence shown by the League in the Manchester City club ought to materially help the officials of the new club in raising all the capital they require. We understand that plenty of good men are applying for positions, and all that is wanted is a little more money. The sooner that is forthcoming and the stronger the team will be, and, consequently, the more certain the prosperity of the club."

Commentary following City's election in May 1894, *The Umpire*

1892-1893 League Leaders

In 1892 Ardwick Association Football Club made a significant move towards the ultimate aim of being one of England's elite teams. The Football League had been in existence for four years without a representative from Manchester. The city was not unique, but by 1892 every ambitious club in the country realised that the League offered potential.

Ardwick's application a year earlier was well received but ultimately rejected mainly because the Brewerymen lacked experience.

The League at this time was very much like a 'gentleman's club'. Ardwick, not being members, were often seen as being working class upstarts with few rights. Ardwick wanted the best and were not afraid to bend the rules to achieve their aims. For instance,

Ardwick tried to sign the best players and felt that financial inducements were an acceptable means of business. The Football League disagreed. They had already put into force maximum signing on fees and had made poaching illegal. None of this seemed to concern Ardwick even after they had been blacklisted during the 1890-91 season for poaching a player. In 1892 Wolverhampton Wanderers supplied the League with strong evidence proving that Ardwick had tried to poach a Wolves player. Fortunately, Ardwick were not alone. Many clubs outside of the League took similar steps to recruit the best.

Despite all of those concerns, it wasn't long before the Brewerymen were in with a chance of achieving their aim of joining the Football League. A decision had been taken in April 1892 to form a second division of twelve clubs and expand the First Division to sixteen. Thirteen clubs, including four sides seeking re-election, applied for First Division status. Three sides were re-elected and Nottingham Forest (9 votes), Wednesday (10 votes) and Newton Heath (6 votes) were accepted into the enlarged division. Interestingly, other applicants to join the League included Newcastle East End (later Newcastle United), Middlesbrough and Middlesbrough Ironopolis. Another aspiring side, Liverpool, were rejected before the vote took place yet another Liverpool side, Liverpool Caledonians, were allowed to stand.

After the First Division election, the Second Division process was considered. It was decided to offer a place to all those clubs that had applied except Liverpool and Liverpool Caledonians (they had not received a single vote in the First Division election). Ardwick joined Darwen, Burton Swifts, Grimsby Town, Bootle, Walsall Town Swifts, Small Heath Alliance, Crewe Alexandra, Lincoln City, Burslem Port Vale, Sheffield United, and Northwich Victoria in the new division.

Much has been made in the years that have followed of the fact that Newton Heath joined the First Division and Ardwick the Second. However, it has to be highlighted that Ardwick did not seek election to the First Division. It is possible that an agreement was reached between the two Manchester sides not to compete directly for election as this may have split the vote. The story of the two aspiring Liverpool clubs suggests that questions may have been raised with ultimately both sides losing out.

Ardwick were by this time the better supported of the Manchester clubs, and seemed to offer more potential, however to be fair Newton Heath had performed better overall in the Alliance.

It does seem very odd that Ardwick did not apply to join the First Division given that they had received four votes the previous year while the Heathens had received none. Ultimately, although many modern day historians incorrectly suggest that the difference between the two sides was vast at that point, the fact is that Ardwick were the side that actually benefited in the longer term. By joining the Second Division, the Club was able over the years that followed to build more of a winning mentality while the Heathens struggled in the top flight. The public preferred winners and by the end of the decade Ardwick/City had become the side that most Mancunians preferred.

As with Ardwick's first game in the Alliance, the Brewerymen made their debut in the Football League at home to Bootle in a game that perhaps helped to set the typical Manchester image for any newcomer. Not only was the Hyde Road ground surrounded by industry, railways, and row after row of terraced housing, but the day itself was particularly grey with heavy rain throughout the match. Maybe this is why Ardwick chose to wear white shirts with navy blue shorts.

Ardwick's first game in the newly formed Second Division was a 7-0 win over Bootle at Hyde Road.

Perhaps those connected with the Club felt a light shirt was needed to ensure the team stood out from its surroundings.

The poor conditions helped to keep the attendance down to around 4,000, even so those brave souls that stood and cheered their heroes on were rewarded with an excellent Ardwick goal feast. The final result was a 7-0 Ardwick victory, putting the Mancunians right at the top of the very first Second Division table on 3rd September 1892, although the following day's *Umpire* newspaper mistakenly put the Club in second place behind Small Heath (later Birmingham City) who had won their game 4-1.

Amongst the goalscorers were Joe Davies, who scored the first Ardwick League hat-trick, and Hugh Morris, who scored the Club's first goal in the League. Interestingly, the Brewerymen were also awarded their first League penalty when Hutchison was adjudged to have fouled 23 year old Bill Angus, who had joined the Club from Third Lanark only two weeks earlier. Ardwick's new captain Dave Russell, a former member of the Preston side which achieved the double in 1888-89, sent the penalty straight into McLaughlin's hands.

Apart from Angus and Russell, most of the Ardwick squad had featured for the Club in the previous campaign, even former captain Davie Weir had chosen to stay despite a few disagreements with the Club prior to the 1892 Manchester Cup Final. Weir had refused to go to Matlock with the team for their build up to the final after it was suggested he would not want to see his old side Bolton lose to Ardwick. The issue was resolved at the time, but during the summer the news broke that Weir had signed for Bolton. A short while later he changed his mind, and returned to Ardwick. Nevertheless, it must have been obvious to his many admirers in both Manchester and Bolton that Weir's heart didn't really lie at Hyde Road. It was no surprise when, in the following January, he returned to the Wanderers.

The fact that the gifted Weir was left out of Bolton's first ever FA Cup final appearance in 1894 because of what has been described as his 'individualistic temperament that caused arguments with other members of the team', may provide an indication to the type of player Weir was. He had the skill, and it appears he had the fight, but he was not the perfect team player, despite being Ardwick captain for two seasons.

Regardless of the Weir situation, Ardwick did make progress during this season. They remained undefeated in their first six games - a feat that saw them head the table - and right up until Christmas looked capable of winning the Division. Sadly, the New Year saw the Club's fortunes change as defeat followed defeat. In fact only two further games were won all season. The first of these was a 3-1 defeat of Crewe on 18th February 1893. This game was significant because one of the goalscorers was debutant Walter Bowman.

Although most Mancunians were unaware at the time, Bowman was actually the first overseas international to play in the Football League. He was born in Canada during 1862, and arrived in the British Isles in August 1888 as a Canadian international.

The Canadians were playing a number of friendly fixtures against sides in Ireland, Scotland and England, and they faced Newton Heath winning 2-0 with Bowman scoring. Whether this appearance was witnessed by any of the Ardwick officials at the time isn't known although it does seem likely that they would have attended.

A second tour followed in 1891 - including a 3-1 Ardwick victory on 12th December 1891 - and Bowman decided to remain behind after the rest of the Canadians had returned home. He joined Accrington, making his debut in January 1892. That match made him the first overseas international to play in the League and on 25th August 1892 he signed for Ardwick. It was almost five months before he made his goalscoring debut.

Bowman remained with the Blues until the close season of 1900, with one of his most significant matches being the 11-3 record victory over Lincoln on 23rd March 1895, although Bowman failed to make the score sheet.

After City little is known of Bowman's life. An article in April 1929 talked of a reunion in Toronto of the touring side but Bowman did not attend. It was believed he was living in the USA in a copper mining city in western Montana called Butte – a town more famous as the birthplace of daredevil Evil Knievel – but he was never traced.

Bowman only managed two appearances in 1892-93, scoring on both occasions, but Ardwick's overall form was not good with seven of the nine League games during 1893 ending in defeat. Despite this loss of form Ardwick still managed to end the season fifth. A top three finish would have seen them enter the end of season Test Matches (play-offs) to determine promotion and relegation. Ardwick could only sit back and ponder what might have been as Hyde Road played host to the play-off game that saw Second Division Darwen overcome Notts County from the First.

As the life of Ardwick, and subsequently Manchester City, always seems to be linked with that of Manchester United it's worth making a comparison of the two clubs' first season in the League. Overall, Ardwick had acquitted themselves well whereas Newton Heath failed, finishing bottom of Division One. They were five points below nearest rivals Accrington who had struggled to raise a team on occasion (they resigned at the end of the season).

The Heathens scraped through the Test Matches to retain their top flight status but the gap between the two Manchester clubs was not significant. In fact records show that a friendly between Ardwick and Newton Heath in January 1893 at the Heathens ground was regarded as one of the "Big Gates in 1892-93" according to the *Athletic News* with receipts of £250 – a very impressive figure.

Ardwick may have been officially a division lower, but in reality it was Ardwick who were winning the plaudits. The general Manchester public were interested in winners and, at the time, Ardwick appealed to an ever growing public.

1893-1894 Ardwick's Last

In May 1893, the League's first officially titled Management Committee was elected with an Ardwick man, Joshua Parlby, becoming one of the two Second Division representatives. Parlby was a rather interesting, 'larger than life' character. His beard, size, and rather loud manner earned him the rather apt nickname Falstaff. The Club's opponents felt he was quite a devious character, but the truth is that he always seemed to know how to achieve what was in the Club's best interests. In later years the great Billy Meredith described his persuasive skills: "There are some men whose silver tongues are said to have the power of charming song-birds from the trees, and I believe Josh Parlby was one of them."

Parlby was a licensee who may have established links with the Hyde Road club through his involvement with Chester's' brewery. He was a knowledgeable football man and had played for Stoke's second team and been a member of their committee.

In 1893 it was felt the smooth talking newcomer

might be able to get a little more out of the team while also providing the Club with a stronger voice in the League's hierarchy. Parlby became Ardwick's first paid secretary, earning a weekly wage of fifty shillings.

Lawrence Furniss, Parlby's predecessor, remained at the Club and was still an important committee member. This was no slight on him, but it is clear that Parlby offered a more authoritative footballing voice and it seems the Club recognised that his name might open a few doors. The *Athletic News* annual recorded Ardwick's contact details as usual but, significantly, Parlby's name appeared as part of the telegraphic address. In previous years Ardwick's telegraphic address was "Football, Manchester", but in 1893 that changed to "Parlby, Football, Manchester" – it seems a minor change, however it highlights Parlby's commitment to the cause and the importance of having him involved. Ardwick were clearly a progressive club. Most of the others did not publicise a telegraphic address.

Ardwick rightly believed Parlby was the man to push them forward. Unfortunately his first season as secretary coincided with a series of amazing failures both on and off the pitch. The season started brightly with a 6-1 victory over Middlesbrough Ironopolis in Ardwick's second game, but apart from that, and the 8-1 thrashing of Burslem Port Vale in October, there were few opportunities to cheer for the Ardwick faithful. New League arrivals Newcastle United, Liverpool, and Royal Arsenal all did the double over a Manchester side that was clearly losing the momentum of the previous four or five seasons.

The lowest moment on the pitch came when Small Heath defeated the Brewerymen 10-2 in Birmingham. Even though Ardwick's goalkeeper, Harry Stones, had to leave the field injured for a while, this was still a major blow to morale. It had all felt so different in August when *The Umpire* newspaper claimed that Ardwick were "making satisfactory progress, and altogether the prospects of the Club are brighter than for some time past."

As early as October, the Ardwick committee were concerned with matters on the pitch and with the financial position of the Club. They called a meeting of season ticket holders to discuss the situation, with the result being that everyone had agreed that the Club must carry on until the end of the season when, it was felt, the Club should be allowed to die. From then until the end of March the committee chose not to hold any official meetings, and Josh Parlby was given the unenviable task of smooth talking his way passed the Club's many creditors. There was also the small matter of completing the League programme, not a simple task when the Club was forced to sell many of its better players to stay alive.

In January 1894 goalkeeper William Douglas, who

had been one of the real Ardwick stars since signing in May 1890, was transferred to First Division strugglers Newton Heath, thus becoming the first player to move directly from Ardwick to the Heathens. In the same month Full back David Robson, another who had been with the Club since May 1890, moved to Wolverhampton Wanderers. Earlier Ardwick had lost the services of Hugh Morris, Joe Davies and England international Jimmy Yates to Sheffield United, leaving the squad exceptionally weak. After leaving Ardwick Yates had a varied career, but sadly life took a turn for the worst for the player once his playing days came to an end. Poor health forced him out of his job at Southampton docks and he became unemployed. In September 1922 it was reported he had committed suicide. He was only 51.

A total of thirty-six players featured in the Club's 28 League matches that season, with the side changing for almost every game. For one game, a 1-1 draw away to Crewe Alexandra, Ardwick were forced to field only ten men when Daniel Whittle and a reserve missed the train. Such was the state of confusion surrounding the Club at the time.

At one point the Club were close to losing their Hyde Road ground when the landlords, the Manchester, Sheffield, and Lincolnshire Railway Company, gave notice to Chesters' Brewery that they wished to close the entrance adjacent to the Hyde Road Hotel. It seems that the railway company had plans to recover the ground from the Club for breaching the agreement - presumably Ardwick were behind in their rent. By this time Chesters' had spent over £2,500 repairing the ground, and investing in the bars, and were not prepared to lose that investment, nor the potential beer sales a popular football club would create. The brewery persuaded the railway company to keep the entrance open for the rest of the season, and at the same time lease the ground to them instead of Ardwick. Chesters' would pay the rates and bear the expense of keeping the ground in a fit state for football. On 25th March 1894 they also agreed and signed a document to underlet the ground to the football club.

Two weeks later, on the 8th April, with still one game to go and Ardwick trapped in the re-election zone, *The Umpire News* reported on the on-going confusion surrounding the finances and future of the Club. The article outlined plans by some season ticket holders to form a new club called Manchester City Football Club. Although evidence does not prove conclusively who came up with the name it does suggest that Joshua Parlby was the most likely member of the committee to have come up with the idea.

It seems that on Wednesday 4th April 1894 Manchester City applied for affiliation to the Lancashire F.A. The Lancashire F.A. stated that it would accept City's application providing that the Club could produce an agreement proving that it had a ground to play on. City immediately stated that they would be using the Ardwick Hyde Road ground and that they would reach an agreement with the landlords within a week. However, John Allison felt that Ardwick themselves should carry on, despite what was agreed in October, and that the Brewerymen would continue to use Hyde Road. The Club now appeared to be split in two with Allison finding support to play on from the bulk of the Ardwick committee, while Joshua Parlby charmed the season ticket holders to back his bold plan for a new 'Manchester' club.

Parlby's enthusiasm persuaded many of the ordinary supporters that the time was right to lay the name Ardwick to rest, and move forward with a more ambitious title. He wanted a club to match the pride that the whole of Manchester was feeling in 1894. The world's first industrial city was still growing at an incredible rate with many ambitious developments taking place. In fact on New Year's Day 1894 the Manchester Ship Canal opened but the official opening, to be performed by Queen Victoria, was scheduled for Monday 21st May 1894 – the same day as the Football League would be meeting in Manchester for the election/re-election of clubs.

Whether Parlby considered the impact of the Queen's visit to Manchester cannot be fully proved, however it seems that the two events were at the forefront of his thoughts. Parlby was, without doubt, one of the greatest orators and visionaries the game possessed. He clearly knew how to promote the causes he believed in and must have felt that the League election meeting and the Queen's visit offered the football team he cared for a great opportunity.

The Ship Canal was a sign that the city's growth would continue for some time as it offered Manchester terrific development possibilities as an inland seaport. There was still great suffering and discomfort in the area - any city developing at the speed Manchester had in the latter half of the nineteenth century would have experienced this - however this was compensated for by the terrific pride the population felt in the city's many achievements. Now Parlby, and his supporters, wanted a football team that could properly represent the whole of Manchester. A team that everybody could feel equally proud of, and a team that truly represented all that was good about the city.

The Umpire News reported that many Mancunians who had not previously supported Ardwick, were sending applications to purchase shares in the new club. Parlby appeared to be achieving part of his aim, he now needed to secure the ground and use his skills of persuasion to bring John Allison and the others round to his way of thinking.

Parlby succeeded. By the time Ardwick played their

PROMOTION OF A FOOTBALL COMPANY AT ARDWICK.

Last night a meeting was held in the Octagon Congregational Schoolroom, Ardwick, for the purpose of bringing before the public a scheme for forming a company to be called "The Manchester City Football Company, Limited." Mr. J. Chapman presided. The room was crowded, and a vote of confidence in the promoters was passed unanimously. It was explained that the company is to be started with a capital of £2,000, in £1 shares, and is to rent the ground now occupied by the Ardwick Football Club.

STOCKPORT COUNTY v. ARDWICK.

At Stockport. The visitors started, and pressed but shot wide. Hughes and Spittall showed fine form for Ardwick, but Chandley cleared all shots. After the visitors had forced several corners Upton handed in the goal mouth, but the ball was got away. Whitehead and Leigh got down, but Steele cleared finely. Milarvie and Milne passed well, but time arrived without any score.

While steps were being taken to form Manchester City Ardwick AFC continued to play. The Club's last known game (above) occurred two weeks after MCFC became established.

next fixture, a friendly with Newton Heath on Monday 9th April, posters were produced recognising the Club's demise. The *Gorton Reporter* recorded: "On Monday evening Newton Heath played Ardwick 'for the last time' as the posters pathetically put it. In future the Manchester City Club which will shortly be affiliated with the Lancashire Association will occupy the old Ardwick venue, arrangements having been made at last with the MS&L Railway Company."

On Thursday 12th April at a rather crowded meeting of the Manchester City supporters, it was formally announced that opposition to the new club had been abandoned, and that everyone was pulling behind the new 'City' club. A couple of days later Ardwick played their last League game - a 5-2 defeat away to Walsall Town Swifts - finishing the season thirteenth out of fifteen.

The following Monday, 16th April, Manchester City Football Club Limited became a registered company, with its registered address given as 31 Halsbury Street, Stockport Road, Manchester – assumed to be Parlby's home at this point.

Making reference to the end of Ardwick A.F.C. the Club's new motto was 'Even in our own ashes live our wonted fires'. The new club wanted to be an outfit far superior to Ardwick, and with Joshua Parlby driving it forward no one could doubt that the City men would achieve their aims. Already Chesters' Brewery had agreed to provide finance to support the new club. That in itself was some achievement as Stephen Chesters-Thompson was having significant financial hardships himself at this stage and in June 1894 the *Gorton Reporter* carried a detailed article on Chesters-Thompson 's bankruptcy and financial issues. Those issues appear to have had no adverse effect on the Club as Chesters' Brewery and the Club, whether Ardwick or City, had a very healthy relationship with both organisations benefitting from the other.

Parlby's first task after the formation of City was to somehow get the Club accepted into the Football League. The League officials had known about Ardwick's plight all season and must have viewed the new club suspiciously. Was Manchester City simply Ardwick in disguise?

1894-1895 Parlby's City

At the League AGM Parlby spoke convincingly of the ambition, finances, and strength of the new club – it is vital to record that Parlby talked of this as a completely new club. It may have taken the best that Ardwick had to offer, but it tried hard to distinguish itself as a separate entity. This is why the football club has continued to record its foundation as 1894. Other clubs, most notably Manchester United, refer to their original formation as Newton Heath in 1878 (some two years before they were known to play football and 24 years before they became Manchester United), but their history is similar to City's in that they reformed as United in 1902.

At the 1894 AGM Parlby used all his persuasive powers to impress the League committee. A newspaper profile of Parlby, written in April 1904, looked back on his contribution in that meeting: "On May 21st 1894, the day on which Queen Victoria opened the Ship Canal, Mr. Parlby applied for and gained admission to the Second Division. On that occasion he was accused of being eloquent, and there was something of that quality in a fine well remembered peroration in which he told the assembled dignitaries of the League that it would be the endeavour of those associated with the club to whose name the club bore. A final hint that the League might add to the gaiety of the city was done. Without doubt it was largely a matter of personal influence."

That statement makes it totally clear that the link between the pride the city was feeling in connection with the Queen's visit and the opening of the Ship Canal was seen by Parlby as a significant factor in Manchester City's own history. For this reason, the view that City are Manchester's side has existed ever since the name was first chosen.

Significantly this League meeting and vote had been held in Manchester at the 18th Century Old Boar's Head Hotel on the corner of Withy Grove and Corporation Street – replaced by the newspaper works, more commonly known as The Printworks today, in the 1920s. Every attendee would have seen the pride and passion Manchester exhibited that night.

Parlby undoubtedly saw Manchester as a major, significant, developing, modern city and he wanted the football club to share in the ambition and progression of the city. If the Connells, William Beastow, Walter Chew and the others had given the Club its community ethos, then Parlby had been the visionary that made City Manchester's side.

As time moves on it is difficult to appreciate how significant the opening of the Manchester Ship Canal was. This was one of the most significant landmarks in the history of Manchester, and to some extent Britain. Manchester City Council set aside £10,000 to decorate and illuminate the city and the route the Queen would take from Manchester London Road station (Piccadilly) to the canal itself, and then back into Manchester to Exchange Station – not too far from the Football League's meeting. As well as the streets, factory owners and ordinary people dressed their buildings and houses throughout the city.

While the focus for many was on the Queen's visit, Parlby's new City gained enough votes to tie with Leicester Fosse in the election vote and were accepted into the Second Division. As Ardwick had finished in the bottom four they would have had to apply for re-election in any case, however it is extremely doubtful that Ardwick would have received the twenty votes City did, even with Parlby's eloquence. It is a fact that Parlby's role in gaining acceptance of a club with no players and little finance was one of, if not the most important moments in the history of the Club. Without Parlby's persuasion the Club would probably have never arisen from the ashes of Ardwick.

Once again, Parlby headed the poll for a place on the League Management Committee.

That night, after the Queen had performed her duties and departed, there were various events tied in with the Ship Canal opening. There were banquets, fireworks and, to put it simply, Manchester partied well into the night. For Parlby and all those connected with football in Manchester the celebrations took on an added significance. It was as if Manchester had not only gained approval from the game of football but that there was now pride in Manchester that until the Queen's royal visit had not been widely exhibited. The football team hoped to tap into that and represent the dynamism of Manchester at its best.

With City's acceptance into the League came the requirement to find top quality replacements for the players that Ardwick had been forced to sell. In June 1894 The Umpire News reported on Joshua Parlby's transfer activity: "The Manchester City Football Club have this week secured M. Calvey, the centre forward of Blackburn Rovers. He played for them in about half the League Matches and all through the cup ties. He is a fine young fellow, who learned his football in the army. He has weight and youth on his side, and should make a big name for himself. R. Jones, the centre half of the Everton Combination team, has also been engaged. He has often taken the place of Holt in League matches. He is a finished player, placing the ball with great judgement, and is a very hard worker. H. Smith, the right full back of Blackpool, has recently thrown in his lot with the new 'City' club, and comes with a big reputation well earned. From the foregoing it will be seen that Mr. Parlby and his colleagues are doing their utmost to secure a strong team."

The report actually got one of the details wrong. H. E. Smith joined City from Blackburn Rovers not Blackpool - perhaps the reporter was looking forward to his own holiday at Manchester's favourite destination!

Ten years later an article viewed Parlby's part in these developments as another major achievement: "With something less than £250 in hand he entered upon the task of getting a team together. It would take too much space to explain how it was done, but that Mr. Parlby had powers of persuasion, if not money, was shown by the fact that he secured C. Williams for £5, H. Smith, G. Mann, M. Calvey and A. Rowan for £10 each, Nash and Williams for something less."

Calvey, Jones, Mann Williams, Nash and Smith all featured in City's first League game. The only player in this opening fixture to have played for Ardwick was full-back Fred Dyer, proving that this club was not simply Ardwick in disguise. The ground, supporters, and bulk of the committee may have been the same, but the playing squad was different. Also different was the Club's kit.

During the early 1890s white had been the predominant shirt colour with shorts/knickers of a navy blue colour, but now Parlby's City chose to wear blue as their main colour. The *Athletic News* annual recorded Manchester City's colours as "Cambridge Blue shirts and grey knickers." Why blue was chosen is not known. During the latter part of the Twentieth Century suggestions were made that the colour was adopted because of a Masonic influence, however there is no evidence that this is true. In fact those that suggested the connection talked of City's selection of the Masonic colours of pale blue and white, but the truth is that the Club selected Cambridge Blue and grey. White came later, although some photographs of the team during this period suggest the shorts are lighter than grey, but that may simply be because of the exposure level of the photographs.

The selection of blue may be connected with Masonic values of loyalty and so on, but it seems more likely Parlby chose the colours because they allowed the Club to have its own distinctive style. Contemporary material talks of various sides wearing blue, such as Small Heath (Birmingham City), however only three League sides included a pale blue as one of their main colours

– Blackburn Rovers & Liverpool (both wore quartered shirts with Cambridge Blue or similar shade forming a front 'half' and a back 'half') and Everton (a slightly darker blue, but lighter than their modern day shade).

City were the only League side wearing a shirt of Cambridge Blue in the manner chosen. The Blues were unique.

It is worth recording that images of the ground during 1894 suggest the paintwork on the stands was striped blue and white. Whether this had lasted from the first known blue and white kit of 1887, the quartered kit of 1890 or highlighted a new attempt at Manchester City branding is not clear. It does seem likely that Parlby would have wanted to provide a bright, fresh image for the Club and ground.

The opening fixture away to Bury on 1st September saw some very talented players appearing for the Blues. These included twenty year old Charlie Williams. He was a rather unorthodox goalkeeper and had joined City from Arsenal, with whom he had featured in over eighty first team games including the club's first ever League fixture (a 2-2 draw with fellow newcomers Newcastle on 2nd September 1893). Williams was to play for City for a total of eight years, winning many admirers with his often unusual displays.

Others appearing included Pat Finnerhan, who had been spotted by City director Lawrence Furniss when he was refereeing a game involving Northwich Victoria, Finnerhan's club. The former Northwich player was a tricky inside right who always seemed to retain the ball until the absolute perfect time to send it to a team member on his way to goal. In his first two seasons with City he was ever present in the League.

Despite the huge influx of players - or indeed because of the creation of a new side - City lost their opening fixture 4-2. The Club fared a little better in their second game, a 1-1 draw at home to Burton Wanderers. It's worth recording that City utilised the Hyde Road Hotel as their main base and changing rooms, while the ground was officially recorded as "Back of the Hyde Road Hotel."

Manchester City 1894-95.

The first taste of success for the new side came on 8th September at Hyde Road when a crowd of around 4,000 saw City defeat Burslem Port Vale 4-1. The goals provided by Calvey (2), Mann, and Finnerhan. A 2-1 away victory the following week against Walsall Town Swifts helped the Club move up the table but, unfortunately, this was to be their last victory until the return match with Walsall (who eventually ended the season third from bottom). Jim Sharples provided the first 'Manchester City' league hat trick to help the Blues win that game 6-1 on 6th October.

A couple of weeks later City made one of their most important signings of all time when the Welsh wizard Billy Meredith was brought to Manchester from Chirk. City had been playing Sandy Rowan out of position on the right wing and some of the players were clearly unhappy with the situation, including one suspects Rowan himself. Pat Finnerhan urged the Club to approach his former colleague Meredith. Finnerhan's views led the Club to seriously consider Meredith whom Lawrence Furniss had spotted originally playing alongside Finnerhan for Northwich. Indeed Meredith had actually played at Hyde Road against Ardwick in January 1894.

Something else that forced the Club to look to strengthen the side was the departure of four players to Baltimore in the New York Soccer League during October. An American football agent had spent considerable effort illegally persuading members of the City squad that their lives would be much better if they moved away from the grime of Manchester to the land of opportunity. Four players - Wallace, Little, Ferguson, and Calvey - believed the agent and left the Blues for the States, forcing secretary Joshua Parlby to strengthen the side.

According to legend, Parlby and Chairman John Chapman, the City representatives who journeyed to Chirk, North Wales, to sign Meredith were chased around the village, forced to disguise themselves, and buy Meredith's mining colleagues drinks in the local pub before being allowed to talk to the gifted Welsh international. It is also said that the City men were ducked in the village pond and given a very rough time by the locals. A report from the early 1900s talked of Meredith as "Parlby's greatest capture" while also saying that "Mr. Chapman has a right to a share of the credit."

Eventually Meredith signed amateur forms with the Club after insisting that he continue to live and work in Wales. His plan was to work in the mine all week, and then travel to Manchester at weekend. City arranged lodging for him in a house on Clowes Street, close to St. Mark's Church, and provided a £5 signing on fee.

Meredith's first game for the Club was an exciting

The Hyde Road Hotel. Headquarters of City in 1880s & 1890s.

5-4 defeat away to Newcastle United on 27th October 1894. Seven days later he changed with his new team mates in the Hyde Road Hotel and then made his home debut in the game that all Mancunians had been looking forward to - the first League meeting between City and Newton Heath. The Heathens had been relegated to Division Two at the end of the 1893-4 season via a defeat in the Test Matches to Second Division Champions Liverpool. While the new City club were trying to build for the future, Newton Heath were able to adjust to life in the Second rather easily. Prior to the derby they had lost only once out of seven games. City on the other hand had played eleven games winning four and drawing one. In spite of the Blues mixed form they were becoming known for excitement. During the course of those eleven games they had both scored and conceded thirty goals.

TRUE BLUE
Joshua Parlby
The visionary who wanted to create Manchester's club.

Although City were hopeful, it was no real surprise when the Heathens defeated the Blues 5-2. By this time games between City and Newton Heath were clearly derby matches using the term as we know it today. The largest Hyde Road crowd of the season - somewhere in the region of 14,000 - viewed the match as the 'Championship of Cottonopolis' and already both sides had their favourite players. Supporters were thrilled to see the young Billy Meredith make a name for himself by scoring both City's goals in this first League derby. Alongside Meredith, Pat Finnerhan was fast becoming a favourite, while supporters also had time for their opponent's goalkeeper William Douglas. Former Ardwickite Douglas was greeted with loud cheers by the Hyde Road regulars - perhaps at the end they regretted giving him such a good welcome!

Sometime later Meredith wrote about his first derby:

Pre-match coverage for the first League derby.

"I got a little cheer to myself as I trotted off and I had the satisfaction of knowing that I had made a good start in my first home match."

By the time of the next derby meeting City were putting together a few decent results, although Boxing Day must have been a particularly bad day for the Blues as Burton Wanderers defeated them 8-0. This was the first game of the season when the Blues failed to score.

The game on 5th January at Newton Heath ended in a 4-1 defeat and, although the scoreline makes the game appear one sided, *The Umpire* match report actually says that the Heathens owed their victory to luck and brilliant 'keeping by Douglas. At one point in the first half City were awarded several free kicks but somehow Douglas kept all attempts out. In the second period the home side were forced to play defensively for a large portion of the half. Nevertheless it was the Heathens who achieved the first League double. No matter how City played, or how successful the Club was becoming in terms of attracting the best players and bigger support, Newton Heath still appeared to be the more successful on the pitch at this point.

By March City had moved up the table and, on 23rd, achieved their best result of the season when they defeated Lincoln City 11-3. This remains City's record scoreline to this day. For the record the City goalscorers were Pat Finnerhan (2), Billy Meredith (2), Sandy Rowan (2), Bob Milarvie, and four from William McReddie, a forward who signed from Stoke in October. Incredibly,

GRAND ECCENTRIC FOOTBALL MATCH
in aid of the "Chronicle" Cinderella Fund, on the
ground of the "City" Football Company, Hyde-road,
THIS DAY (Wednesday), October 2nd, 1895. The City
League Team v. 12 Gentlemen of Ardwick and District.
"City" Team: Rowan and Broad (goal), Robson and Mawn
(backs), M'Bride and Clifford and Milarvie and Moffatt
(halves), Chapman and Little, Hatton and M'Reddie, cap-
tain (forwards). Ardwick and District: A. Wheeldon (goal),
J. E. Chapman and J. Parlby (backs), Shottin, Prouse, and
G. Robinson (halves), S. Ormrod, J. Reed, J. Weiss, A.
Worstencroft, A. Shephard, and S. Holden (forwards). Kick

Officials Chapman, Parlby & Ormerod liked to play the occasional game.

one of Lincoln's goals was an own goal by a Manchester player.

With City's improved form during the second half of the season the Blues eventually ended the season in a creditable ninth place out of sixteen. Their Manchester rivals finished third, missing promotion by losing their Test Match 3-0 to Stoke. City may not have reached the heights that the Heathens had but were certainly in a position to build.

1895-1896 Test Match Special

1895-6 saw City develop further, with Finnerhan, Meredith, and Rowan in outstanding goal scoring form, and ever present goalkeeper Charlie Williams keeping the scores down.

The derby matches with Newton Heath perhaps indicate how the side was moving forward. In October at North Road Sandy Rowan provided City's equaliser after the Blues had gone behind through "a somewhat lucky goal" as *The Umpire* report stated. Two months later, League leaders City defeated their Manchester rivals for the first time in the League. The biggest derby attendance up to that point - somewhere in the region of 20,000 - watched as Robert Hill, the Blues new signing from Sheffield United, scored a beauty in the fourth minute. The Hyde Road crowd had plenty to cheer about as City seemed to have the initiative. They pushed forward in numbers, with Meredith and Rowan supplying most of the Blues' chances. However, the Heathens were better on the break and it was actually from a City attack that the away side found the equaliser. City half-back Thomas Chapman twice found himself able to send in a shot to test the Heathens''keeper Douglas, only to see the ball find the feet of his opponents' defence. Quickly, on the second such attempt, the Heathens sent the ball up field to Joe Cassidy - who four years later would sign for the Blues - who proceeded to send in a fine shot to level the score.

After the Newton Heath equaliser, City continued to dominate the match, playing in fine passing style, and it was no surprise when City regained the lead. This is how *The Umpire* newspaper reported the goal and the final stages of the match:

"The crowd cheered Meredith for dodging Cartwright, and working round Erentz, he beat Douglas with a magnificent shot, the uproar being tremendous. Still keen but fair football continued to be the order, and Williams put out three or four times in quick succession. Though a corner was awarded to Newton Heath in the last minute, it proved ineffectual, and City won a good game, in which much better football was shown than is usual in local contests. That the City won on their merits will be the verdict of fair-minded observers. They combined better, and were quicker on the ball than their rivals, their passing being of a very high order. The coffers of both organisations will benefit largely. The takings amounting to £410."

After the match City remained at the top of the Division with 24 points, with Burton Wanderers one point behind in second place, Liverpool after playing an extra two games were third with the same number of points as Burton. Newton Heath were fourth, seven points behind City. The big test would come in the two games with promotion hopefuls Liverpool. On New Year's Day the Blues travelled to Anfield aiming to bring some meaning to the table. Due to mixed conditions between the Manchester derby and the Liverpool match City hadn't played a game, while both Liverpool and Burton Wanderers had won both the games they played. City had dropped to third place, three points behind both rivals, but with four games in hand over Liverpool and two over Burton. Unfortunately on the day, City were unable to put Liverpool under the kind of pressure they required. The end result being that the Blues went down 3-1 before an Anfield crowd of around 15,000.

In the return fixture at Hyde Road on 3rd April, Good Friday, a huge crowd for the period of 30,000 saw the two sides fight out a 1-1 draw in what was in effect the Championship decider. City needed to win this game to stand any chance of winning the title as prior to the game Liverpool were four points clear of the Blues, with a far superior goal average. This was the Anfield club's last game of the season whereas City still had fixtures against Leicester and Notts County to complete. In the end the draw was not good enough for the Blues, but it did mean that if they won their last two fixtures they would end the season in second place and feature in the Test Match play offs.

Within the next five days City despatched Leicester (2-1) and Notts County (2-0) and ended the season on 46 points level with Liverpool, with Grimsby and Burton Wanderers four points behind in third and fourth spot respectively. All City needed to do now was to play with the same conviction through the Test Matches and they would be in the First Division, alongside the then Lancashire giants Preston, Bolton, Blackburn, Burnley, Bury and Everton.

In 1896 the Test Matches were to be played on a

mini-league basis with Liverpool and City each facing the two bottom clubs in Division One - Small Heath (later Birmingham City), and West Bromwich Albion - home and away. The same points system would operate as in the League (2 for a win, 1 for a draw), and the two teams at the top of the table would play the following season in Division One, the others would be in the Second Division.

City's first Test Match fixture was at home to the First Division's bottom club, West Bromwich Albion, on 18th April. For this special fixture, billed as "the most important Manchester City fixture so far", the directors doubled admission prices for some areas from sixpence to a shilling believing that the Manchester public would pay for the chance to help City into the 'top league'. Despite fantastic weather conditions, the increased admission kept the attendance down to 8,000 according to *The Umpire* newspaper, and 6,000 according to other sources, with gate receipts of £298. It seems many supporters boycotted the game to prove to the management of the Club their anger at the unnecessary increase in price. The directors must have been concerned that their plan backfired totally. As can be seen, the gate receipts were considerably smaller than the December derby game even though the Test Match was much more important, and of a higher profile. Not only did the low attendance affect the Club's balance sheet, it also affected support inside the ground.

By this point City supporters were famous for making a carnival-like atmosphere at big games, something City fans repeated ninety years later with the inflatable banana craze. Regularly during the 1890s supporters played bugles and drums when the Blues attacked and would, occasionally, wear fancy dress. For the right reasons match reports of the period often quoted the fans behaviour as much as the incidents on the pitch. This carnival spirit helped lift many a game for the Blues and the noise and fervour all added to the experience of being a Blue. Without this atmosphere, even on the brightest of days, Hyde Road must have provided a very real picture of gloomy, depressing, industrial Manchester. A tightly packed ground, surrounded by terraced streets, factories, and railway viaducts. Typical Manchester many would say, but then it was always the people, and in particular City supporters, who brightened this part of the industrial city.

Without the great noisy crowd the Blues went a goal down in only the third minute, apparently City's great extrovert 'keeper, Charlie Williams was 'all at sea' as Albion's Perry sent his shot over the heads of the defence. The ball hit the cross bar and rebounded in. The sizeable Albion support in the crowd made all the noise and, at times, it must have seemed as if the game was being played in the Midlands not Manchester.

Nevertheless, City fought back and for much of the game they piled on the pressure. Both Rowan and Finnerhan had shots saved, before Finnerhan scored through a "capital shot." In the second half the pace of the game slowed as the heat started to affect the players. Both sides attacked, but neither could find the goal until virtually the last minute when an Albion forward put the ball in the net only for it to be disallowed. The game ended 1-1. Not a bad result, but not good enough for a home side aiming to achieve promotion.

At Anfield on the same day, Liverpool performed to the level City needed to when they defeated Small Heath 4-0.

In the return fixture, at Stoney Lane, West Bromwich, City suffered a heavy 6-1 defeat two days later. Even with this result all was not lost as Small Heath held Liverpool to a no score draw. If the Blues could win their two games against Small Heath and other results went their way, City could still take one of the two Division One places.

On April 25th at Hyde Road the Blues faced Small Heath in a game they had to win. Something they managed in style. It was a game that the Blues dominated from start to finish and, by the time the final whistle was blown City were the victors by three goals to nil. At Anfield, Liverpool defeated Albion 2-0. The future looked bright again, especially as the directors had returned admission prices to their normal Hyde

Celtic great Willie Maley appeared for City in February 1896.

Road level. City still had to win the return fixture with Small Heath and hope that Liverpool either draw or beat Albion to be certain of promotion. If both Albion and City were to win their final fixtures then goal average would determine the team second to Liverpool. All the ifs and maybes were written about in the local papers, and discussed in the pubs of Manchester leading up to the game. City's attempts to reach the 'top league' was the talking point in the city. Nothing else mattered.

In the end all the permutations were unimportant as City were completely humiliated by Small Heath at Coventry Road, Birmingham. The Blues went down to an 8-0 thrashing and were left to spend the next season in the Second Division. In the other fixture, Liverpool lost 2-0 to Albion – a scoreline that ensured both those sides would meet again the following season in the First Division. The Blues were devastated, as were Small Heath. Their high scoring victory, like City's 5-2 against Stoke in 1998, was too little due to results elsewhere, and the Birmingham side were relegated to the Second Division.

If only City had spent more time planning for their opening fixture against Albion. With normal admission prices, and a City victory, it might have been all so different.

Despite the feeling of failure at the season's end, it had been quite a successful period for the 'Cambridge Blues'. They had achieved their highest position so far, and had made quite a large profit. In the close season they used some of this cash to build dressing rooms, sharing the cost with Chesters' Brewery, who must have been pleased with the profits being generated by the usually large Hyde Road crowds.

1896-1897 Gillespie Arrives

The following season was perhaps a transitional one. The Blues were still suffering from their 'knock-back' in the Test Matches when the season opened. Only two of their opening ten fixtures ended in victory, and a depressing, drizzly, Hyde Road derby ended goalless.

City needed reshaping and secretary Sam Ormerod, who had replaced Josh Parlby some twelve months earlier, was the man to do it. Ormerod, who lived at 1 Beech Grove, Longsight, decided to freshen things up a little. The shorts were changed from grey to white – meaning that the side were wearing blue and white for the first time since the quartered shirts of 1890-91.

Ormerod, who was also a vice-president of the Lancashire FA, brought in some new blood while keeping Pat Finnerhan, George Mann, Billy Meredith, and goalkeeper Charlie Williams as the nucleus of the side. Full back Dick Ray was signed in May 1896 after playing for Burslem Port Vale, half back Charlie Bannister arrived from Newtown, and forward William Townley arrived

from Darwen. Townley was quite a famous player who had scored a hat trick for Blackburn Rovers in the 1890 FA Cup Final. Other players to make their debuts for City during the season were William 'Doc' Holmes, a Matlock born centre-half who had been bought from Chesterfield in the close season, and centre forward Billy Gillespie signed from Lincoln City in January 1897. Gillespie was the brother of Newton Heath's Matthew, and was one of City's first target men. He was the kind of player who always seemed to appear in the penalty box ready to latch onto a Meredith cross, and more often than not would find the target. He was a strong, fearless player. In the 1930s he was remembered in the *Manchester Football News* by J.C. Clegg: "The way he would dive in to head the ball at the risk of maiming himself was enough to make the spectators shudder. At times he would literally hurl himself at the ball and not infrequently did he follow it into the net." No doubt he also forced the opposing goalkeeper into the net!

Gillespie was quite a character. Apart from his skills on the football field he became infamous for off the field activities. The big city life, in particular the brewing industry that seemed to be so closely linked with everybody at Hyde Road, caused Gillespie one or two problems. According to tales handed down through the generations, He liked his drink so much that he was frequently dropped for failing to be sober for matches. Other stories say he actually played while he was drunk. When looking at his career as a whole it can be seen that in his later years at City he did miss the occasional game for reasons that it seems hard to determine, however from the moment he signed in January 1897 through to September 1898 he featured in 44 consecutive League games. During which time he became a hero.

City's great winger Billy Meredith took Gillespie in hand and would regularly take him training or fishing to keep him from the city's distractions. The Welshman would also keep hold of his colleague's money for him, making sure he banked a little each week. Meredith would more or less provide Gillespie with pocket money as and when required to save the centre forward from blowing it all in one go.

In spite of these potential problems, Billy Gillespie was a tremendous buy. He scored on his debut - a 3-1 defeat at Darwen - and provided a further three goals in the ten matches that followed. Unfortunately, his goals and the signing of the other players were not enough to see City achieve the Test Matches as the Blues ended the season in sixth place, seven points behind second placed Newton Heath. Nevertheless there was hope that the next season could provide a real promotion chance. The new players had bedded down and started to play as a team by the end of 1896-97. Incidentally, Manchester rivals Newton Heath found success eluding them, like it had City, in the Test Matches.

1897-1898 Buxton and Stockport

Secretary Sam Ormerod seemed to be planning for the future in both his domestic life and at City. By the start of 1897-98 he had moved to 5 Park Avenue, Longsight, and he had strengthened the City squad. He signed two players by the name William Smith. Fortunately, in those days the chant of "There's only one William Smith" had not been thought of, nevertheless to avoid confusion between the two players a decision was taken to provide both Smiths with nicknames after the towns they had come from. The right-half had signed from Buxton on 24th April 1897, while the inside-right was given the name Stockport after signing from County. Both 'Buxton' and 'Stockport' Smith made their debuts in City's 3-0 Hyde Road victory over Gainsborough Trinity. Billy Meredith, Billy Gillespie, and Fred Williams provided the goals.

City's only point dropped in their first nine games was in the 1-1 draw with Newton Heath at Clayton. The Blues had been behind for much of the game through a Matt Gillespie goal - perhaps brother Billy should have had a quiet word with him. Then, in the last minute Dick Ray scored "a clever goal with a high cross." According to the 'Umpire' report of the game the City faithful cheered loudly and the excitement was intense. It seems this was a typical derby match for tension, atmosphere, and excitement. The 20,000 crowd was also the largest Newton Heath home attendance up to this point.

As the season progressed City's form seemed to falter rather too frequently for a side determined to move out of the division. The Blues finished the season in third place - a point above Newton Heath - but missed the Test Match play offs by six points. They had let themselves down rather too often that season.

1898-1899
Manchester's First National Success

In the close season, City and Chesters combined to form a 'Grand Stand Syndicate' to raise funds to erect a new covered stand. Chesters took 250 £1 shares and advanced more money at a low rate of interest, they also negotiated with the Railway Company to keep the ground rental at the same level for the following five years. Together the Blues and the brewery tried to raise £1,500 for a stand from the Fulham Pageant, transport it to Manchester, and re-erect it on the 'sixpence' side at Hyde Road. Hyde Road was now a ground fit for top class football. It had achieved a few large crowds - regularly achieving 20,000 for derby matches, and the exceedingly large 30,000 for the Good Friday 1896 meeting with Liverpool - and provided decent accommodation. However, it was still not good enough for the large City crowds, even though it had played host to a representative game when on 6th November 1897 the Football League defeated the Irish League 8-1. The Football League side that day included two City players - goalkeeper Charlie Williams, and half-back William 'Doc' Holmes.

1898-99. Front (l to r): Meredith, 'Stockport' Smith, Gillespie, Dougal & Cowie. Stood: Ormerod (manager), Richmond (director), Moffatt, Reed, 'Buxton' Smith, Jones, Holmes & Chapman (chairman) Back (suited): Broad (trainer), F. Williams, Boswell (director), Ray, unknown in doorway and Forrest (director).

The 1898-9 season was to be the first with automatic promotion and relegation. The Test Matches were not to continue after a suspiciously convenient no score draw allowed both Burnley and Stoke to play in the First Division. City were keen to take this opportunity to move out of the Second Division once and for all.

They started the season in style defeating Grimsby 7-2 with hat tricks from Meredith and Gillespie. In fact goal scoring was something City seemed particularly good at as only two games ended without the Blues scoring, while they scored three or more in sixteen of their League matches.

The boys band prepare to play as Meredith takes a corner, 1898-99.

tenths of the hour and a half they never gave the City a chance. Meredith was the only Mancunian who got a chance to do anything worthy of a good cheer."

Glossop seemed invigorated by their victory and they went on to mount a challenge for promotion. As for City, the Blues returned to winning ways in the next match – a 1-0 win at another high-spending club, New Brighton Tower. According to New Brighton historians this game attracted the club's record attendance of 10,000 as thousands of Mancunians travelled to the Wirral seaside town to take in the sights and visit the tower (at that time bigger than Blackpool's).

The Blues tenth League game saw them travel to promotion rivals Glossop North End. According to the *Glossop Dale Chronicle* the attendance was 7,000 with over half the attendance coming from Manchester. City won the match 2-1 with goals from Gillespie and Meredith. The *Chronicle* reporter described the opener as "the softest I have ever seen." He went on: "Williams [Glossop's 'keeper] got down to stop the ball as it rolled quietly goalwards, but he completely missed it, although it was going so slowly it hardly rolled as far as the net."

The Glossop match came in the middle of a 13 match unbeaten run, placing City as comfortable League leaders. Despite a shock 4-1 defeat at Small Heath on 27th December, the Blues led the table by three points at the end of the calendar year. New Brighton Tower were second, followed by Leicester Fosse and then Newton Heath.

On 2nd January a 12,000 crowd witnessed a disappointing 2-0 defeat to Glossop. The Derbyshire side were financed by Samuel Hill-Wood, a wealthy benefactor who ultimately moved to Arsenal and transformed the London club. Back in January 1899 his money had attracted significant stars to Glossop and a number of Manchester-based journalists had criticised the club for its spending. This served to encourage Glossop and the town's *Chronicle* newspaper crowed about their victory: "Monday was the day! We were at Manchester, watching the eleven from the Derbyshire 'village' beating the top of the Division."

The report went on: "right from the start the visitors assumed the upper hand, and for seven-

The highlight of the season came a month after victory at New Brighton. City still led the table and had a game in hand over most teams, but the gap had reduced to a point over New Brighton and Leicester. It was

The programme from the 10-0 win over Darwen.

70

Welsh international Meredith on a contemporary card.

important the side stressed its authority against one of the Division's struggling sides Darwen.

On 18th February the Blues thrashed Darwen 10-0 at Hyde Road. Meredith scored his third hat trick of the season that day but even he was outshone by Fred Williams who scored five. The *Athletic News*, taking a swipe at the so called aristocratic teams like Aston Villa and Stoke, described City's win: "After such a victorious issue you would expect to hear of clock-work movements from wing to wing and all the rest of the Aston-cum-Stokey-Villa class jargon. Such was far from being the case. Gillespie's, Dougal's and Meredith's goals were superb individual efforts - 'aid' in each of which would have been a misfortune."

The newspaper went on to describe individual players with the most interesting comment proving that City's Gillespie was quite a mean player: "His tendency to push the goalkeeper through with the ball was in evidence throughout the game and often he missed the mark and had to find his way out of the network." There's no doubt that Gillespie intimidated more opponents than anyone else on the City side. Although, in the

twenty-first century he would be severely dealt with, during the 1890s he was encouraged to play like this. At least it added grit, determination, and excitement.

Cult hero Gillespie's barging technique had also been seen in another significant game during the season - the Hyde Road derby. In the Boxing Day game the Heathens 'keeper Frank Barrett clearly had the ball in his hands when Gillespie provided his usual party piece by pushing both Barrett and the ball into the net for City's third goal. The Blues eventually defeated the Heathens 4-0 and had a George Dougal effort disallowed for offside.

City's fine form continued and about a month before the end of the season they were certainties for the Second Division title. In their last game of the season they defeated Blackpool 4-1. Gillespie provided the first goal – "a terrific shot" according to *The Umpire News* - but was later penalised for charging the Blackpool 'keeper who was trying to make a save from Buxton Smith. Perhaps Gillespie was now a marked man, or perhaps he'd used the technique once too often. New recruit Jimmy Ross provided the second goal with a 'curling

Billy Gillespie attacks the Stoneyard end in 1898-99.

shot', while City's third came from Meredith. Although the referee had to consult both linesmen before allowing this one to stand.

Blackpool soon pulled one back, but late on in the game Meredith scored his second with a 'high shot'.

The Blues ended the season as Champions, six points above their nearest rivals Glossop (who had performed superbly during March and April to take second place with a point more than Leicester). To celebrate their promotion and provide the players with financial reward, both sides played each other home and away a few days after the season ended. The proceeds of each side's home game were shared between the players of that club.

City's high scoring had been the deciding factor that season. Their 92 goals being far superior to the goals tally for any other club in either division that season. The Welsh winger - by this point football's first true 'star' - Billy Meredith provided 29 goals, the bustling Billy Gillespie a further 17, and Fred Williams 11.

Jimmy Ross, who had played in only nine games had scored seven. Ross, who signed from Burnley for a reported £50, was one of the League's earliest and most influential players. He had been a member of the famous Preston North End 'Invincibles', and had scored an incredible eight goals when Preston beat Hyde 26-0 in the record breaking FA Cup tie of 15th October 1887 - a game in which the referee is reputed to have lost his watch and allowed play to last two hours. In addition, he was the Football League's top scorer in 1890 (24 goals), and was quite a character.

Years later Billy Meredith, looking back on his City days, remembered Ross with great affection: "I must confess that Ross will always be my favourite hero. He was good at everything he put his hand to and what he didn't know about football wasn't worth knowing. At billiards and card games he was an expert. Though he must have been thirty-four at least when he joined us, he was able to win seventy yards handicaps with ease and did so. He could talk like a lawyer and on and off the pitch his comic sayings had us in stitches." It seems the introduction of the experienced Ross at a crucial stage in the season was what City needed to guarantee success.

Although everything was bright on the pitch, there were still a few concerns off it. There was a belief that Hyde Road was not good enough for First Division

Manchester City finished their programme on Saturday by beating Blackpool at Hyde Road by 4 goals to 1, and have the splendid record of 52 points out of a possible 68. Glossop North End also wound up their season's doings by defeating their visitors from Loughbro' by 4 to 0, and can boast of the creditable number of 46 points, which is only two less than sufficed to give Burnley the championship of the second division last season. New Brighton lost their chance by allowing the Fosse to beat them at Leicester by 4 goals to 1, so Manchester and Glossop are safe for the first division, for even if the Fosse should equal the latter in points by winning their remaining match, which is with Small Heath, at Leicester, they would be behind on goal average.

The second division table is now almost complete, only two more matches having to be played, these being Leicester Fosse and Small Heath, on the ground of the latter, and New Brighton and Loughborough, on the ground of the former. Manchester City have scored 52 points, a larger number than has ever previously been obtained, although it must be remembered that the second division is larger now than it used to be, and therefore the opportunities of getting more points have been increased. Their goal average - 92 to 35 - is a really splendid one, and shows how accurate their shooting has been on the whole. It is a pity, however, that they did not reach three figures in goals, and thus equal a record which is in existence.

Record breaking City won Manchester's first national honour.

football. No matter what the Club did to improve the facilities, it would always be a cramped ground. Access was restricted to two sides, and the shape of the enclosure made the erection of huge stands almost impossible. Because of potential problems with the large crowds City expected in the First Division, the Club management looked at what was available further down Hyde Road at Belle Vue.

Belle Vue was a huge pleasure gardens, and entertainment centre. Like City, it offered Mancunians a release from the daily grind - it was hugely popular. Alongside the pleasure gardens was the Belle Vue Athletics track which had played host to the floodlit friendly between Ardwick and Newton Heath in 1889. This ground offered potential. Already it was a popular sporting venue, it was relatively close to City's Hyde Road ground and was within St. Mark's parish.

It had perfect access, was capable of holding between forty and fifty thousand and seemed to offer everything that Hyde Road couldn't. However, for some unknown reason it was decided to stay at Hyde Road and erect the Fulham Pageant stand. Perhaps Chesters were keen to keep their investment in Ardwick. The Belle Vue venue may not have offered the Brewery as many money making opportunities, or may be everyone associated with the Club simply felt that Hyde Road was home, and that it should be given at least one more season. After all, both the Club and the brewery knew that the ground rental could not increase for another four years thanks to the agreement of the previous year, and that Hyde Road had become an established football ground.

Whatever the reason, City decided to refurbish Hyde Road ready for top flight soccer. They wanted to be a real credit to Manchester and, although Newton Heath had featured in the First Division between 1892 to 1894, City were proud of the fact that they were the first of the two Manchester sides to reach Division One on merit. All they needed to do now was prove how a successful Manchester side could benefit football.

1892-1899 SUMMARY

Major Trophies Won: Second Division Champions 1898-99
Highest League Attendance: c.30,000 Liverpool, 03/04/96
Highest Cup Attendance: c.6,000 Wigan County, 29/01/98 (FA Cup)
Secretary/Managers: 1889-93 Lawrence Furniss, 1893-95 Joshua Parlby & 1895-1902 Sam Ormerod

Seasonal Record:

Season	League	Posn	FA Cup	Other	Leading Scorer	Average Attendance
1892-93	FL Div2	5	Q1		Weir 8	3,000
1893-94	FL Div2	13	Q1		Morris 7	4,000
1894-95	FL Div2	9	Did not enter		Finnerhan 14	6,000
1895-96	FL Div2	2	Q1	Failed in Test Matches	Meredith 12	10,000
1896-97	FL Div2	6	Rnd 1		Meredith 10	8,000
1897-98	FL Div2	3	Rnd 2		Gillespie 18	8,000
1898-99	FL Div2	Champions	Rnd 1		Meredith 29	10,000

Future Prime Minister Arthur Balfour stood at the entrance to the players' tunnel, Hyde Road, September 1900.

1899-1902
Meredith –
The First Star

"The City executive, during the close season, has shown commendable enterprise as far as their ground is concerned. Access was inconvenient to thousands who patronised the matches week after week. Much has been done to cope with large crowds."

Commentary prior to the first Division One season in *The Athletic News*, 21st August 1899

1899-1900 First Division

With City's promotion came major interest in Manchester's ability to sustain a top flight club. Newton Heath had spent two seasons in the First Division but had never actually achieved a great deal. City had never featured in this class of football at all. Even in the Club's developing years, prior to joining the League, the Blues' friendlies with the major sides of the day - Preston, Celtic, Blackburn etc., almost always ended with City on the losing side. Occasional victories, such as the 1892 Manchester Cup success against Bolton, made the public notice the Club but were simply one offs. City's arrival in the First Division would test the Club's resolve.

In addition to the strength of the playing side, Hyde Road itself would be tested. Following the decision to

remain at the ground, improvements had been made. The 1887 stand, paid for by Chesters, had been replaced by the new 75 yard long former Fulham pageant stand which, according to *The Umpire* newspaper, could accommodate 4,000 spectators under cover and would help the ground provide a decent view for over 28,000. Over the course of the next year or so other improvements were made including access to the ground which was improved with new turnstiles opened on Bennett Street and behind the Hyde Road Hotel. The dressing rooms now had Russian and Turkish plunge baths and the secretary, Sam Ormerod, even had his own office and telephone. The Club was moving forward.

The opening fixture in the First Division was away to Blackburn Rovers. Blackburn had finished the previous season in sixth place, and had only lost two games at home all season. The game was not going to be an easy one, but then no game in the First could be classed as easy for the Blues.

A crowd of around 10,000, many travelling from Manchester, saw the Blues lose an exciting match by the odd goal in seven. City's scorers that day were Billy Meredith, Jimmy Ross, and Fred Williams. The Blues may not have won the game but their performance satisfied all Mancunians in the crowd. They had put on a fine show and could only have been looking forward to their next game - the first Division One match at Hyde Road. City's opponents on 9th September 1899 for this milestone of a match were the previous season's FA Cup finalists Derby County, captained by legendary England international goalscorer Steve Bloomer.

A 22,000 attendance provided a good atmosphere for the game. When the players entered the field the noise from the City supporters was described as being 'electrifying', and certainly did a great deal to lift the players for what could have been a tense occasion. City Captain Billy Meredith won the toss and elected to play towards the Galloway Works end of the ground, defending the Hyde Road Hotel end.

Within minutes of Derby kicking off, Fred Williams obtained the ball and then provided George Dougal with a chance. Dougal, without hesitation shot at goal, only to see this City's first attempt, go wide. Even though the ball ended some distance from the Galloway net, the crowd gave Dougal a huge cheer and a good round of applause.

According to reports, City dominated play with the visitor's defence having "a particularly warm time". Billy Gillespie forced Derby's Fryer to make a great save from the City forward's header, luckily for Fryer, Gillespie had not been close enough to force both the ball and the player over the line.

City really did pile on the pressure for much of the first half, although Derby did make the occasional surge forward. Interestingly, goal expert Steve Bloomer was unable to get so much as a look in as the Blues' defence managed to curtail any advance he tried to make.

After a short spell of pressure from Derby the first goal came in the twenty-fifth minute. Appropriately it was the home side who took the lead. *The Umpire* newspaper described what was a controversial goal: "Play, however, was again in favour of the City men before very long, and F. Williams and Dougal bustling Methven, the former shot in goal. Fryer saved, but the home forwards coming in a body pushed the ball

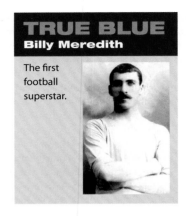

TRUE BLUE
Billy Meredith

The first football superstar.

through. There was apparently a doubt in the mind of the referee as to the legitimacy of the point for, on Derby protesting, he had to consult both linesmen before giving his decision in favour of the home side; and on his pointing to the centre the crowd sent a mighty roar."

The goal was credited to, who else but Billy Gillespie. The old trick seemed to work again.

A few minutes later veteran Jimmy Ross scored City's second. The *Athletic News*, talking about City's right wing players, stressed the importance of Jimmy Ross and his partner the great Billy Meredith: "For real brilliance the right wing took the biscuit....In fact, there are few, if any, better men at outside right (Meredith). His partner, the veteran Ross, of whom it is predicted every season that he has had his day, is in reality taking a second lease of footballing life, despite the paucity of head-covering, and as a wing the two will cause some trouble".

The Blues were still leading 2-0 when the second half commenced. Almost immediately the ageless Ross and dribbling wizard Meredith combined to put Derby under more pressure, but an ankle injury to Ross limited City's chances for a short while. When the former Preston man returned a few minutes later, the Blues resumed the attack.

City soon increased their lead. This time through Meredith, although there is some doubt over whether the 26 year old Meredith actually scored or whether he merely claimed the goal. It seems that Billy Gillespie may have had the final decisive touch but Meredith claimed it. In the Topical Times some twenty years later Meredith provided his view of why the goal was actually his: "From the corner flag I kicked at goal and the ball curled under the bar but, striking the upright bounced back. To save disputes Gillespie promptly headed it into the net but it was agreed that I had scored the goal all right, and at that time I was supposed to have taken out a patent for goals of this kind."

According to *The Umpire* match report the goal came not from a corner, but via a magnificent run by Meredith, and that Gillespie provided the finishing touch as Derby's Fryer was about to save Meredith's shot. Nevertheless, the newspaper did stress Meredith's involvement claiming: "credit must be awarded to the City Captain for the achievement."

A short while later Meredith increased City's lead to four by a rather magnificent solo effort. The following is Meredith's own view of the goal, which unlike his first effort, seems to match almost word for word *The Umpire* description: "A free-kick had been given against us and

I was quite near my own goal when I fastened on to the ball. Carrying it at my toes I galloped down the field, the whole of the Derby team hot upon my heels. Keeping the lead the whole length of the field, I found myself with only Fryer to beat. Giving a mighty kick, I let fly at the goal and the keeper only just managed to touch the ball before it curled itself into the corner of the net, the force sufficient to send Fryer spinning. I rather liked that goal, thinking it above the average, and I can remember the chase I led the field that day."

City's trainer Jimmy Broad was so impressed with Meredith's solo effort he raced up and down the touch line celebrating, and the Club was so pleased with their first home appearance in Division One that they allowed Meredith to claim the match ball. The Blues had not only arrived in the First Division, but they were also providing much excitement. In their following game, City won 4-1 at their Lancashire rivals Bury, with both Meredith and Ross finding the net once again.

Ross followed that by providing two goals in City's 5-1 victory over Notts County at Hyde Road seven days later. By this time secretary Sam Ormerod was delighted with the Club's progress. Sixteen goals and three victories in the Club's opening four fixtures signified that the Blues were more than a match for the big boys of the First Division and, being a big city club, they were able to draw decent sized crowds. Ormerod, pleased by the popularity of his side, told the *Athletic News*: "I really do wish they would stop coming, or else we shall have to make more extensive alterations to the ground. We have taken £350 in season ticket money alone thus far. Our accountant is taxed to the limit and we are contemplating another huge stand to take up the space at the Hyde Road entrance from the railway arch."

Although City's attendances were constant - a regular 20,000 plus - their success did not last. A series of ten games from December to March without victory saw the Blues slip down the table and, for the first time, the press started to point an accusing finger at Meredith and Ross. One article claimed that Meredith was absolutely brilliant when he was being well served by his colleagues but when the going got tough, Meredith disappeared. It seems that at this stage in the Welshman's career he needed the experienced Jimmy Ross more than Ross needed him. One article claimed that Meredith: "doesn't like donkey-work and if his partner is off, Meredith is off too. The worst of it is that, with Meredith off colour, there doesn't seem to be much stuffing left in the City attack - not even when Ross is playing."

Even with this concern over Meredith's playing ability, he still managed to end the season as City's top scorer with fourteen goals in the thirty-three League games he played. The next season, however, saw the player really struggle to find the net as he only managed seven goals from thirty-four games. That may have

been fine for most players but not for City's star player. By this time Meredith was hugely popular with the general public. Even in those days of limited media coverage, you didn't need to come from Manchester or understand football to know who Meredith was. Newspapers provided pen-pictures of the stars with cartoonists providing the face and features for all to see. Unfortunately, Meredith also found that fame could lead to ridicule as cartoonists begun to make fun of the lean spell he was having. In one cartoon marked 'Run Dry', Meredith has placed a bucket marked 'goals' under a tap with the comment: "It's very funny. I can't get anything at all now - look you!"

With the latter half of the 1899-1900 season and 1900-01 seeing Meredith struggle for goals it's no wonder the Blues themselves could not maintain the form they had seen in September 1899. An off form Meredith, regardless of the strength of the rest of the side, was not going to help the Blues. Nor could they drop the clean living Welshman as he, above everybody else, was City's star and the man many supporters had come to watch.

Even with the emerging concerns at the start of the new century, City did manage to end their first Division One season in a satisfying seventh place. The most pleasing part was probably the fact that the Blues ended the season above all their Lancastrian rivals - teams such as Preston, Bury, and Blackburn who had dominated football in the north-west.

Although much was made of the role of players such as Ross and Meredith, City's position was achieved through the hard work of the whole team. Players such as the eccentric goalkeeper Charlie Williams who, not only kept the opposition at bay, he also ended up on the score sheet in one match. This is believed to be the first top flight goal scored by a 'keeper.

The game was the return with Sunderland on 14th April 1900 at Roker Park, played in a windy conditions. City full back, Bert Read, who always had to concentrate when close to Williams because it was often difficult to predict what the goalkeeper would do next, had a perfect view of how the goal was scored. He often recounted the following version of events: "I picked up the ball, placed it, and then just lifted it with my toe into Charlie Williams' hands. He drove it plumb down the centre of the field. It bounced, each time, so it seemed, gaining speed. Porteous and Gow, the Sunderland backs, were taken by surprise. They got in each other's way and the ball sailed towards Doig, the famous Scottish international goalkeeper. He seemed to have it covered, but a sudden gust of wind swung the ball off his fingertips into the net."

Williams was one of the key City players at this time, and many believed that only his unorthodox goalkeeping style prevented him from playing for

England. Another important player during the Blues' first Division One season was the experienced Welsh international full back David Jones. 'DI', as he was known to City supporters, signed for the Blues at the end of September 1898, and made his debut in the 3-0 victory over Luton on 8th October 1898, early in City's promotion season. Although he played a defensive role, he did make it onto City's score sheet a mere six weeks into his Hyde Road career when he combined with Billy Gillespie to give the Blues a 2-0 victory at home to Walsall.

Prior to City, Jones had given Bolton ten years' service, captaining the Trotters 1894 FA Cup Final side. He had also, on several occasions tried to persuade his former Chirk team mate, Billy Meredith, to sign for Bolton. Fortunately for City he failed in his attempts. It was possibly the opportunity of playing with Meredith once more that attracted him to the progressive Hyde Road club in 1898, although he was probably aware of the potential for a successful Manchester side when, over ten years earlier, he featured in a few games for Newton Heath.

Di Jones

During the 1899-1900 season Jones was ever-present in City's thirty-four League games and two FA Cup matches. Charlie Williams, centre-half 'Buxton' Smith, and wing-half 'Doc' Holmes also appeared in every game, helping to provide a little consistency in defence during the Club's inaugural Division One season.

As the Blues adjusted to life in the top flight, Sam Ormerod frequently tried to strengthen the squad. One player he succeeded in bringing to the Club was the well-known Joe Cassidy from neighbours Newton Heath. Cassidy was a 'strong and burly' forward who was 27 by the time he signed for the Blues. For Newton Heath, he had provided much needed fire power during the 1893 Test Matches, helping to prolong the Club's First Division status for one more season, and over the course of the next six years he scored four goals for the Heathens in derby matches against City. The Blues knew only too well what kind of danger he posed in front of goal.

When he moved to City for a weekly wage of £4, the Newton Heath directors admitted that he was the best forward they had ever had, and that it was only because the Club was in such dire financial straits that they were prepared to let him go. According to the Heathens they sold Cassidy to the Blues for £250 to ease their debts.

Cassidy made his debut in the last game of the 1899-1900, but it was the following season when he was able to prove his worth.

1900-1901 Cassidy's Goals

Joe Cassidy ended the 1900-01 season as top scorer with fourteen goals. His opening goal came in City's third game of the season - a 1-0 victory at home to Nottingham Forest.

The Blues next home game was quite a newsworthy event as local M.P. and future Prime Minister Arthur Balfour attended Hyde Road for the visit of Stoke. Naturally, all the newspapers of the day provided reports on his visit, while the *Illustrated London News* went one stage further and sent a photographer. Balfour, accompanied by City Chairman John Chapman, was introduced to the captains and, after City had won the toss to select ends, he was given the task of starting the game for the visitors. Mr. Balfour took a short run before sending the ball some thirty yards towards the City goal. According to reports of the period he quickly left the field as play was going on around him. Whether activity on the pitch was as frenzied as usual at the start of the match isn't known, although the thought of the local M.P. rushing off the pitch as the likes of Meredith and Jones charge around paints an interesting picture. Fortunately, Billy Gillespie was missing from the line-up that day, thus preventing the embarrassing situation of having a City forward 'charging' the future Prime Minister!

Mr. Balfour did actually leave the pitch safely, even

Top: Arthur Balfour with Billy Meredith and the referee (far left). Below left: Balfour entered through a normal turnstile.

though the Blues were quick to obtain the loose ball and attack the Stoke goal. Within the first five minutes both Fred Williams and Joe Cassidy forced Wilkes, the Stoke goalkeeper, to make daring saves, proving that City were keen to win in front of their distinguished visitor.

A mere ten minutes into the game, the Blues rather expectedly took the lead through a Joe Davies effort. According to match reports, the early stages of the game were totally one sided. The *Manchester Evening News* outlined City's domination by describing the action after the opening goal had been scored: "The home players continued to have all the best of the play, Meredith in particular distinguishing himself. With the exception of the occasional breakaway, Stoke were continually on the defensive, and it was not long before a second goal was scored as the result of a fine centre by Meredith. There was no doubt about the way in which the other City forwards were taking their captain's centre. With a lead of two goals the City men still played with dash and vigour. The effective play was not always on the

right wing, Dougal and Williams combining in a way which raised the enthusiasm of the spectators very considerably".

As the game progressed Stoke did get their act together a little, and in the latter stages of the first half they managed to test Charlie Williams a little. City's extrovert 'keeper performed well enough to keep the score at 2-0 into the half-time interval.

The second half was nowhere near as exciting as the first - The *Manchester Evening News* suggested that this may have been because Arthur Balfour had quietly departed from the ground a few moments prior to the interval, although the truth of the matter was that City felt they had done enough. Later in the half the visitors did put the Blues under pressure, although when the Stoke forward, Benbow, was forced to leave the pitch through injury, their chances became limited. Benbow was off the pitch for approximately ten minutes before coming back on, and although he was clearly suffering from the injury and shock he "pluckily played outside

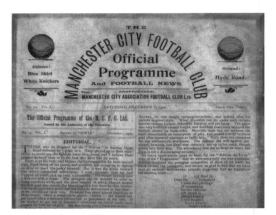

A City match programme from December 1901.

left" according to the report, before retiring three minutes later.

With Stoke down to ten men, City should have increased their lead, however Stoke defended brilliantly to ensure the score remained at 2-0.

The 1900-01 season was perhaps a consolidation season. It was only the Blues second season in the First Division, and the Club were still finding their feet against some of their more illustrious rivals - a fact proved by City's disappointing 7-1 defeat on 1st December at Aston Villa. A number of players had been brought into the Club since promotion and City secretary/manager Sam Ormerod was still trying to mould a team that could live comfortably in the division. Although the likes of Villa were able to embarrass the Blues, it is worth noting that City were certainly better than the Second Division sides they had left behind. In the Manchester Cup final they defeated arch rivals Newton Heath 4-0 in a competition which at this point in football history was still of greater importance to Mancunians than the FA Cup.

Nevertheless, victory over Newton Heath was easy and certainly expected. For Sam Ormerod to build a team that would be remembered nationally he needed full co-operation from the directors and committee of the ever-growing Manchester City.

Ormerod was perhaps handicapped by the fact that City were still a young club, and that many of the directors and business people connected with the side were from the Club's humble origins. Although support and performance on the pitch had improved over the years, there were question marks over the general direction of the Club. Joshua Parlby was still involved, contributing his views whenever they were needed, and often when they were not. While other committee men chipped in with their own perceptions of how the team were performing. Some comments were accurate and needed, while others merely caused confusion, and possibly bitterness. The quiet Ormerod was rarely able

to have the final say over team selection as he formed part of a three man committee, nor could he buy or sell players without reaching full agreement with the committee.

Joe Cassidy was one player affected by this approach when, after scoring fourteen goals in only thirty-one League games the committee - not Ormerod - decided that he was not worth his £4 a week salary. He was sold to Middlesbrough in May 1901 for the ridiculously low figure of £75, thereby creating a loss of £175 on the deal. At Middlesbrough he became a hero when he scored the first ever League goal at Ayresome Park. Sadly, in April 1916 the *Manchester Football News* reported: "Joe Cassidy, whose connection with Manchester football extended over such a long period, has had a mental breakdown."

In addition to their involvement in the buying and selling of players, the City directors would have conversations with their own particular favourite players, and if a player expressed concern at his involvement within the team the directors would act. Likewise, if a director was particularly pleased with the performance of 'his' player, he would pay him a bonus. All of this meddling by the directors and committee caused the knowledgeable and experienced Ormerod many problems. While the team performed well everybody was happy, but when results started to go against the Blues it was Ormerod who would be held accountable.

And so 1900-01 may not have been a successful season but, when the general direction of the Club is taken into consideration, it must clearly be seen as a satisfactory season. Unfortunately the next twelve months would see the Club suffer as the 'committee approach' seriously affected Ormerod's plans.

1901-1902 Ormerod Ousted

To counter the notion that clubs were buying success, the footballing authorities introduced a maximum wage in time for the start of the new season. That maximum was set at £4 a week and would, ultimately, have a major impact on the development of the Blues.

Whether the City management seriously considered the impact of the new maximum is not known, but it is now understood that the Club's biggest star Billy Meredith, who had married his childhood sweetheart Ellen Negus at City's church, St. Mark's, earlier in the year, was already earning more than the authorities allowed as the 1901-02 season opened.

On the pitch the season began with two consecutive away games. The first at Everton ended in a 3-1 defeat - Meredith scored the City consolation goal. The second game also ended in defeat, this time Sunderland won 1-0. A week later Hyde Road witnessed a heavy 4-1 victory by Small Heath. Ormerod was under intense pressure and for the fourth game in a row made significant changes for the trip to Derby on 21st September.

A 2-0 defeat at Derby was the catalyst for widespread criticism of Ormerod. Critics accused him of chopping and changing the team - a point proved by the fact that he had already used nineteen players in four games, with only four ever-present at this early stage.

Before City's next game on 5th October at Notts County, the *Athletic News'* journalist 'Harricus' tried to find out why the Blues were failing: "I had a chat with Sam Ormerod on Friday afternoon; the City secretary is one of the old originals of Lancashire football and a capital referee in his time. Manchester's lowly position formed, of course, the chosen topic for conversation. The genial Sam thinks his club is the victim of circumstance inasmuch as four of the five matches have been played away from home and, being thus handicapped as no other club is, he could hardly be sanguine of success at Nottingham but he thinks City's time will come. When I took him to task on the week to week chopping and changing of the team he said that personally he wasn't in favour of it, but what with letter writers and others, the lot of the directors wasn't a happy one, and no-one was more anxious than they were that City should rank with the best."

Although 'Harricus' had mistakenly stated that City had played one more League fixture than they had, his comments and those of Ormerod, do provide an indication of how Ormerod was not a free man. Not only did the directors contribute to team selection, but it seems that the general public, i.e. letter writers, could also influence team affairs. Even at this early stage in the season it seemed that Ormerod was powerless, and that First Division survival was not within his control.

Results improved over the next month - City somehow achieved two Hyde Road victories and an away draw - but it was not enough to silence the critics. 'Harricus' accused Ormerod of inactivity: "A greater monument to folly and incapacity than the figure of Manchester City this season we have rarely seen. There was a time when we thought the shafts of satire and ridicule would rouse the club to action. But they have availed not. It is quite time the shareholders held a mass meeting and particularly invited the directors and officials. What is Mr. Ormerod doing? IS ANYBODY DOING ANYTHING?"

Three successive defeats - including a 5-0 hammering by Sheffield United - and further team changes throughout November caused 'Harricus' to go on the attack again: "We neither see nor hear of displays of acumen, enterprise and business activity by the directorate and their servants. Two men are badly needed at Hyde Road - one shrewd and commanding personality with the ability to put the finances on the sound basis they ought to be, and to see that affairs are conducted in a business-like manner, and another is a shrewd and sound judge of a player and especially a budding player."

The final comment by 'Harricus' was a deliberate attack on Ormerod who, at this stage in his City career, seemed to be struggling to direct the Club forward. Any team which still included the veteran Jimmy Ross could hardly have been one for the future, despite the player's track record. Ross had been playing in the League since its formation in 1888, and had also been a regular in the Preston side for the four years prior to the League's formation. He was without doubt a veteran, and was an obvious example of City's problems. Ormerod needed to develop the side, but didn't seem capable of creating the situation whereby the older players could move to one side as the newer players fitted in. Under Ormerod there seemed no chance of building the foundations for the future, especially with the directors still meddling in team affairs.

While results went against City on the pitch, off the pitch the likes of John Allison were working hard to put the overall control of the Club into the hands of one or two powerful men. Allison had been involved with City since the Ardwick days - in fact it was Allison who, for a while in 1894, believed the Club should continue as Ardwick A.F.C. Now, after a period off the City board, Allison was convinced he could help create the right environment for a successful City. His contacts included the wealthy newspaper baron Edward Hulton who was easily persuaded to help the Club.

MANCHESTER CITY.

ANNUAL MEETING OF SHAREHOLDERS.

The shareholders of the Manchester City F.C. Company, Limited, held their annual meeting last evening at the Hyde Road Hotel, Mr. John E. Chapman, chairman of directors, presiding. The annual report, which has already been published, was adopted. Mr. H. H. Appleton, the shareholders' auditor, submitted a report which showed that the attendances at the matches last season had reached the total of 257,357. It was decided that certain recommendations in the report should be considered by the new directors. These were reduced by resolution from nine to seven. Messrs. J. Parlby and G. Robinson did not seek re-election. The successful candidates were J. E. Chapman, E. Hulton, jun. George Madders, William Kerr, W. Richmond, J. Healey, and George Shawcroft. Mr. J. R. Prowse, Mr. W. H. Chilton, former members of the directorate, and Messrs. G. H. Dale, S. Boswell, and R. Milarvie were unsuccessful.

In reply to questions the Chairman stated that they were in negotiations for a reserve goalkeeper and a clever forward. The following resolutions, passed at the extraordinary meeting in March, were confirmed:— "That the directors take steps forthwith to secure the services of a first-class outside left forward; that the directors do strengthen the team by the inclusion of high-class players, and adopt a more progressive policy in relation to the club generally; that an assistant secretary be appointed."

At the AGM shareholders urged the Club to strengthen the squad.

It is, we understand, the intention of the gentlemen who have formed themselves into a shareholders' association to secure the election of at least two new directors at the next annual meeting of the club. The names of the gentlemen selected are Councillor John Allison and Mr. Lawrence Furniss. The co-operation of the first-named gentleman is much to be desired, whilst it cannot be said that Mr. Furniss knows nothing about the game. He was secretary of the old Ardwick club for some time.

A crucial period in the re-structuring of the Club saw John Allison and Lawrence Furniss become influential once more.

One of Hulton's newspapers was the *Athletic News*, and looking back one wonders whether the newspaper's attacks on Ormerod and the City directorate had anything to do with this fact. Probably not, but it does make it obvious that once Hulton became involved in the Club, Ormerod's days were numbered, especially with Allison's involvement. Allison had many ideas of how the City side should be shaped and, with results continuing to go against Ormerod during the first weeks of 1902, Allison acted.

Although still at the Club, Ormerod's power was effectively taken from him in February, while John Allison sought to strengthen the side. He had connections with Celtic in Glasgow, and was able to use these links to bolster the City side immediately. Allegedly, Allison used Billy Meredith as bait to tempt the great Celtic manager Willie Maley, but the Welshman remained at City with an improved wage – further breaking the maximum allowed.

Negotiations between Allison and Celtic resulted in City signing Willie McOustra, an inside-forward, and Jimmy Drummond, a twenty year old inside-left. Interestingly, Celtic's Tom Hynds had already signed for the Blues on 27th September 1901, proving the strong links between the two sides.

According to Celtic, the club were offered a transfer fee they simply could not refuse for McOustra and Drummond - approximately £600 - and so reluctantly they allowed the two men to go south. The previous season McOustra had hit the headlines and gained a few admirers by scoring the only goal of a 'Auld Firm' derby match described as "The Cup-tie of the Century", while Drummond had been described as having "passing ability above the average." It is fair to say though, that neither player was vital to Celtic at the time. Drummond had suffered with a number of injuries over the season and after a Celtic game with Hearts on

2nd November had been described as "painfully unfit", nevertheless Allison was right to bring the talent in.

Another player brought in around this time was the sizeable goalkeeper Jack Hillman. Hillman, 6ft tall and weighing 16 stone, arrived at the Club with a reputation for being a little eccentric, and made his debut for City in the 1-0 home victory over Notts County on 1st February. He had been signed from Burnley as a replacement for the equally eccentric Charlie Williams, who remained at the Club until the close season, then moved to Tottenham Hotspur where he became understudy to George Clawley, before moving on to Southampton.

Edward Hulton was backing John Allison all the way by promising to pay for any player Allison needed to strengthen the Blues. As with the arrival of Sheikh Mansour in 2008, this kind of benefactor was extremely useful to the Club, it enabled them to compete for any player and, if City had been better placed in the League, may have helped the Club avoid relegation. As it was City's results did improve enough to give the Club a normally safe 28 points from 34 games, unfortunately in 1902 it wasn't quite enough and the Blues returned to the Second Division to meet their old adversaries Newton Heath.

Relegation provided Allison and Hulton with the perfect opportunity to find a little breathing space to rebuild the team and take stock of the Club's overall situation. Allison and Hulton knew well the financial state of the Blues, but some areas of the press could only see the income streams and not the issues. The *Manchester Evening News*, a rival to Hulton's own newspapers, commented at the season's end: "It is of course generally known that Manchester City Football Club have done remarkably well in the matter of 'gates'

The deaths of Jimmy Ross and Di Jones rocked the Club in 1902.

but few people will be prepared for the astonishing statement that the receipts for the First Division matches at Hyde Road amount to nearly £7,000. There are not two clubs in the League that have done better from this point of view, and the publication of the figures will only intensify the regret that a club which can command such support will have to spend next season in the Second Division."

Hulton and Allison knew the truth of the finances and at the AGM in June, they confirmed that the Club had taken around £7,000 in gate receipts - a tremendous figure – but they explained that even this remarkable figure was not enough to put the Club into profit. When the balance sheet was revealed, the Blues proved to be nearly £1,000 in debt. General criticism of the way the directors had wildly spent money on travelling expenses and on the players' bonuses and wages was made.

Again, the warning signs were there that the Club were too keen to pay the players more than was absolutely necessary, although it seems that many of the big city clubs were a little profligate.

Sam Ormerod was also on the receiving end of much criticism, understandably he resigned. It is obvious that team selection and motivation was not what it should have been during the season, but whether this was entirely Ormerod's fault is not clear. Certainly he was the man officially in charge of the playing side, but the 'selection committee' approach had caused him to alter his side willy-nilly. His first seasons in charge proved what he was capable of, in reality it seems that the Club had lost direction. Nevertheless, it was time for a change and Allison knew who he wanted to bring to the Club.

1899-1902 SUMMARY

Highest League Attendance: c.30,000 The Wednesday, 28/03/02
Highest Cup Attendance: c.22,000 Aston Villa, 27/01/00 (FA Cup)
Secretary/Managers: 1895-1902 Sam Ormerod

Seasonal Record:

Season	League	Posn	FA Cup	Other	Leading Scorer	Average Attendance
1899-1900	FL Div1	7	Rnd 1		Meredith 14	16,000
1900-01	FL Div1	11	Rnd 1		Cassidy 14	18,300
1901-02	FL Div1	18	Rnd 2		Gillespie 15	17,000

MANCHESTER CITY SECURE THE CUP.

Trotters supporters.

Meredith pots Krough the cup winner.

Taylor makes good use of White's clever pass.

Brown distarbs the City attack.

The Premier greets "W.G."

Hillman collars the ball at the finish.

1902-1904
Manchester's Success

"Not a little of the success the City club has achieved is due to the indefatigable labours of the secretary, Mr T.E. Maley, who came to Manchester three years ago, when the City were in the Second Division. He brought to his duties valuable experience gained with the famous Celtic club, and he has had the benefit of being a player, a club official, a legislator, and a selector. His splendid services to the City are reflected in the position they at present occupy – the holders of the English Cup – the most coveted of football prizes, and one of the leading clubs in the League."

The Manchester Evening Chronicle, 12 November 1904

1902-1903 Maley's The Man

John Allison returned to his old friends at Celtic and invited 37 year old Tom Maley, a Celtic director and brother of Celtic Manager Willie, to be the new City Secretary. Tom Maley was a Celtic man through and through and had been involved with the Club since formation in 1888. First as a player (inside-left), then as a director and committee man driving the Club forward. During the latter half of the 1901-2 season he travelled to Hyde Road on a couple of occasions, prompting early

City historians to suggest that Allison had already made a move for Maley before Ormerod resigned.

The Maley family were major influences in the early years of Scottish football, and back in 1890 their connection with Manchester started when Willie Maley guested with Ardwick over Easter. Six years later he returned to Hyde Road again as a guest, playing in City's 5-1 victory over Loughborough in the Second Division. These guest appearances coincided with similar appearances for Everton causing one to suspect that Maley enjoyed some kind of busman's holiday.

During one of Willie's trips to Manchester he would almost certainly have spent time at John Allison's 'Matlock House Hydro' on Hyde Road, where players were provided with the latest treatments for football injuries. Maybe this is where Allison's connections with Celtic stemmed from.

And so with a new manager, and new direction, the Blues prepared for their return to the Second Division, although the news of the deaths of two of Hyde Road's greatest players rocked the Club's preparations. First veteran Jimmy Ross died on 12th June, a mere four and a half months after making his last first team appearance. This last appearance was, appropriately against Preston North End in the First Round of the FA Cup in January 1902. Ross died of an infectious skin condition. City helped his mother, whom he was looking after at the time of his death, financially. They also arranged the funeral.

The second death was Welsh international Di Jones who fell and gashed his knee during the annual public practice match on 16th August. Apparently, he had been tackling a player when he fell to the ground and cut his knee on a piece of glass that had been embedded in the Hyde Road soil. He was treated by the Club and then went to hospital, but the wound turned septic. On the 27th August he died.

At the inquest into his death Tom Maley was asked about the treatment Jones had received and his comments were reported in the local press. He explained that the man who treated him was: "probably as expert in that work as anyone who could have been got. It was a matter of impossibility to dictate to Jones. Moral suasion was no good, and physical force was out of the question with such a man. The stretcher was brought to the chair, but he would not use it. He pushed everyone away and dressed himself. He even wanted to get into an electric car, and at the Infirmary he had to be pressed into the cab."

In 1991 John Harding's *For The Good Of The Game* claimed that City mistreated the Jones family and that the Blues had provided poor support, however this does not appear to be supported by the facts. The coroner recorded a verdict of "death from lockjaw, probably arising from a cut accidentally received" and he made a point of highlighting the Blues' care: "Certainly the football people are not to blame, and I am certain also that the doctors have done all they could." Also the player's family's struggles were alleviated a little when City and Bolton agreed to play a game for the benefit of his widow and children.

The deaths affected everybody at the Club, and Tom Maley did all he could to lift the gloom. He also looked to strengthen the side, and find consistency. He signed inside-forward Sandy Turnbull from Hurlford (Scotland) in July, Full-back Bob Davidson from Celtic (to replace Jones), and outside-left Frank Booth from Stockport County. He also provided Sammy Frost with the opportunity to establish himself in the first team. Frost had been brought to City in May 1901 as an inside-right, but had been found wanting and made only two League appearances during Ormerod's 'season of changes'. Under Maley, Frost was tried at right-half, and quickly made a name for himself. One journalist of the period enthused about Frost's unorthodox style: "Frost at half-back is unique. As a tackler he is a positive 'original'. Along comes the opponent with the ball. Does Frost put out a boot on either side? Not he. His modus operandi is far more certain and far reaching. The ex-Millwallian simply throws himself across and in front of his opponent. 'You can go along as far as you like' quoth Frost, 'but you

Tom Maley, one of Celtic's founders and soon to be City great.

will have to take me with you'. Small wonder that some people assert that Frost will get himself killed someday."

Maley also allowed another half-back, Tom Hynds, to establish himself in the side. Hynds had played in 29 League games the previous season, and so could be regarded as one of Ormerod's regulars, but under Maley he really did prove his ability, establishing himself as probably the best half-back in City's history up until that time. Maley may have been encouraged by the fact that Hynds had been a Celtic player. The player had been with City since 27th September 1901.

Under the new secretary City progressed. Maley was keen on seeing the Scottish passing game as opposed to the traditional English kick and rush, and with his signings, and of course the likes of Meredith, Maley was determined to make City a stylish outfit. He was a great tactician, and clearly chose players who fitted his style, rather than great individuals. Maley's team attacked the Second Division in style. Only five games ended in defeat, unfortunately one of these was the Hyde Road derby with neighbours Manchester United.

During City's period in the First Division their rivals, Newton Heath had struggled to keep alive. City were supported by average crowds of around 17,000 (an average of 18,300 had witnessed the 1901 promotion season) while the Heathens had been watched by an average of 4,650 (5,475 in 1900-01). In 1901-2 they finished the season in their lowest position since formation, and off the pitch the club was in dire financial straits. The only remedy was a re-launch, and on Thursday 24th April the Heathens re-emerged under a new title, Manchester United. The first derby match of the season, Christmas Day 1902, was therefore the first League meeting between two sides with Manchester in their title. That game, which all reports describe as being dominated by the Blues, ended 1-1 at Clayton.

Making his debut in this match was full-back Johnny McMahon, who had been signed from Preston on 17th December. Another new player around this time was, Leyland born, Jimmy Bannister who was signed from Chorley during the close-season, but only made his debut on 6th December. Eventually, Bannister was to become the perfect inside-forward partner to Billy Meredith who described the Lancastrian as "the best partner I ever had. No one fed me better than Jimmy...he was equal to any inside-right playing in League football. I shall always think of him as one of the cleverest and most unselfish partners I have ever been blessed with."

Apart from the five League defeats, City's season was a successful one. They won twenty-five of their thirty-four League games and scored ninety-five goals. Many of these coming during the latter part of the season when table-toppers City achieved crushing victories over Burnley (6-0), Burslem Port Vale (7-1), and Gainsborough Trinity (9-0). With the score at 5-0 at half time in the

City's Promotion in Sight.

By following the example of Small Heath and beating Glossop by an odd goal, Manchester City further strengthened their position; indeed, only two more points are wanted to make promotion to the First Division a matter of certainty. With Stockport County and Barnsley to play away from home, and with Manchester United to meet at Hyde Road City ought not to have the slightest difficulty in not only getting these two points, but in making the championship secure. The only really doubtful match is that with United, but by the time Good Friday is reached City ought to be in the happy position of being able to view the result with equanimity. The game at Glossop was fought with much determination, but City were always the better team. Having scored early in the first half, however, they found the Glossop defence a very sound one afterwards, Clarke, Burgess, and Norgrove making a fine trio. Boden also played a fine game. On the City side, Meredith was not at his best, Bannister being the best forward on his side. The half backs never played better, while Holmes showed still further improvement, and made an admirable partner for the always reliable M'Mahon. Edmondson did exceedingly well as Hillman's substitute, and should have a future before him. He saved one shot which would have beaten a good many goalkeepers.

A 1-0 victory at Glossop in March 1903 set City up for promotion.

home game against Port Vale, the referee is reported to have gone into the Vale dressing room to drag out the reluctant players. Somehow the Gainsborough game remained goalless for the first twenty-five minutes. Top scorer during this season was ace goal poacher Billy Gillespie with thirty goals from thirty-two appearances. Sadly, it's not known exactly how many of these were the result of Gillespie's infamous 'barging' technique.

With the right results, tactical direction, players, and financial backing City were once again promoted into the First Division.

1903-1904 The FA Cup

Manchester needed a top class club and with Edward Hulton's backing the Blues were taking shape. They also received good coverage in the main sporting newspapers of the day. Surely it couldn't have been a coincidence that City's main backer was also the proprietor of several popular 'papers.

Promotion gave the Blues added impetus, and was to spark the first great era for football in Manchester. Tom Maley, recognising that not all of his signings had worked out for the best, made a few changes. The former Celtic inside-left, Jimmy Drummond, failed to impress and, after being described as "awkward and slow", was first dropped into the reserves, then in October 1903 was transferred to Partick Thistle. The player signed alongside him, Willie McOustra, had also struggled to make the right impression mainly through injury, although he remained at the Club and was to play an important role two years later.

Players brought in included the amateur Half-back,

Sam Ashworth, as replacement for McOustra, left-back Herbert Burgess, and inside-forward George Livingstone. Burgess was an Openshaw born player who had made his Football League debut at the age of 18 for Glossop against Liverpool. His original 'trial' game for Glossop was actually a reserve game against City at Hyde Road, but it wasn't until he was 21 that the Blues spotted his real potential. City paid a fee of around £250 for the 5ft 5 inch 'Mighty Atom' who, while with the Blues, became the smallest full-back ever to play for England.

George Livingstone, or 'Geordie' as he was known to the players, must be unique in that, during a career that spanned three decades, he appeared for both Manchester clubs and both Celtic and Rangers. He also had a spell with Liverpool, but never quite made it to Everton to complete the treble. It was actually from Liverpool that he was signed for City in May 1903, although Tom Maley had secured his signature when they met one day in Greenock. Geordie joined the Blues after building a bit of a reputation as a physical player. This started in his days at Celtic where he often found himself involved in 'rough' activity. Nevertheless, it was this kind of forward that would add a bit more steel to Maley's side. Quickly he established himself, prompting the *Athletic News* to comment: "George Livingstone disdains style. He is all utility and a resolute thrusting forward who not only creates openings for Meredith but opens out the game by playing passes to the other wing in the style I used to admire when J. Devey was commander-in-chief of Aston Villa. He makes himself the hub of the game when he is on the ball."

And so with a strengthened side, 1903-04 proved to be the greatest season known in Manchester up to that time. The opening four games in the First Division were all won, with the best result coming in the 4-1 victory over Wolves at Hyde Road, while new boy Livingstone provided one of the goals that helped City to 2-1 victory in their opening fixture at Stoke.

In the 3-1 win at Bury on 7th November, Livingstone again proved his worth when he and Meredith combined perfectly. Another of Maley's buys, Herbert Burgess, proved that it wasn't simply the Scotsman who was value for money as he gave a quite brilliant display.

With fine performances in the League Maley's side really combined perfectly. Until the secretary's arrival the Blues had bought and discovered some great players but, overall, they had not created a great side. Often they had relied on the likes of Meredith, Gillespie, or Ross to find a goal from somewhere...anywhere! Now with the right direction and an increased awareness of tactics they had become a team in the truest sense. The side were determined to achieve something and team spirit was never higher. In at least one newspaper article City's 'grit' had been described as the main reason for the team's rapid rise up the League. The article went on to

At the start of the 1903-04 season City tried to improve crowd congestion.

state that the team 'grafted' for one another and that no matter what the obstacle, the Blues would overcome it.

By the time the FA Cup First Round was played on 6th February 1904, City were well placed for an assault on the League Championship. Something that only a few months earlier had seemed so far away, and something that most Mancunians daren't even dream about, after all City were hardly regarded as one of the famous Lancastrian clubs, let alone one of football's elite. Maley believed in his players though, and with internationals like Meredith and Burgess in the side he had every right to believe that the Blues could do it. Manchester had never once mounted a serious bid for major honours before 1903-04.

The first round of the FA Cup may have come along at the right moment for Maley. It allowed him to divert attention from the League for a short while. It also meant that for the first real occasion in the Cup the Blues could put out a side capable of success. Up until this point City had never really achieved much in the Cup,

A GROWING DIFFICULTY.

Except the ground is the property of the club or is unsuitable for building purposes, football clubs are finding it increasingly difficult to retain possession of their enclosures when they are situated in or near populous centres. This fact is probably best appreciated in Manchester just now, where the all-conquering City club is trembling on the brink of a removal which will be little short of an upheaval. It is an open secret that the directors are in search of a new ground. No one will gainsay the assertion that this search has not been entered upon any too soon. It might with advantage have been begun years ago, but now that there is a serious intent, the followers of the club may well content themselves with saying "Better late than never." Contrasted with the great majority of football grounds, the Hyde Road enclosure is nothing short of an eye-sore. The approach to it is the worst in England. Much has been done to improve both the ground and the approach during the past few years, but the former is still quite inadequate, and the latter is beyond all hope when the weather is wet. In the early days of the season the playing enclosure is surprisingly verdant. Visitors to the ground, after passing the dismal croft, with its background of grimy railway arches, have even been staggered by the scent of new mown hay; but when the damp days of winter soften the ground, the pastoral veneer soon wears off, and long before the end of the season the blades of grass may almost be counted. The absence of turf is, of course, not a fatal objection. Lack of accommodation is the chief complaint against the present enclosure. Thousands were turned away when the opening match was played, and not only did the receipts suffer as a consequence, but when next the club played at home thousands stayed away in the fear that the ground would either be uncomfortably crowded or the gates closed long before the game was advertised to begin. As a matter of fact more than seven thousand more spectators could have been comfortably accommodated on the day of the Wolverhampton Wanderers match. The ground will hold thirty thousand spectators, and now that the arrangements have been vastly improved this number of people may present themselves next Saturday in the certain hope of seeing the game with Sheffield United.

AN ENCOURAGING EXAMPLE.

What is wanted, however, is an enclosure with accommodation for at least fifty thousand spectators, but where can such an enclosure be obtained? That is the rub? It is not permissible to point the direction in which the directors are looking. Suffice it to say that their task is not an easy one, and the fact that they are being helped by an army of irresponsible supporters of the club does not lighten their burden. It is not necessary to state that wherever the new home is made it must, within reasonable limits, be an abiding place. To plant a new club and then have to uproot it again within a few years would be folly. As it is the transplanting of the club from Hyde Road is not unattended with fears, but those concerned may take heart in the example set by the executive of Sheffield Wednesday. This body did not hesitate, when driven from Olive Grove, to transfer the club to the other side of the city where, in spite of the fact that the site is some three miles away from the centre of Sheffield, the attendances have been larger, the players more successful, and the club more prosperous. One thing greatly in favour of Manchester City, and the new ground that is to be, is the greatly improved means of access. No matter where the new site is, it will be within half an hour's run of the centre of the city.

Of necessity the club's centre of interest will be removed, but that is unavoidable, for there is no suitable site in the neighbourhood of the Hyde Road ground, nor is there one within a radius of two miles of the Exchange. Even supposing the new ground was made at a distance of three miles from the Exchange, it would by no means follow that the great majority of the spectators would have much more than a third of that distance to travel which would, of course, mean a penny fare and a quick ride. The two Liverpool grounds are quite three miles from the centre of the city; Aston Park, the home of the Villa, is even further; Owlerton Park is fully three miles; whilst the Derby County, Nottingham, Sunderland, Blackburn, Bury, and Small Heath grounds cannot be reached under twenty minutes from the centre of those places. The bigger the population, the greater the distance. Manchester cannot hope to have its football grounds within such easy reach as towns like Derby, Nottingham, and Bury. In the case of Manchester City the difficulty will have to be faced as it has been elsewhere. One thing is certain and that is that there is no danger of the club becoming a suburban institution. As a matter of fact the contemplated removal ought to remove the slightest suspicion of this. A club bearing the name Manchester City ought to command the interest as well as the support of the whole of Greater Manchester, and not merely of one or two particular districts.

MEETING OF SHAREHOLDERS CALLED.

The committee appointed to confer with the directors as to the terms upon which a new ground would be provided for Manchester City, will present their report at a special meeting of the shareholders to be held at the Devonshire Hotel on Tuesday evening next. It was thought that arrangements might be made whereby the club could retain its present ground, but all idea of this has now been abandoned. The location of the new ground cannot yet be announced, but it may be taken for granted that the site will be the best available, and that the ground, when it is constructed, will be second to none in the country. The directors are not only showing commendable enterprise, but a laudable desire to meet the wishes of the shareholders.

Fans were being turned away on a regular basis as Hyde Road could not cope in the early months of 1903-04. A stadium move was urgently needed and fans pushed the Club to find a bigger home.

MANCHESTER CITY CLUB.

GUARANTORS' PROPOSALS REGARDING NEW GROUND.

THE SCHEME REJECTED.

A meeting of the shareholders of the Manchester City Football Club, convened at a very short notice, was held last evening at the Devonshire Hotel, Stockport-road, to consider the proposals put forward by the directors. There was a large attendance, presided over by Mr. W. Chapman.

The Chairman said the object of the meeting was to safeguard the interests of the shareholders and at the same time the interests of the club. (Hear, hear.) Both of these were threatened by the proposals put forward the previous week nominally on behalf of a majority of the directorate but in reality on behalf of the chairman. Briefly, the offer which was made to the shareholders was that if they would give up their pound share in return for preference shares of one shilling each they would in return be provided with a new ground in some district not made known, and be honoured with a copy of the annual report, post free. (Hear, hear.) He would ask them why had this ridiculous offer been made to them—an offer which was almost beneath contempt (Applause.) If the club were on its last legs, if it were in a financially hopeless condition, and the shareholders threatened with a liability they were unable or disinclined to meet, he could understand such an offer, but all this was far from being the case. (Applause.) The club, he was glad to say, never was in a better position, either from a financial or a playing point of view. (Applause.) It was an insult to the intelligence of the shareholders to treat this club as though it were in the market to be bought at the price of a bankrupt company, or even less. (Applause.) The accommodation at Hyde-road was not what they could wish, but it was now greater than it had ever been before, and it could be still further increased. (Hear, hear.) The railway company, so far from wanting to get rid of the club, assured Messrs. Chesters—from whom the club sub-leased the ground—that there was no likelihood of the land being wanted for at least seven years. That, he submitted, entirely altered the situation. (Applause.) They were no longer hard pressed. (Hear, hear.) They were in the happy position of being able to give many months and even years to an anxious consideration of the question of a new ground, during which time their financial position would be improving. There was no reason why the Manchester City F.C. should ever look back again—(applause)—and there was no reason why, at the end of a few years, they should not be able to provide themselves with a new ground without selling themselves body and soul to anyone. (Applause.) They must all remember that by comparison Manchester City was still a new club. (Applause.) What he would impress upon them was the importance of making it clear to the gentlemen who at present acted as directors that they were quite content to stay at Hyde-road, improving the ground as much as they could, consolidating the position of the club, building up a strong team, and in the meantime saving money for the new enterprise. (Applause.) That, he submitted, was the policy they ought to adopt, for it was the only safe one if they were desirous of maintaining a voice in the management of the club. (Applause.)

Mr. H. Appleton moved the following resolution: "That this meeting is opposed to the scheme put forward at the last extraordinary general meeting of shareholders, believing that it is in the best interests of the club that the present ground should be secured, and that a reserve fund should be created before any attempt is made to launch out in a new direction; the meeting is further of the opinion that the government of the club should remain in the hands of the shareholders, and that it should not be handed over to any one individual." In supporting the resolution, he said the scheme which had been put before them was not only an insult, but a degradation to the ideas of the members of the City Football Club, who wished to see it where it ought to be—at the top. If they analysed the scheme which had been put before them they would see that the club would come into one man's hands. The shares, which ought to be worth £6 each according to the proposals put before them, were to be of the value of a shilling. And they would be aware of the fact that this was a shilling on paper only. (Applause.) He asked them if they were going to allow a syndicate, with the present chairman of directors at the head, to take charge of the City Football Club affairs? (Cries of "No.")

A Shareholder rose to a point of order and said that the scheme put forward at the last meeting was dead. (Cries of "No, no.")

The Chairman, intervening, said that the question had not been settled at the last meeting, and that was the reason why they were called together again.

Mr. Appleton (continuing) asked if they were prepared to sacrifice their pound shares for a shilling? ("No.") In his opinion it was merely another illustration of the fable of the spider and the fly. (Applause.)

Mr. W. Forrest, in seconding the resolution, said that if the shareholders for a single moment ever dreamt of accepting the proposals put before them by the chairman of directors they were bigger fools than ever he dreamt of. (Laughter and applause.) If the City Football Club wanted money they could get it without being tied up in the manner suggested. (Applause.)

Mr. F. Johnson, whilst expressing his sympathy with the first part of the resolution, thought it was asking the shareholders to go over the ground with which they had dealt exhaustively before. In his opinion they had killed the scheme of the chairman of directors at the previous meeting. (Cries of "No," and applause.)

Mr. Forrest pointed out that certain newspapers had stated, after the last meeting, that it was only "a nominal change." (Applause.) They must not forget that point. (Applause.)

Other speakers, including Mr. J. Williams and Mr. Rees, argued both for and against the resolution, which, however, was carried by an overwhelming majority.

TEAMS FOR TO-DAY'S MATCHES.

ASSOCIATION.

THE LEAGUE—FIRST DIVISION.

BLACKBURN ROVERS v. STOKE.—At Stoke.
Blackburn Rovers: Evans, goal; Crompton and Eastham, backs; Blackburn, McDonald, and Bradshaw, half backs; Whittaker, Bow, Pentland, Watson, and Dunkley, forwards.

DERBY COUNTY v. BURY.—At Derby.
Derby County: Whittaker, goal; Methven and Morris, backs; Warren, Hall, and May, half backs; Mercer, Bloomer, Boag, Richards, and Davis, forwards.
Bury: Monteith, goal; Lindsay and McEwan, backs; Johnston, Thorpe, and Ross, half backs; Richards, Lamberton, Wood, Sagar, and J. Plant, forwards.

EVERTON v. NOTTS FOREST.—At Everton.
Everton: Kitchen, goal; Balmer and Crelly, backs; Wolstenholme, Booth, and Abbott, half backs; Sharp, McDermott, Young, Settle, and Hardman, forwards.
Notts Forest: Linacre, goal; Craig and Iremonger, backs; Timmins, Warren, and Norris, half backs; Davies, Shearman, Sugden, Morris, and Spouncer, forwards.

MANCHESTER CITY v. LIVERPOOL.—At Hyde-road.
Manchester City: Hillman, goal; McMahon and Burgess, backs; Frost, Hynds, and Lyon, half backs; Meredith, Livingstone, Gillespie, Turnbull, and Booth, forwards.
Liverpool: Platt, goal; Raisbeck and Hoare, backs; Parry, Fleming, and Hughes, half backs; Goddard, Morris, Parkinson, Chadwick, and Cox, forwards.

Ultimately, the influence of Chesters Brewery meant City were to stay at Hyde Road.

their best seasons had only seen them reach the Second Round (1897-98 and 1901-02).

For the first tie of the 1903-04 season City were at home to Sunderland who over the last four seasons had consistently finished in the top three. This season was not quite as successful, but they had still performed well and had experienced some exciting victories. In their two previous games they had defeated Bury 6-0 and Blackburn Rovers 3-1, while the December meeting of City and Sunderland gave little indication of how the cup meeting would go as it ended in a 1-1 draw.

And so on 6th February a crowd of approximately 23,000, the largest Hyde Road FA Cup attendance so far, looked forward to a great City performance. They were not disappointed. Sunderland were defeated by three goals to two with Billy Meredith in outstanding form, setting up the first two goals. For the first Billy Gillespie sent Meredith forward "like a greyhound from the leash" according to one scribe. The Welshman crossed to Livingstone who forced a corner. From the kick, taken by captain Meredith of course, Gillespie headed past the Sunderland 'keeper Doig.

For City's second goal, the Welsh wizard proved his skills by dribbling past several players before centre-ing to Sandy Turnbull, whose header 'fairly bamboozled Doig', according to the *Athletic News*. Turnbull added the third later in the game when he and Doig both attempted to gain control of a loose ball. With the goalkeeper scrambling on the floor, the City man took the ball out of Doig's reach and forced it goalwards.

Following an hectic game, the Blues received glowing reports in the sporting press over the course of the next three days. Turnbull was praised for two crucial goals, while Meredith once again stole the headlines with his overall performance. According to the *Athletic News*: "The City captain was the raider-in-chief and undoubtedly the most dazzling forward on the field. Assiduously supplied, the famous Welshman hardly ever failed to respond to the calls made upon him. His command of the ball as he threaded his way through the maze of his adversaries commanded admiration. Against a team of such class Meredith has not often given a more dazzling display. R.J. Jackson, hard worker as he is, was quite unable to hold him in check and Rhodes, who

has probably not seen Meredith before and knows not his wary antagonist, was altogether floundering about like an inexperienced schoolboy. I have no wish to be guilty of exaggeration, but Meredith was the King of the Realm."

The draw for the second round pitted City away to Second Division Woolwich Arsenal, who had defeated Fulham 1-0 in the previous round. The Blues defeated the Gunners 2-0 with goals from Sandy Turnbull and Frank Booth, prompting the *Manchester Evening News* to print a cartoon of Billy Meredith leapfrogging over the Gunners while Tom Maley, dressed in kilt, watches.

Outside-left Frank Booth, one of the scorers, had joined City in April 1902 making his first appearance for the Club in a friendly with Celtic on 1st September 1902. That friendly appearance brought a little bad luck to the player as fairly early on in the match he accidentally collided with Celtic's Right-back Hugh Watson causing him to leave the field for twenty minutes or so. When he returned however he seemed more determined than ever to prove what he was capable of and, when a chance came his way, he scored what was described as a "very fine" goal to give City a 1-0 victory.

Throughout Booth's career prior to the Arsenal game he had been rather unlucky with injuries and, at times, must have seriously considered concentrating on a life outside of the sport. He was a hatter by trade, coming from the local hatting areas surrounding the towns of Hyde and Denton, and had only completed his apprenticeship in 1903. Nevertheless a career in football had to be more appealing than life in one of the large hatting factories of east Manchester.

After the tie with Arsenal at Plumstead, George Robey, a very famous music hall comedian with a love of football, took the City team to visit the capital's top music halls. Such light relief was needed in the City camp as the realisation was now dawning that the Blues might seriously be contenders for the League and Cup double that at this point in history had only been achieved by Preston (1889) and Aston Villa (1897). For a side whose only national success so far had been to win the Second Division, this must have felt like an impossible dream but, as the season progressed it became increasingly possible.

In the third round (the quarter-final), City were drawn at home to First Division Middlesbrough. A record 30,022, some sources claim 35,000, paid £1,150 to see how far Maley's determined team could go, unfortunately they went home a little disappointed as the game ended goalless. A few days later the replay at Middlesbrough saw the Blues face a side backed by a fanatical crowd. It seemed that the whole of Middlesbrough packed inside the ground as a partisan crowd of around 33,000 supported their heroes. Local schools and factories closed early to allow fans to attend,

FOOTBALLERS' FUN.
MANCHESTER CITY PLAYERS FINED.
Three of the Manchester City players—Sam Frost, George Livingstone, and John M'Mahon—were each fined 5s. and costs at the City Police Court, this morning, for behaving in a disorderly manner in Oxford Road last night. A police constable said he saw the defendants shouting and jostling passers-by. Frost said they were "only having a bit of fun." Mr. W. J. Crossley, chairman of the Bench: Yes, at the expense of the public.

A cartoon from the Athletic News *depicting City's 3-0 semi-final victory over Wednesday.*

and all the local dignitaries were in evidence. This replay was Middlesbrough's chance of glory, unfortunately for them it was also City's.

In the end the Blues won the game 3-1 with goals from Livingstone, Gillespie, and Turnbull. For the first time ever a Manchester side had reached the semi-final of football's most famous competition.

The draw for the semi brought City and their rivals for the League title Sheffield Wednesday together, while the other tie was to be competed between Bolton and Derby County. Wednesday were reigning League Champions and were defensively strong. Would they be too powerful for the Blues?

A crowd of 53,000 attended a wet Goodison Park, by far the best stadium in the Football League and a fitting venue at the time. Maley was determined that his tactics and style of play would overcome Wednesday's defence.

From the whistle City attacked, completely overpowering the Owls captained by the English international half-back, Tom Crawshaw.

After only twenty-one minutes the Blues took the lead. A Meredith shot hit the crossbar and rebounded to Gillespie who bundled the ball over the line. A cartoon of the game in the *Athletic News* gives the impression that Jack Lyall, the Wednesday 'keeper who later transferred to City, moved out of the way. Possibly he had already experienced Gillespie's method of 'bundling' the ball into the net, and was keen to avoid it at all costs!

By half-time City's domination was rewarded with a second goal, this time Sandy Turnbull hooked in a Meredith cross. In the second half, Turnbull provided a third to guarantee a City victory. This goal was simply a superb effort and was described by the *Athletic News* as the goal of the season: "Livingstone, by really clever

92

dribbling near the centre line, was able to make a very clever pass to Meredith, who spread all sail and steered straight ahead, with Burton hanging on to his left shoulder all the way. But Meredith kept possession, and, although only about a foot in front of his antagonist, he made a marvellous right foot back centre, the ball whizzing past Burton. This was done at a most difficult angle, and Turnbull, who had followed up, volleyed with his instep, and like a flash of lightning, the ball was in the net."

Billy Meredith remembered it as a fantastic goal: "I never saw anything like it. I had centred square and Sandy took the ball first time when it was well off the ground and drove it into the net with marvellous force. The amazing thing was that the ball kept low all the way. You will understand the pace of the shot when I say the ball hit the net at Goodison Park and came out while the goalkeeper was still tumbling!"

The game ended with a fine 3-0 victory to Maley's City. Mancunians were ecstatic. It is extremely difficult to explain exactly how strong the feeling of success was without making it sound too over the top, but it is important that this moment must be seen as one of Manchester's greatest achievements. Until this time the city of Manchester had been famous for cotton, the Ship Canal and industry, and was seen as a grim, sprawling, northern city with little to recommend it to non-Mancunians. Sport, and in particular football, allowed Mancunians to prove that Manchester really had something to offer.

Mancunians united to support the Blues and everyone shared the joy. Tom Maley's 'team' approach was working and long serving trainer Jimmy Broad enjoyed the team atmosphere: "It was a real pleasure to train that team. They were all as keen as mustard and always to be found together... Tom Maley, who understands the players perfectly, was always on the best of terms with his team and joined in any fun that was going on. At our sing-songs, Tom usually contributed a recitation and he did very well too. Turnbull, I think, was our best vocalist but McOustra and Burgess ran him pretty close for that honour. Jack Hillman was past master at making 'stump' speeches. When asked to do something serious he invariably settled back in his chair, lit his pipe and rolled out the tale of 'Young Lochinvar'. Billy Meredith spent most of his leisure-time enjoying the efforts of others. Bill was always very quiet when the others were giving an impromptu concert, but Bill relished it all the same."

With the Cup semi-final over the Blues could concentrate on the League for the following month or so. A couple of days after the semi, City proved that they were one of the most powerful teams of the period as they stretched their unbeaten run by defeating Wolves 6-1 on 21st March. Maley's side had not lost a game since December and were hitting the headlines regularly. Most journalists praised their style, confidence, and team play: "They move with a smartness and precision which could not fail to evoke admiration, the forwards sweeping along like one man brooking no resistance....... backs and half-backs never knew what was going to happen next; now a feint, now a pass, now a short dribble, maybe a shot or a wide pass to the wings, to be followed by a true, insidious centre - all these moves were executed with a perfect understanding and with clockwork precision."

It was incredible that the Blues had managed to keep up the pressure at the top of the League for so long, especially as the cup run had created a fixture pile-up. In March alone City played three cup games and three League games in the space of twenty-one days. This may seem normal for a successful modern day Premier League side, but in 1904 with an eighteen club division and only one cup competition, this was incredible. Nevertheless, the Blues not only survived, they thrived for a period.

On March 26th, however, the pressure increased as they faced their semi-final opponents, Wednesday, away in the League. Unlike the cup match seven days earlier, City were not able to break down the strong Wednesday defence, and when Harry Chapman gave Wednesday the lead, the Blues were unable to fight back. The game ended 1-0, giving Wednesday a four point advantage. Close behind the Blues were Aston Villa and Newcastle, whom City were to face in their next League game.

On April Fool's Day against Newcastle, City suffered a 3-1 defeat at Hyde Road. Was the pressure getting to them? Tom Maley must have been a little worried that the troubles arrived at a time when the Blues needed to be at their best. They certainly needed to be calm. The day after the Newcastle defeat, the Blues beat Sunderland 2-1, with both goals coming from the in-form Sandy Turnbull. Maley was a happy man, especially when he heard that Notts County had beaten Wednesday, and that Villa had lost to Bury. The gap between City and Wednesday was now back to two points, but Villa were close behind and Newcastle had moved above the Blues after victory over Blackburn. Maley knew that he somehow had to keep City's team spirit and attitude right.

On 4th April more good news came when the Blues discovered that Wednesday had lost to Everton, thereby presenting City with a game in hand. There were issues though and a combination of injuries and loss of form forced Maley into the transfer market. On 7th April he purchased Irvine Thornley from Glossop. Whether the urgency made Maley overlook certain issues is not known but the details of this transfer would help to create City's shock downfall.

Thornley's debut was the away game to West

Bromwich Albion on 9th April. Unfortunately, this game resulted in a disappointing 2-1 defeat while Wednesday achieved victory in the Sheffield derby on the same day. The Blues were once again four points behind Wednesday, while Newcastle with only one game to go were one point ahead of City.

Between the 9th April and 16th fixture congestion played its part again as City played four matches to catch up on number of games played with Wednesday. With more necessary team changes it was difficult for Maley to find the right level of team spirit, but somehow he did as the Blues gained points. Frank Norgrove, another player from Glossop whose hurried transfer later caused City much heartache, signed on 15th April and made his debut on 16th. Other squad players such as the long serving William 'Doc' Holmes filled in when required.

By the end of the 4-0 victory over Small Heath, City were on 44 points with one game - away at Everton - to go, while their main Championship rivals, Wednesday, were one point behind with two games to go. Newcastle's season was already over - they finished on 42 points - and Aston Villa were now unable to catch the Blues. City were convinced they could still pull off the double, although they had to ensure they defeated Everton in their last game and hope that Wednesday failed to pick up maximum points.

Before the League programme could reach its conclusion City had the small matter of the FA Cup Final to consider, as this was to be played on St George's Day, Saturday 23rd April - the day Wednesday would face Aston Villa in the crucial League game.

Putting the cliff-hanging League programme to one side for the moment, it's worth considering exactly what Tom Maley had achieved with City so far. He had built a team in the truest sense of the word; he had pushed that side to promotion; and then seen his players dominate most First Division and Cup games since. His team had hit the headlines on several occasions and many of his players had become household names.

By the time Roberto Mancini was managing the side to similar success 107 years later this attention was the norm, but in 1904 this was all very new causing J.J. Bentley to comment in The Umpire newspaper on the eve of the Final: "Since the City have become famous and especially as the Cup Finalists, it has been considered the proper thing to give every detail of their doings and I'm quite expecting to read that, while shaving, Meredith accidentally came across a little wart and the great international actually lost ten drops of his precious blood..."

City's 1904 Cup Final side must be recognised as one of the greatest sides regardless of how the Final or the League programme ended, as this side had come from virtually nothing to be one of true talent and performance. The people of Manchester deserved a little

pleasure after the years of struggle while supporting both City and United and, with a trip to London available, all Mancunians decided to celebrate. Most of the Pubs and Working Men's Clubs in the Ardwick area and in the city, organised excursions to the capital. Many set off early on Friday morning determined to make a holiday of it, and reporters from all the North's leading newspapers journeyed with them.

With City's final opponents being Bolton Wanderers, the whole affair became known as "The Lancastrian Invasion." It sounds crazy today but this really did seem like an Alien invasion to some Londoners. The now defunct, 'Blue-biased', Manchester Evening Chronicle carried a report on the situation in London: "The true character of the London invasion could not be gleaned until midnight and during the early hours of Saturday morning. At Euston, St. Pancras, King's Cross and Marylebone, the trains, heavy laden, steamed in continuously. 'What a cheer!' I heard a jovial porter say, shortly after midnight. 'This is great, ain't it? Blimey! Did you ever see so many pubs in bottles? What, oh! Don't they grub?' And truly, the trippers upheld the tradition of the North. Each little party seemed to have brought their own stack of provisions for the weekend. Nine gallon barrels of beer, stone jars of whisky and big baskets filled with 'baggins' were almost as plentiful as blackberries in Autumn, while there could never have been as many toastmasters on Euston station before, 'Good Health!' rang perpetually in one's ears. 'Hooray!', 'Play up, City!'"

For many Londoners, the excited Lancastrians must have re-enforced their stereotypical view of the North, but who cared? At least they added colour to a rain soaked London morning. For many Blues this would have been their first, and possibly their only, trip to the capital, and no doubt they wanted to take in a few of the sights. Unfortunately, the morning was so miserable that most Mancunians remained at the stations. St. Pancras is reported to have had more people packed onto its platforms that morning than at any other time, while at least sixteen thousand people arrived at Euston during the night with nowhere else to go.

By about seven o'clock some of the more enthusiastic supporters ventured out of the stations to explore the capital. It must have seemed like young birds leaving their nests for the first time as City fans were eager to leave, but uncertain what they would find. Gradually, as more left the security of the station others plucked up the courage. By ten o'clock the sun was shining and most Blues had taken flight. Only the late arrivals remained.

For the directors the journey to London was also a great adventure according to some contemporary reports. Apparently, they obtained a horse-drawn carriage and, with about a dozen on the roof, and around eight inside, they travelled south. Every one of

The City directors and guests on their way to the cup final.

the directors must have been proud, but could any of them have been as proud as Lawrence Furniss who had been connected with the Club since the early 1880s, and secretary/manager when the Club first entered the League? Travelling with Furniss were the Club's two other former secretaries - Josh Parlby and Sam Ormerod. Parlby was, of course, still an important member of the City directorate, whereas Ormerod was actually Stockport County's secretary/manager. By involving Ormerod in City's moment of glory, the Blues proved they did not hold him responsible for City's relegation two years earlier, and that in some way the former manager was being thanked for the work he had put in during his time at Hyde Road.

Another man travelling with the directors was J.J. Bentley, the President of the Football League and former Bolton Secretary/manager. Bentley was also a leading journalist for the Hulton owned *Umpire* newspaper who, only the night before, had made comments about City making the headlines too often.

The players prepared with a break at the Norbreck Hotel, Blackpool. According to one newspaper the team had been training there for several weeks – it seems they did use the hotel in the build-up to most cup ties and some League games that season. On Thursday 21st April they travelled from Blackpool and arrived at their Cup Final base, the Crystal Palace Hotel, West Norwood at 7.30 that evening. They trained on Friday and an assessment was made of all the players' fitness and

injuries. Both Livingstone and Holmes were struggling to be fit, although Holmes had made it clear that he was fully fit and ready for the final before the team had left Blackpool. Livingstone, on the other hand, seemed less likely to play.

The Cup Final was for the tenth consecutive year to be played at the Crystal Palace grounds, at the time a huge pleasure gardens and leisure complex. Although the venue was enormous - over 114,000 attended the 1901 Final - not everybody was guaranteed a good view. Many spectators sought whatever vantage point they could, with the many trees surrounding the ground packed with supporters. Even the journalists searched for the best spots. The *Athletic News* created quite a spectacle by obtaining a gas-filled balloon for the day. They had the intention of providing a bird's eye view of events for their readers.

As the crowd gathered at the Palace ground, Tom Maley selected his team for what was hoped to be the first leg of the double. The team selected was a powerful one: Hillman, McMahon, Burgess, Frost, Hynds, Ashworth, Meredith, Livingstone, Gillespie, Turnbull, and Booth. Livingstone had passed his fitness test but, surprisingly, there was no place for the long serving 'Doc' Holmes, who had played in the quarter-final and semi-final but had suffered injury in the League game with Nottingham Forest on 13th April.

Holmes was bitterly disappointed on hearing the news. He took hold of his boots and threw them out

Scenes from the final including a pitch invading City fan and (opposite bottom) Meredith's goal.

of the dressing room window. Maley had replaced him with the amateur Sam Ashworth and, when considering the cold facts it's easy to understand why. Although Holmes claimed to be fully fit, Maley had doubts. In addition, Holmes was very much a fringe player by this point whereas the hardworking Ashworth was a key member of Maley's team. Nevertheless, Holmes was a City man through and through. He had helped the Club move away from its Second Division roots and now wanted to play a major part in bringing the Cup to Manchester for the first time.

While Maley was attempting to calm the dressing room atmosphere, the *Manchester Evening Chronicle* reporters surveyed the scene prior to the big game: "It was an animated throng, one in which the spirit of partisanship was appreciably more lively than was the case among southern people. The rink was fringed with thousands of ardent Lancastrians, every man a connoisseur. Nearly everyone was willing to back his fancy, win or lose; the dark and the light-blue favours were strongly reminiscent of the University Boat Race. Manchester City seemed the favourites as was only to be expected, but the average Bolton supporters had almost an adoring faith in the potential of the 'Trotters.'"

The article went on to describe that there were a large number of ladies present in the crowd and that the majority of these supported City. It seems that the reporter was quite surprised to find that the female members of the crowd were shouting and making as much noise as the men. Later, he described the now dry conditions and state of the ground: "The ground looked in beautiful condition after the rainfall of the previous day and there was no great amount of wind to make its presence felt on the course of the flying ball.

"Of course, there was the usual crowd wandering on the fringes of the field of play and the tedium of waiting was relieved by the Crystal Palace band, but away on the far terraces, behind the southern goal, the famous Boys Band of St. Joseph's were cheering on their supporters by spirited strains. As the time approached, the policemen in their usual persuasive manner, expeditiously cleared the precincts of the pavilion so that the teams could make their way on to the ground. Several enthusiastic Boltonians were to be noticed with bright parasols and white sleeved hats ornamented with trotters."

The Daily Graphic's report of the moments leading up to the game concentrated on the size of the crowd. The actual attendance was a disappointing 61,374, with receipts totalling £3,000. The reason being that the early morning rain had put off those within a morning's travel of the Palace, and that many Lancastrians simply could not afford the expense of journeying to London and all that entailed. Nevertheless, it did compare with the attendance for the previous year's final (Bury V. Derby County) and the finals pre-1901. Ultimately, any attendance of over sixty thousand for an all-Lancashire final played in London before the days of comfortable wages and multi transport systems has to be significant.

A reporter for the *Graphic* acknowledged the large northern support: "None of the ordinary incidents of such a day were wanting. It would scarcely seem like a Cup tie day now if half the people there were not

Uncovered Stand DD,
CRYSTAL PALACE.

Uncovered Stand DD,
5/-

The Football Association Challenge Cup.
FINAL TIE,
Saturday, April 23rd, 1904.
Kick Off at 3.30 p.m.
The Holder of this Ticket is requested to occupy the Seat by 3.15 p.m.
No. 989 This Ticket does NOT admit to the Palace.

MANCHESTER PLAYER HURT — TRAINER AND
AMBULANCE MAN ANXIOUS TO ASSIST

speaking in a provincial dialect. On Saturday it seemed as though three-fourths of the people were speaking in it, and the remaining fourth were ineffectually trying to imitate them. Then there were the usual crowded trains, the rush for good standing places, the struggles for the refreshment tables, the usual notices imploring you not to climb up into the trees in order to get a view of the match - and the usual number of people who disregarded such notices, and came to no harm for their lawlessness. The only thing wanting was about another fifty thousand people to make the place uncomfortable for everyone.

"Ticket holders were asked to be in their places by a quarter past three, and among the eleven thousand odd people who obeyed this injunction were the Prime-Minister, the Colonial Secretary and Mrs. Lyttleton, the Hon. R. Lyttleton, and Lord Stanley. Mr. Balfour and Mr. Lyttleton were soon recognised by the crowd, and heartily cheered."

Prime-Minister Balfour was, of course, the man who almost four years earlier had visited Hyde Road after being persuaded by Stephen Chester Thompson to become a patron of the Club. Was Balfour the first Prime-Minister to be a Blue? The Manchester Courier implied as much when talking of his interest and on a number of occasions when mentioning Balfour they also stressed: "The Prime Minister (in whose constituency the Manchester City ground is situated)...."

Other celebrities to attend City's first final included the Music Hall stars Harry Lauder and George Robey (who was shouting for City), and cricketers C.B Fry, Wilfred Rhodes, George Jessop, and the larger than life W.G. Grace. Robey, incidentally, had sent the Blues a telegram wishing them well pre-match. The Cup Final was, by this time, established as one of the most important sporting occasions.

In preparation for the 3.30pm kick off, the teams entered the field. Meredith was the first man out, leading the Cambridge Blues as captain. Bolton, dressed in white shirts, followed. Meredith won the toss and elected to play towards the southern goal where the Boy's Band of St. Joseph's entertained the City followers. The band had followed City to most of the key games that season, bringing a little extra atmosphere to the terraces. No game was complete without St. Joseph's musical accompaniment.

Once the game commenced the Palace's slippery pitch helped Bolton keep pace with City. The two sides seemed well matched for a while, but City began to take control according to the *Graphic*: "As the game proceeded the Bolton Wanderers seemed to be getting a little loose in their play, while their opponents were improving. Several times the Manchester forwards quite outplayed the Wanderers, and, passing very neatly, with a great deal of head work, nearly scored. They tried again and again, and anyone could see that if a goal was to be scored, Meredith, the Manchester City Captain, was the man to kick it. The game was getting uncomfortably warm for the Wanderers when Davies, their goalkeeper, was charged over [presumably by Gillespie!], and the free kick put matters right for a time. Manchester returned to the attack, and Davies had a good deal of work to do.

"Eventually Meredith seized the opportunity he had been working for and shot the ball crosswise into the Bolton goal."

Meredith's view of the goal is worth recalling: "I was lying well out on the touch-line, inside my own half. Livingstone whipped out a wide pass. Archie Freebairn, the Wanderers' left-half, touched the ball with his head, but failed to divert it. It landed at my feet. I made off down the wing. I must have dribbled 35 yards before I cut in to beat Bob Struthers, the Bolton back.

THE ONLY GOAL
A BRILLIANT
INDIVIDUAL EFFORT
ON THE PART OF
MEREDITH

AN ENTHUSIASTIC SUPPORTER OF MANCHESTER CITY WANTS TO SHAKE HANDS WITH MEREDITH

"Then I had a clear run to goal and I put the ball into the net just where I wanted. Dai Davies had no chance whatever."

The *Daily Graphic* believed the goal should have been disallowed: "From the seats occupied by representatives of the *DAILY GRAPHIC* Meredith appeared to be off-side when he scored this goal, and one is inclined to think that Davies was of the same opinion, for he but simply held his arms out. However, the goal was not questioned, and, to the accompaniment of loud cheers and the waving of hats and sticks, play began again. The crowds were delighted at the prospect of seeing the match definitely decided, and one of Manchester's supporters was so enthusiastic in his praise of Meredith that he left his seat and attempted to walk out to the field, apparently with the intention of embracing the Manchester captain. Two policemen reasoned with him, but he insisted on going, and at length five policemen escorted him away for a time."

The debate about whether the goal was offside or not raged on for years. Thirty years later, as City prepared for their 1934 FA Cup final appearance, Meredith was quizzed by the *Manchester Evening Chronicle*: "Offside! Nonsense. Not a single Bolton player made a murmur. The crowd took it in the spirit of spectators who have seen a perfectly good goal. The fun began the very next morning. A Sunday newspaper had a contents bill 'Cup won by off-side goal' or something like that. The writer of the story expressed his firm conviction that I was off-side when I received the ball.

"Meat for the Bolton supporters I would say it was. They have quizzed me for 30

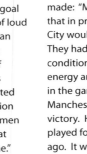

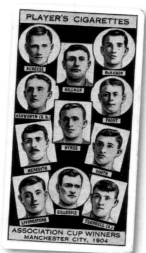

PLAYER'S CIGARETTES

BURGESS McMAHON
HILLMAN
ASHWORTH (S. B.) FROST
HYNDS
MEREDITH BOOTH
LIVINGSTONE TURNBULL (A.)
GILLESPIE

ASSOCIATION CUP WINNERS
MANCHESTER CITY, 1904

years, and I suppose they will till I die. I don't mind. I still think it was one of the best goals I have ever scored."

In 1904 the off-side rule stated that at least three opponents must be goalside of the attacker when the ball was played. According to some journalists at the game that had not been the case.

Interestingly, the players themselves did not appeal, leading to the suspicion that the goal only became controversial as the game progressed and Bolton's chances diminished. According to all reports City certainly deserved their lead and comfortably kept Bolton at a safe distance. In the second half the Blues seemed to relax a little, while still retaining overall control. Some believed City were saving themselves for the important League game against Everton the following Monday. A fact borne out when Meredith seemed to deliberately time waste by moving in to offside positions.

City's relaxed approach did provide Bolton with a few chances, but there was never really any danger. As the game ended thousands swarmed onto the pitch in front of the pavilion to see the Colonial Secretary, Alfred Lyttleton, present the Cup to Maley's City. *The Daily Graphic* reported on the moment and the speeches made: "Mr. Lyttleton, who was loudly cheered, said that in presenting the Cup he was sure Manchester City would not object to his first word being to Bolton. They had played a losing game well, under desperate conditions, and had a given a fine exhibition of pluck, energy and endurance. As one who had taken part in the game of Association Football, he congratulated Manchester City on their well-deserved and splendid victory. He had hardly seen such a good match since he played for England against Scotland six and twenty years ago. It was true that England lost that match, but he would ask the Prime Minister to look up the records and see who it was that scored England's one goal.

"Mr. Balfour, in calling upon the crowd to thank Mr. Lyttleton for coming to present the Cup, said that Mr. Lyttleton had spoken to them as an expert, while he could only speak as an admiring ignoramus. He was glad that the tie had been fought out between two Lancastrian teams, and he was sure they would pardon his satisfaction at the success of Manchester City"

On receiving the Cup Meredith is reported to have said, "I'm sure it has given me great pleasure to win the Cup", although he later denied making those comments as they appeared so amusing to him when he saw them in print. Regardless of the actual words spoken, it must have been an otherwise memorable day for Meredith and everyone connected with City. At Hyde Road a crowd of 8,000 attending a

The original FA Cup, the trophy won by City in 1904.

and hope that Wednesday lose if they were to win their first title and, of course, the coveted double.

The Blues travelled to Liverpool direct from London the day after the final, arriving at 10pm on the Sunday night. The *Manchester Evening Chronicle* revealed the following Monday that this had been a secret operation: "There was no demonstration for the simple reason that their arrival had been kept very quiet, and unlike the heroes of a great English Cup final, they proceeded quietly to the Alexandra Hotel, where they remained overnight."

By the Monday morning rumours had spread across Liverpool that City were in town: "A trip to New Brighton had been arranged and, as the players left the hotel, they were the victims of a cinematograph operator."

This footage was later displayed alongside film of the final itself in Manchester and Salford over the days that followed. Commencing on the Monday after the final, newspapers carried adverts for a film by "New Century Animated Pictures" of the cup final and "the only animated picture taken of the team with the Cup." Two venues, St. James' Hall in the city centre and the Regent Theatre in Salford, had film of the cup tie shown twice a day for at least the following week. St. James' Hall charged a variety of admission prices from sixpence to three shillings depending on distance from the screen, for showings at 3pm and 8pm daily. The Regent Theatre's version was on at 6.50pm and 9pm daily – perhaps this was the same film moved between each location between performances?

One newspaper reviewed the film show at St. James' Hall: "Notwithstanding the many counter attractions, a large and appreciative audience assembled." It went on: "The City football match was replayed and Meredith was actually seen kicking the goal. One could fancy oneself amongst the crowd at the Crystal Palace whilst the game was in progress, so clear and good was the production. To use the football vernacular 'there was not a dull moment from start to finish', for all the most exciting scenes that took place were shown on the screen. The aim of the cinematograph operator is, of course, to secure the best and most exciting incidents, and as far as the City match is concerned this has been done."

Earlier that Monday the City players tried to relax at New Brighton. Billy Meredith chose to reward his team mates by buying them each a hat as celebration for the FA Cup win, however there was great interest in everything the Blues did that day. Presumably, all the players wanted to do was play their final league match and then return home, but one newspaper commented that Meredith and the others had struggled to find a moment's relaxation.

Unfortunately, the exertions of Cup Final weekend and the trip to Merseyside had affected the players and the Everton game became a bit of an anti-climax. The

reserve game, gave a tremendous roar of delight when the score was chalked onto a scoreboard in the stand. Elsewhere in Manchester the news soon spread and the whole city started to celebrate.

The Lancashire FA held a dinner in the Crystal Palace's Garden Hall for both teams after the match. Various speeches were made during which time City expressed their hope that Bolton would win the trophy the following year, while Bolton claimed that City were worthy winners and that they had outperformed their side. Both clubs and Lancashire officials stressed the pride they felt that the county possessed the two greatest sides in the country and that London had been able to see at first hand the passion northerners had for their sides. It is worth noting that the FA Cup was still viewed as the game's greatest prize even though success in the League needed greater consistency.

The only black moment that weekend came when Manchester heard the news that their League rivals, Sheffield Wednesday, had gained a further two points by beating Aston Villa 4-2. This meant that Wednesday were a point ahead of City with one game each remaining. Both matches were to be played away from home with Wednesday at fourteenth placed Derby County on 30th, while City would face fourth placed Everton on Monday 25th at 6pm. The Cambridge Blues knew they had to win same eleven players who had performed so well to win the Cup – on display that evening at Goodison Park - went down to a single goal from Taylor. Wednesday, without playing, were Champions for the second year running, and the Blues were left to consider what might have been. Sheffield Wednesday, incidentally, went on to beat Derby 2-0 and so end the season three points above Maley's City.

Regardless of how the League programme ended, City were the team of the season – a point remembered for years as *The Boys Book Of Soccer 1954* was to prove. An article looking back on the history of the game focused on the Blues 1904 triumph and highlighted: "City were runners up, and that plus the Cup wasn't bad for a young club that had just come up from the Second Division, was it? That's why I call them the team of the year."

Tom Maley's side had won many admirers with their stylish team approach, and had dominated the headlines in the popular sporting press. The manager deserved the success after turning City from a team of individuals going nowhere, into a star-studded team in the truest sense. It would be 2010-11 before another City manager would come as close to FA Cup glory and League success in the same season. Like Maley, Roberto Mancini had transformed talented individuals in to a true team.

Another similarity between the two seasons was the celebratory homecoming. In both 2011 and 1904 this took place on a Monday night. In 1904 the triumphant return had to wait until after the Everton match. Immediately after the final whistle the players changed and rushed to the station for a scheduled departure at 8.30pm. That train was due to bring the Blues back for 9pm.

"That day Manchester recognised the benefits of footballing success, and that day Manchester found its sporting identity."

Understandably, most Mancunians were keen to see the conquering City side bring home the Cup, but the civic leaders and police had been a little out of touch with the mood of the city. Rather surprisingly when a civic reception was first suggested Manchester's leaders gave a response along the lines of 'Manchester is an industrial city and has no time for merriment'. When asked about a special homecoming, the Chief Constable retorted, "I am not interested!"

Some felt too much time had been spent on football and that Manchester simply had to get back to work. Fortunately, the people thought differently. As did City who announced their travel plans from Liverpool and their planned arrival time in Manchester. They also provided details of the route they would take back to Hyde Road. Anyone reading between the lines would be able to work out that City were as keen as anyone to ensure the people were able to celebrate the Cup's arrival in Manchester.

By lunchtime that Monday the Police Chief and councillors were well aware of the interest and plans were revised to ensure proper police involvement.

Ultimately, 150 policemen, mainly from A Division but supplemented by D Division, were "hurriedly organised" (according to the press) for the homecoming. The Lord Mayor announced that he wanted to be at the station when city returned but a prior engagement meant he could not be present. Finally, the authorities were realising how significant this moment was in Manchester's history.

The people of Manchester already knew the significance. The *Manchester Courier*, while referring to some comments from the Prime Minister about football enthusiasts being delighted, explained that it was not simply football fans, but all Mancunians who wanted to see their heroes: "From the Juveniles who had

A gold watch presented to Tom Maley by supporters thanking him for the success.

swarmed the convenient lamp posts in order to obtain a glimpse of all there was to be seen, to the corpulent old dames who encroached on to the tram lines and vigorously clapped their hands."

The press reported on the streets being packed – particularly around Central Station, Peter Street, the whole of Deansgate and beyond – for more than an hour before the team was due to arrive. Reports even claimed that the "entire population" of Manchester had turned out and, if the newspaper articles are anything to go by, this seems highly plausible. Manchester was packed like never before. Only, perhaps, Queen Victoria's visit in 1894 – the day Manchester City officially joined the League – could compare.

This could explain why football eventually got hold of Mancunians in a way that today makes it perhaps the one activity that Manchester is known for more than any other. City's success was the first tangible sporting achievement the people of Manchester could unite behind. Prior to 1904 Lancashire CCC had found success but cricket did not appeal to the greater part of Manchester's population, plus Lancashire was not seen as a pure Manchester institution. Other major activities occurring around the city had focused on one-off events such as major races at the Manchester Racecourse, or festivals lasting several days – a Manchester Wheelers

cycling festival attracted around 50,000 to Alexandra Park in 1883 according to some sources. The FA Cup success was different because it was the first time a major sporting organisation appealing to all areas of society from the city had achieved national acclaim. Promotion in 1899 was an achievement, but winning the English Cup was another level of success altogether.

At 9pm when the Blues were due to arrive back from Goodison Manchester waited. City had missed their scheduled train, putting the whole celebration in doubt. Fortunately, the Cheshire Lines Railway Company came to the rescue and rushed to put on extra trains from Liverpool. As the news spread that the Blues were on the move, people turned out at some of the stations on the route to cheer the side on. At Warrington Station a large crowd gathered and Billy Meredith leaned out of a carriage window holding out the Cup to let everyone see the trophy – scenes replicated on another route to Manchester in 1934 when Sam Cowan performed a similar role to Meredith.

Reports vary on what time the Blues arrived back in Manchester. The most detailed claimed a train pulled up at 9.18pm on one platform and then opposite on the other side of the platform a second train arrived two minutes later. Both had more carriages than anticipated and there was confusion as to which one was City's.

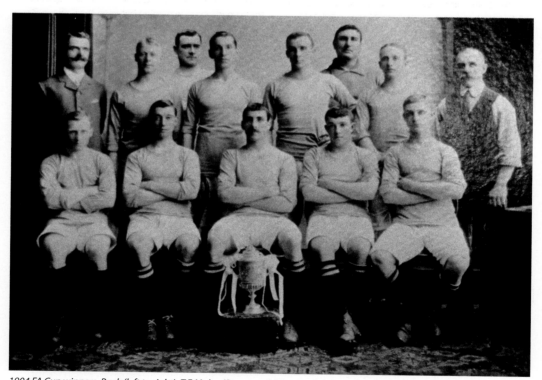

1904 FA Cup winners. Back (left to right): T.E.Maley (Secretary & Manager), S.Frost, W.J.Gillespie, J.McMahon, T.Hynds, J.Hillman, S.B.Ashworth, J.Broad (Trainer). Front: H.Burgess, G.T.Livingstone, W.Meredith, A.Turnbull, F.Booth.

Ultimately, the press revealed that both trains were actually classed as the same train but that the players were on the later section. This was identified when Meredith climbed out carrying the trophy dressed with 'silken ribbons of blue and white'.

A horse drawn carriage, driven by Albert Alexander senior – a man who would later be vice-chairman of the Blues and would temporarily manage the side in 1926 – had pulled up alongside the train and Meredith and the other players climbed on. The first homecoming parade the city had ever known began.

According to newspaper coverage the parade saw a large force of mounted police take the lead; followed by the St. Joseph's Industrial School Band; then came a stage coach dressed in Cambridge Blue and White carrying the players, led by Meredith lifting the Cup at regular intervals; this was followed by a four-in-hand carrying the directors and press. One journalist recorded that the players' coach was greeted with "cries of 'Good Old City' were kept up along the line" before adding that the coach carrying the directors and press was greeted with "Play Up Seconds!" and much laughter.

After the Directors' carriage came the ground committee – an important group of enthusiasts who basically managed City's Hyde Road ground and performed a variety of duties from stewarding to the upkeep of the pitch – then came further mounted police.

The procession travelled from Central Station, to Peter Street, Deansgate, Market Street, Piccadilly, Dale Street, London Road, Ardwick Green, and ended at the Ardwick Conservative Club - not, surprisingly, the Hyde Road ground.

This route was important as it was clearly not the most direct route to Ardwick – Mosley Street or Portland Street would have been a quicker way to Piccadilly/ London Road – but it did cover a significant proportion of the city centre. It also included streets where the Club knew some of the poorer workers lived. The inclusion of Dale Street at this time proved that the Blues knew that this success was one all the people should share in.

Once the procession started the St. Joseph's Band played "See the Conquering Hero Come", but reports told of how they almost lost their instruments as the police struggled to clear a path. According to the *Manchester Evening Chronicle* every building was packed with

TRUE BLUE
John Chapman

A dedicated City chairman, who passed away while still in office in 1920.

onlookers. Special mention was made of the packed windows at the recently opened Midland Hotel.

The *Manchester Courier* talked of the size of the crowd on Peter Street and the streets that followed: "The police had an Herculean task to force the cheering people back, and the same thing happened all along Deansgate."

There were reports of lines of fans, twenty to thirty deep, on both sides of all the main streets. It is no wonder that all the press dedicated considerable space to the parade, including the authoritative *Athletic News*: "As soon as they caught sight of the trophy trimmed with blue and white ribbons which Meredith now and then raised above his head, they gave vent to prodigious cheering. Most of the windows of the upper stories were packed with people whose plaudits, added to by the blowing of a bugle here and there, and the music of the band, made a deafening sound."

The *Manchester Evening Chronicle* followed the procession up Market Street: "In Piccadilly, the scene was one which beggars description. The windows of the hotels were packed, electric standards and the statues on the Infirmary Esplanade [those occupying modern day Piccadilly] were invaded, flags were waved, and bugles were sounded. All vehicular traffic was at a standstill."

The procession turned, presumably up Oldham Street and then turned into Dale Street: The *Athletic News* reported the change in social character: "To the accompaniment of incessant cheering, the procession made its way at walking pace down Dale Street where what might be called the welcome of the middle-classes was exchanged for that of the proletariat. It came from rough working men and larrikins and beshawled women and children in arms and hand, and was hearty if not heartier than had gone before."

As can be seen from that comment, City's homecoming united Mancunians in a way no other success had managed. That day Manchester recognised the benefits of footballing success, and that day Manchester found its sporting identity. Thousands of ordinary people mixed with wealthier citizens on the streets. A Mancunian identity was shared.

The *Manchester Evening Chronicle* reported that the celebrations continued as the team made its way on to London Road, close to the present day Piccadilly

Station: "The tops of the tramcars were utilised as stands for viewing the procession, and all along London Road, Downing Street, and Ardwick Green the same spectacle of indescribable enthusiasm prevailed."

The *Courier* focused on those standing on present day Piccadilly Approach. It reported that 'juveniles' were peering down through the railings and added: "There was no diminuation whatever in size of the crowds lining Downing Street and Ardwick Green was filled with a dense mass of people young and old, of both sexes."

Again the fact that all Mancunians regardless of status, sex and age turned out proved the unifying significance of this night. The wide range of people from different social classes taking to the streets caused the *Manchester Evening Chronicle* to claim: "There is nothing in the annals of football that will compare with the magnificent reception which was accorded the Manchester City football team on the occasion of their return to Manchester last night in the proud position of holders of the English Cup for the first time in Manchester's career. Notwithstanding the lateness of their arrival, the whole population of the city seemed to have turned out to do them honour."

The parade ended at Ardwick Conservative Club. One report claims that a heavy-handed police presence meant that the team had to climb a back-staircase, led by someone holding a candle, to the function room. Once in the room speeches were made by Tom Maley, Billy Meredith, John Chapman and Joshua Parlby.

The City manager summed up the importance of the moment accurately when he told officials and the press that he was deeply moved by the reception and "the appreciation of the people of Manchester of what [City] had been able to achieve."

He added: "Perhaps love of sport had something to do with the bringing together of so great a gathering, but love of Manchester, had much more to do with it."

Later that week the *Manchester Evening Chronicle* claimed that Manchester was now the second city of the Empire. It was a bold statement, but it had to be directly connected with what had occurred earlier that week. Football really had changed the atmosphere for all in the world's first industrial city. The city had achieved a great deal in the world of industry and endeavour and no one could ever question those achievements, but now all Mancunians, regardless of social status, religious background, and length of residency felt they had achieved something together as equals. They were united in their support of the Cup winners and after tasting success for the first time, they were keen to see City find further glory.

1902-1904 SUMMARY

Major Trophies Won: FA Cup 1903-1904 & Second Division Champions 1902-03
Highest League Attendance: c.40,000 Newcastle United, 10/04/03
Highest Cup Attendance: 30,022 (sometimes reported as 35,000) Middlesbrough, 05/03/04 (FA Cup)
Secretary/Managers: 1902-1906 Tom Maley

Seasonal Record:

Season	League	Posn	FA Cup	Other	Leading Scorer	Average Attendance
1902-03	FL Div2	Champions	Rnd 1		Gillespie 28	16,000
1903-04	FL Div1	2	Winners		Gillespie 18	20,000

1904 FA CUP RUN

R1	Sunderland	H	W	3-2
R2	Woolwich Arsenal	A	W	2-0
R3	Middlesbrough	H	D	0-0
	Middlesbrough	A	W	3-1
SF	Sheffield Wednesday	N*	W	3-0
F	Bolton Wanderers	N**	W	1-0

* = Goodison Park   ** = Crystal Palace Ground

	P	W	D	L	F	A
HOME	2	1	1	0	3	2
AWAY	4	4	0	0	9	1
TOTAL	6	5	1	0	12	3

FINAL DETAILS

23 April 1904 at The Crystal Palace
Manchester City 1-0 Bolton Wanderers
CITY: Hillman, McMahon, Burgess, Frost, Hynds, Ashworth, Meredith, Livingstone, Gillespie, Turnbull, Booth
BOLTON: Davies, Brown, Struthers, Clifford, Greenhalgh, Freebairn, Stokes, Marsh, Yenson, White, Taylor
GOALS: Meredith
ATTENDANCE: 61,372
REFEREE: A J Barker (Hanley)

DULCIMER AND BBC RADIO WALES PRESENTS

OCTOBER 30th/HYDREF30
6pm/DRYSAU 6yp

MEREDITH NIGHTS

£5

AN EVENING OF WELSH MUSIC INCLUDING
PLANT DUW, YUCATAN AND TOM EDNEY
WITH EXCLUSIVELY WELSH DJ SETS FROM ADAM WALTON AND DJ FUZZY FELT

The legend continues. In 2011 a night of Welsh music was dedicated to City's star.

1904-1907
Scandal

"Manchester City is becoming too popular to suit some other clubs."

Billy Meredith talking to the press following a determined investigation by the FA, August 1905

1904-1905 Villains

The Cup success and runners up in the League provided City with greater ambition. The Club, under the direction of Edward Hulton, John Allison and, of course, Tom Maley were aiming for the top. City's success proved what was possible.

Unfortunately for the Blues, others were increasingly showing interest in the Club. The Football Association, 'a southern body dominated by amateurs' according to many northerners at the time, were unhappy with City's success. According to John Harding's excellent biography of Billy Meredith, *Football Wizard*, the FA believed that clubs such as City were too professional and that there was a real danger of football's amateur, sporting, nature being lost forever. Before football was lost completely to the northern professionals, the FA decided to teach the main culprits a lesson.

Within two weeks of City's triumphal procession through Manchester, the FA secretary, F.J. Wall, and a member of the FA General Council, John Lewis, arrived at Hyde Road demanding to see the Club's books. They spent the whole close season examining City's accounts determined to find proof of illegal wages and bonuses, yet found nothing tangible. They did discover discrepancies in the transfers of Frank Norgrove and Irvine Thornley from Glossop. The FA had also been investigating Glossop, a northern outfit keen to spend whatever it took to attract the best players as the Blues themselves had suggested in the late 1890s. At Glossop the FA uncovered suspicious information and discrepancies between that and City's books. At Hyde Road they discovered forged receipts for unusual payments that coincided with the players' transfers. The FA determined that these were signing on fees far in excess of the £10 maximum then allowed.

To preserve its amateur image, the FA had insisted on maximum signing on fees in addition to the £4 maximum wage rule. Most First Division clubs broke the rules but some were adept at not bringing due attention to themselves, as Meredith once said, "Of course clubs are not punished for breaking laws. They are punished for being found out."

Meredith's view was accurate - City were a club unable to keep their activities quiet. Right back to their days as Ardwick they had been in trouble with the FA for poaching players, and by 1904 they were seen as a nouveau riche club determined to buy success – an accusation that re-appeared some 104 years later! Back in 1904 the establishment was out to put an end to the Blues' ambitions.

In October City were fined £250, Irvine Thornley was suspended for the rest of the season, and Hyde Road was ordered to be closed for two games. In addition, directors Joshua Parlby, John Chapman, and Lawrence Furniss were banned for three years, while the Finance Director, G. Madders, was suspended for life. This was a major blow.

Furniss and Parlby's places in City's history have always been clear - both managed the Club and both had helped to create Manchester City as we know it today - but what is rarely documented is the role John Chapman played. Chapman had also been involved with the Club since the Ardwick days and, together with Parlby, had signed Meredith. He had also been extremely generous financially, and had helped the Club sign many other players. The FA, in effect, banned the three most influential figures.

Irvine Thornley had only been with the Club since April but was already popular. It was a tremendous disappointment that he was to miss the bulk of the 1904-05 season, especially as he had already scored the only two City goals in the four games he had participated in. Fortunately for Thornley, his enforced absence probably prevented him from getting involved in the bigger scandal that was about to engulf the Club and cause the *Athletic News* journalist James Catton, who

used the pen name Tityrus, to state that City are "like the poor. We always have them with us. It seems we cannot escape from them."

Before those further investigations, City were able to play a little football. Although the opening five fixtures only resulted in one win and two draws, Maley's outfit still had the look of Championship contenders. From 8th October they put together a run of four games without defeat and scored a total of thirteen goals. The bustling Gillespie contributed three of those goals.

In mid-November the *Manchester Evening Chronicle* decided to focus on the steps City had taken to improve facilities for fans: "It is of special interest now that the period of suspension of the Manchester City club has expired, and play is once more permissible at the Hyde Road ground, to draw attention to the nature of the extensive improvements which have been effected, and by which the holding capacity of the enclosure has been so materially increased. Probably few of thousands of spectators who weekly visit our large football grounds have the slightest conception of the care and the thought bestowed in providing for their convenience. Their own enthusiasm is concerned with the play and the players. Football, indeed, has a tremendous hold on the legion of followers."

Whether the article had been created simply to divert attention away from some of the negative aspects of City's development, suspensions and finances is not known, but the fact this appeared in one of Edward Hulton's 'papers suggests it was a great way of diverting attention. Regardless of the motives, the fact was that Hulton's City had invested serious money in ground developments.

Over £2,000 worth of improvements helped increase the capacity by around 10,000 by mid-November 1904. The Main Stand was extended on both ends – it had previously covered a length of about 65 yards – and now stretched the full length of the pitch with an increase in capacity of at least 2,000. The article suggested that the seating accommodation on that side of the ground had more than doubled.

An extraordinary general meeting of shareholders of Manchester City F.C. was held last evening. Resignations of five suspended directors were formally tendered. Mr. Lawrence Furniss, chairman, then read a statement on behalf of his fellow suspended directors. They desired to give an emphatic contradiction to the charges of forgery and burglarious practices, and they desired a full and free investigation by a committee of shareholders. The resignations were then accepted, a rider being added that the directors took with them the confidence and sympathy of the shareholders. The meeting was adjourned until November 3.

In October the FA investigations damaged the Blues.

During the past few weeks, says the "Daily News," a Special Commission appointed by the Football Association has been busy cleaning its stable, and the result is a clean sweep. The Manchester City, Sunderland, and Glossop clubs, all members of the English League, are convicted of grave irregularities in regard to their dealings with players. The three clubs are each fined £250, and a number of officials of each club have received long terms of banishment from the official football world. In addition, the Manchester City club is prohibited from playing on its own ground for a month. During the last two or three years the Football Association has found it necessary to inquire into the conduct of a number of its clubs, and in the majority of cases the revelations have been of a most flagrant character, but never before has the parent body exposed so widespread corruption. A member of the Commission tells us that the cases are the most unpleasant he has ever had to deal with. The sentences are none too severe. Only by enforcing the utmost rigour of its laws can the Football Association hope to stem the tide of corruption which is threatening to destroy a great game.

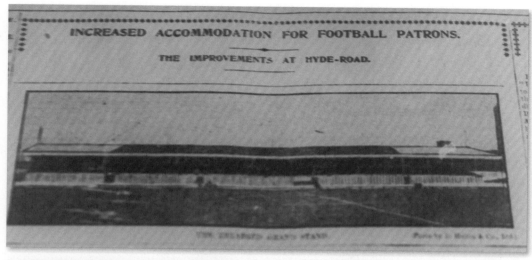

INCREASED ACCOMMODATION FOR FOOTBALL PATRONS.

THE IMPROVEMENTS AT HYDE-ROAD.

After serious ground issues in 1903-04 the Main Stand (top) was extended at both ends and the Stone Yard Stand (bottom) was remodelled. Blue & white painting brightened the ground.

At one end of the ground (the equivalent end to the Etihad Stadium's South Stand) an old stand was demolished and replaced with an uncovered 2,500 capacity "Stone Yard Stand" – twice the previous stand's capacity. At the opposite end, the Galloway Stand was increased to provide 3,000 places, while the Popular Side now contained a small roof providing shelter for about 350 people as well as a vastly improved terraced bank. The article claimed that all the waste ground around the Popular Side's embankment had been filled in to increase accommodation significantly.

As well as the redevelopment of the stands, the Club had improved entrances and exits, particularly on Bennett Street itself. They had also been hard at work with their paintbrushes. Almost every area of the ground had been painted blue and white in a similar manner to a decade earlier. In November 1904 however the blue and white striped paintwork made the ground a wonderful sight in the middle of grim industrial surroundings.

The article stressed the importance of Tom Maley to City's growth and, as the year progressed, his side

recorded convincing victories over Wolves (5-1), Sunderland (5-2), and Derby County (6-0). These results established the Blues in the top half of the table, while the New Year brought official recognition to all the players for their part in the Cup success. At a special commemorative dinner held at the Grand Hotel on Aytoun Street on 9th January, the players, trainer Jimmy Broad, and Secretary/Manager Tom Maley were presented with commemorative gold watches paid for by collections amongst Mancunians.

Mancunians were suffering great hardship at the time, both financially and health wise, and so the fact that fans performed collections and helped raise funds to recognise City's achievement is very significant. This act alone proves how important the game had become to the people of the region. Football really had changed the atmosphere for many in the world's first industrial city.

The winter of 1904/5 was particularly harsh with many locals dying of cold and malnutrition, and unemployment was high. A relief fund was set up

Top: The narrowest part of the ground, close to Bennett Street.

Right: A small shelter on the Popular Side, built in 1904.

and popular music hall entertainer and supporter of City at the final George Robey, brought a 'Team of Internationals' to Hyde Road on 23rd January to raise money. At that game, and others at Hyde Road, blankets were carried around the pitch for people to throw coins into. Although City was viewed as a wealthy and successful club, many Mancunians had little else to cheer. Maybe this is why the Blues mattered so much to Mancunians. It gave them a successful escape from the grim reality of life in Edwardian Manchester.

From the turn of the year through to mid-March City were undefeated in eight League games, taking the Blues back to the top of the League. With Bolton gaining revenge in the second round of the FA Cup - they defeated City 2-1 at Hyde Road - Maley was determined

to see his side capture the title. By mid-April with only four games to go, City, Newcastle, and Everton challenged for top spot.

On the 15th Everton faced Small Heath, a team on the fringe of the title race, at Goodison Park, while City met reigning champions Sheffield Wednesday at Hyde Road. Newcastle, like Maley's Blues the year before, had the small matter of facing Aston Villa in the 1905 FA Cup Final to overcome before turning their attentions back to the League.

At Goodison, Everton defeated Stoke 2-1 to increase their points tally to 45 while City struggled to match Wednesday. After being a goal behind for much of the game, Billy Meredith equalised in the last ten minutes. City had lost their rhythm, but were not out of the race yet. With three games to go they were three points behind Everton and equal with Newcastle, although the Cup finalists had one game in hand and, significantly, had failed in their bid to capture the FA Cup. It was now a question of nerve.

The 21st April was perhaps the most significant date. Newcastle would face Stoke in their first League game since the final while Everton travelled to Hyde Road. A crowd of over 40,000 packed into the ground and, although it is difficult to prove, many believed the attendance that day was City's largest so far and potentially the largest ever at Hyde Road. A game some fifteen years later against Burnley is more likely to be the highest actual attendance however.

The Everton game was an ill-tempered one and, although City won 2-0 with goals from Tom Hynds and George Livingstone, an off the ball incident made the game noteworthy. Everton's Tom Booth brutally 'flattened' City's Frank Booth. Both players were cautioned - inevitably City had retaliated - and Hyde Road became a ground of hate. The police had to escort the players from the pitch and it was perhaps only the fact that City had defeated the League leaders that stopped incidents occurring off the pitch.

In Liverpool the feeling was that City's Booth had provoked his namesake, and that the Everton man was justified in his action. Mancunians on the other hand believed that no amount of provocation could justify the type of brutal attack that had occurred.

With the game ending in controversy, much of the post-match comment concerned the physical side of the game and ignored the fact that the Blues were only one point behind Everton with two games remaining. Unfortunately, Newcastle had levelled with City and had a game in hand - a north-east derby the following day against Sunderland - City needed the Geordies to fail.

By the end of play on the 22nd April, City's position had improved. Newcastle were defeated 3-1 and Everton, who remained a point in front of the two challengers, lost 2-1 at Arsenal. Two days later Newcastle rested as City and Everton played crucial games away from home - Wolves v. City, and Nottingham Forest v. Everton. Both sides achieved convincing victories, with Maley's Blues winning 3-0, to keep up the pressure.

On the 26th Newcastle levelled with City after a 3-1 victory over Sheffield Wednesday, making the final day of the season a tense affair. With the two sides level, a mere one point behind Everton who had already completed their League programme, the title race was wide open. City knew they had to win and hope that Newcastle failed as the Blues' goal average was inferior to the Geordies.

The final fixtures saw Newcastle away at near neighbours Middlesbrough, while the Blues travelled to Villa Park to face the Cup winners. Billy Meredith later recalled: "Aston Villa had no chance of taking the honour. Our officials were very keen on us finishing with level points and we were offered a good bonus if we managed to do this. Our blood was up and the game wasn't the pleasantest."

As Meredith stated the game did not demonstrate the gentlemanly side of football, if anything it showed how physical football could become with numerous off the ball incidents and dangerous tackles. It seems that Villa, who had never really liked playing either Manchester club, wanted to finish the season in the style they had shown at the Palace the week before. They did not want the 'ungentlemanly professionals' from Manchester to achieve further success, especially as they were still regarded as young upstarts with no tradition. Looking back it is difficult to understand exactly how the Blues were viewed, but as an analogy with the 2000s and 2010s it is safe to say that Villa were the early century's equivalent of Manchester United in terms of FA support and media interest, whereas City were similar to Abramovich's Chelsea or even Sheikh Mansour's City. In the eyes of many, they were a side with 'no history' that had appeared from nowhere to challenge the establishment. Sadly, the establishment, especially in the early 1900s, would always win.

With Villa determined to put City in their place, the Blues resorted to tactics many suspected came naturally. Maley's City let themselves down, and conceded goals to Villa's Garraty, Hampton, and Hall. The pressure was on. Two second half goals from George Livingstone and Sandy Turnbull brought the Blues back into it, but it wasn't enough. During the final thirty minutes the game became progressively more violent with Sandy Turnbull seemingly involved in every incident. The Bolton Football Field reported: "Turnbull was in his dourest dribbling mood, dashing about the ball with his whole heart set on victory. Leake found him a real hard opponent and, becoming annoyed at the rough impact, gathered up a handful of dirt and hurled it at the City man. Turnbull was not hurt and responded with an acknowledgement favoured by the bourgeoisie - thrusting two fingers in a figurative manner at the Villa man."

According to the report: "Leake appeared to look towards the referee as though appealing, and not catching his eye, 'gave Turnbull a backhander'. The latter immediately responded with his fists and Leake was restrained by his fellow players from retaliating further."

Although Turnbull had developed a reputation for a rough style of play it appears that he was not the guilty one this time. Unfortunately, Leake was viewed as a gentleman and many were convinced that he would only react, not provoke. The Villa biased Sports Argus tried to convince its readership that Leake was entirely innocent and that he had merely enquired what Turnbull was doing rather than throw dirt at him and give him a 'backhander'. It also claimed the City man had hit Leake at least twice.

The game continued but frequent fights broke out, spoiling any chance the Blues had of equalising. Despite the result and the realisation that City had lost out in the title race, it was a relief when the final whistle went. However, the controversy did not end there as the *Bolton Football Field* reported: "Turnbull was coming off the ground (I think he was almost the first of the City players) and was going down the covered passage to the visitors' dressing room when someone, not a player, sprang out from the urinal and grabbed Turnbull, pulled him inside the Villa dressing room and the door was shut behind him. I thought the whole thing was in fun until, within a few seconds, the door was opened and Turnbull was pitched out heavily, by whom I could not see. He was yelling with pain and fright, and he had obviously been badly handled for his right cheek was grazed with a black mark or dirt (something like a cyclist describes as a cinder rash) and he had a mark on his ribs where he had been kicked."

Nobody disputed that Turnbull had been the victim of a deliberate attack by Villa men, but incredibly the *Birmingham Sports Argus* tried to justify it, thus causing further insults to fly from Manchester to Birmingham and vice versa. Significantly, it wasn't merely the Villa players and employees who were attacking the City men as police had to be called into the ground to protect the Manchester players. An angry mob even stoned the City party. A season that had promised so much ended in disgraceful scenes.

The FA had to act, especially as City's game against Everton had also been viewed as a battle. They set up a special committee to meet in Derby to consider the events at both matches. Meeting behind closed doors, the committee were taking considerable steps to understand everything that surrounded the two games and, as the summer progressed, they interviewed player after player in their quest for the full facts. This seemed rather suspicious, especially to the northern newspapers who were now convinced that the committee were fishing for a bigger catch than merely a disrepute charge against one or two players. With the FA meeting in secret rumour spread throughout football, with most northerners convinced the 'southern' FA would make City the scapegoats.

Sandy Turnbull

1905-1906 An Unjust Ban

On 4th August 1905, a month before the new season started, the FA committee finally produced their surprising findings. Firstly, they suspended J.T. Howcroft and R. T. Johns - the referees of the games at Goodison and Villa respectively - for a month each for failing to control the games. Howcroft in particular was criticised for 'extraordinary feebleness in a critical match'. Then they announced that Tom Booth of Everton and City's Sandy Turnbull were to be suspended for one month, yet no mention was made of Villa's Leake. Also, that Booth's sentence would be suspended because of: "previous good conduct and the provocation received." And finally, the most shocking news of the whole affair: "The Commissioners also reported on statements brought to their notice with regard to W. Meredith of Manchester having offered a sum of money to a player of Aston Villa to let Manchester City win the match. W. Meredith is suspended from football from 4th August until April 1906."

The people of Manchester - and Wales - were outraged that Football's greatest player could be found guilty of bribery. Meredith, staying in Chirk during the close season, spoke to the press: "I am entirely innocent and am suffering for others. Such an allegation as that of bribery is preposterous! I could never risk my reputation and future by such an action and I repeat that I never made such an offer. It is totally unjustifiable and grossly unfair. This sort of thing will demoralise Association Football. Manchester has not many friends among the Association officials and I doubt if the decision will be reversed or the suspension lessened if the whole case is reopened and enquired into."

He added that Aston Villa had too much influence within the FA . The general feeling was that Manchester City had suffered because, as Meredith had stated that summer, City were simply too popular. In Simon Inglis' review of football's major scandals, *Soccer in The Dock*, that theory is followed in more detail: "Alec Leake was not even mentioned, even though it had been plainly stated that Turnbull had been assaulted by Villa players after the game. Small wonder therefore that in the eyes of many neutrals the FA appeared to bear a grudge against Manchester City, a nouveau riche club with no traditions. Villa, in contrast, were solidly reliable, brimming with honours and very much part of the football establishment. Some commentators noted caustically that Leake was an England international while the other players were not. Meredith meanwhile complained, 'Had I been anyone but a Welshman I should have been better dealt with.' But Harricus of *Athletic News* said the FA's methods had seemed 'un-English, most autocratic and arbitrary.'"

It does appear that the Blues had suffered merely

because of who they were and not through the actual actions.

As the weeks passed, further details emerged. It seemed that Leake had laughed off Meredith's bribery attempt at the time, thinking it to be very much a joke, but as the FA commission investigated the Villa-City match a 'responsible gentleman from Birmingham' came forward to state that he had overheard the conversation. Leake was interrogated further and was apparently forced to admit that Meredith had attempted to bribe him. Meredith claimed that he had not attempted to bribe the player but did admit to having a conversation with him. Instead of offering him £10, he claimed to have offered his congratulations to Leake for lifting the FA Cup.

The matter did not end there, however. City's complaints and the anti-FA comments that appeared in the mainly northern sporting press upset the councillors of the FA They felt that their actions were right and, if anything, became more interested in the affairs of City because of the proclamation of innocence. They appointed an auditor, Tom Hindle, to keep a close watch on the Club and report anything out of the ordinary. Because of the state of most leading clubs at the time, not only City, it was not long before Hindle became suspicious.

Meredith, while banned from all football activity, still appeared at Hyde Road asking for his wages and he expected the Blues to look after him: "Though the FA suspended me, I felt strongly that my club would see that I was not the loser financially. At the beginning of the trouble it looked as if the club was going to recognise this, but later I found them shilly-shallying and putting me off until I got tired."

Understandably, for a man who had dedicated over ten years to the Club he expected that club to care for him, especially when on the first day of the ban (4th August 1905) Tom Maley sent him a letter suggesting that he would always be a member of the City, but would have to 'lie low' until Hindle had gone away. The fact was that the Blues were not allowed to support him - the FA had made it quite clear. Because of this, every visit or demand by Meredith caused tremendous embarrassment. There is no doubt that the Club wanted to look after him, however they were forbidden from doing so. Meredith could not accept this and regularly arrived at the ground only to be told he was not welcome. Arguments were witnessed by Tom Hindle, the FA auditor, and the Club were in real danger of being

investigated once again. Hindle persuaded Maley to report Meredith to avoid an FA investigation.

Maley's letter was a difficult one to write: "I am instructed by my directors to bring to the notice of your Association the conduct of William Meredith, a player of this club at present under suspension. This player has been in attendance at almost all the principal matches at our ground and invariably frequented the dressing room and offices despite requests not to do so."

The letter sent on 14th February 1906 went on to say that Meredith had periodically approached the board for his wages, and that when his requests were turned down the player made threats. Basically, the letter gave the impression that Meredith was a parasite. This was something neither Maley nor the City Board believed, however with Hindle's encouragement it seemed the only way to avoid further investigation. Unfortunately, it failed.

Meredith was so appalled by the Club's actions that he started to speak out about the incident with Leake. The FA immediately set up a new commission and started to interview the City players and management not only about the bribe, but also about illegal payments to players. Meredith now claimed that he had in fact offered Leake £10, but told the commission that this was at Tom Maley's suggestion with full approval from the rest of the City team. City were no longer a united team, and with their former captain revealing that he was not the only member involved in the attempted bribe, the rest of the squad were to be interrogated. Any spirit that existed prior to the Villa game must surely have disappeared by this point.

Tom Maley was adamant that he did not have anything to do with the attempted bribery. He was aware that three players had talked about the idea but that one of them clearly stated that he would not stoop so low. He did not reveal who the players were, but it is apparent that Meredith was one of the party. The other issue being pursued by the commission was the question of illegal payments. Maley did not deny that payments had been made to players more than the maximum, but claimed that this seemed common business practice in England and that he only continued to follow the Club's standard practices. He stated that if all First Division clubs were investigated, not four would come out 'scatheless'.

City were certainly guilty of paying above the

maximum but if the FA had carried out a similar investigation at all the leading clubs they would have found the same situation. Unfortunately, City were the team under the spotlight and, as they and their friends in the media, had already criticised the FA they were to be taught a lesson.

The Edward Hulton owned *Athletic News* not only blamed the FA it also pointed the finger at Meredith: "The famous footballer determined not only to admit that he had made an offer to Alec Leake - an offence which ought to have ended his football career - not only that he had been most lavishly and generously paid by the Club which ran dreadful risks to give him all they had except the goalposts, but dragged everyone else he could into the same mess. No sense of gratitude for all the managers who, over the years, remunerated him so that he became comparatively rich, no ideals of friendship for the men who, admitting his enviable playing skills, had done everything they could for him, and no feeling of loyalty for the comrades who had fought side by side with him in many a scrap of hard games restrained this man from divulging the secrets of his masters and colleagues. It would have been honourable to confess his own deeds, to express his sorrow and promise an amendment that he promised to fulfil but he took a course that amounted to revenge after he had been simply killed by kindness by the club whose colours he wore."

On Thursday 31st May 1906 commissioners J.C. Clegg, Charles Crump, and D. B. Woolfall reported on what they had discovered. They were of the opinion that City had been overpaying for years and that the players had actually gained the power and had demanded illegal payments. With the maximum wage at £4, it was revealed that Meredith had been earning £6 and that Livingstone had demanded and received £6 10s. Even the amateur Sam Ashworth had received £50 on top of £25 expenses, and was subsequently declared a professional by the commission.

If all of this wasn't bad enough then came the real shock. A total of seventeen current and former players were to be suspended until 1st January 1907. Tom Maley and former Chairman Waltham Forrest were to be suspended from English football sine die, while directors Allison and Davies were to be suspended for seven months. City were fined £250 and the suspended players had to pay a total of £900 in fines: Meredith (£100), Livingstone (£100), Hynds (£75), McMahon (£75), Hillman, Turnbull, Booth, Burgess, Frost, Bannister, Dearden, Gillespie, and Holmes (all £50), Edmundson, Davidson, Lyon, and Ashworth (all £25).

The Club was virtually dead. No club in the history of football has ever suffered to such an extent, regardless of tragedy or bans, and survived. No matter what irregularities there were, did City really deserve to be treated so harshly? What makes the matter so incredible is that the Club were no worse than most of their big name rivals, any of whom could have been investigated and banned to the same extent.

City's first golden period ended in shame. The 1905-06 season, which had seen the Meredith-less club challenge for the title once again, ended with the Blues in fifth place. Not surprisingly, a loss of form had coincided with the FA investigation. Although it is impossible to say what the Maley inspired City side may have achieved, it still angers many associated with the Blues that the Club were so cruelly attacked at a time when they should have been dominating football. If the side had remained together, would they have won the League? Would the Cup have resided at Hyde Road again? An indication of what City should have achieved appears in the history of Manchester United from 1907 to 1911 when the Reds won two League titles and the FA Cup with some of the former Hyde Road stars. The Blues presented Manchester United with their first opportunity to be successful.

One point worth making is that City were not the only side to suffer as a result of the suspensions. Four of the players were already with other clubs - Ashworth with Everton, Lyon with Preston, Holmes at Clapton Orient, and Davidson at Airdrie. Those clubs felt they should not be penalised for another team's errors, although it was only Airdrie who had the chance of going against the ban. They persuaded the Scottish FA to ignore their English equivalent body and managed to play Davidson whenever necessary.

Three players still left at Hyde Road appealed as they had been reserve players during 1904-05 and, even after bonuses were included, had not received the maximum £208. Their appeal failed, as did a petition signed by 4,128 City supporters against all the suspensions.

With all these players banned from playing for City, the Blues had to find replacements. They also had the small matter of finding a manager and directors.

1906-1907 Newbould's New Boys

The Derby County secretary-manager Harry Newbould was approached and accepted the offer of taking over from Tom Maley. In his younger days, Newbould had made a name for himself as a sprinter, before joining Derby St Luke's as an outside right. In 1896 he joined Derby County as assistant secretary and four years later became the Club's first official secretary-manager. When City approached him about the Hyde Road vacancy they knew he was already becoming disenchanted with the Rams, as he had been forced to sell star player Steve Bloomer to Middlesbrough. The football world were surprised when he took up the Hyde Road offer but, perhaps, he still felt the Club had great potential. He

MANCHESTER C.
1906 - 07

1 BALDWIN. 2 SMITH. 3 BUCHAN. 4 NORGROVE. 5 EADIE. 6 STEEL. 7 DAVIES. 8 DENNISON. 9 KELSO. 10 EVANS. 11 TAYLOR. 12 WHITTAKER.
13 HAMBLETT. 14 GRIEVE. 15 CHRISTIE. 16 CONLIN. 17 YOUNG. 18 BANKS. 19 STEWART. 20 THORNLEY. 21 FISHER. 22 DORSETT.

was aware of the crowd pulling potential of the Blues, and would almost certainly have been aware of how Mancunians had greeted City's 1904 Cup victory, the year after Newbould's Derby had lost 6-0 to Bury at the same stage.

Newbould was actually a qualified accountant. City needed that level of professionalism within their management, even if the rest of the First Division was made up of teams bending the rules as and when they felt fit. From the moment the bans were first discussed, Billy Meredith was fully aware of the 'do as I say, not as I do' approach: "The League met and representatives of each club voted in favour of the punishment meted out to us being enforced. And while their representatives were passing this pious resolution most of them had other representatives busy trying to persuade the 'villains whose punishment had been so well deserved' to sign for them under conditions very much better in most cases than the ones we had been ruled by at Hyde Road."

Regardless of the approaches going on in the background, City still held the banned players' registrations and would do so until the end of December. In the meantime, Newbould tried to find players - any players! - to take City forward. With the Club all but destroyed, his task was an enormous one. To understand how major the task was, imagine the same events occurring in 1991 to Alex Ferguson's Manchester United

a mere year after winning the FA Cup, thus becoming his first successful side. Immediately, United would have lost the bulk of Ferguson's first team squad, they would have lost a potentially great manager, and several influential members of the Board would have been removed. Knowing what United went on to achieve, would the same have happened to City? Could United have recovered? This example is only quoted to give an indication of the task facing Newbould, and the loss that the Blues endured. No one will ever know what the side would have achieved, but neutral observers have always believed that City were treated abysmally. Because of this, avoiding relegation in 1906-07 had to be Newbould's target. Anything more than that could be viewed as real achievement.

When Newbould joined City in July 1906, there were only eleven players available. The northern based Football League tried to encourage clubs to help the Blues, but recruiting players was not an easy task. Newbould approached almost every club, and was regularly confronted with demands for large transfer fees. Walter Smith, the Leicester Fosse goalkeeper, was signed for the relatively high fee of £600 from the Second Division club, while several other players were simply too expensive. Newbould's job was extremely difficult, although he did find an ally in the former Bolton secretary, J.J. Bentley. Bentley, in addition to being President of the League, was Manchester United's chairman and, with one eye on the banned City players who would be available from the end of the year, he offered to help the Blues through the difficult close season. At one point he even directed a Brighton forward called Albert Fisher who was due to sign for United to Hyde Road.

Other players to arrive at Hyde Road included Robert Grieve and Bill Eadie both from Greenock Morton. In addition, Bradford City's England international Jimmy Conlin arrived to take over the outside left position from the suspended Frank Booth, and full-back Tommy Kelso arrived from Third Lanark. Other positions were filled by players who had been signed towards the end of the previous season, such as half-back Alex Steel from Ayr United, and Scottish international George Stewart from Hibernian.

As can clearly be seen, the Blues relied heavily on Scottish imports. Maybe their English counterparts were not keen to join a club that was simply no longer able to make the illegal payments that were part and parcel of the English game. Newbould's first League game in charge was the opening fixture at home to Arsenal on 1st September 1906 refereed by the same man who refereed the 1904 Cup Final, A.J. Barker. City's team included five debutants. In extreme heat, the Blues took the field before a fairly low Hyde Road crowd of around 18,000. The weather at ninety degrees in the shade had a tremendous impact on the game as the players found it difficult to cope, although for some unknown reason the City men suffered more than their opponents.

After thirty minutes Arsenal took the lead as City's large number of debutants struggled. A couple of minutes later Irvine Thornley fell "prostrate and very ill" according to one report and was taken from the field. For the rest of the match he lay flat on his back trying to recover from sunstroke. A few moments after Arsenal found the net for the second time, Jimmy Conlin collapsed. He had adopted the fashionable Blackpool beach method of playing with a handkerchief on his head to protect it from the sun, but even that hadn't been able to save him!

At half time City lost another man when Robert Grieve failed to reappear. Down to eight men, with three forwards missing, the Blues stood no chance of matching the Gunners, but referee Barker refused to abandon the game. Bravely the Blues fought on, and for a while Newbould pushed one of his defenders up front to compensate for the three missing men. This gave the Blues a formation made up of three attackers, three half-backs, one full-back and a goalkeeper. Five minutes into the half, winger Jimmy Conlin bravely returned to the pitch to give City a little more hope.

After a short spell of City pressure, George Dorsett scored for the Blues to make the score 2-1, but the effort was perhaps a little too much for the former West Bromwich player as he collapsed with exhaustion a few moments later. Any hope of equalising disappeared with Dorsett as Arsenal now dominated the match completely. Bravely City played on, but it wasn't long before the Gunners provided a couple of goals to take the score to 4-1. Shortly afterwards City lost Tommy Kelso, then Jimmy Buchan, leaving only six City players on the pitch. Three of whom - including goalkeeper Davies - were making their debuts.

Somehow the six Blues held out until the final whistle. Two days later the new look City travelled to Everton with remarkably only two changes - Fisher replaced Thornley and Kelso made way for Norgrove. Unfortunately, any hope that this game would see the Blues fortunes change were quickly dashed as City suffered their heaviest League defeat of all time as Everton annihilated Newbould's side 9-1. Debutant Fisher provided the consolation goal - at least J.J. Bentley was able to say his 'diversion' technique had saved the Blues from a more humiliating scoreline.

The next match saw the Blues suffer further with a 3-1 defeat at Sheffield Wednesday, but the first real moment of joy for Newbould came in City's next home game on 15th September. With goals from Jones and Thornley the Blues managed a 2-2 draw with Bury before a crowd of approximately 20,000. It may have only brought a point but it was a vital morale booster and gave City hope. After another 2-2 draw, this time away to Newbould's old side Derby, the Blues snatched two points with a 3-2 victory at Middlesbrough. Slowly but surely the team appeared to be getting their act together, although Newbould was still finding it difficult to determine his preferred side as he had already used a total of seventeen players in a mere six games. Consistency was a long way off.

The most satisfying moment of the opening dozen fixtures came on 20th October when City entertained Aston Villa. A crowd of over thirty thousand attended Hyde Road for a game that many spectators saw as a grudge match. The Blues felt they needed to defeat Villa to gain revenge for the problems of the last year or so. The bribery and illegal payments investigations had been caused through the infamous match at Villa Park and many felt that Villa deserved to be taught a lesson on the pitch. Of the players who faced Villa on that fateful day in 1905, only Norgrove and Jones would be playing in the grudge match.

Thanks to two goals from Thornley, and a goal each from Stewart and Conlin City ended the game 4-2 winners. Many felt that justice had been done, although one game could not compensate for the suffering the Blues had endured. Nevertheless, City felt they were able to move forward, unfortunately results over the following six weeks suggested otherwise.

On 1st December the Blues faced newly promoted Manchester United in the first derby match for over three years – this was also the very first Division One Manchester derby match ever staged. Both sides had found the First Division a struggle so far that season with United on fourteen points from the same number of games and City on nine points. The first Division One derby was eagerly awaited: "Football fever raged in Manchester this afternoon. I never saw such unbounded enthusiasm in the City. Starting at Cromwell's monument there was a continuous stream of vehicles right away to Hyde Road and pedestrians in similar processions. Five in a hansom cab was no uncommon sight."

With the backing of a noisy 40,000 crowd, providing receipts of £1,100, at Hyde Road, City wanted to prove that even without Meredith and Co. they were still the dominant Manchester side. According to the *Manchester Guardian*, when the Blues entered the field "a roar rose that will ring in sensitive ears for a week".

In an exciting match, the Blues satisfied all their fans with a convincing 3-0 victory. The City stars that day included Billy Lot Jones, who scored a stylish goal after twenty minutes, George Stewart, who had an effort deflected in for City's second goal and scored the third, goalkeeper Walter Smith, who was chaired from the field, and the lanky Bill Eadie. According to the *Athletic News* cartoon of the game Eadie was 'here, there, and everywhere' - maybe this was an early form of the crude modern day chant.

The game proved City were still the dominant force. Writing in the *Daily Dispatch*, the 'Veteran' believed the Blues were in total control: "The great match is over! City proved themselves to be on the day's play a far superior side; in fact, so far superior that the form can hardly really be true."

Despite the great victory the most noteworthy event of the day actually took place in the Hyde Road offices after the game, when the bargaining for the banned players commenced in earnest. The players' bans were due to be lifted on 1st January, but as there were so many involved, and the purchasing clubs were keen to see the players take the field immediately into the New Year, the transfer deals had to be completed quickly. In reality the bargaining had been going on for some time, especially for the international players, but the FA agreed that deals could be struck in December. For the City management the sooner the event was over the better. It was already twenty months since the infamous game with Villa and the Blues were simply unable to move forward, especially as much needed capital would be gained by the Hyde Road sales. It's worth noting that the main business was carried out at the ground, although some footballing historians have mistakenly located the sale at the Queen's Hotel.

According to reports there were representatives from at least eight clubs at Hyde Road, with the majority interested in the tough England left-back Herbert Burgess, known by City fans as the Mighty Atom. Rumours circulated the north-west that Burgess had signed for Celtic for a sum of around £1,000, but it simply was not true. There were also stories of him signing for Everton in a player exchange. Whether City spread the rumours on purpose to increase the price is not known, but interestingly there were rumours about virtually every player.

Eventually, on 5th December, Burgess signed for Manchester United for the sum of £750, much to the disgust of both Celtic and Everton. The Toffees were so incensed that City had transferred Burgess to their friends at United they complained to the League, causing further heartache. The Manchester Blues had wanted cash for the player and broke the player exchange agreement to make a quick sale instead. Under the heading 'More rumours and a few facts', the *Daily Dispatch* broke the news to Manchester on

Fans at Hyde Road for the first top flight Manchester derby, 1st December 1906. City 3 United 0.

MANCHESTER'S GREAT FOOTBALL DAY: SCENES AT HYDE-ROAD.

6th December, and added: "The inexorable laws of the Football Association have decreed that he shall not play again for City, and therefore it is only fitting that he should go to Clayton. I think the supporters of the City club will be pleased that the matter is definitely settled, for I am sure they would prefer that Burgess remained in Manchester."

In addition to Burgess, United's first great manager, Ernest Mangnall, signed Sandy Turnbull, Jimmy Bannister, and the man who was such a hero to the Mancunian masses Billy Meredith. Each of these signings is officially recorded as 5th December, although there is no doubt that Meredith had signed for the Reds some months earlier on a free transfer. The fact that City received nothing for their brilliant captain angered many, and for a time the Blues had tried to sell him but Meredith, totally bemused by events at Hyde Road, produced an agreement between him and the Club stating that he would be entitled to a benefit match and a minimum sum of £600. This was the main reason he had pursued the Club throughout his suspension.

The FA again became involved and declared that they could force City to honour the agreement. Meredith was adamant that the Blues should not receive a penny for his transfer: "The City club put a transfer of £600 on my head. And United were prepared to pay it. But I refused to let them pay a halfpenny. I had cost no fee and I was determined that I would have no fee placed on my head... I was prepared to fight the matter. The City club were not. I was given a free transfer and, as a result, I got £500 from a gentleman to sign for Manchester United and he also paid the £100 fine to the FA"

In effect Meredith had come out of the whole affair a real winner. With City battle weary he was able to obtain the terms he wanted and had actually managed to pocket the equivalent of well over two years official wages - a vast amount - plus managed to avoid the fine. He was also guaranteed a warm welcome at United because, no matter what had occurred at City, Meredith was still loved by all Mancunians. There was no real animosity between the public and Meredith, nor was there a loathing of United by City fans. In fact, as suggested by the *Daily Dispatch* article, the majority of Blues were delighted that the bulk of their banned side was to remain in Manchester. If nothing else, it gave City's 'poor relations' a chance to match the exploits of the Hyde Road club.

TRUE BLUE
Tom Maley

Manchester's first great manager.

In addition to the transfers to United, it's worth detailing what occurred to a few of the other Hyde Road favourites. Johnny McMahon and Frank Booth signed for Bury for a total of around £750. Tom Hynds moved to Arsenal. Former Celtic man George Livingstone returned to Glasgow with Rangers, although two years later he would travel back to Manchester to join Meredith and Co. at United.

Sammy Frost and goalkeeper Jack Hillman signed for Southern League Millwall, although it was not a particularly good move for the 35 year old 'keeper as, a short while later, an elbow injury ended his career and left one arm permanently crooked. For Frost the move was perfect as it enabled him to return to his chain of sweet shops he had been forced to leave behind when he signed for City in 1901. Sadly, however, business problems later contributed to his suicide in 1926.

Another player worth mentioning is the bustling Billy Gillespie. The controversial player was so disgusted with how he and his colleagues had been treated that he emigrated to the USA in 1905 with his Edinburgh born wife Elizabeth, and settled in Lynn, Massachusetts. He created a new life in the States although football was still important to him. According to his family he coached soccer for a period at Harvard University, and he played for the American company General Electric in Lynn and in the Boston area. He was well known in the area for his soccer activities and sport became important to his family as a result.

Gillespie returned to Manchester and Glasgow on several occasions over the years, often meeting up with Billy Meredith, while newspapers in England occasionally gave information on the whereabouts of Gillespie and the other 1904 stars. These stories seemed to develop over time and supporters at Hyde Road would often talk of Gillespie searching for diamonds in Cape Town, or creating a new life in Canada. These stories were simply not true but they did help to keep his name in the 'papers. Perhaps Gillespie was such a hero to Mancunians that they felt his new life had to be daring, glamorous, and perhaps a little rebellious. Who knows, but the truth is that Gillespie enjoyed a very happy family life in the States. His great-granddaughter was given the middle name Meredith.

After he passed away his widow would wear his 1904 medal on a chain around her neck. Sadly, this was stolen from the nursing home she lived in during her later life.

Clearly, the thief could not possibly have understood the significance of this "English Cup" medal.

Incidentally, Gillespie never paid the £50 fine imposed as a result of the illegal payments investigations. He did this as a protest and this final footballing act did much to reinforce his image with City's loyal supporters. Meredith may have been the biggest star, but Gillespie was certainly the cult figure on the terraces. For comparison purposes think of Gillespie as being a cross between Paul Dickov, Mike Doyle, and Francis Lee.

With the 1905 transfers more or less completed, the City management were able to move away from the politics and the wrangling and concentrate on the League and Cup. Unfortunately City were dogged by inconsistency in the League, and in the Cup the Blues suffered defeat by a single goal in the 1st round replay at home to Blackburn. The game at Ewood Park had ended 2-2.

In February, with proceeds from the transfers of the banned players, City bought Dave Ross, a forward from Norwich. In a complicated deal, they paid the East Anglian club £1,000 with a further £200 going to his former club Bury. The Blues also agreed to play Norwich in a friendly during April. Ross was an eleven stone 22 year old, and it was hoped he would help to give City's attack a little consistency. According to a 1907 'Football Who's Who', Ross was born in Darwen and lived in Bury and away from football his life revolved around the relatively new and expensive hobby of photography. Robert Grieve, a partner of Ross's in the attack was recorded as being a Goss China collector, while William Hall, City's 'keeper for a while late in 1906 was a steeplejack by profession. The Blues certainly had a multi-talented squad.

City's inconsistency remained until the end of the season with the only real newsworthy game being the derby match at Clayton. For the first time the Blues faced Burgess, Meredith, and Turnbull in the new look United in a game that many believed would prove that United now had all the talent. The first half saw City take the initiative and with a strong wind behind them they pushed forward. After approximately ten minutes Burgess, the former City man, raised his hand to block

a centre from George Dorsett. The referee immediately awarded a penalty, which Dorsett converted, and City seemed destined to embarrass their former stars.

Early in the second half the roving Bill Eadie was hurt in a collision with Billy Meredith and was forced to leave the field. Down to ten men the Blues still retained control for a while, but gradually United gained the upper hand and with fifteen minutes to go Charlie Roberts equalised. Walter Smith, in the City goal, was described as being "shocked" that United had actually scored by the *Athletic News*. Whether this was an indication that City had dominated the game, or simply the fact that Smith found it hard to accept that he could concede a goal isn't known. Nevertheless, the ten man City side battled on and a few minutes later Jimmy Conlin put the ball into the United net. Unfortunately the goal was ruled out for offside, although the *Athletic News* reporter was not certain whether it should have been awarded or not: "My view was obscured by a hat fitted on the head of a lady who stood in front of me, and also by one of the thick posts which support the stand. I have by the way a bone to pick with the United club. I arrived an hour and a quarter before the time of starting and was informed that there was no accommodation in the Pressroom, which was largely occupied by people whose business it would be interesting to know." The reporter went on to complain about the poor press facilities and accused United of disrespect towards a reporter from "the recognised national football 'paper."

The game ended level, although ten man City must have gained a moral victory after their fine performance. Nevertheless they secured a much needed point and followed it up seven days later with another draw. This time the Hyde Road return with Stoke ended 2-2 with goals from George Stewart and Billy lot Jones. Unfortunately, the final two games of the season - away to Blackburn, and home to Sunderland - ended in defeat leaving the Blues in 17th position on 32 points - five above the relegation zone. All connected with the Club, especially Manager Newbould, must have been relieved that a difficult season had ended in safety. Back in August anything but relegation would have been viewed as success.

1904-1907 SUMMARY

Highest League Attendance: c.40,000 Everton 21/04/05 & Manchester United 01/12/06
Highest Cup Attendance: c.39,000 Bolton Wanderers, 18/02/05 (FA Cup)
Secretary/Managers: 1902-1906 Tom Maley & 1906-1912 Harry Newbould

Seasonal Record:

Season	League	Posn	FA Cup	Other	Leading Scorer	Average Attendance
1904-05	FL Div1	3	Rnd 2		Turnbull 19	20,000
1905-06	FL Div1	5	Rnd 1		Thornley 21	18,000
1906-07	FL Div1	17	Rnd 1		Thornley 13	22,150

City fans at Hyde Road on 4th April 1911 (City 2 Middlesbrough 1) and at Sheffield United in the FA Cup on 12th March 1914 (goalless game).

1907-1915
Rebuilding The Blues

"The spectators seemed mostly in favour of the City team, and as the play went in favour of the other side they watched it amid constant sweats and fears. This fierce rivalry communicated itself to the players and the play at times was a little too personal to be pleasant. Occasionally one saw a couple of players with their noses close together talking excitedly at each other and obviously explaining by the movements of their hands what they thought the other deserved."

A *Manchester Guardian* report of the first Division One Manchester derby to be viewed as a true grudge match. It ended goalless on 18th April 1908

1907-1908 Respectable Third

After the inconsistency of 1906-07, Harry Newbould was determined his side would find some stability. In his first season in charge he had regularly been forced to make changes and, because of the problems off the pitch, had been introducing players throughout the season. He had also experimented with some positions and players. For example, Jimmy Blair was signed from Arsenal in November as a forward, played in the attack during the December derby, then by the time of the April game with United, Newbould was trying him as a left half-back in place of Willie McOustra. That change was a great success, as was Newbould's purchase of goalkeeper Walter Smith.

Prior to Smith's arrival, City had used four different goalkeepers within the space of a year. Once Newbould bought Smith, he was convinced he could build a consistent side. In 1907-08 Smith became the Club's first ever-present since Meredith in 1903-04, even then Smith played in 44 League and Cup games as opposed to Meredith's 40.

With City's goal safe, and a general feeling of satisfaction within the Club, the season started without any major signings. A 5-2 opening day victory at Sunderland, with Robert Grieve scoring a hat-trick, provided hope and, although results were mixed throughout the opening five months, the Blues were picking up enough points to maintain a healthy position.

In December the Music Hall comedian George Robey

reassembled the 1904 Cup winning side to face the present day side in a charity match at Hyde Road. City supporters were delighted that the triumphal old boys were back in town. The only player missing was the robust Billy Gillespie who was still enjoying life abroad. His place that day was taken by George Robey himself, who managed to score a goal for the old boys. Whether the goal was anything like one of Gillespie's speciality 'push the goalie into the net' variety wasn't recorded by the press of the day, but certainly Robey would have tried to provide a comic touch to the affair.

The charity game ended 4-3 to the City new boys which, if nothing else, would have allowed Newbould the satisfaction of saying his side were moving forward.

By the start of April the Blues had performed well enough to have an outside chance of winning the title, but they were nine points behind eventual champions Manchester United. United, with Meredith & Co., had really combined as a team and City supporters, though delighted that the Championship had arrived in Manchester for the first time, must have wondered what Maley's City side would have achieved if the illegal payments scandal had never erupted. If nothing else, it had put the Blues back several years and given United their first taste of glory. Could City have found title success first?

Regardless of the 'what ifs', City had recovered well enough to challenge in 1907-08 and, by the time of the Hyde Road derby match on 18th April, they were keen to finish runners up to the Reds. Regrettably, the game was not the exciting match that most expected and, with the few chances that came City's way going wide, the game ended goalless. Nevertheless it brought a vital point to take the Blues' total to 41 with two games left, while Newcastle had 42 points with one game remaining. Aston Villa and Sheffield Wednesday were also close behind, but City felt that neither side would pose a real threat, especially Villa who had to face United at Clayton in one of their two final fixtures.

Sadly, the Blues failed to achieve second place by their own failings as their games against Bristol City and Blackburn Rovers both ended goal-less while Aston Villa defeated United 2-1, and Chelsea 3-1 to take second place on goal average. Newcastle had lost their last game away to Middlesbrough, thereby giving the Blues third spot.

Although this was an amazing feat, the popular opinion was that Manchester should have filled the two leading positions to provide much needed civic pride to both sides. It took exactly sixty years before Manchester was able to boast that its clubs were officially the highest two in the League, and a further 44 years to do it again. On both occasions, of course, it was City who celebrated the Championship.

1908-1909 Inconsistency

With City finishing so close to the top of the table in 1907-08, optimism filled Hyde Road and its environs. There was a belief that the Blues could match United's achievement and once again challenge for the title. Unfortunately, the inconsistency of Newbould's first season in charge returned with City putting in some fine performances - the 5-1 victory against the season's Cup finalists Bristol City is a good example - yet in other games the Blues simply conceded too many goals. Prime examples include a 6-3 defeat at Everton, 5-1 at Notts County, and 4-0 at Sheffield United.

On 16th January, City faced Tottenham in the FA Cup first round at Hyde Road. Incredibly, Newbould dropped two of his star players Irvine Thornley and Jimmy Blair. Both were perfectly fit, yet newspaper reports suggested that the two star players had made great bonus demands. The Club denied this, but even so concern was raised.

The Cup-tie crowd of around 20,000 expected a great City victory as the Blues took a two goal lead through the experienced Tom Holford, but it wasn't to be. Tottenham fought their way back into the game and quickly levelled the scores. Then fortune shone City's way as the Blues were awarded a penalty. George Dorsett, playing instead of Jimmy Blair, stepped up to take the kick, but somehow managed to miss the target. After two further goals - one for Spurs and another by Holford for City - Bill Eadie tripped Herbert Middlemass in the area, giving Tottenham the perfect chance to take the lead. The game ended 4-3 to Second Division Spurs and manager Newbould was left to consider where the Blues had failed.

Across at Clayton former Blue George Livingstone joined Meredith and Co. in the red of United. His debut was the eighteenth League Manchester derby on 23rd January 1909. A particularly bad day for City fans as Livingstone scored twice in United's 3-1 home victory. The *Athletic News* made much of the fact that Livingstone was yet another former Blue: "It is a singular coincidence that he should make his debut against his old club, and, by the way, no fewer than three of the famous City forwards were in the United forward line, while another, Booth, was playing the part of a spectator, and I have no doubt that the fifth man, William Gillespie, was anxiously awaiting the result across the Atlantic." No doubt, if he did manage to hear the score, Gillespie would have been as disappointed as all true Blues.

By 9th April City were perilously close to relegation, although with six games to go and 32 points in the bag their future was totally in their hands. Leicester Fosse were bottom on 21 points with seven games left to play, Bradford City were three points ahead of Leicester with the same number of games, while Bury were on 29

MANCHESTER CITY.

G.Baldwin   W.Smith   J.Buchan   P.Norgrove   W.Eadie   A.Steel   Davies   F.Dennison   Kelso   Evans   A.Taylor
F.Whittaker   Hamblett   Grieve   J.Christie   J.Conlin   Young   W.Banks   G.Stewart
I. Thornley   A. Fisher   G. Dorsett

A contemporary postcard from 1908-09.

points with only four games to go, although one of these was at home to the Blues. Below City there was also Nottingham Forest (30 points), and Liverpool (31 points). There were plenty of other teams within reach, including Manchester United who were a mere point above the Blues.

Clearly, City felt safe. A few victories or even a few draws should have been enough, however, it was not that easy. A poor Easter, saw the Blues lose to Sunderland on Good Friday and to relegation favourites Bury the following day, before managing a 2-1 win over fellow strugglers Nottingham Forest on Tuesday 13th

April. City were putting themselves in danger and as only one of their remaining three fixtures was at Hyde Road, they needed to perform at their best, especially as Bury and Bradford were picking up more points.

At Hyde Road on 17th April Irvine Thornley provided his 18th League goal of the season, but it wasn't enough as visitors Sheffield United won 3-1 with two goals from Kitchen and another from Batty. With two games remaining the Blues still remained in control as rivals Bury and Notts County had already completed their campaign, both ending on 36 points, two more than City. Liverpool were level with City but only had one

Thornley opened the score for City.

Irvine Thornley opened the scoring when City faced United on 19th September 1908.

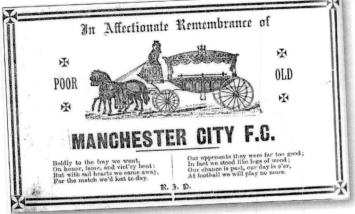

In Affectionate Remembrance of

POOR **OLD**

MANCHESTER CITY F.C.

Boldly to the fray we went,
On honor, fame, and vict'ry bent;
But with sad hearts we came away,
For the match we'd lost to-day.

Our opponents they were far too good;
In fact we stood like logs of wood;
Our chance is past, our day is o'er,
At football we will play no more.

R. J. P.

A card produced by United fans to highlight City's struggles around this time.

game to play, Notts County had 35 points (one match remaining), while Bradford City were by this time a mere two points behind City. Bradford perhaps offered City the most comfort as they had to face Manchester United, who were now safe on 37 points, in their one remaining game.

City's match at Aston Villa on Saturday 26th April was a tense affair, played in a strong wind: "science was thrown to the winds which blew so gustily, and the players went at it hammer and tongs." Significantly, when the first couple of goals arrived they came by means of penalties with Wallace converting for Villa, and James Buchan scoring for the Blues. The tension remained throughout the match then, in the final five minutes, a foul by Bill Eadie gave Villa a free kick. Walters' shot seemed to remain in the air for an eternity before it dropped a fraction under the bar to give Villa the points.

City's final game on Wednesday 28th at Bristol City was vital, especially as both Bradford City and Liverpool had the advantage of playing their final matches after City's season ended, on Thursday 29th and Friday 30th respectively.

As City took to the field at Bristol knowing a point would see them clear. The Blues defended well and, as the game progressed into the final ten minutes, they seemed content to let the game end goalless. That would certainly have given them safety but, as City have since discovered on similar occasions - 1983 and 1996 being prime examples - the Blues should always expect the unexpected. With only two minutes remaining a Bristol effort was diverted past Walter Smith into the City net. Some reports say Bill Eadie diverted the ball, other sources suggest Tommy Kelso was the guilty party. It was immaterial really, what mattered was the fact that

the Blues had fallen from a position of relative safety to near relegation. They had to cross their fingers and hope that either Bradford, against United, or Liverpool, away to Champions Newcastle, would fail to win.

Surprisingly, at Manningham Lane, Bradford, the Cup winners United struggled as Bradford City had overall control of the game. Ultimately, O'Rourke provided Bradford with the only goal of the match. The following day at Newcastle, Liverpool won by the same scoreline. City were down.

The final table put City in nineteenth place on 34 points, nine points more than the bottom club Leicester, but the same as Bradford in the 'safe' eighteenth position. From a position of relative safety the Blues had created a relegation nightmare for themselves. Their goal average was inferior to Bradford City and, quite simply, they had let themselves down in the last month of the season. One more point was all that was needed.

City needed the summer break to take stock of the situation. There would be no panic removal of the manager though. Despite relegation, Newbould had achieved a great deal during his two years at Hyde Road.

1909-1910 Division Two Champions

After a five year period when City's fortunes always seemed to be determined by others, mainly the FA, it was hoped that the next decade would bring the Club a little stability and success. Before the Blues could achieve these aims they somehow had to gain promotion.

Relegation at a time when Manchester United were enjoying their first golden era was difficult to accept, especially as the Reds success came as a result of the Blues' illegal payments scandal. Nevertheless, under City's fifth secretary-manager Harry Newbould, the Blues were not too distraught and quickly set about returning to the First Division. He believed his side to be good enough for promotion, all they lacked was consistency. If they had found that during the previous year, relegation would never have been a possibility.

The only significant signing of 1909 came in April when George Wynn, a former Welsh cup winner, had been signed from Wrexham. Despite being purchased before the end of City's relegation season, inside-forward Wynn was not to make his debut until Christmas Day away to Bradford. Before this moment he remained patiently in the reserves.

City suffered a disappointing 2-1 home defeat to Blackpool in the opening fixture - Irvine Thornley provided the consolation. If Newbould had thought that promotion would be simple then that game convinced him otherwise. He quickly changed his plans.

For the second game there were four team changes, including the return of Bert Jackson and Tom Holford. City looked a much improved side as they defeated Leicester Fosse 3-1. Further joy followed a week later as Lincoln were trounced 6-2. By the time of Wynn's Christmas debut, the Blues were beginning to look more than capable of promotion and had won ten and drawn four of their seventeen games. Captain Irvine Thornley had been the star man, scoring twelve goals in those seventeen matches. Unfortunately, his appearances for the rest of the season would be limited through injury. Billy Lot Jones relished the chance of replacing Thornley as captain and in many games throughout the season he proved his leadership qualities.

Although Wynn's debut was a disappointing 2-0 defeat, he was quickly able to demonstrate his influence as he scored a total of six goals in the same number of matches. In fact, by the end of the season he had netted a total of ten goals in twenty games and had seen the Blues undefeated in every game he scored in.

In addition to Wynn, another man instrumental in City's climb up the table was new goalkeeper Jack Lyall, signed from Sheffield Wednesday in September. Lyall had taken over the number one spot from Walter Smith, although this was far from the end of Smith's Hyde Road career as he managed a deserved return in subsequent seasons.

With Lyall performing well and the whole team performing consistently - something many City teams over the years have struggled to do - Newbould seemed content with the way the Blues were moving forward, and it was not only in the League. In the FA Cup they managed away victories over Workington 2-1, Southampton 5-0, and old adversaries Aston Villa 2-1. As March approached Blues fans started to believe they could win the double of Second Division title and FA Cup. Unfortunately, the world fell apart during a three week spell in March.

On the fifth, Swindon Town defeated City 2-0 in the Cup, before a then record crowd of 14,429 for the Wiltshire club. Up to that point, this was by far the biggest moment in the club's history and caused much embarrassment for City. Four days later, the Blues could only manage a midweek no score draw at home to Barnsley, before a 3-0 victory over Birmingham on the 12th provided a little relief. It did not last though, and on the following Wednesday a real 'four pointer' with Derby ended in defeat. With both sides heading for promotion,

the Blues had once again let themselves down at a crucial stage.

A no score draw away to West Bromwich Albion provided more concern, but then on Good Friday 25th March City captain Billy Lot Jones rekindled City's drive by scoring the only goal of the match at Grimsby.

On Easter Saturday a crowd of over 40,000 made its way for the visit of Promotion hopefuls Oldham Athletic. Irvine Thornley had selected this as his benefit game and could not have picked one better in terms of money raised. According to reports of the period he picked up a total of £1,000 although the directors' report stated: "The amount cannot be now stated with exactitude owing to the fact that there has to be deducted the expenses of the day, in addition to certain sums already paid and yet to be paid as compensation for accidents which occurred on the day of the match."

It appears that Hyde Road ground struggled to cope and that this had caused a few injuries to spectators. In 1910, as with most periods in football history, spectator comfort was not really seen as an issue. It would take minor accidents (including one at Maine Road sixteen years later), and several major disasters over the following eighty years, before the authorities looked seriously into the problems. The idea for many years was to 'pack 'em in', especially for a derby match with promotion rivals Oldham.

Although the attendance provided Thornley with much satisfaction, the result did not as City went down 2-0. Again, they had failed to win a crucial 'four pointer'. Newbould and the team did learn their lesson however, and on Easter Monday they rediscovered their winning ways as Gainsborough were defeated 3-1. From then until the last Saturday of the season the Blues were undefeated, scoring a total of fifteen goals in six games. Billy Lot Jones, in Thornley's absence, had successfully steered the Blues back into Division One.

The final game of the season saw City beaten 3-2 at Wolverhampton, but it hardly mattered. City ended the season as Champions, one point ahead of second placed Oldham. This was the Blues' third Second Division title since 1899, and came after 23 victories, eight draws and only seven defeats.

1910-1911 Ground Work

During the close season, the Club went on a European tour, defeating sides from Hamburg and Gothenburg (twice), while also achieving a victory in one of two games against a Danish XI. This rather successful trip was City's first venture outside of the British Isles, at a time when few travelled abroad in any case.

While City were overseas, Hyde Road was given a

Billy Lot Jones and George Dorsett sent this postcard of themselves back to England from the overseas tour.

in the region of £3,000 on three roofs and other improvements to the ground. Apart from the fact that Hyde Road needed to improve, another reason for the sudden outlay may have been the opening of Manchester United's new Old Trafford ground on 19th February 1910. This move by the Reds provided them with the opportunity of pulling in larger crowds than City. To counteract this, City boasted that the newly refurbished Hyde Road would hold over 35,000 under cover. Old Trafford could only manage about a quarter of that. It's not known whether City's plans were made before Old Trafford opened but, whatever City's reasons, covered accommodation on all four sides of a ground for such a large figure was exceptional in those days. In fact, it was not until the 1970s that first Maine Road, then Old Trafford, would boast roofs on all sides.

Each of the three roofs erected by City were multi-spans. Behind the goal to the right of the Main Stand a multi-span with five spans and six front and six back stanchions was erected. This was merely placed over the irregular sectioned terracing. The same occurred at the opposite end and on the Popular Side, opposite the Main Stand. Here a roof with much larger individual spans was erected.

Multi-span roofs were unusual, even in 1910, but were essential at Hyde Road as they allowed spans of different lengths and depths to be developed if necessary, whereas a traditional single span roof - something like the old Kippax roof - would only really be able to cover a regular shaped area of terracing.

The company contracted to erect these roofs is believed to be Humphreys Ltd of Knightsbridge who worked on Old Trafford and, three years later, Arsenal's new stadium at Highbury. At both these grounds, and at others across the country, they built multi-span roofs, but Hyde Road is probably the only ground in the world which featured three large roofs of this style. Their only problem, as the Blues would later discover, was that this type of roof was relatively expensive to maintain. Nevertheless in 1910 City were justifiably proud of their refurbished home.

The 'new' Hyde Road's first League fixture saw one

much needed facelift. A 1908 Ordnance Survey map shows how primitive Hyde Road was at this point in its history. The developments in 1904 had improved matters considerably, but at that time quantity rather than quality had been the overriding factor. Long term planning had not been made as, perhaps, the long held view that the Blues would one day move to Belle Vue remained at the forefront of thinking.

The 1904 work had provided limited cover – the c.4,000 seater Main Stand and a small shelter on the Popular Side for around 150 standing fans – but the three main banks of terracing were awkwardly shaped. The terracing behind each goal was in irregular sections, while the Popular Side reduced from an extremely large bank at one end to virtually nothing at the other.

The 1910 close season saw City spend somewhere

The Stone Yard Stand, one of three roofs erected in 1910.

of the previous season's stars, George Wynn, hit the headlines with a hat-trick in his First Division debut game. The Blues swamped Bury 5-1 on 1st September 1910 with goalkeeper Jack Lyall proving to be in excellent form. He had been awarded the captaincy for the day and, according to the *Daily Dispatch*, fulfilled the role superbly. His performance was one that inspired the others and brought much joy: "Seasoned fighter though he is Jack Lyall, the City custodian, will doubtless regard the occasion as one of the happiest in his career."

Despite the excellent start, City's form deteriorated over the course of the next few games as, first, they drew 1-1 at Preston, then suffered consecutive defeats against Notts County, Manchester United (the first derby at Old Trafford), and Liverpool. Following the home defeat to the Merseysiders, the Blues travelled to Bury hoping their opening day form returned, despite goals from Wynn and George Dorsett City suffered a 5-2 defeat.

City's poor form continued and by New Year's Day they were bottom of the table after taking a mere fourteen points from twenty-one games. The New Year did bring about a change in fortune, however. The brilliant, but often erratic, Walter Smith was back in goal and the defence was further strengthened by the purchase of full back John Chaplin from Dundee in November. On 3rd January David Ross and Billy Lot Jones scored City's goals in a vital 2-1 home win over Tottenham, and four days later Ross again put his name on the scoresheet when he volleyed home a centre from

Manchester City on New Years' Day wiped off their Christmas Day defeat at Bradford, Dorsett distinguishing himself by scoring two penalty goals.

Joe Dorsett. Dorsett, who had joined his brother George in August, had actually sprinted half the length of the field before crossing to Ross. He also played a hand in City's next game - the Hyde Road derby.

In the first half Dorsett put the Reds under great pressure and, according to *The Umpire* Newspaper, there was one shot in particular which "nine times out of ten he would have scored." Unfortunately, prior to

City c.1910. Manager Harry Newbould is on the far left next to trainer and former Aston Villa star Bob Chatt. John Chapman (back left) and Joshua Parlby (next to Chapman) were once more guiding the Club forward.

the interval he had to leave the field injured. It was a devastating blow as the Blues not only lost their most influential player in the game so far, but they were also to lose him for the next six League games.

Even so, City were already a goal in front, thanks to Billy Lot Jones, when Dorsett left the field: "Stewart took the ball along, and, instead of centre-ing, as the defenders anticipated, he merely tapped it to Ross, who skilfully drew out the defence, crossing with the result that two City forwards had an open goal and Jones took the opportunity of giving his side the lead in a very clever manner."

Down to ten men throughout the second half, City - in particular Tom Holford and Walter Smith - held United at bay. Inevitably, though, City's old partners in crime Billy Meredith and Sandy Turnbull combined to provide United with the equaliser. With the game ending level, *The Umpire* newspaper gave City most of the credit, in particular the play anywhere Holford and the brilliant Smith: "There were none of the United side to compare with Holford and Dorsett. Holford, who seems to have no settled position faced the most dangerous outside-right in the country with a calmness which did him credit. Other players were indulging in horseplay, but Holford, who used to enjoy a rough and tumble affair, played the game and practically held Meredith in check in the first half, even if the old City player was more frisky afterwards.

"But W. Smith was the man above all others on the City side. His goalkeeping in the first half was wonderful, and to his good work, more than anyone else's, is due the fact that City got a point."

Despite the result, City had to be content that they had managed to take a point from a team destined to be champions at the season's end. The directors would also have been pleased that the forty thousand crowd paid impressive receipts of £1,052. Perhaps the refurbished Hyde Road was already playing its part, although it was not all good news as, on the Popular Side, a great deal of crushing occurred with several spectators carried away from the ground by ambulance.

A run of three further draws followed the derby, keeping the Blues in trouble. On April Fool's Day, centre-forward John Smith, who had made his debut in December and had been the only City player criticised by *The Umpire* after the derby, proved he was no fool by scoring a vital goal in the last minute against Oldham to level the scores. The point gave City hope, and the following week, at home to Everton, goals from Wynn and Thornley gave the Blues two further points while Tom Holford entertained the crowd with all kinds of gymnastic feats including a handspring.

That victory against Everton was followed by another fine win - 2-1 against Middlesbrough before a 35,000 Hyde Road crowd. Two defeats and a draw

followed, but they hardly mattered as, at the end of the season, City finished in seventeenth place, six points above Nottingham Forest in twentieth position, and four more than nineteenth placed Bristol City. The Blues would live to fight another day thanks to heroes Smith, Holford, and top scorer Wynn.

1911-1912 Goalkeeping Changes

Another season of struggle saw the Blues fighting to avoid relegation, despite a few new signings. Forward Sid Hoad was signed from Blackpool, full-back Eli Fletcher came from Crewe, and in November another full-back William Henry arrived from Leicester Fosse, while attack was strengthened further by the addition of Sandy Young from Tottenham.

31 year old Sandy Young was an interesting purchase for the Blues. He was a muscular, imposing forward who had enjoyed a successful career with Everton - scoring the only goal of the 1906 Cup Final - and had played international football for Scotland, before moving to Tottenham prior to the 1911-12 season. At Spurs he scored three goals in only five appearances but was then left out of the side, and immediately demanded a transfer. City decided to take a gamble on the player, who was later described as having fits of "temporary insanity." His time at Hyde Road was not particularly enjoyable, and in the close season he moved back to Merseyside, this time with Liverpool.

In 1914 he emigrated to Australia, and the following year was charged with murdering his brother. In June 1916 he was found guilty of manslaughter and sentenced to three years imprisonment, after which he was kept inside for a while longer due to mental instability. Eventually he returned to Scotland, where he died in 1959 at the age of 79. City supporters were already aware of how dangerous Young could be. In 1906 he had managed to score four of Everton's goals in their 9-1 thrashing of City (the Blues' heaviest defeat). It was this goal scoring side of Young's makeup that had convinced Newbould to sign the player.

The opening day fixture, played in extreme heat before 35,000 at Hyde Road, was the twenty-first League Manchester derby. Once again 27 year old Walter Smith played heroically as the Blues managed to match the champions throughout. The game ended goalless, but at least City had obtained a point. By the time the two sides met again, at the end of December, the Blues had only managed fifteen points from nineteen games.

City had improved after the introduction of Young and Henry on 25th November, but their points total was simply not enough. The first couple of months of 1912 gave Newbould little comfort either, as the Blues lost six of their seven games with only a 1-1 draw - thanks to a last minute goal from George Wynn - against Newcastle bringing any joy. Even that game provided a little concern as the Blues were awarded three penalties and somehow missed them all, although Wynn's goal did come from the rebound of the last one. The first two penalties were both taken by the normally reliable Eli Fletcher. The first was saved, with the rebound providing Sid Hoad with an opportunity which was also turned away. The second went several yards wide of the left post, and when the third was awarded Fletcher decided enough was enough and allowed Irvine Thornley to try his luck. Again, goalkeeper Blake saved the effort before Wynn raced in to equalise in the last minute.

Harry Newbould

City's fortunes did change in March, though, on 16th against Young's former club Everton. Tom Holford was moved out of defence to play the role of centre-forward due to injuries to Thornley and a ban following his sending off against Villa on 20th January. Holford had played the role before and, as often quoted in the press of the period, was easily able to adapt to any position. But surely no one could have predicted what kind of an impact he would have as he tore into Everton and scored all of City's goals in their 4-0 Hyde Road victory. No one could believe it, yet twelve days later he was to help the Blues achieve another 4-0 home win. This time he scored twice against Bradford City and, looking back on that period, it appears obvious now that his actions helped kick-start City's season.

Less than a month later, a hat-trick from Wynn against Sheffield Wednesday and another brace against bottom club Bury lifted the Blues out of the bottom two for the first time. With a fine 2-0 victory on the last day of the season at home to Middlesbrough, the Blues finished fifteenth on thirty-five points - a mere two points behind championship favourites United. Fourteen points had been gained in the last eight games to save the Blues with most of the plaudits going to Holford and, once again, Wynn - who scored seventeen goals in thirty-one games.

The star of the previous season, Walter Smith, had only managed to make twelve appearances. He had suffered with fluid on the knee and on 13th January, minutes before the start of City's cup-tie at Preston, he was forced out of the game. Jack Lyall had already moved to Dundee, and so December signing Jim Goodchild hurriedly had to strip and change. The rest of the side had dressed by the time Goodchild was told he was playing and so, in a rush, he made his way onto the field.

During the game he saved a penalty and managed to keep the Preston forwards at bay. His debut ended with Wynn scoring the only goal in the eighty-eighth minute to give City victory. Despite a 1-0 defeat in the second round - at home to Oldham - Goodchild proved he was a good replacement for Smith throughout the last months of the season. The following season would see him start as first choice, although the debate as to who was the better 'keeper would rumble on for the following four years. Fortunately, for the struggling Blues they had two valuable 'keepers.

With so much struggle over the previous couple of seasons it was no surprise when in July Newbould resigned. After holding the Club together in the years following the bans maybe he felt it was time for a different challenge. The following August he assisted a side from Copenhagen called Academicals before becoming the PFA secretary in March 1913.

1912-1913 Mangnall Walks Out On United

Early into the new season announcements appeared in the *Athletic News* and the *Daily Dispatch* stating that Ernest Mangnall - the man who had achieved so much success with United - was to leave Old Trafford and take over from Newbould. This was an enormous surprise to Mancunians and, indeed, the whole of football, and would have been on a par with Alex Ferguson walking out of Old Trafford in the mid-1990s to join the Blues.

At United Mangnall had achieved a great deal and, even today, remains one of the most important men ever to be associated with the Reds. He was the man who purchased Meredith and the other banned City players, he was responsible for turning United from a struggling Second Division side into trophy winners. In 1910 it was mainly due to his ambition and drive that the Reds left the confines of Clayton for the 70,000 capacity Old Trafford.

For City to convince him to leave United was some feat, but what was more remarkable was that he still had to take charge of the Reds in one further derby match prior to moving to Hyde Road. The derby was to be City's second game of the season - five days earlier they travelled to Nottingham to face Notts County. On the morning of the game the *Daily Dispatch* columnist The Observer outlined a pessimistic forecast of City's

1912-13 season: "In Manchester we are chiefly interested, perhaps, in wondering what kind of a season City are going to have. To be perfectly candid, because I do not wish to be told afterwards that I waited the course of events, I do not consider the present team good enough to place City in a good position in the table, unless G.W. Webb makes more difference than one is reasonably entitled to expect.

"All the same, I am hoping that when Mr. J.E. Mangnall takes charge an effort will be made to really strengthen the side, because I am forced to believe there is room for it. By the way, I may mention that it is definitely decided Mr. Mangnall will take up his responsibilities at Hyde-road a week today, and, as a matter of fact, he will be with the team at Nottingham today."

Considering the fact that Mangnall was at Nottingham, not London where United faced Arsenal, it must be obvious that he did actually play a role in City's opening fixture - not officially of course - but he must have offered some advice. At Meadow Lane, William Henry scored his one and only League goal when he netted a forty yard match winner against County. Had he been inspired by the rather negative comments from the *Daily Dispatch*?

The following game was officially Mangnall's last in charge of United, but there has got to be doubt over who decided the tactics to be employed by both sides. It seems crazy to believe that the United players would have listened to future Blue Mangnall, likewise could City afford to take the chance of seeing Mangnall's Old Trafford reign end in victory? As far as the public were concerned, the biggest talking point was not the transfer of Mangnall - that was old news by this point - it was the news that the game was to be classed as a testimonial for everybody's hero Billy Meredith.

A film crew recorded the derby and this was shown in France under the title: "Match De Football Manchester." Around 19 seconds of this film survive today and this is the oldest known surviving Manchester derby footage.

The game itself was not a classic, but a forty thousand crowd satisfied Meredith's bank balance, and a goal by George Wynn satisfied the Blues. Ernest Mangnall must have had mixed feelings about the result but nevertheless *The Umpire* Newspaper reporter summed it up nicely: "United speeded their manager rejoicing with two points to his new club."

Two days later Mangnall officially took charge at Hyde Road. His first task was to check the state of recent signing George Webb. A strict amateur, Webb arrived at Hyde Road from West Ham in July. As the *Daily Dispatch* intimated, he made his debut at Notts County and kept his place at centre-forward for the trip to Old Trafford. Sadly, he was injured early in the derby and left the field in the first half.

By the time he was fully recovered from the injury, he discovered that money had changed hands between City and the Hammers and, because of his strict amateur beliefs, he was horrified. He refused to play for the Club again. In November his retirement was confirmed and new manager Mangnall had to remove him from his long term plans. Sadly, the player died of consumption in 1915 at the age of twenty-eight.

Webb's replacement for Mangnall's first game in charge was another recent signing, Harry Taylor - signed in June from Huddersfield Town. Apart from that essential change, Mangnall selected the same players who had featured at Old Trafford and Meadow Lane for the visit of Aston Villa. George Wynn, once again, provided City with the only goal of the game. A 2-1 victory followed against Liverpool prompting the *Daily Dispatch's* The Observer to question the sudden transformation: "The City deserve credit for all they have accomplished, but one would have more confidence in them carrying on the good work had they, with practically the same team, not made such an inglorious display last season. Either there was a screw very severely loose in 1911-12, or the present form is too good to last. Which is it?"

On the same day as the article, Bolton visited Hyde Road to test City further. In a game watched by a crowd of 33,871 City defeated the Trotters 2-0. Did the The Observer have his answer? The rather more upbeat *Athletic News* believed that Mangnall and the Blues had made it. Under the heading "Manchester's New Wonder" City's position was outlined: "Manchester City stand out boldly as the only first class team in the two divisions of the league, the Southern and the Scottish Leagues, with the highest possible points to their credit.

"The Citizens of Manchester have earned every point in September. Other clubs have remained undefeated, but they have not annexed the maximum marks. Nine years have passed since Manchester City commenced a campaign in this stimulating style."

The article went on to compare previous seasons, quoting 1903-04 as the closest when the Blues opening four games were won, although 1897-98 was actually better with seven straight victories but that was in Division Two.

The *Athletic News*, in a paragraph that could equally apply to the 1980s or 1990s, then paid tribute to City's vast army of loyal supporters: "Such a transformation in their fortunes after nine years will be very welcome and comforting to supporters whose loyalty has often been tested but has never failed.

"Manchester City are probably the only club which can draw huge gates when they are a losing team. Their financial possibilities as a winning team cannot be underestimated, as their gate receipts against Aston Villa were £1009 13s. 3d., representing 32,848 persons, and against Bolton Wanderers £1,131 1s. 6d. paid by 33,871 spectators. Manchester City have had a magnificent Autumn tonic."

On 5th October, after a few poor performances, centre-forward Harry Taylor was dropped for the game against Sheffield United. The feeling amongst City's directors was that he was not quite ready for first team football. In his place Mangnall brought in William Kelly, a former Newcastle player, who had made seven appearances for the Blues the previous season. Despite the change the game ended 1-1. Coincidentally, it was Sheffield United who had ended City's run in 1903. Was this some kind of omen? City fans hoped so. Challenging for the League and reaching the Cup Final would be a great tonic for City's large support.

For the following game, Kelly was dropped along with another forward William Wallace. Joe Dorsett, who had missed the two previous games, returned and Tom Holford was moved up front. Leonard Wall, signed from Glossop in October 1910, filling the vacant centre-half position. Despite the changes appearing perfect on paper, somehow they failed as City succumbed to a 1-0 defeat at home to Newcastle. Mangnall now decided to bring back the player the *Daily Dispatch* claimed the directors did not want, Taylor, in addition to outside-left Wallace. To make way for these changes he dropped Wall and Hoad, pushed Holford back, and moved Joe Dorsett from the left into Hoad's outside right position.

Despite a goal from Wynn, the Blues were beaten 2-1 by Oldham. Mangnall's side had not yet recovered from the folly of changing a winning team at the request of the directors. For the next game, at home to Chelsea, Mangnall dropped Wallace and brought back Sid Hoad. At last, Mangnall had got it right as the Blues achieved a 2-0 victory. Interestingly, Harry Taylor scored one of the goals. Had the directors now changed their minds? Although it's not known whether they made any further comment to Mangnall, it is known that the forward scored twice in the next game - a 4-0 victory at Arsenal

Against Sunderland in the FA Cup crowd control was difficult. Top: The scene when the gates were closed 45 mins before kick-off. Bottom: Police try to move the crowd off the pitch.

- and kept his place for the following twelve League games.

With their form rediscovered, the Blues continued to mount a challenge for the title until December when a total of only three points from a possible twelve caused some concern. After an embarrassing 2-0 Hyde Road derby defeat, Mangnall dropped goalkeeper Jim Goodchild and brought back Walter Smith. His first League game in a year ended in a 4-0 victory over Notts County on 2nd January, with George Wynn, once again, proving to be one of football's greatest strikers as he netted twice.

January also saw the start of what City supporters hoped would be a terrific cup run. On 11th City easily overcame Birmingham 4-0 at Hyde Road with goals from Sid Hoad, Harry Taylor, and another brace from George Wynn. In the next round the Blues again received a home-tie, this time the opponents would be Sunderland for a game it seems everybody wanted to watch.

Early in the day it was obvious to anyone close to Hyde Road that the crowd was going to be huge as Bennett Street, and the other streets in the area, were extremely busy. Indeed by 2pm the City management

City V Oldham, 12th March 1913 with the Popular Side in the background.

had to take the decision to close the gates - even though many ticket-holders remained outside. Naturally, many supporters tried to gain entry by whatever means possible and, by kick off, it was believed there were over fifty thousand in the ground, although the official attendance was recorded as 41,709 (receipts of £1,545). Whatever the actual attendance it was far too high - remember that only two years earlier supporters had been taken away from the ground in ambulances.

In addition to those who had managed to get in, the streets close to the entrances were packed with an estimated fifteen thousand. The Hyde Road ground and its environs simply could not cope. Nevertheless, in scenes that would be repeated at several venues over the years - including Wembley in 1923 - the game kicked off with far too many people in the ground.

Sunderland player, and later founder of *Football Monthly*, Charles Buchan believed the game should not have commenced: "No sooner had the game started than the crowd began to encroach on the field. Before half-time they were three or four yards inside the touchlines."

Somehow the game progressed with Eli Fletcher and Tom Holford being the only City players to make an impression. Indeed, the press claimed Holford played perhaps his best game ever. Nevertheless, five minutes into the second half, Sunderland's Buchan provided the opening goal. Despite people on the pitch, play resumed immediately. According to The Veteran, writing in the following Monday's *Daily Dispatch*, it was Sunderland's second goal, in the fifty-eighth minute that prompted more supporters to enter the pitch: "Eight

minutes later Buchan went through in fine style, and Richardson headed from his centre. It was then the crowd started to encroach again on the Stand side, and the touch judge complained that he could not see the touchline.

"The referee stopped the game, and I thought seemed to be ordering the lines to be re-marked, but then the crowd broke in more, and with the City players obviously appealing for an abandonment this was eventually done."

The report went on to consider the actions of the crowd, the players, and the referee, Mr. Adams, who had already refereed a similar incident at Leeds in the previous season's semi-final. According to The Veteran: "he showed commendable patience, but it was not possible for him to atone for the lack of police."

Much of Monday's press detailed the drama of the events surrounding the game with the Veteran caught in the middle of it: "The crush amongst the thousand odd ticket holders was terrific - I am able to judge, for I was wedged in it for an hour - and the results might have been serious, while hundreds of ticket-holders never got in at all!"

Naturally, as time moved on, the journalists started to consider who was responsible for the near disaster. The two obvious candidates were the City management and the local police: "Assuming that he had charge of the arrangements, I am rather surprised at Mr. Mangnall being caught napping, but it may be that he has been away with the team and had had little to do with the home management. The chief fault was that the ground was never properly policed to start with, for on big occasions like this there should always be mounted police ready on the ground to assist in clearing the playing piece.

"The crowd certainly broke down some of the gates, and the probabilities are that some five or six thousand people got in that way, but it is doubtful if that would have happened if there had been mounted police to guard the gates in the manner that is done at Liverpool."

Most disagreed with the Veteran's view that mounted police should be on the scene 'just in case', but few could disagree with the view that a stronger police presence had been required. In the end the whole question of crowd control should have been debated throughout football but, as with so many other times, the FA chose to consider the Hyde Road invasion in isolation. On Monday 3rd February, without performing any form of detailed investigation, the FA Council met. Unfortunately for City, John Lewis, a member of the Council and one of the FA men who first investigated City's illegal payment scandal seven years earlier, had been present at Hyde Road for the game. He provided the 'official' view of events.

The final result of the meeting, which lasted a little over an hour, was that the Blues were to be fined a record £500 - £350 to go to Manchester charities, the rest to the FA's benevolent fund. They were also ordered to replay the game at Sunderland, much to the disgust of Sunderland's supporters who believed they should have been awarded a victory. Despite being two goals down after about fifty-eight minutes, the Blues still had a chance of progression. If they were to overcome Sunderland, their opponents would be Swindon Town at Hyde Road.

The replay took place on Wednesday 5th when an improved City performance still could not prevent the Blues from leaving the competition. Co-incidentally

Sunderland won 2-0, after Walter Smith had saved a penalty.

In the League, the Blues' form was a little mixed with four defeats in March causing a serious dent in City's bid for the title, and with four successive draws in the final weeks of the season the Blues fell to sixth place on forty-four points - ten behind champions Sunderland. Still a creditable position after a few years of struggle, but not nearly as good as their early season form had suggested. Despite his early season prediction, The *Daily Dispatch's* The Observer chose not to gloat though. After all the Blues, with their ever loyal support, had challenged for most of the season and showed signs of promise and hope for the following season.

George Wynn was once again top scorer, this time with fourteen goals from thirty-one games, while Walkden born centre-forward Fred Howard ended the season on eleven goals from a mere sixteen games. He had even managed to score four goals on his debut on 18th January against Liverpool. Another player making his debut for City that day was Welsh international Edwin Hughes who was signed from Wrexham in December.

1913-1914 Regaining Control

The 1913-14 season commenced with a couple of 1-1 draws, followed by a 3-1 victory over Sheffield United. These results, though not perfect by any means, did offer hope. Unfortunately the following nine games saw City move closer and closer to danger as only three points were gained. Any dream Mangnall may have had of the Blues challenging for the title quickly disappeared as the nightmare of a relegation battle appeared.

With a total of only four victories by New Year, City needed a dramatic turnaround in their fortunes. Fortunately, an impressive spell during January helped

City 2 Tottenham 1, 24th January 1914 with the Main Stand behind.

lift the Blues in the League and progress in the Cup.
Impressive Cup victories over Fulham, Tottenham, and
Blackburn put City into the quarter finals to face Sheffield
United at Hyde Road. That game and the subsequent
replay ended goalless with a third game, played at Villa
Park, finishing 1-0 to Sheffield. For Mangnall's Blues it
was another case of what might have been.

The League programme continued to frustrate
although there were some interesting results. Derby
County were defeated 4-2 with a hat trick coming from
Fred Howard, and Manchester United were defeated by
a single goal. Interestingly, United were also not having
the best of seasons and for this game, which was also
classed as a testimonial for United's Sandy Turnbull and
George Stacey, *The Umpire* newspaper made much of the
fact that City remained the more popular side:

"From the point of view of attendance, Stacey
and Turnbull's benefit match at Old Trafford proved
an unqualified success, for the attendance must have
exceeded 40,000, but the fact that the United were again
beaten, and, worst of all, by their City rivals, should be
distinctly unpalatable to themselves and their well-
wishers. It was easily to be observed which was the most
popular team when the men entered the arena, for the
cheer which greeted United was faint as compared with
that which heralded the appearance of the City."

It should be stressed that this derby was played at
United's Old Trafford.

The victory over the Reds and a further three points
in their remaining three fixtures gave City a total of
thirty-six points and thirteenth position in the table.
They finished one place higher than United for the first
time since the FA ban forced City to lose Meredith and
Co. to the Reds. The Blues were once more the dominant
force.

Significantly, City would only finish below United
on four occasions between 1913 and the end of World
War Two, while the Reds would go a total of 37 years
without major trophy success. This remains the longest
ever trophyless spell for either club (although it should
be remembered that national football competition was
suspended during wartime).

Despite regaining pole position locally, Mangnall
felt the side should have achieved more. Nevertheless
City were making progress and fans loved the changes
the manager was making. Half back Ted Hanney had

*A 1913-14 season ticket
for Hyde Road.*

TRUE BLUE
Ernest Mangnall

A truly great manager who joined City from United
because he felt the Blues offered more potential. He
was right.

arrived from Reading in November 1913 for the sum of
£1,200, and forward Tommy Browell made the move
from Goodison Park for the large fee of £1,780. Browell,
in particular, made a tremendous impression, scoring
thirteen League goals following his November debut,
thereby becoming the Club's leading League marksman.

For George Wynn, the 1913-14 season had not
been a good one. He had struggled with injury and
only managed to appear in twelve games, scoring three
goals. The days of Wynn being City's biggest and best
goalscorer were over. Although he would remain at
Hyde Road until late 1919, he would never again be a
regular fixture in the side.

1914-1915 Uncertain Times

Throughout the early part of 1914 events in Europe
suggested that football was to take a less important
role in the lives of all Europeans. It was obvious that the
major powers were in the middle of a destructive arms
race and, by the time City played their opening fixture on
1st September, Britain was at war.

MAIL, WEDNESDAY, SEPTEMBER 2, 1914.

)TORS IN WAR.

CHIEF ARM OF THE ANSPORT SERVICE.

es other things besides teach to the man in the street. It buries s of ancient ideas and methods reluctantly died out, and which rogress of new systems which have to take their place. In this war transport has received its baptism he component parts of this new e each been "blooded," and their e future is assured. Cycle corps how they can assist our cavalry our horse flesh; they have proved ty as a scouting force. Motor e the couriers of to-day. Motor ry ammunition, forage, provisions, ent with speed and tireless energy at affection will Londoners wel- their motor buses—the elephants hanical transport service. They rto been regarded as necessary

DO THE PUBLIC WANT FOOTBALL?

CITY MATCH INCIDENTS

HOW MANCHESTER WON THE OPENING GAME.

By FREE CRITIC.

Manchester City 4, Bradford City 1.

There was little or nothing at the opening of the football season at the Manchester City ground last evening to remind us that we were in the midst of one of the greatest crises in our history. The only part of the proceedings which served to indicate that the occasion was one not altogether associated with the piping times of peace was the rendering of the British, French, and Russian National Anthems by a local band, and the baring of heads by a crowd of about 14,000 people as the instrumentalists rendered, with telling effect, our national hymn. Certain it is there

ATHLE

WHOLES T

Cricketers a where rallyin Kilner, of Yo stated that di will offer th national serv Mr. P. F. Standard," d most unfair amateurs " c of ordinary "Of the M have alread Saville, M. Littlejohn, Twining, a sionals, Le and other Sir A. W. S. P. Pegl Sharp, M Knight) on Thur urn Mel E. M.

With war breaking out many questioned whether the game should continue.

On 4th August, following Germany's invasion of Belgium, Britain declared war on Germany. The general feeling was that the war would be over by Christmas and that life should continue as normal, wherever possible. Naturally, vast numbers of men volunteered immediately for the armed forces with everybody expected to do their bit for King and Country but, as far as football was concerned, the game had to continue.

City opened with a fine 4-1 victory over Bradford City at Hyde Road but, because of the situation on the Continent, the crowd was significantly lower than for the corresponding fixture the year before. Did football really matter when so many others were already dying? Four days later the Old Trafford derby ended goalless before 20,000. Football, as the FA often stated, would continue, although each club was expected to encourage its own players and supporters to do their bit. City appear to have taken the lead in the north-west with articles appearing in various newspapers. One, entitled "Manchester City's offer", appeared in *The Umpire* stating that the City management would help any player, or his dependants, if that player joined the armed forces,

so long as the Blues were allowed to take attendance money. The players and officials also agreed to give 5% of their wages to the Prince of Wales' Fund.

By Christmas, of course, the Great War, as it was to become known, was not over. Instead, there was deadlock in the despicable, muddy trenches that stretched from the North Sea to Switzerland. Yet in Manchester at times the suffering could be forgotten temporarily as City enjoyed one of their best seasons in years. Walter Smith was back at his best in nets, and with the support of William Henry, Eli Fletcher, Edwin Hughes, and of course Ted Hanney at centre half, the Blues were defensively strong.

In attack Fred Howard, Harry Taylor, and Tommy Browell were joined by Derby County's star forward Horace Barnes for £2,500 (equalling the British transfer record set in February 1914). This impressive forward line helped the Blues challenge all season long. In fact on 5th April, the largest Hyde Road crowd of the season, attended a game that many believed would determine the Championship. Near neighbours Oldham Athletic were the visitors and despite a great deal of pressure at

Top: fans throw coins into a blanket to raise funds for Belgian war victims in September 1914.

Top right: A rare shot of fans stood in the Stone Yard Stand.

Middle: A City shot sails past the Newcastle goal, 10th October 1914.

Bottom: Hague St School score in the Manchester Schools' Shield final against Nelson St at Hyde Road, April 1915.

Opposite: The layout of Hyde Road, 1915.

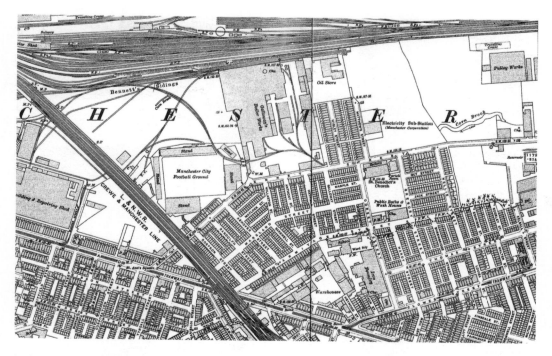

both ends the game between the top two sides ended goalless. For City, on 42 points, the dropped point was significant as the Latics were now only two points behind with two games in hand. The pressure was on.

The next game, away to Bradford City, saw another dropped point and, with only three games left, City had virtually conceded the championship. Oldham had defeated Manchester United to put themselves within a point of the Blues but their two games in hand easily gave them the advantage. Also, City's next opponents Everton had started to climb the table and, although it was not obvious at the time, they were the team that really had to be watched.

Against Everton at Hyde Road City conceded the only goal in the first half and, in effect, the title. Within seven days further defeats at Villa and Bradford (Park Avenue), left the Blues to finish in fifth place. Everton, with their impressive late surge, stole the title from Oldham Athletic who have never been that close since. City's final points tally of 43 was only three points less than Everton and was equalled by Blackburn in third place, and Burnley in fourth.

With the situation in Europe worsening it became obvious that City would have to wait some time before they next had the chance of taking the title.

1907-1915 SUMMARY

Major Trophies Won: Second Division Champions 1909-10
Highest League Attendance: c.40,000 – every season had at least one crowd estimated as 40,000 in the press
Highest Cup Attendance: c.45,000 Oldham Athletic, 03/02/12 (FA Cup)
Secretary/Managers: 1906-1912 Harry Newbould & 1912-24 Ernest Mangnall

Seasonal Record:

Season	League	Posn	FA Cup	League Cup	Other	Leading Scorer	Average Attendance
1907-08	FL Div1	3	Rnd 3			Thornley 14	23,000
1908-09	FL Div1	19	Rnd 1			Thornley 18	20,000
1909-10	FL Div2	Champions	Rnd 4			G. Dorsett 13	18,275
1910-11	FL Div1	17	Rnd 2			Wynn 9	26,000
1911-12	FL Div1	15	Rnd 2			Wynn 17	24,625
1912-13	FL Div1	6	Rnd 2			Wynn 14	24,000
1913-14	FL Div1	13	Rnd 4			Browell 13	27,000
1914-15	FL Div1	5	Rnd 3			Howard 18	21,000

S. COOKSON

MAX WOOSNAM

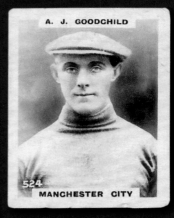

A. J. GOODCHILD

524 MANCHESTER CITY

MICHAEL HAMILL
MANCHESTER CITY

E. FLETCHER

MANCHESTER CITY

FRANK ROBERTS
MANCHESTER CITY

Presented with "Boys' Magazine"

BARNES, Manchester City.

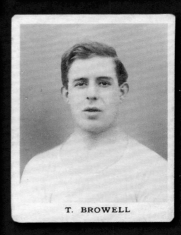

T. BROWELL

1915-1923
Royal City

"Manchester City must have some good friends. They are of course the popular club in Manchester."

The *Glasgow Evening Times* profiled City's recovery after the Hyde Road fire, November 1920

1915-1916 Wartime Champions

At the end of the 1914-15 season the Football League was suspended and, in its place, regional leagues were created with City forming part of the Lancashire section. That section was exceptionally strong, especially as the top five placed clubs in the Football League all formed part of the new fourteen club league. For the Blues it was a successful period and prompted many to wonder what the Club may have achieved had the Football League continued. It always seems petty when references are made to 'what ifs' and 'maybes' but it is a fact that City's first golden era ended prematurely, via the payments scandal, and that City's next big push for the title was also cut short. They were not the only side affected of course. Oldham were at their own peak and never managed to fulfil their potential while League champions Everton missed out in both 1915 and 1939.

The 1915-16 Lancashire section commenced with a 3-1 victory over Stockport County at Hyde Road. Although the result is interesting in itself, one story connected with the game illustrates that everyone had to do their bit for King and Country. Record signing Horace Barnes had been given employment in a munitions factory and, on the day of the Stockport match, found that the only way of guaranteeing he could play in the game was to be absent from work. He played the match, scored a goal, and then had to face the local magistrates who imposed a fine. Naturally, any work connected with the war effort was more important than helping City defeat Stockport.

Despite this Barnes managed to play in every one of City's first twelve games, scoring a total of fifteen goals.

On the final day of the Lancashire section league programme City defeated Preston 8-0 to carry off the title by two points from Burnley. Man of the match was

Hyde Road was used for stabling at times during the war. Here horses are lined up in front of the Popular Side.

undoubtedly Albert Fairclough, who scored five in his first game since 16th October. The other scorers were Joe Cartwright and Horace Barnes, who scored twice to bring his total to 26 from the 24 games he played. Interestingly the Preston side include two Bury players who happened to be at the station when the Preston men arrived in Manchester. Bury's game had been called off and, as Preston only had nine men, the two Bury men quickly accepted Preston's offer to play. Many such incidents occurred throughout football during the First World War.

For the rest of the traditional football season a subsidiary tournament, split into two sections, was organised with City, United, Oldham, Everton, Liverpool, and Stockport County forming the Southern Division. Despite losing their first game 2-0 at Stockport on 4th March, the Blues proved their quality again. The tournament ended with City as champions, proving that Mangnall's men were the most consistent Lancastrian side over the full traditional season. Interestingly, City amassed a total of 48 points from 36 games during the season, compared with Everton's 46 from 38 in their title winning season.

The first true season of wartime football also saw the return of Billy Meredith to City. On 11th March for the visit of Liverpool, Meredith became a Blue again: "After an absence of close on eleven years, Meredith reappeared in the colours of Manchester City and though it was his first game of the season he could

safely take credit to himself that he was unsurpassed by any other forward on the field. Naturally his pace has slackened and he didn't centre with the same facility as of yore. He couldn't lift the somewhat heavy ball, but his feet have not yet lost their cunning and there was none that can back heel with such certainty as he."

Meredith's return to the Blues had been caused through much argument between United and the player – United owed him some of his testimonial money - and the prospect of returning to City where Mangnall was the manager, with Lawrence Furniss back on the Board, did appeal.

With or without Meredith, the Blues could feel proud of what they achieved this season.

1916-1917 Meredith's Patch

For the 1916-17 season Billy Meredith became more or less an ever-present, missing only the opening three games. After a particularly impressive 4-0 victory over Blackpool, the *Athletic News* remembered Meredith's partnership with Sandy Turnbull: "There is a particular spot on the Hyde Road ground which deserves to be known as 'Meredith's patch'. It is the place from where the famous Welshman has made history, and from where on Saturday in the match with Blackpool, he added to the long and glorious line of successes which he inaugurated twenty-two years ago. The master knows to an inch, almost to the blade of grass, and the manner in which he crossed the ball from the old familiar spot and gave Barnes and Brennan the chances from which they won the match vividly recollects the halcyon days of his wonderful association with 'Sandy' Turnbull.

"That profitable relationship has been broken, never, I fear, to be resumed, but Meredith goes on and on, playing though he was when the majority of his colleagues were at school. Not one amongst them had a greater part in the City's opening victory of the season than the still useful 'Wizard of Wales'."

Sadly, the journalist was accurate in his belief that the partnership would not be resumed. In May 1917 came the news that Meredith's former partner, Sandy Turnbull had been killed. He had been taking part in military action in northern France and, on 3rd May 1917, he was killed while serving in the trenches. At the time of his death he was a member of the 8th battalion of the East Surrey Regiment. His death is recorded on the Memorial in the Faubourg-d'Amiens Cemetery at Arras, France. Some historians claim he participated in the famous Christmas Day battlefield match against the Germans.

The 1916-17 season saw City finish fourth in the Lancashire Section, which now included Stoke and Port Vale. In the Subsidiary Tournament City faced both the Potteries clubs and Manchester United home and away, with the results being transferred onto a league table that included all the other clubs in the Lancashire Section. This gave City a position of thirteenth overall out of sixteen clubs.

1917-1918 Third

For the next season City performed reasonably well, finishing fourth in the main tournament and achieving an overall position of third in the Subsidiary Tournament in 1918. Eli Fletcher had appeared in all but two games that season, making 34 appearances, but 32 year old Billy Lomas was the real star. He was an ever present and the Club's top scorer, netting 21 goals in the opening 30 games, but was moved into defence for the remaining six matches. Officially a guest player, Lomas had been on City's books briefly in 1912.

1918-1919 Peace Returns

The Blues ended the main 1918-19 competition in fifth place, while the Subsidiary Section was reorganised to provide section winners - City winning their section - who would then compete on a knockout basis for the Lancashire Cup. The Blues were defeated 1-0 by Oldham, after a 1-1 draw at Hyde Road.

Wartime football was far from perfect, but for City the period was relatively successful, especially as it had helped bring Meredith back to Hyde Road. He was still officially a Manchester United player and, once the war ended and the Football League returned he was expected back at Old Trafford, but he was still in disagreement over payments owed to him. Naturally, Mangnall and the City faithful wanted their hero to remain but, unfortunately, it was not to be.

At Hyde Road, following the ending of the war on 11th November, City's thoughts had to move towards the future. Was the wartime squad strong enough, would all the players return, was Hyde Road still appropriate for staging First Division matches? A lot of these issues had to be considered, especially the future of the ground.

At times during the war Hyde Road had been used to stable horses and the venue was far from perfect. In 1914 the Blues had planned to move to a new site at Mount Street (present day Mount Road), Gorton, but the war had scuppered all thoughts of moving.

Prior to 1914 there had been plenty of problems with crowd control but now, after four years of little maintenance, the stands themselves were not in the best of shape. Surprisingly, in 1917 City pledged their future to their cramped home by taking over the ground lease from Chester's Brewery. It was a significant moment in the history of the Club because it more or less ended the link with the brewery which had gone right back to 1887 with the formation of Ardwick, though some fans had felt the relationship had stunted City's growth at times, particularly on 1904 when supporters urged the Blues to move. Fans were delighted that this was a sign that the successful, rich, football club were aiming to be in total control of their destiny. The annual rent of £500 seemed like a pittance compared with the profit possible from a successful City.

Hyde Road, however, needed improving. In the mid-1970s one supporter born around the time of City's

1904 Cup win remembered an unusual situation which occurred as a result of a railway line which actually ran through the ground, in front of one stand: "One of my memories of City's Hyde Road days was a unique happening during the 1914-18 War and no other club in the history of soccer can equal this one. Behind the 'Lads-only' stand was Galloway Boiler Works and to reach the railway close by, a loop line ran from the sidings into the ground passing in front of the boys stand, and then into the works. Inch-thick ten foot long iron bars kept us back off the pitch.

"During the interval at one game a huge boiler was being brought from the works when the whole contraption stuck on the sharp curved line, blocking the view for everyone in the stand. Considering the howls of protest that went up from all the lads during the twenty minutes it took to get it moving, it's a wonder the boiler didn't burst!"

For City, the immediate post war period required careful planning if the Blues were to remain Manchester's top club.

1919-1920 The King's Blues

After four seasons of relatively successful regional football, the Blues believed they were ready for the return of national competition. Many of the old familiar faces remained and Ernest Mangnall believed that the support of a few younger imports would help City achieve the success that many felt they were ready for four years earlier. It should be noted that the wartime situation had led to City having a total of 31 professionals and 55 amateurs on their books at the start of the season.

Player loyalty was demonstrated when the team for the opening fixture at home to Sheffield United appeared. The only player not to have played pre-war was Stalybridge born Tommy Broad (son of trainer Jimmy), a signing from Bristol City in March 1915. Walter Smith was once again the Club's number one 'keeper, although Jim Goodchild was determined to regain the green shirt, and Barnes, Browell, and Cartwright were there to aid the attack. Even pre-war favourite George Wynn put on the Blue shirt for the Football League's return.

The game ended in a 3-3 draw with Horace Barnes scoring a brace, while Tommy Browell slotted home a late penalty. The next game saw Browell score twice and Cartwright once to defeat Oldham 3-1 at Boundary Park. Five days later George Wynn found the net for the last time in his City career as the Blues were defeated 3-1 by Sheffield United in the return match. Wynn did make one further appearance - another 3-1 against Oldham on 8th September - but his Hyde Road career was now over. In November he moved to Coventry City for £300,

playing in their first season in the League, then after scoring twice in 27 League and Cup appearances he became a bit of a nomad, moving from club to club. He had spells with Llandudno Town, Mansfield and Halifax where, co-incidentally he made an appearance during the Shaymen's inaugural season in the League.

One player who made his debut after Wynn departed was William 'Spud' Murphy who replaced Joe Cartwright on the left wing for the bulk of the season. Murphy was an extremely fast player with terrific stamina - a point proved during the war when he took up cross country running. In February 1918 he joined the Blues, turning professional in May 1919 at the age of twenty-four. His debut was the 4-1 defeat at home to Bolton on 13th September. Seven days later the return game ended 6-2 - this was not a happy period for Walter Smith!

The season saw many unusual results as teams met twice on consecutive Saturdays, creating a feeling of familiarity between sides. Often high scoring victories would be followed by heavy defeats – the games with Notts County were perfect examples. The first ended 4-1 to City at Hyde Road, yet in the return the score was reversed.

In October, the first post war League Manchester derby was a real thriller, with United taking the lead three times before the Blues levelled at 3-3. This was actually the last appearance of Walter Smith who, it must be said, left Hyde Road after an absolutely appalling game. For much of his City career Smith had saved the Blues with a consistently high standard of play, especially in derbies, but for this match it seems he could do nothing right. He was heavily criticised for two of United's goals - for one he hesitated, for the other he was dispossessed while bouncing the ball in his area oblivious to the presence of United's goal poaching star of the period Joe Spence. One newspaper report mentioned his name three times - twice for the goals and then once in the final summary: "The City played a greatly improved game all round, and apart from Smith's mistakes, the defence was most faultless".

Smith left Hyde Road for Port Vale where the nightmare of the Manchester derby was rapidly eclipsed on the morning of his debut. It seems that he was falsely accused of assaulting a hotel chambermaid at South Shields prior to his first game for Vale. He was bailed in time to play, but went through the match knowing that he was constantly being watched by a police detective. Fortunately, it all turned out to be a mistake and Smith remained with Vale until 1922. At Hyde Road the best memories of Smith were his outstanding early derby appearances and his Football League appearance against the Scots in 1915. Like all 'keepers he was a little eccentric - the *Athletic News* once called him: "the only first class goalkeeper in the Country who disdains training" - but he had been a superb player for the Blues.

The King is introduced to the City players at Hyde Road in March 1920.

In addition to the transfer of Smith, the derby also saw the end of Ted Hanney's career at Hyde Road. He was transferred to Coventry for an incredible £2,000. Like Smith, Hanney's debut was not a particularly pleasurable experience - he broke his nose in a collision during the second half - although match reports did state that he played well during his spells on the pitch.

The season progressed with Browell and Barnes providing most of City's fire power, causing many to wonder what the two players may have achieved together had the war not ended national competition. They each scored 22 League goals - making them the Blues' highest scorers since Gillespie's 28 in 1902-3.

These goals, plus the form of Goodchild in goal, helped City reach a respectable seventh place, but the most newsworthy moment of the season came on 27th March 1920 when King George V attended Hyde Road for City's match against Liverpool. The King was on a tour of the Northwest and, as the *Manchester Evening Chronicle* revealed, the Blues received the ultimate honour: "This surely was the greatest day in the history of the City club and the Hyde Road supporters, who are nothing if not enthusiastic, were roused to a fine sense of patriotism by the Royal visit.

"The roads to the ground presented remarkable scenes. The cars were packed to overflowing, and thousands and thousands walked from all directions to Hyde Road. It was expected that a new record would be created as regards attendance."

The Chronicle claimed the attendance had easily exceeded 30,000 a good thirty minutes or so before the King arrived and that officials – at all levels within the Club – focused on organising supporters in an orderly manner to ensure absolute capacity could be reached.

The newspaper also pointed out that City had taken the unusual step of creating a special section of the ground for those less able to watch from the regular stands: "A number of wounded and crippled soldiers were accommodated on the specially arranged seats on the Bennett Street corner of the ground."

With capacity reached, or exceeded if some reports are to be believed, the gates were closed at 2.30 pm – at least 45 minutes before kick-off. According to the majority of reports the attendance that day easily exceeded 40,000. Thirty five minutes later the King was seen: "Shortly after 3.05 a huge cheer from the occupants of the big stand announced the arrival of his Majesty and party, and the Royal Standard was immediately run up a specially improvised flagstaff on the Galloway end stand."

At 3.15pm the players came out, followed by the King. He was accompanied by John Chapman, Ernest Mangnall, the Lord Mayor and council officials. The King was introduced to the players and management, including trainer Jimmy Broad who had been at Hyde Road since the beginning.

Chapman then led the King to his seat in the wooden grandstand and the crowd simultaneously began singing "For He's A Jolly Good Fellow."

The King watched the game from the Royal Box – it seems many Mancunians found humour in the news that the directors' box had been cleaned, spruced up and renamed the Royal Box for the day.

As for the game, Horace Barnes scored two late goals to give the Blues a 2-1 victory, and the King much enjoyment - if Manchester based newspapers are to be believed.

It was a great honour for City and it did prove that

they were one of the most important and famous clubs in Britain, even though Hyde Road was not the grandest of venues. Lifetime City supporter Harry Hughes, born in August 1902, remembered visiting the ground for the first time during this period: "I thought I must go down and see these wonderful creatures called 'CITY', and made my way to the ground off Bennett Street. When I arrived I was mystified as to what to do, there were narrow holes for turnstiles and I didn't know what they were at all. Anyway I eventually paid my shilling and staggered into this vast multitude of people. There must have been 30,000 or more. I could hear the voices - a lovely rustling sound like wheat in the wind. The match was against Bolton Wanderers, I think, they were a real force in the land of course.

"The ground had metal stanchions - the lattice type - holding up the roofs and much of the ground looked similar. There were houses cutting into the Popular Side terracing, overlooking the ground and for years I used to ask my mother if we could flit and move into one of those so we could see the ground. During the games you could always see fellas hanging out of their windows, smoking and drinking pints of beer - a sort of executive box of the day.

"My mother used to say if you're going to the football make sure you don't come home injured and I used to reply 'I'm only watching, I'm not playing' because you didn't think you could get injured watching. Occasionally you'd get crushed a little, but there was never really any trouble.

"The funny part of all these games around this time was the Beswick Prize Band. It was nice to hear the crowd whistling the tunes - 'Oh, Comrades' and tunes like that. There was an old fella there - Patsy Hagan I believe his name was. He wore a great hat and carried a huge beagle stick, marching along, moving his stick, beating time. The band were all right - they played all the tunes and the crowd listened and whistled. Can you imagine the whole crowd whistling more or less all in tune? It was great, but this Patsy Hagan looked to be a staunch teetotaller, very serious. When he marched into the corners with his serious face, he'd wave his stick and turn around, and the crowd would point at him and laugh. It was very funny.

"Another funny thing used to occur with the lads selling 'Batty's Football Tablets'. That was a do in itself! The tablets were sold in little pokey bags - a penny a packet, and I remember that at my first game a fella right at the back threw a penny down and the Batty lad caught it. They used to do it all the time. Anyway, the Batty lad threw the packet back up, right to the man who wanted them! Occasionally, the packets would only go halfway up the terracing and the bag would be knocked to the buyer by the others in the crowd - each one knocking it on. Sometimes the bags would burst

and we'd all get a tablet! That was part of the fun. Every home game you had to buy Batty's tablets.

"I remember that the Hyde Road crowd were always in good humour and, after that first game, I walked home - I don't think I touched the floor until I got home, I was full of it. I said 'that's for me, I'm going there again'. I loved it and couldn't wait for the next game. I dreamt about it all fortnight."

Certainly the atmosphere at Hyde Road was special, even if the venue was inadequate. Already the City management were well aware that the time was fast approaching when the Club would have to move if it was to achieve its potential. It was obvious the policy of make do and mend could not last and that a new venue had to be found as Hyde Road offered little potential for improvement. Bennett Street prevented the popular side from being extended - the stand roof only extended a little over half way because of its irregular shape and the proximity of the houses - while Galloway's Works prevented improvements at that end of the ground. The two other sides could not be enlarged because of railway lines and sidings, and a stone yard. Even access was a problem as two sides offered no opportunity for turnstiles or exit points.

With all this in mind the directors and Ernest Mangnall, the manager, considered other sites. They still wanted to stay in the Gorton/Ardwick area and the most obvious site was Belle Vue, a huge pleasure gardens and zoo a short distance away close to St. Mark's early venues. Ardwick had played a floodlit friendly at the Athletic Ground there against Newton Heath in 1889, and Billy Meredith had lived on Nut Street adjacent to the running track. He used to train on the track during his first City period. It seemed to offer so much potential, as did a site in the Mount Road area that the Blues had considered moving to pre-war. It is believed that site became the modern day Greyhound stadium.

The Blues' management were not entirely convinced that any site offered them more than they already possessed. They had been talking about a move since the turn of the century but Hyde Road always seemed to offer more in terms of familiarity and atmosphere. Hyde Road was home and as the 1920-21 season approached the 40,000 capacity venue was deemed suitable for a while at least.

1920-1921 A Neighbour In Need

Early season capacity crowds caused more headaches for the management - and crushing for a number of supporters. Across the city United, with their 70,000 stadium, felt they could help and John Davies, United's Chairman, offered the use of Old Trafford. The Blues politely turned him down, but by early November drastic measures would change City's view.

On the night of Saturday 6th November, the main stand was destroyed by fire. The cause was eventually announced as a stray cigarette end, not the result of some 'Bonfire night' prank, but the damage was tremendous. *The Daily Dispatch* were quickly on the scene to uncover the facts and mingle with the large crowd of onlookers: "Shortly after 11pm it was discovered that flames were issuing from the buildings underneath the Hyde-road end of the Grand Stand. An alarm was raised, but the outbreak spread with such great rapidity that though the City Fire Brigade answered the call very promptly, the stand and adjacent buildings of the club were almost entirely involved before their arrival.

"The structure, which was built of wood, included the dressing-rooms, offices, baths, and the attendants' rooms. In just over an hour the whole building, which was valued at several thousands of pounds, was razed to the ground.

"The flames could be seen for miles around, and thousands of people were attracted to the ground. A strong body of police was drafted to the scene, but great numbers of people by that time had flocked on to the other stands and made themselves comfortable to watch the rapid progress of the flames. It was an excited crowd, especially when the supports of the roof collapsed. The leaping flames revealed many hundreds of people sitting packed together as on the occasion of some big match.

"The stand was capable of seating about 3,000 people, and in view of the club's difficulties with regard to accommodation the loss is a very serious one."

Over the course of the next few days the *Daily Dispatch* covered City's attempts to recover from the loss and find a venue for the following Saturday's match with Huddersfield. By Wednesday, it was reported that City had tried to negotiate for the use of Old Trafford but that United's terms had become prohibitive. Apparently the Reds wanted a guaranteed income and to keep all receipts in excess of the corresponding fixtures from the previous season. They did state that they would pay City if the receipts did not match those of twelve months previous, but the chances of that actually happening were minimal. Many of City's games had been sell-outs and the Blues felt that, with a bigger venue, the crowds would have been higher. 'It wasn't the ground that attracted the supporters it was the team' was City's main argument.

With the two sides failing to reach agreement, and the Blues determined not to cancel the Huddersfield fixture, the Blues took the only option available to them - they decided to patch up Hyde Road and with typical City spirit 'put on the show'. *The Daily Dispatch* reported that the stand would be replaced by an enclosure with an entrance charge of 1s 9d and that the 'Stoneyard Stand', part of the roofed area behind the Hyde Road goal, would be made available for season ticket holders,

Defender Sammy Sharp made 183 appearances for City. His death at 39 shocked the Club.

All that was left of the Main Stand at Hyde Road after the fire.

officials, and the press. The seated area available was not huge but it was the best the Club could provide.

With the players changing at Galloways, and a little discomfort in the press and officials' section, the game against Huddersfield went ahead as planned. A crowd of over 35,000, according to the *Daily Dispatch*, watched a 3-2 City victory and most Mancunians were pleased with what the Club had managed to achieve in the time, but the real moment of pride came on the 27th when United were the visitors. Harry Hughes remembered the period well: "United in their benign way offered the use of Old Trafford but City politely refused saying 'Don't worry we'll have a grandstand!' and y'know we did! We had one built by the time we played United. It was made of tongue and groove and varnished. In fact you could still smell the varnish all over the ground. It was pretty rough, but it served its purpose, and as it was all new wood it must have been ten times stronger than the old stand.

"As usual the band came out, formed a circle on the pitch and played all the popular songs of the day. Then they started playing 'I wouldn't leave my little wooden hut for you' and the crowd wasn't slow to notice that, and we all started laughing. Then the referee came on, blew his whistle at the band and told them to get off! So as they marched off they played 'Home Sweet Home' - very apt, very witty!"

If United were still in any doubt that City were at home at Hyde Road by the end of the game they must have realised who the masters were, as the Reds were trounced 3-0. Interestingly, even though the crowd reached 40,000 there was still room on the new terracing. The fire had actually provided the Blues with greater opportunity to satisfy their large support.

The star of the derby match was City's amateur centre-half Max Woosnam, who had made his debut the previous March. He was an all-round sportsman, famous for tennis (winning an Olympic Gold at the 1920 Games in Antwerp), football, cricket, and golf. Although United were keen to sign him, he joined City following a recommendation by United player Billy Meredith. Meredith was still experiencing financial issues with United and felt that the Blues would treat Woosnam properly.

By profession he worked at Crossley's - an engine manufacturer with strong links to Gorton and Openshaw - and had to work a five and half day week, which presented serious problems when the Blues were playing some distance away from Manchester. Dutifully he continued to work all morning on the day of a Cup tie at Leicester in March 1920, and was unable to play. When his employers discovered his loyalty to them they insisted that, in future, if City need him to play then he will play no matter how early he has to leave his work. Basically he was threatened "play for City or else....".

According to early club histories Woosnam was a fair, clean player, although he was an "advocate of the healthy shoulder charge."

Other players to arrive around the same time as Woosnam were Sam Cookson, later described as the best uncapped full back of the period, Fred 'Tiny' Fayers, a half-back from Stockport County, and former United player Mick Hamill, signed from Belfast Celtic although City had to pay £1,000 to the Reds as they still held his English registration.

These players, together with fine goalkeeping from Goodchild, and the power of Browell, Barnes, and Murphy enabled the Blues to maintain a strong challenge for the title. Tremendous interest was shown in the Club - 40,000 crowds were the norm - while the Irish FA showed more interest in one of the season's star players - 'Spud' Murphy. They wrote asking if he had been born in Ireland to which Mangnall replied "He comes from St. Helens, where the pills come from."

City's excellent season continued into 1921 and in March they faced fellow challengers Burnley in a game that would severely test the Hyde Road enclosure. Harry Hughes remembered that the crowd for this match was huge, probably the largest Hyde Road crowd ever, and that as a young man it seemed incredible that so many people could pack into the ground: "I managed to get near the front. They had little wooden railings around the pitch to keep the crowd off the turf, but there was never any real danger in those days. Soon the ground became packed beyond ordinary comfort - and we didn't ask for a lot in comfort in those days! Some 'strong arms' lifted me up and put me over the railings onto the turf itself - the holy of holies! Anyway, behind me, right at the back there was a huge wooden door with a padlock on - it would have been one of the large exit gates. While I was safely on the pitch, I heard a tremendous noise and turned to see the gate broken down, all splintered, and the crowd surging in. As I was on the pitch I just missed being involved, just missed being crushed. I was lucky, others were injured."

Some fifty-five years after the event another spectator that day, Joe Carley of Heaton Mersey, provided his memory of how others gained free entry: "I was present perched high up in the Boys' Corner, and from my view point I could see the upper portion of certain houses in Bennett Street. To my amazement I noticed an open window from whence a rope - evidently secured to a bed or other heavy object - crossed the street and was just as securely fastened to a girder supporting the roof over the popular side.

"From the window emerged a youth who swung himself, hand over hand, across Bennett Street and into the ground. Whereupon the rope was quickly untied, or cut, withdrawn into the house and the window slammed shut!

"It was a dangerous procedure which the harassed police had much difficulty in stopping, as they were so busy attending to the jostling, angry and disappointed crowds in the street below."

The Daily Dispatch reported the amazing scenes in full - including the details of a stand fire that was quickly dealt with and the fact that many supporters took up positions on the roof itself. As with the Sunderland game nine years earlier, the tremendous scenes proved that Hyde Road simply was not good enough nor large enough for City. The Blues were extremely popular with an average attendance of 31,020 - the largest up until that point - and Hyde Road was preventing the Club from growing. It was also causing much concern from a health and safety angle, although at this point few seemed that worried if some supporters received minor injuries.

On the day itself, the Blues were simply concerned with winning the game and ending Burnley's tremendous run of thirty games without defeat. Horace

This grainy image shows fans stood on the roof and sat on the girders at City V Burnley, 1921.

Barnes scored twice - one from a free kick forty yards out - and Tommy Johnson provided another to give the Blues an impressive 3-0 win, but within a week hopes of winning the title reduced as both Burnley and Middlesbrough defeated City in their return matches. A fine sequence of five victories and a draw followed but by the final day of the season Mangnall's side had no chance of catching Burnley and, after a 1-1 draw at Newcastle, City ended the season in second place five points behind their Lancastrian rivals.

In addition to their challenge for the title, the Blues did play a part in the relegation battle with Bradford (Park Avenue), though. The Yorkshire club visited Hyde Road on 23rd April needing victory to stand any real chance of avoiding the drop, but fate was not on their side as City were awarded a penalty fifteen minutes from the end. It seems Spud Murphy was tackled, rather innocuously, a fraction inside the box. Harry Hughes remembered Tommy Browell taking the kick: "Bradford's goalkeeper was called 'Scattergood' - I remember the name because it was so unusual - he was leaping about trying to put Browell off his shot and when the player shot, the ball went yards wide of the mark. Scattergood had succeeded and the Bradford people cheered, but the referee ordered it to be retaken. Browell scored with the second shot and some cruel man in the crowd shouted 'how's it going to be in the Second Division next season then?' and Scattergood looked around at the supporter, picked up the ball out of the net and threw it right at this fella's face! The crowd went wild and the players dragged Scattergood away, else he'd have been murdered. That goal basically put Bradford down."

In addition to the Scattergood affair, Harry Hughes clearly recalls the following home game - a 3-1 victory over Newcastle - not for the game itself but for the fact that it was nominated as Jim Goodchild's benefit match: "When it was a player's benefit they'd plaster posters on all the walls in the area. Well, for this one all the posters said 'CITY V. NEWCASTLE UNITED - GOODCHILD'S BENEFIT' and so we all went along because he was a bit of a character. At half time they had about six men carrying this huge sheet around the ground and we all threw some coins in. It must have got very heavy, of course, but they managed to hold it. They went off at the end of the interval and before the end of the game they had counted it all, and sent a lad around with a sign saying 'thank you for £750 15s and 4d ha'penny' or something like that and the crowd all cheered.

"We called him 'naughty boy Goodchild' because of a cartoon that appeared in the 'paper with that caption after some misdemeanour or other."

In the 1970s another City supporter, Mr. B.J. Hill of Hulme, remembered 'naughty boy' Goodchild for another reason: "Jimmy always wore a flat cloth cap when he was playing. Well, in one game, the visitors won a corner, overcame the ball, up jumped Jimmy to gather it, and off flew his cap. I can see him now on his hands and knees frantically searching for that cap among the lethal threshing feet trying to get at the fallen ball.

"The ball was forgotten as far as Jimmy was concerned and he hastily retrieved his cap. But poor Jimmy's secret was out....he was as bald as a billiard ball. You can imagine the reaction of the fans witnessing this amazing episode!"

1921-1922 Meredith Returns

During the close season the major story in Manchester was the incredible news that Billy Meredith, at the age of 47, was leaving United to return to the Blues in a player-coach capacity. His financial disagreements with the Reds had not been resolved. Because of his age and the strength of the City side, few believed he would actually ever play for the Blues, even though he had made a number of appearances for the Reds during 1920-21. Amazingly, he was named in the starting line-up for the opening game of the season though.

A crowd of approximately 35,000 paid to see their hero's return and, after a fine 2-1 victory over Aston Villa, they went home happy, especially as the Blues were now unbeaten in 34 consecutive League games at Hyde Road. This was an astonishing run. The club to break City's run at Hyde Road was Bolton Wanderers who, in a rather scrappy match, ran out winners by the odd goal in five on 3rd December. The Blues' run had been extended to 41 games.

Tommy Browell and Horace Barnes had been in fine form with the two men somewhat overshadowing the exploits of Meredith. For Barnes City's 4-1 victory in the Hyde Road derby of 22nd October was particularly sweet as he became only the second man in history to score a hat-trick in a derby game. In addition to the performance of Barnes, the game was noteworthy as it was the last derby to be played at Hyde Road, although no one realised this at the time, and the last 'home' derby to feature Billy Meredith. The reason for this was that United were relegated at the end of the season and by the time they returned to Division One, in 1925, the Blues had moved to the rather more palatial Maine Road stadium.

Harry Hughes remembered that on the eve of the game a United prankster tried to give the Reds the appearance of home advantage: "The City groundsman arrived very early, about 7am. I don't know why, perhaps like the rest of us the prospect of certain victory over United excited him. It was fortunate that he did arrive because all the railings that went around the pitch used to be blue and white, but on this day some United fan had broken in and painted them all red and white - imagine that at City's ground! It seems that he'd got in in the middle of the night. Well, City weren't having that and by the time of kick off the Club had painted them all blue and white again!

"It caused a great deal of merriment in the crowd. The rivalry was friendly then, but we were still rivals! Arguments used to happen of course, occasionally a scuffle, but that was it. You'd certainly never get a player going into the crowd attacking them of course."

Another match, a 6-1 victory over West Bromwich Albion, during this early part of the season saw Max Woosnam score his first for the Club. A story circulating around Manchester at the time suggested that Woosnam had promised that he would take the whole of the team for a meal at the upmarket Midland Hotel if he ever scored for the Club. According to eye witnesses the moment captain Woosnam scored City's Scottish 'keeper, Tom Blair, threw his gloves into the back of his net and ran the full length of the pitch to congratulate him. Members of the crowd were heard to mutter "he's only interested in that dinner at the Midland." Whether Woosnam paid for the whole team is not known but, being a respectable amateur, no doubt he stood by his word. Within days of the goal one City fan was moved to write a poem of Woosnam's effort.

By the end of another exciting Hyde Road season the Blues found themselves in tenth position. Not as good as the previous years but there had still been a few high spots, especially with Browell and Barnes netting 41 League goals between them. There were also a couple of black moments, with one coming in the very last game of the season when Max Woosnam was "accidentally kicked" according to the *Daily Dispatch*. The player needed an X-ray to determine that the leg was broken, yet he remained as positive as ever and refused to blame anyone else: "I went out to tackle Lowe, the Newcastle winger, pushed the ball into touch and got it just below the knee - as I deserved to do. Entirely my own fault."

In effect the injury would cost Woosnam the rest of his City career, although he did manage to make a further five appearances over the following three years. In his boyhood diary, City supporter Joe Carley wrote about the events that followed that match: "After the game, I made my usual trip to the players' entrance for autographs, and stood amongst a silent crowd of sympathisers as Max, still smiling cheerfully, was carried to the ambulance on a stretcher. A small boy detached himself from the onlookers and calmly asked the injured player to sign his book. Before any of the amazed spectators could shoo the boy away, Max asked the stretcher bearers to stop for a moment so he could sign the book."

Visions of the archetypal English gentleman pausing for a moment, thinking nothing of his own predicament, bring this story to life.

1922-1923 Building A New Stadium

On 9th May 1922, three days after the final game of the 1921-22 season, the local newspapers revealed a story that was to change the direction of the Club completely - City were to move away from the Gorton/Ardwick area to the border of Rusholme and Moss Side. For years it had been known that the Blues were keen to leave Hyde Road, especially after the fire, but many assumed they would stay within a short distance of their birthplace at Clowes Street. Belle Vue, the large zoo and pleasure gardens, seemed the obvious location, especially as there was already a sports ground there. The City management did actively consider that site and another, which ultimately became the greyhound stadium, for some two years. Eventually they rejected Belle Vue on the grounds that the potential sites were too small, and that only a fifty year lease could be obtained from the Jennison family who owned Belle Vue.

Eventually the athletic ground became a major speedway venue - home to the Belle Vue Aces - but, although it lasted longer than the rest of the former pleasure gardens, the ground did not survive into the 1990s, being demolished in 1987. It's destruction was a sad moment for Manchester sport, remember it had staged the 1889 floodlit friendly, and in 1929 Billy Meredith helped a former City director launch an alternative MCFC (Manchester Central) there.

With Belle Vue rejected, City's choice had to offer something special and the press concentrated on the ambitious plans for the new ground. Incredibly, the new sixteen and a quarter acre site was to have an eventual covered capacity of 120,000 developed in two phases. The first phase, to be opened in time for the 1923-4 season, would see the Blues build a grandstand seating somewhere in the region of 15,000 and terracing for 55,000. The plan was to be based on Hampden Park which, in these pre-Wembley days, was the most famous and respected British venue. Once that phase was completed, said the report, City would extend the terracing and erect a roof around the three sides to form a sort of 'C' around the grandstand, thereby reaching the desired 120,000.

Outside the stadium, a 500 space car park was to be developed and, in front of the grand stand, a forecourt that would allow at least twenty thousand to gather. It would also be possible to allow ingress and egress on all four sides and City had asked their architects to design the venue so that 120,000 people could evacuate within a 'very few minutes'.

The land, adjacent to the then unknown minor street of Maine Road, cost £5,500 and had been considered two years earlier but was discounted as part of it was covered by a tip and the rest was a clay pit, excavated for brick making. The Blues called in soil experts and the builders

PRESENTED WITH THE "BOYS' MAGAZINE".

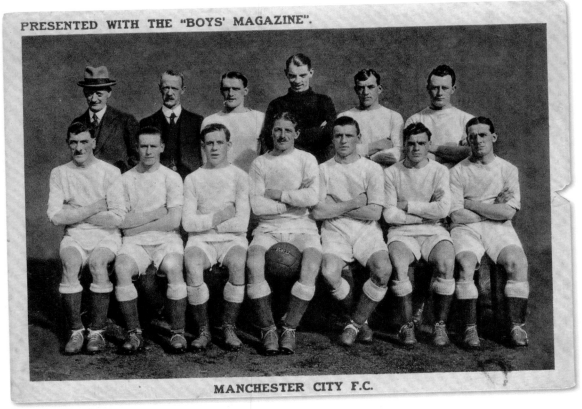

MANCHESTER CITY F.C.

1921-22. The players are (back) Cookson, Blair, Fletcher & Hamill. Front: Meredith, Warner, Browell, Woosnam, Barnes, Murphy & Fayers.

Robert McAlpine to survey the site before making their announcement.

The whole news both surprised and excited the Manchester public, and for those brought up on football the Hyde Road way it seemed incredible to think that such a venue could be built in Manchester. Ernest Mangnall, on the other hand, knew what was possible. He had been instrumental in United's move to Old Trafford and was now confident that the ever popular City could achieve more and, although plans were scaled down a little over the following months, Mangnall helped the Blues develop a stadium that wasn't simply the best in Manchester, it was the biggest and best club ground in England.

Underneath the news of the new stadium, the *Manchester Guardian* carried the story that goalkeeper Tom Blair, who had made 38 League appearances during the 1921-2 season was to give up English football and settle with his relatives at Edmonton, Canada, where he played for Bethlehem Steel. Later he joined two clubs in the USA - Fall River and New Brighton. Although City still had Goodchild on their books, the 30 year old was nearing the end of his Hyde Road career and it was felt

another 'keeper had to be found. Eventually the Blues signed the amateur Jim Mitchell, who had played for Preston in the 1922 Cup final. True to the traditions of eccentric 'keepers Mitchell had hit the headlines for frantically jumping about in goal trying to put Huddersfield's Willy Smith off as he took the Yorkshire club's penalty in the final.

In another game for Preston, Mitchell mistakenly thought a supporter's whistle was the referee's signal for time, and started to walk off the pitch as the other side were attacking. As he walked away, the ball was quickly sent goalward and as it entered the net the 'keeper realised his mistake. He threw his cap in disgust and a short while later chose to leave Preston, convinced they would never forgive him.

In addition to these exploits, Mitchell was also memorable for the fact that he wore spectacles during the game. Despite the proximity of glass, he still bravely coped with the powerful marauding forwards of the day.

Mitchell's debut wasn't until the fifth game of the season - a disappointing 1-0 defeat by Birmingham. The scoreline was bad enough, but even worse was the fact that both Eli Fletcher and Tommy Browell were injured and would be out of action for some time. For Fletcher, who would miss the rest of the season, a Cartilage operation was required, while Browell had badly strained ankle tendons and would be missing until mid-December.

For the next game Tommy Johnson returned to the side in place of Browell, and immediately impressed by providing the only goal of the return match with Birmingham on 16th September. One week later he scored twice while Horace Barnes, who had not been on his best form, provided a third in the Hyde Road victory over Huddersfield.

Between them Barnes and Johnson went on to supply a total of 35 League goals that campaign - not quite as good as the Barnes-Browell partnership, but still acceptable, especially for Barnes who had provided 21 of those goals. To aid the cause Mangnall had purchased Frank Roberts, a forward from Bolton Wanderers, for a club record fee of around £4,000 in October, and he scored a total of ten League goals.

The Blues ended the season - the last at Hyde Road - in eighth place. It had been a strange season following the injuries, with only one player, Charlie Pringle, being ever-present. Half-back Pringle had signed in June from St. Mirren and, together with new captain Mick Hamill in the centre-half position, helped to give the Blues a little consistency. Irish international Hamill was a good all round footballer who could play in a number of positions - he'd been an inside forward at United.

Interestingly, there were five players who only managed single appearances including Meredith, Fred 'Tiny' Fayers (who had been injured in the close season), and Pat Kelly - an October 1920 signing from Belfast Celtic who had struggled to regain fitness following an incident the previous year when he broke his tibia and fibula in a collision with the Chelsea 'keeper.

The final League game at Hyde Road ended goalless

with Newcastle on 28th April before a crowd of around 20,000. On the same date Wembley Stadium, built by the same people who were building Maine Road, hosted its first FA Cup final and, because of the extraordinary scenes, very little space was given over to the City game in the local 'papers. Instead they concentrated on Bolton's performance and the exploits of Billy, the white horse, in clearing the Wembley pitch.

Three months after the last Hyde Road League match, on 18th August, the last ever game, a practice match, was staged on the pitch. Afterwards the goal posts and a few turnstiles were taken from the old ground and erected at Maine Road. One of the stand roofs was dismantled and sold to Halifax Town to be erected at the Shay.

The Shay had opened approximately twelve months before Hyde Road's last League match, and a stand had already been constructed. When this stand was extended it coincided with the demolition of City's ground. Basically, it appears that the metalwork from one of City's multi-span roofs was dismantled and re-erected along the touchline at the Shay. It was linked to the existing roof, and formed one traditional style roof. The roof still existed at the Shay in 2012, although during the early 1990s it was re-clad.

The front stanchions look suspiciously like those at Hyde Road, while investigations in the late 1990s by the author of this book highlighted that the metalwork matched that of similar roofing at a factory in Sale. That factory's roof was also a former stand roof from Hyde Road. Both the Shay roof and that in Sale were so similar that they had to have previously been erected at Hyde Road.

The Sale factory was dismantled and sections of the roof given to Manchester City for possible re-use in a City museum. Sadly, by 2002 the metalwork had vanished from Maine Road and its whereabouts unknown.

Highest League Attendance: c.47,500 Burnley, 26/03/21
Highest Cup Attendance: 28,445 Charlton Athletic, 13/01/23 (FA Cup)
Secretary/Managers: 1912-24 Ernest Mangnall

Seasonal Record:

Season	League	Posn	FA Cup	Other	Leading Scorer	Average Attendance
1915-16	Lancs section champions & Subsidiary Tournament (southern) champions				Barnes 36	10,600
1916-17	4th in Lancs section & 3rd in Subsidiary Tournament				Barnes 16	10,000
1917-18	5th in Lancs section & 3rd in Subsidiary Tournament				Lomas 21	12,200
1918-19	5th in Lancs section & Subsidiary Tournament champions				Browell 14	15,700
1919-20	FL Div1	7	Rnd 2		Barnes & Browell 22	25,240
1920-21	FL Div1	2	Rnd 1		Browell 31	31,020
1921-22	FL Div1	10	Rnd 3		Browell 21	25,000
1922-23	FL Div1	8	Rnd 1		Barnes 21	24,000

The Main Stand under construction at Maine Road, 1923.

1923-1928
Records and Wembley

"The mammoth enclosure will accommodate at least 90,000 people and the first gate is sure to reach enormous proportions, even if that stupendous figure is not reached. Probably two-thirds of the crowd will wish to journey to their Mecca by tram car, and many of them are wondering how to do it."

The *Manchester Evening News* tried to inform fans of travel arrangements for Maine Road's opening match, 21st August 1923

1923-1924 The English Hampden

While Hyde Road's time was coming to an end, Maine Road was having its finishing touches applied. The original scheme had claimed the new venue would be 'The English Hampden', however many historians have fallen for the trap of claiming that Maine Road was designed as the Wembley of the north. This is not true as the City plans had been approved before Wembley had been completed, and certainly a long time before the London stadium gained any positive press coverage. However, it is true that the Blues' ambitions were to develop the best stadium in England. Comparisons with Wembley became inevitable and, for the opening

decade or so, Maine Road received the more positive headlines.

By the time the stadium opened the development had been amended a little. Instead of one 'grandstand' seating around 15,000, City's Main Stand would hold 10,000, while the terracing looping around the pitch would hold somewhere in the region of 75,000 spectators - some 20,000 more than the original plan - thereby giving a capacity of between eighty and ninety thousand. This was a phenomenal figure for a team used to playing in a cramped 40,000 capacity venue and when comparisons with rival venues were made.

The possibility of extending Maine Road to cater for the desired capacity of 120,000 probably did exist as there remained much land behind the popular side, later named the Kippax, and space behind both ends. It is known that behind the scenes over the following seven years City developed a long term plan to extend the stadium in phases.

In almost every respect Maine Road was significantly better than Hyde Road, or indeed the majority of British grounds, although one disappointing area must have been the provision of cover. Hyde Road had, at one time, boasted covered accommodation for 35,000, but all the new ground could offer was one 10,000 seater covered stand. This was still more seats than any other venue and a lot more cover than most.

On the eve of the season most newspapers carried stories of how the grand opening would overshadow all other football that day, including the Birmingham-Aston Villa derby match. The *Manchester Evening News* seemed particularly proud of the stadium's development: "That this vast stadium should have been practically completed between April 24 and August 24 of this year is the subject for wonder and admiration. It unquestionably creates a record in building construction, and it is a splendid testimonial to the organising powers of the contractors, Sir Robert McAlpine and Sons.

"Most people were freely sceptical as to whether the enclosure would be ready for tomorrow. A month ago it did not seem possible that it could be, but by the employment of hundreds of skilled workmen all but the internal work on the huge stand has been completed, and even the remaining task will not occupy more than a fortnight. As already stated the enclosure will accommodate well over 80,000 spectators.

"Sheer curiosity will attract many hundreds of people to this magnificent new ground in Maine Road, Moss Side, but the bulk of the Club's supporters will be keen on participating in what is an historic event in local football activities because of the re-appearance of Max Woosnam, whose career as Captain of the team was so, unluckily suspended for a whole season owing to the fracture of his leg."

Woosnam's return as captain was a fitting tribute to the all-round sportsman. His injury was as a result of an unfortunate accident and had not only deprived him of a year in football, it also prevented him from defending his Wimbledon

Doubles title won with Lycett in 1921. He must have been immensely proud to lead the first City side into the new stadium. Interestingly, Shaun Goater was given a similar honour in the stadium's closing match.

On the opening day the *Manchester Evening News* boasted that this would be a proud moment in "the history of the City's premier football club", although not all Mancunians were convinced the move would be a good one. For many the thirty-six year old Hyde Road was the only venue for the Blues. Some doubted that the unique City atmosphere would survive the transfer away from the Club's birthplace, while others thought the ground was too far away. Harry Hughes was one such sceptic who, although realising that the densely populated Moss Side/Rusholme area offered potential, felt that many Gortonians and Ardwickites would desert the Club: "When they moved to Maine Road I thought it wouldn't be popular. None of us did! But we had to accept it. We were all so sad about it at the time, even though Maine Road was the last word in ground design. Hyde Road was home - it was City's ground and had grown with the Club - and we loved it despite its appearance. United fans used to say that Old Trafford was better than Hyde Road. They'd say 'you can see at Old Trafford!' and we'd respond 'well there's not many people in your way'. They didn't get big crowds then.

"But Maine Road seemed so far away. It wasn't, but sometimes I couldn't afford the fare, even though it was only a penny from Belle Vue to Claremont Road. Sometimes I would get a tram - the little single deckers with seats outside - but when I could afford the fare they always seemed too busy, so I'd give up and walk to the new ground. Even though it wasn't our real home the atmosphere was there and we quickly turned it into City's home. Hyde Road became a thing of the past, never forgotten, but rarely missed."

Maine Road's opening game was covered extensively in the local press with the main reports featuring descriptions of the stadium, not the football. In an otherwise excellent piece, the *Manchester Guardian* covered the entire match in one simple passage and

The greatest club ground of the era during construction. This photo was taken from the spot where the 'Gene Kelly' Stand would later be built in between the Kippax (left) and North Stand.

failed to mention any of the goalscorers, such was their reporter's lack of interest in the playing side of the day's events. In actual fact the City goalscorers were Horace Barnes, who scored the first goal at the ground after about 68 minutes, and Tommy Johnson. In addition Frank Roberts made history by being the first player to miss a penalty at the new ground as his shot went straight to the 'keeper. Sheffield United pulled a goal back two minutes from time, thus providing the Blues with a 2-1 win before a record crowd of 58,159.

Despite the excitement of the first game, the Blues found the League programme offered little in terms of enjoyment. A run in October brought four consecutive victories, but apart from that the majority of games up until the New Year ended in defeat, or disappointing 1-1 draws. Many blamed the pitch which, in parts, became muddy following a rather wet autumn, although only one home game had ended in defeat up to Christmas. There had also been four drawn matches. The stadium was an easy target and architect Charles Swain, by this time a member of City's Board, received much criticism.

While the stadium grabbed all the headlines - positive and negative - during the first period of the season, the second half concentrated on the incredible news that Billy Meredith was back in the side. At the age of 49, the man who had played in City's first season, was preparing to play at Manchester's newest venue. Few could believe it. His return was to come in the FA Cup.

The cup run started with a 2-1 victory at home to Nottingham Forest. In the second round two draws with Halifax Town forced the sides to play a third game at neutral Old Trafford. This time City, thanks to goals from Roberts (2) and Browell, easily overcame the Shaymen.

It was in the aftermath of this game that the rumours of Meredith's return started to spread. On the eve of the third round tie at Brighton the newspapers, both local and national, were full of Meredith stories. Some seemed to ignore the facts, concentrating on the 'human angle' and writing features on this "greying man in his fiftieth year." Ignoring his time at United, one report stated that he'd played for the same club - Manchester City - for thirty years. Perhaps to the general public Manchester only had one newsworthy side.

Deservedly, the story was big news though. Especially as many supporters, and journalists for that matter, had not been alive when he first appeared for the Club. The *Manchester Evening News* reporter, although excited by the prospect of a Meredith winner, viewed the shock news as a last desperate act: "Not until last evening did the Manchester City directors decide upon the team they would like to put in the field against Brighton and Hove Albion. In the end they have sprung a surprise upon the public, inasmuch as they have elected to rely upon the services of a player who has, literally, grown grey in the service of the club - Meredith.

"He is, in the opinion of many good judges of the

game, the best outside right the club have at their disposal. This may be true. It may also be the mere fact that the officials have had to fall back upon a player of his age casts a reflection upon the club management.

"To all intents and purposes, Meredith ceased to be an active member of the first team two seasons ago. Two things have combined to bring him within range of the rather sensational choice now made - sentiment and his own indomitable will to fret his hold on the football stage a little longer. Though he has not been included in the league team so far this season, he has appeared in Lancashire Cup ties, and, as late as Wednesday week last, with the Central League team. His form has been much to be said in favour of the bold experiment now made.

"The chief argument in his favour is that from one of his classic centres any match might be won, just as it was when he scored the goal that served to bring the English Cup to Hyde Road twenty years ago next month."

According to contemporary reports a record crowd of 24,734 packed into the Goldstone Ground to see City trounce the home side 5-1. The inclusion of Meredith seemed to inspire the rest of the team, and in the second half he even supplied one of the goals. Described in John Harding's *Football Wizard*: "In the second half he had taken on Brighton's left-back, darted past him and then lifted a centre into the goalmouth which the goalkeeper had fumbled and somehow palmed into the net."

Meredith himself was generally pleased with his performance and felt that the pace of the game was not too much for him. The following week he played his first League game at Maine Road - a 3-2 defeat of Middlesbrough. This meant that during his career the Welshman had played home games at the first four major Manchester venues - Hyde Road, Maine Road, Clayton, and Old Trafford. No one else could ever match that feat.

The next game was to be the quarter-final tie at home to First Division high flyers Cardiff City. The prospect of the match excited everyone. Cardiff "The Pride Of Wales" against Meredith "The Footballing Prince Of Wales" was how one journalist described it. Thousands of Welshmen made their way to Maine Road for a game that was expected to test the capacity of the new venue, paying rail fare of 21s 2d day return from the valleys. Some had travelled through the night, with a long wait at Shrewsbury, while others had stayed at Manchester's best hotels. According to one report a few Cardiff supporters had booked rooms at the Midland, the Queen's, and at least fifty rooms at the Grand Hotel.

Many of these Welsh fans arrived at Maine Road and started queuing a full five hours before kick-off. By 12.30 the Club decided to open the turnstiles thirty minutes earlier than normal to avoid crowd control problems later. There were also around 150 policemen in the ground, persuading supporters to move from the most congested areas of the popular side. One report concentrated on the size of the crowd and the prospect of whether capacity would be reached. It stated that early indications suggested that the crowd would be huge, but that Maine Road would not be full. It's reporter also witnessed an activity that many people say occurred at many grounds, but few can prove: "Room was made for the foolish late-comers, and in a little while the congestion was so great that boys were extricated from the mass and rolled over the heads of the spectators in order that they might find sanctuary inside the concrete wall."

The official attendance was in fact 76,166, with receipts of £4,909, proving the value of City's new stadium. For a few moments architect Charles Swain must have discussed his plans to increase the capacity.

The game ended goalless - despite City's superstitious wearing of scarlet as at Brighton - with Meredith unable to keep up with the speed of the game at times. Even so, he was still one of the better players on the pitch and his tactical awareness was much needed.

The replay four days later proved to be just as popular, with a large crowd of around fifty thousand. For this match, Cardiff believed they could contain City by marking Meredith out of the game. They failed. The skillful Meredith may not have been the most pacey player on the pitch, but he was the most knowledgeable and in the second half, with the game still goalless, he put together the move that sent City into the semi-finals. The *Topical Times* reporter recorded the event: "Keeping the ball at the end of his toes as surely as though he had it on a piece of string, the veteran glanced in his bird-like fashion to his left, as though he meant to pass in that direction. Blair saw this, and kept his position accordingly; but like a flash the forward darted ahead and leaving the back standing, as it were, he was able to go on and put in a centre which left the Cardiff goal at the mercy of Browell.

"Browell so soon as he had pushed the ball into the net rushed to Meredith to offer his praises; this and that Manchester player surrounded the grand old man for the goal which was designed to take their team to the last round but one of the competition was really his."

The semi-final draw sent City to St. Andrew's, Birmingham to face Newcastle United. The Geordies were not quite the force they had been before the war and City were expected to easily defeat them, especially if they kept faith with their 'lucky' scarlet jerseys. The week before the semi, Meredith played his second League game of the season - a 2-2 home draw with Preston - and prepared to help his side reach Wembley. The media loved the prospect of football's grand old man playing at the relatively new national stadium, and newspaper column after column seemed to concentrate

A Tim Ashmore coloured photo of Billy Meredith, trainer Jimmy Broad and Charlie Pringle.

on the possibility. British Pathe sent a film crew to record the match for posterity.

The fairy tale wasn't to last, however, as City suffered disappointment. Newcastle were a better organised outfit and managed to contain them well. City, and in particular Meredith, barely touched the ball. One reporter summed it up perfectly: "The forwards were never a combined force and, although Roberts made one long dribble, they were not impressive individually. many of the intended passes sent the ball to opponents.

Meredith had many idle moments, although he clapped his hands to tell his colleagues that he was still on the field."

Back in Manchester, many supporters attending a reserve game against Wolves waited eagerly for the latest score to be carried around the ground. Frank Brown was one such supporter who, during the mid-70s, related the tension of the day: "At the reserve match us eagle-eyed youngsters could tell from the slump, or otherwise, of the boardman's shoulders how the big

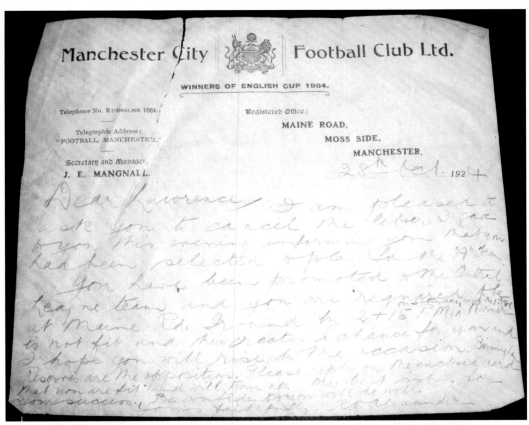

A letter from Albert Alexander snr to a player. Note: Maine Road's telephone number remained the same up to its final years.

match was going as soon as he took the first steps from the tunnel. Facing the tunnel we saw him. And we knew! A sigh from the spectators nearest the players' tunnel confirmed our fears. By the time he reached our part of the ground we knew the worst - City were a goal down. But plenty of time to go, all was by no means lost.

"Then again the figure started his death march down the tunnel, slower than ever this time. A groan, not a sigh, greeted him as chalked on his board appeared the never to be forgotten figures of: Newcastle 2 City 0. That's how it had finished. Goodbye Wembley."

A 2-0 defeat not only ended the prospect of a Wembley final, it also brought to an end thirty years of League and Cup football for Meredith. It was a sad moment, but it was still a fine achievement for the 49 year old who remains the oldest player to have appeared in the FA Cup's senior rounds.

In May, after the Blues finished eleventh in the League, the seven man board of directors decided to end Ernest Mangnall's period of management. His contract was up and the directors felt a change was necessary. In July 1924, he returned to Bolton, his birthplace, to

become a director of Wanderers. For twenty-one years he had been manager of one or other of the Manchester clubs, bringing much joy to both the Reds and the Blues. He was one of the driving forces behind United's move to Old Trafford and City's to Maine Road and, like Tom Maley before him, should be remembered for helping to establish Manchester's trophy winning heritage.

1924-1925 Little Dave

Ernest Mangnall's successor was Oldham Athletic's David Ashworth, who had a get-out clause in his Boundary Park contract which allowed him to leave if 'a better post' became available. This clause worked to City's advantage, sixty-six years later a similar clause went against the Blues during Howard Kendall's time as manager.

Ashworth, known as 'Little Dave' because of his height of only 5ft, was well known throughout football for his bowler hat and waxed moustache. As Liverpool manager he brought the Merseysiders the League title in 1922, yet in January 1923 mysteriously walked out of Anfield to return to Oldham at a time when the Reds were well on their way to winning the title again. At Maine Road, the prospect of being able to challenge for the title once again, encouraged the directors to give 'Little Dave' the job.

As Ashworth's reign began the Blues needed to find the success that their ever loyal supporters and luxurious new stadium required.

Despite the appointment of Ashworth, the 1924-25 season was barely an improvement on the previous one as the Blues struggled to come to terms with the Maine Road mud. Charles Swain was adamant that the drainage was right, but many still criticised his designs. A new groundsman was eventually appointed, but results remained mixed. City ended the season in tenth place on forty-three points, with Frank Roberts top scorer with 31 goals, while another fans' favourite, Horace Barnes, moved to Preston during the season after 235 League and Cup appearances and 125 goals for the Blues.

Other changes included the arrival of centre-half Sam Cowan, signed from Doncaster Rovers, and two new wingers Austin and Hicks. Billy Austin cost City £2,000, while Salford born George Hicks arrived from Droylsden.

All three men quickly made an impression during Ashworth's first season.

On 29th April 1925 Maine Road hosted a benefit match for living legend Billy Meredith, who by this point had retired from first class football. The teams were a Meredith XI, including City's Charlie Pringle and Frank Roberts, and a Rangers & Celtic XI. Johnny McMahon, one of the banned Cup winning City players in 1906, was one of the linesmen for the day. The game was filmed and, in 2012, is the earliest known surviving footage of Maine Road.

1925-1926 Wembley

The 1925-26 season was expected to see City return to the top of the table and challenge for the game's major honours. Sadly, the season developed into one of the Blues most inconsistent seasons. They managed to reach Wembley for the !926 Cup Final, but they also struggled in the League.

The season started well enough with a 3-2 Maine Road victory over Cardiff City, but two successive away defeats followed, causing Ashworth a little concern.

Charlie Pringle (central figure) and other players larking around with the groundsman's wheelbarrow.

Then on 12th September the first derby match at Maine Road provided the Blues with their chance of proving they were still the dominant force in local football. Football League records show that 62,994 paid on the day, while the *Athletic News* reported an attendance of 66,000 (including ticket holders). Whatever the actual figure, this was the record derby crowd at the time. Both sets of fans eagerly looked forward to the first clash for four years. Unfortunately, United took the lead first despite much pressure from City.

As the game progressed the Blues increasingly dominated the game and via a Sam Cowan header from a tight angle, City scored a thoroughly deserved equaliser. The *Athletic News* felt that Cowan's display was the best by far: "Cowan's headwork was a feature of the match. More, he tackled with grim determination and effectiveness, and distributed the ball with discrimination and accuracy.

"Cowan promises to be all that the City club expected when they brought him from Doncaster Rovers last season. He has all the physical requirements for a centre half-back, and, judging by his display in this match, he has the temperament for the big event. His equalising goal was a masterpiece in headwork and judgement".

The following week the Blues achieved another draw, this time an amazing 4-4 at home to Everton with Tommy 'Boy' Browell scoring all four for City. Known as 'Boy' Browell ever since a 1910 match report, when at the age of nineteen he scored three for Hull City stated that "Ten men and a boy beat Stockport." A little over a month after the draw with Everton Browell scored five as City thrashed Burnley 8-3. Together with Frank Roberts, he would end the season on 21 League goals.

Two days after this incredible victory City's great unpredictable streak really displayed itself as that same 8-3 scoreline was repeated. Unfortunately, this time it was Ashworth's team on the losing side as Sheffield United humiliated Manchester's top club. Further defeats followed and by 16th November with the pressure mounting the manager had resigned. Indications are that he was 'pushed' rather than leaving by choice, but the fact is that his year at Maine Road had not been a good one. The Blues were now totally unpredictable, with fine performances one week and abysmal humiliations the next. Ashworth's appointment

was the first to have really failed. Every one of his predecessors enjoyed a little success - the Cup win, runners up in the League, and promotion - and at least a couple of seasons. Before Ashworth's year, Joshua Parlby had managed the Club for the shortest period, although his two years in charge had seen the transformation from Ardwick to City and, to be fair, he also played a role throughout Sam Ormerod's time in charge.

The main problem throughout Ashworth's brief reign was that the Blues looked destined to struggle. His only major signing, £3,000 left back Phil McCloy in the close season, had been brought to England from Ayr United and not only had to adapt to English football, but also to the new offside law, which was helping to create these frequent high scoring games. During 1928 McCloy, incidentally, helped the young Matt Busby settle in Manchester at a time when the future United manager was feeling particularly homesick.

With Ashworth now gone the directors considered the options, looked around for a manager, and then thought, "we'll do the job ourselves!" Something Francis Lee joked was an option seventy years later, as he searched for a replacement for first Alan Ball then Steve Coppell during 1996.

The leading voice was that of Vice-chairman Albert Alexander senior, who took on the larger share of managerial responsibility. League form improved a little during December - two wins, a draw, and two defeats - but consistency remained hard to find.

Albert Alexander Senior

At least in January minds were diverted from the League struggle towards the FA Cup. The Cup run began with a third round visit to the former Cup Final venue, Crystal Palace, to face the famous amateur side Corinthians. A couple of years earlier Corinthians had knocked Blackburn out of the competition and, with City's form of late, it appeared the Blues were heading the same way, especially as they were losing 3-2 with only three minutes to go. Luck was on City's side however, as the Corinthians' keeper caught a centre, and somehow ran into his full-back. This resulted in him taking more than four steps without bouncing the ball. The referee penalised the 'keeper and awarded City an indirect free-kick a mere six yards from goal. The kick was taken and quickly followed by a mad scramble from both sides. Somehow the ball landed at Frank Roberts' feet and the player stabbed home the equaliser.

In the Maine Road replay four days later, the Blues took control and ran out easy 4-0 winners thanks to goals

SPECIAL CARS FOR LADIES.

On Saturday on the occasion of the Manchester City and Huddersfield match, the Manchester Corporation will make the novel experiment of running cars for ladies only after the match. The trial is the result of the growing popularity of football among Manchester women, and it is desired to protect them from the rush that follows at the end of the game.

from Billy Austin (two), Tommy Johnson, and George Hicks. The scoreline was repeated in the next round when the Blues faced high flying Huddersfield Town at Maine Road. The Yorkshire club were enjoying the greatest period in their history as Herbert Chapman led them to three successive League titles, and they should have easily defeated the managerless Blues but, again proving City's unpredictability, the home side could not be beat and goals from Hicks (two), Browell, and Roberts satisfied the 74,789 crowd at the time the second highest footballing crowd in Manchester.

It wasn't all joy for City's spectators though, as late in the game, a crush barrier collapsed causing many injuries with a number of spectators carried away by stretcher. Even at Britain's newest stadium crowd control was far from perfect.

The fifth round tie brought Crystal Palace to Maine Road for, what turned out to be, a fifteen goal thriller. By half-time the score was 7-0 to the Blues, but Palace would not give up and quickly pulled back four goals. City were knocked out of their period of complacency and soon found their goalscoring touch again. By the end it was 11-4 and, according to a number of spectators present on the day, Manchester fans rushed on at the final whistle and carried off the Palace 'keeper shoulder high. Apparently he had played extremely well and, somehow, managed to keep the score down, although one cannot help wondering if he'd have been given such a reception had the scores been reversed.

Frank Roberts was the City star for this particular game, scoring a remarkable five, while Tommy Browell also earned a few plaudits with his hat-trick.

With no management and such a miserable time in the League, no one could believe how City had been able to deliver such strong cup performances. The

quarter-final draw sent the Blues down to London for the second time, this time to face Second Division Clapton Orient on 6th March.

Tommy Johnson provided a hat-trick as City defeated Orient 6-1 to put the Blues into the semi-finals for the second time in three seasons (they had lost to Preston in the first round in 1925). The four semi-final teams included two other Lancastrian sides - Bolton and Manchester United - while Swansea Town seemed to offer the easiest route to the final.

When the draw was made Manchester could not believe it as relegation possibles City and newly promoted United were to face each other. It was the sort of draw that neither side really wanted. Losing in a semi-final is bad enough, but losing to your closest rivals is simply too much.

By the time of the semi, both League derbies had been played. At Maine Road in September the sides played out a 1-1 draw, while the Old Trafford return in January saw the Blues take the lead after eighteen minutes when Roberts headed in Austin's corner. By half-time it was 3-0 with Austin and Roberts combining again for a goal apiece. Johnson added a fourth thirty minutes into the second half, and a little while later Austin added a fifth.

In the last five minutes Hicks scored a sixth from close range. With the score at 6-0 with two minutes remaining the Blues can be forgiven for easing off a little, and allowing Clat Rennox to provide United with a consolation goal from a goalmouth scramble. The game ended 6-1. The biggest derby victory ever, and the most embarrassing home mauling either side has endured in the history of the fixture - matched in 2011-12 by another rampant Blues side.

For the semi-final City hoped they would be able to repeat their performance of two months earlier, although many believed simply gaining victory over the Reds, even by a one goal margin, would suffice. The Blues wanted to become the first Manchester side to reach Wembley.

Despite the hope, the situation looked grim. The Blues were rock bottom with only 8 League games left while the Reds were sixth when they met in the semi-final. The *Manchester Evening Chronicle* headlined: "Most Amazing Team Of The Year: Topsy-Turvy Form Of Manchester City".

City, managerless since November when they sacked David Ashworth, had only managed two League victories in the ten games before the semi – incredibly this included the record-breaking 6-1 defeat of United at Old Trafford.

The Blues seemed capable of attacking at will but offered little defensively. United were the opposite. They knew how to defend and earn victories through physical rather than daring play.

Roberts

When Bramall Lane was selected to stage the semi-final United manager John Chapman was disappointed. His reason was similar to that reportedly made by Sir Alex Ferguson in 2011: "why should Mancunians travel all that way?" Bramall Lane was 40 miles from Old Trafford. Chapman challenged the FA: "What would have been wrong with Bolton? It would have saved both players and spectators from travelling."

The Evening Chronicle described the choice as: "nothing short of deplorable." Amazingly, Sheffield United as hosts were given a third of the tickets – this angered United. Two weeks before the tie the press reported that City's allocation was oversubscribed three times over. However, across at Old Trafford, it was revealed United still had some tickets on open sale at 5 shillings. Inevitably, the publicity meant they soon disappeared - City fans later paid touts 30 shillings (£1.50) for 5s (25p) seat tickets. It seems they were unaware that there would also be cash admission to the terraces on match day.

On the morning of the game special trains were put on from both Manchester Central and Victoria stations. Supporters travelled together amidst "Cheery Banter" according to the *Manchester Evening Chronicle*. It went on to report: "special trains are being run from all parts of the country and enthusiasts are travelling from even as far afield as London. As many saloon parties have been arranged as for a Final."

There were a few minor incidents and, also, one report of a supporter clash. According to the *Chronicle* a "burly man" was talking of how the Blues would win so long as United didn't turn physical. Then a "minute, apologetic man" kicked the City fan before the burly Blue grabbed the smaller man's red rosette and threw it out of the train window. A scuffle broke out before another City fan asked the United man if he had his armour on because: "Tha'll be slashed to ribbons wi' th' gangs at Sheffield!"

Others urged everyone to stick together and watch out for the "Sheffield Blades." It seems all Mancunians made it safely to the ground, although a large number of ticket-holders struggled to see as they were some distance from the match action. At that time Bramall Lane was also a cricket ground and many fans sat in the pavilion. Pre-match a Manchester journalist had suggested: "those who have bought tickets for the cricket pavilion will not be content to witness the game 'from a distance' and will make an invasion of what is regarded as sacred ground."

The journalist also gave his match forecast: "It is generally expected that it will be a duel between a great defence and a clever and penetrative attack. There is no club in the country better served behind than the United, and on their day there is no more clever line of forwards than those of the City."

City's side for the semi included goalkeeper Jim Goodchild, who was only a week away from celebrating his thirty-fourth birthday. He had been with the Blues since October 1911 and was now in the twilight of his career. Since 1921 he had really been City's second choice 'keeper, although he did manage to make a few appearances each season. The rest of the team was: Cookson, McCloy, Pringle, Cowan, McMullan, Austin, Browell, Roberts, Johnson, and Hicks.

When the game kicked off it was City who looked to be the more composed side, United, perhaps mindful of what had occurred at Old Trafford, seemed nervous. They made plenty of mistakes, misplaced passes, hasty shots, and badly timed tackles. City on the other hand seemed composed, with Sam Cowan putting in a fine display in midfield.

In the fourteenth minute the Blues took the lead through a controversial goal. City won a corner kick and, as Hicks curled the ball into the box, Browell jumped above the United defence and headed firmly past goalkeeper Alf Steward. The ball was hooked clear, but the referee immediately signalled for a goal as the ball had clearly crossed the line. In addition to their complaints about the ball not crossing the line, United also claimed that Browell had pushed to gain an advantage. The referee would have none of it, however, and the Blues deservedly took the lead.

Cigarette cards showing scenes from the 1926 FAC semi-final.

Browell's header in the 14th minute brought a goal, but United complained.

The goal was reported differently in various 'papers. Former United star Charlie Roberts seemed to give the most accurate report: "[City's Hicks] shot for the near corner of the goal. Steward saved, but Roberts dashed into him, and the ball went over the line for a corner. This Hicks placed nicely and in the melee Browell headed through."

United's attitude seemed to worsen with petty tackles dominating their play. Frank Barson, the Reds' captain and an extremely tough defender, soon showed what he thought of both the goal and City's dominance by cynically flattening the outstanding Cowan. If that wasn't enough the United man then feigned injury, provoking the crowd further. The referee marched over to him and, after a lengthy talking to, United's captain was allowed to stay on the field, although he was rather subdued for the rest of the match.

According to the locally produced *Athletic News* United's Frank Barson cynically injured a City man: "Cowan was knocked flat down and out! A merciless crash it was, and altogether too vigorous. Cowan lay flat; Barson crouched on his knees and the crowd, suspecting 'the old soldier', roared the more."

In the weeks that followed Barson was investigated and ultimately banned for 8 weeks.

By half-time, despite constant pressure, the Blues remained in the lead by a solitary goal. City's attack seemed rather unlucky on several occasions in both halves as shots from Austin, Johnson, and Browell all

either hit the woodwork, a divot, or scooped away at the last minute by the United 'keeper.

With only fifteen minutes remaining City increased their lead. Hicks sent a though ball to Browell, who struck the ball cleanly first time past Steward into the net. Two minutes later, Roberts broke free down the middle, but his miss-hit shot from fifteen yards did not appear dangerous until Steward, who attempted to turn the ball around the post, diverted it into the net.

In his match report Charlie Roberts claimed that the tie had been better than average for a semi-final and believed: "City played a fine game and I cannot see them being beaten in the final."

With much pride the Blues prepared for their first visit to Wembley stadium. Their opponents would be Bolton, who destroyed Swansea in their semi at Tottenham, for what was a re-run of the 1904 final.

As with 1904 – and indeed 2011 - the final was played before the League programme was completed. In 1926 this meant City went to Wembley with the knowledge that they could still be relegated. Winning the cup was something everybody wanted, but by this time in football history, relegation was something that had to be avoided at all costs. The Blues were well aware that United had struggled to gain promotion for four years, and that a prolonged spell in the Second could seriously affect the future of the Club, especially with United now back in the First. City needed to remain Manchester's dominant club and simply could not afford relegation. Victory at Wembley would also bring much needed cheer to Manchester's loyal supporters, especially as many of them were about to enter a period of struggle through the General Strike.

In the run up, and on the morning of the final everything seemed to go Bolton's way. Firstly, Wanderers had already succeeded at Wembley three years earlier. Secondly, their League form was better - they would eventually finish eighth. Thirdly, the press made them favourites following a cup run that had seen them take part in three replays against lower opposition. According to the 'papers at this time, the team that "struggles most" to reach the final "usually wins." Fourthly, Bolton were able to field ten of the players who had won the Cup in 1923. And finally, Bolton won the toss for choice of dressing room and elected to use room number 11 - the 'lucky' room. Apparently, dressing room 11 had been used by all the teams that had won the Cup at Wembley.

The omens were not good. Perhaps City should have stayed at home.

On the morning of the game the thousands of Lancastrians who arrived at the stadium without a ticket

were surprised to find that they could only buy them from touts. Ever since that first Wembley final three years earlier, the Cup final had been an all-ticket affair to ease crowd control. Unfortunately, this allowed the touts to gain a grip. For this final, 2 shillings (10p) tickets were on sale at 15 shillings (75p) and occasionally £1, while £10 was being demanded for seat tickets. This was an incredible mark-up and angered the many ticketless fans. According to the *Daily Mail* the fans sought retribution: "As though at a command, they descended on the speculators and in many cases chased them out. For nearly an hour the approaches to the field were the scenes of noisy free-fights, and it was the intervention of the police that saved some of the touts from serious injury."

The *Athletic News* believed the final would be the

Lawrence Furniss introduces the King to Billy Austin.

A rare aerial view of the 1926 FA Cup final.

last at Wembley as a result of ticket chaos and the FA's general expenditure to stage the fixture there. The report suggested moving back to the old Crystal Palace ground, or potentially to move the final around the country.

City's captain was Jimmy McMullan, who had signed the preceding February for £4,700 from Partick Thistle. He was a Scottish international left-half and had already made a name for himself with the Blues after a few good performances. For the final itself, journalists suggested he was the most determined of all the City players, popping up anywhere and everywhere on the pitch.

Bolton dominated the opening minutes, while City seemed to be a little nervous. Within the first twenty minutes, the Wanderers had seen three decent chances go astray as the Blues struggled. The *Athletic News* stated that Bolton had obviously planned well, whereas City were "a set of stragglers - earnest but incoherent."

After about twenty-five minutes the Blues started to get into the game: "As soon as the City began to disremember that they had shaken hands with the King and that this was the Cup Final, the fact became apparent to all that there were flaws in the Bolton defence.

"The City did not come to cohesion. They did not take up position so intelligently as the forwards of

Sam Cookson's shirt worn at Wembley. Described as cornflower blue at the time.

163

City on the defensive - Cookson, McCloy and Cowan (l to r).

Bolton. But they were able, by fast, go-ahead methods to bother the backs."

A couple of chances came City's way, but the game remained goalless at half-time. In the second half, Bolton's Pym made a couple of fine saves, at a time when the Blues had the initiative: "For 25 minutes they fought for the decisive goal. Haworth, Greenhalgh, Jennings all wavered. Manchester City sought desperately to deliver the vital blow - a goal would have been sufficient. But it would not come. Hicks shot just over the corner of the goal, Pym had a rare struggle to clear from Hicks' corner-kick, Roberts sent Browell through and, though he overran the ball when gloriously placed, I did not agree with the referee's decision in ruling the inside right out of bounds.

"And just as Bolton were beginning to fight back, in this match of fluctuations, Pym, in their goal, came to the rescue with a match-winning save. There is no exaggeration. When McMullan once again plied Hicks with masterly touch the outside left sustained the high standard of all his previous play by placing the ball precisely in the mouth of goal. Browell's head shot out, and it seemed a score at last.

"As it was very obvious by this stage that a goal would settle all, it is abundantly clear that Pym saved his side when he flung himself full length along the goal-line and turned the ball aside."

Pym received tremendous applause from the Wembley crowd for his fine vital save, but for City this was perhaps the last great chance. The advantage swung back to Bolton, and with twelve minutes remaining the deadlock was broken. The ball, with Bolton seemingly going nowhere in midfield, was sent to Butler on the right wing. He immediately darted forward down the touchline followed by McMullan, according to the *Athletic News*: "The little Scotsman was unable to get to grips. He was never sufficiently close to make the tackle. But he hung on, and his object clearly was to force his opponent into such a position that he would find it extremely difficult to deliver a centre that would endanger the goal. At the same time, McMullan sought to get into a position that would render it imperative that the ball, from Butler's centre, would strike his body and so be kept within the front of goal."

Unfortunately, McMullan failed in his mission as Butler somehow managed to send the ball to Vizard on the opposite wing, who in turn weighed up the situation and centred the ball to an unmarked David Jack in the centre of the City goal. Jack simply banged the ball into the net, leaving Goodchild with no chance to save.

The final few minutes saw plenty of further action as the Blues tried to force an equaliser, but it was not to be. With the final kick of the game, Billy Austin passed the ball to another forward when everybody else expected him to have one final shot. That moment seemed to typify City's season of unpredictability. Nevertheless, the Blues left Wembley a proud side. They had come close to defeating one of the period's leading sides, and had managed a few fine moments.

Manchester's man of the match was undoubtedly McMullan. The *Daily Mail* paid him tribute: "McMullan was the greatest hearted man of the 22. He was half-back, full-back and forward, all combined in one. His attack was as good as his defence, and it was certainly not his fault that his team were beaten."

The result was a fair one, although everybody

associated with the Blues found it difficult to accept. This was the first FA Cup final broadcast live on radio. It was not a national broadcast but the BBC relayed it to public halls in Bolton and Manchester as a test. Back in Manchester, it was also broadcast to fans in Platt Fields close to Maine Road. Large crowds had gathered to listen to this landmark occasion. Loudspeakers had been erected in trees around the park and City fans had listened carefully to an intermittent and rather poor quality commentary. After struggling to listen throughout the game, when the news came through of the goal the fans could not take anymore, and many left immediately for home.

The following Monday's newspapers were full of Bolton's success although, as a sign of the times, both the *Athletic News* and the *Daily Mail* at times seemed more interested in what the King thought of the game. Under the banner headline "The Cup Final That Impressed The King" the *Athletic News* stressed how much he'd enjoyed the game, which seemed remarkably similar to comments made after his visit to Hyde Road in 1920, while the *Daily Mail* commented on the singing of the National Anthem. It stated that 'God Save The King' had never been sung with "such fervour, with such grandeur, with such noble, breath-catching feeling." The 'paper stated that this was a demonstration of affection and loyalty to the King, perhaps the Blues in the crowd sung so well believing they had a royal supporter, after all he had attended a Hyde Road match.

After the final, City had to pick themselves up for a difficult week in the League. On the Tuesday they faced fellow strugglers Leeds United at Maine Road. It was a tense and drawn out affair – with only 22 minutes remaining the game was stopped due to bad light, ultimately play did resume a short while later. The Blues had been leading 2-0 by half time with goals from Austin (after 21 minutes) and Johnson (24 minutes). Jennings

Gallaher's Cigarettes.

JAMES McMULLAN
MANCHESTER CITY

scored for Leeds shortly after half time but the match ended in a 2-1 Blue victory before a crowd of 50,000 according to most reports (the official crowd was later recorded as 43,475 in League records).

The result placed City fourth from bottom on 35 points.

Below them were Leeds (34 points), Burnley (34) and Notts County (31). The Blues possessed the better goal average, but two points from their final game at Newcastle would guarantee survival.

Sadly, within a minute of the start of the Newcastle match, Hughie Gallacher had scored for the home side. Before half-time Frank Roberts equalised, but in the fiftieth minute Gallacher gave Newcastle the lead again. A little while later, City's chance came again as the Blues were awarded a penalty. Billy Austin took the kick, but sent the ball straight at 'keeper Wilson. It was a bitter blow.

After an hour's play Gallacher notched up his hat-trick with a superb header to really end City's chances. Tommy Browell did provide a second three minutes from time, but the damage had already been done. With the game ending 3-2 the Blues still felt they were in with a chance of staying up, after all they had the point advantage and were fourth from bottom, with only two clubs relegated. As they made their way into the dressing room, the news came through that both Leeds and Burnley had won their home games by 4-1 The Blues were down.

For the second week running a few blamed Austin, but there had been plenty of mistakes during an unpredictable, inconsistent season. Perhaps the biggest mistake of all was not having a manager. The directors may have known about football, but a club of City's size and stature needed a true professional in charge. By the season's end, the directors had appointed a new man - Peter Hodge.

There is a little confusion over the date Hodge arrived at Maine Road. Some believe he arrived after the season ended, while others suggest he was at City from the Monday following the Cup final. The 30th April edition of the *Nottingham Evening Mail* – significantly this was after the Leeds game but before the Newcastle match – announced Hodge's shock departure from Leicester and gave the news that he would be taking up his new post at the end of May.

As this appeared in a contemporary report this suggests he played no part in City's final couple of games, however Leicester City historians believe he agreed with their club that he would remain as manager until their season ended. This suggests he arrived in Manchester during the final week of April as Leicester's season ended on 24th April at Bury.

Whatever the truth, Hodge's arrival came too late. The Blues should have appointed a new manager shortly after Ashworth left in November. At least with Hodge at the helm, the Blues could now look towards the future with a little hope. Promotion had to be achieved at the earliest opportunity to ensure City remained a dominant force.

1926-1927 The Narrowest Margin

With the appointment of Peter Hodge, City had found a manager who was capable of building for the future. At his previous club, Leicester City, he constructed a team that won the Second Division in 1925 - two points ahead of second placed Manchester United - and then managed to consolidate during 1925-26. He had been with Leicester since 1919, after managerial spells with Raith Rovers and Stoke, whom he guided to the Southern League title in 1915. At Leicester he is remembered as the club's first great manager, and the first to have real control over team selection, recruitment, and tactics. It came as a shock to the Midlands club when the approach came from Manchester, especially as Leicester were comfortable in the First, while City were heading for Division Two.

Immediately following the end of the 1925-26 season, it was difficult for City supporters to look forward to the future. The General Strike hardly helped. It started at midnight on Monday 3rd May, just two days after City's final game, and caused much tension, friction, and hardship throughout the Country until it ended about ten days later. Some disputes continued throughout the Summer, most notably in the coal mining industry, but gradually life returned to normality, although the Strike had damaged the relationship with former hero Max Woosnam and supporters. Woosnam had broken the Strike at one point and City fans made their opinions known to him in a fairly sour, but typical of the period, incident. It says much about the strength of feeling at that time that some fans never forgave their one-time hero. For the first – but by no means the last - time in City history some supporters suggested 'modern day' footballers were out of touch with the average man.

On 31st July, Hodge made his first major signing when he brought forward Matthew Barrass to City from Sheffield Wednesday. Exactly one week earlier Mancunians had been excited by another sporting first for the city when the country's first greyhound racing track opened at Belle Vue. The Belle Vue stadium was built on one of the possible sites considered by the City management when they were planning to relocate from Hyde Road. It remains in use in 2012 for greyhound racing and since the late 1980s for speedway, and is the only surviving part of the original Belle Vue pleasure gardens.

In addition to the Barrass transfer, Hodge did change his personnel further. 36 year old stalwart Eli Fletcher joined Watford as player-manager after 15 years with the Blues in June, while it was obvious that Hodge believed Tommy 'Boy' Browell's time at Maine Road had now come to an end. At the age of 34 Browell was no longer seen as the deadly attacking player he had once been.

Browell was left out of the team when the new season opened on 28th August, three days before Lancashire C.C.C won the County Championship for the first time since 1904, with the visit of Fulham. Barrass started his career perfectly with a goal on his debut while Austin, Roberts, and Hicks raised the score to 4-2 before a forty thousand crowd. City remained undefeated for the next four games before a 1-0 defeat at Reading on 18th September caused a few worries.

Three days before the Reading fixture, Tommy Browell was transferred to Blackpool for £1,500, where he continued to play until 1930.

After the Reading defeat, a few high scoring victories and draws followed as the Blues began to challenge for promotion. As with the previous season, City were scoring plenty of goals with 35 coming in their first 13 matches. They were also well supported and continued to attract significantly bigger crowds than First Division Manchester United.

At Christmas the Blues faced promotion challengers Middlesbrough home and away on consecutive days. On Christmas Day they suffered a 5-3 Maine Road defeat, with George Camsell scoring all the visitors goals, while on Boxing Day Frank Roberts supplied a

Peter Hodge

consolation goal in a 2-1 defeat. These were significant results as Middlesbrough were in outstanding form and went on to become deserved champions.

The following game, a New Year's day 2-1 defeat at Portsmouth, was also significant as Portsmouth were also a side destined to play a part in the promotion race. It was also the last match to feature Jim 'naughty boy' Goodchild. Although he remained with the Club until August, he was never likely to appear again once City bought Oldham's Welsh international Bert Gray for £2,250. In August, at the age of 35, Goodchild moved back to the Southampton area to become licensee of the Royal Albert Hotel. He also played a couple of seasons for Guildford City. In 1941 he took over the Cricketers Arms in Eastleigh, before passing away in October 1950 at the age of 58. Though his City career was lengthy, he never quite obtained the honours he deserved.

As the season progressed the Blues notched up

several high scores. The best result had to be the 7-0 thrashing of strugglers Darlington on 18th April. Sadly, Portsmouth also kept up the chase and by the last Saturday of the season both sides were level on 52 points, while Middlesbrough were already certain of the title. Importantly, Portsmouth had the better goal average (82 for and 48 against, with an average of 1.708 as opposed to City's 100 for, 61 against at an average of 1.639).

City's final game was at home to bottom club Bradford City, while Preston travelled to Portsmouth. On a beautiful, warm Manchester day City seemed easily capable of destroying Bradford and within six minutes, backed by a noisy 49,343 crowd, the Blues took the lead. The *Athletic News*: "Bell improved upon an inspiring piece of play by Roberts and swung a ball into the goalmouth which Boot caught but failed to hold, the huge assembly was delirious with delight. The cheering was deafening. Ten minutes later another peal of thunder announced a second success, and as fine a goal as anyone could wish to see. All the time in the sweltering heat the City had been playing football of the finest quality, and at an amazing pace. Their manoeuvring was bewildering, and their forwards were as nippy and as virile as they were clever."

The second had been netted by Tommy Johnson.

Shortly afterwards the *Athletic News* noted that tremendous cheering came from City's vast terracing. On investigation, their reporter discovered that Preston had taken the lead at Portsmouth. Then with thirty minutes gone Hicks "coolly and deliberately" placed the ball into the net for the Blues' third. The atmosphere was incredible.

At half time the news came through that the Portsmouth-Preston game had commenced fifteen minutes late and that Preston were winning, so all looked well.

After 52 minutes Broadhurst provided the fourth City goal via a fine long range shot. Roberts made it five six minutes later, then with 24 minutes remaining Johnson made it six. According to The Pilgrim: "[City] were even more dominating than they had been in the first, and one almost felt sorry for Bradford, who were metaphorically torn to ribbons. Their defence was completely disorganised. All they could do was to kick at random, and except for two occasions their forwards never got a look in." Everyone now believed City

were home and dry, although there appeared to be confused messages coming from the south coast. Some heard Portsmouth were leading 4-1 while others thought Preston had increased their lead.

At Maine Road, Johnson completed his hat-trick with a penalty in the 81st minute, awarded after Broadhurst was tripped as he dashed through the box. In the final minute Broadhurst made the total eight. Seconds later the whistle sounded and supporters surged onto the pitch to greet their City heroes. The police helped make a path for the players back to the dressing room as fans congratulated them on "getting back", as the *Athletic News* put it.

As the celebrations continued - the band started playing 'Auld Lang Syne' - news came through that Portsmouth were winning, although nobody seemed to know by how much. To be honest few really cared. Surely 8-0 was enough they thought. This meant Portsmouth needed to win their game 5-1 but, with those vital fifteen minutes play remaining, they had the opportunity to control their own destiny.

While Mancunians pondered the ifs and maybes, on the south coast the Portsmouth management seemed to know specifically what they needed to achieve promotion. The Fratton Park crowd began singing "To Be A Farmer's Boy" – a song sung to their hero the ex-dairy farmer Willie Haines – and in the 78th minute Willie Haines scored his fourth and then Portsmouth's fifth.

About ten minutes later the City directors were informed via ticker-tape that it was all over. Portsmouth were promoted by the narrowest goal average margin in history. Their average equalled 1.7755, while City's was 1.7705. One more City goal would have given the Blues that vital second promotion spot.

Bradford's 'keeper Boot was acclaimed the star of the Maine Road match after pulling off a string of saves, any of which could have provided City with the goal they had desperately needed.

Everybody at Maine Road felt disappointed. It was a terrible blow. The *Athletic News* felt that City had suffered more than most: " By some infinitesimal fraction of a goal they have to go through it all again. Joy was turned to a disappointment that could be felt, but everyone's sympathy was extended to the players and the club. Never has there been such a cruel blow of fate in the history of the League.

"More than once has goal average decided the promotion race, but never has there been a finer fight than this, and never has a club had such a distressing

Tommy Johnson

experience as the City. To lose their position in the First Division by their failure to convert a penalty kick in their concluding match one season, and miss promotion by such a slender margin the next, after running up such a score, is without parallel.

"Another goal would have done it."

1927-1928 The Second Attempt

The annual public practice match on 20th August ended with the first XI defeating the reserves 9-2. Roberts scored five, Broadhurst three, and Johnson netted the other. The Blues followed this up with only one defeat in their opening nine League matches, as they endeavoured to gain promotion. Both games against fellow challengers Leeds ended in Blue victory, while a good away performance against another team challenging, Chelsea, in March helped City keep control. The Citizens, as they were occasionally called in the press, lost the services of Bert Gray for a little while in January and February following the third round cup tie with Leeds. Gray had broken a cheek bone after about thirty minutes and was replaced by winger Billy Austin, who managed to keep Leeds from scoring on a few occasions, as the Blues won 1-0. In the next round they overcame Sunderland 2-1, but Stoke surprised City 1-0 in the fifth round.

While still scoring plenty of goals, manager Hodge decided to increase his firepower further by signing two Barnsley forwards, Eric Brook and Fred Tilson for a combined fee of £6,000. Brook was a roaming, unorthodox outside left who was able to play virtually anywhere, and combined perfectly with Tilson. The two men made their debuts, alongside another newcomer - right winger Alf Horne, in the 2-0 win against Grimsby Town on 17th March. Another recent arrival was Bobby Marshall, who had made his debut two games earlier after signing from Sunderland in March 1928. Marshall started his City career as an inside-forward, but a few years later would forge more or less another career at centre-half. He possessed brilliant ball control, and in his inaugural season would score a total of seven goals in only fourteen appearances.

Brook, Tilson and Marshall would ultimately form

the core of the successful City side that would dominate Manchester football for the following decade.

With considerable fire power the Blues once again scored a century of goals, although this time they had managed to keep the number conceded down to 59. Not a great deal less than the previous year, but their points tally had increased by five. For the fourth time in history City had achieved promotion as champions. They deserved it, as did the Blues' loyal support which had reached an average of 37,468. An incredible figure at this point in football's history, and one which gave the Blues the largest support in the League. Not bad for a Second Division side.

1927-8 was also a successful season in other competitions as the Blues defeated Bury 3-1 in the Lancashire Cup final, and United 4-2 in the Manchester Cup final. At the final of the Lancashire Cup, played at Old Trafford, the local FA brought out all the trophies won by Lancastrian clubs that season. There was the FA Cup (Blackburn Rovers), The League Championship

Bobby Marshall

(Everton), the Second Division Championship Shield (City), and the Lancashire Cup itself. City Chairman Lawrence Furniss, associated with the Club since the early 1880s, proudly posed for photographs with the trophies and directors of the other clubs.

Before the end of the Lancashire Cup Final, City supporters in the crowd of 23,460 moved around Old Trafford and headed for the area closest to the players' tunnel to see the trophy presented. Even with the game still in progress, some supporters ran across the pitch to find the perfect spot. When the referee ended the game, hundreds more invaded the pitch forcing the players to push their way through the dense support. Once the players were all safely off the pitch the presentation was made.

The gate receipts for the final amounted to £1,365 10s. Not quite as large as when City defeated Bolton in 1921 (£1,640 11s), but it was the second highest figure at the time. The competition, considering the strength of Lancashire football at the time, was still regarded as an important one.

Gallaher's Cigarettes.

Swansea's Deacon dribbles between Cookson and McCloy in City's 7-4 victory, 29th August 1927.

1923-1928 SUMMARY

Major Trophies Won: Second Division Champions 1927-28

Highest League Attendance: 62,994 Manchester United, 12/09/25 (often quoted as 66,000)

Highest Cup Attendance: 76,166 Cardiff City, 08/03/24 (FA Cup)

Secretary/Managers: 1912-24 Ernest Mangnall, 1924-25 David Ashworth, 1925-26 Committee led by Albert E Alexander & 1926-32 Peter Hodge

Seasonal Record:

Season	League	Posn	FA Cup	Other	Leading Scorer	Average Attendance
1923-24	FL Div1	11	Semi-Final		Barnes 20	27,400
1924-25	FL Div1	10	Rnd 1		Roberts 31	29,000
1925-26	FL Div1	21	Final		Browell & Roberts 21	32,000
1926-27	FL Div2	3	Rnd 3		Johnson 25	30,848
1927-28	FL Div2	Champions	Rnd 5		Roberts 20	37,468

1926 FA CUP RUN

R3	Corinthians	A	D	3-3
	Corinthians	H	W	4-0
R4	Huddersfield Town	H	W	4-0
R5	Crystal Palace	H	W	11-4
R6	Clapton Orient	A	W	6-1
SF	Manchester United	N*	W	3-0
F	Bolton Wanderers	N**	L	0-1

*= Bramall Lane ** = Wembley Stadium*

	P	W	D	L	F	A
HOME	3	3	0	0	19	4
AWAY	4	2	1	1	12	5
TOTAL	7	5	1	1	31	9

FINAL DETAILS

24 April 1926 at Wembley Stadium

Manchester City 0-1 Bolton Wanderers

CITY: Goodchild, Cookson, McCloy, Pringle, Cowan, McMullan, Austin, Browell, Roberts, Johnson, Hicks

BOLTON: Pym, Haworth, Greenhalgh, Nuttall, Seddon, Jennings, Butler, Jack, Smith (JR), Smith (J), Vizard

GOALS: Jack

ATTENDANCE: 91,447

REFEREE: J. Baker (Crewe)

MANAGER: Directors' committee, mainly vice-chairman Albert Alexander

CAPTAIN: McMullan

When Headachy take
Genasprin
The SAFE Brand

Sunday Dispatch

MARCH 4, 1934

THE ONLY WAY—CUP-TIE VERSION

ARTHUR THOMPSON, the "Sunday Dispatch" photographer, shows in this page of pictures the remarkable adaptability of the Cup-tie fan. These striking photographs were secured during his wanderings among—or behind—yesterday's record crowd of 84,569 at Maine-road, Manchester.

THE MATCH

"FROM A TUNNEL I saw minute headless players and spectators in many weird attitudes."

"HIS WHITE SCARF made an excellent foot support."

"A PRECARIOUS PERCH reminiscent of a pole-squatting record bid."

"NICELY BALANCED on a steel girder at the top of a 30ft. bank."

"TWO MEN ON A BRICK, and a girl's tight-rope act."

"HERE IS INGENUITY—It was only an old perambulator chassis, but it served."

ADVERTISER'S ANNOUNCEMENT

Whilst the nation sleeps....

MILTON
cleans millions of false teeth!

READ THESE TESTIMONIALS

"The cork that Milton performs while one is asleep is marvellous, making the dental plate, no matter how old, to look like new. I have also had excellent results from it when used as a gargle and mouthwash. To my mind, Milton leads all others."
D.V.

"Three months ago I started Milton, using half teaspoonful to tumbler of water, every night, and gradually the stains moved. Of course it took some little time as they were in a bad state, but to-day they are in the same clean state as the day when I received them from the dentist, in fact there is more shine on the gold plate than when it was new."
J.M.

Simply place your false teeth in a tumbler of water overnight—to which a little Milton has been added. Or else for thirty minutes in the morning. When you replace your set, it will be sweet and clean, fresh and free from all grease, film and dirt. Milton cleans immaculately—better than any effort with brushes can. It costs 6d.

"THIS FLEETING GLIMPSE of the ding-dong struggle I obtained by climbing on to a friend's shoulders."

Printed and Published by the ASSOCIATED NEWSPAPERS, LTD., at Northcliffe House and Carmelite House, Carmelite-street, E.C. 4, and Northcliffe House, Deansgate, Manchester 3, March 4, 1934.

1928-1934
Wild Success

"I think Brook played in every position for the Club – he certainly went in nets once – and was a very good player. When the goal went in it was marvellous. Nirvana. On the final whistle I didn't need to use my feet to leave I was wedged in a solid wall of human flesh and swept through the exit gate like a surfboarder."

Supporter Denis Houlston talking in 2003 about Eric Brook's goal in the 1934 FA Cup tie with Stoke which was watched by 84,569.

1928-1929 Johnson The Hero

Despite the success of the previous season, 1928-29 was always going to be testing season for Peter Hodge. He had introduced a number of players towards the end of the previous campaign and was still, very much, trying to build a side for the future. The opening game - a 4-1 defeat at Birmingham - gave Hodge a few headaches. For the following match, the Maine Road derby, Hodge made only one change to his line-up, selecting Frank Roberts instead of centre-forward Tommy Tait, signed the previous March.

Roberts put City ahead with a subtle but fast shot, in a game where United still seemed unable to come to terms with the relatively new offside law. Nevertheless,

United did manage to take the lead by half-time. A point which surprised many as City seemed to have most of the play, but their fire power was seriously lacking. In the second half, Tommy Johnson provided City's equalising goal, before a crowd of 61,007.

A run of good results throughout September gave fans much to cheer - especially the 6-2 defeat of reigning champions Everton at Goodison. Tommy Johnson scored five that day. A feat the Everton directors would remember when the time came to look for a player to support 'Dixie' Dean.

Johnson was idolised by supporters. Harry Hughes, who lived near Johnson in Gorton, remembered that although he was often seen in the Gorton area, he wasn't one for talking about his football: "He lived in Park

171

Avenue, the first house on the right, near Sunny Brow Park. I used to see him quite regularly pushing a pram and, if they'd be playing on the Saturday, he'd be pushing the pram in the morning all around the neighbourhood. You'd all go 'Hello, Tom', and he'd nod his head, and you'd then tell everyone that Tom speaks to you, y'know. Anyway, he was very dignified and always wore a big brimmed trilby - it quickly became very fashionable then! And he always walked with a very deliberate stride, pushing the pram. There was a Billiard Hall on Hyde Road and he used to go in there and get involved with the wrong set - bookies and the like - but it never really affected him. Never dishonest or anything like that. But they were a real rum lot these 'Smiths' I think they were called. Every time he went into the Billiard Hall they'd give him the best table out of the 30 odd there, and we used to go in after work just to watch. Learn a few shots and that.

"Then he'd go in the Plough Hotel on Hyde Road, which I also patronised at times. But unlike me, he never had to buy his own beer. All the toadies would buy it, they'd ask him what he was having and he always replied 'I'll have a draught Bass - a pint'. It was the best, most expensive beer in the house! They would ask him his prediction for the City game, and he always said 'I think we'll lose!' That was his stock answer, as if to say 'shut up, I don't want to talk about football'.

"I never ever mentioned football to him. I'd speak with him occasionally. Usually I'd chat with him at the bank - I was always drawing out, he was always paying in!"

With Johnson in fine scoring form, despite his regular pints of draught Bass, the Blues continued to win more than they lost, but the season was never going to see the Club challenge. In the Cup City were defeated 3-1 in the third round at Birmingham, thereby ending any chance of glory.

Tommy Johnson and Eric Brook.

At the season's end City finished in a creditable eighth place after an unbeaten run in their final eight games. They had also won the Manchester Cup again, this time defeating Bolton 2-0. Hodge had changed the side a few times during the season, with Bert Gray replaced in nets by Lewis Barber, signed from Halifax Town on 6th June 1927. New signings Billy Felton, a full back from Sheffield Wednesday, and Ernie Toseland, a winger from Coventry, were both regulars by the season's close.

Tommy Johnson established a City record of 38 League goals that season.

1929-1930 Supporter Backlash

Tommy Johnson was the star again during the early part of the 1929-30 season, especially at Old Trafford. Against United he scored the first, and would have scored the fourth had the referee not blown for time a second before the ball crossed the line. Nevertheless City's 3-1 October victory proved their dominance once more.

A few weeks after the derby a young Scottish player by the name of Matt Busby made his debut. Busby was about to emigrate with his mother to the USA when Peter Hodge persuaded him to sign in February 1928. His debut, against Middlesbrough, was the first of eleven appearances that season. Signed as an inside-forward, over the course of the next couple of years City would convert him to a stylish half-back.

Fine results followed the October derby, with City moving gradually up the table following an undefeated run of 12 games. Form dipped at Christmas, however. The Boxing Day match with Villa ended 2-1 and was followed by a 4-2 defeat at Burnley two days later.

A season ticket from 1928-29.

On New Year's Day, City competed in a match that even four decades later was still regarded as the greatest ever staged at Maine Road by some fans.

Supporter Joe Carley shared that view and even wrote about it in his diary, reproduced from *Old Friends, Old Times*. Carley wrote about the City-Sheffield Wednesday match: "I remember telling my father after the game that I had never seen a better one, and I don't believe I ever shall. Years later, Ernie Blenkinsop, famous Wednesday full-back, wrote his life story in 'Topical Times' and mentioned this particular game as the finest he had ever been in.

"The pitch was ankle deep in thick mud and, as I watched cameramen gingerly picking their way across it prior to the players' entry, I guessed we would see a real mud-larking match. All the players were roughly at the peak of their careers."

Carley went on: "The game was played at a great pace, but there was only one foul, committed by Seed on McMullan. The players shook hands self-consciously, and no more was the referee worried by 'dirty' play. The players waded through that mud with good open play, switching the point of their attacks about with great ingenuity and bringing their wing-men continually into action. Thrust and counter-thrust. Skill versus skill. I'm sure many of the spectators must have been quite hoarse before one quarter of the match had run its course.

"The speed with which the moves were made on that churned-up mud heap was amazing. Wednesday were the first to draw blood, Allen galloping through to score with a great drive taken on the run. Then came the incident which caused much controversy at the time. McMullan had run through in his own inimitable fashion, shaped to pass out to Brook, and as Walker swerved to intercept the 'pass', Jimmy calmly flicked the ball inwards for Tait to race through and smash into the net as Brown came out and flung himself at the centre-forward's feet. "GOAL!" The crowd's yell was changed to one of indignation as the referee disallowed it on the grounds of offside against Tait.

"Brown was still lying face downwards after his vain attempt to prevent Tait from shooting, and when the players picked him up his face was a mass of blood where Tait's boot had evidently caught the goalkeeper's head as the ball was driven home. A stretcher was summoned, a bandage tied round the unconscious goalkeeper's forehead, and Blenkinsop went into goal. As the stretcher party approached the stand, Brown recovered, looked feebly around, sat up, slipped off the stretcher, and before anyone could stop him he was ambling back to his goal. He staggered like a drunken man, obviously hurt and weak, but he insisted on playing, and certainly helped to provide some further thrills in that hectic afternoon by his daring and clever goalkeeping.

"Shortly before half time, Mark Hooper crossed a high ball for Rimmer to head over Ridley and past Barber into the far corner of the net. City's fans were dismayed, and in spite of the interesting, clever game, a little glum. Twenty minutes after the interval they were even more despondent, for Seed headed another great Hooper centre into the net from close range. 3-0! So the score stood when only 15 minutes of play remained. Then Bobby Marshall wiped off one of the arrears. Five minutes later, with about 8 Wednesday men crowded into their own penalty area, Walker handled the ball. Penalty! Eric Brook, the young City winger drove a powerful shot past Brown. 3-2. How the crowd yelled!

"McMullan had the ball 18 yards from goal and at a bad angle; there was no City player suitably placed. In front of him half a dozen Wednesday players, almost shoulder to shoulder, barred the way. The wily Jimmy put his toe under the heavy, mud-laden ball and calmly lobbed it high over the heads of the astounded defenders to drop into the net by the far post! 3-3.

"The roar when City equalised was great enough to waken my father from his afternoon nap at South Street! Not yet satisfied, City again swept down on the Wednesday defence while the referee looked meaningfully at his watch. Matt Barrass fired in a tremendous drive from 35 yards, knocking the bandaged Brown into the back of the net, but not before the goalkeeper managed to divert the ball over the crossbar. "Corner!" yelled the frenzied crowd. The corner kick was never taken; a long blast on the referee's whistle signalled the end of the game."

The 3-3 draw was followed by a 2-2 against Sunderland on 4th January, and then the Blues faced Tottenham in the FA Cup. Ultimately, City progressed to the fifth round after victory in a replay over Spurs (4-1) and a highly impressive 10-1 mauling of Swindon after another draw.

An advert in the City-Everton programme for travel to Maine Road's nearest station for the 8th February 1930 Manchester derby.

L·N·E·R

CITY
to
UNITED

On Saturday, 8th February

SPECIAL EXCURSION
TO

FALLOWFIELD

		RETURN FARE	
STALYBRIDGE	Dept. 2-5 p.m.	,,	1/-
ASHTON (P.P.)	,, 2-8	,,	10d.
DUKINFIELD	,, 2-10	,,	10d.
GUIDE BRIDGE	,, 2-13	,,	8d.
HYDE ROAD	,, 2-20	,,	5d.
LEVENSHULME	,, 2-25	,,	2d.

Passengers return same day from Fallowfield at 5-15 p.m.

Further particulars from L.N.E.R Stations, Offices and Agencies.

BOOK IN ADVANCE

In the fifth round tie with Second Division strugglers Hull, City failed to perform and paid the price with a 2-1 home defeat before 61,574. City needed to pick themselves up if they wanted to maintain their challenge for the League.

In March, Tommy Johnson was sold by Peter Hodge to Everton for £6,000. The move shocked and angered most supporters. They were not the only ones upset. Alan Johnson, Tommy's son, explained in 2004: "The day he was told he was leaving he was absolutely stunned. He had no idea he was going to leave and he certainly didn't ask to go. We lived in Park Avenue, Gorton, at the time and he didn't want to go, but he had met Dixie Dean, the great Everton star, a few times and, because of Dixie, he felt that if he had to go somewhere it was better to go where he knew someone."

Johnson had been the Club's biggest star for a decade. He had broken all City's goalscoring records - not only did he score more goals in a season than any other player, he was also the Blues' highest overall goalscorer with 166 goals until Eric Brook surpassed his figure.

Hodge tried to silence fans by pointing out that Tommy Tait was in fine form, but the fans would have none of it. Supporters worried that their chance of title success had been scuppered.

Without Johnson, the Blues did achieve a few decent results in March and April, but it wasn't enough to win the title. City ended the season third, 13 points behind champions Sheffield Wednesday. That would normally be quite satisfactory, but after the transfer of Johnson, and the failure in the Cup, supporters felt let down. Selling the Club's brightest star was not something fans would tolerate.

1930-1931

The 1930-31 season did little to convince supporters that Hodge's transfer of Johnson had been right, especially as Tait left for Bolton in November. Another forward, Fred Tilson, struggled with injury, and City failed to score as often as normal. In fact the final tally of 75 helped fuel criticism. Eric Brook, on the wing was the season's top scorer with sixteen, while David Halliday, a November signing from Arsenal, was second after scoring fourteen.

Alongside this supporter anger at Johnson's sale was evident. Club officials had assumed the player would soon be forgotten, but a careful review of attendance figures for the period suggest his departure to Second Division Everton had a detrimental impact on support. During the late 1920s City had at times been the best supported side in the entire League. In 1929-30 they attracted the third highest League average (33,339), but the following season – the first without Tommy – they dropped to fifth position with an average of 26,849. This was the Club's lowest for eight years.

As with the sale of Trevor Francis in 1982 and Shaun Wright-Phillips in 2005, short term monetary gain had a detrimental longer term impact.

Supporter dissatisfaction was a relatively new phenomenon at Maine Road, and even in 1930 it did not reach the levels that perhaps it would have done in later years. Had the Blues been the least successful Manchester side at this point then supporters may have been much more vocal in their criticism, however City did still retain the local bragging rights. In the derbies, the Blues achieved a 4-1 victory at Maine Road and a 3-1 win at Old Trafford. United were eventually relegated, but that was only part of their problem as their financial

City 1930-31. Jimmy McMullan has the ball.

situation was dire, prompting many to suggest that the February derby match might be the last ever as United were to go out of business in the summer. Crowds were down to the low thousands with games against Leicester and Middlesbrough attracting less than four thousand. City supporters felt genuinely sorry for their poor relations, but perhaps relegation would give United a new lease of life, as it had City.

In the mid-90s Harry Hughes remembered the state of United at the time: "I worked in Trafford Park then, and all the locals were United fans. I was working nights and when Saturday morning arrived a couple of them asked 'are you going to see the Rags today?' I didn't know what they meant, and then they explained that United fans had started to call the team the 'Rags' because they were so poor that their kit looked like rags. So after that I knew who they meant, but when I mentioned the Rags, they'd go, 'who the Hell are you talking about?' They didn't like the opposition saying it."

City ended that season in eighth place.

1931-1932 A Minute To Go

During 1931 the Blues embarked on the second phase of their original plan to enlarge the stadium. Maine Road was still regarded as the best club ground, however the directors were still keen to see the venue improve further. Architect Charles Swain's plan saw the corner between the Main Stand and the open Platt Lane end re-profiled with deeper stepped terracing, and a roof installed. New ladies toilets were added to the stand, while bench seating to house 950 was installed on the section closest to the Main Stand. The rest of the corner provided covered terraced accommodation for 6,830.

The provision of covered terracing proved very popular and on 26th August, three days before the opening game, the Club announced: "The new extension to the stand will be ready and those who desire to use it will transfer when they have paid to get into the ground. They will pay a shilling (5p) extra for a seat and 6d (2.5p) for the standing accommodation under cover."

The improvements did not stretch to matters on the pitch however. Although it should be stressed that Hodge had been able to field a consistent eleven for much of the season. Len Langford, signed from Nottingham Forest in June 1930, was first choice 'keeper. Toseland, Marshall, Halliday, Tilson, and Brook provided the attack, while the young Matt Busby was now playing wing-half. A year earlier, United had tried to sign Busby with Peter Hodge allegedly saying "Give me £150 and he's yours." The reply came back that United didn't even have 150 pennies, never mind pounds.

City ended the League campaign in fourteenth position, but it was in the Cup where Hodge's real hopes lay. In the third round at Millwall City, wearing scarlet shirts, conceded a first minute goal. Then two goals from David Halliday gave them the lead, but it wasn't to last as Millwall were awarded a rather dubious penalty. Naturally, they levelled and then in the dying seconds Ernie Toseland provided a vital last minute winner.

Brentford were the visitors in the fourth round when Fred Tilson scored a hat-trick in the 6-1 demolition before 56,190. City certainly knew how to pull in the crowds. In the next round Derby County arrived at Maine Road feeling confident, but were sent home smarting after suffering a 3-0 defeat at the hands of Marshall (2) and Brook. Again the crowd was huge - 62,641 - as City continued their reputation as one of England's best supported clubs.

The quarter-finals produced an all-Lancashire tie with City travelling to Bury. The first half belonged to the Blues as the goals piled in, but shortly after half-time with the score 4-0, Bury fought back. Somehow City managed to hang on as Bury brought the score to 4-3 and continued to pressure. Fortunately, the Blues survived and entered the semi-finals for the third time in eight years.

The Blues' semi-final opponents were to be Arsenal, one of the decade's strongest sides, at Villa Park. It was a game City dominated, yet failed to find the net. The Blues frequently surged forward but they just could not score, while Alex James provided Arsenal with their first chance of the game when his shot was cleared off the line by defender Billy Felton. Sadly, Felton was to have a part to play in Arsenal's only other chance of the game when, in the last minute, Arsenal's centre-forward Lambert took the ball from his feet and sent it across the goal.

The *Manchester Guardian* described what happened next: "Bastin shot, Langford fisted at the ball, it went straight up into the air, hit the cross-bar, dropped back on the line, bounced against the post - and even the spin was in Arsenal's favour, for it broke into instead of away from the net...Lambert and Bastin hugged each other like a family reunion...McMullan stood dumbfounded like some great engineer whose life's masterpiece had been demolished by a paroxysm of nature."

Under the title "A Golden Goal By Bastin" the tie was filmed by Pathe News and shown in cinemas across Britain that week.

The whole of the City team were shocked by what had occurred. Arsenal had been lucky, a tag that seemed to stick with the London club for most of the next three decades, and had not deserved their place at Wembley. Nevertheless City only had themselves to blame. Felton should not have allowed the ball to be taken from him so easily, while the forwards should have converted at least one of the many chances that came their way.

Unfortunately, after three years with the Blues,

Felton was made the scapegoat and was transferred to Tottenham immediately, making his debut the following Saturday away at Swansea Town. After a further two years with Spurs he transferred to Altrincham, and died in the Manchester area on 22nd April 1977 at the age of 76.

Another man to leave in the aftermath of the FA Cup semi-final was Peter Hodge. The City boss had been tempted back to his old club Leicester City who were perilously close to relegation. They had offered Hodge a five year contract and an improved salary, but it had been agreed that Hodge would remain in Manchester until City's FA Cup run came to an end. The manager had announced his return to Filbert Street on 15th February 1932 – almost a month before the FA Cup defeat.

Managerial uncertainty must have had a bearing on the Blues' performances during that period.

It is believed Hodge formally began working at Leicester on Tuesday 15th March after clearing his office at Maine Road in the aftermath of the Arsenal defeat. Wilf Wild, the assistant at Maine Road since 1920, reluctantly took full control of team matters. He was an advocate of splitting the role into two - one purely secretarial/administration duties, the other team management. Though he never quite succeeded to split the role during his time in charge at Maine Road, he did move some of the administration away.

1932-1933 The Number Game

The 1932-33 season was expected to be a difficult one for Wild. He had worked closely with Hodge throughout the previous six years and knew how the former manager had been planning for the future. Many of Wild's first moves seemed to match those of his predecessor, and there was no need for dramatic rebuilding. However, Wild was his own man, and his approach ensured a fine first season.

The Blues finished sixteenth in the League, but for the second year running it was the FA Cup that brought most joy to Manchester. In the third round away at Gateshead, City survived the mud to end the game 1-1 thanks to Toseland. The replay, the following Wednesday banished all thoughts of failure as the Blues swept aside Gateshead 9-0. They'd been leading 8-0 after 63 minutes but, despite calls from the crowd for more, settled for single figures.

The fourth round brought Walsall to Maine Road to endure a 2-0 defeat thanks to Eric Brook, before 52,085 spectators. Then the fifth round draw

sent City to old cup adversaries Bolton. A Burnden Park crowd of 69,920 witnessed a Brook hat-trick and a fourth from Tilson as the Blues overcame the Wanderers 4-2. This remains Bolton's record home crowd and some believe helped inspire artist – and City fan – LS Lowry's "Going To The Match", painted in 1952.

New signing Alec Herd, from Hamilton Academicals, was now appearing as an inside-forward. His arrival guaranteed competition for places.

The quarter-final sent the Blues on another trip across Lancashire, this time to Burnley where a single goal from Fred Tilson was enough to put City into the semi-final again. This time the opponents were hot favourites Derby County at Leeds Road before a crowd of almost 52,000. The first period was extremely difficult as Derby missed a couple of easy chances, while the Blues struggled to find their feet. When they did they had the edge in a closely fought game.

Eric Brook was the main architect providing the opportunity for the game's first two goals. He centred to right-winger Toseland for the first and, in the second half, lobbed beautifully for Tilson to charge between two Derby defenders and head the second. Captain Jimmy McMullan, playing at inside-left to retain his place, provided the third by wriggling past two defenders and the 'keeper before shooting the ball into the net in the 70th minute.

Within a minute Derby had caught Langford off his line, and pulled a goal back. The Rams now had the initiative and with three minutes remaining they scored a second. City managed to hang on though, and the game ended 3-2, sending the Blues to Wembley for the second time in seven years.

City's opponents would be Everton, who overcame

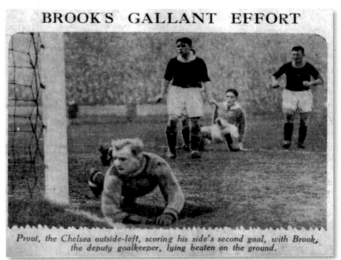

BROOK'S GALLANT EFFORT

Prout, the Chelsea outside-left, scoring his side's second goal, with Brook, the deputy goalkeeper, lying beaten on the ground.

A goalkeeping emergency caused forward Eric Brook to take over in nets as the Blues faced Chelsea in 1932-33.

Fred Tilson netted the only goal of the victory over Sheffield United on 22nd March 1933.

West Ham 2-1 at Molineux. The Blues were determined to bring the cup back to Manchester but everybody knew it was going to be a tough task, especially as Everton had a number of famous, star players - Sagar, Cresswell, Britton, Geldard, Dean, and of course the former City hero Tommy Johnson. Still, City were capable of good performances and at Wembley the two sides would start as equals for the first ever tie between them.

Before the final the question of team colours had to be addressed as both sides traditionally play in blue. In the end both sides changed - Everton wore white while City chose scarlet. City's choice of colour seemed to encourage their supporters who, perhaps, remembered its time as 'lucky scarlet' during 1923-24's FA Cup run. Fans donned red and white hats and scarves and one newspaper commented on the dominance of the colour on the railway specials heading off to Wembley. Ever

since the cup run of 1924, and potentially before that, City tended to adopt either scarlet or more usually maroon as their change strip.

On the morning of the final Wilf Wild, after consultation with Chairman Albert Hughes and Dr. Holmes, shocked supporters and the media by announcing that Fred Tilson was to be dropped from the side. Tilson had been suffering from a mysterious injury to a leg nerve and, although he passed a fitness test, his doctor noticed him wince when his leg was touched in a certain place. Much to the annoyance of the other players, Wild decided he could not risk the centre-forward and so brought Bobby Marshall in at inside-right and moved Herd into the centre.

From the spectators' point of view, one point of good cheer came when the morning's papers announced that the Wembley caterers had altered their menu to take account of the fact that there would be so many Lancastrians in attendance. A spokesman stated that people from the south of England prefer sandwiches, while those from the north prefer meat pies! Wembley increased their order of pies from 14,000 to 17,000, while the number of sandwiches had been reduced in proportion. With their meat pies in their hands, both sets of supporters eagerly awaited the arrival of the two teams.

Fans at the 1933 FA Cup semi-final against Derby.

The 1933 team as depicted in the FA Cup final programme.

R. Marshall is Reserve for Tilson.

City captain Sam Cowan led out his side alongside Dixie Dean of Everton and, together with Jimmy McMullan, spent much of his time trying to calm the nerves of the other City men. The sides were lined up and presented to the Duke of York, who was deputising for his ill father. Interestingly, accompanying the Duke for her first final was his wife, Elizabeth, the mother of Queen Elizabeth II, who also attended the 1981 Cup final.

Within fifteen seconds of the start, City made the first assault with a high centre being caught by the Everton 'keeper Sagar. The save seemed to settle Everton while the Mancunians seemed to suffer from stage fright as they had for the opening period seven years earlier. Cowan and McMullan tried to steady the side, but it was difficult, especially as Cowan began to take on too much.

CUP FINAL PLAYERS TO BE NUMBERED

It was decided yesterday that the clubs competing in the F.A. Cup final at Wembley on April 29 be requested to number their players for that game.

The Everton representatives will be numbered from one to eleven in black on white shirts. The Manchester City men will wear white numbers from 12 to 22 on their scarlet shirts.

The *Daily Mail* noted that: "He was torn between a determination not to leave Dean and a desire to help his forwards. He broke down between the two."

Langford, in the City net, was also struggling. First with nerves, then with the strong sunlight. Every time a high ball came across he appeared blinded by the sun. Corner-kicks brought most concern, especially when Everton realised his predicament. After forty minutes a long centre from Britton forced Langford to look skyward. With Dean close in attendance the City 'keeper tried to keep one eye on the ball and one on the bustling forward. The sun caused the 'keeper to miss the ball, with Dean threatening to charge. The ball landed at Stein's feet and the Everton man simply tapped it in.

Seven minutes after the interval, a similar move caught Langford out again. Britton lobbed the ball into the centre, the 'keeper again considered Dean and the ball. As he tried to catch the ball below the crossbar, Dean barged into him and both players and the ball ended up in the net. Everton were 2-0 up, and City seemed totally out of it.

Ten minutes from time Everton's Geldard placed a corner kick perfectly for Dunn to head a spectacular third goal.

City did have a few exciting moments of their

Sam Cowan introduces the Duke of York to Matt Busby at the 1933 FA Cup final.

Manchester's complete inability to reproduce more than a shadow of the form that had earned them the right to play at Wembley? When are we to see real football in a Cup Final?

"The answer to the first question is Nerves. Wembley gripped and shook Manchester City - as it has done other teams - and reduced them to impotence. Only when - and if - these Cup Final Nerves can be eradicated can there be a hope of playing real football at Wembley."

Sam Cowan's thoughts had already moved forward a year, and the time was now right for all connected with City to learn from their mistakes. If they could find a way of overcoming their nerves, then maybe the *Daily Mail* would see real football played by a classy team. City wanted another chance.

own, but in reality they were never really in the game. Langford made a few saves - it could easily have been four or more - while City's defence failed to help their under pressure 'keeper. The *Daily Mail* gave a truthful assessment: "Cann's efforts were of a negative kind, his kicking a matter of wild conjecture. Dale was more timely in his tackles, but he and his partner had no understanding, and their work was flurried and hesitating.

"Busby made a man's job of it at right half. Cowan was too ambitious and attempted too much. Toseland clung to the idea of following the touchline and the cool and calculating Cresswell was never at a loss in dealing with him. Brook strove in spasms - very good work in making ground, unaccountable lapses in finishing."

And so it was Dixie Dean who went up to receive the Cup from the Duke of York, while the optimistic Sam Cowan started telling anybody who cared to listen that City would be back the following year to win the Cup. He tried to boost morale to the rest of the disconsolate team. The *Daily Mail* reporter noticed: "As Dean triumphantly held the Cup aloft for all to see, a little knot of men moved slowly, almost disconsolately, across the turf not fifty yards away from the celebrations. They were the Manchester players.

"Not for them the cheers and fetings and a line writ large in the record books. Only the torturing thoughts of the Might-Have Been. Watching them, it was impossible to avoid asking two questions: What was the cause of

1933-1934
Record Crowds And Wembley Glory

Sam Cowan's remarks that City would be back to win the Cup gave the Club a little lift in the months following Wembley. Probably exactly what he intended, but it is doubtful whether he really expected the 1933-34 season to be significantly better than in 1932-33, but it was.. In the League, City achieved fifth place, while the Cup run not only took them to Wembley, but saw the Club break many attendance records.

The League programme commenced with a disappointing 3-2 defeat at home to Sheffield Wednesday. Although still with the Club, full back Syd Cann had been replaced by Laurie Barnett, who had made infrequent appearances since Wild took control of the team. Matt Busby's uncle, Jimmy McMullan, had taken the opportunity to move to Oldham as player-manager following the 1933 Cup Final. He had been in tears at the final whistle, realising that after over seven years with the Blues, his City career would end as it began with a loser's medal at Wembley. Immediately on moving to Oldham he signed goalkeeper Fred Swift, elder brother of a young 'keeper called Frank who had paid to watch the 1933 final.

A midweek crowd of 68,614 watched the Blues beat Sheffield Wednesday 2-0 on 21st February 1934.

Nineteen year old Frank Swift's City chance came at Christmas, following a rather surprising 8-0 thrashing at Wolves. Wilf Wild telephoned him on Christmas Eve telling the young 'keeper that he was to keep goal away to Derby the following day. Amazingly, Swift was not even a regular in the reserves at this point, spending most of his time as City's A team 'keeper. The result of his debut game was not a great deal better than the Wolves match - the Blues went down 4-1 - but he had done enough to retain his place, despite admitting he was to blame for two of the goals. The following day he celebrated his twentieth birthday with a 2-0 victory in the Derby return match at Maine Road.

On New Year's Day City suffered another large defeat. The Blues had been leading 2-0 at home to West Bromwich Albion when wing-half Jackie Bray was stretchered off. The rain started coming down in torrents, and City quickly lost their way. Albion went on a goalscoring spree, winning 7-2 by the close. Young Swift was convinced he had blown his chance of becoming the permanent 'keeper. He went home miserable and spent the evening and most of the night going through the details of every goal, looking for mistakes, with his

brother Fred. Fortunately for Swift, Len Langford the regular 'keeper remained out of action with a knee injury, and the only other player available, Nicholls, had been the man who'd conceded eight against Wolves. Swift retained his place.

A 1-1 draw with Leicester followed before the FA Cup run commenced with a home tie against Blackburn. The opening fifteen minutes saw a midfield stalemate, then a Blackburn forward broke through City's defence and made his way to goal. Swift, a little nervous, dived too soon but without knowing how he did it, the 'keeper managed to save the ball. The crowd believed it to be a fantastic reaction save, but Swift rather innocently admitted that he'd made a mistake and that it was merely a chance save.

Regardless of how the save had occurred, it seemed to give the young man a lot of confidence, and from that moment on he seemed to stop more or less everything that came his way. The game ended 3-1 thanks to goals from Toseland (2) and Brook, to send City into the fourth round.

For the second time in five years the Blues were drawn against Hull City, hoping that this time

Manchester's men would get it right. With goals from Herd and Brook the Blues felt comfortable, especially with the score at 2-1 with five minutes to go, but incredibly confusion between Swift and Dale allowed Hull to tap in the equaliser. City could not believe it, but at least they had survived and were now able to bring Hull back to Maine Road for what everybody hoped would be a massacre.

In the replay the Blues defeated Hull 4-1, and looked forward to their next tie away to Sheffield Wednesday on 17th February.

City's huge pulling power at this time guaranteed enormous attendances wherever they played and the fifth round tie at Hillsborough was no exception as City set the ground's attendance record. 72,841 (receipts £5,566) crammed into Wednesday's ground to see what everybody hoped would be a tremendous match, although the attendance was perhaps too much for the venue.

City fan Joe Carley entered his version of the day's events in his diary, starting with his arrival at London Road Railway Station: "I fought my way into a carriage as the train drew in. I say 'fought' because of the crowds that struggled to board the train. I secured a seat in a corridor coach, but the crowds still streamed through the door and overflowed into the passage, which soon became jammed. It was a most unpleasant journey. All I could see was the navy-blue waistcoat of some fellow pushed in front of me, and who leaned on the luggage rack above my head throughout the journey. Just after we started another standing passenger made an effort to divest himself of his overcoat in order to make a little more room, but so tightly packed was the crowd that he only managed to get it off half-way, and had to travel to Sheffield in

W. DALE,
Manchester City F.C.   TOPICAL TIMES.

that condition, being unable to get it either on or off.

"At the ground I joined the queue at one of the 2 shilling turnstiles (the popular side being almost completely filled), and rumours were rife that the gates were being closed. I pushed in with the crowd, paid my two bob, one other person was allowed in after me and then, no more!

"Things were not very comfortable in some parts of the ground and ambulancemen were kept busy. Just before the teams came out a stretcher party passed bearing the blanketed figure of a man killed in the crush."

As with the games at Hyde Road in the early 1920s, few seemed concerned with safety. Hundreds were injured and, as he waited to take his place on the field, the distressed Frank Swift witnessed much of what Joe Carley had seen: "After we had changed, and were ready for the field, we found that the narrow tunnel from the dressing room to the pitch was blocked by ambulance men tending groaning casualties. After forcing my way through with the other players, I had to stand aside to let pass a stretcher bearing a man crushed to death against the railings on the Spion Kop."

It took football another sixty years and a much greater incident at Hillsborough to learn from simple, basic mistakes. All that mattered was the game itself.

Understandably, the early play was not great. Both sets of players made mistakes, but for City a simple miss-kick by Cowan allowed Wednesday's Dewar to nip in and pass the ball to Rimmer to score. Midway through the half Wild's side fought back. Alec Herd received a short pass from a McLuckie free kick, dribbled a considerable length up field, confusing the Wednesday

GROSVENOR HOTEL
DEANSGATE · Facing Victoria and Exchange Stations · MANCHESTER
100 BEDROOMS, RUNNING HOT & COLD WATER IN EACH.
BANQUETS, WEDDING BREAKFASTS, Etc. Catered for.
Blackfriars 7024 (3 lines).   Proprietor: GEORGE HARDMAN.

MANCHESTER CITY F.C. LTD.
BLUE AND WHITE
OFFICIAL PROGRAMME
Vol. 28 No. 31.   March 3rd.   Entered at (Stationers Hall)   TWOPENCE.

PLAY FOR SAFETY!

BEGIN to-day to save for the future. It will be your best defence against life's handicaps. You can open an account with The Manchester & Salford Savings Bank with as small a sum as one shilling.

You can get good interest on the money you save, and your savings are SAFE, for all funds are invested under Government supervision.

Open daily at usual Banking Hours 10—3.
Also on Monday and Friday evenings.
55 branches in Manchester, Salford and district.

MANCHESTER & SALFORD SAVINGS BANK
Head Office:
Booth Street, Albert Square, Manchester.

THE BEST GUIDE TO RACING:
Empire News
RACING HANDBOOK
On Sale Everywhere—Price 2d.

Daily Dispatch

THE NATIONAL NEWSPAPER OF THE NORTH.
MONDAY MARCH 5, 1934

Meet Spring in Radiant Health
1,000
MEDICAL HINT
On Sale Everywhere

THE WAY TO WEMBLEY
BROOK'S AMAZING SHOT BEAT STOKE

STOP PRESS NEWS

Eric Brook, player in the distance closest to the stand, scored an amazing goal in front of 84,569.

defence as he went. Then, about twenty-five yards out, he had a crack at goal, and scored the equaliser.

Early in the second half Dewar gave Wednesday the lead, but it wasn't to last as, twenty-five minutes from time, Alec Herd scored his second of the match and set up a replay for the following Wednesday afternoon.

With thousands taking the afternoon off work, City attracted the incredible attendance of 68,614. Those Mancunians that risked their jobs to attend the game felt it was worth it as City won the match 2-0 with two long range efforts. For the first Fred Tilson waited for the ball to bounce in front of Wednesday's centre-half Millership, then he nipped round the player with the ball and sent a fine effort crashing into the net. The second came from Bobby Marshall who headed in a forty yard free kick taken by Dale.

City were into the quarter-finals again. This time they would face Stoke City - with a young Stanley Matthews in their side - at Maine Road for a game everybody wanted to see. Harry Hughes remembered leaving work early to find a space on the vast terracing: "We went straight from work. There was a gang of us, and I had a cap on. We probably all did. Anyway, I stood with my back to a barrier and I thought I'd be alright. I knew it would be a good crowd but as it filled up I was moved around and couldn't control where I was going. I soon realised that I was behind a barrier with my chest being pushed in - not the best place to be in a huge

crowd. So I decided to duck down under the barrier and come up the other side. As I rose I discovered that I'd come up between a man and his wife or girlfriend and he looked at me in wonderment. Totally astonished that I should have appeared as if by magic between him and his wife. I managed to drop my cap over my eyes and move off before I got myself into trouble!"

The official attendance that day was 84,569 - the largest ever crowd in the provinces and to this day the record for any club fixture. Many supporters had travelled from Stoke and they mingled with City's support on the Popular Side (Kippax). Again, the huge crowd brought a few problems. At least one barrier collapsed and a few supporters were injured, but in the main the worst problem seemed to be actually seeing the action. For much of the game supporters jostled for position, causing many to claim that the attendance was simply too large, but the City management claimed it could have been greater, despite being forced by the police to close the gates some twenty minutes before the game was due to start.

During the game itself, City had a difficult start as Stoke kept them under pressure for most of the first half. It wasn't to be the visitors' day, however, as Eric Brook received a wide pass well out on the wing and raced for the corner flag. Brook then made a speculative lob from the wing, which seemed to change direction in mid-flight. The Stoke 'keeper Roy John appeared to have it

Fred Tilson scores City sixth and his fourth as Aston Villa were defeated 6-1 in the 1934 FA Cup semi-final.

covered, jumped up and somehow missed it as it curled past the 'keeper and into the net for the only goal of the match.

Supporter Fran Parker saw enough of the goal to realise it was something special: "I saw Brooky on the wing and he kicked the ball and it seemed to twist. I don't know how, but it did, and when it went in I closed my eyes tight. It was a great feeling and I was so excited at seeing such an amazing goal!"

Afterwards some claimed the goal had not been an intentional shot but Fran Parker disagreed: "He was a great player. He played for England, and was one of our biggest stars. He knew what he was doing. From where I sat on the edge of the pitch it was as clear as day that he had shot at goal. He may have been on the touchline himself, but goalscorers like that look for openings all the time. Most players probably wouldn't have been able to score it, but Brooky was different."

In the last minute Stoke were awarded a corner and, with everybody bar the 'keeper up field, the Blues really felt the pressure. Swift's vision was blocked for a while as everybody's head went up. Arthur Turner, Stoke's centre-half, was the one to make contact, but fortunately his attempt sent the ball a fraction over the bar. A few seconds later the whistle went and City were into the semi-final for the third consecutive season.

The semi-final took the Blues to Leeds Road, Huddersfield again. This time for a meeting with Aston Villa on a wet and windy day. Villa were favourites for the

cup but City, remembering Cowan's comments following the previous final, were determined to return to Wembley, and quickly set about attacking the Villa goal. Toseland was the first to score for the Blues with a terrific shot past Villa's Morton. Frank Swift in City's net found life a little difficult as Villa immediately tried to level matters but, after 34 minutes Fred Tilson fired in City's second despite the close attention of a Villa defender.

Within a minute Alec Herd added a third, and then almost immediately Tilson banged in City's fourth. Three goals in five minutes had really killed off any hopes Villa

A 1934 London Underground poster advertising the FA Cup final. At that stage they did not know what teams would be appearing in the final.

had of reaching Wembley while Sam Cowan was able to enjoy the half-time break in the knowledge that, barring a major turnaround, his prediction was to come true.

Midway through the second half Fred Tilson added a couple more. Four minutes from time Astley provided Villa with a consolation goal, although one report suggested the City defenders were too bored to tackle him. The game ended 6-1 and despite early pressure from Villa, the Blues made it comfortably into their second consecutive Wembley final. This time they would face Portsmouth - the team that had caused so much promotion heartache in 1927.

In preparation for Wembley, City spent a week at the Palace Hotel, Birkdale, Southport. By co-incidence Portsmouth had preliminary booked the same hotel prior to the semi-final. On hearing that City had no intention of moving elsewhere, the Portsmouth directors chose to cancel their Southport break and look elsewhere. The first battle had been won.

In addition to the first eleven, City took a number of reserves to Southport, including Len Langford. At first this troubled Swift as he was convinced Langford's experience the previous year would give him the edge. Fortunately for Swift there was no question of the young 'keeper being displaced and Langford went to Southport with the intention of helping his colleague prepare.

Another man determined to calm the young Swift was captain Sam Cowan. On the eve of the Cup Final, at their hotel on the edge of Epping Forest the two men shared a room and Cowan did all he could to keep Swift's mind off the final. They talked for hours about everything but football, while Cowan bathed a septic toe he had managed to keep from Wilf Wild and the other club officials. The following morning Cowan allowed Swift to sleep in until 11am, then he took him for a walk away from the media attention and the fans who had gathered at the front of the hotel.

In the press all stories seemed to centre around the players' nerves. If City could overcome them, stressed the *Manchester Evening News*, then the Cup would come to Manchester. As with the 1926 final, many supporters

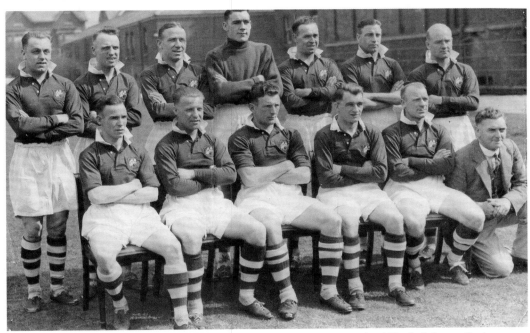

The 1934 team. Back: Tilson, Dale, Busby, Swift, Barnett, Bray & McLuckie. Front: Toseland, Marshall, Cowan, Herd, Brook & Bell (trainer).

arrived without tickets and, once again, challenged the ticket touts who were selling stand tickets for three times face value. A few scuffles broke out but the Evening News claimed it was all good natured.

There were a few incidents that brought sadness to the final, however. A number of coaches had arrived at Leicester Square fairly early in the morning to allow the City fans to spend a morning sightseeing before the final. One supporter, Joseph McGuinness from Simpson Street off Rochdale Road, Manchester, had left his coach to have a look around when another arriving from Manchester hit and killed him. On another journey Mr. John Crossen, a director of Glentoran F.C., had a seizure on the train and died before reaching the capital.

Despite the sad news, generally the City followers were in good spirit. They kidnapped a sailor in Trafalgar Square, believing him to be a Portsmouth follower, and made him climb onto the plinth of Nelson's Column. Once he was up there he defiantly stated that "Pompey will win" before jumping down and disappearing in the crowd.

Other interesting snippets from the newspapers centred around the opening of a new Royal Box, closer to the pitch, and the negotiations between the FA and the film companies. The FA demanded £700 for the rights to film the game while the film companies claimed this was excessive. On the morning of the match, film company officials were caught trying to hide cameras in the most

unlikely places. One intended arriving at Wembley with a camera inside a dummy figure of a sailor, pretending it to be a Portsmouth mascot. Most of the surviving footage of the final comes from the terraces and stands.

In the dressing room, Cowan tried to calm everybody's nerves. By request Eric Brook sang his favourite song, while Alec Herd sat quietly in a corner reading an Edgar Wallace thriller. Frank Swift started to feel the pressure and so trainer Alec Bell dragged him into the washroom, slapped his face and gave him a glass of whisky. In the Portsmouth dressing room, comedian Bud Flanagan entertained City's opponents.

When the time came, City made their way into the tunnel. Once there one of the players noticed that Alec Herd was missing. Alec Bell re-entered the dressing room to find his namesake still reading his thriller, totally at ease.

Wearing maroon, City took the field to a deafening roar. The teams were lined up in front of the new Royal Box and, following the National Anthem, King George V was introduced first to Portsmouth in white shirts, then City.

After the introductions and the kick about referee Stanley Rous, who had been a linesman for the 1926 final, took the captains to the centre for the toss. Portsmouth won the toss and selected ends, then Tilson started the game. Immediately he sent the ball to Toseland and the Mancunians managed their first attack, although it was never really likely to come to anything. Mixed play followed with Portsmouth's first dangerous move bringing an early test for the youthful Swift. Portsmouth were awarded a free kick a yard outside the box after Bray had brought down Worrall. Nicholl took the kick, but fired straight at Swift. Coolly the 'keeper saved just under the bar and then proceeded to send a long kick up field for a City attack.

City failed to keep the ball and Portsmouth were quickly back on the attack. Busby handled, and Portsmouth took another free kick close to the box. Again this was cleared, but the pressure continued.

Gradually City found their own way towards goal and performed a couple of interesting moves before Alec Herd was cynically bowled over by a Portsmouth defender. City fans and neutrals immediately started booing, something so uncommon at the time that the press made comment in most 'papers. Herd was stretchered off, clutching his right leg. A minute later the booing returned as Toseland was fouled. Fans were far from happy with this type of play in a cup final.

Busby took the free kick, but fired over the bar. Just then Herd returned to the field to a fantastic reception, causing the *Manchester Evening News* reporter to state that the City support easily outnumbered that of Portsmouth. Perhaps the two fouls had persuaded neutrals to back the team in maroon.

The King presents the FA Cup to Cowan while Brook and Marshall watch.

In the fourteenth minute Brook missed a superb chance to put City in front. He held on too long and allowed a Portsmouth defender, William Smith, to block his shot.

Frank Swift, though a little nervous, was enjoying himself. A little rain in the opening fifteen minutes had caused him a little concern, but in the main he was content. Because of the drizzle the twenty year old contemplated putting on his gloves but, as he was still learning about first team football, he couldn't make his mind up. He looked across field to his more experienced opposite number, Gilfillan, who had remained gloveless and so the young City man decided to wait. Swift thought: "If Gilfillan put his gloves on then so will I."

After almost thirty minutes the first goal arrived. Portsmouth's centre-forward Weddle had lobbed the ball over Sam Cowan to outside left Rutherford. He moved towards goal, reached about fifteen yards out, noticed Billy Dale moving towards him, moved the ball from his left foot to his right, then shot it towards goal. Swift dived and managed to get his fingers to it, but it was no good, the ball entered the net. The 'keeper believed he would have saved the goal if he'd ignored Gilfillan and put on his gloves. He blamed himself.

At half-time, Swift remained upset by the incident.

Yorkshireman Fred Tilson went up to him and, trying to console the 'keeper, said, "Tha doesn't need to worry. I'll plonk two in the next half."

City, unfortunate to be a goal down, returned to the field determined to win the game. The only player who seemed to be lacking the fight required was Herd, who still appeared shaken following his early injury. He wasn't the only player injured though, as midway through the second half Portsmouth's Worrall and Allen went down. Worrall was attended by the City trainer and made a quick recovery while Allen had to be taken off the field for a while. This gave Wild's side a little more space, and they used it to their advantage.

First Herd saw a fine effort hit the bar and go out of play, then Brook and Tilson combined to bring City the equaliser. Brook took the ball into the middle of the field then crossed to Tilson, who had strengthened the left wing the moment Brook moved infield. Tilson, heavily marked, had one chance to score. Mackie came in to tackle and as the two men came into contact and Tilson was falling, the City man shot with his left foot past Gilfillan. The scores were level.

Allen then returned to the field, but it was too late as Cowan and his team mates had the initiative. Although it didn't all go City's way as frequent Manchester attacks

It is believed that City adopted their own specific round badge as early as the 1930s. This image of Sam Cowan appears to show the City captain wearing it on his lapel in 1934.

were broken up by Portsmouth defenders who then quickly sent the ball up field. At one point almost everybody in the stadium was convinced that Portsmouth were about to take the lead as Worrall sent a powerful header goalward. Swift dived and, with his fists, made the save of the game.

With the tension mounting, the game entered the final five minutes with either side capable of snatching victory. Frantically, both sides applied the pressure, but it was City who were to gain the advantage when Toseland sent a crossfield pass to Tilson who moved towards the Portsmouth goal. The defenders tried to reach him, but it was to no avail as the City man backed up his half time boast and fired in his second of the match. Wembley erupted again.

As the final minutes ticked by, Frank Swift felt the tension. The photographers behind his goal kept shouting the time to him until finally the whistle went. He turned to collect his gloves and fainted. Sam Cowan and Alec Bell rushed over to him, with the trainer immediately pouring cold water on Swift's face. They managed to bring him round but he was still a little dazed as he made his way, with the rest of the team, up to the Royal Box. Fourth in the line up behind Cowan, Brook and Marshall, Swift struggled up the Wembley steps and along to the table set up with the medals. The King enquired how he was feeling and then that was it. Time to celebrate.

City had won the Cup for the second time in their history, and deservedly took time out to celebrate. The team were given a fantastic homecoming with what seemed like the whole of Manchester lining the city's streets. The authoritative Pathe News claimed there were over a million on the streets. The film company was not known for exaggeration and if that figure is accurate – and their footage suggests it is - then this remains the largest homecoming in Mancunian history.

Various speeches were made into a microphone set up on the Town Hall steps, and the players and officials were given a civic reception. The Cup win helped to take minds off the growing problems in Europe where fascism was on the increase, and author H.G. Wells had predicted war by 1940. Mancunians enjoyed the success and wanted more.

In Albert Square Mancunians sang their celebratory songs including "Who Said City Couldn't Play" – the earliest known recording of a City specific song:

> *Who Said City Couldn't Play,*
> *City Couldn't Play, City Couldn't Play,*
> *Who Said City Couldn't Play,*
> *City Couldn't Play football?*

The 1933-34 League programme still had two games left for the Blues. On 2nd May they suffered a 3-2 defeat at Liverpool, and then on 5th May City demolished Wolves 4-0 at Maine Road. Before the game City staff, assisted by a couple of police officers, carried the trophy around the ground on some kind of wooden board. The fans were delighted.

Playing in those final two games was left back Sam Barkas, who joined the Blues from Bradford City on 20th April for a £5,000 fee.

During the week of celebrations an illuminated bus journeyed around the city covered in City's colours. On the front above the bus number, 'City 2 1', was the Manchester coat of arms. On the side the message 'Welcome to the victors' proudly illuminated next to a picture of the FA Cup and a drawing of Sam Cowan. Manchester was proud of its team.

TRUE BLUE
Eric Brook

England international Eric Brook scored 158 goals in 450 League appearances for the Blues. He was with City between 1927 and 1939.

E. BROOK

City's victory was celebrated with an illuminated bus that travelled around the city.

1928-1934 SUMMARY

Major Trophies Won: FA Cup 1933-1934
Highest League Attendance: 68,704 Aston Villa, 26/12/29 (often quoted as 70,000)
Highest Cup Attendance: 84,569 Stoke City, 03/03/34 (FA Cup)
Secretary/Managers: 1926-32 Peter Hodge & 1932-46 Wilf Wild

Seasonal Record:

Season	League	Posn	FA Cup	Other	Leading Scorer	Average Attendance
1928-29	FL Div1	8	Rnd 3		Johnson 38	31715
1929-30	FL Div1	3	Rnd 5		Tait 27	33339
1930-31	FL Div1	8	Rnd 3		Brook 16	26849
1931-32	FL Div1	14	Semi-Final		Halliday 28	24173
1932-33	FL Div1	16	Final		Tilson 17	24254
1933-34	FL Div1	5	Winners		Herd 18	30058

1933 FA CUP RUN

R3	Gateshead	A	D	1-1
	Gateshead	H	W	9-0
R4	Walsall	H	W	2-0
R5	Bolton Wanderers	A	W	4-2
R6	Burnley	A	W	1-0
SF	Derby County	N*	W	3-2
F	Everton	N**	L	0-3

* = Leeds Road, Huddersfield ** = Wembley Stadium

	P	W	D	L	F	A
HOME	2	2	0	0	11	0
AWAY	5	3	1	1	9	8
TOTAL	7	5	1	1	20	8

FINAL DETAILS

29 April 1933 at Wembley Stadium
Everton 3-0 Manchester City
CITY: Langford, Cann, Dale, Busby, Cowan, Bray,
Toseland, Marshall, Herd, McMullan, Brook
EVERTON: Sagar, Cook, Cresswell, Britton, White,
Thomson, Geldard, Dunn, Dean, Johnson, Stein
GOALS: Stein, Dean, Dunn
ATTENDANCE: 92,950
REFEREE: E. Wood (Sheffield)
MANAGER: Wilf Wild
CAPTAIN: Sam Cowan

1934 FA CUP RUN

R3	Blackburn Rovers	H	W	3-1
R4	Hull City	A	D	2-2
	Hull City	H	W	4-1
R5	Sheffield Wednesday	A	D	2-2
	Sheffield Wednesday	H	W	2-0
R6	Stoke City	H	W	1-0
SF	Aston Villa	N*	W	6-1
F	Portsmouth	N**	W	2-1

* = Leeds Road, Huddersfield ** = Wembley Stadium

	P	W	D	L	F	A
HOME	4	4	0	0	10	2
AWAY	4	2	2	0	12	6
TOTAL	8	6	2	0	22	8

FINAL DETAILS

28 April 1934 at Wembley Stadium
Manchester City 2-1 Portsmouth
CITY: Swift, Barnett, Dale, Busby, Cowan, Bray,
Toseland, Marshall, Tilson, Herd, Brook
PORTSMOUTH: Gilfillan, Mackie, Smith (W),
Nichol, Allen, Thackeray, Worrall, Smith (JW),
Weddle, Easson, Rutherford
GOALS: Tilson (2), Rutherford
ATTENDANCE: 93,258
REFEREE: S F Rous (Herts)
MANAGER: Wilf Wild
CAPTAIN: Sam Cowan

MANCHESTER CITY.

CORONATION YEAR CHAMPIONS, 1937

FIRST and foremost in Football fame,
Is Manchester City, who "play the game,"
Right from the start without much luck,
Showing opponents their determined pluck,
They're now "on top" and safely stuck.

DOHERTY, the star, who we praise so loud
In the net placed three against Preston Proud
Valuable points which were 2 of the best,
Inspired his team mates—put Arsenal at rest
Swift in goal, 3 seasons without fail
Is strongly supported by Barkas & Dale,
Our half-backs, Percival, Marshall & Bray,
Noteworthy players, who have won the day.

CENTURY of goals, 'put that in your book'
Helped by Toseland, Herd, Tilson & Brook,
Arsenal of North, our neighbours in distress,
Manchester United have failed to impress,
Perhaps some day they'll have an Eleven,
In Nineteen Hundred and Ninety Seven?
Our Manager & trainer took part in the fight,
No wonder was Wilfred Wild with delight,
Sunderland! Arsenal! Preston!-what a sight!

Fletcher & Son, 41, Tib Street, M/c., 4.   (Copyright)

1934-1939
The Championship Arrives

First and foremost in Football fame,
Is Manchester City, who 'play the game',
Right from the start without much luck,
Showing opponents their determined pluck,
They're now 'on top' and safely stuck.

First verse from a supporter postcard, published following the 1937 Championship success

1934-1935 Topical City

At the beginning of the following season *The Topical Times Sporting Annual* announced its six sportsmen of the year. The leading footballer was Matt Busby, who had performed exceptionally well in the Cup Final. The annual believed that he was the best right half back in Britain. The article went on to stress his strengths, the quality of his ball control and reminded its readers that Busby was at long last winning the kind of international recognition he deserved after appearing for Scotland against Wales during the season.

The Topical Times also raved about another City player Frank Swift, who they rated, alongside Stanley Matthews as one of the best discoveries of the season. The Swift article concentrated on the player's tremendous rise in only four months, stressing that he

seemed to improve with every game. Accurately, they predicted a bright future for the lad from Fleetwood.

Following the success of 1933-34, the following season was always going to be difficult. Expectations were high, especially as the Blues had proved to be good cup fighters for three successive seasons. The League programme commenced with a 1-1 draw at West Bromwich, where Sam Barkas provided the City goal. Barkas was now a regular, with Wild selecting him above Barnett.

The next couple of games, both at home, ended in City victory with both Liverpool (3-1) and Sheffield Wednesday (4-1) finding it difficult to come to terms with a bubbling City. In the match with Wednesday City's outside right Ernie Toseland found himself up against the international Joe Nibloe. Every time Toseland had the ball he seemed to ease past his opponent, prompting

RECORD CROWD I

CITY CATCH ARSENAL NEAR THE END

How Bastin Hoodwinked Defence

By HENRY ROSE

Manchester City 1, Arsenal 1.

CROWD of 80,000—the biggest ever for a League match in England—a crowd out for the Arsenal's body, as it were, roaring at every kick and miskick, gave the game at Maine-road between Manchester City and Arsenal an atmosphere as grim as the grimmest Cup tie.

The game contained all those incidents that make the heart beat faster, though there was little class football.

I think a draw a very fair result. The champions gave us all the football that was going in the first half, and no one would have grumbled had they been one or two up.

A surprise shot by Dougall that just whizzed wide; two of the same sort by Davidson; a header by Davidson; a thrilling run by Drake when he kicked the ball just too far to catch it with Swift out of his goal, were a few of the "nearlies."

the *Manchester Evening News* to report: "Toseland passed Nibloe with the ease of a crack express train passing a stationary object."

City's fine form continued, although injury forced Wild to make a few changes from time to time. Jimmy Heale, signed from Bristol City in January, frequently replaced Marshall. In fact the newcomer finished the season making 27 League appearances - eight more than Marshall.

As usual City were often watched by a few enormous crowds. Wednesday, Leeds, Stoke and Derby each attracted around 50,000, while the game with first placed Arsenal on 23rd February attracted 79,491 – a new Football League record attendance. City, in third place, were only a point behind the Gunners when the two teams met. It is worth noting that the Blues and Arsenal were regarded as the two most significant teams at this point in football history.

The huge crowd witnessed a tense 1-1 draw with Ted Drake scoring for the visitors and Eric Brook for the Blues, but it wasn't enough. City needed the victory, especially when a few weeks later they failed at Blackburn and Huddersfield. Nevertheless, the Blues did manage to achieve a respectable fourth place - one position higher than the previous season. The Cup was a disappointment however, as an away third round tie at Tottenham ended in a 1-0 defeat.

1935-1936 Ten Thousand Pounds

The season commenced without Sam Cowan in the opening day line-up. He was replaced by Robert Donnelly, a summer signing from Partick Thistle, and the former captain moved to Bradford City in October.

During the season other important changes were made, with the most notable being the transfer of the highly rated Busby to Liverpool, and the arrival of

£10,000 man Peter Doherty – at that time the transfer record was only a few pounds more, £10,890. City had converted Busby into a top class wing half and felt unable to turn down Liverpool when the Merseyside Reds put in an offer of £8,000. Doherty on the other hand was a man City desperately wanted and, at his debut on 22nd February against Preston, a crowd of 39,364 couldn't wait to see what the expensive new player could do.

Doherty, in his autobiography, remembered the problems he encountered in his debut match: "It was an uninspiring debut. Preston, giving a wonderful exhibition of football, beat us 3-1, and Bill Shankly, at right-half, blotted me completely out. Bill has always been a wily tactician, but that day he excelled himself. He dogged my footsteps all afternoon, muttering, 'Great wee team, North End; a great wee team,' and subduing me so effectively that I must have been a grave disappointment to the thousands of City fans who had come along to see the Club's expensive capture. During a quiet spell, I heard one of them voices his disapproval very clearly, 'Ten thousand pounds?' he shouted scornfully. 'You mean ten thousand cigarette cards!'"

City ended the season in the rather uninspiring ninth position. Everyone felt dissatisfied.

In the Cup they had reached the fifth round, but even that seemed rather disappointing after the success of two years earlier. The run started with Portsmouth in the third round. A crowd of 53,340 came to see City defeat their old cup rivals again. This time the score was 3-1 thanks to an Eric Brook hat-trick. In the fourth round another large Maine Road crowd, 65,978, witnessed a 2-1 victory over plucky Third Division side Luton Town - Luton's first defeat since 28th September.

The run ended on 15th February before a record Grimsby crowd of around 28,000. Grimsby defeating City 3-2. Two days before that game the rather sad news that twenties' right back Sammy Sharp had died shocked Manchester. The Ardwick-born player was only 39.

1936-1937 Champions

If reaching the fifth round and finishing ninth in 1935-36 was regarded as failure then the 1936-37 season must have brought a real sense of achievement to City's large, loyal support. Sam Barkas was now the Club's established captain, and with Doherty adding a little firepower upfront, the season became a successful one, although it hardly seemed possible during the difficult early months of September and October.

Despite exciting victories over Leeds (4-0) and West Bromwich Albion (6-2) an opening day defeat at Middlesbrough and another at Old Trafford in the first derby since February 1931 caused a little concern amongst City's support. The United defeat was particularly upsetting as the Reds were a side clearly lacking, and destined to return immediately to the Second Division. Further failures occurred, including a 2-1 loss at Wolverhampton. Wolves were in the process of rebuilding and had angered many supporters by selling some of their heroes. On their approach to Molineux the City players couldn't help noticing some graffiti chalked on a wall: "The turf at the ground is now for sale!". Despite the negativity at Molineux, Wolves outplayed the Blues.

A few exciting victories followed in November and December, including 3-1 at Arsenal and 4-1 against Preston, giving the Blues hope, but the real turnaround came at Christmas with a 2-1 victory over Middlesbrough at Maine Road. A couple of draws against Grimsby and West Bromwich followed before the return derby match. A Maine Road crowd of 62,895 watched a rather dull, but important game as City defeated United thanks to a solitary goal from Alec Herd.

In the following League game Toseland, Herd, and Brook each scored as Portsmouth were defeated 3-1 at Maine Road. This had followed City's third round tie away to Wrexham - an easy 3-1 win. In the fourth round City disposed of Accrington Stanley 2-0, before 39,135 at Maine Road to earn a visit to old rivals Bolton in the next round.

The Bolton game was an ill-tempered affair. City eventually won the match 5-0 but at one point, a moment after Herd had scored the Blues' second goal, it looked as if the match would not continue. Bolton vigorously appealed against Herd's goal, and when play recommenced one of their players, Anderson, was sent off. There were further protests and the whole team considered marching off together, but eventually they were persuaded to stay on to finish the rather tense affair.

The draw for the quarter-finals gave City what seemed like an easy route into the semi-finals. The Blues were to travel to Millwall, a Third Division South club. City's thoughts

were starting to turn towards the prospect of a League and Cup Double, although the weaker of the two trophy opportunities seemed to be the League. A simple victory over Millwall seemed likely, despite the Club beating Chelsea and Derby in earlier rounds. It wasn't to be however, as Millwall forced the pace right from the beginning. Dave Mangnall put City under much pressure and by the 51st minute had scored twice for the home club.

At full time, thousands of Millwall fans invaded the pitch to celebrate their 2-0 giant killing victory, and the club's entry into the record books as the first Third Division side to enter the semi-finals. It was a devastating blow for City, but with typical football logic it at least allowed them to concentrate on the League.

The return game with Wolves proved how the Blues had improved during the season as a crowd of 42,133 witnessed Tilson's second hat-trick in two games help to bring a 4-1 victory. Three days earlier he'd scored three against Derby. A big improvement on the October defeat. On 13th March, in City's next League game, two goals from Doherty helped to ensure a 3-0 win over Huddersfield and suggestions that 10th April would be the most vital day in the title race – the day Arsenal were to face City at Maine Road.

A disappointing 1-1 draw at Everton was followed by an excellent Good Friday when City visited Liverpool again. This time they thrilled as they defeated the Merseyside Reds 5-0 with goals from Brook (three), Doherty and Herd on 26th March.

Three days later the return match saw the Blues go goal crazy again as they scored another five, including

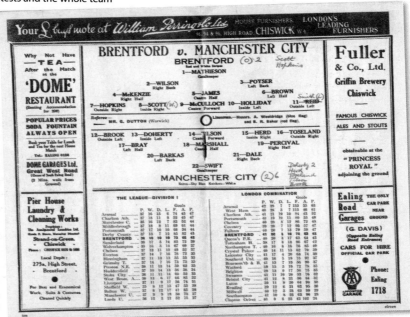

City won 6-2 at Brentford on 3rd April 1937. Earlier in the season the Blues beat West Bromwich Albion by the same score.

a seven minute spell during the second half when they scored four. Liverpool did pull a goal back, but the 10-1 aggregate score was a complete humiliation for the Merseyside club. Almost sixty years later Liverpool inflicted an equally humiliating 10-0 aggregate score over Alan Ball's Blues within a similar time frame.

The Liverpool results, together with a 2-2 draw with Bolton sandwiched in between, meant City were third on 44 points. Above them were Arsenal and Charlton both on 47 points but, importantly, City had two games in hand over both sides.

Away at Brentford on 3rd April, City again seemed the side most capable of success. Shortly after half-time they led 3-0, but then, with the game seemingly won, the Blues sat back a little. In no time at all, Brentford pulled the score back to 3-2. At a time when most teams would have panicked, City regained control and by full-time had increased their lead to 6-2. Four days later, the Maine Road return ended in a 2-1 win, thereby placing City second in the League behind Arsenal, who were due to play the Blues three days later on Saturday 10th April – as the *Evening Chronicle* had predicted this would be a highly significant game in the title race.

Matches between City and Arsenal during the 1930s usually attracted high attendances, and with both teams occupying the top two places in the League there was no doubt what the match of the day - possibly the season - was going to be.

The attendance for this game was quoted in the press as 76,000 - some 13,000 more than the Maine Road derby match (although City submitted a figure of 74,918 to the League) – and local 'papers carried the news that there were over 50,000 on the terraces a full 45 minutes before the game commenced. As with many other popular matches of the period, City officials helped some supporters - most notably young boys - onto the running track around the pitch. Photos clearly show groups of supporters sat in front of Maine Road's white perimeter wall, trying to get a good view of the game.

For the early part of the match City were easily outplayed by the Gunners, but as the game progressed the Blues gradually gained control. In the 35th minute City, now matching Arsenal move for move, seized control and the lead. Arsenal's Bernard Joy sliced a clearance straight to

Peter Doherty

City's Fred Tilson on the left wing. Immediately Tilson steered a long pass to Peter Doherty, who was being closely marked by England captain Eddie Hapgood. With Arsenal's 'keeper Boulton only a yard away and with a very narrow angle, close to the goal line, Doherty somehow hooked the ball into the roof of the net.

Toseland scored a second for the Blues later in the match to bring victory, top spot in the table with 50 points and, crucially, they still had a game in hand over both Arsenal and Charlton (both on 49 points). With a possible eight points left to play for the Blues were confident that the title was at long last on its way to Maine Road.

In mid-week City defeated Sunderland 3-1, despite being a goal down as late as the 67th minute, and then on 17th April the Blues played a memorable game at Preston. Both sides were missing players on International duty – Wild's side were without Sam Barkas and Jackie Bray - and the conditions were poor to say the least. The pitch was an absolute disgrace, following heavy rain, and the Blues found it difficult to cope with the mud. After 12 minutes they were two goals down and later in the half City's left-back, Robert Donnelly was injured. With an obvious limp he moved into the outside-left position, while Eric Brook dropped back into defence.

Doherty and Herd kept switching positions hoping to fool Preston's Milne and Shankly, but the ploy was ineffective and abandoned prior to half-time. Early in the second half, with City very much under pressure, the tactic was tried again. This time it worked and Doherty pulled one back. A minute later Doherty scored again, and then Alec Herd cracked in the third from a Toseland centre. Within three minutes the game had turned. The Blues had surprised themselves by taking the lead.

City were now the masters and playing the kind of football that deserved title success. In another attack, Doherty headed City's fourth goal of the game and hundredth League goal of the season, and, to make Preston's misery complete, a little before the end the limping Donnelly made it 5-2.

The League table made interesting reading. Wild's side were on 54 points, Arsenal 51,

The programme for the final home match of 1936-37 asks an important question.

MANCHESTER CITY F.C.

Hon. President : L. W. FURNISS.
Directors : R. SMITH (Chairman), A. ALEXANDER, J. P. (Vice-Chairman),
Dr. J. B. HOLMES, F. R. JOLLY, W. M. SHAW and H. WOOD,
Secretary Manager : W. WILD, Registered Office: MAINE ROAD GROUND

CLUB GOSSIP

WILL TO-DAY BRING US THE CHAMPIONSHIP ?

TO-DAY we bring our season to an end so far as our home League engagements are concerned, and we are hoping it will be the happiest wind-up we have ever had in the sense that it will consummate our first Championship year.

Two points from the match with Sheffield Wednesday this afternoon and the prize for which we have striven so long and which would complete for us the full round of honours in the game, will be ours.

We have had the F.A. Cup and the Championship of the Second Division of the League, but never the trophy which is now within our grasp.

WE are not counting our chickens before they are hatched. We recognise that we are up against a desperate opposition. The match is of the utmost importance to the Wednesday, to whom defeat might mean the loss of their position, and they are sure to make a tremendous fight.

When we were at Hillsborough in December they inflicted upon us the heaviest defeat we have sustained throughout the season. They had what we should say was their very best day.

They beat us by 5—1, after we had run through six successive matches without a reverse and, except in the following game with Grimsby Town, six

GAS COSTS LESS!

Thousands of consumers can enjoy the comfort of an additional Gas Fire without adding to the cost of their normal gas bill.

THIS IS A BURNING QUESTION !

Mr. Therm
G A S

Enquire for a survey of your account and learn how the optional TWO-PART TARIFF would benefit you.

WHY PAY TOP PRICE?

Enquiries : J. H. SILLITOE, Commercial Manager and Secretary

CITY OF MANCHESTER GAS DEPT.

TOWN HALL   Tel. : CENTRAL 2377   MANCHESTER 2

---

and Charlton were third with 50 points. With each side having two games left to play the Blues knew they simply needed two points to guarantee the title.

At home to Sheffield Wednesday on 24th April, a crowd of 50,985 cheered City on to victory. As with several games that season, the Blues seemed to allow the visitors to dominate the early moves. Gradually, City gained the upper hand and it wasn't long before Eric Brook put them into the lead with a fast, furious drive. Later, Brook told the press, and his City team mates, that he hadn't hit a shot like that for years - if ever!

Within minutes Tilson made it 2-0, then a little while later, Frank Swift provided one of his famous lofty clearances. Doherty gained possession in midfield and he and Tilson charged through the Wednesday defence with a rapid interchange of passes. They travelled well over forty yards, then entered the Wednesday penalty area. Tilson made the final pass, then Doherty whipped it into the net. The Maine Road crowd loved it, and one report described it as "one of the finest goals scored on any ground."

At half-time the crowd gave the team, in particular Tilson and Doherty, a tremendous ovation. They desperately wanted the title, and as the game

progressed they had seen a side whose style of play thoroughly deserved the award.

In the second half, Wednesday fought back and managed to score, but the Blues were simply too good for the Yorkshiremen. In the final minutes of the game Eric Brook finished what he had started and scored City's fourth. At the whistle, thousands rushed onto the pitch in celebration - a scene repeated after a similar success in 2012. The crowd sang, shouted, and cheered, until captain Sam Barkas, manager Wilf Wild, and Chairman Bob Smith appeared.

The Chairman paid tribute to the team: "It has been a fine achievement, especially as they have not been beaten since last Christmas. On behalf of myself and my fellow directors, I take this opportunity of thanking the players. We are tremendously proud of them."

Sam Barkas stressed City's teamwork: "We have all pulled together. We have been a happy family, and that is one of the secrets of our success."

CHAMPIONSHIP GOES NORTH

Manchester City's Strong Finish

BRADFORD FOR THIRD DIVISION

An exciting wind-up to the football season in England is assured next Saturday, as in addition to the Cup final various League positions await settlement. Manchester City crowned a series of 21 League matches without defeat with a victory over Sheffield Wednesday by 4-1.

The victory gave Manchester City the League Championship for the first time in their history, and there were tumultuous scenes at the close among the 55,000 spectators, thousands invading the pitch and shouting their acclamation of the new champions.

WELL DONE, MANCHESTER CITY!

League Champions for First Time: Leicester Go Up With Blackpool: Grim Fight for Honours in Third Division
By RUSSELL STANNARD

Police Stop Crowd From Mobbing New Champions
By GEORGE FITZGERALD

CITY ARE NOW THE MOST POPULAR FOOTBALL TEAM IN EUROPE

Like Barkas and Smith, Wilf Wild was a very happy and proud man. Already during his five years in charge he had seen his team win the League and Cup, and feature in another Cup Final. This made him City's most successful manager, which he remained right up until the arrival of Joe Mercer, although Tom Maley's reign had been destined to achieve a great deal until it was cruelly cut short by the FA's enforced ban.

The following Monday newspapers talked of the increased interest in City. Offers had come for the Blues to tour various European countries and there had also been an offer for the League Championship trophy to be presented on the pitch at the Club's final League game in Birmingham. This was an unusual offer and one City turned down. Surprisingly, considering how trophy presentations evolved in later years, the Blues felt the trophy should be presented at the League's annual dinner the following June. That, it seems, was perceived as the appropriate method.

The final game of the season was away to Birmingham City, and the Blues were determined to increase their unbeaten League run to 22 games. However City were losing 2-1 inside the last couple of minutes. It seemed as if the amazing run would end but then came probably the most unusual goal of the season. Peter Doherty, in his autobiography, remembered the lengths he went to ensure City's record remained: "A high ball was lobbed down the middle, and Harry Hibbs, the Birmingham 'keeper, and myself raced for it. We collided heavily, and at the moment of impact, I fisted the ball through. To my complete surprise, a goal was signalled, and there wasn't even a murmur of protest. Nobody had seen the infringement. I was credited with a perfectly good goal, and our record was intact!"

Champions deserve the luck!

Captain Sam Barkas later talked of how easy it had been to lead this side: "Towards the end of the season the team more or less captained itself. I sometimes thought that I was needed only to spin the coin before the game!"

While City were celebrating, across Manchester, United fans were suffering. The 1930s, so far, had seen the Blues enjoy tremendous success. Although Arsenal were the team of the decade, City were their closest rivals. Not quite as successful, but better than the rest. Since the mid-twenties, the Blues had also been one of the best - occasionally the best - supported clubs of the period while United struggled. The Reds had spent much of the period in the Second Division, had suffered organised boycotts, flirted with many different strips in the hope that they would find a 'lucky' kit, and been very much the underdogs to City. At the end of the Blues Championship season, the Reds were relegated.

When in 1996 the roles were reversed, relegation was seen as the ultimate humiliation. In 1937 humiliation didn't come into it as City supporters genuinely had sympathy for United, and wanted their friends to quickly return to the top flight. Blues wanted the Reds to find a little glory themselves.

While City dominated, United came perilously close to extinction. Nobody found joy in that. Manchester needed two clubs, preferably in the same Division.

Jack Percival's shirt from 1936-37. Although the Manchester coat of arms was added to the shirts for a celebratory team photo no evidence has been identified showing the side wearing the badge during games.

MANCHESTER CITY F.C.
The League Champions. With Championship Cup.

STANDING : McCullough, Dale, T. Chorlton (Trainer), Swift, Marshall, Bray.
SITTING : Toseland, Herd, Tilson, Mr. W. Wild (Manager), Barkas, Doherty, Brook.
FRONT ROW : Heale, Rogers, Clarke, Percival.

City were the first English team to play (above & below) at the Berlin Olympic Stadium. They faced Germany in a highly political match.

1937-1938 Making History

As champions, the Blues were expected to be the team to watch. They were supposed to be the ones who set the football world alight. Sadly, the new season was astounding for all the wrong reasons.

The Blues' dismal season began with three defeats and only two victories in their opening five games. The media and, more worryingly, supporters began to talk of City sliding down the division. The Club went on the defensive and captain Sam Barkas wrote an article for the *Manchester Evening Chronicle* – still regarded at that time as the City 'paper while the *Evening News* was viewed as the United 'paper. Barkas: "Somebody builds a fine structure without certainty of permanence – a football team, of course – and the other fellows say: 'let's have a shot at knocking it down'. Every week somebody has a shot at taking the Champions down a peg or two."

The captain went on to answer specific criticisms. Focusing on the perception that the side was becoming too old he responded: "I do not suppose there is more than a year or two in the aggregate between us and any other team in the League. If our average age in the City team were in the neighbourhood of 30 I should say we were too old to have a chance of the big honours in football. But it is not – and I do not."

Answering criticism about results he countered: "Last season we won only two matches out of the first

The Coronation Loving Cup was presented to City by Stoke City to mark the coronation of King George VI. Each First Division side was presented with a copy which depicted Stoke City and Manchester City on one side.

the Blues win the Charity Shield for the first time in their history. Criticism remained however.

Issues concerning fitness and injury exacerbated the problems and the media made much of the arrival of 19 year old Billy Wardle from Southport for a fee of around £2,200. Newspapers carried stories of how the outside left had gone from schoolboy football to City's first team within a year – not quite accurate but his rise had been meteoric.

Whether Wardle's story was promoted by the Club to divert attention from other issues isn't clear but, possibly for the first time in over two decades, the Blues found that Manchester United upstaged them with their own new 'boy wonder' Jack Rowley. 17 year old Rowley cost £3,000 and made his debut on the same day as Wardle. The United man immediately impressed and comparisons between City's First Division squad and United's Second Division team worked in United's favour. This was highly unusual for the period.

Wardle only managed six appearances – and no goals – during 1937-38 but he wasn't the only player who failed to live up to the Club encouraged hyperbole that season.

A dismal run in December and into the New Year saw four successive defeats, but impressive victories (4-1 at Leicester and 7-1 at Derby), plus the FA Cup run encouraged fans to believe that the Blues would finish in the top half of the table. But it wasn't to be.

February was appalling with only three points gained out of ten. Then came an equally disastrous March. This placed City in severe difficulty and caused Manager Wild to enter the transfer market. He purchased wing-half Les McDowall from Sunderland for a little over £7,000, despite the 6ft player only making 13 appearances in his five years at Roker Park. McDowall made his debut on 16th March in the 1-1 draw at West Bromwich. Around the same time long serving Tilson moved to Northampton Town, as did McCullough and Rodger.

five and we won the Championship. This season we have three wins in six matches and our chances of winning the Championship are as good as anybody else's.

"It is true we have not found our best form yet. The opposition is keener to begin with. Teams pull out just that 'little bit extra' for the satisfaction of beating the Champions. I will go so far as to say that individually the team, for the most part, is playing just as well as it did last season. But the ball has not run quite so kindly for us. Every athlete knows what that means."

Barkas continued to highlight how being champions had affected play, for example increased defensive pressure on City's star man Peter Doherty, and then ended his piece with an admission that his ambition was not now to win the League but to win the FA Cup which, he called, the greatest prize in football. This season Barkas guided City through to the quarter-finals, where they were defeated by Aston Villa. They lost a thrilling game 3-2 before a then Villa Park record crowd of 75,540. One other cup result worth mentioning was the 3-1 defeat of Millwall in the third round replay, which gained revenge for the previous season's disaster.

In the League Barkas' article may have had a direct impact on morale as the Blues thrashed Derby County 6-1 on the very day the newspaper was printed. This was followed by only two defeats in the next seven League games and, on 4th November, a 2-0 victory over Sunderland which saw

With new blood, City made a little progress in April with nine points and twenty-two goals from eight games. On 2nd April the Blues defeated Chelsea 1-0 at Maine Road to lift them to 18th position, then four days later they defeated Charlton 5-3 in a game the *Daily Dispatch* described as 'crazy'. Charlton took the lead as early as the third minute, then a minute later Milsom, who'd signed from Bolton in February, equalised. In the 17th minute he nodded in his second and then five minutes later Bray made it 3-1. It remained 3-1 to the interval then two minutes into the second half Frank Swift was

Sam Barkas

forced to run some distance from his line to save from Charlton's Tadman. Another Charlton man, Robinson, gained control of the rebound and fired past the City 'keeper, who was desperately trying to make his way back, to make it 3-2. Four minutes later Charlton equalised.

In the 65th minute Pritchard regained the lead for City with a left foot shot from Brook's corner, and 18 minutes from time Milsom scored his hat-trick with a clever run, followed by a shot that went a fraction wide of goalkeeper Bartram's left hand.

Despite Milsom's hat trick, the best City attackers were undoubtedly Eric Brook and Peter Doherty. Brook netted four in the 7-1 return with West Bromwich, while Doherty scored a hat-trick as the Blues defeated Leeds 6-2 in their penultimate game.

City were a shade fortunate in their high scoring defeat of West Bromwich as the visitors' goalkeeper, Little, badly bruised his shoulder in the 22nd minute and was forced to leave the field for a while. When he returned he was unable to move his right arm from his side. Another player, Finch, West Bromwich's full back, also left the field with a gashed head following a collision with Eric Brook. When he returned he joined Little out on the wing.

By the time of Little's injury the Blues were already two goals up - a Brook penalty in the second minute and a Doherty header twenty minutes later - but once he'd left the field City could not be stopped.

Despite these victories, the Blues were deep in relegation trouble by 23rd April. With three games left, City lay in 21st position on 33 points, although the four clubs above them were only one point better off. Even Blackpool in 12th place could still be relegated. To boost the attack following a disappointing 2-1 defeat at Bolton, Wilf Wild decided to drop Milsom for the first time since his transfer from Bolton, and replace him with Jimmy Heale for the

ERIC BROOK
in action for Manchester City

———

Illness Ends Footballer's 11-year Record

From Our Own Correspondent

MANCHESTER, Sunday.

ERIC BROOK, the Manchester City and England footballer, missed yesterday his first match for 11 seasons—a record possessed by no other living professional footballer.

It was his birthday, but instead of celebrating it by playing for his club against Grimsby Town, he was undergoing an operation for acute appendicitis and peritonitis.

Late tonight his doctors said he was "more comfortable," but he is permitted no visitors except his wife, who spent two hours with him today.

"Eric is really very ill," Mrs. Brook said to me, "but he refuses to realise it. My only fear is that he will over-tax his strength worrying about being out of the game."

Brook's place in the England team against Czecho-Slovakia will be taken by Ashall, of Wolverhampton Wanderers.

Eric Brook was unfit for City's 3-1 victory over Grimsby on 27th November 1937.

return match at Charlton. The game ended goalless despite considerable City pressure, while Heale performed well enough to retain his place for the home game with Leeds on 30th April.

City won that one 6-2, but they remained in danger.

The final match was away to Huddersfield, who were also struggling. On the final day of the season seven sides remained in danger of the dreaded drop, with both City and Huddersfield only needing a point to survive. A draw seemed the perfect result, but for the home side there was much more at stake. Only a week earlier, the Yorkshiremen had been defeated by Preston in the FA Cup final. The game had been a dramatic one, with Huddersfield losing by a goal scored from a penalty given twenty seconds from the end of extra time.

Huddersfield were still smarting and needed a morale boosting victory. A draw would not be good enough, City realising this went all out for a goal. Despite piling on the pressure luck was not on their side as, in the second half, a magnificent 35 yard drive from Alec Herd proved. The shot hit the cross bar and came down again. The referee waved play on but Peter Doherty, who was fairly close at the time, claimed the ball had entered the net: "In my opinion the ball struck an iron stay at the back of the net and rebounded into play. I could have sworn it was a goal."

In the 78th minute City's luck really did fail when Huddersfield took the lead through a scrappy goal. The Blues continued to push forward but it was no good. As the whistle went the Huddersfield players and supporters celebrated while City had to wait. Memories of the 1927 promotion race came flooding back as the Blues waited to hear how the other results had gone. Eventually the players waiting in the dressing room were given the news that fellow strugglers Grimsby, Portsmouth, Birmingham, and Stoke had all won. If any one of those sides had been defeated the Blues would have been safe on goal average. As it was City ended the season in 21st place despite scoring more goals than any other team in the division.

The agony was compounded by further news relayed to the players and supporters - Manchester United had been promoted on goal average. Although it wasn't known at the time, this reversal in Manchester football - during the City of Manchester's centenary year - would affect sport in the city for decades, right through to at least the late 1960s. Some would argue that repercussions would affect Manchester football right through to the arrival of Sheikh Mansour in 2008.

1938-1939 A Worrying Time

Following Millwall's promotion from the Third Division South, City and their 1937 FA Cup giant killing opponents competed in the same division for the first time. Their inaugural League meeting on 17th September proved that Blues manager Wilf Wild needed to act quickly if he was to fulfil City's dream of an immediate return, as Millwall easily achieved a 6-1 Maine Road victory. For that game Wild had dropped goalkeeper Frank Swift, after three successive defeats. The story was turned into a major news item with journalists from both Manchester evening 'papers, the *News* and the *Chronicle*, and some of the dailies turning up at Swift's house for his view of the affair. Naturally, Swift was far from happy but, with his typical good natured and humorous approach, he laughed at suggestions he was unhappy.

Also missing by this time was Peter Doherty who had damaged ligaments in his right knee during the third game of the season - a 4-2 defeat at Bradford (Park Avenue) - and his absence created an obvious gap in City's attack. When Alec Herd also went down injured in the 3-3 draw at Blackburn on 24th September Wilf Wild could feel the pressure mounting.

By the end of September the Blues were really struggling after amassing a mere five points from nine games. This put City in the bottom four of the Second Division, and caused some supporters to attack the direction of the Club. According to Peter Doherty's

TRUE BLUE
Wilf Wild

Wilf Wild was the first manager to bring the League title to City. He was manager of the Blues from 1932 to 1946.

autobiography letters arrived at Maine Road addressed to "The Blind Asylum" and opened with the line "Dear Blunderers." Something had to be done.

There was a slight upturn in form during the latter weeks of October, when the Blues achieved a no score draw at Plymouth and a 3-2 Maine Road victory over Sheffield United. Defeat at West Bromwich followed but on 5th November a new look City was ready to face Tottenham at Maine Road.

Full back Eric Westwood, who had signed from United in November 1937, was set to make his debut along with a new signing from Spurs, Bert Sproston. Sproston had actually been selected by Tottenham to play against City, but the player had been struggling to settle in the capital after signing for the London club only four months earlier. City negotiated with Tottenham to bring the Sandbach born England international back to the north west, and the day before the game signed him for £9,500 - the same sum Spurs had paid Leeds in June. Unusually Sproston made his debut against his former club.

In addition, Peter Doherty returned to the side, although he was far from fully fit. Wild was determined to gain victory and build a promotion seeking side, no matter what the cost. The Doherty gamble paid off as the Blues won 2-0 with the Irishman supplying one of the goals himself. It was also the kick start City needed as they embarked on a seven game unbeaten run.

From that point on they climbed the table but were never really able to challenge for promotion - the bad spell during September and early October and injuries throughout the season had seen to that.

New signing Sproston had to miss seven games during the crucial spring period, after sustaining an injury in the Spurs return game. This was an incredible match for the former Tottenham man as, after his injury, he was moved to outside left with Eric Brook moving back to defend. While playing as a forward Sproston managed to score to level the game at 2-2 and then, with only a couple of minutes to go, he headed a centre from Maurice Dunkley to give City the victory.

The season ended with a fifth place finish, five points behind second placed Sheffield United. Considering the start this was a respectable position. It was also true that the Blues remained one of the most prolific sides of the period as City's total of 96 League goals was more than any other club in the League.

1934-1939 SUMMARY

Major Trophies Won: The League Championship 1936-1937
Highest League Attendance: 79,491 Arsenal, 23/02/35 (A League record at the time)
Highest Cup Attendance: 71,937 Bury, 22/01/38 (FA Cup)
Managers: 1932-46 Wilf Wild

Seasonal Record:

Season	League	Posn	FA Cup	Other	Leading Scorer	Average Att
1934-35	FL Div1	4	Rnd 3	Charity Shield Runners-up	Tilson 18	34,824
1935-36	FL Div1	9	Rnd 5		Brook 13	33,577
1936-37	FL Div1	Champions	Rnd 6		Doherty 30	35,872
1937-38	FL Div1	21	Rnd 6	Charity Shield Winners	Doherty 23	32,670
1938-39	FL Div2	5	Rnd 4		Herd 20	31,291

1936-37 FOOTBALL LEAGUE CHAMPIONSHIP DETAILS

REGULAR SIDE: Swift, Dale, Barkas, Percival, Marshall, Bray, Toseland, Herd, Tilson, Doherty, Brook.
MANAGER: Wilf Wild

RESULTS	HOME		AWAY	
Middlesbrough	W	2-1	L	0-2
Leeds United	W	4-0	D	1-1
West Bromwich A	W	6-2	D	2-2
Manchester United	W	1-0	L	2-3
Birmingham City	D	1-1	D	2-2
Portsmouth	W	3-1	L	1-2
Chelsea	D	0-0	D	4-4
Stoke City	W	2-1	D	2-2
Charlton Athletic	D	1-1	D	1-1
Derby County	W	3-2	W	5-0
Wolverhampton W	W	4-1	L	1-2
Sunderland	L	2-4	W	3-1
Huddersfield Town	W	3-0	D	1-1
Everton	W	4-1	D	1-1
Bolton Wanderers	D	2-2	W	2-0
Arsenal	W	2-0	W	3-1
Preston North End	W	4-1	W	5-2
Sheffield Wednesday	W	4-1	L	1-5
Grimsby Town	D	1-1	L	3-5
Liverpool	W	5-1	W	5-0
Brentford	W	2-1	W	6-2

LARGEST VICTORY: 6-2 V West Bromwich Albion (H) 5/9/36, Brentford (A) 3/4/37

LARGEST WINNING MARGIN: 5-0 V Derby County (A) 24/2/37, Liverpool (A) 26/3/37

HEAVIEST DEFEAT: 1-5 V Sheffield Wednesday (A) 19/12/36

AVERAGE HOME ATTENDANCE: 35,872

HIGHEST HOME ATTENDANCE: 74,918 V Arsenal 10/4/37

HIGHEST AWAY ATTENDANCE: 68,796 V Manchester United 12/9/36

LEAGUE APPEARANCES: 42 Swift, Percival, Toseland, Brook, 41 Doherty, 40 Bray, 38 Marshall, 36 Dale, 32 Herd, 30 Barkas, 23 Tilson, 13 Clark, 10 Heale, 9 Rodger, 7 Donnelly, 4 Regan, 3 McLeod, 2 McCullough, Neilson, Rogers, 1 Cassidy, Freeman

LEAGUE GOALS: 30 Doherty, 20 Brook, 15 Herd, Tilson, 7 Toseland, Rodger, 6 Heale, 2 Bray, McLeod, 1 Percival, Donnelly, Neilson.

Sam Cowan in his office at Maine Road.

1939-1951
Living With The Enemy

"We would often go together to Maine Road every week to see City and United alternatively. We staunchly insisted we liked the great Frank Swift better than all the United players put together! I am certain it was Frank who single-handedly retained the loyalties of many younger fans."

The Views of City fan James Dowd in 2002, published in *Farewell To Maine Road* 2003

1939-1940 War Reports

With City remaining in Division Two the close season discussions still considered how the Blues could return to the First. Little did anyone realise that their chance of doing this would be delayed for at least another seven years as war was about to sweep Europe. Throughout the summer months, as the prospect of war increased, many players had enlisted in the Territorial Army or other such national service organisations. Liverpool went one stage further than most when they became the first team to join the Territorial Army as a club. West Ham and Bolton followed their example and volunteered en masse, while the directors of Manchester United took a less patriotic view: "It is a matter for the individual to decide."

In growing uncertainty the 1939-40 season opened with City away to Leicester. The line-up was a familiar one: Swift, Sproston, Westwood, McDowall, Cardwell, Bray, Dunkley, Herd, Heale, Doherty, and Brook. The result was a disappointing one as City crashed 4-3 at Filbert Street on Saturday 26th August.

Four days later, as 'The Wizard Of Oz' was making its way around American cinemas for the first time, City entertained Bury in a 1-1 draw at Maine Road. Understandably, the crowd was a rather subdued 20,000. The following day the evacuation of children from British cities began. Within a week over a million children were moved into the Country. For the time being, football was to continue despite the threat of war increasing daily.

On Saturday 2nd September, the day after the Germans commenced their invasion of Poland, the Blues welcomed Chesterfield while Wilf Wild made one alteration to his line-up, replacing Jimmy Heale with Jack Milsom. The change seemed perfect when the former Bolton forward netted twice to give City a 2-0 victory before 15,000. This despite Brook missing a penalty in the tenth minute.

In the Central League the Blues defeated Chesterfield 3-0 while City's 'A' team defeated Accrington Stanley 'A' 6-1 in the Lancashire League. Incidentally, Accrington Stanley's first team, playing in the Third Division (North) were the only team in the four divisions with maximum points from three games.

Later that day news came through that 21 people had died as the result of an air-raid on Warsaw. At noon the following day, as supporters were reading the Sunday reports, Prime Minister Neville Chamberlain announced: "This Country is now at war with Germany. We are ready."

A ban was immediately placed on the assembly of large crowds. City fans joked that the still relatively poorly supported Old Trafford club would have nothing to worry about. Then the announcement was made that the League programme would be cancelled and that all players' contracts would be suspended. City's chance of promotion had ended.

By the end of September, the FA had relaxed their rules and had given permission for the organisation of mini-leagues or competitions consisting of teams within straightforward travelling distance. One proviso was that games could only be played on either Saturdays or Bank Holidays, and that the attendance had to be less than 8,000 or half the capacity of the ground, whichever was the lower figure. Later this was relaxed a little, providing the match was all ticket. In the *Daily Dispatch* for 20th September news appeared that John Maxwell, the Chief Constable of Manchester, had given approval for crowds of between ten and fifteen thousand. He went on to lay down a number of conditions: "Mr. Maxwell explained that the police were anxious not to be unduly restrictive on the management of the public, but that there must be a safety margin to allow dispersal in case of air raid warning. Among the conditions imposed by the police are:-

"Gas masks must be carried by spectators, a look out must be posted outside the ground to listen for sirens or other warnings, loud-speaker equipment must be installed, and a competent speaker appointed to advise the crowd regarding dispersal and the nearest shelter in case of emergency.

"The Manchester United ground, being outside the city boundary, comes under the authority of Lancashire County Constabulary, whose decision regarding play is expected today."

In addition to this news players were told by the FA that they were allowed to receive a wage of 30 shillings a week, with no bonuses, while they played for a club.

During this time of confusion, most of the players who hadn't previously enlisted now joined the forces or obtained work in war supporting industry, although this often caused friction between club and player. Peter Doherty was offered work in Greenock, Scotland and immediately City Chairman Robert Smith told the player he would not be allowed to play in Scotland. Discussions took place for some time before Doherty felt forced to turn down the Scottish job and remain in Manchester. Another director found him work in Manchester for a time, then he joined a few Blackpool players at the ordnance factory at Risley. Early in 1940 he decided to volunteer for the R.A.F. At one point he joined City team mate Jackie Bray training as a PT instructor at Uxbridge.

Frank Swift became a special police constable when war broke out but, according to Swift's biography, he became so confused when directing traffic that he felt it was better to walk away and let the traffic sort itself out. Another player, Les McDowall, returned to Scotland and played for St. Mirren for virtually the whole of the war.

By mid-October the plans for the new mini-leagues had been made. City were to play alongside First Division sides United, Everton, Liverpool, Stoke, and the Third Division's Chester, Crewe, New Brighton, Port Vale, Stockport, Tranmere, and Wrexham in the Western League.

The opening fixture on 21st October was a Manchester derby at Old Trafford before a restricted crowd of 7,000. Regardless of the state of the Nation, or the size of crowd, the players saw this match as the perfect opportunity to show that City were still equal to the Reds despite the official League placings. With goals from Brook, Doherty, Heale, and Herd the Blues defeated United 4-0. The following week 4,000 watched Wrexham defeated 6-1 at Maine Road. Results didn't always go that well for the Blues - a 7-3 Maine Road defeat at the hands of Liverpool in January proves this point - but it was a rather successful season considering the situation in the World at large.

Football was a powerful motivator during these early months of the war and helped boost morale. The 22 game league programme ended with City placed fifth on equal points as United (fourth) and Everton (third). The Western champions were Stoke, with Liverpool second.

City also played a total of 15 first team friendlies. Winning 10, drawing 3, and losing 2. The biggest wins during this sequence both came against Stockport with the Blues winning 5-0 away and 7-2 at home - Jimmy Heale scored four in this match. There was also a War

Cup. The first round was played over two legs and the draw was regionalised. City drew United and in the first leg defeated the Reds 1-0 at Old Trafford. Unfortunately, Wild's side lost the return 2-0 before over 21,000 spectators.

Already teams were having to make use of guest players, with City giving games to ten different guests. Preston's James McIntosh played his one and only league game for City in the February 1940 Manchester derby, while Fred Tilson and Ernie Toseland both returned for single appearances. During the seven wartime seasons a total of 82 guests played for the Blues.

International football also continued throughout the War, although caps were not awarded for these matches. For the Wales England match on 18th November 1939 Swift, Sproston, and Brook helped England to a 3-2 victory. Two weeks later Sam Barkas and Eric Brook were travelling to Newcastle for the clash with Scotland when they were involved in a car crash. Neither was able to make the game and so England fielded a couple of Newcastle men instead. One of them, Tommy Pearson, was actually Scottish. This was typical of the abnormal nature of wartime sport.

Of the two players involved in the crash, Sam Barkas did not manage to play again until February, while Brook was never able to play for the Blues again. It was a tragic end to a wonderful City and England career. In March 1965 Eric passed away at the age of 57.

1940-1941 Guests

For 1940-41 the Leagues were developed further. There would only be two regional leagues with City playing in the Northern section, but for the first time there would be no points awarded at all. Instead the league would be decided on goal average as clubs would be playing an unequal number of matches. Clubs were expected to organise their own fixtures, but each First and Second Division club were asked to play at least two Third Division teams. They were also expected to play over twenty games.

With this rather strange approach to football, where goals were all that mattered, the regularly high scoring Blues were expected to do well. Early in the season City applied to the FA to allow league games to be played on Sundays. Whether this was to squeeze more fixtures in, or simply the hope that Sundays would allow greater attendances isn't known. What is known is that the Blues played a total of 35 league games, winning 18 and drawing 10. But the important figures were the goals scored and conceded with City finding the net an incredible 104 times - more than any other team in the Northern and Southern sections. 55 goals were conceded giving them an average of 1.89, placing the Blues third behind Preston and Chesterfield. Had the

table been decided on goal difference, the high scoring City would have been clear winners.

In the War Cup Wild's Blues progressed past Blackpool, Blackburn, and Everton to face Preston in the fourth round - the northern semi-final. Preston were, without doubt, the real team of the season as they defeated City 2-1 in the first leg and 3-0 in the return, and went on to defeat Arsenal in the national final.

One guest player appearing for the Blues in the Preston games, and for much of the season, was United man Harry McShane, the father of actor Ian McShane who years later would also appear in front of City's supporters during filming of football scenes for the film Yesterday's Hero.

Other guest players included another Red, the future United captain and player of the year Johnny Carey. Both Carey and McShane found the net while with City, with Carey scoring in the 6-4 victory over Bolton while McShane scored twice - once in the 2-2 draw at Burnley on Christmas Day 1940 and once in City's 2-0 defeat of United on 5th October at Old Trafford.

From a regional perspective, one of the most significant wartime events occurred on Tuesday 11th March 1941 when Old Trafford's multi-span Main Stand was hit by a bomb and almost completely wrecked. The pitch was also scorched in the blast. The *Manchester Guardian*, mindful of media restrictions at the time, simply reported: "Slight outbreaks of fire were reported from a football ground and a training institute."

City contacted United immediately and offered to let them use Maine Road. Ultimately, the two clubs agreed an annual rent of around £5,000 plus a share of gate receipts, while the Blues were to use United's Cliff ground for reserve fixtures. Older supporters will have remembered the 1920s prospect of ground sharing which eventually came to nothing.

1941-1942 Regional Football

As the war progressed the regional football programme became more complicated with the league programme split into two with some games counting as War Cup or Lancashire Cup games. In 1941 the Northern League ended on Christmas Day. Each club played against nine other clubs home and away for points rather than goal average. The results for all 38 northern clubs were then compiled into one enormous table. City finished 17th, ten points behind champions Blackpool.

The second half of the season allowed clubs to play as many games as they wish, with the proviso that clubs had to play a minimum of 18 games to be included in the final table. City only managed 17 as Blackpool, who eventually finished runners up in the table, withdrew from two fixtures. The Blues again reached the quarter-final of the War Cup.

1942-1943 The Game Continues

Many footballers became seriously injured or died during the war. Mancunians became used to hearing tragic news. Sometimes the circumstances were odd. According to research by former City historian John Maddocks late 1920s City forward Arthur Bacon was killed in Derby during July 1942 when he fell off his bike during an air raid. The war had an impact everywhere.

On the pitch the format for wartime football followed a similar pattern throughout the conflict. In 1942-43 City finishing 30th out of 48 in the pre-Christmas 1942 league, and 3rd in the post-Christmas championship that followed.

1943-1944 Friendly Fire

The season saw City finish 17th and 19th in the two league competitions. They also reached the semi-final of the northern section of the War Cup.

One of the most significant stories of the war, at least from a City perspective, occurred during this period, although few fans knew the true story at the time. George Smith, who had joined the Blues in 1938 as an inside-forward, joined the armed forces when war broke out and he went on to serve in Africa. There was nothing unusual about young men serving overseas, however Smith's life changed significantly when he was under attack from a plane. A bullet entered his right arm above his elbow, travelled down his arm, past his elbow and came out again after travelling a good six or so inches through his arm. Inevitably, he was in a great deal of pain, but the most shocking aspect of all of this is that the plane that shot at him was actually from the South African Air Force. This meant that Smith was on the receiving end of what would in the 21st century be described as "friendly fire."

He was lucky the bullet had only entered his arm, but he was desperately unlucky to have been fired at by servicemen fighting on the same side. Smith spent some time recovering in Africa before being able to return to Manchester.

Why the South African Air Force chose to shoot at him is a mystery and at the time was not investigated. In fact the whole incident was hushed up and Smith was encouraged not to talk about the specific events. When he eventually returned to Manchester few knew the truth of what happened and, as with so many injured men, it wasn't a subject openly discussed. Even when the war was over the City football guide for 1945 simply stated: "Smith was one of the first casualties when he suffered a permanent injury to his hand sustained in manoeuvres somewhere in South Africa."

The permanent injury caused his hand and fingers to be permanently rigid in a clasping fashion, while his arm

had two large indentations where the bullet entered and exited his flesh. In addition, the path of the bullet down his arm was visible.

Despite the injury, Smith was determined to return to football, but it was felt his injury may prevent him from playing. He knew his arm would present some difficulties, but as a forward it was his feet and head that provided the main aspect of his play, not his arm. Nevertheless, the City management insisted on George performing a number of trials during 1944.

1944-1945 Smith's Return

George Smith passed all the trials and obstacles City presented him with and on 26th August 1944 he celebrated his return to the first team with a hat-trick against Tranmere in the opening match of the new season. This was Smith's first appearance in the first team since 25th April 1942.

By the end of the war he was a key member of the side, although he remained a little self-conscious about his arm. Usually he would cover it up with either the sleeve of his shirt, a sock, or a glove, and for team photos and the like the arm was usually hidden either behind his back or carefully positioned behind another player.

Some supporters and reporters thought his arm had

been amputated. Understandably, Smith wanted his football to do all the talking. He ended the season as top scorer with 22 goals from 36 games, only missing one match.

In the offices another footballer who would ultimately play his part in City's development post war joined the Club in December 1944. 16 year old Johnny Hart was spotted playing for his youth club: "I think it was Billy Williamson – a Scottish centre-forward – who recommended me to City. Billy mentioned me to someone at City – he was guesting for City in the war league. One thing led to another, and I was given an office job.

"It was the last few months of the war and so you have to bear that in mind, but at the time there was me, the secretary-manager Wilf Wild, and Len Parker – he only had one arm - and that was it for office staff! Len and me used to sort out the wages and hand them out and, between the three of us, I guess we ran most of the Club's activities. After each match I used to have to go in the dressing room and pick up all the discarded bandages and tapes and wash them. We always re-used them!"

Hart was signed on professional contracts after the war.

As for the team as a whole a pre-Christmas improved City reached 10th but struggled in the New Year, eventually reaching 47th out of 60 clubs.

1945-1946 The FA Cup Returns

During the summer of 1945, with peace restored across Europe, the FA and the League made plans to bring football back to normality. It was too late to return to a full pre-war programme and so for the last time football was to be divided on a regional basis with all First and Second Division clubs in the North playing each other home and away. The old Third Division North and South were to be recreated as far as possible to play their own competition. City ended the largely satisfactory season in tenth place but in the FA Cup, which had been reinstated at the request of the clubs, the Blues crashed out in the fourth round to Bradford.

The competition largely followed the style of the War Cup with rounds played on a two legged basis. In the third round City defeated Barrow 8-4 on aggregate, and had managed to defeat Bradford 3-1 at Park Avenue in the first leg. The two goal margin was believed to be enough for the Blues and the match programme included the line: "unless something extraordinary happens this afternoon City should be in the hat for the fifth round draw."

Something extraordinary did happen as Bradford cancelled out the Blues' lead with goals in the 21st and 23rd minutes. Cardwell had regained the aggregate lead

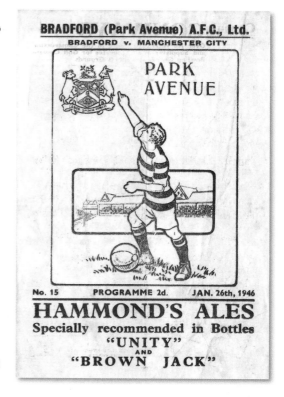

in the 36th minute but the second half saw Bradford in blistering form. They made it 4-4 on aggregate three minutes after the break and then netted three times in nine minutes to make it 6-1 on the night. The Blues pulled a goal back after 78 minutes but Bradford came back again netting a penalty five minutes from time and their eighth in the 87th minute.

The Blues had endured their record home defeat. Logically there was no reason why it should happen on that day. The weather wasn't great and Cardwell was injured during the match, but City's team should have been more than capable of at least holding back Bradford.

As well as the FA Cup matches, the Blues played a total of 42 first team fixtures. One of the highlights was the Manchester derby on 6th April 1946. George Smith netted all four goals as the Blues trounced the Reds 4-1. The match was watched by over 62,000. Scoring four goals - three in seven minutes – made him the undisputed star of the game. Smith: "I wasn't much of a drinker… I never went wild or anything… but beating United in that manner and by scoring four goals was a wonderful moment. I enjoyed the day and enjoyed most of the games against them during this period. It was nice for the landlords to put one over the tenants."

1946-1947 Promotion

The return of the full League programme was eagerly awaited. For City a return to the First Division was vital and, from the moment the season opened on 31st August with a 3-0 victory at Leicester, the Blues entertained their fans. The team was, in the main, a familiar one with the likes of Swift, Sproston, Barkas, McDowall, Herd, and Westwood appearing, but the great Peter Doherty was no longer at Maine Road. Throughout the war the player and club seemed to be at loggerheads with the directors often refusing to let their valuable asset guest for other clubs. They were angry that he'd been unable to play in a few crucial fixtures – they felt it had been impossible for him to get back to Manchester - and so they forbade him from guesting for Derby County. Instead they stated he could play for Manchester United, but as United were playing at Maine Road this seemed to imply that any attempt to turn out for the Reds would bring him into further trouble. Surely he couldn't play for United on City's ground?

In the end the situation became so difficult that Doherty - many claim the greatest League player of all time - asked to be transfer listed. In December 1945 he transferred to Derby County for £7,000. It was a disappointing end to his Maine Road career.

Throughout 1946-47 City, frequently watched by large crowds, challenged for promotion. In November 1946, the no doubt exhausted Wilf Wild ended his fourteen year reign as manager to return to purely secretarial duties. His period in charge had been successful, with more trophies won under him than any predecessor. He remained in office through to his death in December 1950. Keeping City going throughout the war must have taken its toll.

Wild's replacement was former captain Sam Cowan who accepted the position at the start of December 1946. The only problem being that Cowan had set up a rather successful physiotherapy practice in Brighton and felt he could not move away. Much to the directors' annoyance he commuted to Manchester throughout the season. George Smith remembered in 2003 that the team tried to make this work: "We'd have training sessions and meetings certain evenings so that Sam could arrive and talk with us. I don't think we thought there was anything strange, we just went along with it, although I do remember some of the tactical meetings were supposed to be voluntary - well some of the older players didn't like that. They wouldn't volunteer to stay in the evenings for tactical discussions back then!"

On New Year's Day a 4-0 victory over Fulham sent City to the top of the table in style. It also saw the debut of future Liverpool manager Joe

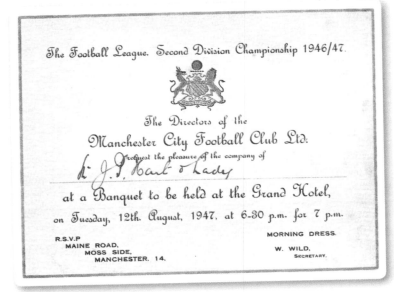

Fagan. The Blues were playing as champions and, more importantly, looked like a typical First Division club. The only problem was the weather. Postponements dragged the season through to mid-June, by which time City started to drop a few points but it hardly mattered.

The Blues won the title with 62 points - four more than second placed Burnley. The popular City were back in the First Division but it had been a long campaign. George Smith: "The season ended in June and on the last day Roy Clarke made his debut and I scored all five goals when we beat Newport County. It was another great day and I was given the match ball. I've still got it because something like that is special, but it didn't matter so much that I scored five. It was good that we won. I ended the season as top scorer but promotion was the main aim."

When Roy Clarke made his debut in that final match he went on to create something of an unusual record by playing in three different divisions of the Football League in three consecutive games. He joined City in May 1947 from Third Division champions Cardiff, made his debut in the last Second Division game, then made his second appearance against Wolves in the First Division.

1947-1948 Cowan's Departure

Despite promotion Sam Cowan was unable to continue as manager. The directors were far from happy with his commuting and so, reluctantly, his brief managerial period was at an end. Most of the players seemed to accept it, however fifties star Johnny Hart, still performing office duties at the Club in 1947, remembered in 2003: "There were a few mutterings around the place. There was one away game – it could have been Southampton in April 1947 – when Sam chose to stay with his family rather than be in the hotel with the players. I think the directors were unhappy with that and I think that's the day when they decided things had to change."

It took some time, however, before the Blues found a replacement and the new season started without a manager in place.

Being managerless at the start of the Club's first post war Division One season was a real issue and may have hampered the Blues' development. This proved to be a significant period in the history of Manchester football. City had been Manchester's best supported and most popular club but the post war period saw United gain support and significant interest. With United in the First Division playing at Maine Road many of City's traditional supporters returning from the war chose to watch both clubs. Those who found it difficult to pay for a game every week started to drift towards the games with the biggest stars - obviously United's games in the First.

For many Blues the fact that United were now playing good football and challenging for the League, as they did in 1946-47, was wonderful news. City fans had seen United as the poor relations - the Reds had been close to relegation to the Third Division and near extinction during the 30s. Many saw any success for United as being good for the whole city, especially as a former Blue hero Matt Busby was helping to bring pride to the Reds. There was only friendly rivalry between the two clubs.

With hindsight, United's stay at Maine Road was bad for the Blues. City had been generous to the Reds at a time when the club could have moved to several venues, such as any of the rugby grounds in the region, the Belle Vue stadium that had staged Manchester Central games in the 30s, or grounds like Burnden Park or Stockport County. The Blues had clearly done the right thing for Manchester as a whole. They could easily have chosen the approach United followed in 1920 when they tried to benefit from City's misfortune following the Hyde Road fire.

In the post war period it was now United who were gaining the upper hand. During the early 1980s City's popular chief scout, Harry Godwin, remembered the turning point: "United played at Maine Road just after the war, and because they were a better team than City they took over a lot of the support of the men whose loyalty had strayed while they were away in the services, and of their youngsters who were just getting interested. United were looking like a team, and they won the Cup in 1948."

Winning the Cup and finishing as runners up to Arsenal in the League, combined with the relatively cheap use of a 80,000 capacity venue, gave United the edge. Pre-war City set the attendance records, but a sign of what was to follow came when the January United-Arsenal game set a new League record crowd of 83,260 – still not Maine Road's best, but huge compared to most venues.

United's use of Maine Road seemed to contrast substantially with City's use of Old Trafford for reserve games. At one fixture the gate receipts were £4 15s. As the *Evening News* put it this was barely enough to cover the transport of the playing kit from Maine Road!

While City's generous support of their neighbours inadvertently damaged the Blues in the long term, it is fair to say that the Club's inability to appoint a replacement for Cowan caused a few short term issues. The most obvious one being consistency. It appears that the directors took it in turns to have ultimate responsibility for all team affairs with one taking responsibility for the first team and another looking after the second team on a rota basis. This situation existed for the opening 16 games of the season – 5 wins, 5 draws and 6 defeats.

On 15th November 1947 the City match programme

SPORTING CHRONICLE
AND ATHLETIC NEWS
Est. 1871 No. 22,087 THURSDAY, APRIL 8, 1948 A KEMSLEY NEWSPAPER THREEPENCE

72,000 ROARED AT RED, BLUE FANATICS
As Manchesters Fought
By EDGAR TURNER

MANCHESTER UNITED .... 1 MANCHESTER CITY 1

FANATICAL fight: a peppy, pulsating, he-man Derby, is the verdict on the battle of Red and Blue before an all-ticket 72,000 crowd at Maine Road, Manchester, last night.

GAVE PEP TO FORWARD LINE

Factors in Fav of Lucky Lo
JOCK SCOT MADE IMPRESSIV
By KETTLEDRUM (Quintin Gil

BILL LINACRE, playing at centre-forward for the first time in Manchester City's team, brought a liveliness which has been missing in the City attack for some time.

The Sporting Chronicle reports on the 1-1 Manchester derby of 7th April 1948. That day City were the away team at Maine Road.

revealed that the search was over: "A secret, as closely-guarded as any budget or atom bomb, has at long last been revealed by the news that 'Jock' Thomson, Everton's coach and former Scottish half-back, has been appointed City manager."

Thomson - who, incidentally, pre-war had lost his place to Joe Mercer at Everton – was a renowned footballer during the early 30s but not noted for his managerial skills. The editor of the City programme revealed that the new manager was delighted with his appointment but surprisingly added: "As Mr. Thomson told me this week he has no set plans for the future, and by that he doesn't mean 'I don't know where to start'. Naturally, he will need a little time to get acclimatised, and, wisely, he does not intend to set the Irwell on fire from the word 'go.'"

Those comments were aimed at setting expectations, but they hardly encouraged fans who had been very supportive of former hero Sam Cowan. Results had to improve if they were to accept the new

manager, and they did initially. Only three points were dropped in the five games following the announcement of his appointment.

Thomson's side did struggle in the final weeks of the campaign, but this proved to be a satisfactory first season back in the First Division as City finished tenth.

There had been some significant player changes. Sam Barkas at the age of 38 had left the Blues at the end of the previous season while newcomers Roy Clarke and Eddie McMorran became regulars. Centre-forward McMorran had signed from Belfast Celtic.

Another player regularly performing well was Scottish international Andy Black, who had joined City in June 1946 from Heart of Midlothian. During 1947-48 Black was City's top scorer with 16 goals, three more than George Smith.

1948-1949 Swift's Retirement

In 1948-49 Thomson's City made an uncertain start to the season. Three victories, two draws (including the first derby of the season), and three defeats in their opening eight games. There had been no major signings, and Frank Swift's announcement that this would be his last season caused a little panic. Swift, who had captained England to an exciting 4-0 defeat over Italy in Turin, wanted to go out at the top. Most agreed with that idea but could not see an obvious replacement. Perhaps Swift's decision had occurred as a result of the first seven seconds of the opening game at Maine Road when Preston kicked off, worked the ball quickly to left winger Bobby Langton. He ran a few yards and then shot. Somehow the ball sneaked in at the near post while Frank Swift was still throwing his cap into the net. The

FRANK SWIFT
*Every Saturday
Special Articles by
Manchester City's
International Skipper*

•

Tom Markland on all City's matches and full reports of all the big games

EVENING CHRONICLE
FOOTBALL EDITION

goal equalled the record for the quickest scored in the League. Even so City won the game 3-2.

As the season progressed Alec Thurlow replaced Swift in nets on occasion, but he never managed to appear for more than two consecutive games. The Blues were always going to find it difficult to replace the world class Swift. Somebody else whose City playing career was to end during this season was Les McDowall, who moved to Wrexham as player-manager. McDowall had captained City for a while pre-war, and was keen to move into management.

In December 1948, perhaps realising the effect United were having on City's gates, the Blues gave their rivals notice to quit. Later that season at Maine Road, United attracted 82,771 for the visit of Bradford Park Avenue, then 81,565 for Yeovil. Still not the record for the stadium but a sure fire warning to the City management that the days of total Blue dominance were over.

For the Reds, the stay at Maine Road was highly profitable. A *Manchester Evening News* article in October 1949 highlighted the huge increase in United's profit while staying at the higher capacity Maine Road. It revealed that United were about to announce an aggregate profit over the three Maine Road League seasons of £75,000 - easily an all-time record. The report noted that the 1949-50 season may not be quite as profitable: "Attendances at remodelled Old Trafford are

limited to 60,000 and, therefore, United may not be able to show such handsome dividends at the end of the current season."

Manchester City were now the ones who needed a lift.

With the Blues ending the season in a creditable seventh place, Frank Swift did retire at the age of 35. His final home game was a highly emotional affair with the goalkeeper chaired from the field at the end, while the final match saw a procession of decorated vehicles travel back across the Pennines. City had lost 1-0 to Huddersfield but that didn't stop the Supporters Club from dressing coaches up for the occasion. They even persuaded Swift to travel back on the lead coach.

1949-1950 Goalkeeping Crisis

Frank Swift's intended replacement Alec Thurlow was taken seriously ill with Tuberculosis and went to Norfolk to convalesce. Ultimately, Thurlow was to die at the age of 34 in 1956. City were desperate. With Thurlow ill and Swift in retirement the Blues were caught without a recognised 'keeper. In desperation they spent a considerable amount of time persuading Swift to come out of retirement. The experienced goalkeeper eventually agreed on condition that the comeback would only last a month or until the Club found a

Manchester City 1949-50. Back row (left to right): Fagan, Emptage, Williams, Powell, Walsh, Smith, Rigby. Front: Linacre, Munro, Westwood, Black, Clarke.

replacement – whichever was soonest. Swift appeared in the opening game of the 1949-50 season - a 3-3 draw with Aston Villa.

Ronnie Powell replaced Swift for the second and third games, but neither were won. and Swift returned. Finally on 7th September Swift kept a clean sheet with his last League performance - the no score draw at home to Everton. Powell then regained his place but it wasn't to last as City were about to set the football world talking by giving a chance to a former German paratrooper by the name of Bernhard Trautmann.

From the moment City gave a trial to the St. Helen's goalkeeper the protests started. The media loved it. Letters were published from writers claiming to be representatives from various ex-servicemen's organisations and Jewish groups. Some fans called for a boycott of the Club if Trautmann was named to play.

At the Club itself, Chairman Robert Smith tried to

BERG TRAUTMANN Joins Manchester C.

Berg Trautmann, 24-year-old German ex-prisoner of war goal-keeper, signed amateur forms for Manchester City late last night.

Trautmann's play with St. Helens in the Lancashire Combination attracted the attention of several Northern clubs.

At present in a bomb disposal unit, Trautmann is expected to resume his former occupation as a motor mechanic.

Trautmann, who has recently been in bed with influenza, is expected to play his first game for Manchester City in the Central League side against Barnsley on Saturday week.

calm the situation: "There is no doubt that many people will be upset by our signing of a German, but I feel we must take the broad view. City need a goalkeeper and we have excellent reports of this German as a goalkeeper and as an individual."

City captain Eric Westwood, who fought at Normandy, also tried to diffuse the situation. He told Trautmann: "There's no war in this dressing room. We welcome you as any other member of the staff. Just make yourself at home - and good luck."

On 17th October the *Manchester Evening News* believed the German gave a satisfactory display for the reserves at Barnsley, despite suffering from boils and a swollen hand. Throughout October the newspaper gave simple one or two line comments on Trautmann's performance, although the 'paper seemed to be confused as to what his first name was. They tried a couple of different spellings before settling for 'Berg'. Perhaps they knew that Berg was German for mountain and believed Trautmann was to be City's defensive rock.

Before Trautmann's debut City struggled on, with struggle being the operative word. On 18th October the *Evening News* provided the distressing news that the injury list was the longest ever experienced at the Club. Manager Jock Thomson was quoted as saying: "It's so bad that we have never been able to field our strongest team in any game this season. Thank goodness Westwood, Fagan, and Walsh have kept clear of injury."

The saddest injury during this period had to be that of Archie Aikman. Aikman was signed by City for £8,000 during the close season from Falkirk and, before he was able to appear for the Blues, he damaged his breast bone in a car accident. The accident took place on 5th August and for the next three months 5ft 10in Aikman visited Manchester Royal Infirmary four days a week for remedial exercises. The centre-forward, who was desperately needed in City's

Manchester City Football Club Ltd.

F. A. CHALLENGE CUP—WINNERS 1904, 1934
FINALISTS 1926, 1933

FOOTBALL LEAGUE CHAMPIONS
1st DIVISION, 1937
2nd DIVISION, 1899, 1903, 1910, 1928, 1947

TELEPHONE No. MOSS SIDE 1191

TELEGRAPHIC ADDRESS:
"FOOTBALL MANCHESTER"

SECRETARY: W. WILD

TEAM MANAGER: J. R. THOMPSON

REGISTERED OFFICE:
MAINE ROAD,
MOSS SIDE,
MANCHESTER. 14

July, 1949

Dear Sir (or Madam),

SEASON TICKETS, 1949-1950

I beg to advise you that Season Tickets are now on sale, and reservation of the seat(s) you occupied last season may be made up to and including Friday, 5th August.

The Prices of the Tickets are :-

CHAIRS. BLOCKS 'B' & 'C'.

£5-5-0 Gents
£4-4-0 Ladies or Boys

RESERVED SEATS. BLOCKS 'A' 'D' 'E' & 'F'

£3-15-0 Gents
£2-15-0 Ladies and Boys

If it is your intention to renew your ticket(s), kindly complete and return the attached form. Postage paid envelope enclosed.

Cheques should be made payable to "Manchester City Football Club Ltd."

Yours faithfully,

W. Wild.

Secretary

City announce season ticket prices for the 1949-50 season.

n **Gets His Chance** | Replaces Ronnie Powell

g **Soccer**

attempt to equal the record
to a football season of 17
hich was successful at Charlton

overed from the injury which
e and Done continues as leader
al 17th match, against Aston
ay.

Balmer, who has been out of the

G OALKEEPER Bert
Trautmann, German
ex-P.o.W., makes his senior
side debut in the Man-
chester City team to visit
Bolton on Saturday.

The first known photograph of Bert Trautmann in action for the Blues. The image was taken at a reserve game.

attack, was keen to regain fitness: "I am fed up being out of the game so long. The doctor says that if I were an ordinary workman I could be back on the job, but my chest is not yet sufficiently sound to take a shoulder charge.

"I've thought sometimes that people might think I wasn't bothering about getting fit, but I am. You want to see the way they've kept me fit at the infirmary, skipping, and bending this way and that. I ache to get into action when I'm watching games, but sometimes I still get a slight clicking in the chest."

Sadly, Aikman never managed to make his League debut for City. He had shown promise when he played in five close season games in Denmark during May 1949, scoring in all but one of those matches, but never made it into the first team. The Blues held his registration until 19th January 1952, after which he returned to Scotland and managed to play in the Scottish League.

With such a large injury list in 1949, City needed to strengthen the squad but the one player who manager Thomson seemed set on simply did not want to come to Maine Road - Don Revie. Thomson had been chasing the Leicester man for much of the season and offered £20,000 in October. He was not alone as interest for the 22 year old inside forward increased almost daily. By the end of October Arsenal, Hull, Fulham and City were all said to be prepared to spend in excess of £20,000 and possibly provide a player in exchange. Jock Thomson told the *Evening News* that City had a house lined up for

Revie and that in talks the player seemed very keen on a transfer to Manchester. Arsenal were second favourites to land him.

The chase for Revie's signature dragged into November with reports suggesting it would take a new transfer record of around £26,000 to bring the player to Maine Road. Eventually, City lost interest and Revie transferred to Hull - said to be the least likely of all the clubs to sign him - for the original sum of £20,000.

On 14th November Eric Thornton, writing in the *Evening News*, shocked the Blues' management by openly stating the Blues would go down if there were no new signings. In a stinging article the City reporter attacked the players he believed were the weak links and outlined what he believed needed to be done to bring respectability back to the Blues. Two days later the newspaper published readers' responses to the article. Most were in agreement with Thornton with the overwhelming theme being that the management simply did not know who to buy, or who to play. There was widespread concern over the transfer stories, in particular the attempted signing of Revie, which supporters believed 'put off' the younger players. It was also felt that Revie's move to Hull indicated that there was something wrong with the management at Maine Road.

In addition to all the negativity, the news that Trautmann was to make his debut appeared. Considering all the anti-German feeling it must have been somewhat surprising to read comments from supporters suggesting the German be 'given a go' in the first team, and that Thornton saw his selection as an extremely wise decision. Considering the plight of the Blues at this point it is clear that Trautmann's inclusion in the squad and then the first team was one of desperation. Anti-German feeling could have overwhelmed the Blues.

Trautmann's debut was not quite the success supporters hoped as the game ended in a 3-0 defeat at Bolton. However he had kept a clean sheet through the first half and been unable to stop two attempts and a penalty in the second. The German was far from happy, but the press viewed the game as a great success for the 'keeper. As did his predecessor. Frank Swift had watched the game and felt he had to welcome his replacement. He told Trautmann that he had put in a great performance and the former England international was genuinely pleased - remember Swift was still officially a City player, but truly had no intention of playing again.

Actually, it was around this time that United tried to lure Swift to Old Trafford. The Reds were struggling to find a replacement for longserving Jack Crompton, and Matt Busby tried to poach his former Blue team mate. With the initial hostility towards Trautmann and the possibility of boycotts, City could not afford to allow one of their all-time most popular players to move to Old Trafford. Not after everything that had happened since 1937.

Fortunately Swift himself turned Busby down, and the Reds' search continued.

At Maine Road, Trautmann prepared for his home debut against Birmingham City. Some 'papers called for a boycott. In the end a crowd of 30,617 watched the new man keep a clean sheet while, at the other end, two goals apiece from Andy Black and Roy Clarke gave City victory. Boycotts were forgotten.

Unfortunately, the next game saw a different City. In dreadful, muddy conditions, Derby County defeated the Blues 7-0 at the Baseball Ground. The Derby fans enjoyed laughing at the City 'keeper. They also took the opportunity to ridicule Trautmann about the war. It was not a good day. Afterwards Swift reassured Trautmann by pointing out that his own second -ever reserve game over 16 years earlier had ended in a 6-1 defeat at home to Blackburn. The occasional humiliating defeat helped develop his character, and he felt certain the new 'keeper would learn from the Derby defeat.

Despite the setbacks - and there were plenty that season - Trautmann won over the Manchester press and, more importantly, the local population. The Rabbi of Manchester, Alexander Altman did much to ease the situation: "Despite the terrible cruelties we suffered at the hands of the Germans, we would not try to punish an individual German, who is unconnected with these

TRUE BLUE
Peter Doherty

Even in the 1970s Peter Doherty was still regarded as the greatest Irish footballer of all time. Some fans were convinced he was also City's greatest star.

crimes, out of hatred. If this footballer is a decent fellow, I would say there is no harm in it. Each case must be judged on its merits."

London was different, though. During the 1990s a City historian, David Whalley, uncovered the story behind City's match at Fulham on 14th January - Trautmann's first in the capital. Whalley believed this was the turning point in the German's relationship with the media in general. Despite the scoreline - City lost 1-0 - Trautmann did much to impress the public and press.

During the early moments of the game Trautmann suffered much abuse though as shouts of 'Kraut' and 'Nazi' rang out. Instead of upsetting the 'keeper, this abuse made the German more determined.

Trautmann's performance that day was brilliant and his approach changed the atmosphere and earned him a standing ovation. All thoughts of him being a 'Nazi' had gone by full time. One young Fulham fan in the crowd that day, Jim Sims remembered the game well: "The effect on us at the Cottage was magnetic. You were watching a supreme professional at the top of his trade.

A real flesh and blood hero. I am absolutely certain that his appearance in the First Division just four years after ceasing hostilities had a major effect on boosting and repairing our relationship with the Germans. He'd been a prisoner of war as a paratrooper, of course, and married an English girl, which all helped. But he gave you that warm glow before the game and you knew you were in for something special.

"After the game, we all clapped like mad as they made the corridor for him. It was unique. It was as though we were trying to wash away the sins of the world and was pretty emotional."

Trautmann had won over the London press and the public and he was able to enjoy his football. Naturally, the player's attitude had helped. He did little to upset the public, and tried to ensure he appeared human - something few Britons at the time believed was possible.

As the season progressed, despite the performances of the agile German, City struggled. The Blues were heading for relegation and the situation looked desperate. On April Fool's Day, City returned to London for another memorable match for the German 'keeper. It was the return with Arsenal, but it was also two days after Trautmann had married Margaret Friar, the daughter of the St. Helen's secretary Jack Friar. The officials allowed the new Mrs. Trautmann to travel with the City party to London as a sort of honeymoon. For the groom, the game was not a happy occasion as he was beaten four times. Perhaps he had other things on his mind.

One week later City defeated Burnley 1-0 - the first win since Christmas Eve - and followed that up with a 2-1 victory over Wolves. There was still hope, but a 3-0 defeat to the same club the next day caused concern.

Away at League leaders Sunderland in the following match, City were winning 2-0 when the referee awarded the home side a penalty. Trautmann was unable to stop the shot and Sunderland gained the momentum. Later another penalty was awarded against the Blues. This time Trautmann saved it, but the referee ordered it to be retaken. The German was far from happy and booted the ball into the crowd. When the ball was eventually retrieved and the penalty retaken, Trautmann saved again. City centre-forward Dennis Westcott rushed up to the referee and jokingly asked: "How did you like that save, ref? Better than the first, wasn't it!"

A couple of draws followed, then City lost the final match at Everton 3-1. Thomson's side were three points behind Charlton, who were safe in 20th place, and the Blues were relegated despite finding an excellent replacement for Swift.

Jock Thomson's rather unexciting period in charge was now over. The directors looked for a man who could inspire the players in the way that Busby had at Old Trafford. It was not going to be easy to find a man

like that. There were few of them in football, although it should be remembered that Cowan had been that type of leader. Perhaps, remembering Cowan's impact they looked for a former captain known to the City faithful?

The man chosen was former half-back Les McDowall who had been Wrexham's manager since leaving City only a year or so earlier.

1950-1951 Paul & Promotion

The Second Division was not the place for one of England's biggest clubs, but it was the appropriate division for a side struggling to come to terms with post war football. Manchester City needed a quick return. Everyone connected with the Club hoped new manager Les McDowall would be able to deliver promotion at the first attempt.

During the close season McDowall entered the transfer market and purchased a man who would go on to become a City legend - wing-half Roy Paul. Paul had found fame while with Swansea and had been first noticed by Arsenal when the two sides met in the fourth round of the 1949-50 FA Cup. Immediately after the game Arsenal manager Tom Whittaker put in a bid for the Welshman, but the Swansea directors refused to sell. It was bad enough losing the tie to 'Lucky Arsenal' never mind the best player.

Somehow, the following July, McDowall did persuade Swansea to sell for £25,000. Joe Mercer, who captained the Arsenal side that beat Swansea always had a high regard for Paul: "Roy Paul was one of the best players I've ever seen. He gave us a hell of a fright when Swansea came to Arsenal in 1950."

Paul made his debut in City's opening fixture - a 4-2 victory at Preston - and managed to appear in all but one League game that season. The one he missed? City's 3-2 away win over his old side Swansea on 21st October, and even that was because he was playing international football for Wales. Roy Clarke was also on international duty.

In the second and third games of the season, both played at Maine Road, City defeated Cardiff 2-1 and Bury 5-1, prompting many to talk about a quick return to the First Division. For those who regularly attended Maine Road, promotion still seemed a long way off. This report summed it up nicely: "To the man who relies on figures Manchester City's 5-1 win over Bury at Maine Road on Saturday promises only a short stay in the Second Division, and in terms of plain arithmetic 6 points from three games confirms this view, but the spectator, who relies on facts rather than figures, is sceptical. He has every reason to be, for Manchester City have not yet shown real strength."

The star of the Bury match was Dennis Westcott who capped his best performance since joining the Blues with a hat-trick. He also had a hand in fourth goal, providing a centre for Johnny Hart.

Two weeks later the Blues achieved another 5-1 Maine Road victory, this time against Chesterfield. A crowd of 43,631 basked in the rather surprising Manchester sunshine as City tore into their visitors. The reporter Don Davies, writing in the *Manchester Guardian* under the name an 'Old International', pointed out a few concerns though. He believed City were a little hesitant in defence and that at times it seemed as if Bert Trautmann and the defenders were struggling to understand each other. He counted three occasions when the Chesterfield forwards had an open net to shoot at, and claimed they had only missed because they were surprised at the gaps. Nevertheless, the game gave City another two points and placed them second on 12 points to Birmingham who had a superior goal average.

By 30th September McDowall's side headed the table. A 1-0 victory against Coventry that day strengthened their lead and set the 'Old International' purring with delight at the way the Blues were now pulling together and performing as a team. His concern about City's defence was rapidly disappearing: "The goal was a triumph of observation and judgement, and set the seal on Spurdle's claims to be rated as a player of the first rank. Paul, too, played beautifully, and with that air of authority one is entitled to expect from a City captain. Behind him, Westwood lent valuable support in a timely return to form. Here was a glimpse of the old campaigner again - speedy, quick-witted, resolute, with a

flair for swift attacking moves on his own. If Westwood's recovery can be maintained, the prospects for City are bright indeed.

"As a result this vied with many a good cup-tie played at Moss Side. For those who like hard shooting, fine goalkeeping, brusque tackling, and 'hair-breadth 'scapes i'th imminent deadly breach' it was ideal. Trautmann, possibly, would win the prize for a flawless performance - his every move is made with such consummate ease and grace - but justice would require a consolation prize for Wood, if only for gallantry under pressure."

The Blues actually remained unbeaten until 7th October - a run of ten games - when Doncaster staged a remarkable recovery. City were winning 3-0 at half-time, but four second half goals for Doncaster gave the Yorkshire club victory. Two City wins followed but postponements and a few poor results from November through to January hampered progress. On 18th November a 4-1 defeat at Blackburn prompted one newspaper to headline the City report with "Bert still disposing the bombs." The German had been released from bomb disposal duties only a few days before, and the report went on to say that he'd been under much more pressure in this game than with his duties. One of Blackburn's goals - scored from a penalty - was hit so hard it actually sailed past Trautmann and went through the net itself!

On 2nd December a 1-1 draw at Barnsley kept City in pole position with 26 points from 19 games. Second

George Smith and Eric Westwood training at Maine Road.

were Blackburn on the same number of points but after playing one additional match.

As the season moved into January the Blues started to lose their way a little, but managed to find themselves challenging for promotion from a 'games in hand' position. Despite setbacks City remained in contention.

A 4-1 victory at Leeds on 24th March boosted morale and then, two days later, 35,149 watched the City-Notts County fixture end goalless. The game was played in appalling conditions witnessed by the 'Old International': "On a fine stretch of water, lashed by incessant rain, Manchester City and Notts County rewarded all who were inquisitive enough to come and watch it by playing, with great heartiness and much good humour, a novel form of aquatic sports which one heard variously described as 'Splash-ball' and 'Foot-polo'. No goals were scored; and fortunately, no lives were lost through drowning."

The draw placed City fourth on 41 points after 34 games. The division leaders were Preston with 52 points from 36 games. At the start of December they had been 8th on 21 points, but a magnificent run had seen them bypass all opposition. Cardiff were eight points behind in second place. City could still achieve promotion, but it now appeared that Preston could not be caught.

A 6-0 thrashing of Barnsley on 21st April was watched by City's third highest crowd of the season - 42,741. The highest had been 45,842 for the no score draw with Hull on 28th October. With only three games left City's destiny was more or less in their own hands, especially when a point was gained away at Sheffield United. That meant that only Cardiff, who were on 49 points from 41 games, could overtake fifty points City.

Preston were already certain of the Second Division championship.

On 30th April another point was gained in the goalless draw at Notts County, and then on 5th May City's final game of the season brought a 2-2 draw at home to Grimsby, who would be relegated to the Third Division (North) that day. Despite the standing of the two clubs it was Grimsby who were the more impressive on the day. The visitors had taken the lead twice, only to see the Blues fight back for the point. City could have changed the game completely, possibly gaining victory, had Roy Paul managed to score from a penalty before the fight back had started.

Despite the result, City were back in Division One - Cardiff had only managed a point from their last game.

McDowall's first season in charge had been a success. To achieve promotion the manager had brought in some new faces. Left-half Frank McCourt was signed from Bristol Rovers after writing to the Club for a trial. He had been keen to move north and fancied his chances at Maine Road. McDowall liked what he saw and gave the player his chance in the first team on 3rd February.

Other newcomers included Ray Haddington - an £8,000 signing from Oldham - and Jimmy Meadows. Haddington was a firm favourite with the Boundary Park support but at Maine Road he featured in only six games, scoring four goals. At the end of the season he was transferred to Stockport County.

The Meadows transfer was different. He was signed from Southport and made his debut on 17th March. From that moment until 5th January he was an ever present.

1939-1951 SUMMARY

Major Trophies Won: Second Division Champions 1946-47

Highest League Attendance: 78,000 Manchester United, 20/09/47 (The record crowd for a Manchester derby in the League)

Highest Cup Attendance: 67,494 Preston North End, 07/02/48 (FA Cup)

Managers: 1932-46 Wilf Wild, 1946–47 Sam Cowan, 1947–50 Jock Thomson & 1950-63 Les McDowall

Seasonal Record:

Season	League	Posn	FA Cup	Leading Scorer	Average Attendance
1939-40	4th in Western Division & War Cup 1st round			Herd 19	4,100
1940-41	3rd in North Regional League & War Cup 4th round			Currier 42	4,000
1941-42	17th & 19th in North Regional League comps & War Cup 3rd round			Boothway 34	4,900
1942-43	3rd & 30th in North Regional League comps & War Cup 3rd round			Currier 26	10,900
1943-44	17th & 19th in North Regional League comps & War Cup semi-final			Doherty 23	14,200
1944-45	10th & 47th in North Regional League comps & War Cup 2nd round			Smith 22	15,400
1945-46	10th in FL North		Rnd 4	Constantine 25	24,000
1946-47	FL Div2	Champions	Rnd 5	Smith 23	39283
1947-48	FL Div1	10	Rnd 5	Black 16	42725
1948-49	FL Div1	7	Rnd 3	Smith 12	38699
1949-50	FL Div1	21	Rnd 3	Clarke 9	39381
1950-51	FL Div2	2	Rnd 3	Westcott 25	35016

Cup winners (l to r) Roy Paul, Roy Clarke, Ken Barnes, Joe Hayes (hidden), Roy Little, Bill Leivers, Bert Trautmann and Dave Ewing.

Wembley Double

"Granada had a great stroke of luck in being able to make quick arrangements to show hundreds of thousands in the North West the triumphant return of Manchester City. The seething crowds, the scenes on the Town Hall steps and the speeches of the players made a brilliant piece of intimate camera work."

The *Manchester Evening Chronicle* reporting on Granada TV's first outside broadcast – City's 1956 homecoming parade.

1951-1952 Revie Signs

For Les McDowall this season was probably seen as a season of consolidation, but the first ten games brought only seven points and the Blues were struggling. The worst moment came on 22nd August when the first away match of the season ended in a 5-1 defeat.

McDowall knew the situation had to improve and he persuaded the directors to break the Club's transfer record twice to sign first Ivor Broadis and then Don Revie. Broadis, a skilful inside forward, cost £25,000 from Sunderland. Earlier in his career he had played wartime football for Tottenham, amongst others, and then in 1946, at the age of 23, he became player-manager of Carlisle. In February 1949 he created history by transferring himself to Sunderland. He made his City

debut at Spurs on 6th October and helped the Blues to a 2-1 victory.

It is worth recording that Broadis was viewed as a great acquisition and shortly after arriving at Maine Road he made his international debut against Austria.

Broadis helped improve matters on the pitch at City immediately, and then McDowall made his second record transfer when he finally persuaded Don Revie to join the Blues.

Revie was already a familiar name to supporters when he signed from Hull on 18th October. The fee was reported as £25,000 – equalling the Broadis record - and almost immediately the player was asked why his planned transfer to the Blues in 1949 never happened: "No player likes a long drawn out transfer serial. Nor for that matter does a football club. It is better for both sides if the parting is swift and sweet. In my case I came in for a lot of unpleasant publicity. It was difficult to make people realise that, although I was determined to leave Leicester, I was not going to do anything rash. I wanted to make sure it was a progressive step."

Revie admitted that at the time a number of clubs were interested in him, with Arsenal being the one he would have most liked to have played for. However, he felt that he wasn't quite ready for the bright lights of London and so had to choose between City and Hull: "'I went over to Manchester with my wife, Elsie, to meet Jock Thomson, the City manager at that time. It was raining when we arrived! Somehow we did not seem to fit the place. However, as we were to discover later, those first impressions that Manchester is a gloomy place were to be proved quite wrong."

With Revie and Broadis in the side McDowall hoped City would be a force, unfortunately the Blues failed to win a game during a dreadful three month period in the new year. The Blues had drawn eight games, but McDowall had to contend with the possibility that City could actually be relegated. Especially as the first three games in April all ended in defeat.

It was not as desperate as it could have been thanks to the ever-impressive Trautmann, who kept the goals against figure respectable, and there were actually enough struggling teams below City. Nevertheless, it was not the successful season fans needed.

The Blues finished 15th on 39 points - 11 more than the relegation zone - and McDowall felt satisfied that the original aim of consolidation was met.

1952-1953 Trautmann The Saviour

The season opened with two successive defeats (Stoke and Tottenham) before the real test - a Manchester derby with reigning champions United. For this game McDowall called up reserve centre-forward Billy Sowden for what turned out to be a promising debut. The player gave United's experienced Allenby Chilton an extremely uncomfortable afternoon and, together with Broadis, Clarke, and Ewing, put goalkeeper Jack Crompton under a lot of pressure. The youngster was also at the centre of a dispute over a possible City penalty after being brought down in the box.

Ivor Broadis was actually the star man as he, first, split the United defence open with a delightful through ball which left Roy Clarke in a great position to score with only the goalkeeper to beat - which he of course did. Then, In a crowded goal mouth, Broadis trapped a loose ball and smashed an unstoppable half volley past the startled Crompton.

At 2-0 the Maine Road faithful loved every minute but, as the game wore on the Reds threw all they could at City. In the final quarter United pulled one back, but in the end it was City's day. Pre-war the Blues had been the dominant local force, post war the initiative had swung to United, causing the 'Old International' to comment in the *Manchester Guardian*: "Manchester City gave their loyal and long suffering supporters that experience for which they have watched and prayed these last five years, namely, the right to do honour to a well merited and clear cut victory over their redoubtable neighbours."

After reporting the major incidents of the game, he suggested there would be plenty to debate in Manchester's bars: "This was a game which will be played over and over again in Manchester club circles for many weeks to come and among the main topics for argument might be these - (1) How do United account for their surprising fall from grace? (2) Why have City kept their real form in hiding for so long? (3) Can anyone deny that Spurdle is City's best left half-back, or that Meadows is wasted at outside right? The question as to whether Crompton did - or did not - grasp Sowden by the ankle and pull him down might be kept in reserve as an enlivener should conversation flag. To City supporters it was as clear as a man pulling rhubarb!"

Despite the derby victory, and a 3-3 draw at Tottenham in the next game, McDowall's side struggled through the Autumn and Winter of 1952. Typical of the period was a 5-4 September defeat at Middlesbrough where both defences seemed particularly poor. One report claimed: "Full-backs lacking in flexibility, centre-halves who were by no means so commanding as usual, and goalkeepers whose jumpiness belied their reputations, were continually extending handsome invitation to the attacks to go in with confidence and have a good time. The invitation was accepted cheerfully.

"It is a long time since any game at Middlesbrough was so full of incident and, although football crowds certainly like goals, neither club is likely to be content with things as they were on Saturday. Four men - one wing half and three forwards - were outstanding on each side and equally deserving, though victory was the reward of one set and defeat of the other. City's four were Paul, Meadows, Revie, and Broadis."

On 20th December City faced Stoke at Maine Road. The sides held the bottom two positions in the division and the game was viewed as a real four point fixture. Coming on the last Saturday before Christmas, it was never going to be a popular fixture, but as the 'Old International' reported the attendance was extremely low – 13,669: "On Saturday, before depressingly broad stretches of unoccupied terracing - for only 13,000 loyalists had braved the elements and the almost certain prospect of a dreary bout of relegation football - Manchester City and Stoke City met to decide which of them should face the strain of a heavy Christmas programme as wooden spoonists. After a close struggle, marred by a serious accident to Robertson, the Stoke City goalkeeper, and yet ennobled to some extent by the gallant bearing of his ten remaining colleagues, Manchester City won 2-1 and so left their friends from the Potteries reluctantly and, as many thought, undeservedly holding the spoon."

Johnny Williamson was one of City's scorers against Stoke. Although he didn't perhaps appreciate it at the time the game was changing with many young managers – the most obvious being Matt Busby at Old Trafford – focusing more on coaching and technique than they had in the past. When looking back on this period in 2003 he felt that the Blues had some very talented former players involved with the entire set up but that the Club didn't really put much attention into coaching. The focus was on natural talent: "Frank Swift was looking after the reserves and being in the same room as someone like that was enough in some ways. I think it was actually Swifty who changed me from being an inside-forward to being a centre-forward. That helped my career, but Swifty was a great influence in that dressing room. He had great humour and there are many stories of pranks played by him – and once in a while on him!

"Coaching didn't really exist though. You were encouraged to play football naturally. It's one of those things that you've either got or you haven't. The two most important things to know are when to give and when to go. That can't be coached. You need a footballer's brain."

On Boxing Day City's natural talent failed them as they were defeated 6-2 at Preston. Not the perfect result to prepare for the following week's derby match at Old Trafford! At United, McDowall gave a derby debut to a raw-boned centre-half called Dave Ewing who had signed from Luncarty Juniors in 1949. His debut was impressive, even though the game itself was rather drab and colourless. It ended 1-1 with City gaining more praise in the media than United. This seemed to give the Blues hope, and seven days later they defeated Swindon Town 7-0 in the FA Cup with Johnny Hart scoring four on a day when Roy Little made his debut. The Blues went out in the next round 5-1 in a replay with Luton, but the

Don Revie

derby draw and Swindon victory had brought a little hope for the rest of the League programme.

On 17th January McDowall's side travelled to Liverpool for the first League game since the derby. It was a memorable day as City - thanks to a goal from Johnny Hart - defeated Liverpool 1-0 to achieve their first away win since the same fixture in April 1952. Although Hart scored, it was Trautmann who was the real hero. He made many brilliant saves, especially in the final minutes when Liverpool had three corners in quick succession. Deservedly, Trautmann made the headlines that day.

City's next game was a 5-1 home win over Middlesbrough, but the Blues away form was still a worry, especially when a trip to Cardiff ended in a 6-0 defeat on 21st February. On that day two players - Eric Webster and Phil Woosnam - both made their only City appearances.

To bolster the attack, McDowall purchased Ken Whitfield from Wolves in time to make his debut in the 2-1 Maine Road defeat of Portsmouth on 28th February before 38,726. A couple of weeks later new winger Harry Anders, signed from Preston on 6th March, made his home debut against Aston Villa: "New signing Harry Anders, playing in his first home game for Manchester City, delighted the fans with his speed and trickery against Aston Villa, topping the day with a goal a few minutes before the end.

"Broadis again was in brilliant form, while Spurdle celebrated his return to the side with a splendid hat-trick and an all-round display which augurs well for the future."

The game ended 4-1 with City relaxing in the final ten minutes, allowing Villa the chance to pull a goal back. The Blues had now been undefeated at Maine Road since 1st November. The problems came on their travels. If they could get their act together away from Manchester then there was a chance they could climb away from the relegation zone.

In the next game City were deservedly leading 3-2 as the game entered its final twenty-five minutes. Then Sunderland piled on the pressure and bombarded Trautmann with so much physical play that the referee had to admonish several home players. In the final minute, Sunderland's approach was simply too much and they snatched an equaliser. Despite the scoreline, the game had been exciting: "Even a score of 3-3 gives little indication of the number of thrills in this hard, keenly-fought game, and City had good reason to feel aggrieved at being robbed of their second away win of the season. Ivor Broadis, captain for the day against his old club, scored two beauties with his left foot in the 22nd and 32nd minutes."

City's home form continued to impress and then, on 4th April, the Blues achieved their second away win of the season when they defeated championship challengers Charlton 2-1. The home side had missed a penalty, and put Bert Trautmann under tremendous pressure, nevertheless the Blues managed to hold on to gain an important victory. Two days later a 1-1 draw at Sheffield brought another vital point, but this was followed by a rare Maine Road defeat when eventual champions Arsenal won 4-2.

Salvation was still in City's hands but they made life difficult for themselves in their final four games. On 18th April a game that on paper should have brought at least a point ended with fellow strugglers Derby gaining an easy 5-0 victory - it could easily have been more – and caused fans to relive the nightmare 7-0 thrashing of December 1949. Both Ewing and Hart were injured during the game, with Hart limping for much of the game. Sadly, the injury prevented him from playing in the vital games that followed.

Ivor Broadis had missed the Derby game as he was on international duty, scoring a couple of goals for England. These were the days when England games clashed with the League programme and those clubs with internationals lost their best players. There was no question of club v country - country won on every occasion to the detriment of the League campaign.

Without Hart, but with Broadis back, City were defeated 2-0 at home to Preston four days after the Derby defeat. Panic was spreading on the Maine Road terraces. With only two matches left the Blues could still be relegated.

Fortunately, the next game ended in a 5-0 Maine Road victory over FA Cup finalists Blackpool. Ultimately, those points saved the Club from relegation. On the final day of the season City played their fourth game in eleven days - a 3-1 defeat at fellow strugglers Chelsea. The result hardly mattered, but statistics would show that McDowall's side had avoided relegation by a solitary point. Stoke and Derby were relegated, with Chelsea's victory lifting them above City on goal average.

Thanks mainly to Bert Trautmann's heroics throughout the season, McDowall's Blues were able to survive for another year. For the City faithful, the situation had to improve. Another relegation struggle would not be tolerated.

1953-1954 Building Blocks

Despite making significant profits in most of the post-war seasons the City directorate seemed keen not to spend cash on expensive new signings for the 1953-54 campaign, even though a season of struggle seemed likely. As early as the opening game fans saw that little had changed during the summer break as Wednesday defeated the Blues 2-0 at Sheffield. Reporters stressed how 'shaky' City's defence looked and how their play never reached a 'high standard'. Three days later a 4-0 home defeat to Wolves caused season ticket holders to consider if their investment had been a wise one.

Johnny Williamson had appeared in both those games at centre-forward. In 2003 he remembered how for most players the match day experience started: "It was a different world! There was always a race on to get into the drying room first because the kit was so old and worn that it really was a case of first up best dressed. The socks were enormous with the heel flapping around near your foot. They'd been washed so many times they'd lost their shape.

"For training we wore thick woolly jumpers – with holes in – and I'm certain some of this kit had been worn by the likes of Swifty and Doherty fifteen years earlier. I'm not saying City were bad because every club was like this. This was normal."

After three successive defeats a trip to Sunderland on 29th August saw the Wearsiders defeated 5-4. However, the next home game, brought City back down to earth. A disappointing crowd of 24,918 found little to excite them. The *Manchester Guardian* reporter 'Old International' knew the Maine Road club well: "Was it scepticism, or empty stomachs, that quelled the high spirits? Those who had built their hopes on a repeat performance in Saturday's vein were sadly disappointed. Villa beat City by the only goal scored. Or would it be true to say that City beat themselves?

"How appropriate it would have been for those whose earnest hope it was that City's sensational win at Sunderland was no mere flash in the pan, if either of the two fierce shots by Spurdle and Clarke in the first phase of the game had been slightly better placed. But Spurdle's hammer blow, delivered after picking up a foolish back pass by Blanchflower, buried itself into somebody's ribs and when Spurdle rolled the rebound deftly in Clarke's direction, Clarke tore in with his head tucked low between his knees, as his manner is, and shot tantalisingly wide of the far post. The only other incidents of note in the next ten minutes or so were two glorious saves by Trautmann - the real hero of the Sunderland battle - and a goalkeeper who can emulate the swift diving grace of a swallow."

The report went on to stress the strength of Trautmann, who by this point in his career was often described as one of, if not the World's greatest 'keeper. He was also being compared to the great Frank Swift, with supporters debating the strengths and weaknesses (if any) of the two City match winners. With City's disappointing early 50s form, Trautmann was at least able to prove his strengths. In every game he seemed to be forced to perform a last ditch miraculous save, to keep the Blues in the game. Without the impressive German it is unlikely the Blues would have survived in 1952-53, and it seemed the 'keeper would be expected to save them again in 1953-54.

Apart from Trautmann, City did have a number of impressive players - Revie, Paul, Spurdle, Anders, and Clarke - but somehow McDowall had not managed to get the team working as a unit. The 'Old International' often commented on this, with the Villa game being a particular worrying one: "There was little method or discernible pattern of play observable - just a formless scramble - and one felt grateful for that fine display of marching and counter-marching by the New Zealand Band at half-time which did remind us that there are still such things in the world as order and precision. But for the time being they seem to be eluding City."

Despite the lack of formation, City defeated Manchester United 2-0 three days later. This result had been achieved without Ivor Broadis who had sensationally been put on the transfer list by Les McDowall. He told reporters: "Following a heart to heart talk between the player and myself, it will be in the best interests of the club and player to part."

The player moved to Newcastle at the end of October for around £18,000.

A couple of 1-1 draws was followed by a 1-0 defeat at home to Huddersfield on 16th September, described by one reporter as "another unbelievably poor display" by the Blues. The struggle continued.

On 24th October Ivor Broadis played his last game for the Club, while young Joe Hayes made his debut. Both were commented on in match reports, with Broadis receiving acclaim for having "intelligent foresight", while Hayes made an impressive debut with two good goalscoring opportunities.

In December 2004 team-mate Johnny Hart looked back on Hayes' debut: "I thought Joe was a great player and a good goalscorer. He was a great guy. I remember when he first signed he had to meet us all at Piccadilly Train Station for the journey down to London. We were going to play Tottenham, and when I got to the station Joe was stood there with a brown paper parcel waiting. I always travelled light – I had my toothbrush in my pocket and that was it. Anyway, Joe said 'where's your pyjamas Harty?' So I told him I never wear them and he said 'Me, neither'. So I asked what was in the parcel, and he said his pyjamas!

"I said 'Didn't you say you don't wear them?' and he said 'Well I've got some just in case I have to share a room with Revie or Trautmann'. He clearly thought he'd be embarrassed in front of the star players. So I ended up sorting out that he could share with me. Anyway, as we were getting to bed I sorted out our alarm call and arranged for some tea to be brought in at 7.30am. We switched the lights off, then he asked 'Harty, who's going to bring the tea?' 'A waitress!' Five minutes later, 'Harty, who's going to open the door?' 'You're nearest, you will!' About ten minutes after that – he must have thought I was asleep – there was a bit of movement in the room. I turned the light on, and caught him practising opening the door, while covering himself up with the blanket!"

Despite Hayes obvious planning skills, Spurs defeated City 3-0. A 3-2 victory over Burnley followed, but the dreaded season of struggle followed.

Improvement came over the Christmas period, then on 2nd January speedy centre-forward Billy McAdams, signed from Distillery on 6th December, made his debut a memorable one by scoring an equaliser in the 49th minute against Sunderland at Maine Road. The game was played in poor, foggy conditions and when Revie scored a winner eleven minutes from time, few knew exactly what had happened. One reporter, Eric Dunster, had problems with another incident, brought to his attention by the groans and cheers of the crowd at the Platt Lane end of the stadium. It seems that the supporters behind the goal were the only ones able to see the action as Sunderland put the ball into the back of the net. Trautmann lay prostrate, the crowd were moaning, and the Sunderland players were celebrating, but within a minute the City supporters began cheering, signalling that the goal had been disallowed. Dunster later discovered that the goal had been disallowed for offside. In his report he questioned whether the game should have been played at all. City fans didn't care. They might not have seen much of the game, but at least the game was won.

A week after the Sunderland game, McAdams scored a hat-trick in City's 5-2 Cup win at Bradford. He followed that with an equaliser in the 56th League derby match at Old Trafford. His arrival and goalscoring streak brought a little encouragement to the Blues, although City's form was not all it should have been. In the Cup City were defeated by Spurs in the fourth round, and in the League convincing victories against Bolton and Spurs were surrounded by heavy defeats. Consistency was an issue.

On 10th April the Blues faced Middlesbrough at Maine Road and, for once, seemed to play perfectly well as a team: "Nothing wrong with City. For once every man made an equal contribution. Their three man success formula of Trautmann, Paul, and Revie which the crowds have come to expect was not needed this time.

"In fact, Clarke, Meadows, and Spurdle stole the show - Spurdle for brilliant runs and centres, and Clarke and Meadows for two goals each. From the moment Revie began the goalscoring at 14 minutes, relegation anxious Middlesbrough got worse. Clarke made it 2-0. And after McPherson and Lawrie missed good heading chances, there was no escape for Borough. They hardly deserved their two goals."

The result and a 1-0 victory over Chelsea six days later more or less brought safety. Defeat at West Bromwich on 17th April hardly mattered as it was followed by a 1-1 draw at home to Chelsea and a Maine Road 3-0 victory over Charlton in the last game of the season. The Blues finished the campaign in 17th place, seven points above the relegation zone.

It had been another season of struggle but Eric Dunster's report brought hope for the future: "City did enough to suggest that they may be more successful next season. McTavish has come on splendidly in recent weeks and Spurdle with his keen anticipation and fine turn of speed looks like making the right wing position his own. Hayes, a terrier for work, will be more than a useful stand by for either inside forward position."

1954-1955 Making Plans

For Les McDowall, the new season was to be one of experimentation. He brought the players back for pre-season training two weeks earlier than normal, and made that training quite tough. 1930s full-back Laurie Barnett, a City coach, really pushed the players to the limit as McDowall strived to develop a successful side. This focus on coaching was about to bring real progress.

For several seasons City had struggled in the League, but McDowall had been making plans. He had been watching and listening to reports coming from the reserves of a new tactical ploy which seemed to be working. Johnny Williamson, playing at centre-forward in the Central League, dropped back behind the other four forwards in one particular game. The plan was based on one used successfully by the Hungarians, who had humbled England twice during the early fifties, and proved totally confusing to the opposition. It also encouraged trainer Fred Tilson. Tilson, it must be remembered, was City's thrilling centre-forward during the 1934 Cup run and, although it seemed to go against the type of play he enjoyed, he recognised the possibilities. He spoke with McDowall, and the reserves tried the technique out during the 1953-54 season.

Johnny Williamson was also enthusiastic. He told Don Revie, in the first team: "It's the answer to all our problems. You just can't stop it when it gets going. This style is ready made for you, Don."

Revie wasn't convinced at this point, but results in the Central League suggested Williamson was right. McDowall also believed the time was right. He called the players together and told them: "We are going to

Les McDowall

were thrashed 5-0 - Trautmann had played brilliantly to keep the score down.

The next game saw Sheffield United arrive at Maine Road hopeful of victory. They left smarting after a thrilling 5-2 City win. Johnny Williamson believed the difference came because the Plan had needed Williamson's reserve colleague Ken Barnes: "The Plan evolved really. It was developed in the reserves but it wasn't one of those ideas that can be pinpointed to one particularly day. In the reserves it was working with me and Ken Barnes, but when it was tried in the first team with Don Revie we got beat 5-0 at Preston. Then they played Ken in the first team with Don and it clicked. You see it needed the two players, and Ken was the difference. Then there was no stopping it."

Williamson was right. Barnes had been unable to command a first team place since arriving in 1950, but had been selected by McDowall to play as an attacking wing-half. With Revie playing as a deep-lying centre-forward, Barnes was used to attack, distribute, and link up with Revie. The two worked together perfectly.

Ken Barnes explained in December 2004 that Les McDowall had actually come close to dropping the Plan: "I remember him talking with Fred Tilson and he wasn't convinced it'd work. He tried it against Preston and City lost 5-0. It was almost scrapped but Don Revie, apparently, stressed to McDowall that it had worked so well in the reserves because of my part in it. He urged him to give me a go. I played against Sheffield United and the Plan worked like a dream. From then on I became a regular and we started to get noticed as a team – it was a true team effort. Other sides had no idea how to combat it. They tried to get their wing half to mark Don but it still seemed to leave a man spare somewhere else."

The plan did not simply involve one or two players, it was a real team strategy. Even Bert Trautmann was expected to play his part by making long, accurate throws to Revie, who would quickly provide a short pass to Barnes. Revie would move forward, with Barnes holding on to the ball while his colleague moved into position, then Barnes would push the ball forward down the touchline for Revie to latch onto. By this point the opposition would already be confused. With Revie unmarked, he would be able to head for goal in relative freedom. It sounds incredibly simple, yet it worked.

The deep-lying role really did confuse the opposition. Few knew how to handle it. Players would be told to mark by numbers, but with a deep number nine confusion reigned. Williamson: "Other teams had no idea how to counteract the plan. It surprised everyone and some of the other teams just could not work it out. Don't forget though that the quality of the players had a lot to do with it. Don and Ken were two exceptional players. Everyone knew that.

"People used to go on about the 'Revie Plan' but Don used to tell them it wasn't 'his' it was the team's. In particularly he used to tell them how vital Ken was. It wouldn't have worked without Ken, and Don made sure they all knew that."

After the Sheffield United game, City began to move up the table, briefly heading it in September. The Revie Plan brought much excitement and interest to the Blues, and for the first time since the war City really did look like a top First Division side. Even United, who by this point were gaining headlines for their brilliant young players, found it difficult to cope. In the Maine Road derby on 25th September the Busby Babes, including the likes of Roger Byrne, Tommy Taylor, and Duncan Edwards, were defeated 3-2. The 'Old International' enjoyed the clash and believed the new approach had brought the Blues back on a level footing with the Reds. While United were a side full of exciting individuals, he liked City's team approach best: "It is a strategy which shows off to perfection the strength and maturity of Paul among his younger defenders, and which gives full scope to the inspired wanderings of Revie. City have staked their all on pure football and they are proving that football pays. What is more, by one of those delicious strokes of irony which play round the uncertainties of sport, the City's forwards helped themselves to three goals, and narrowly missed scoring as many more - without taking into account hot claims for an odd penalty or so - against a defence the three least masterful members of which were to be chosen later in the day as England's bulwark against Ireland."

Fans were pleased to see the Plan work to such effect against their Manchester rivals. City's methods were now bringing out the best in their players. Johnny Hart, for example, was able to use Revie's roaming to his advantage, as he also started to find space. He delighted in confusing the opposition and always seemed to turn up in the right place at the right time.

The team ethos worked well and, although Revie became the headline grabber in many ways, everyone knew that it was the entire team that made it work. Johnny Williamson, the man who had taken the deep-lying role in the reserves, enjoyed occasional opportunities to experience the Plan in action in the first team. One of these he remembered in 2003 as his best match for City: "It's difficult thinking about biggest moments, it's so long ago, but coming into the side for Don when we played at Sheffield Wednesday in November 1954 was great. Not only did I replace Don, but I also scored two goals and we won 4-2. A very good memory that one."

In January, after defeating Derby County in the FA Cup third round, the Blues met United in the fourth round, watched by a Maine Road crowd of 74,723. Again the Babes were defeated by the City men. It was still a great 2-0 victory, thanks to Hayes and Revie, although the Blues were determined not to let the sending off of United's Allenby Chilton be used as a United excuse. Roy Little: "A few of us pleaded with the ref because we didn't want their fans to have the slightest excuse for explaining away a defeat such as 'you only beat ten men', but the ref waved us to one side and Chilton went off. To prove the point about our superiority that season we hammered them 5-0 at Old Trafford!"

Little's 5-0 comment was accurate. Two weeks after the FA Cup tie the Revie Plan once again confused United. By this point the Busby Babes were being acclaimed the best side in Britain, yet they could not defeat City. At Old Trafford the Blues tore into the Reds and with goals from Johnny Hart, Fionan 'Paddy' Fagan (2), and Joe Hayes (2), City won 5-0 equalling the margin of City's emphatic Old Trafford win in 1926 – and matched in 2011 by Roberto Mancini's side.

After the game, United Captain Allenby Chilton was asked what preparations United had made to counter the Revie Plan: "We decided to ignore it. Revie roams so much from midfield and wing to wing that putting one man on him to mark him only results in upsetting the balance of your own side. So we decided to play an all-out attacking game ourselves and by sheer pressure offset the Revie Plan."

Chilton ended by saying the Reds would continue not to change their formation to tackle the Revie Plan. Fans agreed that United's tactics were just about perfect - conceding 10 goals in three derbies seemed about right!

Don Revie attacks the Sunderland goal in the FA Cup semi-final.

After a few seasons of despair, the League programme continued to excite with the Blues ending the season in seventh place, two points behind runners up Wolves, and the best position since the 1937 Championship. City were re-establishing themselves as one of England's leading clubs.

Taking the League on its own it had been a successful season, but it was the Cup run that impressed most. In blizzard conditions, City travelled to Luton for the fifth round tie on 19th February. There Roy Clarke gave McDowall's side the lead after half an hour, following a centre from Paddy Fagan. Fifteen minutes into the second half Luton's Dunne miss-kicked as he tried to clear a Revie centre, leaving the ball free for Roy Clarke to forcefully send home City's second goal.

Following the 2-0 victory, City had to travel to Birmingham City for the sixth round. There, an extremely tough match ended with a City goal late in the game. The Blues were awarded a free-kick outside the Birmingham penalty area. A fierce low shot by Clarke, somehow found Hart who sent the ball into the net, while Merrick, the Birmingham 'keeper, dived.

The semi-final brought City up against Sunderland at Villa Park. Sadly Johnny Hart, who had been a vital member of City's attack, broke his leg in a League game at Huddersfield the week before the semi-final. This was a tremendous blow, and upset City's rhythm. Nevertheless, the Blues were strong enough to overcome Sunderland. They already had a replacement for Hart - Bobby Johnstone. Johnstone had signed for City from Hibernian at the start of March, prompting many

to wonder who would be dropped for the exciting Scot. Hart's injury solved McDowall's selection worries, although it remained a major blow.

In the 56th minute of the semi-final Roy Clarke threw himself at a curling cross from Joe Hayes and headed the only goal of the game. It had been another team victory with Roy Little and Dave Ewing performing extremely well in difficult conditions to hold the defence together.

Sadly, the injury jinx struck again three minutes from time when Roy Clarke injured a knee and was forced to leave the field. It was another set-back for the Blues and terribly upsetting for a player who had done so much to get City to Wembley. In the final weeks of the season Clarke returned to the side, but another knock to the knee in the last League game of the season forced him to miss the final.

City's final opponents were to be Newcastle United who were recognised as a truly successful cup side after defeating Blackpool in 1951 and Arsenal - captained by Joe Mercer - in 1952. They had beaten York City 2-0 in the semi-final replay.

In the week prior to the final, City stayed in Eastbourne while Clarke went to see specialists in Manchester. Injury worries continued to plague the Blues - Dave Ewing twisted an ankle in training, Ken Barnes had what was described as 'violent toothache', and Bert Trautmann suffered from fibrosis and seemed unlikely to make the final. It was not a good week on the south coast, but for one player the week did bring its high points when, on the Thursday before the final, Don Revie travelled to London to receive the Football Writers'

Footballer Of The Year award. He was the first City player to receive the award and told the press that night that the award was really one for the whole of Manchester City. The Revie Plan worked because of the entire team, not one man.

For the rest of the players, moving to Weybridge on the eve of the final lightened the atmosphere. They took part in a TV show with Leslie Welsh, a well-known memory man, and the Millwall squad. Newcastle should have taken part but felt the show would not help their preparation for the final. City, felt the opposite was true and a light-hearted show did much for morale.

After the show - in which little

Prince Philip is introduced to a tracksuited Don Revie by Roy Paul.

Joe Hayes played a starring role - the players returned to the hotel and prepared for City's first final since 1934. During the night Jimmy Meadows took ill, developing a temperature which seemed destined to become a cold. Fortunately, Meadows managed to fight his temperature and, despite calls from a local district nurse for him not to play unless it was absolutely necessary, was determined to play.

At Wembley, captain Roy Paul went around the team saying: "Nothing to beat lads. If we just go out there and play the usual accurate passing game we'll run Jimmy Scholar, Jackie Milburn and the others into the ground." He was nervous himself but played a perfect captain's role.

When the time came to leave the dressing room

and head up the tunnel, City were warned by Walter Winterbottom, the England manager, that Prince Philip was the guest of honour and that: "he doesn't mind players showing natural excitement if they score... but he doesn't want to see any of the players kissing one another after they've scored!" The City players laughed, with Roy Paul shouting that if City scored first he would probably kiss the nearest person: "even if it's the bloody referee!"

Winterbottom left and City trooped out. The Blues were making history that year - the team included the first German to play in a Wembley Cup Final (Trautmann), and the first Channel Islander (Spurdle), also they were the first finalists to enter the field wearing tracksuits. The brilliant Blue tracksuits seemed impressive for the period, but Eric Brook, City's 1930s star, was not pleased. Afterwards in his broad Yorkshire accent he told Roy Paul: "Tha looked nowt more than pansies in pantaloons."

When the game kicked off, Newcastle raced towards the City goal. Milburn forced a corner off Ewing and from the kick White placed the ball perfectly for Milburn who headed in off the cross bar. Incredibly, City were a goal down after only 45 seconds. This remained the fastest goal in a Wembley FA Cup Final until Di Matteo netted for Chelsea after 42 seconds in 1997.

Ken Barnes felt the opening goal was the first of two major blows: "Jackie Milburn wasn't known for his heading ability but the first attack caught us on the hop. He wasn't picked up as he should have been and then he headed home. One goal down in less than a minute. It's very difficult to come back, but we worked hard.

"Then after about 20 minutes Jimmy Meadows went down injured – I remember that the same thing had happened to Arsenal's Walley Barnes in 1952 against Newcastle as well! – and we were down to ten men. You would expect the match to be over, but we came back."

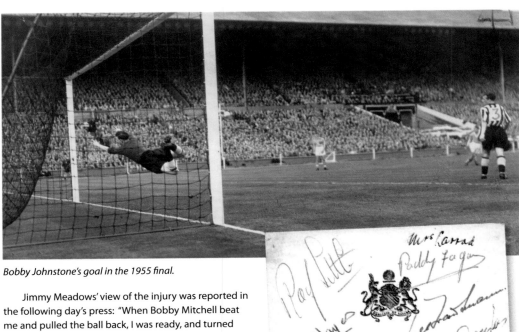

Bobby Johnstone's goal in the 1955 final.

Jimmy Meadows' view of the injury was reported in the following day's press: "When Bobby Mitchell beat me and pulled the ball back, I was ready, and turned with him. I went to push off with my right foot, and my studs caught in the grass. In effect, the top half of my leg moved forward and the rest stayed put. The pain was indescribable."

The *Daily Mail* later revealed that Meadows had torn his cruciate ligaments, and the player spent the next few years in a long painful battle to regain fitness and his place in the City team. The tragic story was similar to what occurred to Paul Lake in the 1990s.

The injury was a huge problem to the Blues and meant they would have to play the remaining seventy minutes with only ten men. Being a goal down, it was always going to be tough, but Roy Paul tried to pull his team together, just as Joe Mercer had done three years earlier with Arsenal.

For a while the tactic worked. City had a twenty minute spell of vintage football and, thanks to a wonderful header from Bobby Johnstone, went into the interval on level terms. The Blues had tried to make the Revie Plan work, but in the second half the odds were very much against McDowall's side. Eight minutes into the second half Bobby Mitchell gave Newcastle the lead. Bert Trautmann felt responsible: "Mitchell had no chance to score from the narrowest possible angle I could cut him down to, so I dived to catch his centre. As I did, he drove the ball straight into the net through the space I had left."

In the 59th minute another Mitchell shot was parried by Trautmann, but George Hannah followed up to score. He told the press: "I just hit it as hard as I could."

City had no way back. The game ended 3-1 with the Blues suffering through injuries to key players throughout the latter stages of the season, not simply on Cup final day itself. Roy Paul was bitterly disappointed. At the City banquet that evening he almost refused to give a speech, feeling that speeches shouldn't be made about losing, but eventually he was persuaded to talk. He stood up, looked around the room at the faces from City's past and present, smiled and predicted: "We'll be back again next year to win it. Sam Cowan knows how I feel. He captained Manchester City's Cup Final team in 1933 and returned a year later to collect the Cup..."

Few at the time believed it, but Paul was determined.

1955-1956 Wembley Again

By the time the 1955-56 season started there appeared to be a major fallout between Don Revie and Les McDowall. McDowall suspended the player for fourteen days, but Revie still played deep for the opening game of the season at home to Aston Villa. The game ended 2-2 with Revie's name making it onto the score sheet with a penalty. The following week he scored another penalty, but this time City suffered a shock 7-2 defeat at the hands of Wolves. Another 2-2 followed at home to Arsenal then came the Maine Road derby with United. Had the Busby Babes changed their plan after the previous season's defeats?

The game was closer than usual, but it still ended in a Blue victory thanks to a solitary goal from Joe Hayes. In addition to Hayes, Bobby Johnstone was fast becoming the player most talked about, gaining headlines for outstanding play. Unfortunately, Johnstone's rise to fame seemed to upset last season's hero Don Revie. Newspapers were full of the conflict between the two players, although everybody attached to the Club played down the story. For a team hoping to improve on their League position, and reach Wembley again it was not the kind of headlines wanted. Nevertheless, the story rumbled on.

On Saturday 19th November 1955 the *Daily Mail* broke the news that Revie had been dropped by McDowall for the game at Everton, and that Bobby Johnstone would be playing the deep lying centre-forward role. Without Revie City managed a 1-1 draw. The previous two games had ended in defeat and so most backed McDowall's decision.

Apart from a defeat in the next game, at home to Newcastle, form did improve with the Blues enjoying an undefeated run of six games throughout December. To bolster City's attack, McDowall had brought in the multi-talented Jack Dyson. In addition to taking over from Bobby Johnstone in the number ten shirt, Dyson was an excellent cricketer who spent the summer months playing at Old Trafford for Lancashire C.C.C. Over the course of the League programme, Dyson was to score 13 goals in 25 appearances to help City move up the table actually mount a serious challenge.

Ultimately, the Blues ended the season in fourth place on 46 points - the same total as the previous season. Again it was the Cup run that impressed most. In the third round City were drawn against Blackpool at Maine Road. Despite poor conditions the game kicked off, and within ten seconds the Seasiders were a goal up thanks to Ernie Taylor. Jack Dyson scored an equaliser, but the conditions deteriorated. After a brief stoppage, play was resumed but in the 56th minute the match was finally abandoned as fog covered the ground.

Four days later, a crowd of over 42,517 - 10,000 more than the original fixture - were present for a 2.15pm Wednesday kick off. The pitch was still in poor condition, but was judged to be satisfactory. Blackpool's goalscorer Ernie Taylor felt otherwise and asked not to play. Without Taylor, Blackpool were defeated 2-1, with all the goals coming in a thrilling eight minute spell early in the second half. Afterwards Roy Paul admitted conditions had made some players, especially Blackpool's Stanley Matthews who had been marooned on the touchline for much of the match, struggle. The mud suited the Blues, in particular Jack Dyson who ploughed through the puddles to score one of the goals. Bobby Johnstone scored the other.

In the fourth round City were drawn away to Southend. It was the first time the two sides met in a major competition - 41 years later they faced each other in the League for the first time - and a giant killing act seemed likely, especially as the Southend management had put sand and shells into the turf to aid drainage. This caused most players to leave the field with skinned knees.

Despite the conditions City won 1-0 - Joe Hayes' shot only just made it over the muddy goal-line - but the star man had been Bert Trautmann. The German had made a number of fine saves. At one point Southend seemed close to being awarded but one of their forwards admitted later: "I didn't bother appealing, that fellow Trautmann would have stopped anything."

The fifth round brought Liverpool to Maine Road. It also brought Revie back into City's attack. McDowall had played him in the two preceding League games, and now thought that he could add something to the Blues' forward play. Roy Clarke was the unfortunate player left out as City again played in difficult conditions. Watched by 70,640, neither side could break the deadlock. The icy conditions prevented either side performing to the level expected.

Four days later the replay was played in similar conditions. This time, with snow on the ground, and Revie replaced by Clarke, City defeated Liverpool 2-1 after being a goal behind. The game wasn't without controversy though. When referee Mervyn Griffiths blew his whistle to end the game few people actually heard it. The players that did were leaving the field, but Liverpool's Billy Liddell continued to play. So did Trautmann and Ewing, and when the Liverpool man sent a shot past the two City players all three of them believed the Reds had equalised. The Kop were also convinced, and it took a brave referee to stand up to a number of irate players, supporters, and local journalists after the match.

City travelled back to Manchester delighted, looking forward to the sixth round visit of Everton to Maine Road. A crowd of 76,129 packed into Maine Road looking forward to a game between two exciting attacking sides.

The Merseysiders spent the first 45 minutes attacking City in style. Trautmann was kept on his toes, finally succumbing to an angled drive from Jimmy Harris. One goal was not a lot to show for the pressure exerted, and in the second half Everton found it difficult maintaining the pressure.

Roy Paul recognised this, and in the 68th minute he took a free-kick a little outside the penalty area and chipped the ball to Joe Hayes, who nodded the ball into the net. Around eight minutes later Johnstone scored the City winner when he threw himself at a Clarke centre. It was a good victory, but for a number of supporters on the vast open popular side terracing the game had not been a comfortable one. Supporter John Lynch: "I remember this match because it was absolutely cram packed. The Kippax was mixed with both City and Everton fans. It was so crowded, you couldn't get out to go to the toilet! Fans were urinating into bottles and passing them down and placing them on the other side of the wall at the front. The police never even batted an eye-lid to this. All I could see was the goal in front of what became the North Stand, but all the goals were scored in the Platt Lane End. City were 1-0 down at half-time and won 2-1, so I missed all three goals!"

City had made it to the semi-finals again, even if many Blues didn't see the goals! The opponents at Villa Park were the struggling Tottenham Hotspur. Spurs were the one team that the Blues did not want to face as they played a similar style to City, with attacking wing-half Danny Blanchflower usually causing most danger.

The players had no need to worry however as Blanchflower really played himself out of the game. He tried to keep close to Bobby Johnstone, who in turn stayed well back behind the other forwards. This upset the Spurs' plan and caused the London club to adapt their attacking policy. In the 40th minute, Roy Clarke received a pass more or less at the very spot where his injury had come the year before. The Welshman held on to the ball, drew the Spurs' full-back towards him, and then centred for Bobby Johnstone to head the ball home.

Tottenham were unable to come back, although in the final minute they threw everything they had at goal and at one point were almost awarded a penalty. The incident became a major talking point over the weeks that followed, but City 'keeper Trautmann remained adamant that he had done nothing wrong: "Tottenham were attacking desperately and there were three men almost on top of me when the ball came over from the right and reached the Spurs' left-winger, George Robb. I managed to divert it with the side of my hand, and then fell headlong. I hadn't the slightest idea where the ball was then, and as I lay on the ground, I groped round frantically with outstretched arms, and Robb seemingly tripped over them. There were frantic appeals for a penalty, but they were unsuccessful and when the

Leivers and Trautmann attempt to clear as City defeat Spurs 1-0 in the semi-final.

final whistle went shortly afterwards, I flung my arms round Bill Leivers' neck and kissed him to his evident embarrassment."

The incident brought back all the old wartime prejudices and prompted a large number of abusive letters to arrive at Maine Road from North London addresses. Trautmann was very upset and when City played at White Hart Lane a week after the semi-final, he dreaded playing in front of an abusive crowd. It didn't help that Spurs were desperate to avoid relegation.

The German took to the field, greeted by abuse from one particular section of the crowd. They greeted every fumble, every mistake with laughter, cheering, and more abuse. Understandably, Trautmann did not have the best game of his life, and the Blues lost 2-1.

After the League game the press got hold of the story and articles appeared across Britain, describing the content of the abusive letters. This prompted more correspondence, although this time Trautmann received over 500 letters of support from all over the country - including London. Shortly afterwards readers of the *Manchester Evening Chronicle* voted him their 'Player of the Year', then the news came through that he was also to be awarded the Football Writers' Player of The Year title. The City 'keeper was overwhelmed by both the awards, and at the Football Writers' ceremony he thanked the press: "I am deeply moved and sincerely grateful - you have made me a proud and very happy man. I hope I can prove myself worthy of the honour."

The build-up to the Cup Final meeting with Birmingham City was full of secrecy and rumour. The secrecy came from Les McDowall who did not tell his players what the final line-up would be until four hours before kick-off. This naturally prompted various rumours about who would be left out, and who would make it. Much of the conjecture surrounded Don Revie - the forgotten man of football. Bobby Johnstone had been struggling with a nagging calf injury, prompting the press to proclaim 'REVIE MUST PLAY'.

Many supporters were against the thought of playing a man who had hardly played a part in getting the Blues to Wembley. Interestingly, inside-right Johnny Hart was now back in contention. After breaking his leg 13 months earlier, he was now back in training and had even played and scored in the final League game of the season.

City spent Cup Final week at Eastbourne and, despite the rumours and doubt, managed to keep their spirits up. There was no animosity between the players, after all it was the manager who would choose the side. He would be the one responsible.

Twenty-four hours before the game McDowall was presented with another conundrum when Bill Spurdle went down with boils. On the Saturday morning Spurdle returned from the doctor with the disappointing news

that it would be impossible to lance the boils, therefore the Channel Islander could not play. A short while later McDowall announced his team:

Trautmann, Leivers, Little, Barnes, Ewing, Paul, Johnstone, Hayes, Revie, Dyson, and Clarke.

The forgotten man, Revie, was back. It was an important decision and one which would lead to City victory.

In the dressing room before the game, captain Roy Paul kept a close watch on his players. He was determined that nerves would not prevent City from playing and checked every player. Trautmann was as cool as ever, while Barnes and Little were keeping everybody amused with Roy Little impersonating Harry Secombe's Goon Show characters. Jack Dyson looked pale, but Paul knew that it was normal for him to suffer a little before an important game. Then the captain looked at Don Revie who seemed to be fiddling around with bits of wood. He watched in astonishment as Revie placed two pieces of old wood in his jacket pocket. Paul had to find out what was happening and listened as Revie explained that an old gypsy woman had given him the wood, saying that it would bring him luck. She had told him that his life was about to take on a drastic change and that he would meet with success in his job, fulfilling a lifetime's ambition.

Paul laughed, but Revie kept to his superstition.

Manager Les McDowall was also checking the players. Ken Barnes remembered: "Birmingham were the cup favourites but we had to win and I think that had an effect on Les McDowall. Before the game I always had a quick smoke and so I was hiding in the toilet having a cigarette when McDowall came storming in. He had a go at me, but I pointed out I always had one, then he told me I had to closely mark Birmingham's Peter Murphy. I said 'When I get the ball I'm attacking, I'm not going to worry about Peter Murphy!' He went on at me and, as he was the manager, I had to do as he said. It wasn't my game but I had no choice."

Barnes followed McDowall's instruction and he joined the rest of the team as they made their way up the tunnel. As City, wearing maroon shirts with thin white stripes, entered the field Manchester supporters on the opposite end to the players' tunnel released thousands of blue balloons. The stadium erupted with cheering and then the players started to hear the City fans singing "She's a Lassie from Lancashire." This had been City's Cup anthem that year with Manchester supporters singing it regularly. Another popular song from City fans around this period was an adaptation of 'Bless 'em all':

THE FOOTBALL ASSOCIATION CHALLENGE CUP COMPETITION

FINAL TIE

BIRMINGHAM CITY
v
MANCHESTER CITY

SATURDAY, MAY 5th, 1956   KICK-OFF 3 pm

EMPIRE STADIUM

WEMBLEY

Chairman and Managing Director   SIR ARTHUR J. ELVIN, MBE
OFFICIAL PROGRAMME   -   ONE SHILLING

Manchester Evening News started to believe McDowall's side would have everything their own way: "Manchester City established themselves as one of the best combinations of soccer artists even that famous Wembley turf has been graced with in post-war years. The million dollar opening which provided Joe Hayes with the leading goal he will never forget spun us into thoughts of a record runaway victory. For it was a magnificent team, finding the right touch at the start and moving beautifully forward."

Despite the early dominance - Four corners in ten minutes and Joe Hayes forced goalkeeper Merrick to make a fine save in another move - Birmingham equalised in the fourteenth minute. It was against the run of play, especially as Don Revie seemed to dominate the game. It was vital City kept their heads. Bill Leivers, Dave Ewing, and Roy Little helped keep Birmingham out with Ewing cheekily singing "Keep Right on to the End of the Road" throughout. The song had been adopted by Birmingham fans throughout the Cup run and Ewing used it to wind up his opponents.

The score remained 1-1 until half-time, prompting many to suggest that the second half would be dominated by Cup favourites Birmingham. Roy Paul

> *Bless 'em all, Bless 'em all,*
> *Bert Trautmann, Dave Ewing and Paul,*
> *Bless Roy Little who blocks out the wing,*
> *Bless Jack Dyson the penalty king,*
> *And with Leivers and Spurdle so tall,*
> *And Johnstone, the Prince of them all,*
> *Come on the light Blues,*
> *It's always the right blue,*
> *So cheer up me lads,*
> *Bless 'em all*

Once again the players were introduced to Prince Philip, then after the toss, Revie kicked off towards the Manchester supporters. Roy Paul watched as City's first move developed. Bill Leivers delicately passed to Revie standing in midfield, who then carried the ball a couple of yards forward, before crossing to Roy Clarke. Revie sprinted towards the penalty area as Clarke held on to the ball. The Welshman then drew the Birmingham full back out, allowing him to slip the ball to Revie, who proceeded to allow the ball to run between his legs before flicking it with his right foot.

Joe Hayes had seen the build-up and was ready as the ball came towards him. He put in a left foot shot and City took the lead after 2 minutes and 47 seconds. The goal rocked nervous Birmingham, just as Newcastle's had affected City the year before. Eric Thornton of the

Bert Trautmann under pressure from Eddie Brown.

Bert Trautmann congratulated by Birmingham goalkeeper Gil Merrick at the final whistle.

TRUE BLUE
Bert Trautmann

Bert Trautmann will always be remembered as a City legend. In the 1956 FA Cup final his bravery became the defining memory of the game.

refused to accept that. He believed that Birmingham were now in the same position as City were the previous year, and thought that a concerted effort in the second half would kill off Birmingham. He felt many of their players were tired. McDowall held the same view and urged his players to keep the ball on the ground.

Ken Barnes listened to his manager of course, but then Don Revie took him to one side: "In the first half we didn't shine as much as we ought. We took the lead, but they came back at us and it was 1-1 at half time. Don Revie had a go at me saying 'where were you in the first half?' I told him about the discussion with McDowall before the match. He told me to ignore that and play my own game. In the second half I did and the Revie Plan started to work. We went on to win a great final 3-1."

Midway through the second half City regained the lead. A throw-in from Barnes reached Revie who played the ball to Johnstone. The ball was then moved between Johnstone, Barnes and Dyson, before Dyson tore through

to send the ball past the advancing Merrick. The players went crazy, before Paul brought a little calm back to the affair.

Within a minute Trautmann was forced to dive at the feet of a Birmingham forward then, with the ball safely gathered, he produced a long kick to Dyson. The cricketer then flicked the ball to Johnstone, who wriggled past two defenders before planting the ball into the net to become the first player to score in consecutive finals. City were leading 3-1 with around 67 minutes gone. The Cup was coming home.

Birmingham still attacked, but there was no way back for them. Then around seventeen minutes from the end Birmingham's Murphy charged forward. Bravely Trautmann threw himself at Murphy's feet, he grabbed the ball but the collision knocked him out. When he was brought round he clutched his neck. It looked serious, but nobody realised how serious until sometime after. Trautmann and his colleagues believed he had displaced a disc. It was sometime after the final that X-rays taken at Manchester Royal Infirmary revealed that he had broken his neck.

For a moment Roy Paul and Les McDowall considered what should be done. Should Roy Little go in goal, or should the big German continue? Trautmann told Paul he wanted to play on. A few minutes after play resumed the German came out to catch a high ball, he collided with Ewing and was knocked out again. Trainer Laurie Barnett, who had played in City's last Cup success when Swift collapsed towards the end of the game, had positioned himself behind the goal ready to help the 'keeper.

For the last ten minutes Dave Ewing did all he could to prevent the Birmingham forwards from getting close to Trautmann's goal. He was magnificent as was captain Roy Paul, who many believed had his finest game that day.

The game ended with City victorious. Roy Paul walked up the famous Wembley steps to take the trophy from the Queen. He thoroughly deserved it. Often his leadership qualities had pushed the Blues forward, through the various rounds of the Cup, and on to Wembley. His confidence had inspired others, but it was the injury to Trautmann and the reappearance of Revie that made the headlines. The *Daily Mail*, under the headline 'Triumph for Revie', stressed Revie's role: "It was Revie, Revie all the way in the FA Cup Final. Within three minutes of the start there could be no doubt he was the man for the job. On the sunlit green carpet of Wembley, Birmingham toiled in his shadow. They could never match the brilliant ball play of the smooth Don."

Revie himself believed Bill Leivers was the star man: "He had two pain killing injections on his sprained ankle, yet he played the game of his life. Many of our attacking moves stemmed from his intelligent passing which switched defence on to attack."

Every one of the City players deserved credit for the success, and the whole of Manchester was able to celebrate as rivals United had managed to win the League. The *Manchester Evening News* brought out a special edition to celebrate the Manchester League and Cup double. Under the headline "City - We're proud of you!" the newspaper boasted about Manchester being 'King Soccer City of Britain'.

At Wembley some City fans even lifted a banner which celebrated both United and City's successes.

For Ken Barnes winning the final meant he could at last have a cigarette: "Well, he may have tried to stop me before the game but there was no way Les McDowall could stop me smoking after we'd won!"

The Monday after the final Manchester prepared for City's homecoming. Every player was touched by the welcome. Trautmann couldn't believe it: "It seemed the whole of Lancashire let alone Manchester had turned

TRUE BLUES
Roy Paul and Roy Clarke

Welsh internationals Roy Paul and Roy Clarke followed in the great tradition of Billy Meredith by winning the FA Cup with the Blues.

out to cheer us as we drove from London Road station to the Town Hall for the civic reception. There was not a spare yard of room to move on the pavements, and even the heftiest policemen had a full time job keeping the milling thousands in check."

The homecoming became a landmark moment in the early history of Granada TV as it was the new station's first live outside broadcast. The FA Cup final itself had also been the first FA Cup final to be broadcast live on both the BBC and ITV.

After a reception at the Town Hall the Blues took the Cup to Belle Vue where a dance was held by the *Manchester Evening Chronicle* as part of City's welcome home. It was a significant moment for many. The huge Belle Vue Pleasure Gardens had almost become the Club's home on several occasions between 1899 and 1923. It was also close to St. Mark's church on Clowes Street where the Club had been founded.

It seemed appropriate that Gorton was able to share in City's glory.

1951-1956 SUMMARY

Major Trophies Won: FA Cup 1955-56
Highest League Attendance: 63,925 Blackpool, 24/09/55
Highest Cup Attendance: 76,129 Everton, 03/03/56 (FA Cup)
Managers: 1950–63 Les McDowall

Seasonal Record:

Season	League	Posn	FA Cup	Other	Leading Scorer	Average Attendance
1951-52	FL Div1	15	Rnd 3		Hart 12	38,302
1952-53	FL Div1	20	Rnd 4		Spurdle 11	34,663
1953-54	FL Div1	17	Rnd 4		Hart & Revie 12	30,155
1954-55	FL Div1	7	Final		Hart 14	35,217
1955-56	FL Div1	4	Winners		Hayes 23	32,198

1955 FA CUP RUN

R3	Derby County	A	W	3-1
R4	Manchester United	H	W	2-0
R5	Luton Town	A	W	2-0
R6	Birmingham City	A	W	1-0
SF	Sunderland	N*	W	1-0
F	Newcastle United	N**	L	1-3

*= Villa Park, Birmingham ** = Wembley Stadium*

	P	W	D	L	F	A
HOME	1	1	0	0	2	0
AWAY	5	4	0	1	8	4
TOTAL	6	5	0	1	10	4

FINAL DETAILS

7 May 1955 at Wembley Stadium
Newcastle United 3-1 Manchester City
CITY: Trautmann, Meadows, Little, Barnes, Ewing, Paul, Spurdle, Hayes, Revie, Johnstone, Fagan
NEWCASTLE UNITED: Simpson, Cowell, Batty, Scoular, Stokeo, Casey, White, Milburn, Keeble, Hannah, Mitchell
GOALS: Milburn, Mitchell, Hannah, Johnstone
ATTENDANCE: 100,000
REFEREE: R J Leafe (Nottingham)
MANAGER: Les McDowall
CAPTAIN: Roy Paul

1956 FA CUP RUN

R3	Blackpool	H	A#	1-1
	Blackpool	H	W	2-1
R4	Southend United	A	W	1-0
R5	Liverpool	H	D	0-0
	Liverpool	A	W	2-1
R6	Everton	H	W	2-1
SF	Tottenham Hotspur	N*	W	1-0
F	Birmingham City	N**	W	3-1

A# = abandoned

*= Villa Park, Birmingham ** = Wembley Stadium*

	P	W	D	L	F	A
HOME	3#	2	1#	0	4	2
AWAY	4	4	0	0	7	2
TOTAL	7#	6	1	0	11	4

 # plus 1 abandoned match

FINAL DETAILS

5 May 1956 at Wembley Stadium
Manchester City 3-1 Birmingham City
CITY: Trautmann, Leivers, Little, Barnes, Ewing, Paul, Johnstone, Hayes, Revie, Dyson, Clarke
BIRMINGHAM CITY: Merrick, Hall, Green, Newman, Smith, Boyd, Astall, Kinsey, Brown, Murphy, Govan
GOALS: Hayes, Dyson, Johnstone, Kinsey
ATTENDANCE: 100,000
REFEREE: A Bond (Fulham)
MANAGER: Les McDowall
CAPTAIN: Roy Paul

TRUE BLUE
Bobby Johnstone

Loved by fans Bobby Johnstone became the first man to score in consecutive finals at Wembley.

WITH THE COLOUR CAMERA AT
MANCHESTER CITY

BILL LEIVERS

JOHN McTAVISH

GEORGE HANNAH

KEN BARNES

BERT TRAUTMANN

ANDY KERR

CLIVE COLBRIDGE

WITH THE COMPLIMENTS OF **Ty·Phoo** TEA LTD., BIRMINGHAM 5

MANCHESTER CITY F.C.

Back row, L to R: Bacuzzi, Doyle, Ogley, Crossan, Gomersall, Young
Front row, L to R: Oakes, Wood, Kennedy, Connor, Pardoe

December 1959's Football Monthly (top) took their colour camera to Maine Road. Bottom: A Typhoo Tea card from 1965.

1956-1965
Losing Supremacy

"If what we have heard is true this is the last straw. We are determined not to let City die as a club. A merger would only go through over our dead bodies."

City supporter Peter Donoghue on hearing the news that City's vice-chairman was in discussion with United about a possible merger, January 1965

1956-1957 Missing Bert

The months that followed the 1956 FA Cup Final were not happy ones for many connected with the Manchester Blues. Bert Trautmann in particular had every reason to feel a little aggrieved. His collision in the final had resulted in a broken neck and the German 'keeper was forced to convalesce, missing the first four months of the season.

Another unhappy player was the unsettled Don Revie. The cunning centre-forward had been disappointed with his treatment at Maine Road for some time and had been considering a move for at least a season. His Cup Final appearance possibly forced a brief change of heart, but in reality he was never going to settle down to life under Les McDowall. By the end of October he told Eric Thompson of the *Daily Mail* that

he wanted to move on, and that he had no intention of coming off the transfer list.

On 3rd November he played his last game for the Blues - a 1-1 draw thanks to a goal from City's Jack Dyson - and by 8th November Sunderland put in a bid of £20,000. The 29 year old decided to grasp the opportunity of resurrecting his career and officially signed for the Roker Park club on 10th for a fee usually quoted as £24,000. It was a sad but inevitable loss. Later in his career Revie found true fame for his highly successful managerial period at Elland Road, when he basically created a football club - taking Leeds United from Second Division football to European competition. He followed that with a brief stint as England manager, before taking a more lucrative position in the United Arab Emirates.

Revie was always trying to find security for him and

his family, hence so many transfer requests throughout his playing career. But his move from England was highly criticised and made the man unpopular at many grounds throughout the country.

By the time of Revie's City departure, the Blues were not enjoying the best of seasons. On the opening day they were trounced 5-1 at Wolves, and it wasn't until their sixth game that City were victorious. A run of six defeats in September and October saw them slip down the table. One of the causes had been the absence of Trautmann.

Throughout the fifties City had felt safe knowing that Trautmann always seemed to produce a miraculous save to prevent defeat, but with the German absent the Blues had to find an alternative. Firstly, the former Preston 'keeper George Thompson was tried, but an injury in only his second game forced another change. For the third game of the season City turned to 6ft 4in Jack Savage, who had been signed from Halifax in November 1953. He had performed well in a couple of games - notably the September Old Trafford derby - but the Blues still suffered. Everybody knew Trautmann was needed back in the side.

Although he was far from fit, the popular German returned to the side on 15th December 1956 after playing two reserve games. The result, a 3-2 defeat by high-flying Wolves, saw manager Les McDowall heavily criticised in the media for bringing the player back too soon. Nevertheless, the 'keeper kept his place and gradually his fitness and mobility improved. He remained City's first choice for the rest of the campaign.

City ended the season in a miserable 18th position and avoided relegation by six points. In the FA Cup third round tie at struggling Newcastle, a crowd of 57,890 were entertained with a performance from both sides that had many pondering why the League was such an issue. The game ended 1-1 at a rain soaked St. James Park, although Bill McAdams missed a relatively simple chance towards the end thanks to the poor conditions.

The following Wednesday 46,988 watched a match that was acclaimed the "game of the year." Playing again in heavy conditions, the Blues were leading 3-0 within thirty minutes thanks to a Bob Stokeo own goal, an excellent header from the reliable Bobby Johnstone, and a minute later a Paddy Fagan effort from a fine through pass by McAdams. Newcastle appeared dead and buried, but the game was far from over.

Three minutes into the second half Newcastle fought back with a penalty from Tommy Casey. Sixteen minutes from time Alex Tait brought Newcastle's tally to two, then with the pressure on City's goal increasing the Geordies seemed destined to find the equaliser. Sure enough, with only five minutes remaining, Newcastle levelled via a Bill Curry header. According to Newcastle based reporters even the City fans applauded!

City had now lost the initiative. The match went into extra time and the Newcastle supporters began singing the "Blaydon Races." The game appeared to be Newcastle's, but with typical City unpredictability the Blues took the lead again. Bobby Johnstone netting his second of the game and third of the tie.

Despite the goal, Newcastle managed to regain control and Len White scored twice to end City's hopes of a decent cup run. For Newcastle this has been recorded as "arguably the club's most thrilling encounter." *The Big Book Of Football Champions* even claimed that this "stirring battle of the giants" ensured the FA Cup remained "the greatest sporting competition in the world."

1957-1958 Goals, Goals, Goals

This season followed a similar vein to the Newcastle game with City supporters witnessing an incredible number of goals. In total 204 goals were scored during City's 42 game League programme - an average of 4.86 goals per match - with the Blues becoming the first side to score and concede 100 goals or more during a season. It was a strange period for the Club with changes occurring both on the pitch and behind the scenes. In November George Poyser joined City from Notts County as Assistant Manager, with a brief to improve the Club's scouting system. After a playing career that had taken him around the country - Plymouth, Brentford, and Wolves are three of the clubs he moved to - he had first started coaching at Wolves before taking the manager's position at Meadow Lane.

On the playing side the Club lost one of its most influential captains, and gained a couple of bright hopes for the future. After seven eventful seasons Roy Paul had decided it was time to move on, joining Worcester on a free transfer as player-manager, while youngsters Colin Barlow and Cliff Sear became established in the side.

Barlow joined City as an amateur in December 1956 and scored on his first team debut at Chelsea on the opening day of the 1957-58 season. He had been recommended to the Blues by former player Billy Walsh who spotted him while coaching at Xaverian College. Barlow played for the 'A' team while on leave from the Royal Dragoon Guards in Germany and was quick to make an impression, especially when he appeared in the first team - a large number of female supporters were delighted every time he ran close to them apparently! During his debut season he scored 17 goals from 39 games.

Full back Cliff Sear was another to make an impression after signing professional forms in January 1957, although he very nearly missed being a City player: "I had previously been a part-timer with the Club. In those days I was a 16 year old who worked down the mines at Bershaw Colliery, near my native Wrexham, travelling over to Manchester at weekends to play for the 'B' team at Crown Point. I played regularly enough, but no one said much to me or gave advice and I didn't think I was making much progress. So I left and linked up with Oswestry Town who were then in the Cheshire League. While playing for them, City manager Les McDowall spotted me and a fee of £1,500 was agreed. Oswestry's manager in those days was Alan Ball senior and he used to bring his son with him to watch us play!"

One game early in the season which both Barlow and Sear were fortunate to miss however was the visit to West Bromwich Albion on 21st September. After an hour of the game City were losing 3-2 but were still in contention, yet the following thirty minutes saw Albion completely overwhelm the Blues 9-2 to register their record win of the century. It was total humiliation. In January Albion also recorded a 5-1 win over the Blues in the FA Cup.

Manager Les McDowall, ever the tactician, had been devising a new plan throughout the early months of the season whereby Keith Marsden, wearing the number ten shirt, would drop back alongside big Dave Ewing to form part of the 'back four' as it became known. Playing with two centre-halves became commonplace over the years but in the late 1950s it was still an innovation. It confused many and after the defeat at Albion, McDowall abandoned it, realising that football wasn't quite ready. The unfortunate Marsden broke a leg shortly afterwards and was unable to establish himself.

Seven days after the League defeat both Barlow and Sear returned to the side. Years later Sear recalled this game and believed it to be one of the Club's greatest team performances: "The game was against Tottenham at Maine Road and on an afternoon of torrential rain we ran out winners by 5-1. It was about my third game in the first team and I got my chance because the regular choice, Roy Little, had been left out. On the right, Ken Branagan was also a last minute choice. In fact, he was in the team so late that he had to be pulled off the reserve team coach that was going to West Bromwich for a Central League game.

"Bobby Johnstone scored a couple for us. So did Joe Hayes, with Colin Barlow getting the other. I can even recall who got the Spurs goal...It was Ken Branagan who turned the ball past John Savage! It was a tremendous all round team performance by City and a good one for me, too, despite a bit of a struggle I had in the first ten minutes or so."

On 7th December Ken Barnes became only the third person to successfully convert three penalties in a Division One game, as City defeated Everton 6-2. Albert Dunlop, who later became a City scout working for Barnes, was the Everton 'keeper that day and Barnes remembered facing Dunlop for each attempt: "I stuck

one to the left, one to the right and he was so confused by the time the third award arrived that I could have back-heeled it in!"

In February revenge over West Brom was gained with a 4-1 victory. A few days later however the whole of Manchester was devastated by the news that a plane carrying Manchester United had crashed at Munich. Seven United players died in the crash on 6th February, with Duncan Edwards succumbing 15 days later, while other casualties included members of United's backroom staff and a number of journalists. The journalists included many names familiar to City supporters - Don Davies - arguably the finest football writer of the period, Eric Thompson, and Alf Clarke. Sadly, the most famous of all the journalists was former City 'keeper Frank Swift.

Swift had been following United's exploits in the European Cup for the *News Of The World* despite his often quoted fear of flying. His death affected many associated with the Blues and football in general. The *News Of The World* received telegrams, letters, and tributes from readers nationwide who had been touched by the Big Fella's love of life and football. The Munich disaster was a devastating blow for the whole of Manchester.

The following day the City players met at Maine Road. Bert Trautmann rushed to see Steve Fleet whose best friend Eddie Colman, a United player, died in the crash: "Bert understood more than anyone how I felt about losing Eddie. He taught me how to handle grief and come to terms with it. It was not easy but Bert had such humility and a caring attitude he helped me tremendously to overcome one of the worst periods of my life. He also offered to help United in any way he could. You see, we all knew the United players. We'd socialise with them, and they were just like us. Bobby Charlton, when he was living in digs, would sometimes come to our house for his tea. We were all close – Red or Blue didn't come into it."

German-national Trautmann contacted United and offered to help with translation, contacts and with whatever the Reds felt they needed.

Despite their grief, the City players were told they had to carry on with their own preparations for the following Saturday's League game at Tottenham. Cliff Lloyd, secretary of the Manchester-based PFA, had called for the suspension of the weekend's games –something City's players desperately wanted – but within 24 hours of the crash the League insisted that only United's game would be called off.

Reluctantly, the Blues travelled to London. That evening they changed their usual routine to visit the Chelsea Gaumont cinema to watch the latest newsreel of events in Germany. The following day, full of emotion, they lined up for a two-minute silence – impeccably observed by all fans. This silence was more personal than any the players had previously been involved with – only four days later Ken Branagan, Dave Ewing, Joe Hayes, Roy Little and others would attend the funeral of Gorton born United captain Roger Byrne. Understandably the crash affected the team that day and the Spurs game ended in a 5-1 defeat.

That evening it was reported that UEFA were speaking with the FA about the selection of a team to replace United in the European Cup. UEFA made it clear they wanted City to take the Reds' place. The Blues immediately made it known that they would not be interested in taking United's place, and that they would do all they could to help the Reds compete in the competition. Eric Alexander, whose grandfather was a City director at the time, remembered: "Our thoughts were with United. They had to take part. Real Madrid had suggested that the Cup be given to United, but that would have been wrong. Part of the recovery process had to be United's return to action – all Mancunians knew that - and we wanted to do all we could to help them go forward."

On 15th February City's match with Birmingham was the first game to be staged in Manchester following the disaster. It was a deeply emotional affair.

As with Spurs seven days earlier, few were in the mood for football and it's clear there was no appetite amongst fans for the Birmingham game. It felt wrong to be playing an important match while friends, fellow Mancunians and public figures were still fighting for their lives, and others were being buried. Significantly, a lower crowd than usual – only 23,461 - attended Maine Road

for this fixture. City's average for the six previous home matches had been 43,000, and the season's average would be around 33,000.

The match programme was full of tributes with every editorial space, other than the Birmingham page and the teamsheet, being given over to the tragedy. There were photographs of all the victims. The programme editor accurately wrote: "Next to Old Trafford, the impact of the Munich air disaster has been felt nowhere more severely nor with more regret than here at Maine Road. Players, officials and sports writers on that ill-fated plane were our friends and yours."

City Chairman Alan Douglas added: "City are convinced United will recover and eventually return to their exalted place in the world of football. And if we can do anything to help them in any way, however small, to achieve that objective, we shall regard it as a privilege to do it."

This was still an emotional time for all Mancunians. The tragedy seemed to touch each and every Mancunian personally, and inevitably the game itself was played in an extremely mournful atmosphere. Abide with Me, with soloist Sylvia Farmer, was played by the Beswick Prize Band pre-match and every fan stood, head bowed to remember Manchester's victims. The weather deteriorated as the game commenced and inevitably the match was abandoned in the 40th minute. The heavy rain and miserable atmosphere proved to all that life was more important than a game of football.

United Chairman Harold Hardman and new

City and Spurs pay their respects to the victims of the Munich air crash.

secretary Les Olive were guests of honour, and they were encouraged by the Blues to approach several City players to fill the gaps left by the crash. The Blues offered the Reds whatever assistance they needed.

Despite the sadness, football had to continue and for City the months that followed were quite entertaining as the Blues moved up the table. The occasional defeat occurred of course - such as the 8-4 at Leicester which ironically followed Trautmann's pre-match comment that he had never had more than seven put past him - but in the main City found a little consistency with the period between 22nd March and 14th April seeing the Blues pick up nine out of ten points. A 2-1 defeat on the last day of the season against Aston Villa resulted in a fifth place finish, although a victory could have placed them third, subject to goal average.

Throughout the season City had once again been well supported with the highest League attendance being 70,493. Interestingly, the ground now boasted covered accommodation for 50,000 after the roofing of the Popular Side, or Kippax St Stand as it now became, during the 1957 close season. This now took Maine Road's covered capacity significantly higher than Old Trafford's and approximately 15,000 more than the old covered capacity of Hyde Road. At last the Manchester footballing public had sufficient shelter, although the noisier element of the City crowd preferred to stand on the still open Scoreboard End (later North Stand). It took a few years for the Kippax to gain its fine reputation for atmosphere.

1958-1959 Consistent Mediocrity

If 1957-58 was a season of high scoring inconsistency, then 1958-59 was one of dismal consistency. Throughout the Club's existence City have strived for consistency, when it arrived in 1958 it saw the Blues plummet down the table rather than challenge for the game's highest honours. 'Consistent mediocrity' is how journalist Arthur Walmsley of the *Manchester Evening Chronicle* described it.

At the start of the season all looked well. The opening game - a 4-3 victory at Burnley after being three down at half time - seemed to indicate that the season would follow the pattern of the previous campaign rather than one of failure. After the opening match, City captain Ken Barnes wrote in one newspaper about his displeasure of seeing City pigeon-holed once again: "The old, old game has started. We extracted ourselves from a nasty half-time predicament at Turf Moor last Saturday, went on to win, and found that besides collecting two points we had picked up the old tag 'The Unpredictables' after only one match!"

Although City scored in each of the opening eleven games they simply did not score enough, despite the

fact that the great Bobby Johnstone was still leading City's attack. Roy Warhurst, the City half-back signed from Birmingham during the 1957 close season, believed the Scotsman was the greatest player he ever saw: "Johnstone was the greatest footballer I ever played with or against. I was 29 when I came to City and I'd seen all Britain's best. But there was nobody to compare with Bobby, when he felt like turning it on. Not even Carter, Doherty, Finney, Billy Steele or Matthews. They couldn't touch him.

"My first game for City was a tour game in Holland. Bobby was brilliant. As the locals cheered him off the park I kept thinking 'this is some great outfit I've joined'. It was the greatest display I've seen from any player that night."

During September City purchased George Hannah, a skilful hardworking inside forward from Lincoln City for £20,000. Hannah had believed his chance of returning to First Division football had long since gone, but when the Blues seemed interested the Liverpool born player couldn't wait to restart his career. Interestingly, his first City goal came in the 4-1 defeat at his former club Newcastle on 25th October. By which time City were struggling at the foot of the table.

Undoubtedly, 1958-59 was a season of transition, highlighted by the number of new players tried, then discarded. One such example was 19 year old Bert Lister who made his debut wearing the number 10 shirt in the 2-0 defeat at Wolves in October. His second appearance came on 31st March at West Bromwich Albion when City succumbed to a 3-0 defeat, but then the youngster was cast aside until he was transferred to Oldham in September 1960. Although neither game had ended successfully, it seems that Lister had done enough during his debut to warrant a decent run. According to one report: "Bert has built his reputation on his ability to grab goals, but though he didn't get one at Molineux, he did quite enough to show that he will play a big part in City's future fortunes."

Another player given an opportunity then discarded was outside left Dennis Fidler, who made one appearance during 1957-58 then four the following season, scoring his solitary goal for the Club in the 4-0 victory at Leeds on 21st February 1959. Fidler was a twenty year old inside forward who had once been a junior with United, but found that with so many more familiar forwards at Maine Road his opportunities were limited. In June 1960 he moved on to Port Vale.

The victory at Leeds had helped boost confidence within the Club, even though the Blues remained in the lower reaches of the First Division. After 29 games City were 18th on 23 points after winning 8, drawing 7, and losing 14. Below were Tottenham (22 points), Leicester (21), Aston Villa (20) and Portsmouth (19). The heroes of the Leeds game included Bert Trautmann, who once

Fog interrupts play during City's 5-1 victory over Chelsea on 15th November 1958.

The Aston Villa manager Joe Mercer felt confident his side would survive, and left the Hawthorns a short while before the end as he had to attend a banquet in Wolverhampton to celebrate Billy Wright's 100th cap. In the 88th minute of the Villa game Ronnie Allen scored an equaliser for West Bromwich Albion condemning Mercer's Villa to the Second Division. The goal was greeted with a great roar at Maine Road where, with seventeen minutes left to play, City were able to relax a little.

At full time the celebrations really began. Bert Trautmann had once again performed heroically for much of the season, saving City on many occasions, and the likes of Colin Barlow and Joe Hayes, both aged 23, were providing a great deal of optimism. Barlow was the season's highest scorer with 17 goals, while Hayes had scored one less.

again seemed to be saving City virtually every week, and defender Ron Phoenix whose skill in breaking up the Leeds attacks excited City fans. His positioning and ultimate tackling kept Leeds at bay and prompted a section of the Elland Road crowd to call out: "give us a chance red head!"

Victories over Portsmouth and Newcastle followed during March, however City's mediocrity reappeared from mid-March onwards. By the time of the last match of the season City were in dire straits. Portsmouth were already down, but the remaining relegation place would either go to Aston Villa or City. Both sides were on 29 points but Villa had a marginally better goal average (City 0.648, Villa 0.662). It was always going to be a tense occasion, but was made a little better by the news that the Blues would kick off at 7.30, whereas Villa's visit to fourth placed West Bromwich Albion would commence fifteen minutes earlier. Put simply, City would be aware of Villa's result and still have time to improve their own situation.

City's opponents were Leicester City, who had also been struggling but were now a good three points above City and Villa. The Maine Road match kicked off with Leicester looking the more impressive side. Indeed the Filbert Street men took the lead in the ninth minute. It wasn't long, however, before Bobby Johnstone took control and after a further sixteen minutes he lobbed the ball up for the diminutive Joe Hayes to head home.

Early in the second half the Blues took the lead with an effort from Ray Sambrook, after significant moves from Johnstone. Then Bill McAdams forced in a third. There was bad news coming from the Midlands, though. Aston Villa were leading 1-0 from a 66th minute Gerry Hitchens goal and if the two scores remained Villa, not City, would be safe thanks to a superior goal average.

There were indications however that 29 year old Bobby Johnstone was nearing the end of his Maine Road career. He had made only 18 League appearances and scored four goals during the 1958-59 season and, although he was vital in a number of games, City were beginning to look to a future without him. Les McDowall had already started looking at a nineteen year old striker playing for Huddersfield. He appeared to offer a great

Groundsman Mike Cassidy marking out in the snow prior to the FA Cup tie with Grimsby, January 1959.

deal, the only problem was the price. City would have to pay a considerable amount to sign the young, exciting forward. His name? Denis Law.

It would take McDowall some time to sign the youngster, but as the close season began he considered City's strengths and weaknesses. They remained in a period of transition. Old campaigners like Johnstone were on their way out. Indeed he would leave the Club for a fee of £7,000 in September 1959, moving to Hibs. Another of the 1956 Cup Final stars Roy Little, who had been with the Club since 1949, had already been transferred, moving to Brighton in October 1958.

In addition Roy Warhurst, who had only been at Maine Road since June 1957 making forty appearances, moved on. He felt that there was too much unhappiness, and a lack of spirit within the Club. He accused the backroom staff of unsettling him and the other players and was desperate to move on: "There was too much back-biting and not enough spirit. I love Manchester but I'd have gone anywhere just to get out of Maine Road. Things just didn't work out."

He actually moved to Crewe, where he made 51 appearances, before moving again seventeen months later to Oldham.

1959-1960 The Law Man

McDowall had already brought in a couple of new faces when the 1959-60 season began, wingers Clive Colbridge and Andy Kerr. Colbridge had signed from Crewe for £10,000 while Kerr arrived from Partick Thistle. Both started the season but by Christmas Kerr had returned to Scotland, signing for Kilmarnock. Colbridge fared considerably better, however, missing only two League games all season.

In October the Blues defeated United 3-0 in their first League derby victory since September 1955. Joe Hayes, who always maintained a fine strike rate against the Reds, was in fine form, scoring twice, with George Hannah providing the other. The match gave the Blues a real boost and the following four games all ended in victory, with Bill McAdams proving to be a prolific marksman. In only eleven appearances he had scored twelve goals. His fine run wasn't to last however as injury forced too many absences. In fact McAdams had been a very unlucky player, suffering more than most with injuries throughout his career. A comparison could be made with 1980s/90s player Paul Lake who, like McAdams, always seemed to be on the verge of something big when injury struck. McAdams was unable to hold down a place in time to appear in either of the mid-fifties finals and, although he made a total of fifteen international appearances for Northern Ireland, his international career suffered.

Another whose international career suffered

because of injury was cricketer/footballer Jack Dyson. He was on the verge of an England call up when, in 1957, he broke his leg in a City pre-season trial match, then late the following March he broke his leg again in a comeback game in the Lancashire Cup. For the following couple of years he endeavoured to return to first team action and, on 14th November, he returned for the visit of Chelsea. The game ended 1-1 with the cricketer securing a successful comeback with a goal.

That game was noteworthy as it also saw the debut of 17 year old Alan Oakes, the man who would ultimately hold the record for most League appearances with the Blues. In later years Oakes felt goalkeeper Trautmann had helped him avoid embarrassment that day: "I gave away a penalty! Fortunately for me Bert Trautmann – the greatest ever keeper – was in nets and he saved the day. As a member of the groundstaff I'd clean Bert's boots and even that felt like a great honour, so you can imagine how grateful I felt when he saved the penalty. The Chelsea game was a one off – I think Ken Barnes was injured – and so it was a few weeks before my chance came again. I felt a lot of satisfaction that I was in the reckoning though. When I arrived at City there were 55 professionals and about five teams to progress through to reach the first team."

In 1959 the appearance record stood at 450 League games, plus 3 expunged at the outbreak of war, and was held by thirties star Eric Brook, but Bert Trautmann was second, making his 400th League appearance on 9th March 1960. Trautmann would end his career on 508 League appearances four years later, while Oakes would finish on an incredible 561 League games plus three appearances as substitute.

The week after Trautmann's 400th League appearance, Manager McDowall finally signed the Scottish striker Denis Law for a British record fee of £55,000 the day before the transfer deadline. It had been a tense negotiation. Law himself had expected to join Arsenal to link up with his Scottish colleague Tommy Docherty, however, Huddersfield were adamant that they could not sell Law for anything less than £55,000.

It all came to a head at Leeds Road where Arsenal had sent coach Ron Greenwood to negotiate a good deal. At the same time City, represented by Les

TRUE BLUE
Alan Oakes

Alan Oakes made his League debut against Chelsea on 14th November 1959 and went on to become City's record appearance holder with 561 (plus 3) League appearances.

Denis Law scores a debut day goal for City at Leeds.

McDowall and Chairman Alan Douglas, were keen to sign the 20 year old Scotsman. The Gunners had only given Greenwood power to offer £25,000 plus David Herd, making a total of £50,000, whereas McDowall and Douglas were able to discuss the pros and cons of offering more. The discussions and negotiations went on while Law himself was playing Table Tennis in the games room. When the young player was summoned he quickly realised that his move to Arsenal was off and, after less than ten minutes, he agreed to join the Blues at a cost that was said to be three times his weight in gold.

Law made his debut a memorable one by scoring in the 4-3 defeat at Leeds on 19th March 1960. Eleven days later he scored again as City defeated West Ham 3-1. He made one other appearance, away at Chelsea, before the player became the subject of his first controversy at the Club. Law was selected to play for Scotland at Hampden Park on 9th April - the date of the vital home game with West Bromwich Albion - and the City management took the view that playing for your country was more important than playing for your club. This angered many supporters, who realised that a Law-less City would struggle and that relegation was still a strong possibility. The Blues were only two points above the relegation zone.

The controversy heightened when other clubs took a different view and refused to release players. The City Board then felt justified in asking the League for a postponement, but the League refused. In the

programme for the game, the Board outlined their views and explained how the circumstance had occurred. The article ended by stressing that the situation of club V. Country cannot be allowed to continue.

As expected, without Law the Blues were defeated 1-0. The return of the Scotsman lifted spirits and helped City achieve successive 1-0 victories over Bolton and Tottenham, although controversy surrounded the game at White Hart Lane. Spurs were awarded a penalty shortly before the half-time interval and winger Cliff Jones's penalty was brilliantly saved by Bert Trautmann. Jones followed up sending the rebound into the net only to find that the referee had blown for half time the moment Trautmann saved. Tottenham supporters believed that decision cost their club the Championship

NO GOAL!

...And this may save City

HERE is the "goal" that wasn't.... and that may save Manchester City from relegation and also cost Tottenham the League championship.

Spurs winger Cliff Jones crashes a follow-up shot into the net after Bert Trautmann had parried the Tottenham man's penalty kick.

But a split-second before the ball crossed the line the referee blew for half-time.

There were only 20 seconds left when the penalty was awarded and time had actually run out when Jones took the kick.

Here, Cliff Sear, City's left back, glances over to referee George Pullin, as he hears the whistle.

The grateful Manchester team went on to win 1—0—one of the shock results of the day.

as, they argued, Spurs would have won the game and the title would have been decided on goal average.

What made the decision worse for Tottenham fans was that City lost 2-1 to Burnley on the last day of the season, thereby guaranteeing the title for the Lancastrian club. By this time, of course, City had reached safety. That had been achieved in their fortieth match - a 2-1 win at home to Preston - with Colin Barlow scoring the vital goal a few minutes before the final whistle on 23rd April.

City ended the 1959-60 season in 16th position, missing 15th place by a marginally worse goal average than Everton. It had been an improvement on the previous season, and with record signing Denis Law in their line-up the Blues eagerly anticipated the 1960-61 season.

1960-1961 More Arrivals

McDowall had made a couple of close season signings, bringing full back Barrie Betts and centre-half Jackie Plenderleith to Maine Road.

Betts had more or less given up all hope of playing in the First Division when a serious spinal injury threatened his career. At the time he was with his home town team, Second Division Barnsley, but once fitness returned a move to Stockport County seemed the only possible way of continuing in the game. In June 1960, after 112 appearances with County Les McDowall thought the time was right to take a gamble on the 28 year old, paying a bargain £8,000. Many questioned the move but Betts quickly established himself, and became the Club's first ever-present for four years. He enjoyed the experience: "I had four seasons at Maine Road - they were the best years of my playing life. I only wish that I'd found my way to City ten years earlier than I did."

Jackie Plenderleith also enjoyed his time at City, although he accepted that the move was not entirely a successful one: "I earned my only Scottish cap with City. I signed from Hibs in July 1960 for £16,500 and by November had won my first cap against Northern Ireland. We won 5-2 but I was dropped. I didn't get picked again simply because I'd lost my place in City's first team.

"Things started to go wrong for me at Maine Road during my second season. I'd asked for a transfer because I thought I was being made a scapegoat and finally it ended with me going back to Scotland to Queen of the South on a free transfer in September 1963. Despite the fact I had my share of reserve team football and also the fact that the first team seemed to be perpetually struggling, I really enjoyed life at Maine Road."

Another player to arrive during 1960 was Gerry Baker, who was signed from St. Mirren on 2nd November,

making his debut three days later in the 3-1 defeat at Bolton. Co-incidentally 16 year old Francis Lee made his Bolton debut in the same game, making a name for himself by both scoring and being booked. Baker had joined a side that had only lost three out of 14 League games, however City's failure following his arrival caused many to criticise McDowall's decision to bring the 22 year old into the side so soon. These comments were similar to those aired when Rodney Marsh first appeared for City in 1972.

Of Baker's opening nine League games, City were defeated in eight. Fortunately he provided two goals in the other game, at home to Fulham, to help bring a 3-2 victory. The other goal came from Clive Colbridge.

The mid-season slump seriously affected City's chance of a top ten place and actually put the Club in serious danger of relegation. On 25th March a goalless draw with Bolton placed the Blues in 18th position and prompted City fans to express their dissatisfaction. Defeats against Preston and Wolves followed, leaving the Blues on equal points with the bottom club.

A little relief came on 8th April when Denis Law helped City to a 2-1 win - only their third victory of 1961 - over Chelsea. Both Denis Law and Colin Barlow had missed the two previous games and their return helped motivate the side. Two 1-1 draws followed, before City demolished Joe Mercer's Aston Villa 4-1 with goals from Law (2), Barlow and Hayes. The game saved the Blues from the dreaded drop and helped make amends for the 5-1 defeat at Villa Park on 3rd December.

City ended the campaign in 13th position, five points above the relegation zone, and City fans pondered another season of 'what might have been'. Apart from the League programme, fans had good cause to wonder about the Blues exploits in both the FA Cup and the newly formed League Cup. In the new competition City defeated Stockport 3-0 then suffered a 2-0 embarrassment at Second Division Portsmouth.

In the FA Cup it took three games and 390 minutes for City to overcome fellow First Division strugglers Cardiff City. In the fourth round, away to Second Division Luton Town on a wet and windy day, City found themselves slipping and sliding on a sodden playing surface. Many doubted whether the game should have been played at all, but it did go ahead. Luton's Alec Ashworth was first to take advantage of the conditions with two goals in the opening 18 minutes. By half-time, however, City had fought back with Denis Law scoring a hat-trick.

By the 67th minute Law had increased his tally to six, although his fifth goal had initially been credited to Joe Hayes. It was an amazing feat but as the conditions were worsening, according to referee K.R. Tuck and the Luton players, the game was abandoned only two minutes later. Les McDowall was furious, as were many of the City team and the supporters who had travelled from Manchester, but the referee would not listen.

Four days later the game was replayed. Denis Law remembers the poor playing conditions: "The pitch was terrible because it was raining all the time. But the annoying part of it was that it was even worse when the game was replayed! We had a feeling that we would lose the replay - and we did, 3-1. And I scored the one!"

The Luton FA Cup tie was the last tie Law would play with City for 23 years. During the summer of 1961 he moved to Italy, signing for Torino for a quoted fee of £125,000. The money, plus the opportunity to follow the likes of John Charles appealed: "Don't forget that in those days in England the maximum wage was only £20 per week. And when the Italians came over and dangled so many carrots in front of me, big money, wine, food, sunshine, it was too good to turn down. John Charles had been out there for a few years and now they were chasing lads like myself and Jimmy Greaves. As it turned out, it wasn't as marvellous

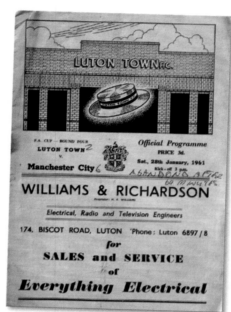

LUTON TOWN F.C.

F.A. CUP — ROUND FOUR
LUTON TOWN 2
v.
Manchester City 6

Official Programme
PRICE 3d.
Sat., 28th January, 1961
Kick-off 3 p.m.
ABANDONED AFTER 60 MINUTES

WILLIAMS & RICHARDSON
Proprietor: H. S. WILLIAMS

Electrical, Radio and Television Engineers

174, BISCOT ROAD, LUTON   'Phone: Luton 6897 / 8

for
SALES and SERVICE
of
Everything Electrical

as we thought it would be. But if I hadn't gone, I might have regretted it for the rest of my life."

By the time of Law's departure, Les McDowall's City were a rather tired, ordinary side, in dire need of new direction. Crowds had started to diminish - the average dipping below 30,000 for the first time since 1933. McDowall was still trying out new ideas and new blood but the time had come for change. Unlike the modern era it was unusual for a team to sack a manager as soon as the struggles began, instead the view was often taken that "he got us in this mess, he can get us out!" Despite four or five seasons of struggle, McDowall's job was safe, even though the time was right for new direction. The belief within the Club was that it was the players who were letting the Club down not the manager of eleven years.

★ The day that the rains came . . . and ruined a six-hit. Referee K. Tuck, ankle deep in water, inspects the Luton pitch and then abandons the match.

1961-1962 Pardoe's Debut

With no pressure to quit, McDowall prepared for the 1961-62 season. He spent the money received from Law's transfer on England Under 23 goalscorer Peter Dobing from Blackburn, and the powerful Bobby Kennedy from Kilmarnock. Both made their debuts against Leicester on 19th August, with Kennedy grabbing a goal: "I couldn't have had a better start. We beat Leicester 3-1 in my first game and I even scored against the great Gordon Banks. The fans loved that and I think they supported me from the beginning, although it was a little tough at first. Denis Law, who was a great hero to the fans, had been sold, and Ken Barnes, another hero, had also moved on, and their replacements were me and Peter Dobing. For a lot of fans – and I can totally understand this – we were not an improvement.

"Usually when you bring players in you try to improve the side, but when we joined I don't think anyone believed the side had improved. Nevertheless the fans took to me and I think they recognised that I always gave 100% - City fans rightly demand that and they will often overlook a player's weaknesses so long as he shows the same commitment to the Club as they do."

As Kennedy mentioned, Ken Barnes had left in May 1961 to become player-manager of Wrexham after over 250 League appearances for the Blues. The team for the Leicester victory was a mix of the old and new and lined up as follows: Trautmann, Betts, Leivers, Cheetham, Ewing, Kennedy, Barlow, Dobing, Baker, Hayes, and Wagstaffe. Wagstaffe believed that the decision to sell Law was to have a major impact on the 1961-62 season: "I actually think that the ambition of the Club had gone when they sold Denis Law. The players still had ambition, but selling Denis seemed to be a backward step. It was the end of the ambition of the Club. It dragged the players down."

Barrie Betts was now the Club captain and under his stewardship six of the opening eight games ended in victory, but City's change of fortune was not to last and by New Year's Day the Blues had slipped alarmingly after gaining only seven points from sixteen games. That was relegation form.

As results worsened, McDowall once again shuffled the pack, bringing in more new players. One player, 17 year old Neil Young, turned out to be the find of the season. Young had signed professional forms in February 1961 and made his League debut in City's 2-1 defeat at Aston Villa. Although he failed to score on that occasion, the youngster remained in the side for the rest of the season, finding the net ten times in only 24 games - a figure that ultimately helped save the Club from relegation.

McDowall also tried wing-half and future manager John Benson, forward Paul Aimson, and goalkeeper Harry Dowd. In 2004 John Benson remembered his first games: "I had appeared in a friendly at Dundee on 17th February, four days before my debut, and I remember there was a lot of talk about me playing in the League. The West Brom match ended in a 3-1 win and then we drew 0-0 at Cardiff - so I'd played in Scotland, England, and Wales all within my debut week!

"I did okay in those games but I knew I was not guaranteed a place – no one was – and I remember looking on the team sheet each week to check if I'd been selected. The manager, Les McDowall, never told you you were in, you had to check the sheet. Actually, you would hide from the manager – he was an authoritarian figure and you simply did not communicate with him.

"In my third game we played Spurs and won 6-2. There was snow on the ground and I'm sure we were a goal up before any of the City players had touched the ball - it was an own goal! We were winning 6-0 with ten minutes to go and Jimmy Greaves netted twice. Bert Trautmann was our 'keeper and he was superb as always. He really saved us at times. I was in awe of him and I remember I'd got on the pitch once as a fan at the end of a 1-0 win over Everton and he lifted me up and carried me off the pitch. An absolutely brilliant 'keeper."

Trautmann's brilliance meant that Harry Dowd was probably the most unfortunate of the new boys at this time as there was never any real possibility of him replacing the living-legend in nets. Dowd was always going to find it difficult making a name during this period at Maine Road, and the two games he played in hardly helped him take the number one spot off the heroic German. His first ended in a 4-1 defeat at Blackburn, while his second saw the Blues lose 6-3 at Burnley. It was no wonder the 23 year old 'keeper had continued to seek a trade outside of football before making his debut: "I played for City as an amateur for a number

TRUE BLUE
Joe Hayes

Joe Hayes was one of the unsung heroes of the 50s and 60s. He netted 142 goals in 331 League games.

of years because I was studying for my City and Guilds to qualify as a plumber. It wasn't so much that I was particularly desperate to become a plumber. They still had conscription in those days, and if I hadn't been learning a trade, I would have been called up. My great pleasure in life was playing football. Simple as that! I got knocked about a bit more in goal, but it was all part of the game."

Another player brought into the side was 15 year old Glyn Pardoe - the youngest player ever to appear in City's first team: "I actually found out I was playing a few days before, so that helped. If I'd have found out on the morning I don't know how I'd have coped. I don't think I ever thought about my age. I'm sure others did, but to me it was just a great opportunity. I can't remember much about the game, except we lost 4-1 at home and I was up against a tough centre-half called Trevor Smith. I wore the number nine shirt for that game – I later played in almost every position! I don't think I did a great deal, but I know I kept my place for the next 3 games."

Pardoe's first game was the 4-1 defeat at home to Birmingham City on 11th April. It had been a quiet debut, but his second match was entirely different. City faced Joe Mercer's youthful Aston Villa side at Maine Road before a pitiful crowd of 18,564. Despite early pressure, the Blues ran out winners thanks to a solitary Neil Young goal. The press the following day were full of praise for the youngsters of both sides, with one report revealing that the Villa manager had wandered around the boardroom after the game with a big, beaming smile. The reporter's view was that Mercer was convinced his youthful side would be world beaters within a couple of years and that the genial manager was full of optimism. City supporters may like to believe that Mercer had been so impressed with the likes of Young and Pardoe that he thought 'this is the club for me!'

Regardless of Mercer's view, the press also detailed the exploits of the young Pardoe: "I must save the last tribute for 15 year old Glyn Pardoe who made two astonishing runs, had two headers and a shot that almost scored and even now is remarkably hard to shift off the ball. Women or no women, soccer is safe for ever in the hands of our young Pardoes."

The City programme was equal in its praise: "The experiment of giving 15 year old Glyn Pardoe an extended trial was also justified in the Villa game. After his quiet debut game against Birmingham, he was seen to much better effect against Villa and if he didn't set Maine Road alight he surely gave promise that he is going to be a menace to opposing defences in the years to come.

"Certainly these end of season games are invaluable in giving young Pardoe the experience of first team football and although there is no intention of rushing him the experience he is gaining now could well see his development stepped up and his challenge for a regular first team place coming sooner or later."

With four games left to play, the Villa result lifted City to 13th position on 37 points - ten above the relegation zone. Although 21st placed Cardiff City still had five games remaining, the Blues were in effect safe. Pardoe played in two further games - a 3-1 win against Sheffield Wednesday and a 3-1 defeat at Blackpool - but missed the last couple of matches. A 3-1 victory on the final day of the season against Blackburn saw City finish in 12th position. A marvellous effort considering their abysmal record from September to January.

In the League Cup City were defeated 4-2 at Ipswich and in the FA Cup the Blues defeated Notts County 1-0 before succumbing to Everton 2-0 at Goodison Park.

Despite the emergence of the likes of Young and Pardoe, the feeling amongst many supporters was that City remained a considerable distance from glory in any competition. Sooner or later personnel had to change at the top.

1962-1963 Paying The Penalty

The 1962-63 season started in the most traumatic way possible with the Blues annihilated 8-1 at Wolves, even City's goal was scored by a Wolves player. Within a week McDowall plunged into the transfer market, purchasing forward Alex Harley from Third Lanark for £18,000. The 26 year old quickly displayed a return on the investment by grabbing both goals in the Blues' first victory, a 2-1 defeat of Ipswich on 5th September. Sadly, three days later City crashed 6-1 at home to West Ham.

Apart from the scoreline, the West Ham defeat was noteworthy for the antics of Bert Trautmann who kicked the ball at the referee while disputing the fifth goal. Then he appeared to rip off his jersey and storm off the field. It later transpired that the brilliant 'keeper had been sent off. Afterwards angry City supporters gathered outside demonstrating.

Seven days later City travelled to Old Trafford to face a United side strengthened by the acquisition of former Blue Denis Law. Despite the hype surrounding a United side that included Nobby Stiles, Johnny Giles, David Herd, Noel Cantwell and, of course Denis Law, City were a little more confident than in previous seasons. The last campaign had ended with the Blues finishing above United for the first time since the 1957-58 season, while the new season had seen the Reds perform only marginally better than City.

Before a rather disappointing derby crowd of 49,193 - the lowest since City's 5-0 win at Old Trafford in February 1955 - the Blues raced into a two goal lead inside 25 minutes. The first was via a penalty from Peter Dobing, the second a superb strike from the regular derby goalscoring king Joe Hayes.

During the second half, however, United fought back with new signing Law reminding his old team why they had broken the British transfer record to bring him to Manchester in the first place. He scored twice to level the scores, but the game was not over until, with virtually the last kick of the game, Alex Harley shot past United's Gaskell to give City the two points.

The game gave the Blues a much needed lift, and over the course of the following seven matches City gathered a total of eight points. Not a huge figure, but enough to relieve a little tension. Unfortunately, City's inconsistency never really disappeared however, and by mid-December the Blues' record read: W5 D7 L9 Pts 17.

They had also progressed to the quarter-finals of the League Cup by beating Blackpool 4-2 in a second round second replay, Newport 2-1 in the third round and Luton 1-0 in the fourth round. However, when City faced Birmingham in the quarter-final on 11th December, the Blues suffered a 6-0 defeat. Birmingham went on to win the League Cup that season.

Within days the worst winter since 1947 made its mark, with many fixtures postponed. The big freeze brought misery across the country and, although from 15th December through to 9th March the Blues did manage to remain unbeaten, they only played three matches. To get match practice City and Burnley flew to Dublin on 15th February where they drew 1-1.

By Easter City were in deep relegation trouble, lying in 21st place on 21 points after 30 games. The programme for the Good Friday fixture with Nottingham Forest outlined the seriousness of the situation: "Welcome this afternoon to Nottingham Forest for the start of a holiday fixture programme which is a critical one for us. The sad run of five successive League defeats in the last few weeks has dangerously heightened the relegation threat and with two home fixtures over the holiday period the chance is there to ease the danger and it calls for the maximum effort from the players to make the most of it."

The article went on to describe how close City had come to defeating the League leaders Leicester six days earlier where only the brilliance of Leicester's reserve 'keeper George Heyes, standing in for Gordon Banks, kept the Blues from scoring a hatful. In actual fact Leicester won 2-0, but City's forwards did manage to put in a large number of accurate shots, only for the 'keeper to deny each effort.

By this time Les McDowall, under intense pressure, had signed Alex Harley's Third Lanark colleague Matt Gray, while Harry Dowd had managed to replace the legendary Bert Trautmann on a more permanent basis. By the end of the season the 'goalkeeping plumber' would appear in a dozen more League games than Trautmann.

The Good Friday fixture with Forest ended in a 1-0 City win with Matt Gray proving to be an important purchase after scoring his fourth in eight matches. The following day Bolton were defeated 2-1 and then on Easter Monday

George Hannah.

the return game with Forest ended 1-1. On 20th April Arsenal were defeated 3-2, with two from Matt Gray and one from Joe Hayes, but the run was not to last.

The following five fixtures ended in defeat, throwing City right back into the relegation dog fight. Years later Glyn Pardoe realised that this had been a particularly bleak period to be a young player at Maine Road: "The great side of the 1950s had disintegrated really. We still had a few of the players in the side like Trautmann and Hayes, but the rest of the side was mainly youngsters finding their feet. It was difficult because there was a general air of despondency. We'd go to places like Blackburn and expect to win. We'd take the lead, but end up losing 4-1 (1st May 1963) and I think that said it all. We didn't know how to win matches. At the time I knew nothing else really, but when you do start to find success you suddenly realise how bleak the atmosphere inside the Club had been just a couple of seasons earlier."

Ten days after the Blackburn defeat a 1-0 home win over Tottenham on 11th May lifted McDowall's side a little, but with only two games left the situation was dire.

City's last two fixtures were a home derby with fellow strugglers United and a trip to mid-table West Ham United. Going into the Maine Road derby City were only one point behind the Reds, although United did have a game in hand. Understandably, the match was an ill-tempered affair with plenty of controversy.

With a crowd of 52,424, and thousands more locked outside, the game began with City playing confidently. In the ninth minute Peter Dobing sent a perfect through ball to Alex Harley who, under considerable pressure, rifled a right foot shot beyond United's Gaskell into the corner of the goal. City continued to dominate with United appearing rather shaky, only the fine goalkeeping of Gaskell and a few timely interceptions from Stiles prevented the Blues from increasing their lead.

After thirty minutes the City crowd roared with delight when Alex Harley appeared to have scored a vital second goal. Incredibly, the referee disallowed the effort on a hair's-breadth off side decision. The City men could not believe it and tempers reached boiling point. Shortly before half-time Pat Crerand and David Wagstaffe were both booked following a brutal confrontation. It was turning into an ugly game, and the fiery Crerand was determined to make his mark: "My first derby game will never be forgotten. It was a knockout. At least it was for City winger David Wagstaffe after I clouted him one on the chin as the teams trooped into the tunnel. I'm not proud of my actions that evening. It wasn't a vicious first half, but I'd become riled with Wagstaffe who I thought had punched me and my Celtic temper boiled up."

Wagstaffe was shocked by Crerand's actions: "I must have upset him or something. As we're walking up the tunnel he's still in a rage. But I didn't think he'd turn round and thump me one! We were walking up

the tunnel and I had my head down. He was about three yards in front of me. I don't know what was going through his mind but he must just have thought 'I'll hit him!' He turned round and did. I thought 'what's all that about'. I didn't get it. I'd been involved with a few altercations on the pitch as you do, but I think he just lost it. I certainly never expected it."

The press later revealed that Wagstaffe had been 'laid out' in the tunnel, yet unbelievably the referee took no action. Maybe he didn't see the incident, but United manager Matt Busby did. He confronted Crerand in the dressing room and by the start of the second half United seemed to be a little less antagonistic towards the Blues. Unfortunately, Wagstaffe had been unsettled by the whole affair.

Alex Harley once again went close, but as the minutes ticked by City's solitary goal seemed to be sufficient. Then disaster struck with only four minutes left. David Wagstaffe, still shaken from his conflict with Crerand, attempted what can only be described as a suicidal back pass: "It really shook me up. I can't remember much about the second half other than at one point I did a back pass and Denis Law, who was playing for them, intercepted it. Somehow Denis got a penalty as Dowd came towards him. It ended 1-1 and soon after we were relegated."

As Wagstaffe mentioned Denis Law, who had been quiet all evening, saw his chance and closed in on Dowd to tussle for the ball. As Dowd dived at the Scotsman's feet, Law fell and the ball ran out of play. The referee pointed to the spot much to the dismay of Dowd and fifty thousand City supporters. Albert Quixall stepped up and calmly slotted the ball past the unfortunate Dowd.

Later Dowd provided his version of the incident: "It was never a penalty; I scooped the ball away from Denis' feet and sent it out of play. I can't remember holding his feet but I did get a kick on the head. I may then have caught hold of him, but the ball was out of play by then, and I'm sure the linesman was signalling for a corner."

Law naturally claimed it was a just penalty but admitted that United would never have scored otherwise: "I was going away from the goal and had lost the ball. It was a lucky break for us."

The game ended 1-1 with City fans feeling deprived of two points by two poor refereeing decisions - three if you include the Crerand-Wagstaffe bout. The two points more or less guaranteed United's survival, but left City needing a better result than Birmingham City from their final game.

In the end Birmingham won, and City were defeated 6-1 at West Ham on 18th May. The Blues were back in the Second Division after an absence of twelve seasons. It was a bitter blow and one which resulted in the departure of long serving manager Les McDowall on 29th May.

1963-1964 Poyser Appointment

After briefly considering the alternatives the City Board took the decision to promote George Poyser, McDowall's assistant, to the post. Alan Douglas, the Chairman, called local journalist Eric Thornton in to explain the appointment: "We've had time against us. If we had appointed a stranger, he would have had a job getting to know the strength of the position before next season opens, but Poyser, having already been with us some time, knows the strength of the playing staff and everything else. We have talked it over with him. He says he knows the positions which need strengthening, and he feels he may be able to take us back into the First Division, so we're going to let him have a go."

Over 30,000 City supporters also knew the positions that needed strengthening, they had paid to witness the decline, but it was Poyser, not them, who became the manager on 12th July 1963. He had become a popular figure around Maine Road since his arrival in 1957, however the appointment hardly excited the City faithful, nor did it excite Alex Harley and Peter Dobing. The two strikers had found it hard to accept relegation and both chose to continue their careers in the First Division. Harley moved to the team that had only narrowly avoided the drop, Birmingham, while Dobing moved to Second Division champions Stoke.

Poyser quickly realised he needed to bring experience and quality to the Club and purchased Derek Kevan from Chelsea. Neil Young was by now a regular, while Joe Hayes continued to make the occasional appearance, as did George Hannah. In goal Poyser had signed Alan Ogley from Barnsley, although it was Harry Dowd who would replace Bert Trautmann on a more permanent basis, with the German making only three League appearances during the 1963-64 season. At the end of the season the legendary 'keeper would retire from first team football after fifteen seasons with the Blues.

The opening fixture of the 1963-64 Second Division started with a depressing 2-0 defeat at home to Portsmouth whose goals were scored by future City manager Ron Saunders, and an own goal from City's number 5, the 17 year old Alf Wood. As you would expect, the programme for that fixture claimed that the Blues would be going all out for promotion, but it also admitted than many supporters were disillusioned with the departure of the two leading scorers Dobing and Harley. It claimed, however, that new manager Poyser had held lengthy talks with the players trying to persuade them to stay, but neither would listen. According to the article, their departures were inevitable.

A 2-2 draw at Cardiff followed the Portsmouth defeat, and then a brace from Derek Kevan gave the Blues victory at Rotherham. Gradually City moved into their stride with December proving to be the most profitable month for the Blues, and for November signing Jimmy Murray who scored ten goals in five games that month. Christmas was particularly pleasing results wise with Murray scoring eight of City's eighteen goals in three victories during Christmas week.

Disappointingly the Christmas period also saw the departure of David Wagstaffe. Wagstaffe was popular with fans and recognised as a good talent, however the manager decided he was no longer needed: "George Poyser called me at home. It was Christmas Eve. I'd been out and I got home and my mum told me the manager had 'phoned and I had to ring him at home. This was highly unusual. I thought this must be very serious because back then no player had the manager's home number. When I spoke with him, he said 'I'll meet you on Boxing Day at the ground at 10 o'clock. You're going to Wolverhampton. If you sign you'll be playing for them. If not you'll be coming back with me and playing against Bury'. That was exactly what he'd said to me. It was a shock."

Wagstaffe was unhappy with the way the Club was stagnating, but he did not want to leave: "There was no ambition there. Once McDowall had gone it faded. Poyser took over. He was a dour man and the atmosphere went. Nothing seemed right. I can't ever remember Poyser being out on the training pitch or anything. I just remember him with his pipe in his mouth.

"Nobody knew anything about the move. There were no papers on Christmas Day or anything, and I went to Wolverhampton. I signed at 12 and played at 3pm. It was amazing and I've heard the stories of people at City thinking I was going to play at Maine Road and then after the game finding out I'd played at Wolves. Very odd.

"I often wonder what would have happened if I'd been able to stay at City until the ambition re-appeared. When Joe Mercer was manager I still knew the lads and Mike Summerbee invited me to his house warming. The place was full of City and United players. It was a great night. Malcolm Allison shouted across to me: 'Hey Waggy!' The place went silent. Malcolm shouted: 'Waggy. It's a pity you left Maine Road before I came'. 'Why's that Malcolm?' He replied: 'I might have made you into a footballer'.

"Everyone laughed, but you know it did make me think. I saw how Young, Doyle, Oakes, Pardoe and so on developed. It was a fabulous team and I used to watch them as often as I could because it was a phenomenal team."

Back in 1963-64 the Christmas period was soon followed by a miserable January and February, with only four points gained in the first nine games of 1964. Alan Oakes felt the cause was an injury to Jimmy Murray in

Bert Trautmann makes an emotional speech in the tunnel at Maine Road after his testimonial game.

the final match of 1963: "After we were relegated in '63 Derek Kevan and Jimmy Murray arrived. We were doing really well, then Jimmy did his cartilage in – that was a major blow - and we tailed off."

The first point of 1964 was earned in a rather remarkable game with Harry Dowd earning the glory. City were losing 1-0 to a debut goal from Bury youngster and future Blue Colin Bell at Maine Road on 8th February when Dowd received a broken finger in the 54th minute. He was unable to continue in nets but stayed on the field and reverted to centre-forward - a role he'd often played as a youngster. Scottish forward Matt Gray replaced Dowd in nets and the game continued with the regular 'keeper keen to impress in attack: "I was restless enough to give it all I'd got. I felt just like a colt on its feet for the first time, pushing and shoving my way through and going for the every ball - many of which I hadn't a hope of getting. But the moment of glory wasn't far away, and it seemed the fans were loving every minute of the action.

"I got the chance to slip the ball to Derek Kevan, his shot hit the bar, and as it bounced down I went lunging in to turn home the equaliser. The newspapers said some very kind things the next day."

With Dowd's efforts up front and a fine performance

in goal from Gray the Blues secured the point. Gray had managed to keep a clean sheet, although Dowd's amazing exploits prevented him from receiving the kind of credit that other emergency City 'keepers Doyle, McDonald, Gleghorn, and Quinn, would over the years.

That game was probably Dowd's highlight of the season as later on, he found himself dropped with Bert Trautmann returning to the side for three games before even he gave way to Alan Ogley for the final five matches of the season.. At one point Dowd asked for a transfer, but he remained at the Club. Trautmann, however, was in his final season and in May he retired. He had been a fine servant, but at the age of 40 with City in Division Two he realised it was time to call it a day. Almost 48,000 paid to attend his testimonial match on 15th April 1964, with many more sneaking in without paying, and thousands locked outside. To many football followers he remains the world's greatest goalkeeper, and City supporters can count themselves fortunate that Bert Trautmann and the popular Frank Swift, England's greatest 'keeper, both played for their club.

Following a run of nine games with only one defeat, the League campaign ended with City finishing in 6th position. The January/February slump had caused them to miss out on promotion by fifteen points, and to drop out of the two Cup competitions. Alan Oakes felt the slump impacted the Club for some time: "We missed promotion and we couldn't get it going again until Joe and Malcolm arrived in '65."

In the FA Cup a 4th January tie at Swindon ended in a 2-1 defeat and a cartilage injury to centre-forward Jimmy Murray, while on 15th January City suffered a 2-0 loss at Stoke in the first leg of the League Cup semi-final.

City had overcome Carlisle (2-0), Hull (3-0), Leeds (3-1) and Notts County (1-0), prior to Christmas, but the semi-final first leg came at what was the most difficult and disappointing period of the season. Sandwiched between defeats at eventual division champions Leeds and at home to second placed Sunderland. The second leg, played on 5th February did end with a Derek Kevan goal giving the Blues a 1-0 victory but it wasn't enough and Stoke went through to face Leicester in the two legged final.

The Blues also reached the two legged semi-final of another competition - the FA Youth Cup where they lost to high flying Manchester United, who included the promising George Best in their line-up.

1964-1965 A Possible Merger

Always optimistic the Club's supporters hoped 1964-65 would bring improvement but few realistically expected it. In fact, attendances had been slipping throughout the early 1960s and City's rate of decline since 1956 was alarming, especially when across in Trafford Matt Busby had almost finished rebuilding United after Munich. In 1963 not only did the Reds help send City down, they also won the FA Cup, and in the season that followed they challenged for the title. Because of their performances, and the effect of Munich on worldwide public consciousness, they were also more popular than at any time in their history up to that point, whereas City were losing support. Also, ground improvements at United in preparation for the 1966 World Cup helped to lift Old Trafford above Maine Road in terms of quality for the first time. It was difficult being a Blue in a world dominated by red.

The media seemed to look at Old Trafford first and the history and traditions of Manchester were being turned on their heads as the Reds replaced the Blues as Manchester's glamour club. Many argue that this is not the case, that United had always been equal with City, but the truth is that City were the glamour club pre-war and that the Reds took the initiative post-war until inevitably, poor management at Maine Road gave United a considerable lead.

Incredibly, the 1964-65 season was to see the news break that at least one of City's directors felt the Blues no longer had a future and that the Club should merge with United. He actually approached the Reds with the idea.

The idea of merging with United shocked supporters. It is a ridiculous idea but throughout the 1964-65 season City appeared to be seriously considering the possibility. Vice-Chairman Frank Johnson had actually come up with the idea. It appears that Johnson had already angered supporters, by proposing the entire Football League should be split into North and South sections, and then he followed this up with the formal approach to United to merge. Furious letters appeared from fans who were absolutely disgusted with Johnson's suggestion.

How far the merger would go was unclear, but at the very least, it was suggested, City and United would share one ground – Old Trafford. The idea that Maine Road with all its history and heritage could be demolished as part of a deal that saw City move into Old Trafford seemed totally ridiculous.

The approach by Johnson came towards the end of the 1963-64 season and was confirmed as being genuine by an Old Trafford director, but the discussions – which seemed to occur several times during 1964 – only became public in January 1965. By that time a group of 'rebel' City shareholders led by Peter Donoghue were pushing for changes at Board level. They had already asked for an Extraordinary General Meeting where they were to demand the resignation of the Board. When he heard the news about the merger, Donoghue was dismayed and told Peter Gardner of the *Manchester Evening News*: "If what we have heard is true this is the last straw. We are determined not to let City die as a club. A merger would only go through over our dead bodies."

Donoghue's group issued a ten point plan to save the Blues. Ultimately, this led to the City board and Donoghue's group announcing they would work together for the good of City.

As for the merger the idea was soon dropped once supporter feelings were known. City's struggles would continue, but at least the Club was independent from United.

The 1964-65 season opened with a 2-1 defeat at Charlton. A 6-0 win at home to perennial strugglers Leyton Orient followed then, after a 2-0 defeat to Northampton Town, Orient won the return game by the odd goal in seven. Dave Bacuzzi, a £20,000 signing from Arsenal, impressed but in reality the Blues were a typical mid table side. Inconsistency reared its head again and games that should have been easy victories ended in defeat.

The month of September saw City follow each victory with a depressing defeat. Unsurprisingly, morale was low. Only one defeat in December provided a minor lift, but January saw the Club sink to its lowest point up to that time. On 13th January, City travelled to Third Division Shrewsbury for an FA Cup third round replay and lost 3-1, then three days later City were at home to

Swindon Town. The attendance was a pitiful 8,015, City's lowest ever for a Maine Road League match, and the vast stadium had an eerie feel.

As well as a general feeling of being let down, there were other mitigating factors that influenced support that day. The Shrewsbury defeat had knocked the stuffing out of many fans, while others had heard the news that snow was forecast. In addition, there was general unease around the city as stories of potential bus strikes were developing. The strikes and snow came later, but on the morning of the game some feared the worst.

During the game, the Blues played some good football at times but went behind to a 19th minute goal from Dennis Brown, and further behind to a goal from 22 year old future Blue Mike Summerbee midway through the second half. City came back with a stunning 30 yard goal from Alan Oakes who, incidentally, was the first player spotted by George Poyser when he joined the Blues as assistant manager in 1957.

The players felt the pain as much as the fans. In 2005 Bobby Kennedy recalled: "That was a miserable day. My strongest recollection is that our groundsman Stan Gibson would put grass seed out at the start of spring to try and get the pitch going for the next season. Growing a pitch then was much more difficult. Anyway, Stan had sown seeds prior to the Swindon game, and during the match the atmosphere was very poor. Pigeons came on to the turf and sat eating the seed in the middle of the pitch. We had to play around them!"

The match ended 2-1 and afterwards the supporters expressed their anger, demonstrating on the Maine Road forecourt. Bricks were hurled at the windows in the Main Stand and City fans claimed they had suffered enough. Kennedy: "After the game there was a bit of a demonstration and one or two bricks were thrown – that was a major disturbance at the time because general disorder was not known – and little Albert Alexander went out to face the fans. It was a brave thing to do but Albert was an absolute Blue and felt the pain of the day himself. I think, after listening to Albert, the fans all just packed up and went home, but in the dressing room some of the players were saying they'd had enough. They wanted to leave… saw no future etc. I didn't feel like that because, even in City's darkest hour, I still couldn't see anywhere better to go. It had been the worst day of my footballing life, but I loved Maine Road, loved the support, and I saw Manchester City as the best club in the world. Why move?"

The attendance that day had been only 615 more than Stockport County, who ended the season bottom of the Fourth Division, and many people felt that the direction of the Club also matched that of their near rivals.

Reporter Eric Cooper, the 'Sports Voice of the North',

considered City's dismal situation and decided: "It isn't soccer experts or players Manchester City need right now so much as a psychologist. A man who might analyse the transitions from optimism to pessimism. A man who by his enthusiasm and drive might fill the gaps between the potential City have shown so often and the failures that have labelled them the most unpredictable team in Soccer. Here is a club that between the wars were Manchester's favourites, reaching the Cup final three times besides winning the League Championship in 1937, while neighbours United were regarded as a music hall joke."

Cooper went on to consider where City's failure began: "Old timers will tell you that the decline at Maine Road set in when they were relegated a year after winning the League title and a cynical fan lowered the flag to half-mast. Since that time City have twice won promotion from the Second Division and twice more returned. They have also won the Cup, but somehow they have never recaptured the old glory. Supporters – and they could probably command more potential fans for a winning team than their successful United rivals – have been buffeted between hope and frustration until they are tired. The image of Manchester City has changed from the glamorous cavalier football of the 30s to one of abject apathy."

Amazingly, George Poyser had missed the Swindon match prompting many to question his commitment. In actual fact, he had been on a scouting trip in a desperate search to bring a saviour to Maine Road. In the *Sunday Express* the next day, James Mossop believed inside left Johnny Crossan was to be the man: "Crisis club Manchester City are to bid this week for Sunderland's inside-left Johnny Crossan. It will be a dire, urgent move, for City lurched deeper into trouble yesterday with another home defeat - and their lowest ever attendance."

On 22nd January Crossan signed for a fee often quoted as £40,000, but sometimes reported as £38,000 or £45,000. Derek Hodgson in the *Daily Express* penned a welcome to the Irishman: "John, you have it in you to be City's greatest player since Denis Law, commanding an adulation, almost an idolatry, that you will never have known before. Half a great footballing city is seeking a hero and you can end the search."

Another journalist believed he had much to offer the Blues but also provided a warning: "Crossan can do it all… the deadly accurate pass… the centre that hangs, spot on… the precise collection and distribution… the eye for a scoring chance. But he must never allow himself to slip into the unhappy ways that lost him his popularity at Sunderland."

As the comment suggested, the new player had not been too popular at Roker Park towards the end of his time there, and his first few performances at Maine Road hardly turned him into the hero that Derek Hodgson had suggested. However, over time the player did impress with his greatest season coming in 1965-66.

Another player appearing in the League team for the first time was Mike Doyle, an 18 year old locally born defender, whose chance came when Alan Oakes was injured. Doyle made his debut in a 2-2 draw at Cardiff on Friday 12th March but these were difficult times for any new player coming into the squad. Often there would be confusion over who would be playing and, for his debut, Doyle had been told rather late on and had to rush via public transport from his home in Reddish to Manchester Airport to catch a flight to Cardiff.

The youngster waited for a bus, but none came and then the panic set in. He wanted to 'phone the Club but realised he didn't know the number then, as he started to feel the world closing in on him, a car pulled up with fellow Blue Vic Gomersall driving. Doyle explained his situation and Gomersall drove him to the airport, arriving with only five minutes to spare. It was no wonder that Doyle was unimpressed with the Club's direction: "The Club, at that stage, was going through one of its worst spells since I had joined, and at times I had the feeling that Manchester City were like a ship without a rudder."

George Poyser's reign was now nearing its end. Demonstrations and poor morale seemed everywhere and the players were also losing respect for their leader. Mike Doyle witnessed an extraordinary event during training one day. The manager rarely took part in training but, as City's situation worsened, Poyser decided to give it a try: "One day he turned up during a training session clad in a tracksuit - and his appearance was the signal for a chorus of laughter, and some ribald remarks

from one or two of the players. I felt annoyed because I believed that this showed a lack of respect for the man in charge, and if players could show such disrespect there was something sadly wrong all the way round."

At Easter Poyser resigned. For the first game after Poyser's departure, Mike Doyle was stood outside Maine Road an hour before kick-off eating fish and chips when Chairman Albert Alexander tapped him on the shoulder and told him to get inside and get changed. Doyle checked with coach Johnny Hart who confirmed that he was to play. It seemed a crazy situation and one that confused the players. They simply didn't know who was in charge, but it would be several months before a new manager would be appointed. In the meantime Fred Tilson took on most of the manager's duties.

City achieved three draws and one victory in their final four games that season. Those results lifted the Blues to 11th, without them the Blues could have finished five places lower. As it was the campaign ended with City in their lowest ever end of season position up to that point.

The Blues were in urgent need of a pick-me-up, especially when the season ended with another meagre crowd, this time only 8,409. Across the city United ended the season as League Champions, FA Cup semi-finalists, and Inter-City Fairs Cup semi-finalists. Something had to be done. The Blues could suffer no more. Albert Alexander had to find the right manager to move City forward and to catch United. Rumours suggested City were after Peter Doherty, others said Bill Shankly, in July the announcement was made.

1956-1965 SUMMARY

Highest League Attendance: 70,483 Manchester United, 28/12/57
Highest Cup Attendance: 46,988 Newcastle United, 09/01/57 (FA Cup)
Managers: 1950–1963 Les McDowall & 1963–1965 George Poyser

Seasonal Record:

Season	League	Posn	FA Cup	League Cup	Other	Leading Scorer	Average Attendance
1956-57	FL Div1	18	Rnd 3		Charity Shield Runners-up	Johnstone 16	30,005
1957-58	FL Div1	5	Rnd 3			Hayes 25	32,765
1958-59	FL Div1	20	Rnd 3			Barlow 17	32,568
1959-60	FL Div1	15	Rnd 3			McAdams 21	35,637
1960-61	FL Div1	13	Rnd 4	Rnd 3		Law 19	29,502
1961-62	FL Div1	12	Rnd 4	Rnd 2		Dobing 22	25,711
1962-63	FL Div1	21	Rnd 5	Rnd 5		Harley 23	24,683
1963-64	FL Div2	6	Rnd 3	Semi-Final		Kevan 30	18,201
1964-65	FL Div2	11	Rnd 3	Rnd 2		Kevan 18	14,753

Mercer and Allison

"Where do you find superlatives to describe the achievements of this brilliant, exciting and breath-taking City side? The Blues again scaled tremendous heights to outclass Spurs on a treacherous ice and snowbound Maine Road pitch."

Manchester Evening News journalist Peter Gardner writing following City's defeat of Spurs, December 1968

1965-1966 A New Beginning

Poyser's resignation gave City the perfect opportunity to get it right and appoint a manager who the players and supporters could respect. Chairman Albert Alexander and the other directors had little experience of appointing managers, after all Poyser had only been the second appointment since 1950, but the pressure to select the right man was immense. The Board looked at all the candidates and then decided that the right man would be the former England and Arsenal Captain Joe Mercer.

Mercer had already proved his ability as a manager turning a rather average Aston Villa side into Second Division champions and League Cup winners. At Villa, and at his previous club Sheffield United, Mercer had developed sides that came within a fraction of reaching Wembley in the FA Cup. His sides always seemed to save their best for cup competition, although it's true to say that he had suffered personally in his last year at Villa Park. The Villa faithful had been presented with promotion and the League Cup in Joe's first two full seasons and naturally expected glory at the highest level. However, the appalling winter of 1962-63 which helped relegate City also affected Mercer's reign at Villa. Twelve months later, his health suffered and Mercer was forced out by the Villa board. Taking the City job was a major gamble.

With concern over his health, Mercer was forced to consider the support he needed from his backroom staff before accepting. At Villa he had taken on too much, at City he knew he needed a strong assistant who would be able to control the training of the players. He remembered a young coach he'd seen at the FA's training centre at Lilleshall: "I 'phoned an extrovert, ebullient, but brilliant coach called Malcolm Allison. Like me he was out of work - sacked by Plymouth Argyle. It took me two days to find him, but he said he would join me if I took the job. Secretly, I met the Manchester board and accepted the job, telling them of my plans for Malcolm."

For Malcolm Allison the opportunity was one not to miss. He had been a player with West Ham in the mid-1950s and had moved into management with Bath City and Plymouth Argyle. He was full of new ideas and when his position at Plymouth became impossible - the directors overruled his team selection - he found there were plenty of other clubs keen to secure his services. For Allison though, there was only one team: "Manchester City had always been my team. When I was a kid I listened to a Cup Final when I was about six or seven. City were beaten by Everton, 3-0, just before Joe played for them. Anyway, from that moment on City were my team. When I went to Manchester I saw Joe and agreed to stay there because that was my team."

Years later Alan Oakes admitted that the players were initially worried: "We were wary of Malcolm at first. He had all these ideas and it seemed so different to what we were used to, but within a week or so he'd won everybody over. The transformation by the two men was so fast – before we'd completed our pre-season games we were convinced we would win promotion. We couldn't wait to get started. The confidence flowed and then Malcolm tackled our fitness."

Glyn Pardoe was another who was uncertain what to expect from Mercer and Allison: "As a player you really worried about where we were heading and who the new guy might be. I was still only about 18 and had no idea how it would all pan out of course. Joe arrived, followed by Malcolm, and everything started to improve. Training improved considerably and so you started to realise how football could be improved and enjoyed. Joe was a very respectable figure. We knew what he'd achieved as a player and he had a great approach. He was quiet but very supportive. A real calming influence. Lovely.

"My first impression of Malcolm – remember I was still only a lad – was that he was very loud. He liked to shout a lot! Naturally, I got used to that, but at first it was a bit of a shock. Malcolm was a terrific coach and we all learnt so much from him. He was fantastic once you got to know him, and together they both turned us into a great side."

In addition to Mercer and Allison, another vital member of the City set up was chief scout Harry Godwin. When Mercer arrived at Maine Road, he put his arm around Godwin and said, "I've heard you're good at nicking one or two youngsters. Nick a few for me, will you?"

It wasn't long before the Mercer-Allison partnership made changes to the City squad. Almost immediately

Malcolm Allison tested inside-forward Derek Kevan: "I used to do these training sessions whereby I'd create a space for him to make runs through, and I used to say to Joe that he just didn't want to make it. I used to work out training schedules whereby if people really wanted to play or work they would do it, whereas if you just play a normal game it's hard to pick out who isn't really trying. I said to Joe, 'We've got to sell Derek Kevan.'"

By the end of July Kevan had been transferred to Crystal Palace. The move surprised many supporters, especially as Kevan had been City's top scorer for the previous two seasons, but Allison had been convinced and, looking at the player's career post-City, indications are that the City coach had perfect judgement. Nevertheless, City's first friendly under the Mercer-Allison partnership was not a pleasant experience and prompted many to again question the departure of Kevan, especially as the Blues had not found a replacement yet.

The game at home to Scottish First Division side Dundee on 7th August ended in a 2-1 defeat and City were even slow handclapped. Journalist Ronald Kennedy was amazed: "The humiliation of a pounding slow handclap in the 65th minute must have been hard for the City's hit seat occupier, Joe Mercer. While Mercer must be given time to sort out a bumper bundle of problems, the paying public has a notoriously short temper. I can recall no ground in twenty years of sports writing where a 'friendly' curtain raiser has got this sort of crowd treatment."

Post match all Mercer would say to the waiting media was: "I've got a lot to say about this!" But

Joe Mercer and Malcolm Allison at their first joint press conference.

July 1965. Back (l to r): Allison, Hart, Doyle, Oakes, Kennedy, Summerbee, Gomersall & Ewing. Middle: Young, Murray, Gray, Pardoe, Crossan, Brand & Connor. Front: Cheetham, Dowd, Ogley & Sear.

presumably he meant to the players, not to the Manchester press, as he stormed off towards the dressing room.

After the game he stepped up his attempts to sign a new striker, but before he could secure the services of a new player City drew 1-1 at Walsall in another friendly. The following day the announcement was made that Mercer had signed the exciting Ralph Brand from Rangers for around £25,000. Unfortunately, Brand's career was to take a nose-dive more or less as soon as he walked into Maine Road. At Rangers he had scored 128 goals in 207 League games and had scored eight goals in eight games with Scotland, but in two seasons at Manchester, Brand could only manage to find the net on two occasions. The player ultimately moved to Sunderland exactly two years to the day after signing for City.

Mercer's second signing occurred after a 3-2 victory at Tranmere and, like the friendly, was rather more successful than the previous one, even if the player's £35,000 arrival brought back painful memories for the majority of City supporters. Mike Summerbee arrived at Maine Road from Swindon after featuring in the infamous 8,015 match earlier in the year. His father George had played with Mercer for Aldershot during the war, and Mercer had kept a close watch on the career of the young Mike, determined that one day he would bring the player to his club. Summerbee was delighted to be in Manchester: "As soon as I drove into Manchester, I could sense something about the place. Even though City were in the Second Division, they were a huge club. The ground is an awe- inspiring place. It reeks of tradition and great players. Although I could

not compare City to anything I had known before, I soon realised what a privilege and pleasure it is to be able to play for a club like that."

In 2005 Bobby Kennedy compared Mercer's first two signings: "Ralph had been a big star in Scotland and was an international player but, I guess, so much was expected of him that it may have put too much pressure. It's difficult to say but he and Mike Summerbee arrived more or less at the same time and Mike succeeded from the start. It was a dream for me to play behind him because he made my life so easy. All I had to do was get the ball and give it to Mike. With Ralph there was a lot of competition for his place – Neil Young and Dave Connor really leaped above him once Malcolm started working with them. I was fortunate when I arrived that there wasn't too much competition but, as time progressed, Tony Book was signed and opportunities became limited for me."

Gradually, Mercer and Allison prepared City for the new season. When they arrived in Manchester they quickly became aware of how dire the situation was. The Club had lacked direction for some time and across the city United were dominant. City supporters had grown tired of playing second fiddle to the Reds and Malcolm Allison quickly became aware of how miserable life had become following the Blues: "United quickly became an object of hatred to me when I moved into the city. I loathed the bumptious, patronising tones of their players, their hangers-on, and many of their supporters. It became a challenge to me when I drove past city parks and saw ninety per cent of them wearing red shirts."

Allison's feelings intensified when his son, Mark, was picked on by an older United supporter who wanted to teach him a lesson for having a father who worked for "that useless team City." Allison admitted in his autobiography that he wanted to punish everyone connected with United, especially after he was forced to listen to the glorification of United at a dinner to celebrate the Reds' championship success: "Matt Busby turned and said, 'I believe there is room for two First Division clubs in Manchester'. And I thought to myself, 'yes, baby, and you're going to get two teams'."

Later he told Matt Busby's son: "Your father has got a 20 year start, but I'll pass him in three."

Allison's approach was typical of the man and he had the kind of attitude that City supporters wanted. His comments may have seemed rather brash and cynical at times, but with the genial Mercer smoothing the way, Allison's views were listened to and respected.

The two men arrived at City when the Club was at an all-time low, even the decimation of the 1904 Cup winning side and subsequent struggles did not leave the Blues as low as in 1965. Of course this low was eclipsed in 1998 when City played in the third tier of the League for one season, however in 1998 support remained loyal – too loyal some would say. In 1965 support had diminished and had caused the new men serious concerns. Allison later admitted that either he, or Mercer, would walk down the tunnel prior to their earliest games to check if anybody had bothered to turn up. Soon the partnership helped to guarantee that the Blues would be rediscovered.

City's first League game under the new partnership was an away trip to Middlesbrough on 21st August. To Allison and Mercer this game was vital as it would help to prove the strengths and weaknesses of the side. Allison's view was that the opening ten games would really demonstrate how right his methods and approach to the game were, and that those matches would put the Blues into a period of strength ready to challenge for promotion. On the training pitch he had been assessing each player and had considered what tactics to employ. He'd been watching David Connor quite closely and decided that he would be the perfect man to block out Ian Gibson, Middlesbrough's chief play-maker. He'd also noticed the aggression of Mike Doyle and felt that he should be in the side immediately. Doyle was also aware that Joe Mercer had been paying him close attention: "I always felt that Joe was more critical of me than he was of others in the team, because I played at wing-half....his position. Joe appreciated my enthusiasm. Whenever I was in action I had the feeling that Joe was watching me more closely than other members of the side."

Allison's plan of using Connor to shut out Gibson worked perfectly, with the Middlesbrough man never really getting into the game. The match ended 1-1 with Jimmy Murray supplying the first League goal under the satisfied Mercer. The following game four days later gave

the Manchester public their first chance of assessing City's promotion chances as they faced a Wolves side relegated the previous season. The crowd of over 25,000 witnessed a hard earned 2-1 victory. A week later the two sides met again with the Blues achieving their first double of the season, winning 4-2. One of City's goals came from the delighted Doyle who, on the coach afterwards, was collared by a laughing Joe Mercer: "You took that goal well, you young devil... but you should never have been in that position in the first place, leaving us open at the back."

No doubt Joe recognised that the young Doyle had played a similar 'attacking wing-half' role to the one he himself had played at Everton. A role in which he'd been admonished many times before.

City's progress continued and the Blues remained undefeated in their first seven games. In fact Mercer and Allison saw their side defeated in only one of the first fifteen League games, although they did steal a few results along the way. Nevertheless the two men were beginning to give the Manchester people what they needed most of all - pride. For years it had been embarrassing supporting the Blues, especially with United doing so well, and City's followers had suffered continual ribbing. Now, as Mercer and Allison stamped their influence on the Club, City supporters were able to walk tall and wear their scarves with pride. Crowds had increased and for the occasional game actually bettered title challenging United. 34,091 attended the Wednesday night visit of Norwich, while United's Saturday game with Fulham in Division One four days earlier was watched by 32,716. These figures are significant as they prove that in attendance terms the Blues were capable of matching the Reds, they were also significant to Malcolm Allison as, at United's Championship banquet, he had been forced to take part in a bet with Pat Crerand, the man remembered for his part in the relegation battle of 1963. According to Allison, Crerand had stated that City were a dying club and that the Blues would never again attract an attendance of over 30,000 at Maine Road. Allison bet him £10 and, only two months into the season, the City coach was proved right.

By this time Mercer had dipped into the transfer market, securing the services of 25 year old George Heslop, Everton's reserve centre-half, and 20 year old Stan Horne, a wing-half Joe had remembered from his time at Villa Park. When Horne was signed Joe turned to Mike Doyle and said: "You'll have to pull your socks up - because Stan's a wing-half too." This was all a bit of psychology on Joe's part to keep his players on their toes, but for a while Horne did replace Doyle.

By the end of October City were top of the division and full of confidence. Gone were the days of fear, confusion and panic. Mercer's steadying influence and

Allison's training methods had brought new life to the Club and everybody connected with the Blues benefited. In 1993 Allison remembered the transformation: "The place was really buzzing. People like Harry Godwin told us how the Club had changed so quickly. It was a fantastic achievement. Years later I also heard that the other staff would eavesdrop on my tactical talks. I've heard that Johnny Hart, my assistant, would gather the youngsters around the door to listen in to my talks. He'd tell them to listen and learn from a real visionary!"

Both Allison and Mercer had brought qualities to the Club that had been lacking for some time. Allison's ideas seemed as revolutionary as McDowall's Revie Plan had been a decade earlier, while Mercer's manner gave the Club dignity and respect. Together they worked well and turned the Club around, although City supporters are divided about who offered most. In reality, they both had strengths and achieved success away from the Club, but when they worked together at City they combined to produce an even greater force.

City maintained a top three position for most of the period leading up to Christmas, then on New Year's Day 1966 a crowd of over 47,000 gave a tremendous ovation as the Blues overcame division leaders Huddersfield Town 2-0. The Blues were now seen as promotion certainties, with a brand of football that excited. But it wasn't simply their performances in the League that grabbed the headlines, it was their progress in the FA Cup.

In the third round the Blues beat Blackpool 3-1 in a replay watched by 52,661 - the largest City crowd for six years - then defeated Third Division Grimsby 2-0. In the fifth round they faced a team they would get to know quite well over the following four seasons Leicester City. The Maine Road tie ended 2-2 with City winning the replay 1-0 thanks to a mistake by England 'keeper Gordon Banks which led to a goal by Neil Young.

The opponents for the quarter-final were Mercer's old club Everton. At Maine Road a crowd of 63,034 - a figure higher than any domestic attendance at Old Trafford that season proving how wrong Crerand had been - watched a tense goalless affair. Three days later a similar result at Goodison forced a second replay to take place at neutral Molineux. Despite the optimism within the camp, Mercer's men were unable to seize the initiative and the game ended with a 2-0 victory to the Merseysiders. Had City won, they would have faced Manchester United in the semi-final.

FA Cup progress would have been nice, but it was promotion that really mattered to the Blues. Both Mercer and Allison realised that the Cup run had stretched their playing resources to the limit and that new blood was still required. Allison, in particular, had an idea of which players to go after, the only problem was a lack of money. City were still relatively short of cash after

the struggles of the late fifties and early sixties and any investment had to be absolutely perfect. For Allison money hardly mattered, whereas Mercer felt he had to keep tight control of the finances.

Despite showing an interest in Bolton's Wyn Davies, it was Bury's Colin Bell that Allison was most interested in. With the knowledge that the Club remained cash strapped, the energetic coach attended a Bury match to watch the young player and determine what kind of a bid the Blues could make. When Allison arrived at the game he realised that there were a few other coaches and scouts from leading First Division clubs ready to watch Bell. This deterred him a little then, once the game started, Allison criticised the player, making out he had little to offer. Every mistake was picked up with Allison screaming that he'd wasted his evening. In actual fact, Allison was considerably impressed with almost everything the player did.

On Allison's recommendation, City managed to raise enough cash and signed the player for a figure of around £42,000 just before the transfer deadline in March. His debut game was against Derby County on 19th March when he scored a goal to help the Blues to a 2-1 victory, although the goal was not the most spectacular one ever seen. Basically, the ball hit him and entered the net.

Over the weeks that followed the rather introverted Bell fitted into the City side, helping the Blues to maintain their challenge for the division title. On 4th May, he provided the only goal of the game at Rotherham which secured promotion for the Blues.

In 2005 Bell looked back on his first few months at Maine Road: "I arrived in March 1966 and it took me the rest of that promotion season to settle. Promotion helped because I was part of the celebrations from the start. The goal I scored at Rotherham guaranteed promotion and afterwards I tasted champagne for the first time. I couldn't believe how quickly I was part of a winning side. Something major I realised at this time was that at Bury we'd go to away matches with the aim of getting a draw – at best – but with City we went expecting to turn over every side. After a couple of games I felt this same level of expectation and I think that's why we became so successful. Malcolm stressed our strengths and used to say that he didn't care how many we concede so long as we win. If ever we won 4-3 he'd never mention the three goals, he'd only mention the four. That was a great way to play and it continued throughout those successful years.

"Even though City was a much bigger club than Bury it still had that homely feel. We were all part of the same family. First team players would pop into the laundry room and have a cup of tea with the ladies in there. Sometimes we'd just love being at the ground. I do think football's lost a lot by having training grounds some distance from the home grounds. We felt part of the

Maine Road furniture. It was my second home and most mornings we'd get in early to get into the gym for head tennis. If ever you arrived at the ground and found you'd arrived too late to make up a head tennis team you'd skulk around and plan to get in even earlier the next day."

Nine days after the Rotherham game City defeated Charlton 3-2 at the Valley to win the Second Division Championship. The Blues had been leading by three goals before allowing Charlton to fight back. Presumably Allison only praised the three City goals and didn't mention those conceded post match.

On 18th May City played their final game of the season before a Maine Road crowd of 34,653. Naturally, this was a day of celebration when the result hardly mattered. Understandably, it was not City's best performance of the season and the game ended goalless, but the celebrations continued throughout the night. In 2005 Alan Oakes viewed promotion as the most important of all the successes Mercer & Allison brought to the Blues: "Because I was there during the dark days, I think the most important one had to be the promotion in 1966. My reason is that without that none of the rest would have followed. Joe and Malcolm didn't just get us promoted, they first stopped the rot. We were going downhill fast and they stopped that, changed gear and pushed us forward quickly, and it wasn't done with negative play. A lot of teams pack the defence and try to ensure they don't lose, we always went out to win and never contemplated holding out for a point."

One of the key players during this season had been City captain Johnny Crossan - a player Mercer had tried to sign in the late fifties for Sheffield United. The skilful

Irishman had played in 40 League games that season, scoring on 13 occasions, and had certainly developed since his arrival in January 1965. He was now one of City's heroes and his natural humour helped mould team spirit in the dressing room. He was an appropriate choice for captain during that season.

1966-1967 A Late Developer

1966 was a good year for English football - England staged and won the World Cup for the first time in its history, and Manchester City regained their rightful place in the First Division. As a result of these two events, Mercer and Allison became instantly recognisable faces throughout the Country commenting on International and domestic football. It was all good publicity for the resurgent Blues and with the World Cup exciting many non-football followers, City's promotion seemed to be perfectly timed to cash in on the positive aspects of the game.

With Manchester buzzing, Mercer and Allison were determined to turn City into a great force. The 1965-66 Cup run had shown that the Blues could live with the best – they had defeated two First Division sides and took a third to two replays before succumbing - but there were still weaknesses. There seemed to be an abundance of talent in attack - Young, Summerbee, Crossan, Doyle and Pardoe had provided a good rate of return - but City needed a stronger defence if they were to stay in the First Division. Heslop had already settled into the centre-half spot, Oakes was a dependable wing-half, and Dowd had overcome the disappointments of

Johnny Crossan, Stan Gibson (lid on head), Joe Mercer & Harry Godwin celebrate.

1964 become City's first choice 'keeper, but Mercer and Allison realised they needed a dependable full-back.

After a short discussion, Malcolm Allison convinced Joe Mercer that he knew the perfect man for the job, a man he had coached before - Plymouth's Tony Book. Mercer had been put off by the player's age, after all he was almost 32, but was reminded that he himself had been a fraction older when he moved from Everton to Arsenal in the 1940s to embark on what became the greatest years of his playing career. Could Book find similar success?

Moving to City was the first chance of Division One football for the £17,000 Book and, despite initial concerns he felt able to perform to the level required: "I felt a bit of an impostor coming into the First Division so late. I was nearly 32 when City signed me. I wasn't exactly a late developer. Long before Malcolm took me to Plymouth, I had trials with Nottingham Forest and Chelsea. In fact, I played for Chelsea's 'A' team and Reserves for 18 months while I was in the Army doing my National Service. Then I got a letter from the manager, Ted Drake, telling me he thought I'd get a living out of the game at a lower level.

"I had a great apprenticeship in the Southern League. I always felt I had a chance of making the grade as a pro, if I could get a break - and Malcolm was the one who gave it to me. Where I was really fortunate was in coming to City just when the place was about to take off! People must have been wondering 'what's this 32 year old going to do for us?'"

Mercer had not needed much convincing about Book. He had seen him play against the Blues and, once in City's colours, Mercer enjoyed watching the player, even if it made him a little envious: "I didn't mind him playing well and having plenty of skill, but what made me green with envy was his speed. I mean, it's not right for the over thirties to be skinning the youngsters. It's meant to be a young man's game! We used to hear these First Division coaches shouting from the bench - 'Take the old man on!' No chance! He was a great athlete."

Book made an impressive debut in City's opening game, a 1-1 draw at Southampton. Johnny Crossan had been missing for that game following a car crash close to Roker Park that resulted in injury, although the player managed to return for the first home game of the season. The fixture provided an enormous test with reigning Champions Liverpool arriving for what looked an easy two points for the Merseysiders. Ominously, two days earlier on home territory Liverpool reserves had defeated their City equivalents 9-0. The footballing public expected the Blues to be humiliated, they were wrong as goals from Bell and Murray helped City to a 2-1 victory before a crowd of 50,923. City were back!

A 1-0 win over Sunderland followed before the Club's first setback - a 3-2 defeat in the return fixture with Liverpool. Two further defeats followed then Glyn Pardoe provided a goal to help City secure a point against Arsenal on 10th September. The following game would provide the biggest test of all for Mercer's men - the Old Trafford derby. To most fans this game mattered more than any other, unfortunately City simply failed to perform. Allison was angry. He believed the players had fallen for the hype that had developed around United since the late fifties and had seen them freeze in the so called 'Theatre of Dreams'. He told them he would never again tolerate any player curling up and dying in front of United's supporters, instead he wanted to see City players go out there to humiliate the Reds.

The game had not been without controversy. As with the last derby in 1963, Denis Law seemed to be at the centre of it all. At one point players squared up to each other, fists flew, and yet referee Jack Taylor took no action. Six minutes later Denis Law upset the City players further by scoring the only goal of the game. It was a major disappointment.

Seven days later City defeated Blackpool 1-0 with a goal from Johnny Crossan, but the visit of Chelsea on 1st October brought City crashing back down to earth. Joe Mercer: "We started well with three good results and seemed set for a fine life among the top-class teams. We were confident. Then Chelsea came north to Maine Road and ripped all our fancy notions to shreds. They took us apart on our own ground. They exposed flaws. They set us thinking. We wanted to survive in the First Division. This became our priority. Tony Book was installed as a sweeper behind the rest of the defence; a negative move that was mere insurance against further good hidings."

Chelsea had humiliated City 4-1 at home, and Mercer and Allison agreed that the positional change was a vital one. In addition the two men discussed ways of improving fitness - an area Allison was determined to see improved. They agreed to bring in Derek Ibbotson, an England athlete, to help develop City as one of the fittest sides in Europe. The move was a good one with Ibbotson taking the players on tortuous nine mile runs, then challenging them to various races. It was all hard work, but each session tried to end in a light-hearted fashion. After one particularly gruelling session Ibbotson challenged any two players, splitting the distance between them, in a 440 yards race. The race started with every City player making what Ibbotson described as a false start, then a dozen of the players boxed the athlete in, resulting in the sub-four minute miler finishing last!

Alongside the improvement in fitness, Allison tried out many of his new coaching methods as the Blues tried to find their feet in the division. A few good results in November helped, especially a win over Everton thanks to a solitary goal from Colin Bell. This was a significant game as, prior to the match, much of the talk centred around the two great midfielders Alan Ball and Colin Bell.

Future City manager Ball had played a significant part in the 1966 World Cup final and had received worldwide recognition, whereas Bell had barely been heard of outside of the north-west. Nevertheless, the media made comparisons. Even the City programme became embroiled in the story: "It will be interesting to compare the two players today. For in the last few weeks Bell has emerged as one of those non-stop players with as much heart as ability and a good helping of both. Ball, with red hair and spectacular skills, will always catch the eye. Bell, with far less First Division experience behind him, and 18 months Ball's junior, is just as priceless an asset to City.

"In the last six months Ball's fame has spread far beyond Britain. The Spanish press after Everton's recent Cup Winners' Cup defeat in Zaragoza called him, 'La bomba con dos piernas' - the bomb on two legs. Colin Bell's are longer - and at 6ft tall he will be out to prove that a good big 'un is better than a good little 'un."

Bell's 73rd minute match winning goal seemed to be enough proof that City possessed a player capable of controlling any game, or any opponent, although the match itself had not been a particularly good advert for English football. Both Bell and Ball received injuries - Bell a cut knee and torn ligaments, Ball was reported to have six stud marks on his thigh after a tackle from Alan Oakes - but they were not the only ones as players from both sides battled throughout the match.

Ten minutes after Bell's goal the protests really began as Everton had an equaliser disallowed. According to the *Daily Mail* the goal, netted by Gabriel from a corner, was disallowed as the referee was busy clearing away toilet rolls behind the goal which the "hooligan Everton supporters" had thrown onto the pitch. *The Mail* report basically stated that the result was a fair one, because of the Evertonians toilet roll throwing. It seemed a perverse comment, but City needed the points, so most Mancunians agreed.

By mid-December, Mercer and Allison were presented with a problem they had always hoped would arise - the question of who to leave out. Mike Summerbee, after missing games against Nottingham Forest and West Bromwich Albion through suspension, was ready for selection, but his replacement Altrincham born Chris Jones had played well and scored his first League goal in the victory at West Brom. There was no way that Jones could be dropped. In the end Mercer and Allison took the difficult decision to drop Neil Young instead, although Young did return for the following game. Allison and Mercer were keen to have players fighting for places and with so many players developing at the same time, it was inevitable that decisions would be taken that would force players to consider their futures.

By the time of the Maine Road derby with United on 21st January City were 19th after 24 games. A pick-me-up was urgently needed. The game was played in atrocious conditions and ended 1-1 with both goals coming in the last fifteen minutes. It had been an exciting match and helped to boost confidence, although Johnny Crossan was far from happy - he'd been dropped. Crossan had not been having the best of times during this season. His pre-season car crash had affected him and foolishly he attempted to disguise an injured knee. He also suffered from a grumbling appendix. This all combined to give the impression that he simply wasn't trying and led to the crowd barracking him. Despite being upset at the time, he remained philosophical about the abuse: "I heard the jeers but that's football. You are king one day, a peasant the next!"

Although Crossan returned to the side for the remainder of the season, his days at Maine Road were numbered, and in August 1967 he was transferred to Middlesbrough for £32,000.

The United game helped the Blues gain momentum. Over the weeks that followed seven points were gained in five games, not championship form but enough to gradually edge City away from the relegation zone. By 19th March the Blues were 17th on 28 points - 7 more than West Brom in 21st position. They had also purchased an exciting forward with a reputation of being a bit of a hell-raiser, Tony Coleman. It was Malcolm Allison who was determined to sign the player, but Joe Mercer was not so sure. Mercer, after all, had been teaching on a course at Lilleshall when the player threw a bed out of the window. He had also heard stories of how the player had caused trouble at every club he'd been to. Stoke City had allegedly thrown him out, Preston said he was 'unmanageable', and at Doncaster it was reported that he had punched a referee in the face. No wonder Mercer was uncertain!

Eventually, Allison convinced Mercer that he could control the player and the two agreed to give him a try. The Coleman signing was proof, if any was needed, that Mercer and Allison worked well together. If one of them was convinced about a player, the other would back that judgement and the player would be signed. Sometimes Mercer would find a player, sometimes Allison. It didn't matter who found the player, all that mattered was that the player could fit into City's plans. Coleman did settle into the City side, although there were a few 'adventures' along the way. In later years Mercer would laughingly boast that he was the only manager Coleman didn't hit!

Coleman's Maine Road debut came on 12th April when a Colin Bell hat-trick defeated one of the new player's former clubs Stoke at Maine Road. Afterwards Liverpudlian Coleman gave his view of the game: "I really enjoyed beating Stoke. They gave me a free transfer - or they sacked me if you look at it another way. The differences that players talk about between the Fourth and First Divisions look to be perfectly true if I can judge from two games. The players here are obviously much better than I ever played with and it makes it more enjoyable.

"My first job is to get fitter. I'm not as fit as the players at Maine Road yet and I'm working on that but it will take a little time. I'm in digs around the corner from the ground which suits me. I don't know Manchester but I've got the feeling I shall be here a long time."

City hovered above the relegation zone for some time, although games in hand gave an unfair position for much of March, April and May. By 19th April the Blues were 17th on 32 points from 36 games with two games in hand over four of the five teams below them. They were still not safe, however a draw against Mercer's former side Aston Villa, and a 3-0 win over Fulham eased the pressure. At the season's end City finished 15th with ten points more than Aston Villa, relegated in 21st place. It was a satisfactory position and one that in later years would be called a vital season of consolidation, although at the time it was more like an end of season fight to avoid relegation. Of the last seventeen games only four ended in defeat and Mercer was content. The turnaround had come as result of yet another fine Cup run.

On 28th January City defeated Leicester 2-1 in the Third Round, then faced Cardiff at Ninian Park. The game ended 1-1, bringing

Stan Ogden (Bernard Youens), Jerry Booth (Graham Haberfield), Len Fairclough (Peter Adamson), Lucille Hewitt (Jennifer Moss) & Annie Walker (Doris Speed) at Maine Road for an episode of Coronation Street broadcast on 29th November 1967.

back memories of the Cup run of 1961 when it took two replays to separate the sides. The replay at Maine Road finished 3-1 with goals from Bell, Crossan and Young. Another replay was needed in the fifth round with the Blues defeating Ipswich 3-0 after a 1-1 draw at Maine Road. Then came the biggest test of all, an away trip to Don Revie's robot-like Leeds.

Mercer looked back on this game as a turning point: "The entire football world expected us to play it tight. But they reckoned wrong. They overlooked the moral courage, the gambling streak, the spirit of adventure that was always just below the surface of the Mercer-Allison partnership. We did precisely the opposite to what was expected. We attacked them! We threw everything in. We decided, in just as few words, 'What the hell have we got to lose?' City were brilliant that day. We gave Leeds a lesson and with the most outrageous luck lost by a

solitary goal that should have been disallowed. We had been so much on top the result was unbelievable. Still, we had found ourselves. We were on our way, we started to stretch defences. Fear was scoffed at!"

City took the game to Leeds. The team that had previously been rooted in a defensive style of play, broke forward and played exciting, attacking football. Revie's Leeds were not used to teams arriving at Elland Road in an attacking frame of mind. The only goal came five minutes into the second half, following Leeds' first corner of the game. When Eddie Gray floated the ball towards the goal, Jack Charlton appeared to impede Harry Dowd, who was playing his first game since November. Charlton headed in, and City complained, unsuccessfully. The media believed it was an unfair result.

Afterwards there was sympathy for the Blues from the Leeds camp. Captain Billy Bremner: "City played magnificently. No honest man would attempt to deny it." Don Revie admitted it was "our toughest game of the season - and that includes our defeats."

ABC TV, producing the match for the ITV network, described it as: "The most exciting match of the season." The *Sunday Mirror* simply stated: "It was City who should have gone into the semi-finals." Another newspaper, the *Sunday Times*, proclaimed: "Leeds were beaten for speed of thought and action from the start. To lucky, lucky Leeds a place in the semi-finals. To magnificent City all the honours in defeat."

Alan Oakes believed the Leeds match, and the previous season's FA Cup tie with Everton, gave City belief: "We had faced a couple of big tests in those first two seasons – We took a strong Everton side to 2 replays in the FA Cup while we were still in Division Two and narrowly lost to Revie's Leeds the following year. We lost 1-0 to Leeds with a Jack Charlton goal that should have been disallowed. So we came away from those games confident we could face any side. There was nothing for us to fear."

The whole football world was beginning to realise that City were edging closer to success. Their style of play was exciting and, with Mercer and Allison, the direction of the Club was near perfect. It was certainly better than at any other time since the mid-fifties. All associated with the game now recognised that Manchester, once again, had two sides worth talking about. United still gained the larger share of headlines, but the Blues were catching up, especially when Malcolm Allison was prepared to speak. Allison's boasts were beginning to excite the City faithful and naturally made great news. The 'papers loved his comments, although it often led to trouble with the FA In November he was given a 28 day ban for 'expressing his feelings' and throughout his time at Maine Road he was regularly in trouble with the establishment. The fans loved it!

1967-1968 Congratulations

During the close season City went on an enjoyable tour to West Germany and Belgium. It seemed to be a laugh a minute with Johnny Crossan spending the whole trip ribbing everybody at one time or other, while Tony Coleman explained that his lack of goals was down to the fact that he doesn't like being kissed by men. At Standard Liege Coleman scored the winner and the rest of the time smothered him with affection!

During a 2-1 victory over Eintracht Braunschweig Chris Jones caused a minor controversy after scoring a fine goal. Apparently, the German announcer stated that the goal had been scored by Mike Summerbee, and so Jones rushed around the pitch pointing to his number 9 to indicate that he'd scored. He wouldn't let the game continue until the announcer corrected himself. The tour was typical of the team spirit Mercer and Allison had striven hard to build.

When the new season commenced on 19th August both Mercer and Allison recognised that the side still needed strengthening, this time in attack. Tony Coleman was an exciting forceful player but the Ralph Brand signing had been a failure, and Johnny

Crossan's time in Manchester had come to an end. Both Glyn Pardoe and Mike Doyle had been pulled back into defence and midfield respectively, leaving Mercer and Allison to try different combinations. As the season got under way, they struggled to find the right blend and results suffered. Only one point - a goalless game with Liverpool - was obtained during the first three games.

After that the youngster Paul Hince was tried at number seven. Hince, who in later years would be the *Manchester Evening News'* City reporter for a while, had made one appearance the year before, scoring twice, and was given his chance to shine again against Southampton at Maine Road. The Blues won 4-2 and Hince kept his place. Malcolm Allison felt Hince particularly enjoyed his next game: "We were playing Nottingham Forest and Hince played quite well at outside-right. In this particular game he absolutely mesmerised the Forest full-back - he was running him inside and outside and totally slaughtering him. Anyway, this full back got involved in an incident and the referee sent him off. Paul Hince went, 'Oh, don't send him off - he's easy! I'm enjoying it!"

The player's arrival coincided with a five match unbeaten run and the Blues moved into the top five, but Allison doubted whether Hince could become a permanent fixture in the side. On 30th September Hince was replaced by the exciting Stan Bowles for the Maine Road derby match. Bowles had already appeared in City's first team, scoring four goals in his first one and a half games (The half was when he came on as substitute, replacing Young, in a League Cup tie against Leicester and scored twice), and was certainly ready for the derby match. Sadly, the game ended 2-1 to the Reds despite the Blues taking the lead in the fifth minute via a low firm shot from Bell.

The game had seen the arrival of goalkeeper Ken Mulhearn. Harry Dowd had dislocated a finger in

Goalscorer Paul Hince in action (left) at Coventry City on 9th September 1967.

training and Mulhearn was forced to make his debut in the derby. He arrived at the ground early and was incredibly tense: "I turned up ridiculously early - it must have been an hour and a half before any of the other players. Malcolm Allison took one look at me and locked me in the medical room! He obviously saw how white faced I was. I must have been the most nervous person ever to appear at a football ground, so he just locked me up out of the way until the rest of the team reported and were getting changed. There were something like 63,000 at the game, and not many days earlier I'd been playing for Stockport in front of a few thousand. The noise and the atmosphere were unbelievable, the first time I'd sampled anything like it."

Despite the result and debut day nerves, Mulhearn retained his place for the rest of the season, and City quickly returned to form. After losing 1-0 at Sunderland the Blues were undefeated in their next eleven League games. This great run coincided with the arrival of Bolton's Francis Lee.

Both Allison and Mercer remembered Lee from his games for Bolton against City in the Second Division, and from a Bolton-City League Cup tie in September 1966, when Lee had scored. The two men went to watch Bolton's game with Liverpool in the same competition during 1967 and the player was outstanding, despite enduring a difficult relationship with the Bolton management.

Lee was dissatisfied with the terms of a new contract he had been offered and was generally disenchanted with the club. On Friday 29th September 1967 he told manager Bill Ridding that he was walking out: "Once they saw how dissatisfied I was with the way they were handling things they said that it'd be best if we made a clean break, and so I said I'd pack the game in. I had my business by then and so I said 'give me my employment cards and I'll pack it in'. They thought I was bluffing."

Bolton began receiving offers for the player while Lee concentrated on his business interests: "I used to drive my lorry during the week and even on the Thursday or Friday before a game I'd be collecting waste paper. I used to put on a flat cap and muffler so that nobody would recognise me! In summer I worked long hours and I was earning more in the summer months than I was playing football in Division One.

"It was getting to be a very good business. My last job was the day before I signed for City! I roped and sheeted about 15 ton of paper and cardboard from a spinning mill in Bolton. Took it to the Sun Paper Mill in Blackburn and when I got back about 5pm I got a call from Joe Mercer. He didn't give his name at first but I recognised him and he said: 'Where've you been?' I told him I'd been playing golf – I couldn't play the game at all then but I couldn't tell him what I had been doing! I asked him 'who is that?' He said, 'Tom Jones'. I said, 'It

George Best and Mike Doyle at the 30th September 1967 Maine Road derby.

doesn't sound like Tom Jones, sounds more like a man called Mercer!'"

Mercer travelled to Bolton to meet Ridding and Lee. The City boss told the player he wanted to sign him. Lee: "The first thing he said to me before we talked it through was 'I'll be honest with you son. We've no money. We're skint!' I said, 'It doesn't matter. I'll just be delighted to start playing again'.

There were problems, however, much to Lee's disbelief: "The next day was a Friday, and I went back to Maine Road and signed. Already Bill Ridding had told the Manchester City officials that I would not get my ten per cent of the transfer fee because I had asked for a move. But even he did not bargain for the Football League reaction. I had my boots with me and was all set to move out with the team to play at Sunderland in a First Division game the following day. But the League refused to rush my registration through, and just as I thought my future had been settled Joe Mercer came out of his office to say, 'It's all off, the League won't accept the registration!' Finally, however, it was ironed out and the following Monday I signed. I remember Joe's words. 'I hope you will sign,' he said when we first met. 'We feel we've got the start of a good side. We are just one player short, and we think you are that player. The odd goal or two will turn us into a great team.

From the moment Lee signed on 9th October City were a more powerful side, and the newcomer slotted in perfectly: "After an unhappy end to my days with Bolton, it was a completely different atmosphere at City. As soon as you got into coaching sessions all they were interested in was attacking. I was used to Bolton's theory of building performances on defence, this was exactly the opposite; we had five great forwards and for a goalscorer such as me, it couldn't have been easier to slip into a side like that."

A tense defensive moment for Doyle, Book Mulhearn and Heslop in the 4-2 victory over Fulham on 21st October 1967.

Despite the great news about Lee there were serious doubts whether the Blues' management team would stay in place as Allison was, at the time of the Lee negotiations, in communication with Coventry City about their vacant manager's position. In fact he met Coventry representatives on the day Lee officially signed for City. This was a major blow to Mercer.

The following day's *Manchester Evening News* carried Allison's views: "I love Manchester City and the atmosphere of the crowd here. Possibly I could sit back and enjoy myself reaping the benefits of some of the work we have done in the last two years. We have a good team here now. But this is such a good offer that I must accept it providing the directors release me from my contract."

Allison had eighteen months of his four year contract left to run, yet the newspaper claimed the City number two would definitely be the manager of Coventry within days. Mercer tried to remain calm during this spell, but Allison's intended move did upset him a great deal. The City boss talked frankly with Allison in private and no details of their actual conversations were ever publicly divulged by either man. However, it is clear that Mercer could not persuade the younger man to stay. Nevertheless, the City manager decided to publicly challenge Coventry over the matter rather than criticise his second-in-command: "What a way to run a club! What a way to carry on. What could this do to our dressing room atmosphere?"

Coventry's chairman Derrick Robins blamed Allison for leaking the story. In response Allison revealed that he had been offered a three year contract and said: "I'll keep that sheet of notepaper for my book – it should make a good chapter."

While the confusion over Allison's on-off move to Coventry continued, the Blues had the small matter of a League Cup tie to play. The game ended in a 1-1 draw at home to Blackpool which, in the circumstances, was

probably an acceptable result. By the time of the replay a week later (18th October) the issue of Allison's move had been resolved.

On 14th October 1967 – the day of Francis Lee's City debut - newspapers carried the news that Allison would not be the new Coventry boss. Allison told reporters: "It's like having a grand on the winner at 10-1 and then the stewards object."

Whether the nature of Allison's potential move had a lasting effect on his role at City is unclear, but it should be remembered that this would have impacted Mercer's view of managerial responsibility. If Mercer had told Allison that 'two years' would be enough for him as manager at the end of August 1965 as Allison later claimed, then clearly those two years were now up, and may have had a bearing on both men's actions. It should be explained however that Allison never made a point of raising the 'two years' issue until after City had found real success, and that Mercer never claimed to have made the initial comment. If Allison seriously considered the move to Coventry, which all the indications say he did, then Mercer must have wondered what would happen if he did actually hand everything over control. Mercer wanted loyalty.

Significantly, Allison's actions in October 1967, just as Mercer was signing Francis Lee, were never referred to by the City boss once success came, but they would have made him think long and hard about the future. Succession planning is all well and good if you can be certain the man succeeding you intends to stay.

Putting the Coventry affair to one side, Mercer focused on the future. Francis Lee proved to be a wonderful acquisition and impressed from the start. In his second game he netted his first City goal and was heralded by the *Manchester Evening News* as a real star: "The £60,000 bundle of energy and enthusiasm crowned a fine game by making two goals and hammering home the fourth after Fulham had kicked their way back to 3-2."

City won that game 4-2 and remained undefeated for a total of eleven consecutive League matches. By the end of that run, the Blues had also reached the Fourth Round of the League Cup after beating Blackpool 2-0 in the third round replay. Unfortunately, a 3-2 reverse at Fulham ended the Blues dreams of success in that competition.

In the League Mercer's side continued to perform well with one match in particular catching the attention of the football world. The game saw City face Tottenham Hotspur on 9th December at Maine Road. It was a real classic, enjoyed by around five million on BBC television's Match Of The Day programme. It was regarded by many as the match of the season. At first many doubted that the game could go ahead as the pitch was covered with snow, however Stan Gibson and the rest of the City groundstaff worked hard to make the pitch playable. Sadly, in the seventh minute Jimmy Greaves snatched the first goal for Tottenham.

Tottenham's lead wasn't to last though, as the Mancunians tore into the Londoners. With the snow still falling, Colin Bell levelled the scores. It was just what City deserved as they mastered the conditions and proved that Malcolm Allison had been wise to really push them hard during training.

Tremendous pressure from Young in particularly almost gave City the lead in the first half, but it wasn't until the second period that the Blues took a deserved lead when Young crossed from the left and Summerbee scored from six yards with a brilliant header.

In the 64th minute, overcoming his fear of being kissed by men, Tony Coleman scored the third when he followed up a Francis Lee shot that had hit the left post. Neil Young made it four with one from close range. City continued to push forward, overwhelming a Spurs side that included internationals Alan Gilzean, Joe Kinnear, Dave Mackay, Pat Jennings, and of course Jimmy Greaves. Shot after shot went towards the Spurs goal with City's forwards in outstanding form. In one attack, Coleman latched on to a pass from Bell. His shot hit the left-hand post, and then Young followed up by hitting the right-hand post. It was a game that proved the strength of the City side.

Afterwards, the Blues made all the headlines and received praise from all over the country. Indeed, almost thirty years later a similar performance by City against Tottenham screened by the BBC prompted the re-showing of the 1967 match. It was one of those games that will never be forgotten.

Letters flooded into Maine Road from all over the Country with one appearing in City's programme from Bobby Greenroyd of Halifax: "Notwithstanding the address, I am a regular Manchester United fan, but after Saturday's game your next home gate will be increased by one."

A group of Tottenham supporters from Walthamstow wrote: "We would like to pay tribute to your team not only for a wonderful display of football but also for the clean and sportsmanlike way you played the game."

Personalities from within the game also contacted

City V Spurs, 9th December 1967 as seen from the Platt Lane Stand by Richard Tucker.

the Club. The great Dixie Dean, a Maine Road regular thanks to his relationship with former Everton team mate Joe Mercer, believed City to be the 'best workmanlike team' he'd seen since his own playing days thirty years earlier. He was also convinced that a number of the City players, in particular Mike Summerbee, were destined to play for England.

Another admirer was Bill Shankly, the Liverpool manager. Prior to City's game at Anfield on 16th December the canny Scotsman turned to Malcolm Allison and proclaimed: "You're not going to tear our team apart like you have torn the others apart, you know!"

That game ended 1-1, prompting the *Liverpool Echo* to concede: "The frequency and power of the City shooting was amazing... This was a game between two of the greatest League clubs in the Country - and it looked like it."

Now, at the half-way stage of the season, City were in third position on 28 points. Liverpool were second with the same tally, while the old foes Manchester United were top with 30 points. The difference between these teams however was that City were still developing as a unit all the time. They were also still learning as two defeats against West Bromwich Albion over the Christmas period proved. Francis Lee remembers the first of these games: "We lost 3-2 at their place on Boxing Day. But even then, we murdered them!"

In the second match City were defeated 2-0 with Malcolm Allison claiming responsibility for the result: "We should have played it as tight as possible, not attacked. This mistake on my part could have cost us the title."

Former Stockport Boys' player John Clay made his first and last full appearance for the Blues in this game, although he had already made a sub appearance against Wolves in October. With so many outstanding players at the Club it was difficult for Clay to become established at City, and he moved on to Macclesfield during the following close season, although he did return to City over twenty years later to perform a public relations role.

On 31st January City once again proved their force, this time with a 7-0 thrashing of Reading at Elm Park in the FA Cup Third Round replay. As the players left the field the tannoy announcer claimed: "Ladies and Gentlemen, you have just seen one of the greatest teams England has produced in a long time."

Again dozens of letters arrived at Maine Road commenting on City's performance. Many Reading fans wrote in saying they could have watched the Blues all night. Other letters arrived commenting on how well behaved the City supporters were, while fans themselves commented on the cheerfulness of the Reading police. These points may seem trivial today, but in 1968 football had already begun to enter its hooligan period. Football

supporters had started to be seen as trouble causers and incidents of violence, or of vandalism, soon found their way into national newspapers. Although City supporters were never totally blameless, during the late 1960s Blues fans continued to gain commendations rather than condemnation.

City's cup run ended in the next round where Leicester City once again faced the Manchester Blues. This time, after a no score draw, Leicester won 4-3 in the Filbert Street replay. This was Leicester's first victory in cup competition over the Blues in six meetings since March 1966. To say the two sides knew each other well is an understatement. In both cities supporters were already making predictions that the two sides would meet again in 1969.

From late February onwards City concentrated on the League where success was now becoming a serious possibility. A 1-0 victory at Burnley on 2nd March left the Blues in third place, four points behind leaders United although City had a game in hand. Apart from the two Manchester clubs Liverpool, Leeds United and Newcastle also posed a threat, and any of these teams were capable of snatching the title. City, however, had the chance of upsetting two of those teams - Leeds and United.

On 23rd March City arrived at Elland Road looking for victory. The Blues were now top of the division on goal average after defeating Fulham 5-1 seven days earlier, and felt they had the initiative. Sadly, a tough, determined approach from Leeds ended with City suffering a 2-0 defeat. It was vital City rediscovered their form in the next game - the 78th Manchester League derby.

The match should originally have been played on 10th February however it was called off as the Old Trafford pitch had been deemed 'unfit'. The re-arranged fixture was played before a crowd of over 63,000 on Wednesday 27th March. To many Reds this was to be the night when City would be humiliated, and taught a footballing lesson by England's so-called biggest club. For City supporters the Manchester derby had become a difficult game to watch, especially at Old Trafford, where the Blues had only won once in twelve years. Malcolm Allison: "The Manchester United thing was still the great barrier across our progress. I was told in the city that we were doing well, but that we would never catch Manchester United!"

The game commenced with Joe Mercer, Matt Busby, and England manager Sir Alf Ramsey sat close to each other in the directors' box. However, the opening moments were not pleasant ones for the City manager as George Best gave United the lead after only 38 seconds. Tony Book felt he was to blame. He believed he should not have allowed Best through, and it affected the City captain for some time, before the rest of the City team brought him back into the game.

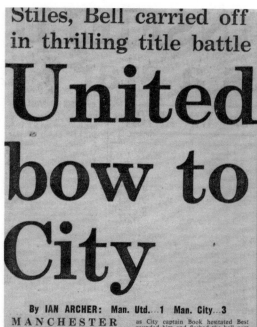

Stiles, Bell carried off in thrilling title battle

United bow to City

By IAN ARCHER: Man. Utd....1   Man. City...3

MANCHESTER CITY made it a three-way deadlock at the top of the First Division when they overwhelmed rivals United at Old Trafford last night.

They ran United into their own ground to proclaim as City captain Book hesitated Best rounded him and flashed the ball past Mulhearn.

This cruel start could have crippled the spirit of many teams, but City are made of sterner stuff. Within 17 minutes they were level.

Again it was a through ball, intelligently placed and instinctively converted, that brought the goal. Doyle passed to Bell, whose fast turn and shot close to the near post beat Stepney.

The second goal for City came from an unexpected source. After Fitzpatrick had fouled Bell, Coleman slung a free-kick across the United goal and bulky

For the first ten minutes all the old concerns came back, then, just when it was needed most, Colin Bell began to control midfield, Mike Doyle won important tackles and City gradually gained the upper hand. After 15 minutes Bell started a right-wing move and then ran yards to reach the final pass and blast the equaliser past United 'keeper, and future City coach, Alex Stepney.

City, in rampant mood, dominated from then on. They pushed forward time and time again, and were appropriately rewarded with a second goal after 57 minutes. Tony Coleman, City's loveable rogue, curled across a free-kick and centre-half George Heslop scored his first goal for the Blues with a firm downward header.

Mercer and Allison were delighted as the Blues powered forward. Colin Bell, by far the best player on display that night, raced clear and headed for goal before being dramatically hauled down by Francis Burns. Francis Lee scored the resultant penalty, but the excellent Bell had to be carried off on a stretcher with an injured knee. City's most important player would miss the next four crucial games.

The game ended 3-1 with Mercer enjoying his post-match discussions with Ramsey and, of course, Busby. Another man who enjoyed his chat with Busby was Allison: "Matt Busby was as urbane as ever. But I sensed

that we were beginning to get through to him. He is a man who hates to be second anywhere, and for it to happen in Manchester was quite a new experience."

Allison also understood the feelings of the City faithful: "There was so much happiness among the City fans that evening. Years of humiliation had been, if not wiped away, at least eased. The balance of power was beginning to swing strongly in our direction. If you are not too tightly involved in football you may discount the feelings of the down trodden supporters. In fact their team becomes an expression of themselves; their moods, their hopes, are tightly interwoven into the fate of the team. And that night at Old Trafford the supporters of Manchester City walked out of the wilderness."

The City assistant manager was right. City fans were able to walk tall and at last felt that their club was capable of great success. The supporters even composed poems about the great night, one 'City's Night Of Glory' had eleven verses and covered almost every incident of the game. It was a truly proud moment for the Blue population of Manchester and one which only people associated with City can understand. In no other British city does the rivalry match that of Manchester. In Glasgow the derby game is a matter of life and death, but it has little to do with football. In any case, neither Glasgow Rangers or Celtic have ever received the national media attention that Busby's United received.

In Liverpool, Sheffield, London, Birmingham and Bristol, no side has ever had to face as much hype as City had encountered with the Reds. When United are dominant, City's suffering seems to be a national joke with media personalities laughing at the Blues simply because they are not United. No other club in British sport suffers in this way. Malcolm Allison recognised this and was determined to turn the situation around. Some of his boasts may have seemed out of place but supporters wanted to hear them. The Blues had suffered enough. Joe Mercer also recognised this but he preferred to play a more diplomatic role. Instead of criticising or humiliating the Reds he would talk about United's strengths before stating the obvious - that City had won. Mercer gave the Club the respect it deserved and realised that the best way to beat the boasts of City's rivals was on the pitch. That attitude, combined with Allison's approach, ensured City were at least on a level with United.

After the derby both Mercer and Allison tried to keep the momentum going. It wasn't easy, especially as many felt that the derby had proven that the Blues were the team of the season. Missing Colin Bell, City lost to Leicester and Chelsea in two of the next four games. Sandwiched in between those defeats were victories on successive days over Chelsea, 1-0 on 12th April, and West Ham, 3-0 the following day.

Whether it was an omen or not the Cliff Richard song

271

"Congratulations" was number one at this stage in the football season. By the season's end the tune was hugely popular at Maine Road.

On 20th April Mercer's men gained a point at Wolves, and some suggested the Blues had lost their chance of League success. There were now four games left - two at home followed by two away.

The Blues were in third place at this stage, four points behind United but with a game in hand. Leeds were second only a point behind United after the same number of games as City. Mike Doyle remembered that both Allison and Mercer were keen to push the players to the limit: "We'd got one point out of two games. From there we went to Southport for four days, and got the biggest bollocking from Mercer we'd ever had. He said, 'The Championship is there to be won, either you want to win it or you don't. You'll train together tomorrow morning and then I don't want to see you again. It's up to you after that.' He knew we'd get together and talk it out. One night there was me, Neil Young, George Heslop, Belly, Mike [Summerbee], Oakesy and Glyn Pardoe discussing the situation. We reckoned we could do it, and I don't think we lost another game from then on."

Against Sheffield Wednesday, a lucky deflection gave the Blues the only goal of the game. At Maine Road, Tony Book and Tony Coleman scored the goals in an easy 2-0 victory over Everton, leaving the Blues a mere two games away from glory. These two matches, however, were tough ones away at Tottenham, then at Newcastle. Both sides had performed well throughout the season, although as the League programme neared its end both were out of contention. Nevertheless, Spurs remained a top six side, while Newcastle were a few places lower. Mercer recognised the difficulties: "It'll be like climbing Everest and K2 in one week."

The first of the games resulted in a terrific 3-1 victory at White Hart Lane. Colin Bell scored twice, Mike Summerbee the other as City first attacked, then defended in numbers. Brian James, in the *Daily Mail*, stressed the Blues' power claiming that their success was down to "bloody hard and selfless running." He also claimed they were "a side of fair quality, brilliantly inspired." He went on to say that "City's output should be rewarded by not less than the title."

Sadly, at least two players were now struggling to be fit for the Newcastle match. Colin Bell and Mike Summerbee had pulled out of England's midweek match against Spain, a game both players were keen to take part in, and were doubtful for the Saturday match at Newcastle. Mercer admitted that many members of City's squad had played when they really were not 100% fit: "This has been true at times of Alan Oakes, Glyn Pardoe, Tony Book, and Mike Doyle as well as Colin Bell and Mike Summerbee. There have been games in which they have gone out with pain-killing injections, games

before which we have left the final decision with the player himself. It has taken moral courage for them to put the good of the side before personal discomfort and, on many occasions, to insist on playing when decisions about their fitness to do so were not easy to arrive at."

Mercer went on to outline his admiration for the City players: "People often talk very disparagingly about modern professionals and try to make out that they don't give quite so much to the job as they did in the old days. They claim that everybody today wants things easier. But never in all my long association with football have I seen greater dedication than that of these Manchester City players. In the old days fear of unemployment was undoubtedly a motivating factor. Today with these players, pride is the driving force - pride in their performances, pride in what they are trying to accomplish."

Despite the fact that City's squad was one of the smallest in the division, the Blues had maintained their challenge right to the end. Mercer was right about the commitment to the Blue cause shown by his players, and with City and United now level on 56 points after the same number of games, the biggest test of all would prove the value of each and every member of the squad.

City and United each had one game to play but the Blues had a better goal average. City's match was at Newcastle. Although it was not reported accurately at the time Newcastle still did not know if they would qualify for Europe. In those days qualification for the Fairs Cup, the predecessor of the UEFA Cup, was a little complicated as it only allowed one team to qualify from a city. So, if City and United finished second and third only the highest placed side would qualify. With Liverpool, Everton, Arsenal, Chelsea and Tottenham, amongst others competing for Europe, there was still a strong possibility that Newcastle could qualify based on the 'one city one club' rule. Newcastle definitely still had something to play for.

United's final match was at home to lowly – but safe from relegation - Sunderland. Because of their pedigree in recent seasons and the fact they were playing a struggling side, United were still viewed as favourites by many, even though City had the better goal average. Also, it has to be remembered that if both City and United failed, Liverpool, with two to play, could leapfrog them and win the Championship by a point. Bill Shankly, the great Liverpool boss, held the view however that City were the side to watch: "I regard City as favourites now. Any team that can do what they did at Tottenham must have a great chance."

Footballer of the Year George Best was another man who believed City were certain to take the trophy from United in style: "When they came to Old Trafford and beat us, I'd only seen them a couple of times before that and didn't think much of them. But that night we never saw the way they went. I've never seen a team run and achieve the work rate they did. I felt like demanding blood tests on them afterwards. They may lack United's individual ability, but if they can keep working and running they must be in with a great chance of beating Newcastle United on Saturday. It won't be easy, but I fancy them to do it."

Best went on to admit that he would love the chance of playing alongside his great friend Mike Summerbee: "I'd like to play a game in the City attack just to see what it's like."

A few years later, when Best was in conflict with the United management for his off the field activities (1972), Malcolm Allison almost brought the player to Maine Road. Naturally, there is no way United would have accepted Best playing for the Blues, but Allison wanted him and Best seemed interested. In the end

the Reds overlooked his refusal to turn up for a game, his failure to go to training and his well-publicised walk out to select him again in 1973. The situation was very similar to the Tevez affair at City in 2011-12 as far as the player's conduct and the club's decisions were concerned.

While neutrals felt certain City would win at Newcastle, those connected with the match itself seemed less convinced. George Heslop: "Frankly, I am a bit prickly about this match. If City win, I think we're going to be among the top teams for years. But I have told my team mates to watch out for Newcastle. The old club hasn't changed. If they are in the mood anything can happen. As for Wyn Davies - the man I will be marking - I think he is absolutely great. We must be on our toes. Newcastle are the most dangerous when you least expect it."

Newcastle's Jim Iley was another convinced that City would find it tough: "This match will be a good opportunity to give ourselves a lift. We've had some disappointing results lately, but it would be a great thing if we could get it out of our system against Manchester City."

As the days passed, the media became more interested in Manchester's Blues. This attention was completely new to the majority of people connected with the Maine Road club. On the Monday following the Tottenham game Mike Summerbee walked into the stadium and noticed that there were considerably more photographers and reporters than normal. He took a long lingering look at the group before calling across to Joe Mercer in a mock serious tone: "What's happened, Boss? Has there been an accident?"

Mercer himself took delight in telling those media men who would listen that City would win the Championship and that he had been practising the walk from Maine Road to Stretford ready for collecting the trophy from the reigning Champions: "I shall personally take great pleasure in walking down to Old Trafford on Sunday morning to pick up the trophy."

On the day of the game over 20,000 City supporters travelled to the North-East for what was to be one of the most significant days in the Club's long history. The Newcastle manager, Joe Harvey, could not believe the size of City's travelling support and prior to

Mike Summerbee scores the opener at Newcastle.

the game he turned to Malcolm Allison: "This is the first time I have been beaten at home before the game has started."

The match commenced with City appearing rather nervous. Heslop, perhaps remembering his own comments about Newcastle, froze for a while, but he was not the only one, especially when Newcastle's Jim Scott hit the crossbar in the third minute. Nine minutes later, however, the Blues made their mark on the game when Mike Doyle took a quick free-kick. Colin Bell raced towards the Newcastle goal, swerving round full-back and future City manager Frank Clark before pulling the ball back. Doyle shot towards goal and Mike Summerbee flicked the ball into the net. The vast City following went wild but, as the celebrations continued, Newcastle came back.

A defensive slip up allowed Jackie Sinclair to gain possession. Sinclair fed a pass across the goal area where Glyn Pardoe found himself facing three Newcastle players. Bryan 'Pop' Robson was the one who scored. The Geordies seemed to have the composure that City desperately needed. Tony Book played a true captain's role and tried to calm his players. After about half an hour Book saved the Blues when he cleared a header from Wyn Davies that looked an absolute certain goal. Then, within two minutes, the Blues took the lead again.

A quickly taken throw-in by Summerbee was pushed goalwards by Colin Bell. Alan Oakes tried a shot, but the ball spun towards leading scorer Neil Young who volleyed a glorious goal with his left foot.

Francis Lee celebrates the goal that clinched the title.

With typical City unpredictability, the Blues allowed Newcastle to fight back. Heslop, still struggling, cleared the ball, but only as far as Jim Iley, the man who'd confidently predicted a Newcastle resurgence. Iley fed Sinclair, who scored with a fine 15 yard shot.

Despite Neil Young getting the ball in the back of the net again - Francis Lee was adjudged offside - the score was still 2-2 at half time. When the interval came, Malcolm Allison was determined to tell the players what he thought. He had not been impressed with City's failure to keep a clean sheet: "I was going to go in at half time and give them a right going over in the dressing room. When I got there, though, I could see that they were all tensed up. So I just told them that they had had 45 minutes to get used to it, and now they had to go out and play."

The second half started with a more composed City side and it wasn't long before the goals came again. After only four minutes Colin Bell slipped the ball across the penalty area to Neil Young, who powered the ball in from 12 yards to give the Blues a 3-2 lead. From then

on City showed the class, determination, and style of football that had thrilled the whole of football. They were perfect in every sense of the word, although Francis Lee had one effort ruled out. Deservedly, he scored with a 12 yard shot in the 63rd minute, after Doyle and Bell had worked well to get the ball to him. Immediately after scoring Lee went straight to the crowd with his arms in the air. Naturally the crowd were delighted, even a few Newcastle fans were hoping the Blues would win the Championship.

However, with the game nearing its end, John McNamee scored Newcastle's third. The Blues were still ahead but with four minutes to go the pressure was on. The final moments were extremely tense and then referee John Thacker put his whistle to his lips and the celebrations began. The supporters chanted, "Champions, Champions", as many of them swarmed onto the pitch to greet their heroes.

Across at Old Trafford, as United were being beaten 2-1 by struggling Sunderland, the Championship trophy vanished. *Daily Express* reporter Alan Thompson set off

City fans celebrate the title in the usual way with a pitch invasion.

Blues clinch it in a blaze of glory

NEWCASTLE UTD... 3   MANCHESTER CITY 4

WHAT a magnificent match to decide a title! What a tremendous climax to a magnificent season as Manchester City waged a thrilling battle with Newcastle United in a game fit to grace Wembley itself at St James's Park.

It was a constant see-saw struggle fought out at helter-skelter pace as City

on a mission to track it down. He started questioning the Old Trafford staff: "Secretary Les Olive was under the impression that a League official had taken it earlier in the week, Matt Busby was not at all sure what had happened to it, and for a minute or two it was lost until a member of the female staff admitted that it had been locked up 'in the vault'. You are at liberty to allow full rein to your imaginations in concluding exactly where the 'vault' is at Old Trafford. But the centre of the boardroom table, where the League Championship Cup has stood proudly for the last 12 months was occupied by five shillings worth of flowers. Sit down the City fan who says symbolic."

Back in Newcastle the celebrations really began. The champagne corks started popping in the dressing room, while the supporters danced in the streets. It really was a remarkable atmosphere on an incredible day. This had been the day that all City supporters had been waiting for, the day when the Mercer-Allison combination helped bring success to a club desperately trying to leap out of the shadows. Life had been particularly grim for City fans for over a decade and only a couple of years earlier supporters had started to desert the Club. The managerial partnership had brought the Blues a new image, and had also brought many exciting players to the Club. Malcolm Allison's coaching techniques had

32

HOW THAT TITLE WAS WON

JAMES MOSSOP reports from Newcastle, Manchester

This team with so many friends are a credit to Joe

WE ARE THE CHAMPIONS

. . . that's the jubilant cry from Manchester City. Just look at those faces — pride, pleasure and jubilation. On the far left, Joe Mercer shows his obvious joy; Albert Alexander, the chairman, next to him, rubs his hands in glee; while the rest of the City board are just jubilant. And no words are needed to describe the feelings of Tony Book, pictured on the right with Joe Mercer.

Allison, Mercer and the players celebrate at a friendly with Bury.

also helped develop some of the younger players into true First Division stars. It was an incredible story.

James Mossop writing in the *Sunday Express* summed it up perfectly: "There could be no more popular, sentimental success story. City are - were - the poor relations of the Manchester clubs. Three years ago discontented fans were throwing stones and abuse at the boardroom windows. The crowds had dwindled to a starvation level of 8,000. But in an amazing spell of hard work and dedication Joe Mercer and Malcolm Allison have lifted ordinary players into the Champions of the Football League. They are just a grand set of lads, mostly young, and the best all-round team in England. It is desperately difficult not to get emotional about Manchester City, about such a major success born out of honesty, bravery and complete dedication. This victory was the pinnacle of the season. An afternoon coloured with skill, blessed with fair play and above all applauded in the end by every man, woman, and child in the 50,000 crowd. These people will never forget it. Many thousands of them swarmed on to the pitch in a dancing, swirling sea of blue and white at the end. They were cheering for the new champions. For 90 minutes City, the team that has won more friends than any other in a season of imaginative attacking football, turned on the style."

Every newspaper was equal in its praise, proving that the Blues really were worthy champions. As the champions journeyed back from Newcastle,

supporters surrounded the team bus to cheer their heroes. Every player deserved the acclaim, for even those that had struggled early on, had improved as the game progressed. Vince Wilson in the *Sunday Mirror* rightly claimed that every player added value to the performance and that the Blues played as a true team. No individual stood out above the rest, nor did any of the players try to claim that they had contributed more. Manchester City won the Championship as a team, together.

Frequently, on the journey away from St. James' Park the team bus struggled to move forward. Understandably, there were queues of traffic on all the major routes out of the city and the bus frequently had to stop. At one point Malcolm Allison jumped out and started to dance in and out of the line of traffic waving to many City supporters along the way. On the bus Joe Mercer orchestrated the singing and everybody joined in.

The following day City held a press conference. It was a light hearted affair with Mercer, Allison and Book talking openly about City's success and about their hopes for the future, in particular their first venture into Europe. Mercer stated that he believed City would do well in the European Cup and that they should survive the first two rounds at least. Allison believed the Blues would go further, stating that he didn't really rate continental coaches: "I think a lot of foreign teams win despite their coaches. If we had played Continental opposition every week we would have won the Championship by 80 points."

He went on to boast that the European coaches were "Cowards" and that City would "terrify Europe to death". Only a few months later, these comments would come back to haunt Allison, but at the time the English footballing public loved his statements. Another quote appeared under the headline "It's Mars Next Stop" in the *Daily Express* the next day: "I think we will be the first team to play on Mars."

A friendly against Bury was hastily arranged for the Tuesday following the Newcastle game to enable the Championship trophy to be presented. Normally, the trophy would be presented at the League's annual dinner but as City would be on tour in America, the League agreed to present it at Maine Road. The presentation took place before the game with Tony Book and the rest of the players going on a lap of honour before Mercer was handed the trophy to lift above his head. The crowd roared with delight and then witnessed a 4-2 victory.

Bury's two goals were scored by Bobby Owen who, two months later signed for the Blues.

The game was noteworthy for it also included an appearance by Malcolm Allison. For much of the game he'd sat, wearing his familiar red tracksuit then, with about ten minutes left he substituted George Heslop and entered the field himself wearing the number 8 shirt. This caused a little confusion as Colin Bell remained on the pitch with the same number but nobody complained, after all it was a night to enjoy especially

A proud chairman - Albert Alexander jnr.

when Allison threw himself into the game. He forced a great save from Neil Ramsbottom, the Bury 'keeper, and had a goal disallowed. The City supporters chanted 'Allison for England', and even called for Mercer to take to the field.

This was a great time to be a Blue. Allison: "I felt acutely that we had come up with some original football. We had thrashed Manchester United, we had become a power in the land."

The players, directors and footballing staff with the trophy.

1965-1968 SUMMARY

Major Trophies Won: The League Championship 1967-1968 & Second Division Champions 1965-66
Highest League Attendance: 62,983 Manchester United, 21/01/67
Highest Cup Attendance: 63,034 Everton, 26/03/66 (FA Cup)
Managers: 1965 – 1971 (continued as General Manager) Joe Mercer

Seasonal Record:

Season	League	Posn	FA Cup	League Cup	Other	Leading Scorer	Average Att
1965-66	FL Div2	Champions	Rnd 6	Rnd 3		Young 14	27,739
1966-67	FL Div1	15	Rnd 6	Rnd 3		Bell 12	31,209
1967-68	FL Div1	Champions	Rnd 4	Rnd 4		Young 19	37,223

1967-68 FOOTBALL LEAGUE CHAMPIONSHIP DETAILS

REGULAR SIDE: Mulhearn, Book, Pardoe, Doyle, Heslop, Oakes, Lee, Bell, Summerbee, Young, Coleman.
MANAGER: Joe Mercer

RESULTS	HOME		AWAY	
Liverpool	D	0-0	D	1-1
Southampton	W	4-2	L	2-3
Stoke City	W	4-2	L	0-3
Nottingham Forest	W	2-0	W	3-0
Newcastle United	W	2-0	W	4-3
Coventry City	W	3-1	W	3-0
Sheffield United	W	5-2	W	3-0
Arsenal	D	1-1	L	0-1
Manchester United	L	1-2	W	3-1
Sunderland	W	1-0	L	0-1
Wolverhampton W	W	2-0	D	0-0
Fulham	W	5-1	W	4-2
Leeds United	W	1-0	L	0-2
Everton	W	2-0	D	1-1
Leicester City	W	6-0	L	0-1
West Ham United	W	3-0	W	3-2
Burnley	W	4-2	W	1-0
Sheffield Wednesday	W	1-0	D	1-1
Tottenham Hotspur	W	4-1	W	3-1
West Bromwich A	L	0-2	L	2-3
Chelsea	W	1-0	L	0-1

LARGEST VICTORY: 6-0 V Leicester City (H) 11/11/67
LARGEST WINNING MARGIN: 6-0 V Leicester City (H) 11/11/67
HEAVIEST DEFEAT: 0-3 V Stoke City (A) 26/8/67
AVERAGE HOME ATTENDANCE: 37,223
HIGHEST HOME ATTENDANCE: 62,942 V Manchester United 30/9/67
HIGHEST AWAY ATTENDANCE: 63,004 V Manchester United 27/3/68
LEAGUE APPEARANCES (substitute appearances in brackets): 42 Book, 41 Pardoe, Heslop, Oakes, Summerbee, 40 Young, 38 Coleman, 37 Doyle (1), 35 Bell, 33 Mulhearn, 31 Lee, 10 Connor (3), 7 Dowd, 6 Hince, 4 Kennedy (2), Horne (1), Bowles, 2 Cheetham (1), Jones, Ogley, 1 Clay (1)
LEAGUE GOALS: 19 Young, 16 Lee, 14 Bell, Summerbee, 8 Coleman, 5 Doyle, 2 Oakes, Hince, Bowles, 1 Book, Heslop, Connor

TRUE BLUE
Joe Mercer

Joe Mercer guided the Blues to incredible success between 1965 and 1971 - the ECWC, the League Championship, FA Cup, League Cup, Charity Shield and Second Division title.

City bring the ECWC to Manchester for the Blues' third homecoming in a year.

1968-1970
European Challenge

"Everybody must respect them. If they don't they are either stupid or blind. Their buys have been good buys. Men like Book. Nobody else seemed to want him or even look at him. Bell is already a tremendous player and will be even better. Lee was floating around for a long time before City stepped in to buy him."

Liverpool's legendary manager Bill Shankly talking of City in May 1969.

1968-1969 The Fourth FA Cup

The close season of 1968 was a great one for supporters. It was a time to reflect on the successes of the first three seasons under the Mercer-Allison combination, and to look forward to the first appearance in European competition. They were right to expect a great deal, after all City's entertaining style of football had helped to create a real buzz around Manchester, and had won many admirers nationwide.

For the players and management however, the Summer of '68 was not as rewarding as it should have been as controversy seemed to follow the Club everywhere. The Blues had now become one of the most talked about teams in Europe with the media following the players and management's every move.

The attention was still relatively new to the majority of players and at times was extremely difficult to handle, added to which a disastrous tour of North America caused a few problems, such as an Achilles tendon injury to Tony Book.

When the Blues returned to England a civic reception at Manchester Town Hall resulted in banner headlines accusing the City players of walking out of the event held in their honour. What made the story more of a 'sensation' as far as the media were concerned was the news that Malcolm Allison was apparently leading the escape party to one of his favourite night clubs. Although the story is a relatively trivial one it did cause much embarrassment at the time, and is significant because it proves that the Blues could no longer expect the media to ignore them. It seems that the public were keen to hear about City and the press were determined to find stories, no matter how trivial. On the one hand the Blues were actively encouraging media attention - Allison's morale boosting boasts, Mercer's cosy chats with his friends in the news industry - but on the other they were trying to keep the negative stories out. It was a difficult balancing act which, fortunately, City usually managed to get right. Throughout the mid to late 1960s the Mercer-Allison inspired Blues managed to gain more positive coverage than bad. If the worst 'sensation' featured the players and Allison sneaking out of a rather formal function then there wasn't too much wrong with the Club.

The 1968-69 season opened with the Charity Shield match against FA Cup Winners West Bromwich Albion. At this point in time the curtain-raiser was played on the home ground of the Champions, with City outplaying West Bromwich to record a convincing 6-1 victory. Everyone connected with the Blues hoped the League campaign would follow in the same style. Sadly, it did not.

City missed Tony Book following his injury on tour, and the Blues struggled in their opening League game - a 2-1 defeat at Liverpool. Neil Young provided the goal that day, but the forward line had now been joined by Bobby Owen - a £35,000 purchase from Bury. Owen scored twice in the Charity Shield victory, but it took the forward some time to settle in the League side.

The first home game was a 3-2 victory over Wolves before a crowd of 36,476 according to the City programmes of the period (officially 35,835). Because of their success in the League, City had been forced to designate certain seating areas purely for season ticket holders. A large section in the popular, if uncomfortable, Platt Lane Stand was marked specifically for this purpose. Similarly, the increase in popularity had forced the Club to make admittance to the Main Stand by ticket only, with the cost of the most expensive seats being 13s 6d per League game.

There were other changes, too. Groundsman Stan Gibson had worked hard to turn the Maine Road pitch into a perfect playing surface, although at times even he could not perform his usual miracles as the Manchester weather and coaching techniques of Allison piled on the pressure: "It will take some pounding again this year. Malcolm likes to get on it and play at the most unlikely times. It might spoil it a bit as a showpiece but if it helps City win I shan't lose any sleep over that."

In addition, Joe Mercer had taken steps to improve the scouting network, boasting that much of Britain had a City man on the lookout for the stars of the future. One of the scouts for Yorkshire knew exactly what it was like to play in a successful City side - Sam Barkas, captain of the League Champions in 1937.

Three days after the Wolves game, City entertained Manchester United, although the game itself lacked any real entertainment. United had come to Maine Road determined not to lose, with their approach somewhat stifling. The game ended goalless and brought much criticism of Manchester football as the public had expected a great performance by the two leading English clubs.

Following the derby an away trip to Leicester ended in a 3-0 defeat as the Champions struggled to find form. Only a further three points were picked up in the following five games and then, with such dismal form, the Blues had to face Turkish Champions Fenerbahce in the European Cup. By this time City were 21st in the First Division after nine matches.

The game played on 18th September was City's first game in European competition and it was the first time an English side had faced a Turkish club competitively, but it was not the first time Fenerbahce had played at Maine Road. In October 1953 the Turks played a friendly under Maine Road's new floodlights which ended in a 5-1 victory to the Blues. Although the tie was expected to be far more difficult than the friendly, the Blues still expected to defeat the Turks. They aimed for a two goal lead. They didn't succeed.

The match ended goalless with the Blues missing chance after chance. Even the normally reliable Summerbee had an off day with a small section of the crowd booing him on occasion: "I was playing centre-forward and thought I was the only man who could play in that position. I ended up struggling - subconsciously I had lowered my standards. We all thought we were unbeatable and lost that edge."

Colin Bell: "It was unfortunate that it was our first experience of Europe and it couldn't have been a bigger tournament. At Maine Road, they kicked us up in the air, picked us up, shook our hands and we accepted it."

Fenerbahce left Maine Road with the advantage, but not a victory. The Turks had to wait another 28 years before they won a game in Manchester, and then it was against United and not City.

The away leg was played on 2nd October, with City flying out on a specially chartered BEA Comet from Ringway at 10 o'clock the day before. The Blues took a squad of sixteen and stayed at the Hilton Hotel in Istanbul.

On arrival at the stadium on the day of the game, the City party soon realised that the match would be a difficult one. The pitch was in an appalling bumpy state while it also appeared that the whole of Istanbul were keen to see the match. The stadium was packed with about 55,000 people hours before the start, although the official attendance was ten thousand lower. A member of the Fenerbahce groundstaff proved to Walter Griffiths, City's secretary, that the figure was significantly higher than 45,000.

When the match commenced, the noise generated by the partisan crowd was deafening. City certainly felt the full force of Turkish devotion. Nevertheless, it was City who first found the net. The popular rebel Tony Coleman latched on to a cross from Francis Lee, controlled the ball, went round Fenerbahce's under 23 international Yavuz Simsek and stroked the ball home.

In the second half, however, it was a different story with Fenerbahce attacking in numbers. Less than a minute after half time they equalised. Although City retained the advantage via the away goals rule, it was Fenerbahce who now had the initiative and twelve minutes from time they took the lead, prompting mass celebrations.

Fans invaded the pitch, fireworks zoomed into the sky, and the City men realised it was virtually impossible to fight back. At full time the Turkish celebrations really began. Over one hundred celebratory fires were lit on the terraces, and for the first time baton-wielding riot police had to clear a path for the players to reach the dressing room. It was a nightmare day for the Blues, but a hugely important one for the Turks. The local press described the result as the most important in the history of the country, boasting of their success over the English Champions.

While the Istanbul press stressed the strengths of the Turks, their English counterparts concentrated on Allison's boasts of "terrifying Europe to death." The City coach actually found it tough saying anything after the defeat. For almost 48 hours after the game a dejected Allison remained silent. When he eventually broke his silence he told the *Manchester Evening News*' Peter Gardner: "'Defeat in Istanbul was the biggest disappointment of my whole career. What made it so particularly frustrating was that in the first half at Fenerbahce we had conquered all the problems that go with playing abroad in the tense atmosphere of the European Cup. The players had silenced the hysterical crowd; they had overcome the different refereeing, poor pitch and the lighter, softer ball."

Looking back in 2010 Francis Lee felt it was simply inexperience that had hampered the Blues progress: "None of us had played in Europe before. Mike Summerbee had only made his England debut against Scotland in February 1968. Colin Bell had played in two England friendlies, but apart from that none of us had any concept of what it could be like in Turkey. Had we played the first leg in Istanbul and the second at Maine Road I think we'd have gone through, but the goalless 1st leg at Maine Road killed us really. We worked hard in Istanbul and it was a creditable result over there but we were out and it was because we were inexperienced. It was a culture shock."

Out of European competition, the Blues were able to concentrate on the domestic scene, although that was

hardly an improvement. City had already been knocked out of the League Cup by Blackpool in the third round, and their League form was mixed. Lee: "Confidence was at a real low after that game. We'd had a bad run and only had a small squad so we struggled. But that was the way it was. Most clubs had small squads but what Shankly used to do at Liverpool was sign a couple of players each season just to ensure that those who were first choice felt the pressure and remained hungry for the game. Back then the motivation for all of us was to be in the team and to keep your place. The money was significantly different if you lost your place – City used to have this thing where we'd get a bonus depending on the size of the attendance as well as goals, wins and so on. That motivated you to ensure you did all you could to entertain as well as win – you wanted the crowds to grow.

"Effectively you could double your wage by simply being in the team. That's a big incentive."

A 2-0 defeat at Everton three days after the Fenerbahce game was probably not a great surprise, but the Champions needed to get their act together to ensure they didn't emulate their 1930s equivalents and find themselves in the relegation zone at the season's end. Significantly, that game at Goodison was the first time City had worn their new away kit of red & black stripes chosen by Malcolm Allison. The defeat brought a lot of complaints from fans about the use of the colours. By the time the season ended however, most fans had accepted Allison's inspired choice.

Inconsistency seemed to dominate the Blues' League Performances. A string of three defeats in November were followed by a 5-1 Maine Road victory over West Bromwich, then a 2-1 defeat at West Ham, and then the impressive 7-0 annihilation of Burnley. City fans did not know what to expect as the campaign seemed to be a complete contrast to the previous season.

On 11th January the 26th League game of the season saw the return of the influential Tony Book for the visit of fifth placed Chelsea. It was an important return as City, lying in 14th position, needed his involvement on the pitch to steady the side. Book returned to his regular number two shirt, with Pardoe moving to number three, displacing £65,000 signing Arthur Mann.

Chelsea were the more accomplished side for the early moments of the game, putting City under considerable pressure, especially when Colin Bell was forced to leave the field for a ten minute spell after receiving a knee injury in the 12th minute.

After 23 minutes Chelsea took the lead, despite a last ditch attempt by Book to keep the ball out. The pensioners continued to attack but, incredibly, it was City who were next to score. Bobby Owen squeezed a ball through a massed defence to Neil Young, who proceeded to turn and hit a perfect shot across into the far corner of Peter Bonetti's goal. The 36th minute goal was very much against the run of play, but the City faithful hardly cared.

At half time Colin Bell, with his knee bandaged, was replaced by Stan Bowles. The injury cost Bell an England cap the following Wednesday - one of many he would lose out on through injury. For Bowles, though, the opportunity was perfect, and ten minutes into the half he helped to transform the match.

A foul on Coleman led to a free-kick taken by Doyle. Bowles and Owen both had shots beaten out, before Bowles sent the ball to Lee, whose shot was rifled into the roof of the net. Then after 63 minutes, Bowles fed Young on the left. Young then ran at speed into the Chelsea penalty area, hit the ball across the goal to Owen who proceeded to score his first League goal for the Club. A minute later he scored his second to give City an important 4-1 win.

For the remainder of the campaign, however, exciting victories like that seemed to be followed by depressing draws or, even worse, defeats. Even so, City gradually picked up enough points to ensure safety and the Blues finished in 13th position. In itself, that was not a terribly high placing, however performances in the FA Cup more than made up for a dismal League campaign.

In the third round City faced Third Division Luton at Maine Road before a crowd of 37,120. The Blues started comfortably, although too many opportunities were wasted. Then in the 26th minute Francis Lee was felled by John Moore in the penalty area, giving City a perfect opportunity to take the lead. Naturally, Lee took the spot kick himself and whacked the ball home to give the Blues the advantage.

City continued to attack with Bell outstanding, but more wasted chances and some rather exciting saves by Luton's Sandy Davie prevented further goals for the Blues. Then, with about ten minutes remaining, Luton started to attack in numbers and Harry Dowd, who at long last had regained the number one shirt from Ken Mulhearn, was forced to make a number of fine saves. Two attempts by Bruce Rioch led to breath-taking saves by the popular Dowd, with other Luton efforts also causing the 'footballing plumber' to ensure the Blues didn't leak any goals.

The game ended 1-0 and gave City a fourth round trip to old Cup adversaries Newcastle United. That match ended goalless but it was still one with plenty of incident. Neil Young came closest to scoring, most thought it was a goal, but Young was unsure: "The shot that everyone thought went in? I was six or seven yards from the by-line, outside the area. I couldn't really see. It was a funny game...Probably better from the spectators' point of view than the players. Control of the game changed very quickly. Both sides had chances...Ours were the more clear cut."

City once again had large support at a ground that had started to seem more like a second home than an away venue. Tony Book felt the Blues fans dominated the terraces: "The City supporters did well for us up there. You could always hear them. And in the last quarter of an hour, which is always a tense time, they really gave us a lift."

Joe Mercer felt that the star of the game was 19 year old Tommy Booth: "We were under a lot of pressure during the match, but did not give them many clear cut openings. Tommy Booth stuck right with Wyn Davies, so that he was not able to turn quickly or break effectively. Both sides must have done a lot of rethinking after Saturday, but there is a great spirit between us and there will be no recriminations after this game."

The replay was a rather exciting affair with City winning 2-0. Alan Thompson writing in the *Daily Express* believed City were superb, especially early on: "They pulverised Newcastle so completely in the first half that it was not so much a match as a massacre. But all they had to show on the ledge was one early goal and half a dozen near misses."

In the *Daily Telegraph* R.H. Williams held a similar view: "Newcastle had no answer to the buoyant City forwards, bouncing at last with optimism who must have been surprised at the obstinate squareness of Newcastle's defence. At any rate, they took obvious delight in drilling holes in it."

The first goal came in the tenth minute with City attacking the Scoreboard End of the stadium. Harry Dowd started the move with a long pump up field which found the head of Lee, who in turn sent the ball to Owen. Owen flicked it on to Young, who then streaked forward in a 30 yard run before firing the ball past McFaul.

Fifty eight minutes later the same players were involved when the lead was increased. This time Young back headed to Lee, who flicked it across to Owen on the right. The former Bury man powered home a shot from about 15 yards out.

Over the two games City easily deserved the victory and proved true value for money for the incredibly large crowds. 60,844 had watched the second game, while the first had been attended by 55,680.

The fifth round draw sent City to Blackburn for an all Lancashire clash, although the match had to be postponed on several occasions as a result of poor weather conditions and a 'flu epidemic in Blackburn. When the game started on 24th February - 16 days after the original date - City proved why they had won the Championship the season before. The first goal came in the 13th minute when Colin Bell, playing his first game since the Chelsea match in January, steered a perfect pass through the Blackburn defence and on to Lee. The forward then charged up field and knocked the ball past Adam Blacklaw in the Blackburn goal.

In the 47th minute the home side equalised, then eleven minutes later Tony Coleman restored the lead: "I'll never forget it if I live to be 100. I hit it with my right foot and it went in like a rocket. That hasn't happened very often!"

Later City increased their lead when Neil Young fed the ball to Lee's feet. The striker stormed through the middle with little opposition and then slammed a searing shot into the net. In the dying minutes Coleman made it four when a mistake by the Blackburn defence allowed him to run in and pinch a cheeky goal.

It was a good all-round performance with Colin Bell the undisputed star: "This was my first game back after injury and I really felt good after my lay-off. The knee which had kept me out of action ended up a little bit sore, but I was ready for a game. I thought the team played extremely well all through the match."

City's quarter-final opponents were Tottenham at Maine Road on 1st March. Again the Blues showed their determination from the very first minute, although Spurs were equally determined. Jimmy Greaves and Alan Gilzean attacked the Blues like no other in the competition so far and City felt the pressure, while defensively the Londoners were determined to stop the Blues no matter what. Johnson was booked for tipping up Bell near the penalty area, then Knowles found the referee taking his name after the player sent Coleman crashing heavily to the ground in another dangerous tackle.

It was a tough match all round but the in the 64th minute City found an opening. A lofted ball from Coleman, out deep on the left, stretched across the penalty area where Bell headed it back untroubled into the middle. Doyle forced his way forward for the ball, then Summerbee turned it forward to Lee. From approximately eight yards out Lee sent the ball scraping in from the inside of the post, with Jennings unable to reach it.

Despite pressure from Greaves & Co. City held on and entered the draw for the semi-final alongside Everton, Leicester, and Cup holders West Bromwich Albion. In the end the draw paired City with Everton at Villa Park. Mercer and Allison perceived that Alan Ball would be the Toffees' most influential player. They discussed how to stop the England international and came to the conclusion that they should simply take him out of the game. They'd seen Ball struggle two years earlier at Maine Road and felt that close marking may actually make his play ineffectual. Dave Connor was brought into the side specifically to stop the threat from Ball and it worked perfectly. Connor managed to annoy the Evertonian so much that he lost his temper, fouled Connor and was booked. Mercer and Allison were delighted that the ploy had proved so effective.

In later years Ball said that he half-expected Connor to be standing next to him in the Everton dressing room toilet at half time!

The early moments of the game were rather mixed, with the Blues appearing rather nervous for much of the opening period. Nevertheless, City playing in their

Lee, Bell and Summerbee congratulate Tommy Booth for his goal in the semi-final.

recently adopted AC Milan style away strip always seemed to have the edge. They ran and fought for everything and managed to keep the Everton attack at bay. Tony Book was outstanding as he managed to bottle up Johnny Morrissey for the entire game. Francis Lee, despite worries about his fitness, proved his ability on many occasions, while Mike Doyle demonstrated his commitment to the Blue cause when he returned to the field after being absent with injury for 18 minutes. On his return, though a little more static, his play hardly seemed to suffer.

Despite City's attacking nature, the game remained goalless right up to the last minute. Then a wonder goal by youngster Tommy Booth set the Blues up for their seventh Cup Final. The ball had been cleared by Harry Dowd and was worked up field in a fluent passing move which started with Young. He fed the ball to Bell before running up field. Bell accurately passed to Lee, who pushed the ball to Young. Quickly, he sent an absolute screamer goalwards, only to see it rebound off the shoulders of Everton's 'keeper Gordon West. The ball went out of play giving City a corner taken by Young. Doyle headed it down to Summerbee who flicked it across the goal face towards the waiting Bell. Booth rushed forward and sent the ball crashing into the net. It was a great moment.

Norman Wynne writing in *The People* was pleased for Booth: "The game was moving with certainty to a replay until Booth came up with his last minute goal. It was fitting that the City centre half should be the goal scoring hero of the day. He was the youngest player on the field, and also the best."

The celebrations began immediately with champagne and cigars passed around the dressing room. Mercer announced that City were going to Wembley to entertain.

By reaching Wembley City had equalled Arsenal's record of six Wembley Finals - a feat which made Mercer immensely proud. Another man full of pride was Malcolm Allison: "It was essentially a great team victory, but I don't think the other players will mind my praising Tony (Book), Tommy (Booth), and Francis (Lee). Tony for his inspirational leadership, especially when we were down to ten men with Doyle undergoing treatment; Francis for his 100% effort when he must have been in considerable pain from his thigh injury and finally Tommy Booth. What can I add to what's already been said about him. He was the 'man of the match' before he did what he stopped Joe Royle from doing - scoring."

City's opponents for the Final were not known until 29th March, a week after the Blues' victory. With an air of inevitability Leicester would face City for the fourth consecutive season. Leicester had defeated West Bromwich 1-0 at Hillsborough to reach Wembley.

In the weeks leading up to the Final City announced that they would be wearing their new change strip of red

An anxious moment as Tommy Booth clears the danger watched by Pardoe, Oakes and Dowd.

and black stripes, rather than the traditional sky blue. It had been Allison's suggestion to wear AC Milan's colours in the first place as he believed it would bring the same kind of invincibility that the Italians enjoyed. He also felt it gave the Mancunians a psychological advantage.

This was not the first time City had worn red at Wembley as in 1933 they had worn their 'lucky scarlet' kit.

The Club also decided to make young Paul Todd, the son of City steward Harry, the first mascot to appear at a Final. They smuggled him in on the players' coach, sitting next to manager Mercer, and then during the game he took Allison's place on the bench as the City assistant had been banned for so called 'excessive coaching'. Allison was forced to watch the game from the stands, although the ban was ineffectual as it actually brought him closer to the pitch than the bench.

One member of the squad had already had a successful week leading up to the Final - Tony Book. City's captain had been voted joint Footballer of the Year (with Dave Mackay of Derby County) by the Football Writers. It was a fitting tribute to a great player, and Book was naturally delighted: "To receive an award that my boss, Joe Mercer, and Stanley Matthews, Tom Finney, and Bert Trautmann, and men of their calibre were given is truly astonishing. It is an honour for which the greatest credit goes to Joe Mercer, Malcolm Allison, and the team. I've had some wonderful help on the way."

The day before the game Book joined the other City players and the management on a trip to Wembley to check out the pitch and facilities. They did not like what they saw, with Mercer describing the pitch as a "cabbage patch." Neil Young remembered that it was an absolute disgrace: "It was terrible. Joe Mercer went berserk when he saw the state of the pitch. They had a Horse Show on it and it was all rutted and bumpy."

The Royal guest for the match was Princess Anne, who had actually participated in the Horse Show. For the final she wore red and black, prompting many to believe she had a bit of a soft spot for City, although the more believable explanation is that her advisors had told her that both finalists traditionally wear blue prompting her to wear neutral colours. She was introduced to the teams and even spent a few moments chatting to mascot Paul Todd. Legend has it that Tony Coleman, who according to Allison had been injured in a fight the weekend before, also made an impression on the Princess. Apparently, as they shook hands he said: "Give my regards to your Mum and Dad."

The game itself was not a classic, although it did produce some fine moments. Leicester's Allan Clarke, at that time the most expensive player in Britain at £150,000, had a superb shot which Dowd finger tipped to safety. The City 'keeper, who had missed out on a League Championship medal, enjoyed making that save and the game itself: "Playing at Wembley has to be

Alan Oakes and Allan Clarke during the final.

the highlight of my career. I can't recall being all that nervous at Wembley. I suppose I was at the start but I soon got into it. I remember making that save from Allan Clarke early on but I was more pleased about smothering the ball at Andy Lochhead's feet when he was through on his own."

Early on both Young and Coleman saw their attempts miss their target as City tried to seize the initiative. Then after 23 minutes, Summerbee gathered a throw-in from Lee, raced down the right, slipped past Leicester player David Nish and centred the ball to Young. The striker crashed the ball past the England under-23 goalkeeper Peter Shilton, into the top corner with his left foot. Young knew he had scored from the second he hit the ball.

Mercer, sat on the bench, was immediately grabbed by a BBC reporter to explain his feelings. This type of intrusion by the media became commonplace in the 1980s but in 1969 it was new to football. It had been brought about by politics between the BBC and London Weekend Television, with each station claiming the other had broken coverage agreements. The BBC claimed it had exclusive rights to interview the Finalists, while LWT claimed they were not getting a fair deal. It was claimed that the LWT men had even disguised themselves in tracksuits to deceive the BBC. A point LWT head of sport Jimmy Hill admitted was true. It was all rather sordid and had created a tension around the Final that should not have been there.

Young, Dowd, Oakes and Bell swamped by fans at Wembley.

Despite the appalling surface both sides did play some fine football at times, but as the game neared its end it was obvious the Cup was on its way back to Manchester. Unfortunately, Leicester combined defeat with relegation to the Second Division, thereby emulating City's feat of 1926. On the pitch Allan Clarke had tried hard to even the score for Leicester. The player was ultimately voted man of the match although Mike Summerbee put it into perspective when he later commented: "I'd rather have my winners' medal."

Tony Book collected the trophy for City, then all the players waited as Leicester collected their medals. The *Daily Mail* applauded City's compassion: "The mood was equal to the match. Fear was hardly evident, bad fouls were few, and the sight of the Manchester men clapping the losers provided a warm afterglow. Manchester City are among the best Cup-winners of past decades. Leicester are far from being the worst losers."

On the pitch Mercer and Allison, laughing and joking with each other, took it in turns to lift the trophy. They also conducted the fans' singing for a while. It was one of the best moments during the successful partnership

Oakes, Young, Pardoe and Dowd – from Division Two in 1965 to major success.

and, while the celebrations continued, Allison turned to Mercer and said: "Boss, I'm worried." Mercer was puzzled after all City had just won the FA Cup to combine with the League, the Charity Shield, and the Second Division Championship since 1966. He asked Allison for an explanation. Allison replied: "Well, Boss, I can't help wondering what went wrong in 1967 when we didn't win anything!" The two men laughed.

It is worth pausing to consider how the Blues compared to football's other successful sides in the competition at this point. City's four FA Cup successes placed them behind Aston Villa (7), Blackburn Rovers (6), Newcastle United (6), Tottenham Hotspur (5), The Wanderers (5) and West Bromwich Albion (5). Bolton, Sheffield United and Wolves had, like City, each won four FA Cups, while Manchester United had only won three, Liverpool one and Chelsea had not yet won the trophy. In fact Chelsea had only won one major trophy (the League Championship) at this point in their history.

In 1969 City's celebrations continued in the dressing room. The Cup was filled with champagne and the media demanded interviews. Allison was asked about Europe. Remembering his boasts of the previous year he replied: "I'll say this - we will at least get through the first round in the Cup Winners' Cup, of that I can promise."

Mercer also remembered the Fenerbahce disappointments: "I believe our Wembley victory is only the start of a truly great future for Manchester City. We go back into Europe still reflecting on our bitter experiences of earlier this season and determined not to make the same mistakes again. Europe is where the lolly is, so instead of being idealistic we have to be more financially minded. Our defeat by Fenerbahce in Istanbul in October taught us a firm lesson in that we should never underestimate the opposition - any opposition. We must get down to basics all the time and I sincerely believe that we have still to see the best of this City team. I don't really like talking about potential but we have

Bringing the FA Cup home to Albert Square.

here a great bunch of players, who are going to become a really great side. Things didn't go well for us earlier this season and, quite naturally, I was disappointed at our results because I knew, Malcolm knew, that the entire team was capable of so much more."

He went on to outline City's strengths, making particular reference to the emerging Tommy Booth. Six months earlier few had heard the player's name, now following his goal in the semi-final and appearance at Wembley everybody seemed to be talking about him. Booth deserved the acclaim.

As the night progressed City moved on to their celebration banquet at the Cafe Royal. The BBC took the opportunity to interview the players and management, and then afterwards many of the players moved on to a West End night club.

The following morning the team and trophy returned to Manchester, travelling by rail from London to Wilmslow. At the usually quiet Cheshire town 25,000 people turned out to see the players board an open-top bus for the 12 mile trip to Manchester's Albert Square. John Humphreys, a City director and a director of Wilmslow-based kit manufacturers Umbro, had suggested the Blues commence their tour from the town. At first it seemed a ridiculous idea, but as that part of Cheshire is strong in its support for City, it was agreed that it would be worth trying.

The journey into Manchester was tremendous with

one newspaper estimating that there were at least 250,000 people lining the route to welcome their heroes back. The bus, loaned by Southport Corporation, and driver Bob Jackson were the same combination that brought United through the streets after their European Cup success twelve months earlier and 52 year old Jackson found City's homecoming moving: "It was fantastic. I would say there were more people about than for United's homecoming, and I was very proud to be in the procession. I saw the game on telly and enjoyed every minute of it."

Tony Book and City's three trophies in a year.

In Albert Square the crowd chanted the names of the players and called for both Mercer and Allison. The supporters listened as both men spoke of the pride they felt bringing the Cup back to Manchester. For Mercer winning the Cup saw him enter the record books as the first man to win the FA Cup and the League Championship as both a player and a manager. It was a special occasion.

1969-1970 Franny's Grand Slam

The Summer of '69 was another good one for supporters as they were able to bask in the glory and the knowledge that their club was now re-established as one of Britain's elite. Fenerbahce had caused a little embarrassment but, apart from Allison's predictions, nobody really expected an entire team of European novices to find success at their first attempt. However, the FA Cup gave the Blues another chance of European glory. This time they would appear in the European Cup Winners' Cup - a competition previously won by Tottenham (1963) and West Ham (1965). The Fenerbahce experience would aid the Blues' preparations.

The season commenced with the Charity Shield match against Don Revie's Leeds United at Elland Road. The result was a disappointing 2-1 defeat, but the game hardly mattered. A week later the 4-1 victory over Sheffield Wednesday did, however, and there was much hope that 1969-70 would see the Blues make an impression on the League.

One young player finding his feet at this time was Ian Bowyer. He had made three League starts the previous season, and appeared in the second League game of 1969-70 at Liverpool. He went on to start a total of 30 consecutive League matches: "It was great period. I scored six goals in the first eight games but the problem was I scored five away from home. So home fans thought that I was rubbish but those that travelled thought I was acceptable! I worked hard but I have to say that for the first 12 months in that side I didn't really have the understanding to play as a striker that I needed."

The more experienced players helped Bowyer settle: "Everyone associated with the Club in those days was part of the family. The other players were brilliant and had so many qualities. Francis Lee was inspiring and would talk about City winning the 'Grand Slam' – the League, FA Cup, ECWC and League Cup! He believed it was possible and as a young player it was great to be in his company when he was telling us that. He truly believed we'd do it. Pre-match he'd say things like 'It's Grand Slam stage 2 today'. After each win he'd say 'that's another step towards the Grand Slam lads'. That shows the ambition of the player and the Club and it was great to be involved with that. It was infectious. For the younger ones seeing the examples of Tony

Book and Alan Oakes was fantastic. Glyn Pardoe was a fabulous skilful footballer. Then of course there's Mike Summerbee and the absolute supreme player Colin Bell.

"The City side back then had so many quality players who were known for their skills. I think actually it's worth remembering that the players back then were talented players who became stars whereas nowadays, it's a generalisation I know, but a lot of the well-known players at the biggest clubs tend to want to be stars who 'happen to play football', not footballers who 'happen to become stars'. It's the wrong emphasis to me."

After Bowyer's eighth League game of the season, a 3-0 victory over Spurs on 13th September, City were eleventh on nine points from nine games. Neil Young had missed all but two of those matches and inconsistency was an issue. Tony Coleman had moved on to Sheffield Wednesday, while Joe Corrigan was now the first choice 'keeper replacing Harry Dowd, but otherwise the team was much the same as the previous season.

September was an extremely busy month as both the League Cup and ECWC campaigns commenced. In the League Cup City defeated Southport 3-0 on 3rd September, then on 17th they faced Atlético Bilbao, managed by the former West Bromwich star Ronnie Allen, in Spain. Bilbao had been forced to change their name from Athletic Bilbao in 1941 following a decree by Spanish dictator Franco.

Determined to avoid an embarrassing defeat, Mercer and Allison sent out a team that included seven of the side that had suffered in Fenerbahce. The others were Tony Book, who'd only missed the Fenerbahce game through injury; Joe Corrigan, who had replaced Ken Mulhearn; Tommy Booth, who had won so many admirers in such a short time; and Ian Bowyer, who had replaced Tony Coleman.

Despite the Blues' determination they were 2-0 down in the opening fifteen minutes. Before half-time Neil Young reduced the deficit and provided the vital away goal which, if the score stood, would mean City simply needed to win 1-0 at Maine Road to go through. Realising this neither Mercer nor Allison panicked and at half-time they calmly spoke with the players. In the second half, however, the Spaniards scored a third.

City fought back and levelled the scores at 3-3 with a goal from youngster Booth and an own goal from the Bilbao captain Luis Echeberria. As the game progressed City appeared the more likely to win the match, sadly they ran out of time prompting Malcolm Allison to forecast victory at Maine Road: "These boys have got the needle tonight because they didn't win. Just wait until we get them back home. We'll give these Spaniards a roasting."

Before the two sides met at Maine Road, City had to play two League games and a League Cup tie.

Their opponents in the League Cup were Bill Shankly's Liverpool at Maine Road. The two sides had already met in the League, with Liverpool achieving a double victory in only eight days, the cup game would be different.

It took City a mere eleven minutes to take the lead when Lee pushed the ball to Doyle. Doyle, from about 35 yards out, hit the ball with tremendous power and sent it rocketing into the net. It was an incredible goal, but ten minutes later it was cancelled out when a Heslop clearance ricocheted off Liverpool's Alun Evans and entered the net.

Neil Young regained the lead for the Blues when Ian Bowyer gathered a loose ball and passed it to Young, who in turn shot past 'keeper Tommy Lawrence. Later Ian Bowyer increased the score to 3-1 but Liverpool pulled one back and the pressure increased. The scorer of the first goal, Mike Doyle then became the match winner as he helped protect the goal from relentless Liverpool pressure, and at the final whistle the score remained 3-2 to the Blues.

Back in Europe, the second leg with Bilbao ended 3-0 with goals from Bell, Oakes, and Bowyer. This set them up for a tie with the Belgian part-timers SK Lierse. The first leg, played on 12th November in Belgium, ended in a 3-0 victory with goals from Bell and two from Lee. The second leg saw City totally outclass their Belgian opponents again, this time two goals apiece from Lee and Bell and another from Summerbee gave City a 5-0 win. The Blues then had to wait until March for their quarter-final tie with Academica Coimbra of Portugal, by which time City had also reached the League Cup Final.

Following the victory over Liverpool, City defeated Everton 2-0 at Maine Road in the fourth round to bring a home tie against Queens Park Rangers in the quarter final. Two goals from Bell and another from Summerbee without reply in that match gave the 42,000 crowd a lot to cheer, and set up a meeting with Manchester United in the two legged semi-final.

The first leg, played on 3rd December, took place at Maine Road with City very much determined to remind the Reds that the Blues were the dominant local force. The game commenced at a frenetic pace and after only 13 minutes Lee helped provide the first goal. City's future Chairman made a typical bustling run down the left and, after avoiding a number of United tackles, sent in a fierce shot which deflected and spun high into the air. Bell, following in, met the loose ball on the half volley and crashed it past United's Alex Stepney.

With their one goal lead City pressed further and Stepney, who in the 1990s became a goalkeeping coach at Maine Road, performed exceptionally well to save from Bell, Lee and Oakes. He managed to keep the score at 1-0 until half-time, by which time the Blues pressure had begun to drop.

Twenty-one minutes into the second half Bobby

Charlton equalised for the Reds. As the game neared its conclusion everyone connected with the Blues felt disappointed that the match had not been killed in the first period when United were there for the taking. However, it wasn't all doom and gloom as, in the 88th minute, Lee set off on another probing run. He entered the penalty area and was promptly felled by United's centre-half Ian Ure. Naturally, Ure complained but referee Jack Taylor remained convinced that the Blues deserved a penalty.

Penalty expert Lee sent the ball low to Stepney's right and the Blues won the match 2-1. As the game ended, George Best exchanged words with Jack Taylor, and appeared to knock the ball out of the referee's hands. The United man was later charged with bringing the game into disrepute, fined £100 and suspended for a month.

City were now confident of a place at Wembley, but they could not allow a complacent attitude to affect the second leg at Old Trafford. The return game started with both sides looking bright and, once again, it was the Blues who were first to gain the upper hand when, after 17 minutes, Summerbee carved an opening for Young in the centre. His shot beat Stepney but was blocked on the line by Ure. Ian Bowyer grabbed the loose ball and slotted it into the net to give City an aggregate two goal lead. It didn't last, however.

Paul Edwards, a 21 year old United full back, pulled one back, but the Blues still seemed the more likely to score again before the interval. Several attempts failed, and then in the second half disaster struck when former Blue Denis Law stabbed home a loose ball. United were now level on aggregate and were pushing forward in numbers. It was looking grim for City, then with only eight minutes remaining the tie was settled in the most unlikely way. Willie Morgan fouled Bowyer some twenty yards from the United net. The referee signalled an indirect free kick. Lee either missed the signal, or simply ignored it, and fired the ball towards the United goal. Stepney had the opportunity to let the ball enter the net knowing that it wouldn't count because the kick had been indirect but, amazingly, he went to catch it. He fumbled the catch and the ball fell loose. Summerbee seized the chance and buried the ball in the net to give City a 4-3 aggregate win. As in the 1930s and 1950s City were to travel to Wembley two years in succession.

The League Cup had already been won by manager Joe Mercer, but it was still a relatively new competition. Many clubs had boycotted it in its early years - indeed 1969-70 was the first season that all League clubs entered - but interest had grown when the final was moved to Wembley and when a place in Europe in the Fairs Cup was promised to the winners. In later years the Fairs Cup was replaced by the UEFA Cup, and the League Cup's significance increased further.

There is no doubt that by 1969-70 the League Cup was regarded as a major trophy. Mercer: "It's an accepted major competition now. The most important part about it though is that it offers a place in Europe. Certainly our programme is a full one, but as a player and as a manager I've always felt that there is only one way to go into a season... and that's to try to win every game, going flat out. When you are three or four goals up then you can think about changing gear. While we are in four major competitions we shall try to win four major competitions."

Mercer was clearly another who believed in Franny's Grand Slam idea of winning everything the Blues competed for.

The League Cup final was scheduled for 7th March against West Bromwich Albion. This was only three days after the Blues next European game and would present the Club with a few significant problems, however before all of that City still had the League campaign and the FA Cup to contemplate.

In the League, results were mixed although by 18th December City had managed to hold on to fourth place on 29 points - nine behind leaders Leeds. The chance of Franny's Grand Slam was still possible at this point.

As City moved into the 1970s the success of the previous few seasons and the prospect of more glory during the season gave everybody connected with the Club hope. Chairman Albert Alexander felt that City were once again one of English football's glamour clubs with tremendous support. He was proud of the turnaround the Club had enjoyed since the arrival of Mercer and Allison, and was pleased with the increased level of support. In the first 18 League and cup games played at Maine Road during the 1969-70 season the Blues averaged almost 40,000 supporters. With further success this was expected to increase further.

Malcolm Allison wanted more, however: "I feel the top average we could expect to get at the moment is 45,000 - and that's getting favourable weather and things like that. The public at the moment are at the stage when they are not quite sure what sort of a side we are. How good are City? It's the sort of question in various ways I'm often asked. People want to be convinced. I'm not upset by this. The big crowd clubs like Liverpool even had to work hard for their numbers. It's only in the last four or five years that they have had exceptionally large gates. To average a 50,000 gate we would have to be at the top for the next five years - and I mean right at the top."

In February, to cater for the ever-growing demand to watch the Blues secretary Walter Griffiths announced plans to redevelop the Scoreboard End terracing. The plan was to completely remove the original terracing and build a new £325,000 'North Stand' with a cantilever roof and space for 22,000 standing spectators in a series of concrete pens. Work would commence in the 1970 close season with the stand ready by August 1971.

In addition, there were plans to extend the Main Stand roof and seating to ensure it reached the corner flag, rather than end mysteriously some yards away. This would have meant an additional section of around 1,000 seats but would also have caused a rather awkward join in the roof, and proved to be rather expensive in relation to the number of spectators it could house. Eventually, the roof extension plan was abandoned, and the section remained roofless until the replacement of the Main Stand roof in the early 1980s.

By the time the development was outlined in the match programme, City had already played two games in the FA Cup. In the first game Hull City were defeated 1-0 with a Neil Young effort, then in the fourth round the Blues had to face Manchester United at Old Trafford. Sadly, the game ended 3-0 to the Reds, although the result may have actually turned out to be a blessing in disguise as City were already experiencing a fixture pile up as they pushed for an incredible hoard of trophies. By the end of the season the Blues played 61 first team games excluding friendlies. Incidentally both League games against United ended in victory, giving fans further proof that City were Manchester's dominant force.

Defeat in the FA Cup meant that Franny's Grand Slam was no longer a possibility. In addition a run of bad results in the League had seen the Blues plummet down the table. By 1st February they lay in 12th position - fifteen points off the bottom, sixteen from the top. All hopes of success lay in the ECWC and in the League Cup. Forty years later Lee remained convinced that City were right to be ambitious: "Well, we wanted to win every game so it seemed natural to me that we should go for all four. In the FA Cup we were odds on to win at Old Trafford because we'd beaten them so many times. We ended up suffering a rare defeat at United, but it was one of those we should really have won based on form and everything. We were doing okay in the League then we had a few injuries – Mike Summerbee, Colin Bell and Neil Young were injured at key times – otherwise I think we would have won three trophies. But the thing about the 'Grand Slam' was that it was the ambition of the place. I remember we were going to London on the train and could see Wembley, and I shouted to the lads to take a look because two of our 'Grand Slam' games would be played there!"

On 4th March City faced Academica Coimbra in the first leg of the European Cup Winners' Cup quarter final in Portugal. The press believed that Mercer and Allison would try to protect their players during this game as the League Cup final would be played only three days later, but Mercer disagreed: "We want to win the League Cup on Saturday, but we also want to win the Cup Winners'

Cup. So it won't be a case of holding anything back for Wembley. A powerful performance can put us on the way to victory against West Bromwich. Defeat tonight could be demoralising."

Coimbra were believed to be a very weak side - a view that many press men held - and their own coach Julio Pereira stated they would be easily outclassed by City, especially as their side was allegedly made up of university students. Mindful of what had occurred with Fenerbahce, the City management refused to listen.

Both Mercer and Allison were right to dismiss the comments as a grim match ended goalless. It was watched by a surprisingly low crowd of only 15,000. When City officials quizzed their Portuguese opposite numbers they discovered that the match was being shown live on local television and that many of the home fans had decided to watch it from the comfort of their own homes.

During the game City's trainer, former player Dave Ewing, was sent from the touch line to the dressing room for shouting. He didn't miss much, and the Coimbra fans sat at home probably felt justified in their decision. As for City, they were happy to get the draw. Mercer smiled afterwards: "It was not a classic, was it?"

If the game itself had brought little joy the following 24 hours or so would bring despair. The City party stayed on in Portugal after the match believing it would help them relax. Unfortunately, the plan backfired. While West Bromwich Albion lay in their Surrey hotel relaxing in preparation for the League Cup Final, the Blues were struggling to get home. An airport strike and appalling weather had caused the flight to be delayed and diverted from London to Birmingham. The players were weary, and eventually arrived back in England a mere thirty-six hours before the Wembley kick-off. The journey from Portugal had taken over ten hours and left everyone tired.

On the Friday, City delayed their pitch inspection until late afternoon to help the players rest. When they arrived at the stadium they could not believe the state of the pitch. The previous year it had been a "cabbage patch", now it was much worse as workmen covered the turf with straw to protect it from the freezing conditions. Although he didn't express his feelings to the players or the media, Mercer felt the conditions would prove too tiring for his players. Nevertheless, he desperately wanted success and told the press: "We are not afraid of the pitch. We've played well on such pitches in the past."

For the Final, Neil Young was dropped. He had spent the previous day celebrating the birth of his daughter and the loss of his Cup Final place was not really a surprise. Glyn Pardoe wore the number seven shirt with George Heslop returning to the side to play alongside Tommy Booth. On paper it appeared a rather defensive

formation, although neither Mercer nor Allison expected the game to be a defensive stalemate.

Once again, Allison was forced to watch the match from the stands. Mercer had asked the FA for a reprieve of the touchline ban, but they would have none of it. City found their outspoken coach a place in the stands, along with those supporters lucky enough to have bought one of the 32,000 tickets allocated to the Blues.

The game commenced with City once again in their successful red and black striped shirts, although the first five minutes hardly proved successful as West Bromwich raced to a one goal lead. Tony Book, continually being harassed by Albion's star man Jeff Astle, pushed a pass back which ended up going for a corner. From Bobby Hope's corner kick the ball was cleared to Ray Wilson, Albion's left back, who then sent a curving cross into the box. City should have cleared the danger, but they hesitated leaving goalkeeper Corrigan exposed.

Amid the City paralysis Jeff Astle, who in the 1990s enjoyed regular appearances as the singer on BBC's Fantasy Football League programme, headed home for Albion. It was a devastating blow for the large army of City supporters, however the men in red and black quickly gained control of the match. Tony Book: "That early goal was a tremendous boost for Albion, but it came so early that it didn't seriously worry us for we had another 85 minutes to wipe it out."

In the 20th minute, Francis Lee crossed to Mike Summerbee right in front of the Albion goal, who seemed certain to score. Sadly, John Talbut dashed in to clear. Then from a Pardoe corner, Albion's 'keeper John Osborne completely missed the ball and Lee sent it narrowly wide with a tumbling header. The equaliser seemed ever closer, especially as Oakes and Doyle were dominating the midfield.

Despite City's efforts the deficit remained into the interval, although in the 27th minute a courageous dive from the developing Corrigan prevented Albion from scoring a second.

In the second half a powerful City searched for an equaliser, then in the 60th minute the inevitable occurred. From a Pardoe corner, Summerbee, who moments earlier had been writhing in agony, got a foot to the ball and hooked it goalwards. Bell headed across to the unmarked Doyle who slid home the equaliser. It was certainly a thoroughly deserved goal.

Shortly afterwards Mike Summerbee was forced to leave the field with a hairline fracture of the leg. He was replaced by Ian Bowyer, while a little later Albion brought on Dick Krzywicki for future Blue Asa Hartford. At one point Tony Book and Jeff Astle were cautioned by the referee as both sides displayed a more physical approach.

Joe Corrigan was keen to prevent Albion from scoring again, as he revealed later: "I was given a real

Glyn Pardoe (11) scores in the League Cup final and later celebrates (below) with Joe Mercer and the other scorer Mike Doyle.

roasting at half time because of that goal but after the equaliser I was determined another shot was not going to pass me."

Francis Lee, playing the game many believe to be the best of his career, came close on a number of occasions, but the Final was forced to enter extra-time. Although the conditions and the events of the previous few days affected the players, extra-time helped to prove that Malcolm Allison had been right to push the players hard in training. His attempts to build up their level of fitness were to prove beneficial at Wembley.

Ian Bowyer remembered Allison's attempts at improving fitness and the psychology of the game: "He brought in renowned, successful athletes and athletic coaches – Joe Lancaster and Derek Ibbotson for example – to make us the fittest side. Totally unheard of at the time, and we'd be worked really hard on a Monday. Mondays at most clubs were 'take it easy' days, but not at City. I remember one Monday being at Maine Road with me and Derek Jeffries tapping the ball to each other across the pitch – not on the pitch that wasn't allowed, so we were on the track with the ball going over the pitch – and then Malcolm came up the tunnel and told us we were off to Wythenshawe Park for training. Our mood dropped. We'd be sat in the car being taken to Wythenshawe and I dreaded it. Before I had my strength it was really hard. Eventually I came through it and was far better for it. Allison's approach was revolutionary. He used to do short, sharp sessions which were unheard of at the time. Malcolm was way ahead of everyone else and it's true that his ideas have only recently become the standard.

"Malcolm had so many ideas. He'd tell us that something he'd come up with was scientifically based and we'd believe him. We'd want to believe him and wouldn't question what he said. One day he came in with some new training shoes. He told us they were specially designed to help you through the last 20 minutes – he was obsessive about ensuring our fitness kicked in for the last 20 minutes when other sides tended to fail. Whether the shoes were any better or not I don't know, but we believed him so I guess from a psychological point of view if nothing else he got the results he wanted."

At Wembley Allison's efforts paid off as the City men dominated the additional thirty minutes. In the 102nd minute Francis Lee was able to chip the ball to Colin Bell, despite being confronted by two Albion defenders. Bell back-heeled to Pardoe, who flicked the ball over the Albion goal line to give City a 2-1 lead.

Pardoe was justifiably pleased with his performance: "Wembley is not a bad place to score your first goal of the season! I feel I am really suited to this midfield role because it gets me more involved in the game. I thought I played one of my best ever games and once the equaliser had gone in there was never any doubt about who would win."

The additional goal was enough, as Pardoe suggested, and at the final whistle the customary celebrations began. Francis Lee deserved more acclaim than most after an absolutely brilliant performance. David Meek, writing in the *Manchester Evening News* was glowing in his praise: "At Wembley we saw just how dangerous Lee in full cry can be. He took a tremendous physical pounding yet never flinched. City just could not have lost the League Cup with such a performance in their midst.

"The ex-Bolton man who made his League debut at the age of 16 is still only 25 and it looks as if his career, in which he has many caps to come, could reach its peak in Mexico this summer. He could play as big a part in England's fortunes as he did for City at Wembley this weekend. Certainly Albion had no answer except a great display by goalkeeper John Osborne."

The City victory gave the Blues a place in the Fairs Cup and meant that Manchester United's only chance of playing in Europe would come if City also found success in the European Cup Winners' Cup. At the time of the League Cup final United were aiming to qualify for Europe via League placing. Once City found success, United would be excluded as, at this time, only one team per city was allowed to enter the Fairs Cup. It was a ludicrous system, but one that well-known Red-hater Mike Doyle was able to joke about: "That's not bad for my new campaign and car stickers...'Keep United out of Europe.'"

Joe Mercer also found the affair amusing: "If we can win the Cup Winners' Cup and so qualify to defend it next season, maybe the authorities will let us flog our Fairs Cup place to the highest bidders."

In the end United's League form prevented them from finishing high enough to reach Europe regardless of City's performance.

On Sunday 8th March City embarked on another tour of Manchester, before a civic reception at the Town Hall. In appalling weather City's loyal fans once again turned out to see their heroes but, unlike the previous seasons, the Blues still had a chance of further success. Many fans must have wondered just how far this great side could go. Within eight weeks they would find the answer.

On 18th March the Blues were due to play Coimbra in the second leg of their Cup Winners' Cup quarter final tie. Before that, however, on 11th they had to entertain Crystal Palace at Maine Road. The game ended in a disappointing 1-0 defeat and was not the kind of preparation the Blues needed for a crucial European tie. Nevertheless they went in to their match with Coimbra believing they held the advantage. A victory at Maine Road seemed almost inevitable, although it was a difficult game.

Colin Bell and George Heslop were injured during the match, and City were prevented from playing the kind of football they enjoyed. Tony Towers and Chris Glennon came on as replacements, but other players went down injured, including Mike Doyle who had to be carried off. Showing his typical fighting spirit Doyle returned to action a little later in the match.

It was looking like another goalless draw as the tie entered extra time, and little separated the sides. Then at around 9.45 pm. Neil Young sent a ball from the left to Towers. Towers had time to control the ball before his right foot shot sent it past the 19 year old Coimbra goalkeeper Cardoso. The goal brought a huge sigh of relief to the City faithful, and was enough to send the Blues into the semi-finals.

The next opponents were Schalke '04 of West Germany on 1st April. Schalke had once tried to sign Bert Trautmann, and rumours circulating during the late 1960s claimed that Schalke had been such a popular and successful club prior to World War Two that they were Adolf Hitler's favourite side. They had been seen by the Nazi regime in the 1930s as an example of their 'new' Germany, in as much as the side were very successful, though the 1960s comments by journalist Peter Gardner and others do not appear to be based on direct evidence that Hitler supported any team.

In 1969-70 Schalke were a formidable side, and in the first leg at Gelsenkirchen they won 1-0. Despite the scoreline, City had played well and were confident of success in the return fixture. The relatively inexperienced Derek Jeffries was drafted into defence and performed at a level better than expected, while Joe Corrigan played one of his best games of his first full season, although even his fine performance had no chance of saving Libuda's magnificent goal in the 77th minute.

In attack Bell, Young, and Lee all came close at one stage or another. In fact, Lee could quite easily have scored an hat trick had luck been on his side. This gave City hope for the second leg.

Before the return game, however, there were three difficult League matches to play in five days. On 4th April City were defeated 1-0 by Sunderland thanks to a strike from future Blue Dennis Tueart, then two days later at Crystal Palace they lost by the same scoreline, although the game was noteworthy as it saw the full League debut of Willie Donachie. Then on 8th the Blues managed to earn a no score draw against a Southampton side who needed the point to stay up. The Southampton defence was rarely troubled with the Blues best effort coming

Schalke's Reinhard Libuda and Tony Book swap gifts prior to their meeting at Gelsenkirchen.

from Lee. Sadly, his shot went wide of the goal and hit a policeman's helmet, providing much amusement but not the goal required.

And so came the vital European match on 15th April. The confidence the players felt after the first leg proved justified as City dominated the match, playing irresistible football. As early as the ninth minute Mike Doyle gave the Blues their opening goal, then five minutes later Neil Young controlled the ball superbly and sent home his first goal since the January FA Cup tie with Hull. In the 27th minute he scored his second, and then seven minutes into the second half Francis Lee scored City's fourth of the night.

Colin Bell made it five late on, and then in the final minute or so Libuda gave Schalke a consolation goal. This was the first real effort to trouble Corrigan, who was playing with a broken nose, all night City were on their way to Vienna for their first European final, although they did not find out who their opponents would be until seven days before the game itself. Gornik Zabrze of Poland eventually beat AS Roma of Italy in a replay in Strasbourg.

Before the final City had two League games left to complete their domestic programme. The first saw them defeat Leeds at Elland Road 3-1 with goals from Bell, Young and Towers. Prior to that match former Blue Don Revie lined up his players to applaud City's European exploits: "I am delighted City have got through and naturally I hope they win the trophy."

The final League game was away to struggling Sheffield Wednesday. The home side still had a chance of avoiding relegation and League records show that 43,893 turned up expecting salvation, they left deflated. City tore Wednesday apart, although the scoreline hardly reflected the true difference in the two sides. Ian Bowyer, replacing the injured Summerbee, scored first, but former Blue Tony Coleman pulled one back for the home side. In the final minute, Bowyer scored his second to send Wednesday down. It was a bitter blow for the Yorkshiremen and was the first in a series of disasters that would see them plummet to 20th position in the Third Division by 1976.

The 2-1 victory gave City a great boost, but it also brought more concern over players' fitness. Mike Summerbee, who had been struggling ever since the League Cup Final, was now unable to play in Vienna while Alan Oakes was to play but was far from fully fit.

The ECWC Final was played in the uncovered Prater Stadium in Vienna. Ian Bowyer: "For City supporters the European trips were great, but I felt so sorry for them that the final was in Vienna in that uncovered stadium with the rain pouring down."

In 2000 *Manchester Evening News* photographer Eric Graham remembered that the weather was an issue: "They only turned on two of the four floodlights for some reason, probably because there were only about 9000 fans in the stadium. The sports writers, in their posh sheepskin coats and expensive mohair suits were falling about laughing on the coach on the way to the stadium in the heavy rain, about how wet us poor 'snappers' were going to get - until they arrived at the ground and discovered that it had no roof!"

One member of the travelling media was the BBC's John Motson: "I was sent to Vienna to cover City's ECWC final against Gornik in 1970. As a rookie reporter desperate for an interview, I interrupted Joe Mercer's pre-match nap! He was kindness itself." Once awake

Mercer worked with Allison to prepare the side. He also had to suffer from the conditions like everybody else: "Managers, directors, press and fans alike had to brave the elements together in the open air. I had to sit there with rain running down my neck, my coat was saturated and my shoes were filled with water. But neither Malcolm Allison nor I would budge from that spot as we watched our players drive home their superiority."

That superiority was evident from the start. Then in the 12th minute Francis Lee's shot proved too much for goalkeeper Kostka to hold and Neil Young followed up to give the Blues the lead. Supporter John Jennings felt that the goal helped calm him and the other fans: "There were some nerves going to the game – Buzzer [Summerbee] was out injured, Oakes was on pain killers… That first goal saw some unbelievable skills from Franny Lee to set Young up."

Ian Bowyer was watching from the bench: "I think we always knew we'd win the game. It was the confidence from the top and the senior players that did it. I was the substitute and Mike Doyle went off injured four minutes after City had taken the lead, so when I came on it felt more of a containment job."

Mike Doyle suffered a badly damaged ankle tendon in a collision with Florenski. He was carried off on the shoulders of Dave Ewing.

Shortly before half-time City increased their lead when Young broke free in the centre. As he attempted to dribble through the penalty area he was brought down by Kostka, the Gornik 'keeper. The Austrian referee Schiller rightly awarded a penalty and inevitably Francis Lee sent a straight, hard shot into the net.

In the 68th minute Gornik's captain Oslizlo pulled one back, but City remained in overall control. This didn't stop some fans from feeling a little nervous late on, especially as the weather had deteriorated. Supporter Les Saul: "It was a big ground but had no cover at all. There were about ten thousand fans present about half being City supporters, the ground looked pretty empty but the City fans gave it some atmosphere. There were only about 300 Gornik fans as that was all that was allowed out of the country at that time.

"As it got near half time with a lead of 2-0 we were highly contented, the lights had gone on as it started to get dark. We thought that we could feel rain drops but as the weather had been so good during the day that we thought it was just a passing cloud, but no it got gradually heavier until it became a downpour. As there was no cover we just had to stay where we were. The second half started and the pitch started to churn up and become waterlogged. City found it hard going in the second half and after Gornik pulled one back we started to have doubts, however we finished winners in the end."

Francis Lee (top left) nets his penalty in the ECWC final. Dave Ewing carried an injured Mike Doyle off the pitch (above) and, on a bad night for photographers, this rare colour image shows a rain-sodden team celebrating.

At the final whistle the City fans, who numbered some four of five thousand in a crowd variously reported as anything from 7,968 to around 12,000, started the now customary celebrations.

Bowyer: "Winning that trophy was a great moment so early in my career. I think all the players just saw the successes as natural. Of course, we didn't win Franny's 'Grand Slam' but we didn't do too badly winning two major trophies in one season. I do remember getting carried away and chatting to Malcolm at the do that night. We were all getting bonuses – peanuts of course – but to a young lad it felt like I'd be a millionaire. I remember asking Malcolm: 'How much are e-type Jags?' Honestly! At that time a couple of players had them and I must have thought it was the thing a footballer should buy."

Goalkeeper Joe Corrigan was another young star: "Playing in the ECWC final was awesome. It was a terribly wet night and the crowd was low, but that didn't detract from the importance at all. To play in such a great side and at that level is a tremendous feeling but you have to keep your feet on the ground."

Many drenched but happy Blues raced onto the field as City became the first English side to achieve the double of winning a major domestic and European trophy in the same season. Leeds United had managed a similar feat in 1968, however Leeds' success had come in the Fairs Cup – with the final held over until 1968-69 – and the League Cup at a time when not all 92 clubs competed in the competition.

City's success was remarkable, especially when you consider the other achievements of the period. The Blues were well and truly a major force in the domestic game, although on the night of the Final the majority of the English public had been more concerned with the replayed FA Cup final between Chelsea and Leeds at Old Trafford. Had the FA Cup been resolved at Wembley, City's success would have been guaranteed major exposure across the nation.

After the game the players and staff enjoyed their end of season party. Mercer and Allison naturally joined in but they were not the main stars of the celebrations. Allison: "It was a great night. Perfect. Back at the hotel Harry Godwin, our Chief Scout, was playing the piano - all the old songs - while Francis Lee was on top, dancing away, in his underpants. It had to be seen to be believed. But that was the type of thing we did."

TRUE BLUE
Malcolm Allison

Regarded as the greatest coach of his generation, he embodied the new spirit that swept through the Club.

Some supporters managed to find their way into these celebrations, including Leicester based John Jennings: "I happened to bump into Tony Heap, a lad I knew from my St Bede's days, who casually mentioned that he was working in Germany and was translating for City that night! Obviously I had to go for a drink with him after the game. That night turned into a supporters dream. Instead of dancing in the fountains of Vienna I got a taxi to the Schonbrunn Park Hotel, and sat there speechless as the team celebrated their win. At one point I was sitting at a table with Joe Mercer, his wife and top sports writer J L Manning, and into the small hours it felt unreal to listen to Allison, Lee and everyone else as they 'relaxed'.

"I couldn't resist getting a few autographs, - the back of my match ticket was signed by Mercer and Allison, and a post card which I had written to my girlfriend in Leicester became much too valuable to post once it had the signatures of Bell, Lee, Summerbee, Mercer and Allison alongside mine!"

Les Saul was also celebrating: "After the game we managed to get a lift on one of the Supporters Club's coaches into the town centre. We took a couple of supporters from Middleton with us into our Hotel so that they could dry out and we could change our clothes. We all went into the centre of Vienna to celebrate after a meal we went into a bar where there was a gang of City supporters, the owner told us that they didn't allow singing in the bar. We were quiet a short time but after a few drinks the singing started, but the owner didn't seem to bother as everyone was in good mood. One of the lads in the bar showed us a shirt that he said Francis Lee had given him after the match, it had a number 11 on it. He cut part of it up and gave pieces to the City fans, I got a piece which I still have and I have checked it out with Francis who did agree that he gave the lad his shirt. I don't know what time we got to bed but it had been a fantastic day."

City returned home to another civic reception - their fourth since May 1968 - and a ten mile tour of the City, starting at the airport. Malcolm Allison was on top form and he made a speech to fans: "We are the greatest club in Manchester. I am only sorry ladies & gentlemen that we were unable to win more than two cups this year. We decided to let a London club (Chelsea) win something for a change!"

Major Trophies Won: The ECWC 1969-70, FA Cup 1968-69 & League Cup 1969-70
Highest League Attendance: 63,052 Manchester United, 17/08/68
Highest Cup Attendance: 60,844 Newcastle United, 29/01/69 (FA Cup)
Managers: 1965 (13 July) – 1971 (7 October, but continued as General Manager) Joe Mercer

Seasonal Record:

Season	League	Posn	FA Cup	League Cup	Other	Leading Scorer	Average Att.
1968-69	FL Div1	13	Winners	Rnd 3	European Cup Rnd 1 & Charity Shield Winners	Bell & Young 14	33,750
1969-70	FL Div1	10	Rnd 4	Winners	ECWC Winners & Charity Shield Runners-up	Lee 13	33,930

1969 FA CUP RUN

R3	Luton Town	H	W	1-0
R4	Newcastle United	A	D	0-0
	Newcastle United	H	W	2-0
R5	Blackburn Rovers	A	W	4-1
R6	Tottenham Hotspur	H	W	1-0
SF	Everton	N*	W	1-0
F	Leicester City	N**	W	1-0

*= Villa Park, Birmingham ** = Wembley Stadium

	P	W	D	L	F	A
HOME	3	3	0	0	4	0
AWAY	4	3	1	0	6	1
TOTAL	7	6	1	0	10	1

1970 LEAGUE CUP RUN

R2	Southport	A	W	3-0
R3	Liverpool	H	W	3-2
R4	Everton	H	W	2-0
R5	Queen's Park R	H	W	3-0
SF1	Manchester United	H	W	2-1
SF2	Manchester United	A	D	2-2
F	West Bromwich A	N**	W	2-1

** = Wembley Stadium

	P	W	D	L	F	A
HOME	4	4	0	0	10	3
AWAY	3	2	1	0	7	3
TOTAL	7	6	1	0	17	6

1970 ECWC CUP RUN

R1(1)	Atlético Bilbao	A	D	3-3
R1(2)	Atlético Bilbao	H	W	3-0
R2(1)	SK Lierse	A	W	3-0
R2(2)	SK Lierse	H	W	5-0
R3(1)	Academica Coimbra	A	D	0-0
R3(2)	Academica Coimbra	H	W	1-0
SF1	Schalke 04	A	L	0-1
SF2	Schalke 04	H	W	5-1
F	Gornik Zabrze	N***	W	2-1

*** = Prater Stadium, Vienna

	P	W	D	L	F	A
HOME	4	4	0	0	14	1
AWAY	5	2	2	1	8	5
TOTAL	9	6	2	1	22	6

FINAL DETAILS

26 April 1969 at Wembley Stadium
Manchester City 1-0 Leicester City
CITY: Dowd, Book, Pardoe, Doyle, Booth, Oakes, Summerbee, Bell, Lee, Young, Coleman. Substitute: Connor
LEICESTER CITY: Shilton, Rodrigues, Nish, Roberts, Woollett, Cross, Fern, Gibson, Lochhead, Clarke, Glover (Manley)
GOALS: Young
ATTENDANCE: 100,000
REFEREE: G McCabe (Sheffield)
MANAGER: Joe Mercer
CAPTAIN: Tony Book

FINAL DETAILS

7 March 1970 at Wembley Stadium
Manchester City 2-1 West Bromwich Albion
CITY: Corrigan, Book, Mann, Doyle, Booth, Oakes, Heslop, Bell, Summerbee (Bowyer), Lee, Pardoe
WEST BROMWICH ALBION: Osborne, Fraser, Wilson, Brown, Talbut, Kaye, Cantello, Suggett, Astle, Hartford (Krzywicki), Hope.
GOALS: Pardoe, Doyle, Astle
ATTENDANCE: 97,963
REFEREE: V James (York)
MANAGER: Joe Mercer
CAPTAIN: Tony Book

FINAL DETAILS

29 April 1970 at Prater Stadium, Vienna
Manchester City 2-1 Gornik Zabrze
CITY: Corrigan, Book, Pardoe, Doyle (Bowyer), Booth, Oakes, Heslop, Bell, Lee, Young, Towers
WEST BROMWICH ALBION: Kostka, Latocha, Oslizlo, Gorgan, Florenski (Deja), Szoltysik, Wilczek (Skowrone), Olek, Banas, Lubanski, Szarynbiski
GOALS: Young, Lee, Oslizlo
ATTENDANCE: Variously reported as anything from 7,968 to 12,000
REFEREE: P Schiller (Austria)
MANAGER: Joe Mercer
CAPTAIN: Tony Book

A full bloodied Maine Road derby. Joe Corrigan dives at the feet of Sammy McIlroy, 6th November 1971.

1970-1973
Premature End

"Had I known these people were involved
I would never have entertained the idea
of transferring my shares. There have
been personality clashes in the past. I am
remaining loyal to the Board."

Vice-chairman Frank Johnson when he discovered some of the people
behind the proposed takeover in November 1970.

1970-1971 Takeover Madness

Following the successes of 1969-70, fans could be
forgiven if they appeared optimistic about the chance
of further glory. City were one of the most attractive,
entertaining sides in Europe and had won many
admirers. Their hard-core support was on the increase
and the media were at long last taking notice of events
in Manchester 14.

It seemed that the Blues just could not fail. However,
the events that followed jeopardised City's position of
dominance and ultimately affected the Club for the
following thirty years or more.

It all started to go wrong shortly after the time of the
European Cup Winner's Cup success. Malcolm Allison
was finding it difficult playing a supporting role. He felt
he deserved the position of Team Manager, and believed

that right at the start of their partnership Joe Mercer had
promised to stand aside by August 1968. That never
occurred, however it must be remembered that Allison
had been intent on leaving City on several occasions
including in October 1967 when he agreed to take the
Coventry City job. Ultimately, he remained at Maine
Road, but his own desire to move was never made an
issue by Mercer. In fact Mercer did all he could to ensure
it was never held against Allison.

Allison felt differently: "I was not satisfied with the
way the Club was being run. I felt the Club had become
big, but that the people in control in the Boardroom had
not grown with it. I liked and admired Albert Alexander,
the little, twinkling Chairman, but some of the people
around him staggered me with their lack of vision. The
secretary Walter Griffiths and I were often in dispute
and the Board would back him on small administrative

matters, like the size of hotel bills. I used to think to myself, 'What is all this, I've helped lift this club from the grave and now I get this sort of treatment.'"

Typical of the attitude that annoyed Allison was Secretary Griffith's response to problems encountered with crowd congestion at the first couple of home matches in August 1971. The Scoreboard End was now closed for redevelopment, reducing the capacity, and putting 18 turnstiles out of action. Naturally, supporters had to endure longer queues than normal and search for new vantage points, but instead of apologising to spectators or offering some kind of assistance, Griffiths felt the responsibility lay entirely with City's loyal fans: "If people could try to get here a little bit earlier it would help everyone, most of all themselves."

Obviously, he had a point, but the approach seemed wrong. Allison felt City were still a small team and believed that the whole attitude of the Club needed to be brought into the 1970s. He wanted City to be the biggest club in the world and felt that a dramatic shake up was the only way this could occur: "I had had enough of being patted on the head. I thought that if I was not going to be given what was my due, I would attempt to take it for myself."

Nothing public occurred for a while, and the new season began with the Blues determined to make an impact on the League. By 10th September after six games City were in second place behind Leeds United, and had earned many positive headlines. Dave Horridge (*Daily Mirror*): "Manchester City have used the experience gained in becoming England's top knock-out trophy experts to emerge as potential League Champions again."

After the 4-1 victory over West Bromwich Albion the *Daily Telegraph's* Frank Green wrote: "So immensely superior were City that, at half time, a colleague in the Press Box forecast a final score of 6-1 - a not unreasonable assessment considering City twice had strong claims for a penalty rejected."

Bob Russell (*Daily Mirror*): "England boss Sir Alf Ramsey, checking among other things the Young England prospects of 18 year old City defender Tony Towers, must have sensed that Bell is already on the brink of greatness."

England Youth player Towers had already received a great deal of praise after a few fine performances, with one reporter comparing him with England's great captain Bobby Moore. Despite the praise Towers himself remained level headed: "I've got to keep working at everything. I get some stick on and off the field, but I don't mind - as long as I am playing. I'm enjoying myself. During games I quite often get players on the other side saying things like, 'How do you manage to get in this team!' and other things to put you off."

With Towers, Bell and the bulk of the side playing

well, the Blues remained undefeated in the League until 26th September when they lost 2-0 at Tottenham. Earlier in the month City's bid to retain the League Cup ended at the first hurdle with a 2-1 defeat at Carlisle. Allison: "We probably made more mistakes against Carlisle than in all our other games put together. I was very disappointed."

On 16th September City faced Linfield of Northern Ireland in the first round of the Cup Winner's Cup, determined to perform better than against Carlisle. The game ended 1-0 in Belfast with a goal from the ever-improving Colin Bell, but the return game caused a little concern especially when it looked likely that Francis Lee would be missing. The England striker was suffering with an inflamed groin and looked doubtful, causing Mercer to consider using youngster Ian Bowyer. Bowyer had first appeared for City during the 1968-69 season and for a period during 1969 deservedly became acclaimed by the press. At one point Alf Ramsey commented favourably about Bowyer's play, however a few poor games and minor setbacks made the player an easy target for sections of the City crowd. In 2010 Bowyer looked back on this period: "I didn't let it get to me particularly. I always thought that fans were entitled to give you a bit of stick. I was about 18 or 19 and didn't really see anything wrong with it. It was part and parcel of the game and, at that age, I didn't think about it in the way older players may have done. Looking back on it now, I don't think it would happen in the same way. I'd played about 50 games at that point and my form was struggling a bit. Nowadays a player would be sent out on loan to get good experience in a different environment before coming back to kick on to the next level. Back then, with less substitutions and fewer opportunities for loans, you'd be dropped – that would be picked up – and then you'd have to return to the side when perhaps someone else was injured."

Bowyer had started his career with a great goalscoring ratio but criticism had begun to come his way during the 1969-70 season: "I couldn't sustain the strike rate of 6 goals in 8 games and so it must have had a bearing. But there was only really one game when I got real stick. West Ham 21st March 1970 – Jimmy Greaves' debut. It was the game Joe Corrigan kicked the ball out and Ronnie Boyce volleyed it back over his head for a goal. So it was a nightmare of a day and we got beat 5-1 with Greaves scoring twice on his debut. The game was shown on Match Of the Day – a rarity in those days – so that highlighted the situation further. I was 18 and didn't have a good game. It never really got to me.

"There was only one time when it did affect me actually and that was on match day but before a game. I parked at the car park at Maine Road and had to walk to the players' entrance. As I walked someone gave me abuse all the way to the door. I went in to the dressing

DAILY EXPRESS Tuesday November 24 1970

TAKE-OVER MEN

PHOTO SPORT ...features the men who seek to take control of Manchester City. From the left: Chris Muir, Simon Cussons, Joe Smith, Michael Horwich and Ian Niven.

How much different would City's history have been had this takeover not occurred? Within three years Mercer & Allison had both gone and Peter Swales was chairman.

room really down – the game hadn't even started and I hadn't even kicked the ball. That hurt."

Bowyer became very much a fringe player and was transferred to Orient during the close season. Later in his career he did find success, spending more or less a decade at Nottingham Forest and winning the European Cup twice: "Personally, I don't think I could have had the success at Forest had it not been for the grounding I got at City at the start of my career. In such a short period of time I saw the highs and lows of the game."

Francis Lee did manage to play against Linfield but City were defeated 2-1 in Belfast with Colin Bell scoring a vital late goal to put them through on the away goals rule. The draw for the next round meant a difficult trip behind the Iron Curtain to Hungary's Honved in the first leg. Francis Lee scored the only goal of the match, but the score should have been considerably better. Derek Potter (*Daily Express*): "Glimpses of high quality skill allied to aggressive running saw Manchester City probe and pound Honved into submission in the Kispest Stadium. It could have been five following one of City's best ever displays."

Another report claimed that City had eight good goal attempts in the first half and a further seven in the second, and were without doubt in full control of the match. Despite the dominance Tony Book felt that the Blues had to be careful in the return match: "I think Honved had a bad day in the first leg. I'm sure that they can be a much better side. Just because we are leading by one goal it would be a mistake to assume that it is all over. It's not over yet by a long chalk."

The official attendance in Budapest was recorded as 14,000, although other sources believed the real gate was closer to 6,000. The City officials agreed and consulted their opposite numbers, but the Hungarians were adamant the crowd was the higher figure, although they did concede that it was considerably lower than expected. They put this down to the fact that the game was shown live on state television, and that the afternoon kick-off prevented many from attending. Whatever the truth, the atmosphere and attendance at Maine Road would be better.

In appalling conditions, a crowd of almost 29,000 witnessed more domination from the Manchester men. Bell and Lee provided the goals as City won 2-0, but at one point there was concern that the game might get abandoned. Tony Book: "I'd been scared right from the start that the referee might call off the game. The rain was getting heavier. That really was our only worry. Of course, we adapted ourselves to the conditions better than they did, but even in the first 15 minutes, when the conditions were comparatively good, we were hitting them with everything. If the ground had stayed reasonably firm I am sure we would have murdered them."

The game had not been without its moments of concern for the faithful, but in the main City were in control. Shortly before the interval Colin Bell and Honved right-winger Sandor Pinter leapt together for the ball, with Bell falling to the ground injured. He was stretchered off but, as the players lined up for the second half, he reappeared to a typical City ovation.

After the game Honved manager Kalman Preiner was asked if he thought the game should have been allowed to continue. He stated that the conditions were appalling but conceded that City were able to adapt superbly, whereas his side could not. He added: "If they go on playing like this they must surely be favourites for the trophy."

City could now have a rest from European football

until March when they would face old adversaries Gornik Zabrze in the quarter final. The draw excited the Manchester public, but before the game could take place politics dominated the Club. Allison, tired of playing second fiddle, wanted control. In his autobiography, *The Colours of My Life*, he claimed to have set the wheels in motion for a takeover of the Blues: "I knew that the City Vice-Chairman Frank Johnson was ready to sell a huge chunk of shares for £100,000 and that the man who bought them had only to make one or two available alliances and he would win control of the Club. So I said to Ian Niven, a fanatical City supporter: 'Find me a man with £100,000, and we will get control of the Club'. Niven came up with the man within a fortnight, Joe Smith, a double glazing tycoon from Oldham."

On Monday 23rd November, two days after a brace from Lee gave City victory over West Ham, the takeover became national news. 78 year old Chairman Albert Alexander awoke to find Joe Smith waiting for him: "I hadn't had my breakfast when he called on me. I told my wife to ask him to wait while I washed and shaved, and then I went downstairs and asked him straight out to put his cards on the table. I didn't recognise him. In effect he came to me as a stranger.

"As far as I know, he has no shares in the Club at the moment. If he had, I would know about them. But I understand he is in a position to acquire the necessary number to gain control. I asked him if he had much support and he said he had, and that his supporters were known to me."

Alexander said he was ready for a fight: "All I can say is that if anyone tries it, they will find I am a very tough nut to crack. We have had similar crises before and I have weathered them."

At this point in history, there were a total of 2,000

Francis Lee in action during the Blues 1-1 draw with Newcastle on 3rd October 1970.

shares in the Club. Alexander possessed 560, his son Eric held 27, while Frank Johnson seemed ready to sell 508 of his 521 allocation. Joe Smith claimed that with Johnson's shares he and his backers could obtain a total of 800 immediately and, as there were around 300 'missing' shares, he would have control. The following day every newspaper covered the story in detail, with Joe Smith quoted everywhere. The *Daily Express* went further than most when it devoted its famous William Hickey page to Smith, in addition to covering the story on both its front and back pages. The takeover was sensational news at the time, with arguably England's most successful club of the period about to be torn apart. The public could not believe it. It wasn't seen as good news, nor was it really viewed as being bad for the Club, it was simply a shock.

Backing Smith were a group of four. They were 46 year old Ian Niven, landlord of the Fletcher's Arms in Denton; 27 year old Simon Cussins, a member of the 'Imperial Leather' soap manufacturing family; 48 year old Michael Horwich, a Manchester solicitor and alleged friend of Malcolm Allison; and 41 year old newsagent Chris Muir, a former City director who had been forced off the Board the year before for what the *Daily Sketch* described as "an illegal action."

In articles about 51 year old Smith he claimed that he came from a poor family and hadn't been able to pay to watch the Blues. Instead, at the age of six, he had waited outside Maine Road until the gates were opened near the end of each game. Then he would rush inside to catch the final ten minutes of action The picture painted was one of a loyal City supporter, and there was no doubt that he loved the Club. He also had a knack for making money but claimed that his life needed a new interest: "I have a lovely house, a £5,500 American car, a luxury caravan and a boat on Windermere. Money is funny. All of a sudden you realise you are rich and for weeks you feel very excited. But it starts getting boring when you realise you can buy anything, there's nothing to fight for. So I go on setting myself challenges. All I want now is to see Manchester City become the greatest club there has ever been or ever will be in the world."

Malcolm Allison liked what he heard, especially when Smith expressed his support for him: "I will do my utmost, everything in my power, to co-operate in any way in any project with Mr. Allison to better the Club. He is the greatest man in football."

Allison's role was one which left him open to criticism from the existing Board. The City coach made no attempt to hide his involvement nor his participation in discussions with the consortium. If Smith's vision was to turn City into the World's greatest club then this matched perfectly with Allison's view. The problem was that the takeover was always more likely to paralyse the Club for a short while at least. Smith's vision may have been perfect, but achieving that would take considerable effort. Ultimately, Smith never succeeded in achieving his vision of turning City into the World's greatest club.

City's ECWC success was something many Mancunians wanted to be a part of. Some had seen how United's quest for the European Cup in the mid to late 1960s had grown their fan base significantly. Crowds had rocketed from 33,358 in 1961-62 to 57,552 in 1967-68 (an all-time high at this point though not bettered until 1999-2000). However, what those desperate for the growth to occur at Maine Road had overlooked was that United's popularity had increased as a result of the ten year journey from the Munich Air Disaster to European Cup winners. The story of United's recovery had added a level of interest throughout the decade.

At Maine Road sustained or continuing success would have the same impact over time, but those desperate for glory could not wait. Player Ian Bowyer, talking in 2010, recognised this: "There was always the thing with United. We'd win the League, they'd get the European Cup, but I have to say that we were the top dogs in Manchester. No question. If City could have sustained that then who knows how great the Club, not just the team, could have become. They wouldn't have needed to sustain it for twenty years. Another five years would have been enough. The spin-offs and so on would have made Manchester City as big as Manchester United are today. A side renowned around the world."

Sadly, although many of the fans and players recognised this, those seeking to gain control felt that the Club was not receiving the kind of support it deserved, nor did they feel that City were a truly great side. Success had increased crowds and City were on a par with Liverpool and Leeds - two of the era's greatest clubs - but some felt more had to be done at Board level to achieve greatness. Mercer was also keen to see City dominate European football, however his comments seemed more achievable and more realistic: "When I first came to City with Malcolm Allison we found everyone was obsessed with a jealousy about Manchester United. We decided that we must emulate them. We have not done too badly, winning everything we have gone in for. But support is a traditional thing. If we can keep winning things for the next five years I would expect our ground to be full every week."

Mercer's views were sensible. He clearly knew what

TRUE BLUE
Albert Alexander

Albert Alexander was the second generation of his family to play a key part in the Blues' history. He was chairman during City's glory years of the late 60s and early 70s and became the President for life. His son Eric became City chairman as well.

he was talking about. The pity was that those seeking to establish control of the Club held different views to the man who had guided City to their greatest successes so far.

On Tuesday 24th November, the Board met to consider the takeover. The meeting was a stormy affair, but the result was a pleasing one for Albert Alexander. Frank Johnson was persuaded not to sell his shares and afterwards he told the media that his about turn was simply because he felt he had been conned into the deal. He was quite prepared to sell to Smith, but was not happy that Michael Horwich and former director Chris Muir were supporting Smith: "Had I known these people were involved I would never have entertained the idea of transferring my shares. There have been personality clashes in the past."

Naturally, Smith was determined and claimed to have a signed agreement from Johnson. It was all becoming very messy and was destined to become a long battle, especially when Chris Muir, with 103 shares, announced: "It may take a day, it may take a week, it may take a few months, but eventually we will be in control."

Little Albert Alexander was particularly disturbed by the situation: "I'm very distressed about the way this thing has been handled. I didn't know the full extent of the other people backing Mr. Smith until this morning. There is no place for them here at Maine Road. When he saw me on Monday to disclose his plans Mr. Smith did not name the others. I now see I was being smooth-talked."

Despite the concern, Alexander still found time to laugh. After a couple of days of being pestered by the media he reminded the reporters of the previous week's top story: "I don't know - it was all Miss World last week, and it's all Albert Alexander this week!"

The comment caused a little amusement at the time, but unlike the story that Jennifer Hosten from Grenada had become Miss World, the Alexander-City takeover story would rumble on for some time. The takeover became a long difficult and confusing battle, and seriously affected the atmosphere within the Club. Allison: "I took the players for a short training session on the Friday afternoon. We were due to play Leeds United at Leeds the following day. The players were a little hostile towards me. Francis Lee, Mike Summerbee, and Colin Bell came to me and said, 'Why try to change the Club, Malcolm? We have done well. You do not change something that works'. I was very much out on a limb."

The Mercer-Allison partnership was also strained with the two men on opposite sides of the takeover. Allison was desperate for change, Mercer remained loyal to Alexander - the man who had given him and Allison the opportunity to prove their abilities. After a night of deep thought, Mercer told Allison he would support him but the comment was too late to really save the relationship.

Understandably after the hassles of the previous week City were defeated 1-0 by Leeds. Afterwards, at around 6pm in an Elland Road corridor Alexander told Allison that the Board had decided to sack him. It was not a shock, but Allison was surprised when Mercer arrived to warn the Chairman: "If he goes, I go!". That threat caused a change of mind and Allison was reinstated, but the partnership could hardly continue for any length of time.

The takeover seriously affected City's chance of League success. Only four of the twenty-four League games that followed the Leeds match ended in victory and the Blues slid down the table. In the FA Cup a 72nd minute goal from Bell brought victory over Wigan in the third round, followed by a 3-0 win at Chelsea. Sadly a home defeat by Arsenal - described by Arsenal captain Frank McLintock as "a 2-1 massacre" - ended all hope of a Wembley appearance. Nevertheless, the Blues were still in Europe.

In March they travelled to Poland, taking their own food supplies, and were defeated 2-0 by an impressive Gornik side. Allison was disappointed but realised: "We didn't play too badly, but nothing went right for us. We were all right at the back but there was nothing coming up front. That was a great goal by Lubanski. The second one was a bit unfortunate.

"I know how good this Polish side is... they are much better than probably the general public appreciate. I would rate Lubanski as a world class player ... one of the best three in the world in his role. He likes to play just behind the centre-forward and go through all the time."

The second leg again ended 2-0 to the home side and so with the aggregate score at 2-2 a replay was arranged in Copenhagen. These were the days before penalty shoot-outs were the norm. Controversy surrounded the match with Gornik's President, Ernest Wyra, demanding that City's players be tested for drugs after the replay. He claimed that they'd taken drugs during the second leg and wanted to see the Blues punished. Mercer became angry and accused the Poles of trying to put City off their game. Nevertheless, UEFA listened to Gornik's gripes and the Blues were forced to accept the tests.

City won the game 3-1 with goals from Booth, Lee and Young. Then came a dope testing fiasco. Colin Bell, David Connor and Derek Jeffries, the three players whose names had been drawn out of a hat, were unable to provide Urine samples. Orange juice was given to the men, but still no luck. Then Allison tried to lighten the atmosphere a little. He picked up a bottle of champagne, demanded entry into the medical room, then returned a few seconds later laughing: "They won't allow them to have this!"

Eventually, samples were produced and the tests were negative, but the whole affair seemed scandalous at the time. Despite the controversy City were through to the semi-finals for the second year in succession. Their opponents would be FA Cup winners' Chelsea on April 14th at Stamford Bridge and 28th at Maine Road.

Around this time Allison had been in trouble once again with the FA and was banned from all football activity for a couple of months, leaving Mercer in total control of the side and causing further friction between the two men.

Immediately prior to the first leg the Blues suffered with an incredible number of injuries. By the time of the match Summerbee, Oakes, Heslop, Bell and Doyle were all on the injury list alongside long term invalid Pardoe. It was always going to be difficult to prepare for the match against such a strong English side, but with so many injuries Mercer had to hope for a bit of luck. In addition to those out of action, other players were suffering. Goalkeeper Joe Corrigan was particularly brave, and actually played against Chelsea with his left eye half-closed and badly bruised.

Understandably, City were forced to play a defensive game and managed to keep the score down to a 1-0 defeat away from home. Mercer was pleased: "We had to play it in a negative way to some extent and it was a very difficult match, but it went more or less as we planned it, and Joe Corrigan in particular was magnificent. We made one mistake and we lost, but we showed that we know a bit about defensive football, and you don't learn it all on the Continent."

More players were missing from the second leg, which was played 48 hours after a 2-2 draw with Liverpool in the League. Corrigan and Booth were both out with Ron Healey taking the goalkeeper's place. Unfortunately, two minutes before half-time, Healey turned an inswinging free kick from Chelsea's Keith Weller into his own net. It was the only goal and Chelsea won 2-0 on aggregate, ending City's dream of becoming the first side to retain the trophy - a feat no side ever managed. Chelsea went on to defeat Real Madrid in the final.

Mercer was disappointed, while Allison was angry. He felt that Mercer should have approached the European games differently, and saw this period as more or less the end of the partnership: "The worst moment was when I was suspended and we were playing Chelsea in the Cup Winners' Cup semi. I said to Joe when we play Newcastle don't play Doyley, and don't play Colin Bell. In

Wearing City's away kit Lee makes his way on to Maine Road's pitch for the ECWC semi-final with Chelsea.

fact I told him to leave out three players for this League match, which wasn't a very important game. Remember I was suspended and Joe was in complete control of the team. In the end Joe played them all because he wanted to win the match. Two of them got injures and they couldn't play in the semi-final, and I was really, really annoyed at him. Really angry. He wanted to win it without my advice because, well, we've all got egos and he perhaps wanted to prove he could do it without me. I told him that he was foolish, but now thinking about it I probably would have done the same thing. Even so, at the time I was really annoyed because those players wouldn't be playing in the semi-final... and it probably cost us the game. It was the blackest moment for me."

A season that promised so much ended trophyless with City in 11th position. Events off the field had dominated too much and it was obvious to all that a solution to the Boardroom wrangles had to be found. For City supporter and Altrincham businessman Peter Swales an opportunity to help the crisis appeared: "I went into a pub in Hale Barns and saw sat in the Lounge City directors John Humphreys and Sidney Rose. I wasn't even 40 then, probably about 38. Full of myself, of course. Knew everything... doing well in business. I'd been at Altrincham Football Club for a couple of years and doing quite well there. I saw these two sat there and I thought 'this is an opportunity'. So I went over to them, and I said, point blank, 'you know all this trouble you're having, I could sort that out for you'. They asked 'how would you do it?' and I just said 'give me the opportunity and I'll do it'.

"Now, I thought that would be the last I'd ever hear, but about three or four days later - they found out about me through business and through football, I'd been involved with the Oldham Premier league and things - I got a call from Albert Alexander and he said 'what's your idea to sort it out?' I had no bloody idea, none whatsoever! So I said 'just let me talk to both parties' and it went from there. I worked with Joe Smith's gang and got on well with them, and with the other side. I did a lot of talking and I managed to settle it. As a result of that I became a director - like the man in between. I had no shares - I think I had ten which they gave me to become a director - for many years. I didn't get any volume of shares until well into the 80s."

It is worth highlighting that some of the other directors, including Eric Alexander, dispute Peter Swales' interpretation of events. In Alexander's biography, published in 2009, he reports that two directors, Sidney Rose and John Humphreys, approached Swales about joining City's Board. Swales became a director in April 1971, but the takeover was not resolved immediately.

1971-1972 Mistreating Mercer

By the time the new season opened on 14th August 1971 Joe Smith and Simon Cussons had become directors. Significantly, there was no place for Michael Horwich, Chris Muir, and Ian Niven, although the latter did make it by the end of February, and Muir followed the following season.

On the playing side Wyn Davies was signed for £52,500 from Newcastle, making his debut in the opening day 1-0 defeat to Leeds, but the Blues were still struggling with injuries. Glyn Pardoe, who had broken his leg after a tackle by George Best in the December 1970 derby match, was still fighting his way back to full fitness. The injury had been quite severe and had almost cost him his leg, but the player tried to remain positive and had attempted to build a routine: "I've been at the ground every day since pre-season training started doing what exercises I could. It's felt pretty good under the plaster. I can get plenty of movement... and the plaster was left on just that little bit longer to make sure. It's not been much of a summer, though."

In 2004 Pardoe talked of the moment when the injury occurred: "I knew very little at the time. It was the December 1970 game at Old Trafford and there was a collision between me and George Best. Apparently I broke my leg and an artery was trapped, but I have no memory of what followed. I've been told that I was within twenty minutes of losing my leg. They had decided that removing my leg would save my life, but fortunately the operation they eventually did meant that

my leg was saved as well. I was in a daze for at least four or five hours and really have no idea of the worry my family and friends went through.

"I missed the rest of that season, all the next, and didn't play again in the first team until November 1972. Even then my appearances were limited. I managed 32 League appearances during 1973-74 and played in the League Cup Final with Wolves, but my career was really over. Even now I still haven't got full movement back, but I do feel fortunate that I am still alive and I still have my leg."

The player was only 24 when the injury occurred and his injury in the Manchester derby ultimately robbed the Blues of a star man, and Pardoe of a long career.

Others struggling to regain fitness included Alan Oakes, who had a cartilage removed from his right knee, and Colin Bell, who had been in considerable pain with a trapped nerve.

Maine Road was also starting to look a little different. The North Stand terracing was finally complete, although the bars, toilets and other internal facilities would not be complete for some time. The new stand included an impressive £11,000 electronic scoreboard supplied by Hird-Brown - the same company who provided Wembley and the organisers of the Munich Olympics with boards.

The pitch itself was different with Groundsman Stan Gibson providing new drainage, and widening it by two yards to give measurements of 117 X 79 yards, and making the overall surface larger than any other ground in England.

Despite the opening day defeat, City's new pitch helped the Blues progress with home victories over Crystal Palace (4-0), Tottenham (4-0), Liverpool (1-0) and Newcastle United (2-1) to leave the Club in fourth place by mid September. The new North Stand had helped crowds to increase on the previous season and the players noticed the difference in atmosphere, especially captain Tony Book: "Against Liverpool I won the toss and because the new North End terraces have got so popular with our

Look hard enough and you might be able to recognise this traumatic trio, usually more familiarly identified in Manchester City's sky blue. From the left, Messrs Tony Book,

Francis Lee and Mike Summerbee. And if you still can't believe it, let us gently inform you that Manchester City's company of strolling players put on Cinderella as their seasonal offering to

Manchester City's Supporters' Club and paraded, without substitutes, Tony Book as a coachman, Francis Lee as the fictitious Lord Lee and moustachioed Mike Summerbee as a postman!

Tony Book, Francis Lee and Mike Summerbee take to the stage for the annual panto.

Joe Mercer always tried to remain positive, but he was treated badly by City's new board.

vocal supporters I decided to play into that goal. The crowd were really tremendous and the lads and myself were spurred on by their support. When we scored just after half-time I think this was due a large extent to our fans from all over the ground rooting for us."

It is worth noting that the North Stand was a very impressive construction for the period and had been developed, primarily, through the vision of Eric Alexander. He had a modern, forward looking approach and plenty of other ideas for developing the stadium and the Club's training facilities. Ultimately, the takeover limited City's ability to plan for the long term and, although Alexander remained a director for several years, his influence became limited as time went by and others who supported the takeover were brought into positions of power.

Back in 1971 City were fourth by the time of Everton's visit on 9th October. A single goal from Francis Lee was enough to bring victory, but the game was significant for another reason. It was the first time Malcolm Allison took control of the side. The changes at Board level affected the positions of both Allison, and Joe Mercer. Mercer was given the title of General Manager, while Allison was moved in as Team Manager. Naturally, Allison was more satisfied with the change than Mercer, but it seemed the only way to keep both men at the Club at the time. After the victory the new manager was asked what kind of a manager he would become. In typically cocksure Allison style he responded: "Probably the best that ever was. And I'll tell you something else, it will be nice to walk out at Wembley ahead of the Cup Final team."

Years later broadcaster and City fanatic Stuart Hall explained his feelings of what was, in effect, the end of the Mercer-Allison partnership: "Joe was the headmaster, Mal was the teacher but Allison could not bear to be placed one pace behind him. For example, when Joe led the team out at Wembley I think, Allison was seething with anger, but what he didn't realise was that the world isn't stupid, everybody recognised Malcolm's contribution and when the next Wembley final came, as sure it would if he'd been a little more patient, Joe would have stepped aside and let Allison enjoy the full spotlight, that he craved so badly.

"I really mistrusted Malcolm from the day Joe was shoved aside. He had this megalomania in those days, where he thought the whole world revolved around Malcolm Allison, and I had this great feeling of resentment towards him. I felt the Club would go downhill, because he wouldn't be capable of managing it. Malcolm was a super coach, and a magnificent motivator of men. In fact he still is, but when it came to actually administering a football club, he had little idea. He's not a bad lad really, deep down, but he needed to be brought into line. He's been misguided, but he's a warm person with so many qualities."

Most people believed that Allison was by far the greatest coach in the world at this point, however the takeover had really caused too many problems in his relationship with Mercer. Both men achieved success outside of the partnership, but at City it was the combination that brought the glory. Mercer had proved during the previous season that he needed Allison's support, and as Team Manager Allison would later demonstrate a similar need. Although it wasn't realised at the time, the takeover cost City a great deal.

Under Allison, the Blues continued to succeed in the League initially and, by the time of the November Maine Road derby match, City were lying third. The derby itself was one of the classic encounters and resulted in a 3-3 draw with Mike Summerbee scoring a last gasp equaliser before 63,326 spectators. The game was a typical derby and was full of incident with Francis Lee involved in a couple of the more newsworthy. The first saw Lee score from a penalty hotly disputed by the Reds, in a season when Lee managed to score a record 13 penalties. The second saw the City man accuse George Best of making a rather theatrical dive when tackled. To prove his point Lee himself demonstrated the dive several times to United players Willie Morgan and David Sadler. The City fans loved it and cheered him on, but the referee was not impressed and booked Lee. In 1989 footage of the game went on sale for the first time, and Lee's demonstrations were enjoyed by a new generation.

Lee's view that Best had dived was a little ironic when much of the press coverage of City during 1971-72 focused on the high total of penalties awarded to City. Many journalists accused Lee of looking for the easy option, something which angered the player at the time. In 2010 he explained: "In those days you used to get some horrendous treatment by the defenders, but I will tell you that the season before those penalties we only had a couple, and before that I think it was one. The reason we got so many in 1971-72 is that they had changed the law, plus we were going for the title so we were putting sides under a lot of pressure and they reacted. I was fouled only five times out of the 13 league penalties we got.

"When I was attacking I used to play the odds. If a defender was coming towards me I'd carry on, or I'd run towards the defender because there were only three things that could happen – he pulls me down, he gets the ball off me - well done, or I get a cracking shot at goal. So the odds were in my favour. You have to play them.

"I think the reason people go on about penalties with me is because I was the one taking them. It didn't seem to matter what they were given for, the headlines were that I had scored from a penalty. The season after I think we only got one penalty. I would say that for every dubious penalty that was awarded there were another twenty that we should have had. There was one game near the end where we should have had a couple of penalties for hand ball but because this was the season when we got that record number of penalties they weren't given."

In addition to the derby draw, Allison's City defeated Arsenal (2-1), West Ham (2-0), and Coventry (4-0) to earn the new manager the Bell's Manager of The Month award. The presentation was made on 11th December before City's 4-0 drubbing of Bobby Robson's Ipswich Town.

It seemed everything was going well on the pitch, off it was a different story. Mercer was far from happy with his role: "The humiliating part of this sad affair is that at one time the Board were saying there was a job for life. But the new regime of directors had no real confidence in me and I finished up by being offered a three year engagement plus a thirty-three and a third per cent cut in salary. However, the thing that hurt most of all was that they just didn't know what to call me. All my life I have been known as Joe Mercer the footballer, or Joe Mercer the manager. Then suddenly they can't find a title for me. That was when my pride was hit most of all."

In 2010 Eric Alexander explained how the directors felt: "Allison and his admirers on the Board decided they did not want Joe to have the title 'manager' in any connotation as, in their opinion, it detracted from Malcolm's position and kept Joe as the ostensible top man. I spent ages trying to convince the other Directors that Joe should stay, even if it was only for his public image and popularity which was all to the advantage of Manchester City. Nothing doing, but eventually they reluctantly agreed that if Joe himself could come up

with a title which was acceptable to both the board and Allison, he would be able to continue at the Club."

Mercer was not dissatisfied that Allison was now team Manager, his quarrel was about his own position, and about the way he was being treated by the new Board. He knew how his great friend Matt Busby was viewed at Old Trafford, and felt that the United directors would never treat Busby in the way that City were treating him. He wasn't alone. Many people at Maine Road were disgusted, especially when one morning they saw him arrive to find his car park space had been taken away and that his name had been removed from his office door without him being consulted. It was a shoddy affair, and proved to many that City were forgetting why the Club had become such a power during the late sixties.

On a different level, Allison was also dissatisfied, especially as he believed he had been promised a twenty year contract when Joe Smith's consortium first went public: "The new Board failed to please either of us. Joe Smith asked me what I wanted. I said I wanted a good contract and that I wanted to be boss... I was terribly disillusioned with Joe Smith when I saw my new contract. It was full of loopholes. My solicitor spent several months working on it and still it wasn't right. I remember saying to the directors, 'My contract isn't worth a light.'"

Changes were still occurring throughout the Club following the takeover battle. By early December Albert Alexander was made President for life – a huge honour considering that the first had been Lawrence Furniss - while his son Eric had been made Chairman the previous April. Joe Smith was now Vice-Chairman. The Board would continue to change throughout the next two seasons.

City continued to progress in the League and by 9th January the Blues were only a point behind league leaders Manchester United. It was a different story in the two cup competitions, though. In the League Cup City defeated Wolves 4-3 in September but were defeated 3-0 at Bolton in the third round, while the FA Cup saw City draw 1-1 with Middlesbrough - thanks to a record breaking 12th penalty from Lee - and then lose the replay 1-0. At least it gave Allison his first chance as City manager to say: "We can now concentrate on the League without any distractions."

He was right as, on 29th January, a 5-2 victory over Wolves put City two points clear at the top. Lee scored an hat-trick that day, and then on 12th February the Match Of The Day cameras travelled to Bramall Lane to see him score his 13th penalty of the season. As if to prove a point, the penalty had been awarded after debutant Mick Speight used his hands to turn away a Lee shot. Who said all City's penalties were awarded through dives by Lee?

Secretary Walter Griffiths, Team Manager Malcolm Allison and Chairman Eric Alexander sign Rodney Marsh.

The game ended 3-3 with Allison claiming that newly promoted Sheffield United were the best side to have come up from the Second Division in 10 years. He'd obviously forgotten about the Blues.

City continued to progress and by mid-March were four points clear at the top. Leeds were second, although they had two games in hand. It seemed that Malcolm Allison had managed to rediscover City's Championship seeking approach, and that nothing could get in the way, then he made a signing that changed everything. It should have been the greatest City signing of the 1970s, Rodney Marsh.

Marsh was a real entertainer, the kind of player that the 1970s footballing public wanted to see, and his £200,000 record signing was seen as a positive move by City to secure the title. Everybody expected him to help the Blues with the final push, and a crowd of 53,322 turned out to see him make his debut against Chelsea on 18th March. In 2009 Marsh talked of his arrival: "The reason I came to City was Malcolm Allison. It's really that simple. I was at QPR and Spurs were interested. I was given permission to speak with City and when I talked with Allison it was clear this was the place I had to go. I have to say that Malcolm was by far the best coach

around. He was decades ahead of the rest and we did things then that are only just becoming part and parcel of football now. Malcolm was very impressive and his enthusiasm was inspiring. He told me that City were the 'best club in Europe' and everything he said was exciting. Coming to Maine Road was something I had to do. I couldn't wait to play there."

His debut was high profile: "It was off the radar! It was absolutely phenomenal and Malcolm orchestrated it all. He told me what to do and how to approach the fans and so on. He made it so easy for me and told me to concentrate on the football and leave him to worry about the rest – I still believe that's how it should be. Footballers should play and leave everything else to the others. I went out on to the pitch and I was surrounded by photographers. I could hardly move. I did everything I was expected to do of course, but I was overwhelmed by the response from the fans."

Despite Marsh's obvious skills, some were not impressed. These included Mike Doyle: "He made his debut against Chelsea. They left Tony Towers out, who'd been playing really well. We should have hammered Chelsea that day. Tommy Booth scored and we managed a 1-0 win. He did mix with the lads to a certain extent, but really it was clear Marsh just wanted to do his own thing. You don't win anything with players like that in your side. But the writing was already on the wall. All we had to do was to win three games to get the Championship. But they persisted in playing Marsh and we just lost all our rhythm and everything."

A no score draw with Newcastle followed the Chelsea victory and all of a sudden the pressure was on. Then came the visit of Stoke on April Fool's Day and another setback, with Gordon Banks performing superbly to help Stoke to a 2-1 victory in the Maine Road mud. Two days later a 2-0 defeat at Southampton left City lying in third place on 50 points. Derby were leading the table on 51 points, with Liverpool second on 50, and Leeds fourth on 49.

The press and some supporters started to blame the recent loss of form on the arrival of Rodney Marsh, but Allison would not accept that viewpoint and kept the player in the side. Years later Marsh confessed: "There'd been some criticism of the fee – it was £200,000 and that was huge for the time. It wasn't the fee that was an issue to me, but I did feel I let everyone down at first. I'd had a groin strain and not trained for about six weeks, so it took a while to get fit."

After the Southampton defeat City won at West Ham 3-1 with Marsh scoring his first and second goals for the Club to silence his critics for a while. Then on 12th April came the Old Trafford derby. City were expected to win, especially as they had not been defeated in the League at Old Trafford since September 1966.

Interestingly, Rodney Marsh was named as substitute - the first time since his arrival he had not been in the starting line-up.

The first half was rather sterile, although City always seemed to have the upper hand. In fact the Blues always seemed the more likely to score, then after about an hour Martin Buchan gave the Reds the lead against the general run of play. It wasn't to last, though, as impressive youngster Willie Donachie galloped down the wing and sent a centre to Lee. The ace goalscorer proceeded to back-head the equaliser. A powerful right foot shot brought lee's second goal of the game and 32nd of the season a few minutes later. Lee was to end the season on 33 League goals - the most since Tommy Johnson's 38 in 1929.

A little while later Allison brought Marsh on for the injured Doyle, and City's expensive forward made it three with a calm, perfect shot into the United net. Marsh: "It was my first Manchester derby and I came on as substitute and scored straight away. As time ticked by we were winning 3-1 and I was holding the ball in the corner. A United player slid towards me hoping to open up play but I stopped and he crashed into the hoardings. I kept the ball at my feet and did an exaggerated look at my watch – the United fans hated me! They tried to give me tremendous abuse but I just kept the ball at my feet. That was my answer. It was typical of me. I always did things because I wanted to."

Afterwards a delighted Allison purred: "Magic, pure magic!" City were back on course.

Rodney Marsh was quick to point out after the match that he was very much happy at Maine Road, despite what the papers were saying: "One ghost I would like to lay immediately is an impression that the papers have given... that the crowd at Maine Road has been getting at me. That's nonsense. I've found them very fair and indeed they have given me a lot of encouragement. If anything surprised me with City, it was the space I was given... probably because our players here seem to think that bit quicker than others. By the time I scored three goals I should really have had eight. Against United I was really surprised at the amount of space created."

Three days after the victory City suffered another setback. This time they only managed a 1-1 draw at Coventry, although Mike Doyle had an effort ruled offside. That game left City second one point behind Derby with both sides having two games left. Importantly, Liverpool and Leeds were also able to snatch the title as both sides had games in hand and were only one and two points behind respectively.

It was vital City defeated Ipswich on 18th April at Portman Road. In the end they suffered a 2-1 defeat which meant that the final game of the season - at home to Derby - wouldn't really give the Blues the opportunity of parading the Championship trophy at Maine Road. The Derby game ended 2-0 but City, despite being top, had to wait a further twelve days before the other sides completed their fixtures. In the end Derby won the title by a point, while City finished fourth on the same number of points as Liverpool and Leeds.

Naturally, the inquests started. Was Marsh to blame? What about Gordon Banks' excellent performance in April? Did the takeover hangover affect the Club? The shoddy treatment of Mercer must have had an impact? And what about the bickering between Mercer and Allison? There seemed to be many theories, but no real answer.

Marsh's view is worth recording. In 2009 he explained: "City were absolutely flying. Before I arrived they were heading for the title and with me playing we missed it by a point. In life you have to be true to yourself and I have to say that I was responsible for City losing that Championship. It wasn't signing me that was the issue, but playing me was. It's something that I feel awful about. City deserved that title and so did the fans.

"City fans were brilliant. They were totally supportive. I remember the first time they sang 'Ooh, Rodney, Rodney...' That was a great feeling. It raised the hairs on the back of my neck. I adored the City fans. Totally adored them. I think I was one of the first to clap the crowd back – and this was something I wanted to do. I did it because it meant something to me. I enjoyed the relationship with the fans and it has to be remembered how important that is."

Someone else who enjoyed the relationship with the fans was Joe Mercer. Sadly, In June 1972 he felt forced out of the Maine Road club and moved to Coventry City as General Manager. He felt he was no longer wanted at Maine Road.

Regrettably for City, the departure of Mercer was not handled well, and brought much criticism of the Club. In fact, the appalling way Mercer was treated turned some against the Blues, and caused others to seriously question the new directors. It appeared to some supporters that the new Board could not recognise what had made the Club great. It wasn't Mercer, it wasn't Allison, it was their partnership. Together they won everything. The first five years of their partnership were perfect, and in 1993 Allison remembered what they achieved together: "We told each other the truth, and we never really fell out. Once he turned to me and said, 'Mal, these have been the best five years of my life. I wouldn't have traded them for anything'. He meant it. We had a great relationship really. I enjoyed it all and I think, like Joe, those first five years were the best-ever for me. I was very lucky when Joe got the City job, and took me there. And we started right from the grass roots, right from the bottom and took them to the top. That is real achievement."

Back in 1972 a hurt Mercer told the press that he believed City could have found him a position at Maine Road similar to that of his old friend Matt Busby at Old Trafford. Instead, all that was offered to him was a public-relations position. If the Board had wanted him to stay then surely they could have found a way of letting him stay on. In 2010 Eric Alexander agreed: "To my simple mind it would have solved all the Board-generated problems if Joe had been a Director. I am certain this would have satisfied all parties and avoided considerable ill feeling and long term problems at the Club."

Alexander recognised Mercer's value to the Blues even if the other directors did not. He stuck his neck out in an attempt to keep both Mercer and Allison at City, and went to see Mercer at home to try and calm things down. He explained the situation and while there he suggested that Mercer and his wife Norah should work out an appropriate job title: "I left it with them both to consider a title that would be acceptable to all parties and departed thinking I had worked a miracle to keep Joe in a job and at City, even if it had hardly increased my popularity with the other Directors and rather put my position at risk."

For Mercer, it did not matter what Alexander said as the problem was not with him. The problem lay elsewhere and, even though Alexander was chairman, Mercer knew the power would ultimately rest with others. Clearly, Alexander's actions were well-intentioned, but the selection of a title was something that hurt the Mercers.

Had Alexander received full support from the other directors and managed to come up with a title before going to see the Mercers, then the situation may have been resolved positively.

Neither Mercer nor Allison should be blamed for the breakdown of the partnership. Allison quite understandably needed the role of Team Manager - Mercer never disputed that - the problem was that the Board was not unified and Mercer recognised that those edging ever closer to full control had little desire in keeping him at Maine Road.

As with the previous season, 1971-72 was impacted by activities in the boardroom. A season when success seemed likely ended with the departure of the Club's most successful manager. What makes this episode shameful however is that, apart from the actions of Eric Alexander, many of the directors and takeover supporters failed to recognise how damaging this would be. It is a fact that the takeover and subsequent disagreements had prematurely killed City's trophy winning period.

Supporters were left to wonder about what might have occurred had the partnership continued to work.

1972-1973 Allison Leaves

The 1972-73 season commenced with City invited to play in the Charity Shield. Playing in a decidedly modern continental strip of white with a blue and red diagonal, they defeated Aston Villa 1-0 at Villa Park to bring the first trophy of Malcolm Allison's reign as City Manager.

By 1972 Allison had become the hugely popular 'Big Mal'.

A week later the League campaign commenced with a 2-0 defeat at Liverpool - in which Wyn Davies and Liverpool's Larry Lloyd were sent off - followed by a 1-0 home defeat against Everton. Allison needed to do something quickly if the Blues were to build on their form of the previous season, but he was adamant he did not need to bring in new faces: "I'm certainly not interested in signing any players. Things might change. I doubt it. The first team squad is 18 strong. Not many clubs can beat that.

"There's a change of style from last season. Now we'll be playing three accepted goalscorers up front - Francis Lee, Wyn Davies and Rodney Marsh with Ian Mellor pushing them all for regular inclusion. We didn't start off last season with this sort of strength. Then we had to adjust. Now we have a settled squad, with everyone knowing what's wanted."

On 19th August the first points arrived with a 3-0 victory over Norwich, but the Blues had to wait until the seventh game for their next points to arrive. By that time City were bottom of the table, one point behind Manchester United.

Off the pitch, there had been further changes to the look of the stadium. As a result of the Ibrox disaster, the decision had been made to install seats on the new North Stand. This now held 7,800 in tip-up plastic seats, paying a mere 70p each per game. Over in the Kippax Stand the admission price was a pleasing 40p for adults and 20p for schoolchildren, although attendees had started to complain about the poor quality of the public address system within the stand – complaints that would last until the stand's demise in 1994.

On 13th September City returned to European action with the first round UEFA Cup tie with Valencia. The game ended 2-2, but the return game was a disappointment as Valencia, managed by the great Alfredo Di Stefano, won 2-1. A week later the Blues were also knocked out of the League Cup by Fourth Division Bury.

During October form did improve, and then November saw exciting victories over Derby (4-0), Everton (3-2) and Manchester United (3-0). By the time of the derby match Allison had sold Wyn Davies to United for a fee of around £60,000 - the largest transfer between the two clubs until Tony Coton moved to Old Trafford over twenty years later.

December brought mainly 1-1 draws with four of

TRUE BLUE
Mike Summerbee

A star of the Mercer-Allison team and, by 2011, City ambassador.

the six games played ending that way, and then the New Year brought Allison hope of glory in the FA Cup. Stoke City were despatched 3-2 in the third round, then Allison 'psyched' out Shankly's Liverpool. Writing in the Daily Express, Allison claimed that City would "bury the myth of Liverpool", and went on to say that the Merseysiders had many limitations. Unusually, Shankly's men fell for the hype and resorted to niggling fouls. The game ended goalless at Anfield, and Allison was happy. City won the replay 2-0 with goals from Bell, after fourteen minutes, and Booth, six minutes into the second half.

In the fifth round City drew Second Division Sunderland at Maine Road. This was the first game to be played following the appointment by the new Board of Bernard Halford as secretary. Halford was responsible for all aspects of ticketing and crowd control amongst other duties. He was, in effect, the most senior figure working at the Club on a daily basis, reporting directly to the Chairman and Board.

Halford, who had been the Oldham secretary for several years working for Ken Bates, was keen to ensure the Sunderland tie went well: "I wanted everybody to see this because being new to the job I didn't want to let any of the fans down. Being a fan I knew how disappointed I'd feel if I couldn't get in to a game, so I suppose I was keen to fill the ground. Nevertheless, we didn't break the safety certificate and everything passed off okay."

The official attendance was 54,478 – the largest at Maine Road since the North Stand became all-seater the previous year and also an attendance that would never be matched at the old stadium again. The old ground's capacity was never viewed that high again, and many, many fans believed there were considerably more in the stadium than the figures claimed. Interestingly, the following summer the capacity was recorded as 52,600 even though there had been no redevelopment.

Four minutes into the match and Rodney Marsh saw his first goal attempt expertly saved by Jim Montgomery, but City did manage to find the net later, when Tony Towers scored with a ground shot. Sadly, an error by Joe Corrigan brought the sides level. He had attempted to send a free-kick to Willie Donachie, but only managed to get the ball to Mick Horswill. The Sunderland player simply lobbed the ball over Corrigan to make it 1-1. Nevertheless, City remained in control for much of the first half, prompting Sunderland manager Bob Stokeo to admit later: "I thought that I would have to throw another ball on the pitch for us to get a kick."

It didn't last, though. In the 67th minute Sunderland took the lead.

City searching desperately for an equaliser were thwarted time and again by the excellent Montgomery, then Summerbee sent the ball into the area from a corner. Marsh did all he could to block the 'keeper, and Montgomery managed to back heel the ball into his own net. City fans were delighted that his luck had finally ran out.

The game continued with both sides determined to win, but the score remained. It had been a fierce encounter with several players booked - indeed goalscorer Towers was sent off. Sunderland won the replay 3-1 despite late pressure from the Blues. Allison was devastated and was now beginning to find it difficult to motivate himself: "I had become disenchanted with the Club. The directors had dragged their feet in giving me the sort of contract I wanted, and had been promised. The urgency and thrill had gone out of my work. It was a desperately unhappy situation to be in after all the great times, the moments when Mercer, the players, and I had between us achieved a sort of working perfection."

On 7th March Allison was forced to sell Ian Mellor to Norwich City: "There are no secrets about why I was forced to encourage clubs who are interested in some of our players - City need to put the financial side of things on a better basis. I can understand that. But I find selling players the toughest part of my job, particularly if it's in a rush. It means you don't get the real value. And I've never liked selling players you've seen come here as kids and develop into top class professionals. That's why I was sorry to see Ian Mellor leave."

Mellor's move should never have occurred and the player himself wanted to stay and develop his career in Manchester. In 2003 he talked about the quality of City's coaching staff around this time: "We were very fortunate at City to have Johnny Hart, Ken Barnes, and Dave Ewing in the coaching set up. They were very knowledgeable and men of real quality. They knew what they were

talking about and they also cared passionately about the game and the Club. They'd all had great careers and as a young player you listened and learned. At times they could be very hard. They pushed you because they knew you had to be hard to survive in football, and they certainly made you work. They gave me the right sort of grounding.

"The biggest coaching influence though has to be Malcolm Allison. In those days he was the best as a coach and motivator and I learnt so much from him. Again he could be tough, but you listened because he had already delivered so much by the time I got into the first team."

Three days after Mellor's departure the visit of Coventry brought Joe Mercer back to Maine Road. Before the game the former City manager received a fantastic ovation, and then witnessed his new side win 2-1. Incredibly, Francis Lee missed a penalty - perhaps he felt the day belonged to Mercer. Allison had already started to consider his own future by the end of that game, before the end of the month he was on his way out of Maine Road. Twenty years later he admitted that he was well and truly shattered after almost eight years of pushing himself, and City, hard. He was in dire need of a break but football rarely allows a manager a sabbatical. If the directors had been able to find a way of giving Allison a short break, he may have been able to return refreshed. Sadly, his first Maine Road career ended with the Blues struggling in the bottom half of the table. He deserved better.

The Board, which now included Peter Swales as Vice-Chairman, promoted Chief Coach and former player Johnny Hart to the Manager's seat and expected him to fill the void left by both Mercer and Allison. It was a tall order. In December 2004 Hart remembered: "I enjoyed being a 'number two', and I loved all my time as a coach. I'd loved my playing career and I felt as if Maine Road was my home. I liked being a second in command. Management was different. I didn't really want the job, but if I'd have turned it down I'd probably have been moved on. It wasn't a job I craved at all."

Despite Hart's reticence, he did help to lift the Blues a little and they ended the season in 11th place.

1970-1973 SUMMARY

Highest League Attendance: 63,326 Manchester United, 6/11/71
Highest Cup Attendance: 54,478 Sunderland, 24/02/73 (FA Cup)
Managers: 1965 – 1971 (continued as General Manager until June 1972) Joe Mercer, 1971 – 1973 Malcolm Allison, 1973 Johnny Hart

Seasonal Record:

Season	League	Posn	FA Cup	League Cup	Other	Leading Scorer	Average Att.
1970-71	FL Div1	11	Rnd 5	Rnd 2	ECWC Semi-final & Anglo-Italian Rnd1	Lee 14	31,041
1971-72	FL Div1	4	Rnd 3	Rnd 3	Texaco Cup Rnd 1	Lee 33	38,573
1972-73	FL Div1	11	Rnd 5	Rnd 3	UEFA Cup Rnd 1 & Charity Shield winners	Lee & Marsh 14	32,351

A blood stained Dave Watson with the League Cup alongside Joe Royle and Joe Corrigan.

1973-1976
Seventies Success

"We were out on the pitch before kick-off and City's coach Ian McFarlane had the ball and was taking shots at Corrigan. You could tell he loved being on the pitch at Wembley and wasn't going to miss his chance to have a kickabout on the turf. We tried to get the ball off him but couldn't. He was like the teacher played by Brian Glover in the film *Kes!* This was his day and we weren't going to stop him. It was really funny. My goal came after about 11 minutes. We were kicking towards the City fans and I remember Doyle knocking it through. I didn't have time to think I just sent it home and ran towards the fans celebrating. I'd already settled and it felt fantastic. We had a great banquet afterwards and Rod Stewart came along to celebrate with us.

1976 League Cup final goalscorer Peter Barnes interviewed in March 2004

1973-1974 Wembley Return

During the close season, manager Hart had made one of City's most amazing transfers when he brought Denis Law back to Maine Road on a free transfer. United fans couldn't believe it, especially as it seemed that manager Tommy Docherty was forcing the player out. At City though, Johnny Hart recognised that the 'King of Old Trafford' still had a lot to offer: "What United decided to do with Law is nothing to do with me, nor am I entitled to comment on it. I feel that a player who was capable of being captain for Scotland around 15 months ago, with the competitive streak which Denis has never lost, would have something to offer. I wouldn't like to think that one of my players could go absolutely sour in such a short period."

The 1973-74 season opened with another invitation to take part in the Charity Shield. This time Burnley defeated the Blues 1-0 at Maine Road, but before the game the City players had made a humorous point when they lined up in the tunnel equipped with a huge pair of sunglasses for referee Gordon Hill. Apparently, Hill had refereed City's goalless League game at Highbury the previous season when he gave a corner instead of a penalty after Jeff Blockley had handled for the home side. At the time general opinion stated that the sun had been in Hill's eyes, thereby prompting the City mickey-take.

The opening League match saw new arrival Denis Law score twice to help City defeat Birmingham 3-1. In the match programme an article by Eric Alexander revealed that he would be relinquishing the Chairmanship of the Club at the AGM on Friday 5th October. He wrote that he was satisfied that his period in control had seen the take-over battle finally resolved, and stated that the Boardroom was now totally democratic: "The majority of these events [the take-over] reached a climax during my term in office and I was delighted that common sense prevailed and differences could be ironed out. To use the expression of a famous politician 'peace in our time' is a milestone I will remember in City history. We have now reached a stage where no one man will ever control Manchester City. This point has been reached by voluntary agreements, and it is the best thing that could have happened to safeguard City and prevent a repetition of our past troubles."

To the outside world all looked well, but it was clear that a few compromises had been reached behind the scenes. Alexander's resignation was one of these and he was quickly replaced by self-styled 'peacemaker' Peter Swales. Joe Smith, who basically had control of the Club, felt comfortable with Swales. He had already made it onto the FA Council and had vast experience of football administration at Altrincham and the Northern Premier League. For Smith, Swales seemed the logical choice. However earlier in the year Swales had already made it clear that his ambition was to take on United. This obsession was ultimately the downfall of the Blues. Had Swales focused on finding success for City first, rather than worry about the Reds, then it's possible he may have guided the Blues to sustained glory rather than long term decline.

On the pitch City's second League game - a 1-0 defeat at Derby - saw the welcome return of Glyn Pardoe. Pardoe was still struggling following his injury in the 1970 match with United, and the derby game was only his seventh appearance in almost three years. It had been a long hard struggle and proved much about Pardoe's character that he had never once given up. He was desperately keen to make sure his return to the first team was not short-lived. His determination helped him make a total of 31 League appearances during 1973-74.

Another player determined was Denis Law, who wanted to prove that United were wrong to discard him. At Stoke in City's third game, the plucky Scotsman scored his third goal of the season as City drew 1-1, while in other games he became chief provider. His opening month at Maine Road was already proving to be rewarding when the news came through that he'd earned a recall to the Scottish squad. Scotland manager Willie Ormond attended Maine Road to see City defeat Coventry 1-0, and afterwards declared: "It's the best centre forward display I have seen so far this season." In addition to Law, Ormond also named left back Willie Donachie in the squad for the World Cup qualifier against Czechoslovakia. Sadly, Donachie, who had played against the same country a couple of years earlier, never actually made it onto the pitch for that game but Law did, partnering the young Kenny Dalglish in attack.

Afterwards every reporter acknowledged that Law was inspirational, and that it was mainly down to him that Scotland had qualified for the 1974 World Cup finals in West Germany. Law was pleased with his own performance, but was willing to share the acclaim, mentioning a player Joe Mercer had signed for Coventry City and who would arrive at Maine Road seven years later: "I have never been happier. After all these years in the wilderness Scotland can now make the rest of the world sit up and take notice in West Germany next summer. We can start playing an established and successful pattern. Some of our youngsters were terrific against the Czechs, particularly Tommy Hutchison. He showed that he is the type of player Scotland have needed for years."

On Friday 5th October City held their Annual General Meeting. As expected Eric Alexander stood down as Chairman with Peter Swales taking control of the Club. Swales was not the major shareholder, indeed he held very few shares, however he had the backing of Joe Smith. Smith was now President – Life President Albert Alexander had passed away by this point - with Simon Cussons holding the position of Vice-Chairman. Two other members of Smith's consortium - Ian Niven and Chris Muir - were also on the Board. Eric Alexander, Sidney Rose, and Umbro's John Humphreys remained on the Board, but the power definitely lay with the former members of Smith's consortium and, of course, Chairman Swales.

Smith saw the appointment of Swales as proof that City was now a democratic club: "In November 1970 I accepted an opportunity to have a closer involvement with my favourite football club, and from this followed an ambition to bring a breath of fresh air into the place. Frankly, it looked to be desperately needed at Maine Road, where a monopoly of power was in existence. Along the way, strewn with obstacles, many unpleasantries and even more in the way of bitter opposition, there were attempts to represent my intentions as a personal grab for power and prestige. I trust that yesterday's meeting proved the truth behind my motives when the Chairmanship passed into the astute care of the best director at present equipped to handle the job, Peter J. Swales. There could be no better choice."

He went on to outline how Swales had managed to bring the two sides in the Boardroom dispute together and how, as Vice-Chairman, Swales had worked hard to help the Club announce the biggest profit in its history.

From his own viewpoint, Swales felt the Club was already moving in the right direction and that the large profit was a culmination of a lot of positive effort by many people at the Club. He outlined his views in the City programme for the game against Southampton on 6th October. He explained about his desire to see the team achieve great success, while maintaining an healthy bank balance. Significantly, in 2003 Eric Alexander highlighted that the Blues had been a highly profitable club for decades but once Swales became Chairman City began to have financial issues.

In 1973 few if any supporters argued against the appointment of a man who clearly loved the Blues, and had the same kind of ambition as the fans on the terraces. He wanted the best, and ended his large programme article as any ambitious man would: "To think of me as a successful chairman, which I dearly want to be, I'm aware that the team has to be successful on the field. There's no reason why it shouldn't be. I will give my best for City, and my best has stood me in reasonable stead before. I will work harder than anyone else. And I cannot promise any more than that."

Swales certainly became the hardest working Chairman throughout the 1970s and 80s, but the success he and City craved was not as great as it should have been. However, in 1973 everybody was hopeful that the new Swales era would be successful, though some probably felt Smith had the controlling voice. Swales: "Well, Joe Smith was the boss. He eventually bought the bulk of the shares, but he didn't have the bottle to do the Chairman's job. He was a wonderful fella, terrific fella. He knew how to make money, but he didn't like the criticism and the rough game that it is. I think he knew that. To be the boss of a football club you've got to have a nerve and a belief in what you're doing. I just took his fancy and that was it. He backed me to the day he died, never once did he go against... even when I made some bad decisions - and there were plenty of those while he was alive! He was great."

One of Swales' first decisions concerned the appointment of a new manager. Johnny Hart had been suffering with ill health due to the pressure of trying

to motivate City's team of expensive stars, and was forced to resign towards the end of November. The whole of his left side was completely numb, and he started experiencing depression around the time of his appointment: "The difficulties, the loss of feeling, was actually just coming on as Malcolm left City. I was offered the job and I took it because I didn't want anybody thinking that I didn't have the guts to have a go at it. And a job like City is the dream of a lifetime coming true for someone like me. A disadvantage I felt was that it came on me suddenly. I never worked myself up, never prepared for the position to be mine."

In 2004 Hart explained: "It just wasn't the role for me. I'm quite a shy person really, and I guess management just wasn't for me. The players were terrific – I had a fantastic squad and they all wanted to play for me. Denis Law arrived back and I was very happy with the players and their motivation, but I just didn't want the role, and it all got to me. I became quite ill. After leaving City I was recuperating for about two years during which time I practically did nothing."

Swales looked around for a man to drive the team forward and found Norwich manager Ron Saunders. Saunders had previously managed Yeovil Town and Oxford United, but it was with Norwich that he first made the headlines, taking the unfashionable club to the Second Division title in 1972, then the League Cup final in 1973. He certainly appeared to be the right man for the job.

Geoffrey Watling, the Norwich director who had been Chairman when Saunders was given the Norwich job, was desperately sad to see Saunders leave Carrow Road, but told the media that he felt it was a perfect move for both the Blues and for the manager: "Manchester City are to be congratulated on their appointment - Ron Saunders can be a Joe Mercer and Malcolm Allison rolled into one, and he will get them

Internationals Law, Lee, Summerbee, Bell & Marsh.

success. Hard but human. That
is a description I give about him.
He would never ask players to do
anything he would not do himself.
I would say he is a physical fitness
fanatic, and he is also dynamic in his
views.

"Dedicated, a players man, he is
all these things. I would recommend
Ron Saunders in every way, an
excellent manager, and he will do
Manchester City a power of good."

Peter Swales felt that Saunders
was the right man for the job: "I
pledge my reputation with Ron
Saunders. I have gambled my future
with him, and I will be proved right.
When I became Chairman it was with
plenty of drumbeats and razzmatazz,
but I know these things are not good
enough to satisfy the City football
public. They want results. When the
appointment was made I thought,
from all the candidates considered
and the interviews conducted, that
he was the right man. Having seen
him at work I now know for sure he's
the right one. If he goes down, I go
with him - it's as blunt as that."

Fans at the top of Wembley Way prior to the 1974 League Cup Final.

As with many other comments made around this
time, this statement was held against Swales during
the 1980s and 90s. It's easy to criticise the comments,
however at the time Swales truly felt he had appointed
the perfect manager. Francis Lee felt the same with Alan
Ball in the 1990s but circumstances, in particular the
relationship between manager and the players, worked
against both managerial appointments.

A lot of what Swales said was probably bravado.
Throughout his career at Maine Road the Chairman
enjoyed letting supporters hear that City would be the
biggest and best. He wanted success, but also wanted
fans to be proud of their club. As Chairman he felt he
was in the perfect place to 'whip up' enthusiasm.

On the pitch itself, the appointment of Saunders
didn't really improve performances in the League at
first. His first game in charge saw the Blues defeated
2-1 at Ipswich, after going a goal down in the eleventh
minute, and by mid-December City were in the lower
half of the table, dropping to sixteenth place at one
point. Gradually during January and February Saunders
brought consistency to the Blues with only one game
ending in defeat. The FA Cup was a little disappointing
though, with a 4-1 defeat at Notts County putting City
out at the fourth round stage.

The League Cup was City's only real chance of

salvaging something out of a rather strange season. In
addition to the changes in personnel, City suffered from
problems resulting from power cuts caused through
a miners' dispute. This affected kick-off times and
attendances, and resulted in the Blues hiring a rather
noisy generator to ensure certain games were played. In
addition petrol shortages restricted the movement of
supporters, further affecting crowd figures. The League
Cup run was severely impacted by the power problems.

Prior to Saunders appointment, the Blues had
defeated Walsall, after two replays, and Carlisle, and
achieved a goalless draw at York. With Saunders - and
the hire of an electric generator for £1,000 - City defeated
York 4-1 and then travelled to Coventry in the fifth round.
An exciting game ended 2-2 witnessed by a crowd of
only 12,661, due to the match kicking off at 2pm on a
Wednesday afternoon. Almost a month later the replay -
another afternoon kick off - saw City score three goals in
the last twelve minutes to win the game 4-2.

On 23rd January the first leg of the semi-final saw
City travel to Plymouth to record a 1-1 draw against the
Third Division side. Tommy Booth had equalised from
a Mike Summerbee corner in the 65th minute. A week
later at Maine Road, a crowd of 40,117 witnessed a 2-0
victory with goals from Lee and Bell to put City through
to their second League Cup Final in four years.

The Final against Wolverhampton Wanderers, played
on 3rd March 1974, gave City the chance to rediscover

success. It also provided Chairman Swales with the perfect start to his career: "I remember sitting in the Royal Box, 100,000 people the Wembley capacity in those days, playing Wolves, thinking 'I've only been in the job a few months, it's a doddle! Absolute doddle! We'll get the First Division, the European Cup... We'll win everything. Ninety minutes later we'd lost, of course, and that was my first taste of bitter disappointment. Defeat - which of course I suffered many times in the years to come - that was a real taste of defeat. I was a young Chairman, and recognised that we had some old players in the team. We had Marshy, Francis Lee, Michael Summerbee, Colin Bell - who was younger than the others, but still an old hand at City - and Ron [Saunders] was a real disciplinarian. He used to get at those players."

According to Swales, Saunders' treatment of the older, more familiar players eventually caused the Chairman a number of problems. Success at Wembley may have changed the course of the rest of the season, but for Swales failure was unbearable. Prior to the game, City had stayed a short distance from Wembley and Saunders ensured the players prepared for the final in

a disciplined, controlled manner. They were not happy. Mike Doyle: "There was no party spirit, and we trained on pitches at the back of the hotel which had more slopes on them than the Alps. All we were allowed to drink was orange juice - not even a glass of wine with our meals. We felt that we were not being treated as men, but as children who might get sick at the party if they ate too much. Frankly, I don't believe any of the players was in the right frame of mind to go out and do his stuff in a Wembley Final. I think we had lost that final before we even went on the park."

The game itself started with City dominating the first half. However, it was Wolves who took the lead in the 43rd minute. Hibbitt's miss hit drive beat 'keeper Keith MacRae - signed by Hart from Motherwell for £100,000 - and crept in at the far post. It should never have occurred, and was very much against the run of play as City had been the more powerful side throughout the half. The Blues' dominance continued into the second half.

Former Blue Dave Wagstaffe appeared for Wolves in the final: "I pulled a thigh muscle on the Wednesday before, but there was no way I was going to miss it. City were odds on because of the quality in the side. Look at the forward like – Summerbee, Law, Lee, Bell, Marsh – you couldn't pick a better forward line. I think it's the best that had ever got to the League Cup final. Our centre-halves were brilliant that day and our 'keeper Gary Pierce was outstanding.

"I came off in that final with ten minutes to go, but it was an incredible game. It was my greatest day as a Wolves player and because only England games and the two finals were played there it meant a lot to be at Wembley. The tunnel seemed to be soundproofed so you'd be in there in silence and then walk out to the noise of about 100,000 Wolves and City fans. What a feeling!"

Opportunities came City's way, but luck seemed to be with Wolves as an effort from Booth was deflected off the goal line, and a header from Lee went over. Luck changed on the hour, though, when Rodney Marsh centred for Colin Bell to shoot the equaliser.

Later, the Wolves 'keeper Pierce was forced to make brilliant saves

Francis Lee and Wolves' right back Geoff Palmer at Wembley.

Colin Bell scores watched by Denis Law and Rodney Marsh (far right).

from Bell, Lee, and Marsh as the Blues tore into Wolves, but once again luck eluded City as Richards scored to put Wolves 2-1 up in the 85th minute. In 2009 Rodney Marsh claimed responsibility: "I felt I let the fans down badly. Wolves' winning goal came from my mistake – the ball hit the back of me and fell perfectly for Richards to score. I was angry with myself and I did not feel it was appropriate for me to get rewarded for losing, so I refused to go up and collect my runners-up tankard. I didn't even shake hands with anyone, I just stormed off.

It wasn't arrogance or anything it was disappointment. I'd let the fans and my team-mates down. That's what it was all about and the fact I let them down still hurts today."

Colin Bell remembered that this game should have brought success: "In my career I've played in two games of this kind. One was when England drew with Poland at Wembley and missed qualifying for the '74 World Cup, and Wolves was the other. If either of those games had been boxing matches, the opposition would have

City applaud Wolves at the end of the final.

thrown the towel in. We were 1-0 down to Wolves at half time but I always felt if we pulled one back we would win. I got the equaliser and we were never out of their half after that. Then, late on, a ball was played across our area; Rodney Marsh just got a toe to it and helped it in the direction of John Richards who scored the Wolves' winner."

Everyone connected with the Blues was saddened by the scoreline, none more than Marsh, who pre-match had told the press: "I will be bitterly disappointed if I don't make an impact." After the final whistle he refused to collect his loser's tankard and walked off, head bowed, towards the dressing room. Later, at the team's hotel, he insisted on drowning his sorrows from a paper cup he had collected in the Wembley dressing room, telling all who cared to listen that it was symbolic of City's - and his - failure. Later he sent a telegram to Wolves apologising for walking out.

For the second time in three seasons, Marsh was seen as costing City a major trophy, but in truth neither occasion was his fault. At Wembley, luck more than anything else, brought Wolves the League Cup. Had any one of the many City chances after the equaliser entered the net, then the Blues would certainly have won the match. Unfortunately, it was not to be.

Wolves appreciated the way Saunders' side acknowledged their opponents however. They City players lined up to applaud Wolves and congratulated them on their success. Dave Wagstaffe believed this was well received by his team mates: "That was great. Wonderful. If you looked at our team none of us had ever won anything. Even Derek Dougan! I think City were saying 'Well done'. We really appreciated that. It meant a lot and said something about City. That night we celebrated at a club after the formal dinner and Franny Lee walked in with bottles of champagne. He gave them to us and said well done. It was a great gesture and said a lot about him and City at that time."

After the Wembley defeat, Saunders set about strengthening the side. On 11th March he signed Sunderland's Dennis Tueart and Mick Horswill, with Tony Towers going in the opposite direction. The Tueart signing turned out to be one of the most important in the history of City although, at the time Chairman Swales was uncertain about what type of a man Tueart was: "I went with Ron Saunders to Sunderland. My first sight of Dennis Tueart was unbelievable. I thought I'd never seen a footballer that looks anything like this - he turned out to be a lovely lad and one of the most intelligent players that have gone through my hands. Highly intelligent. But when I looked at him, he'd got a long coat on. It went from his shoulders right down to the ground. It was a brown leather skin coat with furry lapels and he looked incredible. He was full of himself as well. Sunderland had won the Cup and he was a young hero,

and I remember coming home to my wife and I said, 'Bloody Hell, luv, we've signed a player today and you're not going to believe it when you see him. I don't know what we've signed! My first impression was that he was a real vagabond - he was gonna be more trouble than he's worth. Yet he turned out to be one of my favourite players of all time. I got on with him like an house on fire. I do business with him, and he turned out to be a smashing player. So it shows you that first impressions aren't always right."

Tueart joined a confused City side. Saunders was trying to inject some discipline into the side, but with so many highly successful, international players he was struggling to win over the majority of the squad. Willie Donachie, who at the age of 22 had already appeared for Scotland and played in Europe, remembered the problems: "Ron Saunders obviously had something about him, but he didn't handle the players right. He treated them badly. It was a real split club. He didn't seem to like the stronger, older players. The ones who would stand up to him. He wanted a team that he could totally control. So the younger players, and may be the quieter ones, were okay. But the older ones... he was determined to be rid of. Now, I don't know if that had been influenced by the Chairman. The players we're talking about were Lee, Summerbee, Denis Law... just all of the big strong personalities. It might have been needed, but the way he went about it just alienated him from everybody.

"He used to organise games like the 'old men' against the young players. Not too subtle is it? He just didn't treat them well. Some of his ideas were good. I'm not trying to knock him because, obviously, he went on to win the League with Villa. He knew the game, and knew how it should be played. But he definitely didn't go about turning City around in the right way."

As Saunders' relationship with the players worsened, so did City's performances on the pitch. Tueart's debut saw City fight out a no-score draw with United: "It was a packed house. Docherty and Cavanagh were United's manager and coach at the time and they were screaming blue murder any time the ball came near me, because I was near the wing. They were wanting their players to get near me. It was a tough baptism. I don't remember much about it, but I did realise that there is an awful lot of passion in Manchester!"

The following two games ended in defeat, with a small section at the back of the Kippax chanting "If you're not coming back, clap your hands" during the 1-0 defeat by Sheffield United. Rumours of 'player power' also started to be heard. Donachie: "That was basically true. The players were so unhappy at that time. The performances were bad. The Club was just very unhappy, and I think the Board realised that."

Frank Carrodus, who went on to make 19 League

appearances in 1973-74 and also played for Saunders at Aston Villa later in his career, believed him to be a good manager, but recognised that his style did not work at City: "I have no doubt whatsoever that Ron Saunders was a great manager. He was tactically aware and, for me, a superb manager. At City he had been very tough on the players and the more senior – and more successful – players were treated no differently from the young hopefuls. In fact he was quite harsh at times. By the time he was at Villa he had learnt that you can't treat all players the same. Some need discipline; some need a gentle word every now and then, and I think Ron realised that at City he hadn't got the balance right. Certainly his man-management was much better at Villa. I enjoyed playing for him at both clubs and I also know that when Villa came in for me the fact he was manager helped."

Back in 1974 City had dropped to sixteenth position, then a 2-1 victory over Newcastle on 27th March, courtesy of two goals from Lee, relieved the pressure for a while. 1-1 Draws against Wolves and Everton (Tueart scored his first goal in this match), brought the real possibility that City could be relegated if their form and attitude deteriorated further. Hearing the concern of some of the players, Swales decided to act: "We started slipping down the League a bit, and all the old hands started stirring it up. Now I had no experience at all of player power... We'd got about six games to go with the possibility of being relegated which would have been a tragedy because I'd only been in the bloody job five minutes. So I thought, 'we're not gonna win another match under Ron Saunders', because the players weren't playing for him - the old hands - whether they knew it or not. They definitely weren't.

"Joe Smith knew I was a bit worried and he said, 'you've got to do what you think you've got to do. If you feel you've got to make a change to keep us in the First Division then you've got to do it'. I thought 'right!' - I think I did it when the papers were shut on Good Friday, and he was sacked. I can still see his face now. He said, 'What do you mean sacked? Look, I've just got you to a cup final, and you WON'T be relegated!' He was probably right, but I'd decided that I couldn't take that chance. I wasn't going to stand for that! So he was fired and we put Tony Book in charge."

With Tony Book in charge, City earned a further five points and ended the season in fourteenth place - four points above the relegation zone. This was the first season of three up/three down, hence the pressure. The final match of the season for City was away to struggling Manchester United. United were desperately trying to avoid relegation themselves, and needed to beat the Blues to stand any chance of salvation. It was one of the most crucial derby games of all time.

The game was not a particularly good one, with both sides unable to find any kind of rhythm. United

appeared quite nervous and were making some pretty basic mistakes, but City were hardly better. Then in the 81st minute the game came alive. A sporadic attack by Colin Bell found Lee, who sent the ball into the penalty area. It found Law standing back to goal near the penalty spot. With typical striker's instinct he brilliantly back-heeled the ball past a startled Alex Stepney to give City the lead. Bell went over to congratulate Law, but the former United star was shell-shocked. A number of fans invaded the pitch, and Law was immediately substituted. He later admitted: "It was no more than a reflex action which made me flick out my heel - and as it was I felt sick. I have seldom felt so depressed in my life as I did that weekend. After 19 years of giving everything I had to score goals, I had finally scored one which I almost wished I hadn't."

The final minutes of the match were marred by a second more ugly pitch invasion from disgruntled United supporters and ended with the game abandoned. The League later ruled the score should stand and United were down. It must be made clear, however, that United would have been relegated regardless of Law's goal. Fellow strugglers Birmingham and Southampton both won on the same afternoon, but the story that made the headlines was that Law had relegated his former club.

In 1996 Dennis Tueart remembered Law's disappointment: "In fairness, people keep referring to Denis's back-heeled goal sending United down, but it didn't actually make a difference. That should really go on record, because Denis was sick at the time. Obviously, he had a passionate feeling for both clubs and he was doing a job like any professional. When the ball comes to Denis Law within striking distance of the goal he doesn't think who he is playing against. It's just natural reaction. And I learnt because Denis was one of my schoolboy heroes... Denis Law and Jim Baxter... It was a pleasure to play with him for those couple of months. In training the lad was a genius, and his finishing was tremendous. But he always gets blamed for putting United down, but he knew at the time that United were doomed because the other results had gone against them. Obviously, it's a good line for some, but I don't think Denis appreciated that line.

"After the game it was unbelievable. I think everybody knows the most direct way from Old Trafford to Maine Road to drop us off, was probably via Chorlton at that time. It was certainly the most direct route. On this night there was an insistence from the body of the coach to go the long way round. Into town, around town, then back out to Maine Road via Moss Side. This was so that we could all wave and beep the horn at all the Man. United fans, and tell them they were going down. It was a strange feeling actually."

The Club's only ever-present that season, Willie Donachie, remembered the post-match celebrations:

"Well, I must say, at the time that was fantastic for us. Looking back it was probably a bit childish, but we were delighted because United are such a big club. They get all the publicity and stuff, and because of the local rivalry, it was great. The local lads really hated United - Doyley and Colin Barrett. They were good lads. But it was never really instilled in the players. It was nothing personal. They were just the big rivals. We wanted to beat them for all our fans in the city."

1974-1975 Look At His Face

The new season commenced with the Blues competing in the Texaco Cup. At the time this was regarded as a first team competition and appearance and goalscoring details were included in player records. The tournament's significance reduced over the years, but in 1974-75 the Blues fielded a strong side as they faced Blackpool (1-1 away), Sheffield United (4-2 defeat at Bramall Lane) and Oldham Athletic (2-1 win at Maine Road) in the group stage.

In truth City treated the tournament as part of their pre-season build-up but those games did see a couple of landmark moments that should not be overlooked. When City beat Oldham 2-1 on 10th August both Francis Lee and Denis Law played their last game for City. In fact this was Law's final first team game of any description and 16 days later he announced his retirement. It is often claimed that his last first team appearance had been the 1974 Old Trafford derby, but he did not actually retire until the new 1974-75 season had commenced. Similarly, his final first team goal was not the one scored at Old Trafford, but one he netted against Sheffield United on 6th August.

Francis Lee's final goal had come against Oldham on 10th August, shortly before he moved to Derby

There were other changes. Mike Summerbee was nearing the end of his distinguished City career, but the arrival of Dennis Tueart had impressed many fans. Another exciting player arrived in August 1974 - £250,000 Asa Hartford. He was described by manager Book at the time as his "first piece of gold", and it was no exaggeration. Hartford brought terrific stamina and determination to the side and was a player capable of dictating the course of the game by his actions in midfield. He was the kind of ball player all great sides wanted, and Book was delighted with the purchase. So were the fans on the Kippax when his debut game ended in a 4-0 victory over West Ham, and his second appearance saw him score the only goal to defeat Tottenham. Hartford said at the time: "The fans have made my job easier already by the way they've welcomed me to Maine Road. I'm made up with the kind of reception I've got. I'm desperate to do well for City. I hope for immediate success and I think playing with such

great players as Colin Bell, Rodney Marsh, and Dennis Tueart must make my kind of job easier."

Whether Hartford's arrival and performance played any part in Denis Law's decision to retire is debatable, but it must be remembered that fans loved both Scottish City number tens.

With a side full of entertainers Book's team made their mark on the League, and by the end of September they were in second position. Liverpool had been the pace-setters but a 2-0 victory - with goals from Marsh and Tueart - on 14th September had knocked them off the top, leaving the race wide open.

Rodney Marsh, who had become the new City captain, had at times suffered from his new responsibility, but in the game against QPR on 28th September he produced a particularly memorable goal in the 83rd minute. His involvement up to that point had been disappointing, but somehow he managed to score from a spectacular overhead kick. One reporter stated that he: "attempted an overhead kick that seemed to have as much chance of success as a batsman hitting the pavilion clock."

Marsh's view: "It came from a corner on the right hand side, glanced off Mike Doyle's head and I stuck out my right foot to control it. I swivelled and launched myself into a bicycle kick. The ball hit the net with force… like a shell. It was just perfect and the goalkeeper – Phil Parkes – could do nothing."

The goal put City second, and everyone started to think that the League Championship was a strong possibility.

The Blues maintained their challenge and headed the table on a couple of occasions in November. Then December came, when a couple of disappointing draws, followed by two miserable defeats left City in eighth position. The last game of December had been particularly painful as former Blue hero Francis Lee returned, and proceeded to score a goal at the Platt Lane End to help Derby to a 2-1 victory. The television cameras were there and as the player celebrated commentator Barry Davies uttered a famous piece of commentary: "Look at his face, just look at his face!" Those words were later used to form part of the opening titles of the BBC's Fantasy Football programme in the mid-1990s, but it was clear in 1974 that Lee had proved his point.

For a moment after the goal was scored some City fans even cheered. Francis Lee: "I think they thought 'What have we done, he's playing for them!'

"I enjoyed my football and I loved scoring so when I scored and the film shows me smiling it was because I'd scored what I thought was a good goal. I picked it up with my back to the line, went through two people and on to score the goal. I loved the goal and it is true that everyone applauded. It had nothing to do with City or revenge or anything like that. I think I enjoyed about 95% of every game I ever played. It was fun. A great way to earn a living, so on that day I was happy."

It's doubtful that Chairman Swales ever regretted transferring the player, but it was obvious that Lee still had a lot to offer. In fact, he helped Derby County to the First Division title that season. Lee: "I think if I'd have stayed and Mike Summerbee – remember he was sold a year after me – then I do think we'd have mounted a serious challenge for the title."

The New Year didn't really provide much to lift the crowd as the FA Cup ended in defeat by Newcastle. City had been drawn away, but an FA ruling following crowd disorder at St. James' Park insisted Newcastle played at Maine Road. Earlier in the season there had also been disappointment in the League Cup as Second Division Manchester United won 1-0 to a hotly disputed penalty in the third round.

In the League, City started to hover around eighth place, with their away form preventing them from maintaining the early season challenge. Everton's Joe Royle had been brought to the Club in a bid to boost the attack, although he only managed to score one goal in the sixteen appearances he made that season. Nevertheless, the signing was an important one for both the player and the Club. Royle: "I'd been at Everton for some time, and I was getting over a back injury. Back surgery. Although I was fully fit. Everton had signed Bob Latchford and Billy Bingham told me, down on the training pitch on Christmas Eve '74 that Manchester City wanted to buy me. I said: 'I'm going'. I signed for City within an hour. I think I signed for a tenner rise, but it was actually costing me money because by the time I was driving every day from Ormskirk my petrol bill was

Colin Bell and Leighton James, City V Burnley, April 1975.

more. But I was just desperate to get away and get a fresh start.

"I'd turned down Birmingham. I'd turned down Crystal Palace. There had been interest from United through Tommy Doc. Then of course City. Chelsea were also interested, but I knew people at City. I knew that the Club would suit me. I had 3 terrific years there. Good strong side. When I first went there I played with Rodney Marsh. Mike Summerbee was still around. Great players. We had terrific support. They love their city. It's often said that they have more Manchester supporters than United do. I don't know whether that's true but they love their City and they realise that it was a good time. A good era."

The season ended with an eighth placed finish, seven points behind champions Derby. The final position was a satisfactory one for manager Tony Book. He had introduced a few new faces and had managed to take the Club forward after the upheaval of the previous season. Fans had been provided with plenty of excitement, and there was hope for the future.

Off the pitch, Peter Swales announced yet further changes to the structure of the Club when he brought in three new faces to help shape the Club's direction. He termed the men 'Vice-Presidents', and claimed the idea was based on a model he had seen working successfully at Barcelona. The new men were Fred Pye - who would look after the Youth set up with Chief Scout Ken Barnes, Bill Adams - given the task of raising funds via organising sportsmen's dinners, and Michael Horwich, whose role had not been clearly defined. Horwich had been one of the original members of Joe Smith's consortium and his arrival as Vice-President

MANCHESTER CITY FOOTBALL CLUB
MAINE ROAD, MOSS SIDE, MANCHESTER

F.A. Challenge Cup — 3rd Round
NEWCASTLE UNITED
v
CITY

BLOCK
Y2

Saturday, 4th January 1975
Kick-off 3-15 p.m.

You are advised to take up your position
half an hour before the kick-off

ENTRANCE
ROW
25

J. B. Halford
Secretary

SEAT
24

PLATT LANE STAND
65p
TO BE RETAINED (SEE PLAN AND CONDITIONS ON BACK)

City away at Maine Road in the FA Cup against Newcastle.

meant that every member of that consortium was now involved with the Club. Horwich had also worked with Chris Muir, in the early 1960s, to try and gain control of the Club.

The changes didn't really affect the Club in 1975, but in later years, many would say that these appointments helped increase the size of the Board without really benefiting the Club. The idea seemed a good one, but whether the Club achieved any long term benefits is open to debate.

1975-1976 Overhead

By the start of the 1975-76 season Mike Summerbee had been transferred to Burnley for £25,000, while Tony Book splashed out £200,000 to purchase central defender Dave Watson from Sunderland. Watson immediately pledged his loyalty to the Blue cause by signing a six year contract. He made his debut on 2nd August 1975: "My first game was away at Blackpool in the Anglo-Scottish Cup and Joe Corrigan said to me after that game: 'I don't know how we've coped without you'. I asked him what he meant and he told me about all the things I'd done in that game that would normally be left to him. So that was nice and it made me feel at home immediately. The City fans made me welcome and took to me immediately. They were fantastic."

This transfer brought City's total of internationals to eight, but before the end of the season, the improved form of Joe Corrigan would make the total nine. The Blues were viewed as a wealthy, glamorous club, with somewhere in the region of 15,000 season ticket holders backing Book's bid for success. The media believed City were high spenders and a figure of £1.5 million was quoted as being the amount the Blues had spent under Swales. That figure had been inflated, and in any case seemed to overlook the money brought into the Club from sales, but it was a signal to all in the game that City were prepared and able to compete for star players. Although, they didn't always get their man.

One player who seemed destined to sign for the Blues was England captain and future City manager Alan Ball. In May 1975, Peter Swales felt convinced the Arsenal player would sign for City and seemed prepared to sell Rodney Marsh to raise the funds. *The News Of The World* even suggested that City would be prepared to sell Dennis Tueart if it guaranteed Ball's signature. Eventually, the transfer died and neither Tueart nor Marsh were sold to fund the purchase. Ball remained at Arsenal until December 1976 when he moved on to Southampton. Nevertheless, it was an indication that City were continually being linked with football's most famous stars and that the Blues were perceived as a buying club. Whether they could afford it is another matter altogether.

Rodney Marsh was, by this time, the captain: "It was a major honour. I captained every side I ever played for and I've always been very proud to do so. To be captain of Manchester City… it's not something you can appropriately describe because it's only those selected that fully understand what an accolade it actually is."

The season got off to a flying start with a 3-0 victory over newly promoted Norwich. After the game Norwich manager John Bond told the press that City had been physical and had intimidated his players. The Blues denied it, but the media started to look for negative play.

Whether physical or not, City's poor away form continued from the previous season as the first four away games at Coventry, Aston Villa, West Ham, and Derby all ended in defeat. These defeats left the Blues in mid-table, but progression in the League Cup brought hope. City had been drawn away at Norwich and John Bond was once again complaining. After a 1-1 draw Bond's comments appeared in the newspapers, with the media claiming that Bond was 'anti-City'. That angered the Norwich manager and in City's programme for the replay he tried to defend himself: "I've no anti-feelings towards them at all. My comments after our games were opinions that I felt justified in expressing at the time.

"In the League match at Maine Road I accused them of being physical. And they were. Not everybody in the side, but certain people. And at our place in the League Cup I said they were terribly negative, and I do not sway from this opinion. I don't know whether Tony Book came to our place and might have said, 'sod it', we've got our own priorities. But I can assure you that Manchester City lost a lot of good friends in our area with their tactics last Wednesday. I have a feeling for football generally and the game will disintegrate unless managers and coaches like ourselves do something about it. These feelings were the basis of the views I expressed. I'm not a person who takes any delight at being anti-anything in soccer."

The replay ended 2-2 after extra-time and forced the game to a second replay at neutral Stamford Bridge. That game ended 6-1 and included a hat-trick from Dennis Tueart. In the next round City faced Second Division Nottingham Forest on 8th October at Maine Road. In comments that appeared the total opposite of John Bond's, Clough told the press: "I was praying Manchester City would beat Norwich because I wanted to play the best. City are one of the most entertaining and talented sides in the First Division at home. We have no serious thoughts of shocking City but we hope to give a good account of ourselves against a side that is potentially one of the best in the land.

"When I last came to Maine Road it was with Leeds United and we lost 2-1. If we keep the score down to 2-1 tonight then I think we'll show the strides that Nottingham Forest have taken."

Clough, one of football's most knowledgeable men,

predicted the score accurately with goals from Bell and Royle helping City achieve the 2-1 result. That win put City into the fourth round and set Manchester up for a League Cup derby match for the second successive year. This time the game would be played at Maine Road between two first Division sides. The Blues were determined to win and, by the end of the game, United had been soundly thrashed.

City effectively ended the contest inside the opening thirty minutes when they ran United's defence ragged with some highly skilful and exciting football. As early as the first minute the Blues took the lead when Tueart pulled down a pass and comfortably drove the ball into the net, but five minutes later tragedy struck when Colin Bell did not get up following a tackle from United captain Martin Buchan.

Colin Bell will never forget the entire incident: "I remember Dennis Tueart knocking me through on the inside-right position, and I had three options - the first I was going to have a shot if the ball would sit right, from about 25 to 30 yards out. Or I could even quicken up and go for goal first thing. The third option was to drag the ball inside a defender - and it was Martin Buchan as it happens. I was weight bearing on my right leg as I dragged the ball to let him go past at speed, and he caught my knee - bent the knee backwards, burst a couple of blood vessels, did the ligaments, did the cartilage, and off I went. That was the beginning of the end of my career."

The City fans chanted 'Animal' to Buchan as Bell was stretchered off. They firmly believed the injury was intentional, but Bell holds a different view: "People ask me if the tackle was done on purpose. I don't believe it was and don't believe things like that should happen in the game. No - it's a man's game, you take the knocks. I've only got to be thankful that I was in my late twenties when picking up the injury."

Tueart felt that the injury was a major blow to the Club: "It didn't look anything at the time. It really didn't. I've seen it on tape many, many times. I've watched it in slow motion, slowed it right down still trying to see, and it looks so innocuous. But you knew that when Colin went down there really was a big problem. At the time you had no idea of the extent of the damage. It also left a major hole in our side - a major hole! He would have been a major miss to any side, but ours in particular because we had such a balanced side. Such a settled team. He and I worked quite well together because I used to operate on the right a lot and he did as well. If I drifted off and left the position he would fill it. Then there was his

phenomenal ability to get up and down the field. And of course his goalscoring as well. Although we went on to win the League Cup, that was the biggest setback, and I don't think we were really as good after Colin's injury."

Dave Watson was another to recognise the significance of Bell's injury: "You always want to play in good teams, win trophies and at City I settled very quickly. There was quality all over the place and we were confident of success in the League Cup. Obviously we were missing Colin after that awful tie with United in November. I went to see him in hospital the next day and he was pure white. Someone said you couldn't pick him out from the sheet! There was a lot of gallows humour at the time because we all thought he'd get better. I think his demise then for the England team was bad... it was bad enough for City but with England he was so important and would have been in his position for the following 8 years. He could have gone to Spain in '82 and what a difference he could have made in the qualification for '78. That's how important he was."

At first the story went around that Bell would return within a month or so, but as time went by the realisation set in that Bell would never again be the instrumental figure he had been before.

Tommy Booth was brought on to replace Bell, and with determination the Blues dominated the match. Asa Hartford was the star man as he gave a tremendous display and after 28 minutes he netted from Royle's knock-down. About seven minutes later a mistake by Buchan allowed the ball to reach Tueart who drilled it past Roche for City's third.

In the Second half Royle clipped in a Peter Barnes' cross into the North Stand goal. It was a well-deserved 4-0 thrashing and, once again, proved City's seventies superiority over United. It also helped to prove the ability of manager Tony Book who won the Bell's manager of the month award for November.

In the quarter-finals City faced Third Division Mansfield Town on 3rd December at Maine Road. The game ended 4-2, but the match was not as comfortable as the scoreline suggests. When City were leading 3-2 Mansfield's Terry Eccles missed a chance, and City hung on. Fortunately Hartford scored late on to provide enough of a gap, and the Blues went through

By the mid-1970s City's young supporters' organisation, the Junior Blues, was the largest junior supporters' organisation in the world.

to the two legged semi-final against Jack Charlton's Middlesbrough.

The first game at Ayresome Park ended in a 1-0 defeat, but it was not a poor performance by the Blues. In fact after the match Middlesbrough's local newspaper, the *Evening Gazette*, predicted it would be difficult for their side to overcome City in the second leg. As it was, it had taken Middlesbrough almost 66 minutes to break the deadlock, thanks to City's excellent defence. The majority of the game was played out in midfield with Oakes, Hartford, and the emerging Paul Power putting up a good fight. In attack Royle and Tueart's attempts were impressive, with Tueart doing all he could to silence the Middlesbrough fans who booed his every touch.

Tony Book fired his men up for the second leg. Another man ready for the game was Mike Doyle, who had taken over the captaincy from Rodney Marsh. Marsh had now left the Club for a chance to establish the game in the USA, joining Tampa Bay Rowdies on 12th January, though in October 2009 he pointed out that he had wanted to stay at Maine Road: "I'll tell you the absolute truth. I was captain and we were really flying. I was enjoying my football and I was really, really happy. We beat Norwich 6-1 in the League Cup and Arsenal 3-2 – I scored an header – at the start of October. Our next match was Burnley and although we'd been scoring goals for fun… for example, 4-0 V Newcastle & Middlesbrough… somehow the Burnley game was one of those days when the ball just wouldn't go in. Tony Book and coach Ian McFarlane were apoplectic.

"We came off the pitch and McFarlane went ballistic. As captain I told him to calm down as did one of the other players, but McFarlane lashed out at the player. I became very vocal and told him what I thought and that treating the players like this was an absolute disgrace.

"Somehow the press found out and I was called to see the Chairman Peter Swales. He asked me what had happened and then asked me my views on Book and McFarlane. As captain I told him that I wasn't happy with the way the situation had been handled – sure we didn't beat Burnley, but we got a draw and it was hardly the end of the world. It didn't warrant what happened."

Despite Marsh's comments the decision was taken to place the player on the transfer list: "I never played for City again. I was put on the transfer list. I was at the pinnacle of my career… I was captain of Manchester City… Five years later Peter Swales came up to me in a restaurant in Manchester and sheepishly apologised. He told me he'd had 7,000 letters from fans and that he knew I was right. For me, once I was put on the transfer list that was it I guess. Anderlecht and a few big British sides came in for me and it was all very flattering, but in the end I decided that if I couldn't play for City then I'd rather leave Europe and try something new. I went to the States."

Doyle was the right man to replace Marsh as captain. He had proved, time and time again, his determination.

The second leg of the League Cup tie saw a youthful side tear Middlesbrough apart. In the fifth minute 19 year old Peter Barnes, son of former City Cup winner Ken, crossed the ball to 20 year old Ged Keegan, who proceeded to head home his first senior goal. Immediately the pressure of the first game was lifted and City were able to control the match. Six minutes later Keegan laid the ball off for the experienced Alan Oakes to fire a left-foot shot past the Middlesbrough 'keeper.

In 2005 Alan Oakes admitted that he loved this period of his career, especially playing with Peter Barnes: "I enjoyed it all, and I remember playing a few games with Peter Barnes in front of me. I loved that. He was such a gifted player and it was great for me to play behind someone that exciting at that stage in my career and in his. I know this came a couple of years after I'd moved on, but it irritated me when Peter Barnes was sold because I believe he could have helped City to real success. He was the sort of player you built a team around."

The dominance over Middlesbrough continued and a minute into the second half Barnes scored to bring a 3-1 aggregate lead. One minute from the end Joe Royle made it four, and kept his record of scoring in every round. City were back at Wembley, for their third League Cup Final. Their opponents would be Newcastle United, and the race for Cup Final tickets was a tough one. In 1974 some final tickets had been put on open sale, but in 1976 a large increase in the number of season ticket holders, and a reduction in the amount of tickets available meant that City could not satisfy their average attendance. A large number of fans were disappointed, but secretary Bernard Halford pointed out that the Club had done all it could and that he had even taken the step of writing to all the other League clubs, apart from Newcastle of course, asking for any spare tickets from their allocations.

The final was played on 28th February with City very much the favourites. Newcastle were suffering with injuries and 'flu symptoms and had a poor build up to the match, whereas the Blues were staying at a health farm in the Chilterns with few if any problems. Every member of the side had already played at Wembley except Peter Barnes and Ged Keegan, but they seemed relatively confident in any case.

In preparation for the big game, captain Mike Doyle told the press that the Blues would do all they could to win the trophy. In 1974 City had tried to play with style and found themselves on the losing side, this time Doyle revealed that style didn't matter: "I couldn't care less if the final is rubbish to watch… as long as we win the League Cup. And we will! The success of this City is the complete team work - and individuals don't count. I'm sorry Colin [Bell] hasn't made it, but I'm damned sure it hasn't weakened our chances, because we've proved it. We've been without him for three months and still reached Wembley."

During the interview reporter Alec Johnson suggested that Wembley newcomers Peter Barnes and Ged Keegan would be the ones likely to let City down. Doyle, who was later named 'Man of the Match' by the *Sunday Mirror*, refused to accept that point of view: "Rubbish! Peter is not only a tremendously talented player - he's got his head screwed on the right way. He just isn't the sort to get all worked up. In fact, I'll bet that he could prove the biggest success of the whole match. He's a natural. He does things superbly without having to think or worry.

"Keegan is in the same mould. He'll feel at home, because he's already one of the City first team pool. If he wasn't something special he wouldn't be in it!"

As the game commenced both sides played open, attractive football, although Newcastle seemed to have the edge for a while. Joe Corrigan palmed a 25 yarder from Malcolm Macdonald round the post at one point, then a foul by Newcastle's Keeley on Royle brought an important free-kick. Hartford took the kick and sent the ball to Royle, who headed the ball across the face of the goal. Barnes stormed in to fire a half-volley into the net to give City an eleventh minute lead.

Barnes, who that season won the PFA Young player of the Year award, immediately ran off the pitch in celebration, while the City supporters on the East Terrace danced with delight.

Twenty four minutes later, it was the turn of the Newcastle fans to celebrate when Macdonald sent in a low centre. Watson, Corrigan and Newcastle's Gowling all raced for the ball with the Newcastle man managing to get to it first and stab home for the equaliser. Former Sunderland player Watson was particularly disappointed, but Mike Doyle quickly pulled his side together and ensured Newcastle were kept at bay for the remainder of the half.

As the players came out for the second half, all Blues hoped for an early goal to re-establish control of the game, but few expected it to arrive within a minute of the restart. Naturally Dennis Tueart knows exactly

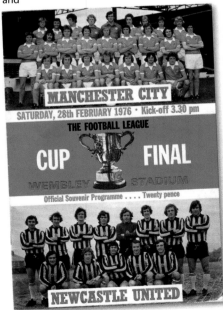

MANCHESTER CITY

SATURDAY, 28th FEBRUARY 1976 · Kick-off 3.30 pm

THE FOOTBALL LEAGUE

CUP FINAL

WEMBLEY STADIUM

Official Souvenir Programme .... Twenty pence

NEWCASTLE UNITED

how the goal came about: "Apart from the style of the finishing, it was a move we'd used an awful lot. When Colin Bell got injured we would try several different players to fit in there and we ended up with Tommy Booth playing right side midfield - Tommy was a centre half but he had a lovely touch, lovely player on the ball, that was the beauty of Manchester City we always had good ball players with ability, right from the back to the front. Tommy came in and did a job on the right side of midfield, and it was no good me going to the far post for crosses with Willie Donachie always marauding down that left side. Always coming out and getting down that left side. He always marauded, did it loads of times, and Willie's always either knocking them short or playing far post. Tommy would get the far post and, as I say, I would drift off and go into the middle to find any bits of spare balls dropping down. I'd try to get on the end of the knock downs not the first one.

"The goal itself, I've seen it on tape. Willie's going, I've gone to the far post, then come away from the far post because Tommy's gone there. But as I've checked back into the centre, I'd gone in too far, the ball's gone over to Tommy. Tommy's got half a head on it, and knocked it back. It just went a wee bit behind me. Well, I'd always been fairly good at volleying right from an early age, and I'd scored a goal, probably it was the first or second game of the season, against Norwich. Which I think was technically a better goal, it flew in the net, overhead kick. I'd scored overhead kicks at school, I'd side volleyed which is slightly different, but timing and volleying had always been a strength, and it just came. Speak to Denis Law and he'll tell you any balls that come to you as a forward, no matter which way they come to you, you just try and twist your body and get some kind of contact onto it. Because you know the general area where the goal is, and I connected pretty well, it went across and bounced in.

"It was important because they'd come back before half time and got the equaliser. We'd worked a good free kick for the first goal. Well worked. Marvellous when I see it on tape. Because we'd tried it on the training pitch, and it worked to perfection. So that gave us the lead. Then they got a good goal back, we'd been caught a little bit square at the back. Then it was important because it was the 46th minute, just after half time, when we got ourselves back in front. I've never known so many people have a go at me for scoring a goal

Dennis Tueart's match-winning overhead kick in the 1976 League Cup Final.

too early, because they were still at the toilet or queuing for a cup of tea! They couldn't get back in time. It was an important goal though, because we'd dominated the majority of the first half. But we went in at 1-1. So, it was important to get quickly back in the lead again, and make them come out again. Which we did. 46th minute you can't have much before that in the Second Half!"

It was very nearly Joe Royle who scored the winner, but his effort had been disallowed. Royle: "It would have been nice. I'd scored in every round and that would have been the full set. The winning was more important though, we just had to contend with Dennis afterwards!" A laughing Royle added: "It would have been nice if I'd scored the winner instead of Dennis. Dennis was always quick to let you know... He's never been short on confidence as our Dennis!"

Tueart and Royle obviously enjoyed playing together and helped foster a good team spirit. Tueart enjoyed Royle's ribbing: "That's the spirit we had in the team. Joe was a great one liner. You need people like that in your side. Joe was a bright lad, and as sharp as a tack. Full of one liners, and that creates good team spirit and a bit of relaxation. We had one or two characters, good one liners, good banter, good team spirit. Joe was an artist at that."

The arrival of Royle had helped Tueart's own career: "Joe was essential for me. People don't appreciate how much skill Joe had. Touch and ability with the ball at his feet was phenomenal. People used to think he was a big, old fashioned centre-forward, but he was far more than that. He had a lovely touch with the ball and good positional ability, and from my point of view, because I used to play off him, he was essential. Lots of people see quite a few of my goals that Joe had a hand in somewhere. He was a good character as well."

During the final Newcastle did have chances to level again later on, but City really were the more dominant side. The goal seemed to kill much of the fight that had pushed the 'flu stricken Newcastle side forward. At the final whistle Tueart swapped shirts with Alan Kennedy and wore his home town colours for the Cup presentation, while Dave Watson's Blue shirt was rapidly becoming blood stained. The big centre half, who had been doubtful for the game right up until three hours before kick-off due to problems with a slipped disc, collided with Alan Gowling when the Newcastle man attempted a glancing back header, and after the match television cameras filmed him having stitches in the dressing room. It was a scene more familiar to viewers of General Hospital, rather than football but City enjoyed

Joe Corrigan and Mike Doyle with famous supporter Helen 'the Bell' Turner.

the attention. Watson remembered in December 2009: "I think that was the first time they'd ever gone into the dressing room for interviews. Our physio Freddie Griffiths saw the camera come through the door and called them in. I was lying on the treatment bed and the doctor was doing my stitches. Before I knew it Brian Moore was stood there with a microphone in front of me interviewing me. He was asking me what I was having done and asking about the game. I'm a bit dazed but I'm answering him. It was all a bit surreal.

"I used to bleed a lot, so there was nothing unusual about that. I'd get cut in most games and I think it was when players threw their arms up when we went up for the ball. Most of my memories of the final are fairly insignificant memories really. Tackling... I can vividly remember tackling Malcolm Macdonald. I can see it. He was a bustling, tough centre-forward who was decent in the air but I could usually beat him. This one time he'd just beaten me in the air and then this tackle came. I used to pride myself that I could tackle with both feet even though I was predominantly right-footed. This time he dropped his shoulder and came the other way. He drifted a bit further left which meant that anyone not competent on their left foot would struggle to get a tackle in. I thought 'no, you bugger! I'll get you'. He moved it again. Then he was about to move it again and I swept him up. Beautiful."

Pre-match Macdonald was tipped to be the star of the final. Watson: "He'd done interviews and said what he would do to City. He would run us ragged. That helped us of course. I'm not saying it made a difference to our planning or anything but it was very satisfying when we won. I remember seeing him on the pitch

crying at the end and I tend to think you should always let your football do the talking. Don't boast about what you're going to do... go out there and do it. We did it at Wembley that day."

As well as Watson's medical treatment, another moment caught by the cameras was the sight of the injured Colin Bell waiting for the winners in the dressing room. He was naturally delighted with City's success, but viewers realised that his loss had been a major one. Then, as the dressing room became more lively, Dennis Tueart filled the League Cup with champagne and walked into the Newcastle dressing room to offer his opponents a drink. Malcolm Macdonald, who over the years suffered a great deal at the hands of City - most notably when his Huddersfield side were defeated 10-1 in 1987 - was the first to drink. It was a gesture appreciated by Newcastle and one which Tueart felt necessary: "What else could I do in the circumstances. They have some wonderful fans up there and I used to be one of them as a kid."

Manager Book, who became the first man to win the trophy as a player and as a manager, was delighted with the result: "This was my greatest moment. It was a tremendous final and Tueart's goal was something special... quite out of this world."

On the Sunday, City returned home to a tour of Manchester, and the whole city appeared to turn out. It was a great day of celebration which most Blues expected to be the first of many during the latter years of the decade. Peter Swales: "As Chairman, the 1976 League Cup was my first trophy, and I certainly didn't think it would be my last! It was great to win it, but the League Cup wasn't the highlight it should have been because, obviously, I thought it was the first of many. I probably felt like Johnson did when Everton won the FA Cup in '95. He would certainly have thought 'this is the first of plenty'."

The rest of the 1975-76 season was a bit of an anti-climax. City had been knocked out of the FA Cup at Stoke in the fourth round, and their League form had not been consistent prior to Wembley, although the Blues managed to hold on to a position of sixth at the time of the final. By winning the League Cup, City had already qualified for the UEFA Cup, so apart from a final push for the title they had little to play for.

On 13th March it was still possible for the Blues to mount a serious challenge for the title as they lay in seventh place, eleven points behind leaders QPR with three games in hand, but they would have had to rely on a number of other powerful sides failing. It never happened as the Blues appeared to stroll along with little interest, although everyone connected with the Club denied this. City ended the season eighth, seventeen points behind champions Liverpool, but Chairman Swales predicted that further glory was on its way.

He held the belief that City would dominate the late seventies, and felt that improvements at Maine Road would help increase attendances. He pointed out that support was already increasing - City averaged 34,281 - and used the visit of Derby County as an example, stating that over 41,000 City supporters were present in a crowd of 42,061 when there was nothing at stake for the home side. He did overlook one significant aspect of that day – the return of Colin Bell. Although Swales may not have recognised the significance, supporters did and the crowd was almost 10,000 more than the previous home game against Wolves.

The Blues defeated Derby 4-3 and Bell survived the full 90 minutes. His next League game came seven days later when he netted City's consolation goal in a 2-1 defeat at Leeds. He played two further games, both at home to Liverpool and Arsenal, and managed to play every minute of all four of his return games, but it was clear that he was not quite ready. Bell himself recognised this: "I tried a comeback towards the end of 1975-76 but after the fourth game (Arsenal) I broke down. It was too soon."

TRUE BLUE
Colin Bell

Regarded by the majority of fans as City's greatest ever player.

1973-1976 SUMMARY

Major Trophies Won: The League Cup 1975-76
Highest League Attendance: 51,331 Manchester United, 13/03/74
Highest Cup Attendance: 50,182 Manchester United, 12/11/75 (League Cup)
Managers: 1973 Johnny Hart, 1973 – 1974 Ron Saunders & 1974 – 1979 (continued as General Manager until 8 October 1980) Tony Book

Seasonal Record:

Season	League	Posn	FA Cup	League Cup	Other	Leading Scorer	Average Attendance
1973-74	FL Div1	14	Rnd 4	Final	Charity Shield Runners-up	Lee 10	30,756
1974-75	FL Div1	8	Rnd 3	Rnd 3	Texaco Cup Grp 1	Bell 15	32,898
1975-76	FL Div1	8	Rnd 4	Winners	Anglo-Scottish Grp 1	Tueart 14	34,281

1976 LEAGUE CUP RUN

R2	Norwich City	A	D	1-1
	Norwich City	H	D	2-2
	Norwich City	N*	W	6-1
R3	Nottingham Forest	H	W	2-1
R4	Manchester United	H	W	4-0
R5	Mansfield Town	H	W	4-2
SF1	Middlesbrough	A	L	0-1
SF2	Middlesbrough	H	W	4-0
F	Newcastle United	N**	W	2-1

*= Stamford Bridge   ** = Wembley Stadium*

	P	W	D	L	F	A
HOME	5	4	1	0	16	5
AWAY	4	2	1	1	9	4
TOTAL	9	6	2	1	25	9

FINAL DETAILS
28 February 1976 at Wembley Stadium
Manchester City 2-1 Newcastle United
CITY: Corrigan, Keegan, Donachie, Doyle, Watson, Oakes, Barnes, Booth, Royle, Hartford, Tueart.
NEWCASTLE UNITED: Mahoney, Nattrass, Kennedy, Barrowclough, Keeley, Howard, Burns, Cassidy, Macdonald, Gowling, Craig.
GOALS: Barnes, Tueart, Gowling
ATTENDANCE: 100,000
REFEREE: J.K Taylor (Wolverhampton)
GUEST OF HONOUR: The Duke of Norfolk
MANAGER: Tony Book
CAPTAIN: Mike Doyle

Dave Watson looking a bit bemused by Milan's Gianni Rivera's gift of flowers, San Siro 1978.

1976-1979
Glamour City

"Nights like Milan are what the game's about. They don't come cheap. A lot of work goes into it. I was immensely proud of that team, and we were so pumped up for it. The Milan crowd were going mad. It was unknown for any team to go to Milan and put them under so much pressure. The crowd were throwing things at us... just like their team was throwing everything at us on the pitch in the second half."

Former captain Dave Watson looking back on the Milan UEFA Cup tie (1978) in 2009

1976-1977 Maintaining A Title Challenge

Everybody had huge expectations for the 1976-77 season, and once again the Club paraded a new expensive signing. This time it was former Red Brian Kidd, signed from Arsenal for £100,000. City also signed Jimmy Conway for £30,000 from Fulham, but he only made eleven League appearances during the season.

There was also one significant departure, Alan Oakes. Oakes signed for Chester for a fee of £15,000, after making 665 appearances plus 3 as substitute for the Blues in a career stretching back to 1958: "I'd had a great season. I'd played 39 League games and won the League Cup and so there was no pressure to leave, but I did think that I may have blocked some other gifted players coming through. I was also aware that I'd be 34 when the new season starts and that I may not be up to it in the way I would normally expect. Chester City were just up the road and for me it was a nice move. I do remember thinking 'what have I done?' because I'd gone from a First Division palace to play at Third Division grounds, but the move was a good one. Looking back though I was perhaps wrong to leave when I did. My advice to any player now is to remain playing at the highest level for as long as you physically can. Those days are precious and should not be cut short."

There were other changes including the introduction of an all blue kit. Ever since City's earliest days the Club had worn white shorts and blue shirts, but the decision was taken in 1976 to make a break with tradition and adopt blue shorts. It was not a popular move and resulted in criticism in the match programme.

The season opened with a 2-2 draw at Leicester and the Blues remained undefeated until their seventh game, by which time they were second to Liverpool. City had already been defeated in the League Cup, losing 3-0 to Ron Saunders Aston Villa, but were a little more hopeful of success in Europe. They faced the Italian giants Juventus on 15th September at Maine Road determined to re-establish their European credentials, while the bulk of the City squad hoped to impress England manager and former Blue Don Revie who was watching from the Main Stand.

The game, watched by 36,955 ended with a narrow victory to the Blues. Brian Kidd netted the only goal of the game and his first for the Club, but it was not a good enough lead. Tony Book had hoped for a two goal advantage, but was still hopeful of glory in the second leg: "I am extremely confident. I do not promise victory in the second leg. Nor do I foresee defeat. The vital thing is going to be the first goal scored - the team that gets it could easily carry off the title."

Book accurately predicted success for the victors, sadly it was Juventus who went on to win both the game and the competition. Before 55,000 in rainy conditions in Turin Juventus defeated City 2-0.

Tueart believes City's failure was simply as a result of inexperience on the continent: "Against Juventus we didn't do too badly in the first game, but we only got the one goal. I think that was because we were a little inexperienced compared to the likes of Liverpool. They had a European head on. They knew how to play in Europe. We didn't. We still went out with all the flair and the creative things that we had in the English League. We just didn't have the ability to play European style at that time. We weren't ready.

"We'd only just come together within 18 months and then we were in Europe. Probably from Tony Book's view as well, he was a little inexperienced as far as Europe was concerned. There wasn't any major change in tactics. We only got the one goal lead which Juventus were happy with. It would have been nice to have been drawn away first - see what we could do there - and then bring them back here. The goal was just before half-time, which is a great time to score, but we couldn't break them down in the second half. They just got behind the ball. Then we went to Juventus, 2-0. They kicked ten bells out of us, unbelievable! Tommy Booth was defending a corner and the ball came over. Tommy went up to head clear, and

this guy came up behind him. I think it was Tardelli, the Italian international, and he came up with six studs in the middle of Tommy's back. Straight through the middle of his back. Tommy went flying... and the referee didn't do anything! He just played on, unbelievable! And that's where we were very inexperienced. Very, very poor in that European tie. No real steel, no European steel."

The defeat could have seriously affected City's motivation but Book, with Chief Coach Bill Taylor, managed to ensure everyone connected with the Club realised how strong a side Juventus were. Defeat was no disgrace. In the League City continued to impress and after a 2-2 draw at Everton on 5th October, the Blues headed the table. A draw against QPR followed and then a 1-0 defeat at Ipswich caused a little concern.

From the Ipswich defeat on 23rd October, through to a 1-0 defeat at Bristol City on 19th February the Blues managed to remain undefeated in 17 League and Cup games. In the FA Cup they defeated West Bromwich Albion 1-0 in a replay, and Newcastle 3-1 at St. James' Park, then on 26th February came the fifth round tie at Leeds. It was a tough, backs to the wall battle, and looked destined to end goalless until Leeds' captain Trevor Cherry managed to score a last gasp winner. City now had to concentrate on the League if 1977 was to be a trophy winning year.

During the unbeaten run the Blues established themselves as a top three side, although they could have seized the initiative themselves had the game with leaders Liverpool on 29th December ended in victory. City were leading through a goal from Royle when, in the 88th minute Dave Watson headed past Corrigan to score an own goal on a slippery, icy Maine Road pitch. The goal levelled the scores, and cost the side a great deal more. Had they won the two points would have made a big difference at the time, but it wasn't to be.

On 2nd April City, lying in third place, entertained fellow challengers Ipswich Town. A crowd of 42,780 witnessed a 2-1 City victory with goals from Kidd and Watson – the Watson goal was talked about for years. Watson: "I'll never forget the goal I scored against Ipswich Town in April 1977. It was such an important one and so many fans over the years have discussed it with me. City and Ipswich were second and third in the League, and were both putting considerable pressure on Liverpool. We couldn't afford to lose, and Peter Barnes sent a great ball in. I met it about eight feet in the air and headed it in from about twelve yards out. Mick Mills said that I'd rose up and headed it in before he'd even had chance to move. It gave me a lot of satisfaction and, of course, we won the match 2-1."

Afterwards Ipswich manager Bobby Robson sportingly told Tony Book: "If we don't win it, I hope you do." Six days later on Good Friday City defeated Leeds by the same scoreline, then the following day travelled to Anfield a point behind Liverpool. Sadly Kevin Keegan scored for the home side just before half-time and Liverpool went on to win 2-1.

Three successive victories against Middlesbrough (1-0), West Bromwich Albion (2-0), and Birmingham (2-1) kept City in with a shout, but a 4-0 defeat at Derby on 30th April was a huge set back, especially as Derby scored all four in the last 25 minutes. In addition Brian Kidd was sent off, and the pitch was in an atrocious state. The Blues remained second however, two points behind reigning champions Liverpool, one point above Ipswich, and Tony Book remained determined. The truth was, however, that with four games to go, time was running out. As with European competition, Liverpool were used to surviving the League marathon, City were not.

At Aston Villa on 4th May, City only managed a 1-1 draw, then three days later they murdered Tottenham 5-0 at Maine Road to keep the pressure on. On the same day, Liverpool scraped a 1-1 draw at QPR after going a goal behind in the first half. The difference was still two points, although the Merseysiders had a game in hand.

On 10th May Book's side could only manage a point against Everton to raise their tally to 54, but Liverpool's game at Coventry ended goalless to more or less guarantee them the title. Liverpool's goal difference was superior, and with a game in hand there seemed no chance of them failing. Four days later City ended their campaign with a 1-0 win at Coventry, while Liverpool played out another no score draw at home to West Ham to guarantee the championship. Two days later, their final game ended in a 2-1 defeat at Bristol, and resulted in City missing the title by a point. Dave Watson felt responsible: "That was a great season and we were really looking good. We missed the title by a point to Liverpool. I scored an own goal against Liverpool that season and that point would have won us the championship. I feel responsible. Most defenders take responsibility whereas forwards don't need to. They miss chances, but our mistakes are noticed. If I was picking a 5-a-side team during training I'd always go for the defenders because the team that's going to win is a team of defenders. We'd chase back... Not take too many chances… whereas the forwards would lose the ball and not chase back. My first rule is always 'If they don't score we can't lose' and that's a good starting point."

Although disappointing at the time, it was a remarkable achievement, especially as Liverpool were at their 70s peak. That same season they narrowly missed out on the treble of the League, FA Cup, and European Cup when they failed to overcome Manchester United in the FA Cup Final. Tueart: "We weren't good enough really. We finished one point behind Liverpool, but their last game was academic. In my opinion they'd won it comfortably."

Peter Swales felt that the injury to Colin Bell, the previous season had cost them the title: "It was the biggest single stroke of bad luck that we had when he was chopped down at the height of his career really. Because you're not going to tell me that we wouldn't have won the League Championship that year without him. He was a brilliant footballer. Terrific speed. Scored plenty of goals. He had everything! Lovely, Belly! He was the greatest player I ever saw. No question. And I include all the greats in that that I saw as a kid. I also include in that George Best. Most people would say that Best was better than Bell, but in my opinion Colin Bell was the best player I've seen in a City shirt, and probably the best I've seen playing for England."

Bell was still trying to fight his way back to fitness as the 1976-77 season ended. It was a long, painful process. One other player who had been struggling to overcome injury caused in a Manchester derby was Glyn Pardoe. Prior to the start of the 1976-77 season he was forced to retire, after almost six years battling to rediscover full fitness. He had managed to make 43 League appearances in the five years that followed the injury, but for a player of his age and ability that total was painfully low considering what he could have achieved. In the history of City, the loss of a fully fit Pardoe should always be bracketed with the loss of Bell. Both careers ended prematurely following serious leg injury against United.

Pardoe's struggle was over, Bell's would continue for two further years.

1977-1978 Bell's Return

The 1976-77 season had ended with City averaging crowds of over forty thousand for the first time since the 1940s. They were the third best supported club behind Liverpool and Manchester United and entered the new season full of optimism. Over 23,000 supporters purchased the superbly priced season tickets with the most expensive ticket costing £37. The Kippax terracing price for 1977-78 was a 'staggering' £11, which would bring a significant saving of £5.80 over the year. Chairman Swales was determined to ensure Maine Road provided quality football at knock down prices, and believed this would help City achieve his ultimate ambition: "My initial ten years in the job was completely motivated by me wanting to get over Manchester United. I'd seen City do well in the late 60s and still couldn't catch United for crowds and support, so my life was devoted to doing them."

Swales continued to travel all over the world to boost City's support, and often created a story for the media to latch on to. Tommy Docherty once joked that Swales liked publicity so much that he carried a card saying: "In case of emergency, please call a press conference." Many believed this demonstrated the

Chairman's desire to see his own name in print, the actual truth was that Swales wanted publicity for City: "I think it's fair that I wanted to see City's name everywhere... in all the papers. I think that's fair. The thing I never calculated was the impact that Munich had on the world at large. There you had a great club whose team was virtually wiped out in a terrible accident, and that really made United. It cemented their name worldwide and we could never overcome that. Nobody will ever catch them now, and that was the thing that I tried to do. Nobody else will ever be able to do that. We came closest... closer than anybody else in the 70s... and we're in the same bloody city!"

Swales tried desperately hard to overtake Manchester United. The Blues gave it their best shot, but a series of major cock-ups leading into the 1980s started to send the Club in the opposite direction.

The 1977-78 season opened with a no score draw with Leicester before an expectant 45,963. That game marked the debut of another big money close season signing. This time the new man was Southampton's Mick Channon, signed for a fee of around £300,000 and reputedly on an expensive six year contract.

The second game saw Tueart bring back happy memories of Wembley when he scored a spectacular overhead kick, during City's demolition of Aston Villa. He provided a further two goals, while Tommy Booth added another to help the Blues record a 4-1 away win. A 1-0 win at West Ham followed - Willie Donachie was attacked by a spectator as hooliganism took hold of the English game - before Channon scored his first couple of goals in the 4-0 Maine Road defeat of Norwich.

Captain Mike Doyle had been dropped for that game with manager Book stating that he wanted to develop a good squad mentality, and that Doyle was not performing to the level required: "I wanted a little more from that area of responsibility which he held. I have spoken to him about the reasons and while I realise he felt another senior game might just play him into his best form, I was sure a change would be the best tonic from the team's point of view.

"Mike in his best form is an impossible player to replace, but when the team needs an injection and a revamp then no past reputation can be sacred and tough decisions have to be made in accordance with the evidence of the most recent matches. No player should be happy at being left out of the first team, and while I have had no bitterness from Mike about my decision I know that he will be fighting mad to get back. I would expect no less from him. I now have 18 players who can be relied upon to serve the first team. It's a squad I am proud of."

The opening four games left City at the top of the table, with the next game at home to arch rivals United. As far as Swales was concerned the game was an important one if he was to realise his dream of upstaging the Reds. United were now managed by the dour Dave Sexton, who had replaced Tommy Docherty during the close season, and were also having a successful start to the season. A crowd of 50,856 witnessed a thrilling City performance with former United man Brian Kidd proving beyond doubt his allegiance to the Blues. He scored twice and helped to pen United in their own half for much of the game. Channon added a third, before celebrating in typical style with his famous cartwheeling arm salute. Jimmy Nicholl scored a late consolation goal, but it was clear to all observers that the Reds had received a mauling. Swales was pleased, so were the fans.

Four days later City faced Widzew Lodz of Poland in the UEFA Cup at Maine Road. Book demanded a three goal margin to take into the second leg, but a crowd of 33,695 witnessed a 2-2 draw. The Blues had been leading 2-0 with goals from Channon and Barnes, and City fans sat in the Platt Lane Stand laughed and joked with a small band of Widzew followers who had been singing throughout the game. Polish international Boniek changed the atmosphere completely when he scored two late goals, a fan ran onto the pitch to confront the player while in the Platt Lane Stand laughter turned to abuse. To cap it all Willie Donachie was sent off and UEFA fined City for the crowd problems.

Dennis Tueart missed the game through hamstring problems but made sure he watched. He did not like what he saw: "We were 2-0 up with ten minutes to go and then Boniek scored from a penalty and a free kick. At 2-0 with ten or fifteen minutes to go we were cruising... justifiably 2-0 up. Then the free kick. He scored direct from it and then got a penalty when one of their guys dived. Suddenly it's 2-2. You go to Poland then - it was an afternoon kick off... park field... and it was awful. The pitch was awful, rock hard, and it was just one of those games. Nil-nil and they were happy because they were through. It was that European knowledge again that let us down. All we needed to say was 'let's not be silly'. 1-0 in a lot of instances like that is enough. We missed a couple of chances and it ended nil-nil. Out again, another bit of inexperience showing through."

Widzew went through on the away goals rule. The out of favour Joe Royle felt he was made the scapegoat: "This is one European game that I was probably never forgiven for. I wasn't even due to be playing in the game, although I was in the squad, because Mike Channon had signed. The day before the game Channon pulled out with an hamstring, and I was told I was playing. So I was going to be thrown into it really. I wasn't due to be anywhere near ready.

"In the game I chased the ball down, challenged the goalkeeper, and the ball dropped. Whilst I was waiting for it to drop and then take it into the empty net, I lost it.

TRUE BLUE
Dennis Tueart

The legendary player later became a City director.

Gary Owen watches as Tueart nets a penalty against Arsenal on 8th October 1977.

I should have volleyed it first time. I was always blamed for that. It was City's way. The fact that we'd lost a 2-0 lead at home was the real reason we went out, but I know what they used to say. The players used to joke about it - Asa would say to me, 'what's it like to cost the Club a quarter of a million pounds?' It was immaterial really. I knew I was on my way out of the Club anyway. I knew that when Mike Channon was signed. I was probably the first of that great side to go.

"I never wanted to leave, but I also didn't want to stay where I was not wanted. As soon as Skip [Tony Book] signed me I think he regretted it because I wasn't an aggressive centre-forward, and I felt that perhaps we just couldn't work together as player and manager. It happens like that sometimes. I still get on with him... great friends... everybody loved Skip... but we just couldn't work together. Bill Taylor, the coach, said to me, 'look, we've got you, we've got Kidd, we've got Tueart... three brilliant forwards who between you scored about fifty goals last season. No way do we want you to go!' But then he said, 'Bristol City are looking to take somebody on loan, why don't you go down there, give it a go, then come back once you've proved yourself again?' It seemed sensible. So I went down and scored four goals on my debut. So that was it then. Great reception... fantastic time... but there was no way of going back to Maine Road because I'd started a new life. I remained great friends with Skip, though."

Royle actually moved on 15th December 1977, but his replacement Channon struggled to make an impact at times.

Following on from the Widzew game, City lost their

way a little in the League. Five defeats in October and November left the Blues lying in ninth position, seven points behind Brian Clough's Nottingham Forest who went on to knock them out of the FA Cup in the fourth round on 31st January.

On 26th November the Blues proved they still had the ability and flair to dominate any match when Chelsea were defeated 6-2 at Maine Road - the transfer listed Dennis Tueart scored a hat-trick. A week later a 2-1 defeat at Derby County ended in controversy when Birmingham referee Derek Civil insisted that he had blown his whistle prior to Dennis Tueart's header entering the net for what should have been the equaliser. What made it worse was that the referee played only about twenty seconds of extra time despite the fact that Derby were frequently time wasting and the referee had indicated that he was to add time. Tony Book was dissatisfied, and when ITV cameras supported Book's argument the manager felt angry: "The ball had gone into the Derby crowd behind the goal as we won our second corner in succession and there was no sign of it being returned by the fans. In full camera shot Mr. Civil could be seen with his arm in the air tapping his watch clearly signalling that he was to add on time for the wasting - and whatever estimate you want to put on the incident, that ball was kept out of play by time-wasting fans for a minimum of 45 seconds. I calculated it at 90 seconds. That was only one of many incidents for which we were entitled to recompense that Mr. Civil kidded us we were going to get. His judgement was diabolical."

A 3-0 victory over Birmingham was followed by a

2-0 defeat at Leeds on 17th December. Then came, for many, the highlight of the season - the Boxing day visit of Newcastle United. The Blues were now in sixth place and still seemed capable of snatching the title, but that wasn't what made the Boxing Day game special. What made it a great day for City fans was the news that Colin Bell had been named as substitute. Apart from four appearances towards the end of 1975-6 season, Bell had not played since his November 1975 injury. There were doubts that he would ever play again.

Peter Swales recognised Bell's strengths at the time: "I consider Colin Bell to be one of the greatest players of all time. And I consider him to be the finest tuned athlete that football has ever seen. So when we talk about Colin Bell, we talk about somebody very special. Our position is very precarious - two years is a long time. But overruling everything is our concern and desire to get the lad playing back in the First Division, and we will try everything that's possible to do that. If it comes to the fact that he's got to quit football, the decision will be taken between Colin and the Club - if he's not going to come back, I'm sure he'll know. There's one thing for sure. He's irreplaceable here!"

On Boxing Day 1977, City's greatest player returned as substitute. The first half ended goalless without an appearance by Bell, although each time he tried to warm up the crowd erupted. Then at half time, Tony Book was forced to change the line-up: "My plan had been to give him [Bell] a twenty minute run at the end of the Boxing Day match, but an injury to Paul Power in the first half forced my hand. It wasn't planned the way it happened."

When the supporters realised that Bell was to play in the second half they again erupted with delight. Some supporters even cried. Peter Swales: "His return game was incredible. It was certainly the best ovation I've ever seen given to any player in any game. I've seen most of the England games over the last twenty years

- you can count on one hand the ones I've missed - and certainly all of City's games, apart from those since the Lee takeover. I've certainly seen plenty of tremendous occasions - players like Dennis Tueart getting hat tricks... United getting beat 5-1 - but the Bell reception the night he came back was far and away the best reception I've ever heard a player get. Terrific... but you knew he would. The supporters loved him. You can never kid supporters. They know great players. It's no good a manager saying, 'this is the best player we've ever had'. The supporters will know after a few weeks whether he really is the best. Bell was the best, no question."

The arrival of Bell totally transformed the game. City immediately dominated the game and by full time had defeated Newcastle 4-0 with Tueart getting an hat-trick and Kidd providing the other, but the real talking point was Bell's return. Tueart clearly remembers the night: "I remember television news had cameras there, but I've never seen the film. Bell came on at half time if I recall, and it was like World War Three. I've never known a noise like it in all my life! The crowd gave him a standing ovation and he hadn't even touched the ball. I've never seen a guy work as hard to get back. The hours and hours he put in. The pain he went through... It was a phenomenal amount of work and he definitely deserved that ovation."

In 2005 Colin Bell talked of how he found the night truly emotional: "There's always been something about Newcastle. That day I came on as substitute and I could not believe the atmosphere. The whole ground – including the Newcastle fans – stood and applauded and chanted my name. I was at the Halifax Supporters Club a month ago and I mentioned the game and almost every person in the room talked of the day and how emotional they got. There were at least two dozen people in the room who said they were crying when I came on. Grown men admitted it and I was deeply touched. On the

Ged Keegan and coach Dave Ewing lift the Central League trophy for season 1977-78.

day you could feel that emotion. I don't believe I did anything of note in the game. I was a passenger, but everyone tells me it was great seeing me there and for me it was and will always be my number one game, and my number one memory of playing football."

Although he was far from the force he'd been before, Bell managed to make it into the starting line-up for the next game - a 2-0 victory at Middlesbrough. By the end of the season he had made a further twenty League and Cup appearances and had scored two League goals, but playing had been a real struggle.

With the reappearance of Bell, City went on a nine game unbeaten run, before a 3-0 defeat at Arsenal brought them down to earth. By mid-March they were third behind Nottingham Forest and Everton, although Forest were six points clear and had a couple of games in hand. Nevertheless, Book remained hopeful: "It would be folly to accept that our interest in the championship quest is at a finish. I haven't got my head in the clouds, but to concede that Nottingham Forest have the whole race stitched up while there are ten games to go for the Blues would be a negative mood to implant upon the team. It's never over until the final whistle is blown."

By this time Dennis Tueart had left City for a career in the States, although he very nearly stayed in the Manchester area: "That first Widzew Lodz game was the start. I'd had a couple of hamstrings. When I came back I wasn't really going to be part of the side. At 28 it was said the manager wasn't going to make me 'an automatic choice'. I felt he didn't know what my capabilities were... my past record... and that I deserved the opportunity to be one of the 4 or 5 that's picked at the start. I didn't get it. I was being subbed, and at 28 I couldn't afford to hang about so I said, 'well, if you don't want me then I'll go, it's as simple as that'. That's normal. At that time I felt I'd proved myself and when I was fit I reckoned I should have been in the side, or at least taken aside and told that I was wanted in the side. I didn't get reassurance like that. I got no encouragement. So I said I cannot accept that and I asked for a transfer. And it was a scramble then. Quite a few clubs came in for me.

"Before I went to the States I'd turned Man United down. It was reported in the press at the time. It was over the Christmas period, and Peter Swales and Tony Book had said, 'Okay we'll let you go, we don't want you to go, but we'll keep you informed of any interest'. Man United came in and I had a meeting with Les Olive and Dave Sexton at Tony Book's house in Sale. They were trying to turn Man United's fortunes around - he was wanting to buy Gerry Francis, and wanted to bring other players in, and I was one of the players he wanted. They'd agreed a fee with the club, and I sat with them and discussed it. Strangely enough that night I was playing in a pro-celebrity squash match at Carriages in Droylsden. I was standing in for John Cleese who had

pulled his calf muscle. I was just going to be a spectator. Then our physio, Freddie Griffiths, who knew these guys, asked me if I would stand in as a celebrity. It ended up that I was playing Leonard Rossiter from Rising Damp. So I was going there that night and Bill Taylor, who was City's coach at the time and who I had a tremendous amount of respect and admiration for, god bless his soul. He asked me what Dave Sexton had said. I said, 'well it looks okay, it's all right'. And I was thinking seriously about going to United, and Bill said to me, 'well think about it, there's two things you need to look at. First of all, are you getting paid more, and secondly are they a better team than us?' Well, I said no not really to both questions and he said 'well there's no argument then is there?' I said, 'No you're right'. So I actually rang Dave Sexton from the squash centre and told him that I'd decided not to go.

"Apart from the transfer call, it turned out to be a bad night though. I got stuffed in the squash game! Leonard Rossiter was a good player. I worked hard but got stuffed!"

Perhaps United should have turned their attention to television's Rigsby instead!

Tueart signed for New York Cosmos for £250,000 and the majority of Blues were disappointed with the departure of their hero.

Joe Royle believes that allowing players of the calibre of Tueart to leave was a big mistake: "There's a famous Rodney Marsh quote which goes something like, 'If ever there was a club capable of making a sow's ear out of a silk purse, then City were it!' Basically, it's true. I was the first to go of a group of great City players. At the time when City won the League Cup and were runners up to Liverpool, there could have only been Alan Oakes who was over thirty. The rest must have been mid to late twenties. What City should have done was what Liverpool did. When City were runners up in the League they should have gradually replaced players. Evolution, not revolution. I went, Dennis went - he got frustrated. Then others followed. That was it. The end of any chance that City may have had."

With Tueart in the States, the Blues continued to challenge for a while, but too many games ended in draws rather than victory. Another season of promise ended with City fourth, twelve points behind Nottingham Forest. Once again there had been positive news on the attendance front with Book's side the third most popular side, watched by 41,687. With United's average decreasing Swales was optimistic that his ambition to overtake the Reds was soon to be achieved. With only two years to go to the end of the decade, he set himself a target to gain the upper hand by the 1980s. He was determined that City would be Britain's biggest club.

1978-1979 Milan Meeting

The post-Argentina World Cup season of 1978-79 was expected to be the one that brought the Blues level with United. City stars Willie Donachie and Asa Hartford had kept the City interest in the competition going for a short while, even if England had failed to qualify, while other countries' players were noticed by scouts from many English clubs for the first time.

During the close season manager Book, backed by Chairman Swales, spent a club record £350,000 to land Luton Town's capable defender Paul Futcher. Futcher had already gained ten England under 21 caps and was viewed at the time as an important signing. City quickly followed that purchase by outlaying a further £80,000 to sign a forward - Paul's twin brother Ron. Both Futcher boys felt delighted, with Paul saying: "It's all been like a dream come true for me. It was the most fantastic month of my life. With all these stars around me in the City side I can't help but improve my game. I've never looked forward to a season so much in my life."

Tony Book lashed out a further £100,000 to sign Colin Viljoen from Ipswich Town. He signed just three hours before the deadline for registering players to appear in City's UEFA Cup match with Twente Enschede on 13th September. The entire purchase was concluded within 12 hours of Book first approaching Ipswich and was seen as a major coup at the time. The midfielder had been on loan to QPR, but once he heard that City were interested he was desperate to move north: "When I was going to move it did seem that financial considerations would be my only priority. But while the finance has still been important, this transfer to City has opened up a whole new world of prospect to share in success. When I heard they were interested in me I just had to come. It's a dream come true."

While it is a fact that the opportunity to play for a big city club was a major factor for the South African born England international, it is true to say that City were now more than willing to pay the best signing on fees and salaries. Money was no object to the Board at this time, although whether there was any long term financial planning is open to debate. Regardless of the directors' financial management, supporters gained a great deal of pride from the news that the Blues were able to outbid most other clubs. Sadly, some of the players purchased were not always of the calibre required to bring success. Interestingly, City had bid to sign Kevin Keegan from SV Hamburg and Gerry Francis from QPR, but both approaches failed.

One star no longer with the Blues was former captain Mike Doyle, who was transferred to Stoke for £50,000 in June. This left only Tommy Booth and Colin Bell at Maine Road from the 1969 FA Cup winning side, and neither of those players were certain to play.

The opening two fixtures ended 1-1 with Brian Kidd scoring both City's goals against Derby County and Arsenal. He followed this with a third in the game against Liverpool, but sadly the Blues succumbed to a 4-1 defeat. Another 1-1 draw followed, this time at Norwich, before Leeds United were defeated 3-0 at Maine Road - a game which saw youngster Roger Palmer score twice.

Interestingly, in the programme for the next game - a 2-0 win over Tottenham Hotspur - Peter Swales wrote in his column about a conversation he had with Norwich manager John Bond after their game at Carrow Road: "We had terrific support at the match and when I heard the attendance was only just over 18,000 - poor, really - I felt there were more Blues fans than Norwich followers. Chatted with Norwich manager John Bond after the game, discussing the Argentinian signings by Spurs. He didn't seem over enthusiastic about them, having watched them closely as a member of the BBC World Cup TV panel. Said he would prefer Ron Futcher in his team rather than the fellow Ricardo Villa, indicating we have got good value for our signing money."

Within three years the opinions of both men would change. The World Cup had proved that English football had much to learn from the Latin countries and from Europe, and the arrival of Villa and Ardiles did much to lift the spirit of Tottenham. Rumours at the time suggested that Ardiles was actually convinced that he had signed for City, not Tottenham. The story goes that City had enquired about the player and that Ardiles was keen to come to a big English club, and quite liked what he had heard from the Blues. The story certainly became a major talking point for a while in Manchester, especially when Ardiles made a big impression at White Hart Lane.

By the time of the game with Spurs, City were already negotiating to purchase another World Cup

A delighted Tony Book and Peter Swales complete the signing of Polish star Kaziu Deyna.

Willie Donachie and Brian Kidd come out for the second half with Coventry in December 1978. Kidd scored in the 2-0 win.

star, Kazimierz Deyna. The negotiations continued for some time, but City were determined to sign the 30 year old Polish international. By the time he did sign on 9th November 1978, City were in sixth position.

Peter Swales felt it was a very peculiar transfer: "I actually went over to Warsaw. This was when it was an oppressive communist state - not like it is now. It was a very hard place and I was frightened to death - I'd only gone to Legia Warsaw to negotiate the signing of a player! All the players were in the army, and I had to see the colonel, or some such commanding officer. And I remember that he brought Deyna in and when he came in he was in his uniform looking very smart. He saluted the colonel and did everything you're supposed to do when you're in the army. Within a short while he was making the excuse that he had to go back to training and I thought, 'this is terrific... got to get back to training... this is what we want from all our players... this is great' And they didn't want a proper fee, there was no money involved. They wanted all sorts. I forget exactly what we sent them... it was all cleared by the FA but it was things like typewriters and medical equipment. There may have been a small amount in cash, but most of it was equipment. It was a strange signing!"

Deyna was never the player he should have been at City, although there were some outstanding moments along the way. He had already won 102 Polish caps and captained his country in two World Cups when he

arrived at Maine Road, but he struggled to settle. Swales: "It looked as if it was the greatest signing ever because he was a great player. But you're suddenly bringing him from a strict regime to a very loose life. I mean... he soon hit the bloody bottle! We were always getting him out of trouble. Kaz was always getting in trouble with the police for speeding or something or other. It was all a new experience for him. And he was towards the end of his career anyway. He did play some good games, but overall he wasn't that good at City, really."

By the time of Deyna's signing City were progressing well in the UEFA Cup. On 13th September they drew 1-1 at Twente Enschede, with captain Dave Watson scoring for the Blues, while Roger Palmer found that his first taste of European football ended in disappointment. An injury sustained in that game forced him to miss City's League game at Chelsea and prevented him from playing for the England Under-21 side in Denmark. He was still missing by the time of the second leg match with Twente.

City won the return 3-2 with Colin Bell finding the net after coming on as substitute for Viljoen for his first appearance of the season. The next round saw City demolish Standard Liege 4-0 at home, although only one goal had separated the clubs up to the 85th minute then a frantic late rally by the Blues made the victory an emphatic one, and caused all those who left the stadium early to realise that no game is over until the final whistle. In the second leg City succumbed to a

TRUE BLUE
Dave Watson

A rock in City's defence and an inspirational leader.

Clements and Corrigan, led by Watson, prepare to face Milan in the San Siro.

2-0 defeat in Belgium - a game which saw the dismissal of Gary Owen resulting in a five match European ban - despite a warning from Tony Book: "We won't sit back and defend that 4-0 lead. Our aim must be to go out and really finish off Liege with an early goal.". The defeat hardly mattered though, as City were through to face Italian giants AC Milan in the third round.

The first leg took place in the impressive San Siro stadium, but didn't actually start as planned. The game should have been played on Wednesday 22nd November, but the conditions were poor with thick, swirling fog forcing the referee to postpone the match. There were already a large number of supporters in the stadium and the atmosphere was incredible, with manager Book admitting that the fervour of the Italian fans shocked the City men to start with. He felt relieved when the referee ordered the game to be played the following afternoon.

Corrigan blocks the ball, watched by Clements during Milan's fightback.

On the Thursday the attendance was 40,000 - significant by English standards, but rather less than the previous night. This reduction helped kill the atmosphere, and lift the Blues. The game commenced in typical European style with City captain Dave Watson swapping pennants with Milan's Gianni Rivera, although the tough City captain looked rather bemused when his opposite number also presented him with a bunch of flowers. Watson: "We were so determined that night and we were immensely proud. We were on a mission. We were focused and that photo of me with the great Gianni Rivera at the handshake shows I don't want any distractions. He's got the flowers to present but I just want to get on with the game.

"Look at their team. They came out with their shirts hanging over their shorts – I hate that. Rivera didn't do that, but once I saw the others I knew we'd do alright. When you see that sort of attitude you think that they might not fancy a tackle, or they might disappear when the pressure's on. So as captain I felt we'd got one up on them already. When the game started we tested them out early on and all my earlier thoughts proved right."

After the first fifteen minutes, City held the upper hand with Tommy Booth and Dave Watson dominating the defence. From then on the Blues seemed the more likely to score, and by the end of an exciting half they led 1-0 thanks to a goal from European Cup winner Brian Kidd. In the 38th minute Hartford sent a carefully flighted cross to the unmarked Kidd, who simply headed home past two Milan defenders and goalkeeper Albertosi. It was just what City deserved, and with a further six decent goal attempts that half, as opposed to two Milan attempts from Collovati and Buriani, the Blues were happy with their performance.

In the 12th minute of the second half City increased their lead with Paul Power - playing his first game since injury in the League Cup at the start of October - making a long, 70 yard run into the penalty area. Once there he cut inside 18 year old defender Franco Baresi, and fired home a low left foot shot over the diving body of Albertosi. It was an important goal and gave the Blues an incredible 2-0 lead. Only two sides had defeated Milan in 52 European meetings at the San Siro, and no British side had ever defeated them there. City now seemed ready to make history. Watson: "I was immensely proud of that team, and we were so pumped up for it. We

took a two goal lead and Paul Power went on a long run and scored. A bit later in the game he did something similar but just missed scoring. He should have scored but to do that twice at Milan shows how much in charge we were. We could have been 3-0 up!

"The Milan crowd were going mad. It was unknown for any team to go to Milan and put them under so much pressure. The crowd were throwing things at us."

Milan soon fought back, however. Derek Wallis of the *Daily Mirror*: "Milan halved the lead two minutes after City scored when Albertino Bigon forced the ball over the line from Walter Novellino's cross and immediately City faced increasing pressure. Three times Corrigan was beaten, but each time the Linesman's flag was raised for offside. The decisions disgusted the crowd, some of whom took out their spite on Corrigan by pelting him with rubbish."

With Milan dominant City defenders Booth and Watson once again proved their worth as they skilfully ended a number of important Milan moves. With only eight minutes remaining Albertino Bigon scored his second for the home side, and the game ended 2-2. Watson: "It would have been nice to have kept the lead, but I remember us being at the airport afterwards and all the English press were buzzing. I just wanted to get home, but suddenly it became obvious that this game was highly significant."

As Watson suggested, the Blues were disappointed with the result at first but, after a while, everyone connected with the Club recognised that a 2-2 draw in

Peter Barnes has control as the Blues beat Milan at Maine Road.

the San Siro fortress was still a remarkable achievement. Tony Book: "The City performance in Milan was the best-ever given by a Blues team in Europe and we were only 8 minutes away from becoming the first British club ever to win in the San Siro stadium. The performance was magnificent. But it still took a lot of the cream from the display that we were pinned to a draw at the finish. So we became the 10th overseas team to take a draw away from Milan - and we not only proved we have come of age in Europe but also learned a lot on the day.

"Had Mike Channon and Peter Barnes played in Milan instead of being injured and on the bench, there's no telling how well we might have done."

The return leg at Maine Road saw City demolish the Italians 3-0 with goals from Booth (14th Minute), Hartford (31st minute), and Kidd (42nd minute). In addition to the goalscorers, the stars of that match were Colin Viljoen - who played his best game since signing - and the ever improving Paul Power. Dave Watson felt that was another remarkable night: "We beat them 3-0 at Maine Road which often gets overshadowed by that first game, but you have to remember that that was a wonderful achievement in its own right."

The result put City through to the quarter finals of a European trophy for the first time since 1971, but the January UEFA draw wasn't kind as it paired City with top German side Borussia Monchengladbach. With West Bromwich Albion, Hertha, Duisberg, Dukla Prague, Honved and Red Star Belgrade all through the Blues had hoped for one of the smaller, less powerful sides. Nevertheless, the Blues were hopeful.

The games were not scheduled to take place until March, leaving City able to concentrate on the domestic scene. Something they desperately needed to think about. Out of eleven games played from mid-October until the end of the year, the Blues had only managed to obtain five points. That run had sent the Blues spiralling down the table from a position of fifth in October down to fifteenth by New Year's Eve. City had also been knocked out of the League Cup in December by Southampton, although their early season form had pushed them through to the fifth round.

In addition to the deterioration in their League form, Chairman Swales was a little perturbed by a disappointing but understandable slump in attendance. City's average attendance by 7th October stood at almost 43,000 but by the end of the year was down to a little over 39,000, and looked destined to drop further the longer the season went on.

Shortly before his death in 1996 Peter Swales admitted that this was the moment when he began to feel action was needed if he was to achieve his aim of toppling United: "I'm a Manchester lad - grew up in Ardwick. I grew up being baited by Manchester United supporters and all through the Busby years. I wouldn't

want to say publicly that I hated them, I didn't. But they were the rivals. In 1977 we were runners up in the First Division by a point and we got to United on support. We averaged 40 odd thousand and we almost caught them, and I thought well next year we'll win the Championship and we'll do it. We didn't - we finished fourth - but I felt we were close. That's when I made my biggest mistake - well I think it was my biggest mistake - Malcolm Allison. Definitely! I got talked into that! Instead of sticking with Tony Book who, when you think of it, gave us second place which today would make him a king, wouldn't it? I think 'no, this is not good enough, we're almost there!' And one or two on the Board started to say 'well, if we could just get Malcolm we could do the final push'. Final bloody push all right!

"Malcolm was probably the best thing to ever happen to Manchester City - him and Joe Mercer as a team. I think Joe was probably a bigger influence than a lot of people think he was, but they were a great team. It doesn't mean though that ten years later you can pick that lad out of the crowd, and bring him back, and expect him to be the manager of the whole set up. I think Malcolm was a terrific motivator and a terrific coach, but he needed Joe. I think Joe made him what he was - he didn't know that, and a lot of his supporters didn't. There are still a lot of them today - even directors of Manchester City. I don't know how old Malcolm is - a lot older than me - he must be 67, but they'd bring him back now! Because they are real fans you see. They can't get over what he did for them in the late 60s. You can't bring old managers back."

In 1979 the news of Mal's return as 'coaching overlord' brought a great deal of delight to the majority of supporters. The news first broke on Friday 5th January with Granada TV revealing that Allison had accepted an offer to return to Maine Road from Tony Book and Peter Swales at an afternoon meeting in London. The following day almost every newspaper carried the story and reasons for Allison's return with the *Manchester Evening News* outlining his views: "I was very happy at Plymouth. Things were happening there and it gave me a good feeling. But I have always had an affinity for Manchester City and I am delighted to be back. My first job will be to get the players together to talk about objectives and aims. I want to find out from them what is wrong, if anything, and how we can put it right together."

When he was asked if he was happy returning to Maine Road as coach he brashly replied: "I am not just a coach I am a scientist. My training is brilliant and, like all scientists, I can make things work."

Supporters loved the hype and felt uplifted by the appointment, although Allison's arrival did not please everyone. City's highly regarded first team coach Bill Taylor had worked harder than most to improve the Blues' status and felt that Allison would undermine his role. Diplomatically he refused to comment openly, although it was obvious he was far from happy with the situation, especially as all the talk seemed to be about how the Club had been failing. It was true that City had plummeted to fifteenth place, but there had been progression in Europe and the Blues had reached the fifth round of the League Cup. Key players, such as Channon, Booth and Kidd, had been missing and results were bound to improve during January and February when City would be free to concentrate on the domestic scene.

The truth was that the directors felt that Book and Taylor were both introverts, and that the Club needed a larger than life character to ensure the Blues received the best media coverage possible. It was all part of the grand master plan to turn City into Britain's most popular club and had little, really, to do with performance on the pitch. The excellent result over AC Milan had proved what the Blues were capable of, and the Book/Taylor combination worked perfectly there but the directors wanted more.

Almost immediately Allison set about toughening up City's training schedule. At the time he told reporters: "City have got a different, vastly improved, approach to soccer. The organisation off the field has got to be the best I have encountered. Now it's the playing side in need of attention and some surgery. I arrived with an open mind. I will give to the players, but I will take from them. I want response. I want excitement. I want the place to jump with liveliness. I cannot have it any other way. I expect each of my players to set 1982 as a target - to be a member of the World Cup squad for their country. You achieve goals by aiming for them. There has got to be ambition and success will breed for it."

He also warned: "Those without that appetite will find it difficult to secure a place at Maine Road. There is a lot of work to be done."

Within a week of Allison's return, City's popular coach Bill Taylor handed in his resignation saying that he felt unable to work under the new set up. It was disappointing news for many of the players who enjoyed working with Taylor both at Maine Road and with England. Joe Royle, who had already been sacrificed at City, rated Taylor highly: "He was a considered coach. Very quiet and was, by his own admission, an ordinary player. Bill was great at organisation on the field and he was a great dovetail with Tony Book. Great appointment for City."

Youngster Gary Owen and most of the other players shared Royle's view: "Malcolm Allison came back and almost immediately it was obvious that he wanted to be the boss. Bill Taylor, who was our coach and England's coach, was suddenly a spare part, even though he was a great guy and a very talented coach. He moved on and that was a big loss to us. Malcolm took over and wanted

to create a new team, even though we were a very good side, competing in Europe and so on."

On 13th January, Allison's first game as coaching overlord ended in a 1-1 draw at Leeds. The next game, his first at home, was also far from successful as the Blues played out a goalless draw with Rotherham in the FA Cup third round. The replay ended to the satisfaction of the new coach with Brian Kidd scoring twice and important goals from Gary Owen and Peter Barnes helping secure a 4-2 victory.

The fourth round saw the Blues face Promotion seeking Third Division side Shrewsbury at snow covered Gay Meadow. It was a nightmare day with City struggling on the icy surface. A tragic mistake by Paul Futcher allowed Shrewsbury to take the lead and the Blues went on to lose 2-0 to the eventual Division Three champions. Allison and Book complained bitterly that the game should never have been played, but it was too late.

Afterwards Swales called an emergency meeting with Allison and Book to determine where the Blues were failing. By that time, Allison had already attempted to change the playing personnel. Only 18 months after signing for £300.000 Mike Channon was transfer listed and immediately brought interest from John Bond at Norwich and from Third Division Swindon Town. The Wiltshire club were the first to make a serious bid, offering £250,000 on 29th January. The player understandably turned down the move stating that he intended to remain in the First Division, but the on-off nature of Channon's departure would continue for several months.

On the same day as the Swindon bid, City offered Allison's former club Plymouth £60,000 for Barry Silkman. Even this relatively straight forward transfer dragged on until 29th March, but Allison was pleased to get his man regardless of the time taken. He was also keen to introduce new ideas into City's training schedule and the 59 year old cabaret dancer and former rock 'n' roll champion Lennie Heppell was brought in to assist the training schedule. He began to teach the players about body co-ordination and suppleness, with one seasoned player suggesting that it might be a good idea to practice playing football once in a while.

In the League form did improve from its November/ December slump and February saw City achieve five points from a possible eight, with only one game ending in defeat. Sadly, that was the Manchester derby. It ended 3-0 with Allison taunted by United supporters. The experienced Colin Bell was used as a sweeper, but the tactic failed and the Blues were well beaten with future City manager Steve Coppell scoring twice. With conditions poor the game had only been staged thanks to magnificent efforts from groundsman Stan Gibson and his groundstaff. Swales admitted in the programme

A Colin Bell shot against QPR in April 1979. Gary Owen (7) scored twice in City's 3-1 win.

later in the season that the rush to improve conditions to stage matches had actually worked against City with the United match and a 3-2 defeat by Chelsea in January hampering progress.

On 3rd March Bolton Wanderers were defeated 2-1 at Maine Road in the last game before the crucial meeting with the highly successful Borussia Monchengladbach in the UEFA Cup quarter final. Liverpool, in particular Bob Paisley, had spent considerable time helping the Blues prepare for this match by providing vital information on the West German side. Liverpool were the most experienced of all English clubs in Europe and had faced Monchengladbach on five occasions, the most recent being in the 1978 European Cup semi-final. Paisley told City that the game would be tough, and outlined the players to watch. He also suggested that Dave Watson and Tommy Booth might be the key men in City's side as the Germans seemed to lack ability to attack the ball in the air.

In the 1977 European Cup final, Liverpool had defeated Monchengladbach by playing to the strengths of players like Tommy Smith and Paisley felt City should do the same. The first leg saw Allison perform one of his many shock moves when he announced that 18 year old Nicky Reid would be making his debut. It was an amazing decision and saw the youngster move virtually from the 'A' team to one of the most important club fixtures of the decade.

Captain Dave Watson was beginning to worry about the direction the Club was heading: "We were good enough to win the UEFA Cup that year and facing Borussia Monchengladbach didn't feel like it'd be a task too far for us. We played Milan at the start of December but the next round didn't come until 7th March. By that time Malcolm was at the Club and everything felt different. He'd messed around with the team… he'd fallen out with Kiddo – a player with great experience of Europe. Some of the younger players couldn't see what we could of course.

"As a player you are powerless. If the manager has the backing of the chairman then it's the player who has to move on. Nicky Reid made his debut and, no matter how good he was, it was asking a lot of him to come in. He played well enough and went on to be a very good player, but for a crucial game in Europe you need experience. I'm not saying it's wrong to throw in young players, but I do think you have to judge the player and the timing."

Reid played well enough to suggest that there would be a bright future for him at Maine Road, while a man who felt he had no future in Manchester, the unhappy Mike Channon, managed to give the Blues a 1-0 lead. Unfortunately, the highly disciplined Germans kept the pressure on and managed to snatch an equaliser and the often vital away goal.

The second leg two weeks later saw Reid retain his place while Allison made yet another surprise selection as Tony Henry - another reserve who up to that point had only featured in two League games (once being substituted by Kenny Clements, once coming on for Asa Hartford) - was included while experienced European campaigners Deyna, Bell, and Kidd were left on the substitutes bench with Paul Futcher. The line-up for what became City's last European match of the Twentieth Century was:

Corrigan; Donachie, Power, Reid, Watson, Booth, Channon, Viljoen, Henry, Hartford, and Barnes.

City were very much the underdogs throughout the match and were losing 3-0 when, late on, Reid was substituted by Deyna. The experienced Pole provided City's only goal of the match, but it was too late and City were out of Europe. All City had left to play for was First Division survival and, of course, pride. On the bench the experienced Kenny Clements and Brian Kidd were left to watch and wonder. Clements: "For the second leg both Brian Kidd and I had to sit it out while Nicky Reid made his debut marking one of the greatest players of all time. When we were two goals down Kiddo threw his shirt at Allison in anger."

Book and Allison experimented with the line up a little, but the season ended with City in fifteenth place, 14 points above the relegation zone. The lowest position reached was 17th at Easter. Attendances had dropped significantly, but the average of 36,638 remained the third highest behind Liverpool and United (46,430). Had City been able to build on the form of the previous season then Swales may have achieved his dream of matching the Reds.

Mike Channon and Gary Owen were joint leading scorers with 11 each in the League, but supporters were angry when it was announced that Owen was to move to West Brom for £450,000 in May. This was the highest fee received by City at the time, but fans felt that was no compensation for losing the England Under 21 team captain. Owen's departure brought much criticism, but further transfer news caused many to consider whether the problems at Maine Road were more fundamental than one or two misplaced players. In addition the player was far from happy.

Both Peter Barnes and Asa Hartford were transfer listed with Barnes joining Owen at Ron Atkinson's West Bromwich Albion in July for £750,000, while player of the year Hartford moved to Nottingham Forest for £500,000 in June. Like Owen Barnes was not happy: "I didn't want to leave. I remember a few months earlier thinking how great the Club was. We'd beaten AC Milan and were doing well in Europe. We had a great side containing internationals Corrigan, Watson, Channon, Kidd, Hartford, Donachie, Bell, Deyna, and me, and then all of a sudden it changed. One day I walked into the main entrance at the ground and saw Ron Atkinson waiting. I couldn't understand why he was there. 'Surely, we're not selling a player' I thought. Then I heard Gary Owen was off to West Brom. I was shocked. Six weeks later I was on my way there as well. Regardless of how things went at West Brom, this was such a major disappointment. I couldn't work out why I wasn't wanted and why the others were transferred."

Other players whom Allison felt were surplus to City's requirements included Brian Kidd - who had been sold to Everton in March for the bargain fee of £150,000 - and captain Dave Watson - sold to Werder Bremen. Watson: "Before Malcolm arrived I'd have said we'd continue to get stronger, harder to beat. The UEFA Cup was well within our grasp. I'd have thought we'd have looked like League champions the next season. I told the chairman that if Malcolm was staying I'd have to go. Peter Swales understood but he made it clear I could not go to another English side. That was wise from City's viewpoint."

Mike Channon had announced that he wanted to stay in April, but in September 1979, after two appearances in the new season, he returned to Southampton claiming he was glad to leave a difficult situation.

These were puzzling times for the majority of Blues supporters, especially as the majority of these players were important heroes, but everyone assumed Allison was working on a grand masterplan and the breakup of City's League Cup winning side, and League challengers was allowed to continue. But who were the replacements? Deyna, Futcher, and Viljoen had hardly lived up to expectations, although each player had suffered with bad luck and had taken time to settle.

The 1978-79 season had started with the Blues hoping for glory, but it ended with the widely held view that the Club was going backwards. Fans could see it every time one of their heroes was sold.

1976-1979 SUMMARY

Highest League Attendance: 50,856 Manchester United, 10/09/77
Highest Cup Attendance: 42,435 Arsenal, 18/01/78 (FA Cup)
Managers: 1974 – 1979 (continued as General Manager until 8 October 1980) Tony Book

Seasonal Record:

Season	League	Posn	FA Cup	League Cup	Other	Leading Scorer	Average Attendance
1976-77	FL Div1	2	Rnd 5	Rnd 2	UEFA Cup Rnd 1 & Tennent-Caledonian Cup (3rd Place)	Kidd 21	40,058
1977-78	FL Div1	4	Rnd 4	Rnd 5	UEFA Cup Rnd 1	Kidd 16	41,687
1978-79	FL Div1	15	Rnd 4	Rnd 5	UEFA Cup Rnd 4	Channon & Owen 11	36,203

Dr Luft, Bobby McDonald, Dave Bennett, Steve Mackenzie, Tommy Hutchison, Nicky Reid and Gerry Gow in their 1981 FA Cup final suits. Note the price tag still on the soles of some of the shoes.

Buy Now Pay Later

"I was desperate to be successful for City. They'd put all this faith in me and I wanted to succeed. I really did. City are a great club. Great club in every way. The size of the fee did affect me. I'm a proud fella and I hated the thought that the Club had spent all of that money on me and I wasn't delivering. I wanted to prove I could play football. I'd love people to say 'great signing, Steve Daley' but as it happens they're saying 'biggest waste of money ever'."

Steve Daley talking honestly in August 2009 about his transfer to City thirty years earlier

1979-1980 Spend, Spend, Spend

By the time the new season started Allison, now Team Manager with Book occupying the role of General Manager, persuaded Swales to open the cheque book and start spending some of the transfer cash received. Allison once again surprised the City faithful as 17 year old Steve Mackenzie was signed from Crystal Palace for a staggering £250,000. The midfielder hadn't even appeared in the League, yet Allison was prepared to make him the costliest teenager in history.

Other players purchased included Preston's striker Mike Robinson, signed for £750,000, and Yugoslavian international Dragoslav Stepanovic, signed for around £140,000. Another striker Bobby Shinton was signed in June from Wrexham, who demanded a fee of £300,000 for the 27 year old.

In addition to these signings General Manager Book told supporters that City were continuing to negotiate for Steve Daley from Wolves, and Kevin Reeves of Norwich. He admitted that Norwich had already turned down £1 million pounds for a player who had been capped once by England, while he had been trying to sign Daley ever since the summer of 1978.

In amongst all this activity came the most difficult announcement of them all - the retirement of Colin Bell. After over three years of determination to regain full fitness the player and the Club realised that the time had come to end the struggle. Even during the years of despair Bell still managed to contribute a great deal to the Blue cause, helping reserve players like Tommy Caton and Nicky Reid develop. In 1978 he was a member of the Reserve side that lifted the Central League Championship.

Bell tried to be positive about his retirement: "I'm pleased that it's with City my career has finished. They have always been the only club for me. I hope they have a great future. I feel as fit as I have ever felt. But I have to face the fact that if I carry on playing and get a knock on the knee I could be crippled for life. It comes to everyone someday. But football has been my life. I don't think I've really had time to let it sink in. It will take a few weeks to get home to me that I'm finished."

Without Bell, the opening fixture against Crystal Palace ended goalless before a Maine Road crowd of 40,681. This was followed by a disappointing 3-0 defeat at Middlesbrough, before City's first victory - 3-2 at home to a Brighton side captained by Brian Horton. Late in the game Joe Corrigan saved a penalty from the future City manager.

A 1-1 draw at Hillsborough followed in the League Cup, and four days later Tottenham won 2-1 at White Hart Lane. The League Cup replay saw City beat Wednesday 2-1, but the result was overshadowed by the news the following day that Book and Allison had finally landed 26 year old Steve Daley. The fee? City boasted that it was an incredible £1,450,277 - the highest in British football. At the time Allison was well pleased with the capture: "I did this deal because the way we play we need a midfield player who is willing to make forward runs, take people on and is a good finisher. Steve is the best in the country at that type of game. I believe he is the only midfield player in the country who can open the game for himself and he's good enough to go through on his own. He will do very well with us."

Ten years later, in City fanzine *Blue Print*, Allison claimed that he had very little to do with the Daley purchase: "Peter Swales signed Steve Daley, not me... Peter Swales and the Chairman of Wolverhampton Wanderers

17 year old Steve Mackenzie.

arranged that deal between themselves. I spoke to John Barnwell before his car accident and I asked him about Daley and I offered £650,000."

Allison went on to say that Swales continued to increase the offer until Wolves accepted. When Swales was interviewed shortly before his death, he felt that he had backed Allison's judgement. It was the judgement that was wrong: "I didn't know Allison like the others did. I knew his reputation and knew what he could do - especially in the late 60s and early 70s - but he'd had an in and out career during the mid-70s. But [at City] it was unbelievable really. He used to talk a language that I was completely alien to. I knew I'd made a mistake [appointing Allison], probably within a month, maybe 2 months. He wasn't right. He'll probably say 'well, they had no bloody money' or something. He would say that it was my fault. He tells that story about Steve Daley. He is completely convinced that it was me who bought Steve Daley and not him. I suppose that's fair enough... he probably believes it was me! We chased him for months and Malcolm polished off the deal, but Daley never did a thing for City. It was unbelievable. I've met Daley several times since and he's one of the most confident men there is. At Maine Road though it was too much for him. He's the only player I've seen where the fear outweighed his ability. He couldn't do a thing, and when I say a thing he didn't do anything!"

For Steve Daley the transfer fee was something he had no control over: "The club you're leaving obviously want the most they can get. The club you're moving to want to pay whatever they have to if they really want you. Aston Villa were definitely in the market to buy me as well, so it wasn't simply a case of City and Wolves negotiating. John Barnwell kept me informed all the way through. City initially bid about £400k and Wolves laughed at it. The market was moving quickly and I was told by someone at City that the offer was increased to £600k plus Colin Viljoen and Mick Channon. Wolves said they wanted the cash. Malcolm was desperate to sign me and City paid what City needed to pay. It's like today. You have to assess how much you want a player and set your limit accordingly.

"When Wolves told me that it was all signed and sealed I was told I had to get up to a pub near the Mere Golf Club to finalise everything with City. I walked out of Molineux, got to my car and realised I didn't have enough petrol to get to Manchester and I didn't have any money. I had to nip back inside and borrow a

Peter Swales (right) chairman from October 1973 to December 1993.

tenner off one of the staff! It was either that or hitch hike to Manchester – can you imagine?"

With hindsight the purchase of Daley should never have happened. Daley: "No one regrets more than me that it didn't work."

Another player signed on the same day as Daley was Stuart Lee from Stockport County. Stockport manager Mike Summerbee and Chairman Freddie Pye (who was also City vice-president) had told Lee about the City interest when he heard that Cambridge United were interested in signing the player. Eventually he joined City for a fee of £80,000, with fans joking that it was the loose change from the Daley deal.

Two players pleased by the conclusion of these deals were Paul Power and Mike Robinson. Power was delighted because at one point he was being lined up in a part exchange deal for Daley which, obviously, never came off, while Daley's arrival removed the pressure from Robinson. "I woke up this morning with that cheap feeling" joked the £750,000 man.

Daley and Lee made their debuts in City's 1-0 home defeat to Southampton on 8th September. An embarrassing 4-0 defeat at West Brom followed - a game which saw rejected men Owen and Barnes perform exceptionally well. Yet still the transfers continued. On 12th September Kenny Clements was transferred to Oldham for £250,000 prompting letters of complaint in the City programme. Allison answered his critics: "The offer from Oldham was too good to turn down. I know that Kenny will do far more for Oldham than he could do

for City. Tony Book did not really want to sell Kenny and pointed out that the lad had done a good job in previous seasons and was a good club player. I'm sure that's true. But when I was working with Kenny I never felt he was my sort of player, was not highly skilled for my needs and would not be what I was searching for in the end. I don't think it's a sound policy to keep players who are stop-gaps."

For Clements the transfer was a chance to get away from the confusion that seemed to surround the Club from the moment Allison returned: "I just wanted to go. I knew it would never be the same again. I'd loved my time under Tony Book and Bill Taylor, and didn't feel I had a future under Allison. Taylor had been pushing me for England. I played in the Queen's jubilee match in 1977 and was on the verge of an England appearance when my leg injury came. One day in training Allison came up to me and said 'Jimmy Frizzell wants to speak to you', and I surprised him by saying 'right, I'll go now'. I went straight to Jimmy and signed. It was a simple deal really because he wanted me and I knew I wasn't going to get back in the side at City. I was never one for sitting on the bench. I wanted to play."

Although Allison probably felt otherwise at this time, fans knew that the transfer of Clements was yet another mistake. As with Owen, Barnes and the others Clements would be missed.

By 4th October City were 14th in the League and out of the League Cup after a 1-0 defeat at Sunderland in the third round replay. On 27th October they were defeated 4-0 by eventual champions Liverpool. Before the game Allison claimed that Paisley's side were far better than any other Liverpool team in history, afterwards he recognised that City remained a long way behind.

A 2-0 defeat at Crystal Palace followed, before the Maine Road derby with United brought Allison delight. City defeated the Reds 2-0 with goals from Tony Henry and Mike Robinson. A week later Steve Daley, said to be insured at a cost of £10,000 a season, scored his first goal for the Club as City defeated Bolton 1-0. It had been a game between two struggling sides and afterwards Bolton supporters called for the dismissal of manager Ian Greaves, despite some bright spells for the home side. The tireless Neil McNab did much to push Bolton forward but on the half hour Dave Bennett crossed towards Robinson. Somehow Robinson missed and Power managed to knock the ball back into the middle. The ball was cleared, then Bennett once again gained possession and fed it to Daley who fired home.

Three consecutive defeats followed, leaving the Blues 18th, before victories over Derby (3-0) and Everton (2-1) lifted the Blues to 12th. Steve Daley netted his second League goal in that match: "It wasn't all doom and gloom and there were some great games. I remember scoring in a great win at Everton in December.

When we were at home the Kippax chanted my name and I loved that. I loved running out towards the fans – as a player charging out of the tunnel towards the Kippax was a thrilling experience."

Then City collapsed. A 1-1 draw at Stoke on Boxing Day was disappointing, but it wasn't the end of the world. Then a 4-1 defeat at First Division newcomers Brighton knocked confidence at an important time. The next game was the third round FA Cup clash against Fourth Division Halifax Town at the Shay.

In his programme notes for the match Halifax Manager George Kirby predicted a shock: "In today's FA Cup 3rd round the only certainty is that there are going to be some surprises, especially with the wintry conditions underfoot. I like to think that we are among one of the possible giant killers. This is because we are playing against one of the certain to be 'top teams' of the 80s. A 4th Div side at home to a 1st Div outfit with such stars as Joe Corrigan, Steve Daley, and Mike Robinson is a possible shock result. It only needs an off day by a key player and Halifax are in the hunt."

Kirby was determined to defeat football's biggest spenders and even brought in an hypnotist to get his players in the right frame of mind. The game itself was played in horrendous conditions, with multi-million pound City struggling to achieve anything. In the 75th minute it was all over as the ex-Birmingham player Paul Hendrie converted a cross from former City schoolboy Andy Stafford to give Halifax a 1-0 victory. It was the biggest result in Halifax history, and the most embarrassing defeat of the Allison period.

Disappointment continued in the League as City endured a run of 17 games without victory. The run had started with that draw at Stoke on Boxing Day, and had included embarrassing defeats at Southampton (4-1) and at home to West Bromwich Albion (3-1). In both games former City players excelled with Channon and Watson finding the net for Southampton, while Barnes scored twice for West Brom. Goalscoring performances of ex-City heroes against the Blues seemed to be a feature of the early 1980s.

These struggles coincided with a dismal run from expensive signing Steve Daley: "I went on a run of games where I just lost form. Around that time I think City had allowed too many established players to leave at once and not replaced them. You can't do that and hope to succeed. The youngsters who came in were all very talented but they needed to be treated like I'd been treated at Wolves. In for a game, then rested. God bless his soul, we had Tommy Caton at centre-half and also Steve Mackenzie in the middle of the park from the start of the season. 16 and 17 year olds. Then there was Nicky Reid. All very good players. Great players. But they were expected to be regulars with no chance of rest or proper development. Normally, the experienced guys would

help the youngsters but when I was suffering from form I had to concentrate on getting my own game right. I couldn't help when I was struggling, and there weren't enough experienced guys to sort it out.

"Tony Book was brilliant. He spent ages with me, working with me on regaining form. A few years ago Joe Royle told me at a Maine Road dinner that if I'd have come to the Club a couple of years earlier when the likes of Royle, Tueart, Doyle and so on were there I'd have been a revelation. The timing would have been right, but 1979-80 the timing was wrong."

At the beginning of March 1980 another hero became a former Blue when Willie Donachie was transferred to North American league side Portland Timbers for £200,000. Donachie: "I needed a change badly. Not because I wanted to leave but because I'd been there too long. If a new coach had've come in at that time... someone who believed in me, and someone who was actually building a new team, then I would have been happy and stayed there forever. But Mal was back and the Club was not a happy place for me anymore. So I wanted to go and at the time Mal wanted to sell me - I was still under contract until the end of the season and Skip [Book] advised me to stay and at the end of the season I would've gone on the freedom of contract thing. But City meant so much to me it hurt me to see it in the state it was. So I wanted to go and going to America was fantastic for me because it was a completely new approach... complete change."

Donachie was dissatisfied with many of the changes introduced since 1978: "I felt players were coming in for vast amounts of money who weren't good enough. But I was only 27 or 28 and, although I was fairly experienced, I was in no position of power to do anything about it. All my best friends like Rod, Joe, Asa and the others were all got rid of. And all I could see were players who were coming in who were not good enough at any price. If somebody's not good enough, they're not worth £200,000 let alone £1 million plus. It doesn't matter.

"I was delighted that Mal came back and it was probably at a time when there had to be some change but, just like Ron Saunders, I think he went about it the wrong way. He gave up on people too fast, and decided too quickly. Instead of bringing people in who were better than the people he had, he would get rid of people and bring in lesser players, in my opinion. So it was just the same problem. The big, great, consistent clubs seem to evolve - they bring a new player in now and again. It's a gradual process. You can't change fast, like Mal tried. I think that was the big problem."

Donachie felt the return of Allison had disrupted the Blues: "The amount of respect we had for Tony Book was incredible. So the start he had as manager was fantastic. Usually you have to earn that respect... he already had it. I think he was well on his way to building a good team when... The pressure came from the top to get Mal back which 'ballsed' it all up. There's no other way of putting it."

Two perfect examples of Donachie's understanding of the situation came during March, when Allison signing Bobby Shinton was sold to Newcastle - signed in June 1979 for £300,000, sold in March 1980 for £175,000 after failing to live up to expectations - and Stuart Lee went to America with Donachie.

Around this time Liverpool signed Ian Rush from Chester. During 1979 the Blues had come close to signing the talented teenager but again City's judgement seemed to fail. Former Blue Alan Oakes was the Chester boss and was keen on Rush moving to Manchester: "I was most satisfied I suppose with Ian Rush – a great find. We knew we had to sell him because of our financial position and, because I am a Blue, I wanted him to go to City. We were having a great cup run and Tony Book and Malcolm Allison came to watch him. Rush scored twice and I met up with Tony and Malcolm afterwards. Tony was keen but Malcolm didn't rate him for some reason and it all collapsed. He later went to Liverpool and the rest is history, but I wanted him to go to Maine Road and I wish that deal had occurred. Of course, you never know how these things would have worked out."

Despite the indications that there were some issues with judgement, Peter Swales continued to back his management team and on 11th March City paid £1,250,000 after VAT and the Football League levy for Norwich's Kevin Reeves. Once again supporters were staggered, but Allison told them that Reeves was a special player: "I'll tell you what we have obtained for our money - a player who has shown the ability to hit the target 9 times out of 10 when striking at goal, though I point out this is merely an indication of accuracy and not goals scored. A player too who has excellent close control and can hold up the ball which is a vital necessity in modern day football."

Reeves had been tracked for some time: "I was signed in March 1980 by Malcolm Allison but that wasn't the first time he'd tried to get me to Maine Road. Just over a year earlier he made a formal offer which would have made me the first million pound player. Although I wanted to join City the time wasn't right. Everything at Norwich was looking good and we were really doing well, so as a young player you can't really give up on something like that, but City was a major attraction to me. I was a Manchester City fan!

"A lot of players claim allegiance to a team to gain popularity but I never really talked about this back then. My interest in City came when I was about ten and first getting seriously keen on football. Malcolm Allison was at Maine Road with Joe Mercer and City were winning everything. The League in '68 and then the FA Cup final in 1969 was the day I really became a

fan. That final was the day I became a Blue I suppose. I wasn't from Manchester but as a young boy interested in playing I had to support the team that played the type of attractive football I wanted to play. When I eventually signed for Malcolm Allison it was a great feeling. Here was I playing for one of the key figures behind the team I loved to support."

Allison made comparisons with City heroes Francis Lee and Mike Summerbee before adding: "He is the nearest thing in today's soccer to Kevin Keegan... A player who will have a reputation just as large and respect just as wide when he matures further the undoubted ability which he has. City fans will soon be delighted. We can all thank the astuteness of our Chairman Peter Swales in finding the ideal moment to re-negotiate, and it has proved conclusively that City's boardroom leader shows more courage than any other Chairman in the country. Mr Swales has backed his beliefs and his management team."

Regardless of the fee Daley's actual contract was ultimately to become a big issue for the Club. Daley: "I signed a ten year contract. Malcolm offered me a five year deal plus a five year option and I told him that I wanted to be at City for the rest of my career. He then made it a straight ten years. I was totally committed and wanted to see out that contract. It would have finished in 1989 and I truly wanted to be at City until retirement."

Daley's loyalty and desire was encouraging but no footballer at this point in history should have been given a straight ten year contract. The manager and, of course, Peter Swales who must have been entirely happy with his manager's judgement, should have considered all possibilities and perhaps been more cautious. The size of Daley's fee, and many of the other transfers of this period, impacted the finances of the Club for many, many years.

Around this time fans laughed about a story doing the rounds that a scout returned from watching a game featuring a player the Blues were interested in. When asked if the player was any good the scout replied: "No better than the rest of the side." Allison said we'll buy the lot then, and Swales started to write a multi-million pound cheque!

Reeves' debut was not as impressive as Allison hoped as the newcomer gave Arsenal a penalty after tackling Devine in the second half. Brady's shot gave the Gunners the lead and they went on to win 3-0. A 1-0 defeat in the 100th Manchester League derby followed, and the Blues were fighting relegation. A 2-2 draw against bottom club Bolton did little to ease the pressure, although City fans were delighted that both goals came from Dennis Tueart, who had re-joined the Blues from New York Cosmos.

Tueart's next goal came in the away fixture at Wolves on 12th April. It was a significant game as it ended a run of 17 games without victory and also saw Kevin Reeves score his first League goal for the Blues. The pressure had been building on the former Norwich man and the goal proved vital as City defeated Wolves 2-1 to climb up to 17th place.

Two of the final three matches were against struggling teams. On 19th April they helped consign Bristol City to Second Division football with a 3-1 defeat, then suffered a 3-1 reverse at Derby. The score hardly mattered as Derby were certain to be relegated in any case. The final game saw Ipswich defeated 2-1 at Maine Road to leave the Blues in 17th position. It had been a nightmare season, and the average attendance had dropped further to 35,272 but it remained the third highest in the League.

1980-1981 Gow, Hutchison & McDonald

The 1980-81 season commenced with a disappointing 2-0 defeat at Southampton - a side that included new signing Kevin Keegan. Four days later newly promoted Sunderland defeated City 4-0 at Maine Road. Three score draws followed against Aston Villa, Middlesbrough, and Arsenal then Nottingham Forest beat the Blues by the odd goal in five. This was followed by the visit of a Stoke side which included Mike Doyle in their number. Doyle's men won 2-1.

The next match was the crucial Manchester derby at Old Trafford. Tueart was missing with a broken wrist sustained in the Stoke game, and few expected the Blues to gain anything from the fixture. City did freeze for a while but, with typical unpredictable style, they amazed everyone with their impressive fighting spirit and despite going 2-1 down to a disputed goal from Arthur Albiston, the players always felt they were in with a chance. In the last minute former Old Trafford ball boy Roger Palmer demonstrated why he was beginning to gain so many admirers when he prodded home a dramatic last minute equaliser.

The 2-2 draw lifted City to 20th, but successive defeats against Liverpool, Leeds, West Bromwich Albion, and Birmingham left the Blues bottom of the division. Before the last couple of defeats Peter Swales had decided it was time for action. He had grown tired of Allison's ideas and wanted results: "He played with a different system every week. He used to have these amazing plans. My big worry for a few months was that the way he was going we were gonna play without a goalkeeper one day, because he'd tried everything else! I was certain he was going to give it a go. I could see him saying, 'let's try without a goalkeeper... we'll have 11 outfield players'. We were virtually bottom of the League after the Leeds match and he had to go. That entire period was a definite mistake. I don't want to come out of this saying he did nothing for Manchester City. He was

great for City. Did a fantastic job, but I maintain that it was a mistake to bring him back and I hold up my hands, I carry the can for that.

"It was the Leeds defeat when it all happened. We were absolutely hopeless and I knew we were going to go down if we continued with Allison. It was hard because he had so many in house supporters. People loved him. They still do. But I knew my big dream of upstaging United was as far away as ever and I sat at Elland Road thinking, 'God strewth, I've had two years of this... three years ago we did so well in the League and almost equalled United's support... look at us now... we're bottom of the League. Haven't won a match this season'. Everything had gone! I knew it had gone and that we were faced with a real struggle. I felt that the die had been cast. When it came to the years when we hadn't any money to spend it was inevitable that we went down."

Swales' big gamble had failed. The late 1970s should have seen City emerge as second only to Liverpool in terms of success, and equal with United in terms of pulling power. The appointment of Allison could have brought terrific reward to the Club but, as was proved with Howard Kendall's return to Everton in 1990, the return of a former managerial hero rarely works.

Looking back City were undoubtedly the under-achievers of the 1970s. From the moment the takeover was announced in November 1970 until the end of the decade City only managed to win one trophy. For a team full of internationals, with better resources than most other clubs, it is not a very impressive tally. Nevertheless, there always seemed to be excitement around the Club. Everybody felt that City's day would come, and much pride was gained from the fact that they were so well supported and that, on the face of it, the Blues could compete in the transfer market.

Although few recognised it at the time the early Seventies takeover had transformed the Club from a position of stability and strong governance to one that would gamble its future in a quest for immediate success. When the success did not arrive the Club struggled to survive.

During 1980 City were helping Granada TV make a documentary about the workings of a football club. It was all part of Swales' bid to boost the media coverage of the Blues but the sacking of Allison and Book gave the TV company a dramatic story and allowed millions to see the reality of life at Maine Road.

Throughout all the interest, one man quickly became the favourite for the manager's job - Norwich City's John Bond. During the mid-1990s Bond gave his view of how the approach first came about. His comments regarding timing give a good indication of how chairman Swales actually viewed his management team: "About six months before I actually took over I met Peter Swales at the Royal Gardens Hotel in London. City at that time were not doing that well under Malcolm, and Swales said, 'I would like you to become our manager. I was at Norwich at the time and so we discussed a few things and he promised he'd be back in touch. Well City started to pick up a little towards the end of the season, and then I got a call saying 'we're not going to do anything now. We're going to keep Malcolm and Tony Book on. We can't do anything at the moment, but rest assured that if I do make a move in the future you will be the first person I speak to'. I understood and I was quite happy at Norwich in any case.

"The new season started and Norwich had been surviving quite easily under me, but this year we were struggling. So both sides were having a bad time. Anyway, I came home from one particular match and my wife said, 'you've had a call from Peter Swales. He's going to ring you at 9 O'clock tomorrow morning he wants you to become his manager'. Norwich had no money and weren't really going anywhere, so to be honest Peter had got me straight away. There was no doubt. It was probably a case of just signing the contract and getting up to Maine Road."

Norwich were determined to keep Bond and promised him a job for life. They also demanded huge compensation from City, and pointed out that Bond had a seven and a half year contract left to run. The wrangling between the two clubs lasted more or less all season but Swales was determined to appoint Bond and the deal was done. The new manager felt that the City Chairman did not have the full support of the Board however: "It wasn't that easy to start with as there were one or two directors on the City Board who didn't really want me as manager, but Peter Swales had the decision and they were unable to object really. So I became manager, but I remember one particular director - Ian Niven - saying 'I don't know where the messiah is who can replace Malcolm Allison!' I sat at the end of the table and he sat immediately on my right and I knew from that day onwards that he was one of my enemies. But he wasn't the only one...

"Another director made a comment about moving from Norwich to Manchester which implied that I was a bumpkin moving into the big city. To be honest I treated that with the contempt that it deserved. The stupidity of the remark said everything about the man really. At that time it didn't really bother me as I knew what I could do. I knew that I was capable of managing Manchester City and doing well enough for the fans.

"Bill Adams made a comment after I'd been there a while and signed my son on, he said 'Now, he will have to prove to me that he can play'. I looked at him and said 'prove to you Mr. Adams? Who the hell do you think you are? You're a director of this club, but it's my job to bring the players in. He hasn't got to prove anything to

you, he has to prove it to me'. I then stormed out of the Boardroom."

The purchase of Kevin Bond did not occur until September 1981, but John Bond later claimed that problems at Board level during his first year or so made him regret leaving Norwich. Not everyone on the Board was against Bond however, Simon Cussins seemed extremely positive about the appointment and felt that Bond was the perfect man to take City forward while Chris Muir said he was very impressed with the man. In general the Board appeared to be in support, although one or two felt unable to make a judgement with Ian Niven stating that he would back the Chairman in whatever decision he made, but refused to give his own opinion.

Bond's meeting with the directors was filmed and broadcast as part of the Granada documentary. Some directors later claimed it had been staged for the cameras but both Swales and Bond were absolutely clear that this was not staged – this was a genuine interview.

Despite any doubts that may or may not have existed at Board level, Bond set about analysing the playing staff and attempted to build confidence: "They'd only got four points out of ten games, hadn't won a match, hadn't got a left full back of any description on their books and the players lacked direction and confidence. To be honest any fool could have turned them around to a limited extent. We lost the first game through a penalty in the last minute against Birmingham, but from then on we climbed and I won the Manager of the Month award for November and December. That set us off."

Bond recognised that the arrival of a small number of experienced players would actually boost confidence. He purchased Bobby McDonald and Tommy Hutchison from Coventry and Gerry Gow from Bristol City and stability appeared. City had already won their second game under Bond - a 3-1 victory over Tottenham at Maine Road - but the arrival of McDonald and Hutchison in the line-up for the game at Brighton on 25th October was an important touch as the Blues won 2-1 with a brace from Tueart. A week later Gerry Gow made his debut in the victory over Bond's old club Norwich. Captain Paul Power scored the only goal of that particular game.

A 1-1 draw at Leicester was followed by a disappointing 2-0 defeat at Sunderland, but mid-November saw Bond's new men bring the Club consistency with three consecutive victories. He was pleased with his purchases: "There isn't a City supporter anywhere who says anything but good about Tommy Hutchison. He was absolutely tremendous, and became a real star. He made everything happen. Gerry Gow stopped everything happening for the opposition, and that rubbed off on the rest of the players. Gow's tenacity rubbed off on Ray Ranson, Tommy Caton and Nicky Reid and the others. Then there was Bobby McDonald. Now I had a few doubts about him when I found out a bit more about him, but he still did a good job for us. He had a streak in him which was a bit wayward, a bit naughty and irresponsible. He loved the glory, but he'd duck out of heading the ball in defence. We didn't see eye to eye and I doubt I'd have bought him if I'd known. But he did a job and the fans loved him. So we'd got a left back who was a real left back, we'd got a midfielder who could tackle, win balls and make things happen, and we had a tremendous fellow up front. It seems a simple concept really."

Bond had almost signed Hutchison for Norwich some time earlier but had felt that the player was too arrogant at the time. According to Bond Hutchison had been persuaded to go in and make demands. This appalled the manager who decided as soon as he heard the words "I want" that he would not be signing the Coventry man. Bond was always a great believer in attitude. Players had to want to play for the Club, not financial reward. Fortunately for City Tommy Hutchison moved to Seattle and was playing in the same side as Kevin Bond. John Bond went to watch his son for a spell and witnessed amazing football from a player who was supposed to be nearing the end of his career. When Bond was given the City job he heard that Hutchison had returned to Coventry and contacted Gordon Milne, the Coventry manager. Hutchison met Bond at Maine Road with the City manager determined not to give in to demands: "I said I'll give you £400 a week, which wasn't the best wage in the world, and I'll give you £50,000 to sign. His attitude had changed and he signed without making a demand."

The figures quoted prove that football clubs in the early 80s were beginning to lose control over payments to players. City were still keen to sign the best and Chairman Swales backed his new manager all the way. There seemed little consideration of what would happen if the Club failed. Apart from the early season panic, City always felt too big a club to be relegated, and Swales continued to ensure that money was available to be spent, whether it was on wages or on transfers.

Of the three signings made, Gerry Gow's was perhaps the most interesting as manager Bond agreed to buy the player, but then discovered that he couldn't give him a medical: "There was no way in the world he would have been able to sustain a medical examination because he would have failed it! I had a chat with Swales and he asked me what I wanted to do and I said that I still wanted to sign him. So he let me pay £175,000 and we just had to take a chance... but what a chance. He was a revelation."

With Gow, Hutchison and McDonald City climbed up the table and reached eleventh place by the middle of January when they defeated Middlesbrough 3-2 at Maine Road. That game was unusual in two respects. The first because it was the last day before the policy of issuing red and yellow cards to signify dismissals and bookings was to be ended. City's Nicky Reid and Middlesbrough's David Hodgson became the last players to receive red cards that day. Ultimately the system was re-introduced but in January 1981 the view was that the card system would end forever.

The other unusual aspect to the game was that City's opponents actually wore Manchester United's home kit. At the time teams playing in games filmed for television were not allowed to wear a sponsor's name. When Middlesbrough set off for Manchester the intention was that the game would not be filmed and so they travelled with their usual home kit which included a sponsor's name. On the morning of the match Granada TV's planned match was called off due to a waterlogged pitch at Burnden Park, Bolton, causing the TV company to select City's match for their highlights programme.

Middlesbrough had to wear a kit without a sponsor's name and so they asked United if they could wear the Reds' sponsorless shirts instead. Someone was sent to Old Trafford to collect the kit and the game went ahead with the Blues of Manchester facing Middlesbrough in the Reds' kit.

Regardless of whether they wore sponsors' names or not, John Bond's side excited the fans regularly by this point as the team started to believe in itself. The turnaround was amazing. Kevin Reeves: "There's no denying that with City struggling under Malcolm there was pressure, but once Bond came in the entire atmosphere changed and the fact I had cost a million didn't matter anymore. I've got to say that I gained most with Bond. He was the biggest managerial influence I suppose. He wanted us to play the way I wanted to play. Everything was geared around the front two players. His philosophy was spot on and very enjoyable. I think if you stand back and study the history of football management you could trace Bond's playing approach to Ron Greenwood. Greenwood was a big influence on Bond at West Ham. I loved playing for Bondy."

During Bond's first game against Birmingham the players seemed confused and worried by tactics, by the end of the year Bond had convinced them that the game could be a simple one, and the result was a group of players who seemed to enjoy playing.

The progression in the League was not the only positive from the remainder of 1980 as the Blues progressed in the League Cup. Allison's City had already passed Stoke City and Luton Town, but Bond's first cup game was the fourth round tie against Second Division promotion hopefuls Notts County at Maine Road. The game had the potential to end in defeat, especially as Bond would be unable to play any of his new signings, nor would the expensive Steve Daley be able to play due to injury.

The match actually ended 5-1 to the Blues with Dave Bennett opening the scoring after 16 minutes. Dennis Tueart was in inspiring form that night scoring the other four City goals, but the result was proof that Bond's whole approach had lifted the Club. Basically, Bond had taken Allison's team and given them belief and confidence. Some of the younger players, like Bennett and Caton, may have been given their chance under Allison, but it was under Bond that they started to achieve their potential.

In the fifth round City were at home to Ron Atkinson's West Bromwich Albion on 3rd December. Again the Bond inspired Allison team managed a victory but it wasn't as emphatic as the County game. The match commenced with an own goal by Tommy Booth, giving Albion the lead in the fourth minute, but an amazing fightback by the Blues brought an equaliser from Dave Bennett only seven minutes later. On the hour a match winning header from Tony Henry, the man who had been severely criticised by Allison only a few months earlier, to make the score 2-1.

Although the result was perfect, in the days before squad rotation Bond felt the chopping and changing nature of team selection was having a detrimental effect on performance. He felt it was counter-productive and wanted to play his preferred eleven week in week out barring injury.

By beating West Brom City were now through to the League Cup semi-final where they met the team everybody feared - Liverpool. The first game of the two legged semi took place at Maine Road on 14th January. It was a night of misfortune for Bond's Blues when in the opening minutes referee Alf Grey disallowed a Kevin Reeves goal for what was described by the referee as 'illegal jumping'. City's players, management team and supporters were furious and convinced that the goal should have stood. All those present were convinced that City were unfairly treated. Bond: "It was scandalous. It was Alf Grey who punished us and I'm sure that, for as long as he lives, he'll never make a worse decision. Ray Clemence came out and never got anywhere near the ball, and Kevin Reeves got up and headed the ball into the net. He never fouled him or anybody else. You bet your life there wasn't a foul in it. It was as simple as that."

Similarly, Kevin Reeves has always believed the goal should have stood. At the time he told reporters: "It was a legitimate jump for a cross from the left. I never climbed on anybody's shoulders. Alan Kennedy, the Liverpool left back, was in there with me and I suspect he thought Clemence was coming to punch the cross clear and just dropped his shoulder to make the way clear for his 'keeper. I had felt Kennedy's shoulder as I went up but I never went to make contact with him, nor

did I feel anything unusual. If I had thought there was doubt about the header after it went in the net I would have been looking at the referee and certainly hesitating with my actions. It's just not the way I would behave to go dashing over to the Kippax to celebrate the goal with them. Like them, I was stunned to see it disallowed."

When interviewed in September 2003 Reeves was still unhappy about the decision: "This was the most controversial incident of my time really. There was absolutely nothing wrong with that goal and the television film proved it. It was perfectly legitimate and the referee could never properly explain why he disallowed it. What made it worse was that after scoring I ran to the Kippax celebrating with the other players unaware of the referee's decision, and then discovered Liverpool were attacking our goal. The entire match changed by a very, very unfair decision. We were all furious. If I'd have known I'd done something wrong then I'd have owned up at the time but, believe me, 22 years later I still know I did nothing wrong that day."

The goal would have changed the entire pattern of the game, instead Liverpool were able to score a late winner through Ray Kennedy. Bond felt at the time that the Blues would have won 2-0 if Reeves' effort had been allowed, instead City had to travel to the Anfield fortress a goal down: "I'm sure we would be in the driving seat, instead of attempting to become the first team to win there for almost three years. I gather Liverpool are unbeaten in 85 home games!"

After the match comedian Eddie Large found himself in a conversation with former Liverpool boss Bill Shankly. The two men discussed City's performance and the quality of Bond's side: "Bill Shankly rated Gerry Gow. Shankly also said 'See that man over there son? The greatest signing of all time. Tommy Hutchison'. I said 'you've made some great signings'. 'Aye, but not like that. The greatest signing ever.'"

Even with the greatest signing of all time it was still a major task to overturn the dominant Anfield side, but Bond believed his players could do it, and he was almost proved correct: "We went to Liverpool, drew 1-1 and played them off the park. We should have won the game and the tie. It was that first leg 'goal' that did us."

Kenny Dalglish had opened the scoring, but at no time during the tie did City really deserve to be losing overall by two goals. The Blues piled on the pressure and in the 59th minute Steve Mackenzie curved a free kick around a defensive wall, Clemence failed to hold the ball and Reeves scored to make it 2-1 to Liverpool on aggregate. Later Bennett hit the bar, but the luck never came and Liverpool went on to Wembley.

The League Cup run had proved so much about the change in atmosphere within the Club during the four months that Bond had been manager. City had gone from a confused team of individuals heading for relegation into a true side, rising up the League, challenging the perennially successful sides like Liverpool. Bond was idolised by the fans and the media loved his approach. He was also the big name, media friendly manager Swales had always wanted. It was a perfect period for Chairman Swales: "For two or three years he was the best manager in the country. At the time I thought we'd really cracked it with John Bond. I got on with him probably better than any other manager we'd ever had. He was a big fella. Dead smart. I remember him saying on some interview or other that it took him ages to decide what he'd wear when he first came to Maine Road because he wanted to look the part. He brought a tremendous confidence to the Club. He could get the players... and we had a bloody good time with Bondy. Terrific time."

Apart from the progress in the League and League Cup, City also managed to challenge for the FA Cup. The run was littered with ties to excite and interest, starting with the third round draw which brought Malcolm Allison back to Maine Road to face his old club. Allison had become the manager of Crystal Palace and eagerly anticipated the chance to put City in their place. Before the kick-off Allison walked on to the pitch and then ran towards the Kippax Stand. He received a fantastic ovation, with City fans chanting "Oh, Malcolm Allison." Afterwards he admitted: "I was overwhelmed with the terrific welcome they gave me when I went over to the Kippax before the kick-off. It was a very emotional moment for me. I was told they would not give me the best of receptions. But knowing them, I could not believe they would treat me any different than when I was their manager.

"I was dead right! They are something special and I have no doubt that they are the most loyal fans in the country. I am pleased that they have now got something to shout about."

The Kippax then chanted the name of Tony Book, before it evolved into "Johnny Bond, Johnny Bond" as the new manager entered the Directors' box. City fans continued to build the atmosphere during the match, although it took some time for the team itself to get going. Possibly because of the involvement of Allison, many of the players seemed ill at ease. It was as if the headmaster had arrived in the middle of a lesson, but as the game progressed City became more comfortable. Then in the 53rd minute the Blues were awarded a penalty at the Platt Lane end for an elbow on City's Phil Boyer by Terry Boyle. From the spot, Kevin Reeves scored his first ever FA Cup goal, and in the 89th minute he scored his second. By which time Power and Boyer had also netted. The game ended 4-0 and Allison was devastated. Television footage shows him speechless. He closed the dressing room door, put an object behind it to block anyone else from entering and sat down

with his players in silence. He was shell-shocked, totally unable to talk to his own players. After a while he stood up, opened the door, moved into the City dressing room, offered his congratulations to Bond, and then returned to the silence. It was a major blow for the former Maine Road boss who, quite rightly, felt that many of the City players were his discoveries.

City's next FA Cup opponents brought more irony to Maine Road. This time it was John Bond's old side Norwich City. In the 16th minute former Norwich player Kevin Reeves volleyed City into the lead and by half time Gerry Gow made it 2-0 following a free kick. In the 74th minute Steve Mackenzie scored a spectacular 25 yarder and then goals from Dave Bennett, Paul Power and Bobby McDonald ensured an emphatic 6-0 victory. The scoreline was impressive, but a serious knee injury to forward Phil Boyer in the 15th minute ensured Bond's fourth signing would take no further part in the season's exploits. Ironically, the injury was inflicted by an innocent tackle from John Bond's son Kevin who had been transfer listed by Norwich and who would sign for City less than eight months later.

At the end of the match, John Bond jumped from the Directors' Box to console his son Kevin. It was a major mistake as the City manager crashed to the ground injured.

With mounting excitement and a belief that this could, at long last, be City's year the draw for the fifth round brought the seemingly simple task of beating Fourth Division Peterborough away. Mindful of recent disappointments at Halifax and Shrewsbury, City looked for safety first with Bond dropping the young centre back Tommy Caton for the first time in his career. In his place returned an influential Cup veteran, Tommy Booth. The selection turned out to be a perfect one as the 31 year old managed to score from a Hutchison corner three minutes before the interval. It was the only goal of the game and provided City with a quarter-final tie away to Everton.

Sadly, Booth was suspended for the quarter final and so Tommy Caton returned, seasoned campaigner Dennis Tueart also returned taking the place of Dave Bennett. The clash at Goodison Park on 7th March was the most difficult of the run so far and took some time to come alive. It was really a midfield dogfight for some time, but gradually Kevin Reeves for City and Imre Varadi for Everton began to break free and attack.

In the 42nd minute Everton took the lead with a goal from Peter Eustoe on the edge of the six yard box. Interestingly, the goal had been made by Asa Hartford and Imre Varadi - two of Everton's four players who at some time in their careers played for City.

In the last minute of the half Gerry Gow equalised for City: "The build up to it was smashing. Bobby McDonald knocked a great ball towards the box. Knowing how

Ray Ranson tackles future Blue Imre Varadi in the FA Cup at Goodison on 7th March 1981.

well Kevin Reeves can get up for the ball and knock it off sweetly I made for the space on the left side - and there was plenty of it as I met the header. I saw the 'keeper coming towards me and knew I had to clip it high over him to have a chance. It was one of those new balls, quite light, and it was caught in the wind. I thought I'd dangled it in the air a little too much as I saw it float upwards and I seemed to be watching it for quite a while before it dropped in at the far end of the net."

Three minutes into the second half a foul by Tommy Caton on Varadi gave Everton a penalty. According to the News of The World: "Tommy Caton blocked Varadi in an enveloping grip in the box." The *Daily Mirror* felt inexperience was to blame for the penalty award: "Tommy Caton, the long, lean youngster at the heart of City's defence, will never know what possessed him to push Imre Varadi so blatantly that referee Peter Willis had no choice than to award the 48th minute penalty from which Trevor Ross reclaimed Everton's lead. That was an example of inexperience which made City regret the absence of the suspended Tommy Booth."

Six minutes from time, with City still trailing 2-1, captain Paul Power managed to equalise. Richard Bott of the Sunday Express: "We had anticipated a super-charged contest and I cannot foresee anything less abrasive when they meet again at Maine Road on Wednesday. City's saviour was their captain, Paul Power. With six minutes left he seized on a pass scooped into Everton's goalmouth by Steve Mackenzie, jabbed out a boot and lobbed the ball over the desperately advancing Jim McDonagh for the equaliser."

In the 85th minute Kevin Ratcliffe was sent off for a rather foolish head butt on Tommy Hutchison. At the time the City man was accused of play acting, but the television footage proved the offence. The game ended 2-2 and forced a replay four days later at Maine Road.

The replay was played on a muddy surface and it took some time for either side to make a real impact. Then in the 65th minute the Blues seized the initiative with Hutchison creating two goals for man of the match McDonald within the space of three minutes. Paul Power added City's third goal of the game and his fourth of the Cup campaign: "Tueart sent the ball through. I had a one on one with the keeper and I sent it home. A very enjoyable moment."

Eastoe scored a consolation in the final minute. The 3-1 scoreline sent City to their tenth FA Cup semi-final, with their opponents being Ipswich Town on 11th April.

Following the excellent result against Everton, League form began to dip with only four points gained in the next seven games. This poor form, together with the excellent progress being made by Ipswich left City as underdogs for the semi-final. Bobby Robson's Ipswich were still chasing the treble of League, FA Cup and UEFA Cup and were a difficult side to beat, whereas Bond's City were still too close to the relegation zone for comfort.

The opening 45 minutes of the Villa Park semi-final really tested City with Ipswich coming close a number of times. In fact during Ipswich's dominant period Alan Brazil made an incredible miskick when he had only Corrigan to beat. A goal then would have guaranteed a City defeat but Bond's men settled down and gradually

The 1981 FAC semi-final. (l to r): Dave Bennett, Steve Mackenzie, Ipswich's Frans Thijssen, Paul Power and Gerry Gow.

assumed control. At the end of full time the match remained goalless, then ten minutes into extra time captain Power scored his then customary cup tie goal: "At the end of ninety minutes we were level and Ipswich's Eric Gates was taking off his boots and heading off the pitch. He had no idea there was going to be extra time and I think that gave us the advantage. We were a fit side and we were ready for the extra half hour. We kept going and when the free kick came one of their players - Gates I guess – should have closed down on me but he didn't, and so I took my chance and from twenty yards out I scored."

Mackenzie had rolled a free kick to Power who sent a swerving left foot drive into the net from 20 yards out. Almost as soon as he kicked the ball he raised his arms to celebrate as he knew, just like the large contingent

City celebrate Paul Power's goal against Ipswich.

of Blues support knew, that City were on their way to Wembley for the 100th FA Cup Final.

Kevin Reeves felt the semi-final was a hugely significant match: "The semi-final victory over Ipswich was a truly memorable game. People forget that Ipswich were challenging for 3 trophies that year and were a major side to beat. I still have photos from the game and my favourite is probably one of the Holte End at Villa Park. It shows the City fans celebrating while the Ipswich supporters are clearly a little miserable to say the least. I loved that day, and after the match it took us hours to get to Manchester. Everywhere we looked there were City fans celebrating and the coach had to crawl through the fans at times. That's the sort of day when players feel the passion of the fans most."

The Cup Final opponents would be Tottenham Hotspur, and Bond knew from the moment the semi-final ended who his preferred starting eleven players would be. Always keen to keep a settled side, Bond was determined to keep the eleven who had faced Ipswich. There would be no place for the experienced Tommy Booth or Dennis Tueart. This was not a surprise to either player, but from a fan's perspective it would have been satisfying to see both players pulling on the famous City shirt for the 100th final.

From the moment Bond arrived at Maine Road Tueart felt his days were numbered: "I said to him 'if you need any help, I've got a two year contract here, I'm still a professional, still want to do well with this club'. Obviously he had his own ideas. He played a certain way and I was operating as a front man at the time and it wasn't really the same as the front men he'd been used to like Phil Boyer, Kevin Reeves and Ted MacDougal. I was then bombed out a few times and I had a few chats with him and asked him what he wanted me to do. Later, one pre-season he got me playing as an attacking midfielder and I really hit it off. One of my best periods. But in '81 I never really felt part of that side. I was part of that squad, but not part of the side."

As part of the squad Tueart helped City reach a creditable 12th place in the League, the League Cup semi-final and the FA Cup final. He wasn't named in the starting line-up for the Cup Final on 9th May 1981, but he had played his part in helping the Blues rediscover their drive.

In the weeks leading up to the final, much was made of the fact that the final would be played in the Chinese Year of the Cockerel and that Spurs had won major competitions in years ending with 1 - 1901, 1921, 1951, 1961, and 1971. There was also 'Ossie's Dream' - the story that Osvaldo Ardiles' dream was to win the FA Cup at Wembley. Basically, everything seemed to indicate that the luck of the cup was on Spurs side and even the supposed impartial BBC delighted in the Tottenham angle. In fact, during the game many City supporters unable to attend the final changed channels midway through to ITV where there appeared to be a more impartial commentary.

These were the days when both the main channels covered the final live with coverage starting mid-morning with offbeat programmes featuring the players, supporters and celebrity fans filling the hours leading up to kick off. Before this final, media friendly John Bond actually appeared as a contestant on a cup final edition of a popular ITV game show Punchlines, proving how desperate the rival channels were getting to attract viewers for the match itself. Fortunately, a minimum of 30,000 City supporters had managed to avoid this television nightmare by actually attending the final. With an average attendance of around 34,000 there remained a lot of dissatisfied fans, however.

Despite the Tottenham hype

Steve Perryman, referee Keith Hackett and Paul Power at Wembley.

John Bond was convinced that his side would win the competition: "Once you arrive at Wembley it is either you or them, and I don't think there is any reason to believe that there are out and out favourites. People always make one side favourites but on the day either side could win at Wembley. Regardless of who were the favourites, we were going to win the game on that day. I have no doubt about that."

Prior to the game itself the FA arranged for a large number of former Cup winning captains to line up on the pitch as part of their 100th final celebrations. 1950 Arsenal captain Joe Mercer received a fantastic reception from City fans, as did City's own Roy Paul, but there was also a great cheer for Tony Book. As with Malcolm Allison's ovation earlier in the Cup run, Book was remembered for his great years at Maine Road and not for the disappointments of 1980.

The City team was a familiar one: Corrigan, Ranson, McDonald, Reid, Power, Caton, Bennett, Gow, Mackenzie, Hutchison, and Reeves with Tony Henry named as substitute. The Tottenham side was captained by Steve Perryman and included the Argentinians Ricardo Villa and Osvaldo Ardiles that in 1978 John Bond had said were overrated. Now was his chance to find out the truth.

Tommy Hutchison's diving header makes it 1-0 to City.

The first half was dominated by the Blues. It opened with four City corners in five minutes while Tottenham defended desperately at times. The value of Bond's three signings was soon proved as, on the odd occasion City were troubled, Gerry Gow did all he could to hold back Ardiles and Hoddle, while Bobby McDonald upset Garth Crooks a few times. Then in the 29th minute an exciting exchange of passes between Dave Bennett and Kevin Reeves near the right corner led to a fine centre by Ray Ranson. Tommy Hutchison dived to head the cross and sent the ball past Aleksic's left hand from some distance out. It was the 150th goal scored in Wembley FA Cup finals and was thoroughly deserved.

City continued to control the majority of play with the mighty Corrigan proving his worth on the odd occasion that Tottenham managed to bypass City's defence. In the 58th minute Steve Mackenzie almost made it two when his effort hit the post.

Ten minutes later John Bond felt justified with his view that the Argentinians were overrated when the ineffectual Ricky Villa was substituted for Garry Brooke. Sadly, the substitution helped to bring Spurs back into the match, then in the 80th minute with City almost home and dry disaster struck. Never the diplomat, Gerry Gow hacked down Ardiles to give Tottenham a free kick twenty yards out. Ardiles

tapped the ball to Hoddle, who curled it around the wall. Corrigan was certain he had the shot covered but Hutchison, who had dropped back behind the wall for the free kick, somehow got in the way. The ball hit his shoulder and was diverted across goal for the Spurs equaliser. It was a tragic moment.

Without wanting to blame Hutchison, John Bond was disappointed that the goal had come off one of his greatest purchases: "The sad thing about this is that both Tommy Hutchison and Gerry Gow were the two biggest influences that made things happen for Manchester City... making us so successful at that point... and the two biggest causes of why we lost the final. Tommy Hutchison scored that excellent first goal and then, only he will ever know why he was in that position

Joe Corrigan saves from Garth Crooks.

for the free kick. He'll take that to his grave why he was there when Hoddle's free kick hit him. Nobody ever told him to get there, and it still haunts me to this day when I see it. And Gerry Gow was the one who caused the free kick because he was on the half way line with the ball and just stood there looking around when he was robbed of the ball. He chased the player right back to the edge of the penalty area and then he did what he normally did in those situations and fouled him. He used to get upset when somebody beat him. He gave a foul away and Hoddle shot at goal."

Goalkeeper Joe Corrigan walked over to a disconsolate Hutchison, helped him up, made a few comments and patted him on the back: "My view was that we still had a few minutes left. We'd still been on top for most of the game. We could still win. I also knew that what had happened to him could have happened to any one of us. So I just told him to 'get up, get on with it. It's only 1-1 and we are still going to win!' He was devastated to be fair, but we did almost win it in the dying minutes. Personally, I believe the game should have been played to a conclusion on that night. The FA Cup is all about the Saturday and I know we would have won had it gone to a conclusion. I never liked facing penalties – I think I only saved two – but that night we'd have won. No question. The Saturday was our day, after that it all switched."

The game went into extra time with both sides trying to summon up that vital goal. Cramp and aching limbs started to affect the players, with Tommy Hutchison replaced by Henry in the 105th minute. Hutchison had been determined to make amends for the own goal, but the game had started to prove too much for the 33 year old. During the second period of extra time Tottenham seemed to suffer more than City with, at one point, three players lying on the ground and two reduced to walking pace. Neutrals felt that the Blues would have regained the lead had the match continued for another five minutes. Obviously it didn't and the two sides were forced to meet again the following Thursday.

The final statistics of the game showed that both sides each made 14 scoring attempts over the two hour period, but that statistic gave a false impression as City dominated the majority of the match. City had 8 corners as opposed to Spurs' 5, while the Blues were caught offside on 12 occasions, nine more than Tottenham. The public knew City had the better game, the media knew it, and the statistics seemed to back it up. Unfortunately, the only thing that mattered was the number of goals scored.

John Bond now felt that the advantage had moved to the London club: "We should have won the FA Cup in that first game, there's no ifs or buts about it. It will haunt me as long as I live. From being convinced we were going to win, to seeing what happened to Tommy Hutchison I began to think that it wasn't going to be ours. It was going to be them and their name was on the Cup. I wouldn't want to cry like a baby about the thing but you've got to feel sorry for yourself, haven't you? Bear in mind as well that Kevin Reeves and Steve Mackenzie, when it was 1-0, they played this magnificent 1-2. Mackenzie got behind the defence, went around the goalkeeper, went to slot the ball into the net and it hit the post and went wide. They'd have been dead and buried!"

The newspapers echoed Bond's comments with the *Daily Mail* stating that Tottenham simply did not deserve a second chance: "For what they are worth to the bewildered Tommy Hutchison, the defiant Joe Corrigan, the prodigious Nicky Reid and the inspiring John Bond, my sympathies are with City. At least they gave their all for 90 minutes and then dredged up a little extra for the additional half-hour. With the heroic exception of Graham Roberts, Tottenham's approach was a disgrace.

"As Keith Burkinshaw and every other manager in the world will tell them, the justification of skill is the effort applied to its expression. Until the second half at Wembley, the hardest work of Tottenham's Cup Final week had been devoted to the myriad of commercial activities undertaken by the players to supplement their meagre income of little more than £1,000 a week over the season. City, at least, were prepared to earn their rewards the hard way, willing to run until the last man dropped to implement the briefing with which Bond gave them the maximum chance of glory. But while City deserved to win on Saturday, Spurs are the team with scope for raising their game. Hopefully, by Thursday, they will remember that their first duty is to Spurs fans paying another fortune to fill Wembley."

Although the sentiments expressed are perfectly true, the sympathy of all should have gone to the City supporters who had to find the money and time to travel back down to Wembley for a mid-week match in addition to purchasing a ticket. Joe Corrigan, always in tune with fans, recognised this as an issue immediately: "Tottenham had no travelling to do; their fans could buy tickets from either Spurs or directly from Wembley's allocation; and our fans were simply outnumbered in the replay even though we were by far a better supported team."

After the match the City contingent returned to their hotel for what was to become an eventful night for John Bond: "That night at the Royal Gardens I experienced a bitter occasion. Unfortunately I don't think Peter Swales, at that particular time, knew how to accept not winning something that he thought he ought to have won. I suppose if you'd have told him in October when I took over that City would avoid relegation, and get to the centenary cup final, he'd have accepted that. But once we got to the final he wanted more. It was a very bitter night for me in many ways. I tried to brush it to one side and get on with having a few drinks, but it was difficult. I remember the attitude of Peter and one or two of the other directors. It wasn't good. They thought we should have won and made sure we knew.

"It was sad really. The lads had played their hearts out and were as unlucky as Hell. They wanted to win more than any of the directors, but it was so unfortunate for them. I just felt very upset about the whole thing, and if I'd have had the thinking and the apparent foresight of a Kevin Keegan I would have walked out on the Club there and then. That's what I should have done. If I'd have done that my future would have been secure in football for ever more. I don't want to boast about what I did in those months to get City to Wembley, because I could also tell you about the things I didn't do, and all the bad things I did. I'm just making a statement of fact about what happened that night. I've thought about it so often, what I should have said. At that particular time I didn't want to be at Manchester City. I'd had enough in those six months I'd been there.

"Funny as it may seem, I got on very well with Peter Swales but I didn't like some of the others. There was a lot of snidiness going on and a lot of talk behind my back. They'd talk about the teams you'd pick. I just didn't like the snidiness about the Club. It was cold. This is the one part of my life I wish I could go back and do again because I would not do what I did that night, that's for sure. If I'd have realised I would actually have walked out before the final. I wouldn't want Peter Swales to think that has any bearing on him because as far as I'm concerned he never interfered and mostly he allowed me to do what I wanted to do. He was okay, it was the rest of them that I had problems with. There were some good office staff there, but the other directors... They never stand up to be counted and are happy to be afforded all the privileges that Manchester City affords them in terms of boardrooms, watching matches,

going to away games, contact with all the big people in the game and so on. That attitude was not for me."

Bond's views say much about how the Club was being run at the time. Had he walked out that night fans would have asked questions about the direction of their Club and later issues may have been avoided. Ultimately, Bond stayed and issues behind the scenes festered for some considerable time.

Seven minutes into the replay Ardiles made an attempt which hit Steve Archibald. The ball fell kindly for the Scotsman who then sent a shot which Corrigan saved. The loose ball somehow found its way to Villa who found more or less an open net waiting for the first goal of the game. City fought back immediately and, within three minutes, Ranson's free kick was met by a half clearance which alloyed Mackenzie to volley home from 20 yards. It was a tremendous goal and the type of effort that should have won the cup, but by full-time it wasn't even regarded by neutrals as the best goal of the game.

For the remainder of the half both sides challenged, forcing referee Keith Hackett to impose stricter control than for the first match. By the end of the match five players were booked, including Tommy Caton who became the first man to be booked twice in one final, after being booked the previous Saturday.

For Tottenham Glenn Hoddle began to prove to millions of television viewers why the Spurs supporters felt he was such a special player, while City's Gerry Gow looked for somebody to kick. It seemed that anybody would do. Then five minutes into the second half City were awarded a penalty after Miller pushed Bennett. Million pound man Kevin Reeves crashed a right footed effort past Aleksic's left hand to give City a 2-1 lead.

In the 70th minute Garth Crooks levelled and City were once again under pressure. Five minutes later Ricky Villa scored the most played Cup Final goal on British television. In an amazing run Villa seemed to pass a million players but, in actual fact, managed to mesmerise Caton twice, Ranson, and then Corrigan. It was a terrific goal, although John Bond felt City let themselves down: "It was a magnificent goal but I bet if Keith Burkinshaw had been in my place he wouldn't have said it was a good goal. He seemed to beat six or seven people in the space of four yards or so, and the ball

Kevin Reeves scores from the penalty spot to put City 2-1 up.

went through Joe's legs, or beneath his body into the back of the net. You score those sort of goals once in a lifetime, and that proved my view that we were never going to win that game once it went to a second match. It was a good goal, but Steve Mackenzie's volley was unbelievable!"

Bond brought on Dennis Tueart in place of Bobby McDonald and the '76 League Cup winner almost levelled, but his shot sailed just outside the post. It was not to be City's day, and it was Perryman, not Power, who collected the Cup. Joe Corrigan was awarded the 'man of the final' award: "Obviously, it does mean a lot to me, but I'd rather have won the final. After the second match I was presented with it by the Spurs manager Keith Burkenshaw. I remember thanking him and then saying something like 'Good luck in Europe next season' and at that very moment it hit home to me what had happened. I suddenly realised that we'd lost and that we wouldn't be playing in Europe. I was devastated. It was an awful feeling. I missed out in another way because the game went to a replay. England were playing Brazil at Wembley on the Wednesday after the final and, although there was nothing official, I understand I was due to play, but the replay (played the following night) meant I couldn't play."

In May 2004 captain Paul Power admitted the defeat continued to upset him: "I'm still very disappointed about the final result, but it was a major honour to be there and to captain the side. Everybody knows the story of the own goal and of the replay, but I still believe that had the game been played to a conclusion on the Saturday then we'd have won. We were still going strong and were still confident. Some of the Spurs players were suffering with cramp and we definitely had the game under our control. Sadly, we put so much into the initial game that we found it difficult matching it in the replay.

"We still had opportunities, and were 2-1 up if you remember, but again we all know about Villa's goal. That goal has been voted the greatest FA Cup final goal of all time so I suppose if you have to get beat it's better to get beat with a goal like that, but I still believe Steve Mackenzie's strike was just as impressive. If that goal had been the match winner it's possible that would have been voted best goal of all time."

Later that night Power followed in the tradition of Cowan and Paul by declaring that City would be back the following year to win the trophy and everybody felt convinced that the '81 final would be the first of many. Sadly, it was the last City FA Cup final for three decades. The 1980-81 season had, however seen a remarkable transformation.

1981-1982 Plans For A Change

Flushed with the funds raised at Wembley, Peter Swales announced during the summer that Maine Road was to be redeveloped at a cost of around £6 million over a five year period, ending by the start of the 1986-87 season. The plan was to see the Kippax and Main Stand roofs replaced by new white barrel style affairs, while the Platt Lane end of the ground would be redeveloped to look identical to the North Stand. The plans included the erection of 36 private boxes to be suspended from the new Main Stand roof, a new television gantry, two lifts, a new restaurant, and a new floodlighting system mounted on the roofs. It would also raise the capacity

Maine Road – a mix of styles at the Platt Lane corner.

from 52,600 to around 54,000. At the time Peter Swales proudly boasted that an increase in the capacity was vital and that nothing would stop the work: "We are committing ourselves to a lot of money, but I'm sure it is the right way to spend it. There's no question of putting the ground before the team. The money for this comes from the Club's Development Association and cannot be used for transfers. The supporters are building this stadium - and I am certain they will be extremely proud of it."

Despite the promises that the playing side would not be affected by the outlay, John Bond was under pressure to keep spending to a minimum. He was keen to improve the squad and felt that the acquisition of a couple of quality players would give City a chance for the title. During the summer he recruited Martin O'Neill from Norwich for £275,000 and attempted to sign United's Joe Jordan. Jordan eventually signed for AC Milan but told Bond that City were the only club he would have signed for had he remained in England. He'd also tried to sign Norwich's Justin Fashanu, who joined Nottingham Forest, and City old boy Peter Barnes. To tempt West Brom to sell Barnes, Bond offered Steve Mackenzie as part payment, but the nature of City's need to part exchange made that transfer, and indeed the Fashanu move fail. Barnes joined Leeds, while West Brom followed up their interest in Mackenzie with a cash offer and City accepted.

In addition to these attempts, Bond was keen to sign the Nottingham Forest striker Trevor Francis. He had been negotiating for some time to bring the international into City's first team, but the negotiations were rather delicate. Francis: "I think that the manager John Bond sold the Club to me really well. He told me of

the plans. Remember City had just been to the FA Cup Final and everything I was told matched my view that City were on the up. I was told other players would be signed to build a quality team capable of challenging for the title.

"When I arrived there I was very impressed with the organisation of the club, the friendliness, the facilities, the people. It was without doubt the best club I had been to as a footballer at that time. I was very impressed and really happy. City were a progressive club. I think it was too good for some of the players. I don't think some of the younger players at the time quite appreciated how well they were looked after in comparison with other clubs."

Bond had also managed to improve the backroom staff with the welcome return of Tony Book. Book became assistant to Chief Scout Ken Barnes, after spending a short period as an advisor to Cardiff City.

In the opening game of the season, City defeated West Brom 2-1 at Maine Road to earn the first three points of the season. This was the first season of three points for a win and opinion was divided as to how it would affect the game. Most seemed to feel it was an experiment that wouldn't last, but it did.

A 1-1 draw at Notts County followed and then on 5th September City travelled to Stoke City for what was to become a memorable occasion. The game saw the debut of new blue hero Trevor Francis, it also saw the new arrival score twice to help City to a 3-1 victory. Thousands of fans had made the journey to the Victoria Ground to welcome their latest £1m player: "I didn't realise at the time how many fans would travel down, so when I saw the crowds and heard the noise I couldn't believe it. It was a strange few days for me. I trained with Forest on the Friday and I only met up with the City players on either Friday night or possibly Saturday morning. But that day was very special to me. It goes down as one of the greatest memories of my career. To see so many fans… magnificent away support. I got a couple of goals and that made an immediate impact for me. It was a great welcome."

The transfer seemed perfect but it almost didn't take place and, according to John Bond, almost forced the manager to resign. Bond and Swales had agreed a fee of around £1.2m for the Forest striker but, at the last minute, Swales told Bond that the Blues could not afford to sign the player. Bond told the Chairman he would resign if Francis was not signed and eventually Swales found the finance to secure the player's signature. But even then there were concerns from Forest and Francis that needed to be ironed out. City also knew that United were keen on the player. To ensure City signed Francis Swales offered a substantial salary which the player felt unable to resist: "To complete the transfer he did all the financial talking with my agent Dennis Roach. The

Trevor Francis signs for John Bond.

tremendous coverage with the Blues appearing to be in the hunt for any player, at any price. John Bond was a media friendly manager who had managed to take the Club to Wembley. Outwardly City were winning the battle and had actually forced United to take action to keep pace with the Blues. The Reds dismissed the dour Dave Sexton and appointed the flamboyant Ron Atkinson to counter the media's interest in City. Swales felt satisfied, but he seemed to be too obsessed with life at Old Trafford. Trevor Francis noticed this unhealthy interest: "Swales was like a man who goes out to buy a Jaguar, and comes home with a Rolls, at the risk of its being repossessed by the finance company. He was always striving to keep pace with United. And it

contract Manchester United had offered me was really excellent. What City offered now was far in excess of United. I couldn't believe it. It was much too high. Over three years it was worth £100,000 a year plus bonuses. Swales, it seems, had put me on a contract the Club could not afford, I can see that now, but who was I to complain? Obviously with hindsight, my contract was at the root of their problems."

The transfer cost City dearly, yet no one seemed unduly concerned at the time. The bank allowed Swales to make the investment, the Board backed the Manager's judgement, and the fans were delighted with the purchase, but the £1.2 million signing was only viable if the Blues could mount a serious challenge for the title, qualify for Europe, and reach the latter stages of a cup. For John Bond the signing was supposed to be the first of a number designed to build a side capable of challenging the ever-dominant Liverpool. Francis turned out to be the only truly great player signed by City during the early 1980s.

City's financial problems were not really common knowledge at the time, although the managers and directors of other clubs were aware of the situation. There appears to have been a perception within football that Peter Swales' ambition to overtake United was seriously affecting his judgement, and that any transfer to City could be performed at an inflated price. There were a number of other clubs caught up in all this crazy transfer activity, each searching for the great player to bring them success.

Despite the obvious flaws in City's strategy it is true that Peter Swales was managing to win the media coverage war with United. Each transfer brought City

would always be difficult, because although City had put tremendous efforts into building up the Junior Blues and other aspects of care for the supporters, United had the bigger following, generating a much bigger income. In one sense, I have to blame Swales for allowing the Club to overreach itself, but at the same time I sympathise. I, too, used to dream about what City might achieve. It ought to be a great club.

"I immediately found at Maine Road that the City supporters are tremendously loyal. In some respects the support is bigger than United's, but it's all within the city, while United draws support from all over the country."

Despite the financial problems, Francis was not the last player to sign that season. Kevin Bond completed his

New £1m man Trevor Francis in action at Maine Road.

John Bond and his coaching staff. (l to r): Tony Scott (youth team), Glyn Pardoe (reserves), John Bond, John Benson (assistant manager), John Sainty (first team coach) and Roy Bailey (physio).

long expected transfer, while the most popular transfer had to be that of Asa Hartford who returned to the Club he loved.

Francis quickly found life at Maine Road far from ideal when, in his fourth League game, a collision with Leeds' John Lukic left the City man limping. He was to miss the following six League games and prompted United supporters to claim the Blues had bought a 'crock'. Blues fans disputed that, but the loss of such an expensive player affected morale. Later in the season his style of play brought further injury, and his first sending off. It also brought more concerns over value for money, especially for Chairman Swales: "It was a good signing. It gave the supporters a lift, but he was a hard man to get playing. You were always trying to get him on the pitch. It always amazed me that he became a manager but, there again, it always amazed me that one of the most successful managers, Don Revie, was one of the most awkward players there was. When Trevor Francis became manager of QPR I thought that was impossible because he didn't want to play unless he was 100% fit... 110% fit! He just wouldn't play. There was one game, in the north-east, where an hour before kick-off we were trying to persuade him to play because he could win us the match.

"He was a great player, and it was a good transfer for City. He was definitely more successful than Steve Daley."

With an experienced side City moved up the table and even reached top spot on 28th December - Goals from Francis and Hartford provided a 2-1 victory over Wolves - although there were a couple of sides with games in hand. Francis: "I loved being at City. I scored a goal at home to Wolves (28/12/81) which I think was

the best goal I scored for City and the win put us top of the League. I think at that time if we'd been able to strengthen the side with perhaps a couple of signings I think we'd have strengthened our position and stayed at the top for some time. I think it would have been the start of a great era but the exact opposite happened (Gow, Hutchison & O'Neill amongst others were sold during the season). We didn't know about financial problems, but clearly looking back City decided the policy had to be to sell instead of strengthen. We fell away and the chance went."

Two days earlier City had defeated Liverpool at Anfield for the first time in 28 years. The 3-1 victory delighted Bond but caused Corrigan a few headaches when a bottle thrown from the Kop knocked him to the ground as he celebrated the third goal.

Optimism swept through Maine Road, but City's position could not be maintained and a serious dip in form during March and April prevented the Blues from challenging. They ended the season in tenth position, 29 points less than the champions Liverpool. In April 2010 Trevor Francis highlighted the December victory over Liverpool as a great victory that should have seen the Blues successful overall: "It's worth remembering that we went to Anfield on Boxing Day and beat Liverpool 3-1. They were about 12th at the time, but they went on an incredible run and won the League by four points. We dropped and finished 10th, but what could we have done? In those days when you started the season there were about 12 teams who could win the title. And we were certainly one of those sides."

Part of the reason for the decline was an ankle injury to Dennis Tueart which prevented him from appearing from mid-December. Tueart had been in incredible form and seemed to enjoy playing with Francis. He'd scored nine goals in only fifteen appearances and was probably at his most potent. Bond had changed the style of play and this seemed to suit Tueart, giving the player a new lease of life. The arrival of Francis had caused many to predict that Tueart was on his way out, but Bond rubbished those suggestions and the City great remained at Maine Road after both Francis and Bond had gone. A fit Tueart throughout 1981-82 would have enabled City to maintain their challenge for the title.

In the Cup competitions City failed to make the progress desired. In the FA Cup a 3-1 win over Cardiff was followed by a 3-1 defeat by Coventry. A game which saw Asa Hartford sent off and future Blue Peter Bodak score a last minute chip for Coventry.

The League Cup was a little more entertaining with the two legged second round against Stoke ending 2-2 on aggregate. Both sides had won the home leg 2-0 and the game eventually became the first domestic match in England to be decided by penalties. But even then it took a long time before the two sides could be separated. In fact it was only when Corrigan saved the 20th penalty that the game ended with City winning by 9 penalties to 8. Northampton Town were defeated 3-1 in the next round, but a 1-0 victory by Barnsley in the fourth round ended City's Wembley dreams.

1982-1983 Selling Francis

During the summer of 1982 City fans arrived daily at Maine Road to view the new all-white Main Stand roof taking shape, but they also witnessed the departure of the expensive Trevor Francis. It was a puzzling departure and one which started the alarm bells ringing for some concerned supporters. Some actually suggested that the player had been transferred to pay for the roof, but others remembered that the Chairman had made it quite clear that the ground developments wouldn't affect the playing squad. Rumours of City's precarious financial state were starting to emerge, but the Club continued to show interest in big name signings. They had also agreed the first shirt sponsorship deal in the Club's history with SAAB promising £400,000 over two years, plus a number of company vehicles.

Swales later admitted that the salary of Francis had made his transfer a financial necessity: "We felt that it was too much to pay for a bloke who wouldn't be playing every week. He knew what he wanted and it was probably 50/50 why he left. He was the highest paid player, and we just didn't fancy paying that for someone who wouldn't be playing every week. Times have changed, but for us it was a tight ship in those days. But it was 50/50. He wanted to go and we probably wanted him to go. We were still friendly with him when he left."

Swales comments in 1995 do not fit with Francis' own views: "After the World Cup I went off on holiday and within a few days I got a call from my agent telling me a transfer had been agreed between City and Sampdoria. It was a real shock. A bolt out of the blue. From what I understand City had overstretched themselves and needed to bring in some cash. It wasn't my doing. I had no inclination or desire to leave City. Absolutely no thoughts, but I was told that City had instigated it. So when it becomes clear the Club are going to sell you there's not much you can do about it really. It all happened after the 1982 World Cup in Spain. I was later told that Sampdoria had been watching me at the World Cup and then it all happened a short time afterwards.

"I'd had a very good relationship with City fans and I was sorry to leave them. City more or less got their money back on my transfer, but that wasn't an issue for me or I guess for the fans. I'd always wanted to play and always thought I'd help City find that success that John Bond had hoped for when he told me of his plans for the squad. I really wish it had been a much longer spell."

Swales sold the player to Italian club Sampdoria but City, rather foolishly, failed to ensure they had first option should he return to the UK.

City did buy during the close season but the purchases hardly inspired the City faithful. Francis was replaced - if that was possible - by West Ham's David Cross, who scored in the opening two games, while midfielder Graham Baker arrived from Southampton.

The first two games ended in victory and then promoted Watford arrived at Maine Road for what became an interesting game. In only the third minute of the game Joe Corrigan collided with Watford's Nigel Callaghan leaving the City 'keeper with a dislocated shoulder. Immediately the City management considered the options with coach John Sainty suggesting that Bobby McDonald could take over in nets. McDonald: "We didn't have anyone named before the game for Joe's job, and it was a shock to see Joe injured. As soon as I was told to go in goal I accepted it, and it seemed the best decision at the time because Paul Power could take over from me at left-back."

For the remaining 87 minutes McDonald performed superbly, making fine saves from Blissett, Callaghan, Jenkins and Armstrong. In fact a Gerry Armstrong shot two minutes from time resulted in a save that any 'keeper would have been delighted to make. He was also a shade fortunate at times with a couple of shots hitting the woodwork.

Fourteen minutes from time Dennis Tueart, who had come on as substitute for his first game since December 1981, headed the only goal of the match. That goal and McDonald's performance put City at the top of the table after three straight victories.

Afterwards McDonald gave his view of the match: "My first touch of the ball in the whole match was the goal-kick after Joe had been taken off and it felt very strange at the time. There was a mark in the middle of the 6 yard box and I kept myself aware of it to help my positional sense. I don't know what came over me at one stage when I started to roll the ball out and chase it. I had taken the regulation 4 steps going after it and I suppose the referee could have blown me up for an offence. But he snapped 'now kick it' and that was all the warning I needed. I was very conscious of the 4 step rule after that and at times I was only taking one step before booting the ball upfield.

"I appreciated the reaction from the supporters. The lads all said 'well done' straight after the whistle went. It was a necessity on the day, but I don't want to go through it again."

During the game the supporters chanted 'Scotland's Number One', while afterwards the press were full of praise. The *Daily Mail* accurately summed up the player's performance: "McDonald managed to look terrified, ham-fisted, courageous and totally unbeatable."

With Corrigan out, City gave 20 year old Alex Williams a run out. He'd actually made his debut on 14th March 1981 against West Bromwich Albion, becoming the first black goalkeeper in the First Division. Williams: "I was wearing a red top because I think West Brom were wearing yellow and green stripes, and of course I'm black, so I certainly stood out! I suppose I became an easy target, but we won the match 2-1 and I was very happy. I knew I was understudy to Joe, but making that first appearance meant so much. My father was so proud. Remember his life had been hard at times. He'd come over from Jamaica and had to take on all sorts of jobs to feed the family. He used to work in Middleton and at one time in Hyde, and would do any job he could. So me playing for City was a great time for him. He was a very proud father, although I have to admit I sometimes worried about how he felt about the abuse and the bananas."

Williams did receive much abuse from opposition fans simply because of his colour: "I tried to block it out, but I kept thinking about how my dad would feel. He did suffer from Asthma and I eventually persuaded him not to come to the game for health reasons but, if I'm honest, the abuse played a part in that decision.

"I was the first black goalkeeper of the modern era, but there was actually a 'keeper called Arthur Wharton at the end of the 1890s who played for Rotherham and Sheffield United who was the first black player in the League. Obviously, society changed completely by the time I was playing 80 years later, so I became recognised as the first. It did bring difficulties, but to me I was a goalkeeper and, on the pitch, that's all that mattered."

Corrigan's injury gave Williams the chance to appear on a regular basis. His first game during 1982-83 ended in a 1-0 defeat at Notts County, but this was followed by a 2-1 win at Spurs with Graham Baker netting twice. Williams: "I received a lot of abuse at the start of the Tottenham game but we won and, at the end, the London fans gave me a very good ovation. That felt nice because my performance won them over. Another difficult place for black players was Leeds but to me it was one of the best grounds to visit. Sure the atmosphere was intimidating but I thrived on it there, and always seemed to be at my best. I never lost at Elland Road and could have played there every week."

Defeat at home to Aston Villa on 18th September was followed by a disastrous trip to Upton Park where City were defeated 4-1. Both Kevin Bond and Asa Hartford were sent off in the second half to add to the pressure, but Alex Williams performed superbly, saving a penalty in addition to a good overall performance. Despite the disappointing results Williams was actually playing well and was certainly not responsible for City's

'Scotland's Number One' – Bobby McDonald took over from an injured Joe Corrigan against Watford.

dip, in fact for the games against Spurs, Villa and West Ham the young 'keeper had been voted City's star player.

These results left City in ninth position, but an upturn in fortunes during October managed to lift the Blues back to second spot on 6th November. John Bond continued to look to change his squad and made bids for 35 year old midfielder Archie Gemmill, 32 year old Ivan Golac, 27 year old Eric Gates, and former Blue hero Peter Barnes, but each transfer required substantial bartering with City offering player exchanges and small amounts of cash. Each bid failed, although Golac did come on a free transfer in March 1983, with City signing him on a month long contract. The Blues were now struggling to compete financially with the rest of the First Division. The transfer market that City had helped to inflate with ridiculous fees paid for average players had collapsed and every club caught up in the power game suffered to some extent. Arsenal were losing £1300 per day and claimed their break even attendance figure was in excess of 30,000 - a good 5,000 more than they were actually attracting. To solve the problem Arsenal Chairman Peter Hill-Wood suggested forming a super league of the 16 major clubs, and many of the leading figures supported him.

At Manchester United Ron Atkinson had been caught up in all the transfer activity and helped the Reds announce a then staggering loss of £2 million. He argued that the side had needed major surgery when he arrived, a United shareholder shouted: "Next time the team needs major surgery, could we have it done on the NHS?"

Football was beginning to suffer, and as City had been the biggest spenders during the period they would suffer more than most. Only sustained success would give the finances a boost, but Swales' Blues already appeared to be on a suicide mission. The transfer of Trevor Francis had seriously affected gates. During Francis' one Maine Road season the Blues averaged 34,063, but the first few months after his departure the crowds had dropped by 6,000 - a figure they could not afford to lose.

Behind the scenes officials at the Club took steps to reduce City's expenditure. Thinking very much about the short term with no focus on what was needed in the long term steps were taken to cut the wage bill without thinking about possible implications.

In October 1982 it was revealed that the contract of first team coach John Sainty had been terminated in a cost cutting measure. Chairman Peter Swales felt eight back room staff was far too many. He also felt the squad was too large and it was cut to 24 professionals and nine apprentices. These actions suggested that Swales and his supporting officials and directors had been following knee-jerk reactions throughout the period since 1979 – how could a Club that had been more than

happy to announce ground redevelopment plans and make significant signings in the months that followed Wembley 1981, be cutting staff and selling players to make ends meet only a year later? The 1981-82 season had seen the Blues challenge for the title for a while, so it's not as if that season had been a disaster.

Despite the impact on the coaching set up and squad, the 1982-83 season continued with a few good results, such as the 4-1 victory over Norwich. Unfortunately, there were also some exceptionally bad moments. In the Milk Cup, in actual fact the League Cup now under sponsorship, City defeated Wigan 3-1 on aggregate then faced Southampton in the third round. A 1-1 Maine Road draw was followed by a demoralising 4-0 drubbing on the south coast. A victory would have given City a meeting with United at Old Trafford.

In the FA Cup the Blues defeated Sunderland 2-1 after a goalless game at Roker Park. Then on 29th January City travelled to Brighton for a fourth round tie that killed any hope of glory. The game ended 4-0 and almost immediately brought the resignation of a frustrated John Bond. The resignation was not simply as a result of the defeat, it had been on the cards for some time. Bond had been uncertain about life at Maine Road ever since the 1981 Cup Final, possibly before. He had not really enjoyed the atmosphere within the Club, in particular his relationship with certain directors was not good. Also, events in his private life complicated matters further, and he later revealed that a certain director had tried to force him to resign by threatening to provide stories to the press. Bond was understandably bitter about this period and the men in power at the time, although he insists that he always maintained a good relationship with Chairman Swales, and that no pressure to resign ever came from him.

These stories of pettiness within the boardroom at that time shock many supporters, yet Bond is convinced that certain influences forced him out, and helped the Club to deteriorate rapidly during the late seventies/early eighties. The departure of Bond sent the Club hurtling down the table. Prior to the Brighton game City had managed to maintain, at worst, a mid-table position, once Bond resigned they were in free fall.

Bond's assistant John Benson was appointed manager but fans felt that he was hardly a credible choice. For Swales the appointment was the easy option, and did not involve any heavy financial compensation to rival clubs. It was not a good move. Despite suggesting the appointment at the time, Bond later felt that Benson was a good number two, but that he was not really capable of the top job. Supporters joked that Benson had only been given the job so that City didn't have to change the initials on the manager's tracksuit. As for Benson, it was not a job he wanted at all: "I had no choice really. Once Bondy had left, either I had to become manager or I would, in all probability have to move on. I had nowhere to go to, so I took the job. I kept my old wage – no increase – and tried my best."

Under Benson City achieved a 2-2 draw with Spurs but followed that with a 4-0 defeat at Coventry. On 19th February a 1-0 defeat at home to Notts County was followed by demonstrations with some supporters actually chanting what was later to become the most popular chant at Maine Road: "Swales Out". These were desperate times. Nine of the following thirteen games ended in defeat and then City entertained fellow strugglers Luton Town for the final game of the season at Maine Road. By that time John Benson had cut the wage bill by selling loyal servant Joe Corrigan to Seattle Sounders for only £30,000, leaving the still inexperienced Alex Williams as City's last line of defence.

Manchester United had defeated Luton 3-0 on the Monday before, leaving City the relatively simple task of obtaining a draw to guarantee survival. Few fans seriously thought that the Blues would be relegated although Luton's manager David Pleat was convinced his side could shock the football world: "The pressure is on City. They have to play well and we know we can produce attacking football as good as anyone in the First Division. If we can do ourselves justice then we can still stay up."

A crowd of 42,843 boosted the post-Francis average to 26,789, leaving City as the fourth best supported club. For much of the match the Blues seemed content to defend - a tactic that left supporters nervous - while Luton attacked with flair. Paul Walsh attacked the City defence, but the Blues managed to hold off any real first half threat.

In the second period Luton were more determined than ever to obtain the three points and Walsh sent a blistering drive towards the City goal. Alex Williams made a magnificent save that time, but fans became more anxious. Luton's Kirk Stephens later saw a shot deflected on to the bar, while the supporters sat in the North Stand panicked every time they saw Luton heading towards them.

David Pleat then made what turned out to be the most important tactical move of the match, when he brought on unpredictable Yugoslav international Raddy Antic in place of the tiring Wayne Turner. Four minutes from the end Luton's Stein, crossed the ball which rebounded off Tommy Caton back to him. The second ball in was pushed out to the edge of the area by Alex Williams. Unfortunately it found its way to the feet of Antic who hit it first time. It deflected past Williams and entered the net. City were shell shocked. In 2003 Alex Williams still pondered if he could have done more: "Could I have stopped the goal? I've asked myself this dozens of times over the years and I can honestly say I could not have done any better. I dived and did actually touch the ball but I couldn't do anything more than that."

For the final four minutes the Blues gave up on defence and went all out for an equaliser, but it wasn't to arrive. When the final whistle was blown Luton's David Pleat jigged across the Maine Road turf straight to Luton's captain and City's future manager Brian Horton. City fans cried, while Dennis Tueart realised that this was the end of his Maine Road career. Tueart was the only player whose contract was close to completion, and as he trudged off the pitch he realised that he was the first player the Club would sell to cut the wage bill, although many would say Corrigan was the first to be sacrificed. Feeling as low as the rest of the City fans, he took a long look around the stadium, thought to himself "this is it, it's all over", and trudged down the tunnel for the last time as a City player. In July he was transferred to First Division Stoke on a free transfer. The wage bill had to be cut.

Another person departing was manager John Benson. Swales felt that a big name manager was required to bring the Blues back on course and so Benson was sacked. Had City remained in the First Division then Benson may still have been looking for another job. Swales: "John Benson was no John Bond that's for sure. I think I always felt he was a caretaker manager. If we'd avoided relegation I think we'd have looked to try and get somebody with more stature really. He never proved himself as a manager before, or since."

Swales' comments were a little harsh as Benson was an excellent number two who never really wanted

TRUE BLUE
Joe Corrigan

After fighting to regain his place in 1974 he became recognised as a truly great 'keeper.

to be a manager. He did ultimately guide Wigan to the play-offs in 2000, but his expertise was working alongside others to help develop the right approach and mentality. In 1983 Benson was dismissed after feeling forced to take on a job he didn't covet. Had Swales brought in an experienced manager relegation may have been avoided. The blame lay with Swales, but that did not make Benson feel any better. In November 2004 he admitted: "When relegation came I felt the pain and hurt all fans did. This was my club and I was manager

when they went down. It was such a painful, horrible, experience, and I still feel that hurt today."

With relegation Swales' dream of upstaging United was as far away as ever. When he became Chairman City were more successful than the Reds, and were not too far behind in terms of support. He had increased support, but the success had disappeared. Within a fortnight of City's relegation, United defeated Brighton in the FA Cup Final replay to bring Ron Atkinson his first trophy at United. The two clubs were going in opposite directions.

1979-1983 SUMMARY

Highest League Attendance: 52,037 Manchester United, 10/10/81
Highest Cup Attendance: 52,532 Everton, 11/03/81 (FA Cup)
Managers: 1979 – 1980 Malcolm Allison, 1980 – 1983 John Bond, 1983 John Benson

Seasonal Record:

Season	League	Posn	FA Cup	League Cup	Other	Leading Scorer	Average Attendance
1979-80	FL Div1	17	Rnd 3	Rnd 3		Robinson 8	35,272
1980-81	FL Div1	12	Final	Semi-Final		Reeves 12	33,587
1981-82	FL Div1	10	Rnd 4	Rnd 4		Reeves 13	34,063
1982-83	FL Div1	20	Rnd 4	Rnd 3		Cross 12	26,789

1981 FA CUP RUN

R3	Crystal Palace	H	W	4-0
R4	Norwich City	H	W	6-0
R5	Peterborough United	A	W	1-0
R6	Everton	A	D	2-2
	Everton	H	W	3-1
SF	Ipswich Town	N*	W	1-0
F	Tottenham Hotspur	N**	D	1-1
	Tottenham Hotspur	N**	L	2-3

*= Villa Park ** = Wembley Stadium*

	P	W	D	L	F	A
HOME	3	3	0	0	13	1
AWAY	5	2	2	1	7	6
TOTAL	8	5	2	1	20	7

The anguish is clear. Hutchison's equalising own goal at Wembley.

FINAL DETAILS

9 May 1981 at Wembley Stadium
Tottenham Hotspur 1-1 Manchester City
CITY: Corrigan, Ranson, McDonald, Reid, Power, Caton, Bennett, Gow, Mackenzie, Hutchison (substitute Henry), Reeves
TOTTENHAM HOTSPUR: Aleksic, Hughton, Miller, Roberts, Perryman, Villa (Substitute Brooke), Ardiles, Archibald, Galvin, Hoddle, Crooks.
GOALS: Hutchison (1 & 1 Own Goal)
ATTENDANCE: 100,000
REFEREE: K Hackett (Sheffield)
GUEST OF HONOUR: Queen Elizabeth, The Queen Mother
MANAGER: John Bond
CAPTAIN: Paul Power

REPLAY DETAILS

14 May 1981 at Wembley Stadium
Tottenham Hotspur 3-2 Manchester City
CITY: Corrigan, Ranson, McDonald (Substitute Tueart), Reid, Power, Caton, Bennett, Gow, Mackenzie, Hutchison, Reeves
TOTTENHAM HOTSPUR: Aleksic, Hughton, Miller, Roberts, Perryman, Villa, Ardiles, Archibald, Galvin, Hoddle, Crooks.
GOALS: Villa (2), Crooks, Mackenzie, Reeves (pen).
ATTENDANCE: 92,500
REFEREE: K Hackett (Sheffield)
MANAGER: John Bond
CAPTAIN: Paul Power

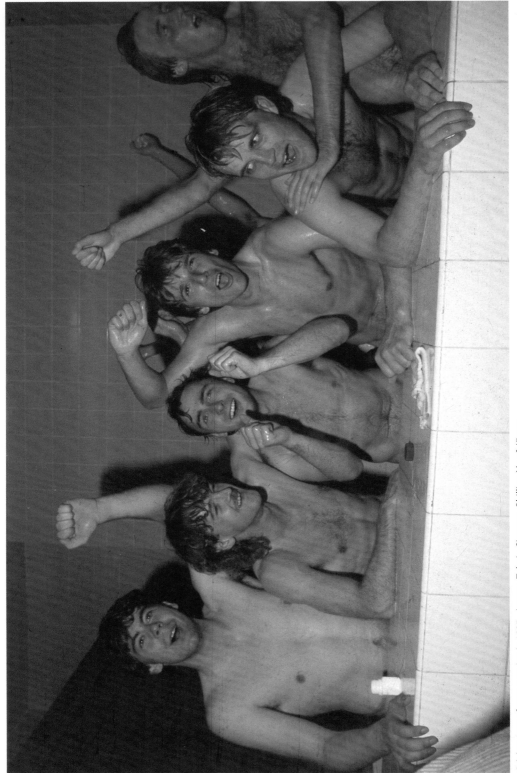

Celebrations after promotion in 1985 – Lomax, Tolmie, Simpson, Phillips, May & Kinsey.

1983-1986
McNeill's
Bargain Buys

"We lived a hand to mouth existence at times, often buying players on the never-never. I also signed players knowing that they wouldn't be there for the duration. I was forced by circumstances to look for quick fix solutions, but if the team lacked star quality, there was no shortage of battlers and we missed out on promotion in my first season after finishing fourth."

Billy McNeill, *Back To Paradise* 1988

1983-1984 Fish Supper

Although it was not public knowledge in the 1983 close season, former City hero Alan Oakes, who was managing at Chester, was considered for the manager's job at Maine Road. Oakes: "I desperately wanted the role because I loved the Club and because I believed I knew exactly what the Club needed. I'd also served what I thought was a good apprenticeship – six years at Chester taught me a great deal about survival and transfer negotiations. I knew City had financial problems and that someone with the right experience was needed – the last thing the Club could cope with was someone who needed to spend – and so I felt I was ideal for the

role. Don't forget what I'd experienced as a player at Maine Road as well. Most importantly, I understood the Club and all about Manchester football fans and their expectations and needs. This remains the greatest club in my eyes.

"I got an interview at Peter Swales' house. A few directors were there and I thought I gave a very good interview. Unfortunately, I didn't get the job. I still wonder what might have happened."

Instead of Oakes, Swales turned to Celtic Manager and 1967 European Cup winning captain Billy McNeill. City approached McNeill, and after discussions in Carlisle the Celtic man told Swales that he would join the Blues. Once in Manchester the new manager felt lonely and made a couple of silly mistakes. McNeill tried to meet the fans: "I invariably forgot myself and referred to them as Celtic fans instead of City. It was all part of me being homesick. I was so fed up when the pre-season training kicked off, and I was still living in a hotel, that I packed everything and drove to Glasgow. I told Liz [his wife] that I wasn't going back, that I had taken enough. I had been in Manchester only a few weeks and was thoroughly homesick."

McNeill was persuaded to return to Manchester, but it took him a long time to settle. Fortunately, he had recognised that he needed to quickly find someone with knowledge of Second Division football and, more importantly, someone who understood what Manchester football was all about. McNeill understood life in Glasgow, and how important football was there, but the Manchester situation was a little different. He appointed Jimmy Frizzell, a fellow Scot who had been Oldham Athletic's manager pre-Joe Royle and significantly knew how to manage on a shoe-string.

City's finances were now in an extremely dire state, with the *Daily Mirror* shocking the Manchester public with an article stating that interest charges alone were costing the Blues £1,000 a day. Relegation had cost the Club, but the biggest causes of City's plight had been the spend, spend years of Allison and Bond and the inability to plan for the long term. Swales' City had simply spent too much money and had rarely seemed to consider what the long term impact would be of any of the Club's actions. In 1983 some sources claimed that the Club was still making payments for Steve Daley who had been sold in February 1981.

Prior to taking the job, McNeill felt that City were still a major player in England. Sure they'd been relegated, but he felt that the finance would be available to gain promotion at the first attempt and then build a successful side. He soon realised that the playing squad was not of the calibre required, nor was there enough money to buy the right players: "Jimmy and I were left with so few players we sat for days on end thinking who we could get for as close to nothing as possible. City had horrendous debts in the wake of their halcyon spending-sprees on players. We could hardly buy a fish supper."

£1.2 million Kevin Reeves had moved on by this time, joining John Bond at Burnley. His last game had been the relegation match the previous season: "It was a very sad day because it was the Luton relegation game. I really didn't think we would get relegated because a week earlier we'd beaten Brighton 1-0 and I'd scored. I didn't think Luton would get anything out of that match but, of course, they managed to get that late goal and we were sunk. It was the worst moment of my City career. The Club needed to cut costs and inevitably I had to leave. A terrible period really."

Reeves felt the departure of Trevor Francis had been

the moment City stopped acting like one of the game's elite: "I know the Club were struggling financially, but selling him resulted in a complete switch of fortune. We were on our way upwards one day and the next he'd gone, and we were going downwards. It didn't necessarily have anything to do with him as a player, it was more the switch in emphasis. One day you're spending millions to buy the best, the next you feel like you're a selling club."

There were inevitably other changes once McNeill took control. Bobby McDonald was transferred to Oxford at the start of the season following well-publicised disciplinary matters during the close season. The majority of supporters were sorry to see the player go, but it was important for McNeill to establish his control.

One player determined to stay was captain Paul Power who loyally said: "I'm staying to lead the fight back to the First Division." He was quickly joined by an army of battling Scotsmen at bargain prices as Frizzell and McNeill boosted their squad. McNeill: "We pulled players out of our memories. Derek Parlane came on a free transfer from Leeds. Jim Tolmie from Lokeren in Belgium, and Neil McNab from Brighton. I had remembered Tolmie with Morton, but was aware he could also be difficult to handle. We weren't in a position to be choosy. We got McNab from Brighton, where he had been a bit of a rebel."

The McNab transfer cost City around £35,000 and proved to be a real bargain, especially when compared to the millions spent over the previous four years for players of uncertain ability. Every one of these signings proved value for money and fans were excited when City defeated Crystal Palace 2-0 on the opening day of the season, with Parlane and youngster Andy May scoring. A disappointing 2-1 defeat at Cardiff followed but then, on 3rd September, the first home game of the season two goals from Tolmie and one from Parlane to bring a 3-2 defeat of Barnsley before 25,105.

A goalless draw against Fulham followed, but then a run of five successive victories left City in second place behind Sheffield Wednesday. The run had included the 6-0 thrashing of perennial promotion also-rans Blackburn Rovers, and a 2-1 defeat of struggling giants Leeds United. McNeill's Scottish bargains were helping City rediscover their pride, but the Club was still struggling for cash. Inevitably the ground redevelopment plans had been put on hold. The only development had been the erection of the Main Stand roof but even that had not reached the level planned and did not add any potential income streams.

Originally, the new Main Stand roof was to have a series of executive boxes installed into it, and they would have raised significant funds, but the plans were put on hold and were never resurrected.

By this time, City's only real saleable asset was

Jimmy Frizzell (assistant), Roy Bailey (physio), Ken Barnes (chief scout), Billy McNeill (manager), and reserve/youth team coaches Glyn Pardoe & Tony Book – their experience was essential.

Tommy Caton, and many of the leading First Division clubs had made approaches. City were determined not to sell the player but with so much interest and a need to balance the books McNeill was forced to listen to any serious offer. In addition the player himself had now started to believe that his international aspirations could not be fulfilled while in the Second Division. On 1st December Caton was sold to Arsenal for a fee of around £450,000. The fee was poor in relation to the transfers of the previous seasons, but City needed the cash.

Within two weeks £200,000 of that fee was spent on Barnsley's strong man Mick McCarthy. It was another important transfer, and one which helped maintain the promotion challenge. With three promotion places available City felt certain they could achieve an immediate return, however they did not account for the role Kevin Keegan would play in Newcastle's fortunes. Newcastle had been struggling to make an impact since relegation in 1978, but then Keegan arrived as a player and the whole place seemed revitalised, indeed he had helped the Geordies achieve a 5-0 thrashing of City in October. McNeill: "There are few players that I have greater respect for than Keegan and this time, I'm referring only to his ability on the pitch, he was the heart and soul of Newcastle. It's a terrible thing to admit,

but every time I read that Kevin had an injury I hoped it would keep him out of the Newcastle side for a game or two. Usually it didn't and I was glad in the end because I have such a high regard for him. He was certainly the difference between City and Newcastle. They had Keegan's inspirational qualities and we didn't."

By 11th February City and Newcastle were level on points with the Blues in third place, and Newcastle fourth with a game in hand. Above them lay Chelsea and Sheffield Wednesday. The four sides were termed the 'Big Four' by the media who regularly chose to feature games from the Second above those in the First. As always Liverpool seemed destined to win the Championship and so much attention turned to the glamour clubs of the Second, especially Newcastle with the charismatic Keegan.

On 18th February came the vital Maine Road clash between the 'Jocks' and the Geordies. A win would put City six points ahead of Newcastle, yet defeat would put the two sides level with Keegan's men also having a game in hand. A crowd of 41,767 - City's and the division's second biggest crowd of the season - saw Steve Kinsey score but fine goals from Beardsley and Keegan gave Newcastle a 2-1 victory. It also gave the Geordies the advantage.

A 0-0 draw at Middlesbrough left McNeill's side in fifth place, with Grimsby nudging above both City and Newcastle for a while. This was the lowest position of the season, but in truth was a fair reflection of the Club's role. Chelsea and Sheffield Wednesday were without doubt the best two sides in the division, while Newcastle had a number of quality players - McDermott, Waddle, Beardsley and Keegan. City still felt capable of promotion though, and entered the Good Friday derby match with struggling Oldham at Boundary Park full of hope.

A crowd recorded by Oldham as 20,320 - their highest League crowd since 1978 - was in high spirits before the match with the local stewards unable to control what was a major fixture for the club. Before the game started a few City fans had climbed over the fences and onto the pitch for their own game of football. As the stewards tried to end that another group of fans grabbed hold of a ladder used by a local television crew to reach the gantry. The supporters raced across the pitch carrying the ladder, and then used it to climb into the upper section of Oldham's Main Stand. It was mayhem, although there was little, if any, actual violence.

Once the game started the off-field activities calmed, but the result - a 2-2 draw - was not the right one for either side and left City in fourth place. A 3-2 defeat against Huddersfield three days later, ensured a miserable Easter and more or less ended the promotion drive, although it was still possible for the Blues to go up.

A 1-0 loss at Derby on 28th April left the Blues in fifth place on 66 points, while Grimsby had a point more. Newcastle had streaked away and were now on 73 points with a far superior goal difference. With three games remaining it was still possible to go up, but highly unlikely, especially as City had to face Chelsea and Sheffield Wednesday. On Friday 4th May at 7.15pm McNeill's side faced second placed Chelsea at Maine Road for the first second Division game ever to be shown live on television.

A victory would have kept City in with a shout, but the game ended in a 2-0 defeat and the dream was over. A goalless game at Sheffield followed, then the final home match of the season ended in a 5-0 thrashing of relegated Cambridge before 20,787. City ended the season fourth, ten points behind third placed Newcastle, while Chelsea snatched the title on goal difference from Wednesday.

Considering the team changes, and the arrival of a manager unfamiliar with life in Manchester the season had been a good one. Goalkeeper Alex Williams was the season's only ever present and had performed exceptionally well, especially in difficult circumstances when the colour of his skin seemed to present the opposition's supporters with an easy target. Williams rarely complained about the abuse and by playing well proved the racists in the crowd would not win. At some grounds bananas were thrown at him and, being so close to the crowd, there were games when he must

City V Newcastle - Two of the Division's 'Big Four' meet in February 1984. Bond heads as Reid and goalscorer Kinsey watch.

have felt sick with the level of the abuse, but he never let it show. Like the great Bert Trautmann before him, he found that some of the London clubs were less than tolerant. Williams tried to excel in these games: "My best performance was at Chelsea when I kept a clean sheet - one of the twelve games in which I haven't conceded a goal. I had a lot to do that day at Stamford Bridge and I got on top of it all - I even coped with some of the verbal abuse from the racist element of the crowd."

In the FA Cup the Blues failed to impress with a 2-1 defeat at Blackpool, while the League Cup saw City defeat Torquay 6-0 in the second round second leg, and then succumb to a 3-0 defeat at First Division Aston Villa.

City, by far the most watched side in the division, needed to achieve promotion the following season. Nothing else would do.

1984-1985 Promotion

On the opening day of the 1984-85 season City took to the field at Plough Lane, for their first ever League game against Wimbledon. It was a new experience, but two shock goals in the first fifteen minutes for the home side proved that the Blues still remained football's great unpredictables. Goals from Derek Parlane and Gordon Smith, signed the previous March, brought the first point of the season. The side that day included Tony Cunningham, signed from Sheffield Wednesday for £100,000 and defender David Phillips who cost £65,000 plus other payments depending on the number of appearances. The arrival of Phillips seemed perfect from an advertisers point of view as the Blues had just agreed a two year sponsorship deal with the electrical company Philips worth around £250,000.

A 3-0 victory over Grimsby in the following match encouraged the faithful, but two successive defeats, and a no score draw against Carlisle raised a few concerns. City did, however, enter October a much better side and after a 1-0 win against Oxford, they lay in 6th position. They dropped a couple of places shortly afterwards but managed to hover around the 8th spot for much of the period leading up to Christmas.

McNeill and Frizzell had managed to add further experience to the side by signing attacker Jim Melrose from Celtic, and bringing central defender Ken McNaught on loan from West Bromwich Albion

Alex Williams, always popular with City fans.

as cover for Nicky Reid and Mick McCarthy. McNaught became the tenth Scottish player signed by McNeill at Maine Road, and should have been one of the best, but West Brom demanded £50,000 to make the transfer a permanent one, and City simply could not afford the outlay, reluctantly letting him return to the Hawthorns in March..

By that time the Blues had climbed up the table and had actually reached top place after an important 1-0 victory at Blackburn. During the match supporters chanted "We'll be top at 5 o'clock." It was the highest City had been under McNeill and coincided with his 45th birthday: "It was a day when the smile seldom left my face. The team's performance was full of character, packed with grit and determination and no shortage of style, which has been apparent for months. There were some excellent contributions at Blackburn. Our skipper, Paul Power, maintained his peak form of late and obliterated the potential danger from their speedy flank man, Ian Miller. Mick McCarthy towered above everyone at the heart of the defence - inspirational stuff. Nicky Reid stood no nonsense and took no prisoners. The whole back four coped comfortably with the problems set by Blackburn, who were then the League leaders with only one home defeat against them and scorers of at least one goal in every one of their home games."

The game wasn't without its disappointment though as, in the 66th minute, Graham Baker fell awkwardly on his left ankle. After treatment from physio Roy Bailey, the player continued but then seven minutes later he crashed to the ground again. This time he landed on his left shoulder, and was led from the pitch clutching his arm. After a visit to the hospital it was revealed that he had dislocated his left shoulder. Baker, who had only just heard that he would be suspended after a booking against Brighton two weeks earlier felt far from happy: "I thought I was going to miss only a fortnight. Now there's no knowing how long it can be. I've got the arm in a sling which I have to keep on for 14 days. The ankle is swollen up with the sprain but that's less of a concern - it's all going to take time. It's such a crucial time in the season. Missing the two home games through suspension is a disappointment but I was contenting myself that at least I'd be available for the real key visits we have to make to Birmingham and Oxford later this month. I've not got any hope at all now."

Another player missing was Clive Wilson who had been excluded from McNeill's plans because of a mystery ankle problem. He had attended training on 11th February and afterwards started to experience pain at the bottom of his left ankle, the next day his right leg began to suffer, by Wednesday he was in hospital with both ankles swollen, then a few days later he was on crutches. Nobody ever found out exactly what caused the condition, although the most likely explanation seemed to be that Wilson had picked up an infection via a cut. The problem managed to end all hope of the player appearing for the rest of the season.

One player who did make it into the first team was Kenny Clements who had returned to the Club after over five years at Oldham. His debut game saw City defeat Middlesbrough 1-0 with a goal from Phillips seven days after the Blackburn match. For Clements it was an emotional return: "The reception I got from the fans when I ran out with the team is really the thing I'll remember from the day. They waved from the Kippax, I waved back, then they started clapping above their heads and chanting my name - and I started clapping them back in a similar manner. It was only briefly but it was getting ridiculous because I was filling up - I had to turn away so that I didn't cry in front of them. It was just so good to be back."

During the match Clements injured his leg and broke his nose, but it was all worth it to be back at Maine Road.

Seven days later Shrewsbury were defeated 4-0 then came a couple of setbacks in crucial away games against opponents challenging for promotion. First City could only manage a goalless draw at Birmingham, then fans endured a 3-0 defeat at Oxford. The Blues were still top on 62 points, but had now played more games than any of the challenging sides. Oxford were second on 58 points with three games in hand, Alan Ball's Portsmouth were third on 57 points with one game in hand, while Birmingham were fourth on the same number of points and games as Portsmouth.

After the Oxford game came draws against Cardiff (2-) and at Barnsley (0-0), and a 2-1 defeat at home to Leeds, leaving the Blues in third position. The Leeds game had been particularly disappointing as Graham Baker, who had only returned to action two days earlier against Barnsley, broke his leg in the 13th minute of the game, thereby ending his season.

City's disappointing form had coincided with a number of injuries to crucial players. Obviously Baker and Wilson were missing, but Jim Melrose (hamstring) and Gordon Smith (knee ligaments) were also out of action. On 13th April City travelled to Grimsby desperate to return to winning ways, but a 4-1 defeat left the Blues in fifth place, one point behind Portsmouth in third position.

An important 2-0 victory over Sheffield United rekindled City's fire and McNeill was determined that three points would be gained in the all-important away trip to Alan Ball's promotion hopefuls Portsmouth. The manager did all he could to coax his side to victory: "I preached confidence and composure. The players responded tremendously, they had the mood and determination to win that last chance available to us at Portsmouth. Nothing less than victory would have served a purpose in my view and we tackled the job correctly. Pompey had a physical approach to the game. They have big lads up front, determined and energetic in their game and it wasn't difficult to anticipate that we would have spells under intense pressure. We played well, tenaciously, defended strongly. Apart from a header which went wide and a very good save early on from Alex Williams, we were every bit in the hunt with them 'till half-time.

"Alex handled cleanly and made one very vital save from Neil Webb when the score was 1-1. Our winner was a classic from Paul Simpson, his third from a handful of first team opportunities. Although it came nine minutes from time it did seem to be scored an eternity away from the final whistle. But imagine the excitement in the closing minutes when City fans stood behind the trainer's bench started hammering for our attention with the news that Blackburn Rovers - possibly the biggest threat to our ambitions then - had lost at Charlton!"

The 2-1 victory lifted City into third place, with every side in the division having played 39 games. The Blues were on 70 points with Blackburn fourth on 67 points. Leeds and Portsmouth were in fifth and sixth place respectively on 65 points.

City's remaining three fixtures looked relatively simple - Oldham Athletic (4th May at Maine Road), Notts County (6th May at Meadow Lane), and Charlton Athletic (Maine Road on 11th May). Oldham and Charlton were both about eight points above the relegation zone, while Notts County were in 21st position with little hope of survival.

Against Oldham City could only manage a draw, but at least it was a point. If City were to beat Notts County then barring a miraculous turnaround in goal difference, the Blues would be up. The Bank Holiday Monday journey to Nottingham was an exciting one for all Blues, with every pub, motorway service station, and cafe on the route full of fans with painted faces and in party mood. It was an amazing exodus and one which pleased manager McNeill. He realised the passion of the Blues fans and finally started to overcome his homesickness. Manchester was not 'his' city, but it was beginning to become a part of him.

Inside the ground the atmosphere made Meadow Lane feel like Maine Road with every side of the then three sided ground housing Blues. In fact, Notts County

Paul Power at Meadow Lane on 6th May 1985. City fans were given Notts County's home terracing.

had been so keen to ensure a big attendance that they had given City the home supporters' section of the Kop. At that time the section held around 10,000 but with County only attracting around 4,000 of their own supporters per game, it was felt the Blues needed the terracing more. The official attendance for the match was 17,812 - almost 5,000 more than their next highest figure which, itself, was a good 4,000 above the third highest.

Despite the large City support, the Blues struggled and County took a three goal lead in the first half. The party atmosphere was replaced by tension with petty scuffles taking place in the stands. At the Kop End City fans started to pull down a section of fencing. At first the stewards, uncertain how to control the fans, allowed them to continue for some time before they tried to stop the vandalism. By the time they acted more supporters had decided to act. Further scuffles broke out around the ground and, although the trouble could be easily quelled, an unfortunate announcement over the tannoy system said that the game would be abandoned and replayed if the fans didn't resume order. This announcement did more to encourage rather than kill the vandalism as some City supporters were encouraged to believe that they could wipe out the three goal margin.

Eventually to ease the situation Billy McNeill walked to the Kop and appealed for calm. A few minutes later peace was restored and the game recommenced, but the atmosphere was strange. During the second half the Blues seemed to be in control and managed to pull two

goals back from Paul Simpson, but the City management felt little satisfaction in the turnaround. Appropriately, the game ended 3-2 to County and a day of fun had been ruined.

The result left City needing a win, but even then Portsmouth could still overtake the Blues if they managed to overturn City's goal difference. The Blues basically held a five goal lead over Alan Ball's side, but Portsmouth had caused City to lose out on goal average back in 1927 and no fan could relax.

On 11th May 1985 the visit of Charlton was watched by an official crowd of 47,285 in a stadium that boasted it could hold 52,600 with 26,500 seats. Many supporters were convinced that there were significantly more in the stadium that day as the Kippax was uncomfortably packed, while in the other three stands fans were forced to sit on the steps to watch the game. It is a fact that fans believed that many of the Blues' attendances during the eighties were under reported.

Whatever the actual attendance it was a day that fans enjoyed, although it didn't start out that way. McNeill remembers the tension: "City were up against it. I put on my best lightweight suit and swept into the ground early in the morning. Everyone was a bag of nerves. But that was the very reason I was there so early and looking, I hoped, a million dollars. I strode around exuding confidence, telling everyone who would listen that we would win. I felt this had been transmitted to the team and that was really all that bothered me. We scored twice early on and eventually led 5-0 before Charlton got a consolation goal which jubilant City fans cheered as well. Our scorers were Andy May, Jim Melrose, Dave Phillips (2), and Paul Simpson. It was a tremendous achievement. There hadn't been so much excitement - or champagne - at Maine Road for years."

At the final whistle fans raced onto the pitch for the biggest and best pitch invasion in years. Andy May and Paul Power were stripped of their shirts immediately while others, Paul Simpson included, lost their shirts to souvenir hunters a little later.

Afterwards the terrible news of fire and tragedy coming from Bradford dampened spirits and caused some supporters to consider what would have happened at Maine Road had fire broken out in the Platt Lane Stand, built up on wood at the back. With so many people sat in the aisles, few would have survived.

In the days that followed naturally the national press covered the news from Bradford, but City still managed to make a few of the back page headlines locally. Each article seemed to concentrate on the view that the Blues remained very much a club in debt. This was no longer a surprise to McNeill, who felt that safety in the First would gradually bring the finance in, but it still disappointed the fans who had remained incredibly loyal. Many questioned where the income had gone and how the Club had fallen so low. Despite promotion many still questioned the management of the Club under Peter Swales.

The Chairman told the press that relegation was the biggest cause of financial hardship: "It cost us half a million, but you must go through terrible pain before you can do really well. The lessons have been learned under a good manager and we don't intend to go down again."

He did admit that he felt responsible for the decline during the early eighties. There had been calls for him to quit prior to relegation, but once the inevitable occurred he told his critics that he'd got City into the mess, so he would get the Club out of it. He added: "I felt destined to go down as a failure. I was beginning to think I was a bit of a Jonah for City. The past two years out of the First Division have been like being in jail - all the time we have been studying and learning."

1985-1986 Trophy Success

Almost immediately following promotion new players were linked with a move to Maine Road. Top of the list seemed to be Mark Lillis from Huddersfield Town. Lillis had been on associate schoolboy forms with City in 1974 but had never really stood a chance of progression at Maine Road and had moved to Huddersfield making his debut in October 1978. During May and June 1985 Birmingham, Chelsea, Oxford, and Sheffield Wednesday had all shown interest in the player, but once the forward spoke with McNeill his mind was made up: "I tried to

speak to everyone with an open mind. I talked to Billy McNeill determined to push to the back of my mind the fact that they were my favourite club, that I'd always wanted to play for them. As you can imagine, that was nigh impossible. So once I assessed the offers I made up my mind. I could have been a little better off going down south.

"I suppose it had to be City. If I had not come here I would probably be looking back on life in five years' time with a lot of regrets."

Lillis had been a City follower since birth. He'd been to Wembley to watch the 1969 Cup Final and in his teens he had been a regular Kippax attendee, while his parents had been season ticket holders for years. He was a true Blue and on his home debut he delighted the Kippax by scoring from the penalty spot, although the kick had to be taken twice after players encroached. After both shots entered the net Lillis turned to his friends on the Kippax to celebrate.

The second penalty helped bring a 1-1 draw with Leicester, while four days earlier another new signing, Sammy McIlroy, helped City achieve the same scoreline at Coventry. McIlroy had signed from Stoke on a free transfer at the start of August. Another new arrival making his debut in that game was Nigel Johnson from Rotherham.

The season was not a particularly successful one but, as far as seasons of consolidation go, it was a satisfactory one. McNeill's men reached ninth place by the start of September, but dropped to 20th in October. This fall down the table coincided with a toe injury to goalkeeper Alex Williams. Williams had played in 112 consecutive games prior to the injury and had hoped for a quick return to action, but a painful back condition caused in a reserve team outing delayed his return to fitness. In fact, the player suffered with a number of troublesome injuries and was never to play in City's first team again. Despite being a passionate Blue he was transferred to Port Vale in January 1987, but suffered further and his career ended all too soon. He did return to Maine Road during the 1990s to play an active role in City's community programme for which he was awarded an MBE.

For City the League campaign had a few high points - the 5-1 defeat of Coventry on 14th December, and the 1-0 victory over championship contenders Liverpool on Boxing Day - but the last two months of the season were a struggle and the Blues ended the season in 15th position, after being 11th at the start of March.

In the League Cup City overcame Bury 2-1 in both legs - the first played at Old Trafford before 11,377 - but were defeated 2-1 at home to Arsenal in the third round. The FA Cup was not much better. The Blues defeated Walsall 3-1, then lost 3-1 to Watford in the second replay after drawing 1-1 and 0-0.

Despite failure in these two competitions, City did have a chance of Wembley glory in a third competition - the Full Members' Cup. This competition had been created as a result of the ban on English clubs playing in Europe following the Heysel European Cup Final of 1985. The teams that would have normally qualified for Europe organised a trophy called the 'Super Cup' to replace continental competition. As a result the Football League decided to organise a tournament for the rest of the top two divisions.

City were placed in a group with two Second Division sides Leeds United and Sheffield United. The winners of that group would progress to a 'northern' semi-final. In the first match City romped home to a 6-1 victory over Leeds at Maine Road, but the attendance was a pitiful 4,029 – at the time the lowest crowd for a first team game at Maine Road.

In the second group game City travelled to Sheffield and defeated United 2-1 with goals from Phillips and Baker, to put them through to the northern semi-final against Sunderland. This time a crowd of 6,642 watched City win 4-3 on penalties after a goalless draw. Immediately afterwards around 200 fans ran onto the pitch to celebrate. Sadly, the pitch invasion came at a time when the government seemed determined to

TRUE BLUE
Paul Power

A quality captain during a time of change, and worthy League title winner with Everton.

clamp down on this kind of activity. Already there were discussions taking place about how to rid the game of the hooligan element and some clubs had already suggested they would ban away supporters altogether. The City management were conscious that they needed to ensure tough sanctions were not imposed at Maine Road and devoted the front cover of the League programme against Coventry to warn supporters that good behaviour was essential. Already Maine Road had fencing built to a height of 2.4 metres on every side, if fans continued to invade the pitch then this would be raised to 4.4 metres, said the Club.

On the pitch, the two legged northern final saw City lose 2-1 at Brian Horton's Hull, then win the second leg 2-0 with goals from Phillips and Melrose before the largest crowd of the entire tournament, excluding the final, of 10,180. That victory gave City a Wembley meeting with Chelsea.

The final was originally scheduled to be played on Saturday 1st March but Oxford, who ironically had been beaten by Chelsea in the Southern final, appealed to the Football League. Oxford were due to face City at Maine Road on that date and Oxford believed the League should take preference over the new trophy. Had Oxford beaten Chelsea in the first place it's doubtful there would have been a complaint, however Robert Maxwell's side did complain and managed to win their appeal. City, Chelsea and the Football League worked hard to find a new date and eventually had to settle for Sunday 23rd March. It was not ideal as both clubs had to play League games the day before. What made it worse was that City had to face Manchester United at Old Trafford.

At Old Trafford McNeill played a City side that really did represent Manchester. By this time everyone connected with the Club boasted that the Blues represented Manchester, whereas United hardly seemed to have anything to do with the city. Old Trafford was outside of the city's boundaries, few

Substitute Jim Melrose came on for Steve Kinsey in the Manchester derby, 14th September 1985.

Mancunians played for the club, and the majority of their support seemed to come from outside the region. City, on the other hand, embodied all that was good - and bad - about Manchester.

The derby match ended with a proud City side drawing 2-2 with Ron Atkinson's multi-million pound United. United had been leading 2-0, although the second of those had been a penalty scored by Strachan. In the 71st minute Clive Wilson sent a bobbling header past goalkeeper Chris Turner, then seven minutes later a misguided back pass by United's Arthur Albiston, who was under tremendous pressure from Paul Simpson, gave City the equaliser. The Blues piled on the pressure and could have taken the lead, but the game ended in a moral victory to the Manchester men.

The City side that day had cost £287,000 whereas United's was over 11 times more expensive. An incredible difference and one that ensured United retained the upper hand. Despite their £2m loss in 1983 the Reds had continued to spend huge amounts to buy the best.

Against the Reds City paraded eight Mancunians as opposed to United's one, and that was Peter Barnes who, ironically, had been discovered by the Blues in the first place. Even United's home grown players could hardly be described as 'local' - Albiston (Scottish), Whiteside (Irish), and Hughes (Welsh). Understandably, City made much of the local angle, but then so did the media especially when later in the season the Blues' youth side defeated the Reds 3-1 on aggregate in the FA Youth Cup Final. City seemed to be the local side, willing to spend time and effort finding and developing its own players, whereas Atkinson's Reds seemed intent on buying success regardless of the financial impact on the rest of football.

After the League draw, supporters left Old Trafford in buoyant mood, chanting the name of own goalscorer Albiston. Some travelled straight to London for the following day's Wembley match, while others soaked up the post-derby atmosphere.

On the morning of the Full Members' Cup Final the press reported on the Manchester derby match, but then spent time criticising the Wembley competition. Brian Madley, writing in the Sunday People, believed the game would be a flop: "Wembley will be half empty this afternoon for the final of the Full Members' Cup, or half full for the final of the Empty Members' Cup. Whichever, the clash between Chelsea and Manchester City will go down as the most anonymous Wembley final of all time."

Other journalists, including the Manchester Evening News' City reporter Peter Gardner, criticised the competition and laughed at both clubs for taking part. Like Madley most stated that Wembley would be empty. They underestimated the loyalty of the City faithful. In the end the final was watched by 68,000 and brought receipts of £508,000. After covering Wembley's costs, and providing financial support to all entrants, City and Chelsea shared a figure of approximately £220,000.

Overall the Full Members' Cup may have been viewed as a 'Mickey Mouse' competition, but the final itself was watched by a crowd comparable with some modern day League Cup Finals – for example the 2006 final between Manchester United and Wigan was watched in Cardiff by 66,866 (8,000 below capacity) - and was attended by greater numbers of partisan support. City's following that day was greater than 30,000, while Chelsea made up the bulk of the rest. Had the two sides played in the FA Cup Final, it's doubtful they would have been allowed so many tickets.

The final was not only well attended, but it also provided entertainment at a level rarely seen at Wembley. It was fitting that City and Chelsea competed the final as the two sides were by far the biggest of all the entrants, certainly City were the club with the biggest following. At the time of the final the Blues' attendance averaged around 26,000, making them the fourth best supported First Division club behind United, Liverpool and Everton.

With Chelsea follower Sir Richard Attenborough as guest of honour the game kicked off. City, playing in their familiar Cup Final outfit of Red and Black stripes, started brightly. In the eighth minute Mick McCarthy miscued an intended shot which

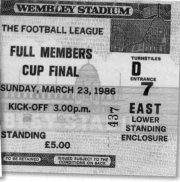

enabled Steve Kinsey to score City's first goal at Wembley for almost five years.

Fans believed the trophy would be coming to Manchester, but an equaliser by David Speedie in the 19th minute gave Chelsea the initiative. In the 36th minute Lee scored Chelsea's second and the score remained 2-1 at the interval. City had struggled defensively for much of the latter period of the first half and Chelsea appeared capable of breaking through at will. Nevertheless within minutes of the restart Steve Kinsey was clearly tripped in the penalty area by Joe Mclaughlin. Fans were convinced a penalty would be awarded but referee Alan Saunders refused City's appeals and the moment was lost.

Shortly afterwards Speedie made it 3-1 for the Pensioners, and then in the 58th minute he became the first person since Stan Mortensen to score a hat-trick in a senior domestic final at Wembley. City now looked dead and buried, and when Lee made it 5-1 in the 79th minute many supporters left for the long journey back to Manchester. Those that were left started singing songs in praise of Arthur Albiston's own goal the day before, and helped encourage City to burst back into life.

McNeill made a double substitution, bringing on Graham Baker and Paul Simpson for Nicky Reid and David Phillips, and the new players quickly moved into action, with Simpson in electrifying form down the wing. A firm header from Lillis five minutes from time inspired the team, and three minutes later the same player seemed to have scored City's third when he and Chelsea's Doug Rougvie headed at the same time. Later Rougvie insisted that he had made the decisive touch which made the score 5-3, but at the time Lillis was convinced it was his goal.

TRUE BLUE
Steve Redmond

Captain of the 1986 FA Youth Cup winning side (below) and soon to be first team captain.

A minute later, Andy May was tripped and Lillis scored the resulting penalty to make the score 5-4. Lillis and the City supporters left in the stadium were convinced that he had scored a hat-trick, but Rougvie's admission that he had scored an own goal ruled out that particular fairy tale.

With City fighting to secure an equaliser, Chelsea fans were relieved to hear the final whistle. Had the game lasted another five minutes then McNeill's side would certainly have equalised, as it was the 5-4 scoreline proved to the football world that Wembley could host entertaining finals.

The fight back brought to an end an amazing weekend where a combined crowd of 119,274 had watched the Blues play with pride.

The 1985-86 season had proved to be more successful than any supporter or official could have hoped, although captain Paul Power had accurately predicted at the start of the season that the Blues would reach Wembley. The Youth Cup success and Wembley appearance had given hope to Chairman Swales and the City faithful, but it was still true that the Club were some £4 million in debt and unable to compete in the transfer market with the mid 80s big five of Liverpool, United, Everton, Arsenal and Tottenham, despite having consistently higher crowds than at least two of those sides.

The period between 1979, when City went transfer crazy, and relegation in 1983 had seen City self-destruct financially and led to a situation whereby the Blues had struggled. By 1986 those financial issues caused City to rely on youth development and youngsters such as Paul Moulden and Steve Redmond (the FA Youth Cup winning captain who had played at Wembley), were now believed to be vital if the Blues were to achieve any form of success.

1983-1986 SUMMARY

Highest League Attendance: 48,773 Manchester United, 14/09/85
Highest Cup Attendance: 31,632 Watford, 25/01/86 (FA Cup)
Managers: 1983 – 1986 Billy McNeill

Seasonal Record:

Season	League	Posn	FA Cup	League Cup	Other	Leading Scorer	Average Attendance
1983-84	FL Div2	4	Rnd 3	Rnd 3		Parlane 16	25,604
1984-85	FL Div2	3	Rnd 3	Rnd 4		Phillips & Smith 12	24,220
1985-86	FL Div1	15	Rnd 4	Rnd 3	Full Members' Final	Lillis 11	24,229

FA Youth Cup winners Ian Brightwell, Steve Redmond and Andy Hinchcliffe. By the end of August 1987 all three were first team regulars.

1986-1989
Relying on Youth

"It was the time of the banana craze and it was really cool to be a City fan. I remember being on the coach to the last game of the promotion season at Bradford. We were all trying to focus and we pulled up in traffic and there in the coach next to us was a group of City fans carrying bananas, inflatable Frankenstein monsters and a paddling pool! It was a great time."

Paul Lake commenting on 1988-89 season in 2010

1986-1987 We Never Win At Home And We Never Win Away

During the summer of 1986 City lost one of its greatest servants when captain Paul Power moved to Everton in what was supposed to be a mainly coaching capacity. It actually resulted in the player appearing so often for the Merseysiders that he helped them to the League title. It was a great moment for the player who also managed to score against City during his return match at Maine Road. Understandably, with City struggling, Power found it hard to celebrate scoring against the club he loved.

By this time, Billy McNeill was well aware of the precarious financial situation and he was finding it difficult motivating himself after the 1985-86 season: "Although we found it hard to win a game we managed to stay in the First Division. When I look back it was a tremendous shoestring achievement, but I knew we had to tighten up for next season - or else!"

In 2009 McNeill looked back and admitted that another season of financial struggle was going to be very difficult: "Our local rivals United could afford to go out and buy the best. I had to wheel and deal on a very tight budget. Not having the resources to buy the players I knew we needed to maintain our First Division status was frustrating."

He was well aware that progress was being made at youth level thanks to the tremendous efforts of former heroes Tony Book, Ken Barnes and Glyn Pardoe who were responsible for youth development: "We were having great success with our youth team. Directors of City and the Club secretary, Bernard Halford, kept telling me to be patient. Bernard was of the opinion that we had to keep cool and hope that the boys developed properly."

Although it was not apparent at the time this 'hope' demonstrated how the Club lacked a long term vision. Those young players were highly talented but needed to progress based on their own developmental needs. McNeill knew this, but the Club's precarious financial state meant he had little opportunity to develop a plan in the manner that Alex Ferguson would later manage at Manchester United. McNeill knew this was always likely to cause long term problems: "My fourth season at Maine Road kicked off with the usual problems of trying to be patient - difficult for me! And dabbling cheap in the transfer market. Apart from the fact that we were always looking for bargain buys, we also had to persuade other clubs to accept payment on the never-never. I tried to convince the Board that dealing like this we would never get the players we really wanted."

There were other nagging issues for McNeill. One problem started to become an issue during the 1985-86 season: "I didn't feel I was under any pressure - at least, not until they appointed Freddie Pye as vice-chairman while I was on holiday. He was given the title of 'Director in Charge of Team Affairs', which I thought was ominous. I never had a relationship with Mr. Pye. After his appointment there was a lot of murmuring in the background. The Chairman tried to encourage me to get together with Mr. Pye, but I couldn't bring myself to do it. He appeared to be working against me in team matters. Maybe I could have made a bigger effort, bit I felt it was a bad appointment and Freddie Pye wanted to dictate policy.

"For instance, I needed a striker but we couldn't afford to buy one. It turned out that Mr. Pye and Ken Bates of Chelsea are friendly, so I was coerced into taking Gordon Davies from Stamford Bridge. The never-never deal worked out was nothing short of astonishing. As a player, Davies had ability but wasn't prepared to be in on the action. I didn't consider Gordon was a strong character either. All this was making me think carefully about my position."

McNeill remained at Maine Road for the first seven games of the season but these issues were omnipresent. Then an offer came from Aston Villa. Villa Chairman Doug Ellis promised McNeill money to buy players and the freedom that he felt he could longer have at City. McNeill: "Peter Swales didn't want me to go and he also thought Villa weren't right for me. However, upsetting influences in the background at Maine Road weren't going away. I spoke with several prominent people and the advice was to keep clear of Villa and Doug Ellis. However, I wasn't happy with the City set up."

Leaving City for Villa was not a popular move: "Others warned me that I could be making a big mistake. Sir Matt Busby said I should be wary and Tommy Docherty said 'you would need to be off yer head.'"

At the end of the season Villa were relegated and McNeill was sacked. After leaving England he remained interested in the fortunes of City and considered what might have been had he not been tempted to move to Villa. Sadly, in 1997 at the age of 57 he was forced to undergo a lifesaving triple heart bypass operation.

Jimmy Frizzell took over as manager. By that time the Blues had been defeated twice, won once, and drawn four - including a difficult away trip to Liverpool. At that time the season was expected to be one of struggle, but no one expected relegation. Frizzell was hopeful that he could build on the progress of the previous season, but by the time of the first derby meeting with United on 26th October, the Blues were bottom of the division.

Frizzell had done much to strengthen the side prior to the derby which, incidentally, was the first to be screened live on television. He'd purchased well-travelled striker Imre Varadi, who immediately delighted the crowd by scoring within six minutes of his debut at Chelsea, and brought Tony Grealish and John Gidman to the Club in time to make their debuts against United. Grealish had been signed for £20,000 from West Bromwich Albion, while Gidman had come on a free transfer direct from the Reds. The former United man, who had been Ron Atkinson's first signing back in July 1981, turned down a lucrative contract with AEK Athens to join the Blues: "Once I knew City were interested that was it. There was nowhere else I wanted to go. As soon as I stepped into Jimmy Frizzell's office and met the lads, I knew I was in the right place with the right people. I am delighted to get this chance to play for City and I hope I will do a good job for Jimmy Frizzell."

Against United Gidman and the other new signings helped the Blues achieve a 1-1 draw. City had played with grit and determination and once again proved that they could match the big spending Reds in one off occasions. Ten days after this draw United dispensed with the services of Ron Atkinson as results and the pressure to win the Championship caused Martin Edwards to act. City, already into their fifth manager of the eighties so far, began to boast that Jimmy Frizzell was now the longest serving manager in Manchester.

The morale boosting draw lifted the Blues into 21st place and brought a little hope. A 1-1 draw at Southampton was followed by a 3-1 victory over Wimbledon in the near-irrelevant Full Members' Cup, and then victories over Billy McNeill's Aston Villa (3-1) and Charlton Athletic (2-1) followed. The Villa game attracted the second highest crowd of the season up to that point as McNeill was forced to endure the taunts of the City faithful. In August 2009 he admitted: "I understand how they felt. They were probably right because I shouldn't have gone to Villa. It turned out to the worst 8 months of my managerial career. Within a fortnight I realised that I had made a huge mistake.

"City supporters were always good to me during my time at Maine Road. Like Celtic fans they are passionate about the Club and they do deserve success. No one should ever underestimate the stature and size of the Club. Like the fans I was desperate for success at City but I knew it wouldn't come because of the financial situation. Had we managed to win a trophy I know the place would have erupted. When City do find sustained success the football world will recognise what anyone connected with the Club already knows. City fans are tremendously loyal and they do deserve real success. They made me feel very welcome during my time in Manchester."

McNeill had left City because of the problems he was having at Board level and because of the Club's exceedingly poor financial position. Had supporters known his reasons at the time and the issues he faced then it is possible they would have exerted more pressure on Chairman Peter Swales and his supporting directors. McNeill's desertion to Villa upset all Blues because they felt that overall he was the right kind of manager to bring the Club success. It's interesting that Atkinson's successor at United was a similarly dour but knowledgeable Scotsman by the name of Alex Ferguson. The difference between McNeill and Ferguson at the time was that United were prepared and able to back their manager with more funds than any other Manchester manager had experienced, whereas City gave their manager less than even his predecessors had been allowed.

The Charlton victory on 15th November 1986 lifted City to 19th but a couple of disappointing defeats against Everton and at Nottingham Forest sent the Blues bottom again. Fans were frustrated and had started to voice their feelings with Peter Swales suffering the majority of the abuse. As the season progressed the anti-Swales contingent grew, and then in April the demonstrations reappeared.

Fans had demonstrated at times during 1983 but those protests were relatively minor compared to what was occurring in April 1987. A 4-2 defeat by 15th placed Southampton on 11th April brought much abuse the Chairman's way, and prompted one group of season ticket holders to produce and distribute a leaflet calling for the Chairman to resign entitled 'The Case Against Peter Swales'.

The hand-out claimed that the Chairman's thirteen and a half years rule had set the Club on a course for

disaster, not success, and questioned what achievements had been made during his reign. Although some of the points had been twisted to win the argument, the leaflet was a damning indictment of what appeared to be years of misrule. It also questioned many of the points Swales believed to have been his best achievements. One area was support: "Peter Swales has consistently claimed credit for improving attendances at Maine road and even repeated the same boast in the *Sunday Mirror* of 12th April 1987 following the 4-2 home defeat by Southampton. Let's examine this claim. When Swales took over City were the third best supported team in the Country and the attendances for the first 4 home matches of the 1973 season before Swales became Chairman were 34,178, 30,931, 31,209 and 32,118, averaging out at 32,109. Present attendances have slipped below the 20,000 mark and will fall even further when we are relegated for a second time. Mr. Swales is either a good liar or a bad mathematician if he thinks a drop of 12,000+ is an improvement in attendances."

The anti-Swales movement was growing and the leaflet summed up the frustrations of a large group of supporters, but no matter how many leaflets were distributed Swales was determined to remain in control. As with the events of 1983 he felt responsible and was still committed to the Blue cause. In '83 he had been as disappointed with relegation as any supporter: "When we got relegated it was the worst day of my life, because there was no way we were going to be relegated before the game and when it actually happened it was as if somebody had hit me over the head with a sledge hammer. It was the only time in my life when I was totally deflated. How I got through the Saturday night and Sunday I'll never know. It took me many months to get over that. We hadn't really got any money, but we got playing again. Got back up. I'd known we were on borrowed time because we didn't have the players to maintain a First Division side, so went down again."

The 1986-87 season was the first to have playoffs to help decide promotion, but in this first season it remained possible for a normally relegated Division One club to enter the play offs and defeat Second Division clubs to retain their status. When the system was announced Peter Swales admitted in an interview that he wouldn't mind being involved in the mini-tournament simply to generate more funds. That statement alone proved how desperate things had got under his chairmanship. Ultimately, City weren't even good enough for that.

The Blues were relegated again in May 1987 after a 2-0 defeat at West Ham. At the end of the game City supporters and West Ham fans who, it must be remembered had an exceptionally poor reputation at this time, climbed over the fences and onto the pitch. Officials thought that the two sets of supporters were about to fight but were surprised to hear the Hammers chanting "You'll be back", and see both groups swapping scarves and souvenirs. It was the kind of moment that should be widely reported in the media but rarely is, and was a sign that the majority of supporters were not the caged wild animals that the government and the media portrayed them to be. City had been relegated, but their supporters did not seek revenge. The West Ham fans could have ridiculed, but they didn't. Perhaps somewhere the Country's leaders had been misinformed? Sadly, it took a major tragedy two years later before they began listening to the truth.

The Blues' form during the season had not been good at all with only eight victories out of 42 matches, and the embarrassment of not winning a game away from home since the 2-0 defeat of Tottenham on 18th January 1986. In the cup competitions City struggled against First Division opponents when Arsenal defeated the Blues 3-1 in the League Cup, while Manchester United won a highly controversial FA Cup third round tie 1-0 at Old Trafford. An Imre Varadi goal was ruled out for a 'pushing offence' by the player, yet no one in the ground could explain when or how the so called pushing had occurred. It was a total mystery and left the City fans feeling cheated - a feeling repeated nine years later at the same venue.

1987-1988 Remember When

During the close season it was no surprise when Chairman Swales decided to act to change the management structure. Stories in the press suggested that Dave Bassett would be offered the manager's job, while other names mentioned included Norwich coach Mel Machin. In the end the Norwich man was given the title Team Manager while Jimmy Frizzell was appointed General Manager. It seemed a strange set up. On the one hand Swales had given Machin authority for team affairs, on the other he retained Frizzell to oversee development. From the supporters' perspective it felt as if Machin was the actual manager, yet the two men seemed to take it in turns to face the press. Even City's match programme alternated the manager's column - one game Frizzell gave his views, the next Machin. It seemed a little strange for two men who had never previously worked together to share these responsibilities, but Swales and his board decided that was the way it was to be.

The side that started the 1987-88 season was a mix of experienced professionals and members of City's impressive youth policy. Gidman, Clements, Varadi and McNab provided the knowledge and know-how while Hinchcliffe, Brightwell, Redmond, White, and Scott proved the value of City's scouting system. The goalkeeper was Eric Nixon who was still determined to prove he was good enough to be City's number one after regularly being replaced by Perry Suckling and Barry Siddall over the previous seasons. The eleventh member of the side that faced Plymouth on the opening day was the exciting Paul Stewart, who had been signed by Jimmy Frizzell the previous year.

City achieved a 2-1 victory over Plymouth that day with Varadi and Stewart combining perfectly. A couple of 1-1 draws followed before the first real setback - a 2-1 defeat at home to Blackburn. The Blues were now 15th in the division and seven days later dropped further when a painful match at Shrewsbury ended goalless. Attendances suffered with a miserly 15,430 (the lowest League crowd since 1965) attending Maine Road for the following game - a midweek 4-0 demolition of Millwall.

By the start of November the Blues had moved up to tenth place, but it was obvious to all that they were simply not good enough for automatic promotion or even a playoff place. Then on Saturday 7th November a crowd of 19,583 attended Maine Road for the visit of Malcolm Macdonald's Huddersfield. After struggling since the start of the season, the Yorkshire side appointed Macdonald to the manager's chair in October. The week before the Maine Road match the team achieved its first win of the season when Millwall were defeated 2-1. Macdonald and his men arrived in Manchester confident of victory, they left shell-shocked.

The game started well enough for Huddersfield with City looking lethargic in defence. Had the away side been more forceful up front then they would undoubtedly have been the first to score. Fortunately, it was the experienced Neil McNab who was first to score when he eased the home supporters' nerves with a clinical 12th minute strike. From then on he dominated midfield and allowed City's forwards to attack in number.

In the 29th minute Paul Stewart scored the second, then five minutes later Tony Adcock, who had signed from Colchester in June made it three. Already Huddersfield seemed dead, but worse was to follow for the Yorkshiremen when youngster David White scored the fourth three minutes before half time.

During the interval City fans joked that their heroes might actually double the score, but no one seriously felt that that was achievable. After the restart, it soon became apparent that Huddersfield had little to offer and that Machin's men were ready to destroy them. Adcock scored his second with a right foot shot in the 52nd minute, then 14 minutes later Paul Stewart made it six. A minute later Adcock scored again to complete his first City hat-trick.

The Kippax now chanted "We want eight!" and in the 80th minute Stewart completed his hat-trick to double the half-time score. Five minutes from time White made it nine, prompting chants of "We want ten!". Before that could happen Huddersfield were awarded a

Hat-trick hero Tony Adcock as Huddersfield suffer a 10-1 defeat. Below: The official team sheet for the game

penalty after John Gidman nudged David Cork. When former City hero Andy May managed to slot the ball home in the 88th minute the City fans cheered and the Huddersfield contingent sat in the Platt Lane stand stood up and started to 'conga' in between the famous old stand's wooden benches. With two minutes remaining could Huddersfield mount a comeback? Even the most seasoned supporter must have realised that the unpredictable Blues had no chance of letting this lead slip.

In the 89th minute White made sure of the result by scoring City's tenth goal. Journalists frantically tried to ascertain what records, if any, were broken by this 10-1 scoreline and the fact that three players had scored their hat-tricks. The result was City's best at Maine Road, but it wasn't the highest Blue score ever. That was 11-3 when Lincoln were defeated in 1895. Whatever the statistics said, it was still a great performance and fortunately for City fans was captured on film by Granada TV for their own highlights programme.

It was unusual in 1987 for quality footage of every game to be made, but within days of the victory City were selling 60 minutes of the Granada footage for £15.

After the match Mel Machin expressed his pleasure at the result and then predicted a bright future: "It may take two or three years to grasp real success, but the

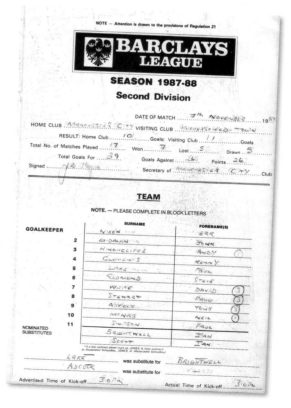

future here at City looks good. The groundwork has been done and we can now start to reach out in keen anticipation of bigger and better things."

What was most remarkable about the game was that leading scorer Imre Varadi had actually missed the goal scoring festival through a recurring thigh muscle injury. The game would have been perfect for the man who seemed to thrive on the adulation of supporters. For a couple of years after the match those same fans were to voice a chant: "Remember when City scored ten."

With the talk of Manchester still focusing on Machin's men, Plymouth arrived at Maine Road for a Full Members' Cup - now sponsored by Simod Sports Shoes - game. Once again City entertained with Plymouth suffering a 6-2 defeat only three days after the Huddersfield massacre. Again the press picked up on City's exploits and for once the rather irrelevant Simod Cup dominated the back page headlines. *The Star* concentrated on the role played by Tony Adcock who had scored his second hat-trick in three days. Under the headline "Adcock's 'Arf Hour" reporter Kevin Francis concentrated on the news that the £80,000 signing from Colchester was only in the side because of injury to Varadi, and suggested that Machin would have a difficult selection problem once Varadi returned to fitness. Machin, who also had the prolific Paul Moulden recovering from injury, looked forward to the time when he would actually be faced with the problem of selecting two of the four decent strikers he had on his books.

Interestingly, City's first goalscorer against Plymouth, Andy Hinchcliffe, was being watched by Liverpool manager Kenny Dalglish. Already the Blues were aware that almost all the wealthy British clubs of the period were keen on City's headline grabbing young players. Only four months later Rangers manager Graeme Souness arrived at Maine Road to watch the game against Swindon. He paid to sit in the North Stand, and watched the exploits of Paul Stewart while covering half his face with a scarf to hide his identity. It didn't work. A *Sunday People* reporter spotted the Rangers manager and his assistant, Walter Smith, and forced the pair to leave before they attracted further attention.

It has to be stressed that Swales' City were totally unable to compete financially with many sides traditionally less wealthy than the Blues at this point. Mismanagement at the highest level had sent the Club on a downward spiral and allowed others to make bids for players that City simply could not compete with. This was totally out of character with the Club's history pre-Swales.

For a while the achievements of City's young players kept interest going, but League form was far from perfect. On 12th December the Blues finally reached fifth position, but then two home League defeats against Oldham and Leeds left City in ninth place. Further

disappointments in January and February caused the Blues to drop as low as 11th at one stage.

It was clear that the only chance of promotion lay with the play offs, but the side would need to find consistency to stand any real hope even then. City did move up the table in March and April with a few significant victories, including a 3-0 defeat of Birmingham City at St. Andrews - a day when Machin gave a debut to 16 year old Neil Lennon. It wasn't a particularly good debut for the youngster as he received constant barracking from the home crowd, and was never to appear in the first team again. Deservedly, in 1997 he played for Leicester in the League Cup Final, by which time he was idolised by the Leicester support and in 2000 moved to Celtic for what became the greatest period of his footballing career.

Apart from a few exciting performances, the regular transfer stories in the press seemed to affect a number of key players, and the Blues ended the campaign a disappointing ninth.

The season was not a complete failure, however, as the two major cup competitions brought much pride to the Club. In the League Cup City defeated Wolves 3-2 on aggregate before First Division Nottingham Forest were despatched 3-0 at Maine Road. The goals were scored by City's perfect partnership, Varadi (2) and Stewart, and brought much praise from Forest manager Brian Clough who admitted: "It could have been four or five on the night."

The fourth round brought another home tie with First Division Watford arriving only ten days after the 10-1 over Huddersfield. The game ended 3-1 in City's favour, prompting Mel Machin to predict a Wembley visit for his side, even if he wasn't too enthusiastic about the performance: "You need a certain amount of luck to go all the way but I know what we are capable of and, with that measure of luck, we could be at Wembley next April. It was a difficult game but in the end I felt we fully deserved our victory over Watford. It was the right result, of course, but I know we are capable of playing better. When we were 1-0 up in the early part of the second half, Watford started to hit long balls behind our full backs and were turning and running at our defenders. We were surrendering territory too much and Eric Nixon must be praised for making two vital saves."

Watford equalised through a controversial goal which was very similar to the infamous Geoff Hurst World Cup Final goal. Few Blues felt the ball had crossed the line, but as with 1966 it counted and City had to withstand a little pressure before they managed to exert their influence again. Machin claimed City's second goal was a 'classic'. It was certainly the best of the match and was scored after Paul Lake turned two defenders brilliantly to create a chance for David White, who'd also scored the first, to fire home. Paul Stewart scored the third via a rebound after his penalty kick had been saved.

The star player was without doubt the ever-improving Paul Lake who, like Hinchcliffe, Stewart, Brightwell, and White, was being watched regularly by scouts from leading First Division clubs. Sooner or later City would have to sell at least one of them, or so the media kept telling the Club's loyal support. Peter Swales was adamant though that none of the Club's brightest stars would be sold.

The opponents for the League Cup quarter-finals were the exceptionally strong Everton, who were third in the First Division at the time of the match. A Goodison Park crowd of 40,014, many from Manchester, witnessed a 2-0 home win. It was a bitterly disappointing Wednesday night for City's well behaved army of fans - many of whom had been abysmally treated by the Merseyside police at the railway station after the match.

The game itself opened with much pressure on Eric Nixon's goal. Fortunately, the relatively inexperienced 'keeper produced some fine saves to keep the score down to 1-0 by half-time, but the rest of City's still developing side appeared a little overawed by the occasion with opportunities at the other end coming to virtually nothing. Paul Lake did have a fine chance to score, but the ball hit the post.

In the second half City played much better, and were edging closer to an equaliser when Graeme Sharp netted Everton's second. Machin's hope of Wembley glory, or at least reaching the semi-finals was over in that competition. He felt the defeat had been caused by having too many players still learning their trade: "We were coming back into the game more and more when Everton suddenly struck with their second goal, and once again it highlighted a problem we have had all season. I can go back over so many games when we have been guilty of making what amount to 'schoolboy errors'. These can be as basic as not playing to the whistle."

By the time of the Goodison defeat City had already progressed in the FA Cup. On 9th January they faced Huddersfield Town at Leeds Road for a game that everyone in Huddersfield seemed fired up for. The Yorkshiremen were determined to avenge the 10-1 November defeat and, despite most early pressure coming from City and an Ian Brightwell goal in the fifth minute, it looked as if the home side would succeed.

Paul Moulden caught in an unusual pose.

Huddersfield grittily fought their way back and, thanks to Duncan Shearer, were leading 2-1 with just seconds to spare. Then City were awarded a free kick from about twenty yards out after Paul Moulden had been pushed in the back. It was a kick John Gidman desperately wanted to take: "I knew it was going to be the last kick of the game and I had to make it count. We had a quick discussion as there was hardly any time left and it was decided I should have a strike at goal. I struck it right and it went round the wall and in off the post."

Although the result brought City a second chance, it wasn't a particularly enjoyable day for the normally quiet Mel Machin. In the 77th minute he was ordered from the dugout for using foul and abusive language during an argument with one of the linesmen. It seemed a strange moment, and was certainly one that displeased Machin. Another dissatisfied City man was Neil McNab who had also been sent off in the closing stages.

The replay three days later at Maine Road was noteworthy for the remarkable performance of Huddersfield's goalkeeper Brian Cox - the same 'keeper who had played in the 10-1. He was outstanding and prevented the Blues from taking the lead. After extra-time the game remained goalless, forcing yet another replay.

At Leeds Road on Monday 25th January City proved once and for all that they possessed the greater strength. Andy Hinchcliffe opened the scoring with a clinical strike from the left. Further goals from White and Varadi - who'd driven straight from hospital where his daughter lay ill to play in the match - ensured a deserved 3-0 result and brought the Blues a nice trip to Blackpool the following Saturday.

At Bloomfield Road a tense game saw Blackpool take the lead in the 82nd minute, despite being outplayed for much of the match. The home side's goal had come from a most unlikely source - 20 year old Richard Sendall. The young player, who had already been told he would be leaving on a free transfer at the end of the season, had come on as substitute for his first senior outing of the season.

As the minutes ticked by it seemed highly unlikely that City would be able to level but then in injury time a mad scramble in the goal area left the home supporters panicking as the Blues piled on the pressure. Suddenly the ball was in the net and the City players were celebrating. On the terraces the large travelling support joined in, but few could claim they actually knew what had happened. Gradually the name of Lake was being muttered as the scorer but how had he managed it?

Some journalists claimed that Lake had sent a shot in off veteran defender Paul Jones, but the player himself had a slightly different view: "I would not have been surprised if the referee had stopped the game. There were so many bodies on the floor and everybody seemed to be having a stab at the ball. But I got my shot in and I was utterly delighted when it went in off the post. There was some confusion when we got back to the dressing room. Two or three of the players were trying to claim it, but I made it clear that it was my goal."

To the supporters it didn't really matter how the goal had been scored, they were just glad to have yet another second chance. City were certainly beginning to behave like a team of escapologists.

Immediately after the game Blackpool manager, and a man who became well known to City supporters a couple of years later, Sam Ellis conceded: "Today was our big chance to win the tie, Wednesday night is just a night out for us."

On the Wednesday Ellis' side came to frustrate as City played their third FA Cup tie in ten days. Despite the spoiling tactics City managed to score first via a Paul Stewart header against his former club. Later Paul Simpson added a second with another header after an effort from White had hit the crossbar. The game ended 2-1 to send City through to the fifth round for the first time since 1981. Their opponents would be Plymouth Argyle.

A Maine Road crowd of 29,206 watched as Ian Scott, Paul Simpson and 85th minute substitute Paul Moulden helped City achieve a 3-1 victory to progress to the quarter-final.

As with the League Cup, the Blues' opponents would be one of the strongest First Division sides of the period. They were also from Merseyside. Liverpool arrived at Maine Road after making their best ever start to a First Division campaign. They had also charged to an impressive 17 point lead in the championship race. If the Everton game was viewed as difficult, this game had to be impossible. Nevertheless, City's players and management were convinced they could achieve a good result against the Liverpool giants.

In addition to the prospect of facing one of Europe's greatest sides, the young Blues would be watched by a Sunday crowd of 44,047, and by millions on terrestrial television. It was a mammoth ordeal for some of the players, yet they started brightly.

For much of the opening half hour City put Liverpool under pressure but then in the 32nd minute the Reds became very fortunate. The referee turned a blind eye as John Barnes gained control of a pass from Peter Beardsley by using his hands. The Liverpool man sprinted past John Gidman to the line, crossed to the near post and Ray Houghton volleyed home. It was a desperate time to concede a goal, especially one so controversial, but the Blues continued to fight.

Almost on the stroke of half-time, Paul Stewart missed a perfect opportunity by driving the ball straight at Bruce Grobbelaar. After 53 minutes City suffered again when Paul Lake was adjudged to have pushed Craig Johnston in the back in the area. A fan ran on to the pitch to argue with referee Allan Gunn before Peter Beardsley fired home the resulting penalty to make it 2-0.

Later Grobbelaar made a dramatic save from a Stewart header, but then Liverpool gained total control of the match. Johnston rounded 'keeper Mike Stowell for the third goal, then Barnes scored with a low shot five minutes from time. A 4-0 defeat at home sounds like humiliation, but the game was not like that. True Liverpool were able to exert their influence on the match whenever they chose, but City gave them a tougher game than most clubs had that season, and had performed well enough to keep the score much lower. In fact Liverpool had managed to achieve victory as a result of two controversial goals.

Jimmy Frizzell was proud of the City performance but angry with the referee: "I have seen the video of Sunday's game and I still believe the referee might have given handball against John Barnes before Liverpool scored their first goal. And I still believe Paul Lake's tackle on Craig Johnston was a good one and that we shouldn't have had a penalty given against us. Referees have to make decisions and we have to accept them. But it's very difficult at times to swallow your disappointment. However, although I made my disappointment obvious to the officials after the game, I was not booked, as reported in some newspapers. Nor was there any reason for me to be."

Reaching the last eight of both major cup competitions was a fine achievement but 1987-88 was a season when the main priority had to have been promotion. The cup exploits had diverted the attention of their young stars, while constant media speculation that almost every one of the youngsters would be sold must have had an effect. Inevitably the following June the most saleable player at that time, Paul Stewart, was transferred to Tottenham Hotspur for £1.7 million. It was a huge amount, and was one Chairman Swales felt unable to turn down. Understandably, the transfer concerned supporters. Would the other exciting players be sold if the right offer came along? Peter Swales was adamant that the now regular players from the 1986 Youth Cup success - Hinchcliffe, Brightwell, Redmond, Moulden and White - would not be sold at any price.

1988-1989 Bananarama

Financially Swales' City could not compete. A point emphasised by the simple fact that whereas Spurs could last out £1.7m on one player (they spent a further £2m on Paul Gascoigne and a further £1.5m on three other players that year) Mel Machin used less than half that amount to buy four players. They were goalkeeper Andy Dibble (£240,000), central defender Brian Gayle (£320,000), striker Wayne Biggins (£160,000), midfielder Nigel Gleghorn (47,500), and forward John Deehan (£10,000). Former FA Youth Cup winner Steve Redmond was now the captain, while Lake, Hinchcliffe, Brightwell, and White all started the season as first team regulars.

The opening fixture saw the Blues create plenty of chances at Hull, but the home side took advantage of a surprising lapse by new signing Dibble to give Hull the only goal of the match. A humiliating 4-1 defeat at home to Oldham followed two days later prompting a large section of City's support to give the season its first hearing of the hardy perennial "Swales Out". The departure of Stewart and inability to compete financially had reminded fans how low they had fallen under the Chairman.

A 2-2 home draw with Walsall brought a point in the next game, prompting further calls for the Chairman to quit. Then at Leeds a penalty by Neil McNab gave City the lead but in typical Blue style with only minutes to go, a lapse in concentration gave Leeds an equaliser. Everyone recognised that two points had been lost rather than one gained.

As if in direct contrast to the events on the field, fans were now making headlines by creating their own entertainment on the terraces. They did this by bringing large inflatable bananas, and other items to every game. The craze had started at Oldham the previous season and had coincided with the arrival of City's first fanzine *Blueprint*. It was a time when supporters of all clubs were fighting against poor publicity and negative media focus. Although City fans were already well known for their frequent attacks on the Chairman, they were out to prove that they were not the animals many believed they were. They started the inflatable craze, and over the course of the next twelve months most other clubs followed in some way.

At Maine Road on 17th September City achieved their first victory by beating Brighton 2-1 before a crowd of 16,033. Peter Swales must have realised that the supporters were losing patience and were keen to see the team move up the table. The possibility of another season in Division Two could have killed many fans faith in the Club and their loyal support for good.

Two away victories followed with City defeating Chelsea 3-1 before a crowd of 8,858 at the Bridge. The low crowd was the result of a ban on away support and the closure of the ground's terracing, not that any of that stopped a large number of Mancunians attending the match. Four days later another away trip - this time to Barnsley - ended in a 2-1 win to lift the Blues to eighth.

On 1st October Division leaders Blackburn arrived at Maine Road with former Blue Nicky Reid as Captain. A mistake from Blackburn's normally reliable

The fans wave bananas and comedian Eddie Large is on the bench. Maine Road in the late 80s.

Colin Hendry gave Wayne 'Bertie' Biggins the chance to score the only goal. City moved up to fifth. Not bad for a team watched by fans carrying inflatable bananas while demonstrating against the chairman, although it is fair to say that protests quelled a little as the Blues moved up the table.

A 4-1 win over Portsmouth followed then on 8th October a difficult trip to Suffolk ended with a 1-0 victory for bogey team Ipswich. Naturally, the Blues felt far from happy with the result, especially as goalscorer Jason Dozzell only received a booking when his late tackle on Mark Seagraves forced the City man to be stretchered off earlier in the match.

After the long trip to East Anglia on the Saturday fans travelled to Plymouth the following Tuesday for the second leg of the League Cup 2nd round. The first game had ended 1-0 to the Blues, prompting many supporters to take the day off work for the long journey to Plymouth yet, incredibly, as they arrived in Devon the news came through that the game had been called off. The supporters who travelled were angry, yet no action was taken to ensure the same wouldn't occur again and in 1997 a similar postponement brought further justifiable criticism from City's travelling fans.

The Plymouth game was only delayed by 24 hours but it caused serious problems for any Blues wanting to attend. Those that managed the journey a second time were in for a treat as City defeated Plymouth 6-3 with Andy Dibble also saving a penalty. It had not been an easy game however. Machin's side were leading 2-0 on the night before allowing the home side back into the game with three goals levelling the aggregate score. After a few minutes panic City fought back to achieve what appeared to be an emphatic win.

After the game many Blues returned to Manchester, but some understandably decided to stay in Devon as the two sides would meet again in the League the following Saturday. It was an incredible week for travelling, yet fans still turned out in large numbers determined to make the Home Park League game a great occasion. It ended in another Blue victory, this time 1-0, but it became more newsworthy because of the party atmosphere of City's support. The Devon press found the inflatable craze puzzling with a photograph from the game carrying the caption: "What's all this?

TRUE BLUE
Paul Lake

Idolised by fans but his career was cut short through injury.

Giant bananas, a huge beer can and even an inflatable Frankenstein monster."

The same photo appeared on the cover of fanzine *Blueprint* later in the season as City's supporters started to plan their next carnival occasion. By November the fans had decided to turn the Boxing Day trip to Stoke into a fancy dress party. Although few, if any, would have realised at the time this was similar to some of the antics their predecessors had been famous for at the turn of the century. Apparently, games at Hyde Road were frequently brightened by supporters in fancy dress playing musical instruments. The 1988 trip to Stoke helped to rekindle that kind of atmosphere.

By the time of the Stoke match, City were fourth. They had led the table after an impressive 4-0 defeat of Bradford on 10th December, but that was only on goal difference. A 2-2 draw with Shrewsbury left them two points behind new leaders Blackburn.

On Boxing Day morning, with little public transport, over 12,000 supporters travelled to the Potteries in party spirit. The newspapers claimed it was City's largest travelling support for a League game outside of Greater Manchester since the 1968 Championship decider, although the Notts County match of 1985 saw a similar, possibly larger Blue support. Once in Stoke there were fans dressed as Laurel & Hardy, Arabs, vicars, hunchbacks, convicts (with the names Lester Piggott and Jan Molby on their backs), Nazi soldiers... basically anything you could imagine. There were even nursery rhyme characters with Humpty Dumpty insisting he sat on a wall inside the ground. Almost every supporter carried an inflatable of some description. It was an incredible sight, and one which proved that the majority of football fans were not hooligans.

When the City players ran onto the pitch they each carried their own banana and threw these into the large crowd. Stoke had generously given over one entire side of the ground and the paddock in front of their family stand. In addition many City families sat with Stoke fans in the family section and, naturally, other Blues found seats in the main stand. It was a fantastic atmosphere and one which should have been seen worldwide to prove the value of positive support. Sadly, the media barely covered the event. Nothing has ever been

Boxing Day 1988 and even the players carried inflatables as over 12,000 fans travelled to Stoke.

shown on television, and little appeared in the press. Even the City match programme failed to highlight the atmosphere of that day. At a time when the Government seemed intent on killing the game by introducing ID cards, positive publicity could have helped the authorities reconsider. Regrettably, it took a major disaster later in the season to make the leaders see sense.

The game itself was a huge disappointment with City losing 3-1 to a side that included former Blues Tony Henry and John Gidman and future star Peter Beagrie. The Manchester men continued to enjoy themselves however. Frank Newton, who had been acclaimed as the man who'd brought the first banana to the Oldham game the previous season, wrote his view of the day for fanzine *Blueprint*: "The match itself has faded from my memory partly because we lost but mainly because there was so much else to take in. The interstellar branch of the City fan club was in evidence with ET sitting on the fence at half time, a crocodile and a canary seemed to be getting on intimate terms, whilst I didn't envy the rear half of the pantomime horse wandering around the ground. I wonder how much of the game he saw? I wish I'd had a week or so to walk round the crowd to take in the humour and imagination displayed by the magnificent City following. When the game ended there was an air of disappointment at the result but still plenty of laughter as new delights appeared at every turn of the head. A rather cold looking fan wandered past wearing

a snorkel and flippers and not much else, a group of pixies were spotted heading towards the car park, whilst Rambo complete with machine gun (with a City scarf tied round it) walked the other way."

The attitude of the supporters lifted spirits, but more than anything else fans needed the team to repay their devotion by winning promotion. After the Stoke match City enjoyed a nine match unbeaten run in the League to leave them second to Chelsea. This run helped give Machin the manager of the month award while captain Steve Redmond was awarded the Young Eagle of the Month award.

After a 1-0 defeat at Watford, the Blues rediscovered their winning ways by beating Leicester 4-2 at Maine Road on 11th March, but it was also a day of despair for many in the crowd. City's greatest hope for the future and Young England star Paul Lake crashed to the ground after an accidental clash of heads with Leicester's Paul Ramsey. The 20 year old lay unconscious and began a series of convulsions clearly showing to the 22,266 crowd the gravity of the situation. Physio Roy Bailey raced on to the field: "It was a very dangerous situation and I had one hell of a job to force open Paul's jaws and hook back his tongue with my finger. In fact his jaw muscles were so tense that John Deehan, who was helping along with Glyn Pardoe, received a nasty bite in the process!"

Lake had swallowed his tongue and was very close to losing his life, only the quick actions of Bailey saved the youngster. Eventually, club doctor Norman Luft arrived on the scene. He had been sitting in the stand and had taken what seemed an eternity to make his way to the injured player, although the entire incident seemed to last longer than the whole game.

Lake himself hardly knew anything about the event: "I can recall the corner coming over and going out to attack the ball, but then the next thing was waking up in the medical room feeling pretty groggy! From what I've heard about it afterwards, I've no doubt that Roy's actions were vital and it is something for which I will owe him for the rest of my life."

When the collision first occurred the stadium fell silent. It was an eerie feeling, and one which proved the seriousness of the situation. Some supporters actually felt sick themselves as Lake's body shuddered, but fortunately Bailey's actions had prevented long term injury. A brain scan the following Monday proved that Lake was not seriously affected.

Sunderland were defeated 4-2 in the next game, then a crucial home meeting against Chelsea ended with a 3-2 defeat. The only bright points being the attendance - 40,070 the highest in the division that season - and the last minute goal for youngster Ged Taggart which made the score look a little respectable.

A week later the game at Walsall gave the travelling support real value for money when Nigel Gleghorn replaced the injured Andy Dibble in goal. City were 2-0 down when Dibble collapsed in agony with a groin problem. Gleghorn put on the green shirt and helped the Blues to fight back with David Oldfield - the fifth most expensive City player up until that point at £600,000 - scoring his first goal for the Club. 'Golden' Moulden equalised and then, early in the second half he scored again to bring a 3-2 lead.

Gleghorn made a couple of good saves and even kicked superbly to keep the pressure off City then a ridiculous back pass from Oldfield gave Walsall opportunity to score, and the game ended 3-3. The substitute 'keeper was certainly the man of the match, winning applause from both sets of supporters after being stand-in for around an hour, yet a mere six weeks later he had to do it all again.

As with the Walsall match, Dibble suffered a groin injury in similar circumstances giving Gleghorn his second chance to grab the headlines. He'd already scored an eighth minute goal in the game against Crystal Palace to give City the lead, then at the start of the second period he replaced Dibble. He managed to keep Steve Coppell's Palace at bay until the 75th minute when a brilliant strike from Ian Wright gave him little chance. Despite constant Palace pressure Gleghorn was able to keep the score down and the match ended 1-1 with the former North East fireman grabbing the headlines again. Gleghorn was pleased with his performance, and

admitted: "I wasn't nervous - the lads are getting used to my positioning! As a kid, I played a lot of basketball and also turned out for Durham's under 19 cricket team as a wicketkeeper. I've got a good pair of hands and enjoy larking about in goal during training."

Interestingly, this was the second consecutive season that City had lost their 'keeper at home to Palace. The previous year Eric Nixon was sent off and replaced by Steve Redmond. On that occasion Redmond was not as fortunate as Gleghorn as the game ended in a 3-1 defeat.

The point kept City in an automatic promotion place on 80 points. Chelsea were already Division Two champions after gaining a lead of 13 points over the Blues, but below Machin's young side lay three teams all on 74 points (Palace, Watford, and Blackburn). With two games to go, it was vital that the Blues did not do anything stupid especially as Palace had a game in hand. It was important that the next game - a home match with mid-table Bournemouth – ended with victory to more or less guarantee promotion.

In party spirits fans prepared for celebration and after only two minutes Paul Moulden gave City the lead. Trevor Morley signed from Northampton in January 1988 made it 2-0, then Moulden hit another to give the Blues an impressive 3-0 lead at half time. Prior to the match and during the interval a band marched across the Maine Road turf as Peter Swales tried to make this a day of celebration, while fans started to talk about the Charlton promotion match of four years earlier. Could the scoreline reach five?

As a beach ball bounced around the stadium - it started in the Kippax and made its way via the North Stand to the Main Stand - play resumed. The atmosphere was one of total celebration with many of the players feeling that their job had been done. As the team relaxed, Bournemouth fought back. A needless corner was given away and then, suddenly, Bournemouth scored. Everybody assumed this was a consolation goal.

A mad scramble failed to clear a loose ball, then Bournemouth scored again. At 3-2 with future Blue Ian Bishop helping the away side attack, fans became exceptionally nervous.

After more than six nervous minutes of injury time (even Alex Ferguson would not have expected that), Andy Hinchcliffe brought down Luther Blissett in the area. The Bournemouth man slotted home the resultant penalty and the game ended 3-3. The 55 away supporters in the 9,000 capacity Platt Lane Stand celebrated while the rest of the officially quoted 30,564 crowd were devastated.

Paul Moulden, the star man in the first half, was not happy with the way he was being treated by the manager during this period. He was hugely popular with fans but not with the manager: "I can't tell you how much I appreciated the support of the fans. That meant everything. Mel Machin was the manager and he just didn't seem to want me. I knew this the previous season – I only got on the team photo because it looked unbalanced and the club photographer insisted I make up the numbers! - and so I asked for a transfer, but he put my request in his drawer and ignored it. I said I wanted to play for City but if I couldn't play I'd have to leave. I didn't want to go, but I felt I had no choice at that age.

"I was on the bench for the Stoke Fancy Dress day – I was angry with that – and then those final weeks of the season were a nightmare. Remember the game at Blackburn in April when I was dropped and City lost 4-0? Mel Machin received so much abuse because he'd left me out. Naturally, I was upset we lost, but I appreciated the support I received. Then the game against Bournemouth. I'd scored twice, we were winning 3-0 and I was taken off. We ended up drawing 3-3 and everyone thought we'd blown it."

By the time of the final match, City remained in second place with a goal difference of 24, but Crystal Palace were now only three points behind with a goal difference of 19 after beating Stoke 1-0 in midweek. The Blues simply had to get a point from their last match to be certain of promotion. A lesser result could still bring success, but after the Bournemouth match nothing could be left to chance, especially as a 3-0 defeat and an easily attainable 3-0 victory to Palace would give the London club the promotion spot.

The remaining match was away at 14th placed Bradford City. It was another fantastic away following with fans in every section of the ground, although the capacity of Valley Parade prevented many Blues from attending what was one of the most crucial games of the period.

Prior to the game fans were in buoyant mood, although they were far from happy when former manager John Bond arrived on the pitch with Mel Machin to record a Granada TV interview. The previous night Bond had criticised City fans for giving abuse to Machin and the team following the pathetic performance against Bournemouth, and had himself gone on to say that the Blues did not deserve automatic promotion as they simply weren't good enough. His comments on the team may have been true, but fans found it hard to accept that the same man could criticise the fans for voicing their own views at Maine Road. At Bradford the former City manager was greeted with abuse, forcing the TV interview to be abandoned.

The former manager was not greeted well by the players either. Paul Lake: "He was at the ground and we snubbed him. He'd been very negative towards us. I will always be positive about what he did for us in 1981 – that was great – but Neil McNab and Gary Megson and some of the other older guys came to us and told us we had to ignore him. We had to refuse the interviews. How could we have been interviewed just before such an important match by someone who was adamant we weren't good enough and still gone out there and given our all? No, it was much better to keep our focus on the game and not be distracted by it. Actually, it sort of galvanised us."

The game commenced with City conceding a goal after 24 minutes. Bradford pressed forward and the Blues simply panicked, although they did manage to get their act together a little before the interval.

At half time various score lines were coming through from the delayed Palace-Birmingham match with the most popular story suggesting that Palace were 4-0

Trevor Morley attacks the Bradford goal.

TRUE BLUE
David White

David White, photographed here celebrating at Bradford, was popular with fans during the late 1980s and early 1990s.

up and in rampant form. Fans feared the worst. The second half commenced with the Blues unable to find the equaliser, despite saves from Moulden and White. Yet, at times, it appeared more likely that Bradford would increase their lead, despite the pressure.

More rumours circulated that Palace had scored again causing many Blues to ponder the prospect of success in the play offs. For one fan the tension was too much and he ran onto the pitch to plead with the players for a little bit more effort. He spoke with Paul Lake for a few moments before three or four policemen led him off the pitch: "He came to me and was a little the worst for wear. He told me the Palace score but he got it wrong. Some have said that this helped us, but in my mind I knew that it didn't matter what was happening elsewhere. We had to do it ourselves. We had to score and, as we've seen so many times with City, it's not worth focusing on results elsewhere because you can get yourself into a false position. The fan coming on is a good story… but I knew we would score. It was just a question of when."

With four minutes remaining experienced goalkeeper Paul Cooper quickly threw to the unmarked Nigel Gleghorn who sent the ball to Paul Moulden. With David White racing down the wing it was inevitable that Moulden would pass to the speedy attacker. Trevor Morley remembers what happened next: "All I can remember is Whitey getting on his left foot and clipping it in. I got goal side of the defender. The ball bobbled and I got very good contact. As soon as I did I knew it was going in. I ran off and waved to the fans and as I turned round to the pitch there were none of my players near me. I suddenly got a feeling the goal wasn't allowed. I looked to the linesman and the referee for about 10 seconds. I was a bit confused why everyone

wasn't jumping up and down. Then I saw a couple of the lads on the floor. It was a horrible few seconds."

The goal did count and City were level. The final minutes provided little opportunity for either side to take the winner, and at full time the Bradford officials wisely allowed City fans onto the pitch to enjoy their celebrations. Following the Hillsborough disaster only

Celebrations at Bradford for fans (top) and Jimmy Frizzell & Mel Machin (with John Bond behind).

Half-naked Gerry Taggart, Paul Moulden and Steve Redmond lead the dressing room celebrations.

four weeks earlier the decision had been taken to keep the gates unlocked.

On the pitch fans greeted their heroes and, as with 1985, a few players lost their shirts to souvenir hunters. The Bradford supporters themselves seemed delighted with the result and many celebrated with the men from Manchester.

As supporters returned to their vehicles the news came through that Palace had won 4-1 not the 5-0 that many believed. Nevertheless, the result was irrelevant as City's point guaranteed promotion.

The Blues were back in Division One and this time, said the much criticised Chairman Swales, it's for keeps: "What happened to Manchester City in the past must never happen again, and my pledge to the loyal band of Maine Road supporters is simply that if I have anything to do with it, it certainly never will."

By the Summer of 1989 Peter Swales was well aware that future failure would certainly apply substantial pressure on him as Chairman. The supporters had proved over the course of two seasons in Division Two that failure would no longer be tolerated. Promotion in 1989 had to be the first step to real success. Even with promotion many fans were critical.

TRUE BLUE
Ian Brightwell

Of all the 1986 FA Youth Cup winners Ian Brightwell was the one with the longest City career.

1986-1989 SUMMARY

Highest League Attendance: 40,070 Chelsea, 18/03/89
Highest Cup Attendance: 44,047 Liverpool, 13/03/88 (FA Cup)
Managers: 1983 – 1986 Billy McNeill, 1986 – 1987 (continued as General Manager until summer 1988) Jimmy Frizzell & 1987 – 1989 Mel Machin

Seasonal Record:

Season	League	Posn	FA Cup	League Cup	Other	Leading Scorer	Average Attendance
1986-87	FL Div1	21	Rnd 3	Rnd 3	Full Members' Rnd 4	Varadi 9	21,922
1987-88	FL Div2	9	Rnd 6	Rnd 6	Full Members' Rnd 2	Stewart 24	19,471
1988-89	FL Div2	2	Rnd 4	Rnd 4	Full Members' Rnd 1	Moulden 13	23,500

In 1990 Crosland Ward snr managed to capture this unique image of Maine Road's floodlights being dismantled behind the North Stand.

1989-1992
Developing City

"I feel we were on the verge of real success, and that changed once Howard left. I also know that Howard has regretted leaving City. I think he realises that the opportunity at Maine Road was greater than anything else that came his way. We finished fifth two years running but I maintain that this was a continuation of Howard's work and the determination of the players. I know the fans gave Howard a great deal of abuse when he left and I guess it's because they felt so let down by his departure. With the quality of young talent at our disposal we would have found success during the early nineties under Howard."

Neil Pointon, commenting in April 2005 about Howard Kendall's departure in 1990

1989-1990 Blue Moon Is Born

Back in Division One City were determined to make an impression. For too many years the Blues had been the laughing stock of northern football and, with Mel Machin in control, they set about taking steps to ensure first of all survival and then an assault on the Championship. Mel Machin told the Blue press: "It's important we have the experience of the first year of First Division football.

But we must look ahead to winning the First Division Championship. Looking at the capabilities of individuals there's no reason why that shouldn't be. It's up to me to strengthen the squad to be able to achieve our ambition - and that is to win trophies.

"With this squad I feel we have got something to build on, something very strong. But first of all we have got to maintain First Division status. That's our prime objective, and then to go on from there."

During the close season Machin was rewarded with an improved contract and took steps to strengthen the squad. Aston Villa's defender Martin Keown interested the manager at first but that deal fell through at the end of May 1989, then Ipswich's unsettled 21-year-old striker and future Blue, Dalian Atkinson was linked with a move to Maine Road at the start of June, as was West Brom's defender Chris Whyte. It was all fairly typical to supporters who were used to hearing about star players but rarely experienced the satisfaction of signing them. Then on 14th June came the shock news that City had agreed to purchase Bournemouth's Ian Bishop for a fee of around £750,000.

Rumours circulated that young hero Paul Moulden was about to go in the opposite direction as part of the deal but Mel Machin reassured fans: "Paul Moulden has nothing to do with the Bishop signing. If he joins them, I would expect the fee to be decided by an independent tribunal."

On 20th June Moulden joined Bournemouth in a deal reportedly worth around £300,000 to the Blues. Around that time there were many stories being circulated about the possible reasons why Moulden was sold. In March 2005 the player explained: "The truth is that I'd never been one of Machin's favourite players and because I had so much support from the fans I think that was an issue. But the biggest issue came at the Player of the Year do after promotion. We were all supposed to wear a shirt and tie, and I turned up in a tee-shirt. He didn't like that at all, and I think that was the night he decided I had to go.

"From my point of view I was also aware of how little I was being paid in comparison with players at other Division Two clubs, never mind sides in the top division. I ended the 1988-89 season as top goalscorer and my pay was £250 a week, and half-heartedly I was offered an increase of £25 to stay. This was a fraction of what other sides were paying their players. It felt as if I wasn't valued and I knew I wasn't wanted. Having said that, it was definitely the Club who made the final decision.

"I loved being with City. I was surrounded by the lads I'd grown up with, and the fans were very, very supportive. I was pleased with most of my performances, and I was always acutely aware that if I didn't give my best I was letting down my colleagues and the lads on the Kippax. I loved playing in front of the Kippax. The support was always great and for me the two best feelings were scoring a goal, and hearing the Kippax. Football's changed, but back then the fact I wasn't being paid much in comparison with the guys I'd played with at young England wasn't an issue – playing for City was everything for me. An opportunity to move had come fairly early on in my career, and the money was better, but I chose to stay at City because I loved the place, loved the fans, and of course appreciated the

efforts of Book, Pardoe, Barnes and also the physio Roy Bailey. By the summer of 1989 I had to move because I knew I wasn't wanted, but that didn't change my feelings for City, the people, and the fans."

It was a sad end to a popular player's City career and upset many supporters. It also caused Ian Bishop a few problems to start with as some fans felt Moulden had been sacrificed to buy Bishop. Nevertheless Bishop was welcomed by the majority to Maine Road and quickly proved a popular man. On arrival he told the press he was delighted with his move north: "I wanted to play in the First Division. Harry Redknapp asked me to stay another year at Bournemouth and he was willing to turn down City's offer for me. But I just felt I wanted to play in the First Division. There was a lot of talk about Arsenal, Liverpool and Manchester United being interested in me, and I heard Chelsea were really keen. Once I realised City were eager though, I made up my mind. They were the only ones to offer the money Harry wanted and I thought there was no point in waiting around and possibly losing the chance of joining City."

The Bishop transfer wasn't actually complete until 4th July, and within a week news started to circulate that the Blues were to purchase their first million pound player since Trevor Francis. Machin was after the brilliant 28 year old Clive Allen. Allen was playing with Bordeaux in France and had been keen to return to England after a year away. Machin heard of Allen's desire and persuaded Peter Swales to go back on his word that "City would never again spend £1 million on one player."

Allen signed for the fourth £1 million move of his career and fans were delighted. They now eagerly awaited the new season, especially the opening game at Anfield. That match would prove more than any other what City would need to do if they were serious about becoming a First Division force.

That opening match of 1989-90 ended in a 3-1 defeat, with City's goal scored by the improving Andy Hinchcliffe, but it was far from a nightmare start. Clive Allen impressed on his debut, as did Ian Bishop, and the Blues had gone in level at the interval. As the City fans left fortress Anfield the first airing of Blue Moon was heard. A couple of supporters had started to sing what was later adopted as the Club's anthem on their way out of the ground. Why they chose that song is a mystery, but it seemed to dovetail neatly with the atmosphere that day. Gradually it was heard more often, and by the end of the season was an important factor behind City's campaign of consolidation.

Another defeat followed the Anfield match when Southampton, led by Jimmy Case, stole a 2-1 Maine Road victory. A 1-1 draw with a Tottenham side that now included Gary Lineker brought the first point of the season and then, on 9th September, Clive Allen netted against his old club, QPR, to give City their first victory

The players take to the pitch for the September 1989 Manchester derby. Notice the narrow segregation (right) in the Kippax.

in the top division since 4th May 1987. A 1-0 defeat at Wimbledon followed, leaving Machin's Blues joint bottom of the division with high-spending Tottenham and Sheffield Wednesday.

A week later the Blues were scheduled to face multi-million pound Manchester United in the Maine Road derby match. Everybody - including even the most biased Blue - expected United to murder Machin's men and it was with a degree of fear and trepidation that fans prepared for the 111th League derby.

While City had struggled to afford players like Allen (who wouldn't be playing against United in any case) and Bishop, Alex Ferguson had brought in Neil Webb (£1.5m), Mike Phelan (£750,000), Gary Pallister (£2.3m), Paul Ince (£1.7m), Mark Hughes (returned for a fee of £1.8m), Mal Donaghy (£650,000), Brian McClair (£850,000) and Danny Wallace (£1.2 million) amongst others. They were football's biggest spenders and seemed able to buy anyone at any price.

They were also the team which appeared most often on television and in the newspapers and had already made headlines at the start of 1989 as a result of a take-over bid by Michael Knighton. It was a story splashed across the tabloids, and Knighton was encouraged to put on a tracksuit prior to their opening fixture against Arsenal, run towards the Stretford End, and score a goal. It all seems a little crazy now, but at the time United gave the impression they wanted to court publicity, any publicity. It is significant that United's inability to win the League – their last success came in 1967 the year before City's – had caused fans to look upon Knighton as

a saviour. There were parallels with Thaksin Shinawatra's arrival at City almost two decades later.

At Maine Road on derby day Knighton, whose take-over eventually floundered, actually stood in the directors' box signing autographs for City's supporters!

The game commenced with United looking fairly bright. In 2004 Andy Hinchcliffe remembered: "All of those involved with City from childhood fully understood the derby. We were City through and through and had spent a good proportion of our life preparing for that day. Nobody needed to tell us how important the game was and I was as determined as ever to play well, however we were also very nervous. The opening ten minutes were difficult."

During those opening minutes a large group of United supporters, who had somehow obtained tickets for the North Stand, tried to cause trouble. The referee took the players off while police and stewards tried to end the violence. Much to the disgust of City's law-abiding supporters in both the North and Main Stands close to the trouble, the United fans were taken from the City section and allowed to find seats in the corner of the old Platt Lane stand, close to Maine Road's Family Section. The trouble-makers should have been removed from the stadium but the official line was they may have caused even more trouble had they been evicted so early in the game.

With the atmosphere tense but peaceful, play resumed. Hinchcliffe believes the short break benefitted the Blues: "It definitely helped us because when we returned we had the upper hand. We then started to tear into them and, I think all fans will agree, we absolutely bombarded them at times."

The bombardment started immediately. David White recognised Mike Duxbury seemed a little ill at ease in United's defence and turned the Red inside out, before spearing in a low centre which the uncomfortable Pallister missed. David Oldfield, following up, managed to crack the ball into the United net for the opening goal after only 11 minutes. City fans could hardly believe it. There was more to follow.

Less than a minute after the first goal Viv Anderson was caught out of position as Paul Lake and Trevor Morley tore a great hole in the Reds' defence. Jim Leighton made a save but it still allowed Morley to fire home the rebound. 2-0!

United attempted to rally but found it impossible to deal with Bishop, Lake and White who by this stage were simply outstanding. Every time United attempted to attack City took the ball off them with ease. Then the Blues made it 3-0 after 36 minutes via Ian Bishop: "Those first two goals set it all up and we didn't relax. We kept on at them because we knew that two early goals in a derby is often not enough. We had to get a third. I remember going for it. At one point I passed Paul Ince and it felt as if he'd given up on me. It looked as if he'd lost there and then. Steve Redmond sent a long ball to David Oldfield, and I saw my chance. I charged in to meet Oldfield's cross. I threw myself at the ball and didn't see it go in. The noise told me we'd scored. That noise! I improvised a celebration."

The score remained 3-0 at half time and the United players trooped off shell-shocked, especially Jim Leighton. Another unhappy man was Mark Hughes who found it hard to accept his side were losing at Maine Road. Throughout the interval City fans simply stood and smiled, rubbing their eyes occasionally. Was it really true that poverty-stricken City were beating the most expensive English squad ever assembled 3-0?

At the start of the second half United came out determined to fight back. Hughes, always looking for the spectacular goal, managed a magnificent bicycle kick to fire the ball past Paul Cooper's left shoulder to make it 3-1. Normally City would panic and allow the Reds back into the match but this day they refused to give United anything and once again seized control of the game.

In the 58th minute City attacked United's right flank where Anderson fatally hesitated. Lake raced through and set the ball up for Oldfield to score easily from close range in front of the United fans in Platt Lane. Chants of "easy, easy" rang out throughout the rest of the match, and then the Blues rubbed it in with another magnificent goal four minutes later. In a sweeping move from the half-way line Bishop found White and, with Duxbury out of position, the City winger swung over a pin-point centre which was met by the on-rushing Andy Hinchcliffe. His bullet header shot past the thoroughly miserable Leighton and the rout was complete. Hinchcliffe: "I'm thankful for TV replays because I can't remember too much about the specifics of the match. Even my goal takes some believing. I don't know why I set off when I did and when I see it I realise how great the build up by the entire team was. For me I suppose it was instinct because I still couldn't tell you why and how it happened. I don't remember heading the ball, but I do remember the feeling when it went in. It was an exhilarating experience."

The player celebrated by holding up five fingers to the United supporters: "I know that has become a defining moment to some supporters. I didn't plan it of course, but I'm glad I did it and I think it helped my relationship with supporters. I'd always been a Blue and that was my way of showing how much I cared. 5-1 is a great scoreline because the '1' proves United tried to get back into it – it wasn't as if we were playing a side incapable of attack - while the '5' shows the overall power of our own side."

United fans had already begun to leave the stadium - some had left as early as the interval. After the goal it was as if a fire alarm had gone off as thousands stood up and walked out en masse. Some even chanted "Fergie Out" as they left. Prior to the match many United fans had boasted this would be their biggest derby win of all time. Instead, it was City's biggest Maine Road derby victory, and best derby win since 1926 when the Blues crushed United 6-1 at Old Trafford. It was also Mel Machin's finest moment as manager and one which no Blue will ever forget.

Goalscorer Andy Hinchcliffe and Paul Lake celebrate City's fifth at the Platt Lane end.

For local broadcaster James H Reeve it was a great moment. He spoke for all Blues when he said on radio after the match: "If the grim reaper came to claim me tonight I wouldn't give a monkeys."

Afterwards Alex Ferguson commented United had missed Bryan Robson and the influential captain would have had a major effect on the result of the game, but City were without their number one 'keeper Andy Dibble, £1m signing Clive Allen, and determined battler Neil McNab.

A week later 'Machin's Marvels', as they were now dubbed, defeated Luton 3-1 at Maine Road with Paul Cooper saving the 56th penalty of his long career. Throughout the game the fans chanted about the 5-1 massacre, while thousands of T-shirts celebrating the event were sold outside the stadium. Sue Mott of the *Sunday Times* soaked up the atmosphere and predicted a bright future for City's young side: "There is evidence beyond wilful optimism that some fine development is going on at the Club. Although the market in blow-up bananas and other items of rubberabilia has deflated, the noisy occupants of the Kippax Stand denoted their joyous solidarity by donning the loud-mouthed tee-shirts. Could be an expensive new trend, this, not to mention a severe run on the polyester trade.

"But while lamenting the potential strain on the cotton boll, those of the green persuasion must be consoled that City's current spurt of form owes nothing at all to crass consumerism. The whole team has been assembled for £1.9 million and much of their talent is home-grown."

The financial state of the Blues meant they could no longer compete financially and many fans pondered what the Club could have achieved had they been as financially secure as they had traditionally been. The derby result was significant but most fans knew that City under Peter Swales stood little chance of matching United's spending power at this stage – a situation so at odds with the Club's pre-Swales history – and therefore success would be difficult to manage.

The trip to Arsenal on 14th October was a sharp reminder. A deeply depressing 4-0 defeat brought back all the old doubts and left Machin and the fans looking for an excuse. They found one - City's shirts. For some reason City had opted to wear a new strip of yellow for the Highbury match, and it was obvious to all that Umbro had hastily made the shirts - even the 'Brother' lettering was peeling off.

The yellow shirts were blamed for the drubbing and disappeared within days of the match. Even so some supporters had already made enquiries at the souvenir shop to purchase replicas!

Eight days after the Arsenal debacle, Aston Villa defeated City 2-0 at Maine Road in a televised match. It was another depressing game and one which saw Trevor Morley dismissed, along with Villa's Stuart Gray, despite being the innocent party. The influential Neil McNab, whose contract would be up in the summer, had not been included in the side at all, while two strikers Clive Allen and Justin Fashanu were named as substitutes. It was all a little perplexing for City's supporters who were trying hard to accept Machin's team selections but found many too confusing to make sense.

Fashanu had been given a chance to resurrect his career by Machin, but that never really proved successful either. On 28th October a superb equaliser from Clive Allen a minute from time gave City a point at fourth placed Chelsea, then the Maine Road visit of Crystal Palace brought the first League victory since Luton in September. Palace were still smarting from a 9-0 hammering at Anfield plus a 5-0 League Cup exit against Forest and, with the Blues making all the early play, it was inevitable City should race into the lead.

David White netted first, in the pouring rain, then Trevor Morley made it 2-0 before the interval. Clive Allen scored the third and final goal in the second half, although the Blues had another effort ruled out. Unlike the previous years, City finished this Palace game without losing their 'keeper, although a confrontation between Mark Bright and Andy Dibble might have turned nasty!

The Blues were now in 14th place and were clearly primed for victory in their next match - a rather easy looking trip to 17th placed Derby County. It proved a major embarrassment as City succumbed to their biggest defeat in 27 years – 6-0. After missing a couple of easy chances the Blues were already two goals down by half-time. In the second half they looked even more nervous and the introduction of two substitutes - Fashanu and Beckford - did not improve City's jitters.

A 3-0 home defeat by Forest followed although the match was more notable for the fact Colin Hendry made his City debut, then four days later Coventry City knocked the Blues out of the League Cup with a 1-0 Maine Road victory in the fourth round. Earlier in that competition the Blues had defeated Brentford 4-1, after a 2-1 reverse at Griffin Park, and Machin's old side Norwich 3-1 at Maine Road.

On 25th November, during the train journey to Charlton Athletic, City fans were told by a club official that Machin was just one game from the sack. It says much about the way the Club was run at times that officials seemed to delight in leaking information throughout the eighties and nineties.

Understandably, neither Machin nor the players were at their best and Charlton took the lead in the sixth minute. Clive Allen netted an equaliser, thanks to a flick by new boy Hendry, a few minutes later. The victory Machin needed did not follow and the match ended 1-1.

Machin paid the price but few understood exactly

why. It was true his team selections frequently looked bizarre with often an unnecessarily defensive style, or occasionally too many forwards sitting on the bench while the team struggled to find the net, but given time he would surely have solved these elementary problems. His purchases had, in the main, been good ones. Who could argue that Clive Allen, Colin Hendry, Ian Bishop, and even Andy Dibble didn't contribute much. Each of these players seemed value for money and would, given time, have helped the Blues achieve some form of success.

Tellingly, Peter Swales claimed two reasons why he had been dismissed. The first was pressure from the fans - total rubbish! The second was that Machin had no 'repartee' with the fans - he meant rapport but at this stage in Swales' career any excuse seemed possible. Visions of Machin and Frizzell being forced to do a song and dance routine to preserve their positions appeared in the press.

Machin had been asked to resign at first but, when he refused, Swales was forced to sack him. At the time Machin was shocked: "I leave Maine Road with my conscience clear. The Club are in a far healthier position than when I arrived, both financially as well as from a playing point of view.... What do they want?"

The fanzine *Blueprint* demanded to know the answer as it clearly expressed its view that Swales, not the fans, had lost faith in Machin: "Peter Swales and his directorate are preparing to wash the blood from their hands in the tide of support which called for the removal of the manager towards the end of last season. Official communiqués from Maine Road will confirm that Mr. Machin has been sacrificed because of his enduring unpopularity with sections of the crowd. If the opinions of supporters counted for anything in the executive decision making process, Peter Swales would not be at Manchester City and in a position to seek scapegoats. There certainly were critics of Machin in the crowd and they made themselves heard in fanzines and on the terraces but this move has come from the massed ranks of nervous directors (not necessarily Swales) anxious to avoid placing their investment in jeopardy."

The fanzine continued to highlight Machin's many achievements at Maine Road: "Mel Machin must be a very disappointed and bitter man: Under his guidance City have been promoted; he has received at least one Bell's Manager of the Month award; he convinced the Board to part with £1 million for one player; and attendances have steadily increased. If only Alex Ferguson could achieve half as much (with infinite resources). As a manager he has done all that was asked of him and will be recorded in the annals of Manchester City history as the manager at the time of the 10-1 and the 5-1 Maine Road Massacre. He brought financial stability to the Club with the sale of Paul Stewart for

an incredibly over-inflated sum of money. He recruited Ian Bishop, Clive Allen and Andy Dibble to the fold and stood by his conviction that Trevor Morley would prove to be a fine player (ironically, Morley's absence in recent weeks is said to be a major factor in the collapse of form). Compared to other League managers he has led the life of a monk and conspicuously failed to bring scandal or ridicule to the club."

The comparison with Alex Ferguson was fair and demonstrated the difference between the clubs. When the 5-1 occurred United fans and the media had expected Ferguson to be sacked, but it seems that instability in the Boardroom during Knighton's proposed takeover was a significant reason why the dismissal never occurred and Ferguson was given time to get it right.

The article ended with concern over City's future: "Perhaps Peter Swales would like to reflect that he cannot appoint another managerial team which does not bring the successes so often promised and so seldom delivered. At the time of writing (27/11/89) no successor has been chosen, rumours are rife and expectations tending to be pessimistic... Don Howe and Dave Bassett have been mentioned in despatches. We could live to regret the passing of that quiet unassuming man from East Anglia, this period could be a very unhappy watershed in the history of Manchester City."

The views of the *Blueprint* writers were consistent with the majority of supporters and the other fanzines. Both *Electric Blue* and *King Of The Kippax* found it hard to accept that the fans could be held responsible. *Electric Blue*: "The worst thing about it though was that Swales blamed us, the fans for getting Mel Machin sacked, which was right out of order. When did Swales ever listen to us? If he did he would have walked out years ago. 'Swales Out!' With a bit of luck he might do that next time, get your banners out!"

Immediately after the Charlton match, rumours circulated Howard Kendall was to be offered the job. Interestingly, he had been in Manchester the night before to present a City shirt to a young girl on Granada's 'Kick Off' programme. The girl expressed concern about the Blues' loss of form and Kendall stated he believed the situation would quickly improve. Whether it was an innocent comment or not hardly mattered as fans began to guess Kendall was lined up as the new manager. Strangely, City denied it and on the following Friday, 1st December, again on 'Kick Off' Peter Swales announced he wanted Oldham supremo Joe Royle to take the Blues forward.

Rather foolishly, Swales released the news only an hour or so before Oldham's important Second Division clash with Blackburn Rovers. The Oldham supporters quickly made their feelings known to Royle and the former City player decided to remain at Boundary Park.

In March 2010 Royle explained what happened and how close he was to taking the job: "There'd be no point denying it now. There had been a conversation with Peter Swales and I had to give it serious consideration. Oldham were in a special position at that time, and I asked Peter for time to think long and hard about it. The talks had gone very well but crucially I hadn't said yes or no. Then I hear the story that I'm leaving and we're about to play an important game at Boundary Park. Peter Swales jumped the gun. The fans put their 'Don't Go Joe' message on the scoreboard and it was a strange atmosphere really.

"The Oldham directors knew the score because there are few surprises in football. They knew Peter Swales had talked with me. I would have loved to have gone to City at that point. Absolutely loved to, but it was the biggest season in Oldham's history at that point. We still hadn't been promoted though and I just thought that I couldn't be the man to duck out of Oldham's biggest ever season. How could I have walked away with the job half done?

"My rejection of City had nothing to do with City. I love City to bits and would have loved to have managed the Club at that point, but I couldn't leave Oldham at that point. I got on well with Peter Swales, but the timing was wrong. I never wanted to let him down, but it wasn't about me or him, it was about Oldham.

"At half time against Blackburn I looked at the players. We'd been awful in the first half and I said to the players 'Hey, this isn't about me. It's about us winning this game. I have to tell you I honestly don't know what's happening. The likelihood is that I'll be staying but I'm not going to make promises. This game is about us not me'. Anyway, we went out and battered Blackburn in the second half."

In 1996, at a time when it looked like Royle had missed the opportunity of ever managing City, he talked of how he would have come later had he been asked: "There were other times later on when the approach would have been welcome, but it never came. That was the end of it. I know that Peter Swales and one or two other directors have always felt it would have been so right at the time for me to have gone there, but it didn't happen. I know Willie was very disappointed that I didn't take it because it was his club. He had great affection for City, like me with Everton. It was his first club."

Royle was also a great friend of Mel Machin and was disgusted at the way he was dismissed: "It annoyed me the way they treated him because we all knew... and they [the directors] certainly knew they weren't too happy with him at the start of the season. There were plenty of rumours. Why did they wait? Bad timing. Exceptionally bad timing!"

After Royle turned the Blues down, City had the small task of facing Liverpool at Maine Road. An official attendance of 31,641 was quoted although *King Of The*

Kippax calculated this meant there were only 7,622 in the busy Kippax Stand which could officially hold around three times that amount at this time. The figure seemed exceptionally low and raised further questions about the direction of the Club.

The Merseysiders defeated City 4-1 although the Blues, guided by caretaker Tony Book, did actually play better than expected. The Liverpool supporters chanted "Swales Out", which was later explained as being a genuine demonstration of support for their Manchester rivals. A Liverpool fanzine believed Swales had "turned a great club into a joke!" The sentiment was appreciated by the fans, but not by the Chairman who was now taking steps to appoint a new manager.

Prior to the Royle fiasco, Swales had considered another former Everton player, Howard Kendall. Kendall, the former Everton and Bilbao manager had planned to take life easy for a while after returning to England from Spain, but with rumours about Alex Ferguson's job at Old Trafford it seemed likely he would return to management rather more quickly than anticipated.

Rumours circulated that he would be the Old Trafford boss by the end of 1989, but he told reporters he had no interest in discussing Ferguson's future. Then events at Maine Road kindled a desire to rebuild his managerial career: "Twenty-four hours after City had sacked Mel Machin I received a 'phone call from a third party asking me if I would be interested in taking over at Maine Road. I had to admit that I was interested because City is a very big club."

Kendall soon met Swales and they discussed terms with the former Everton man insisting on a get-out clause: "As I had done in the past, I simply wanted to protect myself by attempting to cover every eventuality. The clause which I wanted written in to any contract would guarantee my release if another club was to agree to meet a set figure of compensation and would guarantee me a pre-arranged sum in compensation if I was to be dismissed. Obviously, Peter Swales was concerned about the possibility of my taking the City job and then walking out, a few months later, to manage England. He said he felt his club should be entitled to receive compensation if that was to happen. I disagreed and pointed out that my previous employers had been more than happy to insert the disputed clause in my contract. I don't think I was being deceptive or using underhand methods in any way at all. I certainly wasn't looking to use Manchester City as a stepping stone en route to an even more prestigious job."

When Kendall left Swales' home the two men had failed to reach agreement. Swales turned his attention to Royle and Kendall believed his chance had gone. According to Kendall, Royle discovered he had not been first choice and 'phoned Kendall to discover the truth. Kendall: "I suppose I could have paved the way for his appointment by being economical with the truth but I had known Joe for such a long time that I felt it only fair to level with him. Once I confirmed that I had indeed held talks with City, Joe said he was pulling out. He is a very proud man and the idea of only being second-choice did not appeal to him one little bit."

A short while later Kendall was at Manchester airport ready to return to Spain to sort out a few domestic arrangements when a City representative informed him Swales had now agreed to the contractual clauses. Kendall: "I couldn't believe my good fortune, for less than a month after returning home I had been placed in charge of one of the biggest and best-supported clubs in Britain."

On 9th December Kendall flew directly to Southampton from Spain to watch City take on Saints. The Blues, managed by Tony Book and Ken Barnes, were leading 1-0 after 75 minutes. Then Kendall winced as a quickly taken free-kick led to an equaliser from Wallace, before Horne scored a wonder goal five minutes later. The first appearance of Ashley Ward as substitute for David Oldfield was encouraging, but the 2-1 defeat left the Blues struggling.

With typical City irony, Kendall's first game in charge had to be the away trip at Goodison Park. The Blues were bottom of the table on 15 points while Everton were ninth, and the encounter was to be screened live on television. Already Kendall had taken steps to change the City line-up. He'd managed to bring QPR's Peter Reid north on a free transfer to play a vital role in his new managerial team and to instil a bit of confidence on the pitch: "I still thought he had the stamina to perform at the top level and I knew he would be invaluable in terms of motivating and encouraging those players of lesser experience within the dressing room."

With Reid he assessed the squad and believed it too weak to mount a serious attempt at moving off the bottom. He approached Swales for money to enter the transfer market: "Because I was thinking long term, because I was expecting to spend a considerable length of time at the club, because I was determined to transform Manchester City into a team capable of winning the League Championship, I held out my hand and asked for the cash. I knew Alan Harper was having a bad time at Sheffield Wednesday, so I contacted Ron Atkinson and agreed a £150,000 deal. I remember telling my coaching staff at City that if the club was to develop along the same lines as we had at Everton, I wouldn't be happy until Alan was unable to guarantee himself a regular, first team place. I wanted to build a side which was so good Alan would once again have to resort to knocking on my office door to complain about lack of opportunity."

Both Harper and Reid made their debuts in the Everton match. Other former Evertonians in the team included Gary Megson and Ian Bishop, although Bishop had not had a good time at Goodison. The game ended goalless and, though it was not a pretty performance, City were satisfied with a point.

By the time of the next match on Boxing Day, rumours were circulating that Bishop was on his way out. 'Bish' was already a cult figure at Maine Road and seemed to offer so much, yet Kendall was keen to use him as bait to tempt other clubs to part with the players he preferred. Another who looked doomed was promotion hero Trevor Morley.

As both men came out for the Boxing Day clash with Norwich the supporters chanted their names and gave clear notice to the new manager that some players were considered more important than others. A few banners lined the front of the Kippax. One simply stated: "Bish and Trevor don't go."

When Morley was substituted he was given a tremendous ovation, as was Bishop, but it was no use. Both players were soon to leave. The game with fourth placed Norwich ended in a 1-0 victory to lift them off the bottom. Two days later Mark Ward, another former Evertonian, arrived at Maine Road in a deal which sent both Bishop and Morley to West Ham in exchange. Kendall told City's fans the deal was good business for the Club but few actually believed him. Kendall: "When the news of the transfer was made public there was absolute uproar. It wasn't so much that I had bought a third player with Everton connections, nor was it the fact I had sold Morley; it was my decision to let Bishop leave which so angered the general public. When I decided to sell Bishop, I was fully aware the papers would point out that it was the second time I had shown him the door because in 1984, when he was at Everton, I had sold him to Carlisle United. He had nothing more than raw talent and potential in those days and I felt it was best he moved on to gain valuable experience."

Ian Bishop knew his time at City would end once the new manager had been appointed. In September 2009 he explained his feelings at the time: "When I heard the news that Howard had been appointed manager I went to the lads and said 'It's been nice knowing you'. The lads told me not to be daft and said that the fans won't let them sell you. But I knew that Howard had to do what Howard had to do. He later told me that he didn't understand how popular I'd become in such a short time. I think if he'd realised earlier I wouldn't have been sold, but he had a plan that he had to follow and that was it. I understand that, but on the day of my final match it was so emotional. I didn't want to leave the pitch and I was absolutely delighted with the way the fans treated me."

Kendall firmly believed the arrival of Mark Ward and departure of Bishop was vital. He also felt it important to use Clive Allen sparingly, something else which angered the supporters. Allen was the first truly great signing since Trevor Francis and Blues' fans wanted to see him play, yet the manager persisted in naming him only as a substitute. How could a player worth a million only a few months earlier find it so hard to hold down a regular place? These were confusing times for City aficionados.

In January, after a 2-0 victory over Millwall and defeat at Sheffield Wednesday on New Year's Day, Kendall made another shock move when he brought Wayne Clarke from Leicester in exchange for David Oldfield and an amount of cash. Obviously, the move was hardly greeted with delight, especially as Clarke was yet another former Evertonian, but the manager was convinced he had a good deal. He felt particularly unhappy with the furore created: "Those supporters who were still angry about the sale of Ian Bishop did not welcome the arrival of a fourth former Everton player. They seemed to think I was pursuing a policy of jobs for the boys. The fans began to chant 'Everton reserves' during our matches and the suggestion was I was seeking permission to change the colour of City's strip from light blue to royal blue."

Later that month another ex-Evertonian Mick Heaton arrived as Kendall's assistant, and then in February Adrian Heath came from Aston Villa. Kendall: "Adrian was still full of enthusiasm and the passing of the years had not in any way eroded his skill. So I bought him. I must point out that during this period of reconstruction, not once did my Chairman question the wisdom of my transfer deals. He gave me his full support at all times and was always 100 per cent behind me. He deserves great credit for that.

"Like Clarke before him, Adrian endured a baptism of fire. I named him as a substitute for the home game against Charlton Athletic on 24th February and when I sent him on he was jeered all the way from the bench to the pitch. The problem was that to make way for Adrian, I had pulled off Steve Redmond for the first time in his entire career. The whole ground erupted as the supporters chanted, 'What the **** is going on?' The whole thing was getting out of hand."

Earlier in February, Kendall's City arrived at Old Trafford for the return derby match. So much had changed since September the game was always going to be a difficult one to call, but as the Blues were now supposedly a better side it is true to say most fans eagerly awaited this particular match. Disappointingly, United only gave City 600 seats and 4,500 terrace tickets, although even that was considerably more than in the years that followed. The eventual attendance was only 40,274 in a stadium holding a minimum of 48,000, as many disenchanted United fans stayed away.

Although there were noticeable gaps in the United sections, the paddock in front of the Main Stand appeared full of City supporters. They were later joined by Blues evacuated from the Stretford End and estimates

from impartial observers suggested there were around 12,000 City fans in the 40,000 crowd.

The match was the 100th meeting in the First Division and commenced with City tearing into the Reds as they had in September. The Blues were actually two points better off than United in the League and the difference in position prompted City fans to chant "Fergie in" to annoy the home contingent.

Squandering some early chances, City looked the more composed overall but when Clarke missed a sitter some fans still muttered about Everton rejects. It wasn't just the Evertonians who should have given City the lead; Ian Brightwell was also guilty of a shocking miss when, with Leighton off his line, the youngster feebly lobbed the ball wide.

Against the run of play it was actually United who took the lead when Clayton Blackmore was gifted a free header. Fortunately, within five minutes Mark Ward found Brightwell who, from fully 25 yards out, blasted a stunning shot past Leighton for the equaliser. Afterwards the delighted player explained exactly how he'd scored by succinctly telling the media: "I just wellied it!" In May 2010 he remembered how the expression came about: "We totally outplayed them, but Clayton Blackmore scored even though we'd had most of the chances. I had a chance in the first half, but that's a different story. Once they went a goal ahead you'd normally think it's going to be difficult, but we still had a lot of chances and I felt we'd still do it. I remember that the ball was out on the right and Mark Ward sort of half-crossed it. It came to me and I'll never forget this - I heard Steve Redmond on the half way line shout: "Bob…" I'd best not say his exact words, but let's just say he wanted me to have a go in his strong scouse accent! It was on my left foot, which isn't my strongest, but I did what Reddo said. It went in the top corner!

"I ran off and jumped about twenty feet in the air – or at least that's how it looks on the photos. I remember the noise and it was phenomenal.

"When we came to do the post-match TV interview I was asked the usual stuff and then was asked about the goal. So I told him what I just told you, being careful not to say what Reddo actually shouted! Just as I was doing it, someone walked past and we had to do the interview again. But then the same happened again. So we had to do it a third time. By this point I thought I had to say it in a different way – inexperience I guess. I didn't need to, but I ended up saying: 'the ball came out to me and I just wellied it!' It's true I did, but now it's the phrase that people remember. It summed it up nicely, but it wasn't what I'd meant to say."

The match should have brought a City victory, but everyone seemed satisfied with a point.

As the season progressed Kendall's City scraped a few draws (six 1-1 results came in February and March), and achieved a few fine wins, especially during April when five of the seven matches ended in victory. He seemed to be getting it right, in terms of results at least, and was actually starting to win the fans over after so many shock transfers.

In March he paid Arsenal £800,000 for Niall Quinn, and from the moment the lanky Irishman arrived only one game ended in defeat. Quinn: "Howard Kendall came in for me just before the transfer deadline and I jumped at the chance. It was a World Cup year and I needed to prove what I could do. It was a great chance and I remember rushing up to Manchester as soon as I could. I didn't hang about. I wanted that opportunity and couldn't wait to get started. I made my debut against Chelsea and I scored, so it was a great start. The fans took to me immediately and I loved my relationship with them."

The last day of the season was away to FA Cup finalists Crystal Palace. Palace were due to face United at Wembley the following week and, naturally, City fans wished them well. It also created a real carnival atmosphere as thousands of Mancunians travelled to London dressed as 'Blues Brothers'.

The League game ended 2-2 to leave City in 14th place on 48 points. With the season complete, fans now felt able to look forward to a bright spell under Kendall, while the manager felt the Palace match brought him closer to the supporters: "We had guaranteed our First Division future and the thousands of supporters who travelled down to London were in jubilant mood. There was a real carnival atmosphere and, for once, they actually looked as if they were enjoying what they were seeing."

1990-1991 End Of The Affair

During the close season Kendall negotiated new five year contracts for 1986 Youth Cup winners David White and Paul Lake. He also shocked supporters again by transferring another coveted member of that team, Andy Hinchcliffe, to Everton in exchange for Neil Pointon and £600,000. Hinchcliffe admitted in 2004: "I didn't want to leave but if the manager doesn't see a future for you it's difficult to stay. Everton was a good club to go to."

With the arrival of yet another Evertonian came more criticism but there were also a few jokes. At one stage a rumour circulated that David Bowie's Maine Road concert had been called off. The reason? Kendall had discovered Bowie had never played for Everton! New arrival Neil Pointon felt it was the media rather than the fans that made an issue out of the Everton connections. In 2005 he explained: "There were a couple of journalists who deliberately kept trying to stir it up. The fans were superb but the Everton reserves tag appeared in the press and non-City fans grabbed hold of it. For us

players it didn't matter. In the dressing room those of us who had played at Everton obviously had a relationship, but the team spirit grew from everyone in there. White, Redmond, Lake, Brightwell, Hendry, Quinn, Coton and the others joined in with everybody else. I think it was a great mix, and in our dressing room and on the training pitch we were all Manchester City players. The past was the past, and for me the great thing was that with the youngsters White, Redmond, Brightwell, and also Michael Hughes we had a great future ahead of us. I was convinced we were going to win a major trophy with the great mix that Howard put together."

There were other significant transfers - goalkeeper Tony Coton arrived for £900,000 and midfielder Mark Brennan for £400,000 - as Kendall began to build a side he believed was good enough to qualify for Europe.

Despite the new arrivals there was still considerable sadness that a number of Blue heroes had been despatched since Machin's departure. In addition to Morley, Bishop, Oldfield and Hinchcliffe City had also lost Brian Gayle, Gary Fleming and Neil McNab. Nevertheless, after a fine 1990 World Cup, City fans eagerly awaited the opening match of 1990-91 away to Tottenham on 25th August.

This was the first opportunity for Spurs fans to greet their World Cup heroes Lineker and Gascoigne, while City also welcomed back an international star - Niall Quinn. It was also the first match following the death of former manager Joe Mercer. Poignantly City fans chanted several verses of "To see Joe Mercer's aces."

The match ended in a 3-1 defeat with Quinn netting for the Blues while new captain Paul Lake also put in a fine performance. Lake: "He put more responsibility on my shoulders. He gave me the captaincy and I was very happy with it all. I felt so confident because of how Howard was with me, and because he'd achieved so much in the game it meant more. Being captain made me more vocal, so that was good, but we had plenty of captains on the pitch so that made it easier. The day he made me captain he called me into his office and I was convinced I was about to be dropped or sold, and it went the other way. I was so relieved."

A week later Everton were at Maine Road and Kendall's 'old Toffeemen' managed a 1-0 win with Adrian Heath scoring his third League goal for the Club. It was also his only strike of the season. Pointon and Ward supplied the goals four days later as Aston Villa went down 2-1. Andy Dibble had returned for that game while Coton was suffering with a bug.

The Welsh 'keeper was quite impressive and clearly keen to erase the nightmare memory of the Forest match the previous season. At the City Ground Dibble had been preparing for a clearance punt when Gary Crosby ran up behind him and nudged the ball from Dibble's outstretched hand. The City 'keeper stood complaining while the Forest man put the ball in the net for the only goal of the game. Kendall was furious and some claim that goal ultimately led to the purchase of Coton. For Dibble it was a huge embarrassment and unfortunately one repeated several times since with the television footage of the game appearing on A Question of Sport and various sporting blooper shows.

Despite a good performance against Villa, Dibble did not retain his place and Coton was back for the following match, a 1-1 draw at Sheffield United. Someone else missing at Bramall Lane was captain Paul Lake who sustained a knee injury in a rather innocuous challenge with Villa's Tony Cascarino: "We won 2-1 but my foot got stuck in the ground and I twisted it. That was the beginning of the end playing wise." Few ever imagined he would be out for the rest of the season and would struggle against injury for years before retiring early.

A week after the Villa match, Norwich turned up at Maine Road for their customary defeat. This time it was 2-1 thanks to substitute Mark Brennan and the improving Niall Quinn.

A Mark Ward penalty at Chelsea brought a 1-1 draw and left the Club with 11 points from a possible 18. Another 1-1 followed at Wimbledon on 29th September, before Coventry were defeated 2-0. Yet another 1-1 draw arrived at Derby before the first Maine Road meeting with United since the 5-1. As with most derbies of the period City set off determined to prove they were far from the poor relations the media always portrayed them to be. As in 1989 determined City dominated much of the early play and were 2-0 up after a couple of goals from David White in the first 27 minutes. Then in the 79th minute Colin Hendry netted City's third, although Mark Hughes had already pulled one back for the struggling Reds.

Ten minutes away from certain victory, Kendall brought on Ian Brightwell for Peter Reid. Kendall: "I

Colin Hendry celebrates his goal against Burnley in the FA Cup, January 1991.

decided to pull off Peter who, typically, had run himself to a virtual standstill. In layman's terms, the man was knackered. Within a matter of minutes of Peter withdrawing from the action, United had scored twice to draw level. Inevitably, I was blamed for the loss of two points - and local pride. I felt the criticism was unduly harsh because while it was true that United's revival had coincided with my decision to substitute Peter, the goals they scored were down to basic, juvenile defensive errors."

After the 3-3 draw City were defeated 2-1 by Arsenal in the 3rd round of the League Cup. On the same night Everton were beaten by Sheffield United in the same competition prompting the Goodison board to dismiss Colin Harvey.

The media claimed Joe Royle was now hot favourite for the Everton job yet, incredibly Howard Kendall was offered the post. Nine days after the derby he became Everton manager for the second time, upsetting thousands of Mancunians. Captain Paul Lake was stunned: "I was shocked. I got a call from Howard but I thought it was Jason Beckford doing an impression of him! He called me to tell me he was going back to Everton. I said 'Why?' I couldn't get it but he said 'It's heart and head time – City's your love, Everton's mine.'"

The fury which greeted Kendall's desertion puzzled the media and the man himself, but the fact was City supporters had actually started to accept him. They also recognised that more than any other manager since John Bond, possibly before, the Blues actually possessed a leader capable of bringing home the silverware. He was certainly more likely to collect a League Championship than some of the other men appointed by Peter Swales. The departure really did hurt.

When Billy McNeill walked out on City to take up the manager's job at Aston Villa the supporters felt betrayed but they understood. Like Kendall, he had transformed the make up of the side bringing in players he knew, mainly Scots, to do a job but he had also given the Club over three years' hard work and brought promotion and a Wembley appearance.

When Kendall walked out to return to his first love – he had made comments claiming Everton was like a marriage and City was an affair - all the supporters could see were broken dreams. True relegation had been avoided, but they felt Machin may well have achieved that in any case if Swales had not pressed the panic button so early in Machin's First Division reign. The supporters then looked at Kendall's side and though they disagreed with his approach early on, they now saw hope for the future. The Blues were, they felt, destined to find success under Kendall's shrewd guidance, but once he left the dream was shattered.

More worrying for the thousands of loyal supporters was the role of Peter Swales. During the 1980s he could hardly claim to have been the best employer in the world after so many managers had either been sacked or walked out on him. Many felt the Chairman had finally got it right with Kendall but could he be trusted to get it right again? Supporters were painfully aware of the bungled attempt to bring Joe Royle to the Club less than 12 months earlier. Even if Swales were to appoint the right man, what pain would the Blues have to endure for the rest of the season as the new boss reshaped the side? Surely City could not afford to see anyone else come in and transform the line-up as Kendall had?

It was all too much to swallow for many Blues and unfortunately it was Kendall who took the flak. It was understandable, but perhaps more questions should have been asked of the entire boardroom set-up at the Club. Why had City made it so easy for Kendall to use his 'get-out' clause? Why had they failed to appoint Royle in the first place? And why had Machin been so cruelly sacked after bringing some exciting players and a few decent performances to the Club?

Some fans started to consider what had gone wrong since the 5-1 massacre when it was Alex Ferguson, not Mel Machin, who seemed destined for the boot. United kept faith with their high-spending manager and later that season reaped the first reward - the FA Cup. In the years that followed they became the most successful team of the modern era, while City struggled to find consistency.

Once Machin was dismissed, manager followed manager as the Club drifted into the shadows. In 1990, Kendall's departure saw the fans unite in their desire to change the Club. They called for Peter Reid to be appointed manager, and for once Peter Swales appeared to listen.

The reason the supporters backed Reid was simple - they were totally depressed by the chopping and changing nature of life at Maine Road and believed Reid would pursue many of the ideas developed under

Harper, Brennan, Heath and Reid followed by heroic 'goalkeeper' Niall Quinn, 20th April 1991.

Kendall. They felt he had worked closely with his old boss and would be able to maintain the rhythm. It seemed a perfect appointment from the point of view of consistency and, under Reid, City continued to progress.

In December, after victories over QPR and Tottenham, Reid brought in the Bury manager Sam Ellis as his number two. On the surface a sensible move but, over the following three years, it was to cause the new manager much heartache as Ellis's strident views seemed to cramp City's style.

At Goodison, Kendall quickly settled in to life with his old club. As with Malcolm Allison and City, the return was not a successful one yet, in 1997, following the departure of Joe Royle from the Everton manager's chair, Kendall returned yet again to Goodison for a third spell as manager. Under Reid, the Blues progressed up the table.

On 13th January Kendall faced City for the first time since taking over at Everton. Despite the result - a 2-0 Everton win - it was not a pleasant day for the former manager: "The afternoon was soured by the reaction of the City supporters when I took my place on the touchline shortly before kick-off. Some people now refer to that fixture as the 'Judas' game because that short, but hurtful, word was scrawled across numerous banners and flags at the City end of the ground. Actually, this particularly form of Kendall-baiting was initially used in November during City's first game after I had left the club, against Leeds United at Maine Road."

Reid's men made steady progress over the weeks that followed and a run of victories in April helped lift the Blues to fourth. Included in that run was the Maine Road 2-1 defeat of Derby. White and Quinn had both netted for the Blues before Tony Coton was dismissed. Niall Quinn went in goal before Dean Saunders ran up to take the resultant penalty: "I couldn't wait! Tony Coton was sent off for a foul on Dean Saunders, I think. He threw his gloves at the ref in anger and I remember being giddy about it all. I was saying I'd have a go and I rushed to put his gloves and shirt on. I faced the penalty – and I was totally confident about saving it. I managed it, but the ball went out for a corner. Now this is what I am most proud of. The corner came over. I knocked over a couple of players and then caught the ball one-handed. That means more than the penalty to me.

"I loved it. At one point when play was at the other end I started waving to our physio Roy Bailey. I clutched my leg and called for him. He came running around the touchline. He got to the goal in a hurry and asked what was wrong. I said: 'I've got dirt on my shorts'. It was funny. We won the game 2-1 after David White scored an absolutely brilliant goal. It was a wonderful time, but that game had an effect on the Player of the Year award. At the time voting forms appeared in the programme and were handed out, and it just happened

Maine Road in 1991. Within four years the Platt Lane (bottom) and Kippax (right) had been replaced.

that the Derby game was the day when this happened. My performance must have impacted the voting and I remember Jason Beckford having a bit of jokey banter with me. He kept going on about how that one game got me the award, and he was probably right."

The fine April run ended with a marvellous 5-1 win at Villa Park in a game which saw David White become the first City player since the war to score four in an away game.

A disappointing result in the Manchester derby followed (1-0 thanks to Colin Hendry diverting a Giggs' effort past debutant Martyn Margetson), before a 3-2 victory on the last day of the season relegated Sunderland.

Future Sunderland player Niall Quinn netted twice and White scored the other in a game notable for the large away support packed into City's old Platt Lane Stand. It was the last great crowd in a stand that was to be demolished during 1992. The season ended with City in a respectable fifth place on 62 points - three more than Manchester United - and the supporters were delighted even if the final League position seemed a might flattering. At the time there appeared little separating the top clubs and those struggling at the foot of the table, but City had made the most of their determined approach. It was the highest Blues' finish since 1978 and gave everyone a feeling of considerable satisfaction.

1991-1992 Curle Signs

The close season saw Peter Reid smash City's transfer record by over a million with the £2.5m arrival of Wimbledon's powerful defender Keith Curle. It seemed a great deal of money but as the Blues needed to bolster their defence, the pacy England 'B' international seemed perfect. Most were amazed the Club actually had that amount of cash to spare although Reid had been forced

to sell Mark Ward and Alan Harper to Everton for a fee reported to be around £1.3 million. Youngster Ashley Ward had also moved on, joining Leicester.

Curle made his debut in a 1-0 victory at Coventry on the opening day of the season after signing only 11 days earlier. Interestingly, Reid also believed Curle was a good motivator and had immediately appointed him captain.

With Curle strengthening the defence, three points were gained in City's next match - a 2-1 home victory over Liverpool. That game was memorable for yet another penalty by Dean Saunders. Recalling the Derby penalty the season before, fans laughed at Saunders again as the Liverpool man ran up and blasted the ball against the bar!

City now moved into second place and eagerly awaited their third game in seven days. This time the victims were Crystal Palace as the Blues achieved a 3-2 Maine Road victory to put them top of the table, thanks to a Brennan penalty five minutes from time.

A goal-less midweek draw followed at Norwich before City suffered their first defeat of the campaign away at Arsenal. A return to form followed against Nottingham Forest as Quinn and Andy Hill combined to bring a 2-1 victory. Sadly, form deteriorated in September with three successive defeats - including the grudge Maine Road match with Kendall's Everton. In the last minute of that game Michael Hughes appeared the only player courageous enough to take a penalty awarded for a foul on Hendry by Mark Ward, yet the youngster nervously sent the ball over the bar.

Results turned City's way again during October and November as the Blues enjoyed a seven game unbeaten run in the League. In fact they lost only one of their sixteen matches between the start of October and the first week of February. During that sequence the 115th Manchester League derby ended goalless although Adrian Heath performed astonishingly well considering the abuse he now received on a regular basis.

Heath had been involved in a car crash only hours before the game yet still managed a stylish display rarely seen since his arrival at Maine Road. Unfortunately, the diminutive striker received yet more barracking for his role in City's greatest chance to break the deadlock. Mike Sheron had put Heath in the clear. The former Evertonian raced forward, looking certain to score but carelessly the little striker blasted the ball over and the game ended goalless. It proved to be Heath's last season at Maine Road and, although he received large chunks of criticism during his time in Manchester, with hindsight he contributed more than most people realised. Granted his goalscoring record was exceptionally poor but the number of balls he laid on for others was really quite phenomenal.

Footage of the period 1990 to 1992 reveal the numerous goals and chances created by Heath and justify the true value of Kendall's controversial signing as Quinn explained in November 2009: "One player who I have to single out is Adrian Heath. Adrian never got the credit at City that he deserved. I got a lot of credit and support, as did Clive Allen, but it was Adrian who made a lot of my goals. Look at the film of those games. You'll see it's often Adrian who set me up."

Heath was transferred to Stoke City in March 1992.

Other players sold during the season included Colin Hendry, who returned to Second Division Blackburn in November 1991, and Clive Allen, who went to Chelsea in December and scored a beautiful goal against City on New Year's Day. Both transfers greatly disappointed fans, especially Hendry's. However, since the arrival of Keith Curle it had been clear City could not support Hendry, Curle, and Redmond. Blues fans felt Redmond should have been the man sacrificed as Hendry seemed to offer so much more. As substitute he had even featured in attack, netting against West Ham.

One player who arrived during the season was hard man Steve McMahon who had played against the Blues on 21st December at Anfield when it was already certain he would be off to Maine Road. He did little in that game, although City's travelling support made sure he knew he would be welcome in Manchester.

On Christmas Eve he moved for £900,000 and on Boxing Day played in a 2-1 defeat of Norwich. Unfortunately he received a nasty injury during the match and missed the following three League games. He

TRUE BLUE
Niall Quinn

Hugely popular Howard Kendall signing and famous for his 'Disco Pants'.

ended the season with 18 League appearances as City's midfield toughened up, albeit at the expense of mobility.

From February 1992 the Blues lost a little form and a few rumbles began to suggest life behind the scenes was not as it should be. There were reports that Sam Ellis, Reid's assistant, had made a few enemies among the players and there were even suggestions there had been a few training pitch scuffles.

Under the heading "Rumours" the fanzine *King Of The Kippax* surprised fans with this story: "Tony Coton missed a few games early this season because of a damaged hand. The rumour is he damaged it whilst hitting Sam Ellis... what is worse, it appears a few others don't like Sam either - no names though, just remember it is Olympic year."

With disharmony spreading, according to the rumours, supporters began to question whether Reid had been right to draft in Ellis. It appeared many of the problems had arrived with the blunt ex-Bury boss and City's style of play had changed for the worse but was Ellis responsible or Reid? No one seemed able to pinpoint the precise cause but as the Blues were still progressing overall in the League the matter was allowed to simmer away in the background. Had it been tackled there and then, the course of Reid's managerial reign may well have changed for the better. Instead problems mounted and Reid ultimately paid the price.

March 1992 was a miserable month with only one point out of 12 but April proved almost perfect. On the 4th, Championship hopefuls Leeds United arrived at Maine Road expecting the Blues to lie down and surrender the points, especially as United were their nearest rivals for the title. In true City style the Blues murdered Leeds 4-0. It was a result that pleased all but the realisation also dawned that City had basically handed the title to United on a plate.

The following Tuesday City had a chance to further influence events with their visit to Old Trafford, but few really expected a victory this time. After only 21 minutes play the Reds sneaked the lead. Not much else happened until the second half when Niall Quinn headed wide, then a short while later Neil Pointon deliberately sent Ryan Giggs crashing to the ground. A free-for-all followed with Steve Bruce punching Niall Quinn. The referee tried to calm the situation but only managed to send Pointon off. The player had to go, but City fans murmured a United man should have joined him.

The sending off has stayed with Pointon ever since: "I've played this one through many, many times. Prior to the match Ryan Giggs was presented with a young player of the month award and that lodged in my head somewhere. Then in the second half, he fouled me and I went down with my leg bleeding. Our physio Roy Bailey checked me and said I'd need a stitch, but I could carry on. The ref wasn't doing anything so I asked him if he was going to book Giggs. He said no, so I reacted and said a few things about Giggs being the golden boy, the starlet, and about the ref taking it easy because he's at Old Trafford etc. I then said I'd sort it out myself. I shouldn't have said it but I'd lost it a bit.

"Later I was going for the ball and spotted Giggs coming the other way. I thought this was my chance. I was still going to go for the ball, but I'd go in hard and with two feet at the ball. I knew this would knock Giggs over, but I didn't think it'd be too bad. As I committed myself I noticed Paul Ince coming from the other side, and the two of them were going to get me. All the bad tackles that have ever happened to me crossed through my mind. I'd been injured a lot in this way and I decided I couldn't let it happen. I opened my legs and decided – and I know this is totally wrong – that I'd take them both down rather than they get me. We all clattered in to each other. Giggs started to get up and McClair shouted at him to stay down, so he did. I knew I was off, but Ince and others started punching. I knew I was wrong, but there was no need to start fighting. Anyway I was sent off.

"Alex Ferguson said I'd deliberately gone out to maim Giggs, which wasn't true at all, and I received a letter off him apologising afterwards which was very nice. I knew I was wrong and the sending off was right, but it was one of those days when I just thought about everything bad that had happened to me and decided I wouldn't be the victim this time."

As the game progressed, David White's pace proved too much for United and Steve Bruce lunged at him in the area. Amazingly Bruce again stayed on the pitch while captain Keith Curle prepared for the penalty. He ran up and tucked the ball to Schmeichel's left to make the score 1-1.

A fan ran on to the pitch and jumped into the skipper's arms much to the delight of the rest of the jubilant City followers. More pressure followed with White, who had become a father that morning, and £500,000 March signing from Swindon Fitzroy Simpson both going close. At the end the Blue supporters sang "Ten men... you couldn't beat ten men", while Reds' fans insisted they would still win the title.

Less than a month later Leeds dramatically snatched the Championship, while City defeated Oldham 5-2 to end the campaign in fifth place for the second consecutive term. Although much of the season was disappointing because of the loss of several popular players and the largely uninspiring style of play, the final placing at least offered hope that the Blues might soon find real success.

In the two major cup competitions during 1991-92 City were defeated by Middlesbrough 2-1 away from home. In the League Cup they had reached the fourth round, while in the FA Cup they managed only one match.

Reid's side ended the term fairly satisfied. Quinn: "Peter Reid was a novice manager in comparison with Howard but he took the team to fifth twice so everything was positive. We needed a little bit more quality. In fact, I know how close Peter Reid was to signing Ian Wright in August 1991. Arsenal got in there but had Peter been successful – and he almost pulled it off – then Ian Wright would have been a great City hero. We would have found real success. No question."

Supporters were restless about the lack of trophy success and worried by rumours circulating from several cognisant sources within the Club – some officials loved to talk of issues behind the scenes. It seemed, amid all the promise, the Club might be in danger of taking its eye off the ball.

During 1991-92 an article appeared in a leading football magazine which quoted Peter Swales: "City were the last Manchester side to win the Championship, they will also be the next." The comment was vintage Swales. He wanted the best for the Blues and tried to whip up enthusiasm by boasting of what he believed City could achieve. Unfortunately, with United developing so rapidly many felt Swales really had to fulfil this promise.

1989-1992 SUMMARY

Highest League Attendance: 43,246 Manchester United, 23/09/89
Highest Cup Attendance: 26,825 Arsenal, 30/10/90 (League Cup)
Managers: 1987 – 1989 Mel Machin, 1989 – 1990 Howard Kendall & 1990 – Peter Reid

Seasonal Record:

Season	League	Posn	FA Cup	League Cup	Other	Leading Scorer	Average Attendance
1989-90	FL Div1	14	Rnd 3	Rnd 4	Full Members' Rnd 2	Allen 10	27,975
1990-91	FL Div1	5	Rnd 5	Rnd 3	Full Members' Rnd 4	Quinn 20	27,874
1991-92	FL Div1	5	Rnd 3	Rnd 4	Full Members' Rnd 2	White 18	27,691

Steve Worthington captured this scene on the Kippax's final day, 1994.

Premier Blues

"I'd been substituted and was sat watching a monitor. I knew the way the scores were going elsewhere and knew that we were down unless we won. Alan Ball, God bless him, was given incorrect information. I went down there and told him the truth but the announcer guy was down there and he said I was wrong, so nobody accepted it. I saw us holding the ball in the corner and couldn't stand it. I charged down the touchline shouting for them to open up play. I shouldn't have done it in some ways because it made Alan Ball look bad, but I couldn't stand to see us get it wrong."

Niall Quinn talking in 2009 about the relegation decider against Liverpool in 1996

1992-1993 A Whole New Ball Game

In August Peter Reid took steps to strengthen his side. First he signed Oldham's skilful Rick Holden in a deal which saw Neil Pointon and Steve Redmond move to Boundary Park, then paid an incredible £2.5 million for Wimbledon's Terry Phelan, although he did not make his debut until City's fourth match of the season. The Dons' supporters joked their continuing life in the top flight

was down to regular purchases by the Blues. Defenders Gayle, Curle and Phelan had all arrived at Maine Road from Wimbledon in expensive transfers; even Gayle's at £325,000 in June 1988 was considered so at the time.

The loss of Pointon and Redmond was a blow. Pointon: "Both Steve Redmond and I went and I think it's fair to say that neither of us wanted to leave. The management had decided we had to go I guess. I wasn't offered a new contract, and I was on the sidelines for the pre-season training. I didn't ask to leave, nor did I want to leave. I felt I still had a lot to offer City and I wanted to stay for a long, long time. In fact when I was captain of Walsall in 1999 when we faced City in Division Two I remember thinking that I could have still been a City player, and that I'd have loved to have been part of City throughout the nineties."

For some the money spent on Phelan seemed absurd when only a few months earlier the Blues possessed more quality defenders than they actually needed. The talented Hendry had been forced out, while Pointon had won many supporters with his combative nature.

Most were confused by the Club's overall strategy especially as everyone recognised it was in midfield and attack that the Blues were particularly weak. Niall Quinn desperately needed support up front, while a midfield that regularly relied on the 36 year old Peter Reid was hardly classed as one for the future.

Despite the worrying nature of City's transfer activity, few could argue that Terry Phelan was not a useful player. He was certainly a fast left back and had already broken into Jack Charlton's Republic of Ireland squad, winning eight caps. Likewise winger Rick Holden was expected to be a valuable addition, especially as he was the First Division player credited with the most 'assists' the previous season.

Behind the scenes long-serving physio Roy Bailey had been dismissed, while Chief Scout Ken Barnes retired. Worse was to follow as Glyn Pardoe, a very popular and successful youth coach, was also forced out. With Barnes and Pardoe gone, it seemed the Club had forgotten how City had only survived much of the mid-eighties onwards because of youth players brought to the Club by Barnes and trained by Pardoe.

Despite City's changes a new season brought much optimism, especially as this was the first after football's restructure. The Blues were now part of the newly formed FA Premier League with the old Second Division renamed the First. The new League was viewed by those outside

Comedian Norman Wisdom takes to the pitch before the Blues face Oldham in 1992-93. When he first appeared some on the Kippax thought it was Peter Reid wearing a cap!

to have been created by the wealthiest clubs, driven by a desire to make even more money whilst allowing the poorer teams to struggle. City, being a glamour club, were keen to play a major part in the formation of the League and were determined to find success. Chairman Peter Swales said at the time: ""We have entered a new and exciting chapter in the history of football and I am looking forward to being part of it with real optimism. The heated debates which surrounded the introduction of the Premier League concept have long since cooled off and now all of us at Manchester City are eagerly awaiting taking part in the unfolding story."

The Blues were also quick to embrace football's new commercial arrangements by hosting the first Monday night Premier League game shown live on satellite television. The visit of QPR was re-arranged to take place on Monday 17th August as part of the Sky TV deal and City fans were greeted by live music, fireworks, Red Devil parachutists (who were booed because of their name!), and dancing girls. It all seemed a bit excessive for a dark Manchester night but the television viewers probably enjoyed it and the Club made a bit of money, so few complained.

The one truly bright spot of the entire evening was the return of Paul Lake to the City team. Lake had been battling to recover from a cruciate ligament injury since September 1990 and it seemed, as the teams were announced, that Lake had finally won his battle. With him working in midfield alongside Steve McMahon the Blues appeared to have finally gained the right control and blend in an area where they had struggled for two seasons.

City put QPR under considerable pressure and Lake produced an intelligent pass to Niall Quinn. The lanky striker sent in a good shot, but although it was saved the ball rebounded out to David White who scored the first of his 16 that season. In the second half, QPR equalised with a rocket from Andy Sinton, while Lake was understandably substituted by Mike Sheron.

Two days later a disastrous night in Middlesbrough left City defeated 2-0 by their bogey side. It was a night of pain, especially for Paul Lake who, after only eight minutes, fell to the ground clutching his knee. City fans knew immediately it was serious, and the player was carefully helped from the pitch to begin another long battle for fitness.

On the same night Niall Quinn was sent off – he later admitted that the emotion connected with Lake's injury had affected him and caused him to react - to leave a ten man side struggling. Peter Reid severely criticised his players afterwards, yet little changed when City went down to a 1-0 defeat against big spending Blackburn the following Saturday.

The fourth game of the season saw Terry Phelan make his debut in a 3-1 defeat of Norwich. It was City's first Premier League victory and brought much relief to Reid and Ellis, but it wasn't to last. Oldham arrived at Maine Road on 29th August and took part in one of City's inconsistent specials. The Blues had led 2-0 and then 3-1 with goals from Quinn, Vonk and White, but then capitulated as Oldham scored another two and had a Steve Redmond effort disallowed. The 3-3 scoreline brought a point but left most Blues needing tranquilisers as nerves were severely tested.

A David White goal brought victory in September at Wimbledon, but only 4,714 fans witnessed a game which also proved the enduring value of Peter Reid. The City player-manager was the undisputed Man of the Match after starting his first game of the season and instilled a bit of grit into City's game. He replaced himself with Steve McMahon once his legs tired, but selected himself again for the following trip to Sheffield Wednesday.

At Wednesday City, wearing their third strip of white shirts, managed their first Hillsborough League victory since the final day of the 1969-70 season with White scoring twice and Vonk once to provide a 3-0 scoreline.

Three successive 1-0 defeats followed before the next point - 2-2 against Nottingham Forest in early October when the inconsistent Blues twice took the lead only to allow Forest back into the match. By this stage fans were becoming less and less tolerant of Peter Reid and Sam Ellis. They were unhappy with City's sterile style of play and found it difficult to accept the Blues were not playing entertaining football.

Throughout history City had excited their supporters and only resorted to the long ball when the tactic became absolutely vital to avoid relegation or embarrassing defeat. Now, it seemed, the long ball was the preferred method.

In October a *Manchester Evening News* back page story brought an admission that Peter Swales was not prepared to allow his manager to spend any more cash on players. The £2.5 million for Phelan had increased the bank deficit and, quite simply, the Blues could not afford any more. The news hardly surprised City's faithful, but it was a broad hint to Reid and Ellis that the Chairman expected results. Whether Swales had made this clear before Phelan was signed is open to debate, but surely the Chairman and his supporting directors and management team should have had appropriate plans in place?

David White celebrates with goalscorer Mike Sheron, against champions Leeds, November 1992.

A few hours later a third round League Cup tie with Tottenham ended in a 1-0 defeat. Not the kind of result Swales had in mind!

League performances did improve with satisfying victories over Kendall's Everton (3-1), reigning champions Leeds (another 4-0), and Coventry City (3-2) before defeats at Tottenham (1-0) and in the Sky TV live derby match at Old Trafford (2-1).

Another defeat followed on 12th December at Ipswich - a game in which the impressive Garry Flitcroft netted his first League goal for the Club. The Blues were bright one minute but absolutely appalling the next. Fans were increasingly disenchanted with the way the season was developing. Already there had been calls for the Chairman to resign, yet he refused to listen.

At the October 1992 AGM City shareholder Brian Williams asked Swales to do what a large percentage of supporters had wanted since the mid 80s: "You should consider your future as Chairman. Perhaps the greatest service you could give to the club would be to step aside for somebody else. You've been Chairman for 14 years without a major success. You have not been a lucky Chairman and you should give somebody else a chance."

Swales responded in the manner he usually adopted when questioned in this way: "I take your point - but I will not be taking your advice." Earlier in the year the *Electric Blue* fanzine had produced a "Swales Out" special as they tried to make supporters' feelings more widely known. The fans were frustrated with City despite, on the face of it, a decent enough League campaign.

Although results were mixed, the Blues did actually end the first Premier League season in ninth place, which for most clubs would have been regarded as a success. Unfortunately, football at Maine Road has never purely revolved around winning matches, it is also about playing with style. It was something Reid and Ellis ignored at their peril.

On the final day of the season City were humiliated

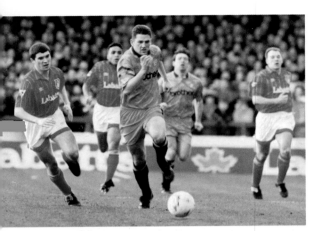

David White surges forward leaving Forest's Roy Keane behind, prior to scoring City's first goal, March 1993.

5-2 by Everton at home. Peter Swales was pelted with eggs and a 'Swales Out' demonstration took place as supporters vented their frustrations. In truth, what made the 1992-93 season so unsatisfactory was that Manchester United were crowned the first Premier League champions. It mocked all the empty boasts and promises made by Swales during the early 90s. The fans felt bitterly betrayed yet no one outside of Manchester could comprehend why Blues were so unhappy.

Two months before the end of the campaign the media had been shocked at the behaviour of City's fans when they invaded the pitch during a sixth round FA Cup tie with Spurs. They condemned the supporters without understanding the background story. To put the record straight it's vital the day's events are covered correctly. The Blues had overcome Reading, QPR, and Barnsley to reach the sixth round for the first time since 1988. Their opponents Tottenham had already knocked them out of the League Cup in October and defeated them in the Maine Road League game. City fans hoped Reid's men had learned a few lessons from these games and everybody connected with the Club believed this was City's year for the cup.

In addition there was a great deal of optimism, particularly as City were to open their new Umbro Stand for the very first time. The stand had replaced the old Platt Lane structure and a large number of fans had already purchased season tickets for the forthcoming 1993-94 season which allowed them into the stand for the remainder of 1992-93. It was not a particularly large or impressive structure, but it was still new and offered supporters the best sightlines of all the seated

sections in the stadium. There was also substantially more leg room than in the North or Main Stands.

Peter Swales was deeply proud of the construction, although supporters were later to dub it 'Swales' folly'. The biggest City crowd of the season, up to that point, of 34,050 plus live terrestrial television in Britain and abroad guaranteed the whole football world would determine exactly how good or bad Reid's side really were. The atmosphere was electric with City fans in good voice; even the chant "There's only one Alan Hansen" rang out as supporters made sure the BBC summariser was thanked for being the only member of the Match of the Day team to publicly back City.

The game kicked off with Maine Road at its noisiest and when Mike Sheron gave the Blues the lead fans started to sing about Wembley. It seemed this really would be City's year for glory; unfortunately the old inconsistencies struck again as Spurs fought back. First Nayim, totally unmarked, scored from 20 yards, then Sedgley ran unopposed on to a through ball to give Tottenham the lead.

At the interval supporters were dejected but still recognised City were in with a chance. Sadly, when Nayim made it 3-1 early in the second half it completely diminished the Blues' hopes. Five minutes from time another totally unopposed effort brought Nayim his hat-trick and left City suffering.

Spurs had another disallowed before Terry Phelan set off on one of his now familiar runs. He roared past several Tottenham players before burying the ball in the net. It was a superb goal but also sparked the moment which brought shame on the Club. Almost immediately supporters from the unfenced Umbro Stand began to run on to the pitch.

The stewards at that end seemed uncertain of how to handle the situation and some allowed the invaders to walk unapprehended onto the pitch. It wasn't long before there were around 20 then, because of the ease of it all, more started to make their way onto the grass. Some climbed over the Kippax fencing to join the Umbro

UMBRO STAND OPENS TODAY

◆ Sunday 7th March is an auspicious date in the recent history of Manchester City as this afternoon's F.A. Cup quarter-final against Tottenham Hotspur co-incides with the culmination of the eleven month project to redevelop the stand at the Platt Lane end of the stadium, which is opened to the public for the first time today as the Umbro Stand.

all the atmosphere of a major sporting occasion, while retaining the exclusivity and sophistication of dining in a private Box before the match action begins.

◆ But this is only part of the story. The club policy has been to provide excellent amenities for ALL the spectators in the new Stand and the thousands of City supporters who file through the men and within a short space of time the BBC claimed there were around 200 City 'hooligans' on the turf.

A few of these supporters were clearly looking for trouble and headed towards the Spurs fans in the North Stand, while others seemed mystified as to why they were on the pitch in the first place. Fans milled around talking, explaining their frustrations to each other.

The police seemed slow to act but when they did they certainly over-reacted, sending about ten officers on horseback onto the pitch to charge the incursors. The tactic worked but gave the media an impression the invasion was much worse than it actually was. Once the pitch was clear the game resumed and Sheringham missed a penalty for Spurs while Quinn fluffed an absolute sitter.

The game ended 4-2 and the media seemed to enjoy the latest footballing sensation, but few connected with the Blues found any enjoyment out of the day. Quinn: "It started well and Mike Sheron gave us the lead. But after that it all fell apart. The pressure was on and we played pitifully. They went in to a 4-1 lead and the fans came on the pitch, then the police horses. Awful. The fans were frustrated – understandably so. It was the worst day I experienced at City. We were on the verge of success and it all fell apart."

Of course the pitch invasion was totally and utterly incorrect, however few in the media actually bothered to understand the underlying reason for the supporters' actions. Some sources claimed it had all been planned before the game even kicked off, but surely even the most organised hooligan could not have plotted a pitch invasion 'just in case' City pulled a goal back to make the score 4-2?

The main reason for the disturbance was undoubtedly frustration. City fans had endured 17 years without success. They had been so stoked up to believe the FA Cup was coming back to Manchester anything less than a victory would have left them feeling depressed. As it was, City's capitulation simply made the supporters angry. They were totally frustrated and, though the manner was wrong, they expressed their feelings in the only way that actually seemed guaranteed to make the Chairman listen.

In *King Of The Kippax* Ged Isaacs wrote: "Swales described it as 'My worst day in football'. A very telling comment as he has presided over two relegations and countless embarrassing team performances. If he's so cut up about a few people on the pitch, why didn't he resign in '83 after the Luton game? Still at least he's confirmed that he doesn't give a shit about the team. As the Moody Blues once put it 'Go now, go now, go now'."

The comment was typical of many made by supporters in the aftermath of this game. While the media liked to portray the image of a rampaging mob running across City's turf, the supporters themselves

were questioning the Chairman and his fellow directors. Peter Reid was blamed for the actual team performance but the real culprits, according to the fans, were the directors. They believed the newly constructed Umbro Stand seemed to typify the attitude of the Club at this point. It was a rather tasteless, small scale construction with too few seats and too many executive boxes. In simple terms it was very much 'small time' as opposed to stands being constructed elsewhere. Even the executive boxes had caused problems at the Tottenham game as, after Sheron's early goal, Spurs supporters lobbed coins and rubbish onto City followers below, causing the first situation that the recently recruited stewards were unable to control.

Throughout the days that followed, fans were made to feel like animals yet the same weekend much worse crowd trouble had occurred at the Blackburn v Sheffield United match. The only difference was City's game was televised. For Peter Swales the whole event had been a nightmare: "I should have gone then! That game was a real low point for me. New stand... Big crowd... Everything right, except the result and the fans on the pitch. I was going to resign but a few friends and other directors persuaded me to stay. They convinced me. I don't know if it was self-preservation or what, but they all convinced me to stay. Now I realise I should definitely have gone... No question! From that point on, it wasn't me. I made a few mistakes and I stopped learning. Stopped listening."

Had Swales gone then the events of the following year would never have occurred. It's impossible to say what might have happened to the Blues, but the nightmare that materialised at the start of the 1993-94 season would have been prevented. In the months that followed the Spurs fiasco, Peter Swales took steps to change the management structure of the Club, while the fans grew increasingly dissatisfied with the overall direction of the team they loved. 1993 was to prove a watershed year in the history of Manchester football.

1993-1994 Don't Save The Swales

The close season of 1993 was not a particularly pleasant one for either the City management team or supporters. Peter Reid and Sam Ellis struggled in their search for quality players. In fact they seemed to be turned down by almost every player approached, while Peter Swales was apparently reluctant to provide enough funds to guarantee any significant signing. Players allegedly on the move to Maine Road included Trevor Sinclair, Paul Stewart, Geoff Thomas, John Barnes and Andy Townsend. Not one of these signed as the summer of '93 became something of a farce.

In addition to the struggle to recruit top quality players, Peter Swales seemed concerned about the effect Manchester United's Championship success was having on football. He had promised City's fans that the Blues would be celebrating League success before the Reds, but that did not occur and as the 1993-94 season approached Swales was feeling the pressure: "Forget the ups and downs... Our two relegations... We had a terrific on-going situation with United for the whole of the 18/19 years because they had not won the Championship. Until they did we were always in with a prayer ... A shout. There was always a battle going on, but the day they won the Championship was the day alarm bells started ringing for me! I understand how a supporter feels when you're losing matches. It's the hardest thing there is, although the hardest thing for me was to keep getting United rammed down my throat!"

The team winning the Championship should never generate a negative impact on other clubs, however the situation in Manchester at the time was unique. While City had struggled during the 1980s United had the occasional FA Cup success, but their own supporters expected more. Their continual failure to win the Championship actually relieved some of the pressure on Peter Swales, but United's success in 1993 brought the focus sharply back onto the failings of Manchester City in a way that no other team has ever been forced to endure.

It was almost a national joke that City had not won a trophy since 1976, even though many other similar sized clubs, for example Newcastle and Chelsea, had been less successful during the period from 1970 to 1993. The pressure resulting from United's success cannot be ignored when analysing the events of 1993. The March '93 derby had already given City's directors something to think about. Peter Swales was forced to accept the Blues were some way behind: "It all struck home to me when United fans were chanting 'you've not won anything for 17 years'. Then you start thinking well we should have won in 1981. Then they'd be chanting that you'd not won anything for 12 years! But winning in '81 would have put us into the European Cup Winners' Cup. Spurs got through to the semi-finals so you never know what might have happened. But that's football. Every club could look back at what could have happened."

For Peter Swales the sad fact was the supporters were now carefully evaluating what had happened during his twenty years as Chairman. They were far from happy and, as the 1993-94 season opened, expected a significant improvement - especially in terms of spectacle - on the previous term. Ninth place in the Premier League would have been much more acceptable if the side had really tried to provide more entertainment.

To ease some of the burden, the Chairman appointed a former newspaper journalist John Maddock as Public Relations Officer. It seemed a most curious move at the time but Swales clearly felt under pressure.

The opening League game was a disappointing 1-1 draw with Leeds at Maine Road. As early as half-time, with City totally outplayed but the game still goalless, supporters voiced their opinions with a series of 'boos'. Flitcroft followed up an effort by Sheron to put the Blues in front in the second half, but no one could argue when Leeds deservedly equalised from a free header at a corner. On paper the 1-1 draw looked a good result, but the truth was City had been very lucky and relied on a series of brilliant saves from Tony Coton. To the supporters nothing, it seemed, had changed.

The following Tuesday City travelled to Everton. A group of fans unveiled a banner at the Park End that referred to an alleged promise made by Swales during the close season. It read: "£6m to spend Swales - you liar." It was patently obvious supporters were losing patience.

During the match the by now familiar chant of "We want Swales out, we want Swales out" rang round Goodison as City failed to get a shot on target until the final few minutes. Earlier Paul Rideout had scored the only goal of the match to give Everton an easy victory.

Prior to the next match on Saturday 21st August the shock news that John Maddock, the former Sunday People journalist, had been promoted to General Manager was announced. Everyone was totally baffled and rumours circulated that Peter Reid would soon be dismissed. Already an unconfirmed story suggested Reid had been asked to sack Sam Ellis in a bid to maintain his own position at Maine Road. Once again City seemed to be shooting themselves in the foot.

It was no surprise when the first game played under the auspices of Maddock ended in a 1-0 defeat at Tottenham. Three days later, Johnny Giles wrote a blistering attack on Swales in the Daily Express. It was an article appreciated by the fans and, at last, it appeared there were some people in the media who actually understood what was really happening at Maine Road. The failure to find success since 1976 could not be blamed solely on Peter Reid. City's directors had to shoulder their share of responsibility.

A large number of injuries were now affecting Reid's plans and he was forced to play both Quinn and Curle despite hamstring problems. Nevertheless the manager did not use injuries as an excuse for the 2-0 humiliation by Blackburn at Maine Road on Tuesday 24th. He simply stated that the Blues did not perform and Blackburn were more determined than City.

Naturally, a 'Swales Out' demonstration followed the defeat with new General Manager John Maddock telling the press the supporters deserved better. Many of his comments appeared to directly undermine Reid and were followed up by an extraordinary interview with Paul Hince of the Manchester Evening News. Basically Maddock told Hince he was the man in charge and he was determined to change the situation: "People had better understand that there is a new regime at Maine Road. I am not a mouthpiece for the chairman Peter Swales. I am the supremo at Maine Road with a specific mandate from the board, and that mandate is to sort out the problem which we have got at the moment."

In a not very thinly veiled warning to Reid and Ellis, Maddock added: "Make no mistake about it. I have the power to hire and fire and whatever has got to be done to put us back on line will be done. There is no point campaigning for the chairman Peter Swales to step down. He has handed control over to me and is as concerned as I am about our current plight. The only thing he has ever wanted is for Manchester City to be one of the major clubs in English soccer and that is the task he has entrusted to me. The future of this club is all that concerns me. I won't duck making decisions, however unpleasant they may be, which is why I attended the press conference after last night's match. I felt after that performance it was my duty as the man in charge to face the music. I wasn't trying to deflect the flak from the chairman. In fact I never even spoke to him after the match.

"I wanted people to know that I am not a puppet or a messenger. I am the man in charge and I will take positive steps to pull this club into shape. You don't have to be a genius to work out that there is something going badly wrong when the team are being booed off the pitch before the end of August. I can only repeat that the necessary steps will be taken to give our supporters the team and the success they deserve."

During this period the players - the only people who could really make a difference to results - were confused. They supported Reid and were frankly appalled by Maddock's comments. Captain Keith Curle: "The only rift here appears to be between the hierarchy and the gaffer. Comments about the lack of team spirit from someone who has travelled only once with us on the team bus is hard to believe."

Niall Quinn agreed: "I signed to play until I am 30, but that was for City not John Maddock. We are all backing Peter 100 per cent. When Mr. Maddock was appointed I thought we would have stability, but things seem to be dragging on. Obviously he has come with a view to clear the place, and right now I don't know if I'll be here next week."

The players probably knew it, but City supporters were now also strongly of the opinion the Reid-Ellis period was about to end. Reid was in a difficult position and, it seemed, in a no-win situation. On the morning of Thursday 26th August *The Sun* newspaper questioned whether Reid would reach his third anniversary as manager in November, while it also included an interview with former boss Malcolm Allison. Allison pointed the finger at Swales and accused him of 20 years of mis-rule. He also queried the role of John Maddock:

"His appointment is bizarre. Why didn't Swales just go to France and get Mickey Mouse? He's a personality who would get the crowds back and give them a laugh. Football is a professional business. How can you put an amateur in a position like that?"

That same day the *Daily Express* printed a letter from Swales complaining about the Johnny Giles article. Throughout the note City's chairman listed the amount of money he had provided to various managers and tried to explain he had never interfered with a manager's decision. He added: "Manchester City were the first club to sign three players valued at £1m. City were recognised as the biggest spenders in football, attracting the best internationals in football. I have often been criticised in the past - on some occasion with justification - but to suggest that I am the chairman who interferes with his managers' dealings in the transfer market is ludicrous. No other chairman in the Premiership has allowed his managers the freedom over the past 19 years as I have given. As a 'failed' manager, there is no doubt you have suffered restrictions from chairmen. I have always allowed mine to get on with their jobs. If that is a fault, then I am guilty. You are guilty of gross misreporting which does neither you, nor your paper any favours."

Giles responded by claiming Swales' letter was a poor attempt at self-justification. He then asked the two questions that the majority of supporters were desperately keen to find answers to: "If you have done so well, why are Manchester City in such a mess? Why did they not make one significant signing during the summer, a time when all the seriously ambitious clubs pushed so hard and successfully to strengthen their squads?"

He went on to attack the appointment of Maddock and some of the other decisions made by Swales over the years. He ended by considering City's plight. He claimed: "Only one man is responsible for that. It is you. You are the chairman. You appoint the managers and, by your own account, say who will be signed. Or, sadly in City's case these days, who will not be signed."

On the same day Peter Reid was due to have a showdown with Swales and Maddock to determine where he stood. In particular Reid wanted to understand what was meant by Maddock's statement about having the power to hire and fire. Reid felt that was part of his role: "It is in my contract that I hire and fire my staff and I expect that contract to be honoured." He was also determined not to leave that role: "There is no way I will resign. I have never run away from a fight in my life and I'm not going to start now."

It wasn't long into the blistering meeting that Reid realised his career at Maine Road had ended a mere 13 days into the new season: "It came as something of a shock. But I'm a professional and I have to get on with life."

City fans were furious. It wasn't so much the dismissal of Reid and his assistant Ellis that angered Blues, it was the way the whole affair had been handled. The supporters had been unhappy with the Club's style of play for some time and it was no secret some wanted the managerial set-up to change during the 1993 close season. Instead they saw Swales hand Reid a new three-year contract, as he had done with Machin, then appoint a journalist as General Manager to "do his dirty work", as the fans put it. It was all too ridiculous for words and quickly made the bungling Blues the laughing stock of British football once more.

The supporters had simply had enough. They blamed the Chairman entirely and were keen to see his role change. For possibly the first time in City history, the majority of newspapers reported the true supporters' views, and each article seemed to list what had occurred during the near 20 years of Chairman Swales' rule. The list was not particularly pleasant reading, although it is true that each newspaper concentrated on the negative aspects of his reign rather than any plus points.

While the anti-Swales movement gained strength, the media also speculated on Reid's replacement; Joe Royle, Steve Coppell, Dave Bassett, and Terry Venables were all tipped for the job. Naturally, the supporters were keen to have either Royle or Venables, but at the time neither Bassett nor Coppell particularly excited them.

For 24 hours everyone speculated, yet local radio station GMR had devised a cunning plan. They knew John Maddock would have to meet either the new man, or his Chairman, before any agreement could be made, and so they tried to follow him on the Friday morning. With live reports throughout the morning, the GMR reporter tailed Maddock and even managed to speak with him. Excited listeners heard Maddock's car was heading south, fuelling speculation the new man would either be Steve Coppell or Terry Venables. The fans' favourite was Venables, but would he really travel north to Manchester? GMR didn't quite manage to discover the answer, but that night's *Manchester Evening News* made it clear Venables was not on City's wanted list.

It then transpired Maddock had already reached agreement with a manager and his existing club, and an announcement would be made the following day, after City's Friday night home game with Coventry. Maddock told the media: "I can tell you that I am delighted to have landed a manager of this pedigree and our fans will feel the same because we have appointed a true professional who is going to help put Manchester City back on the football map."

Earlier that day Maddock also claimed responsibility for bringing Howard Kendall to Maine Road in 1989 and rightly pointed out what City fans expected of the new man: "He must be experienced and do a first-class job.

Fans want someone who can achieve success and has a track record for success." These comments intimated the Blues would be appointing a proven top flight manager, someone who had won trophies; someone who would be respected; and someone who would appeal to what was rapidly becoming the embarrassed generation of Blues.

City's match with Coventry that night (Friday 27th August) took on a rather surreal feel with most fans turning up simply to yell some abuse at City's directors, in particular Swales, rather than enjoy the match.

The game itself ended in a 1-1 draw for Tony Book's men after Sheron had given the Blues the lead in the first half. Five minutes from time a mistake by McMahon allowed Roy Wegerle to equalise. Throughout the match chants of "Swales Out" rang out, while rumours abounded as to who the new boss would be.

In the Main Stand, the beleaguered Chairman visibly suffered in a way that hadn't occurred before and, eventually, Swales left his seat in the directors' box. While all this took place the media, in particular Radio 5, brought the news that the Oxford manager, Brian Horton, had been spotted in one of the Umbro Stand's executive boxes. They tried to gain confirmation that Horton was the new manager and before the game ended clearly stated City had indeed appointed the former Luton player.

Former City player Mike Summerbee was asked for his reaction, and the ex-player was as astonished as the vast majority of supporters. The main comment expressed was "Brian who?" He was certainly not of the calibre suggested by Maddock and, after expecting either a Royle or Venables, supporters felt totally let down by the Club's directors.

Armed with full knowledge of the appointment, fans demonstrated outside the main entrance demanding the resignation of Swales and his board. They were far from satisfied, although many of the following day's newspaper reports grossly overestimated the amount of violence involved. Articles claimed over 1,000 fans rioted with dozens of police being forced to charge the angry mob. It was all a little exaggerated. City's supporters had been demonstrating for years, certainly since the early 1980s, and each protest had always arrived at a natural end.

Temporary crush barriers were pushed over, but there was no actual violence and older supporters remarked that the stone throwing incidents of 1965 were more likely to have caused harm than chants of "Sack The Board" and "Swales Out." Newspaper stories portrayed the Club and its supporters in a very poor light and, potentially, made the situation even worse. It was an extremely distressing time for all connected with Manchester City, especially the supporters and the man everybody loved to hate, Peter Swales.

Ironically, *The Sun* newspaper, which many fans were boycotting due to their ridiculous coverage of the Hillsborough disaster, suddenly became interested in the fans' view and claimed to support their campaign by printing and issuing free "Don't Save The Swales" stickers. For one man this whole period must have been totally bewildering - new manager Brian Horton. In October 2004 he looked back on this period: "I knew I had a job to do. The 'Brian Who' line didn't affect me because those who knew the game knew what I'd done, and in any case I'd managed here for Hull and I'd played in that game for Luton, so I knew what credentials I had. The Board backed me, so it wasn't an issue.

"Arriving at City was like a dream come true! A lot of people have said I'd been approached beforehand; that I was very friendly with key people here etc., but the truth of it all is that when the approach came it was a jolt out of the blue. I hardly knew anyone here – naturally football's a small world and you do know people at most clubs – and when I received the call I had to go for it. I wanted to manage at City, and couldn't wait to get started.

"It was a perfect time in many ways because the team had only two points from five games and were sat at the bottom of the league – I had to turn things around. That focuses your mind on the players, games, training, and results. The situation could only improve on the pitch, and whatever was happening off the pitch couldn't get in the way. The takeover hadn't started when I was given the job, so that wasn't a worry either."

Horton had arrived at Maine Road full of ambition and determined to succeed. In interviews at the time he tried to dismiss all talk that hatchet man John Maddock would be too much of a controlling influence: "I have known John for 20 years, although I don't know all the background of what happened over his new job, I don't expect him to be looking over my shoulder. Remember, I had to work with Kevin Maxwell, who was Oxford chairman, and he let me get on with my job. I am sure the same thing will happen here." He added: "I do have a track record, and that is in keeping Oxford going, especially during the difficult days when the Maxwell family were in charge. And remember, every manager has to step up some time. You have to start somewhere. I believe we can go places. Obviously there are problems but from what I saw from the stand tonight, we have plenty to work with - and I have been promised cash to buy."

On 1st September, Horton's first game in charge brought much relief to the City management and directors as the Blues won at Swindon 3-1. Prior to the game Horton and his assistant David Moss were cheered off the team coach as the supporters tried to convey their criticism was not aimed specifically at them. Understandably Maddock, Public Enemy Number Two,

was jeered when he was first spotted, while Swales did not attend at all. Despite the 3-1 win, there were regular chants of "Swales Out", although it must be stressed the fans also gave the playing staff much support and encouragement. Quite simply, the fans remained loyal to the Blue cause yet were extremely bitter towards the directors.

Five days after that game City's supporters awoke to surprising news. As with the death of Princess Diana, it seems most supporters can remember where they were on the day they heard former player Francis Lee was preparing to bid for the Club. Oldham-based Mark Brown recalled how he first heard the news: "I'd set the radio alarm to go off at 7am and, to be truthful, I was still half asleep when the Radio One news bulletin was being read out. I didn't know if I was dreaming or if it was real, but I vaguely recall hearing 'according to the *Daily Mirror* former hero Franny Lee has mounted a takeover'. I couldn't believe it! I lay in bed waiting for the next bulletin, when it was confirmed. I knew then I hadn't been dreaming! I quickly dressed, drove to work and searched for a copy of the *Mirror* to see what the story really was. For the first time in decades the *Mirror* actually had a City article on its back page! It still seemed like a dream. Then I started to wonder if we'd get a special discount on Lee's toilet rolls - we'd certainly need it if the season continued to be as nerve-wracking as it had begun!"

Veteran *Mirror* reporter Alec Johnson had been given an exclusive story by Francis Lee, and the fans simply loved it. In the article Lee stated his plans: "If we do take over we are going to listen to the fans. They are the most important people of all. This is their club. If they did not come to Maine Road week in and week out, then there simply wouldn't be a Manchester City Football Club.

"This is a real challenge. It is a roll-up-your-sleeves time. My three associates and myself are willing to put big money into the Club to get the best players for the team. But other things are equally important. The most vital thing is that the Club is run from top to bottom just like a winning team. If we are going to make Manchester City the number one team then there is no time for personalities at the Club. Everyone counts."

At a press conference later in the day Lee insisted he was not driven by a desire to take over the Club: "I am not interested in controlling things. The Club should not be run by one man. What I am seeking is a mandate from supporters and shareholders for a place on the board."

Despite Lee's comments, the supporters were now keen to see the former England international as City's driving force, while the existing board of directors seemed reluctant to allow Lee to join their merry band. To give an indication of how he might help the Blues, Lee stated: "I am prepared to make available substantially more funds than have been invested in the Club previously. I don't want to discuss figures but we can start at £1 million and go from there."

For the fans it was now a case of choosing between Lee, a former player who had brought great honour and success to the Club, and Swales, a man whose 20 year reign was rapidly being viewed as a complete and utter disaster. Swales' time as chairman deserved fairer assessment but, with a strong supporter campaign, immense media coverage, and then the arrival of Lee, it was easy to discredit everything the Chairman had achieved.

In simple terms, Swales should have stepped down some time before, possibly in 1989 with the arrival of Howard Kendall, to allow history to correctly record the many achievements of his period at the helm. By remaining in charge into the 1990s he became vilified as a man who appeared stubbornly in love with power. This is untrue, however, in 1993 few Blues were interested in hearing about the real Swales. All they wanted was for him to step down.

Despite the depth of feeling, Swales actually believed the demonstrations would disappear: "I am not panicking, nobody is at this club. And I really don't know what all the fuss is about, even though I do seem to be Public Enemy Number One among our supporters. We'll just wait and see what develops. Some people seem intent on mixing it. There seems to be a vendetta against me, and I would be lying if I said it hasn't affected me."

For the remainder of the week leading up to Horton's first home game in charge on 11th September the media concentrated on the "Swales Out, Lee In" story, particularly the *Daily Mirror*. Each day the *Mirror* reported on Lee's movements and also quoted many supporters, including a vicar who was praying for Swales to stand down, and a group called "Forward with Franny" who seemed keen to bring a little organisation to the fans' demonstrations. The *Mirror* joined *The Sun* by issuing stickers, badges, and posters saying "We Want Franny".

By the day of the Maine Road match with QPR, the newspaper claimed the battle was over and Swales was poised to sell his shares. According to the *Mirror*, Swales had made a statement: "I would love to keep going, but I realise it is probably time for someone else to have a go. We have said if we can get the right deal we will do it. I am sure if we get the right deal it will suit the shareholders. Time marches on, doesn't it?"

The *Mirror* also claimed another leading shareholder and supporter of Swales, Stephen Boler, was prepared to sell his shares if approached. Details of Lee's consortium were now becoming clearer with another former City player, Colin Barlow, playing a leading role. The two men made it clear they were to attend the QPR game, and wanted fans to peacefully make their feelings known. They didn't need to make any special requests as the fans

were desperately keen to tell the world who they wanted to head City's board.

Prior to the QPR match, thousands of supporters stood outside the main entrance in party mood. They had arrived early to celebrate the 'return of the messiah', as it was termed, and when Lee arrived he was mobbed as he tried to make his way into the ground. The fans made all the usual noise and, after Lee's arrival, quickly made their way inside the stadium to enhance the aura further.

In yet another surreal atmosphere the fans cheered and clapped Lee as he made his way into the directors' box, then booed and hissed Swales when he arrived to take his seat five rows behind Lee. It was reminiscent of a pantomime, although it was all much more serious for everyone involved. The arrival of Lee helped to boost the atmosphere with fans giving the team terrific support, although chants of "Come on City" were interspersed with "We want Swales out." In the 17th minute a powerful run by Sheron led to City's first goal, scored by Quinn. Twenty minutes later an impressive corner by £500,000 man Alfons Groenendijk, City's only significant close season signing, was forced into the net by Mike Sheron. In the 70th minute a deflected Garry Flitcroft shot gave the Blues a 3-0 win.

After the match an organised, peaceful sit-in lasted for at least 20 minutes to provide a clear indication to all that the fans would not give in until Swales stepped down. Swales dismissed the demonstration as muted while surprisingly the media, who had stoked the hype throughout the week, failed to cover the event. If they felt the story was now over they were wrong. The takeover tale was to rumble on for some considerable time.

Even as fans welcomed Lee to Maine Road news broke that Peter Swales had been talking to another person keen to seek control of the Club. Swales told the *Manchester Evening News*: "The person in question vigorously pursued his desire to buy Manchester City. This is not a consortium. He is on his own in this and his intentions are serious. I know him and there is no question that he personally has the necessary finances available now to take over this club.

"I have told him to put his offer in writing and this he is prepared to do. When that offer has been received I will invite him back to talk to the whole board."

From this point on the takeover of the Club became extremely bitter, and the facts bewildering. Who was Swales' mystery purchaser? Had Lee spoken with Swales? There were so many questions and such entanglement that supporters struggled to understand what was happening.

At one point it was reported that former newspaper tycoon Eddie Shah was backing Lee, while some had previously suggested he was actually Swales' mystery purchaser. It was all too confusing for most to contemplate, and clearly distracted from the real purpose of the Club - football.

During the battle, Horton tried to develop a side he was comfortable with: "Because I'd watched games here, and knew about the Club's history, I wanted to make sure we played attacking football. City has a great reputation for playing stylish and attractive football, so I wanted to encourage that. We also tried to make sure we had exciting players and then I believe my backroom staff was particularly strong. We had Tony Book – I'm sure he could be still coaching somewhere today if he wanted to – David Moss, Les Chapman, Neil McNab, and Colin Bell. I played with McNab at Brighton and knew his strengths and knew he was well liked here. I tried to get a good mix and because of the strong City names in there I think it was ideal."

On Monday 20th September Horton gave new £1.6m signing Alan Kernaghan his debut in an away match with Wimbledon. Sadly that game, televised by Sky, ended in a 1-0 defeat leaving City in 16th place.

A 1-1 draw with Reading in the League Cup followed two nights later before a crowd of 9,280. The 'Forward With Franny' group had called for a mass boycott, and some supporters did stand outside the ground throughout the match protesting, but the official attendance figure was only a few hundred lower than the Bristol Rovers game the previous season.

Other protests were planned, such as the lighting of candles on the Kippax. Some proved successful while others failed. At the candlelight protest against Oldham on 5th October stewards were ordered to take steps every time they saw the tiniest flicker within the Kippax. Their response was reminiscent of the ARP Warden in Dad's Army demanding: "Put that light out!" Regular tannoy announcements aimed at reminding supporters of potential fire risk were viewed as the directors' last desperate act to end the protest. As a result each announcement was greeted by an increased volume of abuse aimed at Swales and his board.

Once again it all hovered on the brink of farce, and the general public felt City supporters were more concerned with off field activities than the actual play. That wasn't strictly true, although it is fair to say the fans needed to force a change at the top before the action on the pitch could progress.

The Oldham match ended in a 1-1 draw - a remarkable result considering the off-field events and an ever-swelling injury list that Brian Horton somehow had to overcome. The players in the treatment room during Horton's first few weeks included left-winger Rick Holden, defenders Andy Hill and Michel Vonk, and Ian Brightwell and Paul Lake who were suffering from longer term problems. A 2-1 victory over Reading in the League Cup (3-2 on aggregate) eased the tension a little and sent

City through to face Chelsea in the third round, while a dull goalless game at Arsenal in mid-October followed. David White gave City the lead in the next match, but Ian Rush produced an equaliser two minutes from time in a Maine Road draw with Liverpool. The following Tuesday a 1-0 victory sent Chelsea crashing out of the League Cup.

Of more interest afterwards was Stuart Hall, reporting on the match for Radio 5, who revealed a rumour was circulating Maine Road that Francis Lee's bid was doomed to fail because the consortium did not have enough money to buy out Swales and Co. It was then the Swales-Lee takeover tussle took a different turn at the 1993 AGM. It appeared a perfect opportunity to discover some truths, as a large number of supporters would be able to voice opinions and direct questions to the reigning chairman.

Arguably the most controversial AGM in the Club's history took place on Thursday 28th October 1993 at the City Social Club. In previous years the meeting had always been held on a Friday, however as the new date coincided with the Nottingham Forest AGM, some believed the date change had been deliberately altered to ensure less media coverage. The Forest AGM was an equally stormy affair and concerned many allegations about Brian Clough. These gained national media coverage, whereas the City AGM was barely covered - even in the *Manchester Evening News*. In addition, supporters were suspicious that conveniently, the day after the meeting, City at long last bought a striker - Carl Griffiths. The *Evening News* made this the back page story rather than a serious review of the meeting.

Naturally, Peter Swales and his board attended the AGM, as did Francis Lee and Colin Barlow. In addition comedian Eddie Large and Simply Red's manager Elliot Rashman were there. Fanzine editor Noel Bayley was present, with various other *Electric Blue* contributors ready to record the meeting for posterity, while *King Of The Kippax*'s Dave Wallace was refused entry. Apparently some shares had been transferred to Wallace to allow him to attend, but the Club claimed the transaction had not been performed in time. Naturally, the procedural matter was merely seen as a deliberate attempt to dilute the voice of the ordinary supporter.

To fully understand the supporters' feelings at this time it is vital a full and frank review of the meeting is read and understood. The best and most accurate AGM review was the one written by Noel Bayley and Steve Worthington which appeared in the fanzine *Electric Blue*, issue 22.

Over four pages they recorded virtually every exchange of views at what was a stormy meeting. Pro-Swales members who annually, it seems, praised the performance of the Chairman and his Board, were heckled and jeered by their vociferous opponents in the room who were described by one servile speaker as a "disgraceful rent-a-mob."

However, these Francis Lee takeover supporters did represent the views of the vast majority of non-shareholding City fans and posed Peter Swales a string of uncomfortable specific questions to which they received scant or highly unsatisfactory answers.

Looking pale and pressured, the Chairman was full of stubborn resolve despite receiving a vote of no confidence from the floor by 52 votes to 79 to re-elect him as a Director of the Company. It made little difference as a one-share, one-vote ballot was swiftly organised to ensure Swales' re-election.

In a prepared statement the Chairman commented on the proposal received from the consortium led by Francis Lee, who was seated close by: "The proposal contains a number of conditions and does not involve a proposed offer to all shareholders. The board and its advisors consider that this proposal falls well short of reflecting the full value of your club. The board does not view this proposal as forming the basis for any further discussion with this consortium. The board has also had contact with other parties that may be interested in the Club and I will keep you informed should there be any further developments. That's it."

"No, it isn't!" shouted a voice from the floor as others then rose to deliver indictments of Swales' reign. Elliott Rashman, supremo of the rock band Simply Red, was particularly articulate in his condemnation of the regime: "Shareholders are irrelevant. The Club is half-developed - a corner shop in a world of supermarkets. City are a Bovril and Wagon Wheels club. In any other business the Chairman wouldn't still be there after 20 years.

"If you go out on the playing fields of Manchester, what do you see written across kids' shirts? Sharp, more than Brother ... Sharp! And if I was Greenall's and if I was Brother I would be questioning whether you are really capable of taking us into the 21st Century. I suspect not. I'm just an ordinary fan. I'm 41 and I've been supporting City for 31 years. Anyone under 20 doesn't know success."

Swales attempted to halt any further questions but another shareholder hit the mark when he said: "That chair should provide leadership and inspiration and with all due respect, Mr Swales, your reputation is in tatters, your credibility is low and I would urge you, on behalf of all the fans of this football club, and everybody here, that you talk to Mr Lee and his consortium because we do need leadership but we're not getting it at the moment."

And so it went on until the result of the ballot was announced. Swales had won hands down with 688,613 votes in favour of his re-election and 9,270 votes against.

As the meeting failed to satisfy the "Swales Out" contingent the feeling of deflation was enormous. Supporters were asking themselves when the farce would end. To some it seemed never ending and, while prolonged, fortunes on the pitch would continue to be mixed.

A 3-1 defeat at West Ham followed the AGM, then on 7th November came the Maine Road derby with United. It was another first half derby performance that made City look world beaters. The Blues raced to a 2-0 lead, courtesy of Niall Quinn, and seemed a class above the Reds. Unfortunately, a mistake from Michel Vonk early in the second half allowed Eric Cantona to steer the ball past Tony Coton. With 12 minutes to go the controversial Frenchman made it 2-2, then Roy Keane netted another for United three minutes from time to make it a disappointing 3-2 to the Reds.

A couple of draws followed (1-1 at Norwich and 0-0 at Chelsea), before a 3-1 defeat by Sheffield Wednesday at Maine Road brought more pressure for Brian Horton, especially as Niall Quinn crashed to the ground with cruciate ligament damage that would keep him out for the rest of the season. Rumours had circulated for a while that Horton would be

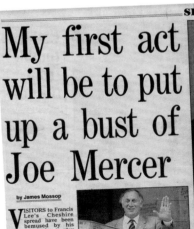

SPORT

My first act will be to put up a bust of Joe Mercer

by James Mossop

JOE MERCER ... a symbol of success

That's Francis Lee's promise to Maine Road fans

FRANCIS LEE ... "happiest days of my life were at Manchester City"

TRUE BLUE
Francis Lee

Francis Lee was a brilliant forward and contributed hugely to City's successes from 1967 to 1974. In 1993 he launched a takeover of the Blues.

one of the first to leave if Lee gained control of the Blues, and as results were working against the manager that story seemed believable, unlike many other newspaper articles at the time. That same match saw chairman Swales protected by three bouncers, dozens of stewards and numerous police as supporters' pleas for him to see sense became more aggressive. Something had to give.

On Monday 29th November Peter Swales announced he was stepping down as chairman of the Club he loved: "This is a very sad day for me. But the situation with supporters has deteriorated to the point where I could see no other solution."

According to reports Swales was to remain on the board but had now resolved to ensure Lee did not gain control of the Blues. However, in an interview later that week he suggested he might be prepared to leave the board entirely, although selling to Lee still looked unlikely: "We are working on bringing a new team to run Manchester City and once everything is in place I may stand down altogether from the board. My time is up as far as running City is concerned. I have reached the stage where I want to relax. The last few months have not been a pleasant episode at Maine Road.

"There are a few options we are examining to make sure that the Club's future is protected. Once we have installed the new team to run the Club there might be a sale of the shares or a partial sale. Another possibility which we are looking at strongly is to go public so that our supporters will have the chance to become part of the set-up at Manchester City. When we have found the right man to become the new chairman within the next couple of weeks he might well feel that it would be in the Club's best interests if I wasn't a director. I can easily appreciate that point of view. The new Chairman wouldn't want it to appear as if I am pulling the strings in the background at the Club. If he wants me to stand down from the board then that is fine by me.

"My involvement in running Manchester City is finished. But I am still a City fan and I would still want to come along to Maine Road on match days to support the team."

As the year moved towards its close, the takeover rumbled on while City's match results worsened. Only one victory occurred during November and December as the Blues struggled. The League Cup run ended with a 2-1 defeat by Forest in a 4th round replay, despite an early goal from Vonk.

Over Christmas and into January Francis Lee and his supporters negotiated with representatives of Peter Swales and Stephen Boler in an attempt to conclude a takeover. Many times during that period it seemed the whole affair was on the brink of a satisfying conclusion, but on every occasion it appeared obstacles were deliberately placed in Lee's way. Nevertheless, in the early hours of Saturday 5th February the takeover

negotiations were completed and Francis Lee and his supporters Colin Barlow and John Dunkerley were welcomed on to the board at Maine Road.

Immediately an exhausted Lee - he'd cut short his annual holiday in Barbados to attend the final negotiations - made an announcement: "I am tired now but it has all been worth it. The supporters have been superb in the way they have backed me in this long fight and the new board will ensure that they have their say in the running of the Club. The immediate priority is to sort out the finances, which may take up to two weeks, and to ensure we remain in the Premiership. We certainly won't be selling any of our top players to help the Club's financial situation. We are facing a relegation battle and you don't win a fight like that by getting rid of your best players."

That afternoon City faced Ipswich Town in the replay of a match abandoned after 39 minutes on 3rd January. The Blues had been leading 2-0 at Maine Road in the original fixture when referee David Elleray angered the City players, especially Tony Coton, by abandoning the tie due to a waterlogged pitch. The pitch had been appalling at the kick-off and perhaps the game should not have commenced. Naturally, it had been a big disappointment, but at least it guaranteed Francis Lee a home fixture for his first match as chairman.

The game was played out amid a carnival atmosphere, so different to a week earlier when the Blues were defeated 1-0 in the FA Cup at Cardiff and whispers the takeover was off circulated around the ground. Prior to the Ipswich game a banner was unveiled welcoming Lee back to Maine Road, while thousands of blue and white balloons were released. City allowed the visitors to take the lead via a mistake. Garry Flitcroft's attempted back pass ended up gifting the former Oldham player Ian Marshall a rather simple opportunity to score.

Fortunately, the men in Blue did not give up thanks mainly to David Rocastle, who had joined City from Leeds in a £1 million exchange for David White on 22nd December 1993. White had been struggling for the Blues ever since his international appearance in September 1992, and many believed he had lost confidence in himself. A move to another high profile club like Leeds seemed sensible, although whether his style would suit the famous defensively-minded Yorkshire side was debatable.

Rocastle had quickly become an important member of Horton's City side, although he did appear at times to lack full fitness. Against Ipswich he was excellent and helped bring the Blue equaliser as he cut through two defenders, charged to the goal-line and sent over a superb cross for Carl Griffiths to flick in a great goal. After the match new chairman Lee suggested Rocastle's display had been reminiscent of skills usually only found in Brazil. He really was that impressive.

The goal seemed to inject more confidence into the side, and with Michel Vonk defending superbly, and Steve Lomas controlling midfield, the Blues dominated. Terry Phelan attempted an overhead shot, before a foul on Lomas brought a free-kick. Keith Curle took it and Vonk knocked down for Garry Flitcroft to touch in the winning goal. It was a great feeling for most Blues that night with a City victory, and the long awaited return of Francis Lee.

Despite the optimism of 5th February, the remainder of the month brought home the realisation that the Blues were still a weak side. A 4-0 defeat at Coventry was a complete and utter shambles. It also made City's search for a decent striker to bolster the attack imperative, especially as Quinn was still missing and the lightweight Carl Griffiths was not fitting in as expected. Fortunately chairman Lee was already taking steps to secure a man who would ultimately become a cult figure at Maine Road - Uwe Rösler.

On 22nd February City endured a goalless match in the snow at Villa Park, although the highlight for all Blues had been yet another penalty miss by Dean

Saunders. Previously, the Aston Villa man had failed to score from the spot against City when playing for Derby County (with emergency 'keeper Niall Quinn in goal), and again while with Liverpool. Immediately after the miss the travelling fans chanted: "Deano is a City fan" which, apparently, he once claimed he was. During the late 80s and early 90s Saunders was tipped to join the Blues on a couple of occasions. Each time he claimed he had stood on the Kippax as a boy and it was reported that he once stated he would walk from Derby to sign for the Blues. He never did. Perhaps he set off, forgot his map, took a wrong turning and ended up at Anfield!

A 2-1 victory at Swindon followed and then on 5th March at QPR Uwe Rösler made his first appearance in a City shirt following his arrival on loan from FC Nurnburg. That game ended 1-1 but before the month was out Rösler was joined by Paul Walsh - a £700,000 buy from Portsmouth - and Peter Beagrie - a £1.1 million arrival from Everton. At Ipswich on 29th March, Rösler and Walsh both demonstrated their value to the new-look Blues with a goal each to help City to a 2-2 draw, then on 2nd April the two men scored again during the comfortable 3-0 victory over Aston Villa at Maine Road. Peter Beagrie bagged number one - prompting his first somersault display while wearing a City shirt.

It was still possible for the Blues to go down and the majority of media pundits reckoned it was a certainty. Only Alan Hansen, who had backed the Blues during the 1993 FA Cup run, believed they were too good to be relegated.

More progress was made in the

The Kippax Last Stand. The huge flag was created by the fanzine Blueprint.

following two games, including an impressive 2-1 victory over Newcastle United before a Maine Road crowd of 33,774. Incredibly, defender David Brightwell - Ian's younger brother - scored the winner. New hero Rösler levelled the scores against Norwich in the next game but a disappointing 2-0 defeat at Old Trafford left City eighth from bottom, only five points clear of the trapdoor after playing more matches than those below.

The final home meeting of the season followed and was truly an emotional day as this was to be the last game played in front of the Kippax terracing. The match became known as "The Kippax Last Stand" and really signalled the end of England's last major terraced area. On the same day the Kop at Liverpool also witnessed its final game but, at this time in football history, the Kippax was actually the largest capacity terraced stand in the country. Understandably, its final day had to be memorable and a number of supporters had worked with the Club to suggest and plan the events.

Prior to the match a steel band played various tunes to welcome supporters into the stadium, while fans handed out balloons and sweets to enliven the atmosphere. City compere Vince Miller, wearing his familiar white suit, joined the steel band and began singing a medley of City's more familiar - and cleaner - chants and songs. Naturally, he sang 'Blue Moon', but there was also a rendition of the ever popular song that outlined the events of 1963 to 1970 - the most memorable line being: "Joe Mercer came we played the game we went to Rotherham."

A large number of former players were introduced to the crowd, and then Francis Lee was brought out to enormous applause. In many ways the Kippax Last Stand also marked the end of one era and the beginning of another. Co-incidentally, Francis Lee had celebrated his fiftieth birthday that week and so, ever the entertainer, Vince Miller burst into voice again to sing 'Happy Birthday To You'.

During the Kippax party, a group of Chelsea supporters dressed, appropriately, as 'Blues Brothers', laid a wreath in the centre against the stand's perimeter fence. It was a gesture much appreciated by the Mancunian Blues.

The game itself ended 2-2 with new heroes Walsh and Rösler both scoring. The point more or less guaranteed City's survival but, on the day, fans seemed more intent on taking souvenirs from the old stand. Small pick-axes had been smuggled into the stadium to hack off pieces of Kippax terracing, while others removed signs - the most notable theft being the 'Colin Bell Bar' sign, which was later seen being carried by two supporters towards Manchester.

The Club cared little about these harmless activities at the time, after all only a few months earlier there had been a much uglier atmosphere at the ground. It

seemed everyone was relieved the takeover had now come to fruition, and relegation had been avoided. The final match saw City draw 1-1 at Sheffield Wednesday, with Rösler scoring his fifth goal in 12 games, and the Blues ended the campaign in 16th place after suffering only two defeats since the arrival of the German.

In February 2010 Francis Lee looked back on these first few months and his return to football. Behind the scenes there were lots of issues, most caused through a lack of planning and quality leadership: "I wasn't really looking to get back into the game at all. I had a good and successful career outside of the game and was happy. But the takeover was one of those things that happened. I should have known that it wouldn't work. The biggest problem we faced at the start was having to build the new Kippax Stand. We ended up spending about £16m in the end – even removing the waste from underneath the old terracing should have cost only £80,000 but ended up costing about £1.8m. I thought then that I'd always been lucky in life and then suddenly my luck had changed. Everything we tried to do became an issue and the Kippax was a bit of a millstone.

"It's extraordinary when you think that at that time Jack Walker had put some money into Blackburn and Everton had had some money put into it, and we put money into City, but prior to that no one ever put money into a football club. They bought shares but never invested, we did invest. But the financial state of the club was appalling. People like John Dunkerley worked very hard during that spell and the training facilities were improved and so on."

1994-1995 Horton's Entertainers

The 1994 close season allowed everyone connected with the Club to reflect on what had been a traumatic campaign from start to finish. For Peter Swales 1993-94 had been an absolute nightmare, but it was also a situation he could easily have avoided. Foolishly he believed City's support would eventually tire of the 'Swales Out' campaign and he attempted to ignore as many of the protests as possible. Although ultimately it was Francis Lee's determination to succeed that forced the takeover, it is important to recognise the vital role supporters played.

Without detracting from Lee, it's also worth making the point that the fans had had enough from the moment the season commenced and would probably have supported anybody who seemed to offer a change at the top. At one stage Swales claimed a number of people had made offers to purchase the Club, although the only one who actually came forward as a potential buyer was wealthy businessman Mike McDonald, a City fan who claimed to have stood on the Kippax as a youngster.

Once it became obvious he could not succeed at Maine Road, McDonald turned his attentions, with some success, to transforming Sheffield United while also retaining strong links with Hyde United on the eastern side of Manchester.

Shortly before his death Peter Swales was asked why the McDonald bid failed: "That was never really serious. Never! Once Francis came in I knew it was a matter of time. He was the only man the fans would accept and I knew that. It had to be Francis. It all got messy though - the threats and hate mail. People giving out my address and that. I was totally stupid at the time. I thought Francis was behind it all! How stupid can you be? But no one could tell me. It's too ridiculous to contemplate, but when it's happening and you have to get security guards and all that you look for someone to blame. Obviously, there's always an element ... A minority that will take the law into their own hands, but for me to believe it was organised was crazy."

There was a lot of hostility from supporters of both groups. When asked about claims that other people had shown interest in buying the Blues, Swales was adamant there had been other offers. Mike McDonald was one such bidder, but who was the first? Swales: "Francis was not the first. Others had been interested, and one wealthy and quite famous man was interested, but he soon scarpered once Francis became interested. I can't tell you who he is, though. It's a pity really because he had a lot of interesting things to say."

As far as all supporters were concerned nothing mattered other than their hero, Francis Lee, was now in control. It was irrelevant to speculate how serious other bids may or may not have been.

Throughout the close season Francis Lee, Colin Barlow and John Dunkerley were kept busy discovering the appalling financial truths of the Club. They were also forced to take a serious look at plans for the future.

The Kippax Stand had to be replaced due to the requirements of government legislation following the Lord Justice Taylor Report, and the new directors were keen to see an improvement on the scheme laid down by former chairman Peter Swales. They also saw the stand's redevelopment as a chance to give the stadium an overall structural design and by the middle of the year plans were released to the public showing a much improved venue. Naturally, the Kippax Stand had to be developed first but the ultimate scheme proposed an extension to each of the other stands to give Maine Road a three tier stadium under one continuous roof. The drawings looked impressive, but the familiar problem of existing so close to a large number of densely populated residential streets always seemed likely to pose a problem.

Away from the ground improvements, Chairman Lee and Managing Director Barlow gave Brian Horton their support, despite media predictions only a few months earlier, and he was able to take stock of the squad and plan for at least another season. Already three of his five major signings had impressed (Rösler, Walsh, and Beagrie), while Carl Griffiths appeared to need only a little further grooming before becoming a permanent fixture in the first team, and defender Alan Kernaghan was prepared to prove his critics wrong. Only time would tell if Griffiths and Kernaghan could match Horton's other signings and become crowd favourites.

During the close season the manager sold Mike Sheron for £1 million to Norwich after 98 appearances, plus 22 as substitute. It was a disappointing transfer of a talented forward, but with the form of Walsh and Rösler it was also one Horton felt would not unduly harm his plans. Another to leave was David Rocastle who joined Chelsea for a reported £1.25 million. Horton: "We have an abundance of midfield players and I think Rocky suspected he was going to be one of the odd men out. Some players are quite happy to be part of the senior squad, but I don't think this would have been the case with David. He was upset when he was left out of a couple of pre-season matches. It is hard to see where I could have accommodated him in the system I have in mind. The offer came out of the blue, and I felt it was good business, but the final decision was his."

A few weeks earlier, the Blues made their only major signing of the summer when they paid Swindon Town £1.5 million for Nicky Summerbee. Understandably, supporters were keen to see if the 23-year-old could compare with his father, the brilliant 60s hero Mike.

Summerbee made his debut in the opening League fixture - a 3-0 defeat at Arsenal. The Blues had conceded as early as the second minute and Rösler was sent off after an hour for dissent. Fortunately a 3-0 win over West Ham in the first League fixture at Maine Road following demolition of the Kippax suggested the campaign might offer more than the previous one, especially as the trio of Blue heroes - Beagrie, Walsh and Rösler - each scored. Three days later it was 4-0 as two goals apiece from Walsh and Rösler humiliated Everton and sent a delighted Brian Horton to face the press. In typical Horton-speak he stated: "It was an excellent team performance, wasn't it?" By this point in his City career the public were finding it a little entertaining that the manager ended every sentence with a question. At least it proved he was human, didn't it?

The only minus point about these two fine Maine Road performances was that too few Blues had been able to view the matches. Because of the Kippax redevelopment, the capacity was severely reduced and both games were attended by more or less sell-out crowds of less than 20,000. Fortunately, City's new Chairman and Managing Director had taken steps to ensure the capacity increased as the season progressed.

The lower level of the new three tier stand would be constructed and seated first allowing the mid-season capacity to reach around 25,000 and the May figure to be almost 28,000. Had the stadium been able to accommodate over 30,000 it's likely this first season under Lee would have seen the Blues watched by their highest average since the 34,000 of 1981-82.

A 3-0 defeat at Chelsea followed on 31st August before September brought five points from three games. The third of those games - a 2-0 win against Norwich - saw Niall Quinn net his

The new Kippax takes shape. The stand was opened in sections with capacity increasing game by game.

first goal since returning from injury. Unfortunately, the Eire international would find himself the odd man out for much of the 1994-95 season as Walsh and Rösler were Horton's preferred strike force. Nevertheless, Quinn did manage to start 24 League games, come on as substitute in a further 11, and score a total of eight League goals - a record considerably better than any of the previous campaign's strikers when Sheron ended as top scorer with a pitiful six.

On 15th October, the away game at QPR proved dramatic; with 30 minutes to go, the Blues were leading 2-0, thanks to Garry Flitcroft and Paul Walsh. QPR fought back and managed to reduce City's lead, although the goal was a controversial one. Andy Dibble, playing his second League game of the season, was adjudged to have punched clear while outside his area. Former City player Clive Wilson took the resultant free-kick and, as he made contact with the ball, the referee appeared to blow his whistle. The City players believed the kick was to be retaken and simply stood motionless, while the ball sailed past Dibble's left hand and into the net. The referee then signalled a goal and, understandably, City complained. Protesting captain Keith Curle was booked, and a shade fortunate to remain on the pitch.

A few minutes later Les Ferdinand charged towards Dibble's net; the City 'keeper put out a leg and Ferdinand crashed to the ground. The linesman flagged and Dibble was sent off for a professional foul, again hotly disputed by the City players. Nicky Summerbee, who was finding it difficult to match the expectations of the fans, was immediately replaced by the still injured Tony Coton. The 'keeper was struggling with a back injury and endured terrible pain as the Blues determined to keep their lead.

It wasn't long before full back Richard Edghill made life even more difficult for the Blues when he was also dismissed for felling Trevor Sinclair once too often. For nine-man City those final fifteen minutes seemed an

eternity as QPR missed a number of chances while Coton, obviously in pain, made a few heroic saves. Yet another match between the two sides had made the headlines. In previous years fixtures between the clubs had marked the commencement of Lee's takeover bid, and the first League game broadcast live by Sky TV. What would the next QPR fixture have in store? The Blues did not have to wait long as the two sides were due to meet in the League Cup on 25th October.

Before that, however, City had the task of facing a Jürgen Klinsmann-inspired Tottenham Hotspur in the League. Much had been made of the arrival of the German World Cup hero and the media proclaimed him as one of the most important foreign players of the period, with much hype following his every move. As a result little had been said about City's own German entertainer Uwe Rösler, still missing following an injury sustained almost a month earlier against Norwich.

In a thrilling match, the Blues tore into Tottenham and after seventeen minutes, Steve Lomas made a run down the right, and sent in an impressive cross to Niall Quinn. Campbell intercepted but Paul Walsh managed to retrieve the ball and fired past goalkeeper Walker.

Spurs, playing a good passing game, levelled the scores on the half hour via Dumitrescu's penalty, but it was obvious the Blues were still controlling much of the action.

A short while later, a City counter-attack led to another goal. Lomas passed out wide to Summerbee who in turn crossed to Walsh. The former Portsmouth player headed powerfully at Walker before Quinn blasted in the rebound to make it 2-1. Five minutes later Terry Phelan knocked the ball to Peter Beagrie who managed to beat two players before releasing Quinn who set Walsh up to score City's third.

A minute into the second half, Klinsmann and Dumitrescu combined for the latter to make it 3-2 via a deflection off Curle. Five minutes later Walsh ran from inside his own half then, as he fell, somehow managed to pass to Beagrie. The former Everton man crossed to the unmarked Lomas who powered home a beautiful header.

With only ten minutes left Walsh made another brilliant run, passing four players on his travels, before turning and crossing to Garry Flitcroft, who netted to make it 5-2 and complete a marvellous performance. It had been a game of memorable quality and was enjoyed by millions on Match Of The Day that night. Commentator John Motson made comparisons with the famous 'Ballet On Ice' from 1967, and the BBC reminded viewers of the skills of that match by showing a few minutes of black and white footage.

Three days later City followed up with another entertaining performance. It was the League Cup encounter at QPR on 25th October. The Blues had already disposed of Barnet 5-2 on aggregate in the second round and clearly expected to put in a good performance at Loftus Road. Sadly, within a minute they conceded a goal just as they had in the earlier League Cup match at Barnet and Horton's side suffered for a while. By the 37th minute they managed to get their act together a little and Summerbee equalised with a 20 yard volley. A minute later Rangers took the lead again.

Fortunately, in the 46th minute Keith Curle netted a penalty to bring City level once again, followed eight minutes later by a magnificent Beagrie volley which made it 3-2 and brought a series of somersaults from the popular ex-Evertonian. Five minutes later, the same player headed through to Lomas who made it 4-2.

In the 87th minute Rangers pulled a goal back to keep City on their toes, but the referee's whistle signalled the start of a party for the fans while their QPR equivalents began to demonstrate against their chairman. Apparently, some unhappy QPR fans were keen to listen to the advice of a few experienced Mancunian demonstrators.

In the next round City overcame Newcastle 2-0 at St. James Park after a 1-1 draw at Maine Road. German import Maurizio Gaudino made his debut in that victory in a match captained by Garry Flitcroft. Afterwards Kevin Keegan admitted City deserved to win and told the press he hoped the Blues would go on to win the trophy. Sadly, a fifth round encounter at Crystal Palace prevented that from happening when, on 11th January, the Blues succumbed to a 4-0 hammering. Horton's side crumbled on a night when the impressive Steve Lomas crashed to the ground with a broken ankle. He also swallowed his tongue, bringing back painful memories of the Paul Lake incident during the 1988-89 season, and went on to miss the rest of the season. It was a huge blow.

Back in the League, City should have defeated Coventry but lost 1-0 in the closing minutes, then a 3-3 draw with Alan Ball's Southampton raised a few concerns. It also brought a little humour as the visitors' 'keeper Bruce Grobbelaar looked as if he was auditioning for a part in Phantom of the Opera as he wore a mask throughout the game to protect his broken cheekbone.

Then on Thursday 10th November came one of the worst nights in the Blue history of Manchester football when City travelled to Trafford for the 121st Manchester League derby. The Blues had only received around 1800 tickets - although this was considerably more than previous years - and were seated in the corner between 'K' Stand and the Main Stand. Among the away contingent was City's biggest hero of the period, Uwe Rösler, who was still out through injury.

As the great German made his way to his seat a few supporters approached and asked for autographs. Naturally he obliged, but an over-zealous United steward marched towards the City player and insisted he sat down. In faltering English Rösler tried to explain but the official didn't seem prepared to listen and started to order the player into his seat.

At this point another, more sensible, steward arrived and explained to the first that this 'fan' was actually Rösler. The first official shouted: "I don't care who he is, he's still got to sit down!" Eventually, the jobsworth saw sense and allowed Rösler to continue signing autographs for the Blues who had formed an orderly queue. The steward walked away muttering: "These City people are all the same. They've got ideas above their station and they won't listen to reason."

The match commenced in typical 1990s derby style with City putting United under considerable pressure throughout the first quarter. Richard Edghill seemed to have the measure of Ryan Giggs and an early challenge by the City man sent his opponent flying to the floor. All Blues - including those of German nationality - seated in the away section cheered, and those opening minutes were a real joy. Sadly, in the 24th minute, very much against the general run of play Eric Cantona gave United the lead. After that the Blues fought back on occasion but the game from thereon was simply a nightmare.

At 4-0 with twenty minutes to go many City supporters drifted off to their Manchester homes. Even Uwe Rösler chose this moment to make his exit - to a fantastic ovation from those Blues remaining. Earlier his already excellent image improved when he attempted to sing a number of City chants including 'Blue Moon' and the ironic 'City is our name', although he struggled to understand many of the words.

For those who were left the agony continued. Every City fan seemed to be praying for an end to the misery. "Don't let it get to five" they muttered over and over again. Then it happened. Kanchelskis scored his third of the match, and the first derby hat-trick since Francis Lee in 1970, to make it 5-0.

Fortunately, the game ended before United could equal the record derby score of six - held by City, of course, since 1926 and matched in 2011-12. Afterwards a shell-shocked Horton faced the media, unlike his opposite number in 1989: "When we needed to stand up and be counted some of our players did not want to know, did they?"

Although he could have taken the easy option and blamed the result on injuries - remember City were missing Rösler, Curle, and both goalkeepers Dibble and Coton - he chose not to. It was a credit to him that he faced the music.

Despite the result City managed to pick themselves up and achieve three successive victories in the following matches, including their first win at Ipswich since 1961. Despite that, December turned out a dismal month with four of the six matches ending in defeat, while January brought two points from a possible nine. It wasn't until 22nd February that the Blues managed their first League victory since the Ipswich match. Co-incidentally, that was the return fixture with the East Anglian club. The goalless draw with Leeds three days later should have ended in victory but somehow dominance could not be turned into goals, although it is fair to say the Blues were still struggling with injury and missed four influential players - Rösler, Walsh, Beagrie, and Flitcroft.

A 1-1 draw at Norwich and a 2-1 defeat at home to Chelsea left City in 16th place and clearly in danger of relegation. It was an extremely tense time for all connected with the Club especially the supporters who had dearly hoped the arrival of Lee might actually propel City towards the top of the table, not the bottom.

A relegation dogfight at Everton on 15th March ended in a 1-1 draw and a sending-off for Terry Phelan for time-wasting, before a 3-2 defeat of Sheffield Wednesday brought a much needed boost to morale. The Blues had been 2-0 down at one point before fighting back courtesy of goals from Walsh and Rösler (2). Despite that result the following three League games all ended in defeat before a Good Friday meeting with Liverpool brought a shock 2-1 victory. Deliberately Horton played a strong attacking formation with Quinn, Rösler and Walsh all present in the starting line-up.

After a bright start, the Blues took the lead in the 18th minute as Summerbee scored his first City League goal following a perfect pass from Gaudino. It was an important goal, especially as Summerbee was still finding it difficult to fit into Horton's side. Although the Blues continued to play with confidence, the impressive McManaman started to bring the Anfield men back into the match.

It was no surprise when the exciting Liverpool youngster scored an absolutely brilliant equaliser and kept his side in the game until a bruising tackle by Flitcroft, early in the second half, sent him limping off. The injury helped City dominate the rest of the encounter and Rösler, in particular, seemed to thrive. He spurned a couple of chances before setting up fellow countryman Gaudino to score fifteen minutes from time. It was a thoroughly deserved goal and victory, and gave Horton confidence relegation could be avoided.

A 3-2 victory against championship favourites Blackburn followed at Ewood Park on Easter Monday. Horton later admitted it was the best performance since his arrival while Blackburn boss Kenny Dalglish was shell-shocked: "Where have Manchester City been all season when they can play like that?"

Where indeed! As all supporters knew, the Blues were the great unpredictables of soccer and defeating the Champions elect while struggling to avoid relegation was not an uncommon occurrence for them. 1994-95 had been an unpredictable, inconsistent season.

Over the weeks that followed, with veteran John Burridge in goal, City achieved a 1-1 draw at Villa. Burridge, who was on loan from Newcastle, came on as a half time substitute against his permanent team Newcastle on 29th April 1995 to make his debut. He was 43 years, 4 months and 26 days and became the oldest player to appear in the Premier League. He started the following three games and ended his City career at home to QPR 15 days after the Newcastle match.

The penultimate game of the campaign saw Horton's side suffer a 1-0 defeat at Nottingham Forest. This was followed by an absolutely appalling 3-2 loss at home to QPR on the final day of the season. That match ensured almost every City-QPR fixture of the 1990s was remembered for one reason or another, but it did little for Brian Horton. Had the side played with more conviction he may have been able to build and develop a team capable of challenging for honours. Unfortunately, it was clear there were still a few problems at Maine Road.

The season wound up with City in 17th place. Had that final match ended on a high note with a win the Blues would have moved five places higher into a position of some respectability. That's how close the League was that season.

The sacking of Brian Horton on 16th May - two days after the final match of the season - was rather confusing to most supporters as newspapers that morning claimed he'd actually been dismissed minutes after the pathetic performance against QPR. On radio at around 8am on the 16th, City secretary Bernard Halford denied the rumours and insisted Horton was still the boss. In St. Albans Horton told the media: "If I've been sacked it's the first I've heard about it. My position certainly wasn't discussed after Saturday's match, but I think an urgent meeting is needed to clarify my position."

A short while later Colin Barlow, City's Managing Director, also dismissed the rumours: "Those stories are totally without foundation. Brian Horton is still the manager of City."

At lunch time, Horton met Lee and the inevitable happened. He was sacked: "There were no arguments. The Chairman was very calm and so was I. The decision wasn't totally unexpected. Every manager is judged on results and we simply didn't win enough matches this season to keep me in a job. But even so it still hurt like hell to be given the sack."

At 2pm Colin Barlow read out a prepared statement at a hastily arranged press conference and wished Horton well for the future. He refused to provide any further information. The media speculated on the reasons for the dismissal.

For most supporters the departure of Horton seemed a might unfair, after all he had made a number of good signings, and there had been quite a few positive points during the season such as reaching the fifth round of the League Cup. City had also reached the same round of the FA Cup, although the peculiar law that surrounds the Blues seems to insist that whenever they draw the same side in both cup competitions they must lose the FA Cup match. Usually they also lose the League Cup match, but this time Newcastle United could only manage to scupper City's chances of a blue Wembley in the FA Cup by winning 3-1 at St. James Park. Despite the positives, it was decided Horton had to go.

In the aftermath of the sacking Lee and Barlow felt certain they could appoint a man who they felt would be a big improvement on Horton, and fans waited eagerly to hear who this new high profile manager would be.

The media were suggesting a number of possibilities including Bruce Rioch, David Pleat, Mick McCarthy,

Bobby Robson, Brian Kidd, and George Graham, plus of course old favourites Dave Bassett and Steve Coppell who seemed destined to always be included in any list of possible Blue managers. By the end of May, Ray Harford, Ron Atkinson and John Toshack were added to this string of prospects.

Earlier Colin Barlow told the public City would be appointing a high profile manager with a proven track record. He added: "Francis and myself, as former players, know exactly what the Club and the fans want and that is a manager who can take us into Europe. Europe next year has to be our target. That means finishing in the top five or six clubs or winning a major cup competition. It means we are not in a position to appoint someone without the necessary experience."

He later added: "There is no immediate pressure on us to appoint a new man. The letters that are coming in are from people with impressive records, while telephone enquiries are from managers quite definitely in the big name category."

Hearing this everyone began to believe the new manager would be one with an impressive c.v. Similar to that of Howard Kendall when he was first appointed in 1989. The official comments certainly seemed aimed at building the supporters up for a major personality with a successful managerial track record and, when it was announced on 29th May City were confident of getting their man within a week, the fans really were filled with optimism. Sadly, an appointment did not materialise and rumours again were rife. Brian Kidd appeared a front runner but it was announced United would deny the Blues permission to speak with Alex Ferguson's assistant. At the time Kidd himself stated: "I have absolutely no

Niall Quinn Scores City's first goal in Brian Horton's last game, 14th May 1995.

intention of leaving United. I have been at the Club since boyhood and I love my job here. I have no desire to go to City or anywhere else. I have told the chairman that I do not wish to speak to any other club."

As the managerial rumours continued, most fans began to doubt that any of the names being suggested that summer would give them more entertainment than Horton's side had. The former manager explained in 2004 how he would have loved to have been there longer: "I believe you need at least three or four years to be given a fair crack, but I have to say I think we did entertain. We didn't always get the results we wanted – or deserved – but I did think we'd be okay.

"There was a time when we hovered about 6th place and that was good – I had an opportunity to move to another Club which I turned down - and there was a game away at Blackburn (17th April 1995) when we won 3-2 but it could easily have been 5-2. Flitcroft had two disallowed and we were unstoppable against the team that ended up winning the League. I guess the best game though was the 5-2 win over Tottenham (22nd October 1994). That was a wonderfully exciting game and I remember John Motson saying something like it was the best game he had ever seen at Maine Road.

"The first season we finished 16th and I had high hopes for the 1994-95 season. We started well with great wins over West Ham (3-0) and Everton (4-0) and we really did think it was the start of something. David Pleat used to watch us and I remember him coming to me after one game and saying 'I really enjoyed that'. It meant a great deal to me.

"We faced Kevin Keegan's Newcastle in both competitions and beat them 2-0 in the fourth round of the League Cup – we had a bit of a patched up side that day as well – and then they beat us 3-1 in the FA Cup. In the League Cup quarter-final against Crystal Palace we struggled in the final 20 minutes or so and ended up losing 4-0! It could have been so much different.

"I loved the twenty months I was here. I loved the supporters, the players, the staff… I'm just sorry that during my time as manager we couldn't win a trophy. We had a lot of excitement, but it would have been great to win something. Having said that we did play good, exciting football in two Premiership seasons."

1995-1996 Managerial Change

By 18th June 1995 it appeared there were two candidates in the running to be City's new manager. Most assumed George Graham was one, especially as he had been seen waiting to be met at Piccadilly station. The other was a complete mystery, although when Huddersfield Town appointed Brian Horton as manager on the 21st some Blues joked the City directors would have to remove him from their short list.

It wasn't long however before the other name became public - World Cup winner Alan Ball. On 30th June, while Ball was on holiday in Spain, an announcement was made that the Southampton manager would be offered the post. The fans were totally unimpressed with the appointment after all the hyperbole throughout the summer. They wanted the promised highly successful, high profile manager with a proven track record and would not accept Ball was that man. The fanzine *Electric Blue* typified the supporters' reactions: "Brian Kidd had embarrassed City by declaring his intention to wallow a while longer at The Sty and George Graham had yet to clear his name, both time and prospective managers were in short supply.

"Hardly surprising then that City should trawl the depths and come up with the name of Alan Ball. Yes, I know, Alan Ball! He of the flame red hair, old bloke's cap and the irritating squeaky voice... I couldn't believe it either. Unlike the previous incumbent of the warm seat, Ball - or Bally as he is known amongst those in the know - is, at least, a household name. No embarrassing cries of 'Alan Who?' were heard in Manchester this time around; instead 'Why Ball?' or words to that effect were in the ascendancy. Of course the answer is almost as simple as the question. Not to put too fine a point on it, there was no one else around. City would doubtless say that they were inundated with prospective managers, most of whom would have been jokers whose only management experience would have been gleaned plying their trade with pub teams the length and breadth of Lancashire anyway!"

Although some supporters did warm to Ball, and others suggested it might be wise to see what improvements he could make to Horton's side before applying a judgement, the majority were clearly sceptical at the appointment. There was a view the other candidate, George Graham, should have been given the job despite his problems with the FA Colin Barlow told the media: "I know George Graham has a lot of fans among our supporters but time was against us as far as he was concerned."

Graham claimed it had been up to him to take the job or not: "It would have been easy for me to have taken the Manchester City job while I was waiting for the FA panel to get their act together, but I did not wish to embarrass City chairman Francis Lee, who had chatted to me about the vacancy at Maine Road before giving the job to my old Arsenal team mate Alan Ball."

On 4th July, with supporter mutterings mounting, Colin Barlow felt it was time to plead for patience: "We would ask fans to reserve their judgement on Alan Ball and give him the time he surely deserves. We will not allow anything to stand in our way. Our aim is and always has been, a team with flair and style playing football on the ground and that will come with Alan

Ball. That's his style and his philosophy. Couple his appointment with the signing of a couple of skilful players and we will be well on the way."

That statement in itself gave the fans another opportunity to attack the appointment. If, as expected, Ball proved unable to bring a 'couple of skilful' players to the Club in the short term then more pressure would be applied.

Barlow went on to compare the appointment with that of Joe Mercer in 1965, stating City's greatest manager had a similar record to Ball before arriving at Maine Road, although Joe had won a trophy.

For many it seemed City's PR machine had failed. Dave Wallace, editor of fanzine *King Of The Kippax*, felt he could have warned the directors how the supporters would react. Wallace had been appointed the Club's first 'Fan on the Board' with a mandate to inform the directors of supporters' concerns and feelings. The role was not an easy one as, no matter who filled the position, it was an impossible task to represent all supporters. In addition, some directors may have felt uncomfortable hearing their views challenged by a 'mere fan'. Nevertheless, the role was an important breakthrough in the relationship between the Club and its followers, even if it was far from perfect. Making use of Wallace at the time of the appointment of Ball could have benefited the City management, or at the very least made them aware of how supporters might react.

Dave Wallace wrote his view in *King Of The Kippax*: "We were led to believe we'd be having a massive name, with a track record, and when Bally's name emerged it was a tremendous anti-climax. I'm astounded the Club didn't anticipate our reaction to the news. Apparently everyone who rang the Chairman thought it was a cracking appointment, and everyone who rang me thought it wasn't! Once their first choice had bit the dust this would have been an ideal opportunity to bounce the idea off the Fans' Rep. I know I couldn't realistically have influenced the decision, but I could have pointed out that we'd need some persuading that this is a good move for City, and that it isn't good enough that he's an old mate, with a liking for the gee gees, as it was presented to us in the press."

As far as Francis Lee was concerned the appointment may have been described in the press as an old pals reunion but in actual fact the relationship between Lee and Ball never came into it: "I had to make a very important and serious decision and old pals' acts simply don't feature in decisions as crucial as the one I had to make. Besides, I have always set out to employ people here who are proud to be associated with the blue shirt of Manchester City, and I know for sure that Alan will feel that pride."

Despite Lee's comments the majority of supporters were still concerned. A quote from former Chairman

Peter Swales later in the year, concerning players, could equally have been applied to the appointment of City's managers: "You can never ever kid supporters. They know great players. It's no good a manager saying, 'this is the best player we've ever had'. The supporters will know after a few weeks whether he really is the best. One thing you can never do is kid supporters. You can build them up, and get them hoping for the future but supporters en bloc will know a player. No question."

Francis Lee was still learning. During his time as a player at Maine Road the supporters were, in the main, perfectly happy with performances on the pitch and the efforts of the players and the management, but after his departure the atmosphere around Maine Road changed, especially during the 1980s and early 90s. The fans were desperate for success and hoped Lee's takeover would totally transform the Club, and bring the success they yearned for. Unfortunately, a transformation of the kind required was always likely to take years rather than months and, unlike his predecessor, Lee was under pressure almost immediately. The honeymoon period was over and the appointment of Alan Ball did little to convince anyone that better days lay ahead.

Despite the scepticism of the fans, the new manager tried to get on with his job and outline his hopes. He firmly believed the squad was of a good quality: "We have got talent here, there's no doubting that. I've got to integrate them into my way of thinking - they've got to be told what I expect from individuals and players. What I've basically said to them up to now is that I've got to earn their respect and they've got to earn mine. I ask every player to train and play to their strengths, and when they can all do that you've got a good team."

He went on to outline what he thought it was possible for the team to achieve: "It's not beyond the realms of possibility to win a cup. Apart from that, I want stability in the Premiership. I want a comfortable season in which we banish any possibilities of relegation. I want the supporters to see young players coming through. And I want them to see that the ship knows what direction it's going in."

There was no doubting Ball's enthusiasm for the job, or his knowledge of the game, however his managerial record had not been the best and a significant improvement at the start of the season would be necessary before the new man gained acceptance. Happily, Ball's assistant was former hero Asa Hartford whose appointment was viewed as a major plus.

On the playing front the close season had seen a few changes. Maurizio Gaudino, the German who seemed to have great potential but also a tendency to grab the headlines for questionable off-field activity, left the Blues despite almost signing permanently in the middle of the managerless period. At the time Colin Barlow stated: "We didn't feel it would be right to sign Maurizio

Gaudino before our new manager was appointed."

Surprisingly, throughout the period prior to Ball's appointment Niall Quinn, one of the Club's biggest stars, almost transferred to Sporting Lisbon. Fortunately the deal fell through, but most agreed it would have been a mistake losing a player of his proven ability prior to any managerial appointment.

Then on 15th July City made a signing that would ultimately become one of the most important in the Club's history - Georgiou Kinkladze. The Georgian international arrived at Maine Road in a £2 million, three year deal. Apparently the Blues had chased him for six months after being tipped off by a European scout. Francis Lee watched him three times, while Jimmy Frizzell and Colin Bell also went to see him play. Alan Ball was most taken after seeing only five minutes of him in action on video.

Kinkladze had also impressed a number of other clubs, including AC Milan and Barcelona, so it was a major coup for the City Chairman to sign him: "I am thrilled that Georgiou has joined us. He is a wonderful young player who will delight our supporters."

Ball added: "His technique is excellent and his passing and vision are first class. We might just have found ourselves a gem."

Kinkladze wasn't the only summer arrival as Portsmouth defender Kit Symons arrived in a £1.5 million deal which also saw Carl Griffiths and Fitzroy Simpson move to Fratton Park. The consistent Symons had previously been coached by Alan Ball at Portsmouth, and the new City manager rated him highly: "Kit is a born winner. He wants to do well, he is the kind of player who belongs here at City. He is good in the air and on the ground, has a first class attitude, and I have no doubt he will do well in the Premier Division."

Two days before the season commenced the Blues signed Eike Immel, a vastly experienced former German international goalkeeper, for £400,000 from VfB Stuttgart. Injuries to Tony Coton and Andy Dibble had left City with a goalkeeping crisis, although Martyn Margetson was still waiting for a decent run in the first team. Immel, Kinkladze and Symons made their debuts against Tottenham on 19th August, the opening day of the 1995-96 season, at Maine Road.

That match ended in a 1-1 draw with Rösler scoring a looping header five minutes into the second half to level the scores. Kinkladze had impressed and, overall, the Blues were happy especially those singing "There's only one German striker" - a reference not only to the goalscorer, but also the fact the talismanic forward Jürgen Klinsmann had deserted Spurs.

City's joy wasn't to last however as eight sorry successive League defeats left the Blues languishing at the bottom of the table. The last of these was the Old Trafford derby, played before 35,707 with no tickets allocated to City. Naturally, some Blues did make it into the venue but the atmosphere was terribly one-sided and left Ball's men under immense pressure. The only goal of the match came after just four minutes when Keith Curle deflected in Paul Scholes' header, but City's marking was exceptionally poor.

The Blues did try to fight back, but Niall Quinn squandered the best effort prompting much ridicule from the United fans behind the goal. A photo of Quinn taken immediately after the miss appeared in many newspapers over the course of the following week. It highlighted City's disappointment, but it also showed a large number of United fans abusing the Irish international. The *Daily Telegraph* followed up, publishing letters criticising the behaviour of those supporters. It was sad to see so much hatred and ridicule, although to many it was a typical derby day reaction.

Following the Manchester derby City played out a goalless match with Leeds at Maine Road and then travelled to Anfield for a third round League Cup tie. The Blues had already beaten Wycombe (4-0 on aggregate), but recognised a meeting with Liverpool was not going to be quite so easy. The match ended in a depressing 4-0 defeat, but even that wasn't as bad as what followed three days later. The Anfield League meeting between the two sides ended in a humiliating 6-0 defeat, prompting ironic chants of "Alan Ball is a football genius." Uwe Rösler threw his boots into the crowd as a protest and now the pressure was on. In 1937 the Blues had defeated Liverpool 10-1 on aggregate over a similar time frame, but nothing could compensate for the feeling of failure felt on 28th October 1995. It was a major disappointment, although Alan Ball told the press he actually enjoyed watching the Liverpool performance!

Results finally did pick up in November lifting City up to 15th and bringing Alan Ball the Manager of the Month award, but by the New Year the Blues were back in the relegation zone.

On Tuesday 12th December, City held their annual AGM. It was not as controversial as in previous years, but it did give shareholders an opportunity to quiz the new manager. Several interesting points were raised and it appeared Ball was keen to tell the truth about his role, City's plight, and the problems of particularly players. His frank, honest approach impressed many and did much to reassure fans his thinking was right. Some of his views looked back to 'the good old days' of the early 70s when football was a completely different game, and many supporters probably agreed with him but the inescapable truth was players of the 90s had an entirely different outlook to those of twenty years earlier. The power base had shifted from the Club to the players and City had to accept it like the rest, even if the principle seemed wrong.

In addition to the frank comments, one moment during Ball's question and answer session lightened the mood. The City manager acknowledged the impressive work of Kinkladze during what had been a difficult time for the player as he tried to adjust to life in England. Ball stated City had got permission and made arrangements to bring the player's mother to England, which prompted one fan to shout: "Why? Can she play a bit? She could fill in at left-back!"

January only brought one defeat - the return fixture with Spurs - but the Blues were not moving up the table. Fortunately, January also saw the start of City's FA Cup run. Ball had suggested at the season's start the Blues were capable of winning one of the cup competitions and with the League Cup campaign over the FA Cup was City's last chance of glory.

The Blues managed to reach the fifth round after home wins over Leicester (5-0 in a replay) and Coventry (2-1 in another replay) and really fancied their chances. Unfortunately the fifth round tie sent the Blues back to Old Trafford for a meeting with United. This time there would be over 8,000 City fans in attendance to ensure the atmosphere was not totally one-sided. If anything the noise generated by the travelling support was far in excess of anything coming from the home fans.

The match kicked off at 4pm with City attacking the end containing their vociferous supporters, and for much of the opening period the Blues made the Reds suffer. Within 30 minutes United were behind as Kinkladze fed a superb pass to the advancing Rösler. The German charged forward and sent an astonishing lob over Schmeichel into the net for the opening goal. It was a thoroughly deserved advantage. The Blues were combining perfectly as a unit and the entire side performed magnificently until disaster struck via one of the FA Cup's more controversial incidents.

Alan Ball: "There could not have been a happier manager in the country at 4.30 on Sunday afternoon, with my team a goal in front, and the United fans silenced as they watched their team run out of ideas very quickly. We were causing a lot of problems, and then came that incident which will be remembered by many at this club for years to come. I am not a person who makes excuses, but it was a bewildering refereeing decision which turned a game upside down."

For a very brief period action had moved to the opposite end of the pitch, where United were struggling to find an opening. There were a number of players in the box but there seemed little danger before referee Alan Wilkie blew his whistle. Roy Keane immediately protested, believing he was to be penalised, but the Irishman's attitude and approach changed rapidly as it dawned Wilkie had given United a penalty. No supporter present could understand why, and much discussion amongst City fans failed to provide a sensible answer.

Those watching live on BBC had the opportunity to see slow motion replays which brought the conclusion it was for an 'incident' between City's German defender Michael Frontzeck and United's Eric Cantona. The two players jumped together but there hardly seemed any contact let alone anything malicious from Frontzeck.

The BBC's Alan Hansen found the whole affair ridiculous: "That decision was absolutely disgraceful." Every journalist felt the same. Henry Winter (*Daily Telegraph*): "Frontzeck, a German international not averse to a touch of rough and tumble, certainly made contact with Cantona but similar scenes are witnessed in the bump and jump of every corner, of every match. The decision incensed City."

The *Manchester Evening News'* United reporter Stuart Mathieson agreed with the general mood: "Luck is a vital ingredient when you are following a recipe for Wembley success and United are enjoying a liberal dollop of it. True the German was manhandling Cantona but it was no more than the kind of argy-bargy going on elsewhere in the penalty area and, at that moment, if Cantona was going to reach the ball he would have had to be standing on Frontzeck's shoulders."

Naturally, with the resultant penalty the Reds equalised and the game ended as a contest. The City players and supporters felt no matter how hard they tried, or how well they performed, the game was going United's way. Had the Blues entered half-time a goal in front, they would more than likely have won the contest. Football did not seem a fair game that weekend for City fans.

In the second half United took the lead and entered the draw for the sixth round. Again, luck worked in their favour as they were presented with the easiest remaining draw - Swindon or Southampton at home - to further anger the City faithful. *The Guardian's* David Lacey held a similar view: "Fate first helped United beat City with the aid of a harshly-judged penalty and then gave them a highly-winnable quarter final at home to Swindon or Southampton. Should United go on to win the Cup ... The sky blue half of Manchester will no doubt be hoping that their celebratory toasts are coupled with the name of Alan Wilkie."

The following week on the BBC's Football Focus the game was analysed in more detail with Gary Lineker stressing how wrong the penalty decision had been. The programme showed a number of other incidents and Lineker made reference to a foul in the area by Steve Bruce on Kit Symons that was considerably worse than the alleged infringement from Frontzeck.

It was difficult for anyone connected with the Blues to pick themselves up that week, but with typical City spirit the following match allowed everyone to begin to erase memories of the game from their minds. League leaders Newcastle arrived at Maine Road expecting to

Kinkladze was always special to fans.

Stands, and inadvertently muted the atmosphere. By the time the players came out the supporters had started to sing again, and the mood seemed right.

A minute's silence was observed for former Chairman Peter Swales who had passed away earlier in the week. His early death was a shock and the fans ensured he was remembered with respect. Of course, the majority of supporters had opposed Swales for most of his final years as Chairman, but they still understood and appreciated his love of and devotion to the Club.

When the game started the fans willed the Blues on, but it was Liverpool who took the lead when a mis-hit pass from Nigel Clough, who had joined City for £1million from Anfield four months earlier, allowed Liverpool to race forward. The Blues conceded a corner and a hopeful effort from McManaman was sliced in by Steve Lomas. It was a terrible time to score an own goal, but the player had been hampered by the pitch which was not in the best of condition following two major concerts by City supporters Oasis a week earlier.

Despite their lead, Liverpool did not appear too interested and to many Blues it felt as if the Merseysiders were keen to see City survive. It appeared Liverpool would have been quite content to allow the Blues to equalise, but the game actually moved further from City when Ian Rush made it 2-0. Surely the Blues could fight back against a side that didn't seem too concerned about the result?

City did retaliate and when Kinkladze was bundled over for a penalty with 20 minutes to go the Blues were presented with their best chance. Rösler blasted the spot kick home to make the score 2-1. Niall Quinn was substituted for 19-year-old Martin 'Buster' Phillips, who had joined City in November from Exeter, and then in the 78th minute he helped fashion the equaliser when he latched on to a Summerbee corner and knocked it back for Kit Symons at the far post to make it 2-2.

Almost immediately rumours spread that Coventry were losing and 2-2 would be enough to guarantee City's survival. Alan Ball, it seemed, was taken in by these and instructed his side to time-waste. Steve Lomas followed his manager's advice much to the annoyance of Niall Quinn who leapt from his seat, raced to the touchline and started shouting at the player and the rest of the side. Seeing this, the crowd grasped the Coventry scoreline had to be wrong and they too urged City to fight on. Quinn: "I'd been substituted and was sat watching a monitor. I knew the way the scores were going elsewhere and knew that we were down unless we won. Alan Ball, God bless him, was given incorrect information. I went down there and told him the truth but the announcer guy was down there and he said I was wrong, so nobody accepted it. I saw us holding the ball in the corner and couldn't stand it. I charged down the touchline shouting for them to open up play. I

leave with three easy points but a stirring battle from the Blues resulted in a 3-3 draw. City had been ahead but allowed Newcastle to score their third in the 81st minute. Keith Curle was cynically head-butted by Newcastle's Colombian maverick Asprilla in the final minutes, while the Blues also had a penalty appeal turned down. If only Alan Wilkie had been refereeing!

Kinkladze was the undisputed Man of the Match, and the BBC delighted in showing the Georgian at his best. City fans had known how special he was all season, the rest of the country were only just beginning to appreciate his silky skills. Despite many impressive performances from Gio, the Blues still struggled in far too many games and on the final day of the season they lay in the relegation zone, third from bottom, on 37 points; the same total as two sides above them used to avoiding the drop, Southampton and Coventry. In simple terms, all City needed to do was earn a point more than either of these sides. Southampton were at home to Wimbledon, while Coventry faced Leeds at Highfield Road. City had the daunting task of a match with Liverpool.

Prior to the game, compere Vince Miller tried to enliven spirits by singing "Blue Moon", and then followed with "Land of Hope and Glory", which drowned out the singing of City fans seated in the Kippax and North

TRUE BLUE
Georgi Kinkladze

An emotional Kinkladze leaves the field after the City-Liverpool match.

shouldn't have done it in some ways because it made Alan Ball look bad, but I couldn't stand to see us get it wrong."

Amazingly, while the Blues played keep-ball in the corner nearest the Family Stand, Liverpool did all they could to open up play. It was bizarre that the side who frankly didn't care about the result were keen to expand the game more than a team who should have been looking for victory. Who says games between Manchester and Merseyside are always bitter affairs?

The crucial amount of time wasted as a result of unsubstantiated rumours left City unable to find the winner, and the match ended in a draw. The Blues were down and that evening Niall Quinn appeared on Match of the Day to apologise to the fans. It wasn't his fault and he, at least, had tried to fire up the players during those fateful final minutes: "I was shell-shocked. Everything had been great and going forward in my life and career. I didn't expect City to fail. I didn't feel able to cope with it but knew that the only thing I could do was apologise. I felt I had to face the music. The fans at least deserved that."

Watching from the stand that day was John Wardle. Wardle, along with David Makin, was one of the founders of JD Sports: "I have a painful memory of being on the Kippax when we were relegated in 1996 and seeing on the opposite touchline Niall Quinn running down shouting at the other players to open up play while the manager Alan Ball just watched. Ian Rush was playing that day for Liverpool and didn't even seem to be trying. It looked as if Liverpool wanted us to win because had we won, then we'd have stayed up. It's a wonder they didn't analyse the Liverpool approach because if that happened now everyone would question it. I was yelling from the Kippax but at that time I was just a fan.

"We floated JD Sports in 1996 and so we had some cash. Francis Lee was City Chairman at the time and there's no doubt about it City were struggling financially. Relegation ultimately made that situation worse. Francis approached us and asked if we could help out. We also had a chat with David Bernstein in London and then we met with everyone and agreed that we could help. City had a Georgian player called Mikhail Kavelashvili and we helped with the funding of that.

"After that we had some shares and our interest in the organisation of the Club grew. Things developed from there."

Wardle and Makin would later play a major part in City's history, but in 1996 they, like the majority of fans, were helpless as the Blues struggled. Relegation was a bitter blow and brought despair almost on a par with 1983. When Francis Lee became Chairman many believed the prospect of relegation was banished forever, but in truth City had slipped too far behind since formation of the Premier League and relegation became inevitable. The appointment of Alan Ball had not encouraged supporters, nor had many of his acquisitions. Nigel Clough had hardly impressed while another brought to Maine Road in a fanfare was Gerry Creaney, who came from Portsmouth in a deal which also saw fans' favourite Paul Walsh transfer south. Creaney came to Manchester to further his international aspirations, according to early reports, but his pallid performances for City caused many to question Ball's wisdom, especially as Uwe Rösler clearly missed the support he received from Walsh.

Other departures included Terry Phelan, Garry Flitcroft and Tony Coton - three players who had achieved a great deal with the Club and had at times been tremendously popular with the fans. The trio were quickly followed by Niall Quinn and Keith Curle as City seemed more intent on reducing the wage bill than considering the strength of the squad. Relegation was a terrible experience, but losing a handful of the most popular players did little to enhance Ball's popularity. Quinn and some of the others had not wanted to leave but felt they had little choice: "The previous year the Club had more or less agreed terms with Sporting Lisbon. In fact I had agreed personal terms and then it all fell through. So when the 1995-96 season started I knew I wasn't in the manager's plans. That was the reality, and I started the season on the bench. So once we were relegated that was it."

Quinn went to Sunderland where the popular City chant "Niall Quinn's Disco Pants" followed him: "It's funny, when I joined Sunderland I thought 'well at least that chant will be left behind at Maine Road' but then they latched on to it! The story of how it started… We were on a pre-season tour of Italy and as always there were quite a few City fans who had made the journey. One night I had a pair of cut-off denims which went high up on my stomach. I must have looked a bit odd! Anyway, that developed into the song. Thinking about it, it's great to have a song with your name in. It doesn't happen to everyone, so it's a real honour, even if it isn't about my playing skills!"

There was concern over the departure of players such as Quinn and Curle. Some of these were documented in the fifth issue of *Bert Trautmann's Helmet*

(the renamed fanzine *Electric Blue*). It was described as a "Ball Out Special" and was produced during the close season following relegation. Understandably, there were a number of comments from different contributors suggesting Ball was clearly not the right man to manage City. This was a view shared by some of the players.

John Foster, who had progressed through City's youth set up and first appeared in the League team during Brian Horton's spell as manager, felt Ball's approach was not appropriate to all the squad: "He gathered the first team squad round the pre-season after we'd been relegated and he stood there and told us what he'd done, about winning the World Cup and so on. It was ridiculous. When he left the room a few things were said and basically he'd lost the players. We had no respect for him. He used to turn up at training with his flat cap on. He'd stand near where the fans could hear him and he'd lambast us. We knew what he was doing. It was all our fault City were struggling nothing to do with him!

"He kept me at the Club and gave me a three year contract, but he also lambasted me at half time in a friendly. He went way over the top and I was the first player to receive a rollicking off him at City. He kept saying 'It's not good enough for AB!' The other players laughed and kept saying 'you're not good enough for AB!'"

With hindsight it is clear that City needed a different approach.

1992-1996 SUMMARY

Highest League Attendance: 37,136 Manchester United, 20/03/93
Highest Cup Attendance: 34,050 Tottenham Hotspur, 07/03/93 (FA Cup)
Managers: 1990 – 1993 Peter Reid, 1993-1995 Brian Horton & 1995 – 1996 Alan Ball

Seasonal Record:

Season	League	Posn	FA Cup	League Cup	Other	Leading Scorer	Average Attendance
1992-93	Premier*	9	Rnd 6	Rnd 3		White 16	24,698
1993-94	Premier	16	Rnd 4	Rnd 4		Sheron 6	26,709
1994-95	Premier	17	Rnd 5	Rnd 5		Rösler 15	22,725
1995-96	Premier	18	Rnd 5	Rnd 3		Rösler 9	27,869

* League restructured with Premier League becoming the top tier of English football

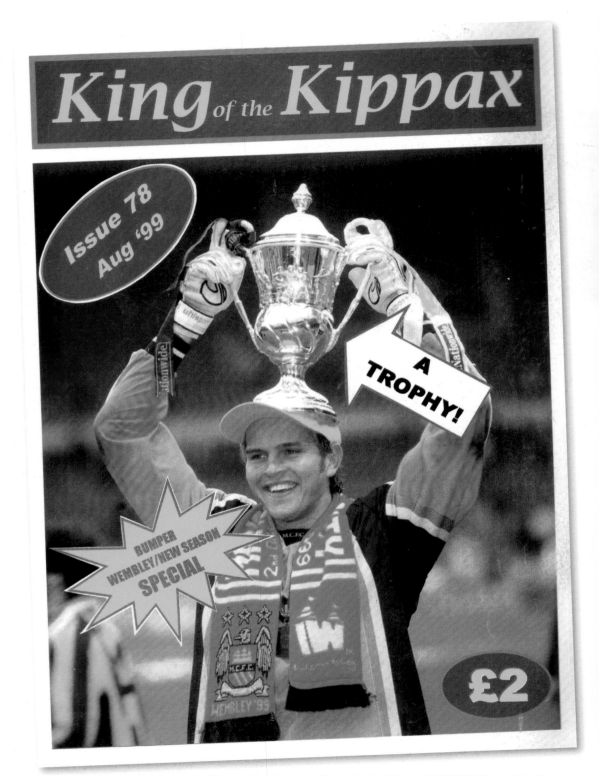

King Of The Kippax *typified the spirit and humour of supporters at this time by highlighting "A TROPHY!" 13 years later the fanzine was still around when the Premier League title was won.*

We're Not Really Here

"I turned to Willie and said 'It looks like Scunny next year' because I'd seen them get promoted the day before. Then Kevin Horlock rifled one in… another strong character for us that year. He grew as the season went on. The Board came up for 5 minutes and Asa Hartford popped up alongside me urging the players on. 'Five minutes, come on'. I looked at Gillingham's bench and they were all downbeat 'what five minutes?' City fans started to roar – and some came back into the stadium after leaving – and then Dicky… Wonderful character. His heart is jammed in that little body it's so big.

Joe Royle commenting on his feelings at the 1999 play-off final, March 2010

1996-1997 Further Managerial Changes

The 1996-97 season needed to see a marked improvement if the majority were to alter their opinion of Ball. It did not. Unfortunately, it became a contender for the most traumatic season in City's history. It was a period of grim managerial struggle with three officially appointed managers and two caretakers, and saw City finish lower than ever before. Yet despite all the negative points, City's vast army of supporters once again proved among the most loyal in the country.

After so much change in such a short period of time it is difficult to recall the mood on the opening night of the season, as City welcomed Ipswich Town for the first Nationwide League game shown live on Sky TV. There was a new captain - Kit Symons - but Alan Ball was still manager despite rumblings at the end of 1995-96 and during the close season. A crowd of 29,126 watched what many would agree was a typical City match of the period. As expected Kinkladze performed exceptionally well, mesmerised the Ipswich defence, and set up the opener for Steve Lomas, who had turned down a move to Wimbledon during the summer. It looked a simple goal but owed much to the efforts of the little Georgian.

Despite that City were never in total control and as the game progressed nerves were severely tested as Michael Frontzeck was sent off for a foul on Paul Mason. Down to ten men, the Blues struggled for the final 25 minutes with Ipswich hitting the woodwork twice. It was a relieved crowd that welcomed the final whistle, and a vital three points. Sky TV's viewers were also probably relieved - it had not been an entertaining Friday evening for neutrals!

The game did, however, give City fans the first opportunity to chant "City, City, top of the League". Sadly, it was their one and only chance.

After the match a buoyant Alan Ball felt it was a good result: "It was the start we wanted and a very solid performance. It was very important we got off to a winning start, so at least this time we have got something to build on."

Four days later the City manager was not so chirpy as he witnessed a 1-0 defeat at eventual champions Bolton. Ball kept his players locked in the dressing room for almost an hour, then refused to speak with journalists. Bolton really made the Blues look appalling that night and brought home the realisation that the two sides were a considerable distance apart. It also raised further concerns over Ball's approach to life at Maine Road. In the next game - away at Stoke - the fans needed to see a much improved performance; they didn't get it.

The opening 45 minutes were a nightmare and left City two goals down. Former Blue hero Sheron netted for the home side making the day even more unbearable and, perhaps understandably, frustrated supporters started to chant "Ball Out". It was something the Stoke fans enjoyed - they'd suffered under Ball a couple of years earlier. Eventually both sets of supporters sang together giving a clear indication to Chairman Francis Lee the time had come for action. The game ended 2-1 (Rösler netted the scant consolation) with Ball groping for positives from the day: "In terms of points we didn't come away with anything, but as the manager I got something out of the match."

Quite what remained a mystery as, before the next game, Ball resigned (26th August 1996). The supporters never really took to the former World Cup winner and only signs of an immediate return to the Premier League might have prolonged his managerial career. His spell at Maine Road ended with a long chat with Chairman Lee who, understandably, did not try to persuade Ball to remain at the Club. The Guardian's David Lacey encapsulated the feelings of City supporters when he considered the achievements of Ball's time at Maine Road before stating: "Ball has taken down more people than the Titanic."

City fan Steve Worthington writing in Bert

Trautmann's Helmet believed he knew where the blame lay for the disastrous start to the new season: "In hindsight, Ball may now recognise that the start of the season was somewhat predictable. Instead of strengthening the team, he allowed it to be weakened. Perhaps he should have stood up to Francis Lee's craving to reduce the wage bill, but he didn't and more senior pros fled the nest. Keith Curle was sold to one of our immediate rivals [Wolves] and Niall Quinn was sacrificed to Sunderland, having been treated like an unsightly boil.

"During a summer visit to Maine Road, the Ed [Noel Bayley] and I met Francis Lee and, judging from the Chairman's incredulous reaction, I felt a bit like Dennis Pennis when I asked, 'Are there any new signings in the pipeline?' To that he somewhat arrogantly replied, 'We don't need any new signings to get out of this League'. The Ed and I looked at each other and feared the worst."

Unknown to the majority, Francis Lee and his board were working hard trying to restructure the Club to ensure a sound financial footing. When they arrived at Maine Road they were absolutely appalled at the financial state of what remained one of the most popular clubs in Britain.

In addition, they felt some of the players signed under Peter Swales had been put on contracts that jeopardised the future of the Club. To allow some of these players to remain would have seriously hampered City's progress and could have created an uneasy situation in the dressing room where there was little comparison between the salaries of the pre-Lee and post-Swales players. Unfortunately, but perhaps understandably, little of this was communicated to the fans. Niall Quinn took exception to some comments that were aired but what was fact and what was fiction? Now Ball had gone, perhaps the new manager would be able to explain.

Former player Asa Hartford filled the void as caretaker for the visit of Charlton on 3rd September. Despite another poor performance, City woke up in the last ten minutes and scraped a 2-1 win. At home to Barnsley four days later the Blues were defeated 2-1 after failing to perform again. Goals from Rösler and Ball's last signing, Paul Dickov, then brought a 2-0 victory at Port Vale, but City came crashing back down to earth with a 3-1 defeat at Crystal Palace and a sending off for captain Symons on 14th September. Hartford: "It was a poor performance and Palace overpowered us. The last thing I said to the players before they went out was that a lot of fans had come down and they deserved 100%. We did not get that from all quarters."

Three days later City faced Lincoln City in the second round of the League Cup. The first match was played away from home and actually started in style with Dickov, who had joined the Club a month earlier, chipping a great cross to Rösler. The German bravely ducked to head home after only 40 seconds and gave the 1,500 travelling fans something to cheer in an otherwise dismal week. However, it wasn't to last. Lincoln were more prepared to battle and John Beck, Lincoln's manager, ensured his men knew how to fight back. They played with a direct approach and, it must be said, dominated the tie. In the 29th minute Lincoln's Terry Fleming had both time and space to fire past Andy Dibble to level the scores, then Steve Holmes was left free to fire home a rather simple second a minute before half-time. Three minutes into the second half, the 6ft 4in Dutch striker Gijsbert Bos managed a back header from Fleming's throw, which skimmed off Michael Brown and entered the net. 3-1 after 48 minutes!

Then Jon Whitney rammed home the fourth in the 79th minute to complete the humiliation. Understandably, City's unhappy fans vented their feelings, but the sad fact was a club which ought to be in the Premier League was annihilated by a modest Third Division outfit.

Caretaker manager Asa Hartford was far from happy: "We were out-fought. We got caught up in a game that did not suit us at all. There were too many silver prizes being picked up by our players. We lost out in the individual contests and when you do that, your chances are slim.

"They wanted it more than us. But you do expect more from our players and you expect them to be able to deal with that sort of situation. The players have let themselves down. I feel sorry for the fans. It's not on."

Lincoln's John Beck told the Yorkshire TV reporter that he felt City were in a confused state: "Manchester City need organising and directing. They need guts and determination to get out of their mini-crisis. They may have to go down to the Second Division to sort themselves out." It was a worrying time for everyone connected with the Blues.

Against Birmingham - captained by former United man Steve Bruce - in the next League game a Kinkladze penalty in the 89th minute brought three vital points, after a Rösler spot-kick in the first half was saved by Birmingham's Ian Bennett. The travelling Midlands fans found it hard to accept and scuffles broke out in their section of the North Stand. Who knows how they'd have reacted had they been supporting City throughout this managerless period!

The second leg of the League Cup tie followed, and once again City started brightly against lowly Lincoln but, with typical unpredictability, the Blues presented their opponents with an opportunity and the game was lost within the first 20 minutes as sloppy defending allowed Gijsbert Bos to tap into an open net.

Again, Asa Hartford was not a happy Blue: "To lose two games against Lincoln City saddens you. Realistically, we lost it in the first leg. But the goal we conceded last night was a comedy of errors, and there were three horrendous mistakes made. It knocked the stuffing out of us.

"There were a lot of corners and knockdowns in their goalmouth for us to feed on, but we were not alive to the possibilities."

City's 5-1 aggregate defeat was the first time the Blues had lost a two-legged League Cup Second Round tie, and was the Club's record defeat over two legs in any competition.

With the Blues losing 5-1 on aggregate at half-time, the following announcement was made: "The match against West Brom will now be played on November 27th ... Dependent on tonight's result."

At the end of September a 2-0 defeat at Sheffield United was the last game of Hartford's caretaker manager period. Ever since Ball's departure City had been frantically searching for a manager - once again George Graham claimed he was interested, then said he wasn't, then took the Leeds job. Dave Bassett accepted the post, then changed his mind. Other names were mentioned on a regular basis, then on 7th October former United player Steve Coppell accepted the challenge saying: "I want to be here a long time."

Coppell brought with him former Liverpool European Cup winner Phil Neal: "I'd been at Cardiff as manager and Stevie Coppell approached me and asked if I'd like to be his assistant at City. Although Cardiff had been good I was very excited about coming to City.

"Stevie was a fantastic manager. Very detailed. He used to scrutinise everything properly and I enjoyed those few short weeks with him. He used video technology and all of the ideas that are fairly routine today, but back then were not used by most managers. He was very precise. Very thorough in his approach and knew exactly how the opposition would perform. I'd train the first team and try to keep them motivated and all part of a happy bunch really, then Steve would get into the specifics of the next game or whatever. We were a good duo, complemented each other well."

Coppell's first game ended 2-2 at QPR prompting a little flutter of optimism throughout the Club, but understandably the manager tried to calm that by saying: "One game means nothing. After six games we will be able to draw more realistic conclusions."

The next five drew mixed results - 2-0 defeat at Reading, 2-0 Maine Road victory over Norwich, 1-0 defeat at home to Wolves, a 3-2 win at Southend, and a frustrating 2-0 defeat at Swindon. Six days after that all important sixth game Coppell stunned everyone when he resigned on medical grounds, prompting various rumours to circulate. The unsatisfactory nature of his departure was merely compounded when, amazingly, a few months later he returned to football management and guided Crystal Palace through the play-offs to the Premiership.

Coppell's assistant Phil Neal was appointed caretaker manager while the search for a new messiah continued. Neal spoke frankly about this period in 2011: "It was all blown apart. It was a shock to me and everybody else when he resigned. I went in on the Monday morning and was told 'Steve's leaving, can you go and take the squad training?' I had no idea whatsoever. He would have contemplated it over the weekend and thought it through properly, but I hadn't a clue. I was left doing the training while he departed.

"I just tried to get on with it. There was a good squad there at the time, but the turmoil had affected them. I became caretaker manager and it was a very hard task, but what I do remember quite vividly and strongly is that it was the supporters who kept me informed. I used to go down to Platt Lane, the training ground back then, and fans would turn up and chat. I always thought it was important to understand the Club and be aware of everything that made up Manchester City, so I really appreciated the information those fans gave me back then. I loved meeting City fans. They were genuine in their support – even when results were working against us - and that helped me enormously. They were fantastic and it was a great education.

"When Steve left, although it was a shock and difficult for us all, I was quite excited. There was no fear, no trepidation… I couldn't wait to get started. I knew I had a different approach to Stevie, but the opportunity was never something I'd walk away from. City was – is – a massive club. I was determined to make it work.

"When you're fulfilling the role of a caretaker manager it's very difficult because you don't know if you'll be there for one day, one month or whatever. I wanted to make long term plans but I never really felt that I'd be given the job on a permanent basis. There were press stories and rumours of discussions between the Club and other managers, so it was never really going to happen."

A pathetic 3-2 home defeat to Oxford brought tremendous criticism from City's battle-weary fans and the question "Have you ever seen a poorer City side?" was asked in the following issue of *King Of The Kippax*. The supporters were still loyal, but how much more could they take? A 2-1 defeat at Portsmouth in mid-November left City in 21st position, afterwards Phil Neal told reporters: "They say Steve Coppell showed courage to leave. It takes more courage to stay!"

A Maine Road goalless draw with Brian Horton's Huddersfield followed, before a 2-1 home defeat by Tranmere caused supporters to leave early and then demonstrate outside the Main Stand. It was another sad day in what was fast becoming City's worst season in history.

Fortunately a 3-2 midweek defeat of West Bromwich Albion, thanks to an early Rösler goal and two Kinkladze

penalties, changed the atmosphere a little on 27th November, but a 3-0 televised humiliation at Wolves the following Sunday brought City crashing back down to earth. The Wolves tannoy system said it all when the Queen record, "Another One Bites the Dust", was played.

A winner from young Jeff Whitley in the next game helped City scrape a 3-2 victory over Bradford City but this was hardly a comforting result as there was still no sign of a new manager. The nightmare continued at Oldham where the struggling Latics won 2-1, and a big Boxing Day crowd of 30,344 witnessed another humiliation when Port Vale beat the Blues 1-0. The *Manchester Evening News* said the incredibly loyal fans felt betrayed. They certainly felt angry.

A third successive defeat and the tenth away setback in 13 games brought a 2-0 embarrassment at Barnsley. Francis Lee was in Barbados on his annual holiday and supporters, whose loyalty to City amazed many in football, chanted: "I'd rather be in Barnsley than Barbados." Only true Blues can understand how and why they perhaps managed to retain a sense of humour.

That game was the end of Neal's period as caretaker - one that lasted considerably longer than Coppell's permanent reign. On 30th December former Forest manager and player Frank Clark arrived and immediately laughed at suggestions City were in crisis: "If you consider that 30,000 people turn up for a home game when you are near the bottom of the First Division and 6,000 fans travel to an away game at Barnsley, it certainly doesn't seem a job from hell to me."

Due to last minute postponements, Clark's first game in charge wasn't until 11th January when Dave Bassett brought Palace to Maine Road for a 1-1 draw. Clark received a tremendous reception before a crowd of over 27,000 prompting Bassett's wife to question her husband's earlier decision to turn City down. Two further draws followed at Huddersfield (1-1) and Sheffield United (0-0) before City's best result of the season - a 4-1 victory at Oxford. The game was a good example of how Clark had brought new life into the Club and started to draw a little confidence out of his players. New signing Kevin Horlock impressed on his debut, while the likes of Rösler and Summerbee were starting to recover from the confidence-sapping days under Ball. City were back, and with a large TV audience watching, the inevitable "Are You Watching Alan Ball?" chant added more enjoyment, especially as Ball had been most unadvisedly criticising the quality of City's players - including those he brought to the Club.

Ball seemed particularly critical of Uwe Rösler, a player whose form dipped alarmingly under Ball: "I think the penny's dropping slowly but surely to the fans that these players they've backed for years are not good enough." As if to prove Ball wrong Rösler's performances improved markedly under Frank Clark. Clark's boys were beginning to excite and many found it hard to accept that many players who had appeared so feeble earlier in the season were now actually displaying real quality. What had Clark brought that Ball, Coppell, Neal and Hartford had been unable to generate?

A run of victories (3-0 at home to Southend and Swindon, and 3-1 at Bradford) began to lift the Blues away from danger and even brought the suggestion Clark's side could reach the play offs. A 1-1 draw with Portsmouth was seen as a failure, even though three months earlier it would have been viewed as a major achievement, but a 1-0 defeat of local rivals Oldham on 8th March was greeted with delight.

A 2-0 reverse at Birmingham was disappointing but it was an odd match, especially as the Birmingham programme was the one produced for the original fixture called off ten weeks earlier! Clark needed to take action to prevent any stall in momentum, especially as Kit Symons was missing for the following game at Grimsby.

That match ended in a 1-1 draw with both managers pleased by the final result. Grimsby's Kenny Swain was impressed with City: "You have to look at the quality in the City side. They are on a roll with one defeat in eleven and they are hard to beat. Frank Clark is a wily old fox and he knows the score." In typical football manager speak he added: "It was a game of three halves. I thought we were okay in the first, shaky in the second, and did well in the third!"

A 1-1 draw at Tranmere followed, then on 22nd March the Blues defeated Stoke 2-0. A small fire in the North Stand delayed the kick-off by 45 minutes, then fans had to wait a further 65 minutes before new arrival Dalian Atkinson headed home for his debut day goal. Steve Lomas added a second three minutes later to see City reach Clark's safety target of 50 points. The manager was relieved, but some were even now hopeful of a play-off place. It was an amazing turnaround from only a few months earlier.

A 74th minute equaliser from Clark signing Ged Brannan brought a 1-1 draw at Charlton, but the play-offs still seemed a distant dream, before a 2-1 home defeat by runaway leaders Bolton more or less ended that fantasy. It also deservedly brought Bolton the Nationwide League title. Two 3-1 victories followed at West Bromwich Albion and at home to Grimsby, before a disappointing 3-0 defeat by QPR at Maine Road on 19th April. It was now reaching the stage when everybody connected with the Club just wanted the roller-coaster campaign to end. It had been another crazy City season and was perhaps time for Clark and his team to take a break and prepare for the following term. Unfortunately there were still three games to go, and the Blues had to soldier on.

A 1-0 defeat at bogey team Ipswich had an air of inevitability and was actually the game that put a mathematical end to any play-off possibility. A no score draw at Norwich followed, and then the final match at home to Reading ended in a 3-2 victory. Those last two games were played without Kinkladze, who had been injured in the England v Georgia international, and speculation was rife the influential Georgian would never play in a City shirt again.

Throughout the match messages from various supporters' groups urging him to stay appeared on the scoreboard and, at the end, he was given a fantastic ovation by City's large crowd. He wasn't the only one as the rest of Clark's side marched around the pitch to much acclaim. Anybody witnessing these positive, joyful scenes would have been convinced the Blues had just won the championship, rather than completed a season of struggle in the First Division. City's final position was 14th – their lowest placing at the time – yet the attitude shown by Frank Clark and his players during this season had done much to convince everyone that the situation could only improve for the Club.

Many felt Frank Clark could bring the Club promotion, particularly as his arrival coincided with an entertaining FA Cup run, although he did have to wait for his first taste of Cup action with the Blues, after the third round tie away to Brentford was postponed twice. This match was originally scheduled for January 4th but was postponed because of the appalling weather that had also wiped out the League game with Birmingham three days earlier.

Had the FA Cup tie been played as planned, it would have been Clark's first match in charge. Instead the 1-1 draw with Crystal Palace on 11th January gave Clark his first real taste of life as a Blue. Three days after that, the Brentford tie was called off for a second time when a late pitch inspection ended the prospect of play a mere two hours before the scheduled start. The large number of City fans who had travelled south were understandably livid.

When the tie was eventually played Kit Symons, with a newly cropped hairstyle, held the defence together superbly as the Blues soaked up a lot of Brentford pressure.

Nicky Summerbee was another who surprised, with a good performance at a time when few supporters actually wanted him in the side. Playing under Frank Clark seemed to give Summerbee a new lease of life and during the Brentford match he combined perfectly with Kinkladze to bring victory.

The two men swapped passes, and then Summerbee powerfully sent a Kinkladze return high into the net for the only goal of the game in the 61st minute. That goal engendered more confidence and, suddenly, the 2,400 City supporters at Griffin Park were anticipating the fourth round tie with Watford.

Frank Clark's first home victory came with a vintage

performance against The Hornets in his sixth game in charge. Since his arrival the Blues had grown in confidence, and the meeting with Watford could not have occurred at a better time. It was the kind of game that sent supporters home dreaming of cup glory, and certainly provided a much needed diversion from the League campaign.

The match was already proving a lively one when Phil Neal purchase Neil Heaney opened the scoring in the 24th minute. This was Heaney's first for the Club and was more than deserved. The Blues continued to dominate, although there were few opportunities for either side.

Then in the 53rd minute Watford's Steve Palmer was dismissed for punching Steve Lomas. This should have allowed the Blues to totally dominate the tie, but actually seemed to present Watford with opportunities.

Five minutes after the sending off, Gifton Noel-Williams netted the equaliser, but Watford's resurgence did not last long as three minutes later Nicky Summerbee, assisted by Kinkladze, restored the lead. In the 71st minute Uwe Rösler - the man Ball was most critical of - latched on to a long ball from Heaney to powerfully drive home an angled shot. Immediately the supporters chanted their hero's name and then, remembering the television criticism from Ball only a few days earlier, they chorused: "Are you watching Alan Ball?" It was a chant that seemed to encompass the whole stadium, and few, if any, supporters failed to voice their opinion.

Later a limping Rösler left the field to a fantastic ovation. It was thoroughly deserved, as was the applause for Summerbee - another player brought to life by Clark. The manager was by then impressing everybody, but he was first to share the accolades: "This is a team effort from the whole club, right down from the Chairman. I and the coaching staff are part of the team and we work hard with the players. The players and everybody at the Club have responded very well. It's another step in the right direction."

On 15th February a crowd of 30,462 arrived at Maine Road for the mouth-watering fifth round clash with Premier League Middlesbrough. The outcome of this tie should have sent City into the next round of the FA Cup, sadly a few dire refereeing decisions sent the Blues crashing out of a competition they could possibly have won. Middlesbrough, somewhat fortuitously, went on to reach the final where they were defeated by Chelsea.

Frank Clark's confident side appeared to look forward more to this clash than any other during the season. It seemed to be the game that would prove that the new approach at Maine Road was destined for success. Sadly, it was not to be.

The game was won and lost as a result of three controversial decisions. The first was when Ian Brightwell timed his move on to Kit Symons' header to perfection, then steered the ball in for what should have been the opening goal. The referee disallowed that effort believing Brightwell to be offside, even though television cameras proved that to be incorrect.

The second error occurred in the 67th minute when £2.75 million import Gianluca Festa punched Steve Lomas (it seemed to be the season for punching Lomas!). He should have been sent off, but the referee merely booked him. Again the cameras proved how erroneous that was. Afterwards Lomas told reporters: "The ref bottled it. The fella gave me a forearm, everyone saw it and the ref told me he didn't. I asked why he'd booked him then and he said maybe TV would prove him wrong."

Error number three arrived when substitute Paul Dickov was clearly tripped in the penalty area by, who else but, Festa. A penalty then would certainly have given City the tie but, with Kinkladze already off as a result of a groin strain, Middlesbrough had the opportunity to control crucial areas of the pitch. In the 78th minute Juninho, with a move created by the fortunate Festa, was left free to drive a shot under goalkeeper Martyn Margetson.

The Blues tried desperately hard to find an equaliser, but it was Middlesbrough's lucky day and the game ended in disappointment. The dream was over for another year. At least it allowed Frank Clark to concentrate on the League - something everyone had tried to forget existed!

1997-1998 A New Low

The 1997-98 season was expected to see an end to the troubles and misery of the previous seasons. It was anticipated Frank Clark would develop a side capable of seeking promotion. During the first few months of Clark's reign, supporters had become excited by his approach to the game. Following the disappointments created by the arrival of first Alan Ball then Steve Coppell - two men never likely to satisfy City's passionate following - Clark appeared to be the right appointment for the Club and, as a result, optimism spread. He was not the most dynamic of football managers, but he did appear knowledgeable and seemed an appropriate appointment to help bring stability to the Blues.

Off the pitch there was further cause for optimism. During 1997 much was done to ensure supporters could be seen across Britain, proud to wear their colours. City's Chief Executive Mike Turner, who had replaced Colin Barlow the previous season, became involved in the redesign of the Club badge and the selection of a new kit manufacturer. He felt City had much to gain from increased awareness of the Blue brand. As a result the Club decided it was time to move away from Umbro after 63 years, to find a company prepared to portray the right image. After considerable time and effort the Blues made what seemed an informed decision and chose Kappa.

The combination was effective immediately with both the new home and away kits appealing to the vast majority of supporters. Within a month of the launch around 60,000 shirts were sold - it would have been more but Kappa had production and distribution problems culminating in a large number of unhappy fans. Perhaps Kappa had underestimated the Blues' pulling power, something many felt their predecessors had done. Umbro had been City's kit manufacturer since the 1930s - this had earlier been acclaimed as the longest sports sponsorship deal in the world - and had developed close links with the Club, however by the mid-1990s the company appeared to be moving elsewhere. They spent considerable time targeting a few high profile clubs, and many fans were simply reluctant to purchase goods that would perhaps indirectly line the pockets of their biggest rivals at Old Trafford. Fans had become hugely critical of the relationship.

In addition to the kit redesign, City also introduced a new club badge. Inscribed with a Latin motto meaning 'Pride in Battle'. The Club initially announced that the Latin text read 'Superbia in proelio' but they also claimed it was 'Superbia in proelia' in the weeks that followed. The style of writing on the badge also brought confusion with some believing the last letter to be an a and some an o.

By 2002 the Club usually stated proelia was the correct version, but in 2012 both City and Umbro (by that time City's kit manufacturer again) claimed it as proelio on their website. As a direct translation of 'Pride in Battle' Superbia in proelio is accurate, as proelia would mean 'pride in battles'. Some fans felt this type of confusion was a sign of wider issues within the Club.

The badge also incorporated the original ship over the three emblazoned lines from the Manchester coat of arms. The three lines had changed colour from the

City of Manchester's coat of arms, becoming white on a blue background rather than the traditional gold on a red background. The new badge also included a golden eagle and three gold stars. This badge received a mixed reaction, particularly as the eagle was identical to the bird worn by Manchester United in the 1958 Cup Final. United's emblem in 1958 was also utilised by City during the late fifties and early sixties and was not, as some United fans still believe, a phoenix. It was an officially produced Manchester city council emblem incorporating an eagle.

City desperately needed to improve and control its merchandising operation and, although many supporters strongly identified with the old badge - four years later a small group of supporters called for the re-instatement of the old one - it was vital the Club made a change.

Other improvements on the merchandising front included the redevelopment of the Social Club into a 3,500 square foot City Superstore. This opened in October 1997 and was a significant improvement on the previous outlet. Previously, the Blues opened new stores in the Kippax Stand and at the Arndale Centre in the city centre. Regrettably, the Arndale shop later closed down. It had been damaged in the 1996 city centre bomb blast.

For many connected with the Blues it felt as if the management finally recognised the enormous size and stature of the Club. Prior to Lee's arrival City had relied on just one rather inadequate franchised shop. Kevin Cummins, writing in *Bert Trautmann's Helmet*, described the old shop: "I was desperate to own anything connected with City. We would visit the shop before every home game, but almost always reluctantly depart empty handed. The problem was that, as with most souvenirs, they were crap. It was impossible to find anything in there that you could possibly want to give house room to. The stock never seemed to change. It was a shoddy enterprise."

The changes made off the pitch certainly improved the merchandising and corporate position, however some felt the focus was wrong. While the whole commercial side of the Club had improved considerably, activities on the pitch remained worrying. City had struggled to find form under each of the managers appointed since the dismissal of Brian Horton in 1995 and former fans' hero Francis Lee was under severe criticism. The 1997-98 season had to see some improvement. Something manager Frank Clark knew only too well: "When clubs do badly, it's customary to blame the manager. That may often be justified but surely it can't explain Manchester City's failure over 25 years. A club might be unlucky with one or two managers, but no club could be so cursed as to appoint 17 duffers. Don't forget many of those duffers have been successful elsewhere. Alan Ball

Despite the struggles the loyalty of fans remained.

had done well with limited resources at Southampton, Peter Reid became a hero at Sunderland, and when I was at Forest I was voted Manager of the Year by my Premier League peers."

Clark had taken steps to strengthen the side during the 1997 close season. Striker Lee Bradbury arrived for an astounding £3m (plus a further £500,000 based on international appearances), while other arrivals included Gerard Wiekens and Tony Vaughan. All three made their debuts in the opening match on 9th August at home to Portsmouth, who fielded former Blue Fitzroy Simpson. A near capacity crowd of 30,474 hoped for a convincing start, but City turned in a rather nervous performance. Aloisi opened the scoring for Portsmouth in the 5th minute, but Uwe Rösler managed an equaliser eleven minutes later.

Ten minutes into the second half debutant Gerard Wiekens made it 2-1 but, City being City, the lead didn't last and only ten minutes from the end Paul Hall equalised. The game ended 2-2. Possibly, expectations were too great. Frank Clark later admitted he felt under too much pressure at this point. Only a few months earlier Mancunians felt City still had an outside chance of reaching the play-offs despite their dreadful inconsistency.

Clark tried to instil confidence and team spirit during this first month, but it wasn't easy, especially when the second match of the campaign was away to Blackpool in the first round of the Coca-Cola-sponsored League Cup. The Blues had been forced to compete in this round after the decision to allow byes to the later rounds for those clubs playing in Europe. Most recognised Blackpool should not pose a threat, however City's low self-esteem at this point was a factor. A 12th August holiday crowd of 8,084 - including many Blues who had chosen to use the game as an opportunity for a mini-break - witnessed a depressing 1-0 defeat. Interestingly, one of City's unused substitutes that day was a young goalkeeper by the name of Nicky Weaver.

In the second leg an 88th minute Kevin Horlock goal levelled the tie, but as the outcome had to be decided on the night, the Blues lost out 4-2 in a penalty shoot-out. Expensive signing Lee Bradbury miscued his penalty, posing early questions about his purchase.

The League campaign was no better. The Blues provided the opposition at the opening of Sunderland's superb Stadium of Light. A huge crowd of 38,827 - the largest in the division since 40,070 watched City v Chelsea on 18th March 1989 - witnessed a 3-1 Sunderland win. Former Blue idol Niall Quinn netted the historic first goal. In the 75th minute Gio Kinkladze also made history by scoring the first penalty at the stadium to level for the Blues. Sadly, Sunderland managed two goals in the final seven minutes.

Another new signing Jason Van Blerk made his

debut in this match, coming on for Uwe Rösler, while Brian Horton signing Alan Kernaghan made his one and only appearance of the season. In September he went on loan to St Johnstone.

Only one point came from the following two games but then City achieved a 3-1 win at League leaders Nottingham Forest with goals from Ged Brannan (2) and Paul Dickov. Ex-Forest chief Frank Clark was delighted.

Unpredictability was a factor throughout the first few months. They could only manage a 1-1 draw at newly promoted Bury; were defeated 1-2 at home by Norwich, but then on 27th September annihilated second placed Swindon 6-0! On the day of the Swindon match the Blues lay in 20th place and were certainly in need of a boost. Fortunately Kinkladze and Dickov were on hand to give supporters a lift. Dickov scored twice and also proved totally selfless when, with the opportunity to complete his hat-trick, he simply squared to misfit Lee Bradbury for a simple tap-in. Bradbury needed the goal more than the bustling striker, but the majority of footballers would surely have grabbed the glory for themselves.

Only one point was gained from the next four matches and the pressure intensified. The Blues lay in the embarrassing position of 22nd out of 24 clubs having amassed only ten points. Only Portsmouth and Huddersfield were below them. Off the pitch there was more embarrassment as Georgi Kinkladze made headlines after crashing his £50,000 Ferrari 355 on Tuesday 28th October. The car allegedly went out of control while leaving a roundabout close to the M56 and A538 at Hale, and crashed into a signpost and motorway bridge support. Photographs of the crumpled vehicle appeared on the front pages of the tabloids while rumours circulated he had been racing against one of his team mates.

Kinkladze was treated for shock, cuts to his back and bruising before being discharged. He received a total of thirty stitches. Understandably he did not appear in City's match with Crewe the following night. His place was taken by Chris Greenacre. Frank Clark's plans had been disrupted: "Georgi was a very, very lucky man. The accident could have been far worse. We were thankful his injuries were only superficial. I was concerned about how the players would react to Georgi's absence. I need not have worried. Their response was excellent with everyone playing their part in what was such an important victory."

This had been Crewe's first visit to Maine Road for a League game, and the old stadium was under severe pressure dealing with crowds of over 30,000. The new temporary stand in the corner between the Kippax and North Stand, later dubbed the 'Gene Kelly Stand' due to the fact its inhabitants became used to singing in the rain, was operational for the first time after being erected during July and August. Supporter Steve Bagley wrote in the fanzine *King Of The Kippax* with an alternative name: "I think the Gene Kelly stand should be renamed the 'Oliver Reed Stand' as it looks like it could fall down at any minute!"

A goalless draw at Oxford followed, but successive home defeats to Port Vale (2-3) and Huddersfield (0-1) sent the Blues back into the relegation zone. The next match was away at Sheffield United - a club whose board of directors was led by former City take-over bidder Mike McDonald and contained former Maine Road director Freddie Pye. David White's father, Stuart, and 1969 FA Cup Final referee George McCabe were also members of the Bramall Lane board.

With City looking extremely sloppy, Brian Deane took the initiative and put the home side into the lead in the 21st minute. After the goal the Blues fought back, although it's fair to say Martyn Margetson was mainly responsible after making a couple of fine saves. Then in the final minute Kevin Horlock netted to give City a much needed point.

This game marked the debut of Craig Russell and a return for Gerry Creaney. Creaney had been on loan at Chris Waddle's Burnley. £1 million rated Russell had arrived from Sunderland, with Nicky Summerbee going in the opposite direction. Clark had high hopes for Russell, but he hardly made an impact.

Against Bradford City Tony Vaughan headed his first goal to give the Blues a surprise 1-0 victory in the final minute - the surprise being that City were always the more likely to concede a goal in the final moments during this season! It was a deeply satisfying result, particularly as the previous home game had been a dire 0-1 defeat by Huddersfield, followed by chants of: "You're not fit to wear the shirt". It was even harder to accept as it was ten years to the day since City had defeated the Terriers 10-1.

The Blues then travelled to Edgeley Park for a game they had to win for all sorts of reasons, not least that defeat by near neighbours Stockport would be seen by many as another nail in City's coffin. Sadly, a humiliation followed.

Within eight minutes County were two up courtesy of poor defending. Time after time loose balls were seized by Stockport while City simply looked weak. In the 30th minute Brett Angell scored County's third.

Kit Symons received considerable abuse, but he wasn't the only City man who seemed incapable of playing football. Virtually the whole team performed feebly during the first half. During the interval the players received a severe roasting from Clark and attitudes improved. Brannan scored in the 49th minute to raise a little hope. Others were also displaying signs City might be able to get back into the match. In particular, Paul Dickov was keen to attack, and substitute

Michael Brown impressed. Sadly, it was all in vain. The game ended 3-1. It was a humiliating experience and increased the pressure on Clark and Chairman Francis Lee.

Noel Bayley, writing in *Bert Trautmann's Helmet*, summed up the feeling well: "Decisions, decisions. Going to work on the Monday after the Stockport game, I needed a placcy bag to put my bits and pieces in. I had a choice - a City souvenir shop bag or a Miss Selfridge bag resplendent with a big heart. Naturally, I chose the latter. It was far less embarrassing!"

A 1-0 victory at West Bromwich Albion followed, before normal service was resumed with a 0-1 defeat at home to a Keith Curle inspired Wolves. The goal was another miserable experience for City, and in particular former captain Symons. He tried to clear a harmless ball and proceeded to slice it high above goalkeeper Martyn Margetson for an own goal in the 42nd minute. Considering the abuse Symons was already suffering it was hardly the highlight of his career, and certainly increased calls for him to be dropped. His confidence appeared at an all-time low, and it seemed no matter how well intentioned, he was always liable to make a mistake. Clark was particularly concerned: "Things got so bad with Kit Symons I felt obliged to remove the captaincy from him. The problem came to a head when we were beaten at Stockport. Kit bore the brunt of the criticism, which was unfair because he wasn't playing that badly. He said he was happy to continue as captain but inwardly I think he was glad to be rid of it."

Captaining the Blues during this period was particularly difficult, and Clark struggled to find the right man: "The captaincy became something of a curse for the players who took it on. Kevin Horlock only lasted five minutes before being injured and ruled out for three months. Gerard Wiekens took over only to suffer a similar fate and missed the next six weeks. Ian Brightwell was next up. He wasn't a great leader but he was happy to do it and at least he managed to survive."

On 13th December City travelled to Birmingham City for what became an exceptionally long match. Very little of note occurred during the first 80 minutes, but from that point the game became lively. Shelia headed home a cross from Russell in the 88th minute, followed shortly afterwards by Birmingham hitting a post. Russell then netted what appeared to be City's second, only to see it disallowed for handball. Nevertheless it still looked as if the points were going to Maine Road and the City players relaxed a little. It was only a matter of moments before the final whistle would be blown, or so they thought.

After two minutes injury time Forster headed Birmingham's equaliser, and the jitters returned. A frantic further five minutes followed before O'Connor netted the home side's winner, proving how cruel the game can be at times. Clark was dumbfounded: "I believe the match went on for far too long. The referee played eight minutes extra at the end, after already playing five minutes more in the first half. I do not know why.

"I can appreciate the extra time played before half-time as there had been two long stoppages, including a clash of heads, and the referee booked four players. But after the interval I can hardly remember either trainer going on to the field and there were only three bookings. Where did the referee get the idea of playing another eight minutes? In that added time we lost the match. I think the time has come for the authorities to examine the whole question of time-keeping."

The following match was considerably better all-round as the Blues defeated Middlesbrough 2-0 at Maine Road. England manager Glenn Hoddle was in attendance to watch the performance of Middlesbrough's Paul Merson, but it was the City players who impressed. Uwe Rösler scored a 17th minute penalty after a foul on Craig Russell, and fifteen minutes later the determined Paul Dickov made it 2-0 after a typical mazy run by Kinkladze.

During the second period City handled the threat of Merson & Co. with ease. Star player for many was Shelia who received a good ovation at the end, while Dickov was proving better value than any of the signings made by Clark. After the game some Middlesbrough fans created havoc in the North Stand.

City's inconsistency shone through again with a 1-0 Boxing Day defeat at Crewe, and two days later a crowd of 31,839 witnessed a 2-3 defeat by eventual Division One champions Nottingham Forest. The better side clearly won with Steve Stone in good form, however two of Forest's goals came from the penalty spot. It was also encouraging to witness City's fight back. At 0-3 it appeared the Blues might be totally over run, however their fighting spirit brought encouraging goals from Shelia (56th minute) and Dickov (77th minute). It didn't encourage Bryan Brett, the *Manchester Evening News* reporter, however. Often local reporters toe the party-line and try to be positive, however Brett was determined to speak truthfully: "The Second Division is staring Manchester City in the face - whether they or the fans like it or not. Yesterday's 3-2 home defeat by Nottingham Forest, when only two late goals masked an embarrassingly heavy defeat, leaves them one point off bottom of the First Division more than halfway through the season.

"It followed the Boxing Day defeat at Crewe, and the Blues head for the New Year embroiled in a

season of misery. It's a relegation battle even their most loyal fans find hard to believe. The Blues are trapped in a quartet of clubs on 24 points - one above rock bottom."

Frank Clark admitted he had changed little at the Club: "A year on from when I came here, we are no better off. We should be doing better. I would have expected us to have done much better. No doubt about that."

The next League match brought improvement as another struggling side, Portsmouth, were beaten 3-0 at Fratton Park. The result lifted the Blues to 17th place, but the points gap between them and bottom club Portsmouth was a mere four. City remained in serious trouble, particularly as the following game ended in a 0-1 defeat to Peter Reid's Sunderland. Three successive draws followed before an embarrassing home defeat by Bury. The Bury scorer, Paul Butler, was a self-confessed City fan: "I was going to go out and celebrate on the town but considering what happened - and me a City fan scoring the goal - I thought I'd better have a quiet night in."

The Club appeared to have hit rock bottom. During the game there were calls for Frank Clark to be sacked and Francis Lee to resign.

At one stage a City fan ran on to the pitch from the Kippax Stand, ripped up his season ticket and marched off. He bravely carried out the threat many fans had been making for years, and was cheered off the pitch by thousands of supporters. In fact it was the loudest cheer of the day and was immediately followed by chants of "What the f**k is going on?" Supporters were totally exasperated by the whole situation.

At the end of the match Uwe Rösler was confronted by angry supporters and had to be escorted from the field by police. Later, when he left the ground, he was again surrounded by disgruntled fans. He spoke sensibly and wisely to the supporters, answering their concerns. He did not criticise his colleagues, although it was clear he was no longer enjoying life at Maine Road.

The defeat coincided with a new issue of the fanzine

The Bury defeat led to players being challenged by fans.

Fury at the gates as City tempers explode

■ Pictures: MARK WAUGH and ANDY YATES

By Pete Spencer

THREE thousand furious Manchester City fans staged the biggest protest of the season after the Blues shock defeat in the Valentine's Day relegation derby against Bury.

Coins, bottles and cans were hurled at police and security guards protecting the club's main gates.

Crash barriers were repeatedly charged by the angry mob and a car parked on the Maine Road forecourt was badly damaged.

Around ten per cent of the 28,000 crowd joined the mass demo, unfurling a giant "Lee Out" banner directed at the chairman.

There were chants calling for manager Frank Clark to be sacked and the crowd

Further turmoil at Maine Road.

Bert Trautmann's Helmet, whose editorial focused on the rumours now engulfing the Club: "The Maine Road rumour mill trundles relentlessly on: if City lose next week, Frank Clark's on his way... Joe Royle and Willie Donachie will be taking over... Dennis Tueart's only here to ease it through... Francis Lee's on the verge of selling out... And so it goes on. Who knows, by the time you read this, Clark may well have gone on his far from merry way. I certainly hope so. But who cares anyway? Well I do and you do. Nearly 30,000 people care enough to turn up to watch a wretched team going through the motions every other week. Somehow I don't think Frank Clark cares; not enough anyway, not as much as you and I care and that might just be the problem.

"At the last AGM he seemed resigned to the fact he'd be on his way sooner or later. Of course, this is a fact of life, especially a fact of a football manager's life, but it was the way in which he casually conceded the point. More recently, in *The Observer* (25/02/98), he was quoted as saying: 'The support is marvellous but the expectation here is unreal.' Unreal! How unreal? My expectation is this: top flight football and a bit of a run in one of the cups. A trip to Europe would be nice too, but let's not get carried away, eh? In my opinion Frank Clark doesn't understand this club or its unique status; he hasn't got a handle on it at all."

The comments were hard to dispute. Clark found

it difficult understanding exactly what sort of club he was managing, while the motives of City's directors seemed unclear. Francis Lee, in particular, was receiving considerable 'stick' from the fans and at least one major shareholder, David Makin. Makin, who earlier in the season had invested around £5 million with his JD sports business partner John Wardle, had been unable to get to the Bury game. Wardle: "David couldn't be at the game that day and he 'phoned me at the end and asked if it was as bad as he'd heard on GMR, the local radio station. I said 'it's worse!' and it was. It was really horrendous. He told me he'd 'phoned GMR and was hopeful of getting on."

At this time, local radio presenter Jimmy Wagg's post-match 'phone-in on BBC GMR was the undisputed preferred listening for City fans. Whenever there was any City news, GMR tended to have it first. Jimmy Wagg remembers that day vividly: "As a Blue I was as despondent as everybody else because it was clear to us all that City were in a desperate state, heading for relegation to the Second Division – the original Third Division! I was listening to a caller and, as was the case back then, there'd be a list of people who had called in and wanted to go on air with their point. I always tried to look out for different angles to get the debate going. As I looked down the list I saw the name 'David Makin' and I thought this could be interesting. I knew he was a

459

shareholder and thought we had to get him on straight away. When he came on it was incredible. He made an unbelievably passionate speech."

Makin telephoned GMR from the Mottram Hall Country Club to air his views on Francis Lee and City's plight: "I think there is a massive chemistry problem within the Club. I really do. He overrides everybody. He tries to be dominant. I am in business and I know if you haven't got a happy work place, then there are problems. I don't think City is a happy workplace."

He added: "I will be doing my best in the next few weeks to remove the chairman because he is staying there. I don't know whether he is bloody minded or what. He is being stubborn. He is being proud. If I was him I think I would put a moustache on and a cap and hide. I know there are people ready behind the scenes, ready to take over. I am not going into any details."

He then outlined what he would do as soon as the board changed: "The first thing I would do when Francis has gone is find that guy who has probably been barred for throwing his ticket away on the pitch and put him in the directors' box. It sums up how the fans feel."

The outburst was an emotional one, but clearly brought many of City's problems out into the open. For a major shareholder who, together with his JD Sports partner John Wardle, was represented on the board by former City hero Dennis Tueart, to make such a statement on local radio proved the disunity within the Club. Ultimately, the outburst led to a greater involvement with the Club for John Wardle: "It was the beginning of the end for Francis as Chairman. It was unfortunate for him that David spoke in that passionate way, but we did all feel that. I won't knock Francis because he was a fantastic player and did his utmost to help City develop while he was Chairman, but I don't think any of us appreciated how bad things had got before he arrived.

"To be fair to Francis he sorted an awful lot out in his first couple of years there and did a terrific job. He did some wonderful things as Chairman but when David made his call, the Club needed a change. We approached David Bernstein and asked him if he would become Chairman if Francis stood down and he was all for it. I think at that time he was the right man to take on the role. I eventually joined the Board to look after mine and David Makin's interests but it was an odd board. There were different parties and interests there and that made it difficult at times. We had people looking after the shareholding that had belonged to Peter Swales and Stephen Boler. We had Greenalls the brewery. We had Francis' representatives, me, David Bernstein and there were others with significant interests as well. So we never had one majority shareholder."

As well as the issues amongst the major shareholders, there were now strong rumours concerning manager Frank Clark's position and the suggested imminent arrival of Joe Royle. The following Monday's *Manchester Evening News* carried more news on the latest crisis at Maine Road. On the front page it's banner headline read "TIME BOMB", while its back page focused on the Lee/Makin affair under the headline "REBELLION". There was also a photo of supporters carrying a "Lee Out" banner. For many it was a painful reminder of the troubles encountered under Lee's predecessor, Peter Swales.

Elsewhere the newspaper featured the Rösler confrontation and the news that the Rochdale branch of the City Centenary Supporters' Association had seconded a vote of no confidence in Francis Lee proposed by their Midlands counterparts. There was also coverage of the demonstration that followed the match. A crowd of around 3,000 gathered on the forecourt to rant at the chairman, manager, and some of the players. After about an hour the police tactical aid group were sent in to break up the demonstration. One supporter was injured as a police horse trampled on his foot. Earlier a club steward had been hit by a coin. It was all extremely depressing.

The events of the following couple of days proved particularly confusing. The Royle rumours grew, while the Lee and Makin debate grabbed much attention. Frank Clark felt the disunity within the boardroom was all becoming too much. He felt sure all the problems within the Club were caused by the different factions within the board. In his autobiography, *Kicking With Both Feet*, he expressed amazement any club could be run that way: "While one faction was planning my downfall another was allowing me to take Peter Beardsley on a month's loan from Bolton. The Club was so short of cash and Beardsley would cost more than £30,000 in wages. It was ridiculous to allow me to do this on the day that I was about to be sacked. Beardsley was a fine player but he didn't feature in the plans of my successor Joe Royle and consequently turned out to be a waste of the Club's money.

"Instead of sacking me, one faction issued a statement to the press on Monday night saying I had been told that results had to improve. I hadn't been told anything of the sort - not that I needed telling since it was obvious. I wasn't even told they were issuing the statement. Consequently, when I was contacted by the local paper asking for my reaction, I didn't know what they were talking about. It was not only embarrassing for me, it made the Club look amateurish and disorganised."

While Clark and the supporters remained confused, the board did hold a meeting on Tuesday 17th February. During this meeting it is believed the decision was made to dismiss the manager. At the same time, Clark was travelling to Sunderland to watch their game with

Reading, City's opponents the following week. During the journey he received a telephone call from Bernard Halford, City's secretary since the early 1970s, saying the chairman wanted to see him. Clark offered to turn round and meet with him immediately but, according to Clark, Halford told him it could wait until the morning. Clark didn't feel the call could be that important and carried on to the Stadium of Light.

After the match, Clark discovered a message on his answerphone from the *Daily Mail's* John Richardson, saying his newspaper were running a story which they had been told was accurate saying Clark had been sacked and Royle was to take his place. The following day GMR's Andy Buckley broke the story to the Greater Manchester public at breakfast time. Shortly after hearing this Clark received a call from Francis Lee. When the two met afterwards the official dismissal was made. It wasn't long before Joe Royle was discussing his appointment with Dennis Tueart.

By this point Tueart had been persuaded to become a director: "Becoming a director was not an ambition at all. I had my business and had no intention of returning. Then I was asked by John Wardle and David Makin if I'd be there nominee and I took a long time to think about it. I turned it down once and then I was asked again and I thought about it. People told me I could do it but I knew that I'd want to put everything in to it and it was at a critical time for my business, and for my family.

"I was frustrated that City were the laughing stock over the previous 15 to 20 years from when I retired. I didn't like it and felt for the fans. I felt I had a relationship with fans and knew what it meant to them, so to see the Club struggle for all those years hurt.

"It was all or nothing – stability, community and team spirit. It's the same with companies as well. I remember my first board meeting at the Club. In Any Other Business I said that I was fed up with people hearing speculation, rumours and gossip from people at the Club. Fans were not being treated respectfully and it's not the way things should be done. So I brought in Chris Bird to manage that side of things."

The Joe Royle appointment was viewed well by the majority of fans. For years they had said City needed to be managed by somebody who understood the fans, the history, and the importance the Club has to Mancunians. Those managers who had got to grips with Manc mentality, such as tough Scotsman Tom Maley in 1904 and Malcolm Allison in the sixties, usually succeeded.

Joe Royle had the right pedigree and he certainly made all the right noises: "When Dennis Tueart, Asa Hartford and myself were in the team we were tops in Manchester - that is the ambition here. We cannot look at that for the moment. This is a 15 game season and we have got to make sure we win half our remaining games. Whatever it takes to make sure this massive club is in the right division we will do.

"The place is awesome and people keep telling me that one day someone will get it right. I want that to be me. Everyone says the potential is fantastic - if you do get it right here, you have lift off. You get 28,000 plus at every game. People turning up to see a team that has been struggling for four or five years."

Interestingly, it was later claimed Royle had been formally approached at around 4.30 the previous afternoon. Like Clark, he too was on his way to Sunderland. He was to go to the game and had planned to meet up with an old friend. "I've just received a rollicking from Peter Reid for not turning up, but that is typical of him," he laughed at the press conference.

Simply to have a manager capable of adding an element of joviality at such a difficult time gave City a sign improvements would follow. For too long there had been an air of negativity. Royle's predecessors - possibly

EXIT CLARK BLAMING 'A VENDETTA'

EXCLUSIVE
By Richard Burgess

SACKED Manchester City boss Frank Clark today lifted the lid on what he decribed as a "vendetta" within the club.

As Joe Royle, the man who dramatically replaced him, began picking up the pieces of City's worst-ever season, Clark wished him luck.

"There seems to be a fifth column on the fringe of the club," said Clark after arriving at the Platt Fields training ground this morning. "It is

the news would be kept quiet and he could tell me himself. But at this club that is impossible and that cannot be right. You can't run a club that way."

Clark has been shown the door along with assistant manager Alan Hill, coach Richard Money and fitness expert Peter Edwards, with another old Blue Willie Donachie expected to be named as Royle's assistant manager.

The dramatic changes sent City shares up 15p to 130p when the Stock Exchange opened today. Man-

Royle Ascent!
Sports special
Pages 52-56

right back to Brian Horton - all appeared to lack the approachability and friendliness of Royle. He knew City; he was passionate about football; and he had also achieved considerably more as a manager than many of the recent incumbents. He saved Everton from relegation when they seemed doomed and won the FA Cup. He promoted Oldham to the Premier League and took them to the League Cup final and to the FA Cup semi-final (twice), and during his eleven month absence from the game he had turned down fourteen jobs before accepting the City post. To many he seemed the only man capable of salvaging the 1997-98 season.

His first game in charge was at home to Ipswich on the day of his appointment. Never the ideal start to the job, but Royle didn't complain. He simply got on with the task and even cut short the press conference to be with his players. One of them, Ian Brightwell had served under 10 different managers (plus numerous caretakers) since his debut only eleven years earlier in August 1986.

That first game was a curious one. Frank Clark's final player, Peter Beardsley, made his debut, while a crowd of 27,156 arrived to witness the fans' favourite boo-boy Kit Symons head home against Ipswich in only the fifth minute. It seemed as if the Blues had already felt the benefit of Royle's arrival, but it didn't last. Opportunities were wasted, and only the defensive expertise of Shelia and another Georgian Kakhaber Tskhadadze kept Ipswich at bay.

Unfortunately, with only seven minutes remaining substitute Bobby Petta managed to evade a clutch of City men to beat the unsighted Tommy Wright. In injury time the Blues relaxed in their typically frustrating Frank Clark manner, and Kieron Dyer swept in their winner.

Off the pitch Royle was keen to bring Willie Donachie back to Maine Road to work as his assistant. Donachie was Nigel Spackman's number two at Sheffield United. They had been impressed with his approach and it was clear their City supporting chairman, Mike McDonald, had no intention of releasing him. In the end McDonald relented and by the end of February Donachie was at Maine Road. At Sheffield, Nigel Spackman saw the departure as the final straw and he resigned as Sheffield United manager claiming the board didn't support him.

Backroom changes at Maine Road during this spell included the departure of former manager Jimmy Frizzell after over 14 years with the Club.

City now had two consecutive away games to overcome. The first ended in a 3-1 victory at Swindon, while the second brought a 3-0 defeat by Reading. Significantly, the third goal was netted in the 89th minute - Royle still needed to get City playing to the final whistle.

Royle started to make a few team changes as he searched for a side capable of staying in the division. Ron Atkinson offered the use of left-back Lee Briscoe,

and he arrived on a month's loan from Sheffield Wednesday.

At home to West Bromwich Albion Rösler netted a 43rd minute winner, prompting talk of a revival. Interestingly, Kinkladze had missed his second consecutive game, and the media focussed on what was in actuality a very simple story to write. Kinkladze was never likely to feature in Royle's survival plans. If the Club needed to fight for victories would City's stylish player be able to cope? Fans thought yes, Royle was not convinced.

Away at fellow strugglers Huddersfield the revival continued with a 3-1 victory to lift the Blues into 17th place. Significantly, City had won two consecutive League games for the first time in eleven months.

Four days later Royle's men succumbed to a 0-2 home defeat by Oxford despite having the majority of play. Oxford had come determined to leave with a point, but somehow managed to take all three. Another defeat followed at Port Vale. City had equalised, thanks to Gerard Wiekens, but in the 73rd minute Ainsworth made it 2-1 to Vale. Surprisingly, Kinkladze re-appeared in the team for that match - his first since Royle's second game in charge. Royle: "I have to say that in terms of innate natural talent it's hard to think of anyone who beats him. The ball was his friend and he was a genius on the ball at times. The issue for me was that I needed to have players I could rely on and I desperately wanted it to be him. I remember willing him on, hoping for a spark. There was a game at Port Vale and we needed to win it and I just hoped for a spark from him. I wanted Gio to keep Manchester City up, but I just couldn't quite trust him. I knew that he was an immense talent, but I also knew that City had struggled. I had to play players that I felt would help us survive. I would never criticise Gio. In absolute pure talent he's right up there. He's still idolised by City fans and I understand why."

Former Oldham player Richard Jobson made his debut at Vale, following a free transfer from Leeds, but Royle continued to struggle to find the right mix. Injuries to players such as Murtaz Shelia hampered progress, but the huge playing squad also caused a few headaches. Royle was desperate to assess them all, but had to make a few snap decisions to reduce the wage bill. Out went David Morley, Rae Ingram, Ray Kelly, Paul Beesley, Eddie McGoldrick, and Tony Scully. Ominously, Kinkladze was also allowed to fly to Amsterdam to have talks with Ajax.

More changes were to follow as £1 million hard-man Jamie Pollock arrived from Bolton in time for the 21st March goalless game with Sheffield United - and was yellow-carded within ten minutes of his debut. Then on transfer deadline day striker Shaun Goater came from Bristol City for £400,000 plus a further £100,000 if City avoided relegation and Ian Bishop returned on a free from West Ham.

The Bishop deal was particularly pleasing for many fans and was further evidence Royle understood the Club and its fans. Bishop was idolised in his previous spell almost nine years earlier, and his departure provoked demonstrations against then manager Howard Kendall. Bishop loved the support he got during his first brief spell: "I remember we were playing Norwich and the crowd sang my name. I cannot describe how that felt. I never wanted to leave but I knew that there was no future for me at City. Ever since then I have hoped I would get another chance at the Club but you begin to wonder if it will ever happen. Whenever I have returned to Maine Road with West Ham the reception has been amazing.

"I feel I have at least three or four good years in me because my game has never been based on pace alone. I want to make up for the time I lost because I have always regretted that my first spell here only lasted six months. Nothing would give me greater pleasure than to end my career here, although I am not planning to hang up my boots for some time."

In the boardroom there were also changes. Francis Lee resigned as both chairman and a director and was replaced at the top by French Connection's David Bernstein. A supporter for over 40 years, Bernstein was keen to find stability: "The last two decades have witnessed constant and damaging speculation about boardroom and change of control issues. We intend to professionalise and stabilise the Club at all levels, diffusing the constant hype that plagues us."

Alongside Bernstein's appointment John Wardle, the chairman of JD Sports joined the board. In addition, the board now consisted of Ashley Lewis, who represented the interests of Stephen Boler and the Peter Swales estate, Andrew Thomas, who represented Greenall's brewery, and Dennis Tueart, who had originally joined the board to represent Wardle and David Makin. Mike Turner was, for the time being at least, still chief executive.

Back on the pitch, both Bishop and Goater made their debuts in a 2-1 defeat at Bradford. All matches were now crucial if the Blues were serious about avoiding relegation, but the next game had extra importance for most associated with the Club. It was the return with Stockport County. County had humiliated Clark's side four months earlier and victory was vital for morale purposes if nothing else. It was also crucial the players kept the momentum going for a full ninety minutes, rather than throw everything into the first half and hope to survive. Royle's considerable planning worked: "The determination against Stockport to put things right was evident throughout the side. We went into the game with the worst home record in the First Division and it is up to us to ensure in the remaining games here we do not slip up again.

"Naturally, I was delighted to see how we kept the pressure on Stockport until the final whistle. I said before the game that it was going to be a massive occasion for everyone, both on and off the pitch. For once in this traumatic season we got it right. The overall display was excellent."

The game ended 4-1 with Goater opening the scoring in the fifth minute. That strike was cancelled out a few seconds later by City fan Aaron Wilbraham, but the Blues' resilience shone through and Jobson made it 2-1 in the 32nd minute. Eight minutes before the break Lee Bradbury scored only his fourth since his expensive transfer, then in the 57th minute he netted his fifth of the season. Royle was delighted: "All strikers go through barren patches - I should know and I was an experienced pro when I hit my worst patch - but when I told Lee in training he was going to be in the side I could see he was raring to go again.

"I decided on a new pairing with Lee linking up with Shaun Goater, who I thought had an excellent home debut. Shaun scored the first goal which obviously settled his nerves and went on to give a superb all-round contribution. Despite all our troubles it shows the potential of this club that quality players like Shaun, Jamie Pollock and Ian Bishop are eager to come here."

Another hero to thousands of fans that day was Stockport 'keeper Eric Nixon. The Former Blue gifted two of the goals to City and was warmly greeted by the chant "Eric's a City fan" from the North Stand. It was not a particularly enjoyable day for Nixon who, at one stage, had to leave the field for stitches in his mouth after an aerial clash with Goater.

Despite this victory City were deep in relegation trouble. They lay in 21st place on 43 points, the same as Portsmouth who were now managed by Alan Ball. Below them lay Reading and Stoke City, but there was little separating the Clubs. Above City were Bury on 46 points and Port Vale, QPR and Norwich each on 45 points. It was going to be a tough final five matches.

Away at play-off seeking Wolves, City managed a 2-2 draw. They had led twice - but an error by Margetson gifted Wolves an equaliser in the 34th minute, then in the final five minutes of the match former Blue and future Rochdale manager Paul Simpson equalised. Two days later Trevor Francis' Birmingham won 0-1 at Maine Road deep into injury time despite a good performance from the Blues. Francis admitted afterwards he would have been delighted if he'd managed to leave with just a point and couldn't believe his luck. Particularly upsetting was that Birmingham's scorer Adebola had performed a nasty tackle on Richard Jobson, putting the City man out of the game. Had he been appropriately sent off he would not have been on the pitch during those final minutes.

After Birmingham came another disappointing blow as Middlesbrough won 1-0 with a strike from Alun

Armstrong shortly before half-time. The Blues rarely threatened, although many felt they deserved a penalty shortly before the end of what was a very controversial televised match on Teesside. One of the major incidents involved Lee Bradbury. The City striker was headbutted by Steve Vickers, who was then sent off. Middlesbrough manager Bryan Robson claimed Bradbury dived and wouldn't accept the television evidence.

Joe Royle wasn't too pleased with the result or the atmosphere: "This is one of the most hostile grounds in the country. The supporters appeal for everything and they generally get their way. I have to say I was not happy with the official's performance, but he was certainly right to send off Vickers. If you head butt someone on the pitch, then you have to go and it is as simple as that."

City remained in 21st place, but with only two games left survival was no longer within their own hands. For the final home match Royle felt it was time to bring Kinkladze back into the side for only his fourth game under the new manager. Many felt he should have been a regular feature in the side, but with his negotiations to join Ajax and Royle's determination to adopt a fighting, never say die attitude it was clear the manager wouldn't play him week in week out. Nevertheless, his arrival provoked a great deal of excitement and, before City's largest crowd of the season 32,040, he netted a first minute goal. Earlier, in the tunnel QPR's Vinnie Jones had an argument with a steward after allegedly intimidating Kinkladze. It was that sort of day.

Immediately after the 43-second goal, the stands were buzzing with discussion on the rights and wrongs of Royle's decision not to play Kinkladze in the other games. The discussions continued, and then in the eighth minute former Blue Mike Sheron netted an equaliser. There seems to be a perverse rule which states that when a former Blue is playing against City he is always going to score. The fans have known this for some time and every season there seem to be at least a couple of examples.

Thirteen minutes later Jamie Pollock intercepted a pass from Sheron, flicked the ball in the air and then, with superb ball control, headed firmly over Margetson into City's net. It felt as if the long running Maine Road farce was never going to end. As a result Pollock was voted Man of the Century in a national poll sabotaged by QPR fans.

Three minutes into the second half Bradbury at last found some accuracy and netted an equaliser. Later Nigel Quashie was sent off for elbowing Dickov. The Blues tried to take the lead but it wasn't to be, and a game they had to win ended in a 2-2 draw.

After the match the players came on to the pitch for their annual lap of honour. It was more a sign of loyalty and gave supporters the chance to urge their players forward for the final battle away to Stoke, but the move was lampooned in the press. The *Independent* reporter Guy Hodgson probably got the balance between humour and tragedy just right: "Like all good farces they kept the best joke until last. After a season in which they have miserably under-performed the Manchester City players returned to the pitch after the game for a mutual saluting session. They applauded the fans, who duly clapped back; the first thoroughly deserving it, the team absolutely not. We were witnessing a novelty, a lap of dishonour in front of 30,000 loyal fans who have been ever-present this season.

"It brought back memories of the best named sports book ever, a history of baseball's New York Mets called *The Worst Team Money Could Buy*, because there before us was an expensive collection of failure that has to live up to its trappings."

Considering City's history and unique ability to make simple tasks difficult he added: "In the pubs of Manchester beforehand there was a curious bonding of optimism and perverse logic which went on the lines that City could relax because their fate was in their own hands. Anybody who has studied the history of the Club would know that is the last place you would want your destiny to be, but just in case City served up a 90 minute reminder.

"It is hard to imagine any team but City conceding two goals that belonged more to black comedy than football yet at 2-1 down they were trailing to strikes from a former player and their own captain, while the one goal they had scored was from an individual they are desperately trying to sell. Laugh? Only the hard-hearted would not weep."

He ended his report explaining City's task was now extremely difficult. Joe Royle had said City needed luck and self-control, Hodgson added: "When did City have any luck, or self-control for that matter? The grand masters of the cock up have a final curtain call."

The final day of the season was an immensely tense affair. City's first visit to Stoke's Britannia Stadium became vitally important to both clubs. Prior to the game the bottom six lined up as follows:

	P	W	D	L	F	A	Pts
QPR	45	10	19	16	51	62	49
Port Vale	45	12	10	23	52	66	46
Portsmouth	45	12	10	23	48	62	46
Stoke	45	11	13	21	42	69	46
City	45	11	12	22	51	55	45
Reading	45	11	9	25	39	77	42

City needed to beat Stoke and hope either Port Vale or Portsmouth failed in their away games at Huddersfield and Bradford respectively. With Alan Ball in charge of Portsmouth, many Blues joked it was a formality. Sadly, Alan Ball's side managed a shock 3-1 victory, while Vale recorded a 4-0 thrashing of a lacklustre Huddersfield. The results stunned those at the Britannia witnessing City's 5-2 rout of Stoke and meant that after a total of 106 years of League football the Blues had plummeted to the third tier for the first time.

The game was played out in a strange almost surreal atmosphere. There had been a significant amount of crowd trouble before, during, and after the game with around 20 casualties and 15 arrests, but the most curious moment came when the teams and some fans realised relegation was a certainty. Both clubs now faced playing derby games with nearby Macclesfield rather than their traditional rivals of Manchester United and Port Vale respectively. The City fans chanted "Are you watching Macclesfield?" before giving Kinkladze a final send off. Everyone realised this would be his final League match for the Club.

Afterwards Chairman David Bernstein apologised to supporters for the disaster. The public apology was a key moment in Bernstein's early reign and supporters were encouraged their rather low-profile Chairman felt as painfully as they did about the nightmare of relegation. He blamed the frequent nature of change that always seemed to block progress. It was something most supporters had been saying for years - the appointment of Peter Reid in 1990 was made because the fans demanded some form of stability when Howard Kendall walked out, likewise the Reid dismissal was viewed as

exceptionally poor timing because of its unsettling nature on the playing squad.

Another consequence of all the constant change was that the playing squad ballooned larger than could be managed effectively. Players were brought in by one manager on high salaries and with promise of regular first team football, only to find the next incumbent preferred someone else.

This mismanagement over a period of years helped turn City into a football laughing stock. As always the fans were forced to suffer the humiliation of it all. Relegation hurt and many Blues found the experience dreadfully painful; some wanted to avoid all mention of football, which was a pretty difficult task considering it was a World Cup year. There were also the regular references to Manchester United that seemed to pop up when least expected. Even the Queen became embroiled in controversy when she was asked to sign a Manchester United football while in Kuala Lumpar for the Commonwealth Games. Mancunians were told it would help their city prepare for their turn as hosts in 2002 but it was difficult to see how. Tommy Muir, one of the leading members of City's Supporters' Club sent a letter and a City ball to Buckingham Palace inviting the Queen to sign for City supporters. He wasn't surprised when he received a diplomatic reply simply wishing the Blues well for the new season.

THE INDEPENDENT
MONDAY
4 MAY 1998

6/FOOTBALL

On the way out: Georgi Kinkladze, who came on as a substitute for Manchester City, leaves the field after his team's hollow victory at Stoke yesterday   Photograph: Ross Kinnaird/Allsport

Surreal tale of two relegated Citys

By Phil Shaw   Thirty years ago next week,   casualties, two with fractured   and Lee Bradbury before City   to the Second Division in seven   games sighed. "It was probably

13 years before they met in the FA Cup final, City and Stoke were relegated to the third tier on a day when no one could forecast a bright future.

1998-1999 The Fightback

Life in Division Two was a totally alien experience when the 1998-99 season commenced. Throughout the Club's history no one had ever seriously contemplated what it would be like to field a team in the equivalent of the old Third Division, beneath the likes of Stockport, Crewe, and Bury. These were worrying times, particularly as heroes Kinkladze and Rösler had moved on. Understandably Kit Symons had also left. Another to go was Ian Brightwell, the playing squad's last link with the mid 80s. These were sad but inevitable losses as the Club made cutbacks.

Despite these departures, City still appeared to be the media's clear favourites for the Division Two title. Supporters, however, knew that if any side was capable of making the simple seem difficult it was City. Promotion may have been a formality as far as the media were concerned but for fans it was hoped for - even demanded - but not expected. Nevertheless, there was a perverse excitement about the new season. Most were looking forward to seeing City stand a chance of winning a significant number of games, while others eagerly anticipated trips to long forgotten footballing venues. There was no doubt City were by far the biggest club in the division, and that gave the Club a certain prestige. It was a somewhat perverse view but the Club and its supporters had to clutch at any positives from the embarrassment of relegation.

Off the pitch season ticket sales were healthy - at the start of August it was revealed nearly 14,000 had been sold - while fans were keen to purchase the new fluorescent yellow and green striped away shirt. Unfortunately, Kappa once again failed to deliver enough shirts to satisfy demand, and a great sales opportunity was missed. Already City's relationship with their kit manufacturer was being questioned. The hyperbole at launch suggested this was a perfect marriage of two forward looking organisations - with City sinking to their lowest position and Kappa failing to deliver the goods, it looked as if marriage guidance was required.

For some supporters the new season was viewed positively. Blackpool on the opening day was acceptable enough; after all the Blues had played them often in cup competitions since the mid 1980s, then an away game at the ambitious Fulham - a club that claimed boldly to be a Premier League club merely playing in Division Two. Burnley and Preston would arrive at Maine Road in October, and then there would be derby matches with Oldham. Even the fixtures with Macclesfield were looked forward to, especially by those Blues with allegiance to both clubs.

On the opening day a crowd of 32,134 squeezed into Maine Road for the Blackpool clash. The Club and fans treated it like a Premier League match. The usual razzmatazz was there. It would have been easy to believe this was not the Second Division - particularly as even the back page of the City programme referred to the game as taking place in "Nationwide League Division One"!

The game itself reassured those with doubts City could storm through the division. Shaun Goater, who had not set the world alight following his arrival the previous season, brought a 24th minute lead when he converted a low cross from the terrier like Paul Dickov. Goater had already set himself the rather ambitious target of 25 goals, and with several chances throughout the match should have increased his tally. He didn't but other players did.

Dickov created many openings and after 62 minutes clipped a pass to the still disappointing Lee Bradbury who netted from about ten yards out. Seventeen minutes later the tricky to pronounce defender Kakhaber Tskhadadze was in the right spot when a Tony Vaughan header rebounded off the post, and the Georgian made it 3-0. It was an impressive performance at times, particularly from young debutants Gary Mason and Nicky Weaver, but there were also a few worrying signs. Despite the goals City did miss too many clear chances and the general feeling was of relief. Joe Royle was glad to get the game out of the way: "I am certainly not kidding myself that it was a marvellous team performance, but it was a promising start. We looked very competitive and our fitness levels were good. Paul (Dickov) and Gary (Mason) showed a great spirit throughout the match and were probably our best players."

Afterwards the Blackpool manager Nigel Worthington was amazed his players had not performed well: "If you do not enjoy playing at Maine Road, you should pack your boots and go home. Before too long Manchester City will be storming back into the First Division."

Three days after the Blackpool victory City travelled to Notts County in the first leg of the first round of the Worthington sponsored League Cup. Tskhadadze opened the scoring from a corner in the 72nd minute, then Australian Danny Allsopp, who had replaced Lee Bradbury, made it 2-0 in injury time. The return match saw a rampaging City annihilate County 7-1. Interestingly, only 123 County supporters travelled to Manchester for a match watched by 10,063.

Royle was delighted: "The Maine Road crowd has not seen a resounding win like that for some time and so I am pleased for them. We played some terrific stuff at times and I thought our young players showed great maturity. There is a great spirit in the camp and to my mind, plenty of reasons to be optimistic at the moment."

The County victory, and Royle's upbeat message, had followed a rather disappointing League game at Fulham on 14th August. Kit Symons, now playing for Fulham, performed well as the home side defeated the Blues 3-0. Inevitably, among the scorers was another City old boy, Peter Beardsley, who opened with a low drive into the bottom left after being given far too much freedom. The result was disappointing, particularly as Fulham, under the guidance of Chief Operating Officer Kevin Keegan, were expected to be one of the main challengers for promotion. A defeat and a couple of draws saw the Blues fall to fourteenth place, the lowest rung on the League ladder in the Club's history.

City desperately needed to take every opportunity presented, but striker Goater was not making the most of his chances. He admitted he had received a rollicking from Jamie Pollock: "Jamie is brilliant at giving the other lads a kick up the backside. If you are not performing, then he will come over and tell you in no uncertain terms. What I admire about him is that he has never allowed his standards to drop. He still trains like a Premiership player and that is important."

A 3-1 defeat of Walsall followed, and then six days later Mel Machin's impressive Bournemouth side were beaten 2-1 at Maine Road. Thankfully Macclesfield, potentially the greatest banana skin of all, were overcome with an 87th minute strike by the overly-criticised Goater. The supporters were still of the view the Club needed a recognised prolific striker, but Royle was convinced Goater was that man. Ultimately the fans grew to love the Bermudan.

Derby won the League Cup second round tie 2-1 on aggregate thanks to a winner from future Blue Paulo Wanchope. Amazingly, Lee Bradbury had put in a sterling performance. When he was substituted near the end he received a good ovation from the crowd who desperately wanted his career to turn the corner. Everyone willed the £3m man to perform well but unfortunately he remained relatively ineffectual. It was no surprise when he went to Crystal Palace in October in a deal worth about £1.5 million, although it was later claimed Palace's financial problems affected the actual transfer of funds.

Three successive score draws against Northampton (2-2), Millwall (1-1), and Burnley (2-2) came in September, but results were overshadowed by events off the pitch. At Millwall the players and fans were faced with a considerable degree of threatening behaviour from the Millwall fans. Royle: "We could have won the match, but it's probably just as well we didn't. I doubt we'd have got out alive. I didn't know supporters were allowed to run on to the pitch and threaten and spit at players. Still, the crowd refereed the game very well. They appealed for everything and got most of it. I am very angry about what I have seen."

The 2,000 City fans in the crowd of 12,726 behaved well but it was extremely difficult at times under the intense provocation of the locals. At the end of the match the City fans were kept behind for over an hour as the police tried to restore law and order. Those travelling by train could see the damage caused outside by Millwall fans who had fought with the police when the area was being cleared. There was glass everywhere. It was all very sad, and revived bad memories of the problems of the mid-80s when City fans travelled to the old Second Division grounds.

After one win in ten City were down in eleventh place and the fans were becoming concerned. Some new faces were needed and with Bradbury moving to Palace and Ged Brannan off to Motherwell for £378,000 the supporters could see no reason why the Club couldn't spend. Royle: "The Club is saddled with a massive debt and I realise that some of the cash must go towards reducing that burden."

Royle did manage to bring a couple of players in however, with the arrival of Michael Branch on loan from Everton, and Andy Morrison from Huddersfield. Morrison joined on loan at first, but soon became a permanent player with City paying Huddersfield £80,000. Town supporters were disappointed with Morrison's departure as he was a bit of a cult figure to some of the club's fans just as he was to become at City. In 2010 Joe Royle looked back on Morrison's arrival with affection: "We were still muddling around mid-table, finding it very hard. We were the team to beat, and we knew that clubs with very small gates were bringing 3,000 to Maine Road. They were making a weekend of it. But we were finding it tough. We needed a leader and that leader was Andy Morrison. His arrival was a seminal moment in the transformation of Manchester City.

"I knew of Andy and Les Chapman had heard that he was available. We got him for about £30 grand. He came in... Scored on his debut. Wrote someone off in a tackle that turned out to be one of his best mates, and a cult hero was born. City love a cult hero and he was it. He was also a quality player. People forget this, but I believe he should have played for Scotland. He was certainly talented enough. They've had a lot of centre-halves who were nowhere near the calibre of Andy Morrison at his best."

With Morrison's input City achieved a 2-1 victory over Colchester on Halloween. The game came to life with the arrival of Ian Bishop in the second period for his first appearance of the season. Horlock netted a 49th minute penalty before Morrison gave City the victory. Morrison scored again in the next match - a 3-0 defeat of neighbours Oldham - but then embarrassment followed at Wycombe. A game, which had little by way of entertainment, ended 1-0 to the home side thanks to a dubious decision.

Three days later City faced Halifax Town in the first round of the FA Cup - another unwelcome

TRUE BLUE
Joe Royle

A man who understood 'City-itis' and turned a failing side into one that had new life and hope.

consequence of relegation to Division Two. It was an embarrassment to play in such an early round, but across the Pennines the people of Calderdale treated the match as a major occasion. The local newspaper ran a full week of articles leading up to the big match. They even produced a special edition paper which included a full colour poster of Paul Hendrie's goal in the 1980 Halifax victory over Malcolm Allison's multi-million pound side. City fans in the area couldn't believe the hype and were fearful of another humiliation. In the end they needn't have worried as the Blues defeated the Shaymen 3-0 with goals from Russell (two) and Goater. Joe Royle was pleased: "As a whole, I thought it was an adequate performance to beat Halifax and at least we are in the hat. Mind you, I won't start getting excited until we are at the semi-final stage of the competition!"

Despite a valiant performance City left the competition at the third round stage with a 1-0 defeat at Premiership Wimbledon. Previously, the Blues had defeated Darlington 1-0 in a second round replay.

Back in the League, City suffered consecutive draws at home to Gillingham (0-0) and at Luton (1-1). After

before dumped out of the Auto Windscreens Shield by Mansfield Town, Bristol Rovers provided more misery in the next League match - a no score draw at Maine Road - then a 2-1 defeat at York left the Blues lying in 12th place, 15 points behind leaders Fulham and second placed Walsall. Royle knew time was running out: "I never expected this job to be easy. It is nine months since I came here and there have been a great deal of changes - mostly for the better. I am still confident things will come right, but I know we have to start winning quickly."

A Boxing Day victory over Wrexham was the first in an unbeaten run of twelve games, although gale force winds made it difficult at times. It was also clear there was a gap where Morrison, missing through influenza, usually dominated. Nevertheless, the Blues withstood the Wrexham pressure, and in the 55th minute Wiekens managed to score via a powerful downwards header from about six yards out. City fans chanted "one-nil to Eng-er-land!"

Michael Brown performed exceptionally well, winning praise from Royle, while a man who was becoming another hero to the City faithful was young goalkeeper Nicky Weaver. With great skill he managed to keep Wrexham's Martyn Chalk and Ian Rush at bay, and left the field to a standing ovation.

The Stoke victory two days later was considerably

more entertaining, enjoyable, and exciting for the Maine Road crowd of 30,478. The most impressive part was City actually came from behind to take the points, something few City sides had managed in recent seasons. The visitors took the lead through Sigurdsson on the half-hour, but earlier a Gareth Taylor header had been disallowed for offside. After a half-time Royle rollicking the Blues attacked like Tasmanian Devils. The crowd, recognising City's fire, burst into life and cheered, applauded, and chanted. All of this led to Paul Dickov netting a rather simple equaliser two minutes into the half. Dickov: "You could feel the confidence flowing through the side once I had scored."

From that point the Blues were unstoppable, but they still had to wait until Taylor headed an 85th minute winner. It's worth noting this was the first time the Blues had won a match after falling behind in nineteen months. 1998 ended with confidence spreading throughout the Club.

On 16th January the Blues achieved a thrilling 3-0 victory over leaders Fulham. Andy Morrison was missing following a cruel dismissal during the Wimbledon cup defeat two weeks earlier, but City coped admirably. Terry Cooke, an exciting young winger, joined the Club on loan from Old Trafford and immediately impressed. He was delighted with his welcome: "It was absolutely unbelievable. The crowd was amazing and their reception gave me such a buzz. It really was totally different from the atmosphere at Old Trafford where a lot of fans simply expect to win and just sit back and enjoy the game. Maine Road is packed with fanatics and they can make such a difference when they get behind you. There's no way you want to lose. I was delighted with the response from the fans."

It wasn't long before Royle started to talk about promotion, although he tried to play down how the Blues would achieve it: "I have never ruled out automatic promotion and that is our objective, but let's not start to get carried away. We are still out of the play off zone and know that we need to keep this run going. I have believed things were coming right for a while and it is nice to be vindicated, but I am not going to start making rash promises now. We cannot look beyond the next game, which is Millwall at home, and will be massive for us. The lads are already talking about that one and there are a few scores to settle."

On the pitch City made Millwall pay for their early season treatment of the Blues with a 3-0 pounding, thanks to goals from Dickov (61), Cooke (71), and Horlock (75). Off the pitch the away supporters ripped up seats in the North Stand, and had earlier created havoc in Stockport fighting with Manchester United followers. For some reason they seemed a trifle upset when the City fans in the North Stand started chanting "1-0 in your cup final"; by the time it was 3-0 the police had total control, although several shops were damaged after the match.

More trouble followed in City's next match, although this time it managed to confine itself to the players. Although the game was a tightly balanced goal less draw at Bournemouth, the referee managed to send off two City men - Pollock and Horlock. Pollock's third dismissal of the season came about eleven minutes from the end when he performed a rather innocuous looking tackle. It was a little late, but it certainly did not appear to be a deliberate foul, and clearly did not warrant a second yellow card. The City captain was furious: "That was an absolute shambles - I have never seen such a poor refereeing performance in my entire career. He seemed intent on turning a good football match into a rugby match. I could appeal against my sending off, but I wouldn't trust that referee to get it right after watching a video. He doesn't need an extra third eye, he needs another five or six."

The Horlock dismissal was equally frustrating for City. In the dying seconds of the match Horlock approached referee Brian Coddington to tell him Nicky Weaver had been clattered by Ian Cox, who came flying in for a last minute corner. That challenge looked considerably more dangerous than the Pollock incident and yet nothing happened. As Horlock approached Coddington, the official waved him away. Then he produced a red card. Afterwards a baffled Royle searched for answers: "The referee said Kevin was walking towards him in an aggressive manner. He admitted that there was no swearing, Kevin just wanted to speak with him. And here was me thinking it was good to talk. Apparently not. In fact, it seems like it's pretty dangerous to even walk on a football pitch nowadays!

"We came here to be positive and win the game, but did not have the cutting edge which we needed. I felt we were strong all over the pitch and on another day, it would have been a great point. But instead we feel bitter and annoyed by the referee's decisions. People are going to look at the stats and think this game was a bloodbath, but I cannot remember a bad tackle."

Victory followed a week later as Macclesfield were defeated 2-0 at Maine Road, with goals from Goater and Gareth Taylor. The match was watched by a crowd of 31,086 including Ajax's Georgi Kinkladze, who viewed from one of the boxes. The Blues moved up to fifth place on 51 points.

Fulham were clearly walking away with the title by this point, but Preston, Walsall, and Gillingham were all within reach, while Bournemouth, Chesterfield, Wigan, and Millwall were all a little too close for comfort. As City had to travel to Chesterfield for their next match, it was clear the Blues still had a grip on their own destiny.

Unfortunately an extremely rare mistake from Wiekens on the half-hour allowed Chris Beaumont to challenge down the left wing. The Chesterfield player then delivered a cross, which caused panic in the City defence. Marcus Ebdon had a shot blocked on the line, but ex-Bolton striker David Reeves drilled the rebound past Weaver.

Several chances to equalise came City's way, but they couldn't capitalise until the 51st minute. 21 year old Lee Crooks surprised everyone - including the City bench who urged him to pass the ball - when he sent an impressive strike from about thirty yards out into the top corner. It was described as "awesome" in the *Manchester Evening News*, and it clearly was a great finish from a player normally seen as rather staid in his approach.

The away draw was a good result, however City's key rivals - Fulham, Preston, Bournemouth, Wigan and Gillingham - all won causing the Blues to drop to sixth, but it was all still close. Then came another of those controversial refereeing days as 22nd placed Northampton scraped a no score draw at Maine Road. Kevin Horlock was sent off for two bookable offences, despite vehement protests from victim Chris Freestone, prompting Royle to talk about the quality of officials once again: "I am fed up talking about referees. I would rather just leave them to get on with their jobs, but sometimes you have to stand up and say 'he is not good enough.'" Quite honestly, the standard of referees in this division deeply disturbs me but I am not sure there is anything we can do about it."

He then spoke briefly about the Horlock incident: "Kevin is gathering quite a collection of bookings which take some believing. First, it was aggressive walking at Bournemouth, and now he has been sent off for having a shot and because another player slipped over."

The game extended City's unbeaten run to 11 matches - their best for 23 years - but it should have been a victory. Once again the main focus had been the referee, but it was clear to the 27,999 paying fans the forwards were missing too many chances. Goater was still the Club's leading striker with eleven goals but was gaining notoriety for missing many more. Had the Club been top of the table there would not have been so much concern, but with City struggling to hold on to a Division Two play-off place fans were unhappy. Fortunately, a confidence booster was just around the corner.

Burnley were annihilated 6-0 with goals from Horlock, Morrison, and Allsopp and a hat-trick from Goater. Royle was happy: "I am delighted for Shaun Goater, who is a lovely man and has never stopped trying during his difficult spell. I only brought him off so he would get a hero's ovation. This has been coming for a while, and there might be one or two more big wins to come before the end of the season."

City's unbeaten run ended on 13th March with a 1-2 defeat by Oldham. It was one of those "expect the unexpected" games the Blues seem to throw up every now and again. As always a large number of chances came City's way, but the frontmen found it difficult to make an impact. Oldham took the lead through a penalty - the first goal conceded at home since the visit of Stoke on 28th December - and Lee Duxbury made it 2-0 in the 56th minute. Before that, however, City had been awarded a spot kick only for Gareth Taylor to send his right foot shot straight at the Oldham 'keeper. Fortunately Taylor did find the net in the 79th minute but it was too little too late. A streaker raced on to the pitch in the final minutes and demonstrated to the players how to score. He then managed to dodge two policemen and a few stewards for a spell before being wrestled to the ground on what was clearly a very cold day. Afterwards City fan Charlie McCormick was quoted as saying: "it was the best tackle I saw all afternoon!" It was that sort of day.

The Oldham match proved to be merely a blip. Successive victories over Notts County (2-1), Colchester (0-1), Reading (1-3), and Wigan (1-0) followed. The Blues now lay in fourth place behind Fulham, Walsall, and Preston and with Preston their next opponents a certain amount of optimism was spreading. The game at Deepdale proved a tense affair. Preston scored in the opening minute, but still City shaded it. Unfortunately, it ended 1-1 despite several key tactical changes by Royle in an attempt to snatch all three points. New arrival Mark Robins came on as substitute, as did Ian Bishop, but Royle wasn't happy: "I am disappointed because I felt we could have won it. All we can do now is focus on winning games and see where it takes us. Take it from me, there are plenty more twists to come in this season."

A 4-0 thrashing of Lincoln followed - Dickov somersaulted in celebration after netting his third goal of the match - and with five games remaining all talk focused on reaching an automatic spot. The teams left to face were having mixed seasons - Luton were mid table; Gillingham were 5th and a serious threat; Wycombe were struggling at the top of the relegation zone; Bristol Rovers were 16th; while York City were 19th. City seemed capable of easily winning those matches, with the only difficult games appearing to be Gillingham and potentially one of the sides hungry to avoid relegation. Of course, football at Maine Road rarely follows the simplistic path and 2-0 victories over Luton and Gillingham were followed by a 1-2 defeat at home to Wycombe.

Victory against Wycombe would have put considerable pressure on second placed Walsall, who were two points ahead of the Blues when the game commenced, and five when it ended.

Sadly a 2-2 draw at Bristol Rovers killed the last hope of automatic promotion. The draw did guarantee a play-off place, but a trip to Wembley couldn't be guaranteed.

Of course all City fans hoped it would happen - even City's Junior Blues magazine had a full colour photograph of the stadium and told its young readers that if automatic promotion was not achieved then there was definitely going to be a day out to remember at Wembley - but nothing could be regarded as a formality. Royle: "We mustn't take anything for granted. This club has a history of standing around corner flags when they need to score. We are in the play offs and that means we have to do it the hard way. We have achieved nothing yet."

The final match of the League campaign saw the Blues defeat York 4-0 before 32,471 at Maine Road. It was the highest crowd of the season, and meant Maine Road had virtually no segregation as the Club crammed supporters into every spot possible. There were still thousands of others who wanted to be there to witness what many hoped would be the Club's last league game in Division Two.

The victory ensured City took third place in the division and brought a play-off semi-final with 6th placed Wigan, who scraped into the play offs on better goals scored than Bournemouth. The first leg was played away at Springfield Park, and became the last competitive match played at the ground before the club's move to the much more impressive JJB stadium. 6,762 paid to watch at Wigan, but a more impressive figure of around ten thousand attended Maine Road to watch via a large screen placed in front of the Main Stand. A surreal atmosphere engulfed Maine Road as the sight of any City player warming up prompted supporters to cheer. Even Moonchester received a massive cheer when he was spotted on the screen.

Shortly before the match kicked off the television cameras showed a large contingent of supporters running through a hole in the Springfield Park fence to take up positions on the terracing. Quickly stewards and police blocked the gap, but at least 100 fans managed to gain free entry.

The positive atmosphere at Maine Road was shattered in the first twenty seconds of the match as the normally dependable Wiekens and Weaver lost all sense of the occasion. Both stood motionless as Stuart Barlow rushed between them to score a very simple goal. Maine Road went silent, while those City fans at Wigan were distraught. Fortunately, Royle's City no longer buckled in these situations and the Blues did dominate the rest of the match. City attacked and attacked, while Wigan tried to withstand the pressure.

After 77 minutes the Blues finally scored the goal they deserved. Michael Brown made a good run down the right. He crossed to Paul Dickov, and City's powerful dynamo swept home a thoroughly deserved equaliser. The cheer from Maine Road was so loud wags joked it could be heard at Springfield Park itself.

As the game wore on City attacked further, but they also kept one eye on defence. This wasn't the time to do anything else stupid. In the sixth minute of injury time Tony Vaughan narrowly missed scoring the winner when he headed fractionally wide, but the Blues felt satisfied. At Maine Road the screen displayed a happy Joe Royle, prompting the City fans to chant, "Royle, Royle, give us a wave." He didn't, and the Kippax supporters gave him a good natured boo as a result.

Four days later Goater gave City a 27th minute lead in the return to send the Blues to Wembley for the first time since 1986. Despite his critics, Goater was still netting enough to be City's top scorer. After the whistle thousands of supporters invaded the pitch to celebrate. It was a terrific sight and seemed to be an outpouring that ended years of hurt. Of course it wasn't, and with Wembley around the corner no one quite knew what to expect, but it was a significant moment. One supporter in a wheelchair found the whole affair particularly entertaining, especially when his friend pushed the chair at a frantic pace across the pitch, and then let go to leave the disabled fan rolling for some distance. He even entered the net at one point as both men laughed.

Director John Wardle was also on the pitch dancing, as the fans partied. Well it was 1999. Life was certainly on the up, and when it was announced City's opponents would be Gillingham and not Preston, most fans assumed there would be absolutely no problem getting tickets. Sadly, the distribution of tickets showed City's organisational skills to be particularly weak.

Confusion, mixed messages, and total lack of understanding led to the biggest ticketing fiasco in the Club's history. Thousands of supporters had to queue in excess of eight hours simply to get tickets their regular season ticket book should have guaranteed. City's queuing system meant fans had to go on a massive tour of the stadium.

During their time inside the North Stand fans were able to read messages left by those that had gone before them such as, "Mummy, where's Daddy? Is he dead? No son he's just gone for his tickets, he'll be back when you're a teenager"; "If anybody finds my body, tell my wife and children that I love them"; "I'm not ringing my wife. I said I'd be home at 11.30, why have two arguments in one day!"; "Here lies the body of an unknown City fan, he bravely queued for six hours before sun stroke and hunger got the better of him."

City fans were disgusted by the Club's total failure. Noel Bayley: "I have been making complaints and advocating suggestions with regard to the piss poor Maine Road ticket office now for longer than I can remember, so I cannot claim to have been surprised by the cock-up when it came to selling Wembley tickets, which was huge even by the ticket office's lowly standards. Instead of a reward for the most loyal fans in the country the Club's legendary amateur antics ensured that Wembley became a huge millstone and then they had the gall to blame the fans. Heads should have rolled."

Eventually, over forty thousand City fans did obtain tickets for the play off final, but there were still a large number disappointed. Meanwhile, Gillingham were able to sell their allocation to more or less anybody from the south east. At one point a Gillingham spokesman even had the 'brass neck' to say the whole of Kent was supporting Gillingham while not even half of Manchester followed the Blues. It was a ridiculous comment and one which upset a large number of Mancunians, particularly as Gillingham's average attendance was some 22,000 less than City's.

The 1999 Play Off Final was scheduled for Sunday 30th May with City clearly the favourites. According to the media Gillingham were going to be swept aside by Royle's men. The trip to Wembley was going to be a great experience for City's followers, although those with longer memories believed this could be yet another of City's famous 'cock-up days'. In the end it became both one of the most tortuous and joyous occasions ever experienced by Blues, and the entire day seemed to sum up exactly what supporting Manchester City was all about.

For many Blues the day began with a long journey down to the capital. Some stayed overnight close by - the Wembley Hilton seemed to have City banners and flags hanging from every window - yet for those arriving early the atmosphere was strange. Supporters wearing suspiciously new Gillingham shirts marched around the stadium, while others encamped close to the ramps on Wembley Way were singing songs glorifying Manchester United, Millwall, and every once in a while Gillingham. Blues arriving via the underground would have been confused as to who City's opponents were early on, but the atmosphere seemed peaceful enough.

The Gillingham fans mainly congregated around the Wembley Way/twin towers area, and cheered every time their Chairman Paul Scally appeared. The pro-Gillingham chanting was abruptly ended when a small group of City supporters lightened the atmosphere by marching through the middle of the Gillingham supporters chanting: "Wem-ber-ley, Wem-ber-ley, it's that shitty place in London that we thought we'd never see!" Everyone laughed, and it said much about the City fans' approach to the match.

Around the stadium close to the players' tunnel end the City supporters gathered en masse. Every song, every flag, every face was blue, and every time a vehicle passed with City merchandise visible the cheering was incredible. At one point a white stretch limousine with City flags sticking out of the sunroof passed. The rumour went around this was Noel and Liam Gallagher, but there had already been a number of other stories concerning the Oasis boys' arrival and nobody seemed to know for certain.

Then a coach appeared with a police escort in the distance. The cheer went up. City were on their way! Except it wasn't City, it was Gillingham, and what was worse was that nobody seemed to realise until the very last moment when the cheering turned into booing. The Gillingham players should have known then the atmosphere would be mainly blue.

When the City coach did arrive, the cheering was incredible and the players couldn't help but be moved by the whole affair. As soon as the coach entered the stadium, City fans rushed to their turnstiles and made their way into the ground. This was the first time many City fans had been since 1986, and the terracing on which they had then stood, close to the Players' tunnel, was now all-seater. As a result the view seemed considerably worse.

The pre-match entertainment was not particularly inspiring with two London based DJs pretending to support Gillingham and City, and then sing songs connected with the clubs. The 'City DJ' chose to sing Oasis songs, surely Blue Moon would have been more appropriate? And even the arrival of Moonchester couldn't save the DJ from embarrassment as his great singalong became singalone. He was eventually drowned out by the sounds of Blue Moon from those in D, E, and F sections amongst others. The Football League even provided opera for the fans, but well known United supporter Russell Watson was booed every time he opened his mouth.

Eventually, the players were brought out on to the pitch for the commencement of play. They were greeted by smoke, fireworks, and inflatable Nationwide Building Society men causing City fans to ponder what had happened to football during City's thirteen-year absence from Wembley.

When the match commenced City were not the great force the media anticipated, instead they slipped their way across a wet surface and relied on the 20 year old Nicky Weaver to keep Gillingham at bay, particularly in the 9th minute when he palmed away an effort from Galloway. As the game wore on confidence grew and in the 26th minute a downward header from Horlock was superbly saved by Gillingham's Bartram.

Mixed play followed a forgettable first half, although it's fair to say City had the better chances and should have taken the lead, especially in the 75th minute when Goater sidefooted a shot against the post. As the game progressed City fans became nervous, then with only nine minutes remaining the Blues were dealt a major blow when Asaba toe-poked a shot into the roof of City's net. There was a feeling of huge disappointment in the stands, but worse was to follow as Robert Taylor made

The scoreboard says it all. 2-0 at 90 minutes. 2-2 after added time and a chance for promotion. Bottom: Gillingham's Bartram at the end of penalties with celebrating City fans behind.

an unlikely equaliser into the top corner. For a few seconds the stadium fell silent as City supporters struggled to comprehend the importance of the goal, and then wild celebrations erupted all over Wembley. Outside those that had left early heard the news and rushed back, and the stadium was full once more.

An extremely tense period of extra time followed, and then came penalties. The City players huddled together as a team, showing a unity previous sides had clearly not enjoyed. This helped City win the penalty shoot-out 3-1, but this score conveys nothing of the drama, the excitement, and the immense feeling of relief experienced at the time. The penalty sequence started with Kevin Horlock scoring the first at the City-filled Players Tunnel end of the stadium. Then Weaver's legs blocked Gillingham's first effort by midfielder Paul Smith.

A confident-looking Paul Dickov marched forward to take City's second, but watched in agony as his attempt bounced off both posts to leave the score at 1-0. Adrian Pennock then shot wide for Gillingham, before Terry Cooke calmly slotted his effort into the bottom corner to make it 2-0.

John Hodge sent Gillingham's third penalty clinically into the roof of the net, then Richard Edghill sent his spot kick in off the bar. The pressure was at long last on Gillingham. Guy Butters looked a little on edge as he prepared for the eighth penalty, while in nets Weaver seemed relatively composed. The young City 'keeper dived the right way and blocked Butters' effort to give City victory. He immediately went on a manic celebratory run, until he was dragged back to reality by Morrison and the other players.

it 2-0 in the 86th minute. Two thirds of the stadium fell silent, then many, many Blues decided enough was enough and left for home. Those that remained were in for a treat, although no-one could possibly have anticipated quite what would follow. Sky TV certainly believed the contest was over as every comment mentioned Gillingham's success and City's embarrassing failure.

Radio Five commentator Alan Green told his listeners about the plight of the thousands of City fans silent at Wembley adding: "That many fans go to every home game. Why do they do it?" It wasn't long before he found the answer.

With a mere 17 seconds of normal time remaining Horlock sidefooted a goal, prompting sparks of optimism from a few supporters. Surely just a consolation, yet four and a half minutes into injury time Dickov fired

Wild celebrations followed, with the players bowing to the supporters to show their appreciation for sticking

473

by the Club through an extremely difficult period. The City fans were in good voice and after several traditional City anthems, they burst into a chant that many may regard as being offensive but at that moment summed up exactly how the supporters felt. For too long City fans had endured abuse from supporters of other clubs and the Blues dismal plight under Alan Ball and others during the 1990s had caused a great deal of pain. Manchester United's success had brought further misery, so when the City fans chanted the obscene but heartfelt "you can stick your f**king treble up your arse!" it was more an indication of how the Blues simply did not care about activity elsewhere, they only cared about their club. Accusations of jealousy were false, City fans were for once singing about their success and nothing else - not even a world-wide headline grabbing treble - was more important.

That chant, though littered with foul language, was actually being sung at Wembley Stadium by supporters of all ages and though, for obvious reasons, it didn't make the headlines, it was a clear indication City fans

TRUE BLUE
Paul Dickov

Although fans tend to focus on his equalising goal in the 1999 play off final, it was Paul Dickov's battling spirit throughout his time at City that made a true hero.

really didn't care about any other team, just the one they had supported through thick and thin. The play-off was the only game that mattered.

Chairman David Bernstein joined fellow director Dennis Tueart and PR guru Chris Bird on the pitch. The normally quiet, unassuming City man later stated: "I just felt it would be wonderful to walk on the Wembley surface... It will be a one off for I won't be making a habit of it, you can be sure of that!"

Bernstein was a very happy man, although he admitted this was not the end of City's struggle: "This is only the first stage. We will clear our heads and take it from there. I'll be working even harder to raise finance, which I've got to say will be easier now we are in the First Division."

Afterwards two men were being seen by most Blues as the real heroes of the day - Nicky Weaver and Paul Dickov. Weaver, in particular, grabbed the headlines and seemed to be the man who impressed the media. Weaver told journalists: "To come from third team football to this in a year is fantastic. To finish the season like this is absolutely incredible. I felt better than I thought I would. Once we got out and started playing it felt like any other game, which helped my nerves. I wasn't overawed by the surroundings at all."

As time progressed the contribution of another man, often pilloried, was highlighted by Andy Noise in *Bert Trautmann's Helmet*: "Richard Edghill - what a star. Never scored a goal in his life. Subject of much (unjustified) criticism, yet he stood up and was counted. He had the bottle, and he bloody did it."

Manager Joe Royle was delighted, although it's fair to say he looked absolutely worn out when he made it into the dressing room after the celebrations. In typically down to earth manner he told the media: "We're not getting too excited about this. A club this size should not be too euphoric about getting out of the old Division Three. And even though we won today, I still think the play offs are a joke. After 46 League games it comes down to a lottery."

Moving on to the performance Joe added: "My players were magnificent, and I never once thought we were beaten. We have now lost just twice in our last 27 matches and I think that tells you everything about their fighting spirit. We have played 49 cup ties this season and this is a very hard division. When fans are hanging off the rafters for you at places like Colchester, it all adds to the pressure. These lads will be better players for this

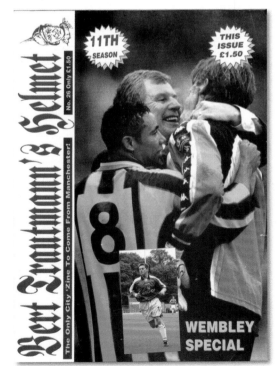

For the first time in years fanzines could be positive about the Club.

experience and the strong nucleus in this side will go forward.

"I think we have gone a long way to curing Man City-itis. We can handle the big games now, even though we weren't at our best today."

That night referee Mark Halsey, who was staying at the nearby Hilton Hotel, witnessed a hotel full of Blues celebrating. They offered to buy him drinks and one or two wags tried to start a collection for the official. It was all light hearted, however Gillingham's chairman Paul Scally didn't see it that way. He made a complaint to the Football League and demanded the game be replayed claiming Halsey had been celebrating. For a couple of days the League deliberated and then, much to City and the referee's relief, announced the result would stand. They did, however, have a word of warning for Halsey: "There is a time and a place for everything and we shall remind him that it is unwise to mix with supporters so soon after an important match."

With the referee chastised and promotion in the bag, City fans looked forward to a season in Division One and were hopeful their new found spirit could lift them higher. Their three season exile from the Premier League had already equalled their longest spell out of the top flight since their first promotion exactly one hundred years earlier.

Promotion at the first attempt from Division Two was greeted by most Blues as a sign Joe Royle was on the right track. The division had been a tough one, and promotion via the play offs, though not the preferred route, had actually helped bind the Club together. Team spirit appeared high and general interest in the Blues increased, but no one was prepared to accept that the job was complete. City had further to go and promotion from Division Two had been a necessity. Royle: "David

TRUE BLUES
Andy Morrison & Nick Weaver

Andy Morrison & Nicky Weaver were important members of the side that gained promotion in dramatic fashion in 1999. Morrison's captaincy gave City a determined approach while Weaver's performance in the play off penalty shoot out enabled City to gain promotion.

Bernstein, the chairman, came up to me on the coach journey back and he told me that the council had been in touch asking us if we wanted a homecoming parade. I said to David 'An open-topped bus for getting out of this division? Are you serious?' And he said, 'I know' but I had to ask."

1996-1999 SUMMARY

Highest League Attendance: 32,471 York City, 08/05/99
Highest Cup Attendance: 31,305 Wigan Athletic, 19/05/99 (Play Off)
Managers: 1995 – 1996 Alan Ball, 1996 Steve Coppell, 1996 – 1998 Frank Clark & 1998 – 2001 Joe Royle

Seasonal Record:

Season	League	Posn	FA Cup	League Cup	Other	Leading Scorer	Average Attendance
1996-97	New 1	14	Rnd 5	Rnd 2		Rösler 15	30,729
1997-98	New 1	22	Rnd 4	Rnd 1		Dickov 9	32,040
1998-99	New 2	3	Rnd 3	Rnd 2	Auto-Windscreens Shield Rnd 1	Goater 18	32,471

The foundations are laid for City's new home. The building came as a result of great co-operation between public and private bodies, including City and Manchester council.

Looking To The Future

"Some supporters had to be asked to leave Maine Road after its final League match on 11th May 2003. They found it hard to say goodbye. This was one of the most significant places in their lives. A place where they had gathered a wealth of memories. This wasn't just a football ground, this was their Utopia."

Farewell To Maine Road by Gary James, published 2003

1999-2000 Back To Back

Immediately after the 1999 promotion season ticket sales had risen to 14,000. Early in the new season the Club were forced to create a waiting list as they had reached their limit of around 22,000. This limit had been set to ensure there would be no problem with potential cup fixture allocations at Maine Road, and was also seen as an effort by the Club to ensure it would still be possible to attend games on a match by match basis.

Alongside the increased interest from spectators, City also found themselves a new sponsor, computer game company Eidos. The Brother sponsorship had come to an end, and City were keen to tie up with an organisation representing the future. Eidos - the company responsible for the bestselling Tomb Raider

and Championship Manager series of games - seemed to offer the Club what they wanted. Eidos' executive chairman and Blue Ian Livingstone was also delighted: "We see Manchester City as a unique property in domestic football with enormous potential for the future. Eidos is impressed with the board's vision for the future and felt it should be part of the new era."

There were other major changes off the field. Chris Bird was promoted to Chief Operating Officer and made a director: "It's unbelievable. When I was a kid I always dreamed of playing for City. Becoming a director is something I never really thought about. I know it sounds cheesy, but this is a real honour." While another change saw kit suppliers Kappa replaced by Le Coq Sportif after only two seasons.

When City's season commenced on Sunday 8th

August they were rated as tenth favourites to win the Division One title, while Blackburn Rovers were the bookies' favourites. As with the 1996-97 season when City were widely tipped following their relegation from the Premier League, the Blackburn prediction was way off the mark. Nevertheless, they did appear to be the team to beat as preparations were made.

The opening game saw the Blues face Wolves at Maine Road before a crowd of 31,755 and a Sky TV audience. 23 year old Mark Kennedy, a signing from Wimbledon, and the on loan left back Danny Granville both made their debuts. City attacked Wolves with force and had plenty of chances, but it wasn't to be. Despite the pressure - according to Sky City had 55% possession in the first half; 80% possession in the second and fourteen corners to Wolves' none - the match ended in a 1-0 defeat.

At half-time Chairman David Bernstein made a move which would help the Club plan for the new millennium when he signed the contract documentation confirming City's move to the new stadium at Eastlands. On the pitch he was joined by council leader Richard Leese and Chief Executive Howard Bernstein for the official signing. The Chairman wrote in City's programme: "The stadium design has benefited from [fans'] feedback at last year's open days. Its capacity should approach 50,000 and its facilities will be fitting for the next Millennium. I would like to thank Manchester City Council and Sport England for the confidence shown in our club. I believe that the City of Manchester, the local community and our club will all derive enormous benefits from this exciting venture"

The signing coincided with an explanation of the plan which would see the stadium built in two phases, with the first concentrating on creating a stadium fit for the Commonwealth Games. Afterwards the athletics track would be removed and the stadium would be squared off to create a traditionally shaped football enclosure. Had City not been promoted in 1999 then it is highly unlikely a permanent stadium of the capacity eventually reached would have been built to house a football team.

All of this was for the future, however, and City's main stadium issue at the time appeared to be how to cram more seats into the existing ground. Additional temporary seating was added to the now infamous 'Gene Kelly Stand' ("singing in the rain", officially block UU in the corner between the Kippax and the North Stand), while the corner between the Kippax and Platt Lane now housed a few hundred seats in front of the scoreboard. Later in the season a further section of seats was added to the Gene Kelly Stand, although these were actually positioned at an awkward viewing angle, and occupants seemed to face the lower tier of the Kippax rather than the pitch. It put some supporters in mind of the old

In 2000 steps were taken to explain how the stadium would develop.

Bernard Manning joke from the mid 80s: "I hear they've built a new stand at Maine Road. Trouble is they've built it the wrong way round - it faces the pitch!"

The new seating was the only way the Club could increase capacity at a stadium that could no longer accommodate City's huge crowds. A year later the Blues sought other ways of increasing the capacity, squeezing seats in to what seemed like every available nook and cranny.

Three days after the Wolves defeat the Blues entertained Burnley in a rather easy 5-0 victory in the League Cup first round first leg. This included two goals from the impressive Mark Kennedy and the first of the season for Shaun Goater. It was hoped victory would spur the Blues on for their match with the Division Two champions Fulham, but sadly the game ended goalless as the two sides cancelled each other out. To further enhance his cult status, Andy Morrison, in a rather bizarre moment, was given a red card for 'licking' Stan Collymore's nose.

On 21st August Adrian Heath's Sheffield United arrived hoping for victory. They left feeling totally demoralised. The game started in frenetic style with both sides having good attempts on goal, although as the first half progressed it was clear City were taking control. Then came a couple of lucky breaks: first a handball led to a penalty easily converted by Horlock, then goalkeeper Tracey - the man who had appeared for the Blues when defeated 5-0 at Old Trafford in November 1994 - pulled down Goater on the edge of the area. Tracey was sent off and Horlock netted his second penalty.

In the second half City tore into the Blades. Kennedy rounded the replacement 'keeper after neat play from Bishop and Dickov to score the third. The fourth came via a cross from Terry Cooke which was neatly headed downwards by the giant Goater. A fifth came from Paul Dickov and then Gareth Taylor, who had replaced Goater in the 70th minute, made it six. The crowd called for ten, but the score remained and afterwards Royle offered the goal feast as a "thank you" to the fans.

Following the thrashing of Sheffield United, the Blues defeated Burnley 1-0 in the second leg of the League Cup, and continued to move up the Division One table by beating Bolton, Nottingham Forest and Crystal Palace. The Palace victory put City second and raised expectations that promotion was attainable, despite the obvious problems associated with mounting a challenge so soon after scraping through the play-offs. As if to test the worth of the City team, the League Cup draw created an interesting two legged tie with Premiership Southampton.

The home leg ended goalless. Not the result hoped for, but still a creditable performance, then a week later the Blues travelled to the Dell for a more entertaining second leg. The match had been re-arranged from the Tuesday night to accommodate Sky TV.

The first few minutes were played at breakneck speed with City creating a flurry of chances in those opening moments. The best effort from terrier Paul Dickov was saved, but then in the eighth minute a Kennedy cross set Dickov up again and this time the 5ft 5in striker made it 1-0 with a well-deserved goal.

Sadly, the lead didn't last as Southampton were awarded a penalty for what was perceived as a foul by the unlucky Edghill. Despite a valiant attempt by Weaver, the Saints equalised. Later an unsighted Weaver was unable to prevent another Southampton goal.

After the interval City had a great deal of possession, but didn't really look capable of scoring. It was no surprise when Oakley sneaked a third for Southampton.

As time progressed the Blues started to fight back. Goater managed to fire home City's second and, shortly afterwards, netted a third. The Blues managed to maintain the pressure on the Saints and came very close to taking the match in the final minutes of normal time. Then former Red Mark Hughes elbowed Edghill and was sent off for his second bookable offence. The City man was concussed for a while, and fans even saw him vomiting on the pitch. He was later stretchered off and spent the night in a Southampton hospital undergoing tests: "Mark came into the dressing room before I went

to hospital. He told me he didn't mean to catch me. Whether he did or not, that's the end of the matter as far as I'm concerned."

Worth noting the day after the game was Edghill's 25th birthday: "I didn't have much of a birthday or much of a week as the doctor down there advised that I should rest for seven days."

Almost immediately Southampton had a goal disallowed for offside, and then two minutes into extra time scrambled a deflected winner. Despite the 4-3 defeat City had proved they were more than a match for Premier League teams of the calibre of Southampton. Joe Royle felt a little aggrieved with the result however: "We didn't get the rub of the green with any of Southampton's goals. One came from a very dubious penalty, one was blatantly offside and the other two were deflected."

Four days before the League Cup defeat a Shaun Goater goal had brought victory at Walsall to help the Blues maintain their promotion challenge. The result lifted City into top spot, but successive defeats to Ipswich and Norwich left the Blues fourth - two points behind leaders Birmingham City.

The following match saw City face the early season promotion favourites Blackburn Rovers, managed by ex-Blue Brian Kidd. It was a match all fans and many neutrals eagerly awaited, even Swedish TV decided this was the right time to show the Blues since relegation from the Premier League. The attendance was 33,027 - the highest since the old Kippax Stand was demolished in 1994 - and only possible because of the increased number of temporary seats squeezed into the corners.

Those watching either in the stadium or in Sweden were in for a treat as Blackburn were defeated 2-0 with goals from Jeff Whitley and the much maligned Richard Edghill - his first in the League. The Blues had been thrilling in the second half and could even afford the luxury of a missed Horlock penalty.

In Sweden supporter Patrik Schèle was impressed with the local TV coverage: "They thought City played a more varying attacking play than Blackburn, who only attacked in the middle. The co-commentator was criticising Kidd for not switching tactics when he saw that Morrison and Jobson took everything in the middle. All in all they thought the win was deserved, but they weren't sure that City would last at the top spot all season. They thought however that Blackburn would be thereabouts when the season ended - from this display I can't figure out why they would be there! Last but not least, the crowd and the atmosphere. They were impressed. They said that they couldn't hear themselves when City were attacking due to the noise from the crowd. Once when 'Blue Moon' started the commentator just went: 'Listen'."

Joe Royle was happy with City's overall

determination: "It was a terrific win for us. We may have been lucky to still be in it at the break but even after we missed that penalty we just kept going forward." He had some sympathy for his under fire former team mate Brian Kidd, stating he believed Blackburn could still challenge. Kidd, on the other hand noticed the difference between the two sides: "They were more determined, their attitude was better and they wanted it more than us. Seeing little Jeff Whitley scoring with a header late on typifies the difference. If City keep showing that sort of spirit there's no reason why they can't go up."

Four days later promotion rivals Ipswich were beaten 1-0 in a closely fought match watched by an incredible midweek crowd of 32,799. The difference between the two sides was in goal where Nicky Weaver seemed desperately keen to prove his England U21 credentials against his main rival Richard Wright. It was a game the young Blue excelled in and clearly ensured City took the three points, but the match was noteworthy for a few other reasons, including an improved defensive performance from Richard Edghill. He even had a hand in the goal. After 58 minutes he sent an accurate long pass to Dickov wide on the right, who sent a cross into the area. The waiting Horlock netted a great goal from about eight yards out.

A 2-1 victory at Brian Horton's Port Vale followed before another former manager, Alan Ball, returned to Maine Road with Portsmouth. By a strange twist of fate Ball's return coincided with the announcement Joe Royle was to be October's Manager of the Month. Many fans remembered how Ball had been the last City manager to win the award back in November 1995. The Ball award came shortly before City plummeted down the divisions and many blamed the former World Cup winner for this demise. Sadly Ball's return in 1999 caused some to threaten the former City manager.

The Portsmouth chief safety officer, Dave Walton, even claimed there had been death threats. He hoped City could control the situation: "We have made the local police aware and they are discussing with their counterparts in Manchester about what safety measures to take. We expect the police and City to have security measures in place."

Chris Bird played down the situation, calmly telling the media: "We have every confidence in the match security already in place."

Ball did receive a significant amount of abuse but managed to shrug much of it off and even raised a laugh from a few City fans when he saluted them by lifting up his familiar flat cap. It must have been an exceptionally difficult time for Ball, particularly as City defeated his Portsmouth side 4-2, but he seemed to cope well.

After that victory City scraped a 1-1 draw at Queens Park Rangers, and then defeated promotion hopefuls Charlton 1-0 at the Valley. A 3-1 victory over Barnsley at

Maine Road followed. Interestingly this match attracted 32,692 despite being played on an appallingly wet Wednesday night. The game also clashed with the official re-opening of Manchester city centre following the 1996 terrorist bomb, with the only impact of a packed city centre being a ten minute delay to the kick off. It's also worth noting the attendance was particularly impressive as it was greater than the crowd at Stamford Bridge for the Chelsea v Feyenoord Champions' League game.

Defeats by Huddersfield (whose supporters saw this as a promotion decider), Wolves, and Stockport County brought further misery. But the disappointment didn't last as over the following weeks City rediscovered their winning ways with victories over Swindon (3-0), West Bromwich Albion (0-2), and Grimsby (2-1). The run was ended by a 1-1 draw at Crewe on 3rd January. The next match, however, would be a real test as City were to face Premiership challengers Leeds United in the FA Cup fourth round. The Blues had already defeated Chester 4-1 in the third round, and now faced David O'Leary's exciting side. The draw brought the largest travelling support of the season to Maine Road - 4,386 - but the increased allocation to Leeds and additional crowd control measures reduced the ground's capacity. In the end the match was watched by 29,240 - some 817 less than the season's lowest League crowd at the stadium - while millions also watched the game live on Sky TV. They witnessed an incredible start.

Shaun Goater looped a perfect header over the Leeds' keeper Martyn to put City in the lead after only two minutes. Television viewers discovered that Goater was clearly offside at the time, but who cared. It was a dream start and all Blues hoped it would set them up nicely for a famous victory. Sadly it did not, and Leeds dominated despite a topsy-turvy goal pattern which saw the visitors go behind twice, with City's second coming from the impressive Ian Bishop. It was a terrific goal and clearly demonstrated Bishop's desire to remain a fixture in Royle's promotion seeking Blues. By half time, however, impressive Leeds had scored three, and at full time the score was 5-2.

David O'Leary hoped City would achieve promotion: "I hope they come up this season and we are back here next term taking points off them. I think they will come up, but I always felt we would score the goals to get us through."

Back in the League the Blues proved their strength with a 4-0 victory over Fulham on Sunday 16th January. The London club, it should be remembered, won the Division Two title in style the previous season and, with strong financial backing from Mohammed Al Fayed, were a very important side to beat. It should also be remembered as the day when Shaun Goater finally silenced his critics with an impressive hat-trick. Perhaps the one o'clock start encouraged him. Royle: "Shaun's game has improved all round. He has won over the crowd and I hope he gets the chance to step up another division with us by the end of the season."

The Blues had been helped by the 68th minute dismissal of Fulham skipper Chris Coleman, and Royle admitted his side were a shade fortunate: "We've played a lot better. At times we were excellent but we were sloppy, too. It was a strange performance but a great win. It was important after the other results, when everybody else seemed to win. There are four in there at the moment at the top and unless we have a massive collapse, it will be hard for Fulham to catch us. We wanted to beat them because they could put together a late run."

After a surprising 1-0 defeat at Sheffield United six days later the Blues beat both Nottingham Forest 1-3 and Norwich City 3-1. Then on 18th February City secured a point at Huddersfield. The Yorkshire club had slipped since the November meeting and were beginning to pay for the surprising transfer of striker Marcus Stewart to promotion rivals Ipswich. Much to the disgust of their fans the Stewart sale had blunted Huddersfield's chance of an automatic promotion spot and, ultimately, the club failed to even make the play-offs.

City also appeared close to losing out on an automatic place, particularly as only four points were gained from the next six matches. Nevertheless, Royle argued that even when the Blues were not at their best they were still gaining some points, and were continuing to score goals, or at least Shaun Goater was. During the eight matches he participated in, following his hat-trick against Fulham, he netted a total of seven. Those goals helped City maintain a play-off place.

Victories for Barnsley and Ipswich put both sides two points ahead of the Blues, but City still had an important game in hand to play. There was also the news Royle had signed Derby's Spencer Prior for £500,000. Prior had turned down Nottingham Forest and Huddersfield, but the 28-year-old viewed the City offer as a good career move, and was keen to help the Blues achieve promotion: "I don't consider this a step down. Manchester City is a Premiership set up. I suppose as I have got older and more confident, so I have been able to take more responsibility. I have learned how to organise and shout a bit but I don't want anyone thinking I have come to City to take over the show. I am here to do my best for the team."

The deal was almost entirely financed by the sale of Tony Vaughan to Forest.

It wasn't long before Prior proved his worth. He made his debut on 25th March as City finally returned to winning ways with a 2-1 victory over Gary Megson's West Bromwich Albion. The fans were immediately impressed with his command of City's defence, and he appeared to fill the void left by Andy Morrison's continuing absence through injury. Royle smiled as he told reporters of Prior's impact: "Spencer is a good talker, he's a great enthusiast. We've found out already that he is a chirpy chappy."

Despite Prior's arrival and the 2-1 victory, the match was a tense affair. The Blues had hit the woodwork twice early on, however it had been Albion who seized the initiative when after an hour Lee Hughes scored. Mark Kennedy levelled via a free-kick in the 77th minute, and then in a frantic final period the Blues bombarded the Albion defence before Shaun Goater scrambled home the winner deep in injury-time.

Results elsewhere left City third, two points behind Ipswich but with a game in hand, although the table rarely provided an accurate view of the situation at this time as City and their main rivals never seemed to play on the same days.

At Swindon the Blues achieved a 2-0 victory on April Fool's Day with goals from the now dependable Goater - his 27th of the campaign - and Kennedy. Royle was delighted, although concerned by City's first half performance: "I am delighted with the victory and I thought we fully deserved the points. It wasn't the best game in the first half, but Shaun Goater did well for the first goal, and we always looked comfortable after the half-time interval and more dangerous after we changed things around."

The game had not been a good one for 25-year-old midfielder Tony Grant who had made his first start since January. He was replaced by Ian Bishop early in the second half and from that point on the game came alive.

Despite the result the Swindon directors were pleased with the match. The Wiltshire club had allowed City fans to occupy both ends of their tiny ground, and it was reported that over half of the 12,397 crowd were supporting the Blues. At £17 per ticket it was calculated the additional gate money was worth over £100,000 to the relegation bound club.

In the table, City still had a game in hand over most clubs, and now lay third on 72 points. The near invincible Charlton (87 points) still headed the League while Barnsley (74 points) were second. Ipswich were fourth - one point behind City after the same number of matches - while Birmingham were fifth on 69 points. The true League position would be clearer once City had played their game in hand against Bolton on Wednesday 5th April.

With eighth-placed Bolton losing to Aston Villa via a penalty shoot-out in the previous Sunday's FA Cup semi-final no one quite knew what to expect from the game. Fortunately, City seized control early on, and after eighteen minutes took the lead through a Kevin Horlock strike. Five minutes later Paul Dickov netted to give City an important 2-0 victory. At long last the Blues had returned to an automatic promotion spot and were now a point clear of Barnsley. They also had a superior goal difference to both Barnsley and Ipswich.

Royle felt City had done enough to kill any Bolton threat with a terrific first half display: "My team knew they needed to win this one - it was our game in hand - and they went for Bolton from the start, and in that first half we played as well as we have done for a very long time." He then told the media of City's target: "Automatic promotion is what we are aiming for and that will be the case until it's mathematically impossible for us."

Bolton's Sam Allardyce viewed City as certainties for automatic promotion: "They have got strength in depth, and that's so crucial at this stage. They had Shaun Goater and Danny Tiatto off injured but could still turn to players of the calibre of Danny Granville and Lee Mills to come on. I think they will hold their nerve and hang on now to one of those top two spots."

City strengthened their position in the top two with a fine 4-0 victory over Crewe at Maine Road three days later. The hero was Paul Dickov who netted twice, although new boy Spencer Prior set the course for victory with a 42nd minute header. Dickov's first came after 68 minutes with Mark Kennedy providing City's third before Dickov completed the rout.

Royle, who celebrated his 51st birthday that weekend, viewed the Crewe match as one of City's best in weeks: "We had 27 attempts on goal and could quite easily have notched double figures. We were terrific today, as fluent as we have been for a long time." Royle was also pleased with the performance of Prior: "After failing to keep a clean sheet for ten matches we have now kept three in a row, and much of that is down to Spencer."

Prior was pleased with his own performance, but was also delighted with the overall team play: "We are winning our battles all over the pitch and when we are on the ball we are as comfortable as many of the Premiership sides I have seen. We are also keeping clean sheets and that is important."

Another man happy with life at Maine Road was Mark Kennedy. Earlier in his career Kennedy had struggled to impress at either Liverpool or Wimbledon, but since his close season move from Wimbledon he had settled well at City. Royle claimed the player had 'come home'. Kennedy wasn't going to argue: "The gaffer is right when he says I have found City a home from home. I cannot say enough about the warmth that has been shown to me here by the fans."

In 2010 Joe Royle explained how Kennedy had not been his first choice, but ultimately proved to be a better acquisition than the man he had tried to sign: "We had tried to sign Lee Sharpe and I spoke with him at Manchester Airport, but somehow a photographer had got wind of the story and he was hanging around.

Sharpe went to Bradford instead, so we signed Mark. It all worked out really well. Mark was fantastic for us in that promotion season."

Royle was also clear that the departure of former hero Georgi Kinkladze a couple of years earlier had indirectly helped finance Kennedy's purchase: "Thinking back to the money we got for Kinkladze... without that money we wouldn't have been able to get some of the players we did, so the £5m we got for him bounced us back up two divisions."

The Crewe victory gave the Blues the perfect opportunity to put rivals Barnsley and Ipswich under severe pressure, particularly as City were to kick off their match at Grimsby at 1pm and could therefore go a morale boosting six points clear before the other sides played.

Again, as with all City fixtures from the period, huge numbers of fans wanted to attend the match. Grimsby were naturally concerned with the possibility City fans could infiltrate the home sections and instigated a policy of testing those purchasing tickets with Grimsby-based trivia. The 'quiz' was even dubbed "who wants to be a Mariner?".

The Grimsby management were determined the safety of their fans came first and even stated they would be prepared to turn away supporters rather than risk mixing fans, or compromising segregation and safety issues. The Blundell Park capacity was quoted as 10,033, but the directors maintained the game would be watched by no more than about 9,000. In the end the attendance was recorded as 8,166 including 2,200 City fans. Unusually for a City away game from their Division Two and Division One days, this was not the home side's highest attendance of the season. As a result Grimsby made around £30,000 less than the revenue they would have taken from a sell-out match.

On the pitch City struggled. Royle: "We were useless! I was disappointed because we were given such a good start. But in the end I was highly delighted to get away with a point. Our passing was poor on a good surface. Only Richard Jobson played anything like his usual standard for us today. If this result jolts us back to our best some good will have come out of it."

The match ended in a 1-1 draw - new hero Prior scored for City in the sixth minute but the lead lasted only ten minutes - but Grimsby had made life exceptionally difficult for the Blues. Royle's opposite number Alan Buckley felt his side could have won: "I was more disappointed with the point than Joe Royle. I thought we deserved all three because we were more than a match for a team knocking on the promotion door. Our start was not good, but the lads got fired up and fully deserved the point if not more."

The result left the promotion race wide open again, and by the time of the next match - at home to Tranmere on 22nd April Ipswich had closed the gap to a point, while Barnsley were still only three points behind. All sides had four games left to play. It started to feel as if the race would go to the very last match of the season away at Blackburn. A game everybody wanted to attend. Not surprisingly City's allocation of 6,157 seats had sold out almost as soon as they went on sale.

At Maine Road the Tranmere match saw a return to winning ways as Jeff Whitley and Shaun Goater ensured a 2-0 victory. Goater scored first, but the Blues remained a little nervous until the 72nd minute when Whitley slotted home a Kennedy cross. Tranmere manager John Aldridge felt the Blues were more than a match for his side, although he was a little disappointed this could be his final chance of facing the Blues for a while: "They've got themselves a great chance of promotion and they deserve it. So do Joe and the fans, but it's a pity for our division. You want to be playing big clubs like City, but we're all a bit selfish."

City were now four points clear of nearest rivals Ipswich and, just as supporters dared to feel confident, two days later, on Easter Monday, came a major jolt to the system. It arrived in the shape of former player Lee Bradbury - a man dubbed 'Lee Badbuy' after becoming City's most expensive signing and one of the Club's biggest flops. Playing once again for Portsmouth, Bradbury somehow helped Pompey to a 2-2 draw.

The Blues had been leading 2-0 after a 26th minute effort from Spencer Prior and a 40th minute flick from Robert Taylor. Unfortunately Portsmouth got back in the match with a penalty from Bradbury deep in first half injury time. Then six minutes from the end he scored again. City fans could barely believe it.

The end of the match was slightly strange as Royle deliberately made a move to acknowledge referee's assistant Wendy Toms. He said she'd had an excellent match and ensured she was the first official he greeted at the whistle. Earlier in the season comments from Royle concerning female officials had been widely quoted - and miss-quoted - as a direct attack on Toms. The meeting was a sign Royle was not anti-Toms had some had claimed.

The result left Ipswich five points behind City but 'The Tractor Boys' now had a game in hand - a Tuesday night match at struggling Crystal Palace. Barnsley still remained a threat as they were only four points behind, although with only two matches left time was running out for the Yorkshire club. Regardless of the threat posed by both Ipswich and Barnsley it was clear promotion was still very much within City's control. Although a home game with Birmingham and an away match at Blackburn were clearly not easy fixtures Royle believed City could grasp success: "We just have to stay calm and make sure we perform at our best and then we will be all right. As I have said before we have no intention of throwing away the top two place we know we have earned by being so consistent all season."

Royle, when quizzed about the tense period to follow, added: "My nerves are OK. I feel fine. I've seen these situations before and I try not to get too high or too low. I keep talking about the rapport between the fans and the team. We had players who could not handle the size of our crowds. Now we have players who thrive on it."

As expected, a tense but very supportive Friday night atmosphere, certainly in the opening period, greeted the Blues. After forty minutes though the atmosphere lightened considerably with Robert Taylor netting the most important goal of his City career. As the match progressed fans became more convinced the Blues were going up and the whole arena was filled with celebratory chants. Even the normally subdued Main Stand joined in with the territorial chants coming from the other three stands by declaring: 'We are the Main Stand, we are the Main Stand'. It's not known whether the directors joined in but the chant was followed by a similar one from the corporate boxes at the back of the Platt Lane Stand, which appeared to be led by Don Price of the Prestwich & Whitefield CSA.

At the whistle the stadium erupted. Ipswich were due to play the following day, but those at Maine Road believed the Club had almost done enough to guarantee promotion. Fans flooded on to the pitch to mob the players, while City's PA system blasted out various uplifting tunes.

Watching the scenes on Sky TV

Fans on the pitch after the Birmingham game, April 2000.

the Ipswich players and management felt determined to make City pay. They felt the celebrations were premature. As did Sky TV who mistakenly saw the invasion as some sort of boast City were back. What they failed to mention was that similar events occur every season, regardless of City's position. When the Blues played their final home match before relegation to Division Two The Independent reported on City's 'lap of dishonour in front of 30,000 loyal fans who have been ever-present this season'. That day the supporters applauded and encouraged their heroes, and the same was true on 28th April against Birmingham. Naturally, the celebrations were a little over the top, but then why not? Royle allowed the players out to receive the fans' acclaim as with every other season, and yet the media criticised him and the Club.

Mark Kennedy defended Royle's actions: "We are all aware it could be misconstrued as arrogance or something like that but it wasn't. Whatever happens next, we believe we can put our hands on our hearts and say it has been a great season."

The next day fans waited for news from the Charlton-Ipswich encounter. Thousands of supporters had already made a vow they would travel to Maine Road and Albert Square to celebrate if Ipswich failed to win, but the news was not good. GMR covered the match extensively, but Ian Cheeseman was unable to report any good news from the Valley. It seemed the champions had coasted and allowed Ipswich to record a 3-1 victory. As with many other seasons, City's future was to be decided by the last match of the season.

Despite the disappointment of that final weekend in April, it was true City's destiny still lay in their own hands. A better result than Ipswich would guarantee promotion, although April Manager of the Month Royle wanted a victory: "We will not be going to Blackburn to defend or looking for just one point, that would be inviting disaster. We will be playing to take three points."

He went on to state he believed his players should go all out to make a name for themselves: "Legends are born in games like this and particularly at a massive club like City with the fan base we have. Someone can be a hero, not just for a day but for a long time."

With Graeme Souness now in charge at Rovers, Royle realised the match would be a tough one: "Graeme, as a friend and a close one, is a totally committed professional and he would have it no other way. He will want to beat us. We neither look for, nor expect any favours."

Off the pitch supporters main concerns all centred around watching the match. Sure the game would be on Sky TV, but it was another of those 'you've got to be here' matches the Blues regularly encountered. The ticket allocation had sold out weeks prior to the match, and the only way of attending the match appeared to be by paying touts a minimum of £80 for a £15 ticket. By match day that figure rose enormously.

At Maine Road the Club disappointed its fans by refusing to screen the big game. Chris Bird explained the decision: "We feel the fact the game is going to be made accessible all over the country rules out the need for the beam-back. In any case it would have been difficult to organise the screening and get the tickets sold in such a short space of time."

Some supporters decided to travel to Blackburn in the hope they would somehow find a way into the ground. As many Blackburn fans seemed determined to cash in on the match, Stuart Caley, Lancashire Police's Football Planning Co-ordinator admitted segregation would be a problem: "This is a very important match for Manchester City and we will be ready for any eventuality. We have tried to prevent away fans from getting tickets in home areas but we cannot possible ensure that 100 per cent, and are saddened to hear some season ticket holders have been selling their seats for the day."

On the day Ewood Park appeared full of City fans, and even a hill which overlooked the stadium seemed to house a few hundred Mancunians. They witnessed an incredible game.

The match kicked off with City in determined mood. Kennedy made several good crosses, but unfortunately the Blues failed to capitalise. Blackburn were then allowed to get into their stride and bombarded Weaver's goal. It was only due to the young 'keeper's brilliance the score remained goalless.

Blackburn hit the bar twice, and just as it started to appear City's luck might hold until the interval a long throw was flicked on to the unmarked Jansen who chested the ball down before volleying home.

One-nil down at half-time was not what Royle wanted, but worse was to follow shortly into the second half when news filtered through there had been a goal in the Ipswich-Walsall match.

At Ewood the news first circulated among some City fans that Walsall had scored - as always one fan's inability to listen to a radio effectively set off a false announcement - then the truth appeared. David Johnson had scored for Ipswich. A tremendous feeling of despair followed, while those watching on Sky were forced to witness several replays of the goal before the cameras zoomed in on several tearful Mancunians. Memories of Liverpool (1996) and Luton (1983) came flooding back, while on the pitch Blackburn again hit the woodwork - twice inside a minute.

Before the fans' depression could deepen any further the game began magically to turn around. A chance came City's way when, with Dickov waiting, Kennedy curled the ball behind the defence. Sadly it flew past Dickov but Goater appeared at the far post. Much to the delight of the thousands of fans wearing the new "Feed the Goat and he will score" Tee shirts, the star striker forced the ball into the roof of the net.

At 1-1 the celebrations were widespread, but fans remained nervous. The Blues could have been four goals down after a shocking first half display, and the logical fear remained Blackburn could yet jeopardise City's promotion bid. A little later, with Blue Moon echoing around Ewood, the nerves were calmed as Edghill sent the ball goalwards with Dickov chasing. Blackburn's Daily decided to end the threat by carefully heading back to his 'keeper, but didn't realise Kelly had already advanced. For a few agonising moments the players and the crowd watched as the ball bobbled goalwards and then wild celebrations commenced as City, playing in their ever-popular red and black stripes, went 2-1 up.

Fans performed a conga in front of the Walkersteel Stand, while those watching from the nearby hill had been fortunate to see both City goals occur on the only part of the pitch actually visible. Martin Lever, watching from the hill, couldn't believe what he was experiencing. He later recalled the opening moments and the atmosphere on the hill as the game turned around: "Fortunately, we could see the goal and goalmouth where all the action was to take place. We were worried about the first half because even though we could only see a limited area of the pitch, we realised through radio commentaries and crowd reactions that City were on the receiving end of a pounding by Rovers. Then came the goal and all went quiet on the hill. Faces looked down. People threw their full cans away in disgust. Half time and back to the off-licence for more refreshments.

"So, suitably refreshed, the second half kicked off and the wall of sound from the hill began again. Congas - some even rolling down the hill and others swinging in the bushes - made this the most unique football watching experience ever. Suddenly news filtered through that Ipswich had scored. Silence? Not likely, the singing just got louder and louder. By this time the gathering on the hill numbered about five hundred.

"Suddenly, cross from the left - couldn't see who - and up pops The Goat - visible to all on the Hill. 1-1 and cue the wildest celebration imaginable - City fans hugging each other; forward rolls down the hill; and complete disorder. Soon after, no danger in the Rovers penalty area and then Christian Dailly decides to assist City karma for the day by giving City the lead - seen by all! Now goal celebration number two was really something. The 15 stone man beside me decided to pick me up and parade me above his head. He and I collapsed in a heap. People were just throwing themselves into a frenzy, flag waving and song after song. By this time one particular chant was really gaining momentum.

"We're on the hill, we're on the hill we're on it, City's on the hill we're on the hill...."

Those on the hill also managed to see the final stages of City's third goal when Kennedy netted from six yards out. He immediately raced to manager Royle and the two men embraced. Nicky Weaver celebrated by performing a cartwheel. Earlier in the season he had been banned from celebrating in that manner to avoid unnecessary injury but with City 3-1 up it seemed right to resurrect it.

Dickov made it 4-1 with a surge through the Blackburn defence. At full time the fans raced on to the pitch to celebrate. Those on the hill had managed by this time to find their way into Ewood Park. The Independent commented on the rather surreal site of supporters charging down the Lancashire hillside: "Hundreds more, ticketless fans, massed on a hillside overlooking the ground, poured down like extras from Zulu to join in the pitch invasion."

All Blues admitted City had been lucky, but in truth it was no more than they deserved after such an enthralling season. At Ipswich, not that it mattered, the home side beat Walsall 2-0 to send the Midlands club into Division Two and Ipswich into the play-offs. Interestingly, City ended the campaign a mere two points behind one-time runaway leaders Charlton - the Blues also had the best goal difference in the division and had equalled their record number of victories in a season (26) and had beaten their record points total (89), although it's fair to say the number of games played was now greater than when those records were set.

In addition, City's reserves were celebrating after winning the Pontin's sponsored Central League. Exciting prospect Shaun Wright-Phillips had appeared in more Central league matches than anybody else as the Blues finished seven points clear of nearest rivals Huddersfield Town.

Academy boss Jim Cassell recognised Wright-Phillips' potential from the start: "I remember in 1998 Joe Royle took a few of the lads across for training and so on, and I said to him 'Joe, you've got a lad there who will play in our first team'. That wasn't arrogance or anything it was

City on the hill at Blackburn.

an obvious fact. Joe came back at the end of the day and said 'Hey, Jim. That lad of yours... he stayed at the front until he dropped. You were right!'

"Wrighty was the making of our Academy. I cannot thank and praise him enough because once you get one in, they all follow. By 2010 31 players had progressed to the Premier League and 12 had played at full international level, while others have appeared in friendlies against the likes of Barcelona which we don't even count. Another 33 had appeared for other clubs in the Championship or below."

The Academy was still in its infancy in 1999-2000 but already it was beginning to pay dividends.

After the Blackburn League match Royle explained how he felt: "If you can't be good be lucky, and we were lucky today. I certainly didn't think it was going to be 4-1. But after the season we have had I feel we deserve this. If nothing else we have resilience, great honesty and team spirit, and that's what saw us through. When they hit the woodwork for the fourth time I thought it would be our day."

He went on to talk of the celebrations at the end: "I felt terror for a minute. I was surrounded by people and it took me back to the old days at Everton when I was a kid and there were sixty thousand fans there - but all's well that ends well. Despite the situation the fans were absolutely phenomenal and they deserve this promotion. We think the world of them and there's a great rapport. They have been superb throughout this last season but they were even better the previous campaign. We averaged 28,000 for our home games, which is a record I think will never be beaten, particularly when you talk about the fact we were playing sides like Lincoln, Wycombe, and Chesterfield. We have known for a while we have Premiership fans, and now we are a Premiership team."

When asked what he thought the turning point was, Royle commented on two substitutions early in the second half. After 47 minutes, he sent on Bishop for Pollock, and followed this six minutes later replacing Taylor with Dickov. Both substitutes played well and Royle was quick to point out that one of the goals had seen the two men work well together: "Ian got the ball down and passed it, and Paul scored a smashing goal."

In the dressing room the players partied. Sky TV viewers witnessed them drenching reporters with water while chanting "Are you watching Alan Brazil?" Sky's Brazil had been rather quick to criticise the Blues throughout the final weeks of the season, and his apparent aversion to everything Blue upset many associated with the Club.

While the high jinks carried on, some Sky viewers noticed Ian Bishop in the background carefully covering his clothes with towels. None of the other players appeared to notice Bishop's desire to protect his property, but his actions raised a few laughs in pubs and clubs around Manchester.

As celebrations continued at Ewood, Manchester also partied. Hundreds travelled to Maine Road and Albert Square to celebrate, and outside every pub fans cheered every City vehicle that passed. Cars, minibuses, and vans streamed towards the city centre with flags and scarves hanging out of their windows. Albert Square quickly became a major area of celebration as high spirited fans took to the fountains. A street festival taking place in the same area seemed to add to the spirit of the day, while for a short period cars circled the square in a celebratory procession.

The police then took the action of controlling vehicle access into the square, and revellers had to choose between parking up and walking into the square or travelling to Maine Road where other celebrations were taking place.

Tom Farrington was one supporter who made his way to Albert Square to celebrate as the evening progressed: "This was finally the day when City reclaimed Manchester - for good! Pubs that were open around Albert Square ran out of beer, and so I think we can safely say that Blues had drunk Manchester dry!!

"At one point there was a cheer from near Central Library so we wandered up to see what was going on. There must have been a couple of thousand Blues outside the Midland Hotel. Then we realised what they were doing there - some of the players and Joe were on the balcony. Bish had a megaphone but we couldn't hear what he was saying above all the noise. 'Blue Moon', 'We're going up', 'City are back' and 'Feed the Goat' drowning Manchester in noise.

"Just before my brother-in-law dropped me off at the station, I recalled to him an incident almost two years ago to the day, when I was sat on the back step of my sister's house looking out into the garden but not really looking anywhere, and not really feeling anything but complete numbness - we had just beaten Stoke but it wasn't enough. Who would have thought that two years on we would be back in the Premiership? I certainly didn't think it would come that quickly and that we would have two memorable days to rank up there with the best of them."

City's promotion may have occurred too soon, but at the time few bothered to question the speed. They simply wanted to look forward and forget about the struggles of the previous five years. It was therefore not a surprise when City refused the City Council's offer of a formal civic reception to celebrate promotion. Most fans dearly wanted some form of official celebration, and for a while the Club and Council officials discussed the options, however a formal parade seemed a little over the top. Understandably, the decision was taken not to have a proper home coming parade. Director Chris

Bird: "While we all agree that the Club's back to back promotion has been a remarkable achievement, we don't feel that it merits a parade through the City."

Instead, City gave a £25,000 donation to charity. The amount represented the cost of organising and holding a parade.

Former Liverpool player Alan Hansen felt the decision was right. The TV pundit, who during the mid-1990s had been asked to become City manager, said ambitions should be much higher than simply moving into the Premier League: "City are a big, big club, and it should not simply stop there. They should not feel the resurrection has reached its completion. How many clubs can boast the support City enjoy? How many clubs could move to a new stadium, as City will do after the 2002 Commonwealth Games, and know the 40-odd thousand seats will be taken for every match? They are a huge football club and within the next few years they should once again be competing for domestic honours as well as looking for a return to Europe."

Hansen's view that City should move upwards following promotion was one shared by thousands of loyal Blues.

2000-2001 A Disappointing Return

Everyone was keen to see the Blues challenge for the game's top honours, sadly the 2000-01 season did not live up to expectations and ended in misery with City relegated.

The signs were clear from the moment the season started when Division One Champions Charlton Athletic crushed the Blues 4-0 at the Valley on the opening day. It was not a pleasant experience, and the agony was compounded in the return match when the visitors won 4-1. City's goal coming in the 90th minute via a Darren Huckerby penalty.

It was an all-round frustrating season, although there were a few high points. New signing Paulo Wanchope scored a hat-trick in only his second appearance as Peter Reid's Sunderland were defeated 4-2, while Royle's former club Everton were humiliated by a 5-0 Maine Road drubbing in December. These however were exceptions as home form was in general quite dreadful.

The Blues achieved a 1-1 draw in the return derby match thanks to a Steve Howey goal in the 84th minute. The match was watched by 67,535 - the highest Old Trafford derby crowd since 1936 - and the game was as heated as any derby. Roy Keane picked up his eighth red card of the season after a particularly nasty over-the-top challenge which pole-axed Alfie Haaland. When questioned Alex Ferguson commented: "I've not seen it, but our secretary says it was a sending-off."

Several players showed flashes of brilliance during the season, but there were very few consistent performers. Former World Player of the Year - and self-confessed City fan - George Weah arrived in a blaze of publicity, but only managed seven appearances and went as quickly as he arrived. The unpredictable Wanchope was leading goalscorer with nine, but he fell in and out of favour with Royle.

Shaun Goater, who it was claimed would never succeed in the Premier League, was kept out of the side until the tenth match, and only made twenty games plus six as substitute. Of the twenty he started he only completed twelve of them. Nevertheless he still managed six goals. A pre-season injury had limited his chances but as soon as he was fit he was named as substitute. It was perhaps the last straw for Weah when Goater warming up received more applause than the former World Player of the Year did for playing.

Unlike City's relegation seasons of 1996 and 1998 flashes of brilliance were few and far between during 2000-01.

After City's final match - a 2-1 defeat at home to Chelsea - Joe Royle was dismissed: "We won at Leeds (2-1 on 5th September) early in the season and I had thoughts of European qualification, but then we had a bad spell. In December we beat Walter Smith's Everton 5-0 and I thought that would be a turning point but the run we had that followed was the sort only relegated sides had. There were goals disallowed like Tiatto's at Middlesbrough where he ran almost the full length of the pitch but was given offside. Goat had one disallowed at Spurs and they scored in the last minute.

"It all went pear-shaped and we were relegated. It was a hard time for us all. My wife had cancer and my father had taken ill, and then relegation."

The departure of Royle became quite messy and at times acrimonious. It was a major shame as Royle had achieved do much for the Blues: "I have to say that I still have a great relationship with City fans and I go to games. I still love the club. I had a great relationship with my chairmen at City. Francis Lee was great to work with, although we only worked together for a few months. People assume he interfered because he knew about the game but he definitely did not. He had opinions like all chairmen, but he left me to manage. I was shocked when he stood down. I know it hurt him a great deal.

"I thought David Bernstein was an excellent chairman and, although he became chairman after I left, I have a lot of time for John Wardle. He's a fan and his love of City was always clear. I love City. There's something magical about the club and I feel fortunate to have played a part in the club's history."

As with so many earlier periods, the media were quick to suggest City had pressed the panic button too soon. Supporters were uncertain what to make of the move. They had been concerned with Royle's dealings in the transfer market during his reign and had worried over his handling of certain players - most notably Wanchope and Kinkladze - but more they feared a return to the chopping and changing of the eighties and nineties.

It was clear the Blues desperately needed to appoint a major figure to reassure the fans. They also needed to find someone who could re-establish the Club as one of England's elite, and with the move to the new 48,000 stadium only two seasons away, City needed to make the right appointment. This would be the most crucial moment in the reign of Chairman David Bernstein. He had to pick the right man.

No, no, the other side!
Where it says
'WELCOME'

2001-2002 Super Kevin Keegan

Only three days after the departure of Joe Royle, City stunned the media with the appointment of former England boss Kevin Keegan as their new manager. At first supporters were uncertain how to greet the former European Player of the Year. They knew he was passionate about football and his record in club management was good. He had helped re-establish Newcastle United as a leading club, and had started to create momentum at Fulham, before he took on the England role. They also knew he might move on if he ever felt he was unwelcome, or his approach was failing. Fortunately, the appointment was to be the catalyst for a great season.

Early in 2002 chairman David Bernstein looked back at the decisions leading up to Keegan's appointment during an interview with Noel Bayley: "When I heard Kevin Keegan was possibly available my personal view

- shared by my colleagues - was we just had to go for him. We had a lot of applications for the job when Joe went. It was a very tight timescale, but we did have a lot of applications.

"We didn't look at the others frankly. I thought we were incredibly fortunate getting hold of Kevin. I thought that his reputation had been affected by the England experience, but that was our gain. That was completely irrelevant to his ability to manage. What he had done at Newcastle and Fulham - and particularly at Newcastle - was quite incredible, and I felt that what this club needed was someone of that stature, someone who had ability, but also glamour and that energy that Kevin has got which, among other things, would have the ability to bring in players to the Club while we were not in the Premier League, which is not the easiest thing to do. Kevin has shown that he can bring in the right players and motivate them. Energise them. Look after them, and get the best out of creative players, and that was my view when we took him on. It's very early days still, but the impact has been made."

Following his arrival Keegan attended a Fans' Forum and outlined his reasons for taking on the job: "This truly is a massive club and it's my job to turn it around. The new stadium is a fantastic incentive for us - not only to get back in the Premiership but to win something as well. It takes very little force to join a club like this. It's a fantastic opportunity. I'm ready for it.

"I'll be judged on what happens from now on. I've got a lot to prove to myself. I've had other opportunities, but this is the only one that appealed. I'm not a fool. I have a real chance here. Hopefully, I can build a successful outfit that people will really want to be part of and I think that's my strength. I think I've already proved that twice at League level at Newcastle and Fulham, and I'm pretty confident that, given that bit of luck everybody needs, we can do it here."

Managerial change (above and left) as reported in the Daily Mail. The appointment turned out to be a very good one for City. Keegan grasped what fans and the Club needed.

Immediately Keegan set about improving the staff. He brought in his former manager Arthur Cox as Chief Scout, and signed former England star Stuart Pearce. Keegan desperately wanted Pearce to be his captain: "He was actually going to quit playing and clean out his horses at home when I saw him this summer, but I told him this club needed a leader. He says more than me in the dressing room and what he says is probably more important as well."

Pearce said at the time: "I had always said that I would not drop out of the Premier League, but this was too good an opportunity to miss. If I was going to drop out of the top flight it could not have been to a bigger club than Manchester City. It is my sort of club, and has my sort of supporters - passionate and knowledgeable about the game."

He made his debut in the opening match with Watford, as did Israeli Eyal Berkovic. Keegan: "Berkovic was a £5.75 million player only two or three years ago, but I bought him for £1.25 million. He is a key signing because we mustn't settle for mediocrity."

Both Pearce and Berkovic shone in the opening match. Watford, managed by Gianluca Vialli, were perceived as strong promotion candidates and so it was important City started their season in the right manner. Pearce was fired up from the start. According to Matt Dickinson in *The Times*: "One feared for Watford from the moment Stuart Pearce led City on to the pitch and performed a little war dance before kick-off."

City won the match 3-0 with both Berkovic and Pearce scoring. The other scorer was Shaun Goater, proving once again he would be an important team member. The result convinced the media City were already on the right track. Matt Dickinson: "Keegan has found a natural home amid the unrelenting fervour of Maine Road. Place your mortgage on Manchester City winning promotion to the FA Barclaycard Premiership. What happens after that is anybody's guess, but even Keegan's arch-doubters would not bet against him riding an open-top bus through Manchester in May."

A week after this victory City were defeated 2-0 at Norwich. It was a nightmare day with the kick-off delayed, three players injured, and Paulo Wanchope sent off after two bookable offences. Fortunately, the visit of Crewe on 25th August gave City an albeit flattering 5-2 win. Stuart Pearce scored his first penalty in a City shirt, while Goater and Wanchope each scored a brace. Wanchope was already proving to be more settled than the previous season when he was alleged to have had a number of confrontations with Joe Royle. Towards the end of the 2000-01 campaign it seemed clear Wanchope would be moving on, but under Keegan the player began to enjoy life at Maine Road again.

Early-season promotion-hopefuls Burnley were defeated 4-2 at Turf Moor with a Goater hat-trick two days later, and then came the first shockwave of the campaign as fellow contenders West Bromwich Albion achieved a 4-0 victory. Other unexpected defeats came in September against Coventry (4-3) and Wimbledon (0-4), but in the main Keegan's City were brushing aside most opponents. The Blues delighted supporters with an entertaining, attacking approach. Occasionally they'd concede more goals than fans would like, however as long as they were winning, conceding the odd goal didn't really matter.

Keegan's approach was refreshing and his transfer dealings seemed perfect. Fringe player Tony Grant was sold to Burnley, but that deal heralded the arrival of a real playmaker, Ali Benarbia. It was a transfer coup that very nearly didn't happen as Benarbia had only called in on his way to Sunderland to have lunch with his agent, who was negotiating a deal for Alione Toure. One thing led to another and by the end of the following day he had signed for the Blues and the next day made a very impressive debut against Birmingham. The transfer was one of the most important of the season. It was also one of the cheapest deals as Paris St. Germain released the 32-year-old Algerian on a free.

On 22nd September the Blues met another fallen giant, Sheffield Wednesday. Three minutes into the game Wednesday took the lead. The City side of the 1990s would have crumbled at this point, but Keegan's Blues simply didn't worry. They got on with the job in hand and the impressive Benarbia squeezed a drive from a little inside the area past Kevin Pressman in the Wednesday goal.

Three minutes later, Pearce launched a long free-kick for Goater to chase. Goater stretched out and lobbed the ball over Pressman for City's second.

When Wednesday levelled two minutes into the second half City decided it was time to seize total control, and by the 68th minute the Blues were leading 4-2 with goals from Granville and Wanchope. Two minutes later Goater skipped around Pressman for the fifth, then twelve minutes from time Wanchope netted a penalty.

Ali Benarbia was the undisputed star after a thrilling performance, but Keegan was not entirely happy with the scoreline: "It may be entertaining, but we are giving away too many goals. I'd honestly be pleased to win our next match 1-0."

The first eight League games had seen an incredible forty goals, but more were to follow. Walsall were defeated 3-0 in the next League match - Benarbia was again the star - and in October Birmingham City were beaten 6-0 in the League Cup. Darren Huckerby scored four that night, and went on to enjoy a terrific season. Possibly the best of his entire career.

By netting four, Huckerby had equalled Dennis Tueart's club scoring record for the competition - Tueart scored four in the 1980-81 5-1 win over Notts County and Huckerby's third was City's 300th goal in the competition. In addition the match had been Birmingham's third visit to Maine Road during 2001 and on each occasion they had gone in 3-0 down at the interval.

Huckerby was quick to praise his colleagues: "When you have got players like Ali Benarbia and Eyal Berkovic in the side, you know you are always going to make chances. Ali is a world class player. You do not get the chance to see the likes of him very often. He is a genius and we are lucky he is here. Hopefully he will be here for another couple of years."

Keegan rightly praised Huckerby: "It wasn't just his goals, his general play was as good as it gets. He held it up well, he turned well and most of the time he made the right choices."

The League Cup run ended with a 2-0 defeat at Blackburn in the fourth round, but in the League City continued to progress with their thrilling, attacking style. One match, however, stunned *Guardian* reporter Andy Wilson. Under the headline "Keegan's City in nil-nil shock" he wrote of his surprise that the meeting with Sheffield United ended goalless. It was the first 0-0 for 35 matches and became newsworthy as a result. That simple headline proved how City had progressed under Keegan. Football is all about goals and, in the main, the Blues were delivering at an incredible rate.

Mixed results followed, including an emotional last game at the City Ground for Stuart Pearce, where he was applauded by both sets of supporters for a typically determined performance. The match ended 1-1 with Goater capitalising on a mistake by defender Riccardo Scimeca to give the Blues the equaliser.

A 2-1 defeat at Portsmouth on 17th November saw the Blues drop to ninth place, while behind the scenes there were changes to Keegan's staff during this period. Willie Donachie, former player and assistant to Joe Royle, decided it was time to move on. He chose to join Terry Yorath at Sheffield Wednesday: "This has been a very difficult decision to make as I have had a lot of very good times at City. However, the new challenge is one that I feel I should accept."

Kevin Keegan was surprised by the move: "The news has come as a great shock to me. Willie has been very important in my first few months at the Club, and he will be missed, but we wish him all the best in his new role."

Derek Fazackerley replaced Donachie as Head Coach at Maine Road, and over the weeks that followed City climbed back up the table reaching third place, four points behind leaders Burnley, after a particularly satisfying 3-2 victory at Millwall. Due to crowd control issues with meetings between the sides in 1999-2000 the clubs agreed away fans would be banned from both fixtures. Shaun Wright-Phillips netted the match-winner - which was also his first League goal - leading to much

praise from Keegan: "It's been a long time coming but it's been worth waiting for. His finish was excellent. He is a very good player and he'll get better. The lad has got a lot of things. Good pace and skill, but the biggest thing he's got is courage. I told him his main job was to defend and anything else was a bonus. Well, the goal was a bonus."

Approximately five thousand watched the game on a screen at Maine Road, and they were delighted when they saw Huckerby score City's second, and then run to the empty away section and applaud the Blues' non-existent travelling support. Mention should be made of the other goalscorer, Shaun Goater. By this time the Bermudan had netted 23 goals in 22 appearances - not bad for a player many had written off two years earlier.

On 11th December a crucial 1-0 win over Wolverhampton Wanderers - thanks to Kevin Horlock - lifted City above Wolves on goal difference. A 3-1 victory over Bradford City and a rare goalless match with promotion hopefuls West Bromwich Albion set City up for their meeting with League leaders Burnley at noon on 29th December. Burnley were convinced they could keep Keegan's City at bay, but a determined performance gave the Blues an extremely satisfying 5-1 victory. Paulo Wanchope netted a hat-trick, with Darren Huckerby and Eyal Berkovic scoring the others.

The result allowed City to head the table for the first time since they won at Burnley on 27th August. It also sowed a few doubts in Burnley's camp, and by the season's end the one time runaway leaders had failed to even make the play-offs.

The real danger now came from Wolves. Dave Jones' side were nipping at City's heels throughout January, but they were not alone. Millwall and West Brom were also chasing hard, and when City faced the Lions on 30th January the Blues were only three points ahead of Wolves and five above Millwall.

The Millwall game proved a real test, especially when Ali Benarbia was sent off in the seventh minute, but City passed with honours. Keegan: "Against Millwall every player did the work of two men after Ali had been sent off. I was tremendously proud of the players. Stuart Pearce had a penalty brilliantly saved and it was beginning to look as if it was not going to be our night, because the Millwall goalkeeper was in outstanding form.

"It got to the stage, with about half an hour to go, when I was so pleased with the actual performance that I didn't care whether we won, drew or lost. I just felt if we could sustain that level of performance for the remainder of the season it would get us where we wanted to go."

City actually won the match with two strikes from Shaun Goater - the first in the 78th minute, the second nine minutes later. According to *The Times'* David McVay: "Even when Shaun Goater scored his 28th goal of the season and his second of the match four minutes from time, created by the admirable Darren Huckerby, it failed to reflect the true nature of this comprehensive victory over one of their closest promotion rivals." City were making a habit of knocking out their rivals. The previous home match had seen fourth-placed Norwich despatched 3-1 despite Tiatto being sent off after ten minutes.

A 2-1 defeat at bogey team Wimbledon followed - again City lost a man when Stuart Pearce was sent off in injury time - before Preston were defeated 3-2 at Maine Road on Sunday 10th February.

The following Sunday - City's sixth Sunday fixture since 13th January - the Blues travelled to Newcastle for a thrilling performance against Keegan's old club in the fifth round of the FA Cup. The media hype focused on Keegan, but the match ended with national recognition that the Blues were clearly a force. Although City lost the match 1-0 after Richard Dunne had been sent off, the general view was that ten-man City were more than a match for the Geordies. City impressed the nation, as they had done three weeks earlier with their spectacular 4-1 fourth round cup demolition of another Premier League side Ipswich Town.

After the Ipswich match Keegan said: "Our fans know we can play but I think we showed the rest of the country that we are a good team. I believe the FA Cup needed a game like our tie with Ipswich where the atmosphere was tremendous and both sides picked their strongest available sides and really set out to win."

The Newcastle tie was another boost for the FA Cup. According to Henry Winter of the *Daily Telegraph*: "Keegan returned with his magnificent Manchester City side whose spirited, defiant football sent the heart rate soaring among Newcastle's nervy support. Making light of Richard Dunne's dismissal and Nolberto Solano's goal, City scared the black-and-white life out of those who still cherish Keegan's name. Shaun Wright-Phillips was marvellous, Eyal Berkovic and Kevin Horlock not far behind with outstanding displays as City narrowly lost a Cup-tie but won countless admirers. If they build on this, they will surely keep the Blue Moon rising and head back to the Premiership, where their noisy supporters belong."

Due to FA Cup commitments City gave Wolves the opportunity to lead the table for a while, and by the time the Blues faced Sheffield Wednesday at home on Wednesday 27th February, Wolves were five points clear after playing two games more than City.

Prior to the match Paul Dickov was invited on to the pitch for a formal farewell. With opportunities at Maine Road limited, Dickov had joined Premiership Leicester City five days earlier. Supporters were sad to see him go, as was Dickov: "Nothing would please me more than City being promoted back to the Premiership. The club is geared up for that and to stay there this time. It will be

a shame I can't be part of it, but that's football. I've had a wonderful time at Maine Road, but my contract would have been up in the summer."

The fantastic ovation given to Dickov was followed by a 4-0 victory over the Owls which included goals from four of the season's most consistent players - Berkovic, Goater, Huckerby and Horlock.

Another quartet were scored four days later when television viewers witnessed a 4-2 defeat of Coventry City with former Coventry man Darren Huckerby netting the opener after fourteen minutes. The Blues remained five points behind Wolves, but that was to change over the course of the next three weeks as City stormed past promotion rivals with a trio of victories at Birmingham (2-1) Bradford (2-0), and Crewe (3-1). The Crewe match put City two points clear of Wolves at the top of the table and still the Blues had a game in hand.

During this run Keegan brought Preston striker Jon Macken to Maine Road for a fee reported as £4m rising to £5m subject to various add-on clauses. As a comparison, Manchester United had signed Veron for £28.1M, van Nistelrooy for £19m and at the season's end Ferdinand for a fee Leeds claimed to be £30m. City simply could not compete with that kind of spending.

City's most expensive signing managed to score a debut goal in the match with Bradford. According to the *Telegraph & Argus*: "Macken was only on ten minutes and could have had a hat-trick. Having hit the post with his first touch the £5m recruit got his debut goal with the final kick of the game."

Despite City's game in hand, Wolves were still a threat. A defeat at bogey-side Stockport County, and a hard-fought draw at Rotherham cancelled out the game in hand and should have given Wolves the initiative, however Dave Jones' side were now feeling the pressure and were unable to capitalise on City's loss of points. With the two sides due to meet on Easter Monday it was clear either side could still win the championship, and Wolves were confident, however a 3-0 City victory against Forest two days earlier meant Wolves were running out of time.

When City took to the field at Molineux they were five points clear with four games remaining. Clearly a Wolves win would hamper City's progress, but a Blue victory would put intense pressure on the Midlands side. In the end the Blues achieved a 2-0 victory in what was described as a physical match, but from Keegan's perspective that owed much to Wolves' determination and was understandable: "There was a lot to play for, especially for Wolves. They eventually had a player sent off, but I don't think the game ever crossed the line between what is acceptable and what is not.

"Our first goal owed a lot to a wicked deflection that took it away from their 'keeper. Even if it wasn't a classic it was the 'Goal of the Season' for me because I always thought the first one would be important. It settled us down and meant Wolves had to come at us even more. It speaks volumes that we were able to control the game for long periods in front of their fans and on their pitch."

Shaun Wright-Phillips claimed the first goal after 36 minutes and immediately took off his tee-shirt to reveal the motto 'Do the Wright thing'. He also scored the second in the eightieth minute to complete Wolves' misery.

According to journalist Ged Scott the Blues were dominant: "City were minus three influential men in Paulo Wanchope, Eyal Berkovic and Danny Tiatto, but with the luxury of 30-goal Shaun Goater sat on the bench, they were still too strong for Wolves. Wolves allowed Ali Benarbia too much freedom and were unable to handle Darren Huckerby's pace, no more so than when Butler took him out once too often. So, on the day when it mattered most, Jones' own expensively assembled side were outclassed."

The victory could have brought City promotion, however West Bromwich Albion achieved their fifth victory in a row and could, mathematically at least, still catch the Blues. Gary Megson's Albion were now level on points with Wolves, eight points behind City. With three games left Blues' destiny lay in their own hands and, for probably the first time in over a decade, supporters felt sure this time there would be no last minute cock-ups. Keegan's City were exciting to watch and, more importantly, they delivered. Wolves and West Brom were no longer perceived as a threat to promotion and, with the Blues at home to 21st-placed Barnsley in the next match, even the League Championship was within reach.

On the eve of the Barnsley match Ali Benarbia was asked about the challenge facing the Blues if promoted. He responded: "If? There is no 'if'. I know we'll go up and win the Championship against Barnsley. No problem for us."

For supporters used to decades of Blue inconsistency the confidence expressed felt refreshing. The Blues had rarely made life easy for themselves, and the impact of Keegan and his staff had supporters walking tall in a similar manner to the early days of the Mercer-Allison partnership.

Benarbia's confidence proved valid later that night; promotion was assured when Wolves were defeated 1-0 at Millwall. The following day, a 1pm kick-off meant supporters arrived bright and early for a day of celebration, and what a celebration. Maine Road was awash with blue and white as ecstatic fans waved their flags and banners and anticipated the Championship. One supporter told Paul Connolly of *The Times*: "I can't believe it. There's nothing that can go wrong. We've already been promoted - we could field a veterans' team and still go up! And the sun's bloody shining."

Despite this refreshing situation the atmosphere was a little muted at the start. Perhaps fans were still nervous of City's past reputation and were fearful of a last-minute failure to secure the Championship. If they were concerned then Darren Huckerby was quickly on hand to reassure them with a twelfth minute strike and another twenty-four minutes later.

Barnsley pulled one back shortly before half-time but a double for Macken and a third for Huckerby gave City a 5-1 lead by the 70th minute. The fourth goal had been the best. Player of the Year Ali Benarbia sent a great pass to Huckerby who proceeded to move quickly forward. Huckerby returned the ball to the Algerian while he continued to move into a goalscoring position, then Benarbia passed back to the ex-Coventry man, who sent the ball crashing into the net. And that was when the celebrations began in earnest.

The cry of 'Champions' bounced around the old stadium, as it had done around St. James' Park in 1968. Throughout the final minutes the fans cheered every player, every move, every moment of the match. Then, when the final whistle blew, the roar was incredible as the Blues finally achieved their first major success since 1976.

The players performed a lap of honour, while Kevin Keegan seemed to delight in bowing to each of the stands in turn. He clearly enjoyed the moment although afterwards he tried to put City's achievement into perspective: "I am not one for getting carried away with celebrations because all we have done so far is return the club to its rightful place."

He did, however, acknowledge the supporters' need to celebrate: "The Barnsley game gave me an insight into the depth of feeling for this club. You all wanted to say 'Thank You' to the players. I sensed many of you had desperately wanted a day like that for years."

He was right, and City's promotion felt like a major success, especially as they would receive the League Championship trophy as a result. So many of City's promotions in the modern era had come via desperate last game of the season victories or draws, but this success was different. Keegan: "There have been a few false dawns here, and the fans have to trust us this isn't going to be another."

The supporters were as convinced as Keegan that this side was better equipped than those promoted during the previous twenty years. For many weeks the Blues had been destined to go up. It may have only become a formality in the final couple of weeks, but City were head and shoulders above the rest. This success was thoroughly deserved. Interestingly, a few of Keegan's predecessors were quick to criticise with the most vocal being Alan Ball: "I couldn't take the club forward because they were in terrible financial difficulties. I had to bear the brunt of what was going wrong by losing my job. Joe Royle had the same thing.

He got them promoted but once he got to the big time they didn't have the money to stay there. Kevin's going to find the same thing."

The criticism may have backed the neutrals' view of City's position, but in truth Keegan's side was already in better shape than any created by Ball or Royle. In addition, City had made it clear Keegan would be supported financially. With a move to the new stadium on the horizon the Blues were keen to attract the best. Before the season's end goalkeeper Peter Schmeichel arrived at Maine Road, while rumours of future major purchases were circulating.

The final away game of the season ended in a 3-1 victory at old foes Gillingham, allowing the Blues to set a new record of 39 points away from home. There was also confirmation the League Championship trophy would be presented at the final match of the season against Portsmouth.

On the last day of the campaign City defeated Portsmouth 3-1 with goals from Howey, Goater and Macken, but the simple facts of the result do not do justice to the achievement felt that day, nor do they portray what actually occurred on the pitch. For many the day belonged to captain Stuart Pearce. It was revealed that Pearce was on 99 career goals and was desperate to reach his century in this his final match. From the moment the game started his every touch of the ball was met with the rousing cry of 'shoot' emanating from the stands. It didn't seem to matter where he was, or how much of a chance he actually had, the cry was always heard.

As the match progressed and City's victory was assured Pearce himself started to push forward, hoping a chance would fall his way. A couple of openings did come - most notably when he sent a Benarbia pass a fraction wide of the post - but then as the game entered its final minute a miracle happened. City were awarded a penalty. Inevitably, Pearce was to take it.

Another veteran, Dave Beasant, was in the Portsmouth goal and dropped a hint to Pearce he wouldn't move, but high drama followed as the City captain blasted the ball into the Platt Lane Stand. Nobody could believe his desperate luck. A goal then would not only have given Pearce his hundredth goal but would also have taken City to 109 League goals - a new season record. The agony was clearly etched on his face but within seconds he was laughing about his misfortune: "There is always a sting in the tail when Stuart Pearce does anything, and that penalty was comical. I have been psyched out by Dave Beasant! The way I missed the goal just about sums me up, but it has been a pleasure and honour to represent the clubs I have, and I am very proud to have won this Championship medal with City."

Musing on his support throughout the match Pearce added: "I couldn't help but smile when the fans were telling me to shoot every time I picked the ball up on the edge of my own box."

Understandably, the stadium remained full right to the end of the match and even then only a small number of Portsmouth fans actually left. While supporters waited for the presentation of the trophy news filtered through that West Bromwich Albion had snatched the second promotion spot, leaving one-time leaders Wolves devastated.

In the end Wolves failed to succeed in the play-offs,

City celebrate with a lap of honour at Maine Road.

493

and the third promotion place went to another Midlands side Birmingham. In Wolverhampton they searched for reasons for their ultimate failure. John Richards, the Wolves match-winner when City were defeated in the 1974 League Cup Final, believed the attitude of his former club was to blame. He felt they had treated promotion as a formality and many neutrals agreed. In February when Wolves led the table, Dave Jones appeared on Football Focus claiming promotion was no longer his club's drive, they wanted the Championship. In March they were selling 'Premiership' season tickets at First Division prices - a move which brought enhanced sales but ultimately little satisfaction. Richards told the press: "Considering all the frustrations we've had here over the last eighteen years, assuming we would go up was tempting fate too much. The form over the last ten matches was clearly not good enough, but the form over the previous thirty-six was. So much so that the meeting with Manchester City on Easter Monday had been billed as a championship decider."

City were grateful another side had taken over their mantle as masters of the cock-up.

The trophy presentation took place in the centre of the pitch. It was a day of celebration for all and the arrival of former player Paul Dickov to tie the blue and white ribbons onto the trophy was greeted with a huge cheer.

The formal presentation began with the players being called out, mainly in pairs, to receive their medals. Once all the players and staff were on the pitch the League Championship trophy was handed to Stuart Pearce and the stadium erupted once more. Wild celebrations followed, as did a special presentation by David Bernstein to Stuart Pearce to mark his long playing career.

It was a moment to enjoy for all, and even the Portsmouth supporters who remained applauded Pearce and the other City men as they performed innumerable laps of honour. This success seemed so much better than previous promotions, partly because of the tremendous football played throughout the season and partly because of the fact City had actually won a recognisable trophy.

2002-2003 Farewell To Maine Road

Most fans, players and pundits felt the Blues stood a very real chance of a mid-table – or higher – finish. Everyone recognised that Kevin Keegan had developed an entertaining side but his moves during the close season brought considerable hope and optimism to all at Maine Road. Together with his management team - in particular Arthur Cox and Derek Fazackerley – Keegan started to prove City were ready for the challenge of the Premier League by signing some of Europe's most

interesting and entertaining players. While other Premiership sides talked about who they might buy the Blues actually bought. Little was heard now from former manager Alan Ball or any of the other pundits who had claimed Keegan would not be supported.

The players brought in included Dutch Under-21 defender Tyrone Loran from FC Volendam; Silvain Distin from Paris St. Germain; Independiente striker Vicente Matias Vuoso; and another Paris St Germain star Nicolas Anelka. There was also the arrival of Cameroon World Cup star Marc Vivien Foe on a year's loan.

Loran was purchased for a low figure reported as 100,000 Euro (around £68,000), while Distin and Vuoso both came for fees speculated to be around £4m, but the highest transfer of them all was ex-Liverpool star Anelka. He arrived for an estimated record fee of £13m, Alioune Toure moving in the opposite direction for about £1m.

Keegan was delighted with each purchase, especially Anelka: "It's a fantastic signing for us. Nicolas is a quality player and we're lucky to have him. We have made a number of good signings this summer but Distin and Anelka are the two I am really excited about."

Director of Football Dennis Tueart explained how happy he was with Distin's arrival: "When it became clear Newcastle were not going to take up their option on the player, Kevin moved very quickly and we are delighted to have Sylvain on board. We looked closely at bringing Sylvain to Maine Road before he went to Newcastle before Christmas but at that stage we were in the First Division and he was understandably looking for a Premiership deal.

"He is a powerful, quick athlete who has already proved himself at the highest level. What is vitally important, too, in the strategy for team building, is that he is a left-sided central defender who is a like-for-like swap for Stuart Pearce who has now, of course, retired."

Off the pitch there were other changes. The sponsorship deal with Eidos came to an end, but a fresh £5m deal with First Advice - a new legal and financial advice company - was announced in May. David Bernstein: "This is the biggest main sponsorship deal in the club's history. First Advice are a Manchester-based company, which we are very pleased about and we think it's a very exciting partnership." Sadly, the deal was doomed as, within twelve months, the company went into receivership and the Blues were forced to wear the company's name even after it collapsed.

Another change about to happen concerned Maine Road. With the Blues due to move in August 2003, focus shifted to the stadium's Road's final season. The manager felt the best way to ensure a positive send off to the stadium was to: "Try to make Maine Road an intimidating place for visiting teams as we did last season."

During the summer steps had been taken to ensure

Extensions to the 'Gene Kelly' stand. Maine Road was simply too small.

as many Blues as possible could attend the final season. Additional temporary seating was placed in the tunnel at the Platt Lane/Main Stand corner and above the police control box next to the Main Stand. This brought the final capacity of the stadium up to 35,150. Still woefully small in comparison with the Blues' history, but the largest capacity the stadium had held since the demise of the terraced Kippax Stand in 1994. Segregation varied game by game, depending on volume and position of away support. They were usually housed in the uncovered Gene Kelly stand (so-called because fans sat in the stand were noted for 'singing in the rain') between the North Stand and the Kippax, and/or in the Kippax end of the North Stand.

An 'End of an Era' memorabilia exhibition was organised by a committee comprising club personnel and supporters. The idea of such an exhibition was first raised by fanzine editor Noel Bayley during the 1999-2000 season. He approached a number of supporters and collectors, and they worked with the Club to put on an exhibition the following October. The May 2002 exhibition followed a similar process.

The exhibition allowed supporters to have their photographs taken with the Championship trophy and tour Maine Road. Both options proved extremely popular with four-hour queues developing for the trophy at one point. Some also took a glimpse into the future by touring the new City of Manchester Stadium. It's fair to say most were impressed, particularly when comparisons were made with Maine Road and other leading Premiership venues.

In June, during the Japan-Korea World Cup, fixture lists for the 2002-03 season were produced and, as anticipated, the Blues' opening matches looked mouth-watering. The season would commence with a trip to Terry Venables' Leeds, while the first home fixture would bring Sir Bobby Robson's Newcastle to Maine Road. The last League visitors to Maine Road would be Southampton.

With a famous trophy safely in the vault at Maine Road, Premier League status assured, a popular manager

in charge, and a move to one of Europe's most impressive venues on the horizon, the summer of 2002 was truly a marvellous time to be a Blue. Or so it seemed.

Behind the scenes steps were being taken to restructure the Blues' finances. City entered into a securitisation deal that released funds in the short term, but whether that helped the long term position of the Club is debateable. In August 2002, when the deal was first announced, Conal Walsh, writing for the *Observer*, questioned whether the move was in City's long term interest or not: "Long derided as one of football's financial basket cases, Manchester City turned full circle last week with the news that it is negotiating to raise £40 million by mortgaging future ticket sales at its new state-of-the-art stadium.

"After being relegated in 1996, the club sank under the financial weight of an over-large playing staff, only to be resurrected by the parsimonious bookkeeping of chairman David Bernstein. But now City is back in the Premiership and Kevin Keegan, the manager, has signalled the club's free-spending intent by splurging £17m on French stars Nicolas Anelka and Sylvain Distin.

"That sort of money is impossible to find on the stock market these days, so the securitisation deal, arranged by bankers Bear Stearns, is a godsend to City's long-suffering fans. Or is it?"

Within his article Walsh quoted a number of financial experts who understood City's short term need but felt

City show fans the transformation, 2002-03.

the Club were not being financially prudent. John Moore, football analyst at Bell Lawrie White, was quoted as saying: "Football clubs have two assets: their ground and the goodwill of their fans, and that is what guarantees the revenue stream. Now clubs are cashing those assets. But you can only sell the crown jewels once. Anelka will probably be middle aged by the time Man City finishes paying off its debt. Football clubs badly need to cut costs. Securitisations just give clubs more money to spend, when many have spent too much already. And if they miss one instalment on their repayments, some could even lose control of their stadiums."

Moore painted an interesting picture showing how individual clubs could often work through

financial issues at a local level due to sentiment, but not with multi-national institutions: "I rather doubt that a big American investment bank like Bear Stearns, or any institutional lender, cares much about what Manchester City fans think."

Another critic quoted was Andrew Lee, football analyst at Dresdner Kleinwort Wasserstein. He felt City were creating a financial headache for years to come: "You give them money up front and they spend it willy-nilly. To recoup what Man City have spent, they'll have to get into Europe or win something. I find some clubs' financial planning comical."

At the time of the securitisation, the Club inevitably talked positively of the arrangement and it was often likened to a mortgage. Alistair Mackintosh frequently talked of a 'well-structured' debt.

Despite the coverage in the financial media, fans remained oblivious in the main to financial issues at City. Most recognised that the struggles of the eighties and nineties had impacted on the Club's ability to compete, but they believed that with a developing Academy set-up, under the direction of Jim Cassell, and a move to the new stadium on the horizon the future would be positive.

Despite the positivity generated by Keegan's promotion winning side and the transfers he had made, the new season kicked off with a 3-0 defeat in the opening game at Leeds. The media viewed this negatively, but the fans felt otherwise and when the Blues won the first Maine Road match of the season 1-0 talk of challenging for Europe filled the air immediately. The victory came against Kevin Keegan's former side Newcastle United, managed by Sir Bobby Robson, with a goal from Darren Huckerby.

TRUE BLUE
Chris Bird

Chris Bird was a dynamic force shaping the Blues behind the scenes during the late 90s and early 2000s. He became Managing Director but resigned during 2002-03.

Four days after defeating Robson's side the Blues travelled to Villa Park where they suffered their second away defeat of the season. The match was also the second game of Peter Schmeichel's Maine Road career – he'd made his debut against Newcastle. Keegan had recognised that City needed a strong 'keeper to help the side stabilise in the Premier League, and Schmeichel was expected to help the defensive record improve. In 2001-02 despite winning the Division One title by ten points the Blues had conceded 52 goals. No one worried at the time as City also netted 108 goals, but in the Premier League Keegan knew it wouldn't be quite as easy to score. A quality 'keeper was crucial.

Another of Keegan's new recruits, Nicolas Anelka, started to prove his value to the Blues when he scored twice against Everton in the fourth game, although everybody had initially assumed he had scored his hat-trick. In fact the player had been presented with the match ball. A few weeks later Keegan explained: "The authorities have taken a goal off him – the first of his 'hat trick'. The Dubious Goals panel later ruled that it was an own goal by Radzinski. He won't want it so why don't they let Nicolas keep it? It means we will have to ask for the ball back!"

The game seemed to be full of odd moments, including the sending off of Shaun Wright-Phillips. Keegan was far from happy with that but the young star's red card was later rescinded to yellow.

A 2-1 defeat at Arsenal followed before the Blues gained another point with a 2-2 draw at home to Blackburn. It had been a remarkable match and caused Keegan to admit: "For 80 minutes we were poor. We were second best all over the pitch."

Danny Tiatto was sent off and the situation looked dire. However, City fans were in full voice that day and the enthusiasm off the pitch encouraged those on the pitch that the game was not lost.

In the 80th minute Anelka scored to provide a little hope and then in the final minute Goater netted the equaliser. In added time the Blues came close to snatching all three points. Keegan felt the fans helped enormously: "The atmosphere inside Maine Road in the closing minutes was probably the best. And one of the main reasons we got the result was because the crowd didn't give up on us. In the end we almost won the game after never being in it."

Despite the support and the Blues' ability to fight back in games like this, the following weeks saw City drop down the table after gaining only one point from a possible 12. These results put the Club close to the relegation zone, but it is fair to say that no one seriously contemplated that the Blues would have to fight for survival.

At the end of October Keegan's side defeated Birmingham 2-0 with goals from Jihai Sun and Nicolas Anelka, and followed this with a 2-1 victory over West Bromwich Albion. Both those games were away from home, but the biggest and most important match of the season so far came on 9th November at Maine Road – the final Manchester derby at the old stadium.

City had been knocked out of the League Cup at Wigan four days earlier and few expected Keegan's Blues to defeat Alex Ferguson's expensively assembled side – the team included five players who cost the Reds more than £7 million while City's team possessed one, Anelka. Those five United players totalled almost £100 million (£7.8m Fabien Barthez, £30m Rio Ferdinand, £28.1m Juan Sebastian Veron, £19m Ruud van Nistelrooy and £7.5m Diego Forlan), and few sides could compete with Ferguson's spending.

With this being the last Maine Road derby the media focused on the significance of the event and past meetings. United captain Gary Neville talked of the hurt he felt when City humiliated the Reds in 1989 with a 5-1 victory: "Even though I was a 14 year old playing for my local club at the time, it still feels part of my United

history. It is a result that hangs over the club. They were embarrassing days. You carry them in the back of your mind on days like this to remind you of what is at stake and how bad you will feel if you don't give it your all and get the right result."

Perhaps thinking of how United fans were joking about City's stature at this point he added: "Any game against City is massive."

Neville's manager seemed to hold different views, or at least he tried to give the impression that activities at M14 7WN did not worry him: "The atmosphere will not be a problem to us. My team has played on the biggest stages and is used to it now. There's more noise when we got to Anfield and Elland Road because they are bigger stadiums."

Despite – or maybe because – Ferguson downplaying the atmosphere Maine Road was rocking. The public address system failed shortly before kick-off and that seemed to allow fans to generate a better atmosphere than usual. Rather than being drowned out by recorded music, fans were able to sing freely. Afterwards many supporters suggested every significant match should see a similar reduction in the use of the public address system.

With passionate support the opening moments were played at a frenetic pace and within the first five minutes the Blues took the lead. The expensive Ferdinand was easily dispossessed by Anelka, who then slotted a wonderful pass to Goater. Goater shot accurately but goalkeeper Barthez parried, and Anelka sent the ball into the United net.

The old stadium erupted but sadly City couldn't keep hold of their lead. Solskjaer equalised within three minutes of Anelka's opener and fans began to feel nervous.

Fortunately, after 25 minutes a seemingly harmless pass into the United area by Foe caused Gary Neville to trot after the ball with the intention of seeing it go out of play for a goal kick. Just as the ball neared the touchline Neville appeared to have second thoughts about letting the ball go out. As he did so Goater, who had been tracking him all the way, took the ball from Neville with ease. He then proceeded to curl the ball past Barthez for his first goal of the match.

From that point on City were in control of the match and deservedly Goater scored a second – and his 100th goal for the Blues – to guarantee a 3-1 victory in the last Manchester derby at Maine Road.

At full time the stadium erupted with "Who let the Goat Out?" and the player admitted: "That was one occasion I wished I'd been out wide on the Kippax side of the ground when the referee blew for time. My walk would have been a lot longer and I could have enjoyed the moment more.

"It was a very special day and a really significant

The last League 'derby' to be played at Maine Road

A perfect final derby match for Maine Road.

occasion but it never struck me until we got back to the dressing room that I had reached the milestone and only then when the lads were saying 'that was your 100th.'"

It is worth noting that the match was noteworthy historically as Peter Schmeichel became only the second player, after Billy Meredith, to captain both City and United.

For most Blues, this was the greatest final moment in the stadium's last season. Unfortunately, it was followed by a 1-0 defeat at home to Charlton and a 3-1 loss at Middlesbrough leaving City in 16th place.

Twenty year old Joey Barton was named as one of the substitutes for the Middlesbrough game. During the second half Keegan told him to get ready to go on, but the player's shirt had mysteriously vanished. Barton later claimed that he had removed his shirt after taking his place on the bench. Somehow the shirt slipped off his seat and couldn't be found when Barton was due to go on. It was a very odd moment and one that annoyed the manager. Keegan had to revise his plans and the youngster had to wait until January to make his debut.

Barton later admitted: "I was gutted and didn't say a word on the coach home. But I am a strong believer in fate and that things happen for a reason. Maybe I just wasn't ready."

On 30th November 18th placed Bolton arrived at Maine Road. Often a thorn in City's side the Wanderers came expecting the opportunity to gain three points, but Keegan's side dominated from the start. Steve Howey brought the lead with a header from an Eyal Berkovic free kick in the 25th minute, and then in the 56th minute Nicolas Anelka set up the Israeli for his first Premier League goal. The game was summed up nicely by *The Times*: "With Bolton managing just two shots on goal throughout, both routinely gathered by Schmeichel, City's victory could hardly be more easily obtained."

The next match saw Keegan's side face another struggling side Sunderland and, despite a good attempt by Kevin Phillips early on, the game was all City's. It was a miserably cold and bitter night, brightened by the exciting play on offer from the Blues. Foe netted first, in the 4th minute, followed by Sun Jihai 17 minutes into the second half and, by the time Goater netted four minutes from time, most of the home sections of the Stadium of Light were empty. The match ended in a comfortable 3-0 win.

Five days later the Blues were losing with 63 minutes gone to Charlton. All seemed lost but Keegan's side would not give up. As pressure mounted Foe netted twice (73 & 87 mins) to ensure a 2-2 draw. In fact *The Times* felt City: "would have won had the referee not failed to punish Rufus's foul on Anelka with a penalty."

In the following match, at home to Tottenham on 23rd December, a Howey header gave City a 29th minute lead. Unfortunately, the Blues somehow allowed Spurs to equalise seven minutes before the interval, and then take the lead three minutes into the second half. By the final minute it was 3-1 to the visitors, however Benarbia managed to score an absolutely beautiful goal in the final minute to make it 3-2. That final minute saw more action as Tottenham's Ziege was sent off for his second offence in quick succession of kicking the ball away. He clearly hoped to preserve his side's lead, but it seemed a ridiculous action – twice - by the player.

On Boxing Day Foe put City in front after 15 minutes against Aston Villa but Dion Dublin netted an equaliser on 41 minutes. In the 65th minute a fairly even game was suddenly transformed when Benarbia was brought on as substitute for Wright-Phillips. Within minutes he had hit the bar, but more was to come when, 13 minutes after coming on, his brilliant diving header put City into the lead. Two minutes later he set Foe up for his second. Already a hero Benarbia's standing at Maine Road was increasing game by game.

Captain Ali Benarbia was one of City's most popular players during this period. Fans loved him and the quality of his play but the player was convinced he could deliver more. At the season's end he admitted: "I have not been happy with how I have played." He added: "We haven't been able to show what we can do on a consistent basis this season. We have been brilliant at times and then given away silly goals to spoil it all."

The Villa win was followed on 28th December with a 1-0 victory at Fulham. Anelka's goal in that match helped lift the Blues to ninth.

On 11th January City defeated Leeds United 2-1 with Niclas Jensen netting an exceptional volleyed goal – many believed this was the finest goal of the season. The victory lifted City to eighth and strengthened Keegan's aim of European football.

Around this time the main player-related story concerned Robbie Fowler. Keegan was desperate to bring the former Liverpool player to Maine Road but there were a number of issues and the on-off transfer rumbled on for some time. It also played a part in unsettling the Club. On 29th January *The Guardian* reported: "The Fowler move leaves the position of David Bernstein at Maine Road unclear. The City chairman has been under scrutiny since it emerged he was culpable for upsetting Fowler, prompting him to change his mind about moving to Maine Road 13 days ago. Fowler had complained he felt 'like damaged goods' after Bernstein, citing reservations about the player's injury problems, went behind Keegan's back to ask Leeds to drop their valuation to £5m, based purely on appearances. In the face of intense pressure from Keegan and the club's directors Bernstein has now indicated he is ready to back down and sanction Fowler's arrival on the original terms."

The following day the media was full of stories confirming that Fowler was now on his way to City.

The BBC reported: "Leeds United's plc confirmed to the Stock Exchange that the former Liverpool striker has completed his move for a £3million fee, with a further £3m payable when the player has made a number of first-team appearances. David Bernstein, chairman of Manchester City, believes that the club is heading onwards and upwards after finally sealing the deal to bring Fowler to Maine Road.

"The England forward is expected to make his debut against West Brom on Saturday. City clinched a deal for the player at the second time of asking but Bernstein denied that there had been a boardroom split. He said: 'We are now looking forward to winning matches and getting this club in the top part of the Premiership.'"

Despite the denial, rumours coming out of Maine Road suggested that all was not well behind the scenes. Fans were openly talking about a split in the boardroom with John Wardle and Chris Bird on one side and David Bernstein and Alistair Mackintosh on the other. There was also talk of an earlier change that had seemed out of place as far as fans were concerned. That change had seen Finance Director Alistair Mackintosh become joint Managing Director with Chris Bird. Bird had been Chief Operating Officer and, in effect, the main figure working at the Club on a daily basis, so the promotion of Mackintosh to give the two men equal billing seemed an odd decision.

The following February the *Manchester Evening News* claimed that City supporting Bird: "felt let down by chairman David Bernstein last December when his role was seemingly divided in two, as finance director Alistair Mackintosh became joint managing director. Bird then felt exposed and embarrassed over the Robbie Fowler transfer saga, as the first signs of boardroom divisions came to light. He allied himself with the John Wardle faction - which wants the club to back Kevin Keegan's ambitions to the hilt - as opposed to the more financially prudent approach favoured by accountants Mackintosh and Bernstein."

While issues behind the scenes rumbled on City defeated Fulham 4-1 at Maine Road on 29th January but then faced Everton in what was to become Robbie Fowler's debut on 1st February. City lost the match 2-1 and only one point was earned in the three games that followed. That point, however, did come in the 1-1 Manchester derby draw at Old Trafford when Goater

TRUE BLUE
David Bernstein

Chairman David Bernstein gave City respectability during an extremely difficult period on the pitch. Together with Chris Bird and the other directors he resurrected the Blues.

scored a mere nine seconds after coming on to the pitch as substitute.

Only earning a point in Fowler's opening four games may or may not have exacerbated issues within the Club, but what is known is that tension behind the scenes did increase. Ian Farrell, writing in *When Saturday Comes*, seemed to have his finger on the pulse: "A mixture of the manager's tenacity and Leeds' desperation reignited the transfer, at a lower price and with the contentious long-term payment plan in place, but the damage was done. The deal had created problems, am-plified others and broadcast the whole thing to a media waiting to laugh. The assurances of boardroom solidarity came thick and fast, but the recent resignation of co-managing director Chris Bird, a major player in City's resurrection and an advocate of a speculate-to-accumulate approach, tells its own story. There are worries that the schism between Bird and JD Sports magnate Wardle on one side and Bernstein and finance director Alistair Mackintosh on the other over spending policy could start a damaging civil war."

By the 5th March both Chris Bird and David Bernstein had resigned. The news stunned fans. Some felt Bernstein was a major loss, some Bird, but the truth was that both men had been instrumental in the transformation of the Blues during the late nineties and early 2000s.

The *Manchester Evening News* outlined the key events: "Bernstein announced that he was quitting 45 minutes before the start of a directors' meeting where

Robbie Fowler in action against Sunderland in the last victory at Maine Road.

he was facing a vote of no-confidence following the resignation of Bird. The board took 90 minutes to discuss the two resignation letters before announcing that Bernstein's resignation will take effect immediately while Bird's will operate from a date to be agreed. They issued a statement saying: 'These resignations have neither been sought nor welcomed by the board. However, faced with the unequivocal determination of both directors to resign, the remaining directors had no choice but to accept this position despite a concerted effort over many days to seek to preserve the board's structure'.

"Bernstein was jogging near his London home as the five directors, deputy chairman and millionaire majority shareholder John Wardle, Alistair Mackintosh, Dennis Tueart, Ashley Lewis and Bryan Bodek made their decision after which they paid tribute to Bernstein and Bird. Early this afternoon City issued a third statement announcing that Wardle will take over as chairman for the immediate future Wardle - the founder of J D Sports who owns a third of the club - was always going to be the most likely to succeed. He is closest to manager Kevin Keegan and is a big supporter of his spend, spend, spend policy to get City into Europe in time for the move to the former Commonwealth Games stadium in the summer.

"Bernstein, 59, who is popular with the fans for bringing in ultra-ambitious Keegan, was unaware of

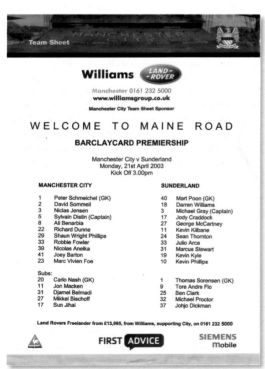

The team sheet for the final win at the old stadium.

talks that went on until the early hours of the morning between Wardle and fellow directors which sealed his fate. He blamed a 'divergence of views on fundamental strategic issues particularly concerning finance and management structure' for his decision to resign. He has been at loggerheads with key directors - particularly Wardle since Bird quit last week."

The newspaper went on: "Bird cited a 'personality clash' as the reason why he was quitting his dream £170,000 a year post. He was angry that the chairman had decided to split his work with finance director Alistair Mackintosh."

Bernstein's statement following resignation gave his reasons for leaving: "It is with regret I have today tendered my resignation as chairman of Manchester City PLC. I emphasise that this decision is entirely my own. On my appointment in 1998 I emphasised three factors required to fulfil the chairman's role effectively - unity, stability and professionalism. Until recently my board, major shareholders and key employees have successfully worked together to achieve these.

"Over the last few months there has been a divergence of views on fundamental strategic issues particularly concerning finance and management structure. I believe this has inhibited my ability to direct the club in the way I would wish."

While supporters pondered the reasons why both Bird and Bernstein left, the fanzine *King Of The Kippax* searched for answers. Wryly it suggested: "As for Bernstein, the most obvious problem was that he'd been sensible for about five years and that's just not acceptable for a City Chairman."

Deputy Chairman John Wardle took on Bernstein's role, although he regularly pointed out that he did not want the position on a permanent basis, while Alistair Mackintosh became City's sole Managing Director.

Almost a decade later John Wardle explained why he took on the role of Chairman: "I was Deputy Chairman at the time so it was automatic that I would take on the role initially. I thought I'd take us to the next meeting and then we'd agree on who the new Chairman would be. I did not think about keeping the role but I started to get letters from fans asking me to do it. I still kept thinking that I wasn't the right man and then one day I saw Kevin Keegan who was such an important figure for us at that time because he had been responsible for putting smiles back on our faces. He had followed Joe Royle who had done an excellent job and had saved the Club when we needed him. Kevin had taken us on to the next level.

"Kevin said to me 'why don't you take it John? We work well together and get on. See how it goes?' Then Arthur Cox called – what a knowledge of football and what a great guy! He was Kevin's assistant at the time and, in that straight talking way of his, he said 'Been talking with Kevin. What's this? You won't be Chairman?

The Kippax Stand, less than eight years old at Maine Road's final game.

Take on the job. It's very important'. I listened to him and then thought 'why not?' So I took it on."

On the pitch Robbie Fowler, playing his fifth League game, netted his first goal for the Club as the Blues beat Birmingham City 1-0 before 34,596 at Maine Road on 16th March, but this was followed by a 5-0 thrashing by Chelsea at Stamford Bridge. Afterwards Kevin Keegan admitted: "It was just about as poor as it gets from our

The match ball from Maine Road's final match.

point of view. At least the players put their hands up and accepted responsibility."

A month to the day earlier Keegan's side had suffered a 5-1 defeat by Arsenal. Although this sounds like a very bleak moment it actually saw the true character of City's support as fans stood to applaud the quality of the Gunners' side. That day Arsenal were sensational and led 4-0 within 19 minutes. Instead of resorting to criticising the home side as others may have done, fans marvelled at the play of Wenger's side and gave them an ovation as they left the pitch at half-time. Future Blue Patrick Vieira netted Arsenal's fifth in the 53rd minute.

Worth noting that before the Arsenal game City had been tenth on 38 points, 19 behind the Gunners, who led the table. The high scoring defeat said more about the quality of the visitors rather than City, and fans recognised they had been beaten by a great side.

On April 5th a 2-0 defeat at Bolton was viewed a little differently, as supporters recognised that a European place was still possible but, they felt, unlikely. The focus for many turned to Maine Road itself. With every game at the stadium a sell-out – only the size of the away support varied – supporters were desperate for the season to see the old venue at its best. They also wanted a few memorable results in those final weeks. Ultimately, the best Maine Road match of the final weeks came on

21st April 2003 when a goal from Robbie Fowler and two from Marc-Vivien Foe brought a 3-0 win over Sunderland. The game became significant as it was to be the last City victory at the old stadium and Foe's 80th minute goal was the last scored there by a City man.

Pre-match Sunderland presented the Blues with a rose bowl commemorating their final visit to the stadium. Significantly, the time span between their first appearance at Maine Road and their last was greater than any other visiting club.

Before the last match at Maine Road City defeated Liverpool 2-1 at Anfield. Always a great place to win but this game was more satisfying than usual because the Blues had conceded the opener in the 59th minute and had to fight back to earn the victory. Former Liverpool player Anelka equalised with a 74th minute penalty and then netted the winner in the final minute.

The last game of the season was Maine Road's final match. The opponents were Southampton, however despite the fact the visitors rarely travelled in vast numbers to matches in the north-west, the football authorities insisted that the Saints should be allocated a couple of thousand seats in the 'Gene Kelly' uncovered stand rather than a few hundred tickets as City had hoped. It had been one of Southampton's greatest seasons and it was understandable that their fans should want a similar allocation to every other League side, however, the discussions between City's officials and those of their rivals were portrayed negatively in the media.

On the day itself fans arrived at Maine Road early to take in all the sights and sounds of the old place. Former players and managers were introduced to the crowd from almost every period of the stadium's history and, without exception, they were welcomed and cheered like never before.

Immediately prior to kick off Colin Bell, Malcolm Allison and Norah Mercer, Joe's widow, were brought out on to the pitch. They were City's chief guests and were introduced to each of the players in turn. Significantly, Malcolm Allison also took time out to shake hands with each of the mascots and, on occasion, he gave them a pat on the head or a gentle ruffle of the hair. So often mascots are ignored by dignitaries but on this day the former City boss made sure he acknowledged them as well as the players.

Shaun Goater had been given the honour of captaining the Blues on this final momentous occasion, just like Max Woosnam had in the opening match in 1923. Paul Connolly, writing in *The Times*, highlighted the crowd's welcome: "The imminent departure of Goater has certainly proved the wellspring for almost as much emotion as the end of Maine Road era. That became obvious when his name was greeted by the crowd before the game with a quite extraordinary tumultuous chorus of 'Feed The Goat.'"

TRUE BLUE
Shaun Goater

Honoured with the captaincy for Maine Road's final game and a true hero.

In 2003, shortly before the Kippax's demolition, Edward Garvey took this unique shot of the new stadium from the old stand.

Unfortunately the game was not the spectacle fans had hoped for or the stadium deserved. In the 34th minute Southampton's Michael Svensson netted the last league goal scored at Maine Road.

At half time three of City's oldest surviving players – Douglas Stewart, George Smith and Billy Walsh – were introduced to the crowd with George receiving the greatest ovation when it was announced he had once scored four goals against Manchester United in a wartime match for the Blues.

In the second half opportunities were few and far between and then, in the 63rd minute, Shaun Goater was substituted to one of Maine Road's greatest ovations. It was as if his departure was the formal signal for the end of the old venue. It wasn't quite the end of course, but the emotion was clearly visible as fans recognised that the last footballing acts were about to be played out.

By the final whistle chants of Blue Moon echoed around the stadium. Where once Billy Meredith had thrilled 76,000 in a FA Cup tie, Eric Brook had scored a

wonder goal before 84,569 and fans had chanted "Who Said City Couldn't Play?" it was time for the final lap of honour by the Blues. Special presentations were made to Goater and Schmeichel, whose careers were officially over that day, while the groundstaff of Roy Rigby, Lee Jackson and Gary Conway removed the goalposts.

Rigby had actually been presented with an award pre-match for the quality of Maine Road's playing surface. Many believed the pitch had been the best it had ever been and the award was thoroughly deserved.

After the formal end to the season a post-match concert, hosted by Marc Riley, was staged. It featured a 'Blues Brothers' band, an Oasis tribute act, Badly Drawn Boy and the Doves. The concert ended with Badly Drawn Boy urging the North Stand to start off the final rendition of Blue Moon.

Once the concert finished many fans simply stayed in the stadium, taking it all in for one last time. Words cannot describe the emotion all Blues felt that day.

1999-2003 SUMMARY

Highest League Attendance: 35,131 Liverpool, 28/09/02
Highest Cup Attendance: 31,252 Ipswich Town, 19/12/01 (League Cup)
Managers: 1998 – 2001 Joe Royle & 2001 – 2005 Kevin Keegan

Seasonal Record:

Season	League	Posn	FA Cup	League Cup	Other	Leading Scorer	Average Attendance
1999-00	New 1	2	Rnd 4	Rnd 2		Goater 23	32,088
2000-01	Premier	18	Rnd 5	Rnd 5		Wanchope 9	34,058
2001-02	New 1	Champions	Rnd 5	Rnd 4		Goater 28	33,059
2002-03	Premier	9	Rnd 3	Rnd 3		Anelka 14	34,564

A worthy home as seen from the south-east corner of the stadium in 2003-04.

2003-2007 Premier Home

"Leaving Maine Road was a huge decision for Manchester City, but we have no doubt that the move to the City Of Manchester Stadium is the right decision for this club. The increased capacity and superb new facilities the stadium will provide will put us amongst the elite of English football, and we are confident that in the City Of Manchester Stadium we will have a home of which our fans can be proud."

City Chairman John Wardle, June 2003

2003-2004 A New Home

The Blues ended the 2002-03 season in a creditable ninth place and also qualified for the UEFA Cup via the Fair Play League. Manager Kevin Keegan had hoped for European qualification at the start of the season, but did not expect to qualify based on a system that rewarded clubs for their disciplinary record.

Sadly, apart from the positive news about Europe, the first few weeks of the 2003 close season brought much sadness to the Club. Clearly the move from Maine Road was an emotional experience, but the stadium's final days were marked with tributes to Marc-Vivien Foe who passed away during an international match for Cameroon. His death was a major shock and for some his loss added to the emotion of moving away from Maine Road. For many supporters leaving the old ground was the biggest emotional upset they had experienced. To some Maine Road was Manchester City.

Despite the sadness of Foe's early death and the departure from Maine Road the new season opened with lots of optimism.

The move to the new stadium brought considerable hope that this would prove to be a memorable season on the pitch as well as off it. Former player Dennis Tueart was a director by this point: "For me the stadium move gave us a chance of looking to the future. It was important we put all the troubles of the past behind us and see the move as a chance to re-establish the Club. For that reason, the opening game against Barcelona was a great moment and I remember sitting there thinking that this is how it should be. City facing top quality European sides in a great stadium with passionate and vocal fans. There were also about five or six Academy lads in the side as well, so I was so proud of how we'd moved on in those few years since relegation to the third level in 1998."

Chairman John Wardle was also a proud man when the stadium opened: "It was a wonderful experience moving. It was as if you'd been living in a terraced house and were then given the keys to a five bedroom mansion. We opened the doors and went in and it was amazing. We were hopping around – 'Look at this', 'what's that?', 'how does this work?' It was great. It was also sad because of leaving Maine Road, but that sadness had to be channelled into the excitement of the new stadium.

"The fans were so important in the move and I was so pleased with the way they supported the move. The opening game was against Barcelona and I have to admit I was overawed with it all that day. The Barcelona President helped and guided me on to the pitch to be introduced to the two teams. Shaking hands with the City players that day in our new home meant so much to me, because it felt we'd achieved something. We were in the Premier League, about to compete in the UEFA Cup, and here we were in our new home facing one of Europe's truly elite clubs."

After the Barcelona friendly, the first competitive game at City's new home was a 5-0 thrashing of Welsh side Total Network Solutions (TNS) in a UEFA Cup qualifying round on 14th August 2003. Despite the fact that this was only the initial stages of the competition the game was eagerly awaited in Manchester and Wales. The TNS manager Ken McKenna was delighted with the draw: "It's a great story. A village team against Manchester City. If you made it up they would lock you up."

The TNS owner Mike Harris was equally excited: "This is fantastic, the best draw we could possibly have had. I am confident we can go up to Manchester and get a good result and then really put the pressure on them in the second leg. If we get the right result I will be looking to relocate the game to the Millennium Stadium - why not?"

The first leg saw the Blues easily overpower the Welsh side. According to journalist Daniel Taylor: "The side with nine Englishman in their starting XI (TNS) were never a serious match for the team with four (City), especially when one of that quartet, Trevor Sinclair, opened the scoring 14 minutes into an uncomfortably one-sided opening half."

City defeated TNS 5-0 in the first leg, but Kevin

Tributes to Marc-Vivien Foe at Maine Road, July 2003.

Keegan felt the victory could have been more impressive: "We could and should have scored more goals."

Three days later the League programme kicked off with a relatively easy 3-0 victory at Charlton. That game saw debuts for David Seaman, Michael Tarnat, Paul Bosvelt and City fan Trevor Sinclair.

The second League game was the first Premier League match to be staged in the new stadium. On 23rd August the historic match ended in a 1-1 draw with Portsmouth's Yakuba Ayegbini scoring the first League goal at the new stadium. David Sommeil netted City's first League goal, but he left it late – the 90th minute. Two days later the Blues headed the table briefly after defeating Blackburn 3-2.

Sadly, the new stadium's second League game ended in a 2-1 defeat to new League leaders Arsenal. Keegan: "We rattled them a bit... If only we could have sustained our form and concentration for the full 90 minutes, we could have been talking about being the top of the League now."

On Sunday 14th September the Blues recorded their first League win at their new home when Aston Villa were defeated 4-1. Villa had actually taken a 31st minute lead before City took control in the second half. A hat trick for Anelka (including the stadium's first – and second - penalty) was greeted with high praise from Keegan: "I was 27 before I learned what the game was all about. If he can continue to develop at the same rate over the next three years, by the time he reaches his peak, he can go on to be the best striker in the world."

The victory over Villa lifted City to third but only five points were gained from the following five matches. This did include a 6-2 win over Bolton though.

The Bolton victory was notable from a stadium perspective as it also marked the sixth consecutive highest record breaking attendance for the venue. Due to seating reconfigurations taking place throughout the early part of the season, a new record crowd for the stadium was set for the first five League games. The first competitive game (TNS, UEFA Cup) saw 34,103 –

capacity had been restricted to about 35,000 due to safety legislation – followed by a record in every one of the following five League games staged – 46,287 (Portsmouth), 46,436 (Arsenal), 46,687 (Villa), 46,842 (Spurs) & 47,101 (Bolton). Each of those matches was watched by a capacity attendance.

Over the following months further changes, such as reducing the size of the Directors' Box, increased capacity further and the record crowd was broken again when Leeds United came on 22nd December (47,126) and then Liverpool (47,201) six days later. Ultimately, the Chelsea game on 28th February became the season's best with an attendance of 47,304.

While attendance records were being set throughout the opening months, Keegan's Blues challenged for a European place. In fact they were still a top six side by mid-November and they were still progressing in the UEFA Cup.

As TNS's Mike Harris had hoped, the second leg of the UEFA Cup qualifier was staged at the Millennium Stadium in Cardiff. This meant City's first two UEFA Cup ties of the new Century were played in Britain's two newest and most impressive venues. Only two of the City players who started the first leg, Eyal Berkovic and Paul Bosvelt, were involved from the start of the second leg, and the match was closer than the first but the Blues were still in control. Two minutes before half time Christian Negouai, the Martinique-born midfielder who was playing his first competitive game in 18 months, stroked the ball passed 'keeper Williams for the opener. Nine minutes from time Darren Huckerby made it 2-0 and ensured a 7-0 aggregate victory.

The Blues went on to face Belgian side Lokeren in the first round proper and Antoine Sibierski opened the scoring with a free kick, but Lokeren's Patrick Zoundi equalised when he latched on to a loose ball. He sent a half-volley flying over a surprisingly hesitant David Seaman and into the net. Five minutes before the break Lokeren took the lead when Distin miss-kicked a clearance and the ball fell to an unmarked Runar Kristinsson, whose first-time shot beat Seaman.

In the second half Robbie Fowler managed to poke home an equaliser after 77 minutes, and then two minutes later the Blues took the lead. City had been awarded a penalty after a foul on Jihai Sun with Nicolas Anelka netting the spot kick.

Interestingly, BBC Three made broadcasting history when it transmitted the first leg live. This was the station's first ever live football match involving an English side.

The Blues won 1-0 in the second leg at Lokeren to ensure a 4-2 aggregate victory. Kevin Keegan gave an honest opinion of the match: "We have done what we had to do here. It was not exciting, it was a workmanlike performance. We were fortunate to get a penalty. If it

had been given at the other end, I would have been disappointed. I think there was an infringement but you don't often get penalties for something like this. Lokeren made it very difficult for us. They pressed us in midfield. They are a good team and I cannot understand why they are bottom of the league. They took the Belgian League by storm last year but they have lost a striker - if they had someone up front they could be a real handful. This was always going to be a difficult game after we won 3-2 in the first leg. But we're in the hat for the next round and we'll meet stronger teams than them now."

The Blues drew Polish side Groclin in the next round. Everyone expected this to be a relatively easy obstacle for Keegan's side, especially as the first leg was in Manchester. The game opened brightly with an attempt from Claudio Reyna going over the bar in the first five minutes. This was quickly followed by Anelka chipping the 'keeper to score the opening goal after a Fowler pass had set the Frenchman up.

Despite the lead, the Polish side gained confidence however and they began to create opportunities for themselves rather than react to City's attempts. David Seaman was forced in to action to make a couple of quality saves. In the 64th minute, with the crowd showing their frustration, Kevin Keegan took the understandable decision to replace a rather ineffective Steve McManaman with the more recognised City battler Danny Tiatto. Unfortunately, despite the change proving a good one, two minutes after the substitution Groclin scored from a set-piece strike twenty yards from goal.

Despite noteworthy efforts from Wanchope and Tarnat the game ended in a 1-1 draw. The away goal inevitably placed great pressure on the Blues, but they were still hopeful of progressing. Over 1,000 fans travelled to Poland in optimistic mood for the game.

When the match commenced the Blues had a number of chances in the opening fifteen minutes or so, but sadly this was not to last. As the game progressed, chances were squandered and in the 73rd minute Keegan substituted both Anelka and Fowler hoping that Jon Macken and Paulo Wanchope would find the much-needed breakthrough. It was not to be however and City were eliminated from Europe on the away goals rule.

After being knocked out of Europe without losing a game manager Kevin Keegan was inevitably disappointed: "I still believed we would have enough to beat [Groclin] in Poland but we couldn't score the goal we needed and Groclin deserved a great deal of credit. We got into the competition through the back door and we are out through the back door. Of course, we'd have liked to have gone out the front door against a bigger team in a bigger stadium but it just wasn't to be."

Being knocked out of Europe in such a manner before Christmas seemed to have a negative impact on City's League form. In fact from the 1-1 draw at home to

Groclin on 6th November until New Year's Day, Keegan's side only gathered three points during an eight game run. This left them thirteenth and caused the manager to admit: "We have the look of a side that has forgotten how to win."

A 1-1 draw at home to Charlton had seen David Seaman save a Paulo Di Canio penalty but there was a definite feeling that, apart from that one incident, fortune was not on City's side. Keegan: "I'm in danger of repeating myself. We're not getting the rub of the green." There was some truth in what Keegan was saying as the *Daily Mail* acknowledged: "Paulo Di Canio had more than 40,000 fans rubbing their eyes in disbelief when he claimed a late equaliser for Charlton... for so long there was real belief that the City team those supporters follow so faithfully would have a victory to celebrate."

The search for a League victory lasted for some considerable time. In fact when Liverpool beat City 2-1 at Anfield on 11th February the Blues had gone 14 consecutive League games without victory, causing the Blues to drop to 16th.

It should be remembered however that Keegan's side did progress in the FA Cup during this time. In the third round City were drawn against Leicester City. Prior to the tie Keegan was questioned about the number of non-English players in the side and whether they would see the competition as being significant. He responded: "Most of our players have been here long enough to know what the FA Cup means and what it means to this club as we are not going to win the League. For them it represents a chance to be part of something very special."

His side defeated Leicester 3-1 after a replay and then drew 1-1 at home to Spurs. The fourth round replay saw one of the most amazing fight backs ever. Tottenham, who had knocked City out of the League Cup in the fourth round before Christmas, had raced to a three goal lead by the 42nd minute and the Blues looked dead and buried by half time. Joey Barton had also been sent off and Keegan's side seemed to only have pride to play for.

Three minutes after the break Distin made it 3-1 and a fight-back began. Bosvelt (61st minute) and Wright-Phillips (80th minute) brought the sides level before Macken scored the winner in injury time.

After the game Keegan admitted: "If I had been a City fan at home or in the pub I would have wanted to kick the television set at half time. We were 3-0 down, we had lost our top goalscorer Nicolas Anelka with a groin strain and had Joey Barton sent off as the players were leaving the pitch. I was already back in the dressing room when I heard about Joey's sending off."

The second half was different: "I told them they had to play for their pride with a capital P, to give our supporters something to go home with."

Actor Kevin Kennedy was on stage in London that night and struggled to keep up to date with events at White Hart Lane: "We were 3-0 down and with only ten men by half time. I was on stage in the show Chicago and a couple of the orchestra were Spurs fans. They made sure I knew how bad it was for City. They were telling me that Keegan would be sacked and that all was lost really. I was pretty despondent and decided I'd avoid them as far as I could. At that point it felt like it could only get worse.

"I went back on stage for the second half. Kept focused on the show and then after the curtain call the two guys from the orchestra were snarling at me. I thought that was odd but when I got into the dressing room I had loads of messages saying City had fought back. I couldn't believe it. I ran out of the theatre, ran down the Strand and was popping in pubs looking for a telly. I was desperate to see what had happened.

"As I'm going down the Strand a figure's coming the other way just as frantic as me. It turned out to be Gary Owen. He confirmed that City had won 4-3. We had a little dance in the middle of the street and then he asked me where London City Hall was. Apparently he'd promised that if City came back in that game he'd bare his backside outside City Hall!"

Sadly, the Blues were knocked out in the fifth round 4-2 by Manchester United on 14th February. Seven days after the FA Cup defeat the search for a League victory finally reached its end as Bolton were beaten 3-1 with a brace from Robbie Fowler and an own goal from Charlton. Pre-match City had dropped to 16th and the victory brought a little relief. Claudio Reyna: "We have moved up a couple of places and it lifts a huge weight off the entire club."

A 1-0 Chelsea defeat followed and then came the first Manchester derby at the new stadium. For pride's sake it was important Keegan's side did not lose that fixture, but with United some 13 places above the Blues pre-match Ferguson's side were clear favourites. It was time for City to upset the form book.

On a wonderful day, perhaps the best the stadium had enjoyed in its inaugural year, a terrific atmosphere helped Keegan's side achieve a memorable victory. Fowler opened the scoring in the third minute and Macken made it 2-0 after 32 minutes. Scholes made it 2-1 three minutes later.

In the second half goals from Mancunian Trevor Sinclair (73) and Shaun Wright-Phillips made it 4-1 to the Blues. Matt Dickinson (*The Times*): "Humiliated by Manchester City last season, Sir Alex Ferguson and his men used the pain to fuel their drive to the title. Humiliated again yesterday, they are condemned to live with the despair for months – perhaps even years."

Keegan felt the win was thoroughly deserved: "We had played better against Chelsea and lost. But against

Mosaic artist Mark Kennedy, Norah Mercer and her son David at the unveiling of mosaic tributes to former manager Joe Mercer in 2005.

The dynamics were different. He felt we should try and get fans in the ground earlier, but I said that performance on the pitch would be the most significant factor.

"When we beat United 4-1 in the first derby at the stadium the atmosphere was incredible. Kevin came to me afterwards and said 'I see what you mean'. That then set the tone of the place. The place was rocking – people were singing as they walked down the spirals at the end of the match and the atmosphere was absolutely superb."

While the atmosphere improved, the success on the pitch could not continue. The derby was followed by a 2-1 defeat at struggling Leeds, causing City to fall to sixteenth and fans began to worry. Their concern intensified when four successive draws, followed by a defeat against Southampton, dragged City into a relegation dogfight.

The opening of the new stadium had brought hope and increased ambition, but suddenly the unthinkable seemed possible. A draw at Leicester on 24th April left City languishing in 17th place, three points above Leeds United. With three games left the Blues survival was in their own hands, but supporters were feeling anxious. There had also been newspaper stories of issues on the training pitch, but the manager put it all in to perspective when he explained that the players actually felt that having two days off, following a 1-1 draw at Spurs on Monday 12th April, was too much. He added: "As a result of their request we made a few changes to our preparation for matches including cancelling days off. I can promise you and them that we are in every day now and will be until the end of the season."

Behind the scenes there was real concern over the Club's financial state. This became public during the season when it was revealed that the Blues were keen to find additional finance. Managing Director Alistair Mackintosh searched the globe looking for someone who would invest. Chairman John Wardle also told the *Manchester Evening News*: "Anyone interested in investing can come and see me any time. If the various Russians who are reputed to be interested want to come to talk or just watch a match, they are more than welcome."

As early as April 2003 journalist David Conn had been critical of City's position: "After the blue moon years of mess, underachievement and bleak farce, City were back, and handed an opportunity unique in football as the extravagant, £110m, 48,000-seat City of Manchester Stadium, built entirely with public money - £77m from the Lottery, £33m from Manchester's council tax payers - was given to City on astonishingly favourable terms.

"City pay no rent up to the old Maine Road capacity of 32,500, then pay the council half the ticket receipts up to 48,000, after deducting their match day costs. The club spent just £20m fitting out corporate boxes, the shop

United we got that important early goal which gave us something to hang on to. We had personnel problems because we had players doing jobs that don't come naturally to them and also had to make two enforced changes at the interval."

Chris Bailey explained the significance of the match in the *Manchester Evening News*: "Maine Road saw some pulsating derbies in its time but few could have matched this first-ever neighbourly spat at Eastlands. And how satisfying that Kevin Keegan's side should choose this day of all days to win their first home game since October 18 and banish all thoughts of the drop."

In 2012 Dennis Tueart remembered that the derby match was an important moment in the stadium's inaugural season: "When we moved to the stadium Kevin Keegan worried about whether the atmosphere would be the same and I told him that fans would take a bit of time getting used to it because they were no longer sat with the people they'd been with for years.

and other moneymakers. Yet out of this windfall, City have somehow managed to fashion another crisis, this one much deeper, financially, than any before."

He went on: "City's official comments that the finances are under control do not square with Wardle's open invitation to the world's wealthy. In the last accounts, City's liabilities exceeded their assets by £10.4m, calculated by valuing the squad at £38.8m, which looks very high for Keegan's collection. Some Premiership clubs have reduced their valuations because of the collapsed transfer market, and with City having announced a loss of £13m for the six months to November 2003, their next accounts, due to be calculated at the end of May, are likely to reveal a loss above £20m and a still larger deficit."

Relegation would have been an enormous blow to the Club from which they may never have recovered, and so it was vital City found enough points somehow to stay up. Against Newcastle on 1st May Paulo Wanchope became City's saviour. He netted the only goal in the 59th minute to bring three points and safety – that weekend results meant that Leicester and Wolves were relegated while Leeds United accepted that they were down exactly three years after appearing in a Champions League semi-final. With two games to go Leeds could still have caught City on points but they were some 36 goals behind the Blues in terms of goal difference.

A 2-1 defeat at Middlesbrough followed and then, on the season's final day, City beat Everton 5-1 with goals from Wanchope (16 & 30), Anelka (41), Sibierski (89) & Wright-Phillips (90). The victory caused the two sides to swap League places. The Blues ended the campaign on 41 points, eight more than relegated Leicester, Leeds and Wolves. A decent enough margin in the end, but that did not change the way most felt about the season.

Prior to that final match Keegan explained truthfully how he felt: "We are just about at the end of the most disappointing season of my managerial career. I haven't enjoyed it and I am sure the same goes for everyone connected with Manchester City."

2004-2005 Keegan Leaves

Unhappy with the way the 2003-04 progressed Kevin Keegan must have hoped the new season saw a significant improvement. However, finance was a major limiting issue. While other major Premier League clubs could go out and spend huge sums on the best players around City were struggling financially. At the start of the new season Keegan admitted: "It has been a strange close season because we knew there would be no money available to buy players unless we moved some out first. Obviously we looked at strengthening the squad without having to spend."

The search for an investor was continuing behind the

scenes, but rumours coming out of the Club suggested that Alistair Mackintosh's trips around the globe were in vain. Serious investors simply could not be found.

While the financial issues dominated much of the Club's activity, the manager did bring in full back Danny Mills and goalkeeper Geert de Vlieger on free transfers, and spent £100,000 on defender Ben Thatcher. These deals hardly encouraged the fans, however. Matters were made worse when the new goalkeeper suffered an Achilles injury in the pre-season meeting with Wolves.

Mills and Thatcher made their League debuts in the 1-1 draw with Fulham on the opening day of the season, when Robbie Fowler netted for the Blues. Sadly, successive away defeats at Liverpool (2-1) and Birmingham (1-0) brought a miserable start to the campaign.

The visit of Charlton on 28th August saw a much more impressive performance as City won 4-0 with goals from Nicolas Anelka (2), Trevor Sinclair and the ever-improving Shaun Wright-Phillips. The manager was delighted: "We were under a bit of pressure after taking only one point from our first three matches and Charlton came here full of confidence after a couple of impressive home wins. But we started brightly, kept up a good tempo, scored four goals without reply and played as well as we have done for a long while in this stadium."

Unfortunately, results were mixed during the weeks that followed with a 2-1 away victory over Crystal Palace proving to be September's best result. By the time Chelsea arrived in Manchester on 16th October the Blues were 12th on 8 points, while the visitors were second, behind Arsenal, on 20 points. Chelsea were also one of only two sides unbeaten in the League and were, without doubt, favourites to win this match. Keegan optimistically told fans pre-match: "It is still 11 against 11 on the day and we are more than capable of beating the top sides."

The manager's views proved correct as City defeated the eventual champions 1-0 with an 11th minute penalty from Nicolas Anelka. It was the first time Jose Mourinho had suffered a defeat at Chelsea and was only the second time his side had conceded a goal during 2004-05. It was also City's first home victory over the London club in the Premier League. Sadly, Jihai Sun suffered cruciate ligament damage and was to miss the rest of the season.

The injury was not the only one affecting Keegan's side during the first half of the season and, as the Blues had one of the smallest squads in the Premier League, the manager found himself with few players to choose from at times. This point was most obvious when City travelled to Old Trafford for the 7th November meeting. Keegan: "We had three kids on the bench [Paddy McCarthy, Bradley Wright-Phillips & Nedum Onuoha) whereas United had Wayne Rooney, Ryan Giggs and Phil Neville even though they had Ruud van Nistelrooy suspended. So it was a 'needs must' against United and we defended magnificently."

Although the derby match ended goalless, it was a morale victory for the Blues under the circumstances and Keegan's men were given a tremendous ovation from the travelling fans at the end of the match. Seven points were gained during the next three games and City's 2-0 defeat of Aston Villa on 27th November marked the first time the Blues had won two successive games in 19 months. Keegan quipped that when he played for Liverpool they'd call it a 'run' when they won ten games in a row, but he'd accept two as a 'run' in the circumstances.

The Villa victory lifted Keegan's side to ninth, their highest position of the campaign so far, and brought an increased belief amongst the team and the fans. Injuries were still an issue, but if the recent form could be maintained the manager believed a top six finish was possible: "Take away the top clubs spending massive sums in the transfer market and paying big wages with huge resources behind them, and we have all got a chance of getting into that sixth position and that includes Manchester City, and I am still looking there."

Keegan's point about high spending, resource rich clubs was accurate. He knew all too well how poor the Blues were in comparison with United, Chelsea and some of the other Premier League sides. Sixth place was the best City, and maybe most of the Premier League, could hope for. Publicly he stated that the most appropriate aim was to finish in the top eight: "My job is to try and set realistic targets for this Club and it is realistic for us to finish in the top eight this year – providing we play to our maximum and get the very best out of everyone and have that bit of luck."

Once again his views were based on a sensible view of the Club's situation and inability to compete financially. However, that did little to encourage fans and as the season progressed some felt aiming for a top eight finish fell short. A decent cup run and a top six finish was what was needed.

The Blues lacked consistency during December and the early weeks of 2005 but they still managed to end January in ninth place. In February Keegan's side managed five points out of a possible 12, including a

Stuart Pearce – City's new leader.

hard-earned point at Chelsea and a newsworthy three points at Carrow Road against Norwich on Monday 28th February.

It had been a real rollercoaster match with Norwich racing to a 2-0 lead before the Blues fought back and won 3-2. Keegan commented: "The important thing was that we never stopped foraging. We kept Norwich on the back foot and Robbie Fowler, who probably foraged more than anyone else, came up with the winning goal after his equaliser had given him his 150th goal in the Premiership."

The City boss did admit that Norwich had impressed and had special praise for one opponent: "Dean Ashton was a real handful and gave as good a centre forward performance against us as I have seen from anybody this season."

The game was given greater TV coverage than anticipated that day following a rallying cry by Norwich's Delia Smith at half-time. She urged Carrow Road fans to improve the atmosphere with a memorable "Where are you?" speech to the Norwich fans that was shown repeatedly on television in the 48 hours that followed. Norwich were ultimately relegated by a point at the season's end.

City's following match ended in a 1-0 home defeat to Bolton Wanderers on 7th March. The game ultimately led to a significant change to the then 12th placed Blues. Manager Kevin Keegan took John Wardle to one side: "There were nine games left and Kevin said 'John, I can't do any more for you'. I didn't believe him. I thought it was a joke at first but with Kevin you knew when he was being serious. He said 'I know when I'm done and it's only right that you put somebody else in'. I sat there shell-shocked. He said that if I wanted him to recommend someone he would. He then recommended Stuart Pearce.

"Stuart had already left Carrington and we had to call him back. I spoke with him, then Kevin talked with him. It was like a handover. Kevin packed his bags and left. We never saw him again at the training ground. That's Kevin. Once he makes a decision to move on, he moves on. Obviously, it stunned me on the day but I have to stress that I cannot speak highly enough about Kevin Keegan. He's a real football person and he also cares about people."

In 2010 City fan Sean Riley looked back on the final year or so of Keegan and the support given by Wardle: "John was great at backing Keegan, and we know that the football at Maine Road under Keegan was really entertaining. He did make some great buys, but after the move, some of the players brought in didn't really deliver. We spent a lot of money for our position at the time and brought in a few players with big names – big histories if you like – but they didn't do it in a Blue shirt. Fortunately, they also brought in David James and I am convinced that he saved us. He brought a quality we had lacked and he made a few penalty saves and other great saves that proved crucial. I think we would have gone down without him."

Keegan was hugely popular with fans, but it is clear that some of the Club's buys had not been popular with fans following the move. Nevertheless, they were sorry to see the manager go and they recognised that he had been responsible for the second stage in City's redevelopment following the disastrous mid-nineties. They also felt that the departure of Nicolas Anelka in January was a sign that financial issues were having a severe impact on the Club. The player was sold for a reported £7m to Fenerbahce. At the time this was City's record sale. Perhaps Keegan felt his hands were tied?

Whether there's any truth in that or not, it is fair to say that Keegan's time brought a great deal of pride back to the Club. Director Dennis Tueart felt that bringing Keegan in during 2002 was absolutely the right move for the Club: "I knew he wouldn't stay for years and years because I knew him. He said to me in 1975 that he would never stay anywhere longer than about five years. People told us he wouldn't stay but I said if he can

have control for a couple of years and get us out of this division then that's fine. That's what we needed. Let's manage first things first and get out of this division. If we can't do that then what hope? So it was no surprise to me when he eventually left us."

Former City and England captain Stuart Pearce guided the Blues through the final nine games of 2004-05. Apart from a 2-1 defeat in his first game, the Blues were unbeaten until the end of the season. This run included victories over Liverpool (1-0), Birmingham (3-0), Portsmouth (2-0) and Villa (2-1).

As a result Stuart Pearce was named the Barclays Premiership Manager of the Month for April. The Club announced he was the first City manager to win the award since the birth of the Premier League. That was not true - Alan Ball had, of course, previously won the award in 1995-96.

Form under Pearce placed the Blues in contention for a UEFA Cup place – this season a seventh place finish would ensure qualification. On the final day City (8th, 51 points), Spurs (9th, 51 points) and Middlesbrough (7th, 54 points) were all in contention but with Pearce's side playing Middlesbrough a Blue victory would give them the edge due to a slightly better goal difference.

Unfortunately, the game ended in a 1-1 draw with Robbie Fowler missing a penalty for the Blues late on. It also brought an unusual substitution when goalkeeper Nicky Weaver came on as replacement for Claudia Reyna, while David James changed out of his 'keeper's shirt to wear an outfield shirt and play up front. James helped put Boro under pressure and it was as a result of his involvement that the Blues were awarded the penalty which should have brought European qualification.

During City's first two seasons at their new home, Maine Road was slowly dismantled. Only the Platt Lane Stand was left when this photo wa s taken.

David James attacks the Middlesbrough goal in City's new away kit.

The game brought a frustrating end to the season, but fans were also angry that the Club had taken the decision to make the team wear a new away kit for the final – all important - home game of the season. Officially launched as the "Dark Side Of The Moon" away kit on 26th May 2005, some supporters were outraged that City's traditional form of Blue was not to be worn in a home game that could bring European qualification on merit for the first time since the late 1970s.

Despite the shirt issue and missing out on Europe with Fowler's missed penalty, the season had ended more positively than some had expected a few weeks earlier when Pearce was first asked to fill a caretaker manager role. Deservedly, Pearce was appointed manager on a permanent basis three days before the final game.

2005-2006 Selling Club

During the close season City sold Shaun Wright-Phillips for a fee quoted as £21m. This disappointed supporters immensely and, in historical terms, was on a par with the departure of Tommy Johnson in the 1930s and Trevor Francis in the 1980s. It was a strong indication that the Blues were no longer able to compete to sign the best players. In effect, for the first time in their history City had become a club more likely to sell stars than sign them.

Wright-Phillips was the Club's rising star and he had just broken in to the England squad, scoring a great goal on his debut. Chelsea were a wealthy club thanks to owner Roman Abramovich, who had taken over the club in 2003. In accounting terms selling a player for £21m was obviously a good move, but from the fans' perspective it was a major blow. Some started to wonder if the player's departure had anything to do with

the securitisation deal signed in 2002-03, while others questioned if City would ever be able to compete for the game's best players again.

The fact that one of City's youngest stars was sold hurt. Wright-Phillips was always regarded by Academy boss Jim Cassell as a key figure in the Club's development in the years prior to his transfer. During the mid-2000s it was the Academy, and the excellent work by Jim Cassell and his team, that kept City competing. Regardless of whatever other financial activities occurred, the determination to keep the Academy funded as a priority during some difficult periods in the nineties and new century was the right one.

The departure of Wright-Phillips coincided and, maybe, influenced an increased desire for further supporter involvement in the direction of the Blues. Colin Savage was a member of a Supporters Trust, set up in the summer of 2005: "A group of us who met online and were concerned about the direction the Club was going and what we saw as the lack of adequate governance, got together to set up a Supporters Trust. With something like 35% of shares in the hands of ordinary fans, we wanted to amass enough of a bloc to enable us to have a proper say in boardroom affairs.

We started talking to major & influential shareholders, including David Bernstein and others, and discovered we were largely pushing at an open door. However our most audacious coup was to find a couple of wealthy backers who were prepared to fund a major share purchase on the fans' behalf. Through a trusted intermediary, we approached Sky, who held just under 10% of the shares (but apparently didn't realise it) and eventually agreed a verbal deal to buy those shares on behalf of the Supporters' Trust."

The developments Savage outlined took place throughout the 2005-06 season and, while they progressed, the new season opened with the visit of Bryan Robson's West Bromwich Albion side after the Blues had faced Tranmere, Macclesfield, Stoke, Sheffield Wednesday and Olympiacos (3-1 City win) in pre-season games. Pearce's side had also competed in the Asia Cup in Thailand.

Andy Cole and Darius Vassell made their League debuts against Albion. Pre-match Stuart Pearce talked of £2m signing Vassell: "Darius has settled in very well since he arrived from Aston Villa last month and I believe he can make a significant contribution to this football club this season and in coming years."

Although the opening match ended goalless Stuart Pearce was full of hope and ambition at the start of the season. On their travels they defeated both Birmingham City and Sunderland 2-1 in August. The Sunderland game ended with City topping the Premier League for the first time since 2003. Stuart Pearce was delighted with the season so far, but admitted: "I think that for the 90 minutes we were probably second best. Mick McCarthy's team were better and deserved to win the game. The players came in having won but there was an air of disappointment, they know they did not deserve to win.

"Sometimes all you can do is take the result, go away and work on it."

Another 2-1, this time at home to Portsmouth in the fourth match, meant Pearce's side would go into the Old Trafford derby undefeated with 10 points from a possible 12. That fine run had deservedly brought Pearce the manager of the month award for the second consecutive month.

At United the Reds took a first half lead. The Blues fought back to make it 1-1 causing the *Manchester Evening News* to report: "Manchester City extended their unbeaten run to 13 games with a hard-fought derby draw. Ruud van Nistelrooy put the Reds ahead just before the break with an opportunist strike but City, with new steel under Stuart Pearce, struck back. Joey Barton was on hand to redirect Darius Vassell's shot into the net to stun Old Trafford.

"The Blues almost snatched a victory late on but Edwin van der Sar saved brilliantly from Andy Cole. A City win might have been tough luck on United… but Pearce is moulding a fiercely determined side at Eastlands."

A shock 1-0 defeat at home to Bolton (City had pounded the Bolton goal throughout the game) on 18th September ended the Blues' impressive run and was followed three days later by a defeat in the League Cup second round. Doncaster Rovers won 3-0 on penalties after the second round tie ended 1-1 after extra time. Both goals had come from penalties in extra time – Vassell in the 95th minute and McIndoe in the 118th minute. Nedum Onuoha received a red card but this was later rescinded.

Doncaster's local newspaper issued a 12 page supplement to mark Rovers' amazing victory and they highlighted the remarkable debut of goalkeeper Jan Budtz who came on in the 105th minute and saved two penalties in the shoot-out.

Back in the League another 1-0 loss, this time at Newcastle, caused City to drop to sixth and Pearce to issue a rallying call: "I told the players 'we stick together and someone's going to pick up the tab for us getting turned over today'."

The players must have listened as Everton, so often a bogey team, were defeated 2-0 in the next game, played on 2nd October. This was the first Sunday morning kick off in the Premier League and the match commenced at 11.15 with some fans making a point of the early start by wearing pyjamas. It was also Stephen Ireland's first full Premiership game. Before the match he admitted to being "very nervous" and post-match he commented

that the rest of the team had supported him: "That helped me ease my nerves and settle in as one of them."

In the following League game West Ham were defeated 2-1, placing the Blues once more in the top four. Talk of European qualification filled Manchester. Whether that encouraged Stuart Pearce to go to Old Trafford to watch United face Lille in the Champions League is not clear, but it is known that he took 18 year old Nedum Onuoha with him to watch the European match: "The manager was attracting a fair bit of attention and I think they just thought I was his bodyguard!"

Unfortunately, City's European ambitions took a tumble in the next League game. A 1-0 defeat at Arsenal – they had been awarded two penalties - caused the Blues to drop to sixth behind Chelsea, Charlton, Tottenham and Wigan. Arsene Wenger commented: "It was a difficult match for us because Manchester City were very organised and they were unlucky to lose."

Although City won the next game 3-1 against Aston Villa, they lacked consistency and the following match at Fulham ended in a 2-1 defeat. A drab goalless draw at home to Blackburn came next, although the day was livened up somewhat by the antics of the City boss. Pearce was so frustrated with Blackburn's timewasting that he twice ran on to the pitch, grabbed the ball and placed it ready to restart the game. Referee Martin Atkinson had a few words with him, while Blackburn's Robbie Savage found it all very amusing. The Blackburn boss Mark Hughes wasn't laughing during the match but seemed content with a point afterwards.

A 1-0 defeat at home to Liverpool came next as the inconsistent streak rumbled on. Impressive victories such as a 5-2 win at Charlton on 4th December – at the time the Blues' biggest away win in the Premier League

Goalscorer Trevor Sinclair celebrating as City beat United 3-1 in January 2006.

- were followed by defeats. On 17th December Birmingham City were defeated 4-1 but City suffered a 4-3 setback at Wigan in the following match.

2006 started poorly with a 2-0 home defeat to Spurs but the next League game saw a much-needed return to winning ways as Manchester United were humbled 3-1. Albert Riera made his debut that day, becoming the first Spaniard to play for City.

Pearce said afterwards: "I was quite simply delighted for the lads and for the fans after the derby match performance. Having taken only one point in twelve from the previous games, it would have been easy for the players to waver. Their response could not have been more different. They stood up to a man, worked as a team from beginning to end and scrapped for absolutely everything. The result was absolutely the right one in my mind."

Ian Ladyman wrote in the *Daily Mail* what most fans had believed since the season commenced: "If ever a team played in the image of their manager this was it."

The derby victory lifted City back to eighth but, unfortunately, the Blues found life away from home tough. A week after the derby they lost 2-0 at Bolton and were to lose seven of the eight away games that followed. The one they won saw a 71st minute goal from Darius Vassell against Aston Villa on 25th April.

Home form was initially better with the Blues defeating Newcastle (3-0), Charlton (3-2) and bottom club Sunderland (2-1). At home to Mick McCarthy's struggling Sunderland, City opened the scoring in the ninth minute with Greek international Samaras powering a shot past goalkeeper Davis from a tight angle. A minute later he volleyed a cross from Trevor Sinclair into the bottom corner for his second goal. McCarthy: "It was two minutes of madness. We conceded two goals that nobody should, to be honest."

With a 2-0 lead Pearce's side eased off. They seemed convinced they had done all they needed to and allowed Sunderland back into the match. Arca took a free-kick which found its way to Breen. He headed across goal for Kyle to apply the final touch to make it 2-1.

Late on Sunderland's Breen was sent off, but the score remained 2-1 at full time.

Neither manager was happy. Pearce talked of his disappointment at allowing Sunderland back into the match and what he thought was City complacency, before adding: "I talked to the players before in the week and I will do so again on Wednesday in respect to where we are going, our targets and where we are at

TRUE BLUE
Jim Cassell

Jim Cassell True Blue – Without City's Academy boss and his team identifying and developing many talented players the Club's fortunes would have been considerably worse.

this moment in time. Some of the games coming up are near enough cup finals and I included the game against Sunderland in that."

McCarthy was generally frustrated: "I'm sick of trying to talk up a lousy position from a lousy season." Those comments seemed appropriate and, for City, the result had been an important victory in the circumstances. Everyone hoped Pearce could build on that result and rekindle the drive that had seen the Blues as title challengers at the season's start. Unfortunately, The Sunderland match marked a very different point as, from then onwards City struggled. Everything seemed to fall apart and the reasons were not clear.

Potentially the FA Cup run may have had something to do with the despondency that filled the terraces. It had all started so well with Pearce's side progressing to the quarter-final after defeating Scunthorpe (3-1) and Wigan (1-0). Robbie Fowler earned his place on the Wigan programme cover for scoring a hat-trick against Scunthorpe, however he made a shock move from the Blues to Liverpool less than 24 hours before the game was actually played. It is worth noting that a few days prior to the FA Cup tie Wigan beat Arsenal to secure an appearance in their first major final – the League Cup.

After Wigan, City defeated Aston Villa 2-1 in a fifth round replay. The initial Villa game became newsworthy as Micah Richards, who had made his debut as an 85th minute substitute at Arsenal on 22nd October, scored a last minute equaliser and then, when grabbed by a television crew immediately as he left the pitch still clearly full of emotion, he used inappropriate language when asked how he felt. Every television viewer knew his feelings and understood, but the BBC insisted on apologising in case anyone took offence at the player's obvious joy and ill-timed comment.

The quarter-final opponents were Alan Pardew's West Ham and fans were full of optimism. They desperately wanted to see the Club progress to at least a semi-final, and they made sure they played their part by getting the early atmosphere very supportive and passionate. Unfortunately, City conceded a goal in the 41st minute, and another after 69 minutes (both by Dean Ashton) and the tie was basically over. Musampa netted a consolation goal five minutes from time to provide a bit of hope but the game ended 2-1 and fans were far from happy.

Supporter Sean Riley was hurt: "Losing at home to West Ham was awful. We always had that habit of falling down at the key stages and when it happens at home, as it did against West Ham, it is doubly disappointing. Away from home, though it's not right, there are often excuses and at least a smaller number of City fans witness it. But at home, playing a side in the same league as you with, on the face of it, a similar if not worse squad, then you have to win.

"Whenever I was in my down moments with City back then I always thought that the Club motto shouldn't be 'pride in battle'. It should be 'never fail to disappoint'. That was my way of dealing with it because we always found a way to fail."

The defeat at home to West Ham sapped the energy out of the Club. Fans were angry at the manner of the Blues' defeat while on the pitch little seemed to go right for the rest of the season. Stuart Pearce recognised the mood change: "The good feeling of the FA Cup run that we had been on and the lift it gave us all, ebbed away following our defeat at home to West Ham and put us under a touch of a cloud."

Five days after the West Ham defeat, City faced Chelsea in a controversial game. It summed up the way the season was falling apart. The Blues lost the match 2-0 on 25th March after a couple of unfortunate incidents. In his regular match programme column Sixties hero Mike Summerbee focused on the odd decision to send off Sylvain Distin in the match. He explained that the captain had been following official protocol when he questioned the referee about a controversial goal: "He went over to the referee, Rob Styles, when he blew for half-time, to ask why he had been booked when Didier Drogba had quite clearly handled the ball before scoring Chelsea's second goal. Everybody in the ground saw the handball except, it seems, the referee and his assistant. Even Drogba admitted he had handled.

"But the referee didn't want to listen to reason or show an ounce of common sense. He just treated Sylvain like a schoolboy, asked for his ball back and then reached for the red card. What absolute nonsense. There are no prizes for guessing which one was the schoolboy."

Ultimately, Pearce's Blues only managed one victory, 1-0 at Aston Villa, in the final ten games of the season with all other matches ending in defeat. That poor end of season run saw City drop from ninth on 5th March to end the season in fifteenth place.

There were some positive signs behind the scenes as the Blues reached the final of the FA Youth Cup. The investment in the Academy was beginning to pay dividends at all levels. Sadly, they were defeated 3-0 in the first leg of the final by Liverpool at Anfield. Supporters felt that the absence of Micah Richards, who it had been decided wouldn't play due to his involvement with the first team, had cost City the match.

The player was recalled for the return game and captained the Blues to a spirited performance. Goals from Daniel Sturridge (32nd & 56th minutes) gave City hope and the pressure they exerted on the Liverpool goal should have brought at least an equaliser. Sadly it wasn't to be and the Merseysiders won the final 3-2 on aggregate.

The Liverpool Way (a Liverpool fans' forum) highlighted Richards' contribution: "City will wonder how they didn't manage to at least force extra time, but ultimately Miki Roque's late goal in the 1st leg proved decisive.

"Steve Heighway named an unchanged side from the 1st leg, whilst City made a couple of changes. In came a striker called Ched something or another [Evans], but more significantly Micah Richards was recalled from 1st team duty and skippered the side. He was outstanding, and looked like a man playing against boys. Powerful, quick, composed on the ball, it's easy to see how he's already made City's first team. His presence seemed to lift the rest of the City side, as they were unrecognisable from the side which lost by three goals at Anfield. In fairness, they played much better at Anfield than we did at Eastlands, and over the two legs they'll feel they were the better side. I can't argue with that."

2006-2007 Unfulfilled Ambition

Three years after the move to the current stadium City fans were feeling a little disheartened that the great leap forward that most had expected had still not occurred. There were many positives, most notably the progression of many impressive youngsters from the Academy into the first team, but behind the scenes the Blues were searching for investment to ensure the side could compete.

The opening League game saw the Blues defeated 3-0 to reigning champions Chelsea with debuts from Ousmane Dabo and Bernardo Corradi. 1999 Wembley hero Paul Dickov also made his first appearance following his return to the Blues during the close season.

A goalless draw at home to Portsmouth followed before the first victory of the season saw City defeat Arsenal 1-0 with a 41st minute penalty from Joey Barton. By the time of the Blues next home game almost a month later, City had endured a worrying run of defeats that included being knocked out of the League Cup and a 1-0 victory by Reading in the League. Manager Stuart Pearce was not happy but held up his hands and claimed full responsibility: "I felt the players gave me everything and at the end of the day, I am the manager and therefore the first person who takes the flak. That's always been the way with me and that will continue to be the case."

Fans loved Pearce for his honesty but they also recognised that City were beginning to lose the optimism and ambition that they needed if they were ever to challenge for a top six finish. Pearce in many ways acted and behaved like the most passionate and dedicated supporter, but without the right financial backing there was a limit to what his side could achieve.

Despite financial issues, the season began positively on the pitch and the Blues set a new Club Premier League record for their opening run of eight home games undefeated. Those eight matches included victories over Arsenal (1-0), West Ham (2-0), Middlesbrough (1-0), and Fulham. The four draws were all goalless against Portsmouth, Sheffield United, Newcastle United and Watford.

Thanks to the best Premier League start, home form was decent during the first half of the season, but Pearce's side could never string together an impressive run of victories home and away. One of the best runs came around the New Year when an unbeaten spell of six games included two FA Cup matches. Then in March and April five consecutive League games brought three victories and two draws, but this was followed by only one point in the final five matches.

After reaching ninth place following the Arsenal game in August, the Blues spent the rest of the season in the lower half of the table never moving higher than tenth. These were frustrating times but one player, who would help City win the FA Cup and Premier League a few years later, was beginning to be seen as one of the Club's most positive assets – Micah Richards. He performed to a consistent standard and, on 30th September, he actually netted an equaliser for the Club in the dying seconds against Everton to ensure an away point. The 18 year old Richards made his first full international appearance a few weeks later when he played for England against Holland on 15th November. Henry Winter, writing for the *Telegraph*, claimed: "England may well have discovered Gary Neville's long term successor." By this stage in his career Richards had only made 23 Premier League starts.

At Everton Richards' goal was very important but City's dominance during the final minutes of the match should have seen the Blues snatch a winner according to goalkeeper Nicky Weaver: "The last five minutes we absolutely battered them and every time the ball went in the box we looked as though we were going to score. Then when [Samaras] hit the post, you're thinking 'is it not going to be our day?' But we kept going and deep, deep into injury time, we got something out of the game."

Everton's captain Phil Neville admitted: "It feels like a defeat... we should have got the second goal and killed off the game."

In the following League goalless draw at home to Sheffield United goalkeeper Weaver was replaced with a future Premier League winner and England 'keeper,

Joe Hart. Hart joined the Blues for £600,000 during the close season and said at the time: "I want to get into the first team picture as soon as I possibly can. I have a four year contract and it would be silly of me to start saying that I want to be number one by this date or that date. I am here to learn, to progress and to give the manager another option if I prove myself."

A first Premier League goal for DaMarcus Beasley, netted in the 83rd minute at West Ham on 30th December, saw City achieve their first back-to-back victories for 14 months. The previous game had ended 1-0 at Sheffield United. Before the West Ham match Stuart Pearce claimed that the Hammers, who had defeated Manchester United a couple of games earlier, were a great side: "I think [Curbishley] has inherited a squad that, if you take the Bobby Moore era out, is certainly the best there has ever been."

It is worth highlighting that earlier in December Chairman John Wardle spoke at the AGM. He commented that talks were progressing with a potential buyer: "The Board is mindful of the need for further investment. Whether or not the current talks succeed, the policy of the Board is to welcome approaches from investors who can demonstrate the capacity and commitment to provide long term benefit for the Club."

The news was viewed suspiciously by some supporters who had heard these kind of comments before. Colin Savage, who was part of a Trust looking at gathering enough supporting shareholders to work as a group, knew that there were a number of deals, including the purchase of shares from Sky TV, coming close to fruition that may have led to the Trust gaining a stronger voice: "As we were making the arrangement, the Club made the announcement on the morning of the 2006 AGM that they were in talks with a potential investor. I still believe this was a stalling tactic designed to forestall our deal with Sky, particularly as they failed to follow proper procedure and announce it through the Stock Exchange. I guess you could say it succeeded, as Sky wanted to see what transpired in case they could get a better deal."

Financial matters were an issue throughout the season. On the pitch League results brought little cheer during the opening months of 2007. A draw and five successive defeats left the Blues languishing slightly above the relegation zone by mid-March. The situation looked dire.

Twelve points were earned in the following seven games to lift City from danger but few were happy with the Blues' progress. The last match of that series was a 1-1 draw at Watford on 21st April. Afterwards Joey Barton was interviewed by the BBC and was highly critical of those in charge of City's long term planning: "There has to be a plan. Everyone seems to have one in place but at the moment it just feels like this club is praying to get the right players this summer. This club and its fans deserve to be at the highest level. If I was a fan I wouldn't have paid to watch us at home this season.

"You have to face facts. We have not brought quality in. One or two have done all right but not enough to take the team onto the next level. We can't gamble on players who have scored six goals in six games in the Pontins League or in Belgium. I know a lot of the supporters are umming and ahhing about whether to buy their season tickets."

Barton may have been a little outspoken, however his views echoed those of supporters. They were very supportive of manager Stuart Pearce but felt the manager wasn't given the resources to compete.

The story in the cup competitions followed a similar pattern to the previous campaign. City suffered a 2-1 defeat at Chesterfield in the League Cup second round, but progressed to the FA Cup quarter-finals where they were defeated 2-0 by Mark Hughes' Blackburn Rovers. As with the West Ham defeat of the previous year, the manner of the defeat added to City's woes. Once again loyal supporters felt let down. These included Sean Riley: "At Blackburn I was astounded. I couldn't understand how any side of Stuart Pearce's could fold in that way. It also must have boosted Mark Hughes, who was the Blackburn manager that day. It must have given him hope. Hughes' side were organised and stuck to the job, but we... we weren't even at the races. There was a feeling that day that it was going to be like this for the rest of our lives.

"Even with Stuart Pearce we couldn't do it and for me that said a lot. If Pearce couldn't motivate them for a game like that then no one could? I knew fans who were starting to drift away. Ticket prices were going up every season, but we had nothing to show for it."

Riley's views are supported by evidence. This season's average attendance became the lowest in the new stadium's brief history with an average some 7,000 below capacity. Riley was never likely to walk away but he understood why some were reluctant to attend every game: "We were getting despondent. We knew then that we were a middle of the road side. Everyone's second team but we would never achieve anything. We weren't a threat. We wanted to be a threat.

"We were totally frustrated and could see no way forward. We all knew then that the 'Big Four' were going

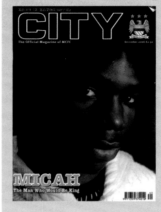

TRUE BLUE
Micah Richards

A popular Academy graduate and worthy FA Cup and Premier League winner.

to be there forever and there was no way we'd shift them. We'd always be on the outside looking in, and that wasn't good enough."

From that point onwards it became clear that the Club was not in a fit position to challenge for the game's top honours, nor were the supporters particularly happy with any activity. They did recognise that financially City were in a different place to Manchester United, Chelsea and some of the other clubs, but they did not know exactly how stark the situation actually was. City Chairman John Wardle knew: "It was grim. I think it's fair to say the situation was grim to the point of there was no money for players. The Club would continue and did continue, but there was no ability to buy the players we needed. So if we'd lost our Premier League status at any point during this time then we'd have had a much bigger financial problem and who knows how that would have ended."

Supporters seemed to understand this, but that did not alter the way they felt. Loyal fan Sean Riley: "I love Pearce. He's a great guy and I thought he showed tremendous loyalty to City and did a wonderful job with what was available. I don't think Pearce was given the luxury of being able to make mistakes, though. City couldn't afford players to fail and so his hands were tied.

"I also think that John Wardle was a Blue through and through but I think that he ended up giving too much freedom to Kevin Keegan and so it put us on rocky ground. John, with of course David Makin, made a big, big commitment to City but with the money in the Premier League going the way it was we couldn't really move up a level."

There is a great deal of merit in what Riley says and, although there were some great moments in the years that followed the stadium move, the Blues never actually progressed to a level where they were able to challenge for trophies. In 2010 John Wardle accepted this: "I am proud of the fact that we were in the Premier League throughout my time as Chairman. I knew we were never really likely to compete in the Champions League because of the way the game had evolved in the nineties and the years we'd been out of the top division, but I thought we were doing okay. From day one my aim was to keep City in the Premier League, but at times during my last few seasons there were real fears that we might get relegated. We didn't, but that was my fear.

"We couldn't challenge because we didn't have

the money. Stuart Pearce was a good manager, but he didn't have the resources to fulfil his potential. Pearcey was – and is – a bloody good manager. I'd be happy to stand on the table and shout this loud and clear. He will succeed. On the training pitch you could see his passion for the game. I felt so sad and very, very guilty that I didn't have the money to give to him to allow us to compete. We didn't have the money to even come close to signing the type of players needed. Had we had the finance we would have taken the Club forward. We had a great manager, superb fans, new stadium, but no finance."

Every time City came close to success in the four years that followed the stadium move, such as the FA Cup quarter-final appearances against West Ham (2006) and Blackburn (2007), the side performed poorly and supporters became vitriolic.

At Blackburn, an extremely poor performance on the pitch was followed by supporters abusing players and, incredibly for City fans, supporters started to take out their anger on each other. Blue against Blue. This was not a normal situation and it had to end. Lifelong fan Keith Durham, who was also working for City's museum at this point, was devastated: "During this period it really affected me. That Blackburn quarter-final remains one of my lowest points as a City fan of almost fifty years. Leaving the ground that day I could see nothing positive. Nothing joined together. That's probably the most aggressive crowd reaction I have seen for some time and that did affect me for some time afterwards. Privately I talked with people about where the Club was going. It felt as if at best we were going to be a club that constantly looked at survival as success. That, as a City fan, hurt.

"We always felt 'we're Manchester City, we're a big club' but that day the realisation dawned that we were some way off. It wasn't about challenging for the title – we knew that wouldn't happen – but it was the realisation that our chance to even scrape a League Cup or FA Cup was some way off."

Understandably, the season ended on a low point with the only positives being the continuing improvement of some of the Club's Academy graduates,

especially Micah Richards. Richards won City's Young Player of the Year: "I'm obviously delighted to win it, and it's the second year running that I've won an award from the supporters. So, I'm grateful to them. Hopefully, I can do it again next year and push on for the senior player of the year award."

Stuart Pearce was delighted with Richards' success: "Micah's rise in the footballing world from Academy player to full England international has been meteoric. It is amazing to think how far he has come in such a short space of time. His athleticism and power in the air are two of his more obvious attributes, but he has so many other qualities to offer. Micah is only going to get better and better and I'm looking forward to working with him over the years as he develops into the finished article."

Richard Dunne won the main Player of the Year award for the third successive season, with Joey Barton second and Sylvain Distin third. The Most Promising Player award went to Ched Evans.

The final League match of the season saw City defeated 2-1 at Tottenham. Sadly, this result brought the end of Pearce's reign as manager. Fans were confused. They obviously wanted the Club to achieve more and had been unhappy with the way the FA Cup campaign had ended two years running, but they liked Pearce and recognised, as John Wardle had, that finance was the issue.

City supporting financial expert Martin Lewis seemed perplexed: "It does remind me somewhat of when Peter Reid was sacked when City were riding high in the top half of the Premiership – soon after we were in Division Two. I hope history won't repeat itself. Yet an injection of cash is needed, and Pearce's departure seems to have hastened that. City's huge debts have crippled its ability in the transfer market for years, and the hope is that'll now change."

Lewis was spot on. No matter what City had achieved in the past, the ability to compete in the modern football world relied upon significant finance and long term planning. By the time of Pearce's departure news was filtering through of a possible takeover.

2003-2007 SUMMARY

Highest League Attendance: 47,304 Chelsea, 28/02/05
Highest Cup Attendance: 39,357 West Ham United, 20/03/06 (FA Cup)
Managers: 2001 – 2005 Kevin Keegan & 2005 – 2007 Stuart Pearce

Seasonal Record:

Season	League	Posn	FA Cup	League Cup	Other	Leading Scorer	Average Attendance
2003-04	Premier	16	Rnd 5	Rnd 4	UEFA Cup Rnd 2	Anelka 16	46,830
2004-05	Premier	8	Rnd 3	Rnd 3		Fowler 11	45,192
2005-06	Premier	15	Rnd 6	Rnd 2		Cole 9	42,856
2006-07	Premier	14	Rnd 6	Rnd 2		Barton 6	39,997

Sven talked of unbelievable support. Here they watch his City beat United, August 2007.

Double Takeover

"City is a big, big club with unbelievable support. It would be an honour for me to be manager, like it would be for all other managers. Every time I visited the club as England coach I was struck by the passion of the fans and was made to feel welcome and at home by nice people.
They have a beautiful stadium and the possibility of a new owner and of course I would talk to them if they indicate they are interested in me becoming coach. City is an established Premiership club with great potential and I know they have ambitions to be challenging higher up the table."

Sven-Göran Eriksson, *Manchester Evening News*, 25th May 2007

2007-2008 The Scent Of Success?

After ending 2006-07 in 14th place with the lowest average support experienced at the stadium, fans were unhappy that the Club seemed destined to stagnate in the lower half of the League. New impetus and investment was needed. Chairman John Wardle admitted in 2010: "We'd been looking for investment for some time because we wanted to create an environment where City could make a challenge. Alistair Mackintosh was talking with various parties around the world. Then we got a call from someone we'd been dealing with who told us that he had a potential buyer."

At this stage it was important that the potential investment was kept a secret. Wardle: "One evening a Harrods helicopter landed on the North Car Park, near the Gasometer, and Thaksin Shinawatra got out. How it was missed by the media and fans I don't know. I had visions of the *Manchester Evening News* front page having a photograph of it and worried that the story would get out. But they missed it. Everybody missed it. In fact they missed it twice because we had another meeting with the helicopter there that wasn't picked up either.

"When I met Thaksin Shinawatra and his entourage I thought he seemed like a pleasant guy. He had security guards with him and it did feel as if he still felt like the Prime Minister of Thailand."

When news did eventually break about the possible takeover some supporters were concerned, especially as Shinawatra had previously been interested in Liverpool. John Wardle discussed this with the former Thai Prime Minister: "I knew it had been well documented but I wanted to hear what he had to say and he told me he couldn't do it because he was still Prime Minister at the time. He said that it wasn't the right thing to do back then. As he was no longer Prime Minister the issues that dogged him then were not an issue. He suggested that he wanted to go back to Thailand but in the meantime he wanted to buy a Premier League football club.

"We talked about everything we needed to talk about and more besides. Lawyers got involved of course and he made a few visits. There was the usual bartering in these situations but eventually we shook on it and that was that."

Wardle knew that Shinawatra's political record and financial history had to be considered. He made sure the Club did all it could to ensure the deal was right and that there was transparency: "We were a PLC and the only way you can sell a PLC is by putting it through all the legal processes. The lawyers checked it all out. Thaksin was checked out. The Premier League checked it out because of their rules. There were the 'fit and proper' tests and all of that. So we went through everything, just as the other PLC clubs would have done when they were sold to overseas owners – or even UK citizens.

"The money was there because before you buy a PLC the money has to be lodged with an independent. So that was there. Everything was done legally because it cannot be done any other way with a PLC. A private company follows different rules, but a PLC has to go through those processes. Everything was there and then we had to go out to shareholders for their approval. Everything was done the right way and in a legitimate way."

Despite the right processes being followed and the legalities adhered to, it is fair to say that Shinawatra's political record in Thailand was always likely to bring criticism to the Blues.

Some fans protested about the takeover and many shareholders chose not to sell their shares. Alongside this those involved with a Trust that was looking to

TRUE BLUE
John Wardle

John Wardle contributed much of his own wealth, along with business partner David Makin, to ensure the Blues became an established Premier League side.

gather enough shares to force greater involvement by fans held mixed views. Some members were delighted, others believed their aims were still the right ones and worried about the future. They had come close to buying Sky TV's holding of almost 10% which, on its own, may have been enough to give them a director.

Regardless of the Trust's well-thought out plans, the majority of fans were delighted that investment now appeared to be on its way. As Sean Riley explains City were so far off success that the majority saw the takeover as an opportunity: "I felt then that if you wanted to compete you needed someone to come in with money. That would come at a price and with strings attached. So the dilemma was, do you sell your shares and help the Club move forward or do you keep hold of them and accept mediocrity?

"I hung on for a long time and was hopeful all the way through that he'd let those of us owning a few shares keep hold of them, but he needed the lot for his plans and ultimately I suppose by having total ownership it then made it easier for him to sell the Club on the year after."

Over time the majority of supporters believed that Shinawatra's purchase of the Blues had more to do with image and public relations for the former Thai Prime Minister, but those do not appear to have been his original aims. His aborted attempt to buy Liverpool while still Prime Minister had suggested that his desire to purchase an English club tied in more with business planning and opportunities.

Shinawatra's human rights record and aspects of his political life often appeared in the news and this did raise some serious concerns for many fans. However, it has to be stressed that the majority of City supporters did view his takeover positively. Why? The obvious answer is that supporters knew exactly how far behind the others they actually were. There were significant comparisons with Manchester United's attempted takeover by Michael Knighton in 1989. Reds fans, though they soon forgot once success came their way, were delighted when Knighton promised to turn United into a team capable of winning the League, and they did little to question his motives, finances or track record.

Within the first few months of his arrival Shinawatra made a big impression. One of his first actions was to bring in the former England manager Sven-Göran

Eriksson. Although some criticised the move, the vast majority of fans saw this as a hugely positive step.

He also held meetings with City's management team and talked of his plans. These plans were not short terms ambitions, these were aims that would take a couple of years at least to come to fruition. He talked of developing the Club's presence around the world, of opening City Stores in London and elsewhere, and of generating interest around the world for Manchester's Blues. There were also a few more crazy ideas, some of which leaked into the media. These included, he told staff, the launch of a City cologne called 'ManCity'. He felt fans, or more importantly their partners, would love the smell of ManCity. That was never produced but at least it proved that he had a vision, even if some of that vision had a more commercial edge to it than fans usually accepted.

Behind the scenes, despite the plans, Shinawatra's personnel found some of City's management obstructive. Some were openly critical, while others chose to ignore the wishes of the owner when it suited them. Others deliberately avoided any contact with his people. This was not in the interests of Manchester City. Fortunately, some personnel felt differently. Academy boss Jim Cassell saw Shinawatra's arrival as an opportunity for the Club to move forward: "Thaksin Shinawatra was like a breath of fresh air. He was different and he was a great supporter of everything we did and were trying to do with the Academy. I remember saying to him that I thought that both he and the manager that he had brought in, Sven-Göran Eriksson, were great for us because Thaksin was a pushy, get things done, sort of guy – a typical politician I guess – while Sven had this air of calm around him. Some of Thaksin's ideas were terrific and he had great plans for the Academy.

Thaksin Shinawatra and Alistair Mackintosh, flanked by a couple of local policemen, prior to City's match with Aston Villa in September 2007.

"He saw the benefit of developing the Manchester City Academy around the world. He was a unique man. Some of his thinking was brilliant but if he did have an Achilles Heel – in terms of the way he acted at City - I think it was the impatience he demonstrated at times. Along with John Wardle and David Makin, Thaksin took us forward to a point where our future could develop."

Shinawatra was, of course, a master politician and he knew that his arrival had received some bad publicity, particularly due to his political record in Thailand. City supporting journalist David Conn highlighted the situation in his column in *The Guardian* on 22nd June 2007. He talked of the corruption charges and so on, but also pointed the finger a little at supporters themselves. The general emphasis was that the fans should be questioning Shinawatra's background more: "Many City fans were rejoicing yesterday as if the club had found another saviour, not caring, as predicted, about Thaksin's background; wanting only his money."

Perhaps banking on the support of fans to help transform some of the negativity, Shinawatra decided to celebrate his takeover in a public manner. His representatives, together with City employees, created a celebratory party in Albert Square, right in the heart of Manchester. The square was significant as this is the location where trophy-winning homecoming parades are held. The party saw members of City's first team, together with Sven, take to the stage, while entertainers performed. One of those entertainers was Shinawatra himself. The new Chairman sang the Club anthem Blue Moon. It was a great PR move for Shinawatra and one which immediately earned him the nickname Frank – a play on the similarity between his surname and that of the American singer Frank Sinatra.

Sean Riley was amongst the thousands of fans who attended the event: "It was surreal. It felt as if we'd won something but someone had forgotten to get the cup! Doing it in Albert Square was significant."

Shinawatra was never likely to be a hands-on Chairman in the mode of Peter Swales or Francis Lee. He needed someone else to take a more pro-active role in the decision making in Manchester. At the time of the takeover, former Chairman John Wardle was approached: "He asked me to stay on and be his representative. I didn't really want to be there full time or anything but we talked. He asked me how he could keep me involved as someone to help take the Club forward. He was a bit naive in some ways with the way football clubs worked and so I suggested that I could be his Deputy Chairman. He suggested I could be the Club President but I told him that Deputy Chairman would be fine.

"Thaksin told me that he couldn't be around all the time and so he'd also like Alistair Mackintosh to stay as Chief Executive. So that was fine."

As Alistair Mackintosh remained Chief Executive it has to be remembered that as the most senior man at the Club on a daily basis he would, in effect, be managing the Club as before. However the former Thai Prime Minister did have his own trusted representatives on site. In particular there was Taweesuk 'Jack' Srisumrid, who was based at the Club on a near full-time basis, and Pairoj Piempongsant. Piempongsant had attended most of the early meetings and spent a bit of time wandering around the stadium, taking in what was happening. Often he was seen wearing a Manchester City shell-suit or other items of City clothing.

Foolishly, some of City's existing management team were not particularly supportive of Shinawatra's representatives. In fact one senior member of the management team openly told another Head of Department not to "volunteer any information to these bloody Thais!" It showed the anxiety some of them faced, but it was also ridiculous and short-sighted. Whatever the personal feelings of that individual were, it was a fact that Shinawatra's representatives were the employers, not a nuisance that could be ignored.

Srisumrid and another member of Shinawatra's staff, a young man who went by the name of Puch, would often engage with staff at lower levels in areas such

as the City Social café bar and the store, and seemed keen on learning about the Club and its fans. Both men borrowed books on the history of the Blues from the Club museum and expressed serious interest in the Club's history.

While everyone tried to come to terms with the takeover and its implications the small matter of playing football had to be considered. The season opened with the Thomas Cook trophy match at Eastlands. Shinawatra was welcomed to the ground like a rock star. Fans saw him as someone who would bring success to the Blues once more and they greeted him as a hero. Of course, some of it was stage managed by Shinawatra's people, but most Mancunians cannot be whipped up into a frenzy simply because someone tells them to, they do it because they believe it. On that day those fans welcoming the new owner believed the good times were around the corner.

Of course, one of the reasons for his popularity was that alongside the general optimism the takeover brought, he had also made a big statement when he appointed former England manager Sven-Göran Eriksson as manager. Sven was loved by fans and, alongside his arrival, he brought some entertaining players to the Club - people like Elano, Geovanni, Corluka and Bojinov. These were not particularly well known at the time, but they were fairly exotic players in comparison to some of City's more recent purchases. There was a real sense of anticipation.

Sven could have gone to a whole host of clubs at this point, but in 2011 he explained why he took the City job: "It is a huge job and a huge club. With new owners

Let battle commence. The Blues beat the Reds 1-0 with a goal from Geovanni.

in place and the club in the Premier League, I felt that they were prepared to match my ambition and invest in new players. I never for one moment regretted taking on the role. We hit the ground running with some excellent football, entertaining the supporters and winning games. I had a very good feeling around that time, and I sensed that the fans shared that feeling."

The situation on the pitch was extremely positive. Under Sven City spent a considerable part of the opening five months in a top four position. His first game, at West Ham on 11th August 2007, had brought a 2-0 victory with goals from Bianchi and Geovanni and seen debuts for eight players. Those eight were: Kasper Schmeichel, Vedran Corluka, Javier Garrido, Elano, Martin Petrov, Rolando Bianchi, Valeri Bojinov (came on as substitute in 61st minute) and Geovanni (came on in 80th minute). The other non-debutants were: Richard Dunne, Micah Richards, Stephen Ireland, Dietmar Hamann, Michael Johnson and Nedum Onuoha (came on as substitute in 62nd minute).

Great results followed including victories over Derby County and Manchester United in the following two games which gave City top spot in the Premier League briefly. Those three victories helped enormously and ensured that Sven had delivered from the start. The manager loved the support the fans were giving him throughout those opening weeks: "They were first-class as they always are. They were great to me then and they will always mean a lot to me."

Sven was also delighted with the way his players had settled: "We had six or seven players who had just signed for us and started very well, playing good, entertaining and attacking football. I remember the Manchester United home game, when Geovanni scored. We may have been a little fortunate, but it was a great result. There were many players we brought in who I thought had a great impact on the team, but I would have to say Elano and Martin Petrov were the best – they were first-class."

Sven also felt that some of the players who had progressed through the Academy were important throughout the season, alongside some of those who had been signed by his predecessors: "A collection of players did very well and impressed me. I would probably pick out Michael Johnson - who was a great talent, Micah Richards, Nedum Onuoha, Richard Dunne and Joe Hart. I also felt that Stephen Ireland was incredible in training, he had such ability."

A trip to Arsenal's Emirates Stadium followed on 25th August. Former Chairman John Wardle remembers that Shinawatra's supporting staff were still trying to get to grips with the game of football: "We'd played Arsenal and went into their directors' area when the match ended. It has a view of the pitch and shortly after we'd gone in there some players came out on to the pitch

for their warm down exercises. As they did so, one of our new owner's group called 'quick everyone, they are coming out for another half. We're going to miss it.' I turned to her and tried to explain but she kept going. It was so embarrassing."

The Arsenal game was one most experts had tipped City to lose by a significant margin. The end result was a 1-0 defeat, perhaps a third 'half' would have helped bring a draw!

Despite the defeat City were playing well and went on a wonderful run in September and October. This allowed supporters and the media to focus on the football rather than the new owners, and by the end of November City were third after winning all eight of their home games. One of the key matches had come at home to Sam Allardyce's Newcastle on 29th September. The visitors were fifth and City third pre-match.

Interestingly, both sides made a goalkeeping change with Allardyce bringing Shay Given into the side and Sven selecting Joe Hart. It was the first Premier League appearance of the season for both 'keepers. Although City and, in particular Elano (who forced a brilliant save from Given in the 11th minute), performed well it

Elano celebrates with Michael Johnson after scoring against Middlesbrough on 7th October 2007. The Blues won the game 3-1.

was actually Newcastle who took the lead in the 29th minute. In years gone by the Blues would have struggled once behind, but Sven's side went on to produce some glorious football.

With pressure on Newcastle mounting City equalised. Star man Elano and Stephen Ireland were involved, with Ireland providing the cross that allowed Petrov to score at the far post eight minutes before the break. Further efforts came close, and then two minutes after the break Petrov sent a perfect pass which Mpenza headed home to make it 2-1.

In the 87th minute Elano deservedly found the net. He simply, or at least he made it look easy, rifled a free-kick from about 25 yards out into the top corner of Given's net. It was a wonderful goal and proved highly popular with fans. Sven soon substituted the player to ensure he received a thoroughly deserved ovation from supporters for his part in the 3-1 win.

Post-match Sven commented: "This team is very good and when they play more games together they will get even better. It's good and I like to see them play football. It was a very good performance so I'm very happy and we could have scored more goals. But I am delighted - good football."

He added: "The third goal from Elano was fantastic. You have to have class feet to score a goal like that from such long range."

Ultimately City's great run was extended to nine successive home wins, but a series of draws during December and January caused Sven's side to drop down the table a little as some of the imported players struggled with the Manchester winter. Nevertheless there was still a great deal of optimism. Around this time Richard Dunne told journalists about the way the season had developed under Sven: "A lot of new lads came in, but the way the manager dealt with people helped everyone settle and the results made it easier. He's brought experience. He believes that keeping the ball

Sven deep in discussion with Hans Backe and Derek Fazackerley during City's match with Everton on 25th February 2008.

allows you to compete with any team and it has served us well. It means we're in with a chance of finishing in the top six and getting into Europe."

Unfortunately, a 1-0 defeat at Everton on 12th January left the Blues in seventh place but there was not much separating the sides and a 1-1 draw at home to West Ham was enough to lift City two places.

Deputy Chairman John Wardle was happy with the way things had progressed: "In many ways those first few months were wonderful. There were a few odd moments like the Albert Square party, but overall Thaksin was getting it right. The football was exciting, Thaksin was getting the support from the fans, and his money had also come through. Sven came in – can't argue with that; the players that came in – can't argue with that, and we had a tremendous first half of the season. You couldn't fault what was happening. I thought we were going to qualify for the Champions League that season.

"At that time, Thaksin did what he said he was going to do. So you can't fault that. He took the Club that was on the brink and shaking a little bit, back up to a level where it was beginning to compete. So I look back on the deal now and still believe that it was absolutely the right thing to do. It was right to sell to Thaksin when we did."

Wardle's views make perfect sense. However, City's public facing staff started to meet Shinawatra's critics on a regular basis. Thai journalists turned up at the ticket office, museum and store asking questions, while television crews would also pull up outside to question fans about the owner's political record. It started to wear some of them down. Every few weeks there would be a story in the media talking of his finance, dealings, politics and so on. As time wore on those stories increased in frequency.

Apart from the background noise, everything else about Shinawatra's ownership seemed positive to fans. Staff views did vary but those that were not directly affected by power struggles tended to be happy. Then, on 27th January 2008 the Blues were knocked out of the FA Cup at Sheffield United in unusual circumstances. Journalist Tim Rich, writing for the *Daily Telegraph*, accurately summed up the bizarre situation that led to a fourth round defeat: "There have been some memorable lows in Manchester City's history, chief of which is getting themselves relegated a year after winning the championship. But they have never, until now, been knocked out of the FA Cup by a balloon.

"The balloons in question were brought by their own supporters and scattered in the City penalty area, making any attempt on Joe Hart's goal resemble something that might have been staged by It's a Knockout. Hart had already successfully distinguished between ball and balloon when saving from Jon Stead's header after Lee Martin's low cross bobbled into the pitted, rutted surface that passes for a penalty box at Bramall Lane. It struck a sky-blue balloon. Michael Ball swung at thin air and Luton Shelton, standing six yards out, tapped it into the net. Hart then began a furious spate of balloon-popping as a whole stable of horses galloped away over the horizon with the door unbolted."

After the game Sven talked with dignity about a defeat that hurt: "I have never seen a goal like that in my life before. We told the fourth official to get a message to the referee to stop the game for one minute so we could clear the balloons. The referee asked Joe Hart to clear them but he has got other things to do and he was trying to clear them when Sheffield attacked and in the end Michael Ball was playing a one-two with a balloon.

"Sometimes you have to stand up and fight. Those who have come from abroad to play for us have learned a pretty good lesson; it is what playing in England is all about. Sometimes, when you meet a team from a lower division, it is not easy at all. People talk about the beauty of the Cup but today the Cup doesn't seem beautiful at all."

The FA Cup defeat hurt fans of course but it was the embarrassing method of defeat that upset them. A year earlier the Blackburn Cup defeat had caused City fans to clash with each other and to hurl abuse at the side. At Sheffield it was a different type of hurt. All-in-all fans knew they could live with this defeat more than that at Blackburn because, overall, the Blues were moving forward under Sven.

Not everyone felt like this however. Some senior management claim discussions took place that day to change manager. It appears that the decision to sack Sven was made that day, if senior figures at the Club at the time are to be believed.

In the wider world, the noise about Shinawatra's political and financial issues was not going away. Alongside this fans were a little concerned with the January transfer window. City made some noise about big signings but, ultimately, little occurred.

One player who did arrive was Benjani. He came in time for a high profile derby match with Manchester United at Old Trafford on 10th February. It was significant as this match was the closest United home League fixture to the fiftieth anniversary of the Munich air crash. To many fans the prospect of allowing the bitter rivalry between Manchester's two sides to be played at this time seemed ridiculous to even contemplate, however once the fixtures had been announced there was little that could be done to alter the situation. City officials had, earlier in the season, sought to have the game moved but their actions brought some ridicule to the Club and even suggested that they felt their fans' behaviour would be poor. This was a gross error on the part of those involved.

The truth was that, prior to the fixtures being

City goalscorer Benjani brushes United's Anderson away during the Blues' victory at Old Trafford in February 2008.

created, City or United could have asked the football authorities to avoid this date for the Manchester derby. The authorities may have rejected that request and that would have been their prerogative. But those responsible for fixtures at City and United did not make the request and so attempts to change the fixture after the lists became common knowledge seemed churlish.

It should be recorded that those responsible at City had also made the mistake of not asking to play their final game of the season away from home. The stadium was to stage the 2008 UEFA Cup final and the Blues had to play away to enable preparation to occur, however when the fixtures were announced City were to play the final game of the season at home.

Inevitably, when City officials asked the Premier League to change both the Old Trafford derby and the final game of the season, they appeared amateurish. It was not as if the Club had not been aware they were staging the UEFA Cup final, nor indeed the date of the anniversary of the Munich disaster. Some supporters worried that if a business whose main interest was football couldn't plan for its core activity in advance then what hope did they actually have of planning for success?

Ultimately, the Manchester derby went ahead on the weekend originally scheduled, while the final game of the season was changed.

As so much had been made of the fiftieth anniversary, there were real fears in the media that City supporters would disturb the minute's silence being held pre-match to remember the 23 victims of the crash. The level of criticism was extremely high and yet – and this is very significant – few national newspapers, television companies and radio stations understood what the disaster actually meant to the majority of Mancunians.

Television and radio debates raged on whether the Blues would be silent. By this time, much was being made of the fact that former City and England captain Frank Swift died in the crash – although the FA had neglected to mention his name as part of their own tribute and focused only on the United players who died.

Many City fans had for several years talked of the Munich disaster as a tragedy for Manchester. The disaster killed 23 people. Inevitably, it was significant that eight of those were United players but it was not simply about those players. Likewise it was not simply about Frank Swift. To limit the focus actually did more damage, and increased resentment amongst fans.

Back in 1958 all Mancunians understood what the disaster meant, but in the years that followed some supporters – both blue and red – felt the disaster was not being recognised for its effect on the whole of Manchester. City fans became angry that the other victims, including Swift, were not included in United's memorial at Old Trafford and never appeared to be remembered when the disaster was discussed.

It is a fact that over the years some City fans have sung about the disaster. Likewise, some United fans have sung about Hillsborough to antagonise Liverpool fans, but this does not mean that all City or United fans feel like that. Supporter Sean Riley: "That day we were under pressure. Everyone expected us to make noise and there was a lot of provocation coming from the stand behind us. It didn't get any coverage at the time but there were missiles thrown into the City section during the minute's silence – food, plastic cups. It didn't get into the 'papers but it did happen. I'm not going to be silly enough to suggest that had the situation been reversed then City fans wouldn't have done it – that's football fans for you. But it did happen. So, considering that provocation I do think City fans were absolutely superb that day.

"I have to add that Alex Ferguson applauding the City fans was great as well. We didn't expect that and it was certainly appreciated. But I do think that the game itself was won the moment that whistle went to signify the minute's silence. I knew that once we'd done that silence and shown proper respect, that City would not let us down. I didn't feel fearful of the game at all and I just knew we'd win. It helped that Joe Hart was excellent that day as well."

City won the match 2-1 after leading 2-0 at half time, with United's consolation goal coming in the final minute. At the end of the Old Trafford derby City fans locked in after the game sang songs in praise of Shinawatra and they seemed genuinely delighted with the Thai takeover. Likewise, the new directors were keen to show their colours. These directors included a rather delighted looking Sasin Monvoisin – one of two women on the City board – and she kept waving her blue and white scarf towards fans. Riley: "We started singing 'Frankie, Frankie, give us a wave' to Thaksin's people. I think that on the day they 'got it'. I like to think that they understood what it was like to be a City fan. It was a huge game and we'd got through it, together."

Sven also felt the togetherness. This match became the highlight of his entire City career: "Yes, that was definitely the game for me. It was a very memorable match. The Club were a little concerned about the fact that it was on the anniversary of the Munich Disaster, but no one needed to worry as the City fans observed the silence perfectly. It was such a silence I seem to remember that I actually felt it, if you know what I mean?"

Following the post-match celebrations, when the time came to be let out of the ground, the Old Trafford's safety announcer thanked City fans for their 'impeccable behaviour'. That led to a chant of "We are impeccable!" as supporters left the ground. Riley: "We lived off that for a while!" Clearly, there should have been no question about this, but as so many people had criticised, abused, and insulted those fans in the build-up to the game, City supporters had every right to stress the point. Sadly, as they left the ground post match many of those fans, including women and children, were abused by people claiming to be United fans on Sir Matt Busby Way and its environs. The spirit of togetherness did not continue outside the ground, nor was there a lasting effect as the rivalry with United became bitter the more the Blues began to challenge their dominance.

During this time Shinawatra was trying to recruit someone to take a more hands-on role at City. He wanted his own man to manage all aspects of the Club and had been in discussion with Garry Cook, based at Nike in the USA, for several months. Cook's appointment was still some way off, but the new man was already excited by the opportunity.

City defeated Chelsea 4-2 on aggregate in 2008 to win the FA Youth Cup for the second time.

The stadium is dressed for the 2008 UEFA Cup final. The fortunes of City and Rangers would change somewhat by summer 2012.

On the pitch City began to slip a little with only one victory coming in an eight game spell after the Manchester derby. At the same time rumours of Sven's possible departure started to leak out of the Club. Some felt the rumours were impacting performance, others suggested that performances were encouraging the rumours. Either way it was a little worrying.

On 12th April the Blues finally ended their winless run with a late 2-1 victory at Sunderland. Both City's goals came in the final eleven minutes with Elano netting a penalty after 79 minutes and Vassell scoring the winner three minutes from time.

Four days later the brightest moment for some came when the Blues won the FA Youth Cup, with a 4-2 aggregate victory over Chelsea, for the first time since 1986 and only the second time in the Club's history. Academy manager Jim Cassell was particularly pleased: "Winning the Youth Cup was something tangible although I have to say that we never saw our work as being one that looked for trophies. Our aim was to develop players for the first team. But winning the Youth Cup was highly significant because it brought a lot of interest our way. It also demonstrated a difference between that season and previous years as our previous final in 2006 against Liverpool had seen us prevented from playing our preferred team because of possible first team needs. Our aim always has to be to support the first team, but I think that had shown that we didn't really have the first team squad that we needed.

"Winning the Youth Cup was a major triumph for the Club – and I mean all the Club. People talk of it as success for me or the Academy, but the truth is that it was a success the entire club shared in and rightly so. It was a fantastic night."

Worth noting though that one newspaper, the *Telegraph*, pointed out its concern for English football by outlining that only nine players who appeared in the final would be eligible to play for England. Significantly, eight of those were in City's side with only one coming from Chelsea.

Regardless of national success, rumours of a possible managerial change continued during the latter stages of the season. Alongside this backdrop, Shinawatra's people were still attempting to bring Garry Cook to Manchester. Cook was delighted when the move was finally resolved: "They put a contract together and it was finalised in late April. I came over to England May 10th and we – City - were playing Middlesbrough away the following day. The news had started to break out."

Cook wanted to go to City immediately and also to the Middlesbrough match but was told not to: "I thought that was a bit strange because I wanted to get started, meet the people and so on, but I had to listen to my employer."

The news was already in the public domain, so Cook's appearance at Middlesbrough would not have been an issue. However, it was also fairly common knowledge that the manager was to be removed from his position. The newspapers included many stories about City, its players, manager and Garry Cook. The *Daily Mail* viewed Cook's appointment as good for the Blues. At the start of May, Journalist Lee Clayton wrote: "Cook will have the responsibility of overseeing City's budget, including their player recruitment programme and expanding their global appeal, specifically across America and Asia where he has expertise of marketing the Nike brand. Cook, 45, has worked in the sports industry for 22 years and is president of Nike's Brand

Jordan, where he has worked closely with basketball legend Michael Jordan. Brand Jordan sales have helped Nike become the world's No 1 seller of sports shoes. Sources in America claimed last night that Jordan himself had tried to persuade the Birmingham-born businessman not to leave the company.

"Cook has worked for Nike in a variety of roles for the past 12 years but has now agreed a three-year contract at the City of Manchester Stadium. He expects to take up his new position by the start of next season after working a short notice period."

It seemed a highly positive move and one which would help the Club develop. According to the *Mail*, Alistair Mackintosh would remain and the two men would work together.

All of that was for the future, however. In the short term the Blues had to finish the season and hope the team did enough to keep Sven in his job.

On the final day of the season, City's game at Middlesbrough ended in a highly embarrassing 8-1 defeat with Elano scoring the consolation in the 87th minute. Supporter Sean Riley was not particularly impressed: "There had been the 2-0 defeat at Chelsea (5th April) which meant automatic qualification for Europe was going to be tough, and then that faint prospect ended when we had the defeats at home to Fulham (26th April) and at Liverpool (4th May). But the biggest disappointment came the week after Liverpool when we played Middlesbrough.

"Before the game we knew that if everything went to plan we would qualify for the UEFA Cup via the Fair Play League. Of course the game starts and by half time we're losing 2-0. Richard Dunne gets himself sent off and we lose 8-1. The result was bad enough but the rumour went around that Dunney's sending off had cost us the place in the UEFA Cup. That was awful! Fortunately, it didn't, but it was a miserable end to the season."

Sven felt he had let the fans down: "Mentally we were not right at all that afternoon and obviously the scoreline reflected that. It was a bad day, one that everyone wanted to forget and no one wanted to be a part of."

On the same day Garry Cook was taken to watch Manchester United's 2-0 victory at Wigan when they won the Premier League title: "Throughout the match my thoughts were in Middlesbrough and I tried to keep in touch with events. It was not pleasant listening to what was happening. After seeing United win and hearing our score I said 'I guess it can't get much worse than this. United winning the championship and City getting beat 8-1 with Richard Dunne being sent off'. There were also the protests for Sven and all that. I said 'If this is the baseline this is the way to kick it off'. I wanted to get things moving. There was a big job to do."

2008-2009 Deadline Day

City ended the 2007-08 season ninth. A victory in that final, eventful game at Middlesbrough would have lifted the Blues one place but the main aim of the season, as far as the media claimed, was for City to qualify for Europe. Sven's side were not in a European place, however qualification for the UEFA Cup did come via the Fair Play League. It was a bit of a bonus and one which should have deterred City's owners from removing Sven, but the decision had already been made.

Sven was dismissed. According to the manager in 2011 he was told during the post-season tour of Thailand: "I was told in Thailand, definitively that my time at the Club was over. Given the choice, of course I would have wanted to stay. We were keen to build on what we had done in the first season and improve in the second season. I had another year on my contract, so for me it was very disappointing the way it all ended.

"I liked the job, the place and I loved the people too, but the weather I could do without. It was too short a time to be there, but a time I look back fondly upon."

Considering the rumours of his dismissal at the Middlesbrough game Sven admitted that it was hard for some to go on the tour: "It was very strange I have to say. A lot of people didn't really want to go, but I urged people to go as we needed to show our professionalism. In the end, I think the staff enjoyed the trip and the time out there was probably welcome given how things had gone at the end of the season."

His views, in 2011, on Shinawatra were interesting: "I hope that one day he may actually explain to me why I was sacked, as he never did at the time." He added that Shinawatra had brought the Blues benefits when he arrived: "He was very good for the Club, no doubt about that. The previous season they were struggling and then he could be seen, perhaps, as the transition between that period and what is going on at the club now."

Garry Cook was by this time preparing for his new role. He attended the stadium for the first time when it staged the 2008 UEFA Cup final and tried to find out as much as he could about the Blues, its structure and so on. He also played a part in the appointment of Mark Hughes as manager during the first week of June. Cook went to City's Carrington training ground for the press conference: "It was all very strange for me, but then Mike Corbett, the security guard at the front gate, put it all into perspective. I'll never forget him. He's been here 20 odd years or something and as I was going through the gate I said to him: 'Hi, Garry Cook here for the press conference'. It was a beautiful sunny day and I asked if everything was okay. He said 'Aye, the press are doing their usual thing'. I said 'All change then?' He said 'Aye, don't worry there'll be another one along next year'.

"It was at that point that I realised that this had

become a habit. Not a good habit, but that was City's habit of replacing their manager every year. It had even become part of the humour which of course City fans have had to develop over the years. We had that. That was my first true impression and I wanted to change that."

There were other early signs that Cook and indeed Mark Hughes had issues to resolve. Some newspapers, such as *The Times*, carried stories suggesting that Mark Hughes had been Alistair Mackintosh's preferred choice a year earlier when Sven was appointed while others, including the *Daily Mirror*, claimed that Mackintosh had been a "lone voice" campaigning to keep Sven in his role.

Whatever the truth, Hughes was given an odd welcome by some. Cook: "There was a very visible comment at Carrington. It was the petition to save Sven. It was pinned up on the notice board at Carrington. Mark Hughes came in there and he said 'This is what we've got'. What a welcome!"

No matter what excuses may have been made for the petition's appearance on the notice board in full view of Hughes and his staff, it was an appalling display and one which may have caused lesser men to question their own position on arrival. Fortunately, the only people Hughes had to keep happy were Garry Cook and Thaksin Shinawatra. The owner believed the appointment was

Newly appointed Garry Cook and Mark Hughes at Carrington.

a good one: "He's an outstanding manager who has achieved many things with Blackburn. Mark was always the first choice of our new executive chairman, Garry Cook. Together they will make a great team. They will both prove to be excellent acquisitions, I'm sure.

He added: "I want this club to advance much, much faster. Sven is a good football general, but we need more. We need a culture of discipline at our club. I want strong leadership from the manager, motivation from young men and I want players who can cope with that.

"These are exciting times for Manchester City and I hope the supporters can understand that I share their goals. That sometimes means making ruthless decisions. Now we can go forward to a new era, with a new management structure and great hope and ambition."

In the second week of June Cook went into City's offices at the stadium for the first time. He was not particularly impressed. Though he recognised that many of the staff were committed and hard working the facilities they had to endure seemed poor: "I went into the basement and I was just horrified. The facilities… it looked like it was beaten up. It looked like there was no hope. One of the things that was going through my mind was gosh, it's a bit like the Wizard Of Oz. You see the Premier League on television. You see the colours, the stadia, the beauty of it all, the glamour, the passion and then you look behind the curtain and it's smoke and mirrors. There's nothing there. Absolutely nothing there. I was horrified. It was depressing. The offices were depressing."

Cook was determined to improve facilities for staff and, of course, for players, supporters and everyone who came in contact with the Blues. Despite moving to the new stadium in 2003 finances had been such that issues had developed. In addition the internal structure of the Club was not what was needed in 2008. For example, the organisation did not have a Human Resources/Personnel department. That may seem like a minor issue, but it was a sign. Changes had to be made.

There was one major change in the structure of the Club at this point. Alistair Mackintosh, who had been Chief Executive, left. Some staff, mostly senior members of the management team, were upset at the departure but others had expected Shinawatra to make a change like this right at the start of his ownership period. A point recognised in Mark Ogden's article for the *Daily Telegraph*: "Mackintosh's departure comes as no surprise, with his role seemingly made redundant with City owner Shinawatra's decision to lure Cook from his Florida-based Nike position in order to drive the club's attempts to take greater advantage of their brand in the developing markets in the Far East."

While changes were being made locally, there were issues internationally. At the start of July, two years after being overthrown as Prime Minister, Shinawatra was back in Thailand facing corruption charges. According to the BBC he had been accused of corruption and abuse of power: "Thaksin has since been living mostly in the UK, but his political allies won democratic elections late last year, facilitating his return to Thailand. He, his family and his aides face a number of different allegations. Millions of dollars of his assets have remained frozen since charges were laid.

"The case now before the Supreme Court relates to the purchase of a plot of land in the Thai capital. The former prime minister is accused of using his political influence to help his wife buy the land from a state agency at a favourable price. The couple, who could face lengthy prison terms if convicted, did not attend court, but their lawyer sounded a positive note."

Whatever the outcome, the freezing of Shinawatra's assets and the accusation of corruption was having a detrimental effect on City. On 9th July it was revealed that former chairman John Wardle was to leave the Club. He told journalists: "I enjoyed every minute of my time here, whatever job I was asked to do. In my time as chairman we never fell out of the top flight and achieved the stability the Club craved for so long.

"It was for this reason that I took the necessary step of selling the club last year, as I believed we had taken Manchester City as far as it could go."

Looking back on that period Wardle felt the optimism of the previous season had disappeared as issues started to surface: "I felt I couldn't continue with the type of environment I was hearing about. I wasn't happy with what had happened with Alistair or with Sven. I was so, so annoyed with what happened with Sven. At Middlesbrough, the 8-1, it was so degrading the way they treated him. Sven was and is a gentleman. In fact he's so much a gentleman that they wanted him to take the team on the tour to Thailand even after what happened at Middlesbrough, and he kept his dignity and did the tour. I thought the way Sven was treated was absolutely disgusting and there was no way I wanted to stay after that. I supported Sven.

"I never had an issue with Mark Hughes coming in. He's a good manager. My feelings were not about that. My feelings were about how Sven was treated and it was totally out of order. We all know managers change but there are ways of doing it. You should always be gentlemen. You should always sit down with someone and talk it through. The way they did it was not like that."

Garry Cook recognised the contribution Wardle himself had made: "Every single City fan owes him an enormous thank you, not just for his financial investment but for the enthusiasm, emotion and wisdom he has imparted to it. He has been the fabric of this football club and quite simply, without his input in the darkest days of the third tier of English football, we would not be in the position in which we find ourselves today."

Wardle's departure was an indication that there were issues with City's owners, but some supporters saw the former Chairman's departure as another inevitable move.

The 2008-09 season opened early for City with a UEFA Cup tie against EB Streymur in the Faroe Islands on 17th July. The Blues had qualified for the competition via the Fair Play League as they had at the time of the move from Maine Road to the new stadium.

Hughes' side defeated Streymur 2-0 in the first leg but the game became more memorable for the lengths a group of hardy fans went to to see the match. The 'Trawler Twelve' as they became known had journeyed across land, sea and air in difficult circumstances to reach the game. This clearly demonstrated that fans were keen to support the Club and, although Sven's departure had upset many, the start of the UEFA Cup campaign was viewed as a new beginning.

The attitude of the fans impressed Garry Cook but behind the scenes both he and Mark Hughes were surprised at how the Club acted at times. The first surprise of the season was that City's initial home UEFA Cup tie of the season had to be played away from Manchester. The stadium, as was often the case during the close season, had staged a concert. The Bon Jovi concert prevented the ground from recovering in time for the Streymur return and so the decision was taken to move the game to Barnsley. Some supporters felt the game could have been staged in Greater Manchester or at least in Lancashire, and so the trip to Barnsley was not viewed particularly positively by fans.

City won that tie but the game raised the concern that football seemed to play second fiddle to other activities. It was understandable that financial considerations had played their part, but supporter Sean Riley was not impressed: "This is why there is no other club like us. What club can have a high profile owner and a new manager in Mark Hughes, and then his first game in charge at City is played at Barnsley because four rockers have messed the pitch up! That can only ever happen at City as Noel Gallagher would say. It was a total lack of professionalism and planning. It suggested that other activities were more important than football at a club that liked to think of itself as a major club.

"I know these things take organising, but we knew we'd be in the UEFA Cup in May and we'd hoped we'd be in it much earlier than that, so we should have thought about this. Mark Hughes and Garry Cook must have thought, 'what the bloody Hell have we come into here?' I know the ground had to have UEFA accreditation or something so that would have limited options, but to be in that situation was poor."

By the time City's first competitive game of the season at the City Of Manchester Stadium took place, Garry Cook had been thrown into the media spotlight. The situation in Thailand with Shinawatra's corruption charge was still in the headlines and much was being made of his role at City. With Cook perceived as his man on the ground, it was inevitable that the media would focus on the man described as City's Executive Chairman.

In the build-up to the 24th August 2008 meeting with West Ham, Daniel Taylor from *The Guardian* wrote of Cook: "headhunted by Thaksin Shinawatra three months ago to become their executive chairman and clearly a man who wants to look at the stars in the sky rather than the mud in the gutter. A man who believes City can be the biggest club in Manchester. 'And we will,' he says. 'Can we be as big, or bigger, than Manchester United? Yes. Can we win the Premier League? Yes. Can we win the Champions League? It will take time, probably 10 years or more. But if I didn't think that, I wouldn't be here'.

"It is a staggering prediction at a time when Thaksin has £800m of assets frozen in Thailand and Mark Hughes's body language is so downbeat. Yet Cook is deadly serious. 'The truth is that this club is not going out of business, it is not bankrupt and we currently have good offers in for four players. I know what's ahead and I know Thaksin's ambitions. He still wants to buy the Ronaldinhos of this world and he knows he can do that only if he has an abundant amount of cash'.

"There is, he admits, a 'cash challenge' in the short term. City have taken out a £30m bank loan to help them through, he confirms. 'Do we have £40m in the bank to buy new players? No'."

Although the suggestion was that Cook's comments were absolutely ridiculous. To even contemplate being bigger than Manchester United or suggest the Club would win the Premier League was staggering, however for fans it was great to hear the ambition of the Club would finally match the desire of the fans. For too long it had felt that City's ambition was simply to survive, not to challenge.

Daniel Taylor was perhaps the first to highlight one of the main reasons for Cook's optimism: "Yet Cook is encouraged because Thaksin is talking to some of the world's richest men about investing in the club. They have had 'Dubai, Saudi Arabia and Kuwait on the phone' and met 'the second richest man in China'. Funding is on its way. 'We have five or six different options and we want to get it done in the transfer window because we need three or four players'."

The article did bring criticism Cook's way in the years that followed. Other media figures jumped on this paragraph: "Not everyone will be satisfied, but Cook is more bothered about the '10-year plan' to become a 'global empire' and bringing in a box-office signing. 'We need a superstar,' he says. 'I've talked about this a lot to Mark and he sort of understands. China and India, 30% of the world population, need a league to watch and we want Manchester City to be their club. To do that, we need a superstar because, no disrespect, Richard Dunne doesn't roll off the tongue in Beijing.'"

This perceived criticism of Dunne became an issue in its own right, but the message Cook was trying to get across was that City needed to raise their sights. It was not meant to be direct criticism of any player, though that is how it was portrayed.

Throughout the piece Cook spoke honestly about how he felt the Premier League needed to change, how City were not in full control of their brand, and his hopes for the future. Many of his comments were ridiculed in the media and that gave fans a false impression of the man. Some of those impressions were to last, even though some of Cook's initial comments proved to be appropriate in the longer term. In fact, many of his predictions and aims came true.

Two of the comments in Taylor's article that received most criticism focused on the growth of the Club and the players: "He sees City becoming a 'global empire' and 'bigger than Manchester United' but feels the club is undermined by leaks to the media and suggests there is 'someone inside the club with a vendetta'. He is unimpressed, too, with some of the footballers he has encountered. 'They don't understand their responsibility to the club,' he says. 'Trying to get them to do something is like dragging them out of bed.'"

Cook was portrayed by some as a man who had been drafted in from the States without a care in the world for the established order. Anyone who had yet to meet him formed an opinion and no matter what would happen in the future, Cook had made the mistake of being open and honest with the media. He had talked passionately about his views and ambitions but, perhaps because the culture in the States was different, he failed to appreciate how his views would come across to the British media and how they in turn would interpret his views.

Cook later recognised this: "Be honest. Alistair Mackintosh had his critics. The fans were critical of him. Very critical at times. There had even been some criticism of John Wardle despite his obvious passion for the Club. So I do think that anyone in this position would have received some negative attention. It comes with the territory. However, the fact is though that we amplified that criticism because we had an ex-Prime Minister who was being pursued by the human rights activists. That was a big story. He was part of the Premier League and that brought attention.

"Now, could I have done a better job? Probably! The piece for me that has always stuck in my mind is that I wasn't going to stand for the status quo. I wasn't going to be a part of the institution. That's not who I am. So, I wanted to tell people what I thought and how I thought it should work.

"I think this is a great football club. It's got great

potential, probably the best in the world. The fans were the best fans and that's what matters. I look at it from a fan's point of view and if somebody says to me 'Thaksin Shinawatra, what's he like?' well I tell him that I run the football club and I've played golf with him. He seems a nice enough bloke. He's alright. But I can't worry about his political career, I've got a football club to worry about. So that's it. That then becomes criticised. That's a mistake."

So what about Cook's views on being 'bigger' than United: "People said you say you're going to be bigger than Man United. I said bigger is relative. They have a big fan base, big revenue... bigger is not necessarily an answer. You would like to think that in the future we will be more successful and you measure that however you want to measure it, but I said that's not a statement of we will be, that's a statement of ambition. We want to be. In turn that means it's a dream, a goal."

In terms of ambition, then surely Garry Cook had the right to say what he wanted City to achieve? Cook: "Didn't Alex Ferguson say that when he took over at United he wanted to beat Liverpool's record? Basically he was saying he wanted United to be the name not Liverpool. I don't think it's any different. It's ambition. People can say well you'll never get there, but it's ambition. If you don't aim for it, then you won't get anywhere. We might get half way which is 50% more than we've got right now."

For fans the ambition was perfect, but some in the media and at other clubs saw Cook's open views and aims as something to ridicule. Maybe they recognised that an ambitious City would be a threat, who knows? It is clear however that some fans formed opinions based on this media coverage. Interestingly, many of his more controversial views on how the Premier League could develop were shared by others in the game.

Some supporters tried to think positively. Sean Riley managed to grab a few minutes with Garry as he arrived at the stadium one day. Riley writes for the long established City fanzine *King Of The Kippax* and took the opportunity to ask a few questions: "I interviewed him – well I knew it was an interview but he didn't because I just stopped him as he was going into the ground. My first impression was that he had to be a good guy because he took the time and trouble to speak with me. It would have been easy for him to walk past or to tell me he was in a rush or whatever, but he didn't. So that was a positive. Then when he spoke he struck me as someone who is very passionate about the game. He told me that he had been to Maine Road to watch Birmingham City play Fulham in the 1975 FA Cup semi-final. It was such a painful experience for him as a fan of Birmingham losing that game, so that encouraged me. He knew what it was like to be a fan and to feel what we feel.

"He also talked of ideas he was coming up with. I now know one of these became 'My First City Game' – a great idea where we share our first experience of being a Blue. It's an innovative idea and a brilliant one too. The fans are the fabric of the Club and we must always remember that. I think Garry understands that, even if the press suggested he didn't. As a fan I was impressed. City were in safe hands."

Behind the scenes Cook and Hughes worked hard to improve everything. Players were brought in but, more significantly, they soon realised that the facilities at the stadium and at the training complex at Carrington were not of a standard either man had expected. Hughes, after managing at Blackburn Rovers and a playing career that took in Barcelona, Bayern Munich, Chelsea and Manchester United, was surprised that City's facilities were at a basic level. In May 2009 Mark Hughes admitted: "One of the things I realised when I came here was that there were not enough things in place to enable this club to be successful in the future."

Hughes added: "Under the Thaksin regime, there were things that you could never anticipate. It was a little bit scattergun and we were flying by the seat of our pants at times, but I never felt as though I had made the wrong move. Absolutely not."

For supporters, the beginning of August 2008 was a little worrying at times. There were rumours that Stephen Ireland and Vedran Corluka were about to be sold. On 9th August City beat AC Milan 1-0 in a friendly at Eastlands, but Corluka did not play and at one point it looked as if Ireland would not appear. Ireland did come on in the 89th minute but there were considerable rumours and stories in the media. Supporters were deeply concerned that confusion seemed to reign.

Around this time Cook was approached by one of Shinawatra's personnel: "He came to me in August and said 'Thaksin needs to look for some investors. He's got some friends and they're looking for investment from them'. On a cash basis we couldn't keep going. Thaksin was finding it harder and harder to put more cash in because of the issues with his funds. I think he didn't want to, or couldn't put in as much cash as we needed. So he was going to his pals and asking them to invest. A Greek shipping tycoon was helping him. We were getting some money in.

"Of course, we were in the transfer window and we were mortgaging what we could. It was all wrong. There was one incident where Pairoj had to go to John Wardle and ask him for a loan to cover the payroll and John gladly accepted that. His heart is truly deeply rooted in this football club and this Club should be grateful, thankful for people like that. People who give up their finances, take a financial risk to put it into something they love emotionally. He accepted it, gladly, and we were very grateful."

The story of former chairman Wardle lending money

to pay the players' wages made its way into the media. Ian Ladyman wrote in the *Daily Mail* on 6th August: "It is believed that Thaksin's cash-flow problems were such last season that he twice had to borrow substantial amounts of money from former owner John Wardle in order to pay the wages. This money has since been repaid to Wardle, who quit his post as deputy chairman a disillusioned man earlier this summer.

"Since Hughes took over, City have spent £3m to sign Israel defender Tal Ben Haim from Chelsea and announced a £19m club record deal for Brazilian striker Jo. Nevertheless, it is understood that the down-payment on Jo was actually a much more modest £4m, with the rest to come in instalments. The club are close to sealing the £7.5m sale of Croatia defender Vedran Corluka to Tottenham as Hughes endeavours to release cash for new players such as Blackburn striker Roque Santa Cruz and West Ham defender Lucas Neill. A recent bid to buy goalkeeper Brad Friedel from Blackburn fell down because City would not match the wages offered by Aston Villa.

"City are committed to significant payments on the eight players - Corluka among them - signed on staggered deals by Hughes' predecessor Sven-Göran Eriksson just prior to last season. The headline investment last summer was £45m but the initial cash outlay was between £15m and £20m."

By this time Shinawatra was trying to find investment. He did not want to sell the Club but he did need an influx of investment. Cook produced a prospectus and, together with some of Shinawatra's closest advisors, he went on the road meeting potential investors: "I had been to the Beijing Olympics and met up with Thaksin there. Pairoj and I were playing golf over there and discussing what was happening. The opening ceremony was on 8th August, and the day before I had a meeting with Thaksin and I said 'You've got to sell'. Thaksin wanted to sell 40% but I said that no one would buy 40%. Who wants 40% of a football club? You have to sell. He didn't agree with me. He thought that somebody might buy 40% but it then morphed on. Whatever happened behind the scenes I don't really know. I was part of the process but I wasn't driving it forward."

Cook arrived back in England and then the news spread that Thaksin Shinawatra had skipped bail and was to all intents and purposes on the run. Ian Herbert of *The Independent* summed it up nicely: "It wasn't quite the pre-season preparation Manchester City had in mind for the man who is supposed to be bankrolling an assault on the upper reaches of the Premier League. The club's chairman, Thaksin Shinawatra, was holed up in a London hotel yesterday after flying directly from Beijing to London to skip bail and avoid corruption charges of which he is now rumoured to be convicted in his

absence over the next few months. The Premier League will then take Home Office advice before deciding whether he is a fit and proper person to own a club. He might even be removed under Britain's 103-year-old extradition treaty with Thailand."

The future looked particularly bleak. However, by this time some supporters had mobilised and were ready to act. Colin Savage was a member of a Supporters Trust, set up in the summer of 2005 with the aim of having a supporter representative on the board. In 2007 the news that Shinawatra was buying the Club caused the Trust to put their plans on hold: "We agreed there was no point in taking the Trust further as there was clearly no desire for it among the fan-base, and we couldn't achieve board representation through control of a bloc of shares. However, early in the following season it became clear that the Club, far from repaying debt, was incurring even more.

"Although Shinawatra had his assets frozen in Thailand, we understood he still had substantial assets that were offshore and out of reach of the Thai authorities. This was enough for us to keep our collective ears to the ground and it was clear that things weren't right behind the scenes. In early summer 2008, it became apparent that the Club was in desperate financial straits and was struggling to meet the second instalment on the previous close season's transfers. A 'Corporate Restructuring' team from one of the major accountants was looking at the books and it seemed administration might well be on the cards so like the Blues Brothers, we decided to re-form the group.

"It's my understanding that the Premier League were so concerned about the prospect of a major club going into administration that they were actively trying to encourage further investment. This was somewhat optimistic as it made far more sense, however much it went against the grain, to pick up what was left of the Club after it had entered administration. There was certainly one person who was actively putting together a proposal on this basis. Eventually, a large loan was arranged, secured on the next few years' season ticket income that enabled that second instalment to be paid and provide some working capital. At the time, it seemed like it was just postponing the evil day a little longer."

Despite the negativity off the pitch, City were making some progress on it. Somehow Mark Hughes was able to motivate his players and, despite defeat at Aston Villa on 17th August, the Blues managed to win their first home League game. West Ham were defeated 3-0 with goals from Daniel Sturridge, a product of City's excellent Academy set-up, and two from Elano, one of Sven's exciting Brazilian imports. For any fan worried about the situation with Shinawatra, then clearly that victory demonstrated a positive. There was also the

European campaign. A shock 1-0 defeat at home to Danish side Midtjylland, at the time only City's second home defeat in Europe, on 14th August had worried many, but the second leg saw a last minute own goal give City parity over the two legs. Extra time followed before the Blues won 4-2 on penalties, four days after the West Ham game.

Off the pitch, fans had been buoyed by the news that Shaun Wright-Phillips was returning. The arrival of the former hero encouraged supporters that all was bright. It should be noted that, despite the worries of the Supporters Trust and those who were aware of how bad finances had got, many fans felt extremely positive with the situation on the evening of 24th August 2009.

Inevitably, some supporters were nervous about the player-related gossip concerning possible moves by Ireland and Corluka, but with typical City optimism most fans tried to concentrate on the good points. Wright-Phillips returning was clearly viewed as a major one. Had supporters known what was going on behind the scenes then those positive feelings would have reached a much more significant high.

Discussions between Shinawatra's personnel and businessmen based in the Middle East led to meetings in the United Arab Emirates and then in Manchester. Garry Cook met representatives at the West Ham game and he performed a presentation on the Club: "We talked about the opportunities for the football club. Why is Manchester City such a unique football club? We talked about several things. We talked about the history and heritage - great club, great history, great opportunity… all of those things. We talked of the support. Big support, valuable support… so you don't have to build everything, that's already here.

"We talked about the property development, because there's no other football club with the opportunity for development around the stadium that we have. It's a great stadium and the opportunity around it is also great. Then the final thing was about where we could go. Nobody had taken their football club and turned it into a brand, other than Man United but that's a bit different."

Often ridiculed in the media for his comments on transforming Manchester City into a world renowned name, Cook's presentation talked of how the Club's strengths could help it achieve like no other if the right investment, planning and success could follow. Cook firmly believed this was the right way forward and he recognised that the interest from the UAE was very serious. However, there were still issues. Thaksin Shinawatra still wanted to have the majority shareholding, but Cook knew that any serious investor would understandably want control.

Within an extremely short period of time events moved at a rapid pace. By the time of the UEFA Cup tie

in Denmark on 28th August the takeover was imminent. Cook knew but few others had any idea. He also knew that there was an intention to buy a world renowned player. Soon the story would emerge in the most public way possible.

On Sunday 31st August the Blues travelled to Sunderland for a Premier League game, winning 3-0 with returning hero Wright-Phillips netting twice. The following day, the final day when it was possible to sign players to compete in the Premier League for the rest of that year, the news of the takeover broke. It was a crazy day by any stretch of the imagination.

Initially there were stories that City were about to sign high value players, and this in itself raised some questions about who was funding the purchases. By lunchtime it was known to be a group from Abu Dhabi, and gradually during the day more news leaked out. Keith Durham was working in the Club's museum at this time. He had heard the news that Corluka had been sold and, like most fans, was initially disappointed that the day had started with departures, and then the world turned upside down: "We had a news website we checked on a regular basis and in amongst the material on Corluka going to Spurs was a one line comment which said 'Manchester City taken over by Middle East consortium'. That was it and none of us knew what that meant, then we heard that Sky Sports News was carrying the early news of the takeover.

"It was absolutely astounding and the point that really grabbed my attention was the fact that this was not coming across as rumour or as a 'if this happens and that happens they will take over the Club'. It came across that this was a done deal. It was amazing and the television focus was on how much money was about to be invested. If I remember right that part was speculation, but it was solid enough for us to start joking 'hey, we can afford to buy Berbatov now. We should do it just to upset United'. It was a joke. I was saying it all tongue in cheek.

"Then at twelve the press websites were hot with news that City had made a bid of about £32m for Berbatov. I honestly thought that our joke had been heard by other fans and that the joke had generated momentum and become a strong rumour. I honestly did not think it could be true, but of course it was."

Around 7.30pm Dr. Sulaiman Al Fahim appeared on television and made bold claims about the money being invested into the side and the players that would be signed. These sensational statements set expectations and created a few myths that dogged City's development over the following two years, probably longer.

In the middle of all the media attention, City still had the small job of actually signing a big name player. For most of the day the news was that Berbatov was the main target but knowing the way transfers panned out efforts were made to sign several players. According to the *Daily Telegraph* these efforts included several other stars: "City sounded out Liverpool about a £45 million deal for Fernando Torres and there were also further bids yesterday for Valencia's David Villa and Stuttgart's Mario Gomez."

For most of the day the story was that City would sign Berbatov. Like all City supporters Sean Riley remembers the day vividly: "I was worried because when you saw Mark Hughes being interviewed he was on a golf course, so I thought it was all a bit of a hoax. Surely Mark would be busy in negotiation if it was true? It felt as if it was all a wind-up. I remember thinking that a United fan had gone out there and created a story. It was like when Michael Knighton launched his takeover of United in 1989 and went out before they played Arsenal, juggling the football. I thought this was going to be our Knighton moment. It was too good to be true.

"We'd waited all that time for a bit of news and then it was non-stop. Every story involved us. It was incredible. I enjoyed every moment of it but I do remember pausing at one point and thinking, 'this is all well and good but we need to beat Chelsea in our next game'. Then we were supposed to be chasing Berbatov – thank God Alex Ferguson put his foot down and got hold of him before we did!"

Jim Cassell and several other Club officials were playing golf with Mark Hughes when the news broke: "It was the annual Club golf day, and I was playing in front of Mark Hughes at the Marriott. The rumours kept growing from tee to tee. Rumours of Berbatov, then the takeover, then Robinho. They just kept coming. Everyone on that golf course – including I would guess Mark – knew that the Club would not be the same again. People have asked me why were we playing golf, but it was the annual golf day and it had been organised in advance."

Activities became more frenzied as the day went on and offers went out for several players, including a bid for Lionel Messi. That bid was made in error and came because some of City's senior figures were based

Most fans spent 1st September glued to their TVs trying to take in an extraordinary day.

in Manchester, others in London and, of course, in other parts of the world. They were communicating via telephone and at one point an official was asked to take a particular action but it seemed contrary to the overall plan. Cook: "He made a comment like 'It's all getting messy'. Via the telephones and other communication lines this somehow was translated to 'get Messi'. An offer was made for Lionel Messi of about £30m. Needless to say it was rejected!"

Ultimately, Robinho became the big signing that day. Immediately, City got their first taste of the criticism that was to come as various footballing figures, including the legendary Pele, suggested that Robinho had signed for City purely for monetary reasons. For many footballing pundits, journalists and so on it was an easy comment to make, but the fans did not care about the money of course. They did, however, care about whether the player would fit into City.

Away from the actual transfer activity, the main focus was clearly on the actual ownership of the Club. Few knew much about the Abu Dhabi United Group and journalists tried to inform fans. Inevitably, because of his public appearance on television, they focused on Sulaiman Al Fahim, but one newspaper, The *Daily Telegraph* appeared to know the real background. Louise Armitstead revealed: "He may be an unknown on the Hyde Road, but Manchester City fans will soon come to recognise Sheikh Mansour bin Zayed Al Nahyan - the real tycoon behind yesterday's extraordinary takeover and one of the world's richest and most powerful men. The brother of the ruler of Abu Dhabi, the biggest of the United Arab Emirates, he has an estimated family fortune of about $1trillion (£555billion) to buy foreign assets alone. Sources said last night he has a personal wealth of 'many, many billions of dollars', apparently putting the £11.7billion firepower of Chelsea's Roman Abramovich in the shade.

"The family's wealth is derived from oil which, when it was discovered in Abu Dhabi in 1958, started the transformation of a nation of fishermen into a powerful state. The burgeoning coffers have been swollen by the recently surging oil price. It is estimated that every time the price of oil goes up by a $1, Abu Dhabi gains as much as $500 million a day.

"The Al Nayhan family is synonymous with Abu Dhabi's wealth and it is with his personal bank account that Sheikh Mansour has spent £210million on buying the 90 per cent Manchester City stake. Sheikh Mansour has a deep love of sport – he is chairman of Al Jazeera Football Club and chairman of the Emirates Horse Racing Authority.

"He is a key political figure and is a member of the UAE Federal Cabinet and Minister of Presidential Affairs. In business, he is chairman of First Gulf Bank and chairman of the International Petroleum Investment

Company. He is married to the similarly fabulously wealthy Sheikha Manal bin Mohammed bin Rashid Al-Maktoum, daughter of Sheikh Mohammed bin Rashid Al-Maktoum, the ruler of Dubai."

Despite this news the majority of the media concentrated on Al Fahim and believed him to be the new public face of the Club. However, the attention that had surrounded Al Fahim was not typical of the approach Abu Dhabi wanted. Sheikh Mansour and the people of Abu Dhabi preferred to show a little more decorum and respect. They wanted to adopt a more low-key approach. They soon put in place a series of moves designed to ensure the right messages were released and that the takeover was viewed accurately. Simon Pearce, who was working for the Abu Dhabi Government and was responsible for the emirate's image, brand and publicity, became involved as did Khaldoon Al Mubarak after the deal to buy City had been brokered by Al Fahim and others. A three page Memorandum Of Understanding was put together under the name the Abu Dhabi United Group (ADUG) – a vehicle for the purchase of the Club. Some still refer to ADUG as the owners of Manchester City but Sheikh Mansour was the actual buyer.

At this time there were obviously some concerns as there would be with any major transaction and so some safeguards were put in place. The Robinho acquisition was based on the fact that if the transaction did not go through ADUG would still loan the money to the Club to make that purchase. There was also an understanding that ADUG could walk away at any point. After a few days Sheikh Mansour decided he wanted Khaldoon Al Mubarak to become the new Chairman: "I was aware that the takeover was going to happen, while it was happening but I was not involved. His Highness Sheikh Mansour, who has been a big fan of football for many years, had been looking to buy a club for some time. So from my perspective I knew it was just a matter of time.

"I think the opportunity came about in the summer of 2008 and I remember sitting with Sheikh Mansour as he told me of his plans. So as soon as the takeover did happen for certain I was asked by His Highness to act on his behalf as Chairman of the Club. To be honest he had caught me by surprise, however I was very much a fan of the game. With my business side of the equation as well it made sense. So I was deeply honoured. I told Sheikh Mansour that as much as it is of interest to me from a business perspective, as a fan this is a dream come true to take the helm of a football team and be part of a journey.

"What makes this experience very unique is that we were not coming in on a finished product. We were not getting involved in something that was already there. We are actually rebuilding. We are dramatically changing a team from a mediocre mid-table team – at best – to

Garry Cook and Khaldoon Al Mubarak relax for a moment before the meeting with Portsmouth. A day when takeover discussions were still progressing, 21st September 2008.

hopefully a serious football team at the highest level of the Premier League. It was an exciting challenge."

With Khaldoon as Chairman the original three page document was turned into about 82 separate takeover documents covering every angle and possibility from the Abu Dhabi perspective.

In the UK newspapers tried to cover every angle. Some talked in negative terms, while others started to wonder if Garry Cook's vision for the Blues was actually now to come true. In one newspaper, *The Times*, journalist James Ducker pointed out that Cook's comments which had been ridiculed a week or so earlier were now vindicated: "Holding court with a group of journalists less than a fortnight ago, Garry Cook was almost laughed out of the room when the Manchester City executive chairman suggested that the club could become the global equal of their sworn rivals, Manchester United, in the next ten years. No one is mocking Cook any more."

At this point Cook's future was in doubt. He had been brought in by Shinawatra but the takeover was likely to see his departure due to conditions in place within his contract. He met with key figures from the takeover group, performed his presentation on the future growth of the Club and its brand and, ultimately, was asked by them to stay on. They were impressed with his vision and ideas, as he was with theirs. Cook was very impressed with everything he was now hearing from Abu Dhabi. There were no boasts, no outlandish statements, and an air of respectability was surrounding those taking over the Club, even if the media and some fans focused on the pre-Khaldoon boasts.

Despite the positivity and a commitment by Khaldoon to ensure the takeover went ahead there were some serious issues along the way. Khaldoon had every faith the transfer would happen: "It could have fallen through at several points, but I think it would have taken a massive issue to ultimately stop it. There had been a handshake and as far as we were concerned, once that happened then it will happen. The lawyers can sort out the legal aspects but the handshake meant it would happen if everything was as agreed. The commercial guys and the lawyers had to work through everything and had something dramatic come up that was either a legal issue or a commercial issue then it would have ended."

On the pitch Robinho had marked his debut with a 13th minute goal ironically against Chelsea, the side he had been expected to sign for. The London club went on to win the game 3-1 in Manchester, but significantly the attendance was 47,331. This was almost 11,000 more than the previous home game against West Ham. Inevitably, the Chelsea game was always likely to attract more fans than West Ham, but the fact is that the attendance was a clear indicator of how fans felt about the ambition of the Club.

The Chelsea game was followed eight days later by the home meeting with Portsmouth. In between those games the due diligence process reached a critical stage. Simon Pearce, Garry Cook, the lawyers, and the rest of the ADUG contingent worked hard. They were desperate to complete activities as quickly as possible. New Chairman Khaldoon Al Mubarak arrived in England in advance of the game and on Saturday 20th September, Khaldoon met with team manager Mark Hughes, Academy manager Jim Cassell, Manchester City Council's Chief Executive Sir Howard Bernstein and various other Club officials. He enjoyed a tour of the stadium; performed in-depth questioning on City's history; assessed the facilities at the Club's training complex at

Carrington; visited the City Store; spent time in the Club's museum and so on. That Saturday, Khaldoon gained a strong understanding of the Blues and their history.

Over the following months and years the media would continually talk of City's Abu Dhabi owners and leaders as having no interest in the Club's history, but this was proved to be incorrect from the beginning. Khaldoon took a real interest in the Club from the start. He was interested in its history, heritage and the dynamics of the place. That was refreshing for everyone at the football club and was so different to most other clubs bought by wealthy businessmen, regardless of nationality. From the outset Khaldoon and the others made it clear that sustainability and long term ambition were their key aims.

The Club's facilities did, however, worry Khaldoon: "I must say I was extremely surprised. I took a tour with Mark [Hughes] and I couldn't believe what I saw. It was not the minimum level of infrastructure required for a top-tier club.

"When I returned [to Abu Dhabi] I immediately went to Sheikh Mansour, showed him pictures of the facility and he was very right to say, 'this is unacceptable'. There were some quick fixes, quick wins, we could do at City, like fixing the gym, the medical facility – we had to do it quickly, because it was simply unacceptable."

There were many areas requiring work, but nothing direct could happen until the ownership was fully resolved. The due diligence process raised a few issues, but to all intents and purposes the Portsmouth game on 21st September 2008 became recognised as the day when the Club changed hands. The transfer, through the 82 documents that had been drafted, reviewed and finally agreed, was actually signed 30 minutes before the game kicked off, with the actual transfer date coming two days later on 23rd September 2008 – interestingly the nineteenth anniversary of a significant 5-1 victory over Manchester United – but visibly Portsmouth was the game when Shinawatra transferred power to Abu Dhabi. He kept hold of ten per cent and was made Honorary President of the Club, although that title was later removed from him.

By retaining a ten per cent stake in City there were a few question marks over long term ambition. If, as seemed totally plausible, the new majority shareholder invested in the Club then surely anyone with a shareholding would also be expected to invest on a proportional basis? With the on-going situation in Thailand, Shinawatra seemed incapable of matching the spending power of the new owner. If he failed to help fund the development of the Club then inevitably the majority shareholder would expect Shinawatra's shareholding to decrease accordingly. Ultimately, this is what happened and eventually resulted in Sheikh Mansour buying out his share.

The camera's on Robinho. City V Twente, 6th November 2008.

TRUE BLUE
Vincent Kompany

Vincent Kompany, here with
Mark Hughes at the time of his
signing in August 2008, went on
to become a great figurehead
for City. In 2012 he deservedly
lifted the Premier League trophy
as captain.

Former Chairman John Wardle was happy that
Shinawatra had sold the Club: "I felt I was right to sell to
Thaksin when I did but I also felt Thaksin was right to sell
when he did. I was ecstatic with the potential the second
takeover offered. It gave us hope and has brought us
a chance to reach the position this Club and the fans
deserve. When I left City I was asked by a couple of clubs
if I would become part of their board or get involved
with them. I was flattered because I have to say that my
involvement with City has changed my life. It truly has.
But I couldn't. I love City. I'm sure I could do a job, but I
wouldn't have the passion. City's my club."

With Khaldoon watching, City won the Portsmouth
game 6-0. The victory included goals from two players
signed shortly before the takeover, Jo and Wright-
Phillips, with another from Robinho.

Behind the scenes in the days that followed, Cook
received tremendous backing from Khaldoon and the
new directors to get to grips with some of the issues
facing the Club. Cook later observed: "Suddenly we had
a plan."

The first physical change that proved that Sheikh
Mansour and Khaldoon meant business came before
the month was out when they brought in Jon Stemp to
tackle some of the infrastructure issues. Stemp's initial
focus was on facilities at Carrington, but in the four years
that followed the new man tackled some of the Club's
biggest infrastructure concerns and helped develop a
long term plan for the growth of the Blues.

The gym development was a strong indication of
how the pace of change at City had to be ramped up. It
was also a clear demonstration that both Mark Hughes
and Garry Cook would now receive the support from the
highest level that had not been there before. Of course,
there was still much to be done but the news that a
fully functioning gym had been created at Carrington
within three weeks of Khaldoon's arrival in Manchester
encouraged those that wanted City to succeed.

Over the course of the season further significant

work was performed at Carrington, while plans were put
into place to build a new office building. Ultimately, that
building, named City@home, was erected during the
2009 close season. Garry Cook: "We knew we had to fix
and build for twelve months and that's what we did, but
our aim was to make sure that each of our 'fixes' would
last."

While the fix process was on-going the Club
benchmarked the best sports, leisure, entertainment and
businesses in the world to ensure that everything they
did from this point on was of the right quality and world-
class. The penny-pinching days of the past were over.

Alongside Jon Stemp there were other arrivals
as time moved on. These included former Arsenal
footballer Brian Marwood as Football Administration
Officer and Graham Wallace as Chief Financial &
Administration Officer.

The transformation Manchester City experienced
during this period was breath-taking. Inevitably, national
and international focus was on the team but Sheikh
Mansour needed the Club to develop across the board.
The ambition of the Blues was now to reach the highest
levels possible. Mediocrity was not where the Club was
heading.

In addition to the buildings and the team there were
significant changes in staffing, reporting lines and the
general organisation of the place. All very important, but
most of this overlooked by the media.

From a football-related perspective there were
negotiations with a variety of sportswear providers to
appoint an appropriate kit supplier. Ultimately, the Blues
struck a deal with Umbro to start in 2009-10. They had
provided the kit for the 1934 FA Cup final and had, until
the mid-nineties, been City's traditional kit provider.

This deal was a nod to City's history and behind the
scenes Club personnel worked with Umbro's design team
to select the appropriate shade of blue, and style of kit.
It may seem a minor point, but the shade of blue worn
during the modern era had varied enormously.

Back on the pitch Mark Hughes' side struggled to match the hope and ambition of the fans and the owner. During a nine game run from the end of October 2008 through to Christmas, the Blues only gathered five points and had plummeted down the division to 18th place by Christmas Day. There was an exciting 3-0 victory at home to Arsenal and draws with Hull and Fulham, but six defeats during that spell hardly impressed. Khaldoon was suddenly faced with the possibility that Sheikh Mansour's Blues could be dragged into a relegation dogfight.

Off the field the new leaders were getting it right, but activities on the pitch were worrying. City had wanted to use the January transfer window to improve the squad for a top four challenge, but instead had to consider damage limitation. Alongside this, as continued to be the case throughout his time as manager, some newspaper reports had suggested that Hughes' position was under threat. There was a suggestion that Mark would be dismissed based on results in December 2008, and that the Blues would appoint a new manager who would be trusted to spend during the January 2009 transfer window.

This was totally ridiculous and out of character with what Khaldoon was trying to achieve. He had no intention whatsoever of replacing the manager at this point, despite the media frenzy suggesting he should. Khaldoon recognised that the squad was not exactly what Hughes had wanted and he chose to back his manager.

Hughes signed Craig Bellamy, Wayne Bridge and

Shay Given. Three players well-known in England. Nigel De Jong was also brought in and Khaldoon backed his manager: "Back then we were heavily scrutinised for what we were doing. Heavily scrutinised for investing in Nigel De Jong who no one knew, but Mark and his team knew what Nigel was about. I trusted them and went along with it and Nigel became a brilliant acquisition for us."

There was one player the Blues could not sign – AC Milan's Kaká. The story was later used against City, and in particular Garry Cook, by those keen to ridicule the Club's aims. Some in the media believed that City had no right whatsoever showing interest in the player, never mind actually meeting his representatives.

On Tuesday 13th January Cook and others met with AC Milan supposedly about the possible purchase of goalkeeper Dida but in truth the City men wanted to talk about Kaká. Pretty soon news was emerging that City and Milan had agreed in principle a fee of approximately €100 million for the player.

Discussions continued without the player's direct involvement. Kaká did, however, talk with a local television crew and commented: "If they want to sell me, I'll sit down and talk. I can say that as long as the club don't want to sell me, I'll definitely stay."

At this time, Kaká was not aware that City had a signed agreement in principle with Milan. Had he known, then the events that followed may have taken a different course. In between the various meetings and discussions, the media in Milan whipped up the local population to make their feelings known. At 6.30pm

Elano's penalty at the end of the first half gave City a 3-0 lead over Blackburn. The match ended 3-1 on 2nd May 2009.

on Thursday 15th January Mauro Suma, AC Milan's TV station director, launched a passionate appeal to supporters: "Nothing has been decided. To all Milan supporters, it's a question of days, if not hours. Please, make your voices heard."

The attention increased pressure on the Milan executives and Kaká's representatives. The City officials felt the situation was being manipulated somewhat and they left. They reached the airport and called the deal off.

City immediately placed a news item on the Club's official website announcing the fact the negotiations were over, with Garry Cook commenting: "Whilst Manchester City Football Club has an obvious interest in world class players of the quality of Kaká, we owe it to our fans that such a transfer must work on every level; commercially, financially, in terms of results on the field and within Manchester City's broader community."

According to *The Independent* newspaper, Silvio Berlusconi swung into action in Milan: "Cue Berlusconi. It was at 11.11pm, by City's reckoning, that the Italian Prime Minister telephoned the first of two football programmes – Il Processo di Biscardi – on the regional channel, to announce that the deal was dead. Once again, his genius for using the media to seize the initiative, set the agenda, suggest the editorial line for newsrooms around the peninsular and, in doing so, to emerge from unfavourable situations as a hero, had come to the fore.

"While admitting that the decision to reject City's world record bid was the player's, the Italian Prime Minister knew that by being the bearer of the good news, he was likely – subliminally, at least – to be perceived as the man responsible for it."

On arrival back in England, Garry Cook was angry but, instead of hiding behind prepared statements and so on, he spoke directly with the media. Television and radio crews spoke with him outside the City Of Manchester Stadium. Listeners to BBC Radio Five Live heard Garry's comments: "The player was clearly for sale. We had entered into a confidentiality agreement weeks ago but, in my personal opinion, they [Milan] bottled it.

"We had gone through a three or four-stage process in which Milan made it quite clear Kaká was for sale and we made it clear we intended to bring him to Manchester City. As we got to the next stage there were questions they could not answer and I think the political and public pressure made them change their conditions."

Over the weeks that followed, Cook received considerable criticism. The 'bottled it' statement was hurled back at him time and time again, but sadly the media were unaware of the facts. City were on the verge of signing him when public pressure caused a change of heart in Milan. The Blues' plan was ambitious but achievable.

Ultimately, Kaká moved to Real Madrid less than six months after City's agreement in principle with Milan. This was despite journalists stressing the loyalty of the player to the Milan cause as the main factor behind City's failed transfer, and the Blues' insistence that they walked away from the deal first.

The British media laughed at City without

Shay Given applauds fans at the end of the UEFA Cup quarter final with Hamburg.

understanding the truth. Brian Viner, writing in *The Independent*, gave a fairly typical response to the Kaká bid: "The City executive chairman, Garry Cook, meanwhile, reckons that Milan 'bottled it'. Would that someone could bottle the loyalty apparently shown by Kaká, in the face of City's flapping chequebook.

"What Kaká appears to have done is nutmeg the belief that money is everything in football, in which case he deserves the respect of everyone who loves the game – even, if they can see past their disappointment, those who support Manchester City."

Journalists writing about Kaká's loyalty had no idea of the level of discussions City had held with the player's father and with Milan, nor were they aware that Kaká was to move clubs only a few months later. City, and in particular Garry Cook, were the ones to criticise. Money was the root of all evil.

Incidentally, Kaká's salary once he moved to Madrid was quoted as £9m a year.

On Tuesday 20th January 2009 the media storm surrounding Cook's 'bottled it' statement seemed out of proportion to all commonsense: "I remember the day when I was sat on the sofa with my wife. We were watching BBC world news and on the news ticker at the bottom it said 'Garry Cook, Executive Chairman of Manchester City, claims AC Milan 'bottled it' over Kaká affair... Barrack Obama is sworn in as the 44th President of the United States of America'. My wife looked at me and said 'are you kidding me?' Sitting there with an American citizen who says 'what? the first black President for one of the biggest nations in the world, and they're more interested in what you said about AC Milan bottling it'."

Over the months that followed a variety of footballing figures talked of City's bid in negative terms. Whether they would have talked so negatively if the purchasing club had been one of the more successful European sides is open to question. The following June Real Madrid paid Manchester United a reported £80m for Cristiano Ronaldo – a figure when exchange rates are considered not much different to the bid City made for Kaká. This was a world record and beat the one

set a few weeks earlier by Madrid's purchase of Kaká. Both transfers, by a big spending club and from two of Europe's giants, should have received a similar level of criticism to City's bid for Kaká, but they did not.

One journalist who was supportive though was Gabriele Marcotti, writing for *The Times*. He put the affair in to perspective: "City should not be viewed as defeated. By approaching Milan and taking it this far, they have shown that they are a real force in global football. With a lesser person than Kaká, they would have triumphed. They'll be back."

Following the addition of Given, De Jong, Bellamy and Bridge, the 2008-09 season ended with City finishing tenth in the Premier League (a drop of one place and five points on the previous campaign), while the two domestic cup competitions ended at the first stage. Although this was disappointing fans felt the future looked considerably brighter than the past. There had also been an excellent run in Europe with Hughes' Blues reaching the quarter-finals of the UEFA Cup.

City had played more competitive games than any other British side, including the Champions League finalists, in European competition during the season. Ultimately, a 4-3 aggregate defeat by Hamburg ended City's chance of glory, but the competition had at least helped develop the Club's name across the continent and provided some experience for the Blues.

After worrying about relegation, the Blues could look forward. For Khaldoon, the signing of Bridge, De Jong, Bellamy and Given had transformed the season into one where Europa League qualification almost came: "Once we made those signings we improved. I wouldn't say that we completely outperformed the sides we faced, but we finished the season on a relatively positive note. It's not where I had hoped to be. My target at the time of the takeover was to make it to the Europa League and being seventh was a target I have to say, but to be fair we fought hard to the last game. It didn't work out how we would have liked but we knew that season would be a building year to get us to the summer."

2007-2009 SUMMARY

Highest League Attendance: 47,331 Chelsea, 13/09/08
Highest Cup Attendance: 47,009 SV Hamburg, 16/04/09 (UEFA Cup)
Managers: 2007 – 2008 Sven-Göran Eriksson & 2008-09 Mark Hughes

Seasonal Record:

Season	League	Posn	FA Cup	League Cup	Other	Leading Scorer	Average Attendance
2007-08	Premier	9	Rnd 4	Quarter-final		Elano 8	42,126
2008-09	Premier	10	Rnd 3	Rnd 2	UEFA Cup quarter-final	Robinho 14	42,899

TRUE BLUE
Roberto Mancini

Mancini with his first piece of English silverware.

2009-2011
Wembley Glory

"We have done a piece of history already by getting into the Champions League. But it is time City won a trophy. I think the fans are happy. We will do everything for them. We have improved over the last year. But we shall continue to work. It's hard to win a trophy but it's even harder to continue to win after that. We want to win the Cup. We want to win the Premier League title and we are working hard for this."

Roberto Mancini interviewed on 12th May 2011

2009-2010 Welcome To Manchester

Previously the close season had been a period for reflection, however City's leaders pushed forward with a number of initiatives. Off the pitch, the Club opened a new box office, extended the City Store, improved Carrington further, dressed the concourse, made improvements to player related areas, and built a new office block to house the majority of administration staff.

All of this was aimed at improving facilities for fans and creating the right environment to allow a successful football club to succeed. Very little of it appeared in the media, but ultimately it was the changes being made behind the scenes that would set the Blues apart from other clubs who had wealthy backers. Sheikh Mansour and his chairman Khaldoon Al Mubarak were determined to make the Club successful in every area, not simply on the pitch.

While the changes were being made, the media focused on player-related activity. The biggest story focused on Carlos Tévez, who had been playing for Manchester United. Throughout the final stages of the 2008-09 season and the month of June there was a great deal of speculation surrounding his planned departure

Carlos Tevez welcomed to City and right to leave the Reds.

from Old Trafford. There were rumours that he would join Liverpool, Chelsea and Real Madrid, but the player actually signed for City on 14th July.

From the moment he arrived, the player had a major impact on the Blues. Arriving at the City Of Manchester Stadium for a few formalities and the press conference, Tévez was mobbed by fans. It was immediately clear that this was a very important transfer and one that caused those that had doubted City's ability to bring in the biggest stars to reconsider. There was no doubt whatsoever that Tévez was a big star and a major transfer for Manchester City. The fact the player left Manchester United for the Blues was also an indication that the balance of power within the game was beginning to change. Sure, United still had the upper hand in so many ways, and most significantly in terms of success, but City were suddenly able to compete. United, for the first time in many years, were perceived as a club who were unable to satisfy their biggest names. With Ronaldo moving on during the close season as well, some fans even suggested the Reds were by necessity a selling club. That was way off the mark, but the summer of 2009 was one which saw Manchester's Blues gain the positive headlines, while some United fans expressed their disbelief at the Reds' inability to keep hold of their stars.

Tévez's transfer was not simply a case of a player moving from one Manchester club to another, it was a sign that the game was changing. The player himself seemed to see City as offering a positive future: "I hope to win many more trophies with City. There is a great feeling of excitement around the club. Look at the quality of the players who have been signed and the prospect of other top-quality players coming, too. Things are happening at this club.

"The owners made it clear to me that they will be doing everything in their power to make this an extraordinary club to play for. I look forward to being part of that experience."

Inevitably, some journalists and fans talked of the fees involved in Tévez's transfer, with *The Times* later claiming the transfer had cost the Blues around £47m. This figure was never accepted by City, but *The Times* quoted it at various points throughout the following seasons, however for the majority of football fans the figure was an irrelevance. The significant fact is that City bought Tévez and even if the fee cost somewhere close to £47m, most fans would argue that the transfer was value for money. Certainly in comparison with Berbatov, Ronaldo, Robinho and Kaka.

A few days after Tévez's arrival, Manchester woke up to discover a new billboard poster adorning a large site on Deansgate close to the Cathedral and, significantly, the border between the twin cities of Manchester and Salford. The new sky blue poster had the words 'Welcome To Manchester' positioned under an unmistakable image of Carlos Tévez with his arms open.

Even though the image was a doctored version of the player celebrating in a United strip, City fans loved everything it stood for. But what did it actually stand for? Some fans said it was simply a welcome to City's new signing. Nothing more nothing less. Others suggested it was a positive step by the Blues to welcome visitors to the city of Manchester, after all it was on a main route through the city. Others thought it was a dig at United for allowing Tévez to leave. The *Telegraph's* Steve Wilson thought it was about local pride: "Manchester City have sought to rub salt in to the wounds of United fans bitter at Carlos Tévez's defection from red to blue by producing a huge city centre poster enforcing their belief that City are the only true Manchester club."

Dave Pullan, a member of City's Executive Leadership Team at the time and responsible for marketing activity, knew what the poster meant to him: "The point of the Tévez poster to me was to think about this from a fan's perspective. Everything is changing at City and the summer was always going to be a busy one with players coming in and going out. The team they had watched was being changed. The biggest risk for the Club as I saw it was that the fans would see this change and feel this was no longer their club. With the Tévez poster it signalled to the fans that we still 'got' them. That was it. It was a very clear signal that we understand your mentality, how you tick and so on. That poster was all about the fans. The positive side of City fans. I loved the idea because it didn't actually say anything other than 'Welcome To Manchester.'"

According to Pullan the advert cost around £50,000 including rights, production and installation. A relatively minor amount but the attention it brought was priceless. It even prompted a scathing attack from United manager Sir Alex Ferguson which then caused the attention to turn global.

Tévez was not the only player who arrived during this period as City sought to strengthen the squad. Emmanuel Adebayor, Gareth Barry, Joleon Lescott and Kolo Touré were all signed as Khaldoon backed his manager with significant investment.

The player investment had surpassed the original plan and as a result the Chairman and Chief Executive were clear that there was a new level of expectation. That expectation, expressed to Mark Hughes, was a top four finish with a target of a minimum of seventy points. As far as the Blues' bosses were concerned there was absolute clarity over the aims and objectives for the campaign.

Despite this significant level of financial backing by the board, there was still media speculation that Hughes would be the first managerial casualty. In fact the view of some reporters was that he would not be in charge by the start of the season. Mark Ogden, writing for the *Daily Telegraph*, recorded at the start of May: "Almost 11 months into the job, barely a day goes by without Hughes's position being placed in doubt with the name of the latest likely successor thrown up by various vested interests that continue to foment the uncertainty around Eastlands. Jose Mourinho, Fabio Capello, Roberto Mancini and Jurgen Klinsmann have all been linked with Hughes's job in recent months, speculation which irks the Welshman."

City fans were also constantly speculating on Hughes' position. Some supported the manager, others were keen for a change. The various blogs and forums carried gossip and rumours, but one blog, mancity. footballblog.co.uk, seemed to accurately judge the situation: "With the majority of modern-day owners willing to sack the manager immediately if anything goes wrong, many fans felt Hughes was walking a managerial tight-rope, with the possibility of falling off at any time. However, fortunately for the fans, and for Hughes in particular, the owners have showed patience when results haven't been great, by allowing Hughes to continue in his job without any interference."

As the blog suggested, City had demonstrated patience even if the media felt he would be dismissed at any point. In fact the season opened with Hughes in the

fantastic position of being backed with more funds and acquisitions than any previous Manchester City manager had been given.

The season opener saw the new look City face Hughes' former club Blackburn Rovers at Ewood Park. Debutant Adebayor scored with an 18 yard drive in the third minute, while Stephen Ireland netted the second in added time to make it 2-0.

It was a thoroughly deserved victory and each of the debutants – Kolo Touré, Gareth Barry, Emmanuel Adebayor and Carlos Tévez had impressed. Tévez had not started the game, but he came on in the 69th minute to replace the previous season's big signing Robinho. Already, some were suggesting Robinho would be on his way out of the Club shortly, but against Blackburn he did have a couple of chances.

Post-match, Mark Hughes spoke to the media and seemed delighted with the victory: "Many people might have been looking to see if we were going to fall flat on our face today and I thought we gave a great response. You saw great character from City today. If we continue to play with the character we showed today then we will keep progressing. We stood up to the challenge and we showed the qualities we will need."

Defensively, City had not been particularly strong – a point noted by the media – but the addition of Kolo Touré was anticipated to resolve some of the issues, while goalkeeper Shay Given was a steadying influence. Worth noting that Mark Hughes replaced Richard Dunne as captain with new arrival Kolo Touré, although the formal announcement did not come until 8th September, after Dunne had moved to Aston Villa. Touré had captained the Blues in two games prior to Dunne's departure.

The new look Blues followed the opening day victory with three further wins in the games that followed - Wolves (1-0), Portsmouth (1-0) and Arsenal (4-2). Of these the Arsenal match brought most headlines. It had been viewed as the first true test of the season, although both Tévez and Robinho were injured.

Despite the weakened strike force, the Blues took the lead in the 20th minute when a Micah Richards' header hit the post and went in off the 'keeper. It was a thoroughly deserved lead, but 17 minutes into the second half Arsenal fought back with van Persie equalising after a tackle from Lescott. Daniel Taylor later wrote in *The Guardian* of the Arsenal player's over the top celebration: "Van Persie made it 1-1 and ran towards the home crowd, mouthing something that led to a complaint being made to the police and the FA writing to the Arsenal striker to remind him of his responsibilities."

For a period, Arsenal seemed the more capable of taking the lead, however City possessed a determination that had not been obvious in previous seasons. This encouraged fans but also put Arsenal under tremendous pressure. Then, in the 74th minute Bellamy made it 2-1 to the Blues, but this was eclipsed six minutes later when Arsenal old boy Adebayor made it 3-1 via a header. It was not the goal that hit the headlines, it was the celebration that followed.

Adebayor's goal was scored at the North Stand end of the stadium, the opposite stand to the away fans. However, the former Arsenal man chose to run the full length of the pitch to celebrate in front of the Gunners' support. Daniel Taylor of *The Independent* accurately portrayed the moment from a media perspective: "Inevitably, a momentous game will be remembered for that astounding moment when Adebayor flashed a header beyond Manuel Almunia and then embarked on a 90-yard dash to arrive in front of the Arsenal fans. Nine minutes earlier was the stamp that left Robin van Persie with a bloodied face and complaining of a 'mindless and malicious' assault. Now, the mind flashed back to David Pleat's gallop across the Maine Road pitch in 1983. Except Pleat never kicked his legs this high. First, Adebayor body swerved Shaun Wright-Phillips, then he evaded Micah Richards, a drop of the shoulder and he was off, head raised, sprinting the full length of the pitch, a one-man runaway embarking on the most provocatively choreographed knee-slide imaginable.

"Everyone knows his grudge by now. Adebayor resents the Arsenal fans for turning on him last season. They had collectively ignored Wenger's request on the morning of the game not to abuse him and, by the time he arrived in front of their stand, there was a concerted effort by some to get on the pitch. Enraged, they threw a car-boot sale's worth of goods, including a plastic stool and several bottles, one knocking a steward unconscious. Police reinforcements were needed as the trouble threatened to escalate."

Adebayor's so-called stamp on van Persie was picked up by the cameras and was obviously an issue, but it was the player's celebration that initially grabbed the headlines. It was criticised severely by the media and rival fans, however the player had received significant abuse throughout the match from his former supporters. Likewise, his celebration was comparable with Gary Neville's over the top celebration against Liverpool in January 2006 when Rio Ferdinand scored the winner in the dying minutes of the game. Footage of both Neville's 60 yard run towards the Liverpool fans at Old Trafford and subsequent celebration and Adebayor's run appeared on YouTube and similar sites. It was very easy to compare the two. Clearly Adebayor's celebration was always going to be seen as a dig at the fans of his former club who had been vitriolic during the game, while Neville's was aimed at rival supporters who often taunted the United player.

Significantly, Adebayor apologised after the game,

Neville did not, and in January 2006 the United man told *The Times*: "I have to put up with Liverpool fans singing plenty of songs about me, none of them tasteful, and I struggle to believe that I have caused them any grave offence with an exuberant celebration. Increasingly people seem to want their footballers to be whiter than white and there are calls for sanctions over every little incident. Do they want a game of robots?"

Neville's comments are important as it provides the most obvious precedent. On 22nd February 2006 Daniel Taylor, writing in *The Guardian*, revealed that the FA had fined Neville £5,000 and issued him with a formal warning. Whether Neville was right or wrong every Blue knew that Adebayor's celebration should have been compared with that of Neville's.

The Adebayor debate overshadowed the game, but it has to be recorded that the City-Arsenal match was highly significant for several reasons. Ultimately, the game ended in a 4-2 victory after Wright-Phillips (84 minutes) and Rosicky (88 minutes) scored for City and Arsenal respectively, but this was City's fourth successive League victory – the Blues best start to the season for almost 50 years – and the attendance was a new stadium record of 47,339.

At the start of the following week, Mark Hughes gave his view of the Adebayor related incidents: "Emmanuel Adebayor sustained a tremendous amount of personal abuse from the kick-off but strongly maintains that there was no malice intended in the challenge on Robin van Persie and apologised to him when he hugged him on leaving the field of play at the end of the game."

Adebayor was given a three match ban for the 'stamp' on van Persie, causing him to miss the Old Trafford derby, but the decision on his celebration was not made until the end of the month. The verdict was that Adebayor should pay a £25,000 fine and receive a suspended ban of two games. It was a harsher verdict than the one imposed on Gary Neville, but City chose not to appeal. Former Arsenal player Perry Groves was reported in *The Sun* as being baffled by the FA's inconsistency: "When Gary Neville got done for celebrating in front of Liverpool fans last year he didn't get a suspended ban, so the FA, who we all want to show consistency, have gone beyond that."

The mention of Neville was important as only eight days after the City-Arsenal game the Blues played the Reds at Old Trafford. The derby was one of high drama and resulted in Michael Owen scoring United's winner in the 51st minute of the second half. When the goal was scored, substitute Neville ran towards City fans in the away section, celebrating before turning the celebration into some form of warm-up routine. It fooled nobody and caused journalist Henry Winter to record "Gary Neville celebrated with typical lack of diplomacy near the enraged away support."

City could have made an issue of this but chose not to. They did question the six extra second half minutes, and much was made in the media over the coming weeks of the concept of 'Fergie Time'. Journalist Tom Bellwood, writing in the *Daily Mail*, commented: "Popular belief has it that Manchester United play 'Fergie Time' at Old Trafford - basically as much injury time as required for the home side to score a winner or draw level. This time around, Sir Alex Ferguson's United side overcame their 'noisy neighbours' in an unforgettable Manchester derby with a Michael Owen goal deep in stoppage time to claim a 4-3 victory.

"City manager Mark Hughes was left bemused at how the referee had played six minutes of injury time when the fourth official had indicated there would be just four added at the end of the 90. United's victory has once again opened the 'Fergie Time' debate and, as this list shows, the Reds do seem to get more than their fair share of luck, late in games at Old Trafford."

Bellwood went on to list several significant 'Fergie Time' moments, while former referee Graham Poll, writing for the same newspaper questioned where the added time came from: "I struggled to see where the additional, additional time came from which enabled United to score the winner. Alan Wiley, the fourth official showed the time allowed - as decided by Atkinson - as four minutes, which I felt was reasonable given the substitutions and number of goals.

"There was one further substitution in the time allowed, Carrick for Anderson, for which 30 seconds is usually allowed. I therefore expected the final whistle at 94.30, as did Mark Hughes. The Owen winning goal was timed at 95.28 and so I could fully understand the City boss's frustration. When you've worked so hard to come back three times and feel that you've earned a point in a key match it must be galling to concede such a goal."

The respected former referee started his article with part of his after dinner speech routine: "In my after dinner speech I often tell how I got the 'hairdryer' from Sir Alex Ferguson on one of my first visits to Old Trafford for not knowing one of the rules of football; at the home of Manchester United you play until they win!"

It is fair to say then that City felt aggrieved with the late, late winner at Old Trafford that gave the Reds a 4-3 win. It should be remembered however that Adebayor, who had scored a goal a game in his opening four League matches, was missing and that Tévez was still not 100% fit.

It is also worth highlighting that the United manager had made comments about City being 'noisy neighbours' which seemed to encourage everyone connected with the Blues. It suggested that they were having an impact and, as most people know, the crucial thing about noisy neighbours is that the neighbours rarely quieten down. In fact often the only way you can stop the noisy

neighbours from impacting your life is by moving away yourself. City fans, in particular, enjoyed being referred to in this manner.

Despite the Old Trafford set back, City, who had moved into third place after the Arsenal match, continued to move forward. Fulham were defeated 2-1 after extra time in the League Cup three days after the United defeat and then another of Tévez's former sides, West Ham, were swept aside with a 3-1 victory. Tévez netted twice.

Adebayor returned for the trip to Aston Villa, another side looking for a top four finish, on 5th October. Bellamy helped City to a 1-1 draw that day as the after effects of the enforced ban seemed to affect Adebayor. The player appeared keen and was certainly entertaining at times, but he was not the same force he had been prior to the ban.

October and November demonstrated a few worrying moments for the Club. Seven successive League draws brought some criticism Mark Hughes' way, but there was also some optimism that the Blues remained undefeated at home and had still only lost one game in all competitions after the opening 16 League and cup games. A 5-1 League Cup victory over Scunthorpe impressed, but that was nothing to the 3-0 humbling of Arsenal in the fifth round which placed the Blues into a major semi-final for the first time since 1981.

City were sixth in the Premier League by this point, but the League draws were causing Hughes' side some concern. Fortunately, a thrilling 2-1 victory over Chelsea on 5th December, watched by another stadium record crowd of 47,348 (the figure surpassed the September Arsenal game by nine people), saw goals from Adebayor and Tévez only three days after the Blues had defeated Arsenal in the League Cup.

The victory, the first of two against the eventual champions, brought encouragement that Hughes' side could finish in the top four. City lay in sixth place with a game in hand over most sides and, apart from the United game, remained undefeated. However, behind the scenes, results were being monitored against an agreed plan created at the start of the season. This plan predicted City's results, game by game, and included a target of seventy points for the season. If seventy points could be accrued, then that would usually be enough for a 'top four finish'.

City had gathered 25 points from 14 games, but seven days after the Chelsea success a 3-3 draw at Bolton raised a few questions. The Blues had fought back three times to earn the point, proving Hughes' side possessed character, but there was criticism of the balance. Craig Bellamy had been sent off in the game, which inevitably caused a disruption to Hughes' tactics, but Graham Chase, writing for The *Daily Telegraph*, felt there were other concerns: "There was plenty to fault in this performance, particularly their slow start and doubts about the defending of £40 million centre-back partnership Kolo Touré and Joleon Lescott. But City provided answers to lingering questions about their character with the good just about cancelling out the bad, though most clubs with Champions League pretensions will hope to leave the Reebok Stadium with three points and they have drawn eight games in that 13-match run without a defeat."

Those draws were beginning to look more like missed opportunities than points gained. Four days later, Hughes' side travelled to another side with ambition, Tottenham Hotspur. The Blues suffered a 3-0 defeat, but it was the manner of the defeat that brought most concern. *The Guardian*'s Kevin McCarra gave his views: "This Tottenham Hotspur victory came with a simplicity that must leave Manchester City in a tangle of anxiety. Some players may have been absent, but there was also a tameness that indicates a lack of appetite or a frustration over their style of play. The danger is that they will not maintain the momentum to realise their grand ambitions. Although Emmanuel Adebayor missed from close range near the end for City, it was the uncomplicated purpose of the victors that separated the sides."

Had the Spurs game ended in a City win, then it's clear the situation would have looked considerably better, but the defeat drew attention to the concerns. It also meant that the Club's results were not in line with the pre-season forecast. City seemed unlikely to meet the seventy points target based on forecasted results, and that was not acceptable.

The City executives saw the Tottenham game as being a sign that something had to be done to halt the number of points being leaked. They were all in agreement and, after a review, the decision was taken to replace Mark Hughes as manager. It was a decision not taken lightly, especially as Khaldoon and Cook had wanted Hughes to succeed. They wanted him to be a hugely successful manager at City, but sadly after all the spending, planning, ambition and hope came the realisation that the Club seemed unlikely to progress in the way everyone had planned at the season's start.

After the decision was made, Hughes was unaware of the process taking place behind the scenes as the City executives searched for a new manager and a process to manage the transition. Although it is perhaps traditional for football clubs to dismiss a manager without any thought of who could follow, City wanted to ensure a smooth changeover. They did not want to create a period of doubt during which the Club would become unsettled and results would suffer. They wanted to ensure that the new manager was in place within a couple of days and couldn't afford to put the Blues at a disadvantage. From a business perspective it made

perfect sense to make the change at a time when it could all be managed in a professional manner.

It was sensible that Khaldoon, Cook and the others knew exactly who they wanted to bring in. The plan had to work for the benefit of Manchester City. It was decided that appointing Roberto Mancini would be in the Club's best interest.

A plan was put together whereby Hughes would manage City's home game with Sunderland on 19th December 2009 and then a meeting would be held between the manager and Khaldoon at 6pm, where the Chairman would explain the situation to Hughes face-to-face. At the same time Cook and other executives would hold meetings with members of Hughes' staff and with the players to ensure everyone got the same story at the same time. At 9.30 on the day of the game a meeting was arranged for Hughes to meet Khaldoon at 6pm.

Regardless of the rights or wrongs of talking with potential managers before dismissing the current manager, it is clear that this plan of communication was significantly more professional and businesslike than the majority of dismissals in the Club's history. Even City's greatest manager, Joe Mercer, discovered he was no longer manager of the Club when he arrived at the ground in 1972 and found his car parking space was no longer his. He then walked into the main corridor at Maine Road and discovered his name had been removed from the manager's door. If in 2009 the communication plan and desire to discuss the matter face to face was somehow unfair then, what does that make the majority of football managerial dismissals?

The problem, however, was not City's plan. It was the way the story was leaked out in the press. Some claim the story sneaked out on mainland Europe, while others are certain a City staff member took a draft press release to Mark Hughes. Whatever the truth, the news leaked out. This led to significant criticism coming the Blues way.

The City executives decided to continue with their plan. They did not want to follow knee-jerk reactions.

By the time the game kicked off, the main television and radio broadcasters were picking up on the story. Sky Sports News claimed Guus Hiddink was to replace Hughes initially. Some fans suggested the new manager would be Jose Mourinho, but it took some time before Roberto Mancini's name started to be mentioned. This added to the view that the leak had occurred within City, not in Italy.

By the end of the game, of course, it seemed fairly common knowledge that Mancini was to be Hughes' replacement. Nevertheless, the City executives stuck to their plan as best as they could. Khaldoon, who was flying in for the sole purpose of talking directly to Hughes, had a great deal of respect for him. He wanted to explain and to thank him for all his work: "I had the talk with Mark. It wasn't easy, but it was respectful. As always Mark was a honourable man."

Afterwards the Welshman told journalists: "I was informed after the match against Sunderland that my contract with Manchester City was being terminated with immediate effect. Notwithstanding media coverage to the contrary, I was given no forewarning as to the club's decision."

It is significant to note that Hughes claimed he did not know about his dismissal until that meeting with Khaldoon. This still did not stop others from claiming the opposite. Manchester United manager Alex Ferguson was quoted by journalist Mark Ogden a few days later as saying: "For Mark, having to go through the [Sunderland] game, knowing what was going to happen at the end of it, must have been terrible."

The leak placed the Blues in a difficult position and brought considerable criticism, however on the face of it the plan had been a good one. Khaldoon wanted to speak with Hughes face-to-face and that meeting had happened.

It should be recorded that City had backed Hughes with more finance than most managers could dream of and, despite him not being the owner's choice as he was already in situ, Hughes had been given a full season, close season and 21 first team games of another season before making the change. His managerial reign lasted about 18 months and 2 weeks. According to Blackburn manager Sam Allardyce in an end of season interview, the average lifespan of a Premier League manager is 1.2 years – a little over 14 months. The fact Hughes was given four months more than the average does not make the lifespan an acceptable one for a football manager, but it does prove that City's executives were not acting out of character with the rest of football. They were certainly not 'trigger happy' as some suggested. If they had been, then Hughes would have gone at least twelve months earlier when newspapers implied he was about to be fired as the Blues hovered around the relegation zone.

Would City have been viewed any differently had Khaldoon insisted Hughes fly out to Abu Dhabi and see him for the news rather than the other way round? At Liverpool in 2012 Kenny Dalglish had to fly to the States for a crucial meeting shortly before his dismissal. For anyone connected with the game that has to be viewed more negatively than Khaldoon's desire to deliver the news face to face in Manchester.

Garry Cook received considerable criticism during this spell: "It was reported that we were classless. That that's how we 'behave', but we did the right thing at the right time. Unfortunately, the outside forces made it a lot worse for everyone than it should have been. Someone leaked it to the press. I didn't leak it. The fact is that we were changing manager because that's what we felt

was in the long term interests of the Club. That was the important thing."

The following Monday after Mark's departure Roberto Mancini was unveiled at a press conference. The media had predicted Cook would not be there. It was suggested by some that he would hide away. Cook did attend but was severely criticised. Instead of focusing on Mancini's appointment, which was what everybody at the Club had hoped, the media fired questions at Cook. Afterwards, message boards and some figures within the media suggested he should have stayed away. With hindsight, it now looks as though whatever Cook did that day he would have been criticised. If he had stayed away he would have been 'hiding'. By attending he was to be 'caught out'.

Cook told the media the story of Mancini's appointment: "The decision to seriously look at other managerial options was taken just three weeks ago following the Hull City game (November 28th). I think it is important to know that Roberto was only offered the job after the Spurs game (December 16th). We negotiated on Thursday, finalised an agreement on Friday and he was not in the stadium on Saturday as was falsely reported."

A few moments later Roberto Mancini was asked when he was first contacted by the Club. The manager replied: "Two weeks ago, I met Khaldoon for the first time. But they called me the day after the Tottenham game. Not before."

The two stories matched, but that did not stop the media from turning this into another storm against the owner, the Chairman and the Chief Executive. When Mancini answered the question, there was a huge intake of breath at the press conference as if everyone thought "ah, we've got them" but in reality the facts were clear and consistent. Both Mancini and Cook were honest that negotiations took place on the Thursday and Friday between Spurs and Sunderland.

The perception that Mancini's story of the approach and Cook's version were different angered City's leaders. Unusually for the Blues, City made sure their own website carried evidence to show that there was no difference in what the two men said.

Although mistakes were undoubtedly made by personnel at the Club during this period, the level of criticism was unfair. Due to the leak the affair became rather messy at times, however this was no worse than had happened at other clubs. Also, it has to be recorded that the media, and some fans, had wanted or expected Hughes to be dismissed at various other points. Cook: "After the takeover we could have dispensed with Mark, but we all kept faith. Then after almost every defeat, every setback, people said we would change our manager. We received letters and emails about it. But we kept faith. Then there was the close season – we could have made a change then and it would probably have been accepted, but again we kept faith.

"But then we started the season and it was okay for a bit but… We could have made the change much earlier but, as I said, we kept faith. Never forget that Mark was a big reason this football club moved forward and did the things it did. He's a good man. And he was incredibly loyal to his people. I always tried to be open and honest with him at all times, which I think I was. And I tried to encourage him to do the right thing with regards to our owners and I think we were relatively close. I always vowed that if he went I would go with him. I don't know whether that's the right thing to say or do. I did talk with Khaldoon about that."

Cook stayed, but the whole Hughes-Mancini change remained an issue for the media. However, it should be considered in comparison with other Premier League clubs. In 2010, only a few months after taking over West Ham United, David Sullivan and David Gold dismissed their manager Gianfranco Zola. The dismissal hit the headlines but the general gist of the media coverage did not portray West Ham's British owners as 'trigger-happy' like they had with City. There was even a suggestion that their decision was inevitable. In Manchester, the fact that City's executives kept faith with Hughes for as long as they did should be remembered, especially as he had not been the owner's choice. Just like Zola had not been Sullivan and Gold's choice.

Another man who received criticism about the managerial change was Brian Marwood. Looking back at the end of the season he had no doubt that Mancini was the right man for City: "I think that in Roberto we have someone who is very well organised. When you speak to people about Roberto Mancini there's a huge amount of respect there. I think that he has achieved at a very high level. I think that he is someone who cares passionately and very deeply. He is not an out and out personality - neither was Mark. I know there were a lot of people clamouring for Mourinho but what we are trying to do is build a football club and I believe Roberto is right for that. If you look at Ferguson and Wenger, Roberto could be the next one. I think he is a great coach and a great thinker about the game. He works hard. I know that later in the season there were mumblings about training sessions. Two sessions or whatever, but that's what the manager wants and that's what's going to bring us success. We need to work hard and Roberto's the man for that.

"Roberto is someone who has been taught well in his own career and with Brian Kidd he has some good English knowledge. I don't know if we'll be successful, but I do know that the indications are there."

Regardless of how Mark Hughes' reign ended, the fact was that City had a new manager and some very important games coming up. The Blues were already through to the League Cup semi-final – City's first major semi-final since 1981.

Mancini's first game in charge ended in a 2-0 victory over Stoke. Petrov and Tévez had put the Blues into a two goal lead by half time but the most interesting development, as far as many fans were concerned, was that City seemed to appear more tactically aware than in previous weeks. In the following day's *Observer*, City fan and *Observer* reader Gavin Slater gave his summary: "I enjoyed that. We had a better balance, and with the midfield three keeping their positions, we just seemed more organised. I've got good vibes about Mancini. When it looked like Stoke would come back into it, he took Sylvinho off, moved Zabaleta to the left, and Richards to the right, which was a good pro-active decision. It was good to have Petrov back too – every time he's had an opportunity he's done well and Barry was outstanding. It was like watching the Barry that plays for England."

Of course, it was early days, but Slater's comments echoed those of many fans and proved that some of the worries following the run of draws under Mark Hughes may have been overcome.

New manager Roberto Mancini celebrates the first goal of his managerial campaign. City went on to defeat Stoke 2-0 with goals from Petrov and Tevez.

Victory over Stoke was followed by a satisfying 3-0 win at Wolverhampton Wanderers with Carlos Tévez scoring twice. Ever since his controversial transfer from Manchester United, the Argentinian had impressed, and by the end of 2009 he was a major Blue hero.

Mancini's next game saw the Blues overcome Middlesbrough 1-0 in the FA Cup. Like many of the other sides with top four ambitions he utilised squad rotation – a move relatively new to City. Some fans were critical, but overall it seemed a sensible approach and one Paul Wilson of *The Guardian* expressed was in keeping with other ambitious sides: "For a chap who has been in the country for a couple of weeks, Roberto Mancini seems to have got the hang of the FA Cup. Craig Bellamy, Carlos Tévez and Gareth Barry began on the bench and Robinho was nowhere in sight."

Wilson added: "With a Carling Cup semi-final against Manchester United coming up on Wednesday, Mancini seemed determined to protect his resources and fully explore the options he has available. Dedryck Boyata and Vladimir Weiss made their first City starts, and there was a rare glimpse of Benjani Mwaruwari, out of action for more than a year, who scored just before the interval to take the sting out of the game for the Premier League side."

Despite the warm feelings about the results and his start at the Club, Mancini was still getting used to an English winter. At times snow had swirled around the stadium during the match and Mancini was asked post-match about his wearing of a blue and white City scarf: "It is a warm scarf. Today I should really have worn two scarves."

The need to wrap up intensified over the following couple of days as a heavy snow fall across the Country threatened fixtures, then on Tuesday 5th January, a day before it was scheduled to be played, the all-Manchester League Cup semi-final was called off. City's pitch was perfectly playable, however traffic chaos in Manchester was an issue.

The Blues had been desperate for the match to be played as the mood seemed perfect for a City victory. There was a great deal of positivity. Similarly, at United a FA Cup defeat to Leeds had increased the pressure on the Reds.

By the time the two sides did face each other the momentum had changed. United suffered a 1-1 draw at Birmingham, but followed this with a comfortable

Mancini's immediate impact was loved by fans.

3-0 victory over struggling Burnley. City's two games saw Blackburn humbled 4-1 – thanks in part to a hat-trick from Carlos Tévez – but the Blues suffered a 2-0 defeat at Everton only three days before the first leg of the League Cup tie.

City's first defeat under Mancini caused some concern, especially as it seemed to delight Everton manager David Moyes – still 'irked' over Lescott's transfer according to the *Liverpool Echo* - so much.

The defeat was not the kind of preparation Mancini had wanted for a semi-final that was suddenly being described as the most important Manchester derby of all time. This was an exaggeration, but the description demonstrated that City had started to become a threat. In the two seasons that followed other games with United would be described as the "most important" derby again.

The game did not disappoint, and supporters left believing for the first time since 1981 that there was a real opportunity of achieving trophy success. It should be noted as well that Manchester United manager Alex Ferguson was now taking City seriously. In September he had described the 4-3 United derby victory as the greatest Manchester derby of all time. Again it was not, but the fact was that the United boss was now seeing City as a serious opponent. The first leg of this League Cup semi-final proved that the Blues were becoming a force once more.

A Tévez penalty had levelled the score at 1-1 following a 16th minute goal from Ryan Giggs. At the time of the United goal it was clear that the Blues were giving the Reds too much respect and were also playing too deep. Supporters urged the side forward and Mancini made a few tactical adjustments to enable the Blues to attack. The new manager's tactical nous paid off and City stormed forward. The penalty came after about 42 minutes and was certainly a valid one, despite the appeals of the Reds.

With the sides level this full-blooded derby seemed to reach new heights. The second half saw the frenetic pace continue and in the 65th minute the Blues deservedly took the lead. Bellamy lifted in a corner which the United 'keeper palmed out. Pablo Zabaleta took up the ball and comfortably delivered a pass into the path of Vincent Kompany who, in turn, lifted the ball across to a waiting Tévez. Tévez headed home and within seconds the stadium erupted into chants of "Fergie, Fergie sign him up" – a reference to the chanting in the Old Trafford League derby of 2008-09 when the United fans urged their manager to sign the brilliant Argentinian.

Regardless of how the League Cup semi-final would ultimately play out the fact that the Blues had come back from a goal down to end the first leg as 2-1 victors showed a spirit and a level of tactical-know-how that many City sides had lacked over the years. It also made it abundantly clear that the Blues were heading in the right direction. Two years earlier the prospect of even being in a semi-final seemed remote, and now the Blues had not only reached that stage but so far they had acquitted themselves well.

Henry Winter, writing in The *Daily Telegraph*, seemed to capture the situation perfectly. In an article which cited Ferguson's comments about City being 'noisy neighbours' he talked of the drama of the game: "As Tévez ran off to celebrate his second, cupping his ears as if challenging the acerbic choir seething in the away pews, any lingering vestiges of restraint disappeared. Two seats were thrown on to the pitch from the visitors' end. The cold night air thickened with sulphurous sounds. This was football at its most viscerally raw, at its most compelling for the 46,067 privileged to be present and the millions more tuning in. Who says the BBC does not make epic dramas any more?"

Winter talked of England's Wayne Rooney playing with determination before adding: "Nothing, not even England's leading player at his buccaneering best, could silence the party raging on the home terraces. Short of Oasis reforming, it does not get much better than this for City fans.

"How they crowed at the sight of their vaunted visitors failing in their late rally. How they loved Tévez's immense contribution and how fitting that great servants of the club, venerated figures like Franny Lee, Mike Summerbee and the peerless Colin Bell, were here to witness such memorable scenes."

Lee, Summerbee and Bell, along with a variety of other former players, were regular attendees throughout the season and, for all of those who suggested that City's Abu Dhabi leaders cared little about the Club's history, this was evidence of how important City's history was to those in control of the Blues. It would have been very easy for the Club to limit the number of former players attending games or to hide them away somewhere, but Cook had given the former players significant involvement in the Club.

As Winter predicted, the second leg was to be a very important game: "Next week's leg of this Carling Cup semi-final promises more fireworks. Welcome to Madchester. When Tévez steps out in front of the Stretford End there will be an explosion of noise that could blow an amp. If Gary Neville, fast becoming one of the great pains of the modern era, and accused of giving

Tévez the finger here, starts next week, the mercury will rise as fast as the noise levels.

"Neville's club know they are locked in a dogfight of gathering danger. Whether United find themselves engaged in a scrap to prevent a shift of power can only be properly assessed after a year or two, but failing to hold on to Tévez now looks an almighty own goal. Whatever the champions' concerns about Tévez's financial demands, whatever Sir Alex Ferguson's scepticism about the Argentine's impact in the major matches, there can now be no doubt that United erred badly in not retaining his substantial services. He makes a difference."

City were not a one-man team, but in Tévez they possessed a talisman.

Ultimately, the Blues were defeated 4-3 on aggregate to Manchester United. Frustratingly, the Reds' winning goal came in added time. There were also worrying scenes on the terraces as missiles were thrown at Craig Bellamy when City had a corner and were well on top in the match. More than one bottle was thrown at Bellamy, while a few coins also rained down on him. Van der Sar rushed over and tried to take the missile from Bellamy with some fans suggesting this was an issue in itself.

After netting a hat trick against Blackburn on 11th January 2010 (4-1 win) Carlos Tevez celebrates with a little dance, later copied by young fans.

The missiles clearly unnerved City and as a result the Blues failed to make the most of their corner. In fact, the Reds managed to get the ball off City and launch a counter-attack. That attack led directly to the first goal of the evening.

Understandably, the Blues felt deflated, but over time this game, and the other derby games of 2009-10 should be seen as significant moments along City's journey. Each game gave them a new experience to learn from, all of which would prove very important in the dying seconds of the 2011-12 season a couple of years later.

Despite the defeat, the Blues had made progress as journalist Henry Winter accurately recorded: "[City] should take pride in defeat. Carlos Tévez never stopped running, never stopped worrying Rio Ferdinand and Jonny Evans. Micah Richards never stopped seeking to break down the right, even bringing an unbelievable save from Edwin van der Sar. On the terraces, City fans were ceaseless in their support. The club will recover from this, pouring their energies into challenging for the fourth Champions League spot and reaching Wembley via the FA Cup. Sadly, if perhaps inevitably, an epic evening was scarred by the bottle and coins thrown at Craig Bellamy, a nasty incident that the FA will doubtless now investigate."

The Blues had much to be positive about at the end of January 2010. Portsmouth were defeated 2-0 via goals from Adebayor and Kompany in the first League game following the United match, prompting Mancini to admit: "I am satisfied for the victory but for the play so-so. The clean sheet is important but it was more important that we won today. It's a good situation for us."

The final days of the month also saw a few moves in the transfer market. Former Arsenal star Patrick Vieira had joined City earlier in the month, and Robinho did return to his original club, Santos, on a six month loan as expected, but it was the arrival of Middlesbrough winger Adam Johnson on transfer deadline day that was to prove the most inspired moment of the transfer window. The winger joined the Blues on a contract lasting until 2014 and he proved to be a popular addition to the side in 2010.

Ultimately, the Blues were only defeated in three of their final 15 League games. They also faced Stoke City three times in February – twice in the FA Cup and once in the League. The first FA Cup meeting on 13th February ended in a 1-1 draw, as did the League meeting three days later.

Stoke had scored in the 72nd minute of the League game, before Gareth Barry saved City's blushes with an 85th minute equaliser. The draw lifted the Blues to fourth place. During the post-match interviews one journalist asked Mancini about an incident in the game.

The Italian claimed he had not seen it, but another journalist said: "You're learning fast." Mancini replied: "Thank you. I have been watching Coronation Street."

The following Sunday, 21st February, presumably after worrying about the situation with Coronation Street's Gail and her missing husband Joe (whose body had just bobbed to the surface of Lake Windermere), Mancini guided City to a goalless draw against Liverpool. The result was satisfactory but some journalists claimed the manager was likely to lose his job at the season's end. Paul Wilson wrote an article on Jose Mourinho for *The Observer* which suggested that the former Chelsea manager could be arriving at either Liverpool or City at the end of the season. In his *Guardian* report Paul McCarra referred indirectly to the rumour: "These clubs have high expectations and Mancini has the added worry of trying to retain his job."

Some supporters saw reports like these as a validation of the rumours that continued to circulate. This contributed to a feeling of anxiety. No matter what was said the rumours were believed. When City travelled to Stoke for the FA Cup replay on 24th February the home fans teased Mancini and City supporters with the chant of "You're getting sacked in the morning." This is fairly normal banter when a side is facing a struggling competitor but the Blues actually lay in fifth place, with a game in hand over most sides, and of course Mancini was only two months into his managerial reign. The chants were premature but when the Stoke-City replay ended in a 3-1 home win, others suggested this would be the final straw for City's Chairman. The fact was, however, City's owner and other executives were not looking to make a change. There was no intention whatsoever to remove Mancini.

In his match report journalist Joe Lovejoy commented: "Mancini's claims after the game that his team had 'played very well and dictated for 80 minutes' will cut no ice with demanding employers who had so little patience with Mark Hughes."

Chairman Khaldoon found the constant speculation about Mancini's future baffling: "It's extremely frustrating. I read the 'papers and see this 'trigger-happy City'. Trigger-happy City based on what? Based on twenty managers fired in our first 18 months? No, this is based on one change. Absolutely one change of an individual that we hadn't even selected to start with, but we had stuck with him. So where does this trigger-happy City come from?

"From day one I have always stated that we would be patient and we have been that way. I cannot see a single contradiction of anything I or 'we' – the team we have put in place - have said since starting out. Not a single one. We said what we would do and we've done it – from A to Z."

With an away game at Chelsea following three

days after the Stoke replay it was important to remain focused on the overall task. Challenging for European Champions League qualification had to be the number one aim.

The Chelsea-City game received considerably more attention than usual simply because of the continued media interest in the private lives of John Terry, Wayne Bridge and Bridge's former girlfriend. The hype was such that the pre-match Premier League handshake was to be as eagerly watched as the game itself. Would Bridge shake Terry's hand? The television cameras zoomed in close as the City players travelled down the line shaking hands. When Bridge came to Terry the City man kept his hand firmly down and did not make any attempt to shake hands with Terry. This in itself became a noteworthy story.

On the pitch City welcomed the return of Carlos Tévez following a period of absence spent with his premature daughter in Argentina, but the side missed Adebayor who was serving a four match suspension brought about by his sending off in the FA Cup tie with Stoke. Tévez's return brought some hope but the statistics pre-match suggested City stood little chance of beating the home side. Those statistics showed that a Chelsea victory would put the Pensioners four points clear at the top of the table; that City had won only once in their last six fixtures; Chelsea were unbeaten at home; and the Blues had not scored at Stamford Bridge in the last decade. If City were to achieve anything they would need to overturn history. And that is exactly what they did, although when they went a goal behind in the 42nd minute few believed Mancini's men could win.

Two minutes after Frank Lampard gave Chelsea the lead the returning Carlos Tévez brought the Blues back into the match. The goal was not Tévez's best of the season but it was one of the most important. The Argentinian picked up the ball, wrong-footed Terry and Carvalho, and then sent a fairly weak shot rolling past the Chelsea 'keeper and into the net. Within a minute Lescott almost made it 2-1 with a header from a free kick by Bellamy.

Six minutes into the second half City launched a counter attack which saw Bellamy wide on the left jink past Mikel and then shoot from a narrow angle. The finish was superb and the ball went in just inside the post.

The goal helped City take control further with Bellamy and Tévez terrorising the Chelsea defence. The Welshman in particular seemed to be on fire as he made several impressive attempts, but it was not until the 76th minute that another goal came. This time Tévez scored from a penalty awarded when Gareth Barry was fouled by Belletti. The Chelsea man was sent off for a professional foul and the advantage had clearly swung City's way with the London side appearing desperate.

Two minutes after the goal Wayne Bridge, who had been booed by the home side, was substituted for Roque Santa Cruz. In spite of the negativity directed at the former Chelsea player by the home crowd, Bridge's performance had been worthy of praise during the match.

City remained in control and then with only nine minutes remaining Ballack went in late on Tévez and the referee, Mike Dean, had no option but to send the German off after his second yellow card of the game. With a two-man advantage the Blues continued to press forward and in the 87th minute Craig Bellamy made it 4-1 after Wright-Phillips had squared the ball to him.

In the 90th minute Gareth Barry caught former Blue Anelka in the area and Frank Lampard scored the resulting penalty. It hardly mattered though as City had won a significant fixture 4-2. It was City's first double over Chelsea since 1957-58 and a clear sign that the Blues could on their day live with the best. Now Mancini's side had to do this game after game.

The victory put City into the top four once again, but with the Tottenham game, originally scheduled for 6th March, moved due to Spurs' FA Cup commitments, the Blues missed the chance to capitalise on the positivity that followed Chelsea. When they did return to action after a break of 15 days, a surprise 1-1 draw at Sunderland – City had been losing for 81 minutes of the match before Adam Johnson salvaged a point in the dying seconds – saw the Blues end the game in fifth place.

The goal gave Roberto Mancini hope that a top four finish was still within City's grasp: "It's going to be very tight but I think we have a good chance of qualifying for the Champions League."

Although this game had ended in a draw and the perceived loss of two points, it is fair to say that Mancini had not been afraid to change tactics in an attempt to find a successful formula. Still learning about the English game, the Italian kept changing formation until he felt satisfied that the Blues were competing. It was this approach to his game that started to impress. Other managers would have blindly stuck to their original plan, perhaps tweaking it with substitutions, but Mancini was different. If his plan was failing then he would take whatever steps he felt necessary to swing the match his way.

Apart from a 2-0 defeat at home to bogey side Everton, Mancini's Blues impressed in the games that followed with confident victories over Fulham (2-1), Wigan (3-0), and Burnley (6-1). Another five goals were scored as City defeated Birmingham 5-1 on Sunday 11th April – a day when 1956 FA Cup Final hero Bert Trautmann, OBE was introduced to the crowd. The former German paratrooper was clearly emotional as a packed stadium sang his name.

Trautmann remained a guest for the next match, and perhaps the biggest test – the return Manchester derby. City's double over Chelsea had helped the Reds in their quest to retain the Premier League title while City were determined to cement their position in the top four – recent results had placed the Blues fourth, one point ahead of Tottenham.

Khaldoon was desperate to see the game but a volcanic eruption in Iceland had brought chaos to the skies and British airspace was closed. Despite the obstacles, the Club looked for options. At one point the Abu Dhabi contingent came close to flying to Geneva and then organising a helicopter to transport them to Manchester, but there were significant issues that had to be overcome from a transport, security and safety viewpoint.

Ultimately, despite the best efforts of those involved, Khaldoon was unable to travel to Manchester, and he sat with Sheikh Mansour, as he often did when he was unable to attend a game in person, to watch the match. Director Simon Pearce: "Never forget that Sheikh Mansour has a real passion for football. He watches every City game and often sits there with other members of his family."

It is known that some senior figures from Abu Dhabi have, at times, sat in the stands and experienced games at the stadium without this becoming common knowledge. They have watched as fans view games, and deliberately not been a focal point for media or fans' attention.

Sheikh Mansour would have been disappointed with what he witnessed on his television. Manchester United defeated the Blues 1-0 with yet another goal in added time – the third derby match of the season to end this way. It was another bitterly frustrating end to a match City hardly deserved to lose.

The disappointment against United was compounded later that night when Spurs beat Chelsea 2-1. Although City's destiny remained in their own hands – win every game and fourth place was guaranteed – the advantage had swung towards Tottenham, and City's following match away at Arsenal was now viewed as one the Blues could not afford to lose.

With great resilience, the Blues managed to earn a vital point from a goalless game with Arsenal. That meant City remained fifth. Unfortunately, the point had come at a high price, as the *Manchester Evening News* reported: "Shay Given was stretchered off in the second half with a serious looking shoulder injury and his involvement in the rest of the season must now be in doubt. He sustained the injury making his only real save of the game from Abou Diaby after 73 minutes and his departure meant a debut for little-known Faroese stopper Gunnar Nielsen.

"Given wasn't City's only casualty, as Wayne Bridge limped off early on with a thigh problem. He was replaced by Micah Richards - himself just fit again following a four-match absence with a knee injury."

These injuries, particularly Given's, had a bearing on the rest of the season. With three matches left to play, Mancini needed to do something about his goalkeeper. With the transfer window closed options were limited, however the Premier League

Adebayor enjoyed scoring his second and City's fifth goal against Birmingham on 11th April 2010. The match ended 5-1.

rules do allow clubs to bring in a replacement 'keeper, subject to their approval, if circumstances are severe. City had debated trying to bring back Joe Hart who was on loan at Birmingham, but Mancini found an answer: "Gunnar Nielsen is not experienced but he came on at the Emirates and did very well. We like him, but I felt it was important to have as much experience as possible in goal for these three really big games and so we brought in Marton Fulop on loan from Sunderland.

"Marton has plenty of experience both of the Premier League and international football, and is a big physical presence. I don't think he will find it hard to fit in with the defenders here."

The new goalkeeper took part in City's training sessions on the Thursday and Friday preceding the Saturday Villa match.

Apart from the goalkeeping worries, Chairman Khaldoon Al Mubarak was happy with City's development and the 2009-10 season at this stage: "We have taken six points off Chelsea, winning home and away. Taken four out of six against Arsenal. And we have lost two games against United in the last 30 seconds – that close. Overall, that is a tremendous season for a team showing intent. It shows that we can compete. It shows that we can compete at that level.

"That's the completion of stage two in our development. In stage three we'll move to the next level. Regardless of where we finish this season, next year will see a concerted effort by us to compete for a top three position. That is our aim."

Khaldoon's feelings prior to the Villa game show, without doubt, that he and the others running the Club were very happy with the way the Blues were progressing. City had achieved a great deal no matter how the final three games would pan out. This was not spin, or hyperbole, this was fact. Already qualification for the Europa League was guaranteed, meaning the Blues had qualified for Europe on merit for the first time in a little over thirty years.

The Villa game saw the visitors take the lead in the sixteenth minute but, as the game progressed City dominated. In the 41st minute Adam Johnson, who was proving to be a real thorn in Villa's side, was brought down in the penalty area and Carlos Tévez equalised for the Blues. Adebayor made it 2-1 two minutes later and then in the 89th minute Bellamy increased the lead. It ended 3-1. Afterwards Mancini commented: "When Aston Villa scored we did not deserve it, but we continued to play well and scored two first-half goals.

The Tottenham game received an incredible amount of hype during its build-up. The attention on this one fixture was significant and greater than the focus on the race for the Premier League title. To most football purists that was a crazy notion, however the game had become so predictable at the highest level that the efforts by City,

Spurs and also Aston Villa had encouraged and excited many.

Ultimately, on the night Tottenham performed better than City and they beat the Blues 1-0 with a goal from Peter Crouch eight minutes from time. It was a disappointing result but most fans accepted that over the course of the full season Spurs had the better record and therefore deserved the Champions League place. The two City-Spurs meetings had both ended in defeat for the Blues and, in the end, no one could complain.

The final game of the campaign ended in a 1-1 draw at West Ham. This brought a fifth place finish on 67 points, three behind Spurs and three ahead of Aston Villa.

City's leaders knew that the Blues were heading in the right direction and, even though fifth place was not what they had hoped for, the signs were clear. City were progressing at a pace.

2010-2011 Yaya's Goals

The close season saw changes to the squad with several players going out on loan and others arriving. Newspapers and sports channels were full of City related transfer stories and the attention was high. Very high.

At the start of July Kolo Touré's younger brother Yaya arrived from Barcelona for a fee of around £24m. Some baulked at the fee – it seemed normal to criticise City's spending but not that of some clubs – but the player would ultimately prove an absolute bargain as he became one of the star men during 2010-11 and 2011-12.

Another star man was World Cup winner David Silva. The Spaniard completed his move to the Blues three days after winning his medal in South Africa. The transfer discussions had taken place before the World Cup finals and the player had been bowled over by the comments of Brian Marwood, Garry Cook and manager Roberto Mancini. They explained the ambition of City and described what the Club meant to the people of Manchester. Silva loved everything he heard: "It's a great project and the Club is signing some great players."

In answer to those who claimed that players were arriving at City simply because of high salaries, Silva explained: "Money is not the main issue here. What is important is trying to win trophies and to get in the Champions League next season."

Silva's emphasis was right. As with the signing of Gareth Barry the previous year, the ambition of turning City into trophy winners was what inspired Silva, not money. It is also worth pointing out that he mentioned trophy success before Champions League qualification. This is significant as many commentators, neutrals and fans believed that City's aim was purely to gain a top four finish. The truth was a little different – the Blues wanted trophy success and a top three finish more than anything else. Simply finishing fourth was not the answer.

Another World Cup international arriving at Eastlands during July 2010 was Serbian defender Aleksandar Kolarov.

Kolarov, Silva and Touré all made their competitive debuts against Tottenham on the opening day of the season. Mancini was still making changes to his squad but it is appropriate to highlight that in the main the team was now taking the shape he had hoped for. Within a few weeks it would be 'his' team, not the side left by Mark Hughes, and so all results from this point on were his responsibility. Whereas some could rightly argue that the previous season's successes and failures were influenced by the work of Hughes, the 2010-11 season could only be viewed as Mancini's. He had to stand or fall by his signings and selections from this point onwards.

Some of his decisions at the commencement of the season raised a few eyebrows. He made Carlos Tévez captain and brought Joe Hart into the side as the preferred goalkeeper over Shay Given. Both moves had their merits, but some fans were not so certain. However, the confidence in Hart was justified during the opening game at Spurs. It ended goalless with Hart pulling off several brilliant saves from Aaron Lennon, Jermaine Defoe and Luka Modric. Man of the Match Hart was modest in his assessment of the day: "I was lucky enough to be playing. But it's not guaranteed that I'll be playing in the coming weeks. I'm just happy to be here, really. It's exciting to be a part of what's going on at the club. The Man of the Match award was a nice touch. My mum will be happy with that!"

Five days later the Blues defeated Romanian side FC Timisoara 1-0 in the Europa League. Mario Balotelli made his debut in that match and another new arrival appeared in City's third competitive game of the season. James Milner signed from Aston Villa with former hero Stephen Ireland going in the opposite direction. Taking into consideration Ireland's value, the fee was estimated to be around £26m. On his debut Milner helped the Blues achieve a very important 3-0 victory over Liverpool when he set his former Villa team-mate Gareth Barry up for the opener. However, despite his high profile transfer Milner did not receive the biggest ovation of the day. That was reserved for Sheikh Mansour.

City's owner flew to Manchester to watch his first live game. Security was high. The security arrangements were, of course, something that had to be fully thought through and were one of the reasons why the Sheikh was not a regular attendee, although he did watch

TRUE BLUE
Garry Cook

Often in the media spotlight, Garry Cook helped transform the club at a rapid pace. Without him City would not have developed at all levels in the manner it did.

games with a passion via television at home. His arrival in Manchester helped boost the atmosphere and when his presence became known a buzz enveloped the stadium. This was already a highly anticipated game and season, but Sheikh Mansour's presence did raise everything a couple of notches.

As he stood taking the applause and cheers from the crowd his pleasure at the experience was thoroughly clear. There were smiles from him, Khaldoon and Garry Cook as they saw and heard the fans publicly show their appreciation for his interest in the Blues.

In the build-up to the match the previous day the *Mail On Sunday* included an article, written from a Liverpool perspective, on the game. The author, Joe Bernstein, quoted an unnamed Liverpool spokesperson: "It makes you wonder why the Abu Dhabi owners bought Manchester City rather than wait to buy Liverpool. If they had spent the £1bn on Liverpool, they would be sitting back now with the best team in the world. When you look at the two clubs, it's King Kong versus Mickey Mouse."

Clearly that spokesperson was unaware of the passion, power and opportunity to create something truly special that existed with City. Liverpool could have been improved at a quicker rate perhaps, but the Blues possessed more potential for growth than the Anfield outlet. Liverpool had dominated English and European football in the past and had even won the European Champions League in recent years, but they had never managed to capitalise fully on their domination. They had a global fan base, but their peak had come at a time when the financial nature of the game was not so significant.

Although the Blues progressed in Europe in the days that followed the Liverpool victory domestically this was a mixed period. Sunderland defeated Mancini's Blues 1-0, and then there was a home 1-1 draw with Blackburn, leaving them eighth in the Premier League.

A 2-0 victory over Wigan on 19th September lifted City back up to fourth place, but then Mancini's squad rotation – some of it forced through injury - came in for severe criticism as the Blues were defeated 2-1 in the League Cup by West Bromwich Albion. Callers to the BBC's 606 claimed that the League Cup was the main competition the Blues stood a chance of winning.

Mancini felt he had played a side capable of winning the tie and was adamant that he had made the right decisions: "I did not regard this as a necessary sacrifice. We wanted to win. That is why I had four senior players on the bench. But I knew there was a chance we could lose because we started with six young players. I am happy with these guys. We might have lost the game but they can improve. If they do not play tonight, when will they ever play?

"I don't regret making the changes. I have big problems at the moment and we couldn't take any risks. If I had more players available it would be a different team, but when you play like us and Chelsea, on Saturday at 12.45, the time to recover is very short. They would need minimum three days so to play tonight would have been dangerous."

Some journalists and fans alike felt the decision had cost City their best chance of glory. The ESPN website written match report expressed those sentiments: "Unless he is intent on winning the Premier League title - and the Blues are already seven points adrift of Chelsea - the Carling Cup was the easiest way of ending the club's 36-year (sic) trophy drought and offer some tangible reward for Sheikh Mansour's £1billion investment in the Eastlands outfit."

Mancini disagreed: "Saturday is more important, the FA Cup is more important. The Europa League is more important."

With hindsight it is clear Mancini made the right decision, but at the time he was seriously criticised by fans and the media.

Three days after the League Cup defeat the Chelsea game proved that Mancini's side had a real chance of glory. It was a tight game but ultimately the Blues swept aside the Pensioners with a powerful performance. Chelsea were undefeated so far. They were already tipped to win the title – even Mancini claimed both before and after the game that they were the best side in England – and so the victory was even more significant than perhaps previous victories over the Londoners. Each time the Blues defeated Chelsea it gained headlines, but in September 2010 the City win brought a recognition that Mancini's side could actually mount a real challenge for the League.

The game ended 1-0 thanks to Carlos Tévez. Describing the 59th minute goal – the first time Chelsea had been behind during the season - superbly for the *Telegraph* Duncan White reported: "The winner was a rapid, lethal counterattack. With much of the Chelsea side committed up field following a corner, John Obi Mikel headed a City clearance down to Ramires. The Brazilian was robbed by James Milner, who found Yaya Touré, who in turn passed to Tévez. The Argentine set off from the halfway line with David Silva peeling to the left, pulling the Chelsea defenders apart. Ashley Cole

was backing off, having to risk the long-range shot. Tévez did not need a second invitation, pushing the ball past Cole and shooting low across Petr Cech and in off the far post."

After the game Mancini was asked about City's title credentials. He claimed Chelsea stood best chance of winning the League and that his side needed to narrow the gap over time: "We must stay a long time at the top, and must try to win something. We must not think we have done it all after today."

His ambition to win a trophy remained clear. The title was a faint possibility but Mancini knew City were not quite ready for that. The League Cup was no longer possible. That meant either Europa League success or FA Cup glory. Mancini's views were clear, but few fully grasped them at this point.

Fourth placed City ended September with a draw at home to Juventus in the Europa League. The following month the Blues moved up the table briefly into second place with victories over Newcastle (2-1) and at Blackpool (3-2), but defeats by Arsenal (3-0) and at Wolverhampton Wanderers (2-1) undid much of the great work performed.

There were reasons for City's struggles in these games. Dedryck Boyata had been sent off against Arsenal after only five minutes, while Carlos Tévez suffered a thigh injury which then meant he was unable to appear against Wolves. However, Mancini preferred not to use these as excuses – nor should he. He admitted he was mystified as to why everything had fallen apart at Wolves: "I can't understand. I need to watch the game again. This is the worst game that we have played. A team like us can lose, it can happen. But we can't play like that for 70 minutes. We lost against Arsenal because we played with one player less, but today we didn't play well. That is the sort of game we must win. You must play all the game 150 per cent, not 50."

With a little optimism he added: "The season is very long so we can recover. We must find a solution. We must try to change our mentality. We have great team spirit."

The media doubted that City had great team spirit. Rumours of issues frequently appeared on websites. In addition, Mancini's own role was being questioned by fans on websites, most notably the forum Bluemoon. There were a few voices of reason but every defeat was greeted with apocalyptic predictions. There was nothing peculiar about this of course, City fans have a habit of taking to extremes. In the nineties fans often felt that victory meant the Blues would win the League. Defeat meant relegation. There was rarely anything in between.

The major difference between the highs and lows predicted by fans in the Nineties to those in 2010-11 was that the media was now demonstrating real interest in City's affairs. Bluemoon and other forums were being utilised to gauge opinions. Those opinions worsened when City were defeated at Poznan in the Europa League. The defeat hardly mattered as the Blues were competing in the Group stage, however it was another sign for those looking for it that all was not well.

In the League, despite victory over West Bromwich Albion (2-0), pressure intensified when the Blues played out goalless draws at Eastlands with United and Birmingham City. Mancini's side were still in the top four – the target as far as some journalists and fans were concerned – so the criticism was a bit extreme to say the least. Then came an away trip to Fulham.

At Craven Cottage Fulham invited Argentinian Diego Maradona as guest of honour. After only five minutes of play Maradona witnessed a wonderful goal from his countryman Carlos Tévez. The City star controlled a through-ball, held off a challenge from Fulham's Salcido on the edge of the penalty box, turned and then sent a low drive zooming past 'keeper Schwarzer and into the bottom left corner.

Twenty-five minutes later another Argentinian, Pablo Zabaleta, made it 2-0 from a corner when he fired the ball screaming into the top right corner. City were totally in control and Maradona seemed to be loving the Blues' – especially the role of the Argentinians – display.

In the 33rd minute, only two minutes after Zabaleta's goal, Yaya Touré made it 3-0. City's dominance had been demonstrated in the build-up to the match as the Blues performed a series of 24 passes before David Silva played a diagonal ball to a typically rampaging Touré who sent a low drive into the bottom left corner of the goal.

Ironic chants of "Boring, Boring City" boomed out from the away section.

Ten minutes into the second half, Tévez netted his second of the game, much to the delight of a celebrating Maradona. It looked like Fulham had picked the wrong day to make Maradona their guest as he seemed to be thoroughly entertained by City's performance.

Although Fulham netted a consolation goal, the 4-1 City win could easily have been more. A penalty decision should have gone the Blues' way, while they also played some wonderful football.

Six days later, Mancini's side were brought back down to earth at Stoke. It was a tough game, but the Blues looked to have won it when Micah Richards scored nine minutes from time. Sadly, Stoke equalised two minutes into added time via Matthew Etherington.

City ended November in fourth place, five points behind the leaders United although they did have a couple of games in hand, but by the end of the following month the Blues had lifted themselves into second place on equal points with the leaders. They had managed this via a wonderful away record and a series of decent results at home. There had been one defeat – 2-1 at Eastlands to bogey side Everton – but there had also been emphatic victories over West Ham, Newcastle and Aston Villa.

The Newcastle game on Boxing Day had seen Tévez in blistering form, scoring twice in the 3-1 victory, while Aston Villa had seen Balotelli gain the headlines with a hat-trick. Tévez had been rested for the Villa game, giving Balotelli the opportunity to prove to his critics his value.

It seemed that whatever Balotelli did he would be criticised. If he gave the impression of not caring about the game he was viewed as being unhappy at City. If he did the opposite and showed a bit more of a fighting spirit or possibly frustration if substituted or the game went away from him, then he was also unhappy at City. It didn't seem to matter what he said or did. He had even been criticised because he didn't smile as much as other players. After the Villa game he was asked about this: "I am always happy, even when I don't smile. I am very happy even if the journalists in Italy say I want to go to Milan. I want to be an important man for this team and the results are on the pitch."

Mancini, ultimately the only man whose views of the player's contribution to the team counted, was very supportive: "Mario is a good guy and I think today he was happy because the supporters supported him throughout the game and he scored three goals. Off the pitch, he is not like he is on the pitch. He is a different guy, but he likes to give this image, this impression, that he doesn't like to play. Maybe it could be that he is homesick because he is 20 years old and it's normal to miss your family at that age.

"Brian Kidd has told me that Cristiano Ronaldo had Mario's same problems when he arrived at United, and needed time to adjust. He knows he has to do more for himself as well as for the team. When he grasps this and makes use of his superior qualities, he will become an important player."

The Villa win placed City top of the Premier League table briefly but the timing of fixtures had played their part. In January a 4-3 victory over Wolves took City to the top again. This time they were a point ahead of second placed United, but the Reds had three games in hand. Although it was morale-boosting to see the Blues head the table, the truth was that the advantage remained with United and third placed Arsenal – the Gunners could also go above City if they won their own game in hand.

On 22nd January the Blues travelled to Birmingham to face Aston Villa in the return game. By this time City were through to the FA Cup fourth round and the Europa League last 32, and seemed capable of mounting a challenge in each of the three competitions. Then came Villa's new £24m signing Darren Bent who scored the only goal of the game in the 18th minute. Immediately City's title aspirations seemed to be written off, but it was actually a training ground incident a few days later that brought more worries Mancini's way.

Adam Johnson, a player Mancini often talked of as a 'game-changer', suffered an ankle injury in training. Scans proved the extent of the damage and caused the manager to explain to the media: "We've lost Adam for three months. He's possibly out for the rest of the season or maybe back for the FA Cup final. It's the same injury Kolarov suffered earlier this season and it's a big problem for us."

Mancini's assessment was fairly accurate. With too little time left in the transfer window to find a suitable replacement the pressure was on. Johnson was an important player but it wasn't so much the individual player that was the issue, it was the fact that despite spending heavily in a determined bid to create a decent squad, the Blues were still not in possession of a squad with the depth of Manchester United or some of the other challengers.

The speed at which the squad had been assembled was impressive, but it also meant that some of the players had not had chance to adjust to Mancunian life. City's critics often focused on the crazy idea that the Blues were buying everybody and anybody without too much overall planning, but the truth was somewhat different. Ever since the arrival of Mancini – and in truth a little earlier – the Blues had tried to develop a plan for player acquisition and development that would see the Club create a squad worthy of trophy success at a rapid rate. Time was always against City. Whereas some, though not all, of their off-the-pitch plans could sensibly take years to come to fruition, activity on the pitch could not be allowed to improve gradually. Success was needed quickly, not because of the whim of a Middle-Eastern Sheikh as some media commentators believed, but to satisfy the aspirations of the fans and to buy time to allow the longer term plans to develop.

City did not want to buy willy-nilly, they wanted to buy based on a phased strategy that would ultimately give them strength in depth. Ironically, had City been keen to buy without making their proper plans then it's possible the Blues would have had several expensive stars for every position waiting in the wings. They could also have hijacked other proposed transfers, but that would have affected the Club's longer term planning and potentially brought issues further down the line.

There were other injury worries as well. Carlos Tévez had a back injury and Mario Balotelli had been missing with damaged knee muscles. Tévez did manage to return to action for the first League game in February – a 2-2 draw at Birmingham – but it was clear as the month progressed that Johnson, in particular, could have added something extra at key moments in a heavily congested month.

By this time the Blues had already reached the last 32 in Europe. However, the reality was that the FA Cup offered the most potential for trophy success.

The Third round draw was made by well-known City fan and musician Noel Gallagher, together with Leicester City supporter Serge Pizzorno from the band Kazabian. Fate decreed that they would ultimately pair City and Leicester in the draw to meet at the Walkers Stadium.

The tie meant so much and had many historical elements to it. Leicester were the defeated finalists when City last won the famous old trophy in 1969 with Neil Young the only goalscorer. Young had recently been diagnosed with a terminal cancer and the pairing of the two sides seemed appropriate. Another added angle was that Leicester were managed by former City manager Sven-Göran Eriksson and included former Blue Darius Vassell in their team. Of course, Sven had also been Roberto Mancini's manager at Lazio, while the current City boss had also enjoyed a brief spell as a Leicester player in 2001: "It was a very good experience for me… short, but enjoyable and it made me want to return to work in England one day. The Leicester fans were wonderful to me."

City had also loaned Leicester two players – Greg Cunningham and Ben Mee.

Four days before the Leicester tie City played out a goalless Premier League game at Arsenal. Chants of 'Boring, Boring City' rang out from Arsenal supporters with short memories – wasn't it the London club that were criticised in this way as they found success during the eighties and nineties? Roberto Mancini admitted afterwards: "We got a good point. People said we went to get a draw but this is not true. It is true we set out not to concede a goal but every team does that in every match it plays."

The Arsenal draw was City's fourth game in ten days, bringing ten points out of a possible twelve. It ensured the Blues held on to second place in the League – two points behind United and two ahead of Arsenal, though the Gunners had a game in hand – and meant Mancini's men were still challenging on three fronts even if the general media focus was on City's chance of qualification for the Champions League.

Prior to the FA Cup tie at Leicester City, with great effort from fan Alex Channon and other supporter representatives, the Blues issued red and black scarfs to anyone buying a ticket for the tie. These scarfs raised funds for a cancer-related charity linked to Neil Young and the idea was that after 24 minutes play the 5,000 City fans attending would turn their backs on the game and perform 'The Poznan' – the newly adopted supporter celebration. The timing was crucial as this was to happen at the point in the game that matched the time when Young scored the only goal of the 1969 final.

The public demonstration was to highlight Young's illness and to prove what the player meant to supporters.

Often regarded as the unsung hero of City's highly successful years under Joe Mercer and Malcolm Allison, Young was one of the biggest contributors to success in those days.

The 2011 FA Cup meeting with Leicester commenced with a desperate opening for City. The home side forced a corner which led to Sol Bamba, making his Leicester debut, stabbing home from about a yard or so out. It was heralded as his first touch in English football and the opening minute goal brought a few concerns City's way but they did not last long.

In the 23rd minute City broke away at speed. James Milner, under great pressure from Bamba, bamboozled the Leicester player before playing a quick one-two with Shaun Wright-Phillips. Milner went on to send a powerful low shot into the bottom corner of the goal.

The timing was perfect, coming a few seconds before the planned Young Poznan commemoration. Within seconds supporters unveiled a large flag/scarf bearing the words "There's only one Neil Young" and the Poznan dance was performed.

The rest of the half saw both sides make significant attempts. City were confident going forward, but Leicester were still a danger. Then in the 45th minute Mancini's side took the lead when Boateng earned a corner. The ball was played short and then Johnson passed to Milner, who threaded the ball through to the six yard area for Tévez to sneak in and send the ball home. It seemed an easy goal, but it was typical of the type of team play Mancini's side had been exhibiting for much of the season.

The second half saw City sit back a little and allow Leicester to have much possession. It appeared that the Blues were already through, but after about nineteen minutes of the half, Leicester equalised and the match ended 2-2.

The replay was staged three days after City had defeated Wolves 4-3 in a League game that lifted the Blues to the top of the table briefly. By the time of the replay City were second on goal difference to United, although the Reds had two games in hand. Nevertheless, reaching top spot did help psychologically.

For the Eastlands replay, the Blues continued their recognition of the life and career of former hero Neil Young. By this time Young's condition was deteriorating and the Club were in regular communication with his wife Carmen and their family. The match programme front contained a head and shoulders image of Young in City's famous red and black striped kit from 1969, while the back cover showed an action image of the player. Profiles and images from his career appeared inside but the most significant aspect came when the present day squad took to the field wearing red and black shirts over their regular playing kit. Those shirts were later signed by the players and auctioned for a Young related cancer charity.

Once the game commenced it was the Manchester side that was the first to get their name on the score sheet. From a throw-in Tévez ran past the Leicester defender Yuki Abe, who tried to dispossess the Argentinian, and charged at Jack Hobbs, the visitors' last defender. The ball bounced off Hobbs' calf and Tévez powered home an unstoppable shot into the far corner of the Leicester goal. It was a trademark great finish from Tévez in the fifteenth minute.

Four minutes later the visitors equalised via a penalty. The pressure was on but the Blues remained in overall control. By half time they had proved their superiority with some excellent football and, more significantly, two further goals. The first came in the 38th minute when a saved shot from David Silva set an unmarked Patrick Vieira up at the far post. The former Arsenal star couldn't miss. A minute later Adam Johnson fired home City's third of the night.

The Blues continued to set the pace and tone of the match and looked to increase their lead further when they were awarded a penalty shortly before the hour mark. Tévez sent the spot kick straight down the middle where it was blocked by goalkeeper Chris Weale's legs.

The saved penalty seemed to give Leicester some hope, but they seemed incapable of making the ultimate breakthrough. City continued to control the match until, with only seven minutes left, Dyer pulled one back for Leicester. The ball had actually been helped in the build-up when a planned pass by Abe hit referee Mark Halsey – well known to City fans for his role in the 1999 Play Off final – and bounced back to the player. Abe then sent it through to Dyer who slotted it to the left of Joe Hart. Television replays later proved that the Leicester scorer had been offside, but fortunately the goal proved to be an irrelevance six minutes later when Kolarov unleashed a left foot strike into the bottom corner of the net during a break which saw City attack in numbers.

The game ended 4-2 to Mancini's side. The pupil had beaten his old master for the right to face Notts County in the fourth round.

In the build-up to the Notts County tie much was made of the fact that County were the World's oldest League team and that they were facing the World's richest club – as usual ignoring the hard fact that it was City's owner that was wealthy not the club itself. Television, in particular, liked to build up the David and Goliath aspect to it. For neutrals it added to the interest perhaps, but for the Blues it continued to give a false impression of the stage they were at in their development. City had yet to win a trophy. Their plans were still in their earliest stages. Success was needed, but the way the Club was perceived at times suggested it was already a successful, and at times arrogant, club. That was unfair.

At County the combination of a poor surface

and determined, battling home side playing with the spirit and style of their manager Paul Ince, caused City significant problems. The match ended 1-1, thanks to an 80th minute equaliser – and first goal – for Edin Dzeko. Afterwards Mancini admitted: "I enjoyed Dzeko's goal. But he needs time to settle into English football."

When asked whether the state of the pitch had a bearing on the result the City manager accepted: "The pitch was another problem." But he also rightly pointed out that this was all part and parcel of the FA Cup: "You must fight for every ball if you want to get to Wembley."

City's goal had been created by Micah Richards who had driven a wonderful cross perfectly into Dzeko's path. Richards was one of City's star men that day and, as the season progressed, he was to prove to be a significant contributor to the Blues' successful campaign. He impressed his manager by always fighting for every ball. As did another key player against County, the experienced Patrick Vieira. After the match Vieira went to talk with Paul Ince and congratulate his team on a good, determined performance.

Although County hoped to repeat their performance in the replay, it was clear from the off that they stood little chance of beating Mancini's side. The Blues, despite at times an hesitant performance, were in control. Deservedly Vieira broke the deadlock in the 37th minute with a headed goal at the North Stand – unusually the Blues lost the toss and attacked the opposite end to normal in the first half. That goal was not exactly pretty but it counted. ITV's Peter Drury commented: "Colchester could score that goal as well as Manchester City could." It seemed an odd and irrelevant way of describing the goal.

Thirteen minutes into the second half Vieira scored his second from a corner. Another header, this time from about ten yards out.

The Blues ultimately won the tie 5-0 with three goals in the final six minutes. Tévez scored the first of these in the 84th minute after a wonderful ball through the middle from Dzeko was chased by Tévez. The energetic Argentinian won the ball, took it wide away from danger, before twisting his body to send the ball home with a trickling shot inside the near post. It was a great finish.

In the 89th minute Gareth Barry flicked a ball into the box. Tévez ran into space, caught up with the pass and then crossed the ball for a headed goal from Dzeko. It all looked very easy, but as most fans already knew, when City were on top form everything tended to look simple.

The fifth and final goal of the night came when a poor clearance from a corner saw the ball land near Micah Richards. After a bit of a spin, Richards gained control of the ball and slammed it into the goal from about eight yards out in the first minute of added time. It was another great finish.

Two minutes later Dzeko had a one-on-one with the 'keeper but his shot was saved. It could easily have been 6-0 on the night, although that score line would have flattered the Blues somewhat.

Mancini talked of the pressure caused by fixture congestion: "When you play every three days, it is difficult to play 100 per cent in every game, but after we scored it changed the game."

Mancini's critics argued, of course, that had his side beaten both Leicester and Notts County in their initial games then there would not have been as much of a congestion issue. The County replay had been played on the weekend of the fifth round, and further progression in Europe and in the FA Cup would exacerbate the issue. Already the fifth round tie was to be played on the date when a replay, if needed, would have been scheduled. It was important the Blues progressed, of course, but they could not afford to take any more ties to replays.

By the time the fifth round tie was eventually played City had dropped to third in the League, ten points behind leaders United after 28 games. A defeat at Old Trafford and draw at home to Fulham in February had meant that the League campaign had faltered a little.

In the Europa League, the Blues had reached the last sixteen but were scheduled to play Dynamo Kyiv. Everyone recognised that would be a difficult tie, and so the hope of trophy success was already beginning to focus on the FA Cup.

The importance of the FA Cup had remained high throughout of course, but many commentators on the game, particularly those with an interest in financial aspects, had believed the FA Cup was an irritant in City's season. They felt that progress in the competition would have a negative impact on the ability of the Blues to finish in the top four. Alongside this the fifth round was expected to provide their biggest test yet, as the opponents were fellow Premier League side Aston Villa.

Villa were having a mixed season and were twelfth, only five points ahead of struggling Wolves and West Ham, and six points above bottom club Wigan. Although the FA Cup offered Villa their only chance of glory, it also had the potential to stretch their resources at a time when safety was more important. In the end Villa manager Houllier picked a more negative side for the tie than his club's supporters had hoped.

Whether Houllier's selections ultimately changed the course of the game or not is open to debate, but Mancini's City were in control throughout. In the fifth minute they took the lead when Vieira flicked on a Kolarov corner. The ball hit Villa's Ciaran Clark before dropping perfectly for Yaya Touré in the penalty area. Inevitably the City man hit an accurate and low ball past Brad Friedel in the Villa goal.

The goal was Touré's first in the competition but it was to be eclipsed by two match-winning efforts later in the campaign. Twenty minutes later the 27 year old played a part in increasing City's lead over Villa when he sent a carefully measured pass through to an advancing Balotelli. The striker calmly side-footed the ball into the top right hand corner of the goal to make it 2-0.

In the second half, David Silva scored the third of the night. It was a fierce twenty yard drive into the bottom corner at the South Stand goal and, as with Touré and indeed Balotelli, it was the Spanish World Cup winner's first FA Cup goal. Silva was later named man of the match by the ITV commentary team.

After the Blues' 3-0 victory much of the media focus was on Houllier's Aston Villa selections, while the man himself tried to talk of City's qualities: "We were beaten by a team that is better than us at the moment and was ruthless in terms of goal opportunities. They were clinical and you must give them credit."

The victory meant City were through to the quarter-finals. The draw had helped play its part with the Blues scheduled to face Reading from the Championship, avoiding all the remaining Premier League sides including the two perceived big guns Arsenal and Manchester United. Promotion seeking Reading had defeated Everton in the fifth round and they definitely contained a spirit, determination, and enough class to compete with any Premier League side. However, from a pure City perspective playing lower league opposition had to be better than facing Everton who, most Mancunians would admit, had been a significant bogey side to the Blues in recent seasons.

Eleven days after beating Villa, City faced Reading at Eastlands. The tie was sandwiched in between two Europa League games with Dynamo Kyiv and there were inevitable concerns that fixture congestion could see the Blues end their campaign trophyless and without the much coveted top four finish. Although City remained in third place in the Premier League Chelsea had a game in hand and could overtake them, while Spurs were also capable of sneaking ahead of the Blues if they won their game in hand and defeated Mancini's side in the still to be re-arranged meeting.

In Europe the first leg of the game at Kyiv ended in a 2-0 defeat. Although not impossible, it was clear a tremendous effort would be needed to overturn the deficit and progress to the last eight.

The added pressure in League and Europe – this was to be City's sixth game in 17 days - meant the Blues could not afford to slip up in any way against Reading

A national magazine pays tribute to Neil Young.

although Mancini made it clear that he was trying to keep everybody's focus on each game rather than on the wider picture. That was something he, Brian Marwood, Garry Cook and Chairman Khaldoon had to focus on. When questioned about the overall chance of success in his pre-game press briefing he simply stated: "We have to make sure we concentrate on one thing at a time."

That was excellent advice, particularly as the peculiarities of modern day football meant that the FA Cup semi-final draw would be made prior to the 4.45pm Sunday afternoon televised City-Reading tie.

The semi-final draw was performed by England manager Fabio Capello and his equivalent from the women's national side Hope Powell. It took place at Wembley Stadium some 45 minutes before the City-Reading tie kicked off.

At the stadium fans packed City Square to see the draw live on the big screens. There was an air of anticipation with most fans muttering that they knew who the opponents would be. To the vast majority of fans outside City's ground there was only one possible opponent – Manchester United.

Hope Powell had the honour of pulling out the first ball and when she did a cheer rang out at Eastlands. The ball was number two and the presenter Jim Rosenthal explained: "That is Manchester City or Reading." Fabio Capello then pulled out ball number four prompting an excited Rosenthal to exclaim: "Manchester United. So the possibility of Manchester City against Manchester United."

Around City Square some fans shouted "Bring it on!" while others focused on the negatives, claiming "just our luck." It certainly had an impact on the atmosphere.

The players soon heard the news. Shaun Wright-Phillips: "We found out in the warm-up. We guessed it would happen. I have been down this road so many times and we always get United, so to me it was inevitable!"

Before the draw fans felt that this could be City's year as usual on these occasions, but after the draw there was a definite feeling that success would have to be worked for. Endeavour was needed.

Ultimately, it was probably better for all-concerned that the draw was made pre-match because it did help to keep everyone's feet on the ground. Supporters inevitably thought about the possibility of facing United at Wembley – the last time City appeared in a FA Cup semi-final the games were played on League grounds around the country. But from a football purist's viewpoint it was disappointing that the draw, which let's be honest was only to decide two games, was not held after the final whistle of all quarter-finals. The hope and anticipation prior to the draw was always an exciting aspect of the FA Cup and, regrettably, the removal of this piece of FA Cup tradition has affected the romance of the competition. Reinstating a Monday draw – perhaps a prime time Monday night show with representatives from each of the competing clubs and other guests, plus highlights of course – could actually increase the interest.

Regardless of the rights and wrongs of the draw, the fact was that Mancini's public strategy of focusing on each game was absolutely spot on. Drawing United brought an edge to the game, but it was absolutely vital his players – and to some extent fans – focused on the Reading game alone.

Ultimately, the Blues did defeat their Berkshire visitors 1-0 with a headed goal from Micah Richards in the 74th minute, but it had been a tough match. Richards: "It was very difficult. As the game went on, it got harder and harder. Reading defended very well."

Mancini recognised that the Blues had been in a real conflict at times: "They made it very difficult. It was not easy. They fought very hard."

On the balance of play City definitely deserved the victory but the tie could so easily have gone Reading's way. In the end however City's overall superiority and control won the match with Spaniard David Silva a consistent thorn to Reading.

Once the Blues were ahead, relieved chants of "Wemberley, Wemberley, We're the famous Man City and we're going to Wem-ber-ley" rang out. At full time the celebrations really began. Playing a semi-final at Wembley still seemed wrong, particularly an all-Manchester match, but the view of many was that a derby match of this significance deserved to be held at the best venue possible.

Ticketing, travel and costs would be significant issues of course, but City were now ready to make the most of the situation.

The 2011 FA Cup semi-final was to be City's first since 1981 and the prospect of facing United worried many fans. Those concerns intensified when City were knocked out of the Europa League 2-1 on aggregate to Dynamo Kyiv and were beaten 3-0 at Anfield (11th April) to a Liverpool side now managed by Kenny Dalglish. There had been a well-deserved and entertaining 5-0 victory over Sunderland on 3rd April, but some fans were nervous.

Wisely, supporters looked to see how they themselves could influence the game. Not in a negative way – throwing bottles at players' taking corners was not an approach City fans preferred – but in a constructive way. This meant, for example, that fans came up with

and promoted the idea of performing their Poznan celebration (which had grown in popularity throughout the season) while the Manchester United team was to be read out. It was a simple but excellent idea and one that would positively get the message across in a highly visible manner.

On semi-final day itself, City fans travelled early. The game wasn't to kick off until 5.15pm but Manchester's Blues seemed keen to get down to Wembley early. The motorways, particularly the M1, seemed to be full of cars with blue scarfs hanging out of windows and flags flying from aerials and roofs.

The supporters in each City car seemed to be laughing, joking and generally in positive mood. Whenever those vehicles passed United fans it seemed as if the Reds were in a much more negative frame of mind. The difference truly was remarkable. Could it be that it was actually United who feared the game more than City? Certainly the fans – or at least those travelling down from Manchester and the north - gave the impression that the Blues had nothing to lose.

This is actually a significant point worth considering further. Had United won the semi-final then clearly that would have hurt the Blues, but ultimately it would not have had much of an effect on City. The 35 years banner at Old Trafford would have rolled on another year no doubt, but that would hardly have been a devastating blow. A City victory, however, would bring the tearing down of that banner a step closer and – more significantly – give the Blues a real chance of glory. Once trophy success followed, City would be able to build further and United's days of local dominance would be nearer to ending.

As fans travelled down to Wembley, there was a lot of debate on the various scenarios. They talked of the 2009-10 League Cup semi-final which had brought hope but deep down fans had known that the Blues were not truly ready to challenge United. One year on, City were ready. This was the day they had dreamed of for some time. That is why so many Blues arrived at Wembley early.

Even a partially closed M1 – there had been a fire under the motorway – was unable to prevent Blues supporters from getting to the stadium in huge numbers earlier than their opponents. It was significant that Wembley Way and the streets around the stadium were noticeably more blue than red. There were pockets of United fans in the area – a bar/Indian restaurant close to the main car park was packed with Reds who had to curb their activities when police vans quelled their attempts at ridiculing City supporters – but visibly Wembley was Blue for some considerable time that morning.

On ITV, as part of their coverage, Roberto Mancini appeared to make an interesting prediction: "This is only the semi-final, after, will be the final." He was actually trying to remind everyone that beating United would not be significant on its own, it was not trophy success in itself. His opposite number, Alex Ferguson, was also interviewed. Interestingly, but perhaps appropriately from a United perspective, the comment that made its way on to the *Telegraph's* match commentary on the day focused on fans: "I hope the supporters behave themselves."

City fans remained, of course, the more positive as the kick off neared. When the teams were announced the Blues cheered each of their players before turning their backs, as planned, to the pitch when the United team was revealed. While United's starting eleven and substitutes were being named City fans bobbed up and down, arms round each other's shoulders, making noise. "Let's all do the Poznan" and other chants drowned out the announcer as the supporters took the attention away from the United players and on to their partying. Any neutral watching at home couldn't fail to be impressed with the attitude and spirit of the Blues.

When the game commenced those supporters of a Blue persuasion were inevitably nervous, but they did all they could to back their team. Journalist Mark Ogden accurately commented on Twitter: "#mcfc fans seem more up for this one than #mufc. More flags in the blue end, nonchalance at the red end."

It's a point the *Telegraph's* Thom Gibbs watching TV coverage agreed with. After five minutes of play his *Telegraph* live commentary included: "All the noise, at least from where I'm sitting in SE1, is coming from the City fans."

The atmosphere within the City sections was certainly extremely positive, although there were several tense moments for supporters in the opening fifteen minutes, including two goal scoring opportunities for Dimitar Berbatov. Duncan White, writing for *The Telegraph*, described the attempts: "The ball was shuttled rapidly from Carrick, to Scholes to Park, who tapped the ball into Berbatov's stride. Unlike the City defence, though, Joe Hart was mobile, sliding upright to reduce Berbatov's options and make an impressive save.

"Sensing vulnerability United pressed on and moments later Nani spun away from Zabaleta and found space on the by-line. His low cross was pretty much perfect for Berbatov, who had got in behind Joleon Lescott, but the United striker got the angle of contact wrong and sent the ball rising steeply above the bar from inside the six yard box. It was an embarrassing miss."

United seemed to have the upper hand and Berbatov's misses were potentially game changing moments. From that point on City improved. David Silva and Adam Johnson – making only his third start in 18 games after injury had side-lined him since January – were picking the ball up at key moments and starting to put the Reds in danger.

As the half wore on City became the side most likely to score. A shot from Gareth Barry hit the side netting, and Mario Balotelli sent another effort rising before dipping down causing United 'keeper Van der Sar to push it over. It was a great save caused by a ferocious effort from a very talented, but occasionally controversial, player. Another significant effort came in the 43rd minute from Yaya Touré, who galloped clear of Paul Scholes, ran twenty yards or so, before shooting powerfully. His attempt was blocked by Vidic and the resulting corner led to a Vincent Kompany shot going a little wide.

It didn't matter whether it was in the highest part of the stadium or the lowest City fans made sure they turned their backs as United's team was announced at the 2011 FA Cup semi-final.

At half time spirits were high. Supporters knew that City had ended brightly and that, apart from one or two of the more experienced players like Scholes, the Blues possessed more spirit and focus. Much had been made pre-match about Wayne Rooney's absence. The player had been suspended after supposedly celebrating a goal by shouting foul language directly into a camera in an aggressive manner. The media and others felt that Rooney's absence would work to City's advantage, but the Blues were also missing a talismanic goalscorer, Carlos Tévez. Despite the obvious investment in City in recent seasons, United were the side with the greater opportunity to fill the void. They had better playing resources and a much stronger squad.

City fans were full of positivity. They believed the Blues had enjoyed a better first half than United, certainly after the opening fifteen minutes, and they genuinely felt pleased with City's efforts. There was the usual concern, but this was already feeling as if it was going to be a successful day. The one downside was actually Wembley Stadium's expensive catering. Many of those that had decided to make a trip to the food outlets in the general supporter areas found themselves still queuing when the players came out for the second half.

United's team was out first and City kept them waiting – perhaps the Blues were stuck in a queue? Whether it was a ploy or not, it is worth recalling that Mancini's side had actually been second out for much of the season.

When play commenced City seemed confident and seven minutes later they were deservedly in front. The Blues were putting United under severe pressure, causing van der Sar to fail to clear the danger. Carrick had the ball but Yaya Touré saw an opportunity. He robbed the player, sped past Vidic and then sent the ball rocketing under the goalkeeper.

Musicians Mike Pickering (back) and Noel Gallager celebrate Yaya's goal in the FA Cup semi final

A deafening and prolonged celebration followed. It was a strange type of cheer and was reminiscent of City's last goal celebration in the old Wembley stadium back in 1999. That day Paul Dickov had brought City level to 2-2 in the Second Division play-off final in added time. The cheer was a mixture of relief, ecstasy, and euphoria. Against United, those same feelings and celebrations heralded Touré's wonderful strike. Thom Gibbs accurately and succinctly wrote for his *Telegraph* commentary: "City's fans make an exceptional noise."

The thoroughly deserved goal brought City added confidence and the Blues attacked at will. Efforts by Johnson and Balotelli followed within minutes. In fact Balotelli had a couple of excellent chances. He also played his part defensively when in the 69th minute he stopped Nani at a crucial point. Little was said at the time, but Balotelli's all-round play in this game was excellent. His critics inevitably focused on the negatives, and at full-time there would be further ammunition aimed in his direction, but his play offered much during this semi-final and should have grabbed the attention.

Eighteen minutes from time United's Paul Scholes, often a thorn in City's backside in earlier meetings, was sent off for a high tackle that hit Pablo Zabaleta in the knee area. Thom Gibbs recorded: "Zabaleta yelps in pain as Scholes nobbles him with a customary awful challenge." That said it all really.

A couple of minutes later Berbatov was substituted for Anderson as recognition that it had not been a great day for United's expensive star and, for a while, the Reds did try to put the Blues under pressure. Unlike the previous season however City remained in control and even as United fans came to life for the final period of added time, it was Mancini's side that seemed destined to hold their nerve.

When the final whistle went Mancini, Brian Kidd and the other members of the coaching team raced on to the pitch while the celebrations began in the stands. As the celebrations took place some tried to imply that Mario Balotelli had been out of order. His crime? He winked at Rio Ferdinand. As Thom Gibbs explained in his commentary: "It looks like Balotelli committed the heinous crime of winking at Rio Ferdinand. This riled Rio tremendously, he ran towards him with the hot blooded vigour of a man that had completely lost his mind, having to be restrained by people from both sides."

This had followed his initial view of the incident: "Ferdinand wants a fight with Balotelli, it appears he said or did something naughty on the final whistle. Ferdinand's eyeballing David Platt now. Possible sore loser syndrome."

Later it was suggested that Balotelli had celebrated by clenching his City badge on the United half of the pitch. Hardly an incident worth Ferdinand's reaction and nothing in comparison with Gary Neville's celebrations at

No matter what he did Mario Balotelli seemed to upset United's Rio Ferdinand.

Old Trafford the previous year, or indeed Wayne Rooney's celebration when he scored against City in the League in February and raced towards the City fans in the away section. Mancini was asked for his view: "I didn't see it. But I want to wait because every time it is Balotelli's fault. Every time." He added: "Maybe we can put him in jail? Next week. For this."

For the fans the semi-final success was a wonderful moment. For the first time since 1981 City had reached the final of the world's oldest knockout footballing competition. They deserved to celebrate. The players, recognising what it meant to supporters as well as to themselves, lined up in front of the goal, turned their back on the fans and performed the Poznan. That moment encapsulated everything that was right about City.

No matter what opponents, the media and neutrals might have said about the Club since its takeover, it had not lost its heart. In fact its heart had grown. It was still Manchester's community club and the players' Poznan performance proved that players and fans alike felt a great bond. That was team spirit.

As the celebrations continued Mancini told the media: "For me, today was important, but I want to win this trophy for this club, the supporters, for everybody who works at Manchester City. For these people."

He went on: "Yes, first we have to play another game. And probably the final will be harder than this. For us it's important to win the first trophies. If we can win the FA Cup, probably next year we can play for the title."

Fans loved the ambition of it all – ambition which ultimately was fulfilled – but, at this point, City were still the team that had not won a major trophy since 1976. The FA Cup had to be won before anyone could seriously accept the Blues had changed.

Mancini was questioned further and was specifically

asked whether he would prefer to win the FA Cup or qualify for the Champions League. For anyone who understood what ambitions the Club had this was a very easy question to answer and one Mancini responded to perfectly: "We want both. I think we deserve to play Champions League. We have spent one year between first and fourth spot. Everything is in our hands. But if we have the same spirit we had today, we will get fourth spot." Of course, Mancini was still targeting a higher finish, but the ambition he described was one that every supporter hoped could be fulfilled.

Beating United was a major step towards achieving City's overall aims. It was a significant progression, but it still caused some to question whether the victory was enough to preserve Mancini's job. Incredibly, there were still some who believed that Mancini would be dismissed at the end of the season. These views – often phrased as if to imply a certain inevitability – seemed at odds with what was actually happening at City.

At no time did Garry Cook, Khaldoon, Sheikh Mansour or any other senior member of the Club suggest Mancini's role would be under threat. Of course, he had targets to meet but, unlike many other clubs, City were not likely to make a knee-jerk reaction. The suggestion that Mancini was under constant pressure to justify his performance and was only a couple of games off being dismissed was inaccurate. One newspaper, *The Telegraph*, suggested the victory: "will buy Mancini valuable breathing space as he aims to secure his future at Eastlands."

The newspaper went on: "However, the City manager denied that Saturday's win eased the pressure on his position."

City's FA Cup final opponents would be Stoke, who beat Bolton 5-0 in their semi-final. Stoke had embarrassed Mancini's City before in the FA Cup when, in 2009-10, they beat the Blues 3-1 after extra time in the fifth round, and they were perceived as a bogey side by many fans. In addition, Tony Pulis' team had enjoyed a decent League campaign and were, by the time of the final, comfortably in the top half of the table free of relegation worries. They had no distractions. Nothing else to worry about. They could go out at Wembley and put everything they had into their game.

For City, the week leading up to the final included a vital League game with Tottenham that would, if they won, determine Champions League qualification. If however the Blues were defeated, the initiative would swing to Spurs.

Some, including author Colin Shindler who had frequently written and developed the impression of City as 'wonderful losers', felt that the Club would sacrifice everything for the Champions League. Shindler was quoted by Brian Viner in *The Independent* as being dissatisfied with the perceived emphasis: "he deplores the fact that the club were manifestly keener to finish fourth or possibly third in the Premier League than they are to win the Cup. 'Playing Champions League group matches on cold November nights against AEK Athens,' he said glumly. 'Is that what it's all about? Opening up a new tranche of money despite already being richer than everybody else?'"

Within the Club itself, however, it was never viewed in this way. Champions League qualification was important of course, but so was the FA Cup. Right from the moment the takeover happened, the Blues knew that success would be measured by fans – and of course across at Old Trafford where the banner on permanent display counted the number of years since City's last major success – by winning trophies. Garry Cook: "The ambition has been there since day one. Qualifying for the Champions League will bring us new opportunities, and the game of football is about finding success. Success can be measured in lots of different ways, but for most of us the obvious way is by silverware. If City qualify for the Champions League it won't be 'job done'. It's only part of our story."

A solitary own goal from Peter Crouch was enough to give City victory over Tottenham and a guarantee of a top four finish, but as Cook pointed out it did not end the ambition. The Blues still wanted to finish as high as possible – mathematically second place was still within grasp although that would require Chelsea to show relegation form in their final two games – and of course the FA Cup brought the opportunity to end the season with tangible trophy winning glory.

Finishing in the top four for the first time since the 1970s was an achievement in its own right, but winning the FA Cup would end 35 years without success at the highest levels of the game. This was what supporters wanted more than anything else, although the likes of Colin Shindler seemed quick to suggest that being in a position to challenge so soon was somehow worthless. He told Brian Viner: "This City team has been cooked in a microwave; very tasty, but if you really want something sumptuous you have to cook it for three hours in red wine, in the oven."

Shindler missed the point. City's leaders knew how long it should take to produce something special and that is exactly what they were planning. However football is such a fickle business at times that the media, fans, general public and sponsors demand immediate success. Realising this, the Blues' bosses searched for a way to bring success while also developing their long term strategy to create a sustainable and successful football club.

Using Shindler's analogy it should therefore be noted that City's exploits during the period following the takeover were like hors d'oeuvres. The owner arrived. He brought in his chef and kitchen staff, but he knew it would take some time for the main meal to be ready – in fact his kitchen wasn't yet suitable to even make a decent meal - and so he sent out a few hors d'oeuvres to ensure everyone had something to whet their appetite while creating the environment that will allow him to make a quality main meal. Hors d'oeuvres are often produced at a faster pace than the main meal and, at City, Champions League qualification and reaching the FA Cup final were City's appetisers while the main meal was being prepared behind the scenes, out of the public glare.

While some continued to snipe and carp about a quickly assembled squad, the fact was that the Blues were, like so many other successful clubs before them, concentrating on the steps needed to make them win their first trophy under Mancini. It was what the fans wanted. But this did not mean they were sacrificing everything else for short term game. It simply meant they were aiming to produce a quick appetiser while preparing something they hoped would prove to be a spell-binding signature dish.

The FA Cup Final was to be played on the same day as several Premier League and other domestic fixtures. National focus was shared, however as City were up against Stoke City the mood amongst both sets of fans was such that this FA Cup Final, more than many others since the dawn of the Premier League, was viewed with enormous significance. This was the top prize. This was the one that mattered.

By the time the players arrived at Wembley Stadium they were well-prepared and were, of course, well-motivated. After the usual cup final rituals, pitch inspections, and so on they walked out on to the turf kitted out in a new limited edition version of the Umbro City 'Mercer' jacket, named after the legendary manager Joe Mercer. This special edition was highly significant and featured the City Of Manchester coat of arms, first worn in a final by the Blues in 1926.

Fans had hoped the crest would appear on the front of the actual cup final shirt, however that space would be occupied by the Club's own crest. Some suggested this was a break with tradition, however the Blues took steps to ensure the City Of Manchester crest did appear on the actual playing shirts by incorporating it in the numbers on the shirt's back. Some traditionalists criticised this move, but the facts were that this was a significant nod to the Club's – and Manchester's – heritage; it was approved by Manchester City Council; and it had been inaccurate to say the Club had always worn Manchester's crest in every final anyway. City did not wear the crest in their first final in 1904, nor did they in 1970 when they represented Manchester in the region's first European Cup Winners' Cup final. The first time a Manchester side had won a European trophy outside of England.

In the stands, as the players made their way on to

the pitch, there was the usual nervousness about the game. City fans recognised that Stoke had been very successful in recent weeks and that they could pose a significant threat, but they also felt delighted to be at Wembley.

In the stands were a variety of former players and celebrity fans alongside normal supporters. Oasis' Liam Gallagher and his family were in a box, while other celebrity fans included an entertaining mix of legendary musicians, including The Smiths' Johnny Marr, comedians (Jason Manford and Eddie of 'Little & Large' fame), and Sportsmen (Ricky Hatton and Andrew Flintoff).

The Club invited over fifty former players including Bill Leivers from the 1956 success, ten members of the 1969 success, and others from every possible period of the Club's history. Significantly, these fifty players not only included some of the Blues' biggest and most successful stars but also those that held a special place in the affection of fans during the dark days of the eighties and nineties. Former FA Youth Cup winners Ian Brightwell and Paul Lake were there, as was 1999 play-off winning captain Andy Morrison. To the outside world the significance of City inviting Andy Morrison was not highlighted or even recognised, but it proved that those in charge of the Club knew the importance of his contribution to the City cause during a decade when the Blues' very existence was under threat.

Andy Morrison is an enormous example of the passion and spirit that makes up Manchester City's DNA. Whereas his achievements in a City shirt may not rank as highly as those of Bert Trautmann, Colin Bell, or Peter Doherty, to fans he represents the spirit and passion of the place. It is highly significant that the Club's leaders invited him and proves that no matter what the general media may claim about the owner and City's leaders, they do recognise the Club's heritage.

This point was further demonstrated when it became clear that several former players, most notably Francis Lee, Tony Book, Mike Summerbee and Colin Bell, were seated in the Royal Box. In previous finals the equivalent seats would have been occupied by directors, their friends, business acquaintances and so on, not former players. Frankly, it seems unlikely that any other club would treat so many players and their wives so well.

When the game commenced it was immediately obvious to the majority watching both at home and in the stadium that the Blues were in control. City seemed able to attack at will and appeared more than capable of keeping Stoke at bay.

Stoke's 'keeper Thomas Sorensen made several good saves, including a brilliant fingertip stop from a wonderful curling shot by Mario Ballotelli that was heading towards the top corner. That could easily have given City the lead, but there were other moments when Manchester's Blues could have scored. Efforts from

David Silva and Carlos Tévez proved City's dominance but, as with so many games during the season, supporters were biting their fingernails and wondering if their dominance would ensure victory.

It was apparent from fairly early on that Balotelli was having an excellent game. He managed to upset Stoke's defenders a little and had come under a great deal of physical pressure, most notably in the 14th minute when Robert Huth ran across his path and jabbed his forearm into Balotelli's chin. Earlier in the season the City man may have reacted, but at Wembley he seemed to take it all in his stride, even though Huth's actions had been crude and deliberate. Perhaps this had much to do with discussions that had taken place between Balotelli and Mancini in the days leading up to the final. The manager had encouraged the player to think about the team and to act more responsibly. It looked as if his words had been listened to.

Despite the youngster's efforts and the overwhelming City pressure, the game remained goalless at the interval.

The second half followed a similar pattern to the first. City remained on top in terms of possession, but it was not until the 74th minute that their superiority became clear in terms of goals. David Silva and Mario Balotelli exchanged passes inside a heavily congested penalty area. Balotelli made an attempt on goal, but his shot flicked off Ryan Shawcross and Marc Wilson before landing in front of the semi-final hero Yaya Touré.

As with his strike against Manchester United Touré ensured this attempt was goal bound. He powered home a left foot shot at speed past Sorensen and into the Stoke net. The goal was scored at the end allocated to City's support and the celebrations – both on the pitch and off it – lasted for what seemed an eternity. Touré found himself at the bottom of a large pile of players while in the stands supporters celebrated in the usual way before the Blues' Poznan celebration took hold.

The Poznan even saw a few former players and officials join in the celebration. In the Club Wembley area former Blue Ian Brightwell and Smith's guitarist Johnny Marr could be seen performing the celebration with other fans, while in the corporate boxes Liam Gallagher and his family were filmed doing it.

For the final fifteen minutes or so Stoke tried to find an equaliser, but the Blues more than matched their every move.

As the game neared its conclusion, goalkeeper Sorensen joined his Stoke team mates as a succession of corners and free-kicks brought a few worries for the Blues. To combat the threat in the dying moments the experienced – and tall - Patrick Vieira was brought on. City had coped well all afternoon with Stoke's set-pieces and balls into their penalty area and, sure enough, they cleared the danger.

From high up in the City section Marie Sharkey photographed Yaya Toure about to make the shot that brought the FA Cup winning goal.

The whistle brought manic celebrations but more significantly it was the end of a fairly barren 35-year period which had seen City fail to win a major trophy. There had been promotions and in 2002 the Club had won the old League Championship trophy, but these were not regarded as major trophies any significant side should be competing for. Roberto Mancini accurately summed up the mood of the Blues: "We have laid down the first brick today. Now we can build a house on it. The first trophy is always important. It is about changing the history of the club and developing the mentality of winners. We have won a very important trophy now, and it was always going to be important for us to get that first win.

"We have made a small piece of history of Manchester City. But we start now."

The trophy presentation saw Stoke first to collect their runners-up medals. City fans applauded vigorously. They recognised that this had been an incredible season for the Potters and also remembered back to 1998 when a match between the two sides resulted in relegation to the third tier of English football for them both. The period since 1998 had seen the two sides work hard to re-establish themselves and, quite simply, competing in a FA Cup final was a remarkable achievement

considering both clubs seemed dead and buried a decade or so earlier.

When City went up to collect their medals the vast majority of Stoke fans stayed behind to witness the presentation. This was unusual. In recent years the losing side's fans have tended to start disappearing from the stadium before their own team had reached the bottom step.

Carlos Tévez was the player to perform the historic trophy raising moment, but he was not the first Blue to get his hands on the famous old trophy. The FA had decided that Corporal Mark Ward, an inspirational soldier who had been awarded the Military Cross for bravery in Afghanistan, would present the FA Cup and co-incidentally he was a Manchester City fan. The former Offerton High School pupil admitted: "I didn't sleep a wink the night before but I was very honoured. Football is a massive part of Army life both playing and supporting. I've always been a big fan and also play in my battalion's football team. When we are away on tour if there is ever a chance to get together and watch a game we do."

The Mercian Regiment soldier brought an important human touch to the whole affair. Despite the general focus on City's perceived wealth, the Blues remained a community club. Although they did not select who would present the trophy they would have been absolutely delighted that the presentation was made by an ordinary person who had experienced an extraordinary life.

Of course, it was also an interesting coincidence that the FA Chairman was David Bernstein, City's former Chairman. Bernstein had been loved by the majority of supporters during his tenure as City's senior official and he, of course, had been well received by fans on Cup final day. Somehow the sight of Bernstein smiling behind Balotelli as Tévez lifted the trophy seemed highly appropriate. Bernstein had helped rescue the Blues in the late 1990s and without his professionalism back then – and of course the drive and focus of Chris Bird who was Managing Director under Bernstein - it is highly unlikely the Club would have recovered from their fall through the divisions.

In the stands some supporters wept with joy as the players embarked on their lap of honour. The fans sang, cheered and celebrated as the long wait finally ended. More significantly however this did not feel as if it was the end of the journey for a trophy, it felt as if this was simply the beginning of City's trophy-winning story.

The last major success in 1976 should have been one of many and City did come close to winning the League the following year, but fate had played its hand and the Blues missed the title by a solitary point. The side of the Seventies had opportunities and it was packed with highly entertaining players, but circumstances meant that Peter Swales, City's Chairman at the time, focused too much on eclipsing Manchester United than making plans that would ensure sustained success for the Blues. He often admitted that was his ambition. Now, however, City's leaders were using their neighbours as a benchmark. When Garry Cook, Roberto Mancini, Brian Marwood and the others first heard of the infamous

Joe Hart and Micah Richards celebrating their first major trophy win.

banner counting the years since City's last major success that was on display at Old Trafford, they did not wallow in self-pity. The banner did not make them think that City's fate was failure. Instead they saw the banner as a challenge. They did not need the banner to motivate them but being able to tear it down did provide the Blues' manager and leaders with an added –and highly visible - incentive.

Victory at Wembley ensured the banner was no longer relevant. To prove the point a banner produced in a similar style somehow found its way on to the pitch and was paraded around reading '00 Years'. The following Monday the real banner was taken down by United officials at Old Trafford amid rumours suggesting that the Reds would create a new version recalling the number of years since City last won the League. Many involved with the Blues hoped the Reds did install something like that as, they felt, this would add further focus to City's ambition, while others suggested that the obsession with the Blues' achievements proved that City continued to impact more on United's psyche than the Reds actually did on the Blues.

Goalkeeper Joe Hart emphasised this point when, on the pitch while celebrating, he was asked by an interviewer about Manchester United: "We couldn't care less what they do at Old Trafford. This has nothing to do with Man United. We're Man City and it's about these players. We're here to win the final and to win the Cup. We had to beat the best to get here and we beat a good side today."

Inevitably, the celebrations went on for some time and words will never do them justice. 1981 FA Cup final captain Paul Power, who had been sat with former Academy boss Jim Cassell, stood in the Club Wembley seated area taking the scene in. A dedicated Blue throughout his playing career – Power was once devastated when he scored for Everton against City and admitted that he had hoped his effort would miss the target - the former star knew what this moment meant and, together with Cassell, he knew how low the Club had actually fallen before the arrival of first Thaksin Shinawatra and then Sheikh Mansour.

Outside the stadium, groups sang and cheered. People danced wildly, waving their flags. Strangers were hugged. Well-known and popular supporter Tommy Muir from the Cheadle branch of the Supporters Club was seen lifting a very good quality replica of the trophy. Later still he was seen at the front of a coach holding it up to let fans see as he drove past crowds heading away from Wembley. Some, no doubt, thought it was the real deal.

Elsewhere former City players were spotted by fans in various pubs, while Kevin Keegan, the manager who had re-established the side as a Premier League outfit almost a decade earlier, was mobbed when he

The winning smile. Carlos Tevez.

crossed the street to a waiting vehicle half a mile from the stadium. Chants of "Super Kevin Keegan" baffled fans further down the road, oblivious to the celebrations taking place at Keegan's corteousy car.

In other parts of the Wembley area, Stoke supporters also celebrated. Sure they were disappointed at losing the final but many of the bars that surrounded the stadium were full of supporters of both teams. The Stoke fans sang songs about Europe, including one to the tune of Yellow Submarine that claimed "We're all going on a European Tour, a European Tour…" They had qualified for the Europa League by finishing as FA Cup runners-up to the Champions League bound City.

Cars, coaches and mini-buses leaving Wembley were decked out with blue flags and scarves, and at almost every motorway service station on the journey north, City supporters were visible. Their celebrations, humour and positivity seemed to bring a smile to the faces of neutrals and others wherever they went.

Manchester City's supporters thoroughly deserved their moment of celebration, but the most significant aspect was that this continued to feel as if the Blues were at the beginning of their trophy-winning journey, not the end. As Micah Richards accurately summed up: "Words can't describe it. This is the start. This is the first one and

it's the most important one. We have got to build from this."

The Tuesday after the final City and Stoke met again. This time in the League. This was, inevitably, an awkward fixture to stage as supporters wanted to see the FA Cup but any celebration could have looked boastful.

Most football clubs would be expected to perform some form of post-match celebration with the trophy on display. It's part and parcel of the game and something that no one could have criticised City for, after all when Manchester United were presented with their Premier League trophy after the game with Blackpool a few days later no one suggested that United's celebrations were out of place even though their opponents were relegated that day. The Reds were champions and deserved their moment and, similarly, City were FA Cup winners and could easily have performed their celebrations after the League game. However, City showed tremendous empathy with Stoke when they deliberately chose not to have the trophy on display or use it in celebrations.

City's decision was admirable and proved that they had respect for the game and their opponents. On the night of the match they also made a point of proving that the FA Cup final had been a friendly one, played between two sides who truly valued it, when they took time out of their normal pre-match schedule to ensure the Club acknowledged the wonderful efforts made by Stoke City and their supporters in making the Cup Final a tremendous occasion.

About twenty minutes before kick-off a long announcement was made thanking Stoke's personnel, players, management and supporters for helping to make the FA Cup Final so special. This was followed by the playing of the Tom Jones' hit Delilah, Stoke's anthem equivalent of Blue Moon.

The game itself was not only an easy victory for Mancini's Blues but it also proved the quality of the side he had assembled and, most newsworthy, demonstrated quite clearly the significance of Carlos Tévez during the season. After fourteen minutes the Argentinian played a one-two with James Milner, then hoodwinked Stoke's Wilkinson and Shawcross as he dummied this way and that, before firing home with a perfect and clinical finish from a tight angle. Ed Ballard, writing for the *Telegraph's* online service gave the most apt description when he explained: "He simply humiliated those defenders."

That goal placed Tévez one behind United's Berbatov at the top of the Premier League goalscoring chart. Fifty or so minutes of action later, City's star equalled the record with an absolutely spell-bounding 35 yard free kick given after a foul on De Jong. Tévez powered a curving, ferocious effort over the wall and into the top right corner. It was an amazing goal – later deemed goal of the month on the BBC's Match Of The Day programme – and voted City's best of the season.

Tévez's second made it 3-0 to the Blues. It had followed a headed goal from Joleon Lescott in the 53rd minute.

After Tévez's second goal fans urged the Argentinian forward. There was a clear desire to see him take the lead in the race for the Premier League's golden boot. In the eightieth minute it appeared the Blues had been awarded a penalty after Milner was brought down. The City captain rushed to take the kick, but it soon became apparent that the referee had actually awarded a free-kick just outside the box. Sadly, the resulting kick missed the target.

In the 89th minute Tévez was substituted for Dedryck Boyata and, deservedly, the striker received a fantastic ovation. A few minutes later the game ended with City lying in third place after leapfrogging over Arsenal. With only one match to go in the Premier League campaign the advantage was now with the Blues. All they needed to do on the final day of the season was to match Arsenal's result and they would finish third. There was also the possibility that Mancini's men could end the season on level points with second placed Chelsea – the London club's goal difference was significantly greater than City's however.

After the full time whistle, the City players left the field to allow their Stoke counterparts to take the applause of the travelling support. Significantly, the vast majority of City fans also applauded and cheered the Stoke side and also their fans. The usual banter had appeared at times during the match – as it should – but post-match the sides seemed to recognise that this had been an incredibly successful season for them both. Significantly, a few Stoke supporters remained behind to watch City's own celebrations and to return the gesture.

Once the Stoke celebrations and acknowledgements had been completed City's players returned to the field. Shaun Wright-Phillips and Micah Richards – two players who had experienced some of City's low points during their careers – held a banner thanking fans for their support as the players walked around the Eastlands turf.

Roberto Mancini and his coaching staff took to the field and walked with the players. For the first time at City's new stadium the end of season lap of honour actually meant something.

As promised, the FA Cup was kept well-hidden. Some suggested the Cup could have been brought out after the majority of Stoke fans had left, but City stuck to their word. Instead, they promised, the FA Cup would appear at the Club's homecoming parade the following Monday. The Blues' dignity and desire to do things the right way was refreshing.

Although the Stoke victory had felt like the end to the season for many fans, it was still not the final Premier League act, that was to come on 'Survival Sunday' as the media were branding the final day. With almost all domestic issues resolved it was inevitable the attention would shift to the six or so clubs involved in the relegation battle, but for Mancunian Blues the focus was on events at Bolton.

In the end City defeated the Trotters 2-0 with goals from Joleon Lescott and Edin Dzeko. Lescott's rather odd headed goal in the 43rd minute from a corner was an example of a player being in the right place at the right time. The ball seemed to hit his forehead and go in. From the stands it looked like a great header with the player deliberately meeting the ball, but television replays brought a few smiles later that night when it was clear he had been unsighted. It looked as if the ball had hit his face with force and then rebounded into the net. It was such an odd goal and brought some laughter from the player.

With City leading 1-0, Dzeko came on as substitute for Johnson and he made an immediate impression. Paul Wilson, writing for *The Guardian*, explained: "The visitors sent on Edin Dzeko after an hour, for the £27m January signing to make the game safe with virtually his first touch. Strictly speaking Dzeko needed two touches to beat Jaaskelainen. His first effort from Barry's left-wing cross was blocked, but the ball bounced kindly and with

The first, but by no means the last, City homecoming of the decade.

the goalkeeper down it was a simple matter for Dzeko to turn and put the ball into an empty net for his second league goal of the season."

When the final whistle was blown the players and manager celebrated once more. Mancini's team was now guaranteed to be competing in the Champions League proper without having to face a potentially tricky qualifying tie during the summer. They had finished third – or joint second as fans dubbed it – on equal points with Chelsea but the London club had a nine goal advantage when it came to goal difference. Arsenal were fourth with three points less than City while Spurs were fifth, nine points behind the Blues.

When everything was taken into consideration and the final acts of the season were recorded, it was clear City had enjoyed a wonderful, record-breaking year. Roberto Mancini became the first manager to guide the Blues to major trophy success in his first full season (Others like Cowan and Keegan had won the second tier title); Joe Hart created a new City goalkeeping record for the number of clean sheets, 29, in a season and won the Premier League's Golden Glove award for 18 clean sheets; the Blues beat their best ever Premier League points tally; achieved their best home record in the Premier League; and Carlos Tévez shared the Golden Boot award for most goals in the Premier League.

No matter which way the season was reviewed, it had been a wonderful and hugely successful campaign.

The night after the Bolton game City staged their first official homecoming victory parade since 1976. Unlike past years where the parade would end at Albert

Square, the historic heart of the city, the idea was to start the homecoming there and travel to the City Of Manchester Stadium for a party within the Club's home. Free tickets for the stadium event were distributed, while other fans chose to position themselves at Albert Square and along the route.

Police and safety officers limited the number of fans allowed in Albert Square – a necessary but unwelcome change from previous parades as far as fans were concerned – but the scenes were still amazing with a sea of blue and white filling the square. At one point the entire square performed the Poznan celebration as Manchester partied.

In total it was estimated that there were around 100,000 fans positioned along the homecoming route and in the stadium.

At the stadium fans waited for the return of their heroes. Music from Kid British, Supra and Badly Drawn Boy kept them entertained. Badly Drawn Boy in particular made a rousing speech in between songs which captured the mood perfectly. This was a time to celebrate the success but it was appropriate that much effort went in to ensuring that the Club's previous FA Cup win in 1969 was also remembered. Tributes to Malcolm Allison and Neil Young – the brilliant coach and the Cup Final goalscorer in 1969 who both passed away during the season – were shown while members of their families, including Young's wife and Allison's daughter, were brought on to the pitch.

A little later four members of the 1969 team were introduced to fans. Francis Lee, Glyn Pardoe, Mike

Summerbee and captain Tony Book came out on to the pitch with the FA Cup. Book, clearly enjoying the moment, placed the trophy carefully on a plinth before he and the others were interviewed. This was all very entertaining and well received by fans as they waited for the present day side to emerge, but the best moment of this period of waiting came when the four 1969 FA Cup winners took part in the Poznan celebration. The entire stadium, including those in the Directors' Box, rose to perform the Poznan but the highlight was seeing Lee, Book, Pardoe and Summerbee stood as a group with their arms across each other's shoulders as they bobbed up and down in the centre of the field. It was a great sight and one replayed on Sky TV the following day.

The four heroes then moved to the side of the stage and lined up, two on either side of the blue carpet that had been placed from the tunnel to the centre. Then the present day team were introduced in groups to wild acclaim, followed by Roberto Mancini and his coaching staff. They all deserved the adulation.

Once everyone was out and on the stage, Tony Book was asked to present the trophy to his 2011 equivalent. It was a fitting touch, one generation of FA Cup winners passing the mantle on to the next. The achievements of the side Book captained – League Champions, FA Cup winners, ECWC winners, and League Cup winners – were of course significantly better than those of the

current team, however whereas the 1969 FA Cup came midway through City's glory years, the 2011 success was anticipated to herald a new era. It was highly possible that Roberto Mancini's men could eclipse the achievements of Joe Mercer's talented team.

After the presentation, the players, management and coaches, plus assorted family members, went on another lap of honour. The night ended with a firework display. Many fans had left the stadium by this time as they simply did not know it was happening and had started to leave once the players disappeared down the tunnel. As the terraces emptied an announcement was made asking fans not to go anywhere and those that stayed were treated to an excellent display. Across in the city centre, those that had remained behind after the parade had left for the stadium, could see the fireworks reaching into the sky from Eastlands.

In future years some may suggest City's commemorations were a little excessive – a week later police and civic leaders estimated that United's Premier League winning parade attracted somewhere between 20,000 to 50,000 - but for fans and the Club in general it was very important to celebrate.

City were trophy winners once more. The big question now was could City mount a serious challenge for League success?

2009-2011 SUMMARY

Highest League Attendance: 47,393 Arsenal, 24/10/10
Highest Cup Attendance: 46,067 Manchester United, 19/01/10 (League Cup)
Managers: 2008 – 2009 Mark Hughes & 2009 – Roberto Mancini

Seasonal Record:

Season	League	Posn	FA Cup	League Cup	Other	Leading Scorer	Average Attendance
2009-10	Premier	5	Rnd 5	Semi-final		Tévez 23	45,512
2010-11	Premier	3	Winners	Rnd 3	Europa League Rnd 3	Tévez 20	45,880

2011 FA CUP RUN

R3	Leicester City	A	D	2-2
	Leicester City	H	W	4-2
R4	Notts County	A	D	1-1
	Notts County	H	W	5-0
R5	Aston Villa	H	W	3-0
R6	Reading	H	W	1-0
SF	Manchester United	N*	W	1-0
F	Stoke City	N*	W	1-0

= Wembley Stadium

	P	W	D	L	F	A
HOME	4	4	0	0	13	2
AWAY	4	2	2	0	5	3
TOTAL	8	6	2	0	18	5

FINAL DETAILS

14 May 2011 at Wembley Stadium
Manchester City 1-0 Stoke City
CITY: Hart, Richards, Kolarov, De Jong, Lescott, Kompany, Barry (Johnson), Yaya Toure, Balotelli, Tevez (Zabaleta) & Silva (Vieira).
STOKE CITY: Sorensen, Wilkinson, Wilson, Huth, Shawcross, Whelan (Pugh), Pennant, Delap (Carew), Jones, Walters & Etherington (Whitehead).
GOAL: Toure
ATTENDANCE: 88,643
REFEREE: M Atkinson (West Yorkshire)
MANAGER: Roberto Mancini
CAPTAIN: Carlos Tevez

Sergio Aguero celebrates scoring the goal that brought the Premier League title.

Worthy Champions

"Whoa! Oh! Oh Jeff! It's 3-2. Oh My God! I've never seen anything like it. It's gone mad. It's gone mad, Jeff. Mancini's on the pitch running about. What a... They're all cuddling each other. They've got love bites and everything... Oh my... Oh my... What a goal by Agüero! Jeff, he gets the ball... so cool. They're all cuddling each other. Jeff, I've played in a League Championship with drama but nothing like this. It's unbelievable. 3-2!"

Former Arsenal star Paul Merson reacting to the final goal of the Premier League season alongside Jeff Stelling in the Sky Sports studio, 13th May 2012

2011-2012 Last Gasp

Winning the FA Cup in 2011 was a landmark moment and one that enabled everyone connected with the Club to feel satisfaction that the investment and commitment was worth it. It was a marvellous achievement but it was important that it was not accepted as the end of the journey. This had to be the starting point. The success had to be followed by further glory if City were to fulfil ambitions. Everyone was hopeful that the FA Cup winners would make a serious challenge for further silverware in 2011-12.

Fans wanted the League title and, after coming third the previous season, it was clear that Mancini's men had the ability to mount a challenge. The wider world still expected Manchester United to be the dominant force but City were hopeful. At the start of the season Mancini made it clear what he thought the Blues needed to do: "To win the title we need to score more than last year." To achieve this the manager had signed Sergio Agüero from Atletico Madrid for a fee reported to be around £38m. During 2010-11 the player had netted 20 league goals for the Spanish side. Mancini: "Agüero can play any position – he can be the main striker, he can play behind the striker, he can play left or right. He is not tall but he is quick and strong and he can score a lot of goals. Now he can play behind Dzeko, Carlos or Mario."

Agüero was on the bench when the season commenced with the second all-Manchester meeting at Wembley in four months. However, unlike the 2011 FA Cup semi-final, the Community Shield match ended in a 3-2 United win. City had raced to a 2-0 lead by half time with goals from Lescott (38 mins) and one from Dzeko a minute into added time. United came back at the Blues and scored their winner four minutes into added time at the end of the match.

The Community Shield defeat hurt of course but, as the season progressed, it became clear that the side had learned another important lesson that day. United, under Alex Ferguson, had become renowned for scoring in the dying seconds of a match. If City were to win the title and find further success they needed to ensure they adopted the same sort of mentality. Losing in added time was not something title winners should experience.

Although the Reds took the plaudits at the annual curtain-raiser it was the Blues who ultimately gained most from the Community Shield result. It was another step towards strengthening City's resolve.

Eight days after the derby match the Premier League campaign opened at the Etihad Stadium – the City Of Manchester Stadium had been renamed during the close season - with the visit of newly promoted Swansea City. New signings Stefan Savic and Sergio Agüero made their debuts as substitutes that day while another summer arrival, Gael Clichy, started the match. Clichy had made his first appearance at Wembley the previous week.

City, wearing their new all-blue kit which had caused some fans to criticise the break with tradition and the loss of white shorts, faced an attacking-minded Swansea side looking to make their mark following promotion.

Swansea pressured the Blues throughout the opening thirty minutes. Mancini's side clearly had the quality but the visitors seemed the more determined. However, the Blues had been soaking up the pressure and taking stock of what Swansea had to offer. Whereas earlier City sides may have become anxious during the period of pressure, the new Blues were more than equipped to deal with a determined opposition.

The game remained goalless until the 57th minute when David Silva dodged past Leon Britton before progressing from City's half and well into Swansea's. He passed to Adam Johnson, who raced forward, cut inside and then tried to curl a shot past the Swansea 'keeper. The shot was saved but the ball dropped in front of Dzeko who, from six yards out, sent the ball home.

A minute or so later Sergio Agüero came on for Nigel De Jong and within nine minutes of his arrival the Argentinian made it 2-0 with a simple tap-in. Three minutes later he played his part in the third goal.

Agüero lifted the ball over the advancing Swansea 'keeper and then managed to hook it back to a waiting Silva on the penalty spot who sent his own shot into the net.

By this time Mancini's side were in total control of the match, although Swansea were still playing decent football themselves and certainly did not adopt negative tactics as many other sides may have done.

Shortly before the end Agüero made it 4-0 with an absolutely brilliant swerving 30 yard shot. Afterwards Mancini was delighted with his new signing: "I'm not surprised by what I saw tonight. Agüero has scored a lot of goals in Spain and Argentina – he's a fantastic striker."

Two debut day goals – significantly he was only on the pitch for around 31 minutes – made Agüero a hero from the start and caused the wider football world to look at City's new signing as a hugely positive arrival to the Premier League. Inevitably, Agüero was in the starting line-up for the following game away at Bolton.

At the Reebok goals from Silva (26th minute) and Barry (37th minute) brought a 2-0 lead, but Bolton pulled one back from Klasnic only two minutes later. Dzeko made it 3-1 two minutes after the break, but Davies made it 3-2 in the 63rd minute. A few minutes later Agüero was replaced by Carlos Tévez. Tévez had appeared to be on his way out of the Club during the summer and once Agüero was signed most assumed the two men would not play together for the Blues, but a week before the Bolton match manager Mancini made the Tévez position perfectly clear: "He is here and he is staying here. It is difficult for him to leave."

Of course, everyone believed Tévez would be on his way before the end of August and if not probably in January. However, as with many comments and rumours during the year no one could predict in August 2011 how the season would develop for City and Tévez.

The Bolton result caused some to suggest that City were not quite the right force for a title challenge even though they had won the match and scored a total of 7 goals in their opening two matches. Some argued that Bolton were destined to struggle – this became fact as the side was ultimately relegated – and that Swansea was another weak side, and so victories had been expected. The view was that Mancini's City would be 'found out' when they faced a strong side capable of mounting a challenge for Champions League qualification.

The critics did not have long to wait as the Blues' third match was away to Tottenham Hotspur. Spurs had lost 3-0 to Manchester United six days earlier at Old Trafford but Harry Redknapp's team had been the better side for the first half and were unlucky to go a goal behind after 60 minutes. All in all Tottenham were recognised as a quality team and a real threat.

At White Hart Lane City soon proved that they

were developing into a formidable side as a thrilling performance brought Mancini's men a superb 5-1 victory. On a day when Samir Nasri made his debut the Blues opened the scoring in the 33rd minute. Nasri played his part by providing a pass from the left wing to Edin Dzeko who scored from close range.

Around 7 minutes later another Nasri cross was headed home by Dzeko to make it 2-0 as City took control of the match. In the second half Dzeko doubled his goals tally with another close range effort nine minutes after the break and one from outside the penalty area two minutes into added time at the end. In between those goals Agüero made it 4-0 after a hour and Spurs pulled one back through Kaboul in the 68th minute.

The game ended in a convincing 5-1 victory with Dzeko understandably gaining most of the praise, although it was clear that Nasri had enjoyed a tremendous debut. Mancini was delighted. He had been keen to sign the player two months earlier but the negotiations had dragged on. On 12th August the manager had expressed concern that the delay in signing Nasri could affect the Blues' progress: "We need this player. I'm worried because I don't have this player today and I probably won't have him tomorrow. We play three games in August. I am worried because every manager wants all the players quickly. I hope we can have this player in the next two or three days."

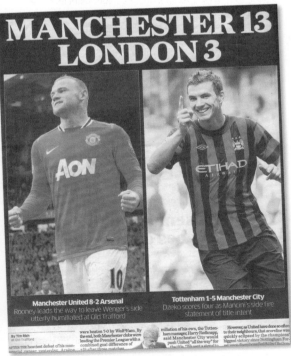

Mancunian supremacy in 2011-12.

Ultimately, Nasri arrived in time for August's third League game and made a wonderful start in a great victory. Defeating Spurs gave supporters a belief that title success was possible. Sure the season had only just started and the Community Shield match had ended in defeat but, when the season commenced, Spurs were viewed as serious contenders and, in truth, the media loved to focus on Harry Redknapp's management style.

Everything appeared to be progressing well for the Blues but then the Club was rocked by a scandal that was ultimately to see the end of Chief Executive Garry Cook's time at the Club. Had the story happened a few years earlier when City were not likely to challenge for the game's top honours then it is likely it would not have received the coverage it did, but the Blues' higher profile meant that any story, particularly one that looked like a cover up, would gain significant coverage.

The story centred around contract negotiations for Nedum Onuoha the previous year. Onuoha's mother was acting for the player during the negotiations but she had also been suffering with cancer. The *Manchester Evening News* revealed that an email sent by her in which she highlighted that she had been "ravaged by cancer" was returned with comments saying: "Brian, Ravaged with it! I don't know how you sleep at night. You used to be such a nice man when I worked with you at Nike. G."

The assumption was that the email had been sent by Garry Cook and meant for Brian Marwood, however Cook initially denied sending the email. An investigation followed and the following Friday, 9th September, Cook resigned. Chairman Khaldoon Al Mubarak issued a statement: "Garry has made a remarkable contribution to Manchester City Football Club over the past three years. His judgement in this matter should in no way lead to his accomplishments being overlooked. On every level, the club is unrecognisable from the organisation which he inherited and our staff and supporter services, community outreach and commercial activity have seen unparalleled growth under his direction with yet more projects to be realised on the horizon.

"On behalf of Sheikh Mansour and the Board, I would like to thank him for his energy and tireless commitment to serving all those connected with the football club. He will always be welcome at Manchester City."

It was appropriate that Khaldoon highlighted the contribution Cook had made. His handling of the email situation was not great. It did cause negative media coverage of the Club and bring some suffering to the Onuoha family, however Cook had improved almost every aspect of the Club since his arrival. He had turned a mid-table side with poor facilities off the pitch into one that had achieved success on the pitch and achieved a great deal of good for the local community.

At the time of his departure Cook issued his own statement: "I am privileged to have held my position at Manchester City Football Club and to have experienced the opportunities that it has presented. The privilege is in part offset however by the significant personal focus which has at times, detracted from the magnificent achievements of those working at the football club.

"It is that factor, together with my error of judgement in this matter that has prompted me to reach this decision, which I believe is in the best interests of the football club.

"I wish Roberto and his team and all of the fans and supportive partners of the Club the very best for exciting times ahead. I would also like to put on record my unreserved thanks to Sheikh Mansour, Khaldoon Al Mubarak and the Board and all of the very talented staff at the Club for their support throughout my tenure at Manchester City. I know the Club will go from strength to strength."

While the Club searched for a new CEO, director John MacBeath took on the role on a temporary basis.

The media tended to focus on the negatives of Garry Cook's time at City, but supporters had mixed views. Some questioned why the email, which the newspapers reported was sent in October 2010, took eleven months to become such an issue. They speculated on the reasons why and the issues behind it. Everyone had sympathy for the Onuoha family and fans were very supportive of Nedum Onuoha during this period, of course.

Some fans did believe that the departure of Cook was something that City's rivals had been after for some time. It was clear that the CEO had made major progress during his time in Manchester and his original aims, though often ridiculed, of turning the Blues into a name renowned around the world and one capable of challenging the game's elite both at home and internationally were looking achievable.

During his time at the Club Cook had become a passionate Blue. He cared, perhaps a little too much at times, about every aspect of the Club. A few weeks before his departure he explained how he wanted to see improvement everywhere and wouldn't rest until the Blues were the best across the board: "We want to be the best in sales, the best in marketing, the best in customer relations and so on. But what do we mean by best? We benchmark around the world, looking at the key factors for success in every area. We don't simply look at other sports clubs in the UK, we benchmark the best clubs and businesses globally."

Cook also made it clear that he believed that right at the heart of everything had to be the Club's supporters and Manchester itself: "Our ethos is that this football club is at the heart of this city, and that the fans are at the heart of this football club. So we talk about heart and soul a lot. We talk about pride and passion as part of our values. They epitomise most of the fans.

"We want anyone who touches the Club at any point, whether it's in the shop, in the stadium, on the website, wherever, to go 'wow' that is really cool. That's different. Better than I've ever seen. This has to be a premium experience whether you are in Abu Dhabi, New York, Beijing or Beswick. We know that fans cannot always get to games, so if you come to us via a digital website then you'll want a positive experience with us as well. If you become involved with our community work you will get a premium experience. That is our aim."

Some of Cook's phraseology throughout his time was not typical football-speak but he did talk with a passion about his determination that City fans would be central to everything the Club did. That was not the case at many other clubs, nor was it always the case at City.

Whether his critics and opponents liked it or not under Garry Cook the Blues had made huge progress. The question now had to be could City continue to progress in all areas without their dynamic CEO?

In 2002-03 Managing Director Chris Bird resigned and, in the years that followed, City missed his dedication, drive and empathy with fans. The departure was also followed by the loss of Chairman David Bernstein. This affected the Club's development at times during the following years. Would Cook's loss have a similar impact or would the Blues progress to plan?

James Ducker, writing for *The Times*, believed Cook's departure would not send the Club into meltdown: "There would have been a time not too long ago when the resignation of their chief executive would have constituted a crisis at City. It is a reflection of the transformation that has taken place that they are able to breeze through this unsavoury chapter with the minimum of fuss.

"City are a far different animal from the one Cook encountered when he joined in 2008. And that has much to do with the achievements of their chief executive."

Ducker also talked of Cook's "tireless work overhauling a club who had become a byword for mediocrity and misdirection."

By the time of Cook's departure the Blues were second in the Premier League on the same number of points as Manchester United, but the Reds had a slightly better goal difference – they had scored one more goal – after three matches. But with fixtures occurring at various times City had the chance to go top briefly if they defeated – or even drew – with Wigan on 10th September.

City managed a 3-0 victory in the 3pm kick-off at home to Wigan with Agüero scoring a hat-trick. Vincent Kompany had been appointed captain by this time, replacing Carlos Tévez, but Agüero, of course, gained all the headlines. Manager Mancini, however, was determined to share the praise and began with the role of Tévez who started the match and lasted 60 minutes: "Carlos Tévez is not at 100% fitness at the moment. He needed this game, it was important to play him and he did well, but he will need maybe two or three more games to get back to 100%. David Silva is a top player, but so is Sergio Agüero and Yaya Touré. For them it is easy to play football. We could have made this game easier for ourselves, I think we must have had 15 chances in the first half and scored one goal."

Wigan's manager, Roberto Martinez, believed the Blues were now a real threat: "City have gone to a different level, they can be regarded as title contenders now." Fans already recognised this, but City's high scoring – they'd netted 15 goals in four games – was making rival players, managers, fans and the media take notice. However, Manchester United beat Bolton 5-0 in the evening match later that day causing some to suggest that whatever City achieved the Reds would still be one step ahead.

It did look as if the two Manchester sides could play leapfrog all season and, to many neutrals, Alex Ferguson's experience would give his side the edge. It was an easy story to create and when the Blues drew 2-2 at Fulham and the Reds beat Chelsea 3-1 in their next League games the media belief that United were to be the dominant force once more intensified. They suggested City were some way off title success with Matt Hughes in *The Times* commenting: "For all their ambition City should set their sights considerably lower, at least in the short term, At an admittedly early stage of the season City trail United by two points, five goals and light years in terms of mentality."

He added: "It is City's misfortune that everything they do is seen in the context of their neighbours' achievements, but the bottom line is there is no way United would have let such a dominant position slip."

Mancini's men had been two goals up – thanks to Agüero – shortly after half time and comfortably ahead in every area, before Fulham equalised through Zamora (55th minute) and Murphy (75th). City had most of the possession and should have comfortably seen off Fulham, but the suggestion that the Blues should not be focusing on a title bid was unfair. City were still undefeated in the League and there had only been five League games. If they were in the same position on the last day of the season fair enough, but this was only mid-September.

The following week City defeated Everton 2-0 with goals from substitute Mario Balotelli and James Milner. It was an important victory over a team that had been a bit of a bogey side in recent seasons, and ensured the Blues were now back on equal points with Ferguson's side who had drawn 1-1 at Stoke despite leading at half time – perhaps United should have set their sights lower?

Three days after beating Everton City faced Bayern Munich in the Champions League. It was to be an eventful night and one which ultimately had a bearing on the entire season.

The Blues' Champions League campaign had seen the Club drawn in the same group as Bayern, Napoli and Villarreal. Both Villarreal and Munich were regular competitors in the Champions League and, on paper, were a real threat while Napoli were, like City, inexperienced but recognised as a very strong side capable of going some distance in the competition. This group was clearly the strongest in the tournament and it would take a tremendous effort to progress, however City were hopeful despite the first group match not going the way they had hoped at home to Napoli.

The pressure had been on the Blues throughout the match with the Italians. They were the home side and expected to win, while Napoli arrived with a determination not to lose. They were well disciplined and tackled hard, and took the lead through Cavani in the 69th minute. Kolarov equalised six minutes later but despite further efforts – substitute Adam Johnson challenged down the wing causing Napoli a few problems – the game ended with a 1-1 draw.

At Bayern Munich on 27th September City were defeated 2-0 by goals from Gomez after 38 minutes and on the stroke of half time, but Mancini's side had looked the more likely to score throughout the opening 20 minutes or so. In fact they should have been awarded a penalty in the first couple of minutes when former Blue Jerome Boateng seemed to take Nasri's legs away. After 20 minutes Boateng made a heavy challenge on Micah Richards in the area that ought to have brought another penalty. Mancini's men were certainly unfortunate at this point in the evening's proceedings.

In the second half Mancini tried to change things around with three substitutions but there was one issue with players on the bench that caused serious concerns. Mancini apparently asked Carlos Tévez to warm up and, according to reports, the player refused. Afterwards the manager faced the media and was clearly angry. When asked about Tévez he suggested the player would never appear for the Blues again. *The Guardian* reported: "If we want to improve like a team, like a squad, Carlos cannot play with us. With me, no – it is finished. It may not be my decision but if I'm deciding then, yes, he goes."

A media storm erupted over the days that followed with Tévez becoming public enemy number one as far as the media were concerned and, in truth, the majority of fans. They were angry at the alleged refusal which added to the disappointment felt with the defeat. Tévez himself was alleged by the media to have issued a comment at the stadium saying: "I didn't feel right to play, so I didn't."

However, the following day the player issued a statement which seemed at odds to those alleged comments: "I would like to apologise to all Manchester City fans, with whom I have always had a strong relationship, for any misunderstanding that occurred in Munich. They understand that when I am on the pitch I have always given my best for the club. In Munich on Tuesday I had warmed up and was ready to play. This is not the right time to get into specific details as to why this did not happen. But I wish to state that I never refused to play.

"There was some confusion on the bench and I believe my position may have been misunderstood. Going forward I am ready to play when required and to fulfil my obligations."

City launched an enquiry, fined and suspended the player, and looked to find a way forward. Many media figures and footballing personalities were quick to suggest that the player should be thrown out immediately, while some also suggested that it was the biggest player-related issue any English club had faced.

Ultimately, the saga ran for most of the season and at times the Club and the player seemed destined never to resolve their differences. Tévez left Manchester. Some said he would never return. In January there were plenty of suggestions of teams he would sign for – these included both Milan clubs, Paris St Germain, Spurs and West Ham – but City rightly determined that the player would only leave if the circumstances were right for the Blues.

At the start of February the manager said that Tévez could play for the Blues once more and he named him as part of his League squad for the rest of the campaign. Criticism came City's way from some who suggested that the Blues had somehow shown a weakness. They argued that Manchester United and other sides would not have allowed the player back and yet those criticising overlooked two simple facts. The first is that City had disciplined the player and ensured that they followed all appropriate procedures. They had taken all the action they were allowed to do – in fact back in October they had been forced to halve the fine they had wanted to impose when the footballers' union, the PFA, explained: "the PFA considers that there is no justification for a fine other than up to the prescribed sanction of two weeks' wages agreed by the FA, the Premier League and PFA. The PFA has informed the Manchester City football club accordingly and Carlos will continue to be supported by the PFA in this regard."

The second fact overlooked was that there had been precedents, including a high profile situation at Manchester United in the early 1970s. Back then George Best failed to turn up for a couple of first team fixtures and had refused to train. He had also walked out on the club and was seen in a variety of locations without, apparently, fulfilling his obligations to the Reds. United

said he would never play for the club again and placed him on the transfer list. However, a year after those issues hit the headlines Best was asked back to play in the 1973-74 season as United fought in vain to avoid relegation.

Although the contributions and significance of Best and Tévez could be debated at length, what is perfectly clear is that the Reds had brought Best back into their side and overlooked his disciplinary issues when they believed it would help them in their bid for survival. Maybe it was a desperate act, but at City in 2011-12 the approach the Blues took was to ensure the player was appropriately punished – subject to the restrictions and agreements in place between the PFA and the football authorities – and then they allowed him the opportunity of redemption. Everyone makes mistakes, and City's approach was admirable.

In March financial expert and City fan Martin Lewis summed up the mood of some fans and of the Club itself: "Earlier this season I felt very sad about Tévez. Like most fans I liked Tévez and then I felt very let down by him. I still think he's a talented player. Even though that experience left a bad taste in the mouth I will add though that I'm a great fan of rehabilitation. You should never give up on anyone and I hope now that when he plays he can put his heart into it fully. If he does we should all cheer him on. To me there's no better story than when someone is rehabilitated like that. It's important to learn from mistakes and not to bear grudges. I think most Mancunians have an ability to forgive and move forward."

Tévez's opportunity to redeem himself would come later in the season, but back in September the Champions League defeat at Munich and the baggage surrounding it had to be put to one side if the Blues were to exert pressure in the race for the League title. At Blackburn on 1st October the home side tried to stifle Mancini's men for some time. In fact City sat back and took stock of the situation throughout the first half as a negative Blackburn team seemed happy to kill the game at every opportunity. In the second half, as often the case during the opening months of the season, the Blues had total control and ten minutes after the interval Johnson made it 1-0. The Observer's Paul Wilson described the goal: "Blackburn were defending so far back they neglected to break out of their penalty area to close down Adam Johnson when a partially cleared corner landed at his feet in the 55th minute. It was obvious what Johnson intended to do, and in fairness to the Rovers defenders there was not much they could have done to prevent such a perfectly executed finish. Controlling with his left foot and then using minimal backlift to shoot with it, Johnson returned the ball almost instantly to find Paul Robinson's top corner from outside the area."

Mario celebrates giving City the lead at home to Newcastle.

Balotelli sent Nasri's cross home three minutes later, before Nasri added a third and Savic headed City's fourth. City fans, who had sung Roberto Mancini's name at various points before and during the match, were in full voice at the end while the Blackburn supporters chanted for the dismissal of their boss Steve Kean. Post match Mancini's assistant David Platt faced the press: "It was the result we were looking for to put Bayern Munich to bed."

After a break for international matches City's next game came two weeks later at home to Aston Villa. Importantly the game ended with the Blues heading the League table after a 4-1 entertaining victory on a sunny Mancunian day. Balotelli opened the scoring with an overhead kick on the edge of the six yard area after 28 minutes – his fourth goal in as many games – with Johnson, Kompany and Milner making it four in the second half. Mancini admitted that his side had not started well before looking forward: "After 15 minutes we played very well. We're happy to go to Old Trafford on top, but the championship will be long and this position can change every week. For us the most important thing is to stay on top or very close to it and fight until the end for the title."

The manager's views were appropriate. The Old Trafford derby, to take place eight days later, was of immense significance and had the Blues gone into that

match two points behind United then a defeat would have placed them five points behind. That in itself may not have been an issue, but United's experience may have helped push them forward. By beating Villa City actually possessed a two point advantage over the Reds and had the better goal difference by two goals. Even if Mancini's men lost to Ferguson's team there would only be a one point difference.

Before the derby City defeated Villarreal 2-1 in the Champions League at the Etihad and fans began to feel optimistic once more about the possibility of European progression.

On the eve of the Old Trafford derby the *Manchester Evening News* proclaimed the game as 'the greatest derby ever' – as with 2009-10 and 2010-11 Manchester's match was being raised another notch once again. For three successive seasons a derby game had been billed as the 'most important' or 'greatest ever' and, even before the match was played, some fans and media figures were already suggesting that the second League derby of the season, scheduled for late April, would be even more significant.

For the October Old Trafford derby all aspects of the media showed interest in the game. Inevitably, the derby was to be shown around the world, but locally the *Manchester Evening News* tried to gauge the feelings of fans and former players. Former Red David Sadler felt that despite City's obvious strengths United could not lose at home: "I don't think we are ready yet for the Blues to get on top. I still think our neighbours will be one position behind us come next May. That will probably mean they are runners-up. I have a gut feeling they will be playing second fiddle on Sunday at Old Trafford as well."

On the morning of the match the newspapers were full of comment about the game, but there was one man who suddenly found himself thrust in to the spotlight for off-the-pitch antics – Mario Balotelli. It was reported that on the eve of the derby fire crews had been called to his house after fire broke out when fireworks were being set off in his bathroom. The fire actually occurred at 1am on Saturday but the player managed to attend training at 10am as planned. The media enjoyed releasing Balotelli related stories by this time and, as the season progressed, the number of stories increased at an incredible rate. Some were clearly fiction, others factual, and supporters often listened to them with incredulity, bewilderment, but also laughter. Did Balotelli really visit a women's prison and ask to have a look around? Did he help a bullied child pluck up the courage to return to school? Was he really carrying a large amount of cash in his car when stopped by police? Did he stop at a school desperate to use the toilet? Was it true that he had paid for several homeless people to spend New Year in a top Manchester hotel?

The stories were often entertaining and caused a French magazine called *So Foot* to question what was true or false in their article: "La Vraie Vie De Mario Balotelli" (the true life of Mario Balotelli).

The Italian player hit the headlines again after the match but this time it was for his antics on the pitch as City thrashed United in the best derby result for generations. In fact the 6-1 Old Trafford victory for Mancini's side was only the second time a team had netted six in the fixture with the previous occasion coming in 1926 when the Blues also defeated the Reds 6-1 at United's home.

Balotelli opened the scoring in the 22nd minute with a terrific shot into the corner of the net out of reach of 'keeper De Gea after Silva and Milner had enjoyed a swift exchange of passes which dumbfounded the Reds' defence. The Blues deserved their lead and Balotelli took that moment to lift up his shirt and show a tee-shirt with the question "Why always me?" Inevitably he was booked for the celebration but fans loved it and the phrase appeared on tee-shirts and other souvenirs as the season progressed.

The Blues continually pushed United but the match remained 1-0 at the break. A minute into the second half Balotelli looked likely to punish the Reds further when he was pulled back on the edge of the area by Evans. The United man was understandably sent off as this was a clear goalscoring opportunity.

In the 60th minute City's dominance brought a second goal for Balotelli. Silva and Milner once again combined, with Milner supplying the final ball for the Italian to push over the line.

Eight minutes later Agüero turned in a low cross from Micah Richards to make it 3-0 as City's domination continued. The Blues did allow United a brief moment of celebration when Darren Fletcher netted in the 80th minute but the final minutes saw Mancini's team attack at will. In the 90th minute Joleon Lescott pulled the ball back after the Reds had failed to clear a corner from Silva, leaving Dzeko with the simple task of tapping the ball home for the fourth.

A minute later Dzeko, who had come on as a substitute for Balotelli in the 70th minute, nutmegged Rio Ferdinand to allow Silva to send a low shot through De Gea's legs for goal number five.

By this point it was clear United were well and truly defeated. Every time they got the ball City looked likely to score and shortly after the fifth Dzeko sent a close range effort over the bar. Inevitably, City fans in the corner away section roared the Blues on time and time again.

The clock was ticking down but there was still just enough time for Dzeko to make it 6-1. David Silva, in outstanding form, volleyed a high ball into the path of the striker. Dzeko raced forward and with total control he easily netted City's third goal in a breathtaking final few minutes. The bizarre nature of football statistics show that all three of the Blues' goals were netted in the 90th minute of the game. Of course they weren't as the fifth and sixth came in added time, but for a team that so often in the past had conceded late to United it was hugely satisfying that this day the Blues played to the end and kept their concentration high. City were worthy victors and the score could easily have been more. Had

The Manchester Evening News *focuses on a great City win.*

City's thrilling 6-1 win deservedly made the headlines.

the game enjoyed a further five minutes or so then undoubtedly Mancini's men would have netted at least a couple more. United were unable to cope with their rivals in exactly the same manner as Huddersfield Town had struggled in 1987. That day it was 10-1 to the Blues and at Old Trafford in 2011 United were fortunate that the game ended when it did. This was a rout in every sense of the word.

Officially that day the Blues had 2,996 fans at Old Trafford but in truth there were many more away fans in the stadium. Some had tickets for the home section, others worked there. One man working inside the ground on derby day was former City Premier League player John Foster. Foster had played for the Blues during the mid-90s but by 2011 his professional football career had been replaced by his new occupation in the

police force. Foster was on duty at Old Trafford: "That was an experience. It was one of the best working days of my life. I was stationed in the stand behind the goal that City were attacking in the second half – unbelievable! When Mario scored the opener at the other end it was dead all around me because I was in a United section, but I was cheering inside. I was on duty so I had to be professional, but every Blue knows how I felt.

"In the second half when City were attacking at will it felt great, and I had a brilliant view of it all. I wanted to be amongst the City fans and at one point I went inside the stand, found a quiet corner and roared my delight! Then I went back all calm and stood there all professional. At 3-1 we had to leave because of how the matchday operation works and so we had to go out on to Matt Busby Way. I had my police radio on of course and anyone passing could hear what was being said.

"The United fans started streaming out at 3-1 and as a group passed me moaning the news came through that it was 4-1… then 5-1… then 6-1. The crowds were streaming out and it was incredible to see and be a part of it. It was one of the best days working I have ever had."

It was an incredible day and the victory ensured City had a five point lead at the top of the League and, ultimately significantly, the goals helped ensure that goal difference was well and truly in City's favour. The Blues had a difference of 12 over United at this point and averaged 3.67 goals per game – a tremendous ratio – while the Reds, who were the second highest scorers, had a ratio of 2.89.

After the match Alex Ferguson claimed it had been his worst day ever, while his opposite number tried to ensure that everyone connected with City kept their feet on the ground and saw this as simply one result – a great one of course – in a long season: "Against Tottenham we played very well and against Bolton, but this is different because we played against a strong team like United. In the end there are three points, finished. We don't take six points for this game.

"I think the season will be very long and probably four or five teams that can win the title. This is important for our confidence. It's important because we showed that we are a good team, but we should appreciate the mentality United had because after 1-0 and the sending off, they continued to play to score. I think that's a very important mentality."

Ferguson was unhappy that his side had continued to try and attack. He admitted: "When we went to 3-1, 4-1 we should have settled for that. We should have just said 'we've had our day.'"

Ominously he added "But we'll come back. By January we'll be okay. We usually get the show on the road in the second half of the season and that will have to be the case."

As the season progressed this line was repeated often by the manager, the media and United fans but analysis on the Bluemoon forum by City fans suggested that the general perception was a false one. United's title-challenging opponents may have been poorer during the second half of the season, but the Reds tended to be consistent with their early season form not better according to the research.

For neutrals the City victory immediately lifted the Blues to the status of title favourites. Alan Hansen, who had often talked positively of City during the 90s and 2000s but had been criticised by fans in recent years as they believed he had been negative towards the Club, was delighted with the Club's resurgence: "Manchester City genuinely now have absolutely everything in place to win the Premier League and that was always

the reality even before their incredible 6-1 win at Old Trafford.

"The title is now City's to lose. They have the squad, their manager is no longer quite so cautious as he was last season and they have the financial power. If City do win the title this season, then the worry for the rest of the League is that they will never get a look-in again."

His views were shared by most neutrals although former England manager Terry Venables seemed to share Mancini's views that there was still a lot further to go in the title race: "Manchester now has two top clubs, make no mistake about that. City are in the ascendency, but United are not finished yet."

Everyone seemed to overlook the fact that there were more than two teams in the title race, afterall both Chelsea and Newcastle were only one point behind the Reds while Spurs had a game in hand and were three points behind United. The season wasn't even a quarter of the way through yet but to the world at large the title was going to be won by one of the Manchester clubs and, on 23rd October 2011, that team was likely to be City.

In the weeks that followed City strengthened their position at the top with victories over Wolves (3-1), Queens Park Rangers (3-2) and Newcastle (3-1). The Newcastle victory was important as Alan Pardew's team were undefeated prior to the match and defensively very tight. This meant City were by this point the only side not to suffer a defeat and, even more significantly, they had now enjoyed the best start any club had experienced in Premier League in history. Out of 12 fixtures the Blues had won 11 and drawn one. They had also scored three goals or more in six consecutive League games. Mancini: "I hope we can continue like this, but I think in 28 [he meant 26] remaining games there will be a time when we lose."

As the Newcastle game kicked off before United's match at Swansea some talked of an eight point gap opening up in the title race but, in truth, this was merely a timing issue. United defeated Swansea 1-0 – though they struggled at times – and the gap at the end of the day remained five points. Later in the season some would talk of the Blues being eight points clear at this time, but it is important that the facts are recorded properly. City were five points clear after the same number of games.

Three days later City were defeated 2-1 at Napoli in the Champions League. It was a disappointing defeat, especially as the Blues had won 3-0 at Villarreal three weeks earlier to bring a real chance of qualification. Losing to Napoli gave the Italian side the advantage.

Prior to the defeat in Italy some fans had talked of City winning four trophies in 2011-12. Similar to Franny Lee's plans for a Grand Slam of trophies in 1969-70 the prospect that City could win four trophies in a season was unlikely, but it did show the ambition both in 1969 and 2011 of the Club. Four trophies was a dream too far, but by simply having that ambition the Blues were back on track. The City of 2011 had a real opportunity of finding the level of success not achieved at the Club since the days of Joe Mercer and Malcolm Allison.

Back in the League the Blues drew 1-1 at Anfield five days after the Champions League defeat. Vincent Kompany, one of the most consistent players since his arrival in 2008 and an inspiring captain, netted the opening goal when he jumped to meet a corner from David Silva and managed to divert the ball into the net in the 31st minute.

Two minutes later a Charlie Adam effort was deflected into the net by Lescott for the equaliser. It was a blow, but worse came when substitute Mario Balotelli was sent off twenty minutes after coming on for his second bookable offence. In the end, considering the Napoli game and the fact that United had also drawn that weekend, the draw was a decent one and ensured the Blues remained in pole position in the title race.

This was a very busy period with games coming thick and fast as the Blues also progressed in the League Cup. Two days after the Liverpool draw Arsenal were defeated by an 83rd minute goal from Agüero at the Emirates in the League Cup quarter final. The resulting cup draw resulted in a City-Liverpool semi-final to be played over two legs in January.

Before facing the Merseysiders again City had several games in the Premier League and, of course, their Champions League meeting with Bayern. On 3rd December Mancini's side defeated Norwich City 5-1 in a rather comfortable game. Agüero opened the scoring after 32 minutes and by full time Nasri (51), Yaya Touré (68), Balotelli (88) and Johnson (one minute into added time) had increased City's lead. This was a day when Samir Nasri once again shone with a delighted David Platt commenting post match: "When he plays with that kind of zest, when he wants to go out and hurt people, he's a handful for anyone."

Nasri's goal came from 43 yards out and was acclaimed that weekend as the longest Premier League goal of the season.

The fact City scored five sent a clear message to all other League clubs. Some may have said the high scoring defeats of Spurs and United were one-offs but the Blues seemed capable of these types of victory game after game in the League. City were delivering.

There was some concern however. David Silva seemed to be tiring at times. He had been the star man so far this season, and every fan wanted to see him play game after game, but it looked as if he needed to be rested a little. Some fans and journalists suggested he could have been substituted in this match to save him for some of the bigger ordeals to come. One of those

would come the following Wednesday with the visit of Bayern.

Against the German side the Blues knew they had to win and hope Villarreal, who had proved to be the weakest side in the group, could stop Napoli from winning their match in Spain. City were hopeful, of course, but Villarreal had not managed a point in any of the previous five games and so it seemed unlikely they could draw even though they were playing at home.

At the Etihad with tremendous backing from fans the Blues knew they had to push forward. They had several chances before David Silva sent a low shot beyond 'keeper Butt to open the scoring in the 37th minute. In the 52nd minute Yaya Touré made it 2-0 with a wonderful goal. He picked up the ball in midfield, laid it off to Agüero and on to Dzeko before it made its way back to Touré. Touré then sent the ball under the 'keeper to complete the move.

City fans celebrated of course, but everyone knew that the result of the Napoli game would ultimately determine whether the Blues' inaugural Champions League campaign would end at the first stage or not.

Across in Spain the news was looking positive at first. Napoli had not been displaying the form they had earlier in the campaign but then everything changed in the 65th minute when Inler netted from 25 yards out. The news made its way to the Etihad and muted the atmosphere somewhat, although the Munich fans had been quite noisy throughout the match. City had taken the decision to place the away fans in level three of the East Stand believing that this may help improve atmosphere and they also gave City the entire South Stand. However, from their new position the Bayern fans seemed to generate more noise than they would have had they been placed directly next to the Etihad's more vocal home fans.

For most of the game the Bayern fans had bobbed up and down in the stand and some on the level below claimed they could feel the stand move. Needless to say the Club decided not to place away fans on level three again in 2011-12.

Napoli went on to beat Villarreal 2-0 and City defeated Bayern by the same score. This meant that Bayern and Napoli qualified with the Blues, who had gathered ten points, missing out. Typically, a total of ten points would have been enough to ensure progression but with Villarreal struggling and the other three sides proving very strong there was little to choose between the sides. Some claimed City's defeat at Munich and the Tévez situation had damaged the Blues' chances, but the truth was that the opening game – a 1-1 draw at home to Napoli – was the difference. Ultimately, it all came down to one goal in that match. Had City kept a clean sheet or scored one more goal in their inaugural Champions League game then they would have progressed.

Some claimed City's inability to progress meant the Blues were far from the finished article, but considering this was their first campaign and that other more knowledgeable and successful European combatants had suffered more embarrassing knock-outs (including United) then this was unfair.

Dropping out of the Champions League gave City a place in the Europa League. In that tournament the Blues defeated Porto 6-1 and then drew 3-3 with Sporting Lisbon on aggregate. Sadly, Sporting had scored twice at the Etihad to knock City out of the competition on the away goals rule. Nevertheless, Mancini's side had reached the last 16 and had ended their entire European season with a combined record most clubs would have been proud of. They had won 6 drawn 1 and lost 3 after scoring 18 and conceding 10. They had defeated the eventual Champions League finalists Bayern Munich and had faced a very strong Napoli side.

The European campaign may not have brought the progress everyone had hoped it would, but it was not the failure that some claimed. If nothing else it gave City more experience and a hunger to ensure that the following season's campaign would be a more successful one.

By the time they were knocked out of the Europa League on 15th March the Blues had also been eliminated from the two domestic cup competitions. In the FA Cup they drew Manchester United at the Etihad in the third round in a game that the *Manchester Evening News* claimed would be "the most important [derby] in living memory" for United though not, obviously, the most important for City. The emphasis in recent years had clearly changed. Whereas in the past United and Ferguson, in particular, had claimed that the derby was more important to the Blues than the Reds, suddenly the reverse was true.

There were a number of reasons why the newspaper made this claim. The most obvious was that United needed to try and get revenge for the 6-1 Old Trafford League game, but more significantly everyone was beginning to realise that the 'noisy neighbours' were not going away. In fact they were getting louder.

The FA Cup tie was hugely important for the Reds but it is also true that many City fans were saying pre-match that, of all the games scheduled in the months to follow, this was the one supporters would be happiest to lose if they had to lose one, or at least they admitted they'd rather lose the FA Cup tie than the planned April League derby. Maybe the manager felt the same as Joe Hart was rested for this game. Also missing were the Touré brothers.

City had hoped they could delay Yaya and Kolo Touré from travelling to compete in the Africa Cup of Nations until after the derby, but the move failed. As Yaya had been one of the star men so far this season the news that he would be missing for several crucial games was not great.

On the pitch against the Reds the Blues opened brightly. In fact they were the dominant force for the opening ten minutes but all of City's dominance and control was undone when Rooney gave United a shock lead. Writing for his online report on the *Telegraph's* website Thom Gibbs recorded the moment: "Wow, where did that come from? Pretty much the first time United have been out of their half."

Less than two minutes later Gibbs was shocked again as Vincent Kompany was sent off for what was supposed to be a two footed challenge: "United players swarmed around Chris Foy, and he wasn't long in producing the red card. Hmm. Watching the replays that is very soft indeed. Kompany's gone in hard, but it's low and not especially dangerous."

Gibbs, watching television coverage of the game, added: "Clive Tyldesley does that rarest of things for a commentator and consults the Actual Rules of Football. 'Reckless is a yellow card, excessive force is a red'. Kompany's challenge plainly sits in the first category for me."

Every City fan and the majority of neutrals agreed with Gibbs assessment but sadly the referee, when surrounded by United players complaining about the tackle, took the action he felt was appropriate. Some fans pointed out that Nani hadn't even appealed himself. From that moment fans knew this was not going to be City's day. Even worse Kompany was to be banned for four games as that was his second red card of the season. It seemed totally unfair. The sending off would inevitably impact the Blues ability to compete in the League and in the League Cup semi-final. The City captain felt the sending off was not justified and appealed: "I appealed because I completely disagreed with the interpretation of the officials on the day. My understanding is that English football prides itself on hardness and fairness."

The immense feeling of frustration at proceedings increased in the 39th minute when United were awarded a penalty. The Reds had scored a second goal nine minutes earlier, but the penalty decision was seen at the time as the moment the game went beyond the Blues. City 'keeper Pantillimon guessed right and saved low to the left, but the ball fell for Rooney and he headed home. Some City fans left at this point while others felt angry at the way the game had progressed.

Mancini's men came out for the second half in seemingly a very positive frame of mind. Sure they were three goals down, but they appeared keen to make amends for the first half disappointment. Two minutes into the half Richards was tackled as he headed towards the box with Kolarov taking the resultant free kick from about 30 yards out. His shot lifted over the wall, bounced on the line and entered the net. It was a wonderful free kick.

In the 64th minute Scholes, who had been brought out of retirement, returned a throw poorly and Nasri pounced to take the ball. He crossed to Agüero who then shot, but the 'keeper palmed the ball back. Agüero made no mistake and fired home. Could City continue the fightback?

As the game progressed United, with the extra man, had most of the possession but the Blues continued to challenge at times. Strong support roared City forward whenever they got the ball and then in the 83rd minute it appeared as if the Blues would get a chance for an equaliser. Kolarov crossed the ball into the area and it hit Jones' leg and then his arm. The majority of people in the stadium believed a penalty was about to be awarded to City but the referee said no. Once again supporters felt dissatisfied and in the weeks that followed there were significant calls for video technology and other improvements to help referees make the right decisions. The feeling of injustice was intensified when a less obvious 'handball' decision went against the Blues in the League Cup semi-final second leg a couple of weeks later.

In added time Pantillimon managed a header when he went up for a corner, but the game ended 3-2 to United. Ultimately, the real winners though were Mancini's men. By the end of added time they had played over 80 minutes with only ten men and come close to equalising. The fight back encouraged everyone that no game was ever lost or beyond them and, unlike the Reds in the 6-1 Old Trafford meeting, Mancini's side seemed to know how to adapt to make the most of any situation.

Three days after defeat in the FA Cup came the first leg of the League Cup semi-final against Liverpool. Unfortunately, City were defeated 1-0 after Gerrard netted a penalty in the 13th minute, but fans were angry when Glen Johnson performed a two-footed tackle but didn't even receive a yellow card.

Over the days that followed some misconstrued this as City fans and officials wanting Johnson sent off, but the truth was that they merely wanted consistency. If Kompany's tackle against United was a sending off offence then so was Johnson's. Consistency was needed as The Guardian's Simon Burnton explained: "Clearly, if Kompany's was a red card Johnson's must also be. The offences are very similar, but Johnson's two feet were travelling at greater pace and therefore were more likely to inflict injury. Both tackles won the ball cleanly, but I can understand if it has been decided that two-footed, studs-up tackles are by nature dangerous and must be eliminated. If that's the case, though, someone should make sure that all the referees know about it, rather than just a couple of them."

In the second leg more refereeing controversy resulted in City suffering further. The Blues were deservedly leading 1-0 and looking more than capable of winning the match and the tie when a Daniel Agger's shot was blocked by Micah Richards and deflected onto the player's arm. It was not deliberate, nor was it something that should have been punished, but Liverpool were awarded a penalty which, as with the first leg, Gerrard converted. Was Richard's unintentional hand ball more significant than Jones' in the FA Cup?

City took the lead again in the 67th minute through Dzeko but Liverpool equalised through former Blue Craig Bellamy seven minutes later. The match ended 2-2 but in a 3-2 aggregate victory for the Merseysiders.

As well as the penalty decision there had been other issues for City during the match with the most worrying being the performance of Savic at centre-half. The player was clearly not able to cope with the quality of Liverpool that night and the Blues were seriously missing both Touré brothers and Vincent Kompany. Kompany's unfair sending off and the Africa Cup of Nations had impacted City's progression in both domestic cups.

City were also stuttering a little in the League although they remained as leaders and had managed to maintain a great record. After the 5-1 victory over Norwich on 3rd December City had lost 2-1 at Chelsea even though Balotelli had opened the scoring in the second minute, but defeated Arsenal (1-0) and Stoke (3-0). Those victories ensured Mancini's side would be top of the Premier League on Christmas Day but the gap was now down to two points. The Blues did still have a better goal difference – ten goals at this point – after scoring an incredible 53 goals in only 17 matches (a Premier League record), and the advantage was firmly with Mancini's side. However, the noises from the media and coming out of Old Trafford about United 'always' having a better second half of the season kept growing louder. City may have been the noisy neighbours but this time it felt as if everybody wanted to talk about how the Blues would come unstuck as the Reds piled on the pressure.

In his match report of United's easy 5-0 victory at Fulham Matt Hughes believed that the Blues: "should resist any temptation to overindulge with their neighbours leaning menacingly over their shoulder. For all their wonderful football, City's players have yet to be tested under real pressure."

Whether his comments were factual or not – Stoke boss Tony Pulis believed "there is more pressure on Manchester City than the other clubs because everybody will be putting them down as favourites" - they were typical of those being stressed throughout the media at this time. Some City fans became affected by this continual belief that the Reds would catch the Blues and that all would be lost. On Boxing Day City and United's results seemed to give the media and rival fans all the evidence they needed.

City suffered a goalless draw at West Bromwich Albion while United won 5-0 at Old Trafford. The Blues were still top – on goal difference – but with Ferguson's side playing their next game on New Year's Eve, the day before City, there was a real chance that his side would be League leaders before the Blues' opening game of 2012. A prospect no City fan could face, nor one United actually deserved. City were the team of 2011 and deserved to be top.

Fortunately, United were defeated 3-2 by a Blackburn side that would ultimately be relegated. Blackburn were bottom of the League before the match and, with widespread unrest amongst fans, they were hardly perceived as a credible threat. Their victory ensured City opened 2012 as League leaders on goal difference – now down to six goals. With a game in hand the advantage was clearly still with City.

At Sunderland the Blues were unable to increase their points tally as Sunderland scored an added time winner. City had plenty of opportunities themselves to win the match, and they certainly deserved at least a point, but as the game neared its conclusion Ji Dong-Won rounded Joe Hart for the only goal while City protested that the Sunderland player was off side. Henry Winter, writing for the *Telegraph* agreed: "Ji was offside. O'Neill ruminated afterwards on the word 'marginally' but marginally is still off. The flag stayed down, infuriating Barry who was clearly appealing for offside."

Two days later Liverpool were defeated 3-0 in the League with goals from Agüero, Yaya Touré (his last appearance before heading off for the Africa Cup of Nations) and a penalty from James Milner. That weekend United lost 3-0 at Newcastle and City's position at the top strengthened, although the Reds equalled the Blues' points tally when they beat Bolton 3-0 before City played their next League match. A 1-0 victory at Wigan ensured a three point lead returned.

On 22nd January title hopefuls Tottenham arrived at the Etihad hoping they could defeat the Blues and sustain a challenge of their own. Spurs were third by this point and were likely to be a major obstacle. In the end City defeated Harry Redknapp's side by the odd goal in five but it had been a tough game.

Samir Nasri opened the scoring in the 56th minute after he had pushed forward following a David Silva pass. Three minutes later Joleon Lescott somehow managed to bundle the ball – and himself – into the net to make it 2-0. However, Spurs pulled a goal back within a minute and in the 65th minute Gareth Bale equalised.

In the third minute of added time Mario Balotelli, who had come on as substitute for Dzeko in the 65th minute, was brought down by Ledley King resulting in a penalty. The Italian took the kick himself and with his usual nonchalance he netted the winner.

It had been quite an eventful few minutes for Balotelli who had received a yellow card about 12 minutes after coming on and had been unpunished when he appeared to stamp on Scott Parker. The referee Howard Webb appeared to be in full view of the incident but he did nothing on the day. An inquiry charged the player with violent conduct and he received a four match ban. Once again the role of referees was seriously questioned as supporters analysed match footage closer to determine whether Webb had or had not seen the incident.

Fans wanted consistency and if Balotelli was guilty then fine, but what about the situation with Glen Johnson's two-footed challenge in the Liverpool game? As football is such a high profile business with an incredible amount of money at risk game after game, it seems only appropriate that technology should be used to help guide referees to the right decisions. Some said that refereeing decisions balanced themselves out over a season, but the majority of fans found it hard to accept that during the opening months of 2012. Consistency at all levels was needed.

After the Spurs game the media inevitably focused on Balotelli's role in the match but the most significant aspect, lost to some extent in the furore, was that the Blues' impressive season was continuing. By this time Tottenham were believed to be the only side who could disrupt the two Manchester clubs and some suggested that while City and United focused on each other Harry's boys would sneak up behind and take the title. Ultimately, that view was far from the truth.

It is fair to say that every League game was now crucial to the Blues. United were still too close for comfort and Spurs, despite the City win, could still be a threat. By the time City faced Everton at Goodison Park Tottenham were third on 48 points, United were second on 51 and the Blues remained top on 54 points. None of those sides could afford to slip up but, with a certain amount of inevitability, Everton managed to beat the Blues 1-0 on 31st January.

The Goodison Park club had often been a bogey side in recent years and the defeat was half-expected by fans who often feared the worst from these encounters. The disappointment intensified as Spurs beat Wigan 3-1 and United won at home to Stoke after the Reds netted two penalties. The three point lead had gone, however the Blues were due to play Fulham at the Etihad before United's next match to restore the advantage.

On 4th February in snowy conditions City were not at their best but they were still some way ahead of Fulham in terms of individual flair. Agüero demonstrated his immense talent from the start and after about nine minutes the Argentinian dodged past Senderos before sending the ball to Adam Johnson. Johnson went past full-back Baird but the Fulham man tripped him giving City a penalty. Agüero smashed the ball past Mark Schwarzer who, around 15 years earlier, had almost signed for the Blues.

After thirty minutes with the snow still falling – Lee Jackson and other members of the groundstaff cleared the lines at regular intervals - the lead increased. Jonathan Northcroft, writing for *The Times*, described the goal: "More footwork from Johnson then produced a second goal when Agüero deflected the ball to him delightfully and he unbalanced Baird with a shuffle before hitting a shot-cum-centre that hit the defender and cannoned in."

In the 72nd minute Dzeko made it 3-0 and Fulham were well and truly beaten. However, by the time City's next game kicked off the Blues had lost top spot briefly to the Reds. United had drawn with Chelsea and then defeated Liverpool, but as City beat Aston Villa 1-0 on Sunday 12th February United's lead only lasted a day. It was however a reminder of how close behind the Reds actually were.

By this time the Blues had managed to survive the period without Yaya Touré (due to his African Nations commitments) and Mario Balotelli, plus of course the four games when Vincent Kompany was unavailable. They had managed to hold on to top spot even though, at times, they clearly missed all those players and had not been on their best form. In addition they had suffered defeats in the two domestic cup competitions and had to contend with a bizarre set of refereeing decisions at times. In January the BBC's summarisers had even talked of City being in crisis – even though they topped the table. If that was a crisis what was losing at home to Bury on Valentine's Day 1998?

Taking everything into consideration, the Blues had coped exceptionally well during a difficult January and early February.

February ended with an easy 3-0 home win over Blackburn which ensured the Blues had not dropped a point at home for almost a year (since a 1-1 draw with Fulham on 27th February 2011). Simon Hart, writing for the *Independent On Sunday* believed it was this form that had enabled City to sustain such an impressive challenge for the title: "It says everything about Manchester City's changed status that in a Premier League season that has thrown up some strange results, the club once famed for unpredictability have become the great dependables. City at the Etihad can only mean one thing these days: a home win. This was their 18th in succession in the League, and there can have been few more comfortable."

Joe Hart only had one save to make and that was a rather tame effort in added time. Goals from Balotelli, Agüero and Dzeko enabled the Blues to maintain their excellent home record, and Balotelli netted again seven days later as City beat Bolton 2-0 in their next match at the Etihad. That weekend United defeated Spurs 3-1 to kill off all hope the London club had of winning the title. City remained top on 66 points with United second on 64 and Spurs third with 53 points – it was now a two horse race.

On Sunday 11th March the two leaders swapped places as United won 2-0 at home to West Bromwich Albion and the Blues suffered a shock 1-0 defeat at Swansea. Vincent Kompany and Joleon Lescott were unable to play through injury and both men were clearly missed. Joe Hart had saved a penalty in the sixth minute, but the Welsh club eventually took the lead in the 83rd minute. Suddenly, everyone claimed that United were now in total control and that their second half of the season form would put City in their place.

The following week United defeated ten man Wolves 5-0, but City followed this with a very important 2-1 defeat of Chelsea on 21st March. It was the Blues 20th consecutive home win – a record for the Premier League – although it took some time before Mancini's men could exert their authority. Despite City being on top the game remained goalless at half time.

In the 60th minute Chelsea took the lead when Gary Cahill's shot was deflected home following a corner. The Blues didn't deserve to be behind but City knew this was a game they had to win if they wanted to maintain a title challenge. Carlos Tévez, who had been back training with the team for over a month was named as a substitute and in the 66th minute Mancini brought him on for his first game since the Munich incident.

Some fans decided not to cheer the player, some actually booed, and others claimed to leave their seats when he appeared, but the vast majority of fans did applaud and support the Argentinian. Regardless of what had gone on before they felt that Tévez, as a City player, would give his all on the pitch and could, potentially, be the difference between title success and second place.

As with the Manchester United fans in 1973 when George Best returned after a much worse series of disciplinary incidents, the majority of fans welcomed Tévez back.

Twelve minutes after Tévez's return Michael Essien was adjudged to have handled in the area, giving the Blues a penalty. Sergio Agüero paused for a moment and appeared to ask Tévez if he wanted to take the spot kick. Wisely the substitute decided it was best for Agüero to have a go. Had Tévez taken the kick and it been saved or missed then it would undoubtedly have been seen as a major issue. In the end Agüero made no mistake and the Blues were level.

In the 85th minute Tévez set up Samir Nasri for the match winner. Post match Mancini was asked about Tévez and the goal: "Carlos is not 100 per cent. He needs more time and that is normal. But he knows the football. That was important because he did an incredible assist for Samir. What happened with him finished one month ago when Carlos came back and everything was finished.

"I have spoken to Carlos every day in the last month. He knew he would be on the bench today and would probably play for 20 minutes. If he can find good form in 10 days that would be important for us. Now it is important for him to play some games, for us, him and his future."

Tévez's return came just in time. This did not stop the media and rival fans from criticising the Blues. A few days after his appearance Hugh McIlvanney wrote in The Times: "The offences Tévez perpetuated against City, against the manager himself and against the simplest principles of how a professional sportsman should behave were too egregious to be conveniently enveloped in tolerance because his abilities are being missed."

Clearly the experienced and knowledgeable McIlvanney could have taken the opportunity to compare the Tévez situation with how Manchester United had welcomed Best back all those years earlier in their fight against relegation. Had he done so he might have seen that the Blues' manager and the Club itself had acted in a significantly more consistent manner than the Reds had, and they ensured that their actions were in the long term interests of the football club. Tévez had been punished. Surely everyone deserves a chance to move forward. What about forgiveness?

City had shown a great deal of control in their handling of the situation.

Some critics did adopt a different tone. Now some were saying that City would probably already have won the title had Tévez stayed. It was an easy comment to make but far from accurate. At the time of the player's disagreement with the Club he was not the Blues' first choice and it had been clear – and often reported – that the player had wanted to leave.

Had Tévez been fully fit and available throughout the season it is highly likely he would have added something to some of the games during the Blues' great run in 2011 but City had been tremendously successful in those matches in any case. Also, it is possible that he may have been transferred in January 2012 and therefore not been available for this crucial period of the season. Whatever ifs and maybes existed it was a fact that Tévez was now back and able to play a part in the final couple of months of the season.

Sadly, despite the optimism the Chelsea game brought, the Blues suffered a 1-1 draw at Stoke in the following game. That day Peter Crouch scored a brilliant volley to give the home side a 59th minute lead but Yaya Touré, often the saviour during 2010-11 and 2011-12, netted the equaliser 17 minutes later. It was a match that once again saw some odd refereeing moments and post match Mancini left the interviews to David Platt who admitted: "He's just worried he might say something that gets him in hot water."

The manager did speak with the media after the following game but the news was not particularly positive. Former Blue Martin O'Neill had managed his Sunderland side to a 3-3 draw during which Balotelli had argued with Kolarov over who should take a free kick. At one point Sunderland had led 3-1 but the Blues had fought back with, appropriately enough, goals from Balotelli (85) and Kolarov (86). With United able to extend their lead to five points if they won their game in hand Mancini admitted that the advantage was well and truly with the Reds. He pointed out that with a Manchester derby scheduled for 30th April: "It is clear we want to win the title and we will fight until the derby with United because I think that will decide our season." He added: "If we go eight points behind, then it is finished."

His comments were interpreted as meaning that if United won their game in hand and the following match and the Blues lost at the Emirates the following Sunday then the title race would be over. In the end that is exactly the scenario that played out with City losing 1-0 with an 87th minute goal to Arsenal and, to make matters worse, Balotelli was sent off in added time for his second bookable offence.

Mancini's side were now eight points behind United and with an inferior goal difference (two goals) after the same number of games. This was much further behind than the Reds had been at any point in the season and, as far as the wider public was concerned, it was only a matter of time before United won the title. Some even suggested it could happen within two weeks due to the number of fixtures.

It was at this point that City's manager began to win the mind games with Alex Ferguson. For so many years the media had talked of the United manager's ability to use psychology to put opponents under pressure with the most obvious example coming in the 1990s when Newcastle boss Kevin Keegan made a passionate speech about how much he'd 'love it' if United failed. In 2012 Ferguson's influence would see United through and help to unsettle the Blues according to various footballing figures, including former United captain Bryan Robson.

Maybe as part of his own attempt at unsettling the Reds, Mancini continually stressed how the advantage was now well and truly with Ferguson's team. United were eight points clear with a two goal advantage and there were only six games left to play. Those games did include the Manchester derby but, as pundits regularly stressed, there was a chance it would all be over by then in any case. City, of course, hoped it wasn't over but even the most optimistic of fans realised that even if the

Toure in action against Sunderland, March 2012.

TRUE BLUE
Yaya Toure

Yaya's determination brought many significant goals City's way in both 2010-11 and 2011-12

derby was won United still had the opportunity to be five points clear.

Even if somehow City managed to catch the Reds on points, goal difference was no longer in the Blues' favour either.

On 11th April Mancini's approach began to pay dividends. At the Etihad, the Blues rediscovered the form that had made them head and shoulders above the rest earlier in the season. They had no fear and fans marvelled at the quality of their team once more.

The Blues took the lead against West Bromwich Albion in the sixth minute when Agüero received a pass from Nasri near the half way line. He raced forward, passing Albion's Keith Andrews with ease, and after travelling around 25 metres he sent a low shot in to the net.

City continued to control the match but it wasn't until the second half that they stressed their superiority. Before the Blues netted their second news filtered through that Wigan had taken the lead against United. A huge cheer went up and a few seconds later Agüero netted his second. Tévez scored the third in the 61st minute – his first since his return to action – and Silva netted the fourth three minutes later.

Ultimately City defeated West Bromwich Albion 4-0 with a thrilling team performance while United suffered a 1-0 defeat at struggling Wigan. Mancini said afterwards: "I fight every day and so do my team, but now I think it's too late. United have a fantastic spirit, we don't have the same spirit and for this reason I think it is difficult."

He added: "United is a really top team and I don't think they can lose the title."

Some fans felt this was defeatist talk but truthfully Mancini was trying to keep expectation at the right level. He was right that United had the advantage and knew that even if City won all their games they would still not be champions unless the pressure got to the Reds. Mancini was determined the pressure would not be on his team. He wanted it on Ferguson's side and, during this period, the Italian proved his strengths as a leader.

Three days later City thrashed Norwich 6-1 at Carrow Road on a day when Carlos Tévez scored a hat-trick. He celebrated his third goal with a cheeky celebration in which he pretended to swing a golf club, thereby making reference to his prolonged absence from the side and the belief that he had spent the time on the golf course.

This was one of the most important victories of the season and narrowed the gap to two points, although United were to win their game in hand the following day.

Despite the performance and the significance Mancini continued to stress that the title race was over. His approach was succeeding in keeping the pressure off and the following week United drew 4-4 with Everton while City defeated Wolves 2-0. Suddenly the points difference was down to three but City's goalscoring exploits had swung goal difference back the Blues' way.

The situation was now clear – beat United in the next match and then better the Reds' results in the final two games and City would be champions. The Manchester derby was, once again, being described as the most important derby ever and for once the hyperbole seemed appropriate. No matter which side won the match it would be an important step towards the League title. The Blues had to win, but a draw would be acceptable for United. With the game taking place at the Etihad City fans were convinced their side would be successful.

As the derby grew near every area of the media seemed focused on the match. It became the most significant topic and even the appointment of Roy Hodgson as England manager that day could not divert attention from Manchester's match. *The New York Times*, in its build up to the match outlined the world view: "Slanting rain and a vicious wind sent ripples and eddies across the puddles forming outside Manchester City's Etihad Stadium on Sunday. Workers spilled out of two satellite television trucks, ferrying cables and cameras into the stadium to prepare for what could be the most anticipated match in Premier League history. On Monday, those cameras will broadcast the game between Manchester United and Manchester City to 650 million homes in 203 territories. Sixteen overseas broadcasters have applied to cover the game, seven more than worked the recent Clásico in Spain between Barcelona and Real Madrid.

"More people are expected to watch Monday's match between City and United than the Champions League final between Chelsea and Bayern Munich in May, and yet this is not even a title decider. With United only 3 points ahead in the standings, and with two matches left for each after Monday's showdown, the winner is not guaranteed the title."

Some talked of the similarity between this game and the 1968 Old Trafford derby. Back then a City victory against the odds set the Blues up for their title success but there were still nine matches left to play and plenty of twists and turns along the way. Now, in 2012, the significance was much higher.

As the *New York Times* had highlighted this was a match everybody wanted to see. As well as the regular 47,000 a number of additional celebrity fans turned up to watch the Blues. In one of the executive boxes was Diego Maradona, accompanying his daughter, to watch his son-in-law Agüero. While in the South Stand in a regular seat was former City owner Thaksin Shinawatra. It seemed an odd location for the former Thai Prime Minister to sit, especially as former directors and personnel from the days of Peter Swales' reign had regular seats in the main VIP area, and some suggested this indicated that City's current owners did not want him to be a distracting influence. Others suggested that his presence proved he remained a Blue and that he was desperate to be there for such a significant match. Whatever the truth his presence there, amongst some of the Blues' most passionate supporters added another angle to the spectacle of it all. Shinawatra was well received throughout the match by those chanting around him, and he even bobbed along to the Poznan at one point.

Ultimately, a tense night – though City fans tried to ensure a positive atmosphere throughout – was settled with a solitary goal. Captain Vincent Kompany proved to be the hero when he headed home from close range from a corner at the end of the first half. Sam Wallace in the *Independent* described the goal: "There were two corners in quick succession in the build up to the goal from Kompany. For the first one David De Gea came off his line but could not get through a crowd of players in front of him to deal with the ball. The United defenders are not in the habit of waiting around for De Gea to deal with trouble but they lost concentration from the second corner in the sequence.

"This time David Silva's ball from the right was met firmly by Kompany at close range and De Gea had no chance. It looked like he was the responsibility of Chris Smalling but Rio Ferdinand will not enjoy watching that one again."

The stadium erupted as the nerves of fans were settled to some extent. In the boxes Maradona was seen celebrating wildly.

City had been on top for most of the game with United offering little up front. In fact they had looked to kill the game at times. It appeared as if they had come for a draw but surely Ferguson would never send his team out to play for a draw against City? The media believed he would always look for a win but for fans the evidence suggested otherwise. Mancini later agreed with that view: "We wanted to win and they wanted a draw. This is the difference. I think that every manager can choose his team and that for them it was important to play for a draw. With a draw they knew the championship was finished."

In the second half City had further chances but the match ended 1-0. There had been some entertaining moments on the touchline when Ferguson and Mancini clashed. *The Independent* reported: "There are not many nights in football when Sir Alex Ferguson has to be dragged away from his opposing manager on the touchline by his longserving kitman. But then there has never been a night when the Manchester United manager has watched what was once an eight-point lead in the title race reduced to nothing by his local city rivals."

Although the match was not the greatest of the season it was one of the most important. Had the Blues lost then it would have been almost impossible for Mancini's men to win the title. Now with City and United level on points the advantage had turned to the Blues as they had the better goal difference.

With two games left to play – away at Newcastle and at home to QPR - the focus increased further. The global audience for the derby had seen that City were a force and capable of success. The reigning FA Cup holders were determined to push United all the way and with the goal difference working in their favour the Blues knew they could do it. Leading the way on the pitch was

Aguero, goalscorer Kompany, Tevez, Toure and Lescott celebrate an important derby goal.

captain Vincent Kompany: "If we win at Newcastle we will win the title. Sir Alex said that, so it must be right. He has far more experience than me."

He added: "We'll give everything we have until the last minute of the season to make sure we finish with no regrets." When he made those comments shortly before the Blues played their penultimate game at Newcastle, he could not have predicted that that was exactly what would happen and the season would be determined by the final moment of the last game.

On 6th May at the newly named Sports Direct Arena, or St James' Park as most football fans still referred to the venue, another of City's inspirational and most dependable players Yaya Touré ensured the Blues remained in pole position in the title race.

It was an extremely tense day – weren't they all during those final weeks of the campaign – and for much of the first half Newcastle had most possession but they hardly threatened the City goal. Nevertheless there was an immense feeling of pressure and nerves high up in the away section and at home for the viewing millions. The Blues had to win as they knew that any slip up would swing the advantage back to the Reds.

As the match progressed it was clear that Newcastle were not going to take it easy. They still had Champions League ambitions of their own and a Geordie win would make them favourites to finish third. This was not an easy game and was, in some ways, tougher than the match against United. Certainly Newcastle fought hard throughout the match and at times it felt as if sooner or later either Cisse or Ba would get a break and put

the Blues in difficulty. David Pleat commented for *The Guardian*: "Newcastle United put in a prodigious effort. No team in any game has grafted harder all season."

City had the greater attacking opportunities, but Newcastle demonstrated a great resilience.

With the match remaining goalless after an hour's play Mancini decided to change things around a little. He brought on Nigel De Jong for Samir Nasri in the 62nd minute and this allowed Yaya Touré to play a much more attacking midfield role. City began to exert their authority and in the 69th minute Dzeko was brought on for Tévez. Within a minute it was 1-0 to City.

Yaya Touré started the move and pushed forward, exchanging passes with Agüero as he progressed. Then he sent a curling shot past the Newcastle 'keeper. It was a great demonstration of the Ivory Coast player at his best and proved that his manager's tactical expertise was once again perfect. Ever since Mancini first arrived in Manchester he had been watching and learning. By May 2012 he had developed his knowledge of the English game and the effort needed to win the Premier League. In the final weeks of the Premier League campaign Mancini's nous was winning the battle for League supremacy.

The goal heralded wild celebrations of course but every Blue knew that the title race was still not over, nor was this match. Concentration had to remain high.

In the 85th minute David Silva was substituted for Micah Richards. Richards, as one of City's best Academy products, was hugely popular on the terraces and his addition with five minutes to go was popular. It was only right that the player appeared at this crucial stage of the season. He had been with the Club at some of its lowest points in the 2000s and now here he was at what was hoped was one of the highest.

Four minutes after Richards appeared Touré netted the second goal of the match with a left foot rising shot from close range after Gael Clichy had set him up nicely.

The celebrations began once more. In the stands, though they didn't realise it, the television cameras picked out Sir Howard Bernstein, the Chief Executive of Manchester City Council. Although his name was not known nationally for involvement with the football team he had been hugely significant in the development of the Club. During the 1990s he fought hard to bring a major sporting festival to the city and was rewarded with the 2002 Commonwealth Games and then he pushed to ensure a suitable venue was built. That venue became the modern day Etihad Stadium and it is fair to report that Sir Howard's involvement enabled both Manchester City and Manchester as a whole to benefit in the way they did.

In addition to his efforts in raising the profile of Manchester, Sir Howard also became a key figure in the development of East Manchester and City following the takeover by Sheikh Mansour. Without Manchester's support – through Bernstein and Council Leader Richard Leese – the transformation of the Club and the area surrounding the stadium would not have occurred. As with engineer and businessman Richard Peacock, who donated money to the football club during its formative years of the mid-1880s, Bernstein's involvement with the Club rarely gets mentioned or the attention it deserves, but it is a fact that he has helped foster a great relationship between the Blues and the city. That's why the sight of him delighted with the performance at Newcastle was highly appropriate.

As for Mancini the victory brought much praise his way. He was described in the *Independent* as a "master puppeteer" for the way he changed the side at Newcastle and managed the Blues to victory and deserved the acclaim. Throughout the season he had juggled his resources and changed tactics when needed. More often than not his approach succeeded and now his side were on the brink of their first top flight title since 1968. Even though he still tried to keep everyone focused on the task in hand he admitted: "If we beat QPR, we are champions. It doesn't depend on what Manchester United do any more. It depends on us."

The manager talked about the significance of the game before adding a word of caution: "It won't be easy because QPR are fighting against relegation. The players need to relax after this game, we have six days and then we have another game, It's not finished yet."

In 1968 a City victory at Newcastle in their last away game of the season brought the Blues the title, in 2012

it gave them one hand – or "two hands" as Ferguson suggested – on the trophy.

On Sunday 13th May 2012 the final games of the Premier League season saw City at home to relegation-battlers QPR and United away to Sunderland. Most assumed the Blues had the easier job, although they did accept that with Mark Hughes as manager the London club would be determined. Rangers needed to defeat the Blues or hope that Bolton were beaten to ensure they survived and so they were clearly a threat.

At the Etihad many fans arrived with painted faces or carrying inflatables, flags and scarves. They were ready to party. This was to be their day. Some arrived very early, desperate to take in every moment while others rigidly stuck to their normal matchday routine, stubbornly believing that any change from the norm no matter how small would wreck City's chances.

Once inside the stadium fans laughed and joked. There were some nerves but overall the mood was one of celebration and shortly before kick off Blue Moon was sung with real passion. The Club's anthem since 1989 the song had, like the Blues' loyal support, become a key part of City's psyche since the struggles of the nineties. At times it had been sung to rally the troops at times of doom and gloom but as the final match began it was being chanted at the beginning of what all fans believed would be a game of pure joy and celebration. The game, like so many moments in the Club's long, eventful and passionate history, was not as straight forward as fans had hoped however.

When the game commenced it was clear that QPR were playing a fairly defensive game. They claimed they would push for a goal, but in truth they seemed to sit back and focus on stopping the Blues from scoring. City had most of the possession – almost all for a significant spell in the first half – but Hughes' side were adept at killing off any threat. Tévez and Agüero worked hard but Rangers were defensively very strong. Then after twenty minutes the news all Blues had dreaded filtered through – Rooney had scored for United at Sunderland.

If the United score remained City had to win. Nothing else would do.

The Blues fought for every ball and searched for an opening but opportunities seemed few and far between and on the terraces the nerves were beginning to tell. Supporters knew what was happening in Sunderland and were desperate for someone, somewhere to make the City breakthrough. Soon though they noticed that Yaya Touré was limping. The player had been such an important member of the team, capable of changing almost any game, and so the sight of him struggling brought serious concerns.

In the 39th minute as Touré hobbled along, Pablo Zabaleta managed an attack down the right wing. He linked up with fellow Argentinian Carlo Tévez who then knocked the ball towards the injured Touré. Despite his struggles, the Ivorian passed to Zabaleta who calmly sent his shot towards the goal. QPR 'keeper Kenny managed to get his hand to it but it wasn't enough to stop the shot entering the net for the opening goal.

Significantly, Carlos Tévez was close by and ready to pounce had Kenny managed to knock the ball down.

Once Zabaleta's goal entered the nets the stadium erupted. The noise was truly special and nerves were settled. Fans sang the goalscorer's name as they partied. The atmosphere remained significantly passionate right through into the half time break and beyond as every fan present in the stadium believed the second half would see the Blues comfortably home.

It was a joy being a Blue at this moment.

During the break confirmation came through of the scores elsewhere – United were still in front but there was bad news for QPR as Bolton were beating Stoke 2-1 after Kevin Davies had netted at the end of the first half. This meant that Rangers knew they had to at least get a draw to survive. Any thoughts that Hughes' side would take it easy in the second half were soon dispelled.

While fans continued their celebrations through the break some did discuss the significance of scoring while Yaya Touré was on the pitch. The player had needed to be substituted shortly after the goal and some fans admitted that had they still been drawing when Touré was taken off then they would have been a little worried. He was a definite game changer and someone fans always wanted on the pitch. However, with City now a

goal up even the most pessimistic of fans felt they would be able to cope without him.

Three minutes into the second half misfortune struck as a hopeful ball from former Blue Shaun Wright-Phillips was hooked forward. Joleon Lescott, often an unsung hero for City, was unlucky when he tried to head the ball to safety only to see it fall into the path of Djibril Cisse. The QPR man fired the ball past Joe Hart for the equaliser. City were stunned and fans stood open mouthed. Had this actually happened?

A few minutes later Carlos Tévez and former Blue Joey Barton tangled on the edge of the area and it appeared as if Barton had swung his arm at the City man. The referee's assistant spotted the issue straight away and explained to referee Mike Dean what he had seen. The referee immediately reached for a red card but Barton seemed determined to inflict more damage. He walked behind Agüero and appeared to knee him, hoping for a reaction no doubt, and then he confronted Vincent Kompany and tried to head butt him. Various players and officials tried to control him before City substitute Micah Richards decided to guide him off the pitch. It was fortunate for Barton that Richards did this as the situation could easily have deteriorated further.

After the match Barton was reported to have said that another member of the QPR side had suggested he should push a City man to react in a bid to have a Blue sent off, although television footage failed to identify which player – if any – actually made that suggestion.

Barton's actions were criticised unreservedly in the

Aguero and Barry celebrate the goal they hoped would bring the title with scorer Zabaleta. The season still had more twists and turns to go.

media in the days that followed. For City fans in the stands at the Etihad however there was now a sense that the Blues couldn't fail to take control. They may have been drawing but surely City possessed enough quality to defeat a ten man QPR side?

In the 66th minute – only 11 after Barton's dismissal – the situation worsened for Mancini's men as Mackie headed QPR into the lead. With United still winning the Blues had to score at least two goals, or hope that Sunderland could transform their match with the Reds.

Mancini immediately tried to change things around. He brought on Dzeko for Gareth Barry in the 69th minute and six minutes later Balotelli replaced Carlos Tévez. For

At 2-1 the tension shows. Some of these young fans are about to experience the beauty of supporting City.

some Balotelli was still on probation after his sending off at Arsenal and this was his first appearance on the pitch since that day. Could the hugely talented but often controversial striker make a difference in the most important final 15 minutes of the season?

Some felt it was a major gamble but Mancini had faith in the young Italian and, together with Dzeko and Agüero, City lay siege to the QPR goal. The Blues pressured like never before but it was all beginning to look in vain. The ball simply would not go in.

Fans on level one were by this time stood watching. The pressure of the day was getting to them and some were even getting angry. Thoughts of the abuse that would come their way if the unthinkable was to come true and City were to lose out to United started to get to them. The pressure was unbearable. For some it was like 1999 and the final moments of normal time in the play off final again except – and this was hugely significant – there were few who truly believed this situation was salvageable whereas in 1999 fans did remain hopeful.

City continued to challenge and threaten but QPR's resilience seemed to intensify. Where was the space that had been expected once Barton had been sent off? Defensively they seemed impenetrable.

As the clock neared 90 minutes some fans felt it was all too much and they left. News crews were outside capturing the thoughts of those leaving. They were hurt and they made their feelings clear, but if 1999 had taught them anything it was that City always had their 'Typical City' mentality. Some always viewed 'Typical City' negatively thinking that the Blues would let them down, but there was another much more positive aspect and that was that whenever City were most in need 'Typical City' would become revitalised and achieve what most thought was beyond them. It had happened at Wembley

in 1999 and Bradford in 1989. At the Etihad in added time in this the last game of the season positive 'Typical City' appeared once more, but this time it was to win one of football's most important prizes. This was the ultimate City moment. Every Blue needed to experience this.

At 90 minutes the fans in the stands stood watching. They of course had no idea what was to follow. No preparation could have made them ready for this. At many times in the past City fans had lifted their team on to triumph or had shown a spirit that encouraged those on the pitch to deliver, but at 90 minutes the fans were dumbstruck. Some tried making noise to encourage the team forward but it was hard.

The fourth official indicated that there was to be five minutes of added time, although many fans felt this was still not enough. The Barton incident had taken what seemed an eternity and there had been two goals in the half so far. Surely a figure of 6 or 7 minutes would have been more appropriate and, they thought, given City a real chance. Five minutes to score two goals still did not seem enough time at that moment on that day. Then came a breakthrough after a minute of added time.

City had a corner, taken by Silva. The ball found its way to Dzeko and the Bosnian headed home to make it 2-2. Fans cheered, of course, but it still felt as if a victory was a step too far. Thoughts turned to Sunderland and some in the North Stand claimed that that game was 1-1. It wasn't and fans that had experienced the Liverpool relegation match in 1996 knew that rumours like this often found their way on to the terraces.

Interestingly, though this was perhaps not universally typical, there seemed to be different reactions from different age groups at this point. Many of the Club's oldest fans felt it was all over, that nothing could be done, while some of the youngest supporters

In added time Dzeko nets the equaliser.

– particularly the teenagers with their parents in the North Stand – felt there was still some hope. Not much maybe, but some nonetheless. Maybe this was because the older fans had been let down too many times during the previous thirty years, while the younger fans had perhaps developed their passion for the Blues during more recent times?

Regardless of whether some fans had hope or not, the fact was that the Sunderland-United game was nearing its conclusion. It ended with a Red victory causing United fans to start celebrating in the north-east and across the country. At the time their match ended they were at the top of the table. On television comments were made prematurely about City's dreams ending in tatters. Ferguson had done it again, or so they thought.

At the Etihad Mancini's side stormed forward hoping for a winner. The manner in which the players continued to challenge was refreshing and their never-say-die attitude had developed over the last couple of seasons under Mancini. Added time defeats to, most often, Manchester United had instilled a new discipline into the side. The season opened with the Blues losing out in the Community Shield to an added time goal but Mancini's men now had the belief and the character to ensure that no matter what City would fight to the end. The fans had been singing "We're Man City, we'll fight to the end"

in the weeks leading up to this game when the Blues were eight points behind the Reds with an inferior goal difference, and against QPR on Sunday 13th May the players did fight to the end.

Four minutes into the added time the last attack of the day ended with Sergio Agüero squeezing a shot inside the near post for the title-winning goal. The stadium erupted with the loudest roar ever known in Manchester 11 while Agüero pulled off his shirt and raced towards the North Stand corner. He of course got booked – when will the authorities realise that fans want entertainment and this type of celebration is what makes football such a passionate and popular sport?

In the stands fans bobbed up and down, roared with delight and generally went crazy. There are no superlatives that can accurately describe how all Blues felt at that specific moment.

A worldwide audience thrilled to the television coverage of the moment and the final drama of that day. No matter how low City fans had felt only a few moments earlier, in the weeks that followed every supporter without question believed that ultimately this was the best way to win the title. Had the Blues been 3-0 up after ten minutes and cruising to victory it would, of course, have been a marvellous achievement and been followed by significant celebrations. But the drama of the last day had taken City's achievement – and

Fighting to the end. Aguero's title winning goal, and the part played by Balotelli, as seen from the third tier of the East Stand. This is what it feels like to be City.

subsequent celebrations – to a new level. The Blues would have been worthy champions no matter how they would have achieved victory on this final day, but City's never-say-die attitude and dramatic finale made this the most thrilling end to a Premier campaign ever.

A day or so before this final match the 2011-12 season had been proclaimed as the greatest ever Premier League season and now City were truly deserving champions of that remarkable campaign.

At Sunderland news filtered through that Agüero had scored as some United fans partied. This prompted the home supporters to celebrate and sing in praise of Manchester's Blues. It seemed supporters of many, many clubs across the nation were delighted for City. Sunderland's fans knew what the Blues had been through and they were genuinely happy for the Club, just as Mancunians would have been happy had the situation been reversed and they had found genuine success in this manner.

Supporters and players of teams like Manchester United, and maybe some journalists who had talked of City as 'buying success', perhaps don't understand that most neutrals and fans of other clubs had empathy with the Blues' plight over the years. Sure City had been transformed by the investment from Abu Dhabi and some were inevitably envious of that, but this had come after years of under investment.

In May 2012 City's success was perceived well by the majority of football fans and neutrals. In future years, of course, continued success is likely to change that view, but it is a fact that genuine football fans were delighted that the Blues had achieved this success. The manner of delivery added to the drama, spectacle and interest of it all.

After Agüero's goal and while fans were celebrating wildly QPR kicked off by booting the ball some way up field. News had filtered through that Bolton had actually drawn guaranteeing Rangers' salvation at the expense of the Trotters and it looked as if everyone on the pitch wanted the match to end. Joe Hart took control of the ball, kept it at his feet and looked as if he'd stay there for ten minutes if he had to without pressure from anybody. The referee blew his whistle, and those five minutes proved to be just enough.

Fans were still bobbing up and down celebrating the goal when the whistle blew, and then the celebrations intensified once more. Some raced on to the pitch to celebrate in the same manner as City fans had at Newcastle in 1968 and at Maine Road in 1937. That seemed appropriate and reminded those watching television screens around the world that this success truly mattered. For much of the season City had been expected to win the title but that did not mean that fans ever became blasé or cocky about the side's prospects. They, of course, enjoyed banter with rival fans, but at the end of the QPR match the pitch invasion proved that for City fans this was like Christmas morning and the big kid in all of them shone through.

Eventually the pitch was cleared and the presentations were made. Members of the 1968 title winning team lined up to applaud the 2012 side as it made its way on to the pitch while City's great former captain Tony Book carried out the trophy. It looked a bit heavy for the septuagenarian to carry but he didn't seem to mind.

After all the present day squad had been welcomed on to the pitch and presented with their own medals the Premier League trophy was presented to Vincent Kompany who, in traditional style, lifted the cup high above his head to start yet another period of wild celebration.

The players performed a lap of honour, posed for photos and generally enjoyed the experience. They were also interviewed. As was the manager. He explained his feelings: "I think it was a crazy finish to a crazy season. I have never seen a final like this. I think we have changed the history of this club. For this we should be proud. We deserve this for our supporters. We deserved to win the title.

"I'm very proud for my players because I think that

Captain Vincent Kompany, looking relaxed after an incredible game.

Headline grabbers once more. Manchester City champions 2011-12.

they wanted to win this title. They worked hard for this and they wanted to win the title until the last second of the last game."

Although Mancini's English was now vastly superior to when he first arrived, this moment found him struggling to find the English superlatives to accurately portray his feelings: "A moment like this… I think in the history of the Club a final like this doesn't exist."

When asked whether City were worthy champions the manager commented: "The best team won the title, sure. I think we played the best football. We conceded less goals and scored more goals. We beat United two times. We scored more goals than them and conceded less goals than them. We deserve to win. To beat a strong team like United is fantastic."

The manager also made sure he talked of Mario Balotelli, the 'enfant terrible' of the City side, and his contribution to Agüero's goal: "I'm happy because Mario did the assist. I think that's important for him to finish this season like this. He did a good assist on the floor for

Sergio. I think that it's right that Sergio scored the last goal. It's difficult to say about one player or two players. It's impossible. All the players are important in this title."

The celebrations continued for some considerable time in the stadium – in fact some fans had to be told to leave. During the celebrations fans were puzzled at first by a loud ticking noise coming through the public address system. As it played some fans began to realise what this signified and then on the video screens the number 44 appeared above the word 'YEARS'. Within seconds this began counting down until it eventually reached 00 YEARS. Fans loved it.

The following day Manchester celebrated the greatest homecoming parade in years as over 100,000 took to the streets to welcome the Champions. Some had to be there simply so that they could come to terms with what had actually occurred in those final moments of the QPR match. They were still finding it difficult to comprehend even though many of them had spent every moment of the previous 24 hours reading

TRUE BLUE
Joe Hart

A tremendous 'keeper at a club with a tradition of brilliant goalies. He has already matched Swift's achievements at club and international level.

newspapers, talking with friends and watching television replays of the key moments. On YouTube and other websites some fans had posted their own reactions while others had created split screen footage showing the actions at the Etihad alongside those at the Stadium of Light. Viewers could see the United fans' celebrations turn to despair as Agüero's goal entered the net.

Unlike City's 1968 success a worldwide audience was able to take in every moment of the Blues' success and analyse it ad infinitum. Those that had actually been amongst the lucky 47,435 at the Etihad had been fortunate to experience the greatest moment in the Club's entire history – it was well worth waiting around 132 years for!

2011-2012 SUMMARY

Highest League Attendance: 47,435 QPR, 13/05/12
Highest Cup Attendance: 46,808 Manchester United, 08/01/12 (FA Cup)
Managers: 2009 – Roberto Mancini

Seasonal Record:

Season	League	Posn	FA Cup	League Cup	Other	Leading Scorer	Average Attendance
2011-12	Premier	1	Rnd 3	Semi-final	3rd in Champions League Group stage & Europa League last 16	Agüero 23	47,044
2012-13	Premier						

2011-12 PREMIER LEAGUE CHAMPIONSHIP DETAILS
MANAGER: Roberto Mancini

RESULTS	HOME		AWAY	
Swansea City	W	4-0	L	0-1
Wigan Athletic	W	3-0	W	1-0
Everton	W	2-0	L	0-1
Aston Villa	W	4-1	W	1-0
Wolverhampton W	W	3-1	W	2-0
Newcastle United	W	3-1	W	2-0
Norwich City	W	5-1	W	6-1
Arsenal	W	1-0	L	0-1
Stoke City	W	3-0	D	1-1
Liverpool	W	3-0	D	1-1
Tottenham Hotspur	W	3-2	W	5-1
Fulham	W	3-0	D	2-2
Blackburn Rovers	W	3-0	W	4-0
Bolton Wanderers	W	2-0	W	3-2
Chelsea	W	2-1	L	1-2
Sunderland	D	3-3	L	0-1
WBA	W	4-0	D	0-0
Manchester United	W	1-0	W	6-1
QPR	W	3-2	W	3-2

LARGEST VICTORY: 6-1 V Manchester United (A) 23/10/11, Norwich City (A) 14/4/12
LARGEST WINNING MARGIN: 6-1 V Manchester United (A) 23/10/11, Norwich City (A) 14/4/12
HEAVIEST DEFEAT: 1-2 V Chelsea (A) 12/12/11
AVERAGE HOME ATTENDANCE: 47,044
HIGHEST HOME ATTENDANCE: 47,435 V QPR 13/5/12
HIGHEST AWAY ATTENDANCE: 75,487 V Manchester United 23/10/11
LEAGUE APPEARANCES (substitute appearances in brackets): 38 Hart, 33 Silva (3), 31 Agüero (3), Barry (3), Yaya Touré (1), Kompany, 30 Lescott (1), 28 Clichy, 26 Nasri (4), 23 Richards (6), 18 Zabaleta (3), 17 Milner (9), 16 Dzeko (14), 14 Balotelli (9), 11 De Jong (10), 10 Johnson (16), 9 Kolarov (3), 8 Kolo Touré (6), 7 Tévez (6), 5 Savic (6), 1 Pizarro (4), 0 Hargreaves (1), Onuoha (1) & Razak (1)
LEAGUE GOALS: 23 Agüero, 14 Dzeko, 13 Balotelli, 6 Johnson, Silva, Touré, 5 Nasri, 4 Tévez, 3 Kompany, Milner, 2 Kolarov, Lescott, 1 Barry, Clichy, Richards, Savic, Zabaleta, & 1 own goals.
Clichy's goal V Bolton sometimes recorded as an own goal.

Subscribers

The author and publisher would like to thank all of the subscribers to this volume. Your support of this project is appreciated. Special thanks to the MCFC Supporters Club, in particular the Denton, Scandinavian, North Bury, Halifax & West Yorkshire branches.

Book	Subscriber Name	City Hero	Book	Subscriber Name	City Hero
1	Khaldoon Al Mubarak		50	Simon Clarke	
2	Manchester City		51	Sean James Riley	Dennis Tueart
3	National Football Museum		52	Trygve Høgebøl	Vincent Kompany
4	Sir Howard Bernstein		53	Martin Waters	Paul Lake
5	Manchester Central Library		54	Matteo Tonna	
6	Trevor Hartley		55	Dave Scull	
7	Gary James	Dave Watson	56	Greg Hughes	Roberto Mancini
8	Edward Garvey		57	Colin Savage	
9	Dave Wallace	Bert Trautmann	58	Adrian Brodkin	Colin Bell
10	Darren Clarke	Mike Doyle	59	David Concannon	
11	Philip Neale	Paul Lake	60	Chris Morris	Niall Quinn
12	Brian Parsons		61	Mark Dootson	
13	Colin Taylor	Dennis Tueart	62	Maria Sammut	
14	David John Fisher	Bert Trautmann	63	Daniel Moorehead	David Silva
15	Graeme Jones	Colin Bell	64	Paul Hughes	Colin Bell
16	Michael Wilson	Colin Bell	65	Dr John E Goldring	Shaun Wright-Phillips
17	Anthony Etches	David White	66	Sem Lima	Vincent Kompany
18	Terry Ashworth	Colin Bell	67	Brian Wainwright	Colin Bell
19	Bob Carney	Mike Doyle	68	Mark Sills	
20	Janakan Seemampillai	Yaya Toure	69	Steve Doohan	Shaun Goater
21	John Robertsson	Richard Dunne	70	Brian White	Colin Bell
22	Matthew Lingard		71	Dominic Brown	Uwe Rosler
23	Nicolas Watts	Colin Bell	72	Douglas Craig	
24	Peter Wilson	Bert Trautmann	73	Mark James	Pablo Zabaleta
25	Thomas West	Sergio Aguero	74	Nik Gardner	Uwe Rosler
26	Tommy Muir	All of them	75	Peter Brophy	Dave Watson
27	Josef 'Joey' Vass	Micah Richards	76	Joe Treglown	Shaun Goater
28	Andrew Patterson		77	Stephen Brocklehurst	
29	Matt Bewley	Colin Bell	78	Russell Askew	Colin Bell
30	Peter Johnson	David Silva	79	Andrew Finnie	Colin Bell
31	Kevin Greaves	Dave Watson	80	Mark 'Tomo' Thomas	Colin Bell
32	Allan Claypole	Paul Lake	81	Ruth Jenkins	Colin Bell
33	Mark Gilligan	Dennis Tueart	82	Philip Jones	
34	Allan Cawley	Mike Summerbee	83	Robert L Dunn	Colin Bell
35	Garry Higgins	Colin Bell	84	Derrol Taylor	Alan Oakes
36	Julian Hardiman	Colin Bell	85	Ryan Walding	Aleksandar Kolarov
37	Benjamin Lee (JMW)		86	Scott Game	Mike Summerbee
38	Paul Francis Hodge	Colin Bell	87	Les McDonald	Bert Trautmann
39	Charlie Adam Hodge	Sergio Aguero	88	Colin Smith	Colin Bell
40	Ian Huddlestone		89	Ann Marie Carty	Niall Quinn
41	Ross Griffin	Vincent Kompany	90	Daniel Corriveau	Shaun Goater
42	Frank McGurdy	Colin Bell	91	Will Edwards	Willie Donachie
43	Gary Douglas	Paul Dickov	92	Colin Aplin	Colin Bell
44	GEM	Vincent Kompany	93	John Lim	Colin Bell
45	Tony Preston	Georgi Kinkladze	94	Martin Bøge	
46	Mark Pilling	Ian Brightwell	95	Andrew Cleaver	Niall Quinn
47	Peter Durkin	Dennis Tueart	96	Chris Hulme	Colin Bell
48	Robert Huyton	Colin Bell	97	Stephen Cheeseborough	
49	Pete Tierney	Peter Barnes	98	John Joyce	Rodney Marsh

Book	Subscriber Name	City Hero	Book	Subscriber Name	City Hero
99	Damian Oatway	Shaun Goater	157	Anne Rees	Sergio Aguero
100	Jack Greenald		158	Kevin Esplin	
101	John Dolman	Shaun Goater	159	Jon Ramsbottom	
102	Jonathan Poole	Colin Bell	160	Andrew Heydeman	Paul Moulden
103	Donald Lowndes Sanderson	Shaun Goater	161	Willy Plumb	Neil Young
104	Ezra Lockey	Sergio Aguero	162	Lee Scott Smith	Shaun Wright-Phillips
105	John O'Connor	Colin Bell	163	Shaun Jenks	Dave Watson
106	Andy Taylor	Colin Bell	164	Mick Henneberry (Tipperary)	Niall Quinn
107	William Leeming		165	Justin Hayes	Paul Lake
108	Del Blades	David Silva	166	Keith Gooch	Colin Bell
109	Nick Dodd	Les Dodd (wartime 1941-43)	167	Lukas Barnes	Vincent Kompany
			168	David Miller	
110	Stanley Burfield	Sergio Aguero	169	Anthony Galloway	
111	Simon Battersby	Peter Barnes	170	Ben Rose	Georgi Kinkladze
112	Mark Reavey	Colin Bell	171	Andrew Morris	
113	Tony Smith	Georgi Kinkladze	172	Stephen Barrow	
114	Thomas William Smith	Sergio Aguero	173	Colin Seaton	Vincent Kompany
115	Tony Burns	Mike Doyle	174	Stuart Carmichael	Uwe Rosler
116	Steve Hardie	Sergio Aguero	175	Stephen Brown	Rodney Marsh
117	David Hollinshead		176	Tom Casey	Shaun Goater/Niall Quinn
118	RJ Mottershead		177	Rob Casey	Mario Balotelli
119	Ian Bell		178	Tuomas Ruikka	Paul Power
120	Ben Hunt	Sergio Aguero	179	Siggi Helgason	Vincent Kompany
121	Harry Moska	Mario Balotelli	180	Peter McNally	Dennis Tueart
122	Cathy Dyster	Colin Bell	181	Anne Marie Bibby	Sergio Aguero
123	Peter Hardman Happy 50th Birthday	Sergio Aguero	182	Rob Lees	David Silva
			183	William Mitchell	
124	Martin Cook	David Seaman	184	James Parkinson	Shaun Goater
125	John C Malone	Vincent Kompany	185	Ian Parkinson	Colin Bell
126	The Pickles Family	Niall Quinn	186	Duncan Walker	
127	Gareth Hamer	Uwe Rosler	187	Adrian Grant	Colin Bell
128	Stanley Ratcliffe		188	Bill Shannon	Bert Trautmann
129	Nick Wright	Niall Quinn	189	Steve Mingle	Colin Bell
130	Robin Harrison		190	Harry Chris Ingham	Colin Bell
131	Keith Hargreaves Happy 50th	Colin Bell	191	Martin Lowry	Bert Trautmann
132	Andrew Phang	Colin Bell	192	Christopher Wagstaffe	
133	Colin James Smith	Colin Bell	193	Darren Page	2011-12 Premier League Champions
134	Mon Miah				
135	Dale Moore		194	Diane & Jack Long	2011-12 Premier League Champions
136	Hugh Dwan	Peter Doherty			
137	Kalle Hallfast	Pablo Zabaleta	195	Manchester Programme Shop	
138	Robert Ball	Glyn Pardoe	196	Peter Marriott	Sergio Aguero
139	Ian Dockry	Dennis Tueart	197	Noel Bayley	
140	Daniel Ball	Paul Dickov	198	Steve & Jamie Bootle	David Silva
141	Norbert & Sophie Hepner	Bert Trautmann	199	Andrew Keegan	
142	Mike Owen	Colin Bell	200	Desmond Miles	
143	Robert Edwards	Colin Bell	201	Jamie Stoddart	Paul Lake
144	Neil Spellman	Georgi Kinkladze	202	Daryl Hickman	Colin Bell
145	Matt Ashworth		203	Mark Pemberton	Vincent Kompany
146	David Brooks	Shaun Goater	204	Roger Brooks	Bert Trautmann
147	Ted, Gordon, Mark, John & Phil Buchan	Colin Bell	205	Andy Noise	Francis Lee
			206	David Kettle	Georgi Kinkladze
148	Paul Newton	Andy Morrison	207	Alex Hardiman	Mario Balotelli
149	Niels Bjerring Hansen		208	Louise Casey	Nicky Weaver
150	Michael Whitehead		209	Helen Casey	Shaun Wright-Phillips
151	Mrs JM Hogg		210	Michael Casey	Shaun Goater
152	Stephen & Susan Casey	Neil Young	211	Daniel Dwan	Sergio Aguero
153	Mike Bennison	Georgi Kinkladze	212	Peter White	
154	Martin McNeil	Joe Corrigan	213	Frank Clarke	Sergio Aguero
155	Nick Ball	Sergio Aguero	214	Mark Poyzer	Dennis Tueart
156	Bob Brindle	Niall Quinn	215	Ian Nickson	

Book	Subscriber Name	City Hero	Book	Subscriber Name	City Hero
216	Joe Carroll	Yaya Toure	274	Ole 'Fisher King' Fuglestad	David Silva
217	Ian R Peat	Dennis Tueart	275	Nils Are Golf	Niall Quinn
218	Joe Doherty	Richard Dunne	276	Jakob Grova	Dennis Tueart
219	John Fielding	Mike Summerbee	277	Morten Hol	Ali Bernarbia
220	Vincent Regan	Vincent Kompany	278	Gjermund Kaldal	Peter Barnes
221	James Valentine Lawlor	Francis Lee	279	Øivind Kopperud	Eyal Berkovic
222	Mark Catlow	Dennis Tueart	280	Tommy Kvarsvik	Georgi Kinkladze
223	Gabriel Knight	Sergio Aguero	281	Harald Larsen	Georgi Kinkladze
224	John Leigh	Bobby Johnstone	282	Andreas Larsson	Shaun Goater
225	Steven Wilson	Joe Corrigan	283	Sven A Ljosland	Joe Corrigan
226	Bartley Ramsay	Joe Corrigan	284	Bjørn H Moen	Francis Lee
227	Dorothy Burgoine	Colin Bell	285	Morten Olesen	Kevin Horlock
228	Mike Jackson-Leafield	Dennis Tueart	286	Per A Rennestraum	Peter Barnes
229	Mel Clegg	Peter Barnes	287	Per Asle Rustad	Colin Bell
230	David Mugford		288	Richard Stott	Mike Doyle
231	John Oxley		289	Tor Sønsteby	Francis lee
232	Leigh Vincent	Vincent Kompany	290	Marius Sørensen	Tony Coton
233	Svein Snekkvik		291	Stein Sørensen	Joe Hart
234	Ian McCleverty	Shaun Goater	292	Thor Sørensen	Dennis Tueart
235	Pam Stevenson	Roberto Mancini	293	Svea	Dennis Tueart
236	Stephen Jacquest		294	Gunnar Talgø	Asa Hartford
237	David Sigsworth	Shaun Goater	295	Espen Vessang-Nielsen	Rodney Marsh
238	Anthony Catterson	Vincent Kompany	296	Terje Nansen	Dennis Tueart
239	Alan G Marsh	Vincent Kompany	297	Branch Scandinavia	
240	Jim O'Connor, RIP Dad	Colin Bell	298	Branch Scandinavia	
241	Phil Hall	Sergio Aguero	299	Branch Scandinavia	
242	Alan Chichester	Kevin Horlock	300	Branch Scandinavia	
243	Phil Goldstone	Colin Bell	301	Branch Scandinavia	
244	Heidi James	2011-12 Premier League Champions	302	Branch Scandinavia	
			303	Andrew Stephenson	Tony Book
245	Hannah Taylor	Joe Hart	304	Alan Potter	Colin Bell
246	Steve Rigby	Trevor Francis	305	Mark Statham	Joe Hart
247	Roni & Barry Foy	Colin Bell	306	Ian Cook	Colin Bell
248	Kim Mitchell	Alan Oakes	307	Roderick Hall	Colin Bell
249	David Glynn Hall	Colin Bell	308	James Curran	Colin Bell
250	Graham Anthony Hall	Dennis Tueart	309	Neil V Buckley	Paul Dickov
251	Neil Boothy Booth	Uwe Rosler	310	David Connor	Shaun Goater
252	Peter Adams	Bert Trautmann	311	Rebecca Slater	Joe Hart
253	Dixie Bourne	Shaun Goater	312	Denton Branch	
254	Gary 'Hovis' Griffin	Colin Bell	313	David Beresford	Colin Bell
255	Darren Russell Taylor	Uwe Rosler	314	Blair I G Martin	Paul Power
256	Michael Grayson		315	Terence Bailey	Joe Mercer
257	Shaun Brendan McGowan	Yaya Toure (My Nickname in the womb)	316	Sue Jack	Vincent Kompany
			317	James Ireland	Colin Bell
			318	Ellis Harry Taylor	Sergio Aguero
258	Howard Croft	Alan Oakes	319	Callum Leon Taylor	Sergio Aguero
259	Stephen Wilson	Colin Bell	320	Paul & Marjorie James	
260	Simon Bevan	Colin Bell	321	Leigh Collis	Joe Royle
261	Barry Maclennan	Paul Lake	322	Sue Wallace	Vincent Kompany
262	Phil Taylor	Colin Bell	323	Anna James	Nigel De Jong
263	Ronald Taylor	Bert Trautmann	324	Eric Fitton	Colin Bell
264	Sofia Peacock	David Silva	325	Colin Johnson	
265	Gareth Jones	Joe Corrigan	326	Mike James	2011-12 Premier League Champions
266	Nigel Goldsmith	Shaun Goater			
267	Phil Banerjee	Paul Lake	327	Duncan Shaw	Colin Bell
268	Morten Anderson	Francis Lee	328	Barbara & Alan Clarke	
269	Ketil Aune	Joe Corrigan	329	Alex Wallace	David Silva
270	Rolf Brown	Dennis Tueart	330	Garry Cook	
271	Eric Duncan	Georgi Kinkladze	331	Philip Alcock	Colin Bell
272	Christian de Lange	Shaun Goater			
273	Ole M Egedal	Tommy Hutchinson			